Frommer's®

France 2011

by Darwin Porter & Danforth Prince

WILEY

Wiley Publishing, Inc.

ABOUT THE AUTHORS

As a team of veteran travel writers, **Darwin Porter** and **Danforth Prince** have produced numerous titles for Frommer's, which have included England, Italy, the Caribbean, Spain, and Germany.

Porter wrote the first ever Frommer's guide to Paris and the first ever Frommer's guide to France. A Francophile, he has lived and worked in Paris on and off for many years. He was joined by Danforth Prince in 1982. Prince was previously employed by the Paris bureau of the *New York Times* and is the president of Blood Moon Productions and other media-related firms. Porter is also a film critic, columnist, broadcaster, and Hollywood biographer.

Published by:

WILEY PUBLISHING, INC.

111 River St.

Hoboken, NJ 07030-5774

ISBN 978-0-470-61438-9 (paper); ISBN 978-0-470-90668-2 (ebk); ISBN 978-0-470-40985-5 (ebk); ISBN 978-0-470-64177-4 (ebk)

Editor: Marc Nadeau
Production Editor: Jana M. Stefanciosa
Cartographer: Nick Trotter
Photo Editor: Richard Fox
Production by Wiley Indianapolis Composition Services

Front cover photo: A field of lavender in Alpes-de-Haute, Provence, France ©Art Kowalsky / Jean-Pierre Lescourret Photos
Back cover photo: Mont St Michel in Normandy, France ©Dallas and John Heaton / SCPhotos / Alamy Images

For information on our other products and services or to obtain technical support, please contact our Customer Care Department within the U.S. at 877/762-2974, outside the U.S. at 317/572-3993 or fax 317/572-4002.

Wiley also publishes its books in a variety of electronic formats. Some content that appears in print may not be available in electronic formats.

Manufactured in the United States of America

5 4 3 2 1

CONTENTS

5 SETTLING INTO PARIS 84

6 EXPLORING PARIS 151

7 SIDE TRIPS FROM PARIS: VERSAILLES, CHARTRES & THE BEST OF THE ILE DE FRANCE 204

8 THE LOIRE VALLEY 241

9 NORMANDY & MONT-ST-MICHEL 287

10 BRITTANY 319

21 THE DORDOGNE & PERIGORD: LAND OF PREHISTORIC CAVES, TRUFFLES & FINE WINE 715

22 THE MASSIF CENTRAL 737

23 FAST FACTS 757

24 USEFUL TERMS & PHRASES 763

LIST OF MAPS

HOW TO CONTACT US

In researching this book, we discovered many wonderful places—hotels, restaurants, shops, and more. We're sure you'll find others. Please tell us about them, so we can share the information with your fellow travelers in upcoming editions. If you were disappointed with a recommendation, we'd love to know that, too. Please write to:

Frommer's France 2011
Wiley Publishing, Inc. • 111 River St. • Hoboken, NJ 07030-5774
frommersfeedback@wiley.com

AN ADDITIONAL NOTE

Please be advised that travel information is subject to change at any time—and this is especially true of prices. We therefore suggest that you write or call ahead for confirmation when making your travel plans. The authors, editors, and publisher cannot be held responsible for the experiences of readers while traveling. Your safety is important to us, however, so we encourage you to stay alert and be aware of your surroundings. Keep a close eye on cameras, purses, and wallets, all favorite targets of thieves and pickpockets.

FROMMER'S STAR RATINGS, ICONS & ABBREVIATIONS

Every hotel, restaurant, and attraction listing in this guide has been ranked for quality, value, service, amenities, and special features using a **star-rating system.** In country, state, and regional guides, we also rate towns and regions to help you narrow down your choices and budget your time accordingly. Hotels and restaurants are rated on a scale of zero (recommended) to three stars (exceptional). Attractions, shopping, nightlife, towns, and regions are rated according to the following scale: zero stars (recommended), one star (highly recommended), two stars (very highly recommended), and three stars (must-see).

In addition to the star-rating system, we also use **seven feature icons** that point you to the great deals, in-the-know advice, and unique experiences that separate travelers from tourists. Throughout the book, look for:

special finds—those places only insiders know about

fun facts—details that make travelers more informed and their trips more fun

kids—best bets for kids and advice for the whole family

special moments—those experiences that memories are made of

overrated—places or experiences not worth your time or money

insider tips—great ways to save time and money

great values—where to get the best deals

The following **abbreviations** are used for credit cards:

AE American Express	**DISC** Discover	**V** Visa	
DC Diners Club	**MC** MasterCard		

TRAVEL RESOURCES AT FROMMERS.COM

Frommer's travel resources don't end with this guide. Frommer's website, **www.frommers. com**, has travel information on more than 4,000 destinations. We update features regularly, giving you access to the most current trip-planning information and the best airfare, lodging, and car-rental bargains. You can also listen to podcasts, connect with other Frommers. com members through our active-reader forums, share your travel photos, read blogs from guidebook editors and fellow travelers, and much more.

THE BEST OF FRANCE

France presents visitors with an embarrassment of riches—you may find yourself bewildered by all the choices. We've tried to make the task easier by compiling a list of our favorite experiences and discoveries. In the following pages, you'll find the kind of candid advice we'd give our closest friends.

THE best TRAVEL EXPERIENCES

- **Hunting for Antiques:** The 18th- and 19th-century French aesthetic was gloriously different from that of England and North America, and many objects bear designs with mythological references to the French experience. France has some 13,000-plus antiques shops throughout the country. Stop where you see the sign ANTIQUAIRE or BROCANTE.

- **Dining Out:** The art of dining is serious business in France. Food is as cerebral as it is sensual. Even casual bistros with affordable menus are likely to offer fresh seasonal ingredients in time-tested recipes that may add up to a memorable meal. For our favorite restaurants in France, see "The Best Upscale Restaurants" and "The Best Affordable Restaurants," later in this chapter.

- **Biking in the Countryside:** The country that invented La Tour de France offers thousands of options for bike trips. For a modest charge, trains in France will carry your bicycle to any point. **Euro-Bike & Walking Tours** (© **800/575-1540;** www.eurobike.com) offers some of the best excursions, including walking and cycling tours of areas such as Provence, Burgundy, and the Loire Valley. See chapter 3.

- **Shopping in Parisian Boutiques:** The French guard their image as Europe's most stylish people. The citadels of Right Bank chic lie on rue du Faubourg St-Honoré and its extension, rue St-Honoré. The most glamorous shops are along these streets, stretching between the Palais Royal to the east and the Palais de l'Elysée to the west. Follow in the footsteps of Coco Chanel, Yves Saint Laurent, and Karl Lagerfeld on the shopper's tour of a lifetime. See chapter 6.

- **Exploring the Loire Valley:** An excursion to the châteaux dotting the valley's rich fields and forests will familiarize you with the French

Renaissance's architectural aesthetics and with the intrigues of the kings and their courts. Nothing conjures up the aristocratic *ancien régime* better than a tour of these landmarks. See chapter 8.

o **Paying Tribute to Fallen Heroes on Normandy's D-Day Beaches:** On June 6, 1944, the largest armada ever assembled departed on rough seas and in dense fog from England. For about a week, the future of the civilized world hung in a bloody and brutal balance between the Nazi and Allied armies. Today you'll find only the sticky sands and wind-torn, gray-green seas of a rather chilly beach. But even if you haven't seen *Saving Private Ryan* or *The Longest Day,* you can picture the struggles of determined soldiers who paid a terrible price to establish a bulkhead on the Continent. See "The D-Day Beaches" in chapter 9.

o **Climbing to the Heights of Mont-St-Michel:** Straddling the tidal flats between Normandy and Brittany, this Gothic marvel is the most spectacular fortress in northern Europe. Said to be protected by the archangel Michael, most of it stands as it did during the 1200s. See "Mont-St-Michel" in chapter 9.

o **Touring Burgundy During the Grape Gathering:** Medieval lore and legend permeate the harvests in Burgundy, where thousands of workers (armed with vintner's shears and baskets) head over the rolling hills to gather the grapes that have made the region's wines so famous. You can sample the local wines in the area restaurants, which always stock impressive collections. See chapter 13.

o **Schussing down the Alps:** France offers world-class skiing and luxurious resorts. Our favorites are Chamonix, Courchevel, and Megève. Here you'll find cliffs only experts should brave, as well as runs for intermediates and beginners. The après-ski scene roars into the wee hours. See chapter 15.

o **Marveling at the Riviera's Modern-Art Museums:** Since the 1890s, when Signac, Bonnard, and Matisse discovered St-Tropez, artists and their patrons have been drawn to the French Riviera. Experience an unforgettable drive across southern Provence, interspersing museum visits with wonderful meals, sunbathing, and stops at the area's architectural and artistic marvels. Highlights are Aix-en-Provence (Cézanne's studio), Biot (the Léger Museum), Cagnes-sur-Mer (the Museum of Modern Mediterranean Art), Cap d'Antibes (the Grimaldi Château's Picasso Museum), La Napoule (the Henry Clews Museum), and Menton (the Cocteau Museum). In addition, Nice, St-Paul-de-Vence, and St-Tropez all have impressive modern-art collections. See chapters 16 and 17.

THE best ROMANTIC ESCAPES

o **Deauville** (Normandy): Using the resort of Deauville to propel herself to stardom, Coco Chanel added greatly to its sense of glamour and romance. Try your hand at the casinos, ride horses, stroll along the elegant boardwalk, or simply revel in the resort's sense of style and nostalgia. See "Deauville" in chapter 9.

o **La Baule** (Brittany): Consider an escape with your significant other to La Baule, a coastal resort in southern Brittany. The salt air; the moody, wind-swept Atlantic; and the Belle Epoque architecture help justify the name of its 8km (5-mile) beach, La Côte d'Amour. See "La Baule" in chapter 10.

o **Talloires** (the French Alps): The bracing climate, the history that goes back to the Middle Ages, and the Gallic flair of the innkeepers make for a memorable stay.

The accommodations include a converted medieval monastery, and the village's cuisine is superb. See "Talloires" in chapter 15.

o **Les Baux** (Provence): During the Middle Ages, troubadours sang ballads to audiences at the fortress of Les Baux. The romantic tradition continues today, with escapists from all over congregating in the rocky, arid landscape. The town has an abundance of romantic hideaways. See "Les Baux" in chapter 16.

o **St-Tropez** (Côte d'Azur): Any blonde feels like Brigitte Bardot in sunny St-Tropez, and the number of scantily clad satyrs and nymphs in town during summer could perk up the most sluggish libido. The real miracle here is that the charm of the place manages to survive its hype and the hordes of visitors. See "St-Tropez" in chapter 17.

THE best DRIVING TOURS

o **La Route des Crêtes** (Alsace-Lorraine): The Vosges, one of the oldest mountain ranges in France, once formed a boundary with Germany. Richly forested with hardwood trees and firs, they skirt the western edge of the Rhine and resemble the Black Forest. La Route des Crêtes (the Crest Road), originally chiseled out of the mountains as a supply line, begins west of Colmar, at the Col du Bonhomme. High points are Münster (home of the cheese), Col de la Schlucht (a resort with panoramas as far as the Jura and the Black Forest), and Markstein. At many points along the way, you can stop and strike out on a well-marked hiking trail. See "La Route des Crêtes" in chapter 12.

o **La Côte d'Or** (Burgundy): Stretching only 60km (37 miles) from Santenay to Dijon, this route is for wine lovers. Rows of terraced vines rise in tiers above the D122/N74/D1138 highways (La Route des Grands Crus), passing through the towns of Puligny-Montrachet, Volnay, Beaune, Nuits-St-Georges, Vosne-Romanée, Gevrey-Chambertin, and Marsannay-la-Côte. Travel at your leisure, stopping to sample the noble vintages (look for the signs sprouting from the sides of the highway). See chapter 13.

o **The Gorges of the Ardèche** (the Rhône Valley): The river that carved these canyons (the Ardèche, a tributary of the Rhône) is the most temperamental French waterway: Its ebbs and flows have created the Grand Canyon of France. Riddled with alluvial deposits, grottoes, caves, and canyons more than 285m (935 ft.) deep, the valley is one of France's most unusual geological spectacles. A panoramic road (D290) runs along one rim of the canyons, providing views over a striking, arid landscape. Plan to park and walk a little on some of the well-marked paths. The drive, which you can do in a day even if you make frequent stops, stretches between Vallon-Pont-d'Arc and Pont St-Esprit. See "The Ardèche" in chapter 14.

o **La Route des Grandes Alpes** (the French Alps): One of the most panoramic drives in western Europe stretches south from the lakefront town of Evian to coastal Nice. You'll see Alpine uplands, larch forests, glaciers, and the foothills of Mont Blanc. Plan on driving 2 to 6 days, stopping in such towns as Morzine, Avoriaz, Chamonix, and Megève. The route covers 740km (460 miles) and crosses many of France's dramatic mountain passes. Some sections are passable only in midsummer. See chapter 15.

THE best CHATEAUX & PALACES

- **Château de Chantilly/Musée Condé** (Ile de France): Anne de Montmorency, a constable of France who advised six monarchs, began this palace in 1560. To save money, he ordered the new building placed atop the foundations of a derelict castle. His descendants enlarged and embellished the premises, added the massive stables, and hired Le Nôtre to design gardens that later inspired Louis XVI to create similar, larger ones at Versailles. See p. 234.

- **Château de Versailles** (Ile de France): Versailles is the most spectacular palace in the world. Its construction was fraught with ironies and tragedies, and its costs were a factor in the bloodbath of the French Revolution. Ringed with world-class gardens and a network of canals whose excavation required an army of laborers, the site also contains the Grand and Petit Trianons as well as miles of ornate corridors lined with the spoils of a vanished era. See p. 208.

- **Palais de Fontainebleau** (Ile de France): Since the days of the earliest Frankish kings, the forest has served as a royal hunting ground. Various dwellings had been erected for medieval kings, but in 1528, François I commissioned the core of the building that subsequent monarchs would enlarge and embellish. Napoleon declared it his favorite château, delivering an emotional farewell to his troops from its exterior staircase after his 1814 abdication. See p. 221.

- **Château d'Azay-le-Rideau** (Loire Valley): Visitors are enthralled by this château's beauty. Poised above the waters of the Indre River, it boasts decorative remnants of medieval fortifications and an atmosphere that prefigures the Renaissance embellishments of later Loire Valley châteaux. See p. 273.

- **Château de Chambord** (Loire Valley): Despite the incorporation (probably by Michelangelo) of feudal trappings in its layout, this château was built for pleasure—a manifestation of the successes of the 21-year-old François I. Begun in 1519 as the Loire Valley's most opulent status symbol, Chambord heralded the end of the feudal age and the dawn of the Renaissance. After military defeats in Italy, a chastened François rarely visited, opting to live in châteaux closer to Paris. See p. 249.

- **Château de Chenonceau** (Loire Valley): Its builders daringly placed this palace, built between 1513 and 1521, on arched stone vaults above the rushing Cher River. Two of France's most influential women, each of whom imposed her will on Renaissance politics and the château's design, fought over Chenonceau. Henri II gave the palace to his mistress, Diane de Poitiers. After the king's death, his widow, Catherine de Médicis, humiliated Diane by forcing her to move to a less prestigious château in nearby Chaumont. See p. 261.

THE best MUSEUMS

- **Centre Pompidou** (Paris): "The most avant-garde building in the world" is a citadel of 20th-century art, with exhibitions drawn from more than 40,000 works. Everything is here, from Calder's 1928 *Josephine Baker* (one of his earliest versions of the mobile) to a re-creation of Brancusi's Jazz Age studio. See p. 156.

o **Musée d'Orsay** (Paris): The spidery glass-and-iron canopies of an abandoned railway station frame one of Europe's most thrilling museums. Devoted to 19th-century art, it contains paintings by most of the French Impressionists, and sculptures and decorative objects whose design forever changed the way Europe interpreted line, movement, and color. See p. 158.

o **Musée du Louvre** (Paris): The Louvre's exterior is a triumph of grand French architecture, while its interior contains an embarrassment of artistic riches, with more paintings (around 300,000) than can be displayed at one time. The collection retains its dignity despite the thousands who traipse through the corridors every day, looking for the *Mona Lisa* and the *Venus de Milo*. I. M. Pei's controversial Great Pyramid neatly offsets the grandeur of its Cour Carrée. See p. 158.

o **Musée de la Tapisserie de Bayeux** (Bayeux, Normandy): This museum's star is a 900-year-old tapestry named in honor of medieval Queen Mathilda. Housed in a glass case, the Bayeux tapestry is a long band of linen embroidered with depictions of the war machine that sailed from Normandy to conquer England in 1066. See p. 310.

o **Musée Historique Lorrain** (Nancy, Alsace-Lorraine): Few other French museums reflect a province as well as this one. Its collections include 16th-century engravings, 17th-century masterpieces by local painters, exhibits on Jewish history in eastern France, antique furniture, wrought iron, and domestic accessories. See p. 395.

o **Foundation Maeght** (St-Paul-de-Vence, Côte d'Azur): Established as a showcase for modern art by collectors Aimé and Marguerite Maeght, this avant-garde museum features works by Giacometti, Chagall, Braque, Miró, Matisse, and Barbara Hepworth. The multilevel design by the architect José Luís Sert boasts glass walls with views of the Provence landscape. See p. 576.

o **Musée Fabre** (Montpellier, Languedoc): This museum occupies a villa where Molière once presented some of his plays. Today it displays one of the worthiest collections of French, Italian, and Spanish paintings in the south of France. See p. 628.

o **Musée Toulouse-Lautrec** (Albi, Languedoc): Henri Toulouse-Lautrec was born in Albi in 1864. Much to his family's horror, he moved to a scandalous area in Paris, where he created depictions of the Belle Epoque scene that are treasures today. Also on view are works by Degas, Bonnard, and Matisse. See p. 647.

o **Musée Ingres** (Montauban, the Dordogne): This museum, in a 17th-century bishops' palace, was created in 1867 when Jean-Auguste-Dominique Ingres (one of the most admired classicists since the Revolution) bequeathed to the city more than 4,000 drawings and paintings. See p. 735.

THE best CATHEDRALS

o **Notre-Dame** (Paris): This structure's stone walls symbolize the power of Paris in the Middle Ages. Begun in 1163, Notre-Dame is the cathedral of the nation and a triumph of medieval architecture. It's dazzling in the morning and at sunset, when its image reflects in the Seine. See p. 160.

o **Cathédrale Notre-Dame de Chartres** (Chartres, Ile de France): No less an artist than Rodin declared this cathedral a French Acropolis. Its site reputedly was holy for the Druids and the ancient Romans. Chartres is one of the world's largest cathedrals, one of the first High Gothic cathedrals, and the first to use flying buttresses. It also has possibly the finest stained-glass windows, more than 2,500 sq. m (26,900 sq. ft.) of glass whose vivid hues and patterns of light are truly mystical. See p. 215.

○ **Cathédrale Notre-Dame de Rouen** (Rouen, Normandy): Consecrated in 1063 and rebuilt after a fire in 1200, parts of it are masterpieces of the Flamboyant Gothic style; others are plainer, though equally dignified. This cathedral was immortalized in the 19th century, when Monet painted a series of impressions of the facade. See p. 288.

○ **Cathédrale Notre-Dame d'Amiens** (Amiens, the Ardennes): A lavishly decorated example of High Gothic architecture, this cathedral boasts a soaring nave whose roof is supported by 126 breathtakingly slender pillars. It was begun in 1220 to house the head of St. John the Baptist, brought back from the Crusades; at 141m (463 ft.) long, it is the largest church in France. It escaped destruction during the world wars, despite fierce fighting nearby. See p. 364.

○ **Cathédrale Notre-Dame de Reims** (Reims, Champagne): One of France's first Christian bishops, St. Rémi, baptized Clovis, king of the Franks, on this site in 496. The church memorializing the event was conceived as a religious sanctuary where the French kings would be anointed; it was large, spectacular, and (in our eyes) rather cold. The coronation of every king between 815 and 1825 was celebrated here. Damaged by World War I bombings, the cathedral was restored by American donations during the 1920s and 1930s. See p. 354.

THE best VINEYARDS & WINERIES

○ **Couly-Dutheil** (12 rue Diderot, Chinon; ℂ 02-47-97-20-20; www.couly dutheil-chinon.com): Many of its medieval cellars are carved into the rock undulating through the area's forests. Most production here involves Chinon wines (mostly reds), though its Bourgueil and St-Nicolas de Bourgueil wines are growing in popularity in North America. See "Chinon" in chapter 8.

○ **Taittinger** (9 place St-Nicaise, Reims; ℂ 03-26-85-45-35; www.taittinger.com): Taittinger is a grand *marque* of French champagne, one of the few still controlled by members of the family that founded it, in 1930. It's one of the most visitor-friendly houses. See p. 355.

○ **Domaines Schlumberger** (100 rue Théodore-Deck, Guebwiller, near Colmar; ℂ 03-89-74-27-00; www.domaines-schlumberger.com): Established in 1810, these cellars blend early-19th-century brickwork and modern stainless steel; a visit will enhance your understanding of the subtle differences among wines produced by the seven varieties of grape cultivated in Alsace. See "Colmar" in chapter 12.

○ **Domaine Maurice Protheau** (Château d'Etroyes, Mercurey; ℂ 03-85-45-10-84; www.domaine-protheau-mercurey.fr): The 50 hectares (124 acres) of grapevines straddle at least two *appellations contrôlées* (a regulation system that ensures a wine has been produced where the bottle says), so you'll have a chance to contrast reds (both pinot noirs and burgundies), whites, and rosés produced under the auspices of both Rully and Mercurey. Headquarters is in a château built in the late 1700s and early 1800s. See "Autun" in chapter 13.

- **The Winegrowing Region around Bordeaux:** This area is among the most glamorous in France, with a strong British influence, thanks to centuries of trade with London- and Bristol-based dealers. One prestigious grower, **Société Duboscq**, Château Haut-Marbuzet, St-Estephe (© 05-56-59-30-54), welcomes visitors who phone in advance of their arrival Monday to Saturday. Free visits to the cellars are followed by a complimentary *dégustation des vins* of whichever of the company's products a visitor requests. See p. 712.

THE best LUXURY HOTELS

- **Hôtel Ritz** (Paris; © 800/223-6800 in the U.S. and Canada, or 01-43-16-30-30; www.ritzparis.com): This hotel occupies a palace overlooking the octagonal borders of one of the most perfect plazas in France: place Vendôme. The decor is pure opulence. Marcel Proust wrote parts of *Remembrance of Things Past* here, and Georges-Auguste Escoffier perfected many of his recipes in its kitchens. See p. 100.
- **Hôtel Meurice** (Paris; © 01-44-58-10-10; www.meuricehotel.com) faces the Jardin des Tuileries close to the Place de la Concorde. Over the course of its career, it has catered to everybody from royalty to Salvador Dalí. Massively restored and still celebrated for its glass-roofed Winter Garden, it's a pocket of posh. See p. 97.
- **Château d'Artigny** (Montbazon, Loire Valley; © 02-47-34-30-30; www.artigny.com): The perfume king François Coty once lived and entertained lavishly at this mansion outside Tours—and you can do the same today in one of the poshest hotels in the Loire Valley. Experience the grandeur once enjoyed by Elizabeth Taylor and other celebs, taking in the weekend soirees and musical evenings. See p. 268.
- **Oustau de Baumanière** (Les Baux, Provence; © 04-90-54-33-07; www.oustaudebaumaniere.com): This Relais & Châteaux property is in the valley at the foot of Les Baux de Provence. Both the cuisine and the accommodations, some of which are in buildings dating from the 16th and 17th centuries, are superb. See p. 509.
- **Grand Hôtel du Cap-Ferrat** (St-Jean-Cap-Ferrat, Côte d'Azur; © 04-93-76-50-50; www.grand-hotel-cap-ferrat.com): The Grand Hôtel occupies 5.6 prime hectares (14 acres) on one of the world's most exclusive peninsulas. In a Belle Epoque palace, it has hosted royals, aristocrats, and wealthy wannabes since the turn of the 20th century. See p. 597.
- **Hôtel du Cap–Eden Roc** (Cap d'Antibes, Côte d'Azur; © 04-93-61-39-01; www.edenroc-hotel.fr): Built during the grand Second Empire and set on 8.9 hectares (22 acres) of splendidly landscaped gardens, this hotel is legendary, evoking the F. Scott Fitzgerald classic *Tender Is the Night.* Swimmers revel in a pool blasted from the dark rock of the glamorous coastline. See p. 569.
- **Hôtel Negresco** (Nice, Côte d'Azur; © 04-93-16-64-00; www.hotel-negresco-nice.com): Built in 1913 as a layered wedding cake in the château style, the Negresco was a lavish escape for the Edwardian era's most respected and most notorious figures, including Lillie Langtry, the longtime mistress of Britain's Edward VII. After her fall from grace, she sat in the lobby, swathed in veils, refusing to utter a word. Following renovations, the hotel is better now than during its Jazz Age heyday. See p. 588.

- **Hôtel du Palais** (Biarritz, Basque Country; ☎ **800/223-6800** in the U.S. and Canada, or 05-59-41-64-00; www.hotel-du-palais.com): Delectably beautiful, this place was built in 1845 as a pink-walled summer palace for Napoleon III and his empress, Eugénie. The Belle Epoque fantasy has entertained such guests as Edward VII of England, Alfonso XIII of Spain, and the duke of Windsor. See p. 678.

THE best AFFORDABLE HOTELS

- **Hôtel de Lutèce** (Paris; ☎ **01-43-26-23-52;** www.paris-hotel-lutece.com): It slumbers on Paris's "other island," the Ile St-Louis, which usually escapes the crush of visitors on the more popular Ile de la Cité, just across the bridge. You're still in the city, but here you can imagine yourself in a country inn. See p. 105.
- **Les Maisons de Léa** (Honfleur, Normandy; ☎ **02-31-14-49-49;** www.les maisonsdelea.com): It overlooks a Norman 18th-century port favored by the French novelist Flaubert. The amenities aren't grand, but the charming setting includes an appealing restaurant, and—more surprising—the price tag is reasonable. See p. 298.
- **Hôtel d'Avaugour** (Dinan, Brittany; ☎ **02-96-39-07-49;** www.avaugourhotel.com): Its exterior looks as antique as the fortifications ringing the medieval harbor, but a major restoration transformed the interior into a cozy getaway on the Norman coast. Add aesthetic appeal, old-time flavor of Dinan's winding alleys, and views of the Channel, and you've got the ingredients for an affordable escape. See p. 329.
- **Ostellerie du Vieux-Pérouges** (Pérouges, Rhône Valley; ☎ **04-74-61-00-88;** www.hostelleriedeperouges.com): This hotel, described as a museum of the 13th century, is one of the most significant in central France. Composed of a group of 13th-century buildings with low ceilings and thick walls, it evokes the France of another day and doesn't overcharge. See p. 441.
- **La Maison Blanche** (Montpellier; ☎ **04-99-58-20-70;** www.hotel-maison-blanche.com): Evokes a French Creole ambience of New Orleans with its gingerbread trim. Bathrooms are spacious for the most part, and the guest rooms are beautifully outfitted in oak. The price is right too. See p. 629.
- **La Réserve** (Albi, Languedoc; ☎ **05-63-60-80-80;** www.relaischateaux.fr/reservealbi): Scrublands, vineyards, groves of olives, and cypresses surround this dignified farmhouse. It's less expensive than many luxurious hideaways along the nearby Côte d'Azur, and its location is just outside the center of one of our favorite fortified sites in Europe, the town of Albi. See p. 648.

THE best HISTORIC PLACES TO STAY

- **Trianon Palace** (Versailles, Ile de France; ☎ **800/937-8461** in the U.S. and Canada, or 01-30-84-50-00; www.westin.com): Louis XIV nearly bankrupted France during the construction of his nearby palace, but this hotel overlooking its gardens might have been even more influential. In 1919, the Versailles Peace Treaty was ratified by delegates who stayed in the same rooms that house guests today. You'll be pampered at this plush, elegant hotel, which boasts its own spa. See p. 211.

○ **Château de Locguénolé** (Hennebont, Brittany; ✆ 02-97-76-76-76; www. chateau-de-locguenole.com): No professional decorator could accumulate the array of furnishings and artifacts that grace this Breton manor house, which has been occupied by the same family for 500 years. Some visitors think it's the most charming hotel in southern Brittany; you may agree. See p. 335.

○ **Manoir du Stang** (La Forêt-Fouesnant, Brittany; ✆ 02-98-56-96-38; www. manoirdustang.com): Even the ivy that twines across the facade of this 16th-century Breton manor house looks as though it was planted by someone very important, very long ago. Formal gardens segue into forested parkland; modern amenities are juxtaposed with enviable antiques—the place is a gem that happens to be a glamorous hotel. See p. 333.

○ **Château de Rochegude** (Rochegude, Provence; ✆ 04-75-97-21-10; www. chateauderochegude.com): During the thousand years of this château's existence, its owners have included popes, dauphins, and less prominent aristocrats who showered it with taste and money. Today each room is outfitted in a style inspired by a specific emperor or king. The setting is 10 hectares (25 acres) of parkland adjacent to the Rhône, outside Orange. See p. 486.

○ **Château des Alpilles** (St-Rémy-de-Provence, Provence; ✆ 04-90-92-03-33; www.chateaudesalpilles.com): The Pichot family built this château in 1827, and it has housed many famous personages, including Chateaubriand. The luxurious hotel, modestly referred to as "a house for paying friends," is a showcase of luxury, refinement, and taste. See p. 498.

○ **Château de la Vallée Bleue** (La Châtre, Massif Central; ✆ 02-54-31-01-91; www.chateauvalleebleue.com): If your room is named for Liszt, Chopin, Flaubert, or Delacroix, it's probably because they slept in the same spot. The château was built by a doctor committed to the well-being of his nearby patient George Sand, the author and feminist trendsetter whose masquerades as a man still provoke curiosity in this part of France. See p. 743.

THE best UPSCALE RESTAURANTS

○ **Restaurant Plaza Athénée** (Alain Ducasse; Paris; ✆ 01-53-67-65-00; www. alain-ducasse.com.): A coveted three-star rating from Michelin hardly seemed to challenge this brash chef. Ducasse is the darling of foodies and the spiritual heir of the legendary Escoffier. No one can outdo his pasta bathed in cream, sweetbreads, truffles, and (get this) the combs and kidneys of a proud, strutting cock. See p. 131.

○ **Le Grand Véfour** (Paris; ✆ 01-42-96-56-27; www.grand-vefour.com): Amid the arcades of the Palais Royal, this has been a dining spot since the reign of Louis XV, attracting such notables as Colette, Victor Hugo, and the forever-loyal Jean Cocteau. Jean Taittinger, of the champagne family, runs it today, and his kitchen brings originality to French classics—everything from pigeon in the style of Rainier of Monaco to French-roasted sole and sea scallops in velvety pumpkin sauce. See p. 124.

○ **Taillevent** (Paris; ✆ **01-44-95-15-01;** www.taillevent.com): Dining here is the social and gastronomic high point of a Paris visit. Its premises (an antique house near the Arc de Triomphe) are suitably grand, and its cuisine as appropriately stylish as the Jackie Onassis look-alikes who dine here. See p. 131.

○ **Les Crayères** (Reims, Champagne; ✆ **03-26-82-80-80;** www.lescrayeres.com): This restaurant's setting is a lavish but dignified château with soaring ceilings and French Empire decor. Built in 1904 as the home of the Pommery family (of champagne fortune) and surrounded by a 5.6-hectare (14-acre) park, it's maintained by a staff that appreciates the nuances of service rituals. You can retire directly to your room after consuming a bottle or two of the region's bubbly. See p. 358.

○ **A la Côte St-Jacques** (Joigny, Burgundy; ✆ **03-86-62-09-70;** www.cotesaint jacques.com): On the edge of Burgundy, beside the river Yonne, this is the quintessential *restaurant avec chambres.* Indulge your taste for well-prepared food and wine, and then totter off to one of the carefully furnished guest rooms in the historic compound. One of our favorite dishes is cassoulet of morels and frogs' legs, sublimely accompanied by a half bottle of red burgundy. See p. 405.

○ **L'Espérance** (Vézelay, Burgundy; ✆ **03-86-33-39-10;** www.marc-meneau-esperance.com): In a farmhouse at the base of a hill (La Colline de Vézelay) that has been a holy site for thousands of years, L'Espérance is run by one of Europe's most famous chefs, Marc Meneau, and his wife, Françoise. The place combines country comforts with great sophistication. See p. 407.

○ **Paul Bocuse** (Collonges-au-Mont-d'Or, near Lyon, Rhône Valley; ✆ **04-72-42-90-90;** www.bocuse.fr.): Bocuse was the *enfant terrible* of French gastronomy through most of his youth. Today he's the world's most famous chef, catering to Europe's hardest-to-please customers. The cuisine is ostensibly Lyonnais, but Bocuse has never been limited by provincialism, and his mind wanders the world for inspiration. His signature dishes range from pigeon in puff pastry with foie gras to his notable black truffle soup. See p. 434.

○ **La Maison Troisgros** (Roanne, Rhône Valley; ✆ **04-77-71-66-97;** www.troisgros. com): The setting is the dining room of a once-nondescript hotel near a train station. The cuisine is a celebration of the agrarian bounty of France. Mingling regional specialties, the menu attracts diners from as far away as Paris. See p. 439.

○ **Auberge du Père-Bise** (Talloires, French Alps; ✆ **04-50-60-72-01;** www. perebise.com): A mysterious alchemy transformed a simple lakeside chalet into an illustrious restaurant. Beside Lac d'Annecy in eastern France, it's outfitted like a provincial home of local gentry, yet it serves elegant food favored by generations of patrons, including the Rothschilds. See p. 458.

○ **Le Moulin de Mougins** (Mougins, Côte d'Azur; ✆ **04-93-75-78-24;** www. moulin-demougins.com): Occupying a 16th-century olive mill in a Provence forest, this long-celebrated destination is a showcase for Riviera foodies. The chef concocts what he calls the "cuisine of the sun," in celebration of sunny Provence. See p. 558.

THE best AFFORDABLE RESTAURANTS

- **Crémerie-Restaurant Polidor** (Paris; ☎ **01-43-26-95-34;** www.polidor.com): For many Parisians, the cuisine here evokes dinners their grandmothers might have cooked in the days after World War II. The unpretentious setting, with lace curtains filtering the sunlight, drew even such iconoclasts as André Gide. See p. 145.

- **Les Vapeurs** (Trouville, Normandy; ☎ **02-31-88-15-24;** www.lesvapeurs.fr): An anomaly among the Norman coast's high-priced brasseries, this restaurant overlooking the port is no-frills, from its Art Deco decor to its fresh, well-priced seafood. Patrons enjoy the festive ambience. See p. 304.

- **L'Auberge de Pélican** (Dinan, Brittany; ☎ **02-96-39-47-05**): Many visitors drive up from Paris for the day, followed by a dinner here in this old-fashioned Breton establishment, where even the bread is homemade. Dishes with an emphasis on fresh fish are based on time-honored recipes. See p. 329.

- **Brasserie de l'Ancienne Douane** (Strasbourg, Alsace-Lorraine; ☎ **03-88-15-78-78;** www.anciennedouane.fr): In a city known for its Alsatian cuisine, this restaurant is a front-runner in the moderate category. In a medieval building, you can feast on the sauerkraut and foie gras of the region, as well as on a succulent specialty, chicken in Riesling wine. See p. 379.

- **Au Chalet de Brou** (Bourg-en-Bresse, Rhône Valley; ☎ **04-74-22-26-28**): In a town famous for its poultry, this restaurant sits across from the village church. It offers the local birds at amazingly low prices, and food critics travel here from all over France for the hearty roast chicken. See p. 443.

- **Le Bistro Latin** (Aix-en-Provence, Provence; ☎ **04-42-38-22-88**): In Paul Cézanne's hometown, seek out its best and most affordable little bistro, serving classic Provençal cuisine in each of its two intimate dining rooms. Its fixed-price menus are the best deal in town. See p. 516.

- **Chez Servais** (Libourne, Bordeaux wine district; ☎ **05-57-51-83-97**): As you're touring the wine district outside Bordeaux, one of your finest and best-value meals is likely to be in this little market town at the junction of the Dordogne and Isle rivers. The cuisine is a savory blend of classical and modern. See p. 711.

FRANCE IN DEPTH

The civilization and history of France and the French way of life—the savoir-faire of its people—lures travelers from all over the world to this country that covers an area smaller than Texas.

You can get lost in France, lost in the sense that each region is so intriguing and varied that you may immerse yourself in one province for so long that you'll never have time to go on to see what's on the other side. France, often referred to as "the garden of Europe," is—perhaps more than any country in the world—a land to be savored. It's better to get to know intimately one, two, or three regions than trying to explore them all. This is not a country to rush through on one of those quick bus tours ("If it's Tuesday, it must be Nice"). It is ideally explored by car, allowing you to stop whenever and wherever you wish.

No European country, not even England, can beat France in its pageantry of personalities, from Madame de Pompadour to Charles de Gaulle, from Jean-Luc Godard to Françoise Hardy, from Catherine de Médicis to Joan of Arc, from Napoleon to Victor Hugo. You'll be introduced to some of these figures in the pages ahead. Seeing where they lived, worked, loved, and became legends is part of the experience of going to France.

This guide is meant to help you decide where to go in France, but ultimately the most gratifying experience will be your own serendipitous discovery of France—sunflowers, a picnic in a poppy field, an hour spent chatting with a small winemaker—whatever it is that stays in your memory for years to come.

FRANCE TODAY

France remains one of the world's most hyped and written-about destinations. It can inspire a masterpiece—and has on countless occasions. Even the cantankerous James McNeill Whistler would allow his masterpiece, a portrait of his mother, to hang in no other city save Paris.

Although not large by North American standards (about the size of the state of Texas, or of Britain and Germany combined), France is densely packed with attractions, both cultural and recreational. Even better, it's permeated with style and known for its *joie de vivre*.

Impressions

I tried to think it out. Why did Paris still draw us to its fascination, why did it draw those who felt themselves creative—talent or no talent? Why had it been, since Franklin, that all of us felt that we were freer there than elsewhere? Why did art, literature, and sex, and the feeding and drinking seem more genuine there? Generations of Americans had run a whole gamut of desires, hopes in Paris—all so opposite to those they had found at home, on the farm, in the city.
—Stephen Longstreet, *We All Went to Paris* (1972)

The French claim credit for developing the Gothic style of architecture and the cathedrals that stand as legacies of soaring stone for future generations. Creators of everything from palaces to subway stations have drawn at least some inspiration from designs inaugurated in France. However, despite the thrilling architectural monuments peppering the country's landscapes, it would be wrong to assume that the culture's main contribution to the world is derived from stone, mortar, stained glass, and gilt. Its contributions to painting, literature, cuisine, fashion, and savoir-faire are staggering.

When other parts of Europe were slumbering through the Dark Ages, Provence was alive with creativity as Provençal poetry evolved into a truly lyrical, evocative, and (in some cases) erotic verse form. Despite the frequent absences of its monarchs, who sequestered themselves with their entourages in remote Loire Valley châteaux, Renaissance Paris developed into one of Europe's most cosmopolitan cities, embellishing itself with majestic buildings and sculpture.

The passionate French tradition of scholarship helped build Europe's university system, synthesized the modern world's interpretation of human rights, helped topple one of the most powerful monarchies of all time, and justified the role of a post-revolutionary emperor (Napoleon) as conqueror of most of Europe.

As for style, it has always been foolhardy to try to compete with the French on their terms. The theatrical backdrops of the sometimes-silly Gallic monarchs have been interpreted by latter-day aesthetes as history's crowning achievement when it comes to conspicuous displays of wealth and prestige.

In politics and ideology, France has always been a leader and remains so today. Fueled by Enlightenment writings, whose most articulate voices were French, the 1789 Revolution toppled Europe's most deeply entrenched regime and cracked the foundations of dozens of other governments. After a period of murky maneuverings by diverse coalitions of strange bedfellows, post-revolutionary Paris became a magnet for the greatest talents of the 19th and early 20th centuries in many fields of endeavor.

Newcomers have commented (often adversely) on the cultural arrogance of the French. But despite its linguistic and cultural rigidity, France has received more immigrants and political exiles than any other European country. Part of this derives from France's status as one of Europe's least densely populated nations per square mile, and part of it from the tendency of the French to let others be until their actions become dangerous or obnoxious, not necessarily in that order.

France

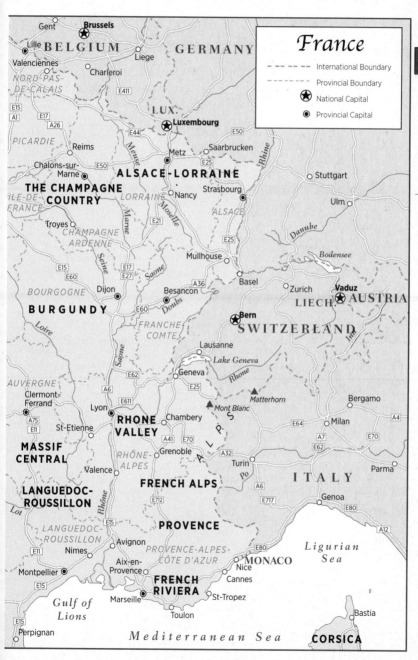

France

- – – – – – International Boundary
- ‑ ‑ ‑ ‑ ‑ Provincial Boundary
- ✪ National Capital
- ◉ Provincial Capital

Gent
Brussels
Lille
BELGIUM
GERMANY
Valenciennes
NORD-PAS-
DE-CALAIS
Charleroi
Liege
E411
E15
A1
E17
A26
LUX.
Luxembourg
E44
E50
PICARDIE
Reims
Saarbrucken
Meuse
Metz
E25
Chalons-sur-
Marne
E50
ALSACE-LORRAINE
Stuttgart
THE CHAMPAGNE
COUNTRY
LORRAINE
Nancy
Strasbourg
Rhine
ILE-DE-
FRANCE
Marne
E21
Moselle
ALSACE
Ulm
Troyes
CHAMPAGNE
ARDENNE
Seine
E17
E27
E25
Danube
Bodensee
E15
E60
Saone
Mullhouse
Basel
BOURGOGNE
Dijon
A36
Besancon
Zurich
Vaduz
LIECH.
AUSTRIA
BURGUNDY
E60
Doubs
Bern
Inn
Loire
FRANCHE-
COMTE
SWITZERLAND
Lausanne
Saone
Lake Geneva
AUVERGNE
E62
Geneva
Rhone
Clermont-
Ferrand
A6
E25
Bergamo
Lyon
E611
Matterhorn
Mont Blanc
A75
E11
RHONE
Chambery
E64
Milan
A4
St-Etienne
VALLEY
A
A41
E70
A7
E70
MASSIF
CENTRAL
RHONE-
ALPES
Grenoble
L
A32
E62
Valence
Rhone
Turin
P
Parma
LANGUEDOC-
ROUSSILLON
FRENCH ALPS
S
Po
ITALY
Lot
E712
A6
Genoa
LANGUEDOC-
ROUSSILLON
E15
PROVENCE
E717
E80
A12
Nimes
Avignon
PROVENCE-ALPES-
CÔTE D'AZUR
E80
Ligurian
Sea
E11
Aix-en-
Provence
Nice
MONACO
Montpellier
FRENCH
Cannes
E15
RIVIERA
St-Tropez
Gulf of
Lions
Marseille
Bastia
E15
Toulon
Perpignan
Mediterranean Sea
CORSICA

This guidebook represents our effort to introduce first-time visitors to France's subtle pleasures and—if possible—to open new doors to those who might have already spent time here. We've set for ourselves the formidable task of seeking out France at its finest and condensing that information so you can access it easily. But the best need not always be the most expensive or the most chic or the most widely publicized.

If you're a first-timer, everything in Paris, of course, is new. But if you've been away for a long time, expect changes. Taxi drivers may no longer correct your fractured French, but address you in English—and that's tantamount to a revolution. More Parisians have a rudimentary knowledge of English, and the country, at least at first glance, seems less hysterically xenophobic than in past years. Part of this derives from Parisians' interest in music, videos, and films from foreign countries, and part from France's growing awareness of its role within a united Europe.

Yet France has never been more concerned about the loss of its unique identity within a landscape that has attracted an increasing number of immigrants from its former colonies. Many have expressed the legitimate concern that France will continue to lose the battle to keep its language strong, distinct, and unadulterated by foreign slang or catchwords. But as the country moves deeper into the millennium, foreign tourists spending much-needed cash are no longer perceived as foes or antagonists. *Au contraire:* The rancor of France's collective xenophobia has been increasingly redirected toward the many immigrants seeking better lives in Paris, where the infrastructure has nearly been stretched to its limits.

LOOKING BACK AT FRANCE

EARLY GAUL   When the ancient Romans considered France part of their empire, their boundaries extended deep into the forests of the Paris basin and up to the edges of the Rhine. Part of Julius Caesar's early reputation came from his defeat of King Vercingetorix at Alésia in 52 B.C., a victory he was quick to publicize in one of the ancient world's literary masterpieces, *The Gallic Wars.* In that year the Roman colony of Lutetia (Paris) was established on an island in the Seine (Ile de la Cité).

As the Roman Empire declined, its armies retreated to the flourishing colonies that had been established along a strip of the Mediterranean coast—among others, these included Orange, Montpellier, Nîmes, Narbonne, and Marseille, which retain some of the best Roman monuments in Europe.

As one of their legacies, the Roman armies left behind the Catholic church, which, for all its abuses, was the only real guardian of civilization during the anarchy following the Roman decline. A form of low Latin was the common language, and it slowly evolved into the archaic French that both delights and confuses today's medieval scholars.

The form of Christianity adopted by many of the chieftains was viewed as heretical by Rome. Consequently, when Clovis (king of northeastern Gaul's Franks and founder of the Merovingian dynasty) astutely converted to Catholicism, he won the approval of the pope, the political support of the powerful archbishop of Reims, and the loyalty of the many Gallic tribes who'd grown disenchanted with anarchy. (Clovis's baptism is viewed as the beginning of a collusion between the Catholic church and the French monarchy that flourished until the 1789 Revolution.) At the Battle of Soissons in 486, Clovis defeated the last vestiges of Roman power in Gaul. Other conquests that followed included expansions westward to the Seine, then to the Loire. After a battle in Dijon in 500, he became the nominal overlord of the king of Burgundy. Seven years later his armies drove the Visigoths into Spain, giving most of Aquitaine, in western France, to his newly founded Merovingian dynasty. Trying to make the best of an earlier humiliation, Anastasius, the Byzantium-based emperor of the Eastern Roman Empire, finally gave the kingdom of the Franks his legal sanction.

After Clovis's death in 511, his kingdom was split among his squabbling heirs. The Merovingian dynasty, however, managed to survive in fragmented form for another 250 years. During this period, the power of the bishops and the great lords grew, firmly entrenching the complex hierarchies and preoccupations of what we today know as feudalism. Although apologists for the Merovingians are quick to point out their achievements, the feudalistic quasi-anarchy of their tenuous reign has been (not altogether unfairly) identified by many historians as the Dark Ages.

THE CAROLINGIANS   From the wreckage of the intrigue-ridden Merovingian court emerged a new dynasty: the Carolingians. One of their leaders, Charles Martel, halted a Muslim invasion of northern Europe at Tours in 743 and left a much-expanded kingdom to his son, Pepin. The Carolingian empire eventually stretched from the Pyrénées to a point deep in the German forests, encompassing much of modern France, Germany, and northern Italy. The heir to this vast land was Charlemagne. Crowned emperor in Rome on Christmas Day in 800, he returned to his capital at Aix-la-Chapelle (Aachen) and created the Holy Roman Empire. Charlemagne's rule saw a revived interest in scholarship, art, and classical texts, defined by scholars as the Carolingian Renaissance.

Despite Charlemagne's magnetism, cultural rifts formed in his sprawling empire, most of which was eventually divided between two of his three squabbling heirs. Charles of Aquitaine annexed the western region; Louis of Bavaria took the east. Historians credit this division with the development of modern France and Germany as separate nations. Shortly after Charlemagne's death, his fragmented empire was invaded by Vikings from the north, Muslim Saracens from the south, and Hungarians from the east.

THE MIDDLE AGES   When the Carolingian dynasty died out in 987, Hugh Capet, comte de Paris and duc de France, officially began the Middle Ages with the establishment of the Capetian dynasty. In 1154, the annulment of Eleanor of Aquitaine's marriage to Louis VII of France and subsequent marriage to Henry II of England placed the western half of France under English control, and vestiges of their power remained for centuries. Meanwhile, vast forests and swamps were cleared for harvesting (often by the Middle Ages' hardest-working ascetics, Cistercian monks), the population grew, great Gothic cathedrals were begun, and monastic life contributed to every level of a rapidly developing social order. Politically driven marriages among the ruling families more than doubled the size of the territory controlled from Paris, a city that was increasingly recognized as the country's capital. Philippe II (reigned 1179–1223) infiltrated more prominent families with his genes than anyone else in France, successfully marrying members of his family into the Valois, Artois, and Vermandois. He also managed to win Normandy and Anjou back from the English.

Louis IX (St. Louis) emerged as the 13th century's most memorable king, though he ceded most of the hard-earned military conquests of his predecessors back to the English. Somewhat of a religious fanatic, he died of illness (along with most of his army) in 1270 in a boat anchored off Tunis. The vainglorious and not-very-wise pretext for his trip was the Eighth Crusade. At the time of his death, Notre-Dame and the Sainte-Chapelle in Paris had been completed, and the arts of tapestry making and stonecutting were flourishing.

During the 1300s, the struggle of French sovereignty against the claims of a rapacious Roman pope tempted Philip the Fair to encourage support for a pope based in Avignon. (The Roman pope, Boniface VIII, whom Philip publicly insulted and then assaulted in his home, is said to have died of the shock.) During one of medieval history's most bizarre episodes, two popes ruled simultaneously, one from Rome and one from Avignon. They competed fiercely for the spiritual and fiscal control of Christendom, until years of political intrigue turned the tables in favor of Rome and Avignon relinquished its claim in 1378.

The 14th century saw an increase in the wealth and power of the French kings, an increase in the general prosperity, and a decrease in the power of the feudal lords. The death of Louis X without an heir in 1316 prompted more than a decade of scheming and plotting before the eventual emergence of the Valois dynasty.

The Black Death began in the summer of 1348, killing an estimated 33% of Europe's population, decimating the population of Paris, and setting the stage for the exodus of the French monarchs to safer climes in such places as the Loire Valley. A financial crisis, coupled with a series of ruinous harvests, almost bankrupted the nation.

During the Hundred Years' War, the English made sweeping inroads into France in an attempt to grab the throne. At their most powerful, they controlled almost all the north (Picardy and Normandy), Champagne, parts of the Loire Valley, and the huge western region called Guyenne. The peasant-born charismatic visionary Joan of Arc rallied the dispirited French troops as well as the timid dauphin (crown prince), whom she managed to have crowned as Charles VII in the cathedral at Reims. As threatening to the Catholic church as she was to the English, she was declared a heretic and burned at the stake in Rouen in 1431. Led by the newly crowned king, a barely cohesive France initiated reforms that strengthened its finances and vigor. After compromises among the quarreling factions, the French army drove the discontented English out, leaving them only the Norman port of Calais.

In the late 1400s, Charles VIII married Brittany's last duchess, Anne, for a unification of France with its Celtic-speaking western outpost. In the early 1500s, the endlessly fascinating François I, through war and diplomacy, strengthened the monarchy, rid it of its dependence on Italian bankers, coped with the intricate policies of the Renaissance, and husbanded the arts into a form of patronage that French monarchs continued to endorse for centuries.

Meanwhile, the growth of Protestantism and the unwillingness of the Catholic church to tolerate it led to civil strife. In 1572, Catherine de Médicis reversed her policy of religious tolerance and ordered the St. Bartholomew's Day Massacre of hundreds of Protestants. Henri IV, tired of the bloodshed and fearful that a fanatically Catholic Spain would meddle in the religious conflicts, converted to Catholicism as a compromise in 1593. Just before being fatally stabbed by a half-crazed monk, he issued the Edict of Nantes in 1598, granting freedom of religion to Protestants in France.

THE PASSING OF FEUDALISM   By now France was a modern state, rid of all but a few of the vestiges of feudalism. In 1624, Louis XIII appointed a Catholic cardinal, the duc de Richelieu, his chief minister. Amassing enormous power, Richelieu virtually ruled the country until his death in 1642. His sole objective was investing the monarchy with total power—he committed a series of truly horrible acts trying to attain this goal and paved the way for the eventual absolutism of Louis XIV.

Although he ascended the throne when he was only 9, with the help of his Sicilian-born chief minister, Cardinal Mazarin, Louis XIV was the most powerful monarch Europe had seen since the Roman emperors. Through first a brilliant military campaign against Spain and then a judicious marriage to one of its royal daughters, he expanded France to include the southern provinces of Artois and Roussillon. Later, a series of diplomatic and military victories along the Flemish border expanded the country toward the north and east. The estimated population of France at this time was 20 million, as opposed to eight million in England and six million in Spain. French colonies in Canada, the West Indies, and America (Louisiana) were stronger than ever. The mercantilism that Louis's brilliant finance minister, Colbert, implemented was one of the era's most important fiscal policies, hugely increasing France's power and wealth. The arts flourished, as did a sense of aristocratic style that's remembered with a bittersweet nostalgia today. Louis's palace of Versailles is the perfect monument to the most flamboyantly consumptive era in French history.

Louis's territorial ambitions so deeply threatened the other nations of Europe that, led by William of Orange, they united to hold him in check. France entered a series of expensive and demoralizing wars that, coupled with high taxes and bad harvests, stirred up much civil discontent. England was viewed as a threat both within Europe and in the global rush for lucrative colonies. The great Atlantic ports, especially Bordeaux, grew and prospered because of France's success in the West Indian slave and sugar trades. Despite the country's power, the total number of French colonies diminished thanks to the naval power of the English. The rise of Prussia as a militaristic neighbor posed an additional problem.

THE REVOLUTION & THE RISE OF NAPOLEON   Meanwhile, the Enlightenment was training a new generation of thinkers for the struggle against absolutism, religious fanaticism, and superstition. Europe was never the same after the Revolution of 1789, though the ideas that engendered it had been brewing for more than 50 years. On August 10, 1792, troops from Marseille, aided by a Parisian mob, threw the dimwitted Louis XVI and his tactless Austrian-born queen, Marie Antoinette, into prison. After months of bloodshed and bickering among violently competing factions, the two thoroughly humiliated monarchs were executed.

France's problems got worse before they got better. In the ensuing bloodbaths, both moderates and radicals were guillotined in full view of a bloodthirsty crowd that included voyeurs like Dickens's Mme. Defarge, who brought her knitting every day to place de la Révolution (later renamed place de la Concorde) to watch the beheadings. The drama surrounding the collapse of the *ancien régime* and the beheadings of Robespierre's Reign of Terror provides the most heroic and horrible anecdotes in the history of France. From all this emerged the Declaration of the Rights of Man, an enlightened document published in 1789; its influence has been cited as a model of democratic ideals ever since. The implications of the collapse of the French aristocracy shook the foundations of every monarchy in Europe.

Only the militaristic fervor of Napoleon Bonaparte could reunite France and bring an end to the revolutionary chaos. A political and military genius who appeared on the landscape at a time when the French were thoroughly sickened by the anarchy following their revolution, he restored a national pride that had been severely tarnished. He also established a bureaucracy and a code of law that has been emulated in other legal systems around the world. In 1799, at the age of 30, he entered Paris and was crowned first consul and master of France. Soon after, a decisive victory in his northern Italian campaign solidified his power at home. A brilliant politician, he made peace through a compromise with the Vatican, quelling the atheistic spirit of the earliest days of the Revolution.

Napoleon's victories made him the envy of Europe. Beethoven dedicated his Eroica symphony to Napoleon—but later retracted the dedication when Napoleon committed what Beethoven considered atrocities. Just as he was poised on the verge of conquering all Europe, Napoleon's famous retreat from Moscow during the winter of 1812 reduced his formerly invincible army to tatters, as 400,000 Frenchmen died in the Russian snows. Napoleon was then defeated at Waterloo by the combined armies of the English, Dutch, and Prussians. Exiled to the British-held island of St. Helena in the South Atlantic, he died in 1821, probably the victim of an unknown poisoner.

THE BOURBONS & THE SECOND EMPIRE   In 1814, following the destruction of Napoleon and his dream, the Congress of Vienna redefined the map of Europe. The new geography was an approximation of the boundaries that had existed in 1792. The Bourbon monarchy was reestablished, with reduced powers for Louis XVIII, an archconservative, and a changing array of leaders who included the prince de Polignac and, later, Charles X. A renewal of the *ancien régime's* oppressions, however, didn't sit well in a France that had already spilled so much blood in favor of egalitarian causes.

In 1830, after censoring the press and dissolving Parliament, Louis XVIII was removed from power after yet more violent uprisings. Louis-Philippe, duc d'Orléans, was elected king under a liberalized constitution. His reign lasted for 18 years of calm prosperity during which England and France more or less collaborated on matters of foreign policy. The establishment of an independent Belgium and the French conquest of Algeria (1840–47) were to have resounding effects on French politics a century later. It was a time of wealth, grace, and expansion of the arts for most French people, though the industrialization of the north and east produced some of the 19th century's most horrific poverty.

A revolution in 1848, fueled by a financial crash and disgruntled workers in Paris, forced Louis-Philippe out of office. That year, Napoleon I's nephew, Napoleon III, was elected president. Appealing to the property-protecting instinct of a nation that hadn't forgotten the violent upheavals of less than a century before, he initiated a repressive right-wing government in which he was awarded the totalitarian status of emperor in 1851. Rebounding from the punishment they'd received during the revolution and the minor role they'd played during the First Empire, the Second Empire's clergy enjoyed great power. Steel production was begun, and a railway system and Indochinese colonies were established. New technologies fostered new kinds of industry, and the bourgeoisie flourished. And the baron Georges-Eugène Haussmann radically altered Paris by laying out the grand boulevards the world knows today.

By 1866, an industrialized France began to see the Second Empire as more of a hindrance than an encouragement to its expansion. The dismal failure of colonizing Mexico and the increasing power of Austria and Prussia were setbacks to the empire's prestige. In 1870, the Prussians defeated Napoleon III at Sedan and held him prisoner with 100,000 of his soldiers. Paris was besieged by an enemy who only just failed to march its vastly superior armies through the capital.

After the Prussians withdrew, a violent revolt ushered in the Third Republic and its elected president, Marshal MacMahon, in 1873. Peace and prosperity slowly returned, France regained its glamour, a mania of building occurred, the Impressionists made their visual statements, and writers like Flaubert redefined the French novel into what today is regarded as the most evocative in the world. As if as a symbol of this period, the Eiffel Tower was built as part of the 1889 Universal Exposition.

By 1890, a new corps of satirists (including Zola) had exposed the country's wretched living conditions, the cruelty of the country's vested interests, and the underlying hypocrisy of late-19th-century French society. The 1894 Dreyfus Affair exposed the corruption of French army officers who had destroyed the career and reputation of a Jewish colleague (Albert Dreyfus), falsely and deliberately punished—as a scapegoat—for treason. The ethnic tensions identified by Zola led to further divisiveness in the rest of the 20th century.

THE WORLD WARS International rivalries, thwarted colonial ambitions, and conflicting alliances led to World War I, which, after decisive German victories for 2 years, degenerated into the mud-slogged horror of trench warfare. Mourning between four and five million casualties, Europe was inflicted with psychological scars that never healed. In 1917, the United States broke the European deadlock by entering the war.

After the Allied victory, grave economic problems, plus the demoralization stemming from years of fighting, encouraged the growth of socialism and communism. The French government, led by a vindictive Georges Clemenceau, demanded every centime of reparations it could wring from a crushed Germany. The humiliation associated with this has often been cited as the origin of the German nation's almost obsessive determination to rise from the ashes of 1918 to a place in the sun.

The worldwide Great Depression had devastating repercussions in France. Poverty and widespread bankruptcies weakened the Third Republic to the point where successive coalition governments rose and fell with alarming regularity. The crises reached a crescendo on June 14, 1940, when Hitler's armies arrogantly marched down the Champs-Elysées, and newsreel cameras recorded French people openly weeping. Under the terms of the armistice, the north of France was occupied by the Nazis, and a puppet French government was established at Vichy under the authority of Marshal Pétain. The immediate collapse of the French army is viewed as one of the most significant humiliations in modern French history.

Pétain and his regime cooperated with the Nazis in unbearably shameful ways. Not the least of their errors included the deportation of more than 75,000 French Jews to German work camps. Pockets of resistance fighters (*le maquis*) waged small-scale guerrilla attacks against the Nazis throughout the course of the war and free-French forces continued to fight along with the Allies on battlegrounds like North Africa. Charles de Gaulle, the irascible giant whose personality is forever associated with the politics of his era, established himself as the head of the French government-in-exile, operating first from London and then from Algiers.

The scenario was radically altered on June 6, 1944, when the largest armada in history successfully established a bulkhead on the beaches of Normandy. Paris rose in rebellion even before the Allied armies arrived, and on August 26, 1944, Charles de Gaulle entered the capital as head of the government. The Fourth Republic was declared even as pockets of Nazi snipers continued to shoot from scattered rooftops throughout the city.

THE POSTWAR YEARS Plagued by the bitter residue of colonial policies that France had established during the 18th and 19th centuries, the Fourth Republic witnessed the rise and fall of 22 governments and 17 premiers. Many French soldiers died on foreign battlefields as once-profitable colonies in North Africa and Indochina rebelled. It took 80,000 French lives, for example, to put down a revolt in Madagascar. After suffering a bitter defeat in 1954, France ended the war in Indochina and freed its former colony. It also granted internal self-rule to Tunisia and (under slightly different circumstances) Morocco.

Algeria was to remain a greater problem. The advent of the 1958 Algerian revolution signaled the end of the much-maligned Fourth Republic. De Gaulle was called back from retirement to initiate a new constitution, the Fifth Republic, with a stronger set of executive controls. To nearly everyone's dissatisfaction, de Gaulle ended the Algerian war in 1962 by granting the country full independence. Screams of protest resounded long and loud, but the sun had set on most of France's far-flung empire. Internal disruption followed as vast numbers of *pieds-noirs* (French-born residents of Algeria recently stripped of their lands) flooded back into metropolitan France, often into makeshift refugee camps in Provence and Languedoc.

> ## Impressions
>
> *Paris is a sphinx. I will drag her secret from her.*
> —Mirabeau

In 1968, major social unrest and a violent coalition hastily formed between the nation's students and blue-collar workers eventually led to the collapse of the government. De Gaulle resigned when his attempts to placate some of the marchers were defeated. The reins of power passed to his second-in-command, Georges Pompidou, and his successor, Valérie Giscard d'Estaing, both of whom continued de Gaulle's policies emphasizing economic development and protection of France as a cultural resource to the world.

THE 1980S & 1990S In 1981, François Mitterrand was elected the first Socialist president of France since World War II (with a close vote of 51%). In almost immediate response, many wealthy French decided to transfer their assets out of the country, much to the delight of banks in Geneva, Monaco, the Cayman Islands, and Vienna. Though reviled by the rich and ridiculed for personal mannerisms that often seemed inspired by Louis XIV, Mitterrand was reelected in 1988. During his two terms he spent billions of francs on his *grands projets* (like the Louvre pyramid, Opéra Bastille, Cité de la Musique, and Grande Arche de La Défense), some of which are now beginning to fall apart or reveal serious weaknesses.

In 1992, France played a leading role in the development of the European Union (E.U.), 15 countries that will ultimately abolish all trade barriers among themselves and share a single currency, the euro. More recent developments include France's interest in developing a central European bank for the regulation of a shared intra-European currency, a ruling that some politicians have interpreted as another block in the foundation of a united Europe.

In April 1993, voters dumped the Socialists and installed a new conservative government. Polls cited corruption scandals, rising unemployment, and urban insecurity as reasons for this. The Conservative premier Edouard Balladur had to "cohabit" the government with Mitterrand, whom he blamed for the country's growing economic problems. Diagnosed with terminal prostate cancer near the end of his second term, Mitterrand continued to represent France with dignity, despite his deterioration. The battle over who would succeed him was waged against Balladur with epic rancor by Jacques Chirac, tenacious survivor of many terms as mayor of Paris. Their public discord was among the most venomous since the days of Pétain.

On his third try, on May 7, 1995, Chirac won the presidency with 52% of the vote and immediately declared war on unemployment. Mitterrand turned over the reins of government on May 17 and died shortly thereafter. But Chirac's popularity soon faded in the wake of unrest caused by an 11.5% unemployment rate, a barrage of terrorist attacks by Algerian Muslims, and a stressed economy struggling to meet European Union entry requirements.

A wave of terrorist attacks from July to September 1995 brought an unfamiliar wariness to Paris. Six bombs were planted, killing 7 people and injuring 115. In light of this, Parisians proved cautious if not fearful. Algerian Islamic militants, the suspected culprits, may have brought military guards to the Eiffel Tower, but they failed to throw France into panic.

Throughout 1995 and early 1996, France infuriated everyone from the members of Greenpeace to the governments of Australia and New Zealand by resuming its long-dormant policy of exploding nuclear bombs on isolated Pacific atolls for testing purposes. This policy continued until public outcry, both in France and outside its borders, exerted massive pressure to end the tests.

In May 1996, thousands of Parisian workers took to the streets, disrupting passenger train service to demand a workweek shorter than the usual 39 hours. They felt that this move would help France's staggering unemployment figures. Employer organizations resisted this idea, claiming that even if the workweek were cut to 35 hours, businesses wouldn't be able to take on many new employees.

The drama of 1996 climaxed with the heat of the summer, when the police took axes to the doors of the Paris church of St-Bernard de la Chapelle. Nearly 300 African immigrants were removed by force from this place of refuge and deported. Strikes and protests continued to plague the country, and Chirac's political horizon became dimmer still—with a 12% unemployment rate and crime on an alarming increase. Terrorist scares continued to flood the borders of France throughout 1997, forcing a highly visible armed police force, as part of a nationwide program known as Vigipirate, to take to the streets of major cities. One of the unusual offshoots of the Vigipirate program involved the closing of the crypts of many of France's medieval churches to visitors, partly in fear of a terrorist bomb attack on national historic treasures.

In the latest power struggle between the Conservatives and the Socialists, in the spring of 1998, Conservatives were ousted in a majority of France's regional provinces, amounting to a powerful endorsement for Prime Minister Lionel Jospin's Socialist-led government.

In 1999, France joined with other European countries in adopting the euro as its standard of currency. The new currency accelerated the creation of a single economy comprising nearly 300 million Europeans, with a combined gross national product approaching 9€ trillion, larger than that of the United States.

France moved into the millennium by testing the practicality of new and progressive social legislation. On October 13, 1999, the French Parliament passed a new law giving legal status to unmarried couples, including homosexual unions. The law allows couples of same sex or not to enter into a union and be entitled to the same rights as married couples in such areas as housing, inheritance, income tax, and social welfare.

THE NEW MILLENNIUM   In February 2005, President George W. Bush flew to Europe to mend fences with some of his worst critics, notably French President Chirac. The two political foes found common ground on such issues as Syria and Lebanon, but Iraq remained a thorny problem. Chirac, a self-styled expert on cows after serving as a former agriculture minister, was not invited to Bush's Texas ranch. When asked why not, Bush enigmatically said, "I'm looking for a good cowboy."

> **Impressions**
>
> *Paris (in each shape and gesture and avenue and cranny of her being) was continuously expressing the humanness of humanity. Everywhere I sensed a miraculous presence, not of mere children and women and men, but of living human beings.*
>
> —e e cummings

Late in 2005, decades of pent-up resentment felt by the children of African immigrants exploded into an orgy of violence and vandalism. Riots began in the suburbs of Paris and spread around the country. Throughout France, gangs of youths battled the French police, torched schools, cars, and businesses, and even attacked commuter trains. Rioting followed in such cities as Dijon, Marseille, and Rouen. Most of the rioters were the sons of Arab and black African immigrants, Muslims living in a mostly Catholic country. The reason for the protests? Leaders of the riots claimed they live "like second-class citizens," even though they are French citizens. Unemployment is 30% higher in the ethnic ghettos of France.

In spring 2006, Jacques Chirac signed a law that made it easier for employers to fire workers, which set off massive demonstrations across France. Some one million protesters staged marches and strikes against the law, which was rescinded on April 10, 2006.

Against a backdrop of discontent regarding issues of unemployment, immigration, and healthcare, the charismatic Nicolas Sarkozy swept into the presidential office in May 2007. It remains to be seen whether his campaign promises to break from "politics as usual" translate into real change, especially for many of France's disenchanted youths.

Sarkozy, the combative son of a Hungarian immigrant, promised to reinvigorate ties with France's traditional ally, the United States. His election was followed by scattered violence throughout the country from anti-Sarkozy protesters. In 2005 he'd called rioters in Paris's immigrant-heavy suburbs "scum," which was blamed for the country's worst violence in 4 decades. Sarkozy has promised to be president of "all the French" during his administration.

In all this muddle, Sarkozy found time to divorce a wife and take a beautiful new bride. A glamorous model-turned-singer, the sexy Carla Bruni is the new first lady of France. "The Carla effect," as it's called in Paris, has decreased Sarkozy's popularity—that, and his failure to revive France's ailing economy. The tabloids have had a field day with the first lady, whose former lovers include Mick Jagger, Eric Clapton, Donald Trump, even Laurent Fabius (a former French prime minister).

Beginning in 2008, a smoking ban in public places came into law throughout Paris and France in general. French authorities estimate that passive smoking kills about 13 people a day in France and ruled the situation unacceptable. Public places include transport stations, museums, government offices, and shops but not streets or private places such as houses or hotel rooms. Those found in breach of the ban will be fined.

Many of the French became uncertain of their future as a European Union member in 2010. The financial instability in Greece, and the continuing woes of debt-ridden Ireland, Italy, Spain, and Portugal, contributed to the drop in the euro's value.

ART & ARCHITECTURE
Art

France's art treasures range from medieval stained glass and Ingres portraits to Monet's Impressionist *Water Lilies;* its architecture encompasses Roman ruins and Gothic cathedrals as well as Renaissance châteaux and postmodern buildings like the Centre Pompidou. This brief overview will help you make sense of it all.

PREHISTORIC, CELTIC & CLASSICAL (25,000 B.C.–A.D. 500)
After England's Stonehenge, Europe's most famous prehistoric remains are France's **Paleolithic cave paintings.** Created 15,000 to 20,000 years ago, they depict mostly hunting scenes and abstract shapes.

The **caves at Lascaux,** the Sistine Chapel of prehistoric art, have been closed since 1963, but experts have created a replica, Lascaux II. To see the real stuff, visit **Les Eyzies-de-Tayac,** which boasts four caves (Font de Gaume is the best). In the neighboring Lot Valley, outside Cahors, is the **Grotte du Pech-Merle,** with France's oldest cave art (about 20,000 years old). Little remains of the art of **Celtic** (ca. 1000 B.C.–A.D. 125) and **Roman** (A.D. 125–500) Gaul. Surviving items—small votive bronzes, statues, jewelry, and engraved weapons and tools—are spread across France's **archaeology museums.** Burgundy preserves the most of Celtic Gaul, including sites at **Dijon, Châtillon-sur-Seine, Alise-Ste-Reine,** and **Auxerre.** To see artifacts of Roman Gaul, visit the southern towns of **Nîmes, Arles, Orange, St-Rémy-de-Provence,** and **Vienne.**

ROMANESQUE (900–1100)
Artistic expression in medieval France was largely church-related. Because Mass was in Latin, images were used to communicate the Bible's lessons to the mostly

illiterate people. **Bas-reliefs** (sculptures that project slightly from a flat surface) were used to illustrate key tales that inspired faith in God and fear of sin (the *Last Judgment* was a favorite). These reliefs were wrapped around column capitals and fitted into the **tympanums,** or arched spaces above doorways (the complete door, tympanum, arch, and supporting pillars assemblage is the **portal**).

The best examples of Romanesque art include a *Last Judgment* tympanum by Gislebertus at **St-Lazare** in Autun; 76 Romanesque cloister capitals and one of France's best-carved 11th-century portals at **St-Pierre Abbey** in Moissac near Montauban; and the tympanum over the inner main portal of huge **Ste-Madeleine** in Vézelay. The **Bayeux Tapestry** (1066–77) is the most notable example of Romanesque artistry, 69m (230 ft.) of embroidered linen telling the story of William the Conqueror's defeat of the English.

GOTHIC (1100–1400)

Paris retains almost no art from the classical or Romanesque eras, but much remains from the medieval Gothic era, when artists created sculpture and stained glass for churches.

Outstanding examples include the **Cathédrale de Chartres** (1194–1220), a day trip from Paris, boasting magnificent sculpture and some of the best stained glass in Europe; the **Cathédrale de Notre-Dame** (1163–1250), with sculpture on the facade, an interior choir screen lined with deep-relief carvings, and three rose windows filled with stained glass; and **Sainte-Chapelle** (1240–50), a tiny chapel adorned with the finest stained glass in the world.

THE RENAISSANCE & BAROQUE (1450–1800)

Humanist thinkers rediscovered the wisdom of ancient Greece and Rome, while artists strove for naturalism, using newly developed techniques like linear perspective. The French had little to do with this movement, which started in Italy and was picked up only in Germany and the Low Countries. However, many Renaissance treasures are in French museums, thanks to collectors such as **François I.**

Not until the 17th-century **baroque** did a few French masters emerge. This period is hard to pin down. In some ways a result of the Catholic Counter-Reformation, it reaffirmed spirituality in a simplified, monumental, and religious version of Renaissance ideals. In other ways, it delved even deeper into classical modes and a kind of super-realism based on using peasants as models and the *chiaroscuro* (contrast of light and dark) of the Italian painter Caravaggio.

Paris's **Louvre** abounds with Renaissance works by Italian, Flemish, and German masters, including **Michelangelo** (1475–1564) and **Leonardo da Vinci** (1452–1519). Leonardo's *Mona Lisa* (1503–05), perhaps the world's most famous painting, hangs there. Great baroque and rococo artists include **Antoine Watteau** (1684–1721), a rococo painter of colorful, theatrical works; and **Jean-Honoré Fragonard** (1732–1806), a master of rococo pastel scenes, including the famous *The Bathers*.

NEOCLASSICAL & ROMANTIC (1770–1890)

As the baroque got excessive, the rococo got cute, and the somber Counter-Reformation got serious about the limits on religious art, several artists looked to the ancients for relief. This gave rise to a **neoclassical** artistic style that emphasized symmetry, austerity, clean lines, and classical themes.

The **romantics,** on the other hand, felt that both the ancients and the Renaissance had gotten it wrong and that the Middle Ages was the place to be. They idealized romantic tales of chivalry and the nobility of peasantry.

Some great artists and movements of the era, all with examples in the **Louvre,** include **Jean Ingres** (1780–1867), who became a defender of the neoclassicists and the Royal French Academy and opposed the romantics; **Theodore Géricault** (1791–1824), one of the great early romantics, who painted *The Raft of the Medusa* (1819), which served as a model for the movement; and **Eugène Delacroix** (1798–1863), whose *Liberty Leading the People* (1830) was painted in the romantic style.

IMPRESSIONISM (1870–1920)

Seeking to capture the *impression* (light made as it reflected off objects), the Impressionists adopted a free, open style; deceptively loose compositions; swift, visible brushwork; and often light colors. For subject matter, they turned to landscapes and scenes of modern life. You'll find some of the best examples of their works in the **Musée d'Orsay.**

Impressionist greats include **Edouard Manet** (1832–1883), whose groundbreaking *Picnic on the Grass* (1863) and *Olympia* (1863) helped inspire the movement with their harsh realism, visible brush strokes, and thick outlines; **Claude Monet** (1840–1926), who launched the movement officially in an 1874 exhibition in which he exhibited his Turner-inspired *Impression, Sunrise* (1874), now in the **Musée Marmottan; Pierre-Auguste Renoir** (1841–1919), known for his figures' ivory skin and chubby pink cheeks; **Edgar Degas** (1834–1917), an accomplished painter, sculptor, and draftsman—his pastels of dancers and bathers are particularly memorable; and **Auguste Rodin** (1840–1917), the greatest Impressionist-era sculptor, who crafted remarkably expressive bronzes. The **Musée Rodin,** his former Paris studio, contains, among other works, his *Burghers of Calais* (1886), *The Kiss* (1886–98), and *The Thinker* (1880).

POST-IMPRESSIONISM (1880–1930)

The smaller movements or styles of Impressionism are usually lumped together as "post-Impressionism." Again, you'll find the best examples of these works at the **Musée d'Orsay,** though you'll find pieces by Matisse, Chagall, and the cubists, including Picasso, in the **Centre Pompidou.** Important post-Impressionists include **Paul Cézanne** (1839–1906), who adopted the short brush strokes, love of landscape, and light color palette of his Impressionist friends; **Paul Gauguin** (1848–1903), who developed **synthetism** (black outlines around solid colors); **Henri de Toulouse-Lautrec** (1864–1901), who created paintings and posters of wispy, fluid lines anticipating Art Nouveau and often depicting the bohemian life of Paris's dance halls and cafes; **Vincent van Gogh** (1853–90), who combined divisionism, synthetism, and a touch of Japanese influence, and painted with thick, short strokes; **Henri Matisse** (1869–1954), who created **fauvism** (a critic described those who used the style as *fauves,* meaning "wild beasts"); and **Pablo Picasso** (1881–1973), a Málaga-born artist who painted objects from all points of view at once, rather than using such optical tricks as perspective to fool viewers into seeing three dimensions. The fractured result was **cubism.** You can see art from all of his periods at the **Musée Picasso** in the Marais.

Church Floor Plan

Architecture

It's worth pointing out that very few buildings (especially churches) were built in one particular architectural style. These massive, expensive structures often took centuries to complete, during which time tastes would change and plans would be altered.

ANCIENT ROMAN (125 B.C.–A.D. 450)

Provence was Rome's first transalpine conquest, and the legions of Julius Caesar quickly subdued the Celtic tribes across France, converting it into Roman Gaul.

Nîmes preserves from the 1st century B.C. a 20,000-seat **amphitheater,** a **Corinthian temple** called the "Square House," a fine **archaeology museum,** and the astounding **pont du Gard,** a 47m-long (158-ft.), three-story aqueduct made of cut stones fitted together without mortar.

Pont du Gard, Nîmes

ROMANESQUE (800–1100)

The Romanesque style took its inspiration from ancient Rome (hence the name). Early Christians in Italy had adapted the basilica (ancient Roman law-court buildings) to become churches.

The **Cathédrale St-Bénigne** in Dijon was the first French Romanesque church, but of that era only the crypt remains. The **Cathédrale St-Pierre** in Angoulême has a single large nave, a rounded apse with small radiating chapels, and a pair of transept mini-apses.

GOTHIC (1100–1500)

By the 12th century, engineering developments freed church architecture from the heavy, thick walls of Romanesque structures and allowed ceilings to soar, walls to thin, and windows to proliferate. Gothic interiors enticed churchgoers' gazes upward to high ceilings filled with light. Graceful buttresses and spires soared above town centers.

The best examples in and around Paris of the Gothic are **Basilique St-Denis** (1140–44), the world's first Gothic cathedral, in a Paris suburb; **Cathédrale de Chartres** (1194–1220), a Gothic masterpiece with some 150 glorious stained-glass windows; and, of course, **Cathédrale de Notre-Dame** (1163–1250), which possesses pinnacled flying buttresses, a trio of France's best rose windows, good portal carvings, a choir screen of deeply carved reliefs, and spiffy gargoyles.

Cross Vault

Cathédrale Notre-Dame de Chartres

Flying Buttress

Cross Section of Gothic Church

RENAISSANCE (1500–1630)

In architecture as in painting, the Renaissance came from Italy and was only slowly Frenchified. And as in painting, its rules stressed proportion, order, classical inspiration, and precision to create unified, balanced structures.

The Loire Valley and Burgundy are home to many Renaissance **châteaux.** Foremost is the Loire's **Château de Chambord,** started in 1519, probably according to plans by Leonardo da Vinci (who may have designed its double helix staircase). In contrast, the **Château de Chenonceau,** home to many a French king's wife or mistress, is a fanciful fairy tale built in the middle of a river. The best example in Burgundy is the **Château de Tanlay,** east of Chablis.

Classical Orders

Château de Chambord

CLASSICISM & ROCOCO (1630–1800)

While Italy and Germany embraced the opulent baroque, France took the funda-
mentals of Renaissance **classicism** even further, becoming more imitative of

Mansard Roof

ancient models. During the reign of Louis XIV,
art and architecture were subservient to political ends. Buildings were grandiose and severely
ordered on the Versailles model. Opulence was
saved for interior decoration, which increasingly (especially from 1715–50, after the death
of Louis XIV) became a detailed and self-
indulgent **rococo** (*rocaille* in French). Exter-
nally, rococo is noticeable only in a greater
elegance and delicacy.

Mansart built town houses, châteaux, and
churches (**Val-de-Grâce** in Paris; the **Palais du Tau** in Reims) and laid out Dijon's
place de la Libération. But the Parisian architect is chiefly remembered for his
steeply sloping namesake, **"mansard" roofs.**

Louis Le Vau (1612–70) was the chief architect of the Louvre from 1650 to
1670 and of the **Château de Vaux-le-Vicomte** (1656–61) outside Paris, a gig that
put him and his collaborators—including Mansart, interior decorator **Charles Le
Brun** (1619–90), and the unparalleled landscape gardener **André Le Nôtre**
(1613–1700)—on Louis XIV's radar and landed them the commission to rebuild
Versailles (1669–85). Versailles is France's—indeed, Europe's—grandest palace.

Château de Versailles

THE 19TH CENTURY

Architectural styles in 19th-century Paris were eclectic, beginning in a severe classical mode and ending with an identity crisis torn between Industrial Age technology and Art Nouveau organic.

Identifiable styles include the neoclassical **First Empire,** with its strong lines often accented with a simple curve—the rage during Napoleon's reign; and **Second Empire,** which occurred during Napoleon III's reign, a reinterpretation of classicism in an ornate mood. During this period Paris became a city of wide boulevards courtesy of **Baron Georges-Eugène Haussmann** (1809–91), commissioned by Napoleon III in 1852 to redesign the city. Haussmann lined the boulevards with simple, six-story apartment blocks, such as elongated 18th-century town houses with continuous balconies wrapping around the third and sixth floors and mansard roofs with dormer windows.

Tour Eiffel, Paris

The **Third Republic** expositions in 1878, 1889, and 1900 used the engineering prowess of the Industrial Revolution to produce such Parisian monuments as the Tour Eiffel and Sacré-Coeur.

Art Nouveau architects and decorators rebelled against the Third Republic era of mass production by creating asymmetrical, curvaceous designs based on organic inspiration (plants and flowers) in such mediums as wrought iron, stained glass, and tile.

The best examples are the **Arc de Triomphe** (1836), Napoleon's oversize imitation of a Roman triumphal arch, the ultimate paean to the classic era; **Tour Eiffel** (1889), which **Gustave Eiffel** (1832–1923), slapped together to form the world's tallest structure at 320m (1,050-ft.); and **Métro station entrances.**

THE 20TH CENTURY

France commissioned some ambitious architectural projects in the last century, most of them the *grand projets* of the late François Mitterrand. The majority were considered controversial or even offensive when completed.

Centre Pompidou, Paris

At **Centre Pompidou** (1977), Britisher Richard Rogers (b. 1933) and Italian Renzo Piano (b. 1937) turned architecture inside out—literally—to craft Paris's eye-popping modern-art museum, with exposed pipes, steel supports, and plastic-tube escalators wrapping around the exterior; **Louvre's glass pyramids** (1989), were created by Chinese-American architect I. M. Pei (b. 1917); **Opéra Bastille** (1989), is a curvaceous, dark glass mound of space designed by Canadian Carlos Ott (b. 1947).

FRANCE IN POPULAR CULTURE: BOOKS, FILMS & MUSIC

Books

There are numerous books on all aspects of French history and society—ranging from the very general, such as the section on France in the *Encyclopedia Americana,* International Edition (Grolier, 1989), which presents an excellent, illustrated overview of the French people and their way of life, to the very specific, such as Judi Culbertson and Tom Randall's *Permanent Parisians: An Illustrated Guide to the Cemeteries of Paris* (Chelsea Green, 1986), which depicts the lives of famous French and expatriates who are buried in Paris.

HISTORY   In addition to the encyclopedia reference above, a broad overview of French history can be found in other encyclopedias and general history books. One very good one is *History of France* by Guillaume de Bertier de Savigny and David H. Pinkney, a comprehensive history with illustrations and plenty of obscure but interesting facts.

Two books that present French life and society in the 17th century are Warren Lewis's *The Splendid Century* and Madame de Sévigné's *Selected Letters,* edited by Leonard W. Tancock, which contains imaginative and witty letters written to her daughter during the reign of Louis XIV. Simon Schama's *Citizens* is a long but enjoyable new history of the French Revolution.

Moving into the 20th century, *Pleasure of the Belle Epoque: Entertainment and Festivity in Turn-of-the-Century France,* by Charles Rearick, depicts public diversions in the changing and troubled times of the Third Republic. *Paris Was Yesterday, 1925–1939* is a fascinating collection of excerpts from Janet Flanner's "Letters from Paris" column of the *New Yorker.* Larry Collins and Dominique Lapierre have written a popular history of the liberation of Paris in 1944 called *Is Paris Burning?*

Finally, two unusual approaches to French history are Rudolph Chleminski's *The French at Table,* a funny and honest history of why the French know how to eat better than anyone and how they go about it, and *Paris: A Century of Change, 1878-1978,* by Normal Evenson, a notable study of the urban development of Paris.

TRAVEL   Since 1323 some 10,000 books have been devoted to exploring Paris. One of the best is *Paris: Capital of the World* by Patrice Higonnet. This book takes a fresh, social, cultural, and political look at this City of Lights. Higonnet even explores Paris as "the capital of sex," and in contrast the "capital of art." The gang's all here from Balzac to Zola.

Showing a greater fondness for gossip is Alistair Horne in his *Seven Ages of Paris.* From the Roman founding up to the student riots of 1968, this is one of the most amusing books on Paris we've ever read. Horne is not a timid writer. He calls the Palais de Chaillot fascistic and hideous, the Pompidou Center a horror. We even learn that a woman once jumped off the Eiffel Tower, bounced off the roof of a parked car, and survived.

In *The Flâneur: A Stroll Through the Paradoxes of Paris,* Edmund White wants the reader to experience Paris as Parisians do. Hard to translate exactly, *a flâneur* is someone who strolls, loafs, or idles. With White, you can circumnavigate Paris as whim dictates.

BIOGRAPHY   You can get a more intimate look at history through biographies of historical figures. The best book yet on the architect who changed the face of Paris is *Haussmann: His Life and Times and the Making of Modern Paris* by Patrick Camiller. Hugh Ross Williamson brings to life Catherine de Médicis in his *Catherine de Medici* by combining text and magnificent illustrations from the art of the 16th century. This queen of France was the dominant personality during her nation's religious wars and mother of three kings of France, a queen of Spain, and a queen of Navarre.

Representing a very different era are *A Moveable Feast,* Ernest Hemingway's recollections of Paris during the 1920s, and Morley Callaghan's *That Summer in Paris: Memories of Tangled Friendships with Hemingway, Fitzgerald and Some Others,* an anecdotal account of the same period. Another great read is *The Autobiography of Alice B. Toklas,* by Gertrude Stein. It's not only the account of 30 years in Paris, but also the autobiography of Gertrude Stein.

Simone de Beauvoir, by Deirdre Bair, was described by one critic as ". . . a biography 'à l'Americaine'—that is to say, long, with all the warts of its subject unsparingly described." The story of the great feminist intellectual was based in part on tape-recorded conversations and unpublished letters.

Colette: A Life, by Herbert R. Lottman, is a painstakingly researched biography of the celebrated French writer and her fascinating life—which included not only writing novels and appearing in cabarets but also dabbling in lesbianism and perhaps even collaborating with the enemy during the Nazi occupation.

THE ARTS   Much of France's beauty can be found in its art. Three books that approach France from this perspective are *The History of Impressionism,* by John Rewald, which is a collection of writings about and quotations from the artists, illuminating this period in art; *The French Through Their Films,* by Robin Buss, an exploration of more than 100 widely circulated films; and *The Studios of Paris: The Capital of Art in the Late Nineteenth Century,* by John Milner. In the last, Milner presents the dynamic forces that made Paris one of the most complex centers of the art world in the early modern era.

Nightlife of Paris: The Art of Toulouse-Lautrec, by Patrick O'Connor, is an enchanting 80-page book with anecdotes about the hedonistic luminaries of Belle Epoque Paris, with paintings, sketches, and lithographs by the artist.

Olympia: Paris in the Age of Manet, by Otto Friedrich, takes its inspiration from the celebrated artwork in the Musée d'Orsay in Paris. From here the book takes off on an anecdote-rich gossipy chain of historical associations, tracing the rise of the Impressionist school of modern painting, but incorporating social commentary, too, such as the pattern of prostitution and venereal disease in 19th-century France.

FICTION The *Chanson de Roland,* edited by F. Whitehead, written between the 11th and 14th centuries, is the earliest and most celebrated of the "songs of heroic exploits." *The Misanthrope* and *Tartuffe* are two masterful satires on the frivolity of the 17th century by the great comic dramatist Molière. François-Marie Arouet Voltaire's *Candide* is a classic satire attacking the philosophy of optimism and the abuses of the ancient regime.

A few of the masterpieces of the 19th century are *Madame Bovary,* by Gustave Flaubert, in which the carefully wrought characters, setting, and plot attest to Flaubert's genius in presenting the tragedy of Emma Bovary; Victor Hugo's *Les Misérables,* a classic tale of social oppression and human courage set in the era of Napoleon I; and *Selected Stories* by the master of short stories, Guy de Maupassant.

Honoré de Balzac's *La comédie humaine* depicts life in France from the fall of Napoleon to 1848. Henry James's *The Ambassadors* and *The American* both take place in Paris. *The Vagabond,* by Colette, evokes the life of a French music-hall performer.

Tropic of Cancer is the semiautobiographical story of Henry Miller's years in Paris. One of France's leading thinkers, Jean-Paul Sartre, shows individuals struggling against their freedom in *No Exit and Three Other Plays.*

For more recent reads you might pick up a tattered copy of *The Da Vinci Code* (if you haven't already read it), or David Sedaris's *Me Talk Pretty One Day,* revealing the viewpoint of an American tourist as he tries to absorb French culture.

Films

Although Americans understood—and very quickly, too—the commercial wealth to be made from films, the French are credited with the scientific and technical inventions that made them possible. French physicists had laid the groundwork for a movie camera as early as the mid-1880s, and the world's first movie was shown in Paris on December 28, 1895. Its makers were the Lumière brothers, who considered filmmaking a scientific oddity and stubbornly confined its use to the production of international newsreels. Later, a vaudevillian actor and illusionist, Georges Méliés, used film to convey plot and drama.

Charles Pathé and Léon Gaumont were the first to exploit filmmaking on a grand scale. Beginning in 1896, they produced and distributed their own films, building their company into a giant before World War I. When Gaumont made his first film, he enlisted his secretary, Alice Guy-Blanché, to create the plot, design the scenery, and direct it. She proved so successful that she was eventually promoted to the head of Paris's largest studio and became the world's first female director.

Before World War I the many talented actors arriving *en scène* included Max Linder, a popular French comic, whose style influenced Charlie Chaplin and helped him develop his keen sense of timing. After World War I a flood of film imports from the United States and an economic depression slowed down the growth of French filmmaking.

By the 1920s the French began to view filmmaking as an art form, and infused it with surreal and dada themes. These were eventually named avant-garde and included experiments viewed (sometimes skeptically, sometimes encouragingly) in Hollywood and around the world. Examples include Man Ray's *Le retour à la raison* (1923), Fernand Léger's *Le ballet mécanique* (1924), and Jean Cocteau's *Le sang d'un poète* (1930).

The golden age of the French silent screen on both sides of the Atlantic was 1927 to 1929. Actors were directed with more sophistication, and technical abilities reached an all-time high. One of our favorite films—despite its mind-numbing length—is Abel Gance's sweepingly evocative masterpiece *Napoleon* (1927); its grisly battle scenes are easily as chilling as any war film made today. Other highlights from this era include René Clair's *Un chapeau de paille d'Italie* (*An Italian Straw Hat*, 1927), Carl Dreyer's *La passion de Jeanne d'Arc* (1928), and an adaptation of Emile Zola's *Thérèse Raguin* (1928) by Jacques Feyder.

Experiments with the early productions of "talkies" were less successful. One popular film director, Pagnol, declared outright that the role of films was to publicize to the masses the benefits of the theatrical stage. During this period, many of the counterculture's most gifted directors either left France altogether (as did René Clair, who emigrated to England in 1934) or died (Jean Vigo, *Zéro de Conduite*).

In 1936 the Cinémathèque Française was established to find and preserve old (usually silent) French films. By that time, French cinematographers had divorced themselves completely from the value system of the stage and had found a style of their own. An average of 130 films a year were made in France, by (among others) Jean Renoir, Charles Spaak, and Marcel Carne. This was also the era that brought such French luminaries as Claudette Colbert and Maurice Chevalier to Hollywood.

During World War II, the best-known (to Americans) of the French directors fled to Hollywood. Those who remained were heavily censored by the Vichy government. Despite that, more than 350 French films, many relating to long past (and therefore uncontroversial) events were produced. Exceptions were Carne's *Les enfants du paradis* (*Children of Paradise*, 1945).

In 1946 France slapped a heavy quota system onto the importation of foreign (especially American) films. A semigovernmental film authority (le Centre national du Cinéma Français) financed independent French film companies and encouraged liaisons between the French and Italian film industries. Many directors who had supported the Vichy government's Nazi collaboration were soon accepted back into the cinematic community.

Two strong traditions—film noir and a return to literary traditions—began to flourish. Film noir included such existentially inspired nihilistic themes as André Cayatte's *Nous sommes tous des assassins* (*We Are All Assassins*, 1952) and Yves Allegret's *Dedée d'Anvers* (1948). Examples of the literary tradition include Bresson's *Journal d'un curé de campagne* (*Diary of a Country Priest*, 1951) and a film rendition of Stendhal's *Le rouge et le noir* (*The Red and the Black*, 1954) by Autant-Lara. By the 1950s comedy adopted a new kind of genre with Jacques Tati's *Les vacances du Monsieur Hulot* (*Mr. Hulot's Holiday*). By the mid-1950s French filmmaking ushered in the era of enormous budgets, à la Hollywood, and the creation of such frothy potboilers as *And God Created Woman*, which helped make Brigitte Bardot a celebrity around the world, contributing greatly to the image in America of France as a kingdom of sexual liberation.

By the late 1950s François Truffaut, widely publicizing his auteur theories, rebelled with a series of short films (the most famous of which was *The 400 Blows*, 1959) that were partly financed by government funds, partly by wealthy benefactors. With Jean-Luc Godard (*A bout de souffle*, or *Breathless*) and Claude Chabrol (*Le beau Serge*, 1959), they pioneered one of the most publicized movements in 20th-century French art, *la nouvelle vague*. In the early 1960s dozens of new directors joined the movement, furiously making films, some of which are considered classics, others of which have been thrown into the dustbin of forgotten artistic endeavors. Enthusiastically endorsed by the counterculture on both sides of the Atlantic, these directors included Renais (*Muriel*), Roger Vadim, Agnès Varda (*Le Bonheur*), Jacques Demy (*Les parapluies de Cherbourg*), Louis Malle, Chris Marker, and Marguerite Duras (*Detruire, dit-elle*).

After a switch to political themes (Costa Gavras's Z) during the 1968 rebellions (and a politically motivated abandonment of the film festival at Cannes by at least a dozen prominent French directors), French cinema turned to comedy in the early 1970s. Examples include Buñuel's *Le charme discret de la bourgeoisie* (1972) and Yanne's *Tout le monde il est beau, tout le monde il est gentil* (1972).

Many American films—still shown rather frequently on TV—were filmed in Paris (or else used sets to simulate Paris). Notable ones have included the classic *An American in Paris,* starring Gene Kelly, and *Moulin Rouge,* starring José Ferrer as Toulouse-Lautrec. Truffaut's *The Last Metro* and Clément's *Is Paris Burning?* gained worldwide audiences, as did *The Sun Also Rises,* an adaptation of Hemingway's celebrated novel, with Ava Gardner and Tyrone Power. *Last Tango in Paris,* with Marlon Brando, was one of the most controversial films set in Paris, and the always provocative Roman Polanski used Paris as a setting for his *Frantic*.

La Belle Noiseuse, in French, with English subtitles, is a 4-hour film that opened in New York in 1991. Director Jacques Rivette tells the story of a once-celebrated painter, Edouard Frenhofer, who attempts to transform a beautiful young woman into his crowning masterpiece.

In 1992, Michael Bene directed *Le ciel de Paris,* about emotional isolation. The film, which opened in New York, starred Sandrine Bonnaire and Marc Fourastier. It was Bene's first and last feature film, as he died of AIDS before its release.

Betty Blue, the stylish Jean-Jacques Beineix film about a torrid summertime love affair, was released in English in 1992. It was first shown in France in 1986 when it was that country's nominee for the Oscar as best foreign film.

One French film that continues to be popular is Jean-Pierre Jeunet's *Amélie,* which tugs at the heart strings. You'll fall in love with those scenes shot in Montmartre. You can also rent *Le Placard* by Francis Veber, starring Gérard Depardieu and dealing with gay life in French society.

The most recent French film to achieve world renown is *La Vie en Rose,* which won Marion Cotillard an Oscar in 2008 for her performance as "The Little Sparrow," Edith Piaf. This film documenting Piaf's tragic life is an astonishing immersion of one performer (Cotillard) into the body and soul of another (Piaf).

Today the transatlantic movie deal is a relatively common occurrence, and movie executives from California, New York, and Paris regularly collaborate and compete on films suitable for both cultures.

Music

You might not immediately think of music when you think of France, but music and France have gone together since the monks in the 12th century sang Gregorian chants in Notre-Dame. Troubadours with their ballads went all over France in the Middle Ages. In the Renaissance era, **Josquin des Prez** (c. 1440–1521) was the first master of the High Renaissance style of polyphonic vocal music. He became the greatest composer of his age, a magnificent virtuoso. **Jean-Baptise Lully**

(1632–87) entertained the decadent court of Versailles with his operas. During the reign of Robespierre, **Claude-Joseph Rouget de Lisle** (1760–1836) immortalized himself in 1792 when he wrote *La Marseillaise,* the French national anthem. Regrettably, he died in poverty.

The rise of the middle class in the 1800s gave birth to both grand opera and *opéra comique.* Both styles merged into a kind of lyric opera, mixing soaring arias and tragedy in such widely popular hits as Bizet's *Carmen* in 1875 and St-Saën's *Samson et Dalila* in 1877.

During the romantic period of the 19th century, foreign composers moving to Paris often dominated the musical scene. **Frédéric Chopin** (1810–49) was half French, half Polish. He became the most influential composer for piano and even invented new musical forms such as the *ballade.* **Félix Mendelssohn** (1809–47) had to fight against anti-Semitism to establish himself with his symphonies, concerti, and chamber music.

At the dawn of the 20th century, music became more impressionistic, as evoked by **Claude Débussy** (1862–1918). In many ways, he helped launch modernist music. His *Prélude à L'Après-midi d'un Faune* in 1894 and *La Mer* in 1905 were performed all over Europe. From Russia came **Igor Stravinsky** (1882–1971), who made *Time* magazine's list of the 100 most influential people of the 20th century. He achieved fame as a pianist, conductor, and composer. His *Le sacre du printemps (The Rite of Spring)* provoked a riot in Paris when it was first performed in 1913, with its pagan rituals.

A revolutionary artist, **Yves Klein** (1928–62) was called a "neo-Dada." His 1960 "The Monotone Symphony" with three naked models became a notorious performance. For 20 minutes he conducted an orchestra on one note. Dying of a heart attack at the age of 34, Klein is considered today an enigmatic postmodernist. **Pierre Boulez** (b. 1925) developed a technique known as integral serialism using a 12-tone system pioneered in the 1920s. As director of the IRCAM institute at the Centre Pompidou, he has influenced young musicians around the world.

France took to American jazz like no other country. Louis Armstrong practically became a national hero to Parisians in the 1930s, and in 1949 Paris welcomed the arrival of Miles Davis. **Stéphane Grappelli** (1908–97), a French jazz violinist, founded the Quintette du Hot Club de France, the most famous of all-string jazz bands. **Django Reinhardt** (1910–53) became one of the most prominent jazz musicians of Europe, known for such works as "Belleville" and "My Sweet."

Some French singers went on to achieve world renown, notably **Edith Piaf** (1915–63), "The Little Sparrow" and France's greatest pop singer. Wherever you go in France, you will hear her "La Vie en Rose," which she first recorded in 1946. Born in 1924, **Charles Aznavour** remains an eternal favorite. He's known for his unique tenor voice with its gravelly and soulful low notes. **Jacques Brel** (1929–78), a singer-songwriter, has seen his songs interpreted by everybody from Frank Sinatra to David Bowie. A popular *chanson* singer, **Juliette Gréco** (b. 1927) became known as "the High Priestess of Existentialism" on Paris's Left Bank and was beloved by Jean-Paul Sartre. She dressed all in black and let her long, black hair hang free before coming to Hollywood and becoming the mistress of mogul Darryl Zanuck.

Among rock stars, the French consider **Johnny Halladay** (b. 1943) their equivalent of Elvis Presley. He has scored 18 platinum albums, selling more than 100 million records. Another pop icon is **Serge Gainsbourg** (1928–91). He was a master of everything from rock to jazz to reggae. Upon his death, President François Mitterrand called him "our Baudelaire, our Apollinaire."

Artists with immigrant backgrounds often are the major names in the vibrant French music scene of today, with influences from French Africa, the French Caribbean, and the Middle East. Along with rap and hip-hop, these sounds rule the nights in the *boîtes* of France's biggest cities. **Khaled** (b. 1960) from Algeria has become known as the "King of Raï." The most loved and influential French rapper today is **MC Solaar** (b. 1969); born in Senegal, he explores racism and ethnic identity in his wordplays.

EATING & DRINKING IN FRANCE

As any French person will tell you, French food is the best in the world. That's as true today as it was during the 19th-century heyday of the master chef Escoffier. A demanding patriarch who codified the rules of French cooking, he ruled the kitchens of the Ritz in Paris, standardizing the complicated preparation and presentation of haute cuisine. Thanks to Escoffier with his legendary flare-ups and those of his French-born colleagues, whose kitchen tantrums have been the bane of many a socialite's life, the French chef for years has been considered a temperamental egomaniac, bearing singlehandedly the burden of diffusing French civilization into the kitchens of the Anglo-Saxon world.

The demands of these chefs, however, aren't as far-fetched as they might seem, considering the intense scrutiny that has surrounded every aspect of France's culinary arts since the start of the Industrial Revolution.

Until the early 1800s, most French citizens didn't eat well. Many diets consisted of turnips, millet, fruits, berries, unpasteurized dairy products, and whatever fish or game could be had. Cooking techniques and equipment were unsanitary and crude, and starvation was a constant threat. Fear of famine was one of the rallying cries of the Revolution; everyone knows Marie Antoinette's "Let them eat cake" response to cries that the poor couldn't afford bread. (However, to be fair to Marie, this comment has been taken out of context. At the time, bread flour was much more expensive than cake flour, so her words weren't as callous as they might seem.)

At the foundation of virtually every culinary theory ever developed in France is a deep-seated respect for the *cuisine des provinces* (also known as *cuisine campagnarde*). Ingredients usually included only what was produced locally, and the rich and hearty result was gradually developed over several generations of *mères cuisinières*. Springing from an agrarian society with a vivid sense of nature's cycles, the cuisine provided appropriate nourishment for bodies that had toiled through a day in the open air. Specific dishes and cooking methods were as varied as the climates, terrains, and crops of France's many regions.

The revolution against Escoffier has been raging for so long that many of the early rebels are now returning to the old style of cookery, as exemplified by the boeuf bourguignon, the *blanquette de veau*, and the *pot-au-feu*.

Cuisine moderne is here to stay, and some restaurants feature both traditional and contemporary. The new cooking is often based on the classic principles of French cookery, but with a big difference. Rich sauces, for example, are eliminated. Cooking times that can destroy the best of fresh ingredients are considerably shortened. The aim is to release the natural flavor of food without covering it with heavy layers of butter and cream. New flavor combinations in this widely expanding repertoire are often inspired.

The most promising trend for those who don't want to sell the family homestead is to patronize one of the *neo-bistrots* springing up across France. Some of the top chefs of Paris, even Guy Martin of Grand Véfour, have opened these more simplified bistros where haute cuisine isn't served, just good-tasting and often regionally inspired dishes. Chefs have fun creating these more affordable menus, perhaps borrowing dishes that their *grande-mère* taught them. We'll feature a number of these bistros in this guide, including those run by the country's most famous chef, Alain Ducasse.

Volumes have been written about French gastronomy—our comments are meant to be a brief introduction only. More than ever, young *chefs du cuisine* are making creative statements in the kitchen, and never in the history of the country has there been such an emphasis on superfresh ingredients. One chef we know in Paris has been known to shut down his restaurant for the day if he doesn't find exactly what he wants in the marketplace that morning.

Of course, you may want to ask, "What will it cost?" France has gained a reputation as being a damnably expensive place in the food department. True, its star-studded, internationally famous establishments—such as Taillevent in Paris—are very expensive indeed. In such culinary cathedrals, you pay not only for superb decor and regal service but also for the art of celebrated chefs on ministerial salaries.

There is also a vast array of expensive restaurants in France that exist almost exclusively for the tourist trade. Their food may be indifferent or downright bad, but they'll also have ice water and ketchup to anesthetize your taste buds, trilingual waiters, and quadrilingual menus. Luckily, there are others—hundreds of others. Paris, which is said to have more restaurants than any other city on earth, has many good, reasonably priced ones. And they aren't hard to find. We've counted 18 of them on a single, narrow Left Bank street.

Once you arrive in the countryside, except for the French Riviera and certain citadels of haute cuisine, food prices become more reasonable.

CUISINE BOURGEOISE & HAUTE CUISINE Cuisine bourgeoise and its pretentious cousin, haute cuisine, were refinements of country cooking that developed from the increased prosperity brought on by 19th-century industrialization. As France grew more affluent, food and the rituals involved in its preparation and presentation became one of the hallmarks of culture. And as refrigerated trucks and railway cars carried meats, fish, and produce from one region to another, associations were formed and entire industries spawned, revolving around specific ingredients produced in specific districts. The country's wines (demarcated with "Appellation d'Origine Contrôlée"); lamb from the salt marshes of Pauillac; poultry from Bresse in Burgundy; and melons, strawberries, apples, and truffles from specific districts command premiums over roughly equivalent ingredients produced in less legendary areas.

France often names a method of preparation (or a particular dish) after its region of origin. Dishes described as *à la normande* are likely to be prepared with milk, cream, or cheese or with Calvados, in honor of the dairy products and apple brandy produced in abundance within Norman borders. **Cassoulet** (a stewed combination of white beans, duck, pork, onions, and carrots) will forever be associated with Toulouse, where the dish originated. And something cooked *à la bordelaise* has probably been flavored with ample doses of red bordeaux (along with bone marrow, shallots, tarragon, and meat juices).

Other than caviar (which the French consume in abundance but don't produce), the world's most elegant garnish is **truffles,** an underground fungus with a woodsy, oaky smell. Thousands of these are unearthed yearly from the Dordogne and Périgord forests, so if your menu proclaims a dish is *à la périgourdine,* you'll almost certainly pay a premium for the truffles and foie gras.

And what's all the fuss about **foie gras?** It comes from either a goose or a duck (the rose-hued gooseliver is the greater delicacy). The much-abused goose, however, has a rough life, being force-fed about a kilogram (2¼ lb.) of corn every day in a process the French call *gavage.* In about 22 days the animal's liver is swollen to about 25 ounces (in many cases far more than that). When prepared by a Périgourdine housewife (some of whom sell the livers directly from their farmhouses to passing motorists), it's truly delicious. Foie gras is most often served with truffles; otherwise, it's called au naturel.

> ### Impressions
>
> *The French will only be united under the threat of danger. Nobody can simply bring together a country that has 265 kinds of cheese.*
> —Charles de Gaulle

Regional Cuisines

What exactly is "French food?" That's a hard question to answer. Even cities have their own specialties.

Gastronomy alone would be good enough reason for going to the Loire Valley. From Nantes to Orléans, the specialties are many, including, for example, shad cooked with sorrel, Loire salmon, chitterling sausage, lark pâté, goat's milk cheese, partridge, rillettes (shredded and potted pork), herb-flavored black pudding, plus good Loire wines, including rosés.

The Normans are known not only as good soldiers but as hearty eaters. Their gastronomic table enjoys world renown. Many Parisians drive up for *le weekend* just to sample the cuisine. Harvested along the seacoast are sole, brill, mackerel, and turbot. Shellfish are also common, especially those fat black mussels, the prawns of Cherbourg, the demoiselles of Dieppe. Try also Madame Poulard's featherweight omelet, sole *normande* (stewed in rich cream), tripe *à la mode de Caen,* chicken from the Auge Valley, and duckling from Rouen. Normandy apples, especially those from the Auge Valley, produce a most potent cider. Matured in oaken casks, the apples also are turned into Calvados, a sort of applejack, a distillation of cider flavored with hazelnuts. A true Norman drinks this cider spirit at breakfast. Benedictine, the liqueur made at Fécamp, also enjoys acclaim. The rich Norman Camembert is imitated but never equaled. Pont l'Evêque cheese has been known here since the 13th century. The Livarot is just fine for those who can get past the smell.

The province of Brittany offers sublime seafood, the mainstay of its diet, including Aulne salmon, pike (best with white butter), scallops, trout, winkles, cockles, spiny lobsters, and Lorient sardines. The *pré-salé* (salt-meadow lamb) is the best meat course, traditionally served with white beans. The finest artichokes come from Roscoff, the most succulent strawberries from Plougastel. Nearly every village has

> ## Impressions
>
> Mummie & I about live in this here kafe. *mummie & I come every day & eat the*
> We feed on choucroute garnie, which *is* *stinkin' stuff, & all our friends hold their*
> *fried sauerkraut trimmed with boiled* *noses & pass us by till we've finished.*
> *potatoes, a large slice of ham & a fat hot* —Edna St. Vincent Millay
> *dog—yum, yum, werry excillint. And*

its own crêperie, specializing in those paper-thin pancakes with an infinite variety of fillings. Buckwheat griddlecakes are another popular item. The food is washed down with Breton cider (admittedly inferior to the Norman variety, but quite good nevertheless). Unlike much of France, the province lacks wine, except for Muscadet, a light white wine produced from the vineyards around the old Breton capital of Nantes in the lower Loire Valley.

The cuisine of Alsace-Lorraine has been influenced by Germany, as reflected by its sauerkraut garni, its most popular dish. It is also the home of foie gras, an expensively delicious treat. The Savoy, in the French Alps, also has many specialties, many using rich cream and milk, which makes the cuisine heavy but tasty. Game such as woodcock is common.

Some of the best food and best wines are found in Burgundy. You'll also see written *"à la Bourgogne"* after a dish, which means bourguignon—cooked in a red-wine sauce and often garnished with buttonhole mushrooms and pearl onions. Lyon is regarded as the gastronomic capital of France. For example, tripe lyonnaise is known around the world. Lyonnais sausage is also well known, and the city's many famous dishes include *quenelles* (fish balls, often made with pike).

The Périgord and Dordogne regions are known for their foie gras and truffles. Many farmers' wives sell foie gras—from goose or duck—directly from their kitchen doors. Even if you don't like foie gras, you'll surely want to try the fish from the rivers of the Dordogne, along with morels, strawberries, and flap mushrooms—called *cèpes*—from the field.

Gourmets, not just beach lovers, go to the Riviera. The food, especially fish, can be exceptionally good. It also tends to be expensive. Bouillabaisse, said to have been invented by Venus, is the area's best-known dish. Each chef has his or her own ideas on the subject. *Rascasse* (rockfish), a fish found only in the Mediterranean, is very popular. One of the best seafood selections, *rouget* (red mullet) sometimes appears on fancy menus as *becasse de mer* (sea woodcock). Yet another is *loup de mer* (bass), cooked with fennel. Aioli, mayonnaise with a garlic-and-olive-oil base, is usually served with hors d'oeuvres or boiled fish. Other specialties include *soupe au pistou* (vegetable soup with basil), *salade Niçoise* (likely to include other items, but traditionally made with tomatoes, green beans, olives, tuna, anchovies, and radishes), *pain bagnat* (bread doused in olive oil and served with olives, anchovies, and tomatoes), and ravioli, which needs no explanation.

MEALS & DINING CUSTOMS In many of the less expensive places described in this guide, the menu will be handwritten, in French only. Don't let that intimidate you. Nor should you be timid about ordering dishes without knowing precisely what they are. You'll get some delightful surprises. We know a woman who wouldn't have dreamed of asking for escargots if she'd realized they were snails cooked in garlic sauce. As it was, she ate this appetizer in a spirit of thrift rather than adventure—and has been addicted to it ever since. As for vegetables, the French regard them as a separate course and eat them apart from the meat or poultry dishes. But we wouldn't advise you to order them especially unless you're an exceptionally hearty eater. Most main courses come with a small helping, or *garni,* of vegetables anyway.

You'll find a large number of specific dishes explained in the "Glossary of Basic Menu Terms" (p. 770), as well as in the restaurant descriptions themselves. No one, however, can explain the subtle nuances of flavor that distinguish them. Those you have to taste for yourself.

As a rule, it's better to order an aperitif—often the house will have a specialty—rather than a heavy drink such as a martini before a classic French dinner. Vodka or scotch can assault your palate, destroying your taste buds for the festive repast to come.

Allow plenty of time for a gourmet dinner. Orders are often prepared individually, and it takes time to absorb the wine and the flavors. Sometimes sorbet is served midway in your meal to cleanse the palate.

Making reservations is important, and please try to show up on time. Too many Americans make reservations and then become a "no-show," which creates ill will, especially since many nine-table restaurants must be filled completely every night in order to make a profit. If you're window-shopping for a restaurant, you'll find the menu most often displayed outside. Parisians read it like a book. It's there for you to study and ponder—so read it in anticipation. Most French people have their main meal during the day; you, too, may want to follow that custom, dining more lightly in the evening.

Most meals consist of several small courses. You can begin, for example, with hors d'oeuvres or a light *potage* (soup). The classic restaurant used to serve a small order of fish after the appetizer, then the meat or poultry course, but nowadays it's likely to be either fish or meat. A salad follows the main course, then a selection of cheese (there are now more than 1,000 registered French cheeses) and dessert (often a fruit concoction or a sorbet). In this book, prices are given for fixed-price or a la carte main courses.

If you find the food "too rich, with too many sauces," that may be because you've been overdoing it. Elaborately prepared gourmet banquets should not be consumed for both lunch and dinner, or even every day. Sometimes an omelet or a roast chicken can make a delightful light meal, and you can "save up" for your big dining experience.

WINE French cookery achieves palate perfection only when lubricated by wine, which is not considered a luxury or even an addition, but rather an integral part of every meal. Certain rules about wine drinking have been long established in France, but no one except traditionalists seems to follow them anymore. "Rules" would dictate that if you're having a roast, steak, or game, a good burgundy should be your choice. If it's chicken, lamb, or veal, you would choose a red from the Bordeaux country, certainly a full-bodied red with cheese such as Camembert, and a blanc-de-blanc with oysters. A light rosé can go with almost anything, especially if enjoyed on a summer terrace overlooking the Seine.

Let your own good taste—and sometimes almost as important, your pocketbook—determine your choice of wine. Most wine stewards, called sommeliers, are there to help you in your choice, and only in the most dishonest of restaurants will they push you toward the most expensive selections. Of course, if you prefer only bottled water, or perhaps a beer, then be firm and order either without embarrassment. In fact, bottled water might be a good idea at lunch if you're planning to drive later. Some restaurants include a beverage in their menu rates (*boisson compris*), but that's only in the cheaper places. Nevertheless, some of the most satisfying wines we've drunk in Paris came from unlabeled house bottles or carafes, called a *vin de la maison*. In general, unless you're a real connoisseur, don't worry about labels and vintages.

When in doubt, you can rarely go wrong with a good burgundy or bordeaux, but you may want to be more adventurous than that. That's when the sommelier can help you, particularly if you tell him or her your taste in wine (semidry or very dry, for example). State frankly how much you're willing to pay and what you plan to order for your meal. If you're dining with others, you may want to order two or three bottles with an entire dinner, selecting a wine to suit each course. However, Parisians at informal meals—and especially if there are only two persons dining—select only one wine to go with all their platters, from hors d'oeuvres to cheese. As a rule of thumb, expect to spend about one-third of the restaurant tab for wine.

WINE LABELS Since the latter part of the 19th century, French wines sold in France (and sometimes elsewhere) have been labeled. The general label is known as *appellations contrôlées*. These controls, for the most part, are by regions such as Bordeaux and the Loire. These are the simple, honest wines of the district. They can be blended from grapes grown at any place in the region. Some are composed of the vintages of different years.

. In most cases, the more specific the label, the better the wine. For example, instead of a Bordeaux, the wine might be labeled MEDOC (pronounced *may*-doc), which is the name of a triangle of land extending some 81km (50 miles) north from Bordeaux. Wine labels can be narrowed down to a particular vine-growing property, such as a Château Haut-Brion, one of the most famous and greatest of red wines of Bordeaux (this château produces only about 10,000 cases a year).

On some burgundies, you are likely to see the word *clos* (pronounced "cloe"). Originally, that meant a walled or otherwise enclosed vineyard, as in Clos-de-Bèze, which is a celebrated Burgundian vineyard producing a superb red wine. *Cru* (pronounced "croo," and meaning "growth") suggests a wine of superior quality when it appears on a label as a *vin-de-cru*. Wines and vineyards are often divided into crus. A grand cru or premier cru should, by implication, be an even superior wine.

Labels are only part of the story. It's the vintage that counts. Essentially vintage is the annual grape harvest and the wine made from those grapes. Therefore, any wine can be a vintage wine unless it is a blend. But there are good vintages and bad vintages. The variation between wine produced in a "good year" and wine produced in a "bad year" can be great, and even noted by the neophyte.

Finally, champagne is the only wine that can be correctly served through all courses of a meal—but only to those who can afford its astronomical cost.

PLANNING YOUR TRIP TO FRANCE

3

Of almost any destination in the world, flying into France is one of the most effortless undertakings in global travel. There are no shots to get, no particular safety precautions, no unusual aspects of planning a trip. With your passport, airline ticket, and enough money, you just go.

Of course, before you lift off the ground in your native country, you can do some advance preparation. In the pages that follow, you'll find everything you need to know about the practicalities of planning your trip: finding the best airfare, deciding when to go, getting around the country, and more.

For additional help in planning your trip and for more on-the-ground resources in France, please see "Fast Facts," on p. 758.

WHEN TO GO

The best time to visit Paris is in the spring (April to June) or fall (September to November), when things are easier to come by—from Métro seats to good-tempered waiters. The weather is temperate year-round. July and August are the worst for crowds. Parisians desert their city, leaving it to the tourists.

Hotels used to charge off-season rates during the cold, rainy period from November to February; now, they're often packed with business travelers, trade fairs, and winter tour groups, and hoteliers have less incentive to offer discounts. Airfares are still cheaper during these months, and more promotions are available. They rise in the spring and fall, peaking in the summer, when tickets cost the most.

In even-numbered years, don't come to Paris during the first 2 weeks of October without a confirmed hotel room. The weather's fine, but the city is jammed for the auto show.

Weather

France's weather varies from region to region and even from town to town. Despite its latitude, Paris never gets very cold; snow is rare. The hands-down winner for wetness is Brittany. Brest (known for the mold—probably caused by the constant damp—that adds flavor to its blue cheeses) receives a staggering amount of rain between October and December. May is the driest month.

The Mediterranean coast in the south has the driest climate. When it does rain, it's heaviest in spring and autumn. (Cannes sometimes receives more rainfall than Paris.) Summers are comfortably dry—beneficial to humans but deadly to vegetation, which (unless it's irrigated) often dries and burns up in the parched months.

Provence dreads *le mistral* (an unrelenting wind), which most often blows in the winter for a few days but can last for up to 2 weeks.

Paris's Average Daytime Temperature & Rainfall

	JAN	FEB	MAR	APR	MAY	JUNE	JULY	AUG	SEPT	OCT	NOV	DEC
TEMP. °F	38	39	46	51	58	64	66	66	61	53	45	40
TEMP. °C	3	4	8	11	14	18	19	19	16	12	7	4
RAINFALL (IN.)	3.2	2.9	2.4	2.7	3.2	3.5	3.3	3.7	3.3	3.0	3.5	3.1

France Calendar of Events

For an exhaustive list of events beyond those listed here, check http://events.frommers.com, where you'll find a searchable, up-to-the-minute roster of what's happening in cities all over the world.

JANUARY

Monte Carlo Motor Rally (Le Rallye de Monte Carlo). The world's most venerable car race. For information, call the Monaco Tourist Office (✆ **377/93-15-26-00;** www.acm.mc). Usually mid-January.

FEBRUARY

Carnival of Nice. Parades, boat races, music, balls, and fireworks are all part of this celebration. The climax is the 114-year tradition of burning King Carnival in effigy, after *Les Batailles des Fleurs* (Battles of the Flowers), when teams pelt each other with blooms. For details, contact the Nice Convention and Visitors Bureau (✆ **08-92-70-74-07;** fax 04-92-14-46-49; www.nicecarnaval.com). Late February to early March.

MARCH

Foire du Trône, on the Reuilly Lawn of the Bois de Vincennes, 12e, Paris. This mammoth amusement park operates daily from 2pm to midnight. Call ✆ **01-46-27-52-29,** or visit www.foiredutrone.com. End of March to end of May.

International Ready-to-Wear Fashion Shows (Le Salon International de Prêt-à-Porter), Parc des Expositions, Porte de Versailles, 15e, Paris. See what you'll be wearing next season. Call ✆ **01-44-94-70-00,** or visit www.pretparis.com. Early March.

APRIL

International Marathon of Paris. Runners from around the world compete. Call ✆ **01-41-33-14-00,** or visit www.parismarathon.com. Early April.

Les 24 Heures du Mans Moto. This motorcycle race is on a grueling 4km (2½-mile) circuit 4.5km (2¾ miles) south of Le Mans. For information, call l'Automobile Club de l'Ouest (✆ **02-43-40-24-24**) or the Le Mans Ticket Office (✆ **04-73-91-85-75;** www.lemans.org). Mid-April.

MAY

Antiques Show. The annual *Cinq Jours de l'Objet Extraordinaire* show features more than 100 galleries and antiques stores displaying their collections in seven streets on the Left Bank, Carré Rive Gauche. For information, call ✆ **01-42-60-70-10,** or visit www.carrerivegauche.com. Mid-May to early June.

Cannes Film Festival (Festival International du Film). Movie madness transforms this city into a media circus. Admission to the films in competition is by invitation only. Other films play 24 hours a day. Contact the Festival International du Film, 3 rue Amélie, 75007 Paris (✆ **01-53-59-61-00;** www.festival-cannes.com). Two weeks before the festival, its administration moves to the Palais des Festivals, esplanade Georges-Pompidou, Cannes 06400. Mid-May.

Monaco Grand Prix de Formule. Hundreds of cars race through the narrow streets and winding roads in a blend of high-tech machinery and medieval architecture. Call ✆ **377/93-15-26-00** or 377/92-16-61-16, or visit www.acm.mc. Mid-May.

French Open Tennis Championship, Stade Roland-Garros, 16e, Paris (Métro: Porte d'Auteuil). The open features 10 days of men's, women's, and doubles tennis on the hot, red, dusty courts. For information, call ✆ **01-47-43-48-00,** or visit www.fft.fr. Late May to early June.

JUNE

Prix du Jockey Club and **Prix Diane-Hermès,** Hippodrome de Chantilly. Thoroughbreds from as far away as Kentucky and Brunei compete in this race. On race days, dozens of trains depart from Paris's Gare du Nord for Chantilly, where racegoers take free shuttle buses to the track. Call ✆ **01-49-10-20-30,** or visit www.france-galop.com for information on these and other Chantilly events. Early June.

Cinéscénie de Puy du Fou, *son-et-lumière,* Château du Puy du Fou, Les Epesses (La Vendée), Brittany. A cast of 2,500 actors, dozens of horses, and laser shows celebrate the achievements of the Middle Ages. Call ✆ **02-51-64-11-11,** or visit www.puydu fou.com. Early June to early September.

Festival de St-Denis. A surge of music in the burial place of the French kings, a grim early Gothic monument in Paris's northern suburb of St-Denis. Call ✆ **01-48-13-06-07,** or visit www.festival-saint-denis.fr. Early June to July.

Paris Air Show. France's military-industrial complex shows off its high-tech hardware. Fans, competitors, and industrial spies mob

Le Bourget Airport. Call ✆ **01-53-23-33-16,** or visit www.paris-air-show.com. Mid-June in alternate years; next is mid-June 2011.

Les 24 Heures du Mans Voitures, for stock cars, is in the same circuit as the April motorcycle rally, but on a 13km (8-mile) radius. For information, call l'Automobile Club de l'Ouest (✆ **02-43-40-25-55**), or contact the Le Mans Ticket Office (✆ **08-92-69-72-24;** www.lemans.org). Mid-June.

Gay Pride Parade, place de la République to place de la Bastille, Paris. A week of expositions and parties climaxes in a parade patterned after those in New York and San Francisco, followed by a dance at the Palais de Bercy. For more information about gay pride and any other aspect of gay, lesbian, and transgendered life in and around Paris, contact Lesbian and Gay Pride Ile de France, 3 rue Perrée, Box 8, Paris 75003 (✆/fax **01-72-70-39-22;** www.inter-lgbt.org). Late June.

JULY

Colmar International Festival, Colmar. Classical concerts are held in public buildings of one of the most folkloric towns in Alsace. Call ✆ **03-89-20-68-97,** or visit www.festival-colmar.com. First 2 weeks of July.

Les Chorégies d'Orange, Orange. One of southern France's most important lyric festivals presents oratorios, operas, and choral works in France's best-preserved Roman amphitheater. Call ✆ **04-90-34-24-24,** or visit www.choregies.asso.fr. Early July to early August.

Fête Chopin, Paris. Everything you've ever wanted to hear by the Polish exile, who lived most of his life in Paris. Piano recitals take place in the Orangerie du Parc de Bagatelle, 16e. Call ✆ **01-45-00-22-19,** or visit www.frederic-chopin.com. Early July.

Les Nocturnes du Mont-St-Michel. This is a sound-and-light tour through the stairways and corridors of one of Europe's most impressive medieval monuments. Call ✆ **02-33-60-14-30,** or check out

Global Tickets can order tickets to many of the musical and theatrical events at the Avignon festival as well as other cultural happenings throughout France. You'll pay a hefty fee (as much as 20%) for the convenience. Contact Global at 234 W. 44th St., Ste. 1000, New York, NY 10036 (📞 **800/669-8687; www.keithprowse.com**).

www.monuments-nationaux.fr for more information. Performances are Monday through Saturday evenings from early July to late August.

Tour de France. Europe's most hotly contested bicycle race sends crews of wind tunnel–tested athletes along an itinerary that detours deep into the Massif Central and ranges across the Alps. The finish line is on the Champs-Elysées. Call 📞 **01-41-33-14-00,** or visit www.letour.fr. First 3 weeks of July.

Festival d'Avignon. This world-class festival has a reputation for exposing new talent to critical scrutiny and acclaim. The focus is usually on avant-garde works in theater, dance, and music. Many of the dance and theater performances take place in either the 14th-century courtyard of the Palais des Pâpes or the medieval Cloître (cloister) des Carmes. For information, call 📞 **04-90-27-66-50,** or visit www.festival-avignon.com. Last 3 weeks of July.

Bastille Day. Celebrating the birth of modern-day France, the nation's festivities reach their peak in Paris with street fairs, pageants, fireworks, and feasts. In Paris, the day begins with a parade down the Champs-Elysées and ends with fireworks at Montmartre. July 14.

Paris Quartier d'Eté. For 4 weeks, music rules the Arènes de Lutèce and the Cour d'Honneur at the Sorbonne, both in the Quartier Latin. The dozen or so concerts are grander than the outdoorsy setting; they include performances by the Orchestre de Paris, the Orchestre National de France, and the Baroque Orchestra of the European Union. Call 📞 **01-44-94-98-00,** or visit www.quartierdete.com. Mid-July to mid-August.

Nice Jazz Festival. The most prestigious jazz festival in Europe. Concerts begin in the afternoon and go on until late at night (sometimes all night) on the Arènes de Cimiez, a hill above the city. Contact the Nice Tourist Office (📞 **08-92-70-75-07;** www.nicejazzfestival.fr). Mid-July.

Festival d'Aix-en-Provence. A musical event par excellence, with everything from Gregorian chant to melodies composed on synthesizers. Recitals are in the medieval cloister of the Cathédrale St-Sauveur. Expect heat, crowds, and traffic. Contact the Festival International d'Art Lyrique et Académie Européenne de Musique (📞 **04-42-17-34-34;** www.festival-aix.com). Throughout July.

AUGUST

Festival Interceltique de Lorient, Brittany. Celtic verse and lore are celebrated in the Celtic heart of France. The 150 concerts include classical and floric musicians, dancers, singers, and painters. Traditional Breton *pardons* (religious processions) take place in the once-independent maritime duchy. Call 📞 **02-97-21-24-29,** or check www.festival-interceltique.com. Early August.

SEPTEMBER

La Villette Jazz Festival. Some 50 concerts are held in churches, auditoriums, and concert halls in the Paris suburb of La Villette. Past festivals have included Herbie Hancock, Shirley Horn, and other international artists. Call 📞 **01-40-03-75-75,** or visit www.lavillette.com. Early to mid-September.

Festival d'Automne, Paris. One of France's most famous festivals is one of its most eclectic, focusing mainly on modern music, ballet, theater, and art. Contact the Festival d'Automne (✆ **01-53-45-17-00;** www. festival-automne.com). Mid-September to late December.

Paris Auto Show, Parc des Expositions, Porte de Versailles, 15e, Paris. This is the showcase for European car design, complete with glistening metal, glitzy attendees, lots of hype, and the latest models. Check *Pariscope* for details, or contact the French Government Tourist Office (see "Fast Facts," p. 758). You can also get information by calling ✆ **01-56-88-22-40** or visiting www.mondial-automobile.com. Two weeks in October (dates vary).

Perpignan Jazz Festival. Musicians from everywhere jam in what many consider Languedoc's most appealing season. Call ✆ **04-68-35-37-46,** or visit www.jazzebre. com. Month of October.

Prix de l'Arc de Triomphe, Hippodrome de Longchamp, 16e, Paris. France's answer to England's Ascot is the country's most prestigious horse race, culminating the equine season in Europe. Call ✆ **01-49-10-20-30,** or visit www.france-galop.com. Early October.

NOVEMBER

Armistice Day, nationwide. In Paris, the signing of the document that ended World War I is celebrated with a military parade from the Arc de Triomphe to the Hôtel des Invalides. November 11.

Les Trois Glorieuses, Clos-de-Vougeot, Beaune, and Meursault. Three Burgundian towns stage the country's most important wine festival. Though you may not gain access to many of the gatherings, tastings and other amusements will keep you occupied. Reserve early, or visit as day trips from nearby villages. Contact the Office de Tourisme de Beaune (✆ **03-80-26-21-30;** www. ot-beaune.fr). Third week in November.

DECEMBER

Christmas Fairs, Alsace (especially Strasbourg). More than 60 villages celebrate a traditional Christmas. The events in Strasbourg have continued for some 430 years. Other towns with celebrations are Münster, Sélestat, Riquewihr, Kaysersberg, Wissembourg, and Thann. Call ✆ **03-89-24-73-50,** or visit www.tourism-alsace.com. Late November to December 24.

The Boat Fair (Le Salon Nautique de Paris). Europe's major exposition of what's afloat, at Salon Nautique de Paris, 52-54 quai de Dion-Bouton, 15e, Paris (✆ **01-47-56-50-00;** www.salonnautiqueparis.com; Métro: Porte de Versailles). Ten days in early December.

Fête des Lumières, Lyon. In honor of the Virgin Mary, lights are placed in windows through the city. Call ✆ **04-72-10-30-30,** or visit www.lumieres.lyon.fr. Early December through early January.

Marché de Noël, Mougins. About 40 merchants, selling all kinds of Christmas ornaments and gifts, descend on this small village in Provence. Call ✆ **04-93-75-87-67,** or visit www.mougins-coteazur.org. Early December.

Fête de St-Sylvestre (New Year's Eve), nationwide. In Paris, this holiday is most boisterously celebrated in the Quartier Latin. At midnight, the city explodes. Strangers kiss and boulevard St-Michel and the Champs-Elysées become virtual pedestrian malls. December 31.

ENTRY REQUIREMENTS

Passports

It's always wise to have plenty of documentation when traveling with children. For changing details on entry requirements for children traveling abroad, keep up-to-date by going to the U.S. State Department website at **www.travel.state.gov**. Children of all ages (from birth) require a passport; children 16 and up follow the same rules for a first-time passport applicant. To obtain a passport, the child *must* be present at the center issuing the passport. Both parents or guardians must be present as well; if not, then a notarized statement from the absent parent or guardian is required.

To prevent international child abduction, E.U. governments have initiated procedures at entry and exit points. These often (but not always) include requiring documentary evidence of relationship and permission for the child's travel from the parent or legal guardian not present. Having such documentation on hand, even if not required, facilitates entries and exits. Any questions parents or guardians might have can be answered by calling the **National Passport Information Center** at ✆ **877/487-2778** Monday to Friday 8am to 8pm Eastern Standard Time.

Customs

WHAT YOU CAN BRING INTO FRANCE

Customs restrictions for visitors entering France differ for citizens of European Union (E.U.) and non-E.U. countries. Non-E.U. nationals can bring in duty-free either 200 cigarettes, 100 cigarillos, 50 cigars, or 250 grams of smoking tobacco. This amount is doubled if you live outside Europe. You can also bring in 2 liters of wine and 1 liter of alcohol over 22%, and 2 liters of wine 22% or under. In addition, you can bring in 60cc of perfume, a quarter liter of eau de toilette. Visitors ages 15 and over can bring in other goods totaling 175€; for those under 15, the limit is 90€. Customs officials tend to be lenient about general merchandise as the limits are very low. Citizens of E.U. countries can bring in any amount of goods as long as the goods are intended for their personal use and not for resale.

WHAT YOU CAN TAKE HOME FROM FRANCE

For information on what you're allowed to bring home, contact one of the following agencies:

U.S. Citizens: U.S. Customs & Border Protection (CBP), 1300 Pennsylvania Ave., NW, Washington, DC 20229 (✆ **877/287-8667;** www.cbp.gov).

Canadian Citizens: Canada Border Services Agency (✆ **800/461-9999** in Canada, or 204/983-3500; www.cbsa-asfc.gc.ca).

U.K. Citizens: HM Customs & Excise at ✆ **0845/010-9000** (from outside the U.K., 020/8929-0152), or consult their website at **www.hmce.gov.uk**.

Australian Citizens: Australian Customs Service at ✆ **1300/363-263,** or log on to **www.customs.gov.au**.

New Zealand Citizens: New Zealand Customs, The Customhouse, 17–21 Whitmore St., Box 2218, Wellington (✆ **04/473-6099** or 0800/428-786; **www. customs.govt.nz**).

Medical Requirements

For information on medical requirements and recommendations, see "Health," p. 58.

GETTING THERE & GETTING AROUND

Getting To France

AIRPORTS

The two Paris airports—Orly (airport code: ORY) and Charles de Gaulle (airport code: CDG)—are about even in terms of convenience to the city's center, though taxi rides from Orly may take less time than those from de Gaulle. Orly, the older of the two, is 13km (8 miles) south of the center; Charles de Gaulle is 22km (14 miles) northeast. Air France serves Charles de Gaulle (Terminal 2C) from North America. U.S. carriers land at both airports.

Most airlines charge their lowest fares between November 1 and March 13. Shoulder season (Oct and mid-Mar to mid-June) is a bit more expensive, though we think it's the ideal time to visit France.

THE MAJOR AIRLINES

American Airlines (© 800/433-7300; www.aa.com) has daily flights to Paris from Dallas–Fort Worth, Chicago, Miami, Boston, and New York.

British Airways (© 800/247-9297; www.britishairways.com) offers flights from 18 U.S. cities to Heathrow and Gatwick airports in England. From there, you can connect to a British Airways flight to Paris.

Continental Airlines (© 800/231-0856; www.continental.com) provides non-stop flights to Paris from Newark and Houston. Flights from Newark depart daily; flights from Houston depart four to seven times a week, depending on the season.

Delta Air Lines (© 800/221-1212; www.delta.com) flies nonstop from Atlanta to Paris every evening and operates daily nonstop flights from Cincinnati and New York. Delta is the only airline offering nonstop service from New York to Nice.

US Airways (© 800/428-4322; www.usairways.com) offers daily nonstop service from Philadelphia to Paris.

The French national carrier, **Air France** (© 800/237-2747; www.airfrance.com), offers daily flights between Paris and such North American cities as Atlanta, Boston, Chicago, Cincinnati, Houston, Los Angeles, Mexico City, Miami, Montreal, New York, Newark, San Francisco, Toronto, and Washington, D.C.

In 2004, Air France acquired control of KLM Royal Dutch Airlines, which led to the creation of **Air France–KLM,** the world's biggest airline in terms of revenue. KLM and Air France have coordinated their schedules and fares and are acting as a unit. The merger has led to better connections between flights.

FLIGHTS FROM AUSTRALIA & NEW ZEALAND

Getting to Paris from Australia is difficult, because **Air France** (© 02-92-44-21-00; www.airfrance.fr) has discontinued direct flights. Qantas flies from Sydney to Singapore and other locations with service to Paris. Consequently, on virtually any route, you have to change planes at least once and sometimes twice. **British Airways** (© 1300-767-177; www.britishairways.com) flies daily from Sydney and Melbourne to London, where you can catch one of several connecting flights to Paris. **Qantas** (© 612/13-13-13; www.qantas.com.au) can route passengers from

Australia into London, where you make connections for the hop across the Channel. Qantas also flies from Auckland to Sydney and on to London.

GETTING THERE FROM THE U.K. & CONTINENTAL EUROPE

By Plane

From London, **Air France** (© 0870/142-4343; www.airfrance.com) and **British Airways** (© 0844/493-0787 in the U.K.; www.britishairways.com) fly frequently to Paris; the trip takes 1 hour. These airlines operate up to 17 flights daily from Heathrow. Many travelers also fly out of the London City Airport in the Docklands.

Direct flights to Paris operate from other U.K. cities such as Manchester and Edinburgh. Contact Air France, British Airways, or **British Midland** (© 0870/607-0555; www.flybmi.com). Daily papers often carry ads for cheap flights. Highly recommended **Trailfinders** (© 0845/058-5858; www.trailfinders.com) sells discount fares.

You can reach Paris from any major European capital. Your best bet is to fly on the national carrier, Air France, which has more connections into Paris from European capitals than any other airline. From Dublin, try **Aer Lingus** (© 800/IRISH-AIR [474-7424]; www.aerlingus.com), which schedules the most flights to Paris from Ireland. From Amsterdam, try **NWA/KLM** (© 800/225-2525; www.nwa.com).

By Train

Paris is one of Europe's busiest rail junctions, with trains arriving at and departing from its many stations every few minutes. If you're in Europe, you may want to go to Paris by train. The cost is relatively low—especially compared to renting a car.

Rail passes as well as individual rail tickets are available at most travel agencies or at any office of **Rail Europe** (© 888/382-7245 in the U.S.; www.raileurope.com) or **Eurostar** (© 800/EUROSAR [387-6782] in the U.S.; www.eurostar.com).

By Bus

Bus travel to Paris is available from London as well as from many cities on the Continent. In the early 1990s, the French government established incentives for longhaul buses not to drive into the center of Paris. The arrival and departure point for Europe's largest operator, **Eurolines France,** 28 av. du Général-de-Gaulle, 93541 Bagnolet (© 08-92-89-90-91; www.eurolines.fr), is a 35-minute Métro ride from central Paris, at the terminus of line no. 3 (Métro: Gallieni), in the eastern suburb of Bagnolet. Despite this inconvenience, many people prefer bus travel.

Long-haul buses are equipped with toilets, and they stop at mealtimes for rest and refreshment.

Because Eurolines does not have a U.S. sales agent, most people buy their ticket in Europe. Any European travel agent can arrange the sale. If you're traveling to Paris from London, contact **Eurolines (U.K.) Ltd.,** 52 Grosvenor Gardens, Victoria, London SW1 0AU (© 0871/781-81-81; www.nationalexpress.com for information or credit card sales).

By Car

The major highways into Paris are A1 from the north (Great Britain and Benelux); A13 from Rouen, Normandy, and northwest France; A10 from Bordeaux, the Pyrénées, the southwest, and Spain; A6 from Lyon, the French Alps, the Riviera, and Italy; and A4 from Metz, Nancy, and Strasbourg in the east.

By Ferry from England

Ferries and hydrofoils operate day and night, with the exception of last-minute cancellations during storms. Many crossings are timed to coincide with the arrival and departure of trains (especially those btw. London and Paris). Trains let you off a short walk from the piers. Most ferries carry cars, trucks, and freight, but some hydrofoils take passengers only. The major routes include at least 12 trips a day between Dover or Folkestone and Calais or Boulogne.

Hovercraft and hydrofoils make the trip from Dover to Calais, the shortest distance across the Channel, in just 40 minutes during good weather. The ferries may take several hours, depending on the weather and tides. If you're bringing a car, it's important to make reservations—space below decks is usually crowded. Timetables can vary depending on weather conditions and many other factors.

The leading operator of ferries across the channel is **P&O Ferries** (🕿 **0871/664-5645** in the U.K.; www.poferries.com). It operates car and passenger ferries between Portsmouth, England, and Cherbourg, France (three departures a day; 4 hr., 15 min. each way during daylight hours, 7 hr. each way at night); and between Portsmouth and Le Havre, France (three a day; 5½ hr. each way). Most popular is the route between Dover, England, and Calais, France (25 sailings a day; 75 min. each way).

Getting Around

BY PLANE

France has few domestic competitors. **Air France** (🕿 **800/237-2747;** www.air-france.com) is the primary carrier, serving about eight cities in France and eight others in Europe. Air travel time from Paris to almost anywhere in France is about an hour.

BY CAR

The most charming châteaux and country hotels always seem to lie away from the main cities and train stations. Renting a car is often the best way to travel around France, especially if you plan to explore it in depth.

But Europe's rail networks are so well developed and inexpensive that we recommend you rent a car only for exploring areas little serviced by rail, such as Brittany, rural Burgundy, and the Dordogne. Or take trains between cities and rent a car on the days when you want to explore independently.

Driving time in Europe is largely a matter of conjecture, urgency, and how much sightseeing you do along the way. Driving time from Paris to Geneva is 5½ hours minimum. It's 2½ hours from Paris to Rouen, 3½ hours to Nantes, and 4 hours to Lyon. The driving time from Marseille to Paris (771km/479 miles) is a matter of national pride, and tall tales abound about how rapidly the French can do it. Flooring it, you may conceivably get there in 7 hours, but we always make a 2-day journey of it.

RENTALS   To rent a car, you'll need to present a passport, a driver's license, and a credit card. You also have to meet the company's minimum-age requirement. (For the least expensive cars, this is 21 at Hertz, 23 at Avis, and 25 at Budget. More expensive cars may require that you be at least 25.) It usually isn't obligatory within France, but certain companies have asked for the presentation of an International

under THE CHANNEL

Queen Elizabeth II and the late French president François Mitterrand opened the Channel Tunnel in 1994, and now the **Eurostar Express** has daily passenger service from London to Paris and Brussels. The $15-billion tunnel, one of the great engineering feats of our time, is the first link between Britain and the Continent since the Ice Age. The 50km (31-mile) journey takes 35 minutes, with actual time spent in the Chunnel 19 minutes.

Eurostar tickets are available through **Rail Europe** (© 888/382-7245; www.raileurope.com). In London, make reservations for Eurostar (or any other train in Europe) at © 0870/518-6186. In Paris, call © 01-70-70-60-88, and in the United States, call © 800/EURO-SAR (387-6782; www.eurostar.com). Chunnel train travel is competitive with air travel, if you calculate door-to-door travel time. Trains leave from London's Waterloo Station and arrive in Paris at Gare du Nord. Fares are complicated

and depend on a number of factors. The cheapest one-way fare is Leisure RT, requiring a purchase at least 14 business days before the date of travel and a minimum 2-night stay. A return ticket must be booked to receive this discounted fare.

The Chunnel accommodates not only trains but also cars, buses, taxis, and motorcycles. **Eurotunnel,** a train carrying vehicles under the Channel (© 0870/535-3535 in the U.K.; www.eurotunnel.com), connects Calais, France, with Folkestone, England. It operates 24 hours a day, 365 days a year, running every 15 minutes during peak travel times and at least once an hour at night.

Before boarding Eurotunnel, you stop at a tollbooth to pay, then pass through Immigration for both countries at one time. During the ride, you travel in air-conditioned carriages, remaining in your car or stepping outside to stretch your legs. An hour later, you simply drive off.

Driver's License, even though this is becoming increasingly superfluous in Western Europe.

Note: The best deal is usually a weekly rental with unlimited mileage. All car-rental bills in France are subject to a 19.6% government tax. Though the rental company won't usually mind if you drive your car into, say, Germany, Switzerland, Italy, or Spain, it's often forbidden to transport your car by ferry, including across the Channel to England.

In France, **collision damage waiver (CDW)** is usually factored into the overall rate quoted, but you should always verify this, of course, before taking a car on the road. At most companies, the CDW provision won't protect you against theft, so if this is the case, ask about purchasing extra theft protection.

Automatic transmission is a luxury in Europe, so if you want it, you'll pay dearly. **Budget** (© 800/472-3325; www.budget.com) has about 30 locations in Paris and at Orly (© 01-49-75-56-05) and Charles de Gaulle (© 01-48-62-70-22). For rentals of more than 7 days, you can usually pick up a car in one French city and drop it off in another, but there are extra charges. Drop-offs in cities within an easy drive of the French border (including Geneva and Frankfurt) incur no extra charge; you can arrange drop-offs in other non-French cities for a reasonable surcharge.

Hertz (✆ **800/654-3001** in the U.S. and Canada; www.hertz.com) maintains about 15 locations in Paris, including offices at the city's airports. The main office is at 27 place St-Ferdinand, 17e (✆ **01-45-74-97-39;** Métro: Argentine). Be sure to ask about promotional discounts.

Avis (✆ **800/331-1084** in the U.S. and Canada; www.avis.com) has offices at both Paris airports and an inner-city headquarters at 5 rue Bixio, 7e (✆ **01-44-18-10-50;** Métro: Ecole Militaire), near the Eiffel Tower.

National (✆ **800/CAR-RENT** [227-7368] in the U.S. and Canada; www.nationalcar.com) is represented in Paris by Europcar, one office is at 78 rue du Rocher, 8e (✆ **01-45-22-77-91;** Métro: St. Philippe du Roule). It has offices at both Paris airports and at about a dozen other locations. For the lowest rates, reserve in advance from North America.

Two U.S.-based agencies that don't have Paris offices but act as booking agents for Paris-based agencies are **Kemwel Drive Europe** (✆ **877/820-0668;** www.kemwel.com) and **Auto Europe** (✆ **888/223-5555;** www.autoeurope.com). They can make bookings in the United States only, so call before your trip.

GASOLINE   Known in France as *essence,* gas is expensive for those accustomed to North American prices. All but the least expensive cars usually require an octane rating that the French classify as *essence super,* the most expensive variety. Depending on your car, you'll need either leaded (*avec plomb*) or unleaded (*sans plomb*).

Beware the mixture of gasoline and oil, called *mélange* or *gasoil,* sold in some rural communities; this mixture is for very old two-cycle engines.

Note: Sometimes you can drive for miles in rural France without encountering a gas station; don't let your tank get dangerously low.

DRIVING RULES   Everyone in the car, in both the front and the back seats, must wear seat belts. Children 11 and under must ride in the back seat. Drivers are supposed to yield to the car on their right, except where signs indicate otherwise, as at traffic circles.

If you violate the speed limit, expect a big fine. Limits are about 130kmph (81 mph) on expressways, about 100kmph (62 mph) on major national highways, and 90kmph (56 mph) on country roads. In towns, don't exceed 60kmph (37 mph).

Note: It's illegal to use a cellphone while you're driving in France; you will be ticketed if you're stopped.

MAPS   For France as a whole, most motorists opt for **Michelin map 989;** www.viamichelin.com. For regions, Michelin publishes a series of **yellow maps** that are quite good. Big travel-book stores in North America carry these maps, and they're commonly available in France (at lower prices). In this age of congested traffic, one useful feature of the Michelin map is its designations of alternative *routes de dégagement,* which let you skirt big cities and avoid traffic-clogged highways.

Another recommended option is *Frommer's Road Atlas Europe.*

BREAKDOWNS/ASSISTANCE   A breakdown is called *une panne* in France. Call the police at ✆ **17** anywhere in France to be put in touch with the nearest garage. Most local garages offer towing. If the breakdown occurs on an expressway, find the nearest roadside emergency phone box, pick up the phone, and put a call through. You'll be connected to the nearest breakdown service facility.

BY TRAIN

The world's fastest trains link some 50 French cities, allowing you to get from Paris to just about anywhere else in the country in hours. With 39,000km (24,200 miles) of track and about 3,000 stations, SNCF (French National Railroads) is fabled for its on-time performance. You can travel in first or second class by day and in couchette by night. Many trains have dining facilities.

INFORMATION   If you plan to travel a lot on European railroads, get the latest copy of the *Thomas Cook Timetable of European Passenger Railroads*. This 500-plus-page book documents all of Europe's main passenger rail services with detail and accuracy. It's available online at www.thomascookpublishing.com.

   In the United States: For more information and to purchase rail passes before you leave, contact **Rail Europe** (© **877/272-RAIL** [272-7245]; www.raileurope. com).

   In Canada: Call Rail Europe at © **800/361-RAIL** (361-7245).

   In London: SNCF has offices at Rail Europe, 179 Piccadilly, London W1V 0BA (© **0870/584-8848**).

   In Paris: For information or reservations, go online (www.sncf.fr). You can also go to any local travel agency. A simpler way to buy tickets is to use the *billetterie* (ticket machine) in every train station. If you know your PIN, you can use a credit card to buy your ticket.

FRANCE RAIL PASSES   Working cooperatively with SNCF, Air Inter Europe, and Avis, Rail Europe (www.railfrance.com) offers three flexible rail passes to North Americans that can reduce travel costs considerably.

   The **France Railpass** provides unlimited rail transport in France for any 3 days within 1 month, at $315 in first class and $269 in second. You can purchase up to 6 more days for an extra $48 per person per day. Children 4 to 11 travel for half-price.

   The **France Rail 'n' Drive Pass,** available only in North America, combines good value on both rail travel and Avis car rentals. It is best used by arriving at a major rail depot and then striking out to explore the countryside by car. It includes the France Railpass (see above) and use of a rental car. A 2-day rail pass (first class) and 2 days' use of the cheapest rental car (with unlimited mileage) is $534 to $612 per person. The best deal if you're traveling in France with a friend—or even three or four friends—is the **France Saverpass,** granting 3 days of unlimited travel in a 1-month period. The cost is $268 per person first class or $231 second class. There's also a **France Youthpass** for travelers 25 or under, granting 3 days of unlimited train travel within a month. The cost is $233 in first class or $200 in second class. For those over 60, the **France Senior Pass** offers all the same features as the France Railpass, but with a savings. You get 3 days of unlimited train travel in 1 month for $288, with additional rail days costing $43 each. Travel days may be used consecutively or nonconsecutively.

   A **France Rail Day Pass** allows you to take day trips from Paris to such cities as Lyon, Reims, Dijon, or Nantes. The cost is $162 in first class or $114 in second class. The pass grants you 1 day of unlimited travel in a 1-month period on the national rail network.

EURAILPASS   The Eurailpass permits unlimited first-class rail travel in any country in western Europe except the British Isles (good in Ireland). Passes are available for purchase online (www.eurail.com) and at various offices/agents around the world. Travel agents and railway agents in such cities as New York, Montreal, and Los Angeles sell Eurailpasses. You can purchase them at the North American offices of CIT Travel Service, the French National Railroads, the German Federal Railroads, and the Swiss Federal Railways. It is strongly recommended that you purchase passes before you leave home as not all passes are available in Europe; also, passes purchased in Europe will cost about 20% more. Numerous options are available for travel in France.

The **Eurail Global Pass** allows you unlimited travel in 20 Eurail-affiliated countries. You can travel on any of the days within the validity period, which is available for 15 days, 21 days, 1 month, 2 months, 3 months, and some other possibilities as well. Prices for first-class adult travel are $798 for 15 days, $1,034 for 21 days, $1,285 for 1 month, $1,813 for 2 months, and $2,236 for 3 months. Children 4 to 11 pay half fare; those 3 and under travel for free.

A **Eurail Global Pass Saver,** also valid for first-class travel in 20 countries, offers a special deal for two or more people traveling together. This pass costs $676 for 15 days, $878 for 21 days, $1,090 for 1 month, $1,541 for 2 months, and $1,908 for 3 months.

A **Eurail Global Youth Pass** for those 12 to 25 allows second-class travel in 18 countries. This pass costs $518 for 15 days, $671 for 21 days, $836 for 1 month, $1,179 for 2 months, and $1,457 for 3 months.

The **Eurail Select Pass** offers unlimited travel on the national rail networks of any three, four, or five bordering countries out of the 22 Eurail nations linked by train or ship. Two or more passengers can travel together for big discounts, getting 5, 6, 8, 10, or 15 days of rail travel within any 2-month period on the national rail networks of any three, four, or five adjoining Eurail countries linked by train or ship. A sample fare: For 5 days in 2 months, you pay $504 for three countries. **Eurail Select Pass Youth** for travelers under 26, allows second-class travel within the same guidelines as Eurail Selectpass, with fees starting at $328. **Eurail Select Pass Saver** offers discounts for one or more people traveling together, first-class travel within the same guidelines as Eurail Selectpass, with fees starting at $428.

MONEY & COSTS

THE VALUE OF THE EURO VS. OTHER POPULAR CURRENCIES

Euro	US$	UK£	C$	A$	NZ$
1.00	1.35	.90	1.40	1.45	1.90

For decades Paris was known as one of the most expensive cities on earth. It still is a pricey destination, but London has surpassed it. Paris is not as expensive as Tokyo or Oslo, but even an average hotel can cost $200 or more—in many cases, much much more.

It's always advisable to bring money in a variety of forms on a vacation: a mix of cash, credit cards, and traveler's checks. You should also exchange enough petty cash to cover airport incidentals, tipping, and transportation to your hotel before you leave home, or withdraw money upon arrival at an airport ATM.

In many international destinations, ATMs offer the best exchange rates. Avoid exchanging money at commercial exchange bureaus and hotels, which often have the highest transaction fees.

Not just Paris, but all of France is a very expensive destination. To compensate, you can often find top-value food and lodging. Part of the cost is the value-added tax (VAT in English, TVA in French), which adds between 6% and 33% to everything.

Rental cars (and fuel) are expensive, and flying within France costs more than within the U.S. Train travel is relatively inexpensive, especially with a rail pass. Prices in Paris and on the Riviera are higher than in the provinces. Three of the most visited areas—Brittany, Normandy, and the Loire Valley—have reasonably priced hotels and restaurants offering superb food at moderate prices.

ATMs

ATMs are widely available in France, certainly in all cities and bigger towns, and even at a bank or two in smaller places. But don't always count on it. If you're venturing into rural France, it's always good to have euros in your pocket.

There are problems involved in the use of ATMs. For example, if you make a mistake and punch your secret code wrong into the machine three times, that machine will swallow your card on the assumption that it is being fraudulently used.

Users with alphabetical rather than numerical PINs may be thrown off by the lack of letters on French cash machines. If your PIN is longer than four digits, check with your bank to see if you can use the first four digits, or if you will have to get a new number for use in France.

To get a cash advance by using a credit card at an ATM, ask for a PIN from your credit card company before leaving your home country.

Note: Remember that many banks impose a fee every time you use a card at another bank's ATM, and that fee can be higher for international transactions (up to $5 or more) than for domestic ones (where they're rarely more than $3). In addition, the bank from which you withdraw cash may charge its own fee. For international withdrawal fees, ask your bank.

Credit Cards

Credit cards are another safe way to carry money. They provide a convenient record of all your expenses, and they generally offer relatively good exchange rates. You can usually withdraw cash advances from your credit cards at banks or ATMs, provided you know your PIN. Keep in mind that you'll pay interest from the moment of your withdrawal, even if you pay your monthly bills on time. Also, note that many banks now assess a 1% to 3% "transaction fee" on *all* charges you incur abroad (whether you're using the local currency or your native currency).

Chip and PIN represents a change in the way that credit and debit cards are used. The program is designed to cut down on the fraudulent use of credit cards. More banks are issuing customers Chip and PIN versions of their debit or credit cards, and more vendors are asking for a four-digit personal identification number, which must be entered into a keypad near the cash register. In some cases, a waiter will bring a hand-held model to your table to verify your credit card.

For the time being, both the new and old cards usually are accepted in shops, hotels, and restaurants regardless of whether they have the new Chip and PIN machines installed. However, some establishments might not accept your credit card unless you have a computer chip imbedded in it; in the changeover in technology, some retailers have falsely concluded that they can no longer accept swipe cards or signature cards without PINs.

HEALTH

General Availability of Healthcare

In general, France is a safe destination. You don't need shots, most food is safe, and the water is potable. It is easy to get a prescription filled, and nearly all destinations have English-speaking doctors at hospitals with well-trained staffs.

Contact the **International Association for Medical Assistance to Travelers** (**IAMAT;** © **716/754-4883** or 416/652-0137 in Canada; www.iamat.org) for tips on travel and health concerns in the countries you're visiting, and for lists of local English-speaking doctors. The United States **Centers for Disease Control and Prevention** (© **800/232-4636;** www.cdc.gov) provides up-to-date information on health hazards by region or country and offers tips on food safety. **Travel Health Online** (www.tripprep.com), sponsored by a consortium of travel medicine practitioners, may also offer helpful advice on traveling abroad. You can find listings of reliable medical clinics overseas at the **International Society of Travel Medicine** (www.istm.org).

The following government websites offer up-to-date health-related travel advice:

- **Australia:** www.smartraveller.gov.au
- **Canada:** www.hc-sc.gc.ca
- **U.K.:** www.nathnac.org
- **U.S.:** www.cdc.gov/travel

WHAT TO DO IF YOU GET SICK AWAY FROM HOME

For travel abroad, you may have to pay all medical costs upfront and be reimbursed later. Medicare and Medicaid do not provide coverage for medical costs outside the U.S. Before leaving home, find out what medical services your health insurance covers. To protect yourself, consider buying medical travel insurance (see "Medical Insurance" under "Insurance" in "Fast Facts," p. 760).

U.K. nationals will need a **European Health Insurance Card** (**EHIC;** © **0845/605-0707;** www.ehic.org.uk) to receive free or reduced-costs health benefits during a visit to a European Economic Area (EEA) country (European Union countries plus Iceland, Liechtenstein, and Norway) or Switzerland.

We list **hospitals** and **emergency numbers** in "Fast Facts" (p. 759).

If you suffer from a chronic illness, consult your doctor before your departure. Pack **prescription medications** in your carry-on luggage and carry them in their original containers, with pharmacy labels—otherwise they might not make it through airport security. Carry the generic name of prescription medicines, in case a local pharmacist is unfamiliar with the brand name.

SAFETY

The most common menace, especially in large cities—particularly Paris—is the plague of pickpockets. Never leave valuables in a car and never travel with your car unlocked.

Much of the country, particularly central France, the northeast, Normandy, and Brittany, remains relatively safe, although no place in the world is crime-free. Those intending to visit the south of France, especially the Riviera, should exercise caution; robberies and muggings are more likely to occur here than in other parts of the country. It's best to check your baggage into a hotel and then go sightseeing instead of leaving it unguarded in the trunk of a car, which can easily be broken into. Marseille is among the most dangerous French cities.

SPECIALIZED TRAVEL RESOURCES

In addition to the destination-specific resources listed below, please visit Frommers. com for additional specialized travel resources.

Gay & Lesbian Travelers

France is one of the world's most tolerant countries toward gays and lesbians. "Gay Paree" boasts a large gay population, with many clubs, restaurants, organizations, and services.

Lesbian or bisexual women can also pick up a copy of *Lesbia.* This publication and others are available at Paris's largest, best-stocked gay bookstore, **Les Mots à la Bouche,** 6 rue Ste-Croix-de-la-Bretonnerie, 4e (*©* **01-42-78-88-30;** www. motsbouche.com; Métro: Hôtel-de-Ville), which carries publications in both French and English.

The **International Gay and Lesbian Travel Association** (IGLTA; *©* **800/448-8550** or 954/630-1637; www.iglta.org) is the trade association for the gay and lesbian travel industry, and offers an online directory of gay- and lesbian-friendly travel businesses and tour operators.

Many agencies offer tours and travel itineraries specifically for gay and lesbian travelers. **Above and Beyond Tours** (*©* 800/397-2681; www.abovebeyondtours.com) are gay Australia tour specialists. San Francisco–based **Now, Voyager** (*©* **800/255-6951;** www.nowvoyager.com) offers worldwide trips and cruises, and **Olivia** (*©* 800/ 631-6277; www.olivia.com) offers lesbian cruises and resort vacations.

Gay.com Travel (*©* **415/834-6500;** www.gay.com/travel), is an excellent online travel resource. It provides regularly updated information about gay-owned, gay-oriented, and gay-friendly lodging, dining, sightseeing, nightlife, and shopping establishments in every important destination worldwide.

The following travel guides are available at many bookstores, or you can order them from any online bookseller: *Spartacus International Gay Guide* (Bruno Gmünder Verlag; www.spartacusworld.com/gayguide); and the *Damron* guides (www.damron.com), with separate annual books for gay men and lesbians. For more gay and lesbian travel resources, visit Frommers.com.

Travelers with Disabilities

Most disabilities shouldn't stop anyone from traveling. There are more options and resources out there than ever before.

Facilities for travelers in France, and nearly all modern hotels, provide accessible rooms. Older hotels (unless they've been renovated) may not provide elevators, special toilet facilities, or wheelchair ramps. The TGVs (high-speed trains) are wheelchair accessible; older trains have compartments for wheelchair boarding. On the Paris Métro, passengers with disabilities are able to sit in wider seats. Guide dogs ride free. However, some stations don't have escalators or elevators.

Knowing which hotels, restaurants, and attractions are accessible can save you a lot of frustration. **Association des Paralysés de France,** 17 bd. Auguste-Blanqui, Paris 75013 (✆ **01-40-78-69-66;** www.apf.asso.fr), provides documentation, moral support, and travel ideas for individuals who use wheelchairs. In addition to the Paris office, it maintains an office in each of the 90 *départements* ("ministates" into which France is divided) and can help find hotels, transportation, sightseeing, house rentals, and (in some cases) companionship for paralyzed or partially paralyzed travelers. It's not, however, a travel agency.

Organizations that offer a vast range of resources and assistance to travelers with disabilities include **MossRehab** (✆ **800/CALL-MOSS** [225-5667]; www.moss resourcenet.org); the **American Foundation for the Blind** (AFB; ✆ **800/232-5463;** www.afb.org); and **Society for Accessible Travel & Hospitality** (**SATH;** ✆ **212/447-7284;** www.sath.org). **AirAmbulanceCard.com** (✆ **877/424-7633**) is now partnered with SATH and allows you to preselect top-notch hospitals in case of an emergency.

Access-Able Travel Source (www.access-able.com) offers a comprehensive database on travel agents from around the world with experience in accessible travel; destination-specific access information; and links to such resources as service animals, equipment rentals, and access guides.

Many travel agencies offer customized tours and itineraries for travelers with disabilities. Among them are **Flying Wheels Travel** (✆ **507/451-5005;** www.flying wheelstravel.com) and **Accessible Journeys** (✆ **800/846-4537** or 610/521-0339; www.disabilitytravel.com).

Flying with Disability (www.flying-with-disability.org) is a comprehensive information source on airplane travel. The "Accessible Travel" link at **Mobility-Advisor. com** (www.mobility-advisor.com) offers a variety of travel resources to persons with disabilities. Also check out the quarterly magazine *Emerging Horizons* (www. emerginghorizons.com), available by subscription.

British travelers should contact **Holiday Care** (✆ **0845-124-9971** in the U.K. only; www.holidaycare.org.uk) to access a wide range of travel information and resources for elderly people and those with disabilities.

For more on organizations that offer resources to travelers with disabilities, go to Frommers.com.

Family Travel

To locate accommodations, restaurants, and attractions that are particularly kid-friendly, refer to the "Kids" icon throughout this guide.

Recommended family travel websites include **Family Travel Forum** (www. familytravelforum.com), a comprehensive site that offers customized trip planning; **Family Travel Network** (www.familytravelnetwork.com), an online magazine providing travel tips; **TravellingInternationallyWithYourKids.com** (www.travel withyourkids.com), a comprehensive site written by parents for parents offering sound advice for long-distance and international travel with children; and Family Travel Files (www.thefamilytravelfiles.com), which offers an online magazine and a directory of off-the-beaten-path tours and tour operators for families. A fun read, for recommendations in France and elsewhere, is *Frommer's 500 Places to Take Your Kids Before They Grow Up* (Wiley Publishing, Inc.). France-specific titles include *Frommer's Brittany with Your Family; Frommer's the Dordogne with Your Family; Frommer's Normandy with Your Family; Frommer's Paris & Disneyland Paris with Your Family;* and *Frommer's Provence & the Côte d'Azur with Your Family.*

For a list of more family-friendly travel resources, turn to the experts at Frommers.com.

Multicultural travelers

Since the days of the celebrated chanteuse Josephine Baker and, later, the author James Baldwin, France has welcomed African-American travelers. That welcome continues today. A good book on the subject is Tyler Stovall's *Paris Noir.* Another worthwhile resource is the website www.cafedelasoul.com.

Regrettably, anti-Semitism has been on the rise in Europe, especially in France, which has registered a significant increase in incidents against Jews. French Jews (not visitors from abroad) have suffered assaults and attacks against synagogues, cemeteries, schools, and other Jewish property. Officials say they believe that attacks in France are linked to the worsening of the Israeli-Palestinian conflict. Some sources—none official—recommend that travelers conceal Star of David jewelry and other such items to ensure personal safety while traveling in France.

Officially, the government of France welcomes Jewish visitors and promises a vigorous defense of their safety and concerns. The French Government Tourist Office website (www.franceguide.com) has a *FranceGuide for the Jewish Traveler* in the "Publications" section with more information.

Senior Travel

Many discounts are available to seniors—men and women of the "third age," as the French say; contact the French Government Tourist Office (see "Visitor Information," in "Fast Facts," p. 764) for information.

Air France offers seniors a 10% reduction on its regular nonexcursion fares within France. Some restrictions apply. Discounts of around 10% are offered to passengers ages 62 and older on select Air France international flights. Be sure to ask for the discount when booking.

Members of **AARP,** 601 E St. NW, Washington, DC 20049 (© 888/687-2277; www.aarp.org), get discounts on hotels, airfares, and car rentals. AARP offers members a wide range of benefits, including *AARP The Magazine* and a monthly newsletter. Anyone over 50 can join.

Many reliable agencies and organizations target the 50-plus market. **Elderhostel** (© 800/454-5768; www.exploritas.org) arranges worldwide study programs for those aged 55 and over.

Recommended publications offering travel resources and discounts for seniors include the quarterly magazine *Travel 50 & Beyond* (www.travel50andbeyond.com). Frommers.com offers more information and resources on travel for seniors.

SPECIAL INTEREST TRIPS & ESCORTED TOURS

Special Interest Trips

In a country as diverse and popular as France, there are numerous options.

BALLOONING The world's largest hot-air-balloon operator is **Buddy Bombard's Private Europe,** 333 Pershing Way, West Palm Beach, FL 33401 (ℂ **800/862-8537** or 561/837-6610; fax 561/837-6623; www.buddybombard. com). It maintains about three dozen hot-air balloons, some in the Loire Valley and Burgundy. The 5-day tours, costing $8,940 per person (double occupancy), incorporate food and wine tasting and all meals, lodging in Relais & Châteaux hotels, sightseeing, rail transfers to and from Paris, and a daily balloon ride over vineyards and fields.

Bonaventura Balloon Co., 133 Wall Rd., Napa Valley, CA 94573 (ℂ **800/ FLY-NAPA** [359-6272] or 707/944-2822; fax 707/944-2220; www.bonaventura balloons.com), meets you in Paris and takes you on the high-speed train to Burgundy, where your balloon tour begins. It carries you over the scenic parts of the region. Guests stay in a 14th-century mill, now an inn owned by a three-star chef.

BARGE CRUISES Before the advent of the railways, many crops, building supplies, raw materials, and finished products were barged through France on a series of rivers, canals, and estuaries. Many of these waterways retain their old-fashioned locks and pumps, allowing shallow-draft barges easy access through the idyllic countryside.

French Country Waterways, Ltd., P.O. Box 2195, Duxbury, MA 02331 (ℂ **800/222-1236** or 781/934-2454; www.fcwl.com), leads 1-week tours through Burgundy and Champagne. For double occupancy, the price ranges from $6,995 to $8,195.

Le Boat, 93 N. Park Place Blvd., Clearwater, FL 33759 (ℂ **800/992-0291** or 800/734-5491; fax 727/530-9747; www.leboat.com), focuses on regions of France not covered by many other operators. The company's luxury crafts fit through the narrow canals and locks of Camargue, Languedoc, and Provence. Each 6-night tour has 10 passengers in five cabins outfitted with mahogany and brass, plus meals prepared by a Cordon Bleu chef. Prices vary widely.

Go Barging (ℂ **800/394-8630;** www.gobarging.com) operates Great Island Voyages, featuring river cruise ships. Fares start at $4,590 per person (double occupancy) for a 6-night cruise, including room, breakfast, and dinner. Bicycles are carried on board for sightseeing trips. This company also offers cruises in the Loire Valley and the south of France.

BICYCLING TOURS Some of the best cycling tours of France are offered by **VBT (Deluxe Bicycle Vacations),** 614 Monkton Rd., Bristol, VT 05443 (ℂ **800/245-3868;** www.vbt.com), which offers trips in five of the most scenic parts of France. These range from Burgundy (which combines a barge tour) to the Loire Valley, even Provence and the Normandy Coast. Packages are priced from $3,295 to $4,170 per person.

Classic Adventures, P.O. Box 143, Hamlin, NY 14464 (ℂ **800/777-8090;** fax 585/964-7297; www.classicadventures.com), sponsors 6- to 10-day spring and fall tours of the Loire Valley and the Dordogne. Accommodations are upscale, and tours are van supported and escorted. The 6-day tour, including room, breakfast, and dinner, is $3,449 per person, for the Loire Valley.

Euro-Bike & Walking Tours, P.O. Box 81025, Billings, MT 59108 (☎ **800/575-1540** or 406/655-4591; www.eurobike.com), offers 10-day tours in the Dordogne ($4,298 per person), 11-day tours in Provence ($4,498 per person), and 8-day tours of the Loire ($3,498 per person). All are escorted and include room, breakfast, and dinner.

Go-today.com (a division of Europe Express), 19021 120th Ave. NE, Ste. 102, Bothell, WA 98011 (☎ **800/227-3235;** www.go-today.com), has biking and walking tours of Bordeaux, Burgundy, the Dordogne, the Loire Valley, and Provence. An 8-day self-guided bike tour is $1,750 per person, double occupancy. All tours include overnight accommodations and most meals. Guided tours include van support and a guide; on nonguided tours, you'll always have the name of an English-speaking local contact.

COOKING SCHOOLS The famous/infamous Georges-Auguste Escoffier (1846–1935) taught the Edwardians how to eat. Today the Hôtel Ritz maintains the **Ritz-Escoffier Ecole de Gastronomie Française,** 38 rue Cambon, Paris 75001 (☎ **01-43-16-30-30;** www.ritzparis.com), which offers demonstration classes of the master's techniques on Saturdays. These cost 135€ to 225€ each. Courses, taught in French and English, start at 1,000€ for 1 week, up to 11,400€ for 6 weeks.

Le Cordon Bleu, 8 rue Léon-Delhomme, 75015 Paris (☎ **800/457-2433** in the U.S., or 01-53-68-22-50; www.cordonbleu.edu), was established in 1895 and is the most famous French cooking school—where Julia Child learned to perfect her *pâté brisée* and *mousse au chocolat.* The best-known courses last 10 weeks, after which you are awarded a certificate. Many enthusiasts prefer a less intense immersion and opt for a 4-day workshop or a 2-hour demonstration class. Enrollment in either is first-come, first-served; costs start at 47€ for a demonstration and start at 920€ for the 4-day workshop. Classes are in English.

LANGUAGE SCHOOLS The **Alliance Française,** 101 bd. Raspail, Paris 75270 (☎ **01-42-84-90-00;** fax 01-42-84-91-01; www.alliancefr.org), a nonprofit organization with a network of 1,100 establishments in 138 countries, offers French-language courses to some 350,000 students. The school in Paris is open all year; month-long courses range from 400€ to 900€, depending on the number of hours per day. Request information and an application at least 1 month before your departure. In North America, the largest branch is the **Alliance Française,** 53 W. Jackson Blvd., Suite 1225, Chicago, IL 60604 (☎ **312/431-1889;** www.afusa.org).

A clearinghouse for information on French-language schools is **Lingua Service Worldwide,** 42 Artillery Dr., Woodbury, CT 06798 (☎ **800/394-LEARN** [5327] or 203/263-6294; www.linguaserviceworldwide.com). Its programs are available in many cities throughout France. They cost $1,043 to $2,940 for 2 weeks, depending on the city, the school, and the accommodations.

MUSIC TOURS One outfit that coordinates hotel stays in Paris with major musical events, usually in at least one (and often both) of the city's opera houses, is **Dailey-Thorp Travel,** P.O. Box 670, Big Horn, Wyoming 82833 (☎ **800/998-4677** or 307/673-1555; fax 307/674-7474; www.daileythorp.com). Sojourns tend to last 3 to 7 days and, in many cases, tie in with performances in other cities (usually

London, Berlin, or Milan). Expect accommodations in deluxe hotels such as the Hôtel du Louvre or the Hôtel Scribe, and a staff that has made arrangements for all the nuts and bolts of your arrival in, and artistic exposure to, Paris.

TENNIS TOURS   Die-hard fans around the world set their calendars by the French Open, held at Paris's Roland-Garros stadium. You can book your hotel and tickets to the event on your own, but if you're unsure about scheduling, consider a California-based company, **Advantage Tennis Tours,** 33 White Sail Dr., Ste. 100, Laguna Niguel, CA 92677 (✆ **800/341-8687** or 949/661-7331; fax 949/489-2837; www.advantagetennistours.com). They typically book packages including 5 or 6 nights of hotel accommodations in Paris, 2 or 3 days on Center Court, and the skills of a bilingual hostess; rates per person, without airfare, begin at $3,455, double occupancy, depending on your choice of hotel and the duration of your visit.

STAYING CONNECTED

Telephones

To call France:

1. Dial the international access code: 011 from the U.S.; 00 from the U.K., Ireland, or New Zealand; or 0011 from Australia.
2. Dial the country code: 33.
3. Dial the city code, which is always two digits, beginning with a zero, but drop that first zero, and then the eight-digit number.

To make international calls from France: First dial 00 and then the country code (U.S. or Canada 1, U.K. 44, Ireland 353, Australia 61, New Zealand 64). Next, dial the area code and number. For example, if you wanted to call the British Embassy in Washington, D.C., you would dial ✆ 00-1-202-588-7800.

For directory assistance: Dial ✆ 12 for assistance in French; in English, dial ✆ 0-800/364-775. For international inquiries, dial ✆ 08-36-59-32-12. This will link you with a bilingual (French and English) phone operator. You are allowed to request only two numbers for which you pay a service charge of 3€.

For operator assistance: If you wish to use an operator to call your home country, you dial the toll-free number of ✆ **08-00-99-00** plus the digits of your country code (for example, ✆ 08-00-99-00-1 for the U.S. and Canada).

Toll-free numbers: Numbers beginning with 08 and followed by 00 are generally toll-free. But be careful: Numbers that begin with 08 followed by 36 carry a .35€ surcharge per minute.

Cellphones

The three letters that define much of the world's wireless capabilities are GSM (Global System for Mobiles), a seamless network that makes for easy cross-border cellphone use throughout France and dozens of other countries worldwide. (In the U.S., T-Mobile and AT&T Wireless use this quasi-universal system; in Canada, Microcell and some Rogers customers are GSM.) In general, reception is good. Unfortunately, per-minute charges can be high—usually $1 to $1.50 in Western Europe and up to $5 in many international destinations. Calls to the U.S. average $1.40 per minute.

Buying a phone can be economically attractive, as many nations have cheap prepaid phone systems. Once you arrive in France, stop by a local cellphone shop and get the cheapest package; you'll probably pay less than $100 for a phone and a starter calling card. Local calls may be as low as 10¢ per minute, and incoming calls are free.

TIPS ON ACCOMMODATIONS

The French government rates hotels on a one- to four-star system. One-star hotels are budget accommodations; two-star lodgings are quality tourist hotels; three stars go to first-class hotels; and four stars are reserved for deluxe accommodations. In some of the lower categories, the rooms may not have private bathrooms; instead, many have what the French call a *cabinet de toilette* (hot and cold running water and maybe a bidet). In such hotels, bathrooms are down the hall. Nearly all hotels in France have central heating, but in some cases, you might wish the owners would turn it up a little on a cold night.

For apartment, farmhouse, or cottage stays of 2 weeks or more, **Idyll Untours** (✆ 888/868-6871; www.untours.com) provides exceptional vacation rentals for a reasonable price—which includes air/ground transportation, cooking facilities, and on-call support from a local resident. Best of all: Untours—named the "Most Generous Company in America" by Newman's Own—donates most profits to provide low-interest loans to underprivileged entrepreneurs around the world (see website for details). At press time, Untour's French offerings included lodging in Alsace, Provence, and Paris. Also check out www.venere.com for more information on accommodations.

RELAIS & CHATEAUX Now known worldwide, this organization of deluxe and first-class hostelries began in France for visitors seeking the ultimate in hotel living and dining in a traditional atmosphere. Relais & Châteaux establishments (there are about 150 in France) are former castles, abbeys, manor houses, and town houses converted into hostelries or inns and elegant hotels. All have a limited number of rooms, so reservations are imperative. Sometimes these owner-run establishments have pools and tennis courts. The Relais part of the organization refers to inns called *relais,* meaning "post house." These tend to be less luxurious than the châteaux, but are often charming. Top-quality restaurants are *relais gourmands.* Throughout this guide, we list our favorite Relais & Châteaux members, but there are many more.

For a $12 catalog of member establishments, contact Relais & Châteaux at ✆ 800/735-2478 or www.relaischateaux.com.

There is also another possibility for châteaux living. For the ultimate in luxury, **Grandes Etapes Françaises,** 21 Square St. Charles in Paris (✆ 01-40-02-99-99; www.grandesetapes.fr), can book you into 10 châteaux or luxury hotels throughout the country. Each hotel or château is unique, and most of them lie only a 1-hour drive from Paris. For example, **Le Château d'Esclimont** in the Ile de France, outside the village of St-Symphorien le Château, is like a fairy-tale castle, lying between Versailles and Chartres.

BED & BREAKFASTS Called *gîtes-chambres d'hôte* in France, these may be one or several bedrooms on a farm or in a village home. Many offer one main meal a day (lunch or dinner).

La Maison des Gîtes de France et du Tourisme Vert, 59 rue St-Lazare, Paris 75439 (☏ **01-49-70-75-75;** www.gites-de-france.fr), lists at least 6,000 *gîtes-chambres d'hôte.* Sometimes these B&Bs aren't as simple as you may think: Instead of a bare-bones farm, you may be in a mansion in the countryside.

CONDOS, VILLAS, HOUSES & APARTMENTS If you can stay for at least a week and don't mind doing your own cooking and cleaning, you may want to rent long-term accommodations. The local French Tourist Board might help you obtain a list of agencies that offer this type of rental (which is popular at ski resorts). In France, one of the best groups of agents is the **Fédération Nationale des Agents Immobiliers,** 106 rue de l'Université, Paris 75007 (☏ **01-47-05-44-36;** www.fnpc.fr).

In the United States, **At Home Abroad, Inc.,** 163 Third Ave., Box 319, New York, NY 10003 (☏ **212/421-9165;** fax 212/228-4860; www.athomeabroadinc.com), specializes in villas on the French Riviera and in the Dordogne as well as places in the Provençal hill towns. Rentals are usually for 2 weeks. You'll receive photographs of the properties and a newsletter.

New York Habitat (☏ **212/255-8018;** fax 212/627-1416; www.nyhabitat.com) rents furnished apartments and vacation accommodations in Paris and the south of France. Bookings should be done at least 3 months in advance (even farther out for the south of France) and can be arranged online or over the phone. Prices in Paris range from 450€ to 8,000€, in the south of France 55€ to 1,350€.

CyberRentals is a worldwide vacation rental website (☏ **512/684-1098;** www.cyberrentals.com) that lists vacation homes, condos, luxury villas, cabins, chalets, and other real estate available for rent by owner. For example, you can find properties such as one typical—and lovely—villa in Gordes in the Provence region that sleeps six and rents for between $2,000 and $4,000 per week, depending on season.

If you want to rent an apartment in Paris, the **Barclay International Group,** 6800 Jericho Turnpike, Syosset, NY 11791 (☏ **800/845-6636** or 516/364-0064; fax 516/364-4468; www.barclayweb.com), can give you access to about 3,000 apartments and villas throughout Paris (and 39 other cities in France), ranging from modest modern units to the most stylish lodgings. Units rent for 1 night to 6 months; all have TVs and kitchenettes, and many have concierge staffs and lobby-level security. The least expensive cost around $170 per night, double occupancy. Discounts are given for a stay of 1 week or longer. Rentals must be prepaid in U.S. dollars or with a U.S. credit or charge card.

Hometours International, Inc., 1108 Scottie Lane, Knoxville, TN 37919 (☏ **865/690-8484;** hometours@aol.com), offers more than 400 moderately priced apartments, apartment hotels, and villas in Paris. On the Riviera, you can rent villas, with pools, at reasonable rates.

Drawbridge to Europe, Inc., 98 Granite St., Ashland, OR 97520 (☏ **888/268-1148;** www.drawbridgetoeurope.com), offers everything from Paris apartments to villas scattered throughout France, including Provence. Rentals are selected for their location, interiors, and possibly historical character.

The aptly named **Homes Away,** 45 St. Clair Ave. W., Ste. 1100, Toronto, Ontario, Canada M4V 1K9 (☏ **800/374-6637;** http://homesaway.com), provides private vacation villas throughout France, including apartments in Paris. Rentals lie in the most tourist-rich provinces of France, including Burgundy, the French Riviera, Provence, and the Dordogne.

Interhome, Inc., 2860 State Rd. 84, Ste. 116 PMB 241, Fort Lauderdale, FL 33312 (© **800/882-6864;** www.interhomeusa.com), offers some 30,000 rental properties in 21 countries, including France. Take your choice, apartment or villa. The agency is especially noted for its villas in Provence and on the Riviera.

Other agencies include **Villanet** (© **877/250-4366** or 206/417-3444; www. rentavilla.com), which in France specializes in rentals in Provence and the Riviera. **Villas & Apartments Abroad** operates out of 183 Madison Ave., Ste. 201, New York, NY 10016 (© **800/433-3020** or 212/213-6436; www.vaanyc.com), and has been satisfying villa seekers for more than 30 years. It seems to have a very personalized service to hook customers up with the right rental.

Worldwide Vacation Rentals, 17 Fox Lane, San Anselmo, CA 94960 (© **800/221-2260;** www.villasintl.com), seems to be doing something right, as it supposedly attracts more repeat customers among villa rentals.

Absolu Living, 236 rue Saint Martin, 75003 Paris (© **01-44-54-97-17;** www. absoluliving.com), is the leader in furnished apartment rentals serving the gay community. Long- or short-term apartment rentals are arranged throughout France. By renting an apartment instead of a hotel, costing from 72€ per night for two persons, you gain more space and freedom—and at a lower price.

HOTEL CHAINS   One good moderately priced choice is the **Mercure** chain, an organization of simple, modern hotels throughout France. Even at the peak of the tourist season, a room at a Mercure in Paris rents for as little as 99€ per night (admittedly, a rarity). For more information on Mercure hotels and its 100-page directory, call © **800/221-4542** in the U.S. (www.mercure.com).

Formule 1 (www.hotelformule1.com) hotels are basic but safe, offering rooms for up to three people for around 40€ per night. Built from prefabricated units, these air-conditioned, soundproof hotels are shipped to a site and assembled, often on the outskirts of cities such as Paris (27 in the suburbs). There are 150 of these throughout the rest of France.

Mercure and Formule 1 are both owned by the French hotel giant Accor, parent of Motel 6, which Formule 1 resembles. Formule 1's low cost makes it unprofitable for the chain to allow customers to reserve rooms from the United States, so you'll have to reserve upon arrival. For a directory, write to Formule 1/ETAP Hotels, c/o Sishe Hotel, 6–8 rue du Bois-Briard, Evry Cedex 91021 (© **08-92-68-56-85;** www.hotelformule1.com).

Other worthwhile economy bets, sometimes with a bit more charm, are the hotels and restaurants of the **Fédération Nationale des Logis de France,** 83 av. d'Italie, Paris 75013 (© **01-45-84-83-84;** www.logis-de-france.fr). This is an association of 3,000 hotels, usually country inns convenient for motorists, most rated one or two stars. The association publishes an annual directory.

SUGGESTED ITINERARIES IN FRANCE

4

When we first launched this guidebook, founding father Arthur Frommer gave us a warning: "You can get lost in France." And we did—and still do on occasion.

If you have unlimited time, one of the world's great pleasures is getting "lost" in France, wandering about at random, making new discoveries every day off the beaten path. But few of us have this luxury, and so below we present both 1- and 2-week itineraries to help you make the most of your time.

France is so vast and so treasure-filled that you can't even skim the surface in 1 or 2 weeks, so relax and don't even try. Instead, we recommend you enjoy the nuggets—Paris, Versailles, and Mont-St-Michel—among other allures, saving the rest for another day. You may also review chapter 1, "The Best of France," to find out what experiences or sights have special appeal to us and then adjust the itineraries to suit your particular travel plans.

France ranks with Germany in offering Europe's fastest and best-maintained superhighways, and it also has one of the fastest and most efficient public transportation systems in the world, especially in its national train system. For example, the highlights of Normandy and the Loire Valley (the château country) are just 1 or 2 hours away from Paris by train. You can travel from Paris to Nice on the Riviera in 5½ hours—or fly much more quickly, of course.

The itineraries that follow take you to some major attractions and some charming towns. The pace may be a bit breathless for some visitors, so skip a town or sight occasionally to have some chill-out time—after all, you're on vacation. Of course, you can use any of these itineraries as a jumping-off point to develop your own custom-made trip.

THE REGIONS IN BRIEF

Though France's 547,030 sq. km (211,209 sq. miles) make it slightly smaller than the American state of Texas, no other country has such a diversity of sights and scenery in such a compact area. A visitor can travel through the north's flat, fertile lands; the Loire Valley's green hills; the east's Alpine ranges; the Pyrénées; the Massif Central's plateaus and rock outcroppings; and the southeast's Mediterranean coast. Even more noteworthy are the cultural and historical differences that define each region.

Destinations in France are within easy reach from Paris and each other. **French National Railroads (SNCF)** offers fast service to and from Paris—though trains tend to crawl on routes that do not serve the capital. The train trip from Paris is 4 hours to Alsace, 5 to the Alps, 7 to the Pyrénées, and 8 to the Côte d'Azur—and the newer TGVs (high-speed trains) cut that travel time dramatically.

You'll find nearly 71,000km (about 44,100 miles) of roads, mostly in good condition. Try not to travel the Route Nationale network all the time. Nearly all of France's scenic splendors are along secondary roads.

A "grand tour" of France is nearly impossible for the visitor who doesn't have a lifetime to explore. If you want to get to know a province, try to devote at least a week to a specific region; you may have a more rewarding trip if you concentrate on getting to know two or three areas at a leisurely pace rather than racing around trying to see everything. To help you decide where to spend your time, we've summarized the highlights of each region for you.

ILE DE FRANCE (EXCLUDING PARIS)   The Ile de France is an island only in the sense that rivers—with odd-sounding names such as Essonne, Epte, Aisne, Eure, and Ourcq—and a handful of canals delineate its boundaries (about an 81km/50-mile radius from the center of Paris). France was born in this temperate basin, where the attractions include **Paris, Versailles, Fontainebleau, Notre-Dame de Chartres,** and **Giverny.** Despite industrialization (and Disneyland Paris), pockets of charm remain, including the forests of Rambouillet and Fontainebleau, and the artists' hamlet of Barbizon. For more information, see chapters 5, 6, and 7.

THE LOIRE VALLEY   This area includes two ancient provinces, Touraine (centered on Tours) and Anjou (centered on Angers). It was beloved by royalty and nobility until Henry IV moved his court to Paris. Head here to see the most magnificent castles in France. Irrigated by the Loire River and its many tributaries, the valley produces many superb wines. For more information, see chapter 8.

NORMANDY   This region will forever be linked to the 1944 D-day invasion. Some readers consider a visit to the D-day beaches the most emotionally worthwhile part of their trip. Normandy boasts 599km (372 miles) of coastline and a maritime tradition. It's a popular weekend getaway from Paris, and many hotels and restaurants thrive here, especially around the casino town of **Deauville.** Normandy's great attractions include the **Rouen** cathedral, the abbey of **Jumièges,** and medieval **Bayeux.** For more information, see chapter 9.

BRITTANY   Jutting into the Atlantic, the westernmost (and one of the poorest) regions of France is known for its rocky coastlines, Celtic roots, frequent rain, and ancient dialect, akin to the Gaelic tongues of Wales and Ireland. Many French vacationers love the seacoast (rivaled only by the Côte d'Azur) for its sandy beaches, cliffs, and relatively modest—by French standards—prices. **Carnac** is home to ancient Celtic dolmens and burial mounds, and the region's most sophisticated resort, **La Baule,** is near some of Brittany's best beaches. For more information, see chapter 10.

CHAMPAGNE Every French monarch since A.D. 496 was crowned at **Reims,** and much of French history is linked with this holy site. In the path of any invader wishing to occupy Paris, Reims and the Champagne district have seen much bloodshed, including the World War I battles of the Somme and the Marne. Industrial sites sit among patches of forest, and vineyards sheath the steep sides of valleys. The 126km (78-mile) road from Reims to Vertus, one of the **Routes du Champagne,** takes in a trio of winegrowing regions that produce 80% of the world's bubbly. For more information, see chapter 11.

THE ARDENNES & NORTHERN BEACHES This northern region is often ignored by North Americans (which is why we feature it as a side trip from Reims). In summer, French families arrive by the thousands to visit Channel beach resorts such as **Le Touquet-Paris-Plage.** This district is quite industrialized and has always suffered in wars. Its best-known port, Calais, was a bitterly contested English stronghold for centuries. Calais is now the port of disembarkation for ferries, hydrofoils, and Channel Tunnel arrivals from Britain. **Notre-Dame Cathedral** in **Amiens,** the medieval capital of Picardy, is a treasure, with a 42m-high (138-ft.) nave—the highest in France. For more information, see chapter 11.

ALSACE LORRAINE Between Germany and the forests of the Vosges is the most Teutonic of France's provinces: Alsace, with cosmopolitan Strasbourg as its capital. Celebrated for its cuisine, particularly its foie gras and choucroute, this area is home to villages with half-timbered designs that make you think of the Black Forest. If you travel the Route de Vin (Wine Road), you can visit towns such as **Colmar, Riquewihr,** and **Illhaeusern,** famous for great food and wine. Lorraine, birthplace of Joan of Arc, witnessed many battles during the world wars. Its capital, **Nancy,** is the guardian of a grand 18th-century plaza, place Stanislas. The much-eroded peaks of the Vosges forest, the closest thing to a wilderness in France, offer lovely hiking. For more information, see chapter 12.

BURGUNDY Few trips will prove as rewarding as several leisurely days spent exploring Burgundy, with its splendid old cities such as **Dijon.** Besides its famous cuisine (*boeuf* and *escargots à la bourguignonne*), the district contains, along its Côte d'Or, hamlets whose names (Mercurey, Beaune, Puligny-Montrachet, Vougeot, and Nuits-St-Georges) are synonymous with great wine. For more information, see chapter 13.

THE RHONE VALLEY A fertile area of Alpine foothills and sloping valleys in eastern and southeastern France, the upper Rhône Valley ranges from the French suburbs of the Swiss city of Geneva to the northern borders of Provence. The district is thoroughly French, unflinchingly bourgeois, and dedicated to preserving the gastronomic and cultural traditions that have produced some of the most celebrated chefs in French history.

Only 2 hours by train from Paris, the region's cultural centerpiece, **Lyon,** is France's "second city." North of here, you can travel the Beaujolais trail or head for Bresse's ancient capital, **Bourg-en-Bresse,** which produces the world's finest poultry. You can explore the Rhône Valley en route to Provence. Try to visit the medieval villages of **Pérouges** and **Vienne,** 27km (17 miles) south of Lyon; the latter is known for its Roman ruins. For more information, see chapter 14.

The Regions in Brief

SUGGESTED ITINERARIES IN FRANCE

THE FRENCH ALPS   This area's resorts rival those of neighboring Switzerland and contain incredible scenery: snowcapped peaks, glaciers, and Alpine lakes. **Chamonix** is a famous ski resort facing **Mont Blanc,** western Europe's highest mountain. **Courchevel** and **Megève** are more chic. During the summer, you can enjoy such spa resorts as **Evian** and the restful 19th-century resorts ringing **Lake Geneva.** For more information, see chapter 15.

PROVENCE   One of France's most fabled regions flanks the Alps and the Italian border along its eastern end, and incorporates a host of sites that have long been frequented by the rich and famous. Premier destinations are **Aix-en-Provence,** associated with Cézanne; **Arles,** "the soul of Provence," captured by van Gogh; **Avignon,** the 14th-century capital of Christendom during the papal schism; and **Marseille,** a port city established by the Phoenicians (in some ways more North African than French). Provence's gems are the small villages, such as **St-Rémy-de-Provence** (Nostradamus's birthplace) and **Les Baux.** The strip of glittering beach towns along Provence's southern edge is known as the **Côte d'Azur,** or the French Riviera (see the following section). For more information, see chapter 16.

THE FRENCH RIVIERA (COTE D'AZUR)   The fabled Côte d'Azur (Azure Coast, or Blue Coast) has become quite overbuilt and spoiled by tourism. Even so, the names of its resorts still evoke glamour: **Cannes, St-Tropez, Cap d'Antibes,** and **St-Jean-Cap-Ferrat.** July and August are the most crowded, but spring and fall can be a delight. **Nice** is the biggest city, and most convenient for exploring the area. The principality of **Monaco** occupies only about 2 sq. km (¾ sq. mile). Along the coast are some sandy beaches, but many are rocky or pebbly. Topless bathing is common, especially in St-Tropez, and some of the restaurants are citadels of conspicuous consumption. Dozens of artists and their patrons have littered the landscape with world-class galleries and art museums. For more information, see chapter 17.

LANGUEDOC-ROUSSILLON   Languedoc may not be as chic as Provence, but it's less frenetic and more affordable. **Roussillon** is the rock-strewn French answer to Catalonia, just across the Spanish border. The **Camargue** is the marshy delta formed by two arms of the Rhône River. Rich in bird life, it's famous for its grassy flats and such fortified medieval sites as **Aigues-Mortes.** Also appealing are **Auch,** the capital of Gascony; **Toulouse,** the bustling pink capital of Languedoc; and the "red city" of **Albi,** birthplace of Toulouse-Lautrec. **Carcassonne,** a marvelous walled city with fortifications begun around A.D. 500, is the region's highlight. For more information, see chapter 18.

THE BASQUE COUNTRY   Since prehistoric times, the rugged Pyrénées have formed a natural boundary between France and Spain. The Basques, one of Europe's most unusual cultures, flourished in the valleys here. In the 19th century, resorts such as **Biarritz** and **St-Jean-de-Luz** attracted the French aristocracy; the empress Eugénie's palace at Biarritz is now a hotel. Four million Catholics make annual pilgrimages to the city of Lourdes. In the villages and towns of the Pyrénées, the old folkloric traditions, permeated with Spanish influences, continue to thrive. For more information, see chapter 19.

BORDEAUX & THE ATLANTIC COAST   Flat, fertile, and frequently ignored by North Americans, this region includes towns pivotal in French history (**Saintes, Poitiers, Angoulême,** and **La Rochelle**), as well as wine- and liquor-producing villages (**Cognac, Margaux, St-Emilion,** and **Sauternes**) whose names are celebrated around the world. **Bordeaux,** the district's largest city, has an economy based on wine merchandising and showcases grand 18th-century architecture. For more information, see chapter 20.

THE DORDOGNE & PERIGORD The land of foie gras and truffles is the site of some of Europe's oldest settlements. For biking or indulging in gourmet meals, the region is among the top vacation spots in France. In the Périgord, the cave paintings at **Les Eyzies** reveal traces of Cro-Magnon settlements. The Dordogne is the second-largest *département* (the French equivalent of an American state). Highlights are the ancient towns of **Périgueux, Les Eyzies-de-Tayac, Sarlat-le-Canéda,** and **Beynac-et-Cazenac.** For more information, see chapter 21.

THE MASSIF CENTRAL The rugged heartland of south-central France, this underpopulated district contains ancient cities, unspoiled scenery, and an abundance of black lava, from which many buildings were created. The largest cities are **Clermont-Ferrand** and **Limoges**—the medieval capitals of the provinces of the Auvergne and the Limousin. **Bourges,** a gateway to the region and once capital of Aquitaine, has a beautiful Gothic cathedral. For more information, see chapter 22.

FRANCE IN 1 WEEK

The title of this tour is a misnomer. There is no way you can see France in 1 week. But, you can have a memorable vacation in Paris and see other highlights of France in a week if you budget your time carefully. One week provides enough time— barely—to visit the major attractions of Paris such as the **Musée du Louvre** (world's greatest art gallery), the **Eiffel Tower,** and **Notre-Dame.** After 2 days in Paris, head for the former royal stamping grounds of **Versailles,** followed by Normandy (an easy commute from Paris), visiting such highlights as **D-day beaches,** the cathedral city of **Rouen** (where Joan of Arc was burned alive), the tapestry of **Bayeux,** and the incredible monastery of **Mont-St-Michel.**

Days 1 & 2: Arrive in Paris ★★★

Take a flight that arrives in Paris as early as possible on **Day 1.** Check into your hotel and hit the nearest cafe for a pick-me-up café au lait and a croissant before sightseeing. Take the Métro to the Palais Royal–Musée du Louvre for a visit to the **Musée du Louvre** (p. 158). Spend at least 2 hours here viewing world-class masterpieces such as Leonardo da Vinci's *Mona Lisa.* After leaving the Louvre, walk south toward the **Quays of the Seine,** spending an hour taking in the tree-shaded banks and panoramic vistas of Paris. Head for that island in the Seine, **Ile de la Cité,** to explore its attractions including **Ste-Chapelle** (p. 162) and the monumental **Notre-Dame** (p. 160) and its gargoyles. As the evening fades, head for the **Eiffel Tower** for the greatest cityscape view in Europe.

On **Day 2,** arrive at the **place de la Concorde** (p. 169) and its Egyptian obelisk, and take a stroll up the 1.8km (1-mile) avenue of French grandeur, the **Champs-Elysées,** until you reach the **Arc de Triomphe** (p. 155), which you can scale for another panoramic view of Paris. After, head for the **Ile St-Louis**

1 Arrive in Paris
2 Paris
3 Day Trip to Versailles
4 Rouen: Normandy's Capital
5 Bayeux & Caen
6 The D-Day Beaches
7 Mont-St-Michel

(p. 125), which, after Cité, is the second island in the Seine. Lacking monumental attractions, this little isle is a sight in itself, with quays to stroll and small side streets where you can discover hidden wonders such as antiques shops and little bistros.

After lunch in one of those bistros, visit **Musée d'Orsay** (p. 158) and the world's greatest collection of Impressionist paintings. After d'Orsay, take a **Bateaux-Mouche** cruise (p. 154) along the Seine. As the afternoon fades, head for **Basilique du Sacré-Coeur** (p. 155) for a crowning view of Paris as the sun sets. Have a final dinner in a Montmartre cafe.

Day 3: A Day Trip to Versailles ★

Having survived 2 days in the capital of France, bid an adieu and take the RER Line C to the **Versailles/Rive Gauche station.** You can spend a full day at Versailles—and then some—or else you can see the highlights in 3 hours, including the Grands and Petits appartements, the glittering Hall of Mirrors, Gabriel's Opera House, the Royal Chapel, and the Gardens of Versailles, which contain the Grand and Petit Trianons.

Day 4: Normandy's Capital of Rouen ★★★

On **Day 4,** take an early train to Rouen and check into a hotel. Spend at least 2 hours exploring the city's ancient core, especially its **Cathédrale Notre-Dame** (p. 288), immortalized in paintings by Monet. Stand at the **place du Vieux-Marché** (p. 292), where Joan of Arc was executed for heresy in 1431, and then visit the **Eglise St-Maclou** (p. 290), a 1432 church in the Flamboyant Gothic style. After lunch, rent a car for the rest of your trip and drive to **Giverny** (p. 232)—it's only 60km (38 miles) southeast of Rouen. At Giverny, visit the **Claude Monet Foundation** (p. 232), returning to your hotel in Rouen for the night.

Day 5: Bayeux ★★ & Caen ★★★

Strike out toward Bayeux, stopping en route to visit **Abbaye de Jumièges**, one of the most evocative ruins in France. Even with a stopover, you can easily be in the city of Caen in time for lunch before visiting **Abbaye aux Hommes** (p. 305), founded by William the Conqueror. After Caen, continue west to the city of **Bayeux,** where you can arrive in time to view the celebrated **Musée de la Tapisserie de Bayeux** (p. 310). Stay overnight in Bayeux.

Day 6: The D-Day Beaches ★★

Reserve **Day 6** for exploring the D-day beaches, where Allied forces launched "the Longest Day," the mammoth invasion of Normandy in June 1944 that signaled the beginning of the end of Hitler's Third Reich.

From Bayeux, head east to explore the coastline. Your voyage of discovery can begin at the seaside resort of Arromanches-les-Bains, where you can visit the **Musée du Débarquement** (p. 313), **Omaha Beach** (p. 314), and the **Normandy American Cemetery** (p. 314). You can have lunch in the town of Grandcamp-Maisy (p. 315), later checking out **Utah Beach.**

That evening, drive to **Mont-St-Michel** (less than 2 hr. away) and overnight in the pedestrian village on "the Rock," giving you plenty of time for an early-morning visit to this popular attraction. If it's summer, you can also take an illuminated night tour.

Day 7: Mont-St-Michel ★★★

You can explore one of the great attractions of Europe, **Mont-St-Michel** (p. 315), in a minimum of 3 hours. This great Benedictine monastery, founded in 966, is best enjoyed by taking an English-language tour that covers the highlights. After viewing the abbey, drop in at **La Mère Poulard** (p. 318) for a legendary omelet. After lunch, return your car to Rouen, where you'll find frequent train service back to Paris and your flight home the following day.

FRANCE IN 2 WEEKS

With 2 weeks to explore France, you'll have time to visit several regions—not only Paris, but also the best of the Loire Valley châteaux, the most history-rich town of Provence (Avignon), and several resorts on the Riviera, taking in the beaches, modern-art galleries, and even the principality of Monaco.

France in 2 Weeks

0 ——————————— 200 mi

0 ——————————— 200 km

English Channel

D-Day Beaches

6 **Rouen**
Bayeaux **4**
5 **Caen** **Paris**
NORMANDY **1-2**
7 **3**
Mont-St-Michel **Versailles**

Orléans
8

THE LOIRE VALLEY **9** **Amboise**
Chenonceau

F R A N C E

1 Arrive in Paris
2 Paris
3 Day Trip to Versailles
4 Rouen: Normandy's Capital
5 Bayeux & Caen
6 The D-Day Beaches
7 Mont-St-Michel
8 Orléans
9 Amboise & Chenonceau
10 Avignon
11 Avignon to St-Tropez
12 Cannes
13 Nice
14 Nice to Monaco

Avignon **10** *PROVENCE* **MONACO**
RIVIERA **14**
13 **Nice**
12 **Cannes**
St-Tropez
11

Mediterranean Sea

For **days 1 through 7,** follow the "France in 1 Week" itinerary, above.

Day 8: Orléans—Gateway to the Loire Valley ★

On **Day 8,** leave Paris on an early train to **Orléans** (trip time: 1 hr., 15 min.). Heavily bombed in World War II, Orléans is a fairly dull town. Rent a car here and drive west to the **Château de Chambord** (p. 249), the largest château in the Loire Valley, representing the apogee of the French Renaissance architectural style. Allow 2 hours for a visit. Back on the road again, continue southwest to the **Château de Blois** (p. 250), called "the Versailles of the Renaissance" and a virtual illustrated storybook of French architecture. Stay overnight in Blois.

Day 9: Amboise ★★ & Chenonceau ★★★

On the morning of **Day 9,** continue southeast from Blois to **Amboise,** where you can check into a hotel for the night. Visit the 15th-century **Château d'Amboise** (p. 257), in the Italian Renaissance style, and also **Clos-Lucé** (p. 258), last residence of Leonardo da Vinci. In the afternoon, drive southeast to the **Château de Chenonceau** (p. 261), famous for the French dames who have occupied its precincts, including Diane de Poitiers (mistress of the king) and Catherine de Médicis. You can spend 2 hours at the château before driving back to Amboise for the night.

Day 10: Avignon, Gateway to Provence ★★★

From Amboise, get an early start on **Day 10** and drive east to Orléans to return your rental car. You now face a choice: You can take a morning train from Orléans to Paris's Gare d'Austerlitz and then catch the Métro or a taxi to the Gare de Lyon, where you can hop aboard a TGV (fast train) that will put you in Avignon in about 2½ hours. Or, you can take a train from Orléans to Lyon and change trains for Avignon.

Check into a hotel in **Avignon,** capital of Provence. Before the day fades, you should have time to wander through the old city to get your bearings, buy some colorful Provençal fabrics, and see one of the smaller sights such as the **Pont St-Bénézet** (also known as the Bridge of Avignon). See p. 488.

Day 11: Avignon to St-Tropez ★★

In the morning, spend 2 hours touring the **Palais des Papes** (p. 490), which was the capital of Christendom during the 14th century when the popes lived here during the so-called "Babylonian Captivity." After lunch in one of Europe's most beautiful medieval cities, rent a car and drive to **St-Tropez** (p. 533). If it's summer, get in some beach time and spend a good part of the early evening in one of the cafes along the harbor, indulging in that favorite French pastime of people-watching.

Day 12: Cannes, Capital of the Riviera Chic ★★★

Before leaving St-Tropez in the morning, check out the Impressionist paintings at **Musée de l'Annonciade** (p. 538). Drive 50km (31 miles) east along the coast until you reach Cannes.

Assuming it's summer, get in some time at the beach, notably at **Plage de la Croisette** (p. 545), and feel free to wear your most revealing swimwear. In the afternoon, take the ferry to **Ile Ste-Marguerite** (p. 550), where the "Man in the Iron Mask" was imprisoned. You can visit his cell. That evening, you may want to flirt with Lady Luck at one of the plush **casinos** (p. 555).

Day 13: Nice, Capital of the Riviera ★★★

It's only a 32km (20-mile) drive east from Cannes to **Nice,** the Riviera's largest city. After checking into a hotel (the most affordable along the Riviera), stroll through **Vieille Ville** (p. 584), the old town, beginning at the foot of "the Rock." Enjoy a snack of *socca,* a round crepe made with chickpea flour that's sold steaming hot by street vendors. Then head for the **promenade des Anglais** (p. 584), the wide boulevard along the waterfront. Stop in at one of the grand cafes along the water for a light lunch. In the afternoon, head for the best of the hill towns above Nice, notably **St-Paul-de-Vence,** only 31km (19 miles) to the north. Here you can wander its ramparts in about 30 minutes before descending on the greatest modern-art museum in the Riviera, the **Foundation Maeght** (p. 576).

Continue over to Vence (p. 578) for a visit to **Chapelle du Rosaire** (p. 578), where the great Henri Matisse created his artistic masterpiece for some Dominican nuns. From there, it's just 24km (15 miles) southeast to Nice.

Have dinner at a typical bistro, serving a traditional Niçoise cuisine with its inevitable Italian influences.

Day 14: Nice to Monaco ★★★

While still overnighting in Nice, head east for the most hair-raising but thrilling drive in all of France, a trip along the **Grande Corniche** highway that stretches 31km (19 miles) east from Nice to the little resort of **Menton** near the Italian border. Allow 3 hours for this trip. Highlights along this road include **Roquebrune-Cap Martin** and **La Turbie.** The greatest view along the Riviera is at the **Eze Belvedere** at 1,200m (3,937 ft.).

FRANCE FOR FAMILIES

France offers many attractions for kids. Perhaps your main concern with having children along is pacing yourself with museum time. Our suggestion is to limit **Paris** to 2 days and then spend a day wandering the spectacular grounds and glittering interiors of **Versailles,** 2 days in **Disneyland Paris,** and 2 days on the **Riviera.**

Days 1 & 2: Paris ★★★

Take the kids for a morning visit to **Notre-Dame** (p. 160). The highlight is climbing the 387 narrow and winding steps to the top of one of the towers for a fabulously Quasimodo view of the gargoyles and Paris. After a visit, head for the **Eiffel Tower** (p. 156). In addition to scaling this fantastic monument, you can also order lunch—allow at least 2 hours for your visit, one just to access the elevators on levels one and two. Food is available at the Altitude 95 restaurant on the first floor, but it's a bit pricey for most families. A first-floor snack bar and a second-floor cafeteria offer the best values for the family on a budget.

After touring the tower, take the kids for a donkey ride in the nearby **Champ de Mars,** which also stages the best puppet shows.

In the afternoon, take the children for a stroll through the **Jardin des Tuileries** (p. 163), where there are more donkey rides, ice-cream stands, and a marionette show. At the circular pond, you can rent a toy boat.

Climax your day with a ride along the Seine on the famous **Bateaux-Mouche** (p. 154). Boats have open sun decks.

On **Day 2,** visit the **Musée du Louvre** (p. 158). Even if your child is not a museum buff and bores easily, he or she will surely be intrigued by the many displays. Over the years, we've observed that, even more than the paintings, kids are fascinated by the Egyptian art and antiquities displayed in the Sully and Denon wings, a total of 7,000 items, the largest exhibition of such artifacts outside of Cairo.

After the Louvre, take the Métro to Porte de la Villette, where you can spend 2 or 3 hours at **Cité des Sciences et de l'Industrie** (p. 170). The mammoth structure is home to a planetarium, a 3-D cinema, video workshops, and interactive exhibits.

Space is too tight in this book to document all activities in Paris of interest to children, but you'll want to spend a good 2 hours in the **Jardin d'Acclimatation** in the northern part of the Bois de Boulogne. The visit starts with a ride on a narrow-gauge train through a stretch of wooded park, and attractions include a zoo, a house of mirrors, a puppet theater, a playground, and kiosks selling waffles.

As the afternoon fades, head for **Butte Montmartre** with its fiesta atmosphere. Take the Métro to Anvers and walk to the funicular, the cable car that carries you to the **Basilique du Sacré-Coeur** (p. 155). Once you arrive at "the top of Paris," follow the crowds to the **place du Tertre,** where a Sergeant Pepper–style band often blasts off-key, and you can have a local artist create a sketch of your kids. Finally, reward your brood with ice cream sold on the square.

Day 3: Versailles ★

Tear yourself away from the glories of Paris for a day spent at the **Château de Versailles** (p. 208). Take the RER line C to the Versailles/Rive Gauche station. Kids delight in the Hall of Mirrors and in the grand apartments. Take the children for a walk through the garden, where they can visit the hamlet where the ill-fated Marie Antoinette strolled with her lambs. You can buy the makings of a picnic lunch in Paris and enjoy it on the grounds, or else you can purchase fast food at one of the stalls placed in discreet corners of the garden.

Return to Paris in time to visit **Parc Zoologique de Paris,** in the Bois de Vincennes on the southeastern outskirts of Paris. Quickly reachable by Métro, this is one of France's greatest zoos, complete with playful animals in natural habitats as well as lions roaming a veldt. There's even a cement mountain similar to Disneyland's Matterhorn.

Days 4 & 5: Disneyland Paris ★★★

Disneyland Paris is the top family-vacation destination in France. Allow a full day to see the highlights of the park, plus another day to absorb its secondary adventures. Our recommendation is to visit **Main Street, U.S.A., Frontierland,** and **Adventureland** on the first day, saving **Fantasyland, Discoveryland,** the entertainment center at **Village Disney,** and **Sleeping Beauty Castle** for the second day. You can stay in the Disney hotels on-site, coming in various price ranges from very expensive to budget. The RER commuter express train A takes you from Etoile in Paris to Marne-la-Vallée/Chessy in 45 minutes.

Day 6: Nice ★★★

Return to Paris and fly to Nice, capital of the French Riviera. If you flew Air France transatlantic, Nice can often be attached as a low-cost extension of your round-trip fare.

In Nice you can check into your hotel for 2 nights, as the city has the most affordable hotels on the Riviera. Set out to explore this old city. The people-watching on the Riviera alone is likely to leave your kids wide-eyed. Beware that they'll see plenty of skin, as topless bathing is rampant. There's always a lot of free entertainment in summer along the boardwalk in Nice, called the **promenade des Anglais** (p. 584).

1 & 2 Paris
3 Versailles
4 & 5 Disneyland Paris
6 Nice
7 Monaco

In the afternoon, journey to the hill town of **St-Paul-de-Vence** (p. 574). This is the most evocative of the hill towns of Nice, and children delight in touring the ramparts and strolling along the pedestrian-only rue Grande. You can have a late lunch in the cafeteria of the **Foundation Maeght** (p. 576), the Riviera's greatest modern-art museum.

Return to Nice for the evening and take your kids for a stroll through the Old Town, dining in a typical Niçoise bistro.

Day 7: Monaco ★★★

While still based in Nice, head for the tiny principality of Monaco, which lies only 18km (11 miles) east of Nice.

Children will enjoy the changing-of-the-guard ceremony at **Les Grands Appartements du Palais** (p. 608), where Prince Rainier took his young bride, film star Grace Kelly, years ago. But the best part of Monaco for kids is the **Musée Océanographique de Monaco** (p. 609), one of Europe's biggest aquariums with sharks and other exotic sea creatures. Monaco also has the

Collection des Voitures Anciennes de S.A.S. le Prince de Monaco (p. 608) and the **Musée National de Monaco** (p. 608), with a mammoth antique doll collection.

Return to Nice that night and prepare for your flight home in the morning.

A WINE LOVER'S TOUR OF BURGUNDY

For the aficionado or even the lover of French landscapes, a tour of Burgundy, one of the world's greatest wine-producing regions, is one of the highlights of France. Burgundian vintages have been called *le vin des rois, le roi des vins* (the wine of kings, the king of wines). You can tour the winemaking towns and sample the finest of chardonnays and pinot noirs along the way. The best centers are **Dijon** (capital of Burgundy), **Beaune, Auxerre,** and **Autun.**

Day 1: Chablis to Auxerre ★★

Begin at **Chablis** in Burgundy's northwestern edge. Vineyards surround Chablis, the capital of Basse Bourgogne (Lower Burgundy). The town is now more famous for its wine than for its monuments, but it has two historic churches: the Eglise St-Martin and the Eglise St-Pierre. Chablis is not worth an overnight stop, though 15km (9⅓ miles) to the west along D965, in the hamlet of **Tonnerre,** is **Saint-Père,** one of the best restaurants in the province. After a meal, backtrack about 24km (15 miles) west on D965 (passing through Chablis) to **Auxerre** (p. 402).

Scene of many pivotal moments in French history, Auxerre is the site of one of France's most impressive churches, the Gothic **Cathédrale St-Etienne** (p. 403). Stay overnight in Auxerre.

Day 2: Vézelay ★★

Drive south from Auxerre along N151 and then east on D951 to the hamlet of **Vézelay** (p. 405). If there's one must-see Romanesque church in France, it's here. Park at the bottom of the village and climb the cobblestone main street. At the base of the hill is **L'Espérance** (p. 407), one of the best restaurants in the world. It's closed Tuesday and at lunch Wednesday, so plan your itinerary accordingly.

You can spend the night in Vézelay, drive 9.5km (6 miles) east on D957 to **Avallon,** or continue south for 56km (35 miles) on well-signposted country roads to **Château-Chinon.** Wherever you spend the night, plan an early departure the following day.

Day 3: Autun ★★

From Château-Chinon, drive east 32km (20 miles) on D978 to visit one of the oldest towns in France, **Autun** (p. 409).

En route, you may wish to take this detour: Heading east on D978 toward Autun, turn right (south) at Arleuf, going right onto D500. At a fork, turn right toward Glux and follow arrows to Mont Beuvray on D18. Take D274 to reach the summit. After 3km (1¾ miles) of climbing, you'll be at **Oppidum of Bibracte,** home of Eduens, a Gallic tribe. Here Vercingetorix organized the

A Wine Lover's Tour of Burgundy

1 Chablis to Auxerre
2 Vézelay
3 Autun
4 En Route to Beaune
5 Routes des Grands Crus
6 Dijon
7 En Route to Paris

Gauls to fight Caesar's legions in A.D. 52. At this altitude (840m/2,756 ft.), you'll have a splendid view of the wine country of Autun and Mont St-Vincent. Leave Mont Beuvray on D274 and continue northeast to Autun.

At Autun, you'll find a historic town with ruins left by the ancient Romans, as well as a cathedral built in 1120 to hold the remains of St. Lazarus. Spend the night here.

Day 4: En Route to Beaune ★★

Start early in Autun and be prepared for tours of châteaux, fortresses, vineyards, and other historic sites. Your route will be loaded with appealing detours, so be as flexible as possible as you negotiate a labyrinth of country roads toward Beaune.

Leave Autun on D973 east. After 9.5km (6 miles), turn left onto D326 toward Sully. Here you'll find the **Château de Sully,** once known as the Fontainebleau of Burgundy; it's closed to the public, but a view from the outside may satisfy you. The gardens are open Easter to September daily 8am to 6pm.

Leave Sully, following signs to the village of **Nolay.** About 4km (2½ miles) past Nolay, you'll reach the **Château de La Rochepot** (✆ **03-80-21-71-37;** www.larochepot.com), a medieval-style fortress built during the Renaissance (July–Aug daily 10am–noon and 2–6pm; Apr–June and Sept daily 10–11:30am and 2–5:30pm; Oct daily 10–11:30am and 2–4:30pm). Admission is 6€ for adults and 3.50€ for children ages 6 to 14.

Now head toward **Beaune** on D973, passing some well-known vineyards: Chassagne-Montrachet, Puligny-Montrachet, Meursault, Auxey Durresses, Volnay, and Pommard. En route, you can detour to a restaurant whose setting is as intriguing as its food. **Chagny,** 43km (27 miles) east of Autun and 18km (11 miles) southwest of Beaune, rarely attracts sightseers, and serious foodies from all over stop at **Lameloise,** 36 place d'Arnes (✆ **03-85-87-65-65**), for lamb filet in a rice crepe, Bresse pigeon, lemon soufflé, and one of the broadest selections of burgundies in France. Reservations are required. It's closed Wednesday all day and at lunch on Tuesday and Thursday.

Continue north to Beaune on D973, which changes to N741. You can overnight in Beaune (p. 411). If you arrive early enough in the day, you can explore Beaune's historic attractions in 2½ hours, including **Musée des Beaux-Arts** (p. 412).

Even more intriguing for the wine connoisseur is a visit to one of the cellars for a tour and a tasting. Our favorite is **Marché aux Vins** (p. 412), housed in a former church. Its cellars are in ancient tombs under the 14th-century church.

Day 5: Route des Grands Crus ★★★

The road visited on this trip is called the Route des Grands Crus, or road of the great wines.

Route N74 continues north 44km (27 miles) to Dijon, but you can make a full day of it because of the stopovers along the way.

This route takes you along the most celebrated vineyards of the **Côte d'Or,** which actually stretch from Dijon in the north to Santenay southwest of Beaune, a distance of 60km (37 miles). This is a region of France's greatest wines, and each village has some claim to fame.

As you head north from Beaune, the first village is **Aloxe-Corton,** where Charlemagne once owned vineyards. The emperor is still honored with "a white wine of great character," Corton-Charlemagne, which is still produced here.

The N74 continues north to the village of **Vougeot,** known for the quality of its red wines.

In Vougeot, you can visit the **Château du Clos-de-Vougeot** (✆ **03-80-62-86-09**), surrounded by France's most celebrated vineyards. The 12th-century château maintains a cellar, open for visits year-round (Apr–Sept Mon–Fri 9am–6:30pm and Sat–Sun 9am–5pm; Oct–Mar Mon–Fri 9am–5pm, Sat–Sun 9–11:30am and 2–5pm). Admission is 3.50€ for adults and 2.60€ for students and children 8 and older.

The N74 continues north to Dijon, but you can branch off onto D122 to Chambolle-Musigny, where you'll see signs directing you to the town of **Gevrey-Chambertin,** which lies only 10km (6¼ miles) south of Dijon. Nine of the region's 33 Grands Crus are produced here.

Visit the village's main attraction, **Le Château de Gevrey-Chambertin,** constructed by the lords of Vergy in the 10th century. In the 13th century, the decaying castle was expanded by the powerful monks of Cluny. The great hall is impressive, with exposed ceiling beams. Look for the guards' room in the watchtower and the collection of vintage wines in the vaulted cellars. English-language tours, ending with a tasting of the prize vintages, cost 14€. The château is open Monday, Thursday, and Friday 10am to noon and 2 to 5pm, Saturday and Sunday 11am to noon and 2 to 6pm. For more information, call © **03-80-51-84-85.**

The D122 takes you north into **Dijon** (p. 415), where you can spend the night (or a second night if your schedule allows). It takes 4 hours to explore Dijon. If you arrive early enough in the day, you can see half of the town's attractions, visiting the rest of the sights the next morning.

Day 6: Dijon ★★★

Surrounded by some of the world's most splendid vineyards, Dijon was the former seat of the powerful dukes of Burgundy. A university town and regional center today, it has had a long and rich history. Its monumental attraction is the **Musée des Beaux-Arts** (p. 416), housed in an old palace and showcasing a stunning collection of European art from the 14th to the 19th centuries. Next, pick up a map at the **Office de Tourisme** (p. 415) and walk through the historic core of this ancient city. Or, better yet, in our view, spend the day touring the magnificent wine country around Dijon (see "Side Trips from Dijon," p. 420).

Day 7: En Route to Paris

Dijon is one of the major transportation hubs in this part of France, and you can easily return to Paris from here. If you're driving, the distance is 312km (194 miles), which you can do in a morning, reaching Paris to the northwest in time for lunch.

SETTLING INTO PARIS

The City of Light always lives up to its reputation as one of the world's most romantic cities. Ernest Hemingway referred to the splendors of Paris as a "moveable feast" and wrote, "There is never any ending to Paris, and the memory of each person who has lived in it differs from that of any other."

Here you can stroll along the Seine and the broad tree-lined boulevards; browse the chic shops and relax over coffee or wine at a cafe; visit the museums, monuments, and cathedrals; and savor the cuisine.

5

ORIENTATION

Arriving

BY PLANE

Paris has two international airports: **Aéroport d'Orly,** 13km (8 miles) south of the city, and **Aéroport Roissy–Charles de Gaulle,** 22km (14 miles) northeast. A shuttle (19€) makes the 50- to 75-minute journey between the two airports about every 30 minutes.

CHARLES DE GAULLE AIRPORT (ROISSY) At Charles de Gaulle (✆ **01-48-62-12-12,** or 39-50 from France only), foreign carriers use Aérogare 1, while Air France uses Aérogare 2. From Aérogare 1, you take a moving walkway to the passport checkpoint and the Customs area. A *navette* (shuttle bus) links the two terminals.

Fast RER (Réseau Express Régional) trains depart the airport and **Roissy rail station** every 10 minutes between 5am and midnight for Métro stations including Gare du Nord, Châtelet, Luxembourg, Port-Royal, and Denfert-Rochereau. A typical fare from Roissy to any point in central Paris is 8.20€ per person (5.60€ children 4–10). Travel time from the airport to central Paris is around 35 to 40 minutes.

You can also take an **Air France shuttle bus** (✆ **08-92-35-08-20** or 01-48-64-14-24; www.cars-airfrance.com) to central Paris for 15€ one-way. It stops at the Palais des Congrès (Port Maillot) and continues to place Charles-de-Gaulle–Etoile, where subway lines can carry you to any point in Paris. That ride, depending on traffic, takes 45 to 55 minutes. The shuttle departs about every 20 minutes between 5:40am and 11pm.

The Paris Airport Shuttle

The **Paris Airport Shuttle** (✆ **01-53-39-18-18;** fax 01-53-39-13-13; www.paris shuttle.com) is the best option. It charges 25€ for one person or 19€ per person for two or more going to and from Charles de Gaulle or Orly. Service is daily 6am to 11pm. Both shuttles accept American Express, Visa, and MasterCard, with 1-day advance reservations required.

The **Roissybus** (✆ **01-58-76-16-16**), operated by the RATP, departs from the airport daily 6am to 11:45pm and costs 8.60€ for the 45- to 50-minute ride. Departures are about every 15 minutes, and the bus leaves you near the corner of rue Scribe and place de l'Opéra in the heart of Paris.

A **taxi** from Roissy into the city will cost about 47€ to 60€; from 8pm to 7am the fare is 40% higher. Long orderly lines for taxis form outside each of the airport's terminals.

ORLY AIRPORT   Orly (✆ **01-49-75-52-52,** or 39-50 from France only) has two terminals—Orly Sud (south) for international flights and Orly Ouest (west) for domestic flights. A free shuttle bus connects them in 3 minutes.

Air France buses leave from Exit E of Orly Sud and from Exit F of Orly Ouest every 12 minutes between 6am and 11:30pm for Gare des Invalides; the fare is 9€ one-way, 14€ round-trip. Returning to the airport (about 30 min.), buses leave both the Montparnasse and the Invalides terminal for Orly Sud or Orly Ouest every 15 minutes.

Another way to get to central Paris is to take the RER from points throughout central Paris to the station at Pont-de-Rungis/Aéroport d'Orly for a per-person one-way fare of 6€, and from here, take the free shuttle bus that departs every 15 minutes from Pont-de-Rungis to both of Orly's terminals. Combined travel time is about 45 to 55 minutes.

A **taxi** from Orly to central Paris costs about 30€ to 50€, more at night. Don't take a meterless taxi from Orly; it's much safer (and usually cheaper) to hire one of the metered cabs, which are under the scrutiny of a police officer.

BY TRAIN

Paris has six major stations: **Gare d'Austerlitz,** 55 quai d'Austerlitz, 13e (serving the southwest, with trains to and from the Loire Valley, Bordeaux, the Pyrénées, and Spain); **Gare de l'Est,** place du 11-Novembre-1918, 10e (serving the east, with trains to and from Strasbourg, Reims, and beyond, to Zurich and Austria); **Gare de Lyon,** 20 bd. Diderot, 12e (serving the southeast, with trains to and from the Côte d'Azur [Nice, Cannes, St-Tropez], Provence, and beyond, to Geneva and Italy); **Gare Montparnasse,** 17 bd. Vaugirard, 15e (serving the west, with trains to and from Brittany); **Gare du Nord,** 18 rue de Dunkerque, 15e (serving the north, with trains to and from London, Holland, Denmark, and northern Germany); and **Gare St-Lazare,** 13 rue d'Amsterdam, 8e (serving the northwest, with trains to and from Normandy). Buses operate between the stations, and each station has a Métro stop. For train information and to make reservations, call ✆ **08-92-35-35-35** from abroad, **36-35** from France between 8am and 8pm daily. From Paris, one-way rail

5

SETTLING INTO PARIS

Orientation

Paris Arrondissements

passage to Tours costs 30€ to 51€; one-way to Strasbourg costs 55€ or 80€, depending on the routing.

Warning: The stations and surrounding areas are usually seedy and frequented by pickpockets, hustlers, hookers, and addicts. Be alert, especially at night.

BY BUS

Most buses arrive at the **Eurolines France** station, 28 av. du Général-de-Gaulle, Bagnolet (© **08-92-89-90-91;** www.eurolines.fr; Métro: Gallieni).

BY CAR

Driving in Paris is *not* recommended. Parking is difficult and traffic dense. If you drive, remember that Paris is encircled by a ring road, the *périphérique*. Always obtain detailed directions to your destination, including the name of the exit on the *périphérique* (exits aren't numbered). Avoid rush hours.

The major highways into Paris are A1 from the north; A13 from Rouen, Normandy, and other points northwest; A10 from Spain and the southwest; A6 and A7 from the French Alps, the Riviera, and Italy; and A4 from eastern France.

Visitor Information

The **Paris Convention and Visitors Bureau** (© **08-92-68-30-00;** .35€ per minute; www.paris-info.com) has offices throughout the city, with the main headquarters at 25–27 rue des Pyramides, 1er (Métro: Pyramides). It's open Monday through Saturday 10am to 7pm (June–Oct from 9am), Sunday and holidays from 11am to 7pm. Less comprehensive branch offices include Clémenceau Welcome Center, corner of avenue Champs-Elysées and avenue Marigny (8e; Métro: Champs-Elysées), open April 6 to October 20 daily 9am to 7pm. **Espace Tourisme Ile-de-France,** in the Carrousel du Louvre, 99 rue de Rivoli, 1er (Métro: Palais-Royal–Louvre), open daily 10am to 6pm; in the **Gare de Lyon,** 20 bd. Diderot, Paris 12e (Métro: Gare de Lyon), open Monday through Saturday 8am to 6pm; in the **Gare du Nord,** 18 rue de Dunkerque, 10e (Métro: Gare du Nord), open daily 8am to 6pm; and in **Montmartre,** 21 place du Tertre, 18e (Métro: Abbesses or Lamarck-Caulaincourt), open daily 10am to 7pm. You can walk in at any branch to make a hotel reservation; the service charge is free. The offices are extremely busy year-round, especially in midsummer, so be prepared to wait in line.

City Layout

Paris is surprisingly compact. Occupying 2,723 sq. km (1,051 sq. miles), its urban area is home to more than 11 million people. The river Seine divides Paris into the **Rive Droite (Right Bank)** to the north and the **Rive Gauche (Left Bank)** to the south. These designations make sense when you stand on a bridge and face downstream (west)—to your right is the north bank, to your left the south. A total of 32 bridges link the Right Bank and the Left Bank. Some provide access to the two islands at the heart of the city: **Ile de la Cité,** the city's birthplace and site of Notre-Dame; and **Ile St-Louis,** a moat-guarded oasis of 17th-century mansions.

The "main street" on the Right Bank is **avenue des Champs-Elysées,** beginning at the Arc de Triomphe and running to place de la Concorde. Avenue des Champs-Elysées and 11 other avenues radiate like the arms of an asterisk from the Arc de Triomphe, giving it its original name, place de l'Etoile (*étoile* means "star"). It was renamed place Charles-de-Gaulle following the general's death; today, it's often referred to as place Charles-de-Gaulle–Etoile.

FINDING AN ADDRESS Paris is divided into 20 municipal wards called *arrondissements,* each with its own city hall, police station, and post office; some have remnants of market squares. *Arrondissements* spiral out clockwise from the 1st, in the geographical center of the city. The 2nd through the 8th form a ring around the 1st, and the 9th through the 17th form an outer ring around the inner ring. The 18th, 19th, and 20th are at the far northern and eastern reaches of the Right Bank. Arrondissements 5, 6, 7, 13, 14, and 15 are on the Left Bank.

Most city maps are divided by *arrondissement,* and addresses include the *arrondissement* number (in Roman or Arabic numerals and followed by "e," or "1er" for the 1st arrondissement). Paris also has its own version of a zip code. The mailing address for a hotel is written as, for example, "Paris 75014." The last two digits, 14, indicate that the address is in the 14th arrondissement—in this case, Montparnasse.

Numbers on buildings running parallel to the Seine usually follow the course of the river—east to west. On perpendicular streets, building numbers begin low closer to the river.

MAPS If you're staying more than 2 or 3 days, purchase an inexpensive pocket-size book called *Paris par arrondissement,* available at newsstands and bookshops; prices start at 6.50€. This guide provides you with a Métro map, a foldout map of the city, and maps of each *arrondissement,* with all streets listed and keyed.

The Arrondissements in Brief

Each of Paris's 20 *arrondissements* possesses a unique style and flavor. Do note, however, that in this guide we cover hotels in central Paris only; for a wider selection of accommodations in the outer *arrondissements,* see the latest edition of *Frommer's Paris.*

1er (Musée du Louvre/Les Halles) The **Louvre** lures hordes to the 1st arrondissement, on the Right Bank. This area is home to rue de Rivoli and the **Jeu de Paume** and **Orangerie** museums. Walk through the **Jardin des Tuileries,** laid out by Louis XIV's gardener. Pause to take in the beauty of **place Vendôme.** Zola's "belly of Paris" (Les Halles) is no longer the food-and-meat market; it's now the **Forum des Halles,** a shopping center.

2e (La Bourse) Home to the **Bourse (stock exchange),** this Right Bank district lies between the *grands boulevards* and rue Etienne-Marcel. On weekdays, the shouts of brokers echo across place de la Bourse. Much of the east end of the 2nd is devoted to the **garment district (Le Sentier).** You'll find gems amid the commercialism, and none finer than the **Musée Cognacq-Jay,** 25 bd. des Capucines, featuring work by artists from Watteau to Fragonard.

3e (Le Marais) This district embraces much of **Le Marais (the Swamp),** one of the best loved of the old Right Bank neighborhoods. Kings have called Le Marais home, and its salons have echoed with the remarks of Racine, Voltaire, Molière, and Mme. de Sévigné. It enjoyed a renewal in the 1990s, with galleries and boutiques. One of its chief draws is **Musée Picasso,** a repository of 20th-century art. Le Marais is also the center of Paris's gay and lesbian scene. Rue des Rosiers, with its Jewish restaurants, preserves the memory of the hundreds of Jewish residents who used to reside in Le Marais.

4e (Ile de la Cité/Ile St-Louis & Beaubourg) The 4th has it all: not only the Ile de la Cité, with **Notre-Dame,** the **Sainte-Chapelle,** and the **Conciergerie,** but also the Ile St-Louis, with town houses, courtyards, and antiques shops. Ile St-Louis, a former cow pasture and dueling ground, is home to 6,000 Louisiens, its permanent residents. The area is touristy and crowded.

As the heart of medieval Paris, the 4th evokes memories of Danton, of Robespierre, even of Charlotte Corday stabbing Marat in his bathroom. Here are France's finest **bird and flower markets,** plus the **Centre Pompidou.** After all this, you can retreat to **place des Vosges,** a square of perfect harmony where Victor Hugo penned many masterpieces from 1832 to 1848.

5e (Latin Quarter) The Quartier Latin is Paris's intellectual soul, featuring bookstores, schools, churches, jazz clubs, student dives, Roman ruins, and boutiques. The area got its name because students and professors at the **Sorbonne** (founded in 1253) spoke Latin. As the center of "bohemian Paris," it was the setting for Henry Murger's novel La Vie Bohème (later the Puccini opera La Bohème).

Changing times have brought immigrants offering everything from couscous to spring rolls. The 5th borders the Seine, so you'll want to stroll along **quai de Montebello,** where vendors sell everything from antique Daumier prints to copies of Balzac's Père Goriot. The 5th also stretches to the **Panthéon,** the resting place of Rousseau, Zola, Hugo, Voltaire, and Jean Moulin, the Resistance leader tortured to death by the Gestapo. Marie Curie is buried here as well.

6e (St-Germain/Luxembourg) For some, this is the most colorful Left Bank quarter. You can see young artists emerging from the **Ecole des Beaux-Arts.** Strolling the boulevards of the 6th, including **St-Germain,** has its own rewards, but the secret of the district lies in its narrow streets, hidden squares, and the **Jardin du Luxembourg,** near Marie de Médicis' **Palais du Luxembourg.** To be authentic, stroll these streets with a loaf of bread from the ovens of **Poilâne,** 8 rue du Cherche-Midi. You'll encounter historical and literary associations, as on **rue Jacob,** where Racine, Ingres, and Hemingway lived. Today's big name could be Spike Lee checking into **La Villa Hôtel** at 29 rue Jacob.

7e (Eiffel Tower/Musée d'Orsay) The **Eiffel Tower** dominates the 7th on the Left Bank. The tower is one of the most recognizable landmarks in the world, but many hated it when it opened in 1889. The 7th is also home to the **Hôtel des Invalides,** which contains Napoleon's Tomb and the Musée de l'Armée. Even visitors with no time to explore should visit the **Musée d'Orsay,** the world's premier showcase of 19th-century French art and culture.

8e (Champs-Elysées/Madeleine) The 8th is the heart of the Right Bank, and its showcase is **avenue des Champs-Elysées,** linking the **Arc de Triomphe** with the obelisk on **place de la Concorde.** Here you'll find fashion houses, hotels, restaurants, and shops. The area is known for having France's (perhaps the world's) superlatives: the best restaurant **(Taillevent),** the sexiest strip joint **(Crazy Horse Saloon),** the most splendid square **(place de la Concorde),** the grandest hotel **(Crillon),** the most impressive arch **(Arc de Triomphe),** the oldest Métro station **(Franklin-D-Roosevelt),** and the most ancient monument **(Obelisk of Luxor,** 3,300 years old). Also here is **La Madeleine** church, which looks like a Greek temple.

9e (Opéra Garnier/Pigalle) Everything from the Quartier de l'Opéra to the strip joints of Pigalle (the infamous "Pig Alley" for World War II GIs) is in the 9th, on the Right Bank. Baron Haussmann's 19th-century redevelopment radically altered it, and the grands boulevards are among the most obvious of his works. Another attraction is the **Folies-Bergère,** where cancan dancers have been kicking since 1868 and such entertainers as Mistinguett, Edith Piaf, and Josephine Baker appeared. The **Opéra** (now the Opéra Garnier or Palais Garnier), once the haunt of the Phantom, made the 9th the last hurrah of Second Empire opulence.

10e (Gare du Nord/Gare de l'Est) The two stations, along with cinemas, porno houses, and commercial zones, make the 10th one of the least desirable tourist districts. We avoid it, except for **Brasserie Flo,**

for *la formidable choucroute*—sauerkraut with everything.

11e (Opéra Bastille) The **Opéra Bastille,** opened in 1989, is the center of this district. The "people's opera house" stands on the **place de la Bastille,** where on July 14, 1789, Parisians stormed the fortress and released the prisoners.

This area between the Marais, Ménilmontant, and République is "blue-collar chic," and *artistes* walk the sidewalks of rue Oberkampf. Hip Parisians live and work among decaying 19th-century apartments and 1960s public housing with graffiti-spattered walls.

12e (Bois de Vincennes/Gare de Lyon) The 12th is experiencing a renaissance, with new housing, shops, and restaurants. Few out-of-towners came here until the opening of famed restaurant **Au Trou Gascon.** The major attraction is the **Bois de Vincennes,** a sprawling park on the eastern periphery of Paris. It is a favorite of families, who enjoy its zoos and museums, its château and lakes, and the Parc Floral de Paris, with springtime rhododendrons and autumn dahlias. The **Gare de Lyon** is in the 12th, but going here is worthwhile even if you don't have to take a train, as the building is a great architectural monument of Belle Epoque France. The ceiling frescoes and Art Nouveau decor of the station's restaurant, **Le Train Bleu,** are national treasures—and the food's good, too.

13e (Gare d'Austerlitz) Centering on the Gare d'Austerlitz, the 13th may have its fans, though we've yet to meet one. But worth seeing is the **Manufacture des Gobelins,** 42 av. des Gobelins, which makes the famous Gobelins tapestries.

14e (Montparnasse) The northern end of this district on the Left Bank is **Montparnasse,** home of the Lost Generation. One of its monuments is the Rodin statue of Balzac at boulevard Montparnasse and boulevard Raspail. At this corner are **literary cafes** such as La Rotonde, Le Sélect, La Dôme, and La Coupole. Perhaps Gertrude Stein didn't frequent them (she loathed cafes), but other American expats such as Hemingway and Fitzgerald came for a drink or four. At 27 rue de Fleurus, Stein and Alice B. Toklas collected paintings and entertained T. S. Eliot and Matisse.

15e (Gare Montparnasse/Institut Pasteur) A mostly residential district beginning at Gare Montparnasse, the 15th, on the Left Bank, stretches west to the Seine. It's the largest *arrondissement* but has few attractions, except for the **Parc des Expositions,** a fairground that stages special exhibitions, and the **Institut Pasteur,** a biochemical research center founded by Louis Pasteur in 1887.

16e (Trocadéro/Bois de Boulogne) Highlights of the 16th, on the Right Bank, are the **Bois de Boulogne, Jardins du Trocadéro, Musée de Balzac, Musée Guimet** (famous for its Asian collections), and **Cimetière de Passy,** resting place of Manet, Giraudoux, and Debussy. This large *arrondissement* is known for its well-heeled bourgeoisie, high rents, and posh boulevards. Prosperous, conservative addresses include **avenue d'Iéna** and **avenue Victor-Hugo.** The 16th also includes the best place in Paris to view the Eiffel Tower: **place du Trocadéro.**

17e (Parc Monceau/Place Clichy) One of the most spread-out *arrondissements,* the 17th, on the Right Bank, flanks the northern periphery of Paris. It incorporates the northern edge of place Charles-de-Gaulle–Etoile in the west, the place Wagram at its center, and the tawdry place Clichy in the east. Highlights are **Parc Monceau,** the **Palais des Congrès** (of interest only if you're attending a convention), and the **Porte Maillot Air Terminal.** The 17th does contain two great restaurants: **Guy Savoy** and **Michel Rostang.**

18e (Montmartre) The 18th, at the far end of the Right Bank, is associated with such names as the **Marché aux Puces de Clignancourt** flea market, **Moulin Rouge, Sacré-Coeur,** and **place du Tertre** (a tourist trap if ever there was one). Utrillo was its native son, Renoir lived here, and Toulouse-Lautrec adopted the area as his own. Today, place Blanche is known for its prostitutes, and Montmartre is filled with honky-tonks, souvenir shops, and bad restaurants.

19e (La Villette) Visitors come to what was once the village of La Villette to see the **Cité des Sciences et de l'Industrie,** a science museum and park. Mostly residential, this district is one of the most ethnic in Paris, home to workers from all parts of the former empire. A highlight is **Les Buttes Chaumont,** where kids can enjoy puppet shows and donkey rides.

20e (Père-Lachaise Cemetery) This district's greatest landmark is the **Père-Lachaise Cemetery,** resting place of Piaf, Proust, Wilde, Duncan, Stein and Toklas, Bernhardt, Colette, Jim Morrison, and many others. The district is home to Muslims and members of Paris's Sephardic Jewish community, many of whom fled Algeria or Tunisia. With turbaned men selling dates and grains on the street, this *arrondissement* seems more North African than French.

GETTING AROUND

BY METRO (SUBWAY) The Métro (📞 **32-46** in France, or 08-92-69-32-46 from abroad; www.ratp.fr) is the most efficient and fastest way to get around Paris. All lines are numbered, and the final destination of each line is clearly marked on subway maps, in the system's underground passageways, and on the train cars. The Métro runs daily from 5:30am to 1:15am (last departure at 2am on Sat). It's reasonably safe at any hour, but beware of pickpockets.

To familiarize yourself with the Métro, see the color map on the inside back cover of this book. Most stations display a map of the Métro at the entrance. To locate your correct train on a map, find your destination, follow the line to the end of its route, and note the name of the final stop, which is that line's direction. In the station, follow the signs for your direction in the passageways until you see the label on a train. Many larger stations have maps with push-button indicators that light up your route when you press the button for your destination.

Transfer stations are *correspondances,* and some require long walks; Châtelet is the most difficult—but most trips require only one transfer. When transferring, follow the orange CORRESPONDANCE signs to the proper platform. Don't follow a SORTIE (exit) sign, or you'll have to pay again to get back on the train.

On the urban lines, one ticket for 1.60€ lets you travel to any point. On the Sceaux, Boissy-St-Léger, and St-Germain-en-Laye lines to the suburbs, fares are based on distance. A *carnet* is the best buy—10 tickets for about 11.60€.

At the turnstile entrances to the station, insert your ticket and pass through. At some exits, tickets are also checked, so hold onto yours. There are occasional ticket checks on trains and platforms and in passageways, too.

RER TRAINS A suburban train system, RER (Réseau Express Régional), passes through the heart of Paris, traveling faster than the Métro and running daily from 5:30am to 1am. This system works like the Métro and requires the same tickets. Beware that on trips outside of central Paris (including to the airports), the RER costs more than the Métro, ranging from 1.60€ to 11€. The major stops within central Paris, linking the RER to the Métro, are Nation, Gare de Lyon, Charles de Gaulle–Etoile, Gare-Etoile, and Gare du Nord as well as Châtelet-Les-Halles. All of these stops are on the Right Bank. On the Left Bank, RER stops include Denfert-Rochereau and St-Michel. The five RER lines are marked A through E. Different

discount TRANSIT PASSES

The **Paris-Visite pass** (*©* **32-46**) is valid for 1, 2, 3, or 5 days on public transport, including the Métro, buses, the funicular ride to Montmartre, and RER trains. For access to zones 1 to 3, which include central Paris and its nearby suburbs, its cost ranges from 8.80€ for 1 day to 28.30€ for 5 days. Get it at RATP (Régie Autonome des Transports Parisiens) offices, the tourist office, and Métro stations.

branches are labeled by a number, the C5 Line serving Versailles–Rive Gauche, for example. Electric signboards next to each track outline all the possible stops along the way. Make sure that the little square next to your intended stop is lit.

BY BUS   Buses are much slower than the Métro. The majority run Monday through Saturday from 6:30am to 9:30pm (a few operate until 12:30am, and 10 operate during early morning hours). Service is limited on Sundays and holidays. Bus and Métro fares are the same; you can use the same tickets on both. Most bus rides require one ticket, but some destinations require two (never more than two within the city limits).

At certain stops, signs list destinations and bus numbers serving that point. Destinations are usually listed north to south and east to west. Most stops are also posted on the sides of the buses. During rush hours, you may have to take a ticket from a dispensing machine, indicating your position in the line at the stop.

If you intend to use the buses a lot, pick up an RATP bus map at the office on place de la Madeleine, 8e, or at the tourist offices at RATP headquarters, 54 Quai de La Rapée, 12e. For detailed recorded information (in English) on bus and Métro routes, call *©* **32-46,** open Monday to Friday 7am to 9pm.

The RATP also operates the **Balabus,** big-windowed orange-and-white motorcoaches that run only during limited hours: Sunday and national holidays from noon to 8:30pm, from April 15 to the end of September. Itineraries run in both directions between Gare de Lyon and the Grande Arche de La Défense, encompassing some of the city's most beautiful vistas. It's a great deal—three Métro tickets, for 1.60€ each, will carry you the entire route. You'll recognize the bus and the route it follows by the BB symbol emblazoned on each bus's side and on signs posted beside the route it follows.

BY TAXI   It's virtually impossible to get a taxi at rush hour, so don't even try. Taxi drivers are organized into a lobby that limits their number to 15,000.

Watch out for common rip-offs: Always check the meter to make sure you're not paying the previous passenger's fare; beware of cabs without meters, which often wait outside nightclubs for tipsy patrons; and settle the tab in advance.

You can hail regular cabs on the street when their signs read LIBRE. Taxis are easier to find at the many stands near Métro stations. The flag drops at 5.50€, and from 10am to 5pm, you pay .89€ per kilometer. From 5pm to 10pm, you pay 1.14€ per kilometer. On airport trips, you're not required to pay for the driver's empty return ride.

You're allowed several pieces of luggage free if they're transported inside and are less than 5 kilograms (11 lb.). Heavier suitcases carried in the trunk cost 1€ to 1.50€

apiece. Tip 12% to 15%—the latter usually elicits a *merci*. For radio cabs, call **Les Taxis Bleus** (☎ 08-25-16-10-10) or **Taxi G7** (☎ 01-47-39-47-39)—but note that you'll be charged from the point where the taxi begins the drive to pick you up.

BY BOAT   The **Batobus** (☎ 08-25-05-01-01; www.batobus.com) is a 150-passenger ferry with big windows. Every day between April and December, the boats operate along the Seine, stopping at such points of interest as the **Eiffel Tower, Musée d'Orsay,** the **Louvre, Notre-Dame,** and the **Hôtel de Ville.** Unlike the Bateaux-Mouche (see chapter 6), the Batobus does not provide recorded commentary. The only fare option available is a day pass valid for either 1, 2, or 5 days, each allowing as many entrances and exits as you want. A 1-day pass costs 12€ for adults, 6€ for children 15 and under; a 2-day pass costs 16€ for adults, 8€ for children 15 and under; a 5-day pass costs 19€ for adults, 9€ for children 15 and under. Boats operate daily April through December (closed most of Jan) every 15 to 30 minutes, starting between 10 and 10:30am and ending between 4:30 and 10:30pm, depending on the season of the year.

[Fast FACTS] PARIS

For additional practical information, see "Fast Facts: France" (p. 758).

Currency Exchange
American Express can fill most banking needs. Most banks in Paris are open Monday through Friday from 9am to 4:30pm; ask at your hotel for the location of the one nearest you. For the best exchange rate, cash your traveler's checks at banks or foreign-exchange offices, not at shops and hotels. Most post offices will change traveler's checks or convert currency. Currency exchanges are also at Paris airports and train stations and along most of the major boulevards. They charge a small commission.

Some exchange places charge favorable rates to lure you into their stores. For example, **Paris Vision,** 214 rue de Rivoli, 1er (☎ 01-42-60-30-01;

Métro: Tuileries), maintains a minibank in the back of a travel agency, open daily 6:30am to 9pm. Its rates are a fraction less favorable than those offered for large blocks of money as listed by the Paris stock exchange.

Dentists   For emergency dental service, call **S.O.S. Dentaire,** 87 bd. du Port-Royal, 13e (☎ 01-43-37-51-00 or 01-43-36-36-00; Métro: Gobelins), Monday through Friday from 6 to 11:30pm and Saturday and Sunday from 9am to midnight. Staff members will arrange an appointment with a qualified dentist either on the day of your call or for early in the morning of the following day. You can also call or visit the **American Hospital** (see "Doctors," below).

Doctors   Some large hotels have a doctor on staff. You can also try the

American Hospital, 63 bd. Victor-Hugo, in the suburb of Neuilly-sur-Seine (☎ 01-46-41-25-25; www.american-hospital.org; Métro: Pont-de-Levallois or Pont-de-Neuilly; bus no. 82), which operates a 24-hour emergency service. The bilingual staff accepts Blue Cross and other American insurance plans.

Drugstores   After hours, have your concierge contact the Commissariat de Police for the nearest 24-hour pharmacy. French law requires one pharmacy in any given neighborhood to stay open 24 hours. You'll find the address posted on the doors or windows of all other drugstores. One of the most central all-nighters is **Pharmacie Les Champs "Derhy,"** 84 av. des Champs-Elysées, 8e (☎ 01-45-62-02-41; Métro: George V).

Emergencies For the police, call 📞 **17;** to report a fire, call 📞 **18.** For an ambulance, call 📞 **15** or 01-45-67-50-50.

Police In an emergency, call 📞 **17.** For nonemergency situations, the principal *préfecture* is at 9 bd. du Palais, 4e (📞 **01-53-73-53-73;** Métro: Cité).

Post Offices Most post offices in Paris are open Monday through Friday from 8am to 7pm and every Saturday from 8am to noon. One of the biggest and most central is the main post office for the 1st arrondissement, at 52 rue du Louvre (📞 **01-40-28-76-00;** Métro: Musée du Louvre). It maintains the hours noted above for services that include sale of postal money orders, mail collection and distribution, and expedition of faxes. For buying stamps and accepting packages, it's open on a limited basis 24 hours a day. If you find it inconvenient to go to the post office just to buy stamps, they're sold at the reception desks of many hotels and at cafes designated with red TABAC signs.

Safety Beware of child pickpockets, who prey on visitors around sites such as the Louvre, Eiffel Tower, Notre-Dame, and Montmartre, and who like to pick pockets in the Métro, often blocking the entrances and exits to the escalator. Women should hang onto their purses.

WHERE TO STAY

Although Paris hotels are quite expensive, there is some good news. Scores of lackluster lodgings, where the wallpaper dated from the Napoleonic era, have been renovated and offer much better value in the moderate-to-inexpensive price range. The most outstanding examples are in the **7th arrondissement,** where several good-value hotels have blossomed from dives.

By now, the "season" has almost ceased to exist. Most visitors, at least those from North America, visit in July and August. Because many French are on vacation, and trade fairs and conventions come to a halt, there are usually plenty of rooms, even though these months have traditionally been the peak season for European travel. In most hotels, February is just as busy as April or September because of the volume of business travelers and the increasing number of tourists who've learned to take advantage of off-season discount airfares.

Hot weather doesn't last long in Paris, so most hotels, except the deluxe ones, don't provide air-conditioning. To avoid the noise problem when you have to open windows, request a room in the back when making a reservation.

Some hotels offer a continental breakfast of coffee, tea, or hot chocolate; a freshly baked croissant and roll; and butter and jam or jelly. Though nowhere near as filling as a traditional English or American breakfast, it is quick to prepare—it'll be at your door moments after you request it—and can be served at almost any hour. The word "breakfast" in these entries refers to this version.

Rates quoted include service and value-added tax unless otherwise specified. Unless otherwise noted, all hotel rooms have private bathrooms.

Alternatives to Hotels

If you want to stay somewhere more intimate (and in some cases, more restrictive) than a hotel, consider booking a room within a private home.

An agency promoting upmarket B&B accommodations in Paris is **Alcôve & Agapes,** 8 bis rue Coysevox, Paris 75018 (📞/fax **01-44-85-06-05;** www.bed-and-breakfast-in-paris.com). Reservations are made through the Internet only. This outfit is a bridge between travelers who seek rooms in private homes and Parisians who wish to welcome visitors. Most hosts speak at least some English, range in age from 30 to 75, and have at least some points of view about entertainment and dining options within the neighborhood. Available options include individual bedrooms, usually within large, old-fashioned private apartments, as well as "unhosted" accommodations where the apartment is otherwise empty and without the benefit (or restrictions) of a live-in host.

Rates for occupancy by either one or two persons, with breakfast included, range from 65€ to 195€ per unit, depending on the apartment, the neighborhood, the setup, and the plumbing. In cases where a client occupies an unhosted apartment, the refrigerators will be stocked with sufficient breakfast supplies for the number of days you are staying (3-night minimum stay).

Hotes Qualité Paris (www.hqp.fr), a program run by the Paris city government that seeks residents willing to rent rooms in their homes like a B&B, encourages locals to make available their spare rooms at prices that begin around 100€ a night. It's strictly potluck; you might end up on a house barge docked between the Louvre and the place de la Concorde, or else in an old-fashioned bedroom near the Bois de Boulogne with a host who happens to be a passionate history lecturer, as you'll find out at breakfast the next morning.

Coach House Rentals (www.rentals.chsparis.com) has expanded its private homes for rent to include addresses in Paris. Its website has pictures and full descriptions of the properties, with an English-speaking reservation team to handle bookings and to deal with any questions. A company representative will meet guests at their rental to show them the ropes. The company can usually arrange a car to meet guests at the airport and take them to their prearranged rental.

The aptly named **Good Morning Paris,** 43 rue Lacépède, 75005 (www.good morningparis.fr), is yet another bed-and-breakfast agency with carefully inspected rooms to rent. Prices can range from 69€ for two people with a shared bathroom or 90€ for two with private bathroom, including breakfast. A few apartments are also rented, housing two to four people from 106€ a night. A minimum of 2 nights is required for all rentals. Flats are possible right in the heart of Paris off the Champs-Elysées or in more romantic sectors, including the Latin Quarter, even Montmartre.

Though a bit more risky than the previously inspected and approved recommendations, a budget option for rental apartments can be pursued by checking out the classified ads in **FUSAC** (France-USA Contacts), a free biweekly magazine that is widely distributed in bookstores, cafes, or restaurants catering to English-speaking visitors.

FUSAC is taking potluck if you want an apartment. A safer bet is **Paris Attitude** at 6 rue de Sentier, 75002 (© **01-42-96-31-46;** fax 01-42-96-27-86; www.paris attitude.com). Apartments are centrally located and are furnished and well equipped; short- or long-term rentals are available. A studio for two people right off the Champs-Elysées might rent for 550€ per week or 1,150€ per month.

Parisian Home, 12 rue Mandar, 75002 (© **01-45-08-03-37;** www.parisian home.com), has a large selection of apartments available in central Paris, ranging from cramped studios to spacious three-bedroom apartments for more luxurious and expensive living. Don't expect elegant furnishings, however, though the rentals, both short- or long-term, are well equipped with linen, dishes, and the like. The agency's website is detailed with lots of pictures and descriptions of the services available. You deal with the agency, not the owners. The minimum stay is 1 week.

Unlike Parisian Home, **France Lodge,** 2 rue Meissonier, 75017 (✆ **01-56-33-85-85;** www.francelodge.fr), has both hosted and unhosted apartments, some 100 in all sprinkled all over the central *arrondissements* of Paris. The agency's roster ranges from B&Bs to small studios, or even luxurious five-room apartments if you want to spread out or have a big family. The cheapest rentals, rather cramped, begin at 400€ a week, but 900€ would be more average.

Parisian Home and France Lodge rent apartments that owners use only occasionally. However, **Appartement de Ville** (✆ **01-42-45-09-08;** www.appartement deville.com) rents more upmarket apartments that owners use as their primary residence. Lodgings under this agency have more atmosphere and give you a feeling that you're living more like a Parisian—which you are, of course. Many of the apartments are owned by those in the arts, including actors and dancers who have to be away from Paris for extended periods for engagements. There are some 200 apartments, most of them quite unusual, in the agency's roster. Although most apartments are in the very heart of Paris, you can make better deals by booking into one of the unchic *arrondissements,* including the 10th, 11th, and 12th. Studios can range from 450€ to 840€ per week, with larger apartments costing much more, perhaps 2,000€ for a three-bedroom.

Finally, some good deals are possible if you go for an "aparthotel," a cross between a hotel and an apartment. Short on charm, these rentals are good on convenience, each with a kitchenette. Although rates are more than short-term studios (see above), you get more of the services of a hotel, including fresh towels and a reception desk. The best known of agencies renting aparthotels is **Citadines** (✆ **08-25-33-33-32;** www.citadines.com). The cheapest rentals are the studios with pullout beds. A studio for two might range from 140€ to 250€—even more—per night in such highly prized locations as the Louvre area or St-Germain-des-Prés on the Left Bank.

Right Bank: 1st Arrondissement (Musée du Louvre/Les Halles)
VERY EXPENSIVE

Hôtel de Vendôme ★★ This jewel box was once the embassy of Texas when that state was a nation. The hotel opened in 1998 at one of the world's most prestigious addresses. It is comparable to the Hôtel Costes but with a less flashy clientele. Though the guest rooms are moderate in size, they're opulent and designed in classic Second Empire style, with luxurious beds and well-upholstered, hand-carved furnishings. Suites have generous space and such extras as blackout draperies and quadruple-glazed windows. The security is fantastic, with TV intercoms.

1 place Vendôme, Paris 75001. ✆ **01-55-04-55-00.** Fax 01-49-27-97-89. www.hoteldevendome.com. 29 units. High season 780€–865€ double, from 1,130€ junior suite, from 1,525€ suite; winter 550€–620€ double, from 830€ junior suite, from 970€ suite. AE, DC, MC, V. Parking 27€. Métro: Concorde or Opéra. **Amenities:** Restaurant; piano bar; babysitting; room service. *In room:* A/C, TV, hair dryer, minibar, Wi-Fi (free).

Hôtel Meurice ★★★ This landmark lies between the place de la Concorde and the Grand Louvre, facing the Tuileries Gardens. The hotel is more media-hip, style-conscious, and better located than the George V. Since the 1800s, it has welcomed the royal, the rich, and even the radical. The mad genius Salvador Dalí made the

Where to Stay on the Right Bank

Hôtel Amour **2**
Hôtel Banke **3**
Hôtel Bellevue & du Chariot d'Or **15**
Hôtel Britannique **21**
Hôtel du 7e Art **22**

Hôtel du Bourg Tibourg **20**
Hôtel Chopin **5**
Hôtel Duo **19**
Hôtel de Lutèce **25**
Hôtel de Vendôme **8**

Hôtel des Chevaliers **16**
Hôtel des Deux-Iles **23**
Hôtel du Petit Moulin **14**
Hôtel Langlois **4**
Hôtel Meurice **10**

Gare de l'Est

Hôtel Ritz **6**
Hôtel Saint-Louis en l'Isle **24**
Hôtel Saint-Merry **18**
Hôtel Thérèse **7**
Le Relais du Louvre **12**

Murano Urban Resort **13**
Pavillon de la Reine **17**
Timhotel Le Louvre **11**
Villa Royale **1**
Westin Paris **9**

Ⓜ Métro Stop

0   1/5 mi
0   0.2 km

5

SETTLING INTO PARIS | Where to Stay

Meurice his headquarters. The mosaic floors, plaster ceilings, hand-carved moldings, and Art Nouveau glass roof atop the Winter Garden look new. Each room is individually decorated with period pieces, fine carpets, Italian and French fabrics, marble bathrooms, and modern features such as fax and Internet access. Our favorites and the least expensive are the sixth-floor rooms. Some have painted ceilings of puffy clouds and blue skies, along with canopy beds. Suites are among the most lavish in France.

228 rue de Rivoli, Paris 75001. © **01-44-58-10-10.** Fax 01-44-58-10-15. www.meuricehotel.com. 160 units. 640€–980€ double; from 1,050€ junior suite; from 1,700€ suite. AE, DC, MC, V. Parking 27€. Métro: Tuileries or Concorde. **Amenities:** 2 restaurants; bar; babysitting; room service; full-service spa. *In room:* A/C, TV, hair dryer, minibar, Wi-Fi (20€ per day).

Hôtel Ritz ★★★   The Ritz is Europe's greatest hotel, an enduring symbol of elegance on one of Paris's most beautiful and historic squares. César Ritz, the "little shepherd boy from Niederwald," converted the Hôtel de Lazun into a luxury hotel in 1898. With the help of the culinary master Escoffier, he made the Ritz a miracle of luxury. In 1979, the Ritz family sold the hotel to Mohammed al Fayed, who refurbished it and added a cooking school. The hotel annexed two town houses, joined by an arcade lined with display cases representing 125 of Paris's leading boutiques. The public salons are furnished with museum-caliber antiques. Each guest room is uniquely decorated, most with Louis XIV or XV reproductions; all have fine rugs, marble fireplaces, tapestries, brass beds, and more. Ever since Edward VII got stuck in a too-narrow bathtub with his lover, the tubs at the Ritz have been deep and big.

15 place Vendôme, Paris 75001. © **800/223-6800** in the U.S. and Canada, or 01-43-16-30-30. Fax 01-43-16-31-78. www.ritzparis.com. 159 units. 770€–870€ double; from 1,020€ suite. AE, DC, MC, V. Parking 48€. Métro: Opéra, Concorde, or Madeleine. **Amenities:** Restaurant; 4 bars; nightclub; babysitting; health club; indoor pool; room service; sauna. *In room:* A/C, TV, hair dryer, minibar, Wi-Fi (25€ per day).

EXPENSIVE

Westin Paris ★ ☺   It's location, location, location. You're 30 seconds from the Tuileries Gardens, 3 minutes from the place Vendôme, 5 minutes from place de la Concorde, and 7 minutes from the Louvre. Renovations have breathed new life into most of the rooms, which are a bit small for the most part but comfortably furnished and well maintained. Some patrons have written in the guest book that they found the beds "heavenly." Two connecting rooms can be blocked off for families, and family rates are available. Many of the units overlook an inner courtyard.

3 rue de Castiglione, Paris 75001. © **800/454-6835** in the U.S., or 01-44-77-11-11. Fax 01-44-77-14-60. www.starwoodhotels.com. 440 units. 350€–410€ double; from 630€ suite. AE, DC, MC, V. Métro: Tuileries. **Amenities:** 2 restaurants; bar; babysitting; health club; room service. *In room:* A/C, TV, hair dryer, minibar, Wi-Fi (25€ per day).

MODERATE

Hôtel Britannique ✒   Conservatively modern and plush, this is a much-renovated 19th-century hotel near Les Halles and Notre-Dame. The place is not only British in name, but also seems to cultivate English graciousness. The guest rooms are small, but immaculate and soundproof, with comfortable beds. A satellite receiver gets U.S. and U.K. television shows. The reading room is a cozy retreat.

20 av. Victoria, Paris 75001. © **01-42-33-74-59.** Fax 01-42-33-82-65. www.hotel-britannique.fr. 39 units. 190€–221€ double; 279€–325€ suite. AE, DC, MC, V. Métro: Châtelet. **Amenities:** Bar; room service. *In room:* A/C, TV, hair dryer, minibar, Wi-Fi (free).

Hôtel Thérèse   Close to the Louvre, place Vendôme, and the Tuileries Gardens, this hotel combines French charm with English classicism. For example, the wood library and bar evokes a London club with its wood-paneled walls and plush arm-chairs, but the lounge is adorned with Parisian art. It's government-rated three stars but seems more like four stars in ambience, style, and comfort. Owner Sylvia de Lattre, who likes shades of pistachio and royal blue, trolled the flea markets for paintings and prints to personalize each bedroom. The rooms are unpretentious but filled with quality furnishings from the soft efficient lighting by Philippe Starck to the natural wool quilts.

5–7 rue Thérèse, Paris 75001. ☏ **01-42-96-10-01.** Fax 01-42-96-15-22. www.hoteltherese.com. 43 units. 185€–320€ double. AE, MC, V. Métro: Musée du Louvre. **Amenities:** Library/bar; room service. *In room:* A/C, TV, hair dryer, minibar, Wi-Fi (free).

Le Relais du Louvre   One of the neighborhood's most up-to-date hotels, Relais du Louvre overlooks the neoclassical colonnade at the eastern end of the Louvre. Between 1800 and 1941, its upper floors contained the printing presses that recorded the goings-on in Paris's House of Representatives. Its street level held the Café Momus, favored by Voltaire, Hugo, and intellectuals of the day, and is where Puccini set one of the pivotal scenes of *La Bohème*. Bedrooms are outfitted in mono-chromatic schemes of blue, yellow, pink, or soft reds, usually with copies of Direc-toire-style (French 1830s) furniture. Many rooms are a bit small, but others contain roomy sitting areas.

19 rue des Prêtres-St-Germain-l'Auxerrois, Paris 75001. ☏ **01-40-41-96-42.** Fax 01-40-41-96-44. www.relaisdulouvre.com. 21 units. 145€–215€ double; 220€–435€ suite. AE, DC, MC, V. Parking 25€. Métro: Louvre or Pont Neuf. **Amenities:** Babysitting; room service; smoke-free rooms. *In room:* A/C, TV, hair dryer, minibar, Wi-Fi.

INEXPENSIVE

Timhôtel Le Louvre ☺   This hotel and its sibling in the 2nd arrondissement, the Timhôtel Palais-Royal, are part of a new breed of government-rated, two-star, family-friendly hotels cropping up in France. These Timhôtels share the same manager and temperament. Though the rooms at the Palais-Royal branch are a bit larger than the ones here, this branch is so close to the Louvre that it's almost irresistible. The ambi-ence is modern, with monochromatic rooms and wall-to-wall carpeting.

Timhôtel Le Louvre: 4 rue Croix des Petits-Champs, Paris 75001. ☏ **01-42-60-34-86.** Fax 01-42-60-10-39. www.timhotel.fr. 56 units. Métro: Palais-Royal. Timhôtel Palais-Royal: 3 rue de la Banque, 75002 Paris. ☏ **01-42-61-53-90.** fax 01-42-60-05-39. 46 units. Métro: Bourse. 119€–170€ double. AE, DC, MC, V. **Amenities** (at both branches): Restaurant (breakfast only); rooms for those w/limited mobility; smoke-free rooms. *In room:* A/C, TV, Wi-Fi (free).

Right Bank: 3rd Arrondissement (Le Marais)
EXPENSIVE

Murano Urban Resort ★ 👶   This hotel oddity, not everyone's cup of tea but charming for some, was created when two abandoned buildings—one a run-down five-story apartment house, the other a three-story parking garage—were intercon-nected and upgraded into a coherent whole. The result is a trendsetting, aggressively minimalist hotel with an angular sense of design. The decorative theme revolves around the transparency of Murano glass. You'll find a Murano glass chandelier in the green-toned lobby, another in a key spot on the ground floor, and very large glass-framed mirrors in some of the upper hallways. The mirrors and chandeliers are metaphors for the games that residents can play with light in their respective, and otherwise sparsely furnished, units: Up to three sets of curtains in any room filter sunlight in patterns that range from gauzy and bright to complete blackout. Additionally, individual settings switch on and off a spectrum of lights in up to six colors. Collectively, they create the semblance of noonday sun; individually and separately, they create moods that range from cheerful to pensive, depending (in theory) on an occupant's mood. Two of the suites have small (about 14-sq.-m/151-sq.-ft.) swimming pools on their private terraces.

13 bd. du Temple, Paris 75003. ✆ **01-42-71-20-00.** Fax 01-42-71-21-01. www.muranoresort.com. 52 units. 400€–650€ double; from 750€ suite. AE, DC, MC, V. Métro: Filles du Calvaire. **Amenities:** Restaurant; bar; health club; Jacuzzi; room service; spa. *In room:* A/C, TV, hair dryer, Wi-Fi (free).

Pavillon de la Reine ★★ 🎁 This is the kind of hidden gem that Frommer's readers love, opening as it does onto the most romantic square in Paris. In days of yore the 1612 mansion was a gathering place for the likes of Racine, La Fontaine, Molière, and Madame de Sévigné. You enter through an arcade that opens onto a small formal garden. The Louis XIII decor evokes the heyday of the square itself, and iron-banded Spanish antiques create a rustic aura. Each guest room is individually furnished in a historical or modern style—take your pick. Some units are duplexes with sleeping lofts above cozy salons.

28 place des Vosges, Paris 75003. ✆ **01-40-29-19-19.** Fax 01-40-29-19-20. www.pavillon-de-la-reine.com. 56 units. 380€–490€ double; 610€–710€ duplex; 610€ junior suite; 710€–950€ suite. AE, MC, V. Métro: Bastille. **Amenities:** Bar; babysitting; room service. *In room:* A/C, TV, minibar, Wi-Fi (free).

MODERATE

Hotel du Petit Moulin ★ 🎁 In the heart of the Marais, this hotel, an enclave of bohemian chic, used to be a *boulangerie* where Victor Hugo came every morning to buy freshly baked baguettes. No more. Designer Christian Lacroix has gone behind the unpretentious facade and turned it into an idiosyncratic hotel with bold, daring designs in the bedrooms, which range in price from the Comfort rooms to the Superior or Executive rooms. A well-heeled array of international guests meet in the trendy bar or can be seen making their way through the lounge and halls with period tapestries and Flemish frescoes.

29-31 rue du Poitous, Paris 75003. ✆ **01-42-74-10-10.** www.hoteldupetitmoulin.com. 17 units. 250€–350€ double. AE, MC, V. Métro: Bastille or Filles du Calvaire. **Amenities:** Bar; room service. *In room:* TV, minibar, Wi-Fi (free).

INEXPENSIVE

Hôtel Bellevue & du Chariot d'Or Originally built in 1860 as part of the majestic redevelopment of central Paris by Baron Haussmann, this hotel has a grand facade and inexpensive, relatively comfortable and cozy, simple bedrooms. The hotel has become more desirable because of its location in the once-neglected Arts et Métiers district north of the Pompidou Center. The second part of its name—"Chariot d'Or" (Golden Carriage)—derives from the medieval custom of placing brides-to-be (along with their dowries) in a flower-draped ceremonial carriage. During the occupation of Paris during World War II, the site was commandeered as a garrison for rank-and-file Nazi troops.

39 rue de Turbigo, Paris 75003. ✆ **01-48-87-45-60.** Fax 01-48-87-95-04. www.hotelbellevue75.com.
59 units. 72€–75€ double; 87€ triple; 98€ quad. AE, DC, MC, V. Métro: Châtelet–Les Halles or Réaumur-
Sebastopol. **Amenities:** Bar; babysitting. *In room:* TV, Wi-Fi (free).

Hôtel des Chevaliers   Half a block from the place des Vosges, this hotel occupies a corner building whose 17th-century vestiges have been elevated to high art.
These include the remnants of a well in the cellar, a stone barrel vault covering the
breakfast area, and Louis XIII accessories that will remind you of the hotel's origins.
Each guest room is comfortable and well maintained. Units on the top floor have
exposed ceiling beams. Some are larger than others, with an extra bed making them
suitable for those traveling with a child or for three people on the road together.

30 rue de Turenne, Paris 75003. ✆ **01-42-72-73-47.** Fax 01-42-72-54-10. www.chevaliers-paris-hotel.
com. 24 units. 94€–190€ double. AE, MC, V. Métro: Chemin Vert or St-Paul. **Amenities:** Bar. *In room:*
A/C, TV, hair dryer, minibar, Wi-Fi (free).

Right Bank: 9th Arrondissement (Opéra Garnier/Pigalle)

EXPENSIVE

Hôtel Amour   This is the kind of hotel that services the needs of suburbanites
looking for lodgings in the town center, or young business travelers seeking a "nouveau
chic" address. One critic even claimed that thanks to the hotel bar being frequented
by young European fashionistas, each flaunting their respective allure and neurosis,
"waiting in a queue for the toilets has never been so entertaining." Each bedroom is
outfitted in ways radically different from its neighbors: Each has a very comfortable
mattress—they come from the same company that supplies the (much more expensive) Hotel Ritz—and no TV and no telephone. (The assumption being that anyone
hip enough to check in here already has a working cellphone of his or her own.)

8 rue Navarin, Paris 75009. ✆ **01-48-78-31-80.** 20 units. 140€–165€ double; 250€ duplex. AE, MC, V.
Métro: St-Georges. **Amenities:** Restaurant; bar; room service. *In room:* A/C, minibar, no phone, Wi-Fi
(free).

Villa Royale ★ 🛎   Paris can be many things to many people, and if your vision of
the city involves the scarlet-toned settings once associated with the Moulin Rouge,
and the paintings of Toulouse-Lautrec, this designer hotel might be for you. It does a
flourishing business renting small but carefully decorated rooms, each of which
evokes Paris's sometimes kitschy world of glitzy and risqué nightlife entertainment.
Expect rooms outfitted Liberace style, with rococo gewgaws, velvet and velour upholsteries, jewel-toned walls, and TV screens that are sometimes encased in gilded
frames. Each is named after someone from the world of French entertainment,
including namesakes inspired by La Bardot, La Deneuve—even Claude Debussy.

2 rue Duperré, Paris 75009. ✆ **01-55-31-78-78.** Fax 01-55-31-78-70. www.leshotelsdeparis.com. 31
units. 160€–350€ double. AE, DC, MC, V. Métro: Pigalle. Bus: 30 or 54. **Amenities:** Room service.
In room: A/C, TV, hair dryer, Wi-Fi (in some; free).

MODERATE

Hotel Banke ★   In the tradition of Derby Hotels Collection, this luxurious boutique hotel is art oriented. Works of art adorn both the public rooms and the accommodations. The building dates from the Belle Epoque era and contains a majestic
hall from that time, which is embellished with a great mosaic. Bedrooms are midsize

to spacious and decorated with antique art and an avant-garde design. The on-site spa focuses on a self-styled "purification and regeneration of your internal ecology." Bathrooms, for the most part, are very spacious. The staff is also extremely friendly, a rarity in Paris. The terrace opens onto a panoramic view of Sacré-Coeur and the Opéra.

20 rue Lafayette, 75009 Paris. © **01-55-33-22-22.** 94 units. 220€–300€ double; 380€ suite. AE, DC, MC, V. Métro: Opéra. **Amenities:** 2 restaurants; bar; exercise room; room service; spa. *In room:* A/C, TV, hair dryer, minibar, Wi-Fi (free).

Hôtel Langlois   This hotel used to be known as Hôtel des Croises, but when it was used as a setting for the Jonathan Demme film *The Truth About Charlie,* the hotel owners changed the name to match the one used in the film. It's a well-proportioned, restored town house with a main stairwell and spacious landing. An antique wrought-iron elevator running up the center of the building adds an old-fashioned Parisian touch. The rooms are well proportioned but not overly large; those in the front get the most light. Units in the rear are darker but quieter. Rooms, with their aura of Ecole de Nancy (a florid Art Nouveau style), have well-chosen antiques, tasteful rugs and fabrics, even an occasional fireplace. Bathrooms are modernized, with tub and shower. We suggest avoiding the upper floors in summer: There's no air-conditioning, and the heat is often stifling.

63 rue St-Lazare, Paris 75009. © **01-48-74-78-24.** Fax 01-49-95-04-43. www.hotel-langlois.com. 27 units. 140€–150€ double; 190€ suite. MC, V. Métro: Trinité. **Amenities:** Breakfast room; room service. *In room:* TV, hair dryer, minibar, Wi-Fi (free).

INEXPENSIVE

Hôtel Chopin ✒   Enter this intimate, offbeat hotel through a passageway that includes a toy store, a bookstore, the exit from the Musée Grevin, and the architectural trappings of its original construction in 1846. Just off the Grands Boulevards, this old-fashioned hotel evokes the charm of yesteryear. In honor of its namesake, the Chopin has a piano in its reception area. The inviting lobby welcomes you behind its 1850s facade of elegant woodwork and Victorian-era glass. In the style of Paris of long ago, the comfortably furnished bedrooms open onto a glass-topped arcade instead of the hysterically busy street, so they are rather tranquil. We prefer the bedrooms on the top floor, as they are larger and quieter, with views over the rooftops of Paris. The least expensive bedrooms lie behind the elevator bank and get less light.

10 bd. Montmartre or 46 passage Jouffroy, Paris 75009. © **01-47-70-58-10.** www.hotel-chopin.com. Fax 01-42-47-00-70. 36 units. 92€–106€ double; 125€ triple. AE, MC, V. Métro: Grands-Boulevards. *In room:* TV, hair dryer, Wi-Fi (free).

Right Bank: 4th Arrondissement (Ile de la Cite/Ile St-Louis & Beaubourg)

EXPENSIVE

Hôtel du Bourg Tibourg ★ 🎒   Don't come here expecting large rooms with lots of elbowroom. What you get is a sophisticated and supercharged color palette, a sense of high-profile design, and a deliberately cluttered venue that looks like an Edwardian town house decorated by an obsessive-compulsive individual on psychedelic drugs. It is set behind an uncomplicated, cream-colored facade in the Marais and marked only with a discreet brass plaque and a pair of carriage lamps. Its rooms have been radically overhauled by superstar decorator Jacques Garcia. Bedrooms are genuinely tiny, but rich with neoromantic, neo-Gothic, and in some cases neo-Venetian swirls and curlicues. Each is quirky, idiosyncratic, richly upholstered, and supercharged with tassels, faux leopard skin, contrasting stripes, fringes, and lavish window treatments. Rooms facing the front get more sunlight; rooms facing the courtyard tend to be quieter.

19 rue du Bourg-Tibourg, Paris 75004. © **01-42-78-47-39.** Fax 01-40-29-07-00. www.hotelbourg tibourg.com. 30 units. 230€–260€ double; 360€ suite. AE, DC, MC, V. Parking 26€. Métro: Hôtel de Ville. **Amenities:** Room service. *In room:* A/C, TV, hair dryer, minibar, Wi-Fi (free).

MODERATE

Hôtel de Lutèce ★   This 17th-century hotel feels like a country house in Brittany. The lounge, with its old fireplace, is furnished with antiques and contemporary paintings. Each of the guest rooms boasts antiques, adding to a refined atmosphere that attracts celebrities such as the duke and duchess of Bedford. The suites, though larger than the doubles, are often like doubles with extended sitting areas. Each is tastefully furnished, with an antique or two. The hotel is comparable in style and amenities to the Deux-Iles (see below), under the same ownership.

65 rue St-Louis-en-l'Ile, Paris 75004. © **01-43-26-23-52.** Fax 01-43-29-60-25. www.paris-hotel-lutece. com. 23 units. 195€ double; 230€ triple. AE, MC, V. Métro: Pont Marie or Cité. **Amenities:** Smoke-free room. *In room:* A/C, TV, hair dryer, Wi-Fi (free).

Hôtel des Deux-Iles ★   This is an unpretentious but charming choice in a great location. In a restored 18th-century town house, the hotel has elaborate decor, with bamboo and reed furniture and French Provincial touches. The guest rooms are on the small side, but the beds are very comfortable and the bathrooms well maintained, with tubs or shower units. A garden off the lobby leads to a basement breakfast room that has a fireplace.

59 rue St-Louis-en-l'Ile, Paris 75004. © **01-43-26-13-35.** Fax 01-43-29-60-25. www.deuxiles-paris-hotel.com. 17 units. 195€ double. AE, MC, V. Métro: Pont Marie. **Amenities:** Room service; smoke-free rooms. *In room:* A/C, TV, hair dryer, Wi-Fi (free).

Hôtel Duo ★ 👔   Fashionistas flock to this restored hotel in the Marais, which is one of the cutting-edge places to stay in Paris. The location is convenient to the Centre Pompidou, Notre-Dame, the Louvre, and the Picasso Museum. The building has been in the family of Veronique Turmel since 1918. In 2002, she decided to completely convert the interior while retaining the facade. She hired Jean-Philippe Nuel, who kept many of the original architectural features, including exposed beams, old stones, and hardwood floors. He created a medieval look graced with Wengé-wood furnishings, white walls, and bronzed sconces—old-world charm in a tasteful and refined setting. The midsize bedrooms are completely up-to-date, with beautiful and comfortable furnishings. The so-called breakfast "cave" is a charming room with slipcovered chairs and sea-grass matting.

11 rue du Temple, Paris 75004. © **01-42-72-72-22.** Fax 01-42-72-03-53. www.parishotelleduo.com. 58 units. 200€–340€ double; 480€ suite. AE, DC, MC, V. Métro: Hôtel-de-Ville. **Amenities:** Lounge for drinks; exercise room; room service. *In room:* A/C, TV, hair dryer, minibar, Wi-Fi (free).

Hôtel du 7e Art   The hotel occupies one of many 17th-century buildings classified as historic monuments in this neighborhood. Don't expect grand luxury: Rooms are cramped and outfitted with the simplest furniture, relieved by 1950s-era movie posters. Each has white walls, and some of them—including those under the sloping mansard-style roof—have exposed ceiling beams. The five-story building has a lobby bar and a breakfast room but no elevator. The "7th Art" is a reference to filmmaking.

20 rue St-Paul, Paris 75004. ℂ **01-44-54-85-00.** Fax 01-42-77-69-10. www.paris-hotel-7art.com. 23 units. 95€–150€ double. AE, DC, MC, V. Métro: St-Paul. **Amenities:** Bar. *In room:* A/C, TV, hair dryer.

Hôtel Saint-Louis en l'Isle ★ ✦ Proprietors Guy and Andrée Record maintain a charming family atmosphere at this antiques-filled hotel in a 17th-century town house. The hotel represents an incredible value, considering its prime location on Ile St-Louis. Expect cozy, slightly cramped rooms, each with a small bathroom containing a tub/shower combination. With mansard roofs and old-fashioned moldings, the top-floor units sport tiny balconies that afford sweeping views. The breakfast room is in the cellar, which has 17th-century stone vaulting.

75 rue St-Louis-en-l'Ile, Paris 75004. ℂ **01-46-34-04-80.** Fax 01-46-34-02-13. www.saintlouisenlisle. com. 19 units. 140€–220€ double. MC, V. Métro: Pont Marie or St-Michel-Notre-Dame. **Amenities:** Babysitting. *In room:* TV, hair dryer, Wi-Fi (free).

Hôtel Saint-Merry ★ ▥ The rebirth of this once-notorious brothel as a charming, upscale hotel is an example of how the area has been gentrified. It contains only a dozen rooms, each relatively small but accented with neo-Gothic detail: exposed stone, 18th-century ceiling beams, and lots of quirky architecture. A suite, much larger than a double, has upgraded furnishings. The clientele here is about 50% gay males; the other half is straight and tends to be involved in the arts scene in the surrounding neighborhood. Before it became a bordello, it was conceived as the presbytery of the nearby Church of Saint-Merry.

78 rue de la Verrerie, Paris 75004. ℂ **01-42-78-14-15.** Fax 01-40-29-06-82. www.hotel-saintmerry. com. 12 units. 110€–180€ double; from 250€–407€ suite. AE, MC, V. Métro: Hôtel de Ville or Châtelet. **Amenities:** Babysitting; room service. *In room:* A/C,TV (in suite), hair dryer, Wi-Fi (2€ per day).

Right Bank: 8th Arrondissement (Champs-Elysées/Madeleine)

VERY EXPENSIVE

Fouquet's Barrière ★★★ This deluxe boutique hotel on the corner of the Champs-Elysées may lack the historic cachet of the neighboring George V or Plaza Athénée. It's a more contemporary brand of glitz and glamour. Standing alongside its namesake, the legendary restaurant, Fouquet's, it offers some of the most luxurious and spacious bedrooms in Paris, with a decor with ceiling-high padded headboards in shiny gold. The hotel contains such novel features as waterproof floating TV remotes in the bathtub, and a bedside button to let your butler inside. There's one butler to every eight guests, and the service is the best in Paris. That butler even arrives to unpack your luggage and serve you champagne.

46 av. George V, Paris 75008. ℂ **01-40-69-60-00.** Fax 01-40-69-60-05. www.fouquets-barriere.com. 107 units. 730€–950€ double; from 1,000€ junior suite; from 1,190€ suite. AE, MC, V. Parking 45€. Métro: George V. **Amenities:** 2 restaurants; 2 bars; health club; indoor pool; room service; spa. *In room:* A/C, TV, hair dryer, minibar, Wi-Fi (free).

Four Seasons Hotel George V ★★★ ☺ In its latest reincarnation, with all its glitz and glamour, this hotel is one of the best in the world. The George V opened in 1928 in honor of George V of England, grandfather of Queen Elizabeth. During the liberation of Paris, it housed Dwight D. Eisenhower. The guest rooms are about as close as you'll come to residency in a well-upholstered private home where teams of decorators have lavished vast amounts of attention and money. The beds rival those at the Ritz and Meurice in comfort. The largest units are magnificent; the smallest are, in the words of a spokesperson, *"très agréable."* Security is tight—a fact appreciated by sometimes-notorious guests. The staff pampers children with bathrobes, bedtime milk and cookies, and even special menus.

31 av. George V, Paris 75008. ℭ **800/332-3442** in the U.S. and Canada, or 01-49-52-70-00. Fax 01-49-52-70-10. www.fourseasons.com. 245 units. 750€–1,095€ double, from 1,795€ suite. AE, DC, MC, V. Parking 40€. Métro: George V. **Amenities:** Restaurant; 2 bar lounges; babysitting; health club; room service; spa; sauna. *In room:* A/C, TV, hair dryer, minibar, Wi-Fi (22€ per day).

Hôtel de Crillon ★★★   The Crillon, one of Europe's grand hotels, sits across from the U.S. Embassy. Although some international CEOs and diplomats treat it as a shrine, those seeking less pomposity might prefer the Plaza Athénée or the Ritz. The 200-plus-year-old building, once the palace of the duc de Crillon, is owned by Jean Taittinger, of the champagne family. The salons are appointed with 17th- and 18th-century tapestries, gilt-and-brocade furniture, chandeliers, fine sculpture, and Louis XVI chests and chairs. The guest rooms are luxurious. Think Madame Pompadour meets Louis XV. Some are spectacular, like the Leonard Bernstein suite, which has one of the maestro's pianos. The furniture, including the beds, offers grand comfort.

10 place de la Concorde, Paris 75008. ℭ **01-44-71-15-00.** Fax 01-44-71-15-02. www.crillon.com. 147 units. 770€–950€ double; from 1,220€ junior suite; from 1,620€ suite. AE, DC, MC, V. Free parking. **Amenities:** 2 restaurants; bar; tearoom; babysitting; health club; room service. *In room:* A/C, TV, hair dryer, minibar, Wi-Fi (free).

Plaza Athénée ★★★   The Plaza Athénée, an 1889 Art Nouveau marvel, is a landmark of discretion and style. In the 8th Arrondissement, only the Bristol can compare. About half the celebrities visiting Paris have been pampered here; in the old days, Mata Hari used to frequent the place. The **Salon Gobelins** (with tapestries against rich paneling) and the **Salon Marie Antoinette,** a richly paneled and grand room, are two public rooms that add to the ambience of this lavish hotel. There's also a calm, quiet interior courtyard draped with vines and dotted with geraniums. The quietest guest rooms overlook a courtyard with awnings and parasol-shaded tables; they have ample closet space. Some rooms overlooking avenue Montaigne have views of the Eiffel Tower. The hotel is also home to **Restaurant Plaza Athénée** (p. 131), where Alain Ducasse presents an award-winning menu focusing on "rare and precious ingredients."

25 av. Montaigne, Paris 75008. ℭ **866/732-1106** in the U.S. and Canada, or 01-53-67-66-65. Fax 01-53-67-66-66. www.plaza-athenee-paris.com. 191 units. 860€–920€ double; from 1,060€ junior suite. AE, MC, V. Parking 28€. Métro: Franklin-D.-Roosevelt or Alma-Marceau. **Amenities:** 3 restaurants; bar; tearoom; babysitting; health club; sauna; room service; smoke-free rooms; rooms for those w/limited mobility. *In room:* A/C, TV, hair dryer, minibar, Wi-Fi (25€ per day).

EXPENSIVE

Hotel Balzac ★★★   Built for the director of the Paris Opera in 1853, and once home to Balzac himself, this luxurious, intimate town-house hotel overlooks the Champs-Elysées. Vibrant, warm colors such as plum and copper prevail throughout the elegant bedrooms furnished with tasteful contemporary pieces of varying styles.

The hotel manages to recapture the romantic era but with a cutting modern edge. It underwent a multimillion-dollar restoration to attract guests who like five-star comfort but not one of the more commercial palace hotels. For atmosphere, the hotel has lithographs depicting Balzac and scenes from his works including *La Comédie Humaine*.

6 rue Balzac, 75008 Paris. (℃ **01-44-35-18-00.** Fax 01-44-35-18-05. www.hotelbalzac.com. 70 units. 350€–600€ double; 790€–870€ junior suite; from 870€ suite. AE, MC, V. Parking 23€. Métro: Champs-Elysées. **Amenities:** Restaurant; bar; health club; indoor pool; room service; spa. *In room:* A/C, TV, hair dryer, minibar, Wi-Fi (22€ per day).

Hôtel La Trémoille ★   In the heart of Paris and a 2-minute walk from the Champs-Elysées, this is a preferred Right Bank address for fashionistas, as it lies in the heart of the haute couture district. Built in the 19th century, the hotel opened again following a massive renovation that returned the swank address to much of its original elegance and charm. It blends modern and traditional styles. Originally a private residence, the hotel is outfitted in a Louis XV style, all in woodwork, mosaics, and tapestries. Rooms are cozy and comfortable, each decorated in harmonies of tawny ocher, gray, and white, with much use of silks, synthetic furs, and mohair.

14 rue de la Trémoille, Paris 75008. (℃ **01-56-52-14-00.** Fax 01-40-70-01-08. www.hotel-tremoille.com. 93 units. 485€–630€ double; from 700€–1,150€ suite. AE, DC, MC, V. Métro: Alma-Marceau. **Amenities:** Restaurant; bar; health club; room service; sauna. *In room:* A/C, TV, hair dryer, minibar, Wi-Fi (free).

Hôtel Le A ★   Lying only 2 blocks from the Champs-Elysées, this town house has been converted to an elegant enclave. It's true the rooms are a bit small—the staff refers to them as cozy—but the overall comfort may still entice your soul. Decorations in the lobby, hall, and bar were by artist Fabrice Hybert, who also painted one unique work for each guest room. The abstract paintings are both modern and figurative. A spacious lounge with a library is filled with books on art and design. Walls are painted with bold abstractions. The hotel bar under a 19th-century glass roof, with a tasteful black-and-white decor, has become a favorite rendezvous with the fashionistas of the era. Rooms represent supreme comfort with adjustable lights, electronic blinds, and other modern amenities. The elevator ceiling that changes color every few seconds is a bit much, however.

4 rue d'Artois, Paris 75008. (℃ **01-42-56-99-99.** Fax 01-42-56-99-90. www.paris-hotel-a.com. 26 units. 365€ double; 499€ junior suite. Rates include continental breakfast. AE, DC, MC, V. Parking 24€. Métro: St-Philippe du Roule. **Amenities:** Lounge; bar; smoke-free rooms. *In room:* A/C, TV, hair dryer, minibar, Wi-Fi (free).

MODERATE

Galileo Hotel ★ 🏨   This is one of the 8th's most charming hotels. Proprietors Roland and Elisabeth Buffat have won friends from all over with their Hôtel des Deux-Iles and Hôtel de Lutèce on St-Louis-en-l'Ile (p. 105). A short walk from the Champs-Elysées, this town house epitomizes French elegance and charm. The medium-size rooms are a study in understated taste. Within this hotel, rooms with numbers ending in 3 (for example, nos. 103, 203, 303, 403, and 503) are more spacious than the others. Room nos. 501 and 502 have private glassed-in verandas that you can use even in winter.

54 rue Galilée, Paris 75008. (℃ **01-47-20-66-06.** Fax 01-47-20-67-17. www.galileo-paris-hotel.com. 27 units. 185€ double. AE, DC, MC, V. Métro: Charles-de-Gaulle–Etoile or George V. **Amenities:** Rooms for those w/limited mobility. *In room:* A/C, TV, hair dryer, minibar, Wi-Fi (free).

Right Bank: 11th Arrondissement (Opéra/Bastille)

MODERATE

Gabriel Paris Marais ★ 🛏 This boutique hotel calls itself Paris's first "detox hotel," a concept devoted to a "regeneration of your body." One example of this is that some accommodations are outfitted with "Night Cove," a system that uses sound and light to encourage natural sleeping patterns. Near the Picasso Museum in the Marais, the hotel is rated only two stars, but is most comfortable, with modern technology and comfortably furnished bedrooms that range from small to midsize. In the surrealist but harmoniously decorated bar, guests can order a large choice of antioxidant drinks and teas.

25 rue du Grand-Prieure, 75011 Paris. ☎ **01-47-00-13-38.** www.hotel-gabriel-paris. 41 units. 240€–280€ double. AE, DC, MC, V. Métro: République. **Amenities:** Cafeteria; room service. *In room:* A/C, TV/DVD, MP3 docking station, hair dryer, minibar, Wi-Fi (free).

Right Bank: 16th Arrondissement (Trocadéro/Bois de Boulogne)

MODERATE

Radisson Blu Le Metropolitan Paris Eiffel ★★ This stylish boutique hotel occupies a former private residence, a Haussmanian style building that is just a few steps from Trocadéro and Palais de Chaillot, or a 10-minute walk to the Eiffel Tower. Surrounding the hotel are restaurants, boutiques, flower shops, and cafes, a real Parisian atmosphere. In spite of its 18th-century facade, all the glamorous interiors are modern. Many of the rooms open onto a view of the Eiffel Tower. Stylish bedrooms range from midsize to spacious; each room was designer decorated in a soothing palette of beige, white, and black.

10 place de Mexico, 75016 Paris. ☎ **01-56-90-40-04.** www.radissonblu.com. 48 units. 260€–290€ double; 500€ suite. AE, DC, MC, V. Métro: Trocadéro. **Amenities:** Restaurant; bar; concierge; indoor pool; room service. *In room:* A/C, TV/DVD, hair dryer, minibar, Wi-Fi (free).

INEXPENSIVE

Au Palais de Chaillot Hôtel When American-trained brothers Thierry and Cyrille Pien opened this hotel, budget travelers flocked here. Located between the Champs-Elysées and Trocadéro, the town house was restored from top to bottom, and the result is a contemporary yet informal variation on Parisian chic. The guest rooms come in various shapes and sizes, and are furnished with a light touch, with bright colors and wicker. Room nos. 61, 62, and 63 afford partial views of the Eiffel Tower.

35 av. Raymond-Poincaré, Paris 75116. ☎ **01-53-70-09-09.** Fax 01-53-70-09-08. www.hotelpalaisde chaillot.com. 28 units. 134€–154€ double; 179€ junior suite. 20€ extra bed. AE, DC, MC, V. Métro: Victor Hugo or Trocadéro. **Amenities:** Room service. *In room:* A/C, TV, hair dryer, Wi-Fi (free).

Right Bank: 18th Arrondissement (Parc Monceau/Place Clichy)

EXPENSIVE

Renaissance Paris Arc de Triomphe ★★ On the site of the once-famous Theatre de l'Empire, this cutting-edge hotel with its intriguing modern interiors lies only steps from the Arc de Triomphe and the Champs-Elysées. The top-floor rooms and suites open onto large terraces with panoramic views over the heart of Paris. The upscale hotel rooms and suites are spacious, tastefully decorated, and outfitted with the latest in-room technology. Its all-glass exterior has made this a distinctive landmark, even though it opened only in 2009. This is definitely a trendy and hip hotel, so is probably not the best for kids. The on-site Makassar Lounge & restaurant blends French bistro flavors with authentic Indonesian dishes.

39 av. de Wagram, 75017 Paris. ✆ **01-55-37-55-37.** fax 01-55-37-55-38. www.marriott.com. 108 units. 289€–599€ double, from 429€ suite. Parking: 35€. Métro: Charles-de-Gaulle-Etoile. **Amenities:** Restaurant; bar; concierge; exercise room; room service. *In room:* A/C, TV/DVD, hair dryer, minibar, Wi-Fi (free).

Right Bank: 18th Arrondissement (Montmartre)

EXPENSIVE

Hotel Particulier ★★★ No hotel in Paris seems quite as special as this one, lying between avenue Junot and rue Lepic and nestled in a "secret" passageway called *le passage du rocher de la sorcière*, or the witch's rock passage. Modern Paris meets Old Montmartre in this Directoire mansion from the 18th century, and the wedding is harmonious. Louis Bénech, one of the landscape architects who renovated the Tuileries, created the intimate gardens of the hotel. Each suite has a different personality, appointed with the work of various artists that range in decor from an erotic window by Philippe Mayaux to hat lamps by Olivier Saillard. The most unusual is the suite "Curtain of Hair," a loft created in the attic with photographs of the long hair of Natacha Lesueur, a photo artist.

23 av. Junot, 75018 Paris. ✆ **01-53-41-81-40.** Fax 01-42-58-00-87. www.hotel-particulier-montmartre. com. 5 units. 290€–590€ suite. AE, DC, MC, V. Métro: Blanche. **Amenities:** Breakfast room. *In room:* A/C, TV, hair dryer, Wi-Fi (free).

Kube Rooms & Bars ★ 🍴🛏 Design-savvy clients appreciate the way the architect Raymond Morel made repeated use of the cube, a form that the owners refer to as "the most modern of shapes." It occupies the six-story premises of what was built in the late 1800s as the administrative headquarters of a now-defunct brewery (Les bières de la Meuse), which we remember from beer fests of yesteryear. There's a restaurant and a dance lounge on the street level, where a DJ spins tunes. Bedrooms (and everything else about the place) seem to revel in the concept of the rectangular cube. Rectangular beds are lit from below and appear to float. Expect shag-covered sofas, fuzzy faux-fur slippers in tones of high-voltage yellow, and a sense of compact efficiency. On the premises is the Ice Kube Bar, a deep-cooled conversational oddity whose bar top is fashioned from—you guessed it—ice.

3-5 passage Ruelle, Paris 75018. ✆ **01-42-05-20-00.** Fax 01-42-05-21-01. www.kubehotel.com. 41 units. 250€–400€ double; 400€–750€ suite. MC, V. Parking 30€. Métro: La Chapelle. **Amenities:** Restaurant; bar/lounge w/DJ several nights a week; exercise room. *In room:* A/C, TV, hair dryer, Wi-Fi (free).

MODERATE

Hotel des Arts ★ In the center of Montmartre between place du Tertre and the Moulin Rouge, this hotel lies in a delightful quarter of Paris once made famous by poets and painters. It has a warm, welcoming atmosphere and in a former life it was a dormitory for the dancers of the Moulin Rouge. As you might expect, the rooms are small yet comfortable with country-style curtains and bedspreads. Opt for one of the four bedrooms on the sixth floor for a panoramic view of Paris. *Warning:* As night falls, the area around the hotel often has its share of sex workers, although the hotel itself is a fine destination.

5 rue Tholozé, Paris 75018. ☎ **01-46-06-30-52.** Fax 01-46-06-10-83. www.arts-hotel-paris.com. 50 units. 95€–155€ double. AE, MC, V. Métro: Blanche. **Amenities:** Breakfast room. *In room:* TV, Wi-Fi (20€ per day).

INEXPENSIVE

Hôtel Ermitage　Built in 1870 of chiseled limestone in the Napoleon III style, this hotel's facade evokes a perfectly proportioned small villa. It's set in a calm area, a brief uphill stroll from Sacré-Coeur. Views extend over Paris, and there's a garden in the back courtyard. The small guest rooms are like those in a countryside *auberge* (inn), with exposed ceiling beams, flowered wallpaper, and casement windows opening onto the garden or a street seemingly airlifted from the provinces. All the bedrooms come with small tub/shower combinations.

24 rue Lamarck, Paris 75018. ☎ **01-42-64-79-22.** Fax 01-42-64-10-33. www.ermitagesacrecoeur.fr. 12 units. 96€–100€ double; 145€ quad. Rates include breakfast. No credit cards. Parking 15€. Métro: Lamarck-Caulaincourt. **Amenities:** Babysitting; room service. *In room:* Wi-Fi (free).

Left Bank: 5th Arrondissement (Latin Quarter)

MODERATE

The Five Hotel ★ 🎁　A charmer among Left Bank boutique hotels, the Five is named for the 5th Arrondissement (Latin Quarter) and lies in a restored 1800s town house on a U-shaped street off boulevard de Port-Royal. The interior design is not to everyone's taste, including a red-leather-paneled hall or a red-painted gas fireplace. The rooms are individually designed in various colors (blood red or Halloween orange, for example), and tiny white lights evoke a planetarium. Of course, if you want a room the color of a prune, that too is available. A Chinese lacquer artist, Isabelle Emmerique, has certainly been busy here. Some rooms are minuscule, but all the beds are exceedingly comfortable.

3 rue Flatters, Paris 75005. ☎ **01-43-31-74-21.** Fax 01-43-31-51-96. www.thefivehotel.com. 24 units. 198€–353€ double; 392€ suite. AE, DC, MC, V. Métro: Bastille or Gobelins. **Amenities:** Luggage room; room service. *In room:* A/C, TV, hair dryer, Wi-Fi (free).

Grand Hôtel Saint-Michel　Built in the 19th century, this hotel is larger and more businesslike than many town house–style inns nearby. It basks in the reflected glow of Brazilian dissident Georges Amado, whose memoirs recorded his 2-year sojourn in one of the rooms. The public areas are tasteful, appointed with portraits and rich upholsteries. Improvements have enlarged some rooms, lowering their ceilings and adding amenities, but retained old-fashioned touches such as wrought-iron balconies (on the fifth floor). Triple rooms have an extra bed and are suitable for families who share a private bathroom with tub and shower. Sixth-floor rooms have views over the rooftops.

19 rue Cujas, Paris 75005. ☎ **01-46-33-33-02.** Fax 01-40-46-96-33. www.grand-hotel-st-michel.com. 47 units. 290€–350€ double; 400€ suite. AE, DC, MC, V. Métro: Cluny–La Sorbonne. RER: Luxembourg or St-Michel. **Amenities:** Bar; babysitting; exercise room; room service. *In room:* A/C, TV, hair dryer, minibar, Wi-Fi (free).

Hôtel des Jardins du Luxembourg　Built during Baron Haussmann's 19th-century overhaul of Paris, this hotel boasts an imposing facade of honey-colored stone accented with ornate iron balconies. The interior is outfitted in strong, clean lines, often with groupings of Art Deco furnishings. The high-ceilinged guest rooms,

Where to Stay on the Left Bank

5

SETTLING INTO PARIS | Where to Stay

113

some with Provençal tiles and ornate moldings, are well maintained, the sizes ranging from small to medium. Best of all, they overlook a quiet dead-end alley, ensuring relatively peaceful nights. Some have balconies overlooking the rooftops. Ongoing renovations have kept the bedrooms looking spiffy.

5 impasse Royer-Collard, Paris 75005. ℂ **01-40-46-08-88.** Fax 01-40-46-02-28. www.les-jardins-du-luxembourg.com. 26 units. 143€–153€ double. AE, DC, MC, V. RER: Luxembourg. **Amenities:** Bar; babysitting; room service; sauna. *In room:* A/C, TV, hair dryer, minibar, Wi-Fi (10€ per day).

INEXPENSIVE

Familia-Hôtel   As the name implies, this hotel has been family run for decades. Many personal touches make the place unique. Finely executed sepia-colored frescoes of Parisian scenes grace the walls of 14 rooms. Eight units have restored stone walls, and seven have balconies with delightful views over the Latin Quarter. The dynamic owners renovate the rooms as often as needed to maintain the highest level of comfort.

11 rue des Ecoles, Paris 75005. ℂ **01-43-54-55-27.** Fax 01-43-29-61-77. www.hotel-paris-familia.com. 30 units. 99€–122€ double; 167€ triple; 179€ quad. Rates include breakfast. AE, DC, MC, V. Parking 20€. Métro: Jussieu or Maubert-Mutualité. *In room:* TV, hair dryer, minibar, Wi-Fi (free).

Hôtel des Grandes Ecoles ♦   Few hotels in the neighborhood offer so much low-key charm at such reasonable prices. It's composed of a trio of high-ceilinged buildings, interconnected via a sheltered courtyard, where in warm weather, singing birds provide a worthy substitute for the TVs deliberately missing from the rooms. Accommodations, as reflected by the price, range from snug, cozy doubles to more spacious chambers. Each room is comfortable, but with a lot of luggage, the very smallest would be cramped. The decor is old-fashioned, with feminine touches such as flowered upholsteries and ruffles. Many have views of a garden whose trellises and flower beds evoke the countryside.

75 rue de Cardinal-Lemoine, Paris 75005. ℂ **01-43-26-79-23.** Fax 01-47-47-65-48. www.hotel-grandes-ecoles.com. 51 units. 115€–140€ double. Extra bed 20€. MC, V. Parking 30€. Métro: Cardinal Lemoine, Jussieu, or Monge. RER: Port-Royal or Luxembourg. **Amenities:** Babysitting; room service. *In room:* Hair dryer, Wi-Fi (free).

Hôtel Moderne Saint-Germain ★   In the heart of the Latin Quarter, between the Pantheon and Saint-Michel, the Hôtel Moderne is better than ever since it ended the 20th century with a complete overhaul. Though the rooms are small, this is still one of the neighborhood's better three-star hotels. Its charming owner, Mr. Gibon, welcomes guests to her spotless accommodations. In units fronting rue des Ecoles, double-glazed windows hush the traffic.

33 rue des Ecoles, Paris 75005. ℂ **01-43-54-37-78.** Fax 01-43-29-91-31. www.hotel-paris-stgermain. com. 45 units. 150€ double; 190€ triple. AE, DC, MC, V. Parking 26€. Métro: Maubert-Mutualité. **Amenities:** Fitness center; room service; smoke-free rooms. *In room:* A/C, TV, hair dryer, Wi-Fi (free).

Left Bank: 6th Arrondissement (St-Germain/Luxembourg)

VERY EXPENSIVE

Hôtel d'Aubusson ★★★   This mansion in the heart of St-Germain-des-Prés was the site of the city's first literary salon. Fully restored, it is today one of the best of the luxe boutique hotels of Paris. It's graced with original Aubusson tapestries.

Lying 2 blocks south of pont Neuf and the Seine, the hotel has taken over a former private residence from the 1600s, to which is attached a 1950s building. You enter a grand hall under a beamed ceiling with a baronial fireplace and furnishings in the style of Louis XV. There are also a number of smaller, more intimate lounges. The bedrooms are midsize to large, each attractively and comfortably furnished, often in a Directoire style and sometimes with exposed ceiling beams. Antiques are often placed in front of the original stone walls. For the most traditional flair, ask for one of the rooms on the top two floors.

33 rue Dauphine, Paris 75006. ℰ **01-43-29-43-43.** Fax 01-43-29-12-62. www.hoteldaubusson.com. 49 units. 305€–535€ double. AE, DC, MC, V. Parking 25€. Métro: Odéon. **Amenities:** Bar; cafe; babysitting; room service. *In room:* A/C, TV, hair dryer, minibar, Wi-Fi (free).

Hôtel de Fleurie ★ ☺
Off the boulevard St-Germain on a colorful little street, the Fleurie is one of the best of the city's "new" old hotels; its statuary-studded facade recaptures 17th-century elegance, and the stone walls in the salon have been exposed. Many of the guest rooms have elaborate draperies and antique reproductions. All of the bedrooms were renovated early in the millennium. Because some rooms are larger than others and contain an extra bed for one or two children, the hotel has long been a family favorite.

32–34 rue Grégoire-de-Tours, Paris 75006. ℰ **01-53-73-70-00.** Fax 01-53-73-70-20. www.fleurie-hotel-paris.com. 29 units. 250€–320€ double; 465€ family room. Children 12 and under stay free in parent's room. AE, DC, MC, V. Métro: Odéon or Mabillon. **Amenities:** Bar; babysitting; room service; rooms for those w/limited mobility. *In room:* A/C, TV, hair dryer, minibar, Wi-Fi (free).

Hôtel de l'Abbaye Saint-Germain ★
This is one of the district's most charming boutique hotels, built as a convent in the early 18th century. Its brightly colored rooms have traditional furniture, plus touches of sophisticated flair. In front is a small garden and in back is a verdant courtyard with a fountain, raised flower beds, and masses of ivy and climbing vines. If you don't mind the expense, one of the most charming rooms has a terrace overlooking the upper floors of neighboring buildings. Guest rooms are midsize to large and are continually maintained. Suites are generous in size and full of Left Bank charm, often with antique reproductions.

10 rue Cassette, Paris 75006. ℰ **01-45-44-38-11.** Fax 01-45-48-07-86. www.hotelabbayeparis.com. 44 units. 251€–367€ double; 461€–519€ suite. Rates include breakfast. AE, MC, V. Métro: St-Sulpice. **Amenities:** Bar; room service. *In room:* A/C, TV, hair dryer, Wi-Fi (free).

Hotel Le Six ★ 👬
This boutique hotel is a bastion of restrained charm and low-key luxury with harmonious tones and soft lighting. Its major feature is an elegant spa offering the same products as the swank Ritz Hotel. The staff promises to leave you "gorgeous." Sturdy oak furnishings and autumnal colors fill the hotel; the best accommodations are the upper suites, opening onto views of the Paris skyline. All the accommodations are imbued with a high comfort level, made more so by the soundproofing. Guests gather in the library and lounge, sheltered under a glass roof and evoking a winter garden.

14 rue Stanislas, 75006 Paris. ℰ **01-42-22-00-75.** Fax 01-42-22-00-95. http://hotel-le-six.com. 41 units. 231€–552€ double; 402€–600€ junior suite; 552€–802€ suite. AE, DC, MC, V. Métro: Notre-Dame-des-Champs Vavin. **Amenities:** Room service; spa. *In room:* A/C, TV, minibar, Wi-Fi (free).

L'Hôtel ★
Ranking just a notch below the Relais Christine, this is one of the Left Bank's most charming boutique hotels. It was once a 19th-century fleabag whose

major distinction was that Oscar Wilde died in one of its bedrooms, but today's guests aren't anywhere near destitution. In 2000, superstar aesthete Jacques Garcia redecorated the hotel, retaining its Victorian-baroque sense. Other than for maintenance purposes, the decor has remained virtually intact ever since. Guest rooms vary in size, style, and price; all have decorative fireplaces and fabric-covered walls. All the sumptuous beds have tasteful fabrics and crisp linens. About half the bathrooms are small, tubless nooks. Room themes reflect China, Russia, Japan, India, or high-camp Victorian. The Cardinal room is all scarlet, the Viollet-le-Duc room is neo-Gothic, and the room where Wilde died is Victorian. One spacious room contains the furnishings (including multiple mirrors) and memorabilia of stage star Mistinguett.

13 rue des Beaux-Arts, Paris 75006. ✆ **01-44-41-99-00.** Fax 01-43-25-64-81. www.l-hotel.com. 20 units. 280€–740€ double; 640€–740€ suite. AE, DC, MC, V. Métro: St-Germain-des-Prés. **Amenities:** Restaurant; bar; babysitting; indoor pool; room service; steam room. *In room:* A/C, TV, hair dryer, mini-bar, Wi-Fi (free).

Odéon Hôtel ★   Reminiscent of a modernized Norman country inn, the Odéon has such rustic touches as exposed beams, stone walls, high ceilings, and tapestries mixed with contemporary fabrics, mirrored ceilings, and black-leather furnishings. Near the Théâtre de l'Odéon and boulevard St-Germain, the Odéon stands on the first street in Paris to have pavements (ca. 1779). By the 20th century, this area began attracting such writers as Gertrude Stein and her coterie. The guest rooms are small to medium in size and well furnished. The beds are excellent, with reading lamps and bedside controls.

3 rue de l'Odéon, Paris 75006. ✆ **01-43-25-90-67.** Fax 01-43-25-55-98. www.odeonhotel.fr. 33 units. 190€–270€ double. AE, DC, MC, V. Métro: Odéon. **Amenities:** Bar; babysitting; room service; smoke-free rooms. *In room:* A/C, TV, hair dryer, Wi-Fi (free).

MODERATE

Hôtel des Deux Continents   Built from three interconnected historic buildings, each between three and six stories high, this hotel is a reliable choice with a sense of Latin Quarter style. The carefully coordinated guest rooms range from small to medium-size and include reproductions of antique furnishings and soundproof upholstered walls.

25 rue Jacob, Paris 75006. ✆ **01-43-26-72-46.** Fax 01-43-26-67-80. www.2continents-hotel.com. 41 units. 118€–185€ double; 230€ triple. MC, V. Métro: St-Germain-des-Prés. *In room:* A/C, TV, hair dryer, Wi-Fi (8€ per day).

Hôtel du Pas-de-Calais   The Pas-de-Calais dates from the 17th century. It retains its elegant facade, with wooden doors. Novelist Chateaubriand lived here from 1811 to 1814, but its most famous guest was Jean-Paul Sartre, who struggled with the play *Les Mains Sales (Dirty Hands)* in room no. 41. The hotel is a bit weak on style, but as one longtime guest confided, "We still stay here for the memories." Rooms are small; inner units surround a courtyard with two garden tables and several trellises. From January until the end of March, the hotel often grants very good discounts.

59 rue des Sts-Pères, Paris 75006. ✆ **01-45-48-78-74.** Fax 01-45-44-94-57. www.hotelpasdecalais.com. 38 units. 185€–315€ double; 300€ suite. AE, DC, MC, V. Parking 25€. Métro: St-Germain-des-Prés or Sèvres-Babylone. **Amenities:** Bar; babysitting; room service. *In room:* A/C, TV, hair dryer, Wi-Fi (free).

L'Apostrophe ★ 🛏 This Rive Gauche boutique hotel lies near the Café de Flore and Café des Deux-Magots, once the favorite literary haunts of some of France's most celebrated writers. This hotel pays homage to that tradition, becoming the first Parisian "poem hotel," an establishment devoted to the aesthetic, the beauty, and the mysteries of writing. On the ground floor is painted the story of *One Thousand and One Nights*. The first floor is devoted to the markings that pre-date writing. On the second floor are signs indicating the alphabet, calligraphy, and music. The third floor is devoted to books and posters. A stay here is like no other in Paris. Bedrooms are beautifully decorated and comfortable, though a bit small. Be aware that the shower and water basin are actually in the room—there is no separate bathroom (with the exception of the toilet).

3 rue de Chevreuse, 75006 Paris.© **01-56-54-31-31.** http://apostrophe-hotel.com. 16 units. 162€–290€ standard double; 210€–350€ double with a Jacuzzi. Métro: Vavin. **Amenities:** Bar. *In room:* A/C, TV/ DVD, CD player, hair dryer, Wi-Fi (free).

Le Placide ★★ 🛏 Converted from a former family home in the 19th century, Le Placide has the aura of a private club. This small boutique hotel in St-Germain lies just steps from the chic Bon Marché Department Store. It was designed by a member of Philippe Starck's firm, who brought a 21st-century style of luxury and comfort to the interior, featuring white Moroccan leather, lots of glass, a bit of chrome, and a crystal pedestal table. Fresh flowers adorn each room, and rose petals are placed on your bed at night. The spacious bathrooms provide much natural light.

6 rue St-Placide, 75006 Paris. © **01-42-84-34-60.** www.leplacidehotel.com. 11 units. 179€ double; 300€ suite. AE, MC, V. Métro: St-Placide. **Amenities:** Bar. *In room:* A/C, TV/DVD, CD player, MP3 docking station, hair dryer, minibar, Wi-Fi (free).

Prince de Condè ★ In the heart of St-Germain-des-Prés, with all its art galleries, this 18th-century building has been restored and turned into the epitome of Left Bank charm. Guests gather in the elegant lounge with its cozy ambience, carved stone walls, and arches. The wallpapered bedrooms, small to midsize, are comfortably furnished and intimate, each tidily maintained with double-glaze windows.

39 rue de Seine, Paris 75006.© **01-43-26-71-56.** Fax 01-46-34-27-95. www.prince-de-conde.com. 11 units. 195€ double; 280€ suite. AE, MC, V. Métro: St-Germain-des-Prés. **Amenities:** Breakfast lounge. *In room:* A/C, TV, hair dryer, minibar, Wi-Fi (free).

Villa Madame ★ In the heart of St-Germain-des-Prés, this hotel has a smart Left Bank address, set in a neighborhood filled with tony boutiques and fashionable hair salons, and just a short walk from Jardin du Luxembourg. It reopened late in 2008 after 2 years of major renovations. The bedrooms are sleek and modern with the latest gadgets. We prefer the accommodations on the top floor, with their balconies overlooking the rooftops of Paris. There is an inside courtyard, where you can order breakfast or else drinks in the evening. The Big Salon is actually a tearoom with a fireplace.

44 rue Madame, Paris 75006.© **01-45-48-02-81.** Fax 01-45-44-85-73. www.hotelvillamadameparis. com. 28 units. 220€–320€ double; 500€ suite. AE, DC, MC. Métro: Rennes or St-Sulpice. RER: Luxembourg. **Amenities:** Babysitting. *In room:* A/C, TV, minibar, Wi-Fi (free).

INEXPENSIVE

Grand Hôtel des Balcons ★ 🏷 The Corroyer-André family welcomes you to this restored 19th-century building, once patronized by Baudelaire and the poets

Henri Michaux and Endré Ady. You enter an Art Nouveau setting with stained-glass windows and tulip-shaped molten glass lamps and chandeliers. The hotel lies behind a restored facade studded with small balconies—hence, its name. Bedrooms are not only affordable, but harmonious in decor and big on comfort and good maintenance. Close to the gardens of Luxembourg, the rooms are not large but ample enough for big closets and full-length dressing mirrors.

3 Casimir Delavigne, Paris 75006. ☎ **01-46-34-78-50.** Fax 01-46-34-06-27. www.balcons.com. 50 units. 125€ double; 220€ triple or quad. AE, MC, V. Métro: Odéon. RER: Luxembourg. **Amenities:** Breakfast room. *In room:* TV, hair dryer, Wi-Fi (5€ per day).

Left Bank: 7th Arrondissement (Eiffel Tower/Musée d'Orsay)

VERY EXPENSIVE

Hôtel Montalembert ★★   Unusually elegant for the Left Bank, the Montalembert dates from 1926, when it was built in the Beaux Arts style. Its beige, cream, and gold decor borrows elements of Bauhaus and postmodern design. The guest rooms are spacious except for some standard doubles that are small unless you're a very thin model. Frette linens decorate roomy beds topped with cabana-stripe duvets that crown deluxe French mattresses.

3 rue de Montalembert, Paris 75007. ☎**800/786-6397** in the U.S. and Canada, or 01-45-49-68-68. Fax 01-45-49-69-49. www.montalembert.com. 56 units. 410€–520€ double; 650€–900€ suite. AE, DC, MC, V. Parking 33€. Métro: Rue du Bac. **Amenities:** Restaurant; bar; access to nearby health club; room service. *In room:* A/C, TV, hair dryer, minibar, Wi-Fi (29€ per day).

EXPENSIVE

Bourgogne & Montana   Across from the Palais Bourbon and just 2 blocks from the Seine, this boutique hotel resides in the same tony neighborhood as such famous Parisian residents as Karl Lagerfeld. It is only a short walk to the landmark place du Palais-Bourbon and the boulevard St-Germain. A six-floor hotel, the building itself dates from 1791. Two of the bedrooms open onto the Grand Palais or the Assemblée Nationale. A 1924 cage elevator takes visitors to the accommodations, which are mid-size for the most part, although some are small and have no view whatsoever. Each room is individually decorated, often in Empire style or with Empire reproductions.

3 rue de Bourgogne, Paris 75007. ☎ **01-45-51-20-22.** Fax 01-45-56-11-98. www.bourgogne-montana. com. 32 units. 190€–290€ double; 360€–380€ junior suite. Rates include breakfast. AE, DC, MC, V. Métro: Invalides. **Amenities:** Bar; babysitting; room service. *In room:* A/C, TV, hair dryer, minibar, Wi-Fi (free).

MODERATE

Derby Eiffel   This hotel faces the Ecole Militaire and contains airy public areas. Our favorite is a glass-roofed conservatory in back, filled year-round with plants and used as a breakfast area. The soundproof and modern guest rooms employ thick fabrics and soothing neutral colors. Most front-facing rooms have views of the Eiffel Tower. In 1998, enormous sums were spent upgrading the rooms and bathrooms and improving the hotel's interior aesthetics, and renovations have been going on ever since. All bathrooms have showers and half-tubs.

5 av. Duquesne, Paris 75007. ☎ **01-47-05-12-05.** www.hotelsderby.com. Fax 01-47-05-43-43. 43 units. 135€–155€ double; 196€ triple. AE, DC, MC, V. Métro: Ecole Militaire. **Amenities:** Bar; babysitting; room service. *In room:* A/C, TV, hair dryer, minibar, Wi-Fi (5€ per day).

INEXPENSIVE

Hôtel à l'Eiffel Rive Gauche   The charm of this family-owned and -run, intimate hotel derives from a very small on-site team and the sense that you've entered a distinctive universe that's very closely linked to the surrounding upscale residential neighborhood. Built around 1900, the hotel retains such original touches as the black-and-white, checkerboard-patterned floor tiles from the 1930s. Bedrooms are outfitted in tones of off-white and dark bordeaux, with vaguely French Empire themes scattered with some angular furniture from the 1960s and 1970s. The hotel lies on a tranquil street in the heart of the so-called "Triangle" (Eiffel, Invalides, and Champs-Elysées).

6 rue du Gros Caillou, Paris 75007. ✆ **01-45-51-51-51.** Fax 01-45-51-11-77. www.hotel-eiffel.com. 29 units. 105€–155€ double; 115€–175€ triple; 135€–205€ quad. MC, V. Métro: Ecole Militaire. *In room:* TV, fridge, hair dryer, Wi-Fi (free).

Hôtel de Londres Eiffel   Small and charming, this independently run hotel is just a 2-minute walk from the Eiffel Tower. Completely renovated, it is "dressed" in colors of yellow and raspberry, which is far more harmonious and elegant than the combination sounds. In a residential district (one of the best in Paris), the bedrooms are midsize and tastefully decorated, each with an individual decoration. The top floors open onto views of the illuminated Eiffel Tower at night. Bathrooms are small but well equipped, with either a tub or shower.

1 rue Augereau, Paris 75007. ✆ **01-45-51-63-02.** Fax 01-47-05-28-96. www.londres-eiffel.com. 30 units. 185€–220€ double; 380€ suite. AE, DC, MC. Parking 34€. Métro: Ecole Militaire. *In room:* A/C, TV, hair dryer, minibar, Wi-Fi (free).

Hôtel du Quai Voltaire   Built in the 1600s as an abbey and transformed into a hotel in 1856, the Quai Voltaire is best known for such illustrious guests as Wilde, Richard Wagner, and Baudelaire, who occupied room nos. 47, 55, and 56, respectively. Camille Pissarro painted *Le Pont Royal* from the window of his fourth-floor room. Guest rooms in this modest inn were renovated in 2008; most overlook the bookstalls and boats of the Seine.

19 quai Voltaire, Paris 75007. ✆ **01-42-61-50-91.** Fax 01-42-61-62-26. www.quaivoltaire.fr. 33 units. 150€–160€ double; 180€ triple. AE, DC, MC, V. Parking 14€. Métro: Musée d'Orsay or Rue du Bac. **Amenities:** Bar; room service. *In room:* Hair dryer, Wi-Fi (free).

Hôtel Lindbergh   A 5-minute walk from St-Germain-des-Prés, this hotel provides streamlined, simple guest rooms. About two-thirds of the bathrooms contain tubs as well as showers. Breakfast is the only meal served, but the staff will point out good restaurants nearby—an inexpensive bistro, Le Cigale, is quite close.

5 rue Chomel, Paris 75007. ✆ **01-45-48-35-53.** Fax 01-45-49-31-48. www.hotellindbergh.com. 26 units. 136€–160€ double; 180€ triple. AE, DC, MC, V. Parking 18€. Métro: Sèvres-Babylone or St-Sulpice. **Amenities:** Limited room service (breakfast only). *In room:* TV, hair dryer, Internet (free).

Near Orly Airport
MODERATE

Hilton Paris Orly Airport ★   Boxy and bland, the Hilton at Orly is a well-maintained, especially convenient business hotel. Noise from incoming planes can't penetrate the guest rooms' sound barriers, giving you a decent shot at a night's sleep. (Unlike the 24-hr. Charles de Gaulle Airport, Orly is closed to arriving flights from midnight–6am.) The midsize rooms are standard for a chain hotel; each has been renovated.

Aéroport Orly, 267 Orly Sud, Orly Aérogare Cedex 94544. **800/445-8667** in the U.S. and Canada, or 01-45-12-45-12. Fax 01-45-12-45-00. www.hilton.com. 351 units. 90€–250€ double; 300€ suite. AE, DC, MC, V. Parking 14€. Free shuttle bus btw. hotel and both Orly terminals. **Amenities:** Restaurant; bar; babysitting; exercise room; room service; sauna. *In room:* A/C, TV, hair dryer, Wi-Fi (free).

INEXPENSIVE

Air Plus Also boxy and contemporary-looking, and connected with Orly by frequent 10-minute complimentary shuttle-bus rides, this 1990s hotel provides standard bedrooms. Rooms are comfortable, insulated against airport noise, and a bit larger than you might expect. The location is in a leafy residential zone.

58 voie Nouvelle (near the Parc Georges Méliès), Orly 94310. **01-41-80-75-75.** Fax 01-41-80-12-12. airplus@club-internet.fr. 72 units. 82€ double. AE, DC, MC, V. Free parking. Transit to and from airport by complimentary shuttle bus. **Amenities:** Restaurant; room service. *In room:* A/C, TV, hair dryer, Wi-Fi.

Near Charles De Gaulle Airport

EXPENSIVE

Hyatt Regency Paris–Charles de Gaulle ★ This property is adjacent to the Charles de Gaulle Airport. Lying only a 25-minute drive from Disneyland Paris and a half-hour from the attractions of central Paris, the Roissy property was designed by the renowned architect Helmut Jahn. He created a stunning five-story structure of sleek design and tech-smart features. Inaugurated in 1994, this is the first hotel of its size to be built in Paris since 1975, and as airport hotels go, the cutting-edge architecture puts it in a class by itself. The builder allowed natural glass to flow into the hotel, with a spectacular glass atrium overlooking the lobby. Jet-lagged passengers find ultimate comfort in the elegantly furnished and soundproof guest rooms, which meld American convenience with European style.

351 av. du Bois de la Pie, Roissy 95912. **01-48-17-12-34.** Fax 01-48-17-17-17. http://paris.charlesde gaulle.hyatt.fr. 388 units. 155€–255€ double; 365€–400€ suite. AE, DC, MC, V. Parking 29€. RER1 train to airport, and then Hyatt shuttle. **Amenities:** Restaurant; bar; babysitting; exercise room; nearby jogging track; indoor pool; room service; sauna; 2 tennis courts. *In room:* A/C, TV, hair dryer, minibar, Wi-Fi (free).

Pullman Paris Aéroport CDG ★ Many travelers pass happily through this bustling, somewhat anonymous member of the French chain. It employs a multilingual staff accustomed to accommodating international business travelers. The conservatively furnished guest rooms are soundproof havens against the all-night roar of jets. Suites are larger and more comfortable, although they are not especially elegant and are consistent with the chain format.

Aéroport Charles de Gaulle, Zone Central, B.P. 20248, Roissy 95713. **800/221-4542** in the U.S. and Canada, or 01-49-19-29-29. Fax 01-49-19-29-00. www.sofitel.com. 350 units. 140€–370€ double; 450€–1,100€ suite. AE, DC, MC, V. Parking 12€. Free shuttle to and from airport. **Amenities:** Restaurant; bar; indoor pool; exercise room; room service. *In room:* A/C, TV, hair dryer, minibar, Wi-Fi (free).

INEXPENSIVE

Hôtel Campanile de Roissy This hotel is less expensive than most other lodgings near the airport. Its cement-and-glass design is barely masked by a thin overlay of cheerful-looking and rustic artifacts. Generally, this is an efficiently decorated, but not particularly stylish, place to stay, with a well-meaning but overworked staff.

Parc de Roissy, 95700 Val-d'Oise 95700. **01-34-29-80-40.** Fax 01-34-29-80-39. www.campanile.fr. 258 units. 91€–131€ double; 131€–189€ quad. AE, DC, MC, V. Free shuttle to and from Roissy. **Amenities:** Restaurant; bar; rooms for those w/limited mobility; smoke-free rooms. *In room:* TV, hair dryer, Wi-Fi (free).

WHERE TO DINE

Our best piece of advice—even if your budget is lean—is to splurge on one grand French meal (and to make reservations well in advance). A meal at a place such as **Taillevent, Alain Ducasse,** or **Carré des Feuillants** is something you'll always remember.

Three-star dining remains quite expensive. The 100€ main course (*entrée* means "appetizer" in French; don't confuse entrees with main courses) is no longer a novelty, and first courses can exceed 50€; in the top dining rooms, the total bill easily surpasses 175€ to 200€ per person. You can get around that high price tag in many places by ordering a fixed-price menu, perhaps for a "mere" 90€, or by heading for one of the not-so-celebrated but equally stellar dining rooms—**Pierre Gagnaire,** for example, instead of the legendary Alain Ducasse.

One question we're often asked is whether you can dine badly in Paris. The answer is an emphatic yes. We get complaints from readers who cite haughty service and mediocre food at outrageous prices. Often, complaints are about places catering mostly to tourists. We'll help you avoid them by sharing our favorite discoveries. While others are fighting it out for a table at one of the less-than-wonderful places, you can enjoy finer fare off the beaten track.

In the past, suits and ties were a given, and women always wore smart dresses or suits. Well, you can kiss your suits au revoir. Except in first-class and deluxe places, attire is more relaxed, but that doesn't mean sloppy jeans and workout clothes. Parisians still value style, even when dressing informally.

Restaurants are required by law to post their menus outside, so peruse them carefully. The fixed-price menu remains a solid choice if you want to have some idea of what your bill will be when it's presented by the waiter (whom you call *monsieur,* never *garçon*).

Part of the fun of a trip to Paris is enjoying the experience of an old-fashioned, family-run bistro. Just when bistros seemed to be dying, new-wave chefs started moving in, reviving them with excellent food at affordable prices.

Right Bank: 1st Arrondissement (Musée du Louvre/Les Halles)

VERY EXPENSIVE

Carré des Feuillants ★★★ MODERN FRENCH   This is a bastion of perfection, an enclave of haute gastronomy. When chef Alain Dutournier turned this 17th-century convent between the place Vendôme and the Tuileries into a restaurant, it was an overnight success. The interior is artfully simple and even, in the eyes of some diners, spartan-looking. It has a vaguely Asian feel, shared by a series of small, monochromatic dining rooms that are mostly outfitted in tones of off-white, black, and beige, and that overlook a flowering courtyard and a glass-enclosed kitchen. You'll find a sophisticated reinterpretation of cuisine from France's southwest, using seasonal ingredients and lots of know-how. Some of the best dishes include roasted rack of milk-fed Pyrénées lamb cooked in a clay pot, or slices of John Dory with potatoes and a tender cabbage lasagna. Milk-fed veal with flap mushrooms and purple artichokes is yet another specialty. For dessert try the mango and passion-fruit ravioli.

14 rue de Castiglione (near place Vendôme and the Tuileries), 1er. © **01-42-86-82-82.** Fax 01-42-86-07-71. www.carredesfeuillants.fr. Reservations required far in advance. Main courses 62€–85€; fixed-price lunch 85€–175€, dinner 175€. AE, DC, MC, V. Mon–Fri noon–2:30pm and 7:30–10pm. Closed Aug. Métro: Tuileries, Concorde, Opéra, or Madeleine.

Where to Dine on the Right Bank

Angélina **18**	Benoit **33**	Chez Jean **6**	Juveniles **10**
Au Bascou **26**	Bofinger **23**	Chez Jenny **24**	L'Absinthe **16**
Au Pied de Cochon **12**	Brasserie Flo **4**	Chez Vong **28**	La Famille **2**
Au Petit Monsieur **30**	Carré des Feuillants **19**	Goumard **20**	L'Ambassade
Aux Lyonnais **7**	Casa Olympe **5**	Joe Allen **13**	d'Auvergne **27**

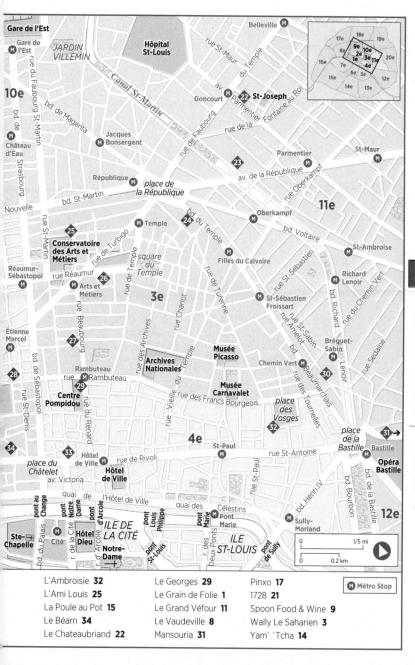

Gare de l'Est

Gare de l'Est

JARDIN VILLEMIN

Hôpital St-Louis

rue St-Maur

du Temple

Belleville

10e

bd. de Magenta

Canal St-Martin

Goncourt

St-Joseph

22

rue St-Maur

av.

Parmentier

Fontaine au Roi

bd. de Strasbourg

rue du Faubourg St-Martin

Château d'Eau

Jacques Bonsergent

rue du Faubourg

rue de la

Parmentier

St-Maur

Nouvelle

Réaumur-Sébastopol

République

place de la République

bd. St-Martin

av. de la République

rue Oberkampf

11e

23

rue St-Denis

Temple

bd. du Temple

24

Oberkampf

bd. Voltaire

St-Ambroise

25

Conservatoire des Arts et Métiers

rue de Turbigo

square du Temple

Filles du Calvaire

rue St-Sébastien

Richard Lenoir

rue Réaumur

26

Arts et Métiers

rue de Temple

3e

rue de Turenne

St-Sébastien Froissart

rue St-Sabin

bd. Richard

rue du Chemin Vert

Étienne Marcel

rue Beaubourg

rue des Archives

rue Charlot

Musée Picasso

rue Amelot

Bréguet-Sabin

rue Sedaine

27

Rambuteau

Archives Nationales

rue Vieille du Temple

Chemin Vert

Beaumarchais

28

rue de Sébastopol

Rambuteau

29

Centre Pompidou

rue du Renard

rue des Francs Bourgeois

Musée Carnavalet

place des Vosges

32

bd. des Tournelles

bd. Beaumarchais

place de la Bastille

30

31

Bastille

34

33

Hôtel de Ville

rue de Rivoli

4e

St-Paul

rue St-Antoine

Opéra Bastille

place du Châtelet

av. Victoria

Hôtel de Ville

rue St-Paul

bd. Henri IV

bd. Bourbon

bd. de la Bastille

12e

pont au Change

pont Notre-Dame

quai de l'Hôtel de Ville

quai des

Célestins

Sully-Morland

pont d'Arcole

pont Louis Philippe

pont Marie

Pont Marie

Ste-Chapelle

Cité

Hôtel Dieu

ILE DE LA CITÉ

Notre-Dame

r. des Deux Ponts

ILE ST-LOUIS

pont de Sully

0   1/5 mi

0   0.2 km

L'Ambroisie **32**	Le Georges **29**	Pinxo **17**
L'Ami Louis **25**	Le Grain de Folie **1**	1728 **21**
La Poule au Pot **15**	Le Grand Véfour **11**	Spoon Food & Wine **9**
Le Béarn **34**	Le Vaudeville **8**	Wally Le Saharien **3**
Le Chateaubriand **22**	Mansouria **31**	Yam' `Tcha **14**

[M] Métro Stop

Le Grand Véfour ★★★ TRADITIONAL FRENCH   This is the all-time winner: a great chef, the most beautiful restaurant decor in Paris, and a history-infused citadel of classic French cuisine. This restaurant has been around since the reign of Louis XV. Napoleon, Danton, Hugo, Colette, and Cocteau dined here—as the brass plaques on the tables testify—and it's still a gastronomic experience. Guy Martin, chef for the past decade, bases many items on recipes from the French Alps. He prepares such heavenly dishes as filet of lamb with wasabi, carved into rib sections and served with the smoked essence of its own juice. Other specialties are noisettes of lamb with star anise, Breton lobster with fennel, and cabbage sorbet in dark-chocolate sauce. The desserts are often grand, such as the *gourmandises au chocolat* (medley of chocolate), served with chocolate sorbet.

17 rue de Beaujolais, 1er. ✆ **01-42-96-56-27.** Fax 01-42-86-80-71. Reservations required far in advance. Main courses 75€–125€; fixed-price menu 88€ lunch, 268€ dinner. AE, DC, MC, V. Mon–Fri 12:30–1:45pm; Mon–Thurs 8–9:30pm. Closed July 25–Aug 22, last week of Dec, and 5 days in Apr. Métro: Louvre–Palais-Royal or Pyramides.

EXPENSIVE

Chez Vong ★ CANTONESE   This is the kind of Les Halles restaurant you head for when you've had your fill of grand cuisine and pretensions. The decor is a soothing mix of greens and browns, steeped in a Chinese-colonial ambience that evokes early-1900s Shanghai. The chef's specialty is lacquered Peking duck with shrimp. Other menu items feature shrimp and scallops served as spicy as you like, including a superhot version with garlic and red peppers; Peking duck; chicken in puff pastry with ginger; and an array of fish dishes. The whims of fashion have deemed this one of the restaurants of the moment, so it's full of folks from the worlds of entertainment and the arts.

10 rue de la Grande-Truanderie, 1er. ✆ **01-40-26-09-36.** www.chez-vong.com. Reservations recommended. Main courses 25€–60€; fixed-price lunch Mon–Fri 25€. AE, DC, MC, V. Mon–Sat noon–2:30pm and 7–11:15pm. Closed 3 weeks in Aug. Métro: Etienne-Marcel or Les Halles.

Goumard ★★★ SEAFOOD   Opened in 1872, this landmark is one of Paris's leading seafood restaurants. It's so devoted to the fine art of preparing fish that other food is banned from the menu (the staff will verbally present a limited roster of meat dishes). The decor consists of a collection of Lalique crystal fish in artificial aquariums. Even more unusual are the restrooms, classified as historic monuments; the Art Nouveau master cabinetmaker Majorelle designed the commodes in the early 1900s. Much of the seafood is flown in from Brittany daily. Examples include flaky crab cakes, flash-fried scallops with black truffles, sautéed wild squid, and grilled John Dory. Nothing (no excess butter, spices, or salt) is allowed to interfere with the natural flavor of the sea.

9 rue Duphot, 1er. ✆ **01-42-60-36-07.** Fax 01-42-60-04-54. www.goumard.com. Reservations required far in advance. Main courses 19€–79€; fixed-price menu 59€. AE, DC, MC, V. Daily 11:30am–12:30am. Métro: Madeleine or Concorde.

MODERATE

Au Pied de Cochon ★★ LATE NIGHT/TRADITIONAL FRENCH   Their famous onion soup and namesake specialty (grilled pigs' feet with Béarnaise sauce) still lure visitors, and where else in Paris can you get such a good meal at 3am? Other specialties include a platter named after the medieval patron saint of sausage makers, *la temptation de St-Antoine,* which includes grilled pig's tail, pig's snout, and half a pig's foot, all served with Béarnaise and *pommes frites;* and *andouillettes* (chitterling sausages) with Béarnaise. Two flavorful but less unusual dishes: a *jarret* (shin) of pork, caramelized in honey and served on a bed of sauerkraut, and grilled pork ribs with sage sauce. On the street outside, you can buy some of the freshest oysters in town.

6 rue Coquillière, 1er. ☎ **01-40-13-77-00.** www.piedecochon.com. Reservations recommended for lunch and dinner hours. Main courses 17€–48€. AE, DC, MC, V. Daily 24 hr. Métro: Les Halles or Louvre.

Joe Allen ★ ☺ AMERICAN   The first American restaurant in Les Halles is aging well. Joe Allen long ago invaded the place with his hamburger. Though the New York restaurateur admits "it's a silly idea," it works, and this place serves Paris's best burger. While listening to the jukebox, you can order black-bean soup, chili, sirloin steak, ribs, or apple pie. Joe Allen is getting more sophisticated, catering to modern tastes with dishes such as grilled salmon with coconut rice and sun-dried tomatoes. His saloon is the only place in Paris serving New York cheesecake and real pecan pie. A very popular brunch is served Saturday and Sunday from noon to 4pm, costing 18€. Without a dinner reservation, expect a 30-minute wait at the New York Bar.

30 rue Pierre-Lescot, 1er. ☎ **01-42-36-70-13.** www.joeallenrestaurant.com. Reservations recommended for dinner. Main courses 13€–21€; fixed-price menu 14€–26€. AE, MC, V. Daily noon–2am (Sat–Sun brunch noon–4pm). Métro: Etienne-Marcel.

L'Absinthe MODERN FRENCH   Charming and airy, its pair (upstairs/downstairs) of dining rooms are gracefully paneled, and an enormous antique clock dominates a panorama over the chattering and animated dining room. Best of all for foodies who follow this sort of thing, this upscale bistro is associated with one of the mightiest names of megacelebrity French gastronomy: It's owned and its dining room is supervised by Caroline, daughter of Michel Rostang. In summer, tables spill outside onto an all-pedestrian, see-and-be-seen stretch of street with dauntingly upscale boutiques. Come here for well-prepared, but not particularly innovative, bistro-style food. The best examples are tender veal in a red-wine sauce, scallops sautéed with bacon and sherry, poached codfish with a garlicky aioli sauce, and a served-pink version of standing rack of veal. Service is quirky, a wee bit judgmental, and at its worst a bit cranky.

24 place du Marché St-Honoré, 1er. ☎ **01-49-26-90-04.** www.restaurantabsinthe.com. Reservations recommended. Main courses 22€; fixed-price menu 31€–39€. AE, DC, MC, V. Mon–Fri noon–2pm; Mon–Sat 7:15–10:30pm. Métro: Tuileries.

La Poule au Pot LATE NIGHT/TRADITIONAL FRENCH   Established in 1935, this bistro welcomes late-night carousers and showbiz personalities looking for a meal after a performance. (Past aficionados have included the Rolling Stones, Prince, and Dustin Hoffman.) The decor is authentically Art Deco; the ambience, nurturing. Time-tested and savory menu items include salmon with champagne sauce; onion soup; a tripe casserole Norman style; Burgundy-style snails; country pâté on a bed of onion marmalade; and a succulent version of the restaurant's namesake—chicken in a pot, with slices of pâté and fresh vegetables.

9 rue Vauvilliers, 1er. ☎ **01-42-36-32-96.** www.lapouleaupot.fr. Reservations recommended. Main courses 21€–36€; fixed-price menu 35€. MC, V. Tues–Sun 7pm–5am. Métro: Louvre or Les Halles.

Pinxo ★ 🎁 SOUTHWESERN FRENCH   This is the cost-conscious brasserie that's associated with megachef Alain Dutournier's terribly stylish, and much more expensive, Carré des Feuillants, which is on a nearby street. Within Pinxo, a good-looking waitstaff encourages clients to share their starters and platters with their tablemates. This becomes relatively easy because anytime something appears on a plate, it's replicated, sometimes with variations, three times. The setting manages to elevate kitchen drudgery to a high, and high-tech, art form. Expect a wooden floor, white walls, and views that extend directly into an all-black open kitchen-cum-the-ater. Most foods here are grilled or at least prepared with heart-healthy cooking oils. Examples include a mixture of Aquitaine beef on the same plate as a steak, a tartare, and a blood sausage, all of them accompanied by a slice of foie gras. Other dishes to sample include rare sesame-glazed tuna and sautéed squid with garlic chips.

In the Plaza-Paris-Vendôme Hôtel, 9 rue d'Alger, 1er. ☎ **01-40-20-72-00.** www.pinxo.fr. Reservations recommended. Main courses 13€–28€; fixed-price lunch 21€. AE, MC, V. Daily 12:15–2:30pm and 7:15–11:30pm. Métro: Tuileries.

Yam' 'Tcha ★★★ TRADITIONAL FRENCH/CHINESE   This sweet little res-taurant lies on an ancient side street in Les Halles, feeding only 20 diners at a time. In spite of its lack of pretension, it is one of the hottest dining tickets in Paris, so try to reserve a table as far in advance as possible. French food critics have made chef Adeline Grattard the queen of Les Halles and a darling of the media, including *Le Figaro,* whose reporters first discovered her amazing talents. Her prix-fixe menus are regularly changing and adjusted to the season. You might begin with such delights as an appetizer of broad beans with sautéed pork dressed with ginger, garlic, and ses-ame-seed oil. Try also the fat Mozambique shrimp or the sublime duckling with sautéed eggplant (aubergine). Finish, perhaps, with a delightful dessert of home-made ginger ice cream with avocado slices and passion fruit.

4 rue Sauval, 1er. ☎ **01-40-26-08-07.** Reservations required. Fixed-price lunch 30€–65€; fixed-price dinner 65€. AE, MC, V. Métro: Louvre-Rivoli.

INEXPENSIVE

Angélina ★★ TEA/TRADITIONAL FRENCH   In the high-rent area near the InterContinental, this *salon de thé* (tea salon) combines fashion-industry glitter and bourgeois respectability. The carpets are plush, the ceilings high, and the accessories have the right amount of patina. This place has no equal when it comes to viewing the lionesses of haute couture over tea and sandwiches. The waitresses bear silver trays with pastries, drinks, and tea or coffee to marble-topped tables. Lunch usually offers a salad and a *plat du jour* (dish of the day) such as *salade gourmande* (gourmet salad) with foie gras and smoked breast of duck on a bed of fresh salad greens. An enduring specialty here is hot chocolate, as well as Mont Blanc, a combination of chestnut cream and meringue.

226 rue de Rivoli, 1er. ☎ **01-42-60-82-00.** Reservations not accepted for tea. Pot of tea (for 1) 7€; sandwiches and salads 10€–15€; main courses 16€–30€. AE, MC, V. Mon–Fri 8am–7pm; Sun 9am–7pm. Métro: Tuileries or Concorde.

Le Béarn COUNTRY FRENCH   This is the most famous of the workingman's "zinc cafes" of the 1st arrondissement. It was created in 1945 at the end of the war and installed in what had been a butcher's shop. For those who like to dine in the scruffy, gritty zincs of Paris, the kitchen and the Art Nouveau flower tiles are still here from the day it opened. Patrons squeeze together on burgundy leather banquettes at Formica tables. The menu is based on regional products, and the food is prepared country style. Familiar fare to Parisians for decades includes veal kidneys in Madeira sauce and fresh mushrooms, perch with a white butter sauce, or strip steak with Béarnaise sauce. For an appetizer, try the old-fashioned hard-boiled eggs with mayonnaise or smoked herring marinated in oil. The french fries are homemade.

8 rue Halles, 1er. ✆ **01-42-36-93-35.** Reservations advised. Main courses 8€–16€; fixed-price menu 17€. AE, DC, MC, V. Mon–Sat 8am–11pm. Métro: Châtelet.

Juveniles SCOTTISH/INTERNATIONAL   A short stroll from the Louvre and the Opéra, Juveniles is the domain of Tim Johnston, a Scot, who has opened this tiny wine bar, featuring the best Australian wine *carte* in Paris. You can even order that famous (notorious?) Scottish dish, haggis here—it's a delicacy for some. The menu also includes sausages and mashed potatoes, Puy lentils (the best in the world), and charcuterie plates. He even serves Indian chicken tikka masala. The cheeses are pungent, the staff bilingual and friendly.

47 rue de Richelieu, 1er. ✆ **01-42-97-46-49.** reservations recommended. Set-lunch menu 17€; fixed-price dinner 28€; main dishes 17€; tapas from 7€. MC, V. Tues–Sat noon–3pm and 7–11pm. Métro: Pyramide or Palais Royal.

Right Bank: 2nd Arrondissment (La Bourse)
MODERATE

Aux Lyonnais ★ LYONNAIS/TRADITIONAL FRENCH   After a meal here, you'll know why Lyon is called the gastronomic capital of France. There is no better Lyonnais bistro in Paris than this time-mellowed place vaguely associated with Alain Ducasse. The day's menu is based on the freshest produce in the market that morning. It's offered against an 1890s bistro backdrop of potted palms, etched glass, and globe lamps. Inventiveness and solid technique characterize such dishes as parsleyed calves' liver, pike dumplings (the best in Paris), skate meunière, and peppery coq au vin (chicken stewed in red wine) with *crème fraîche* (fresh cream) macaroni. Foie gras is a starter, or you can opt for a charcuterie (deli meat) platter. The best for last: a heaven-sent Grand Marnier soufflé.

32 rue St-Marc, 2e. ✆ **01-42-96-65-04.** www.auxlyonnais.com. Reservations required. Main courses 22€–25€; 3-course fixed-price menu 26€–34€. AE, DC, MC, V. Tues–Fri noon–1:30pm; Tues–Sat 7:30–10pm. Métro: Grands-Boulevards.

Le Vaudeville LATE NIGHT/TRADITIONAL FRENCH   Adjacent to La Bourse (stock exchange), this bistro retains its marble walls and Art Deco carvings from 1918. In summer, tables dot a terrace among banks of geraniums. The place is boisterous and informal, often welcoming groups of six or eight diners at a time. The roster of platters includes a salad of crayfish and asparagus points, grilled Dover sole, smoked salmon, sauerkraut, and grilled meats, even stewed calf's head. Three dishes reign as enduring favorites: fresh grilled codfish with mashed potatoes and truffle juice, fresh escalope of warm foie gras with grapes or raspberries, and fresh pasta with morels. The prix-fixe menu is a good deal.

29 rue Vivienne, 2e. ✆ **01-40-20-04-62.** www.vaudevilleparis.com. Reservations recommended in the evenings. Main courses 16€–30€; fixed-price menu 40€–50€. AE, DC, MC, V. Daily noon–3pm and 7pm–midnight. Métro: Bourse.

Right Bank: 3rd Arrondissement (Le Marais)

EXPENSIVE

L'Ami Louis ★ TRADITIONAL FRENCH   L'Ami Louis is in one of central Paris's least fashionable neighborhoods, far removed from the part of the Marais that has become chic, and its facade has seen better days. It was one of Paris's most famous brasseries in the 1930s, thanks to its excellent food served in copious portions and its old-fashioned decor. Its traditions, even the hostile waiters, are fervently maintained today, and Bill Clinton loves it. Amid a "brown gravy" decor (the walls retain a smoky patina), dishes such as game in season, grilled veal kidneys, milk-fed lamb, confit of duckling, and slices of foie gras are served on marble-topped tables. The whole roasted chicken is served with a mountain of french fries. Though some say the ingredients aren't as good as in the restaurant's heyday, the sauces are as thick as they were between the wars.

32 rue du Vertbois, 3e. ✆ **01-48-87-77-48.** Reservations required far in advance. Main courses 36€–60€. AE, DC, MC, V. Wed–Sun noon–1:30pm and 8–11:30pm. Closed July 19–Aug 25. Métro: Temple.

INEXPENSIVE

Au Bascou ★ 🍴BASQUE   The succulent cuisine of France's "deep southwest" is the specialty here, where art objects, paintings, and tones of ocher celebrate the beauty of the region, and hanging clusters of pimentos add spice to the air. For a ray of sunshine, try *pipérade basquaise* (a spicy omelet loaded with peppers and onions); pimentos stuffed with purée of codfish; and *axoa* of veal (shoulder of calf served with pimento-and-pepper-based green sauce). Also noteworthy is sautéed shrimp with fennel salad.

38 rue Réaumur, 3e. ✆ **01-42-72-69-25.** Reservations recommended. Main courses 17€; fixed-price lunch menu 19€. AE, DC, MC, V. Mon–Sat noon–2pm and 7:30–10:30pm. Closed Aug and week of Christmas. Métro: Arts-et-Métiers.

Chez Jenny 🍴 ALSATIAN   One of the city's most famous Alsatian restaurants was established in 1930 by members of the Jenny family. Little has changed since its inauguration except that the clientele is a lot more contemporary-looking than in the old days. Up to 220 diners can fit into this nostalgia-laden setting, where Alsatian *Gemütlichkeit* prevails. An ongoing specialty is the *choucroute de chez Jenny*, sauerkraut piled high with sausages, tender pork knuckles, and slices of ham. Also available are salmon with sorrel, grilled meats, grilled fish, and chicken supreme flavored with Riesling. Any of these tastes wonderful accompanied by one of the Alsatian wines that fill the wine list.

39 bd. du Temple, 3e. ✆ **01-44-54-39-00.** www.chez-jenny.com. Reservations recommended. Main courses 20€–25€; fixed-price menu 24€. AE, DC, MC, V. Sun–Thurs noon–midnight; Fri–Sat noon–1am. Métro: République.

L'Ambassade d'Auvergne ★ AUVERGNAT/TRADITIONAL FRENCH   You enter this rustic tavern through a bar with heavy oak beams, hanging hams, and ceramic plates. It showcases the culinary bounty of France's most isolated region, the Auvergne, whose pork products are widely celebrated. Try chicory salad with apples and pieces of country ham; pork braised with cabbage, turnips, and white beans; or grilled tripe sausages with mashed potatoes and cantal cheese with garlic. Nonpork specialties are pan-fried duck liver with gingerbread, perch steamed in verbena tea, and roasted rack of lamb with wild mushrooms.

22 rue de Grenier St-Lazare, 3e. © **01-42-72-31-22.** www.ambassade-auvergne.com. Reservations recommended. Main courses 14€–23€; fixed-price menu 28€. AE, MC, V. Daily noon–2pm and 7:30–10:30pm. Métro: Rambuteau.

Right Bank: 4th Arrondissement (Ile de la Cite/Ile St-Louis & Beaubourg)

VERY EXPENSIVE

L'Ambroisie ★ ✋ FRENCH One of Paris's most talented chefs, Bernard Pacaud, drew attention with his vivid flavors and gastronomic skill, but culinary standards here are declining. At this 17th-century town house, the decor resembles an Italian palazzo. Pacaud's tables are nearly always filled with diners drawn here by all that praise in Michelin. The dishes change seasonally and may include escargot cannelloni in a creamy star anise–flavored broth, or roasted foie gras glazed with onion caramels, lobster gazpacho, or *poulard de Bresse demi-deuil homage à la Mère Brazier* (chicken roasted with black truffles and truffled vegetables). There is a rather snobby attitude here: It's a bit shocking when one calls for a reservation to be asked to state one's nationality.

9 place des Vosges, 4e. © **01-42-78-51-45.** www.ambroisie-placedesvosges.com. Reservations required far in advance. Main courses 100€–140€. AE, MC, V. Tues–Sat noon–1:30pm and 8–9:30pm. Métro: St-Paul or Chemin Vert.

EXPENSIVE

Benoit ★ TRADITIONAL FRENCH There's something weighty about this historical monument; every mayor of Paris has dined here since the restaurant was founded in 1912. Today Benoit is owned by the Alain Ducasse Group. This fabled chef claims that "I want to use more products from the soil." The setting is theatrical, and the service can be attentive or arrogant, depending on a delicate chemistry that only longtime fans of this place understand. Prices are higher than you'd expect for bistro fare, but it all seems part of the self-satisfied norm here, and clients keep coming back for more. The satisfying cuisine is full of flavor, based on time-tested classics. Traditional crowd pleasers include turbot roasted in the Basque style; filet of sole Nantua; or a traditional head of veal with a ravigote sauce. One of the best dishes is a filet of beef in a Bordelaise sauce served with macaroni and cheese. The chefs make a satisfying cassoulet of the house with white beans.

20 rue St-Martin, 4e. © **01-42-72-25-76.** Reservations required. Main courses 24€–43€; fixed-price lunch 38€. AE, DC, MC, V. Daily noon–2pm and 7:30–10pm. Métro: Hôtel de Ville.

MODERATE

Bofinger ✋ ALSATIAN/FRENCH Opened in the 1860s, Bofinger is the oldest Alsatian brasserie in town, but it's grown tired and stale over the years. Nonetheless, it's packed every night with visitors because of its world fame. If the food isn't what it used to be, the atmosphere for some will be worth trekking over here. It's a Belle Epoque dining palace, resplendent with brass and stained glass. Affiliated with La Coupole, Julien, and Brasserie Flo, the restaurant has updated its menu, retaining the most popular traditional dishes, such as sauerkraut and sole meunière (sole in lemon-butter sauce). Other items include roasted leg of lamb with fondant of artichoke hearts and parsley purée, grilled turbot with a fennel sauce, and bouillabaisse

Bofinger. Shellfish, including fresh oysters and lobster, is almost always available in season. Weather permitting, you can dine on the terrace. In light of the restaurant's rich history, a staff member conducts brief complimentary tours.

5-7 rue de la Bastille, 4e. ☎ **01-42-72-87-82.** www.bofingerparis.com. Reservations recommended. Main courses 15€–35€; fixed-price menu 25€–32€. AE, DC, MC, V. Mon–Fri noon–3pm and 6:30pm–1am; Sat–Sun noon–1am. Métro: Bastille.

Le Georges ★ INTERNATIONAL   The Centre Pompidou is again in the spotlight; all of artsy Paris has been talking about this place. Georges is in a large space on the top floor of Paris's most comprehensive arts complex, with views through bay windows over most of the city. The decor is minimalist and postmodern, with lots of brushed aluminum and stainless steel. Tables are made from sandblasted glass, lit from below, and accessorized with hypermodern cutlery. Menu items are mostly Continental, with hints of Asia. Some combinations surprise—macaroni with lobster, for example. Others seem exotic, including roasted ostrich steak. Aside from these dishes, some of the best items on the menu are king crab with coconut milk and curry. To get here, head for the exterior elevator to the left of the Centre Pompidou's main entrance. Tell the guard you have a reservation; otherwise, you might not be allowed up.

Centre Pompidou, 6th Floor, 19 rue Beaubourg, 4e. ☎ **01-44-78-47-99.** www.centrepompidou.fr. Reservations required for dinner, recommended for lunch. Main courses 37€–47€. AE, DC, MC, V. Wed–Mon noon–2am. Métro: Rambuteau.

Right Bank: 8th Arrondissement (Champs-Elysées/Madeleine)

VERY EXPENSIVE

Lasserre ★★★ FRENCH   It's so old, it's new again. This elegant restaurant was a bistro before World War II and has since become a legend. The main salon stretches two stories high, with a mezzanine on each side. Tall, silk-draped, arched windows frame the tables set with fine porcelain, gold-edged crystal glasses, and silver candelabras. The ceiling is painted with white clouds and a cerulean sky, but in good weather, the staff slides back the roof to reveal the real sky. The faces of Audrey Hepburn, Maria Callas, and Marlene Dietrich have given way to young British royals and statuesque models from Brazil. A spectacular chef, Jean-Louis Nomicos, is a master of taste and texture, and he's brought renewed life to this swank citadel. The appetizers are among Paris's finest, including macaroni with black truffles and foie gras, or marinated scallops with caviar. The main course specialty is poached sole filets *Club de la Casserole,* in puff pastry with asparagus tips and asparagus-flavored cream sauce; also wonderful are the veal kidneys flambé and pigeon André Malraux. The wine cellar, with some 160,000 bottles, is one of Paris's most remarkable.

17 av. Franklin D. Roosevelt, 8e. © **01-43-59-02-13.** Fax 01-45-63-72-23. www.restaurant-lasserre.com. Reservations required far in advance. Main courses 56€–95€; fixed-price lunch 75€, dinner 185€. AE, MC, V. Thurs–Fri noon–2pm; Mon–Sat 7–10pm. Closed Aug. Métro: Franklin-D-Roosevelt.

Pierre Gagnaire ★★★ MODERN FRENCH   If you're able to get a reservation, it's worth the effort. The menus are seasonal to take advantage of France's rich bounty; owner Pierre Gagnaire demands perfection, and the chef has a dazzling way with flavors and textures. Stellar examples are roast duck; and turbot cooked in a bag and served with fennel and Provençal lemons. Chicken with truffles comes in two stages—first the breast in wine-based aspic and then the thighs, chopped into roughly textured pieces.

6 rue Balzac, 8e. © **01-58-36-12-50.** Fax 01-58-36-12-51. www.pierre-gagnaire.com. Reservations required. Main courses 65€–165€; fixed-price menu 105€ lunch, 255€ dinner. AE, DC, MC, V. Mon–Fri noon–1:30pm; Sun–Fri 7:30–10pm. Métro: George V.

Restaurant Plaza Athénée (Alain Ducasse) ★★★ FRENCH   Few other chefs have been catapulted to international fame as quickly as Alain Ducasse. There's a lot of marketing and glitter involved, but what you'll find in this world-renowned hotel is a lobby-level hideaway that top-notch decorator Patrick Jouin originally decorated around the turn of the millennium and then artfully redecorated, much to the fascination of haute Paris. The six-star chef, Alain Ducasse, who supervises the kitchens here, divides his time between Paris, Monaco, Las Vegas, New York, and Tokyo. In this, his Parisian stronghold, he places a special emphasis on "rare and precious ingredients," whipping up flavorful and very expensive combinations of caviar, lobster, crayfish, truffles (both black and white), and shellfish. Cuisine is vaguely Mediterranean and decidedly contemporary, yet based on traditional models. Some of the best examples include smoked, tea-glazed pigeon or line-caught sea bass with flap mushrooms. For appetizers, try the creamy pasta with truffles and giblets. Desserts are perhaps the finest in all of Paris's luxe restaurants. The wine list is superb, with some selections deriving from the best vintages of France, Germany, Switzerland, Spain, California, and Italy.

In the Hôtel Plaza Athénée, 25 av. Montaigne, 8e. © **01-53-67-65-00.** Fax 01-53-67-65-12. www.alain-ducasse.com. Reservations required 3–4 weeks in advance. Main courses 70€–175€; fixed-price menus 260€–360€. AE, DC, MC, V. Thurs–Fri 12:45–2:15pm; Mon–Fri 7:45–10:15pm. Closed mid-July to Aug 25 and 10 days in late Dec. Métro: Alma-Marceau or FDR.

Taillevent ★★★ FRENCH   This is the Parisian ne plus ultra of gastronomy. Taillevent opened in 1946 and has climbed steadily in excellence; today it ranks as Paris's outstanding all-around restaurant, challenged only by Lucas-Carton and Pierre Gagnaire. It's in a grand 19th-century town house off the Champs-Elysées, with paneled rooms and crystal chandeliers. The place is small, which permits the owner to give personal attention to every facet of the operation and maintain a discreet atmosphere. Each dish is supreme in flavor, including John Dory with olives or lamb saddle seasoned with wild herbs. A cassoulet of crayfish, if featured, is also divine. Chefs dare serve that old standard, *baba au rhum,* but it's perhaps the best you'll ever taste. The wine list is among the best in Paris.

15 rue Lamennais, 8e. © **01-44-95-15-01.** Fax 01-42-25-95-18. www.taillevent.com. Reservations required 3-4 weeks in advance. Main courses 34€–90€; fixed-price lunch 80€; dégustation 190€. AE, DC, MC, V. Mon–Fri 12:15–2:30pm and 7:15–10pm. Closed Aug. Métro: George V.

EXPENSIVE

La Maison Blanche ★★ PROVENÇAL/TRADITIONAL FRENCH   Jacques and his twin brother, Lauren Pourcel, were two of the most famous chefs in the southerly province of Languedoc before heading north to Paris. The setting would be the envy of any restaurant in the world: Positioned on the uppermost (seventh) floor of the Art Deco–style Theatre des Champs-Elysées, it has contemporary, all-white-and-purple decor, sweeping views across the Seine, and two dining rooms. Clientele tends to be rich, non-French, and a bit pretentious, but in light of the brilliant food and the sublime setting, who cares? The menu changes with the inspiration of the chefs and the seasons, but stellar examples include such starters as crispy filet of red mullet with coriander-flavored baby vegetables or a small tart of duck foie gras with roasted rhubarb and peach. An especially good fish specialty is filet of John Dory in a candied lemon vinaigrette with stuffed olives, or else a rack of Aveyron lamb with cracked wheat and a mushroom compote.

15 av. Montaigne, 8e. © **01-47-23-55-99.** Reservations required. Main courses 38€–73€; fixed-price lunch 55€. AE, DC, MC, V. Mon–Fri noon–2pm; daily 8–11pm. Métro: Alma-Marceau.

L'Angle du Faubourg ★★ TRADITIONAL FRENCH   Throughout the 1980s and early 1990s, a reservation at the ultra-upscale Taillevent was sought after by diplomats, billionaires, and *demi-mondains* from around Europe. In 2001, Taillevent's owner, M. Vrinat, opened a cost-conscious bistro that capitalizes on Taillevent's reputation, but at much lower prices. Lunches here tend to be efficient, relatively quick, and businesslike; dinners are more leisurely, even romantic. The restaurant has an ultramodern dining room, additional seating in the cellar, and a menu that simplifies Taillevent's lofty culinary ideas. The best examples include braised lamb with the juice of black olives; risotto with ingredients that change weekly (during our visit, it was studded with braised radicchio); and a grilled, low-fat version of *daurade* (bream), served with artichokes and a reduction of mushrooms, appreciated by the many diet-conscious *photo-modèles* who stop in.

195 rue du Faubourg St-Honoré, 8e. © **01-40-74-20-20.** www.taillevent.com. Reservations required. Main courses 25€–47€; fixed-price menu 38€–75€. AE, DC, MC, V. Mon–Fri noon–2:30pm and 7–10:30pm. Closed Aug. Métro: Terne or Etoile.

1728 ★ 🍴 JAPANESE/MODERN FRENCH   An 18th-century town house, just off Faubourg-St-Honoré where the Marquis de Lafayette lived, has been turned into this chic rendezvous. The decor is sumptuous, just like it was in the 1700s, with paintings on the wall—each for sale—and low marble dining tables and chairs. Call the place what you like—upmarket tea salon or cafe. Start with the tuna tartare or even a well-stuffed club sandwich at lunch. The tiger shrimp is savory and is scented with malt whiskey. For a main course, one of the most delightful offerings is steamed sea bass, flavored with ginger and served with snow peas and zucchini. Other fine selections include filet of sole with a saffron-laced sauce and filet of beef in a sauce made of Chinese truffles. The pastries are supplied from the famous Pierre Hermé bakeries.

8 rue d'Anjou, 8e. ✆ **01-40-17-04-77.** www.restaurant-1728.com. Reservations recommended for main meals. Main courses 15€–48€; fixed-price lunch 45€. AE, MC, V. Mon–Fri noon–midnight; Sat 2:30pm–midnight. Closed 3 weeks in Aug. Métro: Concorde.

Spoon, Food & Wine ★ INTERNATIONAL   This hypermodern venture by star chef Alain Ducasse is both hailed as a "restaurant for the millennium" and condemned as surreal and a bit absurd. Despite that, there can be a 2-week wait for a dinner reservation. This upscale but affordable restaurant may be the least pretentious and most hip of Ducasse's ventures. The somewhat claustrophobic dining room blends Parisian and Californian references, and the menu (which changes every 2 months) roams the world. Examples include deliberately undercooked grilled squid (part of it evokes sushi) with curry sauce; grilled lamb cutlets; and spareribs with a devil's marmalade. Vegetarians appreciate stir-fried dishes in which you can mix and match up to 15 ingredients.

In the Hôtel Marignan-Elysée, 14 rue Marignan, 8e. ✆ **01-40-76-34-44.** www.spoon.tm.fr. Reservations recommended 1–2 weeks in advance. Main courses 29€–47€; fixed-price lunch 36€. AE, DC, MC, V. Mon–Fri 12:15–2:30pm and 7:30–10:30pm. Closed Aug and last week of Dec. Métro: Franklin-D-Roosevelt.

MODERATE

Citrus Etoile ★ FRENCH   It's a good example of a hip, well-connected, and stylish restaurant of the minute, where part of the fun involves seeing and being seen by the politically connected and trend-conscious crowd. The decor is minimalist black, white, and orange, a bemused blend of the best of California (former home of the owners and inspiration for some of the cuisine) and France. If you opt for a meal here, you'll be in good hands: Chef Gilles Epié used to be a caterer and private chef in Hollywood before returning to Paris with his fashion-model wife Elizabeth (an American, who supervises the dining room) to open this in-vogue dining venue near the Arc de Triomphe. Menu items are health conscious, artfully simple, "uncluttered," and flavorful. Try such delights as rabbit leg, grilled tuna with foie gras, plumb oysters with fresh asparagus, or lobster cooked in tarragon-flavored bouillon.

6 rue Arsène Houssaye, 8e. ✆ **01-42-89-15-51.** www.citrusetoile.fr. Reservations recommended. Main courses 42€–69€; set menus 45€–85€. AE, MC, V. Mon–Fri noon–3pm and 7:30–10:30pm. Métro: Etoile.

Market ★ FUSION   The creative force here is Alsatian Jean-Georges Vongerichten, whose restaurants in New York, Hong Kong, London, and Las Vegas are classified by local critics as both megahip and top tier. The Paris gemstone in the Vongerichten empire holds 130 diners in a richly paneled postmodern decor, designed by decorating mogul Christian Liaigre, dotted with carved masks from Oceania (Polynesia) and Borneo and with art objects on loan from the Paris branch of Christie's auction house. Menu items include a pizza with black truffles and fontina cheese; foie gras with a purée of quince, corn pancakes, and wild cranberries; or crabmeat salad with mango. Main courses might feature *daurade* (bream or porgy) baked in a salt crust; a faux-filet (sirloin) with exotic mushrooms; or a "black plate" for two diners, loaded high with shellfish and their garnishes. There's a wine list that most oenophiles consider extremely interesting.

15 av. Matignon, 8e. ✆ **01-56-43-40-90.** Reservations required. Fixed-price lunch 34€; pizzas 19€–29€; main courses 29€–46€. AE, MC, V. Daily noon–3pm and 7:30–11:30pm (Sat–Sun brunch noon–6pm). Métro: Champs-Elysées–Clémenceau.

5

SETTLING INTO PARIS

Where to Dine

INEXPENSIVE

Bar des Théâtres TRADITIONAL FRENCH Its local patrons in the 8th arrondissement have long called this bar/restaurant "the Temple of the God Steak Tartare." For those daring souls who still eat this blood-rare red meat specialty, this long-established restaurant is said to make the best dish. Even though it's situated in the most lethally priced district of Paris, it has kept its prices reasonable over the years. Across the street is the Théâtre des Champs-Elysées, and many of its performers, especially actors and musicians, make the bar their "local" while appearing here. The chef also specializes in a delectable *magret de canard* (breast of duckling), and you can even order caviar and foie gras, but those items would put this into a very expensive category. Better settle for the sauerkraut.

6 av. Montaigne, 8e. ☎ **01-47-23-34-63.** Reservations recommended. Main courses 13€–22€. AE, DC, MC, V. Daily noon–1am. Closed in Aug. Métro: Alma Marceau.

Right Bank: 9th Arrondissement (Opéra Garnier/Pigalle)

EXPENSIVE

Casa Olympe ★★ 🏛 PROVENÇAL/CORSICAN Serious Paris foodies and peripathetic gourmands such as Francis Ford Coppola make their way to the 9th to feast on the wares of an original cook. Olympe Versini earned a Michelin star at the age of 29 and dazzled some of the most discerning palates of *tout* Paris in Montparnasse before opening this unassuming 32-seat dining room. Critics cite the earthiness of her cooking as evoked by her duck ravioli bathed in a *jus* reduction, or her heavenly foie gras terrine brazenly studded with split vanilla beans. From head to hoof, she serves most parts of the pig—and does so with gustiness. Her langoustine ravioli is modish but not excessively so, and her beef tenderloin with peppercorn sauce is one of the best versions of this time-honored dish.

48 rue St-Georges, 9e. ☎ **01-42-85-26-01.** Reservations required. Fixed-price menus 28€–37€. MC, V. Mon–Fri noon–2pm and 8–11pm. Closed 3 weeks in Aug, 1 week in May, and 10 days in Dec. Métro: St-Georges or Notre-Dame-de-Lorette.

Chez Jean ★ TRADITIONAL FRENCH The crowd is young, the food is sophisticated, and the vintage 1950s aura makes you think that American expatriate novelist James Baldwin will arrive any minute. Surrounded by well-oiled pine panels and polished copper, you can choose from some of Grandmother's favorites as well as more modern dishes. Owner Jean-Frederic Guidoni worked for more than 20 years at one of the world's most expensive restaurants, Taillevent, but within his own milieu, he demonstrates his own innovative touch at much more reasonable prices. For starters, consider a chicken consommé with endives and chorizo; a savory version of a cheesy alpine staple, raclette, made with mustard sauce and *Curé Nantais* cheese; and slow-braised pork cooked for 7 hours and served on a bed of carrots, apricots, and confit of lemon.

8 rue St-Lazare, 9e. ☎ **01-48-78-62-73.** www.restaurantjean.fr. Reservations recommended far in advance. Main courses 27€–38€; fixed-price menu 70€–95€; fixed-price lunch 46€. AE, DC, MC, V. Mon–Fri noon–2:30pm and 7:30–10:30pm. Métro: Notre-Dame de Lorette, or Saint-Georges.

Wally Le Saharien ALGERIAN Head to this dining room—lined with desert photos and tribal artifacts crafted from ceramics, wood, and weavings—for an insight into the spicy, slow-cooked cuisine that fueled the colonial expansion of

France into North Africa. The prix-fixe dinner menu begins with a trio of starters: spicy soup, stuffed and grilled sardines, and a savory *pastilla* of pigeon in puff pastry. Next comes any of several kinds of couscous or a *méchouia* (slow-cooked tart) of lamb dusted with an optional coating of sugar. *Merguez,* the cumin-laden spicy sausage of the North African world, factors importantly into any meal, as do homemade pastries.

36 rue Rodier, 9e. (?) **01-42-85-51-90.** Reservations recommended. Main courses (lunch only) 35€–57€; fixed-price dinner 45€. MC, V. Tues–Sat noon–2pm and 7–10:30pm. Closed in Aug. Métro: Anvers.

Right Bank: 10th Arrondissement (Gare du Nord/Gare de l'Est)

MODERATE

Brasserie Flo ★ ALSATIAN   This remote restaurant is hard to find, but once you arrive (after walking through passageway after passageway), you'll see that *fin de siècle* Paris lives on. The restaurant opened in 1860 and has changed its decor very little. The specialty is *la formidable choucroute* (a mound of sauerkraut with boiled ham, bacon, and sausage) for two. Onion soup and sole meunière are always good, as are warm foie gras and guinea hen with lentils. Look for the *plats du jour,* ranging from roast pigeon to tuna steak with hot peppers.

7 cour des Petites-Ecuries, 10e. (?) **01-47-70-13-59.** Reservations recommended. Main courses 18€–36€; fixed-price dinner 28€; fixed-price lunch 19€. AE, DC, MC, V. Daily noon–3pm and 7pm–1am. Métro: Château d'Eau or Strasbourg-St-Denis.

Right Bank: 11th Arrondissement (Opéra Bastille)

MODERATE

Au Petit Monsieur ★ 🍴 TRADITIONAL FRENCH   A meal at this restaurant, tucked away in the 11th arrondissement, is like dining in the French countryside. Under wooden beams and held up by old stone walls, the three dining rooms are decorated with country crockery. Patrons dine at bare wooden tables, using kitchen towels as napkins. Both modernists and upholders of French culinary tradition find a happy home here. Everything is served by a capable staff sensitive to your needs and orders. The fixed-price lunch and dinner menus are changed every day. Appetizers often begin with a tureen of soup from which you help yourself. Appetizers feature such dishes as a risotto with artichokes and tomatoes, followed by a tournedos of duckling in the Provençal style, or else delicate veal in a white sauce.

50 rue Amelot, 11e. (?) **01-43-55-54-04.** Reservations required. Fixed-price lunch 12€–22€; dinner 35€. AE, MC, V. Mon–Fri noon–2pm; Mon–Sat 7–10pm. Closed in Aug and last week of Dec. Métro: Chemin Vert.

Mansouria   MOROCCAN   One of Paris's most charming Moroccan restaurants occupies a much-restored building midway between place de la Bastille and place de la Nation. The minimalist decor combines futuristic architecture with bare sand-colored walls, accented only with sets of antique doors and portals from the sub-Sahara. Look for seven kinds of couscous, including versions with chicken, beef brochettes, or lamb, onions, and almonds. *Tagines* are succulent dishes of chicken or fish prepared with aromatic herbs and slow-cooked in clay pots that are carried to your table.

11 rue Faidherbe, 11e. (?) **01-43-71-00-16.** Reservations recommended. Main courses 15€–24€; fixed-price lunch 29€–45€, dinner 30€–46€. AE, MC, V. Wed–Sun noon–2pm; Mon–Sat 7–11pm. Métro: Faidherbe-Chaligny.

INEXPENSIVE

Le Chateaubriand ★ 🍴 MODERN FRENCH   The owner, Inaki Aizpitarte, calls this time-tested old eatery a "neo bistro," and so it is. The dark 1930s decor is relatively intact, but this native of the Basque Country, where he learned his culinary skills, has completely changed the cuisine. Today instead of the classic coq au vin or steak frites, you are treated to rare tuna slices in pink beet foam flavored with pomegranate seeds or steamed cod with Moroccan spices. At dinner the only choice is a prix-fixe and it's a winner, perhaps featuring such dishes as eel flavored with orange juice and olive oil, warm cockles and mussels, teriyaki salmon, or mint lamb tagine. Some of the dishes are very daring indeed, including pork belly flavored with licorice.

129 av. Parmentier, 11e. ✆ **01-43-57-45-95.** Reservations required. Main courses at lunch 12€–35€; fixed-price lunch 16€; 5-course set-price dinner 30€–39€. AE, DC, MC, V. Tues–Fri noon–2pm; Tues–Sat 8-10:30pm. Métro: Goncourt.

Mélac TRADITIONAL FRENCH   This is one of the most time-honored zinc bars and cafes in Paris. Emile Zola in *The Belly of Paris* may have coined the term zinc bar, which by 1880 came into common usage. One of our all-time favorites dates from 1938, and not much has changed here since. You still have to walk through the kitchen to get to the main dining room. Many of the hearty dishes of Jacque Mélac's Aveyron (a department of the Auvergne) are served, including the likes of confit of pig's liver, veal tripe bundles, fresh and cured sausages, and a *poêlon aveyronnais* (a casserole of chicken liver and fried eggs in a sauce made with red wine and shallots). Of course, you get the great tasting wines of the Aveyron served here.

42 rue Léon-Frot, 11e. ✆ **01-43-70-59-27.** www.melac.fr. Reservations recommended. Main courses 15€–20€; set-price lunch (Tues–Fri) 15€. AE, DC, MC, V. Tues–Sat noon–4pm and 8-11pm. Closed Aug. Métro: Charonne.

Right Bank: 12th Arrondissement (Bois de Vincennes/Gare de Lyon)

EXPENSIVE

Au Trou Gascon ★★★ GASCONY   One of Paris's most acclaimed chefs, Alain Dutournier, lures fashionable palates to an unchic area. He launched his career in southwest France's Gascony region. His parents mortgaged their inn to allow Dutournier to open an early-1900s bistro in a little-known part of the 12th arrondissement. Word spread of a savant in the kitchen who practiced authentic *cuisine moderne*. His wife, Nicole, is the welcoming hostess, and the wine steward has distinguished himself for his exciting cave containing several little-known wines along with a fabulous collection of Armagnacs. You can start with duck foie gras cooked in a terrine or Gascony-cured ham. The best main courses include a casserole of scallops with endive, tender lamb from the Pyrénées, or the chef's favorite dish, the cassoulet, made with duckling, pork, lamb, and sausage. Starters feature foie gras with raisins or else grilled shrimp.

40 rue Taine, 12e. ✆ **01-43-44-34-26.** www.autrougascon.fr. Reservations recommended a day in advance. Main courses 28€–42€; fixed-price lunch 38€, dinner 49€. AE, DC, MC, V. Mon–Fri noon–2pm and 8-10pm. Closed Aug and 6 days in Nov. Métro: Daumesnil.

INEXPENSIVE

L'Ebauchoir ★ 🍴 TRADITIONAL FRENCH   Tucked into a neighborhood rarely visited by foreigners and featuring a 1950s decor that is so out it's in, this bistro attracts carpenters, plumbers, and electricians, as well as an occasional journalist and screenwriter. With buffed aluminum trim and plaster-and-stucco walls tinted dark orange-yellow and bordeaux, the place might remind you of a factory canteen. You can order surprisingly generous and well-prepared smoked herring and potato salad for starters, even tuna tartare. One of the most unusual main courses is a grilled tuna steak with white chocolate. Too much for you? There's always the more traditional roast chicken (flavored with thyme) or a rack of lamb with turmeric, along with red snapper filet with olive oil and fresh garlic.

43–45 rue de Citeaux, 12e. ℰ **01-43-42-49-31.** Reservations recommended for dinner. Main courses 14€–25€; fixed-price lunch 14€, dinner 23€. AE, MC, V. Tues–Sat noon–2:30pm; Mon–Sat 8–11pm. Métro: Faidherbe-Chaligny.

Right Bank: 16th Arrondissement (Trocadéro/Bois de Boulougne)

EXPENSIVE

Le Relais du Parc ★★ MODERN FRENCH The two most celebrated chefs of France, Alain Ducasse and Joël Robuchon, buried the hatchet and launched this joint venture. The Parisian press hailed them as the dynamic duo. But Batman and Robin they aren't. The marriage did not last: Ducasse is still in charge, though not the actual chef. In fair weather, you dine alfresco among white magnolia trees in the inner courtyard, or else in the intimate and elegant dining room in neutral hues. Each dish is a delight, including pigeon with cabbage and foie gras, or langoustines from southern Brittany enhanced by Iranian caviar. The wild hare from the Loire Valley is stuffed with foie gras and roasted. You can also enjoy Ducasse's signature baked macaroni with butter, ham, and truffles, or his Pompadour potato casserole with crispy bacon.

In the Hotel Sofitel Le Parc, 55–57 av. Raymond-Poincaré, 16e. ℰ **01-44-05-66-10.** Reservations required. Main courses 36€–49€; set lunch 49€–59€, dinner 85€. AE, DC, MC, V. Tues–Sat noon–2pm and 7:30–10pm. Closed Aug. Métro: Trocadéro or Victor Hugo.

MODERATE

La Butte Chaillot ★ 🍴 TRADITIONAL FRENCH · This baby bistro showcases culinary high priest Guy Savoy and draws a crowd from the affluent neighborhood's corporate offices. Diners congregate in posh but congested areas. Menu items change weekly (sometimes daily) and betray a strange sense of mass production not unlike that found in a luxury cruise ship's dining room. You might begin with a terrine of rabbit studded with nuts and served with a red-onion compote, or perhaps crayfish tartare flavored with lemon. For main dishes, filet of sea bass is served with green lentils from the Pyrénées, or else you might go for the duckling confit with mushrooms.

110 bis av. Kléber, 16e. ℰ **01-47-27-88-88.** www.guysavoy.com. Reservations recommended. Main courses 16€–28€; fixed-price menus 36€. AE, DC, MC, V. Sun–Fri noon–2pm; daily 7–11pm. Métro: Trocadéro or Boissière.

Right Bank: 17th Arrondissement (Parc Monceau/Place Clichy)

EXPENSIVE

Rech ★ TRADITIONAL FRENCH/SEAFOOD The fabled chef Alain Ducasse has brought new life to this fish brasserie founded in 1925 and specializing in shellfish. The original Alsatian brasserie features have been retained, including the Art

Deco furnishings and even the oyster shucker on the sidewalk. The previous owner, August Rech, believed in keeping the menu limited but choice, a tradition that has been respected. Ducasse was inspired to create some of the recipes here while vacationing in Brittany. The *pièce de résistance* is a platter of *fruits de mer*, but you can also order half a dozen different kinds of succulent fresh oysters. Poached skate wing appears with garlic and caper butter, and you can also order a grilled entrecote with Béarnaise sauce. For dessert, patrons order the largest éclair served in Paris.

62 av. des Ternes, 17th. ℰ **01-45-72-29-47.** Reservations required. Main courses 24€–45€; fixed-price lunch 34€; fixed-price dinner 53€. AE, DC, MC, V. Mon–Sat noon–3pm and 7–10pm. Closed July 25–Aug 15. Métro: Ternes.

MODERATE

Restaurant Caïus ★ ✂ TRADITIONAL FRENCH   This chic place, popular for business lunches and dinners, also draws residents and shoppers. It's ringed with wood paneling, banquettes, and teakwood chairs. The new owner, Jean-Marc Note-let, has brought renewed vigor to the kitchen. His cuisine, however, remains tradi-tionally French and is based on spices and a judicious use of pepper. The dining room is a showcase for the chef's enticing cuisine, which is based on authentically flavor-filled local foodstuffs. To whet your appetite, try such dishes as grilled flap mushrooms or duckling foie gras. Among other recent masterful offerings were dorado braised with Belgian endives and root vegetables, and a confit of beef with fava beans and aged vinegar along with celery whipped into almond milk.

6 rue d'Armaillé, 17e. ℰ **01-42-27-19-20.** Reservations recommended. Main courses 19€–31€; fixed-price lunch 23€, dinner 39€. AE, DC, MC, V. Mon–Sat noon–2:30pm; Mon–Sat 7:30–11pm. Métro: Argentine.

Right Bank: 18th Arrondissement (Montmartre)

MODERATE

La Famille ★ MODERN FRENCH   The ambience is like New York's East Vil-lage, and this place attracts fashionistas and photographers who climb the hill to Montmartre to sample the tasty food. The bartender makes mojitos like Hemingway drank them, while Edith Piaf records spin in the background. Each dish arrives like a sensation, including the oyster terrine made with seaweed, cappuccino, and cilan-tro mousse. Other unusual sensations include a terrine of duck confit or a special mackerel dish. For dessert, finish off, perhaps, with a lemon tart with lemon verbena *jus*. Always count on the chefs offering some surprise combinations every night.

41 rue des Trois Freres, 18e. ℰ **01-42-52-11-12.** Reservations required. Set-price menus 29€–50€. MC, V. Tues–Sat 8–11:30pm. Closed 3 weeks in Aug. Métro: Abesses.

INEXPENSIVE

Au Grain de Folie ORGANIC/VEGETARIAN   Simple and wholesome, this cuisine is inspired by France, Greece, California, Turkey, and India. The menu includes an array of theme salads, cereals, tarts, terrines, and casseroles. Dessert selections might include an old-fashioned tart or a fruit salad. The decor includes potted plants and exposed stone. You can choose one of an array of wines or a frothy glass of vegetable juice to accompany your meal. This place may be a bit difficult to find, but it's worth the search. Marie-Cécite is the charming owner.

24 rue de La Vieuville, 18e. ℰ **01-42-58-15-57.** Reservations recommended. Main courses 11€–14€; fixed-price menus 8€–15€. No credit cards. Daily 12:30–2:30pm and 7–11pm. Métro: Abesses.

Left Bank: 5th Arrondissement (Latin Quarter)

MODERATE

Brasserie Balzar ★ TRADITIONAL FRENCH   Opened in 1898, Brasserie Balzar is battered but cheerful, with some of Paris's most colorful waiters. The menu makes almost no concessions to modern cuisine; it includes onion soup, pepper steak, sole meunière, sauerkraut with ham and sausage, pigs' feet, and fried calves' liver served without garnish. Be warned that if you want just coffee or a drink, you probably won't get a table at mealtimes. But the staff, accustomed to many patrons' odd hours, will be happy to serve you dinner in the midafternoon. Guests have included Sartre and Camus (who often got into arguments), James Thurber, and countless professors from the nearby Sorbonne.

49 rue des Ecoles, 5e. © **01-43-54-13-67.** www.brasseriebalzar.com. Reservations strongly recommended. Main courses 18€–35€. AE, DC, MC, V. Daily noon–midnight. Métro: Odéon or Cluny–La Sorbonne.

Itineraire ★ TRADITIONAL FRENCH   There's always a danger when a successful restaurant moves and expands. Often its original charm and patrons are lost. Not so with acclaimed chef Sylvain Sendra and his wife, Sarah, who closed their 26-seat Le Temps au Temps in the 11th arrondissement and opened another restaurant in the Latin Quarter. Their new place is twice as large, and the cuisine is just as good as it always was. Specialties include everything from Jerusalem artichoke soup to pheasant breast accompanied by dates, pistachios, fruit compote, and the odd nugget of buckshot.

One specialty is morchella mushrooms served with bacon crisps and a soft-boiled egg. They have a distinctive strong taste and come in a creamy sauce. Salmon is cooked on one side only and served with cannelloni stuffed with risotto. You might also order a delightful sea bass stuffed with white asparagus and served with a creamy parmesan vanilla sauce.

5 rue de Pontoise, 5e. © **01-46-33-60-11.** Reservations required. Fixed-price menu 36€. AE, MC, V. Tues–Sat noon–2pm and 7:30–10:30pm (11:30pm Fri–Sat). Métro: Maubert-Mutualité.

Le Pré Verre ★ 🍴 ASIAN/TRADITIONAL FRENCH   Around the corner from the Sorbonne in the heart of the Latin Quarter comes a refreshing restaurant where you can get seriously good food—all for an affordable price. Even if this is not an earth-shattering gastronomic experience, it is solid and reliable, with good cooking and market-fresh ingredients. The Delacourcelle brothers are firmly based in the French tradition, but they have added innovative modern twists by giving extra spicing to the food, many of the flavorings inspired by Asia. In a welcoming, relaxed, and convivial atmosphere, tables are placed so close together that you're literally dining and rubbing elbows with the same people. For something bourgeois, dig into the well-flavored terrines for starters. One of these—and the most delectable—is made with layers of foie gras and mashed potatoes. Your meal might begin with oysters marinated with ginger and poppy seeds or scallops with cinnamon. Main courses might include suckling pig with aromatic spices and crisp-cooked cabbage, or roasted codfish.

8 rue Thenard, 5e. © **01-43-54-59-47.** www.lepreverre.com. Reservations required. Main courses 18€; fixed-price menu at lunch 14€–29€, at dinner 29€. MC, V. Tues–Sat noon–2pm and 7:30–10:30pm. Closed Aug. Métro: Maubert-Mutualité.

Where to Dine on the Left Bank

Alcazar Restaurant **4**
Allard **5**
Au Pied de Fouet **13**
Aux Charpentiers **9**
Brasserie Balzar **19**
Breakfast in America **20**
Coco de Mer **22**
Crémerie-Restaurant
    Polidor **8**
Itineraire **17**
La Cigale Récamier **10**
La Crémerie **7**
L'Arpége **12**
La Petite Chaise **11**
La Rôtisserie d'en Face **3**
L'Avant Comptoir **6**
Le Pre Verre **18**
Les Papilles **21**
Le Timbre **14**
Marty **23**
Restaurant du Musée
    d'Orsay **1**
Ribouldingue **16**
Sensing **15**
Ze Kitchen Galerie **2**

Les Papilles ★ 🍴 One of the most exciting additions to Paris's culinary scene is **Les Papilles,** a deli, bistro, and wine shop all at one address. It features an appetizer (called entrée in French), a plat du jour, and dessert for an affordable price. Wine is available by the glass, but patrons are encouraged to order by the bottle since these bottles have some of the cheapest retail prices in France. Near Jardin de Luxembourg, Les Papilles offers superb food, including a four-course dégustation menu at night that blends the cookery of the Garonne with the chef's imaginative creation of the day.

30 rue Gay-Lussac, 5e. Ⓒ **01-43-25-20-79.** Reservations not needed. Market menu 31€; fixed-price dinner 80€. AE, MC, V. Mon–Sat noon–3pm and 7–11pm. Métro: Luxembourg.

Marty ★ 🍴 MODERN FRENCH   Charming, with a stone-trimmed decor that's authentic to the era (1913) when it was established, this restaurant has been "discovered" by new generations of restaurantgoers. Named after its founders, Etienne and Marthe Marty, its fame now extends beyond the 5th arrondissement. Service is attentive, and lots of Jazz Age murals grace the walls. Food is savory, satisfying, and unfussy. Views from the hideaway tables on the mezzanine sweep over the entire human comedy, which is loud, large, and animated, unfolding above and below you. Begin a meal with duckling terrine or Andalusian gazpacho. Continue with *suprême* of guinea fowl with vegetable moussaka, a rump steak in black-pepper sauce, or perhaps fried scallops sautéed in the Provençal style.

20 av. des Gobelins, 5e. Ⓒ **01-43-31-39-51.** www.marty-restaurant.com. Main courses 21€–35€; fixed-price menu 35€. AE, DC, MC, V. Daily noon–midnight. Métro: Gobelins.

Ribouldingue TRADITIONAL FRENCH   Offal lovers flock to this bistro near St-Julien-le-Pauvre church to enjoy such old-fashioned fare as the tip of a pig's snout or thinly breaded and sautéed slices of a cow's udder. What about lamb's brain meunière or tripe cooked in white wine, even veal kidneys in garlic sauce? If you're offal timid, you can opt for many other dishes, including veal rib with fried potatoes, Pollock with eggplant caviar and crispy lardoons (bacon cubes), or even a blanquette of monkfish. We adore their mascarpone crumble, but you might want the ice cream made of ewe's milk. This Latin Quarter bistro is the creation of Nadège Varigny, the daughter of a butcher in the French Alps. She'll seat you in one of the two cozy rooms, and will do so with a great sense of humor.

10 rue Saint-Julien-le-Pauvre, 5e. Ⓒ **01-46-33-98-80.** Reservations required. Fixed-price lunch 27€; fixed-price dinner 29€; main courses 17€–26€. MC, V. Tues–Fri noon–2:30pm; Tues–Sat 7:30–10:30pm. Closed 3 weeks in Aug. Métro: Cluny La Sorbonne or St-Michel.

INEXPENSIVE

Breakfast in America AMERICAN   Connecticut-born Hollywood screenwriter Craig Carlson opened this replica of a down-home U.S.-based diner in 2003, building it with funds from members of the California film community who donated memorabilia from their films. Its self-proclaimed mission involves dispensing proper, rib-sticking American breakfasts and diner food to a generation of Parisians who assume, prior to their visits here, that coffee comes only as espresso, and that quantities per meal are rigidly limited. The venue replicates a 1950s-era railway car, replete with scarlet-and-black Naugahyde banquettes, faux windows with mirrored insets, and an unabashedly Americanized staff. Breakfast (heaping portions of the egg-and-waffle-and-bacon combinations, as well as omelets) is served throughout the day and evening. Also available are a dozen variations of burgers, as well as tacos, club sandwiches, and BLTs.

17 rue des Ecoles, 5e. ℰ **01-43-54-50-28.** Reservations not accepted. Breakfast platters 7€–11€; fixed-price Sun brunch 16€; lunch and dinner platters and "blue-plate specials" 8€–12€. MC, V. Daily 8:30am–10:30pm. Métro: Cardinal Lemoine or Jussieu.

Coco de Mer ★ 🏠 SEYCHELLE ISLANDS   The theme of this restaurant tugs at the emotions of Parisians who have spent their holidays on the beaches of the Seychelles, in the Indian Ocean. It contains several dining rooms, one of which is outfitted like a beach, with a sand-covered floor, replicas of palm trees, and a scattering of conch shells. Menu items feature such exotic dishes as tartare of tuna flavored with ginger, olive oil, salt, and pepper; and smoked swordfish, served as carpaccio or in thin slices with mango mousse and spicy sauce. Main courses focus on fish, including a species of red snapper (*boirzoes*) imported from the Seychelles.

34 bd. St-Marcel, 5e. ℰ **01-47-07-06-64.** Reservations recommended. Main courses 14€–17€; fixed-price menus 23€–30€. AE, DC, MC, V. Tues–Sat noon–3pm; Mon–Sat 7:30pm–midnight. Métro: Les Gobelins or St-Marcel.

Left Bank: 6th Arrondissement (St-Germain/Luxembourg)

EXPENSIVE
Sensing ★★ MODERN FRENCH   This eatery is devoted to the five senses. One of the most famous chefs in Paris, Guy Martin, who continues to enjoy his three stars granted by Michelin at Grand Véfour, is also the inspiration for this chicly modern Left Bank restaurant. Wisely, he's hired a talented on-site chef, Rémy Van Péthegem, to rattle those pots and pans, and he's full of innovative surprises.

The decor relies on video projections on the walls and blond sycamore tables. Videos celebrate a woman's beauty, showing lips, curvature of the shoulder, hairdos, and eyes, as well as fields of blooming flowers. When plates are served, they are like statements from a museum of modern art—geometric arrangements of rectangles and cylinders along with Miró-like squiggles of sauce. Dishes are sublime, ranging from herb-crusted veal with tubes of macaroni stuffed with fresh mushrooms to fresh squab coated with a muscovado sugar caramel crust.

19 rue Bréa, 6e. ℰ **01-43-27-08-80.** www.restaurantsensing.com. Reservations required. Main courses 29€–36€; fixed-price lunch 25€–55€; 7-course fixed-price dinner 75€–95€. AE, MC, V. Tues–Sat noon–2:30pm; Mon–Sat 7:30-10:30pm. Closed Aug. Métro: Vavin.

MODERATE
Alcazar Restaurant ★ MODERN FRENCH   Paris's highest-profile *brasserie de luxe* is this high-tech place funded by British restaurateur Sir Terence Conran. It features a red-and-white futuristic decor in a street-level dining room and a busy upstairs bar (La Mezzanine de l'Alcazar). The menu includes rack of veal sautéed with wild mushrooms, roasted rack of lamb with thyme, and shellfish and oysters from the waters of Brittany. The wines are as stylish and diverse as you'd expect.

62 rue Mazarine, 6e. ℰ **01-53-10-19-99.** Reservations recommended. Main courses 17€–33€; fixed-price lunch 20€–32€, dinner 43€; Sun brunch 32€. AE, DC, MC, V. Daily noon–2:30pm and 7pm–1am. Métro: Odéon.

Allard ★ TRADITIONAL FRENCH   This old-time bistro, opened in 1931, is still going strong. It was once the city's leading bistro, although today the competition is too great for it to re-claim that reputation. Over the years, the front room's zinc bar has been a haven for many celebrities, including Mme. Pompidou, actor Alain Delon, and, since then, a gaggle of French celebrities. Allard serves all the old specialties, with quality ingredients deftly handled by the kitchen. Try snails, foie gras, Challans duck with olives, or frogs' legs or turbot in a beurre blanc sauce. We head here on Monday for the cassoulet Toulousian (casserole of white beans and goose and other meats) and on Saturday for coq au vin.

41 rue St-André-des-Arts, 6e. ☎ **01-43-26-48-23.** Reservations required. Main courses 19€–39€; fixed-price lunch 25€, dinner 34€. AE, DC, MC, V. Daily noon–2:30pm and 7:30–11:30pm. Métro: St-Michel or Odéon.

Aux Charpentiers TRADITIONAL FRENCH   This old bistro, which opened more than 130 years ago, attracts those seeking the Left Bank of yesteryear. It was once the rendezvous spot of the master carpenters, whose guild was next door. Nowadays, it's where young men take dates. Though the food isn't imaginative, it's well prepared in the best tradition of *cuisine bourgeoise*—hearty but not effete. Appetizers include pâté of duck and rabbit terrine. Recommended as a main course is roast duck with olives. The *plats du jour* recall French home cooking: salt pork with lentils, *pot-au-feu*, and stuffed cabbage. The wine list has a selection of bordeaux, including Château Gaussens.

10 rue Mabillon, 6e. ☎ **01-43-26-30-05.** Reservations required. Main courses 18€–31€; fixed-price lunch 21€, dinner 28€. AE, DC, MC, V. Daily noon–3pm and 7–11:30pm. Métro: St-Germain-des-Prés or Mabillon.

La Rôtisserie d'en Face ★ 🍴 TRADITIONAL FRENCH   This is Paris's most popular baby bistro, operated by Jacques Cagna, whose expensive namesake restaurant is across the street. The informal place features a postmodern decor with high-tech lighting, yellow walls, and red banquettes. The simply prepared food is very good and employs high-quality ingredients. Tantalizing starters include red tuna and sea bream tartare flavored with ginger and soya, or else rabbit pâté with pine kernels. Main dish favorites include the signature spit-roasted, free-range chicken served with the traditional buttery mashed potatoes. Other mains include cold grilled salmon with coriander-marinated fresh vegetables. Few desserts top "the red berry bowl," with Cassis sauce and whipped cream.

2 rue Christine, 6e. ☎ **01-43-26-40-98.** Reservations recommended. Main courses 22€–27€; fixed-price lunch 25€–31€. AE, DC, MC, V. Mon–Fri noon–2:30pm; Mon–Sat 7–11pm. Métro: Odéon or St-Michel.

Le Timbre ★ 🏨 TRADITIONAL FRENCH   A Brit running a restaurant in Paris? That's practically unheard of, at least to former president Jacques Chirac, who once denounced British cooking as the worst in the world. Surprisingly, a Brit, Chris Wright, has opened the tiniest restaurant on the tiniest street in Paris, lying near Montparnasse. The Manchester-born chef shops for only the finest of French regional products, including truffles and foie gras, and he gets by with no microwave and no freezer. He is a skilled French chef, ranking up there with the best of them. In this postage stamp restaurant near Luxembourg Gardens, Wright prepares faultless dishes, including trout stuffed with fresh fava beans and country ham, andouillette sausages with lentils, or a filet of whitefish with olives. In spite of all these *à la française* dishes, he likes to put English cheddar on his cheeseboard. If not the cheese, you might end your meal with the ruby-red strawberry soup.

3 rue Sainte Beuve, 6e. ✆ **01-45-49-10-40.** www.restaurantletimbre.com. Reservations required. Main courses 15€–21€; fixed-price lunch 24€–28€. MC, V. Tues–Sat noon–2pm and 7:30–10:30pm. Closed 3 weeks in Aug. Métro: Notre-Dame-des-Champs or Vavin.

Ze Kitchen Galerie ★ 🎁 INTERNATIONAL/MODERN FRENCH   The owner and head chef of this restaurant, William Ledeuil, trained in haute Parisian gastronomy under culinary czar Guy Savoy. The setting is a colorful loft space in an antique building, with an open-to-view showcase kitchen. Most of the paintings on display are for sale (the place doubles as an art gallery). Menu items, like the paintings, change about every 5 weeks; appetizers are subdivided into pastas, soups, and fish; and main courses are divided into meats and fish that are usually *à la plancha* (grilled). For starters, ever had beet gazpacho with candied ginger, cucumber, and fresh shrimp? The grilled chicken and veal sweetbreads with a carrot-and-mustard *jus* (flavored with ginger) is heavenly, as are platters of oysters, mussels, and sea urchins. Sometimes grilled shoulder of wild boar with tamarind sauce is featured. A meal might also be followed with the restaurant's "cappuccino of the month," a frothy dessert concoction whose ingredients change with the seasons.

4 rue des Grands-Augustins, 6e. ✆ **01-44-32-00-32.** www.zekitchengalerie.fr. Reservations recommended. Main courses 30€–35€; fixed-price lunch with wine 24€–39€; fixed-price dinner 76€. AE, DC, MC, V. Mon–Fri noon–2:30pm; Mon–Sat 7–11pm. Métro: St-Michel or Pont-Neuf.

INEXPENSIVE

Crémerie-Restaurant Polidor ★ ☺ TRADITIONAL FRENCH   Crémerie Polidor is the most traditional bistro in the Odéon area, serving *cuisine familiale*. Its name dates from the early 1900s, when it specialized in frosted cream desserts, but the restaurant can trace its history from 1845. The Crémerie was André Gide's favorite, and Joyce, Hemingway, Valéry, Artaud, and Kerouac also dined here. Peer beyond the lace curtains and brass hat racks to see drawers where, in olden days, regular customers used to lock up their cloth napkins. Try the day's soup followed by kidneys in Madeira sauce, boeuf bourguignon, *confit de canard*, or *blanquette de veau*. For dessert, order a chocolate, raspberry, or lemon tart.

39 rue Monsieur-le-Prince, 6e. ✆ **01-43-26-95-34.** www.polidor.com. Main courses 11€–48€; fixed-price menus 22€–32€. No credit cards. Daily noon–2:30pm; Mon–Sat 7pm–12:30am; Sun 7–11pm. Métro: Odéon.

La Crèmerie ★ 🎁 TRADITIONAL FRENCH   A New Yorker, Serge Mathieu was an architect when he first entered La Crèmerie. But after one dinner here, he decided to buy the joint and transform this tiny 19th-century "creamery" in the Latin Quarter into his own place. He has done so admirably. Today under a ceiling of handpainted silk under glass, he attracts the neighborhood locals to his precincts. They know they can get great bargains from his wine cellar, which showcases artisanal bottlings from all over the country. His charcuterie and cheeses are also exceptional. You can dine on foie gras, oysters, delicately smoked tuna, and a spectacular chocolate fondant, the creation of Mathieu's wife, Hélène. Take note that La Crèmerie doesn't serve any hot food except for grilled vegetables. The cost, of course, depends on what you order.

9 rue des Quatre Vents, 6e. ✆ **01-43-54-99-30.** www.lacremerie.fr. Reservations not needed. Meals from 20€. MC, V. Tues–Sat 10:30am–10pm; Sun 11am–2:30pm; Mon 2–8pm. Métro: Odéon.

L'Avant Comptoir ★ FRENCH/SPANISH   This hole-in-the-wall is just steps from the Odéon. Here you will encounter bistro maestro Yves Camdeborde, who operates a crêperie by day and a cocktail and hors d'oeuvres bar by night. Next door to his seminal restaurant Le Comptoir, his latest business lies in a short, narrow, standing-room space with an open kitchen. His small plates are Basque and Béarnais-inspired "nibbles." There's a great selection of French wines by the glass. Try such hearty fare as a shellfish bouillon with octopus; deep-fried pig's foot croquettes; oxtail canapés with horseradish cream, or chicken hearts grilled with garlic and parsley. No more than a dozen people can crowd into this place at a time. It's really narrow.

3 carrefour de l'Odéon, 6e. © **08-26-10-10-87.** No reservations accepted. Main courses 12€–22€. MC, V. Daily 9am–1am. Métro: Odéon.

Left Bank: 7th Arrondissement (Eiffel Tower/Musée d'Orsay)

If you're in the 7th arrondissement for breakfast or lunch, perhaps visiting the Musée d'Orsay, a good refueling stop is the bakery, bar, and cafe, **Eric Kayser ★★**, 18 rue du Bac, 7e (© **01-42-61-27-63**; Métro: Bac or Musée d'Orsay). Kayser's forte is bread-making, and he is known for the long fermentation of his dough. He is always coming up with new ideas for his breads, including one made with apricots and pistachios or else chorizo. This Alsatian baker offers many *luxe* breads and pastries, and breakfast is a delight here. At lunch you have a choice of 20 different combinations of *tartines* (open-faced sandwiches), and at teatime there are gourmet snacks such as a sweet tartine with meringue and chestnuts. Open Tuesday to Sunday from 7am to 8pm.

VERY EXPENSIVE

L'Arpège ★★★ MODERN FRENCH   L'Arpège is best known for Alain Passard's specialties—no restaurant in the 7th serves better food. Surrounded by etched glass, burnished steel, and pearwood paneling, you can enjoy such specialties as couscous of vegetables and shellfish, lobster braised in the yellow wine of the Jura, braised monkfish in an Orléans mustard sauce, pigeon roasted with almonds and honey-flavored mead, and carpaccio of crayfish with caviar-flavored cream sauce. Although Passard is loath to include red meat on his menus, Kobe beef and venison sometimes appear. He focuses on fish, shellfish, poultry, and—his passion—vegetables. These he elevates to levels unequaled by any other chef in Paris.

84 rue de Varenne, 7e. © **01-47-05-09-06.** Fax 01-44-18-98-39. www.alain-passard.com. Reservations required 2 weeks in advance. Main courses 48€–180€; fixed-price lunch 135€; fixed-price dinner 420€. AE, DC, MC, V. Mon–Fri 12:30–2:30pm and 8–10:30pm. Métro: Varenne.

EXPENSIVE

La Fontaine de Mars ★ TRADITIONAL FRENCH   When President Obama and his First Lady dined at the classic French bistrot, **La Fontaine de Mars,** visiting Americans began booking tables here. One of the "ancient" bistrots of Paris, it's been a venerable institution since it first opened in 1908, but it's never had this kind of business before. The menu is about the same as it was when your French grandfather (if you had one) may have dined here before WWI. Believe it or not, the chef still cooks that Burgundian appetizer of two eggs baked in red wine with shallots and served with a bacon sauce. Homemade duck foie gras is on the menu, with such main dishes as free range chicken breast with fresh morels or the classic sole menu-ière. Obama went for the black chocolate mousse.

129 rue Saint Dominique, 7e. © **01-47-05-46-44.** www.fontainedemars.com. Reservations required. Main courses 32€–45€. AE, MC, V. Daily noon–3pm and 7:30–11pm. Métro: École Militaire.

Le Violon d'Ingres ★★★ MODERN FRENCH   This restaurant is Paris's *pièce de résistance*. Chef-owner Christian Constant is "the new Robuchon." Those fortunate enough to dine in Violon's warm atmosphere rave about the artistic dishes. They range from wood pigeon cooked on the grill and served with a fricassee of mushrooms to such hearty fare as veal's head with the tongue and brain poached in a sauce of capers and hard-boiled eggs. If you're not steely enough for that, you can opt for the sea bass under a crust of almonds. The service is charming and discreet; the wine selection, well chosen. The Constant family has tied up the dining rituals along this street, with less expensive, less formal restaurants flanking Le Violon d'Ingres.

135 rue St-Dominique, 7e. ✆ **01-45-55-15-05.** Fax 01-45-55-48-42. www.leviolingres.com. Reservations required at least 2 days in advance. All main courses 27€; fixed-price menu 49€. AE, DC, MC, V. Tues–Sat noon–2:30pm and 7–10:30pm. Métro: Invalides or Ecole-Militaire.

Les Ombres ★ MODERN FRENCH/INTERNATIONAL   Les Ombres in French means "the shadows." Architect Jean Nouvel named this museum rooftop restaurant for the shadows cast by the Eiffel Tower looming nearby. A late dinner is practically a spectacle, as the tower twinkles for the first 10 minutes of every hour. Fortunately, the chefs don't just rely on the view. The head chef, Arno Busquet, trained under the great Joël Robuchon, and for his ingenious cuisine he sails the seas, from Oceania to Asia and the Americas. You dine under a canopy of "metallic lace" inspired by the tower itself. Feast on such dishes as foie gras with spiced mango chutney, or guinea fowl stuffed with Creole sausage and served with an apple cabbage purée. Other delights include a shellfish risotto flavored with lemon, duck seasoned with rosemary, or seared tuna belly with onion rings flavored with sesame. The cuisine is invariably based on fresh produce.

Musée du Quai Branly, 27 quai Branly, 7e. ✆ **01-47-53-68-00.** www.lesombres-restaurant.com. Reservations required. Main courses 32€–45€; fixed-price menus 38€–145€. MC, V. Daily noon–2:30pm and 7–10:30pm. Métro: Pont de l'Alma.

MODERATE

La Cigale Récamier ★ 🍴 TRADITIONAL FRENCH   The Obamas dined at La Fontaine de Mars (see p. 146), but the following day, which was a Sunday, Mrs. Obama dined with her daughters at La Cigale Récamier, a Left Bank bistro that had been recommended to her by some members of the American Embassy. A former First Lady, Laura Bush, had also dined here. Once news spread of Mrs. Obama's visit, this humble Left Bank bistro was put on the culinary map. Chef Ferard Idoux visited the White House in 2008. Idous is a new chef, having taken over from a man who ran the place for 3 decades. He served the Obama women his famous Camembert soufflé and beef filet grilled in fresh basil.

4 rue Récamier, 7e. ✆ **01-45-48-86-58.** Reservations required. Main courses 21€–35€. AE, MC, V. Mon–Sat noon–3pm and 7–11pm. Métro: Sévres-Babylone.

La Petite Chaise TRADITIONAL FRENCH   This is Paris's oldest restaurant, opened as an inn in 1680 by the baron de la Chaise at the edge of a hunting preserve. (According to lore, the baron used the upstairs bedrooms for afternoon dalliances, between fox and pheasant hunts.) Very Parisian, the "Little Chair" invites you into a world of cramped but attractive tables, old wood paneling, and ornate wall sconces. A vigorous chef has brought renewed taste and flavor to this longtime favorite, and the four-course set menu offers a large choice of dishes in each category.

Examples are *magret* of duck with sweet-and-sour sauce, *pot-au-feu* whose ingredients change with the seasons, and grilled sea bass on a bed of fennel with a light butter sauce.

36 rue de Grenelle, 7e. ✆ **01-42-22-13-35.** www.alapetitechaise.fr. Reservations recommended. Main courses all 20€; fixed-price menu 31€. MC, V. Daily noon–2pm and 7–11pm. Métro: Sèvres-Babylone or Rue du Bac.

Restaurant du Musée d'Orsay ★ MODERN FRENCH   If you can overlook the hysterical and rude staff—a big if—you can treat yourself to a sumptuous Belle Epoque dining room overlooking the Seine. Perhaps Marcel Proust and his gay comrades once sat under the magnificent frescoed ceiling. In such a glamorous setting, you can enjoy a traditional cuisine, though it has been given a decidedly modern interpretation. Escoffier it isn't. The best bargain is the two-course prix-fixe lunch. (If not lunch, you can use the romantic setting for afternoon tea once you've had a feast of the Impressionists.) The menu is ever changing, but basically it consists of a more simplified version of traditional French cuisine. Expect such savory dishes as grilled sea bream filet or perhaps duck and peaches supreme served with *gratin dauphinois*.

1 rue de Bellechasse, 7e. ✆ **01-45-49-42-33.** Reservations recommended. 2-course lunch 17€; Sun brunch 23€; Thurs evening gourmet menu 42€; children's menu 7.60€. AE, MC, V. Tues–Sun lunch 11:45am and 2:30pm, tea 3:30–5:30pm; dinner only Thurs 7–9:30pm. Métro: Solférino. RER: Musée d'Orsay.

INEXPENSIVE

Au Pied de Fouet TRADITIONAL FRENCH   This is one of the neighborhood's oldest and most reasonably priced restaurants. In the 1700s, it was a stopover for carriages en route to Paris, offering wine, food, and stables. Don't expect a leisurely or attentive meal: Food and drink will disappear quickly from your table, under the gaze of others waiting their turn. The dishes are solid and unpretentious and include *blanquette de veau* (veal stew), chicken in vinegar sauce (a house specialty), *petit salé* (a savory family-style stew made from pork and vegetables and served with lentils), and filet of sea wolf or filet of codfish. If you demand a polite staff, go elsewhere: The waiters are among the rudest in Paris. Some visitors claim that's part of the charm of this place. You decide.

45 rue de Babylone, 7e. ✆ **01-47-05-12-27.** www.aupieddefouet.com. Main courses 7.90€–13€. MC, V. Mon–Sat noon–2:30pm; Mon–Fri 7–9:30pm. Métro: Vaneau.

Left Bank: 14th Arrondissement (Gare Montparnasse)

EXPENSIVE

La Cagouille ★ 🏛 TRADITIONAL FRENCH/SEAFOOD   Don't expect to find meat at this temple of seafood—owner Gérard Allamandou refuses to feature it. Everything about La Cagouille is a testimonial to a modern version of the culinary arts of La Charente, the flat sandy district on the Atlantic south of Bordeaux. In a trio of oak-sheathed dining rooms, you'll sample seafood prepared as naturally as possible, with no fancy sauces or elaborate techniques. Try such dishes as fried filet of sole, grilled John Dory, or warm cockles. Red mullet might be sautéed in oil or baked in rock salt. The name derives from the regional symbol of La Charente, the sea snail, whose preparation the restaurant elevates to a fine culinary art. Look for a vast assemblage of wines and cognacs.

10 place Constantin-Brancusi, 14e. © **01-43-22-09-01.** www.la-cagouille.fr. Reservations recommended. Main courses 16€–60€; fixed-price menu 23€–38€. MC, V. Daily noon–2:30pm and 7:30–10:30pm. Métro: Gaîté.

MODERATE

L'Assiette MODERN FRENCH   Everything here appeals to a nostalgic crowd seeking down-to-earth prices and flavorful food. The place was a charcuterie (pork butcher's shop) in the 1930s and maintains some of its old accessories. Mitterrand used to drop in for oysters, crayfish, sea urchins, and clams. The food is inspired by Paris's long tradition of bistro cuisine, with a few twists. The new chef and owner was once a student of Alain Ducasse, the master chef. You might begin with an appetizer of smoked ham or else sardines marinated in citrus. The chef also makes a tasty *pot-au-feu* or stew, and does wonders with pepper steak. Escargot arrives in a pot sprinkled with homemade croutons. The duck pâté is another good choice, followed by such desserts as crème caramel or *riz au lait* (rice with milk).

181 rue du Château, 14e. © **01-43-22-64-86.** www.restaurant-lassiette.com. Reservations recommended. Main courses 21€–37€; fixed-price lunch 23€. AE, MC, V. Wed–Sun noon–2:30pm and 7:30–10:30pm. Closed Aug. Métro: Gaîté.

Le Severo ★ TRADITIONAL FRENCH   This is the carnivore's delight—in fact, its owner was a butcher from Nivernaises before turning restaurateur. Come here to experience the way Parisians ate back in the 1890s. No one seems to do fried pigs' feet, crunchy crisp, as the cooks here do. It's served with hand cut and expertly cooked french fries. On the blackboard menu, you are likely to encounter some of the choicest cuts of meats in Paris. Farmhouse blood pudding (*boudin noir*), steak tartare, and grilled rib-eye steaks are just some of the offerings in this joint. Most beef arrives blood rare and beautifully marbled. Parisians order their steak *saignant* (underdone). If you want it medium rare, ask for it *à point*.

8 rue des Plantes, 14e. © **01-40-44-73-09.** Reservations required. Main courses 20€–27€. MC, V. Mon–Sat noon–2pm; Tues–Fri 7:30–10pm. Closed Aug. Métro: Mouton-Duvernet or Alésia.

15th Arrondissement (Gare Montparnasse)
MODERATE

Jadis ★★ 🍴 TRADITIONAL FRENCH   In the autumn of 2009, *Le Figaro* hailed Jadis as "the best bistrot of the autumn." *Le Fooding* went even further, calling it "the best bistrot in Paris." We won't go that far except to say that Jadis still has the same high standards that brought it so much early acclaim. In the up-and-coming 15th arrondissement, Chef Guillaume Delage in his culinary showroom dazzles some of the finest palates of Paris. He is known for giving his own interpretation to what some food critics call "soulful Neoclassical flavors." A typical example of that is his *épaule d'agneau* (a shoulder of lamb for two). Cooked with flat mogette beans, the lamb is served in a copper casserole. His set menu is based on the classic "snout-to-tail" type of cooking, so he's not afraid to use an animal's brains and feet.

208 rue de la Croix Nivert, 15e. © **01-45-57-73-20.** Reservations required. Fixed-price lunch or dinner 32€. AE, MC, V. Mon–Fri 12:15–2:30pm and 7:15–10:30pm. Métro: Convention.

THE TOP CAFES

Whatever your pleasure—reading, meeting a lover, writing your memoirs, nibbling a hard-boiled egg, or drinking yourself into oblivion—you can do it at a French cafe. (For the top wine bars, see "Paris After Dark," in chapter 6.)

Across from the Centre Pompidou is avant-garde **Café Beaubourg,** 100 rue St-Martin, 4e (✆ **01-48-87-63-96;** Métro: Rambuteau or Hôtel-de-Ville), with its soaring concrete columns and minimalist decor by the architect Christian de Portzamparc. The food is passable, but it's the location that keeps this cafe humming. In summer, tables spill onto the sprawling terrace, providing a panoramic view of the neighborhood's goings-on. Open Sunday through Wednesday 8am to 1am, Thursday through Saturday 8am to 2am.

Jean-Paul Sartre came to **Café de Flore,** 172 bd. St-Germain, 6e (✆ **01-45-48-55-26;** www.cafe-de-flore.com; Métro: St-Germain-des-Prés), where it's said he wrote his trilogy *Les Chemins de la Liberté (The Roads to Freedom).* The cafe is still going strong, though celebrities have moved on. Open daily from 7:30am to 1:30am.

Next door, the legendary **Deux Magots,** 6 place St-Germain-des-Prés, 6e (✆ **01-45-48-55-25;** www.lesdeuxmagots.fr; Métro: St-Germain-des-Prés), is still the hangout for sophisticated residents and a tourist favorite in summer. Inside are two Asian statues that give the cafe its name. It's open daily from 7:30am to 1am.

Fouquet's, 99 av. des Champs-Elysées, 8e (✆ **01-47-23-50-00;** Métro: George V), is the premier cafe on the Champs-Elysées. Outside, a barricade of potted flowers separates cafe tables from the sidewalk. Inside are a grill room, private rooms, and a restaurant. The cafe and grill room are open daily from 8am to 2am; the restaurant and the slightly less formal grill are open daily noon to 3pm and 7pm to 1am.

At **La Coupole,** 102 bd. Montparnasse, 14e (✆ **01-43-20-14-20;** Métro: Vavin), the crowd ranges from artists' models to young men dressed like Rasputin. People come here to see and be seen. Perhaps order a coffee or cognac VSOP at a sidewalk table, repeating a ritual that has continued since the place was established in 1927. The dining room serves food that is sometimes good, sometimes indifferent. It serves a buffet breakfast Monday through Friday from 8:30 to 10:30am. Open daily 8am to 1am (until 1:30am Friday to Saturday).

Café de la Musique, in the Cité de la Musique, place Fontaine Aux Lions, 213 av. Jean-Jaurès, 19e (✆ **01-48-03-15-91;** Métro: Porte de Pantin), attracts a crowd devoted to music. The recorded sounds in the background are likely to be more diverse and eclectic than in any other cafe in Paris. The red-and-green-velour setting may remind you of a modern opera house. On the menu you'll find pasta with shellfish, pork in cider sauce, and stingray in black-butter sauce. Open daily 8am to 2am (until 1am only Sunday to Monday).

In the Marais, **La Belle Hortense,** 31 rue Vieille du Temple, 4e (✆ **01-48-04-71-60;** Métro: Hôtel de Ville or St-Paul), is the most literary cafe in a legendary literary neighborhood. It offers an erudite and accessible staff; an inventory of French literary classics as well as modern tomes about art, psychoanalysis, history, and culture; and two high-ceilinged, 19th-century rooms little changed since the days of Baudelaire and Balzac. The zinc-covered bar serves wine for 3€ to 9€ a glass. Open daily as a cafe and bookstore from 5pm to 2am.

EXPLORING PARIS

Paris is one of those cities where the street life—shopping, strolling, and hanging out—should claim as much time as sightseeing. A gourmet picnic in the Bois de Boulogne, a sunrise pilgrimage to the Seine, an afternoon at a flea market—Paris bewitches you with these experiences. For all the Louvre's beauty, you'll probably remember the Latin Quarter's crooked alleyways better than the 370th oil painting of your visit.

The best way to discover Paris is on foot. Walk along the avenue des Champs-Elysées, tour the quays of the Seine, wander the Ile de la Cité and Ile St-Louis, browse the shops and stalls, and stroll the squares and parks. A walk at dawn can be enthralling as you see the city come to life: Merchants wash shop fronts, cafes begin serving coffee and croissants, and vegetable and fruit vendors start setting up their stalls and arranging their produce.

Paris is also a shopper's city—with everything from tony boutiques to colorful street markets. We've covered the best of the best in this chapter.

For sheer variety, there's nothing like Paris nightlife. Nowhere else will you find such bars, clubs, cabarets, jazz dives, music halls, and honky-tonks. (For information about the cafe scene, see chapter 5.)

ORGANIZED TOURS

Before plunging into sightseeing on your own, you may want to take the most popular get-acquainted tour in Paris: **Cityrama,** 149 rue St-Honoré, 1er (© **01-44-55-61-00;** www.pariscityrama.com; Métro: Louvre-Rivoli). On a double-decker bus with enough windows for Versailles, you take a 1½-hour ride through the city. While you don't go inside any attractions, you get a look at the outside of Notre-Dame and the Eiffel Tower, among other sites, and a good feel for the city. Earphones provide commentary in 16 languages. Tours depart daily at 10am, 11:30am, 1pm, and 2:30pm. A 1½-hour orientation tour is 22€ adults and 10€ children. A morning tour with interior visits to the Louvre costs 44€. Half-day tours to Versailles are 64€, or 63€ to Chartres. A joint ticket that includes

Top Paris Attractions

Versailles and Chartres costs 110€. A tour of the nighttime illuminations leaves daily at 10pm in summer, 7pm in winter, and costs 30€; it tends to be tame and touristy.

The **RATP** (© 08-92-68-77-14; www.ratp.fr), which runs regular public transportation, also operates the **Balabus,** a fleet of orange-and-white big-windowed motorcoaches. The only drawback is their limited operating times: Sunday and national holidays from 12:30 to 8:30pm, from April to the end of September. Itineraries run in both directions between Gare de Lyon and the Grande Arche de La Défense. Three Métro tickets will carry you along the entire route. You'll recognize the bus, and the route it follows, by the Bb symbol on its side and on signs posted along its route.

A boat tour on the Seine provides vistas of the riverbanks and some of the best views of Notre-Dame. Many boats have sun decks, bars, and restaurants. **Bateaux-Mouche** (© 01-42-25-96-10; www.bateaux-mouches.fr; Métro: Alma-Marceau) cruises depart from the Right Bank of the Seine, adjacent to pont de l'Alma, and last about 75 minutes. Tours leave daily at 20-minute intervals from 10:15am to 11pm between April and September. Between October and March, there are at least five departures daily between 11am and 9pm, with a schedule that changes according to demand and the weather. Fares are 10€ for adults and 5€ for children 4 to 13. Dinner cruises depart daily at 8:30pm, last 2 hours, and cost 95€ to 135€. On dinner cruises, jackets and ties are required for men. There are also lunch cruises Saturday and Sunday departing at 1pm, costing 50€ or else 25€ for kids 11 and under.

The amusingly named **Fat Tire Bike Tours–Paris,** 24 rue Edgar Faure, 15e (© 01-56-58-10-54; www.fattirebiketoursparis.com), is a Texas-based company that leads guided English-speaking bike tours of the City of Light. This is a great way to get oriented to Paris, as you cycle by such monuments as the Eiffel Tower or Napoleon's impressive tomb. Night tours are also available. Day tours start daily at 11am from mid-February to mid-December; a second tour starts daily at 3pm April to October. Night tours run daily at 7pm March to October; from mid-February to mid-March and in November night tours run Tuesday, Thursday, Saturday, and Sunday at 7pm. Day tours cost 26€ adults, or 24€ for students and children, with night tours, starting at 6pm, going for 28€ for adults or 26€ for students and children.

Context:Paris (© 215/609-4471 in the U.S., or 01-72-81-36-35; www.context paris.com) is an organization of graduate students and art-history professors who lead thematic walking tours of the city. Tours range from 1-hour orientation "chats" to 4-hour in-depth visits of the Louvre. Being academics, the guides try to create a college seminar feeling without being too obtuse and scholarly. Context:Paris also rents cellphones, arranges transportation, and organizes culinary excursions. Prices vary widely depending on what itinerary you select, with tours ranging in price from 35€ to 85€.

The Museum Discount Card

If you're a culture buff, consider buying a **Paris Museum Pass,** which admits you to some 70 museums in Paris and its environs. You do the math—if you plan to visit three or four museums, the card is usually worth the investment. A pass good for 2 days costs 32€; for 4 consecutive days, 48€; and for 6 consecutive days, 64€. Cards are available at all major museums and Métro stations. For more information, contact **Association InterMusees,** 4 rue Brantôme, 3e (© 01-44-61-96-60; www.parismuseumpass. fr; Métro: Rambuteau).

THE TOP ATTRACTIONS

Arc de Triomphe ★★★ At the western end of the Champs-Elysées, the Arc de Triomphe is the largest triumphal arch in the world, about 49m (161 ft.) high and 44m (144 ft.) wide. Don't cross the square to reach it! With a dozen streets radiating from the "Star," the traffic circle is vehicular roulette. It's the busiest traffic hub in Paris. Instead, take the underground passage.

The arch has witnessed some of France's proudest moments—and some of its more humiliating defeats, as in 1871 (when Paris capitulated in the Franco-Prussian War) and 1940, when news cameras captured the memory of German troops marching under the arch.

Commissioned by Napoleon in 1806 to commemorate his Grande Armée's victories, the arch wasn't completed until 1836, under Louis-Philippe. Four years later, Napoleon's remains—brought from his grave on St. Helena—passed under the arch en route to his tomb at the Hôtel des Invalides. Since then it has become the focal point for state funerals. It's also the site of the Tomb of the Unknown Soldier, where an eternal flame burns.

Of the sculptures decorating the monument, the best known is Rude's *Marseillaise,* also called *The Departure of the Volunteers.* J. P. Cortot's *Triumph of Napoleon in 1810,* along with the *Resistance of 1814* and *Peace of 1815,* both by Etex, also adorn the facade. The arch is engraved with the names of hundreds of generals who commanded troops in Napoleonic victories.

You can take an elevator or climb the stairway to the top, where there's an exhibition hall with lithographs and photos depicting the arch throughout its history. From the observation deck, you have a panoramic view of the Champs-Elysées as well as such landmarks as the Louvre, Eiffel Tower, and Sacré-Coeur.

Place Charles-de-Gaulle-Etoile, 8e. ✆**01-55-37-73-77.** www.monum.fr. Admission 9€ adults, 5.50€ for those 18–24, free for children 17 and under. Apr–Sept daily 10am–11pm; Oct–Mar daily 10am–10:30pm. Métro: Charles-de-Gaulle-Etoile. Bus: 22, 30, 31, 52, 73, or 92.

Basilique du Sacré-Coeur ★★★ Montmartre's crowning achievement is Sacré-Coeur, with its gleaming white domes and *campanile* (bell tower), though its view of Paris takes precedence over the basilica itself. Like other Parisian landmarks, it has been the subject of much controversy. It was attacked for its ornate architecture, which was denounced in the Parisian press as more of a wedding cake than a church.

After France's defeat by the Prussians in 1870, the basilica was planned as an offering to cure the country's misfortunes; rich and poor alike contributed. Construction began in 1873, but the church wasn't consecrated until 1919. The interior is decorated with mosaics, the most striking of which are the ceiling depiction of Christ and the mural of the Passion at the back of the altar. The crypt contains what some believe is a piece of the sacred heart of Christ—hence the church's name.

On a clear day, the vista from the dome can extend for 56km (35 miles). You can also walk around the inner dome of the church, peering down like a pigeon (a few of which will likely be there to keep you company).

Place St-Pierre, 18e. ✆**01-53-41-89-00.** www.sacre-coeur-montmartre.com. Free admission to basilica; joint ticket to dome and crypt 5€ adults. Basilica daily 6am–11pm; dome and crypt daily 9am–6pm. Métro: Abbesses; take elevator to surface and follow signs to funicular.

Centre Pompidou ★★★ The dream of former president Georges Pompidou, this center for 20th-century art, designed by Richard Rogers and Renzo Piano, opened in 1977 in the old Beaubourg neighborhood and became the focus of controversy. Its bold exoskeletal architecture and the brightly painted pipes and ducts crisscrossing its transparent facade (green for water, red for heat, blue for air, and yellow for electricity) were jarring. Perhaps the detractors were right all along—within 20 years, the building began to deteriorate so badly that a major restoration was called for. The center was relaunched in 2000.

The Centre Pompidou encompasses four separate attractions. The **Musée National d'Art Moderne (National Museum of Modern Art)** displays a large collection of 20th-century art. With some 40,000 works, this is the big draw, although it can show only about 850 works at one time. If you want to view some real charmers, see Alexander Calder's 1926 *Josephine Baker,* one of his earlier versions of the mobile, an art form he invented. Marcel Duchamp's *Valise* is a collection of miniature reproductions of his fabled dada sculptures and drawings; they're displayed in a carrying case. Every time we visit we have to see Salvador Dalí's *Portrait of Lenin Dancing on Piano Keys.*

In the **Public Information Library,** the public has free access to a million French and foreign books, periodicals, films, records, slides, and microfilms in nearly every area of knowledge. The **Center for Industrial Design** emphasizes contributions in the fields of architecture, visual communications, publishing, and community planning; and the **Institute for Research and Coordination of Acoustics/Music** brings together musicians and composers interested in furthering the cause of music, both contemporary and traditional.

Finally, you can visit a re-creation of the Jazz Age studio of Romanian sculptor **Brancusi (l'Atelier Brancusi),** which is configured as a minimuseum that's slightly separate from the rest of the action; this attraction is open Wednesday to Monday from 2 to 6pm.

Place Georges-Pompidou, 4e. ✆ **01-44-78-12-33.** www.centrepompidou.fr. Admission 12€ adults, 9€ students, free for children 17 and under. Wed–Mon 11am–10pm. Métro: Rambuteau, Hôtel de Ville, or Châtelet–Les Halles.

Eiffel Tower ★★★ This may be the single most recognizable structure in the world—it's the symbol of Paris. Weighing 7,000 tons but exerting about the same pressure on the ground as a person sitting in a chair, the tower was not meant to be permanent. Gustave-Alexandre Eiffel, the engineer whose fame rested mainly on his iron bridges, built it for the Universal Exhibition of 1889. (He also designed the framework for the Statue of Liberty.)

The tower, including its 17m (56-ft.) TV antenna, is 317m (1,040 ft.) tall. (The advent of wireless communication in the early 1890s preserved the tower from destruction, because it was the best place in the city for antennas.) On a clear day you can see it from 64km (40 miles) away. Its open-framework construction ushered in the almost-unlimited possibilities of steel construction, paving the way for skyscrapers. Skeptics said it couldn't be built, and Eiffel wanted to make it soar higher. For years it remained the tallest man-made structure on earth.

You can visit the tower in three stages: Taking the elevator to the first landing, you'll have a view over the rooftops of Paris. A cinema, museum, restaurants, and bar are open year-round. The second landing provides a panoramic look at the city (on this level is Le Jules Verne restaurant, a great place for lunch or dinner). The third landing offers the best view, allowing you to identify monuments and buildings. On the ground level, in the eastern and western pillars, you can visit the 1899 elevator machinery when the tower is open.

To get to **Le Jules Verne** (✆ **01-45-55-61-44**), take the private south foundation elevator. You can enjoy an aperitif in the piano bar and then take a seat at one of the dining room's tables, all of which provide an inspiring view. The menu changes seasonally, offering fish and meat dishes that range from filet of turbot with seaweed and buttered sea urchins to veal chops with truffled vegetables. Reservations are recommended and a fixed-price luncheon menu goes for 85€, set dinners for 200€.

You can ice-skate inside the Eiffel Tower, doing figure eights while taking in views of the rooftops of Paris. Skating takes place on an observation deck 57m (187 ft.) aboveground. The rectangular rink is a bit larger than an average tennis court, holding 80 skaters at once—half the capacity of New York City's Rockefeller Center rink. Admission to the rink and skate rentals are free once you pay the initial entry fee below. The rink is open for 6 weeks during December and January.

Insider tip: The least expensive way to visit the tower is to walk up the first two floors for 4€ adults or 3.10€ ages 25 and under. With this route, you also bypass the long lines for the elevator.

Champ de Mars, 7e. ✆ **01-44-11-23-23.** www.tour-eiffel.fr. Admission to 2nd landing 8€, 3rd landing 13€. Stairs to 2nd floor 4.50€. Sept–May daily 9:30am–11:45pm; June–Aug daily 9am–12:45am. Oct–June stairs open only to 6:30pm. Métro: Trocadéro, Ecole Militaire, or Bir Hakeim. RER: Champ de Mars-Tour Eiffel.

Hôtel des Invalides (Napoleon's Tomb) ★★★ The glory of the French military lives on in the Musée de l'Armée. The Sun King decided to build the "hotel" to house soldiers with disabilities. It wasn't entirely a benevolent gesture, because the veterans had been injured, crippled, or blinded while fighting Louis's battles. This massive building program was launched in 1670. Eventually a Jules Hardouin-Mansart gilded dome crowned the structure.

The best way to approach the Invalides is from the Right Bank across the pont Alexandre-III. Included in the collections (begun in 1794) are Viking swords, Burgundian basinets, 14th-century blunderbusses, Balkan khandjars, American Browning machine guns, war pitchforks, salamander-engraved Renaissance serpentines, musketoons, and grenadiers. You can even see General Daumesnil's wooden leg. There are suits of armor worn by kings and dignitaries, including the famous "armor suit of the lion" that was made for François I. The displays of swords are among the world's finest.

Crossing the Cour d'Honneur (Court of Honor), you'll come to **Eglise du Dôme,** designed by Hardouin-Mansart for Louis XIV. He began work on the church in 1677, though he died before its completion. In the Napoleon Chapel is the hearse used at the emperor's funeral on May 9, 1821.

To accommodate the Tomb of Napoleon—made of red porphyry, with a green granite base—architect Visconti had to redesign the high altar. First buried at St. Helena, Napoleon's remains were returned to Paris in 1840 and then locked inside six coffins. Surrounding the tomb are a dozen Amazon-like figures representing his victories. Almost lampooning the smallness of the man, everything is awesome: You'd think a real giant was buried here, not a symbolic one. The statue of Napoleon in his coronation robes stands 2.5m (8¼ ft.) tall.

Place des Invalides, 7e. © **01-44-42-37-72.** www.invalides.org. Admission to Musée de l'Armée, Napoleon's Tomb, and Musée des Plans-Reliefs 8.50€ adults, 6.50€ students, free for children 17 and under. Oct–Mar daily 10am–5pm; Dome Apr–Sept daily 10am–6pm. Closed Jan 1, May 1, Nov 1, and Dec 25. Métro: Latour-Maubourg, Varenne, Invalides, or St-Francois-Xavier.

Musée d'Orsay ★★★   The neoclassical Gare d'Orsay train station has been transformed into one of the world's great museums. It contains an important collection devoted to the pivotal years from 1848 to 1914. Across the Seine from the Louvre and the Tuileries, it is a repository of works by the Impressionists as well as the Symbolists, Pointillists, Realists, and late Romantics. Artists represented include van Gogh, Manet, Monet, Degas, and Renoir. It houses thousands of sculptures and paintings across 80 galleries, plus Belle Epoque furniture, photographs, objets d'art, architectural models, and a cinema.

One of Renoir's most joyous paintings is here: *Moulin de la Galette* (1876). Another celebrated work is by the American James McNeill Whistler—*Arrangement in Gray and Black: Portrait of the Painter's Mother.* The most famous piece in the museum is Manet's 1863 *Déjeuner sur l'herbe* (Picnic on the Grass), which created a scandal when it was first exhibited; it depicts a nude woman picnicking with two fully clothed men in a forest. Two years later, his *Olympia,* lounging on her bed wearing nothing but a flower in her hair and high-heeled shoes, met with the same response.

1 rue de Bellechasse or 62 rue de Lille, 7e. © **01-40-49-48-14.** www.musee-orsay.fr. Admission 8€ adults, 5.50€ ages 18–24, free ages 17 and under. Tues–Wed and Fri–Sun 9:30am–6pm; Thurs 9:30am–9:45pm. Closed Dec 25, Jan 1. Métro: Solférino. RER: Musée d'Orsay.

Musée du Louvre ★★★   The Louvre is one of the world's largest and greatest museums—and now more beautiful than ever since the facade has been thoroughly cleaned. The $1.2-billion Grand Louvre Project, a 15-year undertaking, is officially complete, but refurbishment of individual galleries and paintings continues. For up-to-the-minute data on what is open and about to open, check out the museum's website (www.louvre.fr).

The collection is staggering. You'll have to resign yourself to missing some masterpieces; you simply can't see everything. People on one of those Paris-in-a-day tours race to glimpse the *Mona Lisa* (in her own special room) and the *Venus de Milo.* Those with an extra 5 minutes go in pursuit of *Winged Victory,* the headless statue discovered at Samothrace that dates from about 200 B.C.

To enter the Louvre, you pass through the 21m (69-ft.) **I. M. Pei glass pyramid** in the courtyard. Commissioned by Mitterrand and completed in 1989, it received mixed reviews. The pyramid allows sunlight to shine on an underground reception area and shelters shops and restaurants beneath the Jardin du Carrousel.

Pressed for time? Take a **guided tour** (in English), which lasts about 90 minutes. The short tour, which is your only option if you visit on Monday, covers the "highlights of the highlights." Tours start under the pyramid at the station marked ACCUEIL DES GROUPES.

The collections are divided into eight departments: Asian antiquities; Egyptian antiquities; Greek, Etruscan, and Roman antiquities; Islamic art; sculpture; paintings; prints and drawings; and objets d'art. In 1997, President Jacques Chirac inaugurated nearly 10,000 sq. m (about 107,000 sq. ft.) of gallery space, most of it in the Sully wing, including a new presentation of Egyptian antiquities. It gave 60% more

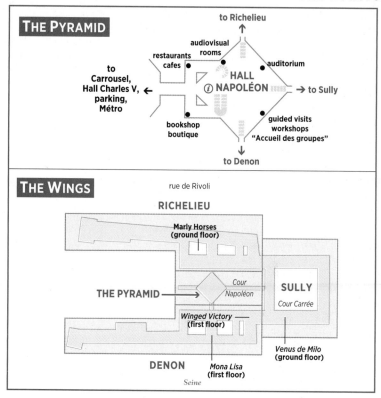

space to the world of the Pharaohs, a culture that has fascinated the French since Napoleon's occupation of Egypt in 1798.

Other areas include restored rooms of Greek, Etruscan, and Roman antiquities. The **Grand Galerie,** a 180m (591-ft.) hall opening onto the Seine, is dedicated to mostly Italian paintings from the 1400s to the 1700s, including works by Raphael and Leonardo da Vinci.

The **Richelieu Wing** houses the collection of northern European and French paintings, decorative arts, French sculpture, Oriental antiquities (a rich collection of Islamic art), and the grand salons of Napoleon III. Originally constructed from 1852 to 1857, this wing has been virtually rebuilt. In its 165 rooms, plus three covered courtyards, some 12,000 works of art are displayed. Of the Greek and Roman antiquities, the most notable (aside from *Venus* and *Winged Victory*) are fragments of the Parthenon's frieze.

We love Mona and Venus, but our eternal passion burns for Jacques-Louis David's *Portrait of Madame Récamier,* depicting Napoleon's opponent at age 23; on her comfortable sofa, she reclines in the style of classical antiquity. Other favorites of ours

Leaping over the Louvre Line

If you don't want to wait in line at the entrance to the Louvre pyramid, or use the automatic ticket machines, you can order tickets over the phone (📞 **08-92-68-46-94**) with a credit card. You can also order advance tickets and take a virtual tour at www. louvre.fr. Tickets can be mailed to you in the U.S., or you can pick them up at any Paris branch of the FNAC electronics chain.

are *Ship of Fools,* by Hieronymus Bosch, in the Flemish galleries; *Four Seasons,* by Nicolas Poussin, the canonical work of French classicism; Eugène Delacroix's *Liberty Leading the People,* perhaps the ultimate endorsement of revolution (Louis-Philippe purchased the painting and hid it during his reign); and Paolo Veronese's gigantic *Wedding Feast at Cana,* showing (if nothing else) how stunning color can be when applied by a master.

When you tire of strolling the galleries, you may like a pick-me-up at the Richelieu Wing's **Café Richelieu** (📞 **01-47-03-99-68**) or at **Café Marly,** 93 rue de Rivoli, 1er (📞 **01-49-26-06-60**), where we suggest a cafe crème, a club sandwich, a pastry, or something from the bistro menu.

34–36 quai du Louvre, 1er. Main entrance in the glass pyramid, Cour Napoleon. 📞 **01-40-20-53-17,** 01-40-20-50-50 for operator, or 08-92-68-46-94 for advance credit card sales. www.louvre.fr. Admission 9€, free for children 17 and under; free to all 1st Sun of every month. Sat–Mon and Thurs 9am–6pm; Wed and Fri 9am–10pm. 1½-hr. English-language tours (Mon and Wed–Sun) 6€, free for children 12 and under with museum ticket. Métro: Palais-Royal–Musée du Louvre.

Notre-Dame ★★★

For 6 centuries, it has stood as a Gothic masterpiece of the Middle Ages. We actually feel that Notre-Dame is more interesting outside than in. You'll have to walk around the entire structure to appreciate this "vast symphony of stone" with its classic flying buttresses. Better yet, cross the bridge to the Left Bank and view it from the quay.

From the square parvis (the courtyard in front), you can view the trio of 13th-century sculpted portals. On the left, the Portal of the Virgin depicts the signs of the zodiac and the Virgin's coronation. The central Portal of the Last Judgment is in three levels: The first shows Vices and Virtues; the second, Christ and his Apostles; and the third, Christ in triumph after the Resurrection. On the right is the Portal of Ste-Anne, depicting such scenes as the Virgin enthroned with Child. Over the central portal is a remarkable rose window, 9m (30 ft.) in diameter, forming a showcase for a statue of the Virgin and Child. Equally interesting is the Cloister Portal (around on the left), with its 13th-century Virgin, a unique survivor of many that originally adorned the facade. (Unfortunately, the Child she's holding is decapitated.)

If possible, view the interior at sunset. Of the three giant medallions that warm the austere cathedral, the north rose window in the transept, from the mid–13th century, is best. The interior is typical Gothic, with slender, graceful columns. The carved-stone choir screen from the early 14th century depicts biblical scenes. Near the altar stands the 14th-century Virgin and Child. Behind glass in the treasury is a

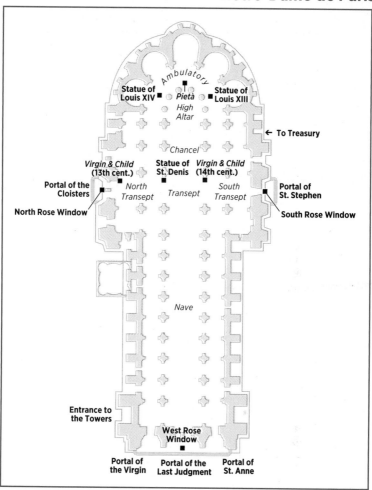

display of vestments and gold objects, including crowns. Notre-Dame is especially proud of its relic of the True Cross and the Crown of Thorns.

To visit the gargoyles immortalized by Victor Hugo (where Quasimodo lurked), you have to scale steps leading to the twin square towers, rising to a height of 68m (223 ft.). Once here, you can inspect those devils (some sticking out their tongues), hobgoblins, and birds of prey.

Approached through a garden behind Notre-Dame is the **Memorial des Martyrs Français de la Déportation** (© **01-46-33-87-56**), jutting out on the tip of the Ile de la Cité. This memorial honors the French martyrs of World War II, who

A Nighttime Walk & an "Abomination"

When Viollet-le-Duc designed the fly-ing buttresses of the cathedral of Notre-Dame, they were denounced as "horrendous," "a blight of Paris," and an "abomination." Now they are one of the structure's most interesting archi-tectural features. On the Ile de la Cité, wander through the garden in the rear of the cathedral. Near the square Jean XXIII, cross the pont de l'Archevêche and follow quai de Montebello along the Left Bank of the Seine for a won-derful perspective, especially when the Bateaux-Mouches light up the but-tresses as they pass along. You'll end up at the place St-Michel, where you can order a nightcap in a cafe.

were deported to camps such as Auschwitz and Buchenwald. In blood red are the words (in French): FORGIVE, BUT DON'T FORGET. It's open June to September daily from 10am to noon and from 2 to 7pm, and off season daily from 10am to noon and 2 to 5pm; admission is free.

6 place du parvis Notre-Dame, 4e. ☎ **01-53-10-07-02.** www.notredamedeparis.fr. Free admission to the cathedral. Towers 8€ adults, 5€ seniors and ages 13–25, free for children 17 and under. Treasury 3€ adults, 2€ ages 12–25, 1€ ages 6–12, free for children 5 and under. Cathedral year-round daily 8am–6:45pm (until 7:15pm Sat–Sun). Towers and crypt year-round Tues–Sun 10am–6pm (until 11pm Sat–Sun June–Aug). Museum Wed and Sat–Sun 2–5pm. Treasury Mon–Fri 9:30am–6pm, Sat 9:30am–6:30pm, Sun 1:30–6:30pm. Métro: Cité or St-Michel. RER: St-Michel.

Ste-Chapelle ★★★   Come here to see one of the world's greatest examples of Flamboyant Gothic architecture—"the pearl among them all," as Proust called it—and brilliant stained-glass windows with a lacelike delicacy. The reds are so red that Parisians have been known to use the phrase "wine the color of Ste-Chapelle's win-dows." Ste-Chapelle is Paris's second-most important monument from the Middle Ages (after Notre-Dame); it was erected to enshrine relics from the First Crusade, including the Crown of Thorns, two pieces from the True Cross, and the Roman lance that pierced the side of Christ. St. Louis (Louis IX) acquired the relics from the emperor of Constantinople and is said to have paid heavily for them, raising money through unscrupulous means.

Viewed on a bright day, the 15 stained-glass windows depicting Bible scenes seem to glow ruby red and Chartres blue. The walls consist almost entirely of the glass. Built in only 5 years, beginning in 1246, the chapel has two levels. You enter through the lower chapel, supported by flying buttresses and ornamented with fleurs-de-lis. The servants of the palace used the lower chapel, and the upper chamber was for the king and his courtiers; the latter is reached by ascending a narrow spiral staircase.

Ste-Chapelle stages **concerts** in March to November (daily at 7 and 8:30pm); tickets cost 19€ to 25€. Call ☎ **01-44-07-12-38** from 11am to 6pm daily for details.

Ste. Chapelle, 6 bd. du Palais, 1er. ☎ **01-53-40-60-80.** www.monum.fr. 8€ adults, 5€ ages 18–25, free 17 and under. Mar–Oct daily 9:30am–6pm; Nov–Feb daily 9am–5pm. Métro: Cité, St-Michel, or Châte-let-Les Halles. RER: St-Michel.

MUSÉE DU LOUVRE/LES HALLES: THE 1ST ARRONDISSEMENT (RIGHT BANK)

The 1st arrondissement is first for a reason: Several of the city's top attractions are here, including the **Louvre** and the Tuileries. It's also home to **Les Halles,** the major fruit, meat, and vegetable market of Paris for 8 centuries. But the smock-clad vendors, carcasses of beef, and baskets of vegetables all belong to the past. Today, the action has moved to a modern steel-and-glass structure at Rungis, a suburb near Orly. Here is **Les Forum des Halles** (Métro: Les Halles; RER: Châtelet–Les Halles), which opened in 1979. This large complex, much of it underground, houses dozens of shops, restaurants, and movie theaters.

For many visitors, a night on the town still ends in the wee hours with the traditional bowl of onion soup at Les Halles, usually at **Au Pied de Cochon (Pig's Foot;** ✆ **01-40-13-77-00;** www.pieddecochon.com) or **Au Chien Qui Fume** (**Smoking Dog;** ✆ **01-42-36-07-42;** www.auchienquifume.fr).

There's much to see in Les Halles, beginning with the **Eglise St-Eustache,** 2 rue du Jour, 1er (✆ **01-42-36-31-05;** www.saint-eustache.org; Métro: Les Halles), with another entrance on rue Rambuteau. In the old days, cabbage vendors came here to pray for their produce. The Gothic-Renaissance church dates from the mid–16th century, yet wasn't completed until 1637. It has been known for its organ recitals since Liszt played here in 1866. Inside is the black marble tomb of Jean-Baptiste Colbert, minister of state under Louis XIV. A statue of the statesman rests on top of his tomb, flanked by Coysevox's *Abundance* (a horn of flowers) and J. B. Tuby's *Fidelity.* The church is open Monday to Friday 9:30am to 7pm, Saturday 10am to 7pm, and Sunday 9am to 7pm. There's an organ concert Sunday at 6pm.

Jardin des Tuileries ★★ These spectacular, statue-studded gardens are as much a part of Paris as the Seine. Le Nôtre, Louis XIV's gardener and planner of the Versailles grounds, designed them. Some of the gardens' most distinctive statues are the 18 enormous bronzes by Maillol in the Jardin du Carrousel, a subdivision of the Jardins des Tuileries placed there in 1964 and 1965, under the direction of then Culture Minister André Malraux. About 400 years before that, Catherine de Médicis ordered a palace built here, connected to the Louvre; other occupants have included Louis XVI and Napoleon. Twice attacked by Parisians, it was burned to the ground in 1871 and never rebuilt. The trees are arranged according to designs, and the paths are arrow straight. Breaking the sense of order and formality are bubbling fountains.

Seemingly half of Paris wanders the Tuileries on a warm spring day, admiring the daffodils and tulips. As you walk toward the Louvre, you'll enter the **Jardin du Carrousel,** dominated by the **Arc de Triomphe du Carrousel.** Pierced with three walkways and supported by marble columns, the monument honors Napoleon's Grande Armée, celebrating its victory at Austerlitz on December 5, 1805. The arch is surmounted by statuary, a chariot, and four bronze horses, and is open daily as follows: April, May, and September 7am to 9pm, June to August 7am to 11pm, and October to March 7:30am to 7:30pm.

Bordering place de la Concorde, 1er. ✆ **01-40-20-90-43.** Métro: Tuileries.

Jeu de Paume   After knowing many roles, this museum has become a center for photography and video, exploring "the world of images, their uses, and the issues they raise." Its exhibitions not only display photography but mechanical or electronic images. It is now one of the finest museums of its type in the world and presents ever-changing exhibitions, many of them daringly avant-garde.

For years the national gallery in the Jeu de Paume, in the northeast corner of the Tuileries Gardens, was one of the treasures of Paris, displaying some of the finest works of the Impressionists. In 1986 that collection was hauled off to the Musée d'Orsay, to the regret of many. Following a $12.6-million face-lift, this Second Empire building has been transformed into a series of state-of-the-art galleries.

Originally, in this part of the gardens, Napoleon III built a ball court on which *jeu de paume,* an antecedent of tennis, was played—hence the museum's name. The most infamous period in the national gallery's history came during the Nazi occupation, when it served as an "evaluation center" for works of modern art. Paintings from all over France were shipped to the Jeu de Paume; art condemned by the Nazis as "degenerate" was burned.

1 place de la Concorde, 8e. © **01-47-03-12-50.** www.jeudepaume.org. Admission 7€ adults, 5€ students and children. Tues noon–9pm; Wed–Fri noon–7pm; Sat–Sun 10am–7pm. Métro: Concorde.

Musée de l'Orangerie ★   In the Tuileries stands this gem among galleries. It has an outstanding collection of art and one celebrated painting on display: Claude Monet's exquisite *Nymphéas* (1915–27), in which waterlilies float amorphously on the canvas. The waterlilies are displayed as the artist intended them to be—lit by sunlight in large oval galleries that evoke the shape of the garden ponds at his former Giverny estate.

Creating his effects with hundreds and hundreds of minute strokes of his brush (one irate 19th-c. critic called them "tongue lickings"), Monet achieved unity and harmony, as he did in his Rouen Cathedral series and his haystacks. Monet continued to paint his water landscapes right up until his death in 1926, although he was greatly hampered by failing eyesight.

The renovated building also houses the art collections of two men, John Walter and Paul Guillaume, who are not connected to each other, except that they were both married at different times to the same woman. Their collection includes more than 24 Renoirs, including *Young Girl at a Piano.* Cézanne is represented by 14 works, notably *The Red Rock,* and Matisse by 11 paintings. The highlight of Rousseau's nine works displayed here is *The Wedding,* and the dozen paintings by Picasso reach the pinnacle of their brilliance in *The Female Bathers.* Other outstanding paintings are by Utrillo (10 works in all), Soutine (22), and Derain (28).

Jardin des Tuileries, 1er. © **01-44-77-80-07.** www.musee-orangerie.fr. Admission 7.50€ adults, 5.50€ students 25 and under. Free 1st Sun of every month. Wed–Mon 9am–6pm. Closed May 1–Dec 25. Métro: Concorde.

Musée des Arts Décoratifs   In the northwest wing of the Louvre's Pavillon de Marsan, this museum holds a treasury of furnishings, fabrics, wallpaper, objets d'art, and items displaying living styles from the Middle Ages to the present. Notable are the 1920s Art Deco boudoir, bathroom, and bedroom done for couturier Jeanne Lanvin by the designer Rateau, plus a collection of the works donated by Jean Dubuffet. Decorative art from the Middle Ages to the Renaissance is on the second floor; collections from the 17th, 18th, and 19th centuries occupy the third and fourth floors. The fifth floor has specialized centers, such as wallpaper and drawings, and exhibits detailing fashion, textiles, toys, crafts, and glass trends.

Palais du Louvre, 107 rue de Rivoli, 1er. © **01-44-55-57-50.** www.lesartsdecoratifs.fr. Admission 8€ adults, 6.50€ ages 18–25, free for children 17 and under. Tues–Fri 11am–6pm (Thurs until 9pm); Sat–Sun 10am–6pm. Métro: Palais-Royal or Tuileries.

Palais Royal   At the demolished Café Foy in the Palais Royal, the outraged Camille Desmoulins jumped on a table and shouted for the mob "to fight to the death." The date was July 13, 1789. The renown of the Palais Royal goes back even farther. The gardens were planted in 1634 for Cardinal Richelieu. It later became the residence of the ducs d'Orléans. Philippe-Egalité, a cousin of Louis XVI, built his apartments on the grounds and later rented them to prostitutes. By the 20th century, such artists as Cocteau and Colette rented the apartments. (A plaque at 9 rue Beaujolais marks the entrance to Colette's apartment.) Today, the Palais Royal contains apartments, shops, and a few restaurants such as **Le Grand Véfour** (© **01-42-96-56-27;** www.grand-vefour.com; p. 124). Note sculptor Daniel Buren's prison-striped columns, added in 1986, and Pol Bury's steel-ball sculptures decorating the fountains.

Rue St-Honoré, on place du Palais-Royal, 1er. No phone. Free admission. Métro: Palais-Royal–Musée du Louvre.

LE MARAIS: THE 3RD ARRONDISSEMENT (RIGHT BANK)

When Paris began to overflow the confines of the Ile de la Cité in the 13th century, the citizenry settled in Le Marais, a marsh flooded regularly by the Seine. By the 17th century, the Marais had reached the pinnacle of fashion, becoming the center of aristocratic Paris. At that time, most of its great *hôtels particuliers* (mansions)—many now restored or being spruced up—were built by the finest craftsmen in France.

In the 18th and 19th centuries, the fashionable deserted the Marais in favor of Faubourg St-Germain and Faubourg St-Honoré. Industry took over the quarter, and the once-elegant hôtels became tenements. There was talk of demolishing this sector, but in 1962, the Comité de Sauvegarde du Marais saved the district. The Centre Pompidou sparked the neighborhood's regeneration.

No longer "the Swamp" (its English name), the Marais, in the 3rd arrondissement and part of the 4th, is trendy once again, filled with tiny twisting streets, gay and straight bars, and cutting-edge designer shops.

In **place de la Bastille** on July 14, 1789, a mob attacked the Bastille and sparked the French Revolution. Nothing remains of the Bastille, built in 1369. Many prisoners—some sentenced by Louis XIV for "witchcraft"—were kept within; the best known was the "Man in the Iron Mask." When the fortress was stormed, only seven prisoners were discovered (the marquis de Sade had been transferred to an asylum 10 days earlier). Authorities had discussed razing it anyway, so the attack was more symbolic than anything else. What it started will never be forgotten. Bastille Day is celebrated every July 14. In the center of the square is the **Colonne de Juillet (July Column),** honoring the victims of the 1830 July Revolution, which put

Louis-Philippe on the throne. The God of Liberty, a winged nude with a star emerging from his head, crowns the tower.

Not far away, **place des Vosges ★★★**, 4e (Métro: St-Paul or Chemin Vert), is Paris's oldest square and once its most fashionable. It was called the Palais Royal in the days of Henri IV, who planned to live here—but his assassin, Ravaillac, had other ideas. Henri II was killed while jousting on the square in 1559, in the shadow of the Hôtel des Tournelles. His widow, Catherine de Médicis, had the place torn down. Place des Vosges, once a dueling ground, was one of Europe's first planned squares. Its *grand siècle* red-brick houses are ornamented with white stone, and its covered arcades allowed people to shop even in the rain—an innovation at the time. In the 18th century, chestnut trees were added, sparking a controversy that continues to this day: Critics say that the addition spoils the perspective.

As you stroll the Marais, you might want to seek out the **Hôtel de Rohan,** 87 rue Vieille-du-Temple (℄ **01-40-27-60-96**), once occupied by the fourth Cardinal Rohan, who was involved in the scandal that framed Marie Antoinette for buying a priceless diamond necklace. The main attraction is the 18th-century Salon des Singes (Monkey Room). In the courtyard is a stunning bas-relief of a nude Apollo and four horses against exploding sunbursts. The hotel (mansion), which is administered by France's National Archives, can be visited only during special exhibitions announced in Paris newspapers.

At 47 rue Vieille-du-Temple is the **Hôtel des Ambassadeurs de Hollande,** where Beaumarchais wrote *The Marriage of Figaro.* Never occupied by the Dutch embassy, it is one of the most splendid mansions in the area and is closed to the public.

Although the facade of the 17th-century **Hôtel de Beauvais,** 68 rue François-Miron, was damaged during the Revolution, it remains one of the most charming in Paris. A plaque commemorates the fact that Mozart inhabited the mansion in 1763. To visit inside, speak to the Association du Paris Historique, on the ground floor of the building, any afternoon.

Hôtel de Sens, 1 rue de Figuier (℄ **01-42-78-14-60**), was built from the 1470s to 1519 for the archbishops of Sens. Along with the Hôtel de Cluny, it's the only domestic architecture remaining from the 15th century. Long after the archbishops had departed in 1605, the scandalous Queen Margot, wife of Henri IV, occupied it. Her "younger and more virile" new lover slew the discarded one as she looked on. Today, the mansion houses the Bibliothèque Forney. The gate is open Tuesday to Saturday 1:30 to 8:30pm.

Work began on the **Hôtel de Bethune-Sully,** 62 rue St-Antoine (℄ **01-44-61-21-50**), in 1625. In 1634, the duc de Sully, who had been Henri IV's minister of finance, acquired it. After a strait-laced early life, Sully broke loose, adorning himself with diamonds and garish rings—and a bride who had a preference for younger men. The mansion was acquired by the government after World War II and holds the National Office of Historical Monuments and Sites. Recently restored, the relief-studded facade is appealing. There's daily admittance from 9am to 7pm to the courtyard and the garden that opens onto place des Vosges.

The **rue des Rosiers (Street of the Rosebushes)** is one of the most colorful of the streets remaining from the old Jewish quarter. The Star of David shines here,

Hebrew letters flash (in neon), shops run by Moroccan or Algerian Jews sell cous-cous, bearded men sit in doorways, restaurants serve kosher meals, and signs appeal for Jewish liberation.

Shoppers will delight in such places as **Passage de Retz,** 9 rue Charlot (© **01-48-04-37-99;** www.passagederetz.com), an avant-garde gallery that was established in 1994 and has the most amusing exhibitions in the Marais. At **Hier, Aujourd'hui, et Demain,** 14 rue de Bretagne (© **01-42-77-69-02**), you'll fall in love with 1930s Art Deco.

Musée Carnavalet–Histoire de Paris ★★ The history of Paris comes alive here in intimate terms—down to the chessmen Louis XVI used to distract himself in the days before he went to the guillotine. A renowned Renaissance palace, the mansion was built in 1544 by Pierre Lescot and Jean Goujon and acquired by Mme. de Carnavalet. The great François Mansart transformed it between 1655 and 1661. It's best known because one of history's most famous letter writers, Mme. de Sévigné, moved here in 1677. Fanatically devoted to her daughter (until she had to live with her), she poured out nearly every detail of her life in letters, virtually ignoring her son. A native of the Marais, she died at her daughter's château in 1696. In 1866 the city turned the building into a museum.

23 rue de Sévigné, 3e. © **01-44-59-58-58.** www.carnavalet.paris.fr. Free admission. Special exhibits 5€ adults, 4.20€ students. Tues–Sun 10am–6pm. Métro: St-Paul or Chemin Vert.

WHERE PARIS WAS BORN: ILE DE LA CITE & THE 4TH ARRONDISSEMENT

Medieval Paris, that architectural blending of grotesquerie and Gothic beauty, began on this island in the Seine. Explore as much of it as you can, but at least visit **Notre-Dame** (see "The Top Attractions," earlier in this chapter), the Ste-Chapelle, and the Conciergerie. The 4th arrondissement is on the Right Bank, opposite the island.

Conciergerie ★★ This is the most sinister building in France. Though it had a long, regal history before the Revolution, it's visited today chiefly by those wishing to bask in the Reign of Terror's horrors. The Conciergerie conjures images of the days when tumbrels hauled victims to the guillotine. You approach the Conciergerie through its twin towers, the Tour d'Argent and Tour de César, though the 14th-century vaulted Guard Room is the actual entrance. Also from the 14th century is the vast, dark, foreboding Salle des Gens d'Armes (People at Arms), transformed from the days when the king used it as a banquet hall.

Few of the prisoners in the Conciergerie's history endured tortures as severe as those inflicted on Ravaillac, who assassinated Henri IV in 1610. He got the full treatment: pincers in the flesh, hot lead and boiling oil poured on him. This was also where Marie Antoinette awaited her trial and eventual beheading.

1 quai de l'Horloge, 4e. © **01-53-40-60-80.** www.monum.fr. Admission 7€ adults, 4.50€ ages 18–25, free for children 17 and under. Mar–Oct daily 9:30am–6pm; Nov–Feb daily 9am–5pm. Métro: Cité, Châtelet, or St-Michel. RER: St-Michel.

THE CHAMPS-ELYSEES, PARIS'S GRAND PROMENADE: THE 8TH ARRONDISSEMENT (RIGHT BANK)

In late 1995, after two hard, dusty, and costly years of construction, great improvements in Paris's most prominent triumphal promenade were unveiled. The *contre-allées* (side lanes that had always been clogged with parked cars) were removed (new underground garages alleviate the parking problem), lighting was added, pedestrian sidewalks were widened, and new trees were planted. Now the Grand Promenade truly is grand again—with the exception of all of those fast-food joints.

Musée Jacquemart-André ★★ 🎁 This is the best decorative-arts museum in Paris, though it's no place to take the kids (unless they're aspiring decorators). Plan at least 2 hours. The museum is the legacy of the André family, prominent Protestants in the 19th century. The family's last scion, Edouard André, spent most of his adult life stationed abroad in the French army, returning to marry Nélie Jacquemart, a well-known portraitist. They compiled a collection of French 18th-century decorative art and European paintings in an 1850s town house, which they continually redecorated according to the fashions of their time.

In 1912, Mme. André willed the house and its collections to the Institut de France, which paid for extensive renovations and enlargements completed in 1996. The collection's highlights are works by Bellini, Carpaccio, and Uccelo; Houdon busts; Gobelin tapestries; Savonnerie carpets; della Robbia terra cottas; awesome antiques; and works by Rembrandt (*The Pilgrim of Emmaus*), Van Dyck, Rubens, Watteau, Fragonard, and Boucher. After a major restoration, one of the most outstanding exhibits is a group of three mid-18th-century frescoes by Giambattista Tiepolo; this is the only museum in France with frescoes by the Venetian master. The works depict spectators on balconies viewing Henri III's arrival in Venice in 1574. Take a break from the Gilded Age opulence with a cup of tea or a tart in Mme. André's dining room, hung with 18th-century tapestries.

158 bd. Haussmann, 8e. 🕻 **01-45-62-11-59.** www.musee-jacquemart-andre.com. Admission 10€ adults, 7.50€ children 7–17, free for children 6 and under. Daily 10am–6pm. Métro: Miromesnil or St-Philippe-du-Roule.

Place Vendôme ★★ Always aristocratic and often royal, place Vendôme enjoyed its golden age during the Second Empire. Fashion designers such as Worth introduced the crinoline here. Louis Napoleon lived here, wooing his empress, Eugénie de Montijo, at the Hôtel du Rhin. In its halcyon days, Strauss waltzes echoed across the plaza. In time they were replaced by cannon fire. A column crowned by Napoleon dominates the square. There was a statue of the Sun King until the Revolution, when it was replaced by *Liberty.*

Then came Napoleon, who ordered that a sort of Trajan's Column be erected in honor of his victory at Austerlitz. It was made of bronze from captured Russian and Austrian cannons. After Napoleon's downfall, the statue was replaced by one of Henri IV, everybody's favorite king and every woman's favorite man. Later Napoleon mounted it again, in uniform and without the pose of a Caesar.

WHERE ROYAL HEADS rolled

The eastern end of the Champs-Elysées is one of the world's grand squares, **place de la Concorde,** an octagonal traffic hub built in 1757 to honor Louis XV. The statue of the king was torn down in 1792 and the name changed to place de la Révolution. It's dominated by an **Egyptian obelisk** from Luxor, the oldest man-made object in Paris; it was carved around 1200 B.C. and given to France in 1829 by the viceroy of Egypt.

During the Reign of Terror, Dr. Guillotin's invention was erected on this spot, where it claimed thousands of lives—from Louis XVI, who died bravely, to Mme. du Barry, who went kicking and screaming. Before the leering crowds, Marie Antoinette, Robespierre, Danton, Mlle. Roland, and Charlotte Corday lost their heads. (You can still lose your life on place de la Concorde if you chance the frantic traffic and try to cross over.)

For a spectacular sight, look down the Champs-Elysées—the view is framed by Coustou's Marly horses, which once graced the gardens at Louis XIV's Château de Marly. (These are copies; the originals are in the Louvre.) On the opposite side, Coysevox's winged horses flank the gateway to the Tuileries. On each side of the obelisk are fountains with bronze-tailed mermaids and bare-breasted sea nymphs. Gray-beige statues ring the square, honoring the cities of France. To symbolize Strasbourg's fall to Germany in 1871, that city's statue was covered with a black drape that wasn't lifted until the end of World War I. Two of the palaces on place de la Concorde are today the Ministry of the Marine and the deluxe Hôtel de Crillon. Jacques-Ange Gabriel designed them in the 1760s.

The Communards of 1871, who detested royalty, pulled down the statue. Courbet is said to have led the raid, for which he was jailed and fined the cost of restoring the statue. He couldn't pay it and was forced into exile in Switzerland. Eventually, the statue of Napoleon, wrapped in a Roman toga, won out.

Place Vendôme, 8e. Métro: Opéra.

MONTMARTRE: THE 18TH ARRONDISSEMENT (RIGHT BANK)

From the 1880s to just before World War I, Montmartre enjoyed its golden age as the world's best-known art colony, where *la vie de bohème* reigned supreme. Following World War I, pseudo-artists flocked here, with tourists hot on their heels. The real artists had long gone to such places as Montparnasse.

Before its discovery, Montmartre was a sleepy farming community, with windmills dotting the landscape. Those who find the trek up to Paris's highest elevations too much of a climb may prefer to ride **Le Petit Train de Montmartre,** which passes all the major landmarks; it seats 55 passengers and offers English commentary. Board at place Blanche (near the Moulin Rouge); the fare is 6€ adults, 3.50€ children 10 and under, free under 4. Trains run daily 10am to 6pm, until midnight in

July and August. For information, contact **Promotrain,** 131 rue de Clignancourt, 18e (✆ **01-42-62-24-00**).

The simplest way to reach Montmartre is to take the Métro to Anvers and then walk up rue du Steinkerque to the **funicular,** which runs to the precincts of Sacré-Coeur every day 6:15am to 12:45am. The fare is one Métro ticket. Except for Sacré-Coeur (see "The Top Attractions," earlier in this chapter), Montmartre has only minor attractions; it's the historic architecture and the atmosphere that are compelling.

Specific attractions to look for include the **Bateau-Lavoir (Boat Warehouse),** on place Emile-Goudeau. Gutted by fire in 1970, it has been reconstructed. Picasso once lived here and, in the winter of 1905 and 1906, painted one of the world's most famous portraits, *The Third Rose* (Gertrude Stein).

L'Espace Montmartre Salvador-Dalí, 11 rue Poulbot, 18e (✆ **01-42-64-40-10;** www.daliparis.com), presents Dalí's phantasmagorical world with 330 original works, including his 1956 *Don Quixote* lithograph. It's open daily from 10am to 6pm (July to August until 8pm); admission is 10€ for adults, 7€ seniors, 6€ for ages 8 to 18 and students, and free for children 7 and under.

One of the most famous churches here is the **Eglise St-Pierre** on rue du Mont-Cenis. The church was consecrated in 1147; two columns in the choir stall are the remains of a Roman temple. Among the sculptured works, note the nun with the head of a pig, a symbol of sensual vice. At the entrance are three bronze doors sculpted by Gismondi in 1980: The middle door depicts the life of St. Peter; the left is dedicated to St. Denis; and the right honors the Holy Virgin.

Musée de Vieux Montmartre, 12 rue Cortot, 18e (✆ **01-49-25-89-37;** www.museedemontmartre.fr), exhibits a wide collection of mementos. Dufy, van Gogh, Renoir, and Suzanne Valadon and her son, Utrillo, once occupied this 17th-century house. It's open Tuesday to Sunday 11am to 6pm; admission is 7€ for adults, 5.50€ for students and ages 12 to 26. Free for children 11 and under.

Cimetière de Montmartre ★ Novelist Alexandre Dumas and Russian dancer Vaslav Nijinsky are just a few of the famous composers, writers, and artists interred here. The remains of the great Stendhal are here, as are Hector Berlioz, Heinrich Heine, Edgar Degas, Jacques Offenbach, and even François Truffaut. We like to pay our respects at the tomb of Alphonsine Plessis, the courtesan on whom Dumas based his Marguerite Gautier in *La Dame aux Camélias*. Emile Zola was interred here, but his corpse was taken to the Panthéon in 1908. In 1871, the cemetery became the site of the mass burials of victims of the Siege and the Commune.

20 av. Rachel (west of the Butte Montmartre and north of bd. de Clichy), 18e. ✆ **01-53-42-36-30.** Mon–Fri 8am–6pm; Sat 8:30am–6pm; Sun 9am–6pm (until 5:30pm in winter). Métro: La Fourche.

LA VILLETTE: THE 19TH ARRONDISSEMENT (RIGHT BANK)

Cité des Sciences et de l'Industrie ★★ ☺ Opened in 1986, this science complex, designed to "modernize mentalities" as part of the process of modernizing society, is so vast that a single visit gives only a glimpse of its scope. Some exhibits have an overlay of Gallic humor, including seismographic activity presented as the comic-strip adventures of a jungle explorer. The silver-skinned Géode (a geodesic dome) is a 34m (112-ft.) sphere with a 370-seat theater. Explora, a permanent exhibit, spreads over the three upper levels; its displays revolve around four themes: the universe, life, matter, and communication. The Cité has a multimedia library, a planetarium, and an "inventorium" for children.

At Cinaxe, sophisticated audio systems and oversize screens combine to enhance the sensations of film scenes. The experience includes episodes representing what you'd see, for example, in an airplane flying over mountains or if you were on the nose cone of a rocket.

The *Argonaute* is a submarine built in 1905 as part of a scientific experiment and a forerunner of the giant nuclear subs whose construction was partially based on ideas developed here. It was disarmed in 1982 and would have been demolished but for its purchase by the Musée de la Villette. Today, it's a source of pride, although it's firmly mounted on concrete and is never submerged.

La Cité des Enfants consists of three sections, one each for ages 3 to 5 and ages 6 to 12, plus a special section about electricity. This is an adventure playground, with watersports, a butterfly greenhouse, robots, an ant farm, interactive TVs, and even a Techno Cité that explains the workings of computers and other machines.

The Cité is in **Parc de La Villette,** Paris's largest park, with 54 hectares (133 acres) of greenery. You'll find a belvedere, a video workshop for children, and information about exhibitions, along with a cafe and restaurant.

In the Parc de La Villette, 30 av. Corentine-Cariou, La Villette, 19e. ✆ **01-40-05-70-00.** www.cite-sciences.fr. Ticket options 8€–20€ adults, 6€–16€ ages 7–24, free for 6 and under. Tues–Sat 10am–6pm; Sun 10am–7pm. Métro: Porte de La Villette.

Musée de la Musique   Housed in the stone-and-glass Cité de la Musique, this museum is a tribute to the rich musical traditions of many ages and cultures. You can view 4,500 instruments, as well as paintings, engravings, and sculptures that relate to musical history. One appealing section of mandolins, lutes, and zithers evokes music from the 17th century. It's all here: cornets disguised as snakes, antique music boxes, even an electric guitar. As part of the permanent collection, models of the world's great concert halls and interactive display areas give you a chance to hear and better understand the art and technology of musical heritage.

In the Cité de la Musique, 221 av. Jean-Jaurès, 19e. ✆ **01-44-84-45-00.** www.cite-musique.fr. Admission 8€ adults, 6€ students 19–25, 6€ children 18 and under. Tues–Sat noon–6pm; Sun 10am–7pm. Métro: Porte de Pantin.

TROCADERO: THE 16TH ARRONDISSEMENT (RIGHT BANK)

La Cité de l'Architecture et du Patrimoine ★ ☺   After a decade-long make-over, the City of Architecture and Heritage was opened by President Nicolas Sarkozy in 2007. With its trio of galleries and vast space, the museum is the largest architectural museum in the world. It lies in the east wing of the Palais de Chaillot on a hill overlooking a curve of the Seine, with panoramic views of Paris in all directions. The Eiffel Tower looms just across the river.

Exhibits are devoted to 12 centuries of French architecture, the most stunning of which is the **reproduction of the stained-glass window ★★** in the Gothic cathedral at Chartres. Other exhibits include a walk-in replica of Le Corbusier's mid-20th-century Cité Radieuse in Marseille.

In all there are 350 plaster cast reproductions of some of the greatest achievements in French architecture, going back to the Middle Ages. One gallery reproduces France's remarkable paintings and frescoes from the 12th to the 16th centuries. A third gallery is devoted to modern architecture right up to a turn-of-the-millennium cultural center in New Caledonia in the South Pacific. Children can build their own architectural masterpieces with LEGOS and other materials.

1 place du Trocadéro, 16è. ℂ **01-58-51-52-00.** www.citechaillot.fr. Admission 8€ adults, 5€ students, free for ages 18 and under. Wed–Mon 11am–7pm (9pm Thurs). Métro: Trocadéro.

THE LATIN QUARTER: THE 5TH ARRONDISSEMENT (LEFT BANK)

This is the precinct of the **University of Paris (the Sorbonne),** where students meet and fall in love over coffee and croissants. Rabelais called it the Quartier Latin because the students and professors spoke Latin in the classrooms and on the streets. The sector teems with belly dancers, restaurants from Vietnamese to Balkan, cafes, bookstalls, and *caveaux* (basement clubs).

A good starting point is **place St-Michel** (Métro: St-Michel), where Balzac used to get water from the fountain when he was a youth. This center was the scene of much Resistance fighting in the summer of 1944. The quarter centers on **boulevard St-Michel** (known as "Boul' Mich"), to the south.

La Sorbonne   The University of Paris—everybody calls it the Sorbonne—was founded in the 13th century, and by the 14th century it had become the most prestigious university in the West, drawing such professors as Thomas Aquinas. Reorganized by Napoleon in 1806, the Sorbonne today is the premier university of France. At first glance it may seem architecturally undistinguished; it was rather indiscriminately reconstructed at the turn of the 20th century. Not so the **Eglise de la Sorbonne,** built in 1635 by Le Mercier at the center of the Sorbonne. It contains the marble tomb of Cardinal Richelieu, a work by Girardon based on a Le Brun design. At his feet is the remarkable statue *Science in Tears.*

Bd. St-Michel. Métro: St-Michel.

Musée National du Moyen Age (Thermes de Cluny) ★★   This museum has two draws: the world's finest collection of art from the Middle Ages, including jewelry and tapestries; and the well-preserved manor house, built atop Roman baths, that holds the collection. In the cobblestone **Cour d'Honneur,** you can admire the Flamboyant Gothic building, with its clinging vines, turreted walls, gargoyles, and dormers with seashell motifs. Along with the Hôtel de Sens in the Marais, this is all that remains in Paris of domestic medieval architecture.

The Cluny was the mansion of a 15th-century abbot. By 1515, it was the home of Mary Tudor, the widow of Louis XII and daughter of Henry VII of England and

Elizabeth of York. Seized during the Revolution, it was rented in 1833 to Alexandre du Sommerard, who adorned it with medieval works of art. After his death in 1842, the government bought the building and the collection.

Most people come to see the **Unicorn Tapestries ★★★**, the world's most outstanding tapestries. They were discovered a century ago in the Château de Boussac in the Auvergne. Five of the six tapestries seem to deal with the senses (one depicts a unicorn looking into a mirror held by a maiden). The sixth shows a woman under an elaborate tent, her pet dog resting on an embroidered cushion beside her. The lovable unicorn and its friendly companion, a lion, hold back the flaps. The red-and-green background forms a rich carpet of spring flowers, fruit-laden trees, birds, rabbits, donkeys, dogs, goats, lambs, and monkeys.

Downstairs are the ruins of the Roman baths, dating from around A.D. 200. You can wander through a display of Gallic and Roman sculptures and an interesting marble bathtub engraved with lions.

Insider tip: The garden represents a return to the Middle Ages. It was inspired by the luxuriant detail of the museum's most fabled treasure, the 15th-century tapestry of *The Lady of the Unicorn*. It's small but richly planted.

In the Hôtel de Cluny, 6 place Paul-Painlevé, 5e. © **01-53-73-78-00** or 01-53-73-78-16. www.museemoyenage.fr. Admission 8€ adults, free 25 and under. Wed–Mon 9:15am–5:45pm. Métro: Cluny-La Sorbonne, Saint-Michel, or Odéon.

Panthéon ★★ Some of the most famous men in the history of France (Victor Hugo, for one) are buried in austere grandeur here, on the crest of the mount of Ste-Geneviève. In 1744, Louis XV vowed that if he recovered from a mysterious illness, he would build a church to replace the Abbaye de Ste-Geneviève. He recovered—and Mme. de Pompadour's brother hired Soufflot for the job. He designed the church in the form of a Greek cross, with a dome reminiscent of St. Paul's in London. When Soufflot died, his pupil Rondelet carried out the work, completing the structure 9 years after his master's death.

After the Revolution, the church was converted into a "Temple of Fame," a pantheon for great men. Mirabeau was buried here, though his remains were later removed. Marat was another temporary tenant. Voltaire's body was exhumed and placed here—and allowed to remain. In the 19th century, the building changed roles many times—it was a church, then a pantheon, and again a church. After Hugo was buried here, it became a pantheon once more. Other men entombed include Jean-Jacques Rousseau, Emile Zola, and Louis Braille.

In 1995, the ashes of scientist Marie Curie were entombed, "the first lady so honored in our history for her own merits," in the words of François Mitterrand. Another woman, Sophie Bertholet, was buried here first, alongside her chemist husband, Marcellin, but not as a personal honor to her.

The finest frescoes, by Puvis de Chavannes, are at the end of the left wall before you enter the crypt. One illustrates Ste-Geneviève bringing supplies to relieve the victims of the famine. The best depicts her white-draped head looking out over moonlit medieval Paris, the city whose patroness she became.

Place du Panthéon, 5e. © **01-44-32-18-00.** www.monum.fr. Admission 8€ adults, 5€ ages 18–25, free for children 17 and under. Apr–Sept daily 10am–6:30pm; Oct–Mar daily 10am–6pm (last entrance 45 min. before closing). Métro: Cardinal Lemoine or Maubert-Mutualité.

ST-GERMAIN-DES-PRES: THE 6TH ARRONDISSEMENT (LEFT BANK)

This area was the postwar home of existentialism, associated with Jean-Paul Sartre, Simone de Beauvoir, Albert Camus, and the intellectual, bohemian crowd that gathered at the Café de Flore, the Brasserie Lipp, and Les Deux-Magots. The black-clad poet Juliette Greco was known as *la muse de St-Germain-des-Prés,* and to Sartre she was the woman with "millions of poems in her throat." Her long hair and uniform of black slacks, black turtleneck sweater, and sandals launched a fashion trend adopted by young women from Paris to California.

In the 1950s, new names appeared—Françoise Sagan, Gore Vidal, and James Baldwin—but by the 1960s, tourists had become entrenched at the cafes. Today, St-Germain-des-Prés retains a bohemian street life, full of bookshops, art galleries, *caveaux* nightclubs, bistros, and coffeehouses.

Eglise St-Germain-des-Prés ★★   Outside, it's a handsome early-17th-century town house; inside, it's one of Paris's oldest churches, dating from the 6th century when a Benedictine abbey was founded on the site. The columns in the triforium are all that remain from that period. Restoration of the Chapelle St-Symphorien— the site of a pantheon for Merovingian kings—began in 1981. During that work, unknown Romanesque paintings were discovered on the chapel's triumphal arch. The Romanesque tower, topped by a 19th-century spire, is the most enduring landmark in St-Germain-des-Prés. Patrons of Les Deux-Magots, across the way, hardly notice the church bells.

 Gregorians Unplugged

Eglise St-Germain-des-Prés stages concerts on the Left Bank. With fantastic acoustics and a medieval atmosphere, the unamplified sound will thrill you. Call ✆ **01-42-64-83-16.** Arrive about 45 minutes before a performance for a good seat. Tickets range from 20€ to 45€.

The Normans nearly destroyed the abbey at least four times. The present building has a Romanesque nave and a Gothic choir with fine capitals. Among the people interred at the church are Descartes (well, his heart at least) and Jean-Casimir, the king of Poland who abdicated his throne.

When you leave the church, turn right onto rue de l'Abbaye and have a look at the 17th-century (and very pink) Palais Abbatial.

3 place St-Germain-des-Prés, 6e. ✆ **01-55-42-81-33.** www.eglise-sgp.org. Free admission. Mon–Sat 8am–7:45pm; Sun 9am–8pm. Métro: St-Germain-des-Prés.

Eglise St-Sulpice ★★   Pause first on the rue St-Sulpice. The 1844 fountain by Visconti displays the likenesses of four bishops of the Louis XIV era: Fenelon, Massillon, Bossuet, and Flechier. Work on the church itself, once Paris's largest, began in 1646 as part of the Catholic revival in France. Although the body of the church was completed in 1745, work on the bell towers continued until 1780, when one was finished and the other left incomplete. One of its most notable treasures is Servandoni's rococo Chapelle de la Vierge (Chapel of the Madonna), which contains a Pigalle statue of the Virgin. The church houses one of the world's largest organs; it has 6,700 pipes and has been played by such musicians as Charles-Marie Widor and Marcel Dupré.

The main draw is the Delacroix frescoes in the Chapel of the Angels (on your right as you enter). Seek out his Jacob wrestling (or is he dancing?) with an angel. On the ceiling, St. Michael has his own troubles with the devil, and another mural depicts Heliodorus being driven from the temple. Painted in the final years of his life, the frescoes were a high point in the baffling career of Delacroix.

Rue St-Sulpice, 6e. ✆ **01-46-33-21-78.** www.paroisse-saint-sulpice-paris.org. Free admission. Daily 7:30am–7:30pm. Métro: St-Sulpice.

THE EIFFEL TOWER/ MUSEE D'ORSAY: THE 7TH ARRONDISSEMENT (LEFT BANK)

From place du Trocadéro, you can stand between the two curved wings of the Palais de Chaillot and gaze out on a panoramic view. At your feet are the Jardins du Trocadéro, centered by fountains. Directly in front, pont d'Iéna spans the Seine, leading to the **Eiffel Tower.** Beyond, stretching as far as your eye can see, is the **Champ-de-Mars,** once a military parade ground and now a garden with arches, grottoes, and cascades. Also in this area are the **Musée d'Orsay** (p. 158) and the **Musée Rodin** (see below).

Le Musée du Quai Branly ★★★   The architect Jean Nouvel said he wanted to create something "unique, poetic, and disturbing." And so he did with the opening of this $265-million museum in 2006, which took a decade to launch. There was even scandal: The terra-cotta figures from Nigeria turned out to be smuggled. At long last under one roof nearly 300,000 tribal artifacts from Africa, Asia, Oceania, and the Americas have been assembled. Galleries stand on sculpted pillars that evoke totem poles. Set in a lush, rambling garden on the Left Bank in the shadow of the Eiffel Tower, this is the greatest monument to popular culture to open in Paris since Pompidou.

Housed in four spectacular buildings with a garden walled off from the quai Branly are the art, sculpture, and cultural materials of a vast range of non-Western civilizations, separating into different sections that represent the traditional cultures of Africa, East and Southeast Asia, Oceania, Australia, the Americas, and New Zealand. The pieces here come from the now-defunct Musée des Arts Africains et Oceaniens, the Louvre, and the Musée de l'Homme. Temporary exhibits are shown off in boxes all along the 180m (600-ft.) exhibition hall. Incredible masterpieces are on display made by some very advanced traditional civilizations; some of the most impressive exhibits present lifelike tribal masks of different cultures, whose emotional expressions are described in English. Allow 2 hours for a full visit; also take a stroll in the carefully manicured garden, or have a coffee in the small cafeteria across from the main building. There are numerous entrances to the museum grounds from the area near the Eiffel Tower; the main entrance is on quai Branly.

27–37 quai Branly and 206–208 rue de Université, 7e. ✆ **01-56-61-70-00.** www.quaibranly.fr. Admission 8.50€ adults, 6€ students 18–26 and seniors, free for children 17 and under. Tues–Wed and Sun 11am–7pm; Thurs–Sat 11am–9pm. Métro: Alma-Marceau. RER: Pont d'Alma.

Musée National Auguste Rodin ★★   This beautiful house and its gardens are a repository of the work of Auguste Rodin (1840–1917). Though his works were first thought obscene, he is considered the master of French 19th-century sculpture. After his death, the government purchased Rodin's 18th-century mansion, where he had his studio from 1910 to 1917. The rose gardens were restored to their original splendor, making a perfect setting for Rodin's most memorable works.

In the courtyard are three world-famous creations: *The Gates of Hell, The Thinker,* and *The Burghers of Calais.* Rodin's first major public commission, *The Burghers* commemorated the heroism of six burghers who in 1347 offered themselves as hostages to Edward III in return for his ending the siege of their port. *The Thinker,* in Rodin's own words, "thinks with every muscle of his arms, back, and legs, with his clenched fist and gripping toes." Inside the mansion, the sculptures, plaster casts, reproductions, originals, and sketches reveal the freshness and vitality of this remarkable man. Upstairs are two versions of the celebrated and condemned nude of Balzac, his bulky torso rising from a tree trunk. Also here are many versions of Rodin's last major work, his *Monument to Balzac* (a large one stands in the garden). Generally overlooked is a room devoted to Camille Claudel, Rodin's mistress and a towering artist in her own right. His pupil, model, and lover, she created such works as *Maturity, Clotho, The Waltz,* and the *Gossips.*

Looking for a Quick Escape?

The little alley behind the Musée Rodin winds down to a pond with fountains, flower beds, and even sandboxes for children. It's one of the most idyllic hidden spots in Paris.

In the Hôtel Biron, 79 rue de Varenne, 7e. ✆ **01-44-18-61-10.** www.musee-rodin.fr. Admission 6€ adults, 5€ ages 18–25, free for children 17 and under; 10€ adults, 7€ ages 18–25 combo ticket with access to temporary exhibits. Apr–Sept Tues–Sun 10am–5:45pm; Oct–Mar Tues and Thurs–Sun 10am–5:45pm, Wed 10am–8:45pm. Métro: Varenne, Invalides, or Saint-Francois-Xavier.

MONTPARNASSE: THE 14TH ARRONDISSEMENT (LEFT BANK)

For the Lost Generation, life centered on the Left Bank cafes. Hangouts such as the Dôme, Coupole, Rotonde, and Sélect became legendary. Artists, especially American expatriates, turned their backs on touristy Montmartre. Picasso, Modigliani, Hemingway, and Man Ray came this way. Fitzgerald was here when he was poor (when he was in the chips, he hung out at Le Ritz). Faulkner, Isadora Duncan, Miró, Joyce, Ford Madox Ford, and even Trotsky came here.

The life of Montparnasse still centers on its cafes and nightclubs, many only a shadow of what they used to be. Its heart is at the crossroads of boulevards Raspail and de Montparnasse, one of the settings of Hemingway's *The Sun Also Rises.* Rodin's controversial statue of Balzac swathed in a large cape stands guard over the prostitutes who cluster around the pedestal. Balzac seems to be the only one in Montparnasse who doesn't feel the impact of time and change.

Cimetière de Montparnasse ★   In the shadow of the Tour Montparnasse lies this burial ground of yesterday's celebrities, debris-littered and badly maintained. A

A Museum in the 15th (Left Bank)

Musée Bourdelle ★, 18 rue Antoine-Bourdelle, 15e (✆ **01-49-54-73-73**; Métro: Montparnasse-Bienvenüe, www.bourdelle.paris.fr), is devoted to the work of Emile-Antoine Bourdelle (1861–1929), a student of Rodin. The museum displays his drawings, paintings, and sculptures, and you can wander through his studio, garden, and house. The most notable exhibits are the 21 studies he did of Beethoven. The original plaster casts of some of his greatest works are also on display. Though some exhibits are badly captioned, you'll still feel the impact of Bourdelle's genius. Admission to the permanent collection is 7€ adults, 3.50€ ages 14 to 25, and free for kids 13 and under. It's open Tuesday to Sunday from 10am to 6pm.

map (to the left of the main gateway) directs you to the most famous occupants: Simone de Beauvoir and Jean-Paul Sartre, who share a gravesite. Others buried here include Samuel Beckett, Guy de Maupassant, Alfred Dreyfus, auto tycoon André Citroën, Camille Saint-Saëns, and Man Ray.

3 bd. Edgar-Quinet, 14e. ✆ **01-44-10-86-50.** Mon–Fri 8am–5:45pm; Sat 8:30am–5:45pm; Sun 9am–5:45pm (until 5:15pm Nov–Mar). Métro: Edgar-Quinet.

Tour Montparnasse ★★ Towering over the entire *arrondissement* is the Tour Montparnasse, rising 206m (676 ft.)—like the Eiffel Tower, a landmark on the Paris skyline. Completed in 1973, it was denounced by some critics as "bringing Manhattan to Paris." The city passed an ordinance outlawing any more structures of this size in the heart of Paris. Today, the tower houses a mammoth underground shopping mall and a train station. You can ride an elevator to the 56th floor and then climb three flights to the rooftop terrace. At viewing tables, you can pick out all the landmarks, from Sacré-Coeur to the Défense area in the distance. A bar and restaurant are also on this floor.

33 av. du Maine, 14e. ✆ **01-45-38-52-56.** www.tourmontparnasse56.com. Admission 11€ adults, 7.50€ students 16–20, 4.50€ children 7–15, free for children 6 and under. Apr–Sept daily 9:30am–11:30pm; Oct–Mar daily 9:30am–10:30pm (Fri–Sat until 11pm). Métro: Montparnasse-Bienvenüe.

PARKS, GARDENS & CEMETERIES

See p. 163 for details on the **Tuileries. Cimetière de Montmartre** can be found on p. 170, and the **Cimetière de Montparnasse** on p. 176.

Bois de Boulogne ★★ ☺ This is one of the most spectacular parks in Europe. If you had a week, you could spend it all in the Bois de Boulogne and still not see everything. Spend your time strolling along the many hidden pathways or traversing the park in a horse-drawn carriage.

Porte-Dauphine is the main entrance, but you can take the Métro to Porte-Maillot as well. West of Paris, the park was once a forest for royal hunts. In the 19th century, carriages bearing elegant damsels with their escorts rumbled along avenue Foch. Nowadays, it's more likely to attract middle-class picnickers.

EXPLORING PARIS

Parks, Gardens & Cemeteries

6

When Napoleon III gave the grounds to the city in 1852, Baron Haussmann developed them. Separating Lac Inférieur from Lac Supérieur is the Carrefour des Cascades (you can stroll under its waterfall). The Lower Lake contains two islands connected by a footbridge. From the east bank, you can take a boat there, perhaps stopping at the cafe-restaurant on one of them. Restaurants in the Bois are numerous, elegant, and expensive. The Pré-Catelan contains a deluxe restaurant of the same name and a Shakespearean theater in a garden said to have been planted with trees mentioned in the Bard's plays.

The **Jardin d'Acclimatation** (© 01-40-67-90-82; www.jardindacclimatation. fr), at the northern edge of the park, is for children, with a small zoo, an amusement park, and a narrow-gauge railway. Two racetracks, **Longchamp** and **Auteuil,** are in the park. The annual Grand Prix is run in June at Longchamp (site of a medieval abbey). Fashionable Parisians turn out, the women attired in their finest haute couture and hats. North of Longchamp is the Grand Cascade, the artificial waterfall of the Bois de Boulogne.

In the 24-hectare (59-acre) **Bagatelle Park** (© 01-43-28-47-63), the comte d'Artois (later Charles X) made a wager with Marie Antoinette that he could erect a small palace in less than 3 months. He hired nearly 1,000 craftsmen and irritated the local populace by requisitioning all shipments of stone and plaster arriving through the west gates of Paris. He hired *ébenistes* (cabinetmakers), painters, and the Scottish landscape architect Thomas Blaikie—and won his bet. If you're in Paris in late April, go to the Bagatelle to look at the tulips. In late May, one of the finest rose collections in Europe is in full bloom. If you can, visit in September, when the light is less harsh than in summer, or even in February, when, stripped of much of its greenery, the park assumes its true shape. From June to September hours are daily 9:30am to 8pm (closes at 5pm in winter). Admission is 2.90€; free under 3.

Porte-Dauphine, 16e.© **01-40-67-97-00.** Métro: Les-Sablons, Porte-Maillot, or Porte-Dauphine.

Cimetière du Père-Lachaise ★★

This cemetery has been called the "grandest address in Paris." Everybody from Sarah Bernhardt to Oscar Wilde (his tomb is by Epstein) was buried here. So were Balzac, Delacroix, and Bizet, as well as Chopin and Molière. Rock star Jim Morrison's tombstone usually draws the most visitors—and causes the most disruption. If you search hard enough, you can find the tombs of Abélard and Héloïse, the ill-fated lovers of the 12th century.

Spreading over more than 44 hectares (109 acres), Père-Lachaise was acquired by the city in 1804. Nineteenth-century French sculpture abounds, recalling a time when families tried to outdo others in ornamentation and cherubic ostentation. Some French socialists still pay tribute at the Mur des Fédérés, the anonymous gravesite of the Communards who were executed on May 28, 1871. Several monuments honor the French who died in the Resistance or in Nazi concentration camps.

Note: A free map is available at the newsstand across from the main entrance; it will help you find the well-known gravesites.

16 rue de Repos, 20e.© **01-55-25-82-10.** www.pere-lachaise.com. Mon–Fri 8am–6pm; Sat–Sun 9am–6pm (until 5pm Nov to early Mar). Métro: Père-Lachaise or Philippe Auguste.

Jardin du Luxembourg ★★ ☺

Hemingway told a friend that the Jardin du Luxembourg "kept us from starvation." In his poverty-stricken days in Paris, he wheeled a baby carriage through the gardens because it was known "for the classiness

ROYAL remains AT ST-DENIS

In the 12th century, Abbot Suger placed an inscription on the bronze doors of Basilique St-Denis: MARVEL NOT AT THE GOLD AND EXPENSE, BUT AT THE CRAFTSMANSHIP OF THE WORK. The first Gothic building in France that can be dated precisely, St-Denis was the "spiritual defender of the State" during the reign of Louis VI ("the Fat"). The facade, with its crenelated parapet similar to the fortifications of a castle, has a rose window. The windows, in stunning colors—mauve, purple, blue, and rose—were restored in the 19th century.

St-Denis, the first bishop of Paris, was patron saint of the French monarchy. Royal burials began here in the 6th century and continued until the Revolution. The sculptures around the four tombs—some two stories high—span the country's artistic development from the Middle Ages to the Renaissance. The guided tour (in French only) takes you through the crypt. François I was entombed at St-Denis. His funeral statue is nude, although he demurely covers himself with his hand.

Other kings and queens here include Louis XII and Anne of Brittany, Henri II, and Catherine de Médicis. Revolutionaries stormed through, smashing many statues and dumping royal remains in a ditch in the garden. They were reburied under the main altar during the 19th century. In a bizarre twist, following a Mass in 2004, the heart of the 10-year-old heir to the French throne, Louis XVII, was buried at St-Denis, near the graves of his parents, Marie Antoinette and Louis XVI. Ceremonies recognizing the royal heart put to rest decades of rumor and legend surrounding the child's death. Genetic testing has persuaded even the most cynical historians that the person who might have been the future King Louis XVII never escaped prison. The boy died of tuberculosis in 1795, his body ravaged by tumors. The child's corpse was dumped into a common grave, but not before a doctor secretly carved out his heart and smuggled it out of prison in a handkerchief. The heart was compared to DNA from hair trimmed from Marie-Antoinette during her childhood in Austria. It was a perfect match.

The Basilique St-Denis is in a northern suburb of Paris at place de l'Hôtel-de-Ville, 2 rue de Strasbourg (✆ 01-48-09-83-54; Métro: Basilique St-Denis). Admission is 6.50€ for adults, 4.50€ for ages 18 to 25, and free for children 17 and under. It's open April to September Monday to Saturday 10am to 6:15pm and Sunday from noon to 6:15pm, and October to March Monday to Saturday 10am to 5pm and Sunday noon to 5:15pm. Free organ concerts are presented on Sundays at 10am (✆ 01-48-20-20-98 for more information). It's closed January 1, May 1, and December 25.

of its pigeons." When the gendarme left to get a glass of wine, the writer would eye his victim, lure it with corn, and snatch it. "We got a little tired of pigeon that year," he confessed, "but they filled many a void."

Before it became a feeding ground for struggling artists, the Luxembourg Gardens knew greater days. They are the finest formal gardens on the Left Bank (some say in all of Paris). Marie de Médicis, the much-neglected wife and later widow of the roving Henri IV, ordered the **Palais du Luxembourg** built on this site in 1612. She planned to live here with her "witch" friend, Leonora Galigäi.

The queen didn't get to enjoy the Luxembourg Palace for very long. Her son, Louis XIII, forced her into exile after he discovered that she was plotting to overthrow him. She died in Cologne in poverty. (The 21 paintings she commissioned from Rubens for her palace are now in the Louvre.) Call ✆ **01-44-54-19-49** to make a reservation for 8€, but don't count on getting one. It is almost impossible unless you personally know one of the politicians. On any given day, only 30 tickets are allotted.

The gardens are the main draw. They're mostly in the classic French style: well groomed and laid out, the trees planted in designs. Urns and statuary encircle the central water basin. One statue honors Ste-Geneviève, the patroness of Paris, depicted with pigtails reaching to her thighs. Bring the kids and soak in the atmosphere. You can sail a toy boat, ride a pony, attend a Grand Guignol puppet show, or even play boules with a group of elderly men who aren't afraid of looking like a cliché from 1928, complete with black berets and Gauloises.

6e. ✆ **01-42-34-23-62** (garden). Métro: Odéon. RER: Luxembourg.

Parc Monceau   Eighteenth- and 19th-century mansions, some evoking Proust's *Remembrance of Things Past,* ring much of the park. It was built in 1778 by the duc d'Orléans, or Philippe-Egalité, as he became known, and opened to the public during Napoleon III's Second Empire. Today you'll find mothers and nurses wheeling baby carriages around the park.

Parc Monceau originally held an Egyptian-style obelisk, a medieval dungeon, an Alpine farmhouse, a Chinese pagoda, a Roman temple, an enchanted grotto, various chinoiseries, and a waterfall. The fairy-tale touches have largely disappeared, except for a pyramid and an oval *naumachie* (a place for a mock sea battle) fringed by a colonnade. Solid statuary and monuments, one honoring Chopin, have replaced many of the fantasies. In spring, the tulips and magnolias alone are worth the airfare to Paris.

8e. ✆ **01-42-27-39-56.** www.parcmonceau.org. Free admission. Métro: Monceau or Villiers.

PARIS UNDERGROUND

Les Catacombes ★   Every year an estimated 50,000 tourists explore some 900m (3,000 ft.) of underground tunnel to look at six million ghoulishly arranged skeletons. First opened to the public in 1810, this "empire of the dead" is now illuminated by overhead electric lights.

In the Middle Ages, the Catacombs were quarries; in 1785, city officials decided to use them as a burial ground. The bones of several million persons were moved here from their previous resting places, because the overcrowded cemeteries were considered health menaces. In 1830, the prefect of Paris closed the Catacombs to the viewing public, considering them obscene and indecent. In World War II, the Catacombs were the headquarters of the French Resistance.

1 place Denfert-Rochereau, 14e. ✆ **01-43-22-47-63.** www.catacombes-de-paris.fr. Admission 8€ adults, 6€ seniors, 4€ ages 14–25, free for children 13 and under. Tues–Sun 10am–5pm. Métro: Denfert-Rochereau.

The Sewers of Paris (Les Egouts) ★   Some sociologists assert that the sophistication of a society can be judged by the way it disposes of waste. If that's true, Paris receives good marks for its network of sewers. Victor Hugo is credited with making them famous in *Les Misérables.* "All dripping with slime, his soul filled with a strange light," Jean Valjean makes his flight through the sewers of Paris. Hugo also wrote,

Memorial to a Princess

Place de l'Alma (Métro: Alma-Marceau) is still a tribute to the late Diana, princess of Wales, who was killed in an auto accident August 31, 1997, in a nearby underpass. The bronze flame in the center is a replica of the one in the Statue of Liberty and was a gift from the *International Herald Tribune* to honor Franco-American friendship. Many bouquets and messages (and even graffiti) still surround the flame.

Paris has also opened the **Center for Nature Discovery, Garden in Memory of Diana, Princess of Wales,** 21 rue des Blancs-Manteaux, 7e. The small park, which you can visit during the day on weekends, is devoted to teaching children about nature and gardening, and contains flowers, vegetables, and decorative plants. Admission is free.

"Paris has beneath it another Paris, a Paris of sewers, which has its own streets, squares, lanes, arteries, and circulation."

In the early Middle Ages, drinking water was taken directly from the Seine, while wastewater was poured onto fields or thrown onto the unpaved streets, transforming the urban landscape into a sea of smelly mud.

Around 1200, the streets of Paris were paved with cobblestones, with open sewers down the center. These helped spread the Black Death, which devastated the city. In 1370, a vaulted sewer was built in the rue Montmartre, draining effluents into a tributary of the Seine. During the reign of Louis XIV, improvements were made, but waste disposal in Paris remained deplorable.

During the early 1800s, 30km (19 miles) of sewer were added beneath the Parisian landscape. By 1850, the Industrial Revolution made the manufacturing of iron pipe and digging equipment more practical. Baron Haussmann developed a system that used separate underground channels for drinking water and sewage. By 1878, it was 580km (360 miles) long. Beginning in 1894, under the guidance of Belgrand, the network was enlarged, and new laws required that discharge of all waste and storm-water runoff be funneled into the sewers. Between 1914 and 1977, 966km (600 miles) of sewers were added beneath the pavements of Paris.

Today, the network of sewers is 2,093km (1,300 miles) long. Within its cavities, it contains freshwater mains, compressed-air pipes, telephone cables, and pneumatic tubes. Every day, a plant in the suburb of Achères processes 1.3 million cubic yards of wastewater.

The *égouts* (sewers), as well as telephone and telegraph pneumatic tubes, are built around four principal tunnels, one 5.5m (18 ft.) wide and 4.5m (15 ft.) high. It's like an underground city, with the street names clearly labeled. Each branch pipe bears the number of the building to which it is connected.

Tours of the sewers begin at Pont de l'Alma on the Left Bank, where a stairway leads into the bowels of the city. However, you often have to wait in line as long as 30 minutes. Visiting times may change in bad weather, when a storm can make the sewers dangerous. The tour consists of a movie on sewer history, a visit to a small museum, and a short trip through the maze.

Pont de l'Alma, 7e. © **01-53-68-27-81.** Admission 4.20€ adults; 3.40€ seniors, students, and children 5-16; free for children 4 and under. May-Sept Sat-Wed 11am-5pm; Oct-Apr Sat-Wed 11am-4pm. Métro: Alma-Marceau. RER: Pont de l'Alma.

SHOPPING

Shopping is the local pastime. The City of Light is one of the rare places in the world where shopping surrounds you on almost every street. The windows, stores, and people (and even their dogs) brim with energy, creativity, and a sense of expression. You don't have to buy anything, just peer in the *vitrines* (display windows), absorb cutting-edge ideas, witness new trends, and take home an education in style.

Business Hours

Shops are usually open Monday to Saturday from 9:30 or 10am to 8pm, but hours vary, and Paris doesn't run at full throttle on Monday morning. Small shops sometimes take a 2-hour lunch break and may not open until after lunch on Monday. While most stores open at 10am, some open at 9:30am or even 11am. Thursday is the best day for late-night shopping, with stores open until 9 or 10pm.

Sunday shopping is currently limited to tourist areas and flea markets, though there's growing demand for full-scale Sunday hours, à la the United States and the United Kingdom. The big department stores are now open for the five Sundays before Christmas; otherwise, they're dead on *dimanche.*

The **Carrousel du Louvre** (© **01-43-16-47-10**), an underground mall adjacent to the Louvre, is open daily 10am to 8pm. The tourist shops that line rue de Rivoli across from the Louvre are open Sunday, as are antiques villages, flea markets, and several food markets. The Virgin Megastore on the Champs-Elysées pays a fine in order to stay open on Sunday. It's *the* teen hangout.

Great Shopping Areas

1ER & 8E   These two *quartiers* adjoin each other and form the heart of Paris's best Right Bank shopping neighborhood. This area includes the famed **rue du Faubourg St-Honoré,** with the big designer houses, and **avenue des Champs-Elysées,** where the mass-market and teen scenes are hot. At one end of the 1er is the **Palais Royal**—one of the city's best-kept shopping secrets, where an arcade of boutiques flanks the garden of the former palace.

On the other side of town, at the end of the 8e, is **avenue Montaigne,** 2 blocks of the fanciest shops in the world, where you float from one big name to another.

2E   Behind the Palais Royal lies the **Garment District (Sentier)** and a few upscale shopping secrets such as **place des Victoires.** This area also holds a few *passages,* alleys filled with tiny stores such as **Galerie Vivienne** on rue Vivienne.

3E & 4E   The difference between these two *arrondissements* gets fuzzy, especially around **place des Vosges,** center stage of the Marais. Even so, they offer several dramatically different shopping experiences.

On the surface, the shopping includes the real-people stretch of **rue de Rivoli** (which becomes **rue St-Antoine**). **BHV (Bazar de l'Hôtel de Ville),** which opened in 1856, is the major department store in this area; it has seven floors and lies adjacent to Paris's City Hall at 52–64 rue de Rivoli (© **01-42-74-90-00;** www. bhv.fr). Many shoppers will also be looking for **La Samaritaine,** 19 rue de la Monnaie, once the most famous department store in France. It occupied four noteworthy buildings erected between 1870 and 1927. These buildings have been sold and are undergoing renovation to be completed in 2012. The new owner has not made his intentions clear about the future of this Parisian landmark.

Hidden in the **Marais** is a medieval warren of tiny, twisting streets chockablock with cutting-edge designers and up-to-the-minute fashions and trends. Start by walking around place des Vosges to see galleries, designer shops, and fabulous finds, and then dive in and get lost in the area leading to the Musée Picasso.

Finally, the 4e is also the home of **place de la Bastille,** an up-and-coming area for artists and galleries where you'll find the newest entry on the retail scene, the **Viaduc des Arts** (which stretches into the 12e).

6E & 7E Whereas the 6e is one of the most famous shopping districts in Paris— it's the soul of the Left Bank—much of the good stuff is hidden in the zone that becomes the wealthy residential 7e. **Rue du Bac,** stretching from the 6e to the 7e in a few blocks, stands for all that wealth and glamour can buy. The street is jammed with art galleries, home-decor stores, and gourmet food shops.

9E To add to the fun of shopping the Right Bank, the 9e sneaks in behind the 1er, so if you choose not to walk toward the Champs-Elysées and the 8e, you can head to the big department stores in a row along **boulevard Haussmann** in the 9e. Here you'll find the two big French icons, **Au Printemps** and **Galeries Lafayette,** and a large branch of Britain's **Marks & Spencer.**

Shopping A to Z
ANTIQUES

Directly across from the Louvre, **Le Louvre des Antiquaires,** 2 place du Palais-Royal, 1er (② **01-42-97-27-27;** www.louvre-antiquaires.com; Métro: Palais-Royal), is the largest repository of antiques in central Paris. More than 250 dealers display their wares on three floors, specializing in objets d'art and small-scale furniture of the type that Mme. de Pompadour might have favored. You may find 30 matching Baccarat crystal champagne flutes from the 1930s, a Sèvres tea service dated 1773, or a small Jean Fouquet pin of gold and diamonds. Too stuffy? No problem. There's always the 1940 Rolex with the eggplant crocodile strap.

Village St-Paul, 23–27 rue St-Paul, 4e (no phone; www.village-saint-paul.com; Métro: St-Paul), isn't an antiques center but a cluster of dealers in a hole-in-the-wall hide-out; the rest of the street, stretching from the river to the Marais, is lined with dealers, most of whom close on Sunday. The Village St-Paul *is* open on Sunday, and hopping. Inside the courtyards and alleys are every dreamer's visions of hidden Paris: dealers selling furniture and other decorative items in French Provincial and, to a much lesser extent, formal styles.

ART

Galerie Adrien Maeght, 42 rue du Bac, 7e (② **01-45-48-45-15;** www.maeght.com; Métro: Rue-du-Bac), is among the most famous names, selling contemporary art on a Left Bank street. In addition to major works, it sells posters beginning at 8€, signed and numbered lithographs, and books on art and artists.

The **Viaduc des Arts,** 119 av. Daumesnil (btw. rue de Lyon and av. Diderot), 12e (② **01-44-75-80-66;** www.viaduc-des-arts.com; Métro: Bastille, Ledru-Rollin, Reuilly-Diderot, or Gare-de-Lyon), occupies the vaulted spaces beneath one of the 19th-century railway access routes into the Gare de Lyon. Around 1990, crafts artists, including furniture makers, potters, glass blowers, and weavers, began occupying the niches beneath the viaduct, selling their wares to homeowners and representatives of Paris's decorating trades. Trendsetting home-furnishing outfits have since rented additional space. Stretching for more than 2 blocks between the Opéra Bastille and the Gare de Lyon, it offers the possibility of seeing what Parisians consider chic in home decorating.

BOOKS

The most famous bookstore on the Left Bank was **Shakespeare and Company,** home to the legendary Sylvia Beach, "mother confessor to the Lost Generation." Hemingway, Fitzgerald, and Gertrude Stein were all patrons. Anaïs Nin often stopped in. At one point Beach helped Henry Miller publish *Tropic of Cancer,* a book so notorious in its day that returning Americans trying to slip a copy through Customs often had it confiscated as pornography. Long ago, the shop moved from rue de l'Odéon to 37 rue de la Bûcherie, 5e (© **01-43-25-40-93**; www.shakespeareco. org; Métro: St-Michel), where expatriates swap books and literary gossip.

Scattered over two floors of tightly packed inventory, the **Village Voice Bookshop,** 6 rue Princesse, 6e (© **01-46-33-36-47**; www.villagevoicebookshop.com; Métro: Mabillon), specializes in new English-language books, so it's a favorite among expatriate Yankees and Brits. It's near some of the Left Bank gathering places described in Gertrude Stein's *The Autobiography of Alice B. Toklas.*

Taschen, 2 rue de Buci, 6e (© **01-40-51-79-22**; www.taschen.com; Métro: Odéon), is a Germany-based publishing house that's known for coffee-table books. Erudite, high-profile, and glossy, most of them focus on architecture, art, photography, or eroticism. If you're in the market for a sweeping overview of the organization's past projects, this is the store for you.

W. H. Smith France, 248 rue de Rivoli, 1er (© **01-44-77-88-99**; www. whsmith.fr; Métro: Concorde), is France's largest store devoted to English and American books, magazines, and periodicals. You can get the *Times* of London and the Sunday *New York Times,* available Monday afternoon. There's a fine selection of maps and travel guides.

CHILDREN'S CLOTHES, SHOES & TOYS

Au Nain Bleu, 5 bd. Malesherbes, 8e (© **01-42-65-20-00**; www.aunainbleu.com; Métro: Concorde or Madeleine), is the world's fanciest toy store. But don't panic: In addition to the expensive stuff, there are rows of cheaper penny candy–style toys in jars.

Bonpoint, 15 rue Royale, 8e (© **01-47-42-52-63**; Métro: Monceau or Villiers), is part of a chain that helps parents transform their darlings into models of well-tailored conspicuous consumption. Though you'll find some garments for real life, the primary allure of the place lies in its tailored, traditional—and expensive—garments by the "Coco Chanel of the children's garment industry," Marie-France Cohen. The shop sells clothes for boys and girls from newborn to age 16.

Prices are a whole lot lower at **Orchestra Kazibao,** 18 rue Vignon, 9e (© **01-42-66-24-74** or 01-42-66-24-72; Métro: Madeleine), which carries selections for toddlers to 14-year-olds. Kids will love the fashions, which are wearable, washable, and affordable. It's only a short walk from place de la Madeleine.

CHINA & CRYSTAL

Purveyor to kings and presidents of France since 1764, **Baccarat** (www.baccarat. fr), 11 place des Etats-Unis, 16e (© **01-40-22-11-22;** Métro: Boissiere or Iéna), and 11 place de la Madeleine, 8e (© **01-42-65-36-26;** Métro: Madeleine), produces world-renowned full-lead crystal dinnerware, jewelry, chandeliers, and statuary. The Madeleine branch is more glamorous but not as well stocked. It carries porcelain and crystal from other manufacturers, such as Christofle.

Lalique, 11 rue Royale, 8e (© **01-53-05-12-81;** www.cristallalique.fr; Métro: Concorde), famous for its clear- and frosted-glass sculpture, Art Deco crystal, and perfume bottles, has recently branched out into other merchandise—for example, silk scarves meant to compete with Hermès and leather belts with Lalique buckles.

And then there's **Limoges-Unic & Madronet,** 34 rue de Paradis, 10e (© **01-47-70-34-59;** Métro: Gare-de-l'Est). In two shops a 3-minute walk from each other, you'll find Limoges china and anything else you might need for the table—glass, crystal, and silver. It pays to drop into both stores, whose inventories vary according to the season and the whims of the buyers.

CHOCOLATE

Some of Paris's most delicious chocolates can be found at **Christian Constant,** 37 rue d'Assas, 6e (© **01-53-63-15-15;** Métro: St-Placide; www.christianconstant. com). Particularly appealing are combinations of chocolate meringue, chocolate mousse, and bitter chocolate *feuilles d'automne* (autumn leaves).

Racks and racks of chocolates are priced individually or by the kilo at **La Maison du Chocolat,** 225 rue du Faubourg St-Honoré, 8e (© **01-42-27-39-44;** www. lamaisonduchocolat.com; Métro: Ternes), though it'll cost you about 100€ for a kilo (2.5 lb). Note the similarity to Hermès when it comes to the wrapping and ribbon (and prices). The chocolate pastries are affordable; the store even has its own chocolate milk. There are five other branches around Paris.

CRAFTS

One of the few regional handicrafts stores in Paris worth going out of your way to find, **La Tuile à Loup,** 35 rue Daubenton, 5e (© **01-47-07-28-90;** www.latuile aloup.com; Métro: Censier-Daubenton), carries beautiful pottery and faïence from many regions of France. Look for figures of Breton folk on the faïence of Quimper, as well as garlands of fruits and flowers from the *terre vernissée* (varnished earth, a charming way to define stoneware) from Normandy, Savoy, Alsace, and Provence.

DEPARTMENT & DIME STORES

After you've admired the architecture of one of Europe's most famous department stores, step inside **Au Printemps,** 64 bd. Haussmann, 9e (© **01-42-82-50-00;**

www.printemps.com; Métro: Havre-Caumartin; RER: Auber). Inside the main building is **Printemps de la Mode,** which occupies the bulk of the structure, and a housewares shop, **Printemps de la Maison.** Upstairs are wares of every sort, especially clothing. An affiliated store across the street is **Le Printemps de l'Homme,** the menswear division. Behind the main store is a branch of **Monoprix,** Printemps's workaday but serviceable dime store, which contains a grocery. Check out the magnificent stained-glass dome, built in 1923, through which kaleidoscopic light cascades into the sixth-floor cafe. English-speaking interpreters are stationed throughout the store and at the welcome desk in the basement of the main building.

A two-part department store, **Au Bon Marché,** 24 rue de Sèvres, 7e (✆ **01-44-39-80-00;** www.lebonmarche.fr; Métro: Sèvres-Babylone), is on the Left Bank in the midst of all the chic boutiques. No. 38 houses a gourmet grocery store; no. 22 is a source for your general shopping needs.

Colette, 213 rue St-Honoré, 1er (✆ **01-55-35-33-90;** www.colette.fr; Métro: Pyramides), is a swank citadel for a la mode fashion that has made the elegant but staid rue St-Honoré less stuffy. For cutting-edge design, this is the place to go; you'll see fashions by young talents such as Marni and Lucien Pellat-Finet, furnishings by such designers as Tom Dixon, and even zany Japanese accessories. Here's a tip: Even if you don't buy anything, head for the tea salon downstairs for fresh quiches, salads, and cakes.

At **Galeries Lafayette,** 40 bd. Haussmann, 9e (✆ **01-42-82-34-56;** Métro: Chaussée-d'Antin; RER: Auber), stand under "the Dome"—a stained-glass cupola that towers above the arcaded store. Built in 1912, Galeries Lafayette consists of several stores: **Lafayette Hommes** men's store, **Lafayette Sports, Galeries Lafayette Mariage** (for wedding accessories), and two other general-merchandise stores, both known simply as **"GL."** One floor above street level is one of the fanciest grocery stores in town, **Gourmet Lafayette,** with prices that are slightly less than those at Fauchon.

FASHION

CUTTING EDGE CHIC **Azzedine Alaïa,** 18 rue Verrerie, 4e (✆ **01-42-72-54-97;** Métro: Hôtel-de-Ville), showcases the collection of the darling of 1970s French fashion. Alaïa revived body consciousness and put the ooh-la-la in Paris chic; he specializes in evening dresses. If you can't afford the current collection, try the stock shop around the corner at 18 rue de Verrerie, which sells last year's leftovers at serious discounts.

Dolce & Gabbana, 54 av. Montaigne, 8e (✆ **01-42-25-68-78;** Métro: Alma-Marceau), occupies most of the ground floor of a soaring skyscraper that houses the executive offices of the LVMH (Louis Vuitton/Moët Hennessy) group. It showcases the entire line of sexy, sporty, haute men's and women's clothing.

Supporters of the high-camp, high-fashion mogul **Jean-Paul Gaultier** describe him as an avant-garde classicist without allegiance to the aesthetic restrictions of the French bourgeoisie. Detractors call him a glorified punk rocker with a gimmicky allegiance to futurist models as interpreted by *Star Trek.* Whatever your opinion, it's always refreshing and insightful for a fashion buff to check out what France's most iconoclastic designer is doing. There's a branch of his store at 6 rue Vivienne, 2e (✆ **01-42-86-05-05;** Métro: Bourse), but the main branch, and biggest inventory, is at 44 av. George V, 8e (✆ **01-44-43-00-44;** Métro: George V).

DISCOUNT & RESALE **Anna Lowe,** 104 rue du Faubourg St-Honoré, 8e (📞 01-42-66-11-32 or 01-40-06-02-42; www.annalowe.com; Métro: Miromesnil), is one of the top boutiques for women who wish to purchase Chanel or Versace at a discount. Many clothes are runway samples; some have been gently worn.

The inventory at **Réciproque,** 88–123 rue de la Pompe (btw. av. Victor-Hugo and av. Georges-Mandel), 16e (📞 **01-47-04-30-28;** Métro: Pompe), is scattered over five buildings. Everything is secondhand, in sections devoted to Chanel, Versace, Lacroix, Hermès, and Mugler. Women will find gowns, suits, sportswear, and shoes. Men should go to no. 101. Everything has been worn, but in some cases that means only on runways or during photo shoots.

French film stars often shop at **Défilé des Marques,** 171 rue de Grenelles, 7e (📞 01-45-55-63-47; Métro: Latour-Maubourg), but anyone can pick up Laurent, Dior, Lacroix, Prada, Chanel, Versace, Hermès, and others at a fraction of the original price. Hermès scarves are sold here as well. Low prices derive from the owners' skill at picking up used clothing in good condition from last year's collections, from collections of many years ago, or from estate sales.

FLAGSHIPS The **Chanel** boutique, 29 rue Cambon, 1er (📞 **01-42-86-28-00;** www.chanel.fr; Métro: Concorde or Tuileries), carries classic Chanel as well as pieces with Karl Lagerfeld's interesting twist.

During the decade (1947–57) that he directed his empire, **Christian Dior,** 30 av. Montaigne, 8e (📞 **01-40-73-73-73;** www.dior.fr; Métro: Franklin-D-Roosevelt), was the only couturier whose name was known throughout the Western Hemisphere. The house has continued to thrive since its reorganization into a small-scale version of a department store, with sections devoted to men's, women's, and children's clothing; gift items; makeup and perfume; and so on. Unlike some of the other big-name fashion houses, Dior is very approachable.

One of the most recognizable accessories in France is an opulent silk scarf or tie from **Hermès,** 24 rue du Faubourg St-Honoré, 8e (📞 **01-40-17-46-00** or 01-40-17-47-17; www.hermes.com; Métro: Concorde). You'll find them in abundance, along with everything else (bags, purses, and so forth) endorsed by the legendary saddle maker, at the flagship branch.

Louis Vuitton, 6 place St-Germain-des-Prés, 6e (📞 **01-45-49-62-32;** www.louisvuitton.fr; Métro: St-Germain-des-Prés), is the most interestingly decorated branch of Vuitton in Paris. Antiques and fine hardwoods evoke the grand age of travel, when steamships and railway cars hauled the affluent to exotic places. It

---

A Discount Shopping Village Outside Paris

Just 35 minutes from the center of Paris, **La Vallée Village,** 3 Cours de la Garonne, Serris 77700 (📞 **01-60-42-35-00;** www.lavalleevillage.com), is home to some 90 boutiques in this chic outlet shopping village. Sometimes brand names such as Lacoste or Waterford are sold at 70% less than retail prices in the center of Paris—just ask such patrons as Sir Mick Jagger, Victoria Beckham (Posh Spice), or even the Duchess of York. From the center of Paris you can take RER A to the Val d'Europe station; by car, follow the A4 motorway out of Paris to exit 12.1 (signposted from there).

stocks a wide inventory of purses, suitcases, and trunks with the traditional mono-gram, plus new lines of Vuitton leather goods crafted from beige cowhide. The store also sells writing instruments as well as a Carnet du Voyage, a do-it-yourself scrap-book with watercolors and space to preserve your memories.

VINTAGE COUTURE   At **Didier Ludot,** 20–24 Galerie de Montpensier, in the arcades surrounding the courtyard of the Palais Royal, 1er (📞 **01-42-96-06-56;** www.didierludot.com; Métro: Palais-Royal), fashion historians salivate at the inven-tory of the haute couture of yesteryear. In this stylish shop, at prices that rival what you'd expect to pay for a serious antique, you'll find a selection of gowns and dresses created between 1900 and 1980 for women who looked fabulous at Maxim's, at cocktail parties on the avenue Foch, in Deauville, or wherever.

FOOD

At place de la Madeleine stands one of the most popular sights in the city—not La Madeleine church but **Fauchon,** 26 place de la Madeleine, 8e (📞 **01-70-39-38-00;** www.fauchon.com; Métro: Madeleine). It stocks a wider choice of upscale gourmet products than anyplace else in the world. Areas are devoted to candy, pas-tries, and bread; fresh fruits and veggies; dry and canned goods; fresh fish and meats; awe-inspiring takeout food; and wine.

Fauchon's main competitor, **Hédiard,** 21 place de la Madeleine, 8e (📞 **01-43-12-88-88;** www.hediard.fr; Métro: Madeleine), opened in 1854. It's a series of salons filled with almost Disney-esque displays meant to give the store the look of an old-fashioned spice emporium. Hédiard is also rich in coffees, teas, and jams. Upstairs is a superb restaurant, **La Table d'Hédiard** (📞 **01-43-12-88-99**), open Monday to Friday 8:30am to 10pm, Saturday noon to 10:30pm.

Le Maison du Miel (the House of Honey), 24 rue Vignon, 9e (📞 **01-47-42-26-70;** www.lamaisondumiel.com; Métro: Madeleine, Havre-Caumartin, or Opéra), has been a family tradition since before World War I. The entire store is devoted to products made from honey: vinegar, mustard, soap, regional varieties of nougat, and various edible honeys. It's around the corner from Fauchon and worth the walk.

JEWELRY

Well-dressed women around the world wear fabulous gemstones from **Van Cleef & Arpels,** 22 place Vendôme, 1er (📞 **01-53-45-35-50;** www.vancleef-arpels.com; Métro: Opéra or Tuileries). One of the firm's specialties is yellow diamonds, whose color resembles amber but whose fire is unmistakably brilliant. Floral motifs, in platinum or gold with vibrant hues, are also a trademark.

LEATHER

One of the most glamorous leather purveyors, established by an Italian entrepreneur on place Vendôme in 1905, is **Morabito,** 259 rue St-Honoré, 1er (📞 **01-53-23-90-40;** Métro: George V). Today it sells chicer-than-thou handbags at prices that begin at 480€, as well as suitcases—some of the best in Paris—for men and women.

LINGERIE

Undergarments manufactured and sold by **Cadolle,** 4 rue Cambon, 1er (📞 **01-42-60-94-22;** www.cadolle.com; Métro: Concorde), are among the world's most com-fortable and opulent. Herminie Cadolle invented the brassiere in 1889, and in 1911, she moved to this location near the former headquarters of Coco Chanel, whose "emaciated" styles she disliked. Today, her great-granddaughters manage the store. What's new here? The magic word is corsets, preferably in black, worn with long skirts or slacks. Fashioned out of everything from velvet to satin, they're almost guaranteed to turn heads day or night.

MALLS

Carrousel du Louvre, 99 rue de Rivoli, 1er (ⓒ **01-43-16-47-10;** www.carrousel dulouvre.com; Métro: Palais-Royal–Musée du Louvre), combines a convenient location, a food court, handy boutiques, and plenty of museum gift shops with a touch of culture. Always mobbed, this is one of the few shopping venues allowed to open on Sunday. The easiest way to get here is to enter from rue de Rivoli. It has a Virgin Megastore, the Body Shop, and several big-name boutiques, such as Courrèges and Lalique. Check out Diane Claire for the fanciest souvenirs you've ever seen. A branch of the Paris Convention and Visitors Bureau is next door to Virgin.

Forget about the street address of **Forum des Halles,** 1–7 rue Pierre-Lescot, 1er (ⓒ **01-44-76-96-56;** www.forumdeshalles.com; Métro: Etienne-Marcel or Châtelet–Les Halles). This mall fills an entire block where the old produce market, Les Halles, once stood. Now it's a crater of modern metal with layers of boutiques around a courtyard. There's one of everything here—but the feel is sterile, without a hint of *joie de vivre.* Shops are open Monday to Saturday 10am to 8pm, with restaurants and movie theaters remaining open at night and on Sunday.

MARKETS

Artists love to paint the **Marché aux Fleurs,** place Louis-Lépine, Ile de la Cité, 4e (Métro: Cité); photographers love to click away. The stalls are ablaze with color, each a showcase of flowers (most of which escaped the fate of being hauled to the perfume factories of Grasse in the French Riviera). The Flower Market is along the Seine, behind the Tribunal de Commerce. On Sunday, this is a bird market.

Paris's famous flea market, **Marché aux Puces de Clignancourt,** avenue de la Porte de Clignancourt (no phone; www.marchesauxpuces.fr; Métro: Porte-de-Clignancourt; then turn left, cross bd. Ney, and walk north on av. de la Porte de Clignancourt), is a complex of almost 3,000 stalls and shops in St-Ouen, a suburb north of the 18th arrondissement. It sells everything from antiques to junk, new to vintage clothing. Beware of pickpockets and troublemakers while shopping the market.

The first clues that you're here are the stalls of cheap clothing along avenue de la Porte de Clignancourt. Hold off spending until you get to rue des Rosiers, and then turn left. Vendors start bringing out their offerings around 9am Saturday to Monday and take them in around 6pm. Hours are a tad flexible, depending on weather and crowds. Monday is traditionally the best day for bargain seekers—attendance is smaller and merchants demonstrate a greater desire to sell.

First-timers at the flea market always ask two things: "Will I get any real bargains here?" and "Will I get fleeced?" It's all relative. Obviously dealers have already skimmed the best. And it's true that the same merchandise displayed here will sell for less out in the provinces. But for the visitor who has only a few days to spend in Paris—and only half a day for shopping—the flea market is worth the experience. Vintage French postcards, old buttons, and bistro ware are quite affordable; each market has its own personality and an aura of Parisian glamour that can't be found elsewhere. Most of the markets have toilets; some have a central office to arrange shipping. Cafes, pizza joints, and even a few restaurants are scattered throughout. Almost without exception, they are bad. The exception is **Le Soleil,** 109 av. Michelet, St. Ouen (☎ **01-40-10-08-08;** www.restaurantlesoleil.com); it was converted from a cafe into a family-run restaurant by Louis-Jacques Vannucci. Catering to flea-market shoppers, the restaurant looks flea-market decorated as well. The food is excellent, especially the sautéed chicken in light cream sauce, green bean salad with tomato cubes, and fresh Norman cod and the tiny mussels cooked in a rich broth. Charging 36€ for a fixed-price menu, it is open Monday to Friday for lunch noon to 2:30pm, Saturday noon to 3pm, and Sunday noon to 4pm.

Then there's the **Marché aux Puces de la Porte de Vanves,** avenue Georges-Lafenestre, 14e (Métro: Porte-de-Vanves). Like a giant yard sale, this bazaar sprawls along two streets. It's Paris's best flea market—dealers swear by it. There's little in terms of formal antiques, and few large pieces of furniture. You'll do better if you collect old linens, secondhand Hermès scarves, toys, costume jewelry, or perfume bottles. Asking prices tend to be high, because dealers prefer to sell to nontourists. On Sundays, there's a food market one street over. It's open Tuesday to Sunday 7am to either 3 or 5pm.

Marché Buci, rue de Buci, 6e (Métro: St-Germain-des-Prés, or Mabillon), is a traditional French food market held at the intersection of two streets. It's only 1 block long, but what a block it is. Seasonal fruits and vegetables dance across tabletops while chickens spin on the rotisserie. One stall is devoted to big bunches of fresh flowers. Avoid Monday morning, when very little is open (the best day is Sun).

MUSIC
The chain called **FNAC,** with a branch at 136 rue de Rennes, 6e (☎ **08-25-02-00-20;** www.fnac.com; Métro: St-Placide), is for anyone looking for CDs, records and tapes, computers, photo equipment, TVs, and stereos. It's known for its wide selection and competitive prices. The ticket service sells tickets for most of the venues and concerts in the city. There are eight other locations in Paris.

Virgin Megastore, 52–60 av. des Champs-Elysées, 8e (☎ **01-49-53-50-00;** Métro: Franklin-D-Roosevelt), is one of the anchors that helped rejuvenate the Champs-Elysées. The landmark building houses the city's largest music store as well as a bookstore and cafe. The ticket service can make reservations for plays, concerts, and sporting events. Other branches are in the Carrousel du Louvre (see "Malls," above), at both airports, and in Gare Montparnasse. It's open daily until midnight.

PERFUME, COSMETICS & TOILETRIES
Almost every working woman around place de la Madeleine shops at **Catherine,** 7 rue Castiglione, 1er (☎ **01-42-61-02-89;** Métro: Concorde). They appreciate its discounts and lack of pretension. It resembles a high-volume pharmacy more than a boutique; *flacons* of perfume move in and out fast. You get a 30% discount on most makeup and perfume and a 20% discount on brands such as Chanel and Dior.

You'll find some of the best deals in cosmetics at **maki,** 9 rue Mansart, 9e (☎ **01-42-81-33-76;** Métro: Blanche). In the middle of a theater area, it's where actors and models come for quality products at discounted prices. The staff will often give advice on makeup.

Though you can buy its scents in any discount *parfumerie,* we recommend visiting the source of some of the world's most famous perfumes: **Parfums Caron,** 34 av.

Montaigne, 8e (📞 **01-47-23-40-82;** www.parfumscaron.com; Métro: Franklin-D-Roosevelt). Established in 1904, it quickly gained a reputation as the choice of temptresses.

WINES

Les Caves Taillevent, 199 rue du Faubourg St-Honoré, 8e (📞 **01-45-61-14-09;** www.taillevent.com; Métro: Charles de Gaulle–Etoile), is a temple to the art of making fine French wine. Associated with one of Paris's grandest restaurants, Taillevent (p. 131), it occupies the street level and cellar of an antique building in a neighborhood awash with memories of the French empire. Stored here are more than 25,000 bottles of wine.

PARIS AFTER DARK
The Performing Arts
LISTINGS & TICKETS

Announcements of shows, concerts, and operas are on kiosks all over town. You can find listings in *Pariscope,* a weekly entertainment guide, and in the English-language *Boulevard,* a bimonthly magazine. Performances start later in Paris than in London or New York—anywhere from 8 to 9pm—and Parisians tend to dine after the theater. (But you may not want to follow suit, because many of the less expensive restaurants close as early as 9pm.)

There are many ticket agencies in Paris, mostly near the Right Bank hotels. *Avoid them if possible.* You can buy the cheapest tickets at the theater box office. Tip the usher who shows you to your seat in a theater or movie house.

For information and tickets to just about any show in Paris (also Dijon, Lyon, and Nice), **Keith Prowse** has a New York office if you'd like to make arrangements before you go. It's at 234 W. 44th St., Ste. 1000, New York, NY 10036 (📞 **800/669-8687;** www.keithprowse.com). The Paris office is at 7 rue de Clichy, 9e (📞 **01-42-81-88-98;** Métro: Place de Clichy). They will mail tickets to your home, fax confirmation, or leave tickets at the box office in Paris. There's a markup of 20% (excluding opera and ballet) over box-office price, plus a U.S. handling charge of $8. Hotel and theater packages are also available.

Several agencies sell tickets for cultural events and plays at discounts of up to 50%. One is the **Kiosque Théâtre,** 15 place de la Madeleine, 8e (no phone; www.kiosquetheatre.com; Métro: Madeleine), offering day-of-performance tickets for about half-price (average price is 20€). Tickets for evening performances and matinees are sold Tuesday to Saturday 12:30 to 8pm; Sunday 12:30 to 4pm.

For easy access to tickets for festivals, concerts, and the theater, try one of two locations of the **FNAC** electronics-store chain: 136 rue de Rennes, 6e (📞 **08-25-02-00-20;** Métro: St. Placide); or 1–7 rue Pierre-Lescot, in the Forum des Halles, 1er (📞 **08-25-02-00-20;** Métro: Châtelet–Les Halles).

THE TOP VENUES

Opéra Garnier ★★★, place de l'Opéra, 9e (📞 **08-92-89-90-90;** www.operadeparis.fr; Métro: Opéra), is the premier stage for dance and opera. Because of competition from the Opéra Bastille, the original opera has made great efforts to present more up-to-date works, including choreography by Jerome Robbins, Twyla Tharp, and George Balanchine. The architect Charles Garnier designed this rococo wonder in the heyday of the empire. The facade is adorned with marble and sculpture, including *The Dance* by Carpeaux. Restoration has returned the Garnier to its former glory: Its boxes and walls are lined with flowing red and blue damask, the ceiling (painted by Marc Chagall) has been cleaned, and air-conditioning has been added. The box office is open Monday to Saturday 10:30am to 6:30pm.

The controversial building known as the **Opéra Bastille ★★★**, place de la Bastille, 120 rue de Lyon (② **08-92-89-90-90** or 01-40-01-17-89; www.operade paris.fr; Métro: Bastille), was designed by the Canadian architect Carlos Ott, with curtains created by fashion designer Issey Miyake. The showplace was inaugurated in July 1989 (for the Revolution's bicentennial), and on March 17, 1990, the curtain rose on Hector Berlioz's *Les Troyens.* Since its much-publicized opening, the opera house has presented works such as Mozart's *Marriage of Figaro* and Tchaikovsky's *Queen of Spades.* The main hall is the largest French opera house, with 2,700 seats, but music critics have lambasted the acoustics. The building contains two additional concert halls, including an intimate room seating 250, usually used for chamber music. Both traditional opera performances and symphony concerts are presented here. Call to find out about occasional free concerts on French holidays.

New York has its Carnegie Hall, but for years Paris lacked a permanent home for its orchestra. That is, until 2006 when the restored **Salle Pleyel ★★★**, 252 rue du Faubourg-St-Honoré, 8e (② **01-42-56-13-13;** www.sallepleyel.fr; Métro: Miro-mesnil), opened once again. Built in 1927 by the piano-making firm of the same name, Pleyel was the world's first concert hall designed exclusively for a symphony orchestra. Ravel, Debussy, and Stravinsky performed their masterpieces here, only to see the hall devastated by fire less than 9 months after its opening. The original sound quality was never recovered because of an economic downturn. In 1998, real estate developer Hubert Martigny purchased the concert hall, restoring the Art Deco spirit of the original and also refining the acoustics it once knew. Nearly 500 seats were removed to make those that remained more comfortable. The Orchestre Philarmonique de Radio France and the Orchestre de Paris now have a home worthy of their reputations, and the London Symphony Orchestra makes Pleyel its venue in Paris. Tickets range from 10€ to 145€, and seniors and young people 26 and under can arrive an hour before a concert and fill any available seat for just 10€. Reservations are made by phone Monday to Saturday 11am to 7pm.

The Art Deco **Théâtre des Champs-Elysées,** 15 av. Montaigne, 8e (② **01-49-52-50-50;** www.theatrechampselysees.fr; Métro: Alma-Marceau), which attracts the haute couture crowd, books both national and international orchestras as well as operas and ballets. Events are held year-round, except in August. The box office is open Monday to Saturday 1 to 7pm.

Conceived by the Mitterrand administration, **Cité de la Musique ★★★**, 221 av. Jean-Jaurès, 19e (② **01-44-84-45-00,** or 01-44-84-44-84 for tickets and information; www.cite-musique.fr; Métro: Porte-de-Pantin), has been widely applauded. At the city's northeastern edge in what used to be a run-down neighborhood, the $120-million stone-and-glass structure, designed by Christian de Portzamparc, incorporates a network of concert halls, a library and research center, and a museum. The complex stages a variety of concerts, ranging from Renaissance to 20th-century programs.

Even those with only a modest understanding of French can delight in a sparkling production of Molière at the **Comédie-Française,** 2 rue de Richelieu, 1er (② **08-25-10-16-80;** www.comedie-francaise.fr; Métro: Palais-Royal–Musée du Louvre), established to keep the classics alive and to promote important contemporary authors. The box office is open daily from 11am to 6pm; the hall is dark from July 21 to September 5. The Left Bank annex is the **Comédie-Française-Théâtre du Vieux-Colombier,** 21 rue du Vieux-Colombier, 4e (② **01-44-39-87-00;** Métro: Sèvres-Babylone or Saint-Sulpice). Although its repertoire can vary, it's known for presenting some of the most serious French dramas in town.

International stars appear in the cavernous **Olympia,** 28 bd. des Capucines, 9e (② **01-55-27-10-00** or 08-92-68-33-68; www.olympiahall.com; Métro: Opéra or Madeleine). Yves Montand appeared once—the performance sold out 4 months in advance—but today you're more likely to catch Gloria Estefan. A typical lineup may include an English rock group, Italian acrobats, a well-known French singer, a dance troupe, an American juggler or comedy team (doing much of their work in English), plus the featured star. A witty emcee and an onstage band provide smooth transitions between acts.

CHANSON (FOLK MUSIC)

Au Lapin Agile ★   Picasso and Utrillo patronized this little cottage near the top of Montmartre, then known as the Cabaret des Assassins, and it has been painted by many artists, including Utrillo. You'll sit at carved wooden tables in a dimly lit room with walls covered by bohemian memorabilia and listen to French folk tunes, love ballads, army songs, sea chanteys, and music-hall ditties. You're encouraged to sing along, even if it's only the *"oui, oui, oui—non, non, non,"* the refrain of "Les Chevaliers de la Table Ronde." Open Tuesday to Sunday 9pm to 2am. 22 rue des Saules, 18e. ② **01-46-06-85-87.** www.au-lapin-agile.com. Cover (includes 1 drink) 24€, 17€ students. Métro: Lamarck Caulaincourt.

Cabarets

These places are all outrageously expensive, but they provide some of the most lavish, spectacular floor shows anywhere.

Crazy Horse Saloon   Since 1951, this sophisticated strip joint has thrived, thanks to good choreography and a sly, coquettish celebration of the female form. The theme binding each of the 5-minute numbers (featuring gorgeous dancers in erotic costumes) is La Femme in her various states: temperamental, sad, dancing/ bouncy, or joyful. Dance numbers that endure season after season include "Le Laser" and "The Erotic Lesson." Dinner is served at Chez Francis, a restaurant under separate management a few steps away. Shows last just under 2 hours. You'll find a small number of women among the audience of mainly businessmen. Shows Sunday to Friday 8:15 and 10:45pm; Saturday at 7, 9:30, and 11:45pm. 12 av. George V, 8e. ② **01-47-23-32-32.** www.lecrazyhorseparis.com. Reservations recommended. Cover (includes 2 drinks) 65€ for seat at the bar, 100€–150€ for table (dinner spectacle). Métro: George V or Alma Marceau.

Folies-Bergère   The Folies-Bergère has been an institution since 1869. Josephine Baker, the African-American singer who danced in a banana skirt and threw bananas into the audience, became the toast of Paris here. According to legend, the first GI to reach Paris at the 1944 Liberation asked for directions to the club. Don't expect the naughty and slyly permissive, skin-and-glitter revue that used to be the trademark of this place. In 1993, that all ended with a radical restoration of the theater and a reopening under new management. Today, it's a conventional 1,600-seat theater devoted to a frequently changing roster of big-stage performances in French, many of which are adaptations of Broadway blockbusters. True, there's always an acknowledgment of the nostalgia value of the old-time, much naughtier Folies-Bergère, and endless nods to the stars of yesterday (especially Josephine Baker and her topless act with bananas), but if you're looking for artful nudity presented with unabashed Parisian permissiveness, head for the Crazy Horse Saloon or the Lido. Shows are usually given Tuesday to Saturday at 9pm and Sunday at 3pm. 32 rue Richer, 9e. ✆ **01-44-79-98-60** or 08-92-68-16-50. www.foliesbergere.com. Tickets 25€–84€. Métro: Grands Boulevards or Cadet.

Lido de Paris   The Lido competes with the best Las Vegas has to offer. Its $15-million production, *C'est Magique*, reflects a dramatic reworking of the classic Parisian cabaret show, with eye-popping special effects, water technology using more than 60,000 gallons per minute, and even aerial and aquatic ballet. The show, the most expensive ever produced in Europe, uses 70 performers, $4 million in costumes, and a $2-million lighting design with lasers. There's even an ice rink and swimming pool that appears and disappears. The 45 topless Bluebell Girls, those legendary showgirls, are still here. 16 bis av. des Champs-Elysées, 8e. ✆ **800/227-4884** in the U.S., or 01-40-76-56-10. www.lido.fr. Dinner dance (7pm) and show (11:30pm) 140€–210€; show only (9:30 and 11:30pm) 90€. Price includes half-bottle of champagne per person. Métro: George V.

Moulin Rouge   This is a camp classic. The establishment that Toulouse-Lautrec immortalized is still here, but the artist would probably have a hard time recognizing it. Colette created a scandal here by offering an onstage kiss to Mme. de Morny, but shows today have a harder time shocking audiences. Try to get a table; the view is much better on the main floor than from the bar. What's the theme? It's strip routines and the saucy sexiness of *la Belle Epoque,* and of permissive Paris between the wars. Handsome men and girls, girls, girls, virtually all topless, keep the place going. Dance finales usually include two dozen of the belles doing a topless cancan. Revues begin nightly at 9 and 11pm. 82 bd. Clichy, place Blanche, 18e. ✆ **01-53-09-82-82.** www.moulinrouge.fr. Cover including champagne 92€–102€; 7pm dinner and show 150€–180€. Métro: Blanche.

Le Cool Jazz

The great jazz revival that long ago swept America is still going strong here, with Dixieland or Chicago rhythms pounding out in dozens of jazz cellars, mostly called *caveaux.* Most clubs are on the Left Bank near the Seine, between rue Bonaparte and rue St-Jacques. For the latest details, look for publications such as *Jazz Hot, Jazz Magazine,* or *Pariscope.*

Baiser Salé   In a cellar lined with jazz-related paintings, a large bar, and videos that show jazz greats of the past (Charlie Parker, Miles Davis), this is an appealing club. Everything is mellow and laid-back, with an emphasis on the music. Genres include Afro-Caribbean, Afro-Latino, salsa, merengue, rhythm and blues, and sometimes fusion. 58 rue des Lombards, 1er. © **01-42-33-37-71.** www.lebaisersale.com. Cover Tues–Sun 8€ or 18€ after 10pm. Free Mon. Métro: Châtelet.

Bizz'art   On the Canal St-Martin, this is a venue for live jazz and other music concerts, including R&B, house, and funk. Live jazz begins the evening, which turns into an eclectic dance party. Happy hour is Wednesday to Saturday from 8 to 10pm, and there's also an on-site restaurant serving a three-course "Menu Bizz'art" for 34€. One group appearing here is called Dance Your Ass Off. Open daily from 8pm to 1am (only Fri–Sat in Aug). 167 quai de Valmy, 10e. © **01-40-34-70-00.** www.bizzartclub.com. Cover 10€–12€. Métro: Louis Blanc.

Caveau des Oubliettes ★   It's hard to say which is more intriguing—the entertainment and drinking or the setting. An *oubliette* is a dungeon with a trapdoor at the top as its only opening, and the name is accurate. Located in the Latin Quarter, just across the river from Notre-Dame, this nightspot is housed in a genuine 12th-century prison, complete with dungeons, spine-tingling passages, and scattered skulls, where prisoners were tortured and sometimes pushed through portholes to drown in the Seine. The *caveau* is beneath the subterranean vaults that many centuries ago linked it with the fortress prison of Petit Châtelet. Today patrons laugh, drink, talk, and flirt in the narrow *caveau,* or else retreat to the smoke-filled jazz lounge. There's a free jam session every night, perhaps Latin jazz or rock. At some point on Friday and Saturday nights concerts are staged (a cover is assessed at this time). It's open daily 5pm to 2am. 52 rue Galande, 5e. © **01-46-34-23-09.** www.caveaudesoubliettes.fr. Cover 15€ Fri–Sat. Métro: St-Michel.

La Chapelle des Lombards 🎁   The club's proximity to the Opéra Bastille seems incongruous, considering the African/Caribbean jazz and Brazilian samba that's the norm. It's a magnet for South American and African expatriates, and the rhythms and fire of the music propel everyone onto the dance floor. Open Tuesday to Sunday 11:30pm to 6am, June to August daily 11:30pm to 6am. 19 rue de Lappe, 11e. © **01-43-57-24-24.** www.la-chapelle-des-lombards.com. Cover 15€–19€ including first drink. Free for women Thurs before midnight. Métro: Bastille.

Le Petit Journal   Sometimes French jazz aficionados refer to this jazz club and restaurant by its English name—"The Small Newspaper of Saint-Michel." The club lies in the center of the Latin Quarter, opposite the Garden of Luxembourg. Created in 1971, it is the "high temple" in Paris for the jazz of New Orleans. Some of the country's top artists appear here, including Claude Bolling. The music is downstairs in the cellar. Open Monday to Saturday 9:15pm to 2am. 71 bd. St-Michel, 5e. © **01-43-26-28-59.** www.petitjournalsaintmichel.com. Cover 17€–20€ including a drink; dinner and show 48€–53€. Closed Aug. RER: Luxembourg.

Dance Clubs

The area around the Eglise St-Germain-des-Prés is full of dance clubs. They come and go so quickly that last year's disco inferno could be a hardware store by now—but new ones will spring up to take the place of the old. For the most up-to-date information, look for publications such as *Time Out, Pariscope,* or *L'Officiel des Spectacles.*

Batofar ★   Self-consciously proud of its status as a club that virtually everybody views as hip, Batofar sits on a converted barge that floats on the Seine, sometimes attracting hundreds of gyrating dancers, most of whom are in their 20s and 30s. House, garage, techno, and live jazz by groups that hail from (among other places) Morocco, Senegal, and Germany sometimes add to the mix. Come here for an insight into late-night Paris at its most raffish and countercultural, and don't even try to categorize the patrons. Beer will cost around 8.50€ a bottle. Open Tuesday to Saturday 10pm to 6am. Closed November to March. Facing 11 quai François Mauriac, 13e. ℂ **01-53-14-76-59.** www.batofar.org. Cover 10€–14€. Métro: Quai de la Gare.

Cab ★★ If you've ever wanted to dance in a basement under the Louvre, it doesn't get much classier than this joint patronized by French models, Arab businessmen, women with a past, and children of the rich. Dim lighting illuminates black leather furniture and two bars with shiny black or glass surfaces. There is also a trio of different seating areas. Music is house and electro, with various hip-hop songs and other American hits mixed in. We even heard Michael Jackson one night (remember him?). Open Wednesday to Saturday 11:30pm to 6am. 2 place du Palais Royal, 1er. ℂ **01-58-62-56-25.** www.cabaret.fr. Cover 20€, including 1 drink. Métro: Palais Royal-Musée du Louvre.

Chacha Club ★★ For the chic and sophisticated of all ages, this hot spot draws a crowd that the French press labeled "international slutterati." In addition to a cavernous bar and dance hall, there are several small salons, even a passcode-restricted bedroom. The *über*-trendy place is also a restaurant serving a range of finger foods such as tapas and antipasti. DJs keep the sound track on high throughout the night. Some of the most beautiful models in Paris arrange themselves on the leather armchairs. It's better to go early if you want to get in: the doorman is one tough bully. Open Monday to Saturday 8pm to 6am for the club, 8pm to midnight for the restaurant. 47 rue Berger. ℂ **01-40-13-12-12.** www.chachaclub.fr. Food platters 15€–25€. Metro: Louvre-Rivoli.

Club Zed 🎁 Hip, breezy, and very French, this popular nightspot in a former bakery with a vaulted masonry ceiling may surprise you with its mix of musical offerings, including samba, rock 'n' roll, 1960s pop, and jazz. Specific theme parties, such as the one at Halloween where virtually everyone comes in costume, are a delight. Open Thursday 9:30pm to 2:30am, Friday and Saturday 11pm to 5:30am. 2 rue des Anglais, 5e. ℂ **01-43-54-93-78.** Cover 10€ Thurs, 18€ Fri–Sat, including 1st drink. Métro: Maubert-Mutualité.

Favela Chic The hot sounds of Brazil permeate this nighttime party at this bar and restaurant, which makes the best mojitos in town (surely even Ernesto Hemingway would approve). Weekends are packed with an under-35 crowd. At times you'll think you've been transplanted to Rio de Janeiro. Bossa jazz and samba rap are also heard on some nights. A *favela*, incidentally, is a ghetto in Brazil. Open Tuesday to Thursday 7:30pm to 2am, Friday to Sunday 8pm to 4am. 18 rue du Faubourg du Temple, 11e. ℂ **01-40-21-38-14.** www.favelachic.com. Cover 10€ Fri–Sat. Métro: République.

La Balajo Established in 1936, this dance club is where Edith Piaf won the hearts of Parisian music lovers. Today, it's easy to compare La Balajo with New York City's Roseland—an old-fashioned venue steeped in big-band nostalgia, which sometimes manages to shake the dust out for special parties and events. Afternoon sessions focus on tangos, *paso dobles*, and waltzes, and are more staid than their late-night counterparts. Evenings attract a younger crowd (age 20 to 35-ish), who groove to a mixture, depending on the DJ, of house, garage, techno, and old-fashioned disco. Open Tuesday to Thursday 7pm to 2am, Friday and Saturday 11pm to 6am, and Sunday 3 to 7pm. 9 rue de Lappe, 11e. ℰ **01-47-00-07-87.** www.balajo.fr. Cover (includes 1 drink) 8€ for afternoon sessions, 16€–20€ for night sessions. Métro: Bastille.

La Java   This bal-musette dance hall was once one of the most important in Paris; Piaf and Maurice Chevalier made their names here. Today, you can still waltz on what one critic called "retro fetish night," or even tango on Sunday afternoon. Brazilian and Latin themes predominate on some nights. Overall, it's one of the best places in Paris for the old-fashioned pleasures of couples arm in arm on a dance floor. 105 rue du Faubourg du Temple, 11e. ℰ **01-42-02-20-52.** www.la-java.fr. Cover 17€. Métro: Belleville or Goncourt.

La Machine du Moulin Rouge   Opened in 2010, this is one of the largest clubs in Paris on the same premises as the defunct La Loco, which became known all over Europe. Today, La Machine remains one of the most popular techno clubs. On this site years ago, The Beatles stormed Paris. The sounds of electronic music are heard across three floors of cavernous space. Ticket prices can vary, depending on the event. Open daily 7pm to 6am. 90 bd. de Clichy, 18e. ℰ **01-53-41-88-89.** www.lamachine dumoulinrouge.com. Métro: Blanche.

Le Baron ★   If there's such a thing as a speak-easy in the 21st century, this bastion of cool is it. Once it was the most expensive brothel in Paris, and much of its original decor remains, including the 1920s-era tile of frolicking nude ladies, the sexy red walls, and the tasseled lamps. Today, however, the Gucci crowd in thick shades turns up, an equal mix of both sexes, including some customers who haven't decided which sex to be. The dance floor is one of the most packed in Paris with some of the world's most beautiful people. Drinks are costly—but so is being trendy. Open daily 11pm to 6am, though they can vary. 6 av. Marceau, 8e. ℰ **01-47-20-04-01.** www.clublebaron.com. Métro: Champs-Elysées.

Les Bains Douches   The name "the Baths" comes from this hot spot's former function as a Turkish bath that attracted gay clients, none more notable than Marcel Proust. It may be hard to get in if the doorman doesn't think you're trendy and *très chic.* Yes, that was Jennifer Lopez we saw whirling around the floor. Dancing begins at midnight, and a supper club–like restaurant is upstairs. Meals cost 32€ to 120€. On certain nights this is the hottest party atmosphere in Paris, and Mondays are increasingly gay, although sexual preference is hardly an issue at this club. "We all walk the waterfront," one DJ enigmatically told us. Open from 9pm to 2am. 7 rue du Bourg-l'Abbé, 3e. ℰ **01-53-01-40-60.** www.lesbainsdouches.net. Cover 10€–20€. Métro: Etienne Marcel.

Nouveau Casino   Some Paris watchers consider this the epitome of the hyperhip countercultural scene that blossoms along the rue Oberkampf every night. In a former movie theater adjacent to the Café Charbon, it's a large, drafty space centered on a dance floor and an enormous bar crafted to resemble an iceberg. Live concerts take place nightly between 8pm and 1am; on Friday and Saturday, the party continues from 1am till dawn, with a DJ who spins some of the most avant-garde dance music in Paris. Celebrity spotters have picked out Prince Albert of Monaco and such French-language film stars as Vincent Cassel and Mathieu Kassovitz. 109 rue Oberkampf, 9e. ℰ **01-43-57-57-40.** www.nouveaucasino.net. Admission to concerts 16€–27€; to disco 7€–20€. Métro: St-Maur, Parmentier, or Ménilmontant.

Rock

Bus Palladium A single room with a very long bar, this rock-'n'-roll temple has varnished hardwoods and fabric-covered walls that barely absorb the reverberations of nonstop recorded music. You won't find techno, punk, jazz, blues, or soul here. It appeals to hard-core, mostly heterosexual, rock wannabes ages 25 to 35. It's open Tuesday to Saturday 11pm to 5am (sometimes Mon or Sun for special events; check out schedules on the Internet). 6 rue Fontaine, 9e. ✆ **01-45-26-80-55.** www. lebuspalladiumparis.com. Métro: Blanche or Pigalle.

Wine Bars

Many Parisians prefer the wine bar to the traditional cafe or bistro—the food is often better and the ambience more inviting.

Au Sauvignon This tiny spot has tables overflowing onto a covered terrace and a decor that features old ceramic tiles and frescoes done by Left Bank artists. Wines range from the cheapest Beaujolais to the most expensive Puligny-Montrachet. A glass of wine costs 4.50€ to 6€. To go with your wine, choose an Auvergne specialty, such as goat cheese or a terrine. Fresh Poilâne bread is ideal with ham, pâté, or goat cheese. Open Monday to Saturday 8am to 10pm. Closed in August. 80 rue des Sts-Pères, 7e. ✆ **01-45-48-49-02.** Métro: Sèvres-Babylone or Saint Sulpice.

Le Sancerre Engagingly old-fashioned, with an agreeable staff and food prepared fresh every day, this wine bar specializes in vintages from the Loire Valley and Sancerre. The latter, produced in red, rosé, and white, is known for its not-too-dry fruity aroma and legions of fans who believe it should be more celebrated. Other wine choices include chinon and saumur wine (both from the Loire Valley), as well as pinot de Bourgogne (from Burgundy), gamay (from the Ardèche Valley in France's southwest), and chenas (from the Beaujolais). Food items usually include *andouillettes* (chitterling sausages), omelets with flap mushrooms, fresh oysters, and quiche. Glasses of wine cost 3€ to 6€; simple platters of food cost 8€ to 10€ each. Open Monday to Friday 8am to 4pm and 6:30 to 11pm, Saturday 8:30am to 4pm. 22 av. Rapp, 7e. ✆ **01-45-51-75-91.** Métro: Alma-Marceau.

Willi's Wine Bar ★★ Journalists and stockbrokers head for this popular wine bar in the financial district. It offers about 300 kinds of wine, including a dozen specials you can taste by the glass for 4€ to 18€. Lunch is the busiest time; on quiet evenings, you can better enjoy the warm ambience. Daily specials are likely to include lamb brochette with cumin or Lyonnais sausage in truffled vinaigrette, plus a spectacular dessert such as chocolate terrine. A fixed-price menu costs 21€ to 27€ at lunch, 33€ to 35€ at dinner. The restaurant is open Monday to Saturday noon to 2:30pm and 7 to 11pm; the bar, Monday to Saturday noon to midnight. 13 rue des Petits-Champs, 1er. ✆ **01-42-61-05-09.** www.williswinebar.com. Métro: Bourse, Pyramides, or Palais-Royal.

Bars & Pubs

Académie de la Bière ✔ The decor is paneled and rustic, an appropriate foil for an "academy" whose curriculum includes more than 153 kinds of beer from microbreweries. More than half of the dozen beers on tap are from small-scale breweries in Belgium that deserve to be better known than that country's bestseller, Stella Artois. Snack-style food is available, including platters of mussels, assorted

AFTER-DARK diversions: DIVES, DRAG & MORE

On a Paris night, the cheapest entertainment, especially if you're young, is "the show" at the tip of Ile de la Cité, behind Notre-Dame. A sort of Gallic version of the Sundowner Festival in Key West, Florida, it attracts just about everyone who ever wanted to try his or her hand at performance. The spontaneous entertainment usually includes magicians, fire-eaters, jugglers, mimes, and music makers from all over, performing against the backdrop of the illuminated cathedral. This is one of the greatest places in Paris to meet young people in a sometimes-euphoric setting.

Also popular is a stroll along the Seine after 10pm. Take a graveled pathway down to the river from the Left Bank side of pont de Sully, close to the Institut du Monde Arabe, and walk to the right, away from Notre-Dame. This walk, which ends near place Valhubert, is the best place to see spontaneous Paris in action at night. Joggers and saxophone players come here, and many Parisians arrive for impromptu dance parties.

To quench your thirst, wander onto Ile St-Louis and head for the **Café-Brasserie St-Regis,** 6 rue Jean-du-Bellay, 4e; across from pont St-Louis (✆ **01-43-54-59-41;** Métro: Pont Marie). If you want to linger, you can order a *plat du jour* or a coffee at the bar. But try doing as the Parisians do: Get a 3€ beer to go *(une bière à emporter)* in a cup and take it with you on a stroll around the island. The cafe is open daily until midnight.

If you're caught waiting for the Métro to start running again at 5am, try the **Sous-Bock Tavern,** 49 rue St-Honoré, 1er (✆ **01-40-26-46-61;** Métro: Les Halles or Louvres-Rivoli), open Monday to Saturday from 11am to 5am, Sunday 5pm to 5am. Young drinkers gather here to sample from 250 varieties of beer or 20 varieties of whiskey. The dish to order is a platter of mussels—curried, with white wine, or with cream sauce; they go well with the brasserie-style fries.

If drag shows aren't your cup of tea, how about *Last Tango in Paris*? At **Le Tango,** 11 rue au Maire, 3e (✆ **01-42-72-17-78;** Métro: Arts et Métiers), memories of Evita and Argentina live on. On-site is a ballroom called La Boîte à Frissons. The evening starts at 10:30pm, with couples dancing until 12:30am, featuring the waltz, the tango, *paso doble,* the polka, rock 'n' roll, and cha-cha. After that, the dance floor turns into a disco. The cover is 8€. It's open Friday and Saturday from midnight to 5am.

If you're looking for a sophisticated, laid-back venue, consider the **Sanz-Sans,** 49 rue du Faubourg St-Antoine, 4e (✆ **01-44-75-78-78;** www.sanzsans.com; Métro: Bastille or Ledru Rollin), a multiethnic playground where the children of prominent Parisians mingle, testifying to the unifying power of jazz. In this redvelvet duplex, the most important conversations seem to occur over margaritas on the stairway or the back-room couches. The later it gets, the sexier the scene becomes. No cover is charged.

cheeses, and sausages with mustard. Open Sunday to Thursday 10am to 2am and Friday and Saturday 10am to 3am. 88 bis bd. du Port-Royal, 5e. ✆ **01-43-54-66-65.** www.academie-biere.com. RER: Port Royal.

Andy Whaloo   A play on Andy Warhol's name, this bar would be at home in Marrakesh, the chicest city today in North Africa. Enjoy tapas Mediterranean or smoke a hookah. The background music might be raï from old Algers. Patterned Moroccan rugs are thrown over banquettes, which fill up nightly with some of the most fashionable young people of Paris. The stools are made from paint barrels. The ambience is definitely of the *souk*. Open daily 4pm to 2am. 69 rue des Gravilliers, 3e. © **01-42-71-20-38.** Métro: Opéra.

Barrio Latino This multilevel emporium of good times, Gallic flair, and Latin charm occupies a space designed by Gustav Eiffel in the 19th century. Tapas bars and dance floors are on the street level (*rez-de-chaussée*) and third floor (*3ème étage*); a Latin restaurant is on the second floor (*2ème étage*). Staff members roll carts loaded with tapas around the floors, selling them like hot dogs at an American baseball game. The restaurant specializes in food that French palates find refreshing: Argentine steaks, Brazilian *feijoada* (a bean-based dish that's similar to cassoulet), and Mexican chili, all of which taste wonderful with beer, caipirinhas, *Cuba libres,* or rum punches. The clientele is mixed, mostly straight, partly gay, and 100% blasé about matters such as an individual's sexuality. 46 rue du Faubourg St-Antoine, 12e. © **01-55-78-84-75.** Cover 20€ for nondiners daily noon–2am. Métro: Bastille.

Buddha Bar The food is mediocre, but that doesn't seem to matter to the fashionistas on the see-and-be-seen circuit. A giant Buddha presides over the vast dining room, where a combination of Japanese sashimi, Vietnamese spring rolls, Chinese lacquered duck, and various Asian fusion dishes are served. Many patrons come here to drink at the lacquered bar, found upstairs from the street-level dining room. From the upper perch you can observe the action of the swanky international patrons below. The music is spacey, the atmosphere electric, and some of the prettiest women and handsomest hunks in Paris are in attendance nightly. The location is near the Champs-Elysées and place de la Concorde. Open Monday to Friday, from noon to 2am, and Saturday and Sunday, from 4pm to 2am. 8 rue Boissy Anglas, 8e. © **01-53-05-90-00.** www.buddhabar.com. Métro: Concorde.

Café de l'Industrie This is a bizarre, only-in-Paris type of complex—a restaurant, cafe, and shop of provocative lingerie. The original cafe branched out with a second restaurant across the street known as Cafés de l'Industrie as well as a shop called L'Industrie Lingerie. Good Parisian food and drink are served in the main branch with an interior decorated with photos of movie stars. Live jazz is played Sunday to Tuesday nights. This retro-style neighborhood cafe and restaurant lie next to place de la Bastille. Open daily 9:30am to 2am. 16 rue Saint-Sabin, 11e. © **01-47-00-13-53.** www.cafedelindustrie.com. Métro: Bréguet-Savin or Bastille.

Experimental Cocktail Club The bar's name is written on a brass plate like that of a private club. Once you pass inspection from an ill-tempered doorman and go through heavy curtains at the entrance, you enter a small, overcrowded room where patrons, mostly those in their 30s, are drinking some of the most divine cocktails in Paris, costing from 9€. The rustic chic place was designed by New Yorker Cuoco Black. Open daily 5pm to 5am. 37 rue Saint Sauveur, 2e. © **01-45-08-88-09.** www.experimentalcocktailclub.com. Métro: Sentier or Reaumur-Sebastopol.

La Belle Hortense There are dozens of other bars and cafes near this one, but none maintains a bookstore in back, and few seem so self-consciously aware of their roles as ersatz literary salons. Come for a glass of wine and participate in a discussion at what's defined as "a literary bar." It's named after a pulpy 19th-century romance (*La Belle Hortense*) set within the neighborhood. Glasses of wine cost 3€ to 7€. Open daily 5pm to 2am. 31 rue Vieille-du-Temple, 4e. © **01-48-04-71-60.** Métro: Saint-Paul.

Le China   There's been a club on this site for years. Back in the 1930s, it was an opium den and jazz club. Today, in its latest incarnation, it is all dark colors, candles, soft lights, and intimacy. Upstairs, backgammon games are played, and there is also a fireplace and library plus a winter garden with big rattan chairs. The on-site restaurant evokes 1930s Shanghai with red-painted walls. A long zinc bar is on the ground floor, and in the basement is a bar that stages jazz concerts. It's an ideal place to have a drink. Cocktails cost from 10€. Open daily 6pm to 2am. 50 rue de Charenton, 12e. ✆ **01-43-46-08-09.** www.lechina.eu. Métro: Ledru Rollin.

Le Piano Vache   A student hangout since the uprising of 1969, this enduring Latin Quarter favorite attracts a counterculture clientele; even Johnny Depp has been known to show up. You can lose yourself here in a "lasso" of blue smoke around the old *déglingué* piano. It's where the Paris of yesterday meets the Paris of today. Piano music graces the night. There's music on most nights beginning after 8pm. DJs play everything from punk to rock; the '80s often live again. Open daily 9pm to 2am. 8 rue Laplace, 5e. ✆ **01-46-33-75-03.** www.lepianovache.com. Métro: Maubert Mutualité.

Le Paris Paris ★   This is a chic bar operated by the owners of Le Baron. The atmosphere is sexy and at times a bit intoxicating (or is that the champagne talking?). This subterranean club is installed in a former Chinese restaurant, and attracts *Parisiens aristo-branchés* (plugged in jet-setters). DJs rule over the intimate dance space. If you get by the doormen, you descend a staircase lit by red lights as in an old bordello. Drinks range from 9€ to 17€, and the music is a bit electro. Open Tuesday to Sunday 8pm to 2am. 5 av. de l'Opéra, 5e. ✆ **01-42-60-64-65.** Métro: Palais Royal or Pyramides Ligne.

Louis Bar & Lounge ★   In the swanky Hotel de Trémoille, this bar since 1883 has always been a chic rendezvous for a drink. In its latest restoration, it still evokes the 1930s with thick carpets and embroidered fabrics. With its private alcoves, the bar is intimate with both a library and a fireplace, with seating around a live piano player. Near the Champs-Elysées, the bar attracts chic Parisians. Cocktails range in price from 18€ to 20€. Open Monday to Saturday 7pm to midnight, Sunday 7 to 11pm. 16 rue de la Trémoille, 18e. ✆ **01-56-52-14-14.** Métro: George V or Franklin D. Roosevelt.

Mojito Habana   Amid a decor that evokes colonial Havana under Batista, with lots of green upholsteries, wood panels, and deep sofas, you'll find a three-tiered place with a restaurant (it charges around 50€ for a full meal); a piano bar (music begins at 11pm every night the place is open, and at 10pm on Tues); and a cigar lounge. Jazz concerts are featured Tuesday night. Cocktails, including *Cuba libres*, cost 13€ each. Entrance is always free. And the music that's in the background is international rock and pop, not solely salsa and merengue. It's open Monday to Saturday noon to 5am. And it attracts a lot of nattily dressed business travelers. 19 rue de Presbourg, 16e. ✆ **01-45-00-84-84.** Métro: Etoile.

Literary Haunts

Harry's New York Bar ★   At *sank roo doe noo,* as the ads tell you to instruct your cabdriver, is the most famous bar in Europe—possibly in the world. Opened on Thanksgiving Day 1911 by an expatriate named MacElhone, it's where members of the World War I ambulance corps drank themselves silly. In addition to being Hemingway's favorite, Harry's is where the white lady and sidecar cocktails were invented; it's also the reputed birthplace of the bloody mary and the headquarters of a loosely organized fraternity of drinkers known as the International Bar Flies.

The historic core is the street-level bar, where CEOs and office workers loosen their ties on more or less equal footing. Daytime crowds are from the neighborhood's insurance, banking, and travel industries; evening crowds include pre- and post-theater groupies and night owls who aren't bothered by the gritty setting and unflattering lighting. A softer, somewhat less macho ambience reigns in the cellar, where a pianist provides music. Open daily noon to 2am. 5 rue Daunou, 2e. ℂ **01-42-61-71-14.** www.harrys-bar.fr. Métro: Opéra.

Rosebud   The popularity of this place known for a bemused and indulgent attitude toward anyone looking for a drink and some talk hasn't diminished since the 1950s. The name refers to the beloved sled of Orson Welles's *Citizen Kane.* Around the corner from Montparnasse's famous cafes and thick in associations with Sartre and de Beauvoir, Ionesco, and Duras, Rosebud draws a crowd ages 35 to 65, though the staff has noticed the appearance of literary-minded students. Drop in at night for a glass of wine, a shot of whiskey, or a hamburger or chili con carne. Open daily 7pm to 2am. 11 bis rue Delambre, 14e. ℂ **01-43-35-38-54** or 01-43-20-44-13. Métro: Vavin.

Gay & Lesbian Bars & Clubs

Gay life is centered on **Les Halles** and **Le Marais,** with the greatest concentration of gay and lesbian clubs, restaurants, bars, and shops between the Hôtel de Ville and Rambuteau Métro stops. Gay dance clubs come and go so fast that even the magazines devoted to them, such as *Illico*—distributed free in the gay bars and bookstores—have a hard time keeping up. For lesbians, there is *Lesbian Magazine.* Also look for Gai Pied's *Guide Gai* and *Pariscope*'s regularly featured English-language section, "A Week of Gay Outings." Also important for both men and women is *Têtu Magazine,* sold at most newsstands.

Banana Café   This popular bar is a stop for gays visiting or doing business in Paris. Occupying two floors of a 19th-century building, it has walls the color of an overripe banana, dim lighting, and a policy of raising the drink prices after 10pm, when things become really interesting. There's a street-level bar and a cellar dance floor that features a live pianist and recorded music—sometimes with dancing. On many nights, go-go dancers perform from spotlit platforms in the cellar. Open daily from 5:30pm to 4 or 5am. 13 rue de la Ferronnerie, 1er. ℂ **01-42-33-35-31.** www.banana cafeparis.com. Métro: Châtelet–Les Halles.

La Champmeslé   With dim lighting, background music, and comfortable banquettes, La Champmeslé provides a cozy meeting place for women and a few (about 5%) "well-behaved" men. Paris's leading women's bar is in a 300-year-old building with exposed stone, ceiling beams, and 1950s-style furnishings. Thursday night, one of the premier lesbian events in Paris, a cabaret, begins at 10pm. Open daily 4pm to 6am. 4 rue Chabanais, 2e. ℂ **01-42-96-85-20.** www.lachampmesle.com. Métro: Pyramides or Bourse.

Le Depot   This gay pleasure palace stages everything from Queer Mother Nights to Putanas at Work. Patrons wander the rooms downstairs searching for their companion of the night. The pickup area and best cruising grounds are in the section where porno flicks are being shown on television sets mounted on the walls. The many back rooms allow you to get better acquainted with your catch of the evening.

After 11pm, lesbians patronize the upstairs dance floor. The age range here is from 18 to 50. The post-Sunday-brunch gay tea dance, starting at 5pm, is one of the happening events of Paris. Open daily from 2pm to 8am. 10 rue aux Ours, 3e. ✆ **01-44-54-96-96.** Cover 8.50€–13€. Métro: Etienne-Marcel.

Le Queen   Should you miss gay life à la New York, seek out the flashing purple sign near the corner of avenue George V. This place is often mobbed, primarily by gay men and, to a lesser degree, chic women who work in fashion and film. Look for drag shows, muscle shows, striptease by danseurs atop the bars, and everything from '70s-style disco nights to foam parties (only in summer), when cascades of suds descend onto the dance floor. Go very, very late: The place opens at 11pm and stays open until 6 or 7am. 102 av. des Champs-Elysées, 8e. ✆ **01-53-89-08-90.** www.queen.fr. Cover Fri–Sat 15€–20€. Métro: Franklin-D-Roosevelt or George V.

Le 3w Kafe   The 3w means "Woman with Woman." This is the best-known lesbian bar in the Marais, where an unattached female can usually find a drinking buddy. On weekends there's dancing downstairs with a DJ in control of the sounds. Straight men are welcome but only if accompanied by a female. Gay men are admitted without any problem. At this dive, theme evenings are often presented. Open Tuesday to Sunday 7pm to 6am. 8 rue des Ecouffes, 4e. ✆ **01-48-87-39-26.** Métro: St. Paul.

Open Café/Café Cox   Although this side-by-side pair of gay men's bars are independent, their clienteles are so interconnected, and there's such traffic between them, that we—like many other residents of this neighborhood—usually jumble them together. Both define themselves as bars rather than dance clubs, but on particularly busy nights, one or another couple might actually begin to dance. Simple cafe-style food is served from noon to around 5pm. Don't come here with preconceptions about what type of guy you're likely to find; patrons can include just about every type of man that roams the streets of gay Europe today. Open Sunday to Thursday 11am to 2am, Friday and Saturday to 4am. 15 rue des Archives, 4e. ✆ **01-42-72-26-18** or 01-42-72-08-00. Métro: Hôtel de Ville.

SIDE TRIPS FROM PARIS: VERSAILLES, CHARTRES & THE BEST OF THE ILE DE FRANCE

Château de Versailles, the Cathédrale Notre-Dame de Chartres, and the Palais de Fontainebleau draw countless tour buses to this region. They're the stars of the Ile de France. Some lesser known but equally stunning spots also await you. You can find everything from Romanesque ruins, Gothic cathedrals, and feudal castles to 18th-century châteaux, forests such as Fontainebleau and Chantilly, sleepy villages, and an African game reserve. For kids of all ages, there's Disneyland Paris. Finally, this region is a haven for artists, so you can visit the painted worlds of Corot, Renoir, Degas, Monet, and Cézanne.

You can experience everything we describe here on a day trip or an overnight from Paris. For even more day trips, check out the latest edition of *Frommer's Paris.*

VERSAILLES ★

21km (13 miles) SW of Paris; 71km (44 miles) NE of Chartres

Back in the *grand siècle,* all you needed was a sword, a hat, and a bribe for the guard at the gate. Provided you didn't look as if you had smallpox, you'd be admitted to the Château de Versailles, where you could stroll through salon after glittering salon and watch the Sun King, gossiping, dancing, plotting, and flirting. Louis XIV was accorded about as much privacy as an institution.

Today, Versailles would welcome the return of Louis XIV and his fat treasury. You wouldn't believe it to look at the glittering Hall of Mirrors, but Versailles is down at the heels. You get to see only half its treasures; the rest—including the Musée de France, with its 6,000 paintings and 2,000 statues—are closed to the public. Some 3.2 million visitors arrive annually, spending about 2 hours here.

Essentials

GETTING THERE To get to Versailles, catch the **RER** line C1 to Versailles–Rive Gauche at the Gare d'Austerlitz, St-Michel, Musée d'Orsay, Invalides, Ponte de l'Alma, Champ de Mars, or Javel stop, and take it to the Versailles/Rive Gauche station. The trip takes 35 to 40 minutes. Do not get off at Versailles Chantier, which will leave you on the other end of town, a long walk from the château. The round-trip fare is 5.60€; Eurailpass holders travel free on the RER but need to show the pass at the ticket kiosk to receive an RER ticket. **SNCF trains** make frequent runs from Gare

St-Lazare and Gare Montparnasse in Paris to Versailles. Trains departing from Gare St-Lazare arrive at the Versailles/Rive Droite railway station; trains departing from Gare Montparnasse arrive at Versailles/Chantiers station, a long walk as mentioned.

You can purchase the **Château Passeport,** which from April to October costs 20€ Monday to Friday, rising to 25€ Saturday and Sunday. From November to March its daily cost is 16€. The pass is sold at the tourist office in Versailles and with it you can avoid the long lines at the château itself.

The tourist office doesn't sell tickets to each of the sights, so you should purchase it if you want to see the whole Versailles complex. If you hold the **Paris Museum Pass** (see "The Museum Discount Card" box in chapter 6), admission is free to the château. You can also avoid the long ticket lines with the Paris Museum Pass.

An even better deal to consider is a combined RER train fare and château entrance ticket. These are sold at any SNCF (train) or Transilien (RER) station. Called *forfait,* the packet costs 22€, including the round-trip train fare from Paris and a 1-day Passeport. This is a great deal considering the cost of the Passeport itself (see above). The combined deal also allows you to avoid the long lines at the palace entrance.

Both Versailles stations are within a 10-minute walk of the château, and we recommend the walk as a means of orienting yourself to the town, its geography, its scale, and its architecture. If you can't or don't want to walk, you can take bus B, or (in midsummer) a shuttle bus marked CHATEAU from either station to the château for either a cash payment of around 2€ (drop the coins directly into the coin box near the driver) or the insertion of a valid ticket for the Paris Métro. Because of the vagaries of the bus schedules, we highly recommend the walk. Directions to the château are clearly signposted from each railway station.

If you're **driving,** exit the *périphérique* (the ring road around Paris) on N10 (av. du Général-Leclerc), which will take you to Versailles; park on place d'Armes in front of the château.

VISITOR INFORMATION   The **Office de Tourisme** is at 2 bis av. de Paris (© **01-39-24-88-88;** fax 01-39-24-88-89; www.versailles-tourisme.com). The office is closed Sunday and Monday.

EVENING SPECTACLES   Recognizing the value of the palace as a national symbol, the French government offers a program of fireworks and illuminated fountains, "Les Fêtes de Nuit de Versailles," on about 7 to 10 widely publicized dates between late August and early September, usually beginning at 9:30pm. Observers, who sit in bleachers near the palace's boulevard de la Reine entrance, close to the Fountain *(Bassin)* of Neptune, are treated to a display of fireworks, prerecorded classical music, and up to 200 players (none of whom utters a line) in period costume, portraying the glories of France as symbolized by Louis XIV and the courtiers of the *ancien régime.* Shows are big on pomp and strong on visuals, and last about 90 minutes. Tickets range from 35€ to 85€. Gates open around 90 minutes before showtime. For information, call © **01-30-83-78-89.**

DAYTIME SPECTACLES   Saturdays and Sundays from April to early October, between 11:30am and noon and 3:30 and 5pm, the French government broadcasts classical music throughout the park and opens the valves on as many fountains as are currently in operation as part of a program known as "Les Grandes Eaux Musicales de Versailles." The spectacles showcase the landscaping vision of the palace's designers and encourage participants to walk, promenade, or meander the vast park, enjoying the juxtaposition of supremely grand architecture with lavish waterworks. Afternoon events include water coming out of more jets than during the somewhat less lavish morning events. Admission to any part of the park during these spectacles can vary from 6€ to 10€. For information, call ☎ **01-30-83-78-88.**

You can purchase tickets to all spectacles at Versailles up until about a half-hour before the day or night of any performance from the ticket office in the Accueil-Billeterie on Place d'Armes, immediately across from the main facade of the palace, or from any French branch of the **FNAC** department store (FNAC's central phone number is ☎ **01-55-21-57-93**).

A RETURN TO FADED glory

The French government will pour the equivalent of $455 million into a grand restoration of Versailles and its splendid gardens. The project has gotten off to a slow start and is estimated to continue until 2024, but the attraction—one of the most visited in Europe—will remain open during the restoration. The grand design of the architects is to make the palace, dating from the 17th century, look much as it did when it was home to Louis XIV, XV, and the ill-fated XVI. Some features will be removed, such as a wide staircase ordered built by King Louis-Philippe in the château's last major rebuilding in the 1830s. Other features will be added, including a replica of the *grille royale* (a gilded royal insignia that was part of the entrance gate) that was torn out after the 1789 Revolution. Facilities for visitors with disabilities will also improve.

Exploring the Château & Gardens

Château de Versailles ★★★   Within 50 years, the Château de Versailles was transformed from Louis XIII's hunting lodge into an extravagant palace. Begun in 1661, its construction involved 32,000 to 45,000 workmen, some of whom had to drain marshes and move forests. Louis XIV set out to build a palace that would be the envy of Europe and created a symbol of opulence copied, yet never duplicated, the world over.

Wishing (with good reason) to keep an eye on the nobles of France, Louis XIV summoned them to live at his court. Here he amused them with constant entertainment and lavish banquets. To some he awarded such tasks as holding the hem of his robe. While the aristocrats played at often-silly intrigues and games, the peasants on the estates sowed the seeds of the Revolution.

When Louis XIV died in 1715, his great-grandson Louis XV succeeded him and continued the outrageous pomp, though he is said to have predicted the outcome: *"Après moi le déluge"* (After me, the deluge). His wife, Marie Leszczynska, was shocked by the blatant immorality at Versailles.

The next monarch, Louis XVI, found his grandfather's behavior scandalous—in fact, on gaining the throne he ordered that the "stairway of indiscretion" (secret stairs leading to the king's bedchamber) be removed. The well-intentioned but weak king and his queen, Marie Antoinette, were well liked at first, but the queen's frivolity and spending led to her downfall. Louis and Marie Antoinette were at Versailles on October 6, 1789, when they were notified that mobs were marching on the palace. As predicted, *le déluge* had arrived.

Napoleon stayed at Versailles but never seemed fond of it. Louis-Philippe (who reigned 1830–48) prevented the destruction of the palace by converting it into a museum dedicated to the glory of France. To do that, he had to surrender some of his own riches. Decades later, John D. Rockefeller contributed toward the restoration of Versailles, and work continues today.

The magnificent **Grands Appartements** ★★★ are in the Louis XIV style; each bears the name of the allegorical painting on the ceiling. The best known and largest is the **Hercules Salon** ★★, with a ceiling painted by François Lemoine, depicting the Apotheosis of Hercules. In the **Mercury Salon** (with a ceiling by Jean-Baptiste Champaigne), the body of Louis XIV was put on display in 1715; his 72-year reign was one of the longest in history.

The most famous room at Versailles is the 71m-long (233-ft.) **Hall of Mirrors ★★★**. Begun by Mansart in 1678 in the Louis XIV style, it was decorated by Le Brun with 17 arched windows faced by beveled mirrors in simulated arcades. On June 28, 1919, the treaty ending World War I was signed in this corridor. The German Empire was proclaimed here in 1871. In 2007, a $16-million makeover was completed, returning the Hall of Mirrors to much as it was during the reign of the Sun King. The restoration marked the first time in more than 3 centuries that the hall was restored from top to bottom. Even so, hawk-eyes will notice nips and tucks. But Frédéric Didier, the chief architect of France's monuments, claimed, "All the wrinkles in her face tell a story."

The royal apartments were for show, but Louis XV and Louis XVI retired to the **Petits Appartements ★★** to escape the demands of court etiquette. Louis XV died in his bedchamber in 1774, a victim of smallpox. In a second-floor apartment, which you can visit only with a guide, he stashed away first Mme. de Pompadour, and then Mme. du Barry.

Louis XVI had a sumptuous **Library,** designed by Jacques-Ange Gabriel. Its panels are delicately carved, and the room has been restored and refurnished. The **Clock Room** contains Passement's astronomical clock, encased in gilded bronze. Twenty years in the making, it was completed in 1753. The clock is supposed to keep time until the year 9999. At age 7, Mozart played for the court in this room.

Gabriel designed the **Opéra ★★** for Louis XV in 1748, though it wasn't completed until 1770. In its heyday, it took 3,000 candles to light the place. Hardouin-Mansart built the harmoniously gold-and-white **Royal Chapel** in 1699, dying before its completion. Louis XVI married Marie Antoinette here in 1770, while he was the dauphin.

In 2005, a previously off-limits section of the vast palace was opened to the public for the first time by an act of the Parliament. The decision adds some 25,085 sq. m (270,000 sq. ft.) of the south wing to public access. Up to now, the area had been reserved for use by Parliament itself. Among the rooms opened up is the mammoth **Battle Gallery,** which at 119m (390 ft.) is the longest hall at Versailles. The gallery displays monumental paintings depicting all of France's great battles, ranging from the founding of the monarchy by Clovis, who reigned in the 5th and 6th centuries, through the Napoleonic wars in the early 19th century.

Spread across 100 hectares (247 acres), the **Gardens of Versailles ★★★** were laid out by landscape artist André Le Nôtre. At the peak of their glory, 1,400 fountains spewed forth. *The Buffet* is an exceptional fountain, designed by Mansart. One fountain depicts Apollo in his chariot pulled by four horses, surrounded by Tritons rising from the water. Le Nôtre created a Garden of Eden using ornamental lakes and canals, geometrically designed flower beds, and avenues bordered with statuary. On the mile-long Grand Canal, Louis XV used to take gondola rides with his favorite of the moment.

A walk across the park takes you to the pink-and-white-marble **Grand Trianon ★★**, designed by Hardouin-Mansart for Louis XIV in 1687. Traditionally it has been lodging for VIPs, though de Gaulle wanted to turn it into a weekend retreat. Nixon slept here in the room where Mme. de Pompadour died. The original furnishings are gone, replaced today by mostly Empire pieces.

Gabriel, the designer of place de la Concorde in Paris, built the **Petit Trianon ★★** in 1768 for Louis XV. Louis used it for his trysts with Mme. du Barry. In time, Marie Antoinette adopted it as her favorite residence, a place to escape the rigid life at the main palace. Many of the current furnishings, including a few in her rather modest bedchamber, belonged to the ill-fated queen. Many other sites on the 34-hectare (86-acre) "Domaine" of Marie Antoinette have been opened to the public, including a delicate wooden and papier-mâché minitheater where she performed playing a shepherdess and an artificial grotto where she held private encounters. Other sites opened for the first time include a French pavilion where she often dined and a marble columned structure known as the Temple of Love, as well as Belvédère Hall where small recitals were held.

Les Grandes Ecuries (the Stables) stand immediately opposite the château's main front facade, where horses and carriages of the kings were housed. Visitors can watch a team of up to a dozen students, with their mounts, strut their stuff during hour-long riding demonstrations within the covered 17th-century amphitheater of the historic stables. However, don't go with any expectations that the horsemanship will re-create exclusively 17th- and 18th-century styles. The focus is on showmanship and equestrian razzmatazz rather than exact period replication. Hour-long demonstrations are conducted Thursday to Sunday at 11:15am. There's an additional presentation every Saturday and Sunday at 3pm. Depending on what's happening, the price of tickets can vary, perhaps 20€ to 25€. Admission to this event provides the only official way a visitor to Versailles can easily gain entrance to the stables.

© **01-30-83-78-00.** www.chateauversailles.fr. Palace 14€ adults or 12€ after 3pm; free for ages 26 and under. Both Trianons 10€ adults; free 26 and under. Palace: Apr–Oct Tues–Sun 9am–6pm; Nov–Mar Tues–Sun 9am–5pm. Trianons Tues–Sun noon–6pm. Grounds daily dawn to dusk.

Musée Lambinet ★ 🏛 Often overlooked by visitors to Versailles, the Musée Lambinet is filled with treasures seized from the French court during the Revolution. Here are all the antiques, the carved wood paneling, even religious art and other objets d'art so beloved by Marie Antoinette and the mistresses of Louis XV. The sumptuous mansion from 1751 is also filled with paintings (no great masterpieces, however), weaponry, and rare porcelain (look for the Du Barry rose). Also on view are rare displays illustrating the lives of Jean-Paul Marat, the radical journalist, and his murderer, Charlotte Corday, as depicted in stage plays and films.

54 bd. de la Reine. © **01-39-50-30-32.** www.musee-lambinet.com. Admission 5.50€ adults, 2.50€ ages 6–18. Tues–Sun 2–5:45pm.

Shopping

Founded by the Sun King himself, Louis XIV, **Marché Notre-Dame,** place du Marché Notre-Dame (© **01-30-97-84-89**), is the major public market in Versailles, housed in a series of red-brick buildings. The present look dates from the 19th century. Indoor shops selling local cheeses and fresh fruits are open daily, but the outdoor stalls in the center of the square flourish only on Tuesday, Friday, and Sunday, from about 9am to 2pm. It's best to go before noon; some of the stalls start shutting down in the early afternoon.

Close to the mammoth market, **Passage de la Geôle** (© **01-30-21-15-13**) is open Friday to Sunday 10am to 7pm, housing antiques shops selling furniture and objets d'art at "all prices."

Where to Stay

VERY EXPENSIVE

Trianon Palace ★★★ This luxe hotel is the grandest in the Ile de France, and after its 2008 renovation it has a more modern feel, with redesigned public and private rooms. A Westin property, it was built in 1910 on land that had sheltered a Capucine monastery during the *ancien régime*. The setting is lovely—the 2-hectare (5-acre) garden borders the gardens of the Petit Trianon at Versailles. In 1919, it was the head-quarters of the peace conference of Woodrow Wilson, Lloyd George, Georges Clemenceau, and other world leaders. Since then, guests have included John D. Rockefeller, Queen Elizabeth II, and Marlene Dietrich, who made headlines by wearing pants in the dining room. The hotel is in a classically designed palace, last restored in the early 1990s and connected to a late-20th-century annex (Le Pavillon) by an underground tunnel. Accommodations in both buildings are decorated in traditional style with reference to château living, using rich fabrics and a mixture of antiques and reproductions. Amenities and electronic accessories are top of the line. The hotel has joined with Phytomer, a top name in French beauty care, to create an outstanding spa.

1 bd. de la Reine, Versailles 78000. ✆ **800/937-8461** in the U.S. and Canada, or 01-30-84-50-00. Fax 01-30-84-50-01. www.trianonpalace.com. 199 units. 200€–300€ double; from 500€ suite. AE, DC, DISC, MC, V. Parking 20€. **Amenities:** 2 restaurants; cafe; bar; babysitting; health club; indoor pool; room service; sauna; spa; tennis courts. *In room:* A/C, TV, hair dryer, minibar, Wi-Fi (4.50€ per hr.).

MODERATE

Novotel Château de Versailles A 15-minute walk north of one of the side wings of the château, this chain hotel, built in 1988, has a modern facade with columns and large windows. It's not too expensive and is a convenient choice for visitors to Versailles. The renovated bedrooms come in two different styles—the classically French Harmonie or the far more contemporary Novation.

4 bd. St-Antoine, Le Chesnay 78152. ✆ **01-39-54-96-96.** Fax 01-39-54-94-40. www.accor-hotels.com. 105 units. 99€–159€ double; 165€–185€ suite. Children 16 and under stay free in parent's room. AE, DC, MC, V. Parking 11€. **Amenities:** Restaurant; bar; room service. *In room:* A/C, TV, hair dryer, minibar, Wi-Fi (4.50€ per hr.).

Where to Dine

La Flottille (✆ **01-39-51-41-58**) is the only restaurant inside the park (at the head of the Grand Canal), with a sweeping view over some of Europe's most famous landscaping. Both restaurant and snack-bar service are available. In warm weather, the traditional French cuisine is also served at outside tables. Reservations are recommended.

VERY EXPENSIVE

Gordon Ramsay au Trianon ★★★ FRENCH/INTERNATIONAL The *enfant terrible* of chefs, Gordon Ramsay, has invaded Versailles and is king of the roost at this Art Deco restaurant inside the swanky Trianon Palace Hotel. He is a master at traditional French cooking done in a modern style, and changes his menu frequently to take advantage of the best and the freshest in any season. No one does filet of turbot like Ramsay. But the same could be said of his roast sea bass with asparagus cooked in foie gras butter. He stuffs delectable ravioli with langoustines, and you can toss a pork belly his way, and he'll create a culinary masterpiece for you. The service, the setting, everything here is a delight. The food is of the highest order—and so are the prices. In summer, you can dine under the canopy on the front terrace.

In the Hotel Trianon Palace, 1 bd. de la Reine. ✆ **01-30-84-55-55.** www.trianonpalace.fr. Reservations required. Main courses 55€–72€; fixed-price menu 150€. AE, DC, MC, V. Fri–Sat 12:30–2:30pm; Tues–Sat 7–10:30pm. Closed 1 week in Jan, 1 week in Mar.

MODERATE

Le Potager du Roy ★ MODERN FRENCH   Philippe Letourneur spent years perfecting a distinctive cuisine that now adds novelty to the dining scene in Versailles. Letourneur rotates his skillfully prepared menu with the seasons. Examples are fresh foie gras, roasted duck with *navarin* of vegetables, and roasted codfish with roasted peppers in the style of Provence. Looking for something unusual and earthier? Try fondant of pork jowls with confit of fresh vegetables.

1 rue du Maréchal-Joffre. ✆ **01-39-50-35-34.** Reservations required. Fixed-price menu 34€–42€. AE, MC, V. Tues–Sat 12:30–1:30pm and 7:30–9:30pm.

INEXPENSIVE

Le Resto du Roi ★ 🍴 PROVENÇAL SEAFOOD/FRENCH   This informal seafood bistro is in an 18th-century building overlooking the western facade of Versailles. Though the cuisine isn't opulent, it's charming and very French. Specialties include a gratin of scallops and shrimp in fish broth, filet of sea wolf grilled with caramelized onions, and sautéed scallops with vinegar crafted from aged banyuls dessert wine. Carnivores will appreciate the main courses, the best of which is *magret* of duckling dressed with caramelized peach. Care and imagination go into the cuisine, and the service is professional and polite.

1 av. de St-Cloud. ✆ **01-39-50-42-26.** Reservations required. Main courses 15€; fixed-price menus 20€–36€. AE, MC, V. Daily 11:45am–2:30pm and 7–10:30pm.

Versailles After Dark

O'Paris Pub, 15 rue Colbert, off place d'Armes (✆ **01-39-50-36-12**), is an Irish pub where you can order the best brews in town. A bit more upmarket, **Bar à Vins-Restaurant Le Ducis,** 13 rue Ducis (✆ **01-30-21-93-76**), provides a mellow atmosphere on a summer evening, with tables spilling onto a side street. A bottle of wine and a good companion should get you through an evening, enhanced perhaps by a plate of food selected from the chalkboard menu.

THE FOREST & CHATEAU OF RAMBOUILLET

55km (34 miles) SW of Paris; 42km (26 miles) NE of Chartres

Once known as La Forêt d'Yveline, the **Forest of Rambouillet** ★ is one of the loveliest forests in France. More than 19,000 hectares (46,930 acres) of greenery stretch from the valley of the Eure to the high valley of Chevreuse, the latter rich in medieval and royal abbeys. Lakes, copses of deer, and even wild boar are some of the attractions of this "green lung." Most people, however, come here to see the château, which you can visit when it's not in use as a "Camp David" for French presidents.

Essentials

GETTING THERE **Trains** depart from Paris's Gare Montparnasse every 20 minutes throughout the day for a 35-minute ride. Information and train schedules can be obtained by contacting **La Gare de Rambouillet,** place Prud'homme (✆ **08-91-36-20-20**). By **car,** take N10 southwest from Paris, passing Versailles along the way.

VISITOR INFORMATION The **tourist office** is at the Hôtel de Ville, place de la Libération (✆ **01-34-83-21-21;** www.ot-rambouillet.fr).

Seeing the Château

Château de Rambouillet ★ Dating from 1375, the château is surrounded by a park in one of the most famous forests in France. Superb woodwork is used throughout, and the walls are adorned with tapestries, many from the era of Louis XV. Before it became a royal residence, the marquise de Rambouillet kept a house here; it's said she taught Paris's cultured ladies and gentlemen how to talk, introducing them to poets and painters. François I, the Chevalier king, died of a fever here in 1547 at age 52. When the château was later occupied by the comte de Toulouse, Rambouillet was often visited by Louis XV, who was amused (in more ways than one) by the comte's high-spirited wife. Louis XVI eventually acquired the château, but Marie Antoinette found it boring and called it "the toad." In his surprisingly modest boudoir are four panels representing the continents.

In 1814, Napoleon's second wife, Marie-Louise (daughter of Francis II, emperor of Austria), met at Rambouillet with her father, who convinced her to abandon Napoleon and France after her husband's defeats at Moscow and Leipzig. Afterward, she fled to her original home, the royal court in Vienna, with Napoleon's 3-year-old son, François-Charles-Joseph Bonaparte (also known as l'Aiglon—the Young Eagle—and, at least in title, the king of Rome). Before his death in Vienna at age 21, his claim on the Napoleonic legacy was rejected by France's enemies, despite the fact that his father had had a special annex to the château at Rambouillet built especially for his use. Before his final exile to the remote island of St. Helena, Napoleon insisted on spending a final night at Rambouillet, where he secluded himself with his meditations and memories.

 Through an Enchanted Forest

Rambouillet and its forests can provide a verdant interlude. If you've exhausted the idea of a ramble through the gardens that surround the château (or if they're closed because of a visit from the president of France), consider a visit to the **Rochers d'Angennes,** rocky hillocks that remain as leftovers from the Ice Age. To reach them, park your car on the D107, where you'll see a sign pointing to the **Rochers et Etang** **d'Angennes,** about 4km (2½ miles) north of the hamlet of Epernon. Walk along a clearly marked trail through a pine forest before you eventually reach a rocky plateau overlooking the hills and a pond (*l'Etang d'Angennes*) nestled into the surrounding countryside. Round-trip, from the site of your parked car to the plateau and back, your promenade should take between 30 and 45 minutes.

In 1830, the elderly Charles X, Louis XVI's brother, abdicated the throne at Rambouillet as a mob marched on the château and his troops began to desert him. From Rambouillet, he embarked for a safe but controversial haven in England. Afterward, Rambouillet fell into private hands. At one time it was a fashionable restaurant attracting Parisians by offering gondola rides. Napoleon III returned it to the Crown. In 1897, it was designated a residence for the presidents of the republic. In 1944, Charles de Gaulle lived here briefly before giving the order for what was left of the French army to join the Americans in liberating Paris.

It takes about 2 hours to see the château at Rambouillet.

Parc du Château. ✆ **01-34-83-00-25.** Admission 5€ adults, 3.50€ students 18–25, free for children 17 and under. Apr–Sept Wed–Mon 10am–noon and 2–6pm; Oct–Mar Wed–Mon 10am–noon and 2–5pm.

Where to Dine

La Poste TRADITIONAL FRENCH   On a street corner in the town's historic center, this restaurant dates from the mid-19th century, when it provided meals and shelter for the region's mail carriers. The two dining rooms have rustic beams and old-fashioned accents that complement the flavorful old-fashioned food. Tasty menu items include a fricassee of chicken and crayfish; noisettes of lamb "prepared in the style of a roebuck," with a *grand Veneur* sauce (that's made with red wine, autumn berries, a touch of vinegar "to make it acidic," and crème fraîche). Also popular are civets of both *une biche* (female venison) and rabbit during hunting season.

101 rue du Général-de-Gaulle. ✆ **01-34-83-03-01.** Reservations recommended Sat–Sun. Main courses 18€–20€; fixed-price menus 23€–40€. AE, MC, V. Tues–Sun noon–2pm; Fri–Sat and Tues–Wed 7–9:30pm. Closed 1st week of Jan and Sept.

THE GLORIOUS CATHEDRAL OF CHARTRES ★★★

98km (61 miles) SW of Paris; 76km (47 miles) NW of Orléans

Many observers feel that medieval architecture reached its pinnacle in the world-renowned cathedral at Chartres. Come to see its architecture, its sculpture, and—most of all—its stained glass, which gave the world a new color, Chartres blue.

The ancient town of Chartres also played a role in World War II. Jean Moulin, a Resistance hero and friend of de Gaulle, refused to sign a document under torture stating that French troops committed atrocities. The Gestapo killed him in 1943 (he's buried in the Panthéon in Paris). To view the town's monument to Moulin, head down rue du Cheval-Blanc from the cathedral until it becomes rue Jean-Moulin (the monument is ahead on your right). Other street names, including boulevard de la Résistance, commemorate the World War II resistance movement. Allow 1 hour for the cathedral, 1½ hours for the town.

Essentials

GETTING THERE   From Paris's Gare Montparnasse, **trains** run directly to Chartres, taking less than an hour. Tickets cost 27€ round-trip. Call ✆ **08-92-35-35-35.** If **driving,** take A10/A11 southwest from the *périphérique,* and follow signs to Le Mans and Chartres. (The Chartres exit is clearly marked.)

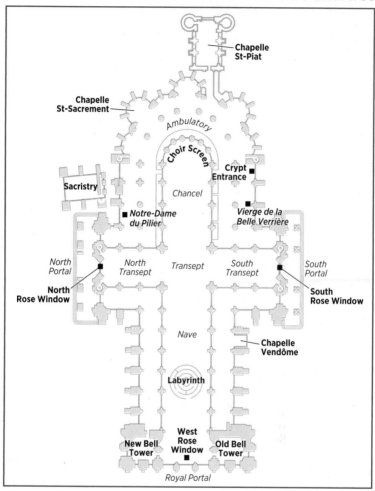

Chapelle St-Piat

Chapelle St-Sacrement

Ambulatory

Choir Screen

Crypt Entrance

Sacristy

Chancel

Notre-Dame du Pilier

Vierge de la Belle Verrière

North Portal

North Transept

Transept

South Transept

South Portal

North Rose Window

South Rose Window

Nave

Chapelle Vendôme

Labyrinth

New Bell Tower

West Rose Window

Old Bell Tower

Royal Portal

VISITOR INFORMATION   The **Office de Tourisme** is on place de la Cathédrale (☎ **02-37-18-26-26;** fax 02-37-21-51-91; www.chartres-tourisme.com).

Seeing the Cathedral

Cathédrale Notre-Dame de Chartres ★★★   Rodin reputedly once sat for hours on the sidewalk, admiring the cathedral's Romanesque sculpture. His opinion: Chartres is the French Acropolis. When it began to rain, a kind soul offered him an umbrella—which he declined, so transfixed was he.

The cathedral's origins are uncertain; some suggest it grew up over a Druid site that later became a Roman temple. As early as the 4th century, a Christian basilica was here. A fire in 1194 destroyed most of what had then become a Romanesque cathedral, sparing the western facade and crypt. The cathedral today dates principally from the 13th century, when it was rebuilt with the efforts of kings, princes, churchmen, and pilgrims from all over Europe. One of the world's greatest High Gothic cathedrals, it was the first to use flying buttresses.

French sculpture in the 12th century broke into full bloom when the **Royal Portal ★★★** was added. The portal is a landmark in Romanesque art. The sculptured bodies are elongated, often formalized beyond reality, in long, flowing robes. But the faces are amazingly (for the time) lifelike, occasionally betraying Mona Lisa smiles. In the central tympanum, Christ is shown at the Second Coming, with his descent depicted on the right, his ascent on the left. Before you enter, admire the Royal Portal and walk around to both the North Portal and the South Portal; both date from the 13th century. They depict such scenes as the expulsion of Adam and Eve from the Garden of Eden.

Inside is a celebrated choir screen (parclose); work on it began in the 16th century and lasted until 1714. The niches, 40 in all, contain statues illustrating scenes from the life of the Madonna and Christ—everything from the Massacre of the Innocents to the Coronation of the Virgin.

But few rushed visitors ever notice the screen; they're too transfixed by the light from the **stained glass ★★★**. Covering an expanse of more than 2,500 sq. m (26,900 sq. ft.), the peerless glass is truly mystical. It was spared in both world wars because of a decision to remove it piece by piece. Most of it dates from the 12th and 13th centuries. It's difficult to single out one panel or window—depending on the position of the sun, the images change constantly; however, an exceptional one is the 12th-century *Vierge de la Belle Verrière* (*Virgin of the Beautiful Window*) on the south side. Of course, there are three fiery rose windows, but you couldn't miss those even if you tried.

The nave—the widest in France—still contains its ancient labyrinth. The wooden *Notre-Dame du Pilier* (*Our Lady of the Pillar*), to the left of the choir, dates from the 14th century. The crypt was built over 2 centuries, beginning in the 9th. Enshrined within is *Notre-Dame de Sous Terre* (*Our Lady of the Crypt*), a 1976 Madonna that replaced one destroyed during the Revolution.

 A Free Concert

If you visit Chartres on a Sunday afternoon in July or August, the church features free organ concerts at 4:45pm, when the filtered light brings the cathedral's western windows to life.

Try to take a tour conducted by Malcolm Miller (✆ **02-37-28-15-58;** fax 02-37-28-33-03; millerchartres@aol.com), an Englishman who has spent 3 decades studying the cathedral and giving tours in English. His rare blend of scholarship, enthusiasm, and humor will help you understand and appreciate the cathedral. He usually conducts 75-minute tours at noon and 2:45pm Monday to Saturday for 10€ per person or 5€ per student. Tours are canceled during pilgrimages, religious celebrations, and large funerals.

If you're fit enough, don't miss the opportunity, especially in summer, to climb to the top of the tower. You can visit the crypt, gloomy and somber but rich with medieval history, only as part of a French-language tour. The cost is 2.70€ per person.

16 Cloître Notre-Dame. ✆ **02-37-21-22-07.** www.monum.fr. Free admission to cathedral. Daily 8:30am–7:30pm. There are 2 tours daily, 1 at 11am, another at 4:15pm.

Exploring the Town

Next to the cathedral is the **Musée des Beaux-Arts de Chartres ★**, 29 Cloître Notre-Dame (✆ **02-37-90-45-80**), open May 2 through October 3 Wednesday to Monday 10am to noon and 2 to 6pm (closed Sunday morning); the rest of the year, it's open only until 5pm. Admission is 3€ for adults, 1.50€ for children 18 and under. In a former Episcopal palace, the building at times competes with its exhibitions. The collection covers mainly the 16th to the 20th centuries and includes works by old masters such as Zurbarán, Watteau, and Brosamer. Of particular interest is David Ténier's *Le Concert.*

At the foot of the cathedral, the lanes contain gabled houses. Humped bridges span the Eure River. From the Bouju Bridge, you can see the lofty spires in the background. Our favorite stroll is along **rue du Pont-St-Hilaire ★**, where you get the best views of the old rooftops that lie beneath the towering cathedral. The street of St-Hilaire is east of the Gothic **church of St-Pierre**, on rue St-Pierre, a 10-min-ute stroll south of the cathedral. Two evocative streets of old Chartres, each a 3-minute walk south of the cathedral, are **rue du Cygne** and **rue des Ecuyers.** To the east, the most charming old *quartier* is **St. André,** once home to cobblers and tanners. Most of the buildings are restored but date from the 1700s and are known for their embossed doorways crowned by bull's-eye glass.

Shopping

Your best shopping bet in Chartres is place des Epars. This pedestrian area is home to most of the apparel shops and even some haute couture boutiques. Many shops selling regional items line the narrow streets that fan southeast from the cathedral. Along rue Noël-Balay is a small mall with about 15 interesting shops, which can also provide a dry respite if it's raining.

At **Galerie du Vitrail,** 17 Cloître Notre-Dame (✆ **02-37-36-10-03**), you'll find a huge selection of stained glass. **Lassaussois Antiquités,** 17 rue des Changes (✆ **02-37-21-37-74**), specializes in antique objets d'art and contemporary furnishings.

Where to Stay

Grand Monarque Best Western The most appealing and desirable hotel in Chartres occupies an imposing civic monument whose 600-year-old foundations and infrastructures were "gentrified" sometime in the 19th century with white stucco, neoclassical detailing, and touches of the baroque. Functioning as an inn since its original construction in the 15th century, and expanded and improved many times since then, the hotel remains under the direction of a local family. It attracts guests who enjoy its old-world charm—such as Art Nouveau stained glass and Louis XV chairs in the dining room. The guest rooms are decorated with reproductions of antiques; most have sitting areas.

22 place des Epars, Chartres 28005. ✆ **800/528-1234** in the U.S., or 02-37-18-15-15. Fax 02-37-36-34-18. www.bw-grand-monarque.com. 60 units. 104€–180€ double; 210€–240€ suite. AE, DC, MC, V. Parking 8€. **Amenities:** 2 restaurants; brasserie; bar; room service; smoke-free rooms. *In room:* A/C (in some), TV, hair dryer, minibar, Wi-Fi (free).

TO TASTE A madeleine

And suddenly the memory returns. The taste was that of the little crumb of madeleine which on Sunday mornings at Combray (because on those mornings I did not go out before church-time), when I went to say good day to her in her bedroom, my aunt Léonie used to give me, dipping it first in her own cup of real or of lime-flower tea.

—Marcel Proust, *Remembrance of Things Past*

Illiers-Combray, a small town 87km (54 miles) southwest of Paris and 24km (15 miles) southwest of Chartres, was once known simply as Illiers. Then Proust groupies started to come and signs were posted: ILLIERS, LE COMBRAY DE MARCEL PROUST. Illiers was and is a real town, but Proust made it world famous as Combray in his masterpiece, *A la recherche du temps perdu (Remembrance of Things Past).* So today the town is known as Illiers-Combray.

The taste of a madeleine launched Proust on his immortal recollection. To this day, readers from all over the world flock to the pastry shops to eat a madeleine dipped in lime-flower tea. Following the Proustian canon, you can explore the gardens, streets, and houses he wrote about and visited. The town is epitomized by its Eglise St-Jacques, where as a boy, Proust placed hawthorn on the altar, which he later referred to in his novels as l'Eglise St-Hilaire.

Members of Proust's family had lived in Illiers for centuries. His grandfather, François, was born on rue du Cheval-Blanc. At 11 place du Marché, opposite the church (now headquarters for a local insurance company), François ran a candle shop. His daughter, Elisabeth, married Jules Amiot, who ran a shop a few doors away. Down from Paris, young Marcel would visit his aunt at 4 rue du St-Esprit, which has been renamed rue du Docteur-Proust, honoring Marcel's grandfather.

Musée Marcel Proust/Maison de Tante Léonie, 4 rue du Docteur-Proust (✆ **02-37-24-30-97**), contains the world's most concentrated dose of Proust memorabilia and the objects and memories that helped spark his creative vision. In his novels, this was Aunt Léonie's home, filled with antimacassars and antiques, and typical of the bourgeois comforts of its day. Upstairs are the bedrooms where the young Marcel and his Aunt Léonie slept. Today they contain souvenirs of key episodes in his novels. Also important is a re-creation of the Salon Rouge, which Proust maintained at 102 bd. Haussmann, Paris, 8e, filled with furniture owned by his parents and grandparents. Especially significant are the documents and objects, some of them particularly emotive and evocative, left to the museum by Celeste Albaret, wife of Proust's chauffeur, and his protector, guardian, and "handler" the last 9 years of his life. The museum is open for English-language guided tours Tuesday to Sunday only, at 2:30 and 4pm. During July and August, there's an additional tour Tuesday through Sunday at 11am. Tours are 7€ for adults, 5€ for students, free for children 11 and under. The museum is closed from mid-December to mid-January.

In the center of town, a sign guides you to other Proustian sights, all open 24 hours a day without charge.

Hôtel Châtelet   This modern hotel has many traditional touches. The rustic guest rooms are inviting, with reproductions of Louis XV and Louis XVI furniture. The larger, more expensive units face a garden and avoid street noise. But many windows along the front (street) side of the hotel open onto a view of the cathedral. Each room comes with a tidy, tiled bathroom with shower and tub. In chilly weather, there's usually a fire burning in one of the salons. Breakfast is the only meal served, but numerous restaurants are close by.

6-8 av. Jehan-de-Beauce, Chartres 28000. ℂ **02-37-21-78-00.** Fax 02-37-36-23-01. www.hotel chatelet.com. 48 units. 104€–129€ double. Extra person 25€. AE, DC, MC, V. Parking 8€. **Amenities:** Bar; room service. *In room:* TV, hair dryer, minibar, Wi-Fi (free).

Where to Dine

La Vieille Maison ★★ MODERN FRENCH   Even if the food here wasn't superb, the 14th-century building could be visited for its historical value. The dining room, outfitted in the Louis XIII style, is centered on a narrow ceiling vault, less than 2m (6 ft.) across, crafted of chiseled white stone blocks during the 800s. Bruno Letartre, the only *maître cuisinier de France* in Chartres, supervises the cuisine. The menu changes four or five times a year, reflecting the seasonality of the Ile de France and its produce. Some good examples include foie gras of duckling; bar roasted in its skin with black pepper; foie gras served on sliced rye bread; a lasagna with lobster and scallops, or beef in a Bordeaux wine sauce. Dessert raves go to a hot Grand Marnier soufflé.

5 rue au Lait. ℂ **02-37-34-10-67.** www.lavieillemaison.fr. Reservations recommended. Main courses 32€–38€; fixed-price menu 20€–45€. MC, V. Tues–Sun noon–2:15pm; Tues–Sat 7–10pm.

Le Geôrges ★★ FRENCH   The best food, and the most upscale dining ambience, in Chartres is now featured by the town's best hotel, an also-recommended establishment with roots that date from the 15th century, when the site served food and drink (not as elegant as what you'll find today) to weary travelers and postal workers. Set on the hotel's street level, within a formal, high-ceilinged dining room outfitted in soft reds and grays, it contains an unusual collection of cast-iron/board models, each about as big as a laptop computer, of antique ovens, bigger versions of which might have fed the masons who labored on the nearby cathedral. Menu items change with the seasons, but usually include savory portions of *pâté de Chartres,* made with a combination of minced meats (including wild duck) baked in a giant puff pastry, freshly grilled scallops, and a superb version of roasted veal Grand Monarque, served with a casserole of mushrooms and cheese. Another specialty is turbot served with wild mushrooms and a risotto. Desserts are sumptuous, and the chef is known locally for his Grand-Marnier soufflé.

In the Grand Monarque Best Western, 22 place des Epars. ℂ **02-37-18-15-15.** Reservations recommended. Main courses 18€–36€; fixed-price menus 48€–85€. AE, DC, MC, V. Tues–Sun noon–2pm; Tues–Sat 7–10pm.

Chartres After Dark

For an evening of theater or modern dance from September to June, try the **Théâtre Municipal,** boulevard Chasles (ℂ **02-37-23-42-79**). For dancing, go to **Le Privilège,** 1 place St-Pierre (ℂ **02-37-35-52-02**), where you'll find a range of dance music from zouk to disco.

BARBIZON: THE SCHOOL OF ROUSSEAU ★★

56km (35 miles) SE of Paris; 9.5km (6 miles) NW of Fontainebleau

In the 19th century, this village on the edge of the forest of Fontainebleau was a refuge for artists such as Rousseau, Millet, and Corot, many of whom couldn't find acceptance in conservative Paris salons. In Barbizon, they turned to nature, and painted realistic pastoral scenes. These artists attracted a school of lesser painters, including Daubigny, Diaz, Charles Jacques, Decamps, Paul Huet, Troyon, and others. Today, Barbizon attracts fashionable Parisians for *le weekend*. Some complain about its prices, but others just enjoy the sunshine and clean air. Even with hordes of galleries and souvenir shops, the town retains much of its traditional atmosphere.

Essentials

GETTING THERE Barbizon doesn't have a railway station, so the most direct **train** route is from Paris to Fontainebleau (see below), doubling back to Barbizon on one of two buses a day. The round-trip fare to Fontainebleau is 15€. Bus fare to Barbizon costs 1.50€. For information and schedules, call ✆ **01-64-10-29-20.**

VISITOR INFORMATION The **Office de Tourisme** is at 41 Grande Rue (✆ **01-60-66-41-87;** www.barbizon-tourisme.com).

Museums

Maison et Atelier de Jean-François Millet This museum is devoted to the best-known Barbizon painter, who settled here in 1849. Millet painted religious, classical, and especially peasant subjects. Here you'll see his etching of *The Man with the Hoe,* as well as some original furnishings.

27 Grande rue. ✆ **01-60-66-21-55.** Admission 4€ (free for children 11 and under). Daily 9:30am–12:30pm and 2–5:30pm.

Musée Auberge Ganne The inn that housed most of the Barbizon artists during their late-19th-century sojourns here was L'Auberge du Père-Gannes. In the mid-1990s, through collaboration with Paris's Musée d'Orsay, it became the Musée Ganne, a showcase for Rousseau, who began painting landscapes directly from nature (novel at the time) and settled in Barbizon in the 1840s.

92 Grande rue. ✆ **01-60-66-22-27.** Admission 3€ adults, 2€ students, free for ages 19 and under. Mon and Wed–Sun 10am–12:30pm and 2–5:30pm.

Where to Stay

Hostellerie du Bas-Bréau ★★★ This member of Relais & Châteaux is one of France's great old inns (it opened in the 1840s), set amid shade trees and courtyards. Many artists and writers stayed here, notably Robert Louis Stevenson, who scattered anecdotes of the inn throughout his novels. Napoleon III and his empress, Eugénie, came in 1868 to purchase some paintings. Since then, the hotel has maintained its role as a glamorous competitor in the district through several enlargements and refurbishments. It's furnished with antiques and reproductions. In the colder months, guests gather around the fireplace in the living room. Guest rooms contain antiques and comfortable beds; units in the rear open directly onto semiprivate terraces.

22 Grande rue, Barbizon 77630. ✆ **01-60-66-40-05.** Fax 01-60-69-22-89. www.bas-breau.com. 21 units. 190€–390€ double; 350€–480€ suite. AE, DC, MC, V. **Amenities:** Restaurant; bar; babysitting; outdoor pool; room service. *In room:* A/C, TV, hair dryer, minibar, Wi-Fi (free).

Hostellerie La Clé d'Or ★ 🛏🛏 Encircled by a stone wall, the grounds of this century-old hotel include a garden and a stone terrace full of plants that flower in a wash of pinks and yellows in spring and summer. The terrace leads to many of the guest rooms, which are cozy, a bit small, and outfitted in an unglitzy, country-comfortable style that incorporates traditional furniture and subtly patterned upholstery. Other units provide a bit more architectural flair under A-frame ceilings with exposed heavy wooden beams. Note that in some units, a curtain of sorts replaces the bathroom door.

73 Grande rue, Barbizon 77360. ✆ **01-60-66-40-96.** Fax 01-60-66-42-71. www.hotel-restaurant-cledor.com. 16 units. 75€–97€ double; 128€ suite. AE, DC, MC, V. **Amenities:** Restaurant; room service. *In room:* TV, hair dryer, minibar, Wi-Fi (free).

Where to Dine

We recommend the restaurant at the **Hostellerie du Bas-Bréau** (see "Where to Stay," above).

L'Angélus ★ FRENCH   If you don't dine at the hotels, Barbizon has at least one good independent restaurant, and it lies right in the center of the village. A little English is spoken, and the food is prepared from fresh ingredients, and it's generally excellent, as is the service. Try such specialties as supreme of guinea fowl with fresh mushrooms, or scallops in a savory tomato sauce. Tenderloin of beef comes with foie gras, the salmon with hollandaise sauce. Shrimp in a whisky sauce is yet another delight.

31 Grande rue, ✆ **01-60-66-40-30.** www.langelus-restaurant.com. Set menus 29€–36€. AE, MC, V. Wed–Sun 12:15–2:30pm and 7:15–9:30pm.

FONTAINEBLEAU: REFUGE OF KINGS ★★★

60km (37 miles) S of Paris; 74km (46 miles) NE of Orléans

Napoleon called the Palais de Fontainebleau the house of the centuries. Napoleon stood on its horseshoe-shaped exterior staircase and bade farewell to his army before his departure to exile on Elba. That scene has been the subject of countless paintings, including Vernet's *Les Adieux.*

After Versailles, a visit to Fontainebleau can be a bit of a letdown. French kings originally came to Fontainebleau because of its proximity to great hunting. François I converted it from a hunting lodge into a palace fit for a king. Versailles, on the other hand, is the creation of the French monarchy at its pinnacle of splendor, prestige, and power.

Set in 20,000 hectares (49,400 acres) of verdant forest, Fontainebleau remains a country retreat for Parisians who come for horseback riding, picnicking, and hiking. It's not as crowded with tourists, so it's more peaceful than Versailles. Allow 2½ hours to see everything in Fontainebleau.

Essentials

GETTING THERE **Trains** to Fontainebleau depart from the Gare de Lyon in Paris. The trip takes 45 minutes each way and costs 7.50€ one-way. Fontainebleau's railway station lies 3km (1¾ miles) north of the château, in the suburb of Avon. A local bus (marked simply CHATEAU and part of line A) makes the trip to the château at 15-minute intervals Monday through Saturday and at 30-minute intervals on Sunday; the fare is 1.40€ each way. If you're **driving,** take A6 south from Paris, exit onto N191, and follow signs.

VISITOR INFORMATION The **Office de Tourisme** is at 4 rue Royale, Fontainebleau (© **01-60-74-99-99;** www.fontainebleau-tourisme.com), opposite the main entrance to the château.

Seeing the Château & Gardens

Musée National du Château de Fontainebleau ★★★ Napoleon joined the parade of French rulers who used the Palais de Fontainebleau as a resort, hunting in its magnificent forest. Under François I (who reigned 1515–47), the hunting lodge was enlarged into a royal palace in the Italian Renaissance style. The style got botched, but many artists, including Cellini, came from Italy to work for the French monarch.

Under François I's patronage, the School of Fontainebleau (led by the painters Rosso, Fiorentino, and Primaticcio) increased in prestige. These artists adorned one of the most outstanding rooms at Fontainebleau: the 63m-long (207-ft.) **Gallery of François I ★★★**. (Restorers under Louis-Philippe didn't completely succeed in ruining it.) Surrounded by pomp, François I walked the length of his gallery while artisans tempted him with their wares, job seekers asked favors, and courtesans attempted to lure him from the duchesse d'Etampes. The stucco-framed panels depict such scenes as Jupiter carrying off Europa, the Nymph of Fontainebleau (with a lecherous dog peering through the reeds), and the king holding a pomegranate, a symbol of unity. However, the frames compete with the pictures. Everywhere is the salamander, symbol of the Chevalier King.

If it's true that François I built Fontainebleau for his mistress, then Henri II, his successor, left a memorial to the woman he loved, Diane de Poitiers. Sometimes called the Gallery of Henri II, the **Ballroom (La Salle de Bal) ★★★** is the château's second splendid interior. The monograms H & D are interlaced in the decoration. At one end of the room is a monumental fireplace supported by two bronze satyrs, reproduced in 1966 (the originals were melted down during the Revolution). A series of 16th-century frescoes depict mythological subjects.

An architectural curiosity is the **Louis XV Staircase ★★**. Primaticcio originally decorated the ceiling for the bedroom of the duchesse d'Etampes. When an architect added the stairway, he simply ripped out her bedroom floor and used the ceiling to cover the stairway. Of the preserved Italian frescoes, one depicts the Queen of the Amazons climbing into Alexander the Great's bed.

Fontainebleau found renewed glory under Napoleon. You can wander much of the palace on your own, visiting sites that evoke his 19th-century heyday. They include the throne room, the room where he abdicated (the abdication document displayed is a copy), his offices, his bedroom (look for his symbol, a bee), and his bathroom. Some of the smaller rooms, especially those containing his personal mementos and

Hiking Along Trails Left by French Kings

The Forest of Fontainebleau is riddled with *sentiers* (hiking trails) made by French kings and their entourages who went hunting in the forest. A *Guide des Sentiers* is available at the tourist information center (see above). Bike paths also cut through the forest. You can rent bikes at the Fontainebleau-Avon rail depot. At the station, go to the kiosk, **La Petite Reine** (② 01-60-74-57-57). The cost of a regular bike is 13€ per half-day, 16€ for a full day. The kiosk is open Monday through Friday from 9:30am to 6pm, Saturday and Sunday from 10am to 7pm.

artifacts, are accessible by guided tour only. The furnishings in the grand apartments of Napoleon and Joséphine are marvelous.

The **Musée Chinois (Chinese Museum),** which is open only erratically, usually, but not always, on weekends (a function of staff shortages), holds the Empress Eugénie's collection of Chinese treasures, including Far Eastern porcelain, jade, and crystal.

After your trek through the palace, visit the **gardens** and especially the carp pond; the gardens, however, are only a prelude to the forest of Fontainebleau and not nearly as spectacular as those surrounding Versailles.

Place du Général-de-Gaulle. ② **01-60-71-50-70.** www.musee-chateau-fontainebleau.fr. Combination ticket including private *appartements* 8€ adults, 6€ students 18–25; ticket to *petits appartements* and Napoleonic rooms 4.50€ adults, 3€ students 18–25, free for children 13 and under. Apr–Sept Wed–Mon 9:30am–6pm; Oct–Mar Wed–Mon 9:30am–5pm.

Where to Stay

Grand Hôtel de l'Aigle-Noir (The Black Eagle) ★   This mansion, once the home of Cardinal de Retz, sits opposite the château. The formal courtyard entrance has a high iron/board grille and pillars crowned by black eagles. It became a hotel in 1720 and is the finest lodging in Fontainebleau, far superior in amenities and style to the Hôtel Napoleon (see below). The rooms are decorated with Louis XVI, Empire, or Régence-era antiques or reproductions, with plush beds and elegant bathroom amenities. Enjoy a drink in the Napoleon III–style piano bar before dinner.

27 place Napoleon-Bonaparte, Fontainebleau 77300. ② **01-60-74-60-00.** Fax 01-60-74-60-01. www. hotelaiglenoir.fr. 15 units. 170€–240€ double; 280€–380€ suite. AE, DC, MC, V. Parking 10€. Closed last 2 weeks of Dec. **Amenities:** Restaurant; bar; exercise room; room service. *In room:* A/C, hair dryer, minibar, Wi-Fi (free).

Hôtel de Londres   With a historic 1850s-era facade, and owned and managed since 1932 by generations of the same family, this hotel enjoys one of the best locations in town for anyone who's fascinated by the architecture of the château of Fontainebleau. It's directly in front of the cour des Adieux, site of Napoleon's farewell to his troops before his exile to Elba. The hotel occupies two of the building's three floors. The well-maintained rooms are tastefully and cozily outfitted, mostly with Louis XVI furniture, and have extralong beds and tiled bathrooms. Other than breakfast, no meals are served.

1 place du Général-de-Gaulle, Fontainebleau 77300. ② **01-64-22-20-21.** Fax 01-60-72-39-16. www. hoteldelondres.com. 16 units. 100€–170€ double; 180€–320€ suite. AE, MC, V. Closed 1 week in Aug and Dec 23–Jan 9. **Amenities:** Bar. *In room:* TV, hair dryer, Wi-Fi (free).

Hôtel Napoleon This classically designed hotel—the number-two choice in Fontainebleau—is a short walk from the château. The lobby has Oriental rugs, arched windows, and a garden tearoom. An inviting bar features an ornate oval ceiling, Louis-Philippe chairs, and a neoclassical fireplace. The renovated guest rooms are filled with reproductions of antiques and flowered headboards. All are comfortable, but those facing the courtyard are larger and more tranquil. All units have full bathrooms.

9 rue Grande, Fontainebleau 77300. ✆ **01-60-39-50-50.** Fax 01-64-22-20-87. www.hotelnapoleon-fontainebleau.com. 57 units. 165€ double; 270€ suite. AE, DC, MC, V. Parking 9€. **Amenities:** Restaurant; bar; room service. *In room:* TV, hair dryer, minibar, Wi-Fi (5€ per 45 min.).

Where to Dine

In addition to the options below, **La Table des Maréchaux,** in the Hôtel Napoleon (see above), is a superb choice.

Le Caveau des Ducs TRADITIONAL FRENCH This reasonably priced restaurant occupies a former storage cellar. It sits underground, beneath a series of 17th-century stone vaults built by the same masons who laid the cobblestones of rue de Ferrare. Although the food is simple, the setting—with lots of wood and flickering candles—is dramatic. Menu items include staples such as snails in garlic butter, roast leg of lamb with garlic-and-rosemary sauce, and virtually everything that can be concocted from the body of a duck (terrines, *magret,* and confits). Filet of rump steak with brie sauce is tasty, as are platters of sole, crayfish tails, and salmon on a bed of pasta. Especially flavorful are strips of veal in morel-studded cream sauce on a bed of pasta.

24 rue de Ferrare. ✆ **01-64-22-05-05.** www.caveaudesducs.com. Reservations recommended. Main courses 15€–23€; fixed-price menu 22€–41€. AE, MC, V. Daily noon–2pm and 7–10pm.

Le François-1er (Chez Bernard) ★ TRADITIONAL FRENCH The premier dining choice in Fontainebleau has Louis XIII decor, winemaking memorabilia, and walls that the owners think are about 200 years old. If weather permits, sit on the terrace overlooking the château and the cour des Adieux. In game season, the menu features hare, duck liver, and partridge. Other choices include a cassoulet of snails with flap mushrooms and garlic-flavored cream sauce, *magret* of duckling with cassis sauce, *rognon de veau* (veal kidneys) with mustard sauce, and scallops à la Provençale. Chef Bernard Crogiez's cuisine is meticulous, with an undeniable flair.

3 rue Royale. ✆ **01-64-22-24-68.** Reservations required. Main courses 14€–29€; fixed-price lunch Mon–Fri only 15€; fixed-price dinner 25€. AE, MC, V. Tues–Sun noon–2pm; Mon–Sat 7:30–10pm. Closed 2 weeks in Aug and 1 week in Dec.

VAUX-LE-VICOMTE: LIFE BEFORE VERSAILLES

47km (29 miles) SE of Paris; 19km (12 miles) NE of Fontainebleau

Though it's close to Paris, Vaux-le-Vicomte is hard to reach by mass transit. By **car,** take N6 southeast from Paris to Melun, which is 6km (3¾ miles) west of the château. By **train,** take the 45-minute ride from Gare de Lyon to Melun (14€ round-trip), and then a taxi from the station 6.5km (4 miles) to Vaux-le-Vicomte (14€ each way). Once there, allow 2 hours to see the château.

The nearest **tourist office** is in the Hotel de Ville, 18 rue Paul Doumer, Melun (☎ **01-64-52-64-52**); it's open Tuesday to Saturday 9:15am to 12:15pm and 1 to 5pm.

Seeing the Château

Château de Vaux-le-Vicomte ★★★ The château was built in 1656 for Nicolas Fouquet, Louis XIV's finance minister. The king wasn't pleased that Fouquet was able to live so extravagantly, and then he discovered that the minister had embezzled funds from the treasury. Fouquet was arrested, and Louis hired the same artists and architects who had built Vaux-le-Vicomte to begin creating Versailles. If you visit both, you'll see the striking similarities.

One of the stateliest French châteaux that's still privately owned, Vaux-le-Vicomte belongs to Patrice, comte de Vogüé, whose ownership dates back many generations. He lives in one of the outbuildings, not in the main building, which is open for tours.

The view of the château from the main gate reveals the splendor of 17th-century France. On the south side, a majestic staircase sweeps toward the gardens, designed by Le Nôtre. The Grand Canal, flanked by waterfalls, divides the greenery. The château is furnished with 17th-century pieces. The entrance hall leads to 12 staterooms, including the oval rotunda. Many rooms are hung with Gobelin tapestries and decorated with painted ceiling and wall panels by Le Brun, with sculpture by Girardon. A self-guided tour of the interior includes Fouquet's personal suite, the huge basement and wine cellar, the servants' dining room, and the copper-filled kitchen.

Included in the admission fee is entrance to the château's carriage museum, **Musée des Equipages,** in the stables. Some 25 restored 18th- and 19th-century carriages are on display, each accessorized with mannequin horses and people.

Candlelight evenings, **Des Soirées à Chandelles,** take place every Saturday from May to mid-October between 6pm and midnight, and every Friday in July and August from 6pm to midnight. During the events, all electricity to the château is cut off, and thousands of candles illuminate both the château and its gardens. The effect has been called mystical, a memorable re-creation of the way of life that prevailed during the building's heyday. Admission during candlelight evenings is 17€ for adults, 15€ for students and children 6 to 15, free for children 5 and under.

77950 Maincy. ☎ **01-64-14-41-90.** www.vaux-le-vicomte.com. Admission 14€ adults, 11€ students and children 6–16, free for children 5 and under. Sept–June Thurs–Tues 10am–5:30pm; July–Aug daily 10am–5:30pm. Closed Nov and last 2 weeks of Dec.

Where to Dine

Auberge de Crisenoy MODERN FRENCH You are more likely to find locals from Melun than fellow visitors at this *auberge,* and that's part of its charm. Behind the solid stone walls of a former private home, the two dining rooms (on separate floors), plus an additional 10 tables on a mezzanine, overlook a garden. The menu items are based on modern interpretations of French classics and change every 3 months. The best examples include foie gras with white grapes, toast, and compote of apples; *filet l'agneau* stuffed with onions, pears, and new onions; and well-seasoned cassoulet of snails and sweetbreads, served in a copper pot placed directly on the table.

23 Grande Rue, Crisenoy. ☎ **01-64-38-83-06.** Reservations recommended. Fixed-price lunch Tues–Fri only 21€; fixed-price dinner 32€ and 49€. MC, V. Tues–Sun noon–1:30pm; Tues and Thurs–Sat 7:30–9pm. Closed 1 week at Christmas, 1 week in Mar, and 3 weeks in Aug. From Vaux-le-Vicomte, follow N36 toward Meaux for 2.5km (1½ miles).

La Table de Saint Just TRADITIONAL FRENCH Dine here, and you're bound to be charmed. The original masonry from the 17th-century farmhouse, including artfully crafted oak beams, is intact. It occupies one of the farmhouses once associated with the **Château de Vaux-le-Pénil,** a Renaissance castle that today is privately occupied. It is widely known in the region, but closed to casual visitors and is only a few steps away. Menu items change with the seasons, but may include foie gras with figs served with confit of celery and acidified apples; lobster salad with orange sauce; scallops roasted with truffles; and roasted rack of lamb with moussaka of fresh vegetables.

11 rue de Libération, Ferme Saint Just, Vaux-le-Pénil. ☎ **01-64-52-09-09.** Reservations recommended. Main courses 30€–40€; fixed-price menu 45€–90€. AE, MC, V. Tues–Sat noon–1:30pm and 7:30–9pm. Closed 3 weeks in Aug, 2 weeks at Christmas, and 1 week in May. From Vaux-le-Vicomte, drive 5.5km (3½ miles) west, following signs to Melun, then to Maincy, and then to Vaux-le-Pénil.

DISNEYLAND PARIS ★★★

32km (20 miles) E of Paris

After provoking some of the most enthusiastic and controversial reactions in recent French history, the multimillion-dollar Disneyland Paris opened in 1992. It's one of the world's most lavish theme parks, conceived on a scale rivaling that of Versailles. European journalists initially accused it of everything from cultural imperialism to the death knell of French culture.

But after godly amounts of public relations and financial juggling, Disneyland Paris has become France's number-one tourist attraction, with 50 million visitors annually. It accounts for 4% of the French tourism industry's foreign-currency sales. About 40% of the visitors are French, half from Paris. Disneyland Paris looks, tastes, and feels like the ones in California and Florida.

Situated on a 2,000-hectare (4,940-acre) site (about one-fifth the size of Paris) in the suburb of Marne-la-Vallée, the park incorporates the most successful elements of its Disney predecessors and European flair. The park in Florida is larger than the Paris property, with a greater number of attractions and rides, but Disneyland Paris does a decent job of re-creating the Magic Kingdom. In 2002, the Paris park added **Walt Disney Studios,** focusing on the role of movies in popular culture. Take 1 day for the highlights, 2 days for more depth.

Essentials

GETTING THERE The RER commuter express **rail** network (Line A) stops within walking distance of the park. Board the RER in Paris at Charles-de-Gaulle–Etoile, Châtelet–Les Halles, or Nation. Get off at Line A's last stop, Marne-la-Vallée/Chessy, 45 minutes from central Paris. The round-trip fare is 12€. Trains run daily, every 10 to 20 minutes from 5:30am to midnight.

Shuttle buses connect Orly and Charles de Gaulle airports with each hotel in the resort. Buses depart the airports every 30 to 45 minutes. One-way transport to the park from either airport is 14€ for adults, 12€ for children 3 to 11.

If you're **driving,** take A4 east from Paris and get off at exit 14, DISNEYLAND PARIS. Parking begins at 8€ per day, but is free if you stay at one of the park hotels. A series of moving sidewalks speeds up pedestrian transit from parking areas to the park entrance.

VISITOR INFORMATION   All the hotels we recommend offer general information on the theme park. For details and reservations at any of its hotels, contact the **Disneyland Paris Guest Relations Office,** located in City Hall on Main Street, U.S.A. (© **01-60-30-60-53** in English, or 08-25-30-60-30 in French; www.disneylandparis.com). For information on Disneyland Paris and specific details on the many other attractions and monuments in the Ile de France and the rest of the country, contact the **Maison du Tourisme,** Disney Village (B.P. 77705), Marne-la-Vallée (© **01-60-43-33-33**).

ADMISSION   Admission varies depending on the season. In peak season, a 1-day park ticket costs 52€ for adults, 44€ for children 3 to 12, free for children 2 and under; a 2-day park-hopper ticket is 110€ for adults, 96€ for kids; and a 3-day park-hopper ticket is 159€ for adults, 117€ for kids. Peak season is from mid-June to mid-September as well as Christmas and Easter weeks. Entrance to Disney Village is free, though there's usually a cover charge at the dance clubs.

HOURS   Hours vary throughout the year, but most frequently are 10am to 7pm. Be warned that autumn and winter hours vary the most; it depends on the weather. It's good to phone ahead if you're contemplating a visit at this time.

Seeing Disneyland

Disneyland Paris is a total vacation destination. In one enormous unit, the park includes five "lands" of entertainment; a dozen hotels; a campground; an entertainment center (**Disney Village,** with six restaurants of its own); a 27-hole golf course; and dozens of restaurants, shows, and shops. The Disney Village entertainment center is illuminated inside by a spectacular gridwork of lights suspended 18m (59 ft.) above the ground. The complex contains dance clubs, shops, restaurants (one of which stages a dinner spectacle based on the original *Buffalo Bill's Wild West Show*), bars for adults trying to escape their children, a French Government Tourist Office, a post office, and a marina.

Visitors stroll amid flower beds, trees, reflecting ponds, fountains, and a large artificial lake flanked with hotels. An army of smiling employees and Disney characters—many of whom are multilingual, including Buffalo Bill, Mickey and Minnie Mouse, and, of course, the French-born Caribbean pirate Jean Laffite—are on hand to greet the thousands of *enfants.* You'll see characters from *Aladdin, The Lion King, Pocahontas,* and *Toy Story.* As Disney continues to churn out animated blockbusters, look for the newest stars to appear in the theme park.

Main Street, U.S.A., abounds with horse-drawn carriages and barbershop quartets. Steam-powered railway cars embark from the Main Street Station for a trip

 FASTPASS Those Long Lines

Disneyland Paris has instituted a program that's done well at the other parks. With the **FASTPASS** system, visitors to the various rides reserve a 1-hour time block. Within that block, the waiting is usually no more than 8 minutes.

FOR THOSE WITH another DAY:
WALT DISNEY STUDIOS

Next to Disneyland Paris, **Walt Disney Studios** takes guests on a behind-the-scenes interactive discovery of film, animation, and television.

The main entrance to the studios, called the **Front Lot,** consists of "Sunset Boulevard," an elaborate sound stage complete with hundreds of film props. The **Animation Courtyard** allows visitors to learn the trade secrets of Disney animators, and the **Production Courtyard** lets guests take a look behind the scenes of film and TV production. At **Catastrophe Canyon,** guests are plunged into the heart of a film shoot. Finally, the **Back Lot** is home to special effects and stunt workshops. A live stunt show features cars, motorbikes, and jet skis.

This ode to Hollywood and the films it produced since the end of its "golden age" has a roller coaster, the Rock 'n' Roller Coaster, featuring the music of Aerosmith, which combines rock memorabilia with high-speed scary twists and turns (completely in the dark); and a reconstruction of one of the explosion scenes in the Hollywood action film *Armageddon.*

Admission is 51€ for adults, 43€ for children. Hours are daily from 10am to 7pm.

through a Grand Canyon diorama to **Frontierland,** with its paddle-wheel steamers reminiscent of Mark Twain's Mississippi River. Other attractions are the Critter Corral petting zoo and the Lucky Nugget Saloon, which is inspired by the gold-rush era, with the steps and costumes of the cancan show originated in the cabarets of turn-of-the-20th-century Paris.

The park's steam trains chug past **Adventureland**—with its swashbuckling pirates, Swiss Family Robinson treehouse, and reenacted *Arabian Nights* legends—to **Fantasyland.** Here you'll find the **Sleeping Beauty's Castle (Le Château de la Belle au Bois Dormant),** whose pinnacles and turrets are an idealized (and spectacular) interpretation of French châteaux. In its shadow are Europeanized versions of *Blanche Neige et les Sept Nains* (Snow White and the Seven Dwarfs), Peter Pan, Dumbo, Alice (from Wonderland), the Mad Hatter's Teacups, and Sir Lancelot's Magic Carousel.

Visions of the future are in **Discoveryland,** where tributes to invention and imagination draw from the works of Leonardo da Vinci, Jules Verne, H. G. Wells, the modern masters of science fiction, and the *Star Wars* series.

Where to Stay

You can easily make Disney a day trip from Paris—the transportation links are excellent—or you can spend the night.

The resort's six theme hotels share a reservation service. In North America, call ✆ **407/W-DISNEY** (934-7639). In France, contact the **Central Reservations Office,** Euro Disney Resort, S.C.A., B.P. 105, F-77777 Marne-la-Vallée Cedex 4 (✆ **08-25-30-60-30;** www.disneylandparis.com).

VERY EXPENSIVE

Disneyland Hotel ★★   At the park entrance, this flagship four-story hotel is Victorian, with red-tile turrets and jutting balconies. The spacious guest rooms are plushly furnished but evoke the image of Disney, with cartoon depictions and candy-stripe decor. The beds are king-size, double, or twin; in some rooms armchairs convert to beds. Accommodations in the rear overlook Sleeping Beauty's Castle and Big Thunder Mountain. Some less desirable units open onto a parking lot. The luxurious bathrooms have marble vanities, showers and tubs, and twin basins. On the Castle Club floor, you get free newspapers, all-day beverages, and access to a well-equipped private lounge.

Disneyland Paris, B.P. 111, F-77777 Marne-la-Vallée Cedex 4. ✆ **01-60-45-65-89.** Fax 01-60-45-65-33. www.disneylandparis.com. 495 units. 526€–853€ double; from 770€ suite. AE, DC, MC, V. **Amenities:** 2 restaurants; bar; cafe; babysitting; health club w/indoor pool; room service; sauna; spa. *In room:* A/C, TV, hair dryer, Internet (5€ per 15 min.), minibar.

EXPENSIVE

Hotel New York ★   Inspired by the Big Apple, this hotel centers on a nine-story "skyscraper" flanked by the Gramercy Park Wing and the Brownstones Wing. (Their exteriors resemble row houses.) This convention hotel is less family friendly than others at the resort. Guest rooms are comfortable, with Art Deco accessories, New York–inspired memorabilia, and roomy combination bathrooms with twin basins and tub/shower combos. Try for one of the units fronting Lake Buena Vista.

Disneyland Paris, B.P. 100, F-77777 Marne-la-Vallée Cedex 4. ✆ **01-60-45-75-92.** Fax 01-60-45-73-33. www.disneylandparis.com. 565 units. 280€–470€ double; from 360€–610€ suite. AE, DC, MC, V. **Amenities:** 2 restaurants; bar; babysitting; exercise room; indoor and outdoor pools; room service; sauna. *In room:* A/C, TV, hair dryer, minibar, Wi-Fi (4.50€ per hr.).

Newport Bay Club ★★   You expect to see the reincarnation of Joe Kennedy walking along the veranda with its slated roofs, awnings, and pergolas. It's very Hyannisport here. It's also the biggest hotel in France. With a central cupola, balconies, and a blue-and-cream color scheme, it recalls a harborfront New England hotel (ca. 1900). The layout features nautically decorated rooms in various shapes and sizes. The most spacious are the corner units.

Disneyland Paris, B.P. 105, F-77777 Marne-la-Vallée Cedex 4. ✆ **01-60-45-55-00.** Fax 01-60-45-55-33. www.disneylandparis.com. 1,093 units. 240€–454€ double; 500€–840€ suite. AE, DC, MC, V. **Amenities:** 2 restaurants; bar; health club; indoor and outdoor pools; room service; sauna. *In room:* A/C, TV, minibar, Wi-Fi (15€ per day).

MODERATE

Hotel Cheyenne/Hotel Santa Fe ☺   Next door to each other near a re-creation of Texas's Rio Grande, these Old West–style lodgings are the resort's least expensive hotels. The Cheyenne consists of 14 two-story buildings along Desperado Street; the desert-themed Santa Fe encompasses four "nature trails" winding among 42 adobe-style pueblos. The Cheyenne is a favorite among families, offering a double bed and bunk beds. Children have an array of activities, including a play area in a log cabin with a lookout tower and a section where you can explore the "ruins" of an ancient Anasazi village. The only disadvantage, according to some parents, is the absence of a pool.

More recently constructed, but charging the same prices, is the nearby **Kyriad Hotel,** a government-rated two-star hotel designed for families that evokes the aesthetics and layout of a French country inn. Whenever the Cheyenne and the Santa Fe are full, Disney usually directs the overflow to the Kyriad.

Disneyland Paris, B.P. 115, F-77777 Marne-la-Vallée Cedex 4. ✆ **01-60-45-63-12** (Cheyenne) or 01-60-45-79-22 (Santa Fe). Fax 01-60-45-62-33 (Cheyenne) or 01-60-45-78-33 (Santa Fe). www.disneyland paris.com. 2,000 units. Hotel Cheyenne 131€–279€ double; Hotel Santa Fe 112€–249€ double. AE, DC, MC, V. **Amenities:** Restaurant; bar; Internet (15€ per 100 min.). *In room:* A/C, TV.

Where to Dine

Disneyland Paris offers a gamut of cuisine in more than 45 restaurants and snack bars. You can live on burgers and fries, or you can experiment at the following upscale restaurants.

Auberge de Cendrillon TRADITIONAL FRENCH   This is a fairy-tale version of Cinderella's country inn, with a glass couch in the center. A master of ceremonies wearing a plumed tricorn hat, embroidered tunic, and lace ruffles welcomes you. There are corny elements, but the chefs go out of their way to make a big deal of French cuisine. For the most part, they succeed admirably. The appetizers set the tone. Our favorites are warm goat-cheese salad with lardons and the smoked salmon platter. Either will put you in the mood for a French classic such as loin of lamb roasted under a zesty mustard coating or flavorful sautéed veal medallions. There is a choice of courses on the fixed-price menu. Because the restaurant follows the park's seasonal schedule, lunch is usually easier to arrange than dinner.

Fantasyland. ✆ **01-64-74-24-02.** Reservations recommended. Fixed-price menu 56€ adults, 21€ children. AE, DC, MC, V. Mid-July to Aug daily 11am–9pm; rest of the year daily 11am–6pm.

California Grill ★★ ☺ CALIFORNIAN/FRENCH   The resort's showcase restaurant serves cuisine that's the equivalent of the fare at a one-Michelin-star restaurant. Focusing on the lighter specialties for which the Golden State is famous, with many concessions to French palates, the elegant restaurant accommodates both adults and children gracefully. Even French food critics are impressed with oysters prepared with leeks and salmon. We also embrace the appetizer of foie gras with roasted red peppers and the roasted pigeon with braised Chinese cabbage and black-rice vinegar. Another winning selection is fresh salmon roasted over beechwood and served with a sprinkling of walnut oil, sage sauce, asparagus, and fricassee of forest mushrooms. Many items are specifically for children. If you want a quiet, mostly adult venue, go here as late as your hunger pangs will allow.

In the Disneyland Hotel. ✆ **01-60-45-65-76.** Reservations required. Fixed-price menu 55€–71€; children's menu 17€–20€. AE, DC, MC, V. Daily 6:30–10:30pm.

Inventions ✦ INTERNATIONAL   This may be the only buffet restaurant in Europe where animated characters from the Disney films (including Mickey and Minnie) go table-hopping. With views over a park, the restaurant contains four enormous buffet tables devoted to starters, shellfish, main courses, and desserts. Selections are wide, portions can be copious, and no one leaves hungry. Don't expect *grande cuisine*—that's the domain of the more upscale California Grill (see above), in the same hotel. What you'll get is a sense of American bounty and culinary generosity, with ample doses of cartoon fantasy.

In the Disneyland Hotel. ✆ **01-60-45-65-83.** Buffet 49€ adults, 25€ children 7–11, 19€ children 3–6. AE, DC, MC, V. Daily 12:30–3pm and 6–10:30pm.

Disneyland After Dark

The premier theatrical venue is **Le Legende de Buffalo Bill** in Disney Village (✆ **01-60-45-71-00**). The twice-per-night stampede of entertainment recalls the show that once traveled the West with Buffalo Bill and Annie Oakley. You'll dine at tables arranged amphitheater-style around a rink where sharpshooters, runaway stagecoaches, and dozens of horses and Indians ride fast and perform alarmingly realistic acrobatics. A Texas-style barbecue, served in an assembly line by waiters in 10-gallon hats, is part of the experience. Despite its corny elements, it's not without its charm. Wild Bill is dignified and the Indians are suitably brave. Shows start at 6:30 and 9:30pm; the cost (dinner included) is 65€ for adults and 48€ for children 3 to 11.

THE REMARKABLE ZOO OF CHATEAU DE THOIRY

40km (25 miles) W of Paris

Château et Parc Zoologique de Thoiry ★★   Known throughout Europe for its synthesis of the French Renaissance and modern pop culture, this attraction draws more visitors in a year than the Louvre or Versailles. The centerpiece of the estate is a 16th-century château, owned for generations by the family of the vicomte de la Panouse. Its architect, Philibert de L'Orme, conceived it as a transparent bridge of light, with the sun rising or setting in the center of its central archway during the summer and winter solstices. The creative and hardworking caretakers are Paul de la Panouse and his Minnesota-born wife, Annabelle. Displays include two original manuscripts of unpublished waltzes by Chopin; antique paintings and furniture; at least 600 letters exchanged during the *ancien régime* between the monarchs of France and Spain; letters to French aristocrats from Benjamin Franklin; and the financial records of France from 1745 to 1750. But despite its status as a treasure-trove of culture and documentation, the château is not as popular as the 485 hectares (1,200 acres) of land around it, 121 hectares (300 acres) of which have been transformed into a safari-inspired nature preserve.

Many of the more than 1,000 animals in the park—including elephants, giraffes, zebras, monkeys, rhinoceroses, alligators, lions, tigers, kangaroos, bears, and wolves—roam wild over fenced-off fields. Others, including many birds, are more ornamental, strutting peacefully in or near beautiful formal gardens. For part of your exploration, you'll drive, slowly, in your own (nonconvertible) car over a network of roads. Other subdivisions, including a lion park, require strolling through a Plexiglas tunnel, parts of which are aboveground, parts of which are buried to allow migrations of wildlife from one part of the park to another.

Thoiry-en-Yvelines 78770. ✆ **01-34-87-52-25.** www.thoiry.tm.fr. Admission to château, nature reserve, and park 25€ adults, 22€ seniors and students, and 18€ ages 3–14. May–Aug daily 10am–7pm; Sept–Apr daily 10am–5pm. Take Autoroute de l'Ouest (A13) toward Dreux. Exit at Bois-d'Arcy onto the N12 and follow signs on N12 and D11 to Thoiry.

Where to Stay & Dine

Auberge de Thoiry ★ ☺   In the heart of the village of Thoiry, some 183m (600 ft.) from the entrance to the safari park, this establishment dates from about 1890, when it was a postal relay station. It was later renovated into a charming hotel. Owner Jean-Paul le Moal decorated each guest room to evoke an animal (dog, tortoise, hippopotamus, and so forth). The hotel's low-key charm, its appeal to adults and children, its reasonable rates, and its restaurant—the best in town—make it quite enjoyable. Many of the original structure's stone walls and ceiling beams were preserved during renovations in the late 1990s, and painting techniques make the walls look much older than they really are. The restaurant's fixed-price menus cost 20€ to 25€.

38 rue de la porte St-Martin, Thoiry 78770. ℂ **01-34-87-40-21.** Fax 01-34-87-49-57. 12 units. 59€–69€ double; 81€ triple; 128€ family suite. DC, MC, V. Free parking. **Amenities:** Restaurant; bar; room service. *In room:* TV.

GIVERNY: IN THE FOOTSTEPS OF MONET

81km (50 miles) NW of Paris

On the border between Normandy and the Ile de France, the Claude Monet Foundation preserves the estate where the great painter lived for 43 years. The restored house and its gardens are open to the public. Budget 2 hours to explore the museum and gardens at Giverny.

Essentials

GETTING THERE   It takes a morning to get to Giverny and to see its sights. Take the Paris-Rouen **train** from Paris's Gare St-Lazare to the Vernon station, where a taxi can take you the 5km (3 miles) to Giverny. Vernon itself lies 40km (25 miles) southeast of Rouen. Perhaps the easiest way to get there is on a 5-hour **bus tour,** for 67€ per person, which focuses on Monet's house and garden. For ages 3 to 11, the fare is 34€. Tours depart at 1:45pm Tuesday to Saturday between April and October from 2, rue des Pyramides, first arrondissement (www.pariscityrama.com). You can arrange tours in the summer through **Cityrama,** 149 rue St-Honoré, 1er (ℂ **01-44-55-61-00;** Métro: Palais-Royal–Musée du Louvre), or year-round through **American Express,** 11 rue Scribe, 9e (ℂ **01-47-14-50-00;** Métro: Opéra).

If you're **driving,** take the Autoroute de l'Ouest (Port de St-Cloud) toward Rouen. Leave the autoroute at Bonnières, and then cross the Seine on the Bonnières Bridge. From here, a direct road with signs leads to Giverny. Expect it to take about an hour; try to avoid weekends. Another approach is to leave the highway at the Bonnières exit and go toward Vernon. Once there, cross the bridge over the Seine and follow signs to Giverny or Gasny (Giverny is before Gasny). This is easier than going through Bonnières, where there aren't many signs.

Show me the Monet

Claude Monet Foundation ★★★   Born in 1840, the French Impressionist was a brilliant innovator, excelling in presenting the effects of light at different times of day. Some critics claim that he "invented light." His paintings of the Rouen cathedral and of waterlilies, which one critic called "vertical interpretations of horizontal lines," are just a few of his masterpieces.

Monet came to Giverny in 1883. Many of his friends visited him at this house (known as Le Pressoir), including Clemenceau, Cézanne, Rodin, Renoir, Degas, and Sisley. When Monet died in 1926, his son, Michel, inherited the house but left it abandoned. The gardens became almost a jungle, inhabited by river rats. In 1966, Michel died and left house and gardens to the Académie des Beaux-Arts. It wasn't until 1977 that Gerald van der Kemp, who restored Versailles, decided to work on Giverny. A large part of it was restored with gifts from U.S. benefactors, notably the late Lila Acheson Wallace, former head of *Reader's Digest*.

The house is open to the public. It contains Monet's collection of 18th- and 19th-century Japanese prints as well as antique (though not original) furnishings. From the painter's bedroom window, you'll have a stunning view of the gardens. You can stroll the garden and view the thousands of flowers, including the *nymphéas*. The Japanese bridge, hung with wisteria, leads to a setting of weeping willows and rhododendrons. Monet's studio barge was installed on the pond.

84 rue Claude-Monet Parc Gasny. ℂ **02-32-51-28-21.** www.fondation-monet.com. Admission 6€ adults, 4.50€ students, 3.50€ children 7–12, free for children 6 and under. Daily 9:30am–6pm. Closed Nov–Mar.

Where to Stay

La Musardiere Giverny is becoming so popular with visitors that many local homes are opening as B&Bs. We find this small inn to be the best of the lot. A short walk from Monet's museum and gardens, it is a former manor house. An attraction in summer is the terraced and arbored garden.

A scenic park filled with ancient trees surrounds the hotel and restaurant. The mansard-roofed building dates from 1880 and was around in Monet's time. Many of the antique features and architectural adornments are still in place. *Musardiere* is French for a place for "idling or dawdling along," and that is just what you do here. Each medium-size guest room, attractively and comfortably furnished, has a small bathroom with tub or shower. The hotel also operates its own restaurant and crêperie where fixed-price menus cost 26€ to 36€.

123 rue Claude-Monet, Giverny 27620. ℂ **02-32-21-03-18.** Fax 02-32-21-60-00. www.lamusardiere.fr. 10 units. 81€–89€ double; 130€ suite. AE, DC, MC, V. Free parking. Closed Jan. **Amenities:** Restaurant; bar. *In room:* TV, hair dryer, Wi-Fi (free).

Where to Dine

Baudy FRENCH We hesitate to recommend this place because of the never-ending buses arriving from Paris, but it's a local legend and deserves a look. During the town's 19th-century heyday, the American painters used the pink villa as their lodging. In Monet's time, this place was an *epicerie-buvette* (casual hangout) run by the painter's friends, Angelina and Gaston Baudy. Metcalf was the first artist to arrive on Mme. Baudy's doorstep, and in time a string of other painters followed. Artists such as Cézanne could be found wandering around the rose garden here. The place no longer has its "legendary two tables," at which Mme. Baudy fed the artists, but it plays host to virtually all visitors to Giverny, feeding them simply prepared, traditional French cuisine, including big, freshly made salads and a changing array of hot food.

81 rue Claude-Monet. ℂ **02-32-21-10-03.** Reservations recommended. Main courses 14€–21€; fixed-price menu 24€. MC, V. Daily 10am–9:30pm; Sun 10am–3pm. Closed Nov–Mar.

Restaurant Les Fleurs ★ FRENCH   Capably managed by Bernard Lefebvre, this pleasant, popular restaurant does a large percentage of its business with art lovers. The Claude Monet Foundation is just across the river in Giverny. On the main street of Vernon, 4.8km (3 miles) southwest of the museum, the restaurant focuses on flavorful, familiar *cuisine bourgeoise* that many diners remember fondly from their childhood. Menu items include fresh fish, such as sea bass served with saffron sauce; a flavorful risotto of the day; and sweetbreads braised with Parmesan. Other dishes include fresh scallops with cocoa; a platter devoted to different preparations of duckling; and a variety of meats grilled, simply and flavorfully, *à la plancha.*

71 rue Sadi-Carnot, Vernon. ✆ **02-32-51-16-80.** Reservations recommended. Main courses 18€–30€; fixed-price menu 18€–47€. AE, MC, V. Wed–Sun noon–2pm; Tues–Sat 7:30–10pm. From the Claude Monet Foundation in Giverny, drive 5km (3 miles) southwest, crossing the Seine, and follow signs to Vernon.

CHANTILLY: A DAY AT THE RACES ★★★

42km (26 miles) N of Paris; 50km (31 miles) SE of Beauvais

This is a resort town for Parisians who want a quick weekend getaway. Known for its frothy whipped cream and its black lace, it also draws visitors to its racetrack and château.

Two of the great French horse races, **Le Prix du Jockey Club** and the **Prix Diane-Hermès,** take place at the Hippodrome on the first and second Sundays of June, respectively. Thoroughbreds from as far away as Kentucky and Brunei, as well as entrants sponsored by old and new European money, compete in a very civil format that's broadcast throughout France.

Essentials

GETTING THERE   **Trains** depart frequently for Chantilly from Gare du Nord in Paris. The ride takes about 30 minutes; the round-trip cost is 16€. On race days, free shuttle buses take fans from the Chantilly station to the track. Alternatively, RER line D will get you from Métro stop Châtelet–Les Halles to Chantilly in about 45 minutes.

VISITOR INFORMATION   The **Office Tourisme** is at 60 av. du Maréchal-Joffre (✆ **03-44-67-37-37;** www.chantilly-tourisme.com).

Seeing the Château & Museums

Château de Chantilly/Musée Condé ★★★   Once the seat of the grand Condé, head of the Bourbon-Condé dynasty, this château and the museum within it are on an artificial lake. Approach on the same forested drive that Louis XIV rode for a banquet prepared by his chef, Vatel. (One day when the fish didn't arrive on time, Vatel committed suicide.) The château is French Renaissance, with gables and towers, but part was rebuilt in the 19th century. A forest once filled with stag and boar skirts it.

In 1886, the château's owner, the duc d'Aumale, bequeathed the park and palace to the Institut de France, along with his art collection and library. The château houses sumptuous furnishings as well as works by artists such as Memling, Van Dyck, Botticelli, Poussin, Watteau, Ingres, Delacroix, Corot, Rubens, and Vernet. See Raphael's

Madonna of Lorette, Virgin of the House d'Orléans, and *Three Graces* (sometimes called the *Three Ages of Woman*). A series of about 40 miniatures represents the foremost French painter of the 15th century, Jean Fouquet. A copy of the rose diamond that received worldwide attention when it was stolen in 1926 is occasionally on display in the jewel collection. One of the most celebrated Condé acquisitions is the Limbourg brothers' *Les Très Riches Heures du Duc de Berry,* a 15th-century illuminated manuscript illustrating the months of the year, which is not always on view.

The château was built about 1560 by Jean Bullant for a member of the Montmorency family. The stables (see below), a hallmark of French 18th-century architecture, were constructed to house 240 horses, with adjacent kennels for 500 hounds. If you have time, take a walk in the garden laid out by Le Nôtre. A hamlet of rustic cottages and the Maison de Sylvie, a graceful building constructed in 1604 and rebuilt by Maria-Felice Orsini, are in the park.

If you don't want to see the château and its museum, you can visit the gardens (5€; free for 17 and under). Once you're in the garden, you can ride a narrow-gauge electric railway (touristy and loaded with children) through the park, or take a boat ride with lots of other passengers on the château's ornamental lake. Either of these requires a supplement of 5€.

Chantilly. ✆ **03-44-62-62-62.** www.chateaudechantilly.com. Admission to the château, museum, and gardens 11€ adults, 9€ children 13-17, free for children 4-12. Nov-Mar Wed-Mon 10:30am-5pm (park until 6pm); Apr-Oct Wed-Mon 10am-6pm (park until 8pm).

Les Grandes Ecuries/Musée Vivant du Cheval ★★   This museum occupies the restored Grandes Ecuries, the stables built between 1719 and 1735 for Louis-Henri, prince de Bourbon and prince de Condé, who occupied the château. Besides being fond of horses, he believed in reincarnation and expected to come back as a horse in his next life, so he built stables fit for a king.

The stables and an adjoining kennel fell into ruin, but they've been restored as a museum of the living horse, with thoroughbreds housed alongside old breeds of draft horses, Arabs and Hispano-Arabs, and farm horses. Exhibits trace the horse's association with humans and include a blacksmith shop and displays of saddles, equipment for the care of horses, and horse-race memorabilia.

Daily equestrian displays (Apr–Oct) last about 30 minutes and explain how the horse is ridden and trained (11:30am, 3pm, and occasionally 4:30pm).

Chantilly. ✆ **03-44-27-31-63.** www.museevivantducheval.fr. Admission 10€, 8€ for children 17 and under. Mar 22-Nov 2 Wed-Mon 10am-6pm; off season Wed-Mon 10:30am-5pm.

Where to Stay

Best Western Hôtel du Parc   This 1987 hotel is in the center of town, close to a host of restaurants and sights. There are grander châteaux in Chantilly, but if you want a midtown location, this is your finest choice. The contemporary lobby, dominated by mirrors and chrome, gives way to an inviting English-style bar, with plenty of dark wood and leather. The medium-size guest rooms have built-in furnishings and glass doors that open onto private balconies. About half of the small bathrooms have both tub and shower. Overall, expect a no-frills experience that's pleasant but nothing special.

36 av. du Maréchal-Joffre, Chantilly 60500. ✆ **800/528-1234** in the U.S. and Canada, or 03-44-58-20-00. Fax 03-44-57-31-10. www.bestwestern.fr. 57 units. 130€-150€ double; 160€-180€ suite. AE, DC, MC, V. Parking 10€. **Amenities:** Bar; room service. *In room:* TV, hair dryer, Wi-Fi (free).

Château de la Tour ★★ A wealthy Parisian banking family built this elegant turn-of-the-20th-century château with a 4.8-hectare (12-acre) park as a weekend getaway. During World War II, it was the home of the German l'Etat Major, and in 1946, it became a luxury hotel. The likes of Edith Piaf, Tino Rossi, and Jean Gabin met and mingled in the restaurant. Today, celebrities and sports personalities still frequent the château. In 1990, it gained a new wing; guests can choose rooms with a modern flavor or a more traditional ambience. All units are large and feature hardwood floors, high ceilings, and first-class furnishings, and half of the units are air-conditioned. Public areas feature two wood-burning fireplaces.

Chemin de la Chaussée, Chantilly-Gouvieux 60270. ✆ **03-44-62-38-38.** Fax 03-44-57-31-97. www. lechateaudelatour.fr. 41 units. 160€–190€ double; 180€–230€ suite. AE, DC, MC, V. Free parking. **Amenities:** Restaurant; bar; babysitting; bike rentals; outdoor pool; room service; tennis court. *In room:* A/C, TV, hair dryer, minibar, Wi-Fi (free).

Where to Dine

The restaurant at the **Château de la Tour** (see above) is open to the public for lunch and dinner.

La Ferme de Condé TRADITIONAL FRENCH The most appealing restaurant in Chantilly is in a 100-year-old stone-sided former Anglican church. It's on the periphery of town, about 1.6km (1 mile) north of the château. Antique farm implements, racks of wine bottles, and barrels give the space a cozy feel. The cuisine is old-fashioned, with variations based on seasonal ingredients and the chef's inspiration. Look for fresh oysters from Brittany or homemade foie gras, followed by succulent sweetbreads with morels, and, a major treat, suckling pig roasted on a spit. Two other delights include a fresh lobster salad and a "trio" of salmon.

42 av. du Maréchal-Joffre. ✆ **03-44-57-32-31.** Reservations recommended. Main courses 19€–44€; fixed-price menus 25€–45€. AE, DC, MC, V. Daily noon–2pm and 7–10:30pm.

SENLIS ★★

52km (32 miles) S of Paris; 100km (62 miles) S of Amiens

Sleepy Senlis, which some Parisians treat as a suburb, is a quiet township surrounded by forests. Its memories are many and regal. Barbarians no longer threaten its walls as they did in the 3rd century, and gone are the kings of France, from Clovis to Louis XIV, who passed through or took up temporary residence. You can tie a visit to this town with a trek to Chantilly (see above). Today, the core of Vieux Senlis is an archaeological bonanza that attracts visitors from all over the world. Budget 2 hours to see Senlis.

Essentials

GETTING THERE Approximately 20 **trains** daily depart from Paris's Gare du Nord for Chantilly (see above). In front of the railway station in Chantilly, **bus** no. 15 (marked SENLIS) has a schedule that coincides with the arrival of trains from Paris. The round-trip bus and train fare is 16€. Total travel time from downtown Paris to Senlis is 45 to 60 minutes.

VISITOR INFORMATION The **Office de Tourisme** is on place parvis Notre-Dame (✆ **03-44-53-06-40;** www.ville-senlis.fr).

Seeing the Sights

Medieval streets loaded with antique masonry and evocative doorways run throughout the city. One of the most interesting is the **rue du Chat-Harét;** from its center, it affords a view over the ruined château and the Gallo-Roman foundations. The **rue des Cordeliers** is the site of a (since demolished) medieval convent, and nos. 14 and 10 on that street are particularly beautiful and old, but neither is open to the public.

Cathédrale Notre-Dame de Senlis ★★ This cathedral has a 13th-century spire that rises 77m (253 ft.) and dominates the countryside. The severe western facade contrasts with the Flamboyant Gothic southern portal. A fire swept the structure in 1504, and much rebuilding followed. A 19th-century overlay was applied to the original structure, begun in 1153. Before you enter, walk around to the western porch to see the sculptures. Depicted in stone is a calendar of the seasons, along with scenes showing the ascension of the Virgin. The builders of the main portal imitated the work at Chartres. In the forecourt are memorials to Joan of Arc and Marshal Foch.

3 place Notre-Dame. ✆ **03-44-53-01-59.** Free admission. Daily 8:30am-7pm.

Château Royal et Parc and Musée de la Vénerie (Hunting Museum) ★ A short walk from the cathedral stands this curious archaeological ruin. Its stones have more royal associations than virtually anywhere else in France. The most impressive aspect remaining today is a massive Gallo-Roman wall, in some places more than 6m (20 ft.) tall. It encircles an area of about 6 hectares (15 acres), some of them occupied by parts of medieval Senlis. Of the wall's 28 original watchtowers, 16 remain. Within the circumference, the best-preserved fortification of its kind in France, are the ruins of a château that was occupied, or at least visited, by virtually every monarch of France from Hughes Capet (in the 10th c.) to Henri IV (late Renaissance). Abandoned by the monarchs around 1600, the château was demolished after the French Revolution. Today, you can wander freely among the ruins, imagining the grandeur of life as it used to be.

The complex's highlight, in the verdant park that surrounds the ruin, is the **Prieuré St-Mauritius,** a monastery that not only honors a saint but also was founded by one, Louis IX. It houses the **Musée de la Vénerie (Hunting Museum),** where you'll see hunting-related works of art from the 15th century to the present. Exhibits include arms, horns, trophies, drawings, engravings, and old hunting suits and costumes, all of which evoke the passion and pageantry that used to surround royal hunting expeditions. You can visit the museum only as part of a 1-hour tour (in French); tours begin every hour on the hour.

Senlis. ✆ **03-44-32-00-81.** Free admission to the park. Admission to the Hunting Museum including guided tour 2€ adults, 1€ students and children 12-18, free for children 15 and under. Mon and Wed-Fri 10am-noon and 2-6pm; Sat-Sun 11am-1pm and 2-6pm.

Musée des Spahis No other site in Senlis depicts the ancient Roman occupation of Gaul in such vivid terms. In the partially Gothic former home of the local bishop, the museum, which opened in 1989, contains most of the archaeological artifacts of the Gallo-Romans in the region. It also includes rare sculptures and church art from the Middle Ages. One floor above street level, you'll find paintings, some by local artists working in an untrained style that art historians refer to as "naive," executed between the 17th and 20th century.

Place du Parvis. ℂ **03-44-32-00-83.** Admission 2€ adults, 1€ students and children 16–18, free for children 15 and under. Mon and Thurs–Fri 10am–noon and 2–6pm; Wed 2–6pm; Sat–Sun 11am–1pm and 2–6pm. Closed Tues and at 5pm Nov 1–Feb 1.

Where to Stay & Dine

Hostellerie de la Porte Bellon   In a town of lackluster inns, this is a good oasis for the night. The stately but relatively inexpensive hotel was built as a convent 300 years ago and later functioned as a coaching inn. A short walk east of Senlis's historic core, it has three floors of big-windowed guest rooms and a facade dotted with old-fashioned shutters and window boxes filled with pansies and geraniums. At the entrance is an unusual 19th-century glass vestibule inspired by an English greenhouse. Accommodations have comfortable beds and cheerful wallpaper, but are a bit spartan.

51 rue Bellon, Senlis 60300. ℂ **03-44-53-03-05.** Fax 03-44-53-29-94. 19 units. 89€ double; 239€ 3-bedroom suite. AE, MC, V. Closed Dec 18–Jan 8. **Amenities:** Restaurant; bar. *In room:* TV, Wi-Fi (free).

La Vieille Auberge TRADITIONAL FRENCH   This building has held a restaurant since 1558, when it served burned and greasy food to wayfarers and pilgrims headed for the nearby cathedral. Today, considerably cleaned up, it has Louis-Philippe furniture and one large candlelit dining room that consists of three separate spaces. The refined, rustic dining areas have stone walls and heavy tables. During warm months, guests can sit on a small terrace. The staff takes pride in serving classic French dishes, which may include such favorites as filet of beef *rossini* with foie gras or fricassée of sweetbreads in a sauce made with fresh morels. The best pasta is the spaghetti with fresh shrimp.

8 rue Long Filet. ℂ **03-44-60-95-50.** www.lavieilleauberge-senlis.com. Reservations recommended Fri–Sat. Main courses 16€–44€; fixed-price menu 19€–40€. AE, DC, MC, V. Wed–Mon noon–1:45pm; Wed–Sat and Mon 7–9:30pm. Closed 3 weeks in Jan and 3 weeks in July.

COMPIEGNE ★★★

81km (50 miles) N of Paris

A visit to this Oise River valley town is usually combined with an excursion to Senlis, a quiet township with medieval streets surrounded by forests, some 32km (20 miles) away. The most famous dance step of all time was photographed in a forest about 6.5km (4 miles) from town: Hitler's "jig of joy" on June 22, 1940, heralded the ultimate humiliation of France and shocked the world.

Like Senlis, this town north of Paris lives for its memories—not all pleasant. Many come to visit the 14,160-hectare (35,000-acre) forest of Compiègne. With its majestic vistas, venerable trees, and ponds, it merits exploration.

Essentials

GETTING THERE   Trains run frequently from the Gare du Nord in Paris. The ride takes 50 minutes. The station is across the river from the town center. A round-trip ticket costs 23€. If you're **driving,** take the Paris-Lille motorway (A1 or the less convenient E15) for 81km (50 miles).

VISITOR INFORMATION   The **Office de Tourisme** is located at 28 Hôtel-de-Ville (ℂ **03-44-40-01-00;** www.compiegne-tourisme.fr).

Seeing the Sights

An imposing statue of **Joan of Arc,** who was taken prisoner at Compiègne by the Burgundians on May 23, 1430, stands in the town square.

Château de Pierrefonds ★★ One of the Compiègne forest's most evocative medieval buildings lies 12km (7½ miles) north of the town. (To reach it from the center, follow signs to Soissons.) Originally built in the 1100s as a château-fortress, it was later bought by Napoleon. Surrounded by a moat, it looks feudal, with rounded towers capped by funnel-shaped pointed roofs. Artifacts from the Middle Ages are displayed inside. Save time for a stroll through the tiny village of Pierrefonds at the base of the château. Here, half-timbered houses recall the château's medieval heyday.

Rue Viollet-Le-Duc in the Forêt de Compiègne. ℂ **03-44-42-72-72.** Admission 7€ adults, 4.50€ students 18–25, free for ages 17 and under. May–Aug daily 9:30am–6pm; Sept–Apr Tues–Sun 10am–1pm and 2–5:30pm.

Musée de la Figurine Historique (Museum of Historical Figurines) ★ Housed in one of Compiègne's finest monuments, the Flamboyant Gothic Hôtel de Ville, built from 1499 to 1503, this museum showcases a collection of about 100,000 tin soldiers, from a Louis XIV trumpeter to a World War II soldier. The Battle of Waterloo, staged in miniature on a landscape with thousands of figurines, is depicted in all its gore.

28 place de l'Hôtel-de-Ville. ℂ **03-44-40-72-55.** Admission 3€ adults, 1.50€ seniors and students, free for ages 17 and under. Tues–Sat 9am–noon; Tues–Sun 2–6pm (until 5pm Nov–Feb).

Musée National du Château de Compiègne ★★★ In its heyday, Compiègne attracted royalty and two Bonaparte emperors. But this wasn't always a place of pageantry. Louis XIV once said: "In Versailles, I live in the style befitting a monarch. In Fontainebleau, more like a prince. At Compiègne, like a peasant." But the Sun King returned again and again. His successor, Louis XV, started rebuilding the château, based on plans by Gabriel. The king died before work was completed, and Louis XVI and Marie Antoinette expanded it.

Napoleon's second wife, Marie-Louise, arrived at Compiègne to marry him; in a dining room, which you can visit only on the guided tour, she had her first meal with the emperor. Accounts maintain that she was paralyzed with fear of the older man (Napoleon was in his 40s; she was 19). After dinner, he seduced her and is said to have only increased her anxiety.

During the Second Empire, Compiègne reached its pinnacle. Under Napoleon III and Eugénie, the hunting season was the occasion for balls and parties. Women in elegant hoop skirts danced to Strauss waltzes; Offenbach's operas echoed through the chambers and salons; and Eugénie, who fancied herself an actress, performed in the palace theater for her guests.

On the tour, you'll see the gold-and-scarlet Empire Room, where Napoleon spent many a troubled night, and his library, known for its secret door. In the Queen's Chamber, Marie-Louise used the "horn of plenty" bed.

Various wings of the château hold museums. They include the **Musée National de la Voiture (National Automobile Museum),** which exhibits about 150 vehicles, from Ben-Hur chariots to a Citroën "chain-track" vehicle. The château also contains a series of rooms defined as either the **Musée de l'Imperatrice Eugénie,** the Musée du Second Empire, or the Musée Napoleon III, depending on who happens to be talking about it. It's devoted to sculpture, paintings (including some by Carpeaux), and furniture, as well as mementos and documents showcasing life, politics, values, and morals of France's Industrial Revolution and its Gilded Age.

Place du Général de Gaulle. ⓒ **03-44-38-47-02.** www.musee-chateau-compiegne.fr. Admission (including access to museums) 6.50€ adults, 4.50€ student, free for children 17 and under. Wed–Mon 10am–6pm.

Wagon de l'Armistice (Wagon du Maréchal-Foch) ★★ In 1940, in one of the most perverse twists of fate in European history, Hitler forced the vanquished French to capitulate in the same rail coach where German officials signed the Armistice on November 11, 1918. The triumphant Nazis transported the coach to Berlin, and then to Ordüff in the Thuringian Forest, where an Allied bomb destroyed it in April 1945. In Compiègne's suburb of Rethondes, 6.5km (4 miles) to the south, you can visit a replica that recounts the events of 1918 and 1940 in graphic detail, assisted by newspapers, photos, maps, and slide shows.

Rte. de Soissons, Rethondes. ⓒ **03-44-85-14-18.** Admission 4€ adults, 2€ children 7–14, free for children 6 and under. Apr to mid-Oct Wed–Mon 10am–6pm; mid-Oct to Mar Wed–Mon 10am–5:30pm.

Where to Stay

Hostellerie du Royal-Lieu ★ This half-timbered inn is the best choice for food and lodging close to the town, about 2km (1¼ miles) away. Guest rooms are medium in size, sleekly designed, and the bathrooms are tidily organized. The rooms and the restaurant's terrace overlook a garden. Meals in the elegantly rustic dining room may include four-fish stew with red butter, or brochette of quail with black olives and polenta. Dinners range from 30€ to 75€. Dessert soufflés are available if you order them 30 minutes in advance.

9 rue de Senlis, Compiègne 60200. ⓒ **03-44-20-10-24.** Fax 03-44-86-82-27. www.host-royallieu.com. 15 units. 138€ double; 159€ suite. AE, DC, MC, V. Follow signs southwest toward Senlis until you reach rue de Senlis, a 5-min. drive east of the town center. Free parking. **Amenities:** Restaurant; bar; room service. In room: TV, hair dryer, Wi-Fi (free).

Where to Dine

The restaurant at the **Hostellerie du Royal-Lieu** (see above) is also open to the public.

La Part des Anges ★ 🍴 FRENCH Our favorite restaurant in Compiègne occupies two warmly decorated dining rooms within a tile-roofed building from the early 1990s in the commercial center of town. Jean-Jacques Moissinac tends to the kitchen (and as such might never be seen by most diners) while his English-speaking wife Marie-Hélène tends to service in the dining room. The decor shows many successful efforts to create an old-fashioned warmth, including tapestry fabrics, indirect lighting, and a floor covered with antique beige-and-brown ceramic tiles that were salvaged from a much older building. Menu items represent good quality for the price; items likely to appear include lobster-stuffed ravioli; sea scallops poillé; filet of roebuck with peppercorn sauce; and a selection of seasonal meats and vegetables. The place lies within a 10-minute walk of the château, the Hôtel-de-Ville, and most of the town's historic monuments.

18 rue de Bouvines. ⓒ **03-44-86-00-00.** www.lapartdesanges60.com. Reservations recommended. Main courses 20€; set-price menus 30€–60€. AE, MC, V. Tues–Fri and Sun noon–1:30pm; Tues–Sat 7:30–9pm. Closed 4 weeks July–Aug.

THE LOIRE VALLEY

B ordered by vineyards, the winding Loire Valley cuts through the land of castles deep in France's heart. Medieval crusaders returning here brought news of the opulence of the East, and soon they began rethinking their surroundings. Later, word came from Italy of an artistic flowering led by Leonardo and Michelangelo. Royalty and nobility built châteaux in this valley during the French Renaissance, and an era of pomp reigned until Henri IV moved his court to Paris, marking the Loire's decline.

The Loire is blessed with attractions, including medieval, Renaissance, and classical châteaux, Romanesque and Gothic churches, and treasures such as the Apocalypse Tapestries. There's even the castle that inspired *Sleeping Beauty.* Trains serve some towns, but the best way to see this region is by car.

ORLEANS ★

119km (74 miles) SW of Paris; 72km (45 miles) SE of Chartres

After suffering damage in World War II, many Orléans neighborhoods were rebuilt in dull styles, so visitors who hope to see how it looked when the Maid of Orléans (Joan of Arc) was here are likely to be disappointed. Today, this city of 200,000 has lost a lot of its prominence to Tours, but signs of restoration bring hope for the future.

Essentials

GETTING THERE Ten **trains** per day arrive from Paris's Gare d'Austerlitz (trip time: 1 hr., 15 min.); there are also a dozen connections from Tours (trip time: 50 min.). The one-way fare from Tours to Orléans is 17€ to 25€. Orléans lies on the road between Paris and Tours. If you're **driving** from Paris, take A10 south; from Tours, take A10 north.

VISITOR INFORMATION The **Office de Tourisme** is at 2 place de L'Etape (𝄐 **02-38-24-05-05;** www.tourisme-orleans.com).

BIKING YOUR WAY through THE LOIRE

Once you're in Tours, you can rely on public transport to see much of the Loire. You can also rent a bicycle, a great way to see the region, as it's relatively flat. **Detours de Loire,** 35, rue Charles Gille, Tours (© **02-47-61-22-23;** www.locationdevelos.com), rents mountain bikes and all-purpose bikes for 14€ to 21€ per day. A 300€ deposit (usually a credit card imprint) is required. The shop is only 46m (150 ft.) from the rail station. A full-day excursion that may interest some experienced mountain bikers involves a 35km (22-mile) jaunt from Tours to Chenonceaux, following a rugged path that mostly meanders beside the Cher River. Amstercycles provides a map for this itinerary and advice about how best to navigate the bumps. The railway station at Tours doesn't check baggage, so the shop guards bags. The service, available to customers and noncustomers, costs 2€ per day and is available from May to September Monday to Saturday 9am to 12:30pm and 2 to 7pm, and Sunday 6 to 7pm only. Off-season hours are erratic.

An excellent itinerary involves riding 17km (11 miles) west of Tours to the Jardins de Villandry. The relatively flat and scenic road takes you along the bank of the Cher River. From here, continue 8km (5 miles) to the Château de Langeais, also a lovely route. If you want to head east from Tours, consider the 24km (15-mile) excursion to Amboise. This route is more densely trafficked and not as bucolic. The tourist office provides maps.

BikeToursDirect, 1638 Berkley Circle, Chattanooga, TN (© **877/462-2423**), has expanded its Loire Valley tours to 10, including 3-week-long programs that when linked together take cyclists from the headwaters of the Loire through to the Atlantic. BikeToursDirect represents overseas bike tour operators whose low overhead and frequent departures allow them to offer prices as much as 70% below those of United States bike tour companies. Self-guided tours start at less than $750 per person, based on double occupancy, and include hotels, breakfasts, rental bikes, luggage transfers, and detailed route information.

Exploring the Town

Orléans is the chief town of Loiret, on the Loire, and beneficiary of many associations with the French aristocracy. It gave its name to ducs and duchesses of Orléans. In 1429, **Joan of Arc** relieved the city from attacks by the Burgundians and the English. That deliverance is celebrated every year on May 8, the anniversary of her victory. An equestrian statue of Jeanne d'Arc stands on place du Martroi. From the square, you can drive down rue Royal (rebuilt in 18th-c. style) across pont George-V (erected in 1760). A simple cross marks the site of the Fort des Tourelles, which Joan of Arc and her men captured.

Near rue Royale is **place du Châtelet,** with many boutiques, including a Galeries Lafayette. Look for fashionable clothing, jewelry, books, and leather goods. For antiques, walk along **rue de Bourgogne,** where a host of dealers sell everything from objets d'art to furniture.

Cathédrale Ste-Croix ★   Begun in 1287, after an earlier Romanesque church here collapsed from old age, the cathedral was burned by the Huguenots in 1568. Henri IV laid the first stone of the present building in 1601, and work continued until 1829. The cathedral boasts a 17th-century organ and woodwork from the early 18th century in its chancel, the masterpiece of Jules Hardouin-Mansart and other artists associated with Louis XIV. You'll need to take the guided tour to see the chancel, the crypt, and the treasury, with its Byzantine enamels, gold work from the 15th and 16th centuries, and Limoges enamels.

Place Ste-Croix. **02-38-77-87-50.** Free admission; tip the guide 1€ if you take a guided tour. May–Sept daily 9:15am–6pm; Oct–Apr daily 9:15am–noon and 2:15–5pm.

Eglise St-Aignan One of the most frequently altered churches in the Loire Valley, St-Aignan was consecrated in 1509 in the form you see today. It possesses one of France's earliest vaulted hall crypts, complete with polychromed capitals. Scholars of pre-Romanesque art view the place with interest; its 10th- and 11th-century aesthetics are rare. Aboveground, the church's Renaissance-era choir and transept remain, but the Protestants burned the nave during the Wars of Religion. In a wood-carved shrine are the remains of the church's patron saint.

Place St-Aignan. No phone; ask at tourist office. Free admission. Only Sun noon–6pm.

Hôtel Groslot   This Renaissance mansion was begun in 1550 and embellished in the 19th century. François II (first husband of Mary, Queen of Scots) lived here during the fall of 1560 and died on December 5. Between the Revolution and the mid-1970s, it functioned as the town hall. Marriage ceremonies, performed by the town's magistrates, still occur here. It was here that Charles IX met his lovely Marie Touchet. The statue of Joan of Arc praying was the work of Louis Philippe's daughter, Princesse Marie d'Orléans. In the garden you can see the remains of the 15th-century Chapelle St-Jacques.

Place de l'Etape (northwest of the cathedral). (C) **02-38-79-22-30.** Free admission. July–Sept Mon–Fri 9am–6pm; Oct–June Mon–Fri and Sun 10am–noon and 2–6pm.

Musée des Beaux-Arts ★★   This is primarily a picture gallery of French and some Dutch and Flemish works from the 16th to the late 19th centuries. Some of the works once hung in Cardinal Richelieu's château. The collection includes busts by Pigalle and a fine array of portraits, including one of Mme. de Pompadour. Among non-French works, the undisputed star is a lovely Velázquez commemorating the Apostle St. Thomas.

Place Ste. Croix. (C) **02-38-79-21-55.** Admission 3€ adults, 1.50€ students, free for children 15 and under. Tues–Sun 10am–6pm.

Shopping

One of the city's main industries, from the Middle Ages well into the 20th century, was vinegar making. You can buy some of the famous Orléans vinegar north of town at **Martin Pouret,** 236 Faubourg Bannier, Fleury-les-Aubrais ((C) **02-38-88-78-49**). The family-owned business dates from 1797. The current M. Pouret is the only person in the region carrying on the slow, traditional vinegar-making method. You can do a wine tasting at one of the region's most comprehensive wine merchants, **Cave de Marc & Sebastien,** 7 place du Châtelet ((C) **02-38-62-94-11**), in the heart of the commercial center, just north of the Loire and west of rue Royale.

Orléans

place de Gambetta · Gare · To Chartres & Paris · To Etampes · PARC LOUIS PASTEUR · bd. de Verdun · Bus Station · place Albert-1er · rue E. Vignat · rue Jules Lemaître · rue du Faubourg St-Vincent · Paris · Orléans · FRANCE · 0 100 mi · 0 100 km · rue Bannier · rue de la République · bd. de Aléxandre Martin · rue d'Alsace-Lorraine · rue de la Bretonnerie · rue R. Chollet · bd. A. Briand · rue Bellebat · bd. St-Euverte · place de l'Etape · rue d'Escures · place du Martroi · Hôtel Groslot · rue Dupanloup · place Ste-Croix · rue du Bourdon Blanc · Cathédrale Ste-Croix · place du Gén de Gaulle · rue Jeanne d'Arc · place Abbé Desnoyes · Musée Historique · Maison Jeanne d'Arc · Musée des Beaux-Arts · rue de Bourgogne · rue de Bourgogne · To Sens & Gien · rue de la Tour Neuve · rue Royale · place du Châtelet · Eglise St-Aignan · To Blois & Tours · quai Cypierre · Nouvelle Halle · quai du Châtelet · quai du Fort-Alleaume · pont George-V · Loire · 0 1/5 mi · 0 0.2 km · Church · Information · Post Office

Where to Stay

D'Orléans   This is one of the top five hotels of Orléans, where the competition is not very keen. It is for those who prefer simplicity to opulence and think of a hotel room only as a place in which to sleep and shower. Each room is midsize and furnished in a minimalist way, yet all the accommodations are comfortable and well maintained. Two buildings are linked around a courtyard and bound by the joint breakfast room. The beds have been renewed and slowly the interior is being renovated.

6 rue Adolphe Crespin, Orléans 4500. ✆ **02-38-53-35-34.** Fax 02-38-53-68-20. http://hotelorleans.fr. 18 units. 68€–86€ double; 92€ triple. AE, DC, MC, V. Parking 9€. **Amenities:** Breakfast room; room service. *In room:* TV, hair dryer, Wi-Fi (free).

Hôtel d'Arc   This four-story hotel, built in the 1920s, with an Art Deco facade and old-fashioned elevator, sits in the middle of the town and is close to the railway station and the pedestrian-only shopping streets. The guest rooms feature ceiling moldings and paneling. Most are of average size; the largest units have numbers that end in 2. Most rooms are peaceful, but avoid those that face rue de la République, which tend to be noisy. Although the hotel has no restaurant, it serves breakfast in an ornate room with a carved marble fireplace.

37 rue de la République, Orléans 45000. © **02-38-53-10-94.** Fax 02-38-81-77-47. www.hoteldarc.fr. 35 units. 99€–163€ double. AE, DC, MC, V. *In room:* TV, hair dryer, minibar, Wi-Fi (free).

Hôtel Mercure Orléans ★ If you seek modern comfort, this is the town's finest address. Along the river, adjacent to pont Joffre, the eight-story bandbox structure is within walking distance of place du Martroi and its Joan of Arc statue. Though rather impersonal—it's favored by businesspeople—it provides the best rooms in the city. Most units are in chain-hotel style and of medium size. The on-site restaurant serves French and Loire Valley specialties.

44–46 quai Barentin, Orléans 45000. © **02-38-62-17-39.** Fax 02-38-53-95-34. www.accorhotels.com. 111 units. 133€–163€ double; 195€ suite. AE, DC, MC, V. Parking 5€. **Amenities:** Restaurant; bar; babysitting; outdoor pool; room service. *In room:* A/C, TV, hair dryer, minibar, Wi-Fi (10€ per 3 hr.).

Where to Dine

Chez Jules ★ 🍴 TRADITIONAL FRENCH This small bistro serves one of the best regional cuisines in the city and gives you the warmest welcome. Tables are limited so it's important to reserve in advance. The prices are among the most affordable in Orléans. Try the eggplant caviar with ratatouille for openers, perhaps marinated mussels and beets, or else a goat cheese pastry. Look for a changing array of seafood dishes, depending on availability. One specialty is parmentier of pigeon with foie gras. The menu is seasonally adjusted.

136 rue de Bourgogne. © **02-38-54-30-80.** Reservations required. Fixed-price menus 15€ at lunch, 22€–31€ at dinner. Main courses 18€–22€. AE, MC, V. Tues–Fri noon–2pm and Mon–Sat 7–10pm. Closed 3 weeks in July.

La Vieille Auberge ★ MODERN FRENCH You can dine inside in a stylish interior, or, if the weather's right, order your food in a lovely garden. The restaurant is housed in a building from the 17th century, and all the food is prepared fresh daily by skilled chefs. The menu changes with the season to take advantage of the best of seasonal produce, including on occasion lobster, oysters, game (in autumn), shellfish, and country lamb.

2 rue du Faubourg St-Vincent. © **02-38-53-55-81.** http://lavieilleauberge.net. Reservations recommended. Main courses 18€–35€; fixed-price lunch 25€; fixed-price dinner 35€–49€. AE, MC, V. Mon–Thurs noon–2pm and 7–9:30pm; Fri–Sat noon–2pm and 7–10pm; Sun noon–2pm.

Orleans After Dark

You'll find most of the action in the bars along **rue de Bourgogne** and a handful of places on **rue Bannier.** A trendy young crowd drinks the night away at **Le Moog,** 38 rue de l'Empereur (© **02-38-54-93-23**), in a modern setting of stainless steel and bordello red lighting, with pop music playing in the background. There's also a terrace for fair weather. A few streets over is one of the better jazz clubs, **Paxton's Head,** 264 rue de Bourgogne (© **02-38-81-23-29**), with a down-home English pub feel. **Havana,** 29 rue Bourgogne (© **02-38-52-16-00**), crawls with some of the city's most attractive and available 20- to 30-year-olds. This joint serves strong, party-colored drinks and loud music.

CHATEAUDUN

103km (64 miles) SW of Paris; 43km (27 miles) SW of Chartres

Austere and foreboding, **Château de Châteaudun ★★**, place Jean-de-Dunois (② **02-37-94-02-90**), rises on a stone table over a tributary of the Loire. Begun in the Middle Ages, the château is a mix of medieval and Renaissance architecture, with towering chimneys and dormers. After a fire in the 18th century, Hardouin, Louis XV's architect, directed the town's reconstruction and turned over the castle to the homeless, who stripped it of its finery. In 1935, the government acquired the fortress and launched a restoration. Even today, it's not richly furnished, but fine tapestries depicting scenes such as the worship of the golden calf now cover its walls. The château's most admirable features are two carved staircases. Inside the Ste-Chapelle, dating from the Middle Ages, are more than a dozen 15th-century robed statues. In 2002, the curators added a permanent exhibit honoring Jean Dunois, a comrade in arms to Joan of Arc.

The château is open daily: May 2 to June 30 10am to 1pm and 2 to 6pm; July 1 to September 4 10am to 1pm and 2 to 6:15pm; September 5 to April 30 10am to 12:30pm and 2 to 5:30pm. Admission is 7€ for adults, free for children 17 and under. Allow 1½ hours to see the château.

Essentials

GETTING THERE   Four to 15 **Transbeauce buses** (② **02-37-18-59-00**) per day arrive from Chartres (trip time: 1 hr.), depending on the day of the week and the season. The one-way fare is about 7.40€. For schedules, call the station, Gare Routière, Chartres, at ② **02-37-18-59-00.** There are five **trains** per day, departing from Paris's Gare d'Austerlitz, charging around 19€ each way, and arriving 90 minutes later in Châteaudun. If you're **driving** from Paris, head southwest along A10 and exit at Phivars. Then take N10, following signs for Châteaudun.

VISITOR INFORMATION   The **Office de Tourisme** is at 1 rue de Luynes (② **02-37-45-22-46;** www.ville-chateaudun.com).

Where to Stay

Hôtel St-Michel   This hotel's tradition of housing guests dates from the early 19th century, when it was a coaching inn. Today it is Châteaudun's best inn, although that's not saying a lot. The staff is less than helpful, but the place is decent. Guest rooms are functional in design and simply, though comfortably, furnished. Breakfast is served in the lounge, in your room, or in the greenhouse-style winter garden.

28 place du 18-Octobre and 5 rue Péan, Châteaudun 28200. ② **02-37-45-15-70.** Fax 02-37-45-83-39. www.hotelstmichel.net. 19 units. 51€–58€ double. AE, DC, MC, V. Parking 7€. **Amenities:** Bar; exercise room; room service; sauna. *In room:* TV, minibar, Wi-Fi (free).

BEAUGENCY ★

150km (93 miles) SW of Paris; 85km (53 miles) NE of Tours

On the right bank of the Loire, the town of Beaugency boasts a 14th-century bridge that's unusual because each of its 26 arches is in a different style. The heart of town is an archaeological garden called the **City of the Lords,** named after the counts who enjoyed great power in the Middle Ages. A major medieval event took place here: the 1152 annulment of the marriage of Eleanor of Aquitaine and her cousin, Louis VII. This remarkable woman later became queen consort of Henry II of England, bringing southwestern France as her dowry. She was the mother of Richard the Lion-Hearted. (The film *The Lion in Winter* dramatizes these events.) Allow 2 hours to see Beaugency.

The 15th-century **Château Dunois** is currently closed for renovations and may not reopen again until 2011 or beyond. You have to see it from its exterior. The château is brooding, foreboding, and impressive, its historical links stretching back to almost-mystical medieval antecedents. It was built on the foundations of an earlier château from about A.D. 1000, known as the Château des Sires de Beaugency (château of the lords of Beaugency), whose feudal power extended throughout the region. Astride the street (la rue du Pont) that leads to one of the château's secondary entrances, the Voûte St-Georges (St. George's Vault) is an arched gateway from the earlier château.

Eglise Notre-Dame, place Saint-Fermin, would have been a good example of 12th-century Romanesque architecture if Gothic touches hadn't been added. Originally, it was attached to a Benedictine abbey. Nearby, the **Tour St-Fermin,** with a panoramic view of the valley, is all that remains of a church that stood on place Saint-Fermin. A trio of bells is in this tower, whose spire rises 54m (177 ft.). These attractions are open daily from 7am to 7pm; admission is free.

The 10th-century **Eglise St-Etienne,** place du Martroi, is one of the oldest churches in France. Now deconsecrated, it is owned by the municipality and is open only for temporary exhibitions of painting and sculpture.

Essentials

GETTING THERE If you're **driving** from Blois to Beaugency, take D951 northeast. About 20 **trains** per day run between Beaugency and either Blois or Orléans; each trip takes 20 minutes, and the one-way fare starts at 5.80€. For railway information, call ☏ **08-92-35-35-35.** From Orléans, about eight **buses** a day make the trip to Beaugency. For bus schedules and information, call the station in Orléans (☏ **02-38-61-90-00**).

VISITOR INFORMATION The **Office de Tourisme** is at 3 place du Dr.-Hyvernaud (☏ **02-38-44-54-42**).

Where to Stay & Dine

Abbaye de Beaugency ★ This government-rated three-star hotel offers the most historic accommodations in Beaugency. Built in 1640 as a monastery, it retains the stone window and door frames of its original construction, and an elegant brick facade that may remind you of a château. A hotel since 1935, it sits beside the Loire, within view of the town's oldest bridge. Guest rooms are large and bright, and each bathroom has both a tub and shower.

2 quai de l'Abbaye, Beaugency 45190. ☏ **02-38-45-10-10.** Fax 02-38-44-98-14. www.hotel-abbaye-beaugency.com. 19 units. 100€–150€ double. DC, MC, V. **Amenities:** Restaurant; bar; room service. *In room:* TV, minibar, Wi-Fi (free).

La Tonnellerie ★ 🎁 About 1.5km (1 mile) south of the center of Beaugency, this well-managed hotel is intimate and charming. It was originally built as a manor house in the 19th century, and it retains its original L-shaped design, walled garden, and sense of the era of Balzac and Flaubert. The Laura Ashley–furnished rooms are comfortable and traditional. The Pouey family can arrange visits to the château, golf, hiking, cycling, or a trip to a winery.

12 rue des Eaux-Bleues, Tavers, Beaugency 45190. © **02-38-44-68-15.** Fax 02-38-44-10-01. www. tonelri.com. 20 units. 158€–230€ double; 174€–210€ apt or suite. AE, DC, MC, V. Closed Dec 16–Jan 14. Take A10, exit at Beaugency, and then take N152 to Beaugency/Tavers. **Amenities:** Restaurant; guests-only bar; babysitting; outdoor pool. *In room:* TV, Wi-Fi (free).

CHAMBORD

191km (119 miles) SW of Paris; 18km (11 miles) E of Blois

When François I said, "Come on up to my place," he meant the **Château de Chambord ★★★**, 41250 Bracieux (© **02-54-50-40-00;** www.chambord.org). Some 2,000 workers began "the pile" in 1519. What emerged after 20 years was the pinnacle of the French Renaissance, the largest château in the Loire Valley. It was ready for the visit of Charles V of Germany, who was welcomed by nymphets in transparent veils tossing wildflowers in his path. Monarchs such as Henri II and Catherine de Médicis, Louis XIII, and Henri III came and went from Chambord, but none loved it like François I. The state acquired Chambord in 1932.

The château is in a park of more than 5,260 hectares (13,000 acres), enclosed by a wall stretching some 32km (20 miles). Four monumental towers dominate Chambord's facade. The three-story keep has a spectacular terrace from which the ladies of the court used to watch the return of their men from the hunt. The keep also encloses a corkscrew staircase, superimposed upon itself so that one person may descend and a second ascend without ever meeting. The apartments of Louis XIV, including his redecorated bedchamber, are also in the keep.

The château is open daily April to September 9am to 6:15pm, and October to March 9am to 5:15pm (until 7pm July to August). Admission is 9.50€ for adults and free for ages 25 and under. At the tourist office, you can pick up tickets for the summer *son-et-lumière* presentation, "Jours et Siècles" ("Days and Centuries"). The price is 10€. Allow 1½ hours to visit the château.

Essentials

GETTING THERE   It's best to **drive** to Chambord. Take D951 northeast from Blois to Ménars, turning onto the rural road to Chambord. You can also rent a **bicycle** in Blois and ride the 18km (11 miles) to Chambord, or take a **tour** to Chambord from Blois in summer. From June 15 to September 2, **Transports du Loir et Cher** (© **02-54-58-55-44**) operates bus service to Chambord, leaving Blois at 9am and 1:30pm with return trips at 1 and 6pm.

VISITOR INFORMATION   The **Office de Tourisme** on place St-Michel (© **02-54-33-39-16**) is open mid-June to October.

Where to Stay & Dine

Hôtel du Grand-St-Michel   Across from the château, and originally built as a kennel for the royal hounds, this inn is the only one of any substance in town. Try for a front room overlooking the château, which is dramatically floodlighted at night. Accommodations are plain but comfortable with provincial decor. Most visitors arrive for lunch, which in summer is served on a terrace. The marvelous collection of Loire wines is so good that it almost overshadows the regional cooking. High points from the menu include stew of wild boar (in late autumn and winter), breast of duckling in green-peppercorn sauce, and several local pâtés and terrines, including coarsely textured, flavorful rillettes of regional pork.

103 place St-Louis, Chambord 41250, near Bracieux. © **02-54-20-31-31.** Fax 02-54-20-36-40. www. saintmichel-chambord.com. 40 units. 54€–90€ double. MC, V. Free parking. Closed mid-Nov to mid-Dec. **Amenities:** Restaurant; Internet; tennis court. *In room:* TV.

BLOIS

180km (112 miles) SW of Paris; 60km (37 miles) NE of Tours

This town of 55,000 receives half a million visitors yearly, primarily to visit the **Château de Blois ★★★**. If time remains after a visit to the château, you may want to walk around the town. It's a piece of living history, with cobblestone streets and restored white houses with slate roofs and red-brick chimneys. Blois (pronounce it "Blwah") hugs a hillside overlooking the Loire. Some of its "streets" are mere alleyways originally laid out in the Middle Ages, or lanes linked by a series of stairs. Allow 1½ hours to see Blois.

Essentials

GETTING THERE The Paris-Austerlitz line via Orléans runs six **trains** per day from Paris (trip time: 1½ hr. plus transfer waiting time at Orléans), costing 24€ one-way; from Tours, 8 to 13 trains arrive per day (trip time: 40 min.) at a cost of 10€ one-way. For information and schedules, call © **08-92-35-35-35.** The train station is at place de la Gare. From June to September, you can take a **bus** (© **02-54-58-55-44**) from the Blois train station to tour châteaux in the area, including Chambord, Chaumont, Chenonceau, and Amboise. If you're **driving** from Tours, take RN152 east to Blois. If you'd like to explore the area by **bike,** check out **Traineurs de Loire,** place St-Louis L'Embarcadaire (© **02-54-33-37-54;** www.traineursde loire.com). Rentals start at 13€ per day.

VISITOR INFORMATION The **Office de Tourisme** is at 23 place du Château (© **02-54-90-41-41;** www.bloispaysdechambord.com).

Exploring the Town & the Château

If you have time for **shopping,** head for the area around **rue St-Martin** and **rue du Commerce** for high-end items such as clothing, perfume, shoes, and jewelry. Find a one-of-a-kind piece of jewelry or have something created by the master jeweler **Philippe Denies,** 3 rue St-Martin (© **02-54-74-78-24**). If you prefer antique jewelry, stop by **Antebellum,** 12 rue St-Lubin (© **02-54-78-38-78**), and browse its selection of precious and semiprecious stones set in gold and silver. If you want to acquire a copy of the tapestries at nearby châteaux, you'll find a wide range at **Tapisserie Langlois,** Voûte du Château (© **02-54-78-04-43**). Chocoholics flock to **Jeff de Bruges,** 77 rue du Commerce (© **02-54-74-26-44**), and **Max Vauché,** 50 rue du Commerce (© **02-54-78-23-55**). On Saturday all day, a **food market** is on rue St-Lubin and place de la Republique, lining several blocks in the center of town at the foot of the château.

Château de Blois ★★★ A wound in battle earned him the name Balafré (Scarface), but he was quite a ladies' man. In fact, on the misty morning of December 23, 1588, the duc de Guise had just left a warm bed and the arms of one of Catherine de Médicis's ladies-in-waiting. His archrival, King Henri III, had summoned him, but when the duke arrived, only the king's minions were about. The guards approached with daggers. Wounded, the duke made for the door, where more guards awaited him. Staggering, he fell to the floor in a pool of his own blood. Only then did Henri emerge from behind the curtains. "Mon Dieu," he reputedly exclaimed, "he's taller dead than alive!" The body couldn't be shown: The duke was too popular. Quartered, it was burned in a fireplace.

The murder of the duc de Guise is only one of the events associated with the Château de Blois, begun in the 13th century by the comte de Blois. Blois reached the apex of its power in 1515, when François I moved to the château. For that reason, Blois is often called the "Versailles of the Renaissance," the second capital of France, and the "city of kings." Blois soon became a palace of exile. Louis XIII banished his mother, Marie de Médicis, to the château, but she escaped by sliding into the moat down a mound of dirt left by the builders.

If you stand in the courtyard, you'll find the château is like an illustrated storybook of French architecture. The Hall of the Estates-General is a beautiful 13th-century work; Louis XII built the Charles d'Orléans gallery and the Louis XII wing from 1498 to 1501. Mansart constructed the Gaston d'Orléans wing between 1635 and 1637. Most remarkable is the François I wing, a French Renaissance masterpiece, containing a spiral staircase with ornamented balustrades and the king's symbol, the salamander.

Let the Horse Lead the Way

You can take a 25-minute **horse-and-buggy ride** through the old town of Blois for 6.50€ for adults and 4.50€ for children 2 to 12. The carriage departs from place du Château during April, May, June, and September on weekends and holidays from 2 to 6pm; in July and August, it leaves daily from 11am to 7pm. For more details, call the tourist office.

The château presents a *son-et-lumière* show in French from May to September, usually beginning at 10:30pm (but sometimes earlier, depending on the school calendar). As a taped lecture plays, colored lights and readings evoke the age in which the château was built. The show costs 7€ for adults, 3€ for children 7 to 15, and is free for children 6 and under.

41000 Blois. ✆ **02-54-90-33-33.** www.chateaudeblois.fr. Admission 8€ adults, 6.50€ students 12–25, 4€ children 6–17, free for children 5 and under. July–Aug daily 9am–7pm; Apr–June and Sept daily 9am–5:30pm; Oct–Mar daily 9am–12:30pm and 1:30–5:30pm.

Where to Stay

Some of the best rooms in town are at **Le Médicis** (see "Where to Dine," below).

Holiday Inn Garden Court ★ ☺ This leading hotel, built in 1996, sits in the heart of town. It has all the modern amenities and a certain traditional charm. The rooms are furnished with contemporary flair and provide chain-hotel standardized comfort. In summer, guests flock to a terrace overlooking the hotel garden.

26 av. Maunoury, Blois 41000. ℰ **800/465-4329** in the U.S. and Canada, or 02-54-55-44-88. Fax 02-54-74-57-97. www.holiday-inn.com. 78 units. 110€–160€ double. Children 11 and under stay free in parent's room. AE, DC, MC, V. Free parking. Bus: 1. **Amenities:** 2 restaurants; bar; babysitting; room service. *In room:* A/C, TV, hair dryer, minibar, Wi-Fi (7€ per day).

Hôtel le Savoie This modern 1930s-era hotel is both inviting and livable, from its courteous staff to its guest rooms, which are small but quiet and cozy. Bathrooms are small but have sufficient shelf space; each has a shower. In the morning, a breakfast buffet is set up in the bright dining room.

6-8 rue du Docteur-Ducoux, Blois 41000. ℰ **02-54-74-32-21.** Fax 02-54-74-29-58. www.hotel-blois. com. 24 units. 49€–55€ double. MC, V. **Amenities:** Bar; babysitting; room service. *In room:* TV, minibar, Wi-Fi (free).

Mercure Centre ★ This is one of the best-located hotels in Blois—three stories of reinforced concrete and big windows beside the quays of the Loire, a 5-minute walk from the château. Rooms never rise above the chain format and roadside-motel look, but they are roomy and soundproof.

28 quai St-Jean, Blois 41000. ℰ **02-54-56-66-66.** Fax 02-54-56-67-00. www.mercure.com. 96 units. 95€–240€ double. AE, DC, MC, V. Parking 7€. Bus: Quayside marked PISCINE. **Amenities:** Restaurant; bar; babysitting; Jacuzzi; indoor pool; room service; sauna. *In room:* A/C, TV, hair dryer, minibar, Wi-Fi (10€ per 3 hr.).

Where to Dine

Au Rendez-vous des Pêcheurs ★★ TOURAINE/SEAFOOD This restaurant occupies a 16th-century house and old grocery a short walk from the château. Chef Christophe Cosme enjoys a reputation for quality, generous portions, and creativity. He prepares two or three meat dishes, including roasted Sologne pigeon on a caramelized cauliflower pancake, and succulent line-caught whitefish in puff pastry. These appear alongside a longer roster of seafood dishes, such as poached filet of *sandre* (a freshwater fish; "zander" in English) served with fresh oysters, and freshwater eel in puff pastry with figs.

27 rue du Foix. ℰ **02-54-74-67-48.** www.rendezvousdespecheurs.com. Reservations required. Main courses 29€–35€; fixed-price menu 30€–69€. AE, MC, V. Tues–Sat 12–2:30pm; Mon–Sat 7–10pm. Closed 2 weeks in Jan and 3 weeks in Aug.

Le Médicis ★ TRADITIONAL FRENCH Members of the Garanger family maintain one of the most sophisticated inns in Blois, just 1km (⅔ mile) from the château. It's ideal for a gourmet meal or an overnight stop. Fresh fish is the chef's specialty. Typical main courses are asparagus in mousseline sauce, scampi ravioli with saffron sauce, and *suprême* of perch with morels. Chocolate in many manifestations is the dessert specialty. The Garangers rent 12 elegant rooms with air-conditioning, TV, minibar, and hair dryer. Double rates are 87€ to 150€.

2 allée François 1er, Blois 41000. ℰ **02-54-43-94-04.** Fax 02-54-42-04-05. www.le-medicis.com. Reservations required. Main courses 18€–36€; fixed-price menu 22€–60€. AE, MC, V. Daily noon–1:30pm and 7–9pm. Closed Jan and Sun night Nov–Mar. Bus: 2.

L'Orangerie du Château ★★★ ☺ TOURAINE Next to the château, one of the castle's former outbuildings holds the grandest and best restaurant in the area. Chef Jean-Marc Molveaux presides over a floral-themed dining room. Faithful customers and the most discerning foodies visiting Blois delight in his filet mignon with truffles. You can also sample his lovely waffle of potatoes with marinated salmon, or perfectly roasted monkfish flavored with fresh thyme. Everything tastes better with a Sauvignon de Touraine. For dessert, our favorite is melted chocolate and pistachio with crème fraîche.

1 av. Jean-Laigret. ℭ **02-54-78-05-36.** www.orangerie-du-chateau-fr. Reservations required. Main courses 23€–37€; fixed-price menu 33€–77€; children's menu 15€. AE, MC, V. Thurs–Tues noon–1:45pm; Thurs–Sat and Mon–Tues 7:15–9:15pm. Closed mid-Feb to mid-Mar.

Blois After Dark

There's not much in the way of nightlife in Blois, but you could saunter down to the fun and friendly **L'Hendrix Café,** 1 rue du Puits-Châtel (ℭ **02-54-58-82-73**), for a drink. Another possibility is **Le Velvet Jazz Lounge,** 15 bis rue Haute (ℭ **02-54-78-36-32**), off rue Denis Papin. This is part of a 13th-century abbey but is now a venue for weekly jazz concerts. Otherwise, this is a classy joint for a drink. From Tuesday to Sunday it becomes a *salon de thé* from 3 to 7pm, becoming a bar after that (usually open until 2am).

CHEVERNY

192km (119 miles) SW of Paris; 19km (12 miles) SE of Blois

The upper crust heads to the Sologne area for the hunt as if the 17th century had never ended. However, 21st-century realities—like formidable taxes—can't be entirely avoided, so the **Château de Cheverny ★★★** (ℭ **02-54-79-96-29;** www. chateau-cheverny.fr) must open some of its rooms to visitors.

Unlike most of the Loire châteaux, Cheverny is the residence of the original owner's descendants. The family of the vicomte de Sigalas can trace its lineage from Henri Hurault, the son of the chancellor of Henri III and Henri IV, who built the first château in 1634. Upon finding his wife carrying on with a page, he killed the page and offered his spouse a choice: She could swallow poison or have his sword plunged into her heart. She elected the less bloody method. Then he had the castle torn down and the present one built for his second wife. Designed in classic Louis XIII style, it has square pavilions flanking the central pile.

You'll be impressed by the antique furnishings, tapestries, and objets d'art. A 17th-century French artist, Jean Mosnier, decorated the fireplace with motifs from the legend of Adonis. The Guards' Room contains a collection of medieval armor; also on display is a Gobelin tapestry depicting the abduction of Helen of Troy. In the king's bedchamber, another Gobelin traces the trials of Ulysses. Most impressive is the stone stairway of carved fruit and flowers.

The château is open daily November to March 9:45am to 5pm, April to June and September 9:15am to 6:15pm, July and August 9:15am to 6:45pm, and October 9:45am to 5:30pm. Admission is 7.50€ for adults, 5.40€ for students, 3.60€ for children 7 to 14, and free for children 6 and under. Allow 2 hours for your visit.

Essentials

GETTING THERE   Cheverny is 19km (12 miles) south of Blois, along D765. It's best reached by **car** or on a **bus tour** from Blois with **Transports du Loir et Cher** (ℭ **02-54-58-55-55**). From the railway station at Blois, a bus departs for Cheverny once a day at noon, returning to Blois 4 hours later, according to an oft-changing schedule. Most visitors find it a lot easier to take their own car or a **taxi** from the railway station at Blois.

Where to Stay & Dine

Les Trois Marchands TRADITIONAL FRENCH   This coaching inn, more comfortable than St-Hubert (see below), has been handed down for many generations. Jean-Jacques Bricault owns the three-story building, which has awnings, a mansard roof, a glassed-in courtyard, and sidewalk tables under umbrellas. In the tavern-style main dining room, the menu may include foie gras, lobster salad, frogs' legs, fresh asparagus in mousseline sauce, game dishes, or fish cooked in a salt crust. The inn rents 24 well-furnished, comfortable rooms with TVs for 42€ to 55€ for a double.

60 place de l'Eglise, Cour-Cheverny 41700. ℂ **02-54-79-96-44.** Fax 02-54-79-25-60. www.hoteldes 3marchands.com. Dining room main courses 17€–40€. Fixed-price menu 26€–45€. AE, DC, MC, V. Tues–Sun 7am–11pm. Closed mid-Feb to mid-Mar.

St-Hubert TRADITIONAL FRENCH   About 457m (1,500 ft.) from the château, this inn was built in the 1950s in the provincial style. The least expensive menu may include terrine of quail, pikeperch with beurre blanc, cheeses, and a fruit tart. The most expensive menu may list lobster; an aiguillette of duckling prepared with grapes; casserole of seafood with shellfish sauce; and, in season, thigh of roebuck in pepper sauce. The St-Hubert offers 20 conservatively decorated rooms with TVs for 55€ to 90€ for a double. Each accommodation comes with free Wi-Fi.

122 rte. Nationale, Cour-Cheverny 41700. ℂ **02-54-79-96-60.** Fax 02-54-79-21-17. www.hotel-sthubert. com. Main courses 16€–22€; fixed-price menu 17€–29€. AE, MC, V. Daily noon–2pm and 7–9pm. Closed Sun night off season.

VALENÇAY

233km (145 miles) SW of Paris; 56km (35 miles) S of Blois

Château de Valençay ★★ (ℂ **02-54-00-10-66;** www.chateau-valencay.com) is one of the Loire's most handsome Renaissance châteaux. Talleyrand acquired it in 1803 on the orders of Napoleon, who wanted his minister of foreign affairs to receive dignitaries in style. The d'Estampes family built Valençay in 1550. The dungeon and west tower are of this period, as is the main body of the building, but other wings were added in the 17th and 18th centuries. The effect is grandiose, with domes and turrets.

The private apartments are open to the public; they're sumptuously furnished, mostly in the Empire style but with Louis XV and Louis XVI trappings as well. A star-footed table in the main drawing room is said to have been the one on which the final agreement of the Congress of Vienna was signed in June 1815 (Talleyrand represented France).

Visits to Valençay are more detailed (and last about 45 min. longer) than those to other châteaux in the valley. The Musée de Talleyrand that used to stand here is closed, but some of the collection is displayed in the new rooms of the castle. After your visit to the château, you can walk through the garden and deer park.

Admission to the castle, car museum, and park is 11€ for adults, 8€ for students, and free for children 6 and under. The château is open daily March 22 to April 10:30am to 6pm, May 10am to 6pm, June 9:30am to 6:30pm, July and August 9:30am to 7pm, September 10am to 6pm, October to November 9 10:30am to 5:30pm. Allow 1½ hours to see the castle. The museum is open daily: June 10am to 12:30pm and 2 to 6:30pm, July and August 10am to 12:30pm and 1:30 to 7pm, off season 10am to 12:30pm and 1:30 to 7pm. Admission is 5.50€ for adults or 4.50€ students and children.

Within 183m (600 ft.) of the château, the **Musée de l'Automobile,** route du Blois, 12 av. de la Résistance (☎ **02-54-00-07-74**), features a collection of more than 60 antique automobiles. Of special interest is a Bédélia (ca. 1914). The tandem-style automobile (the driver rode behind the passenger) with a pulley-operated two-speed gearshift is the rarest in the collection. The Bédélia, like 80% of the cars in the collection, was made in France.

Essentials

GETTING THERE If you're **driving** from Tours, take N76 east, turning south on D956 to Valençay. From Blois, follow D956 south. SNCF operates **rail** service from Blois. For information, call ☎ **36-35** or 08-92-35-35-35.

VISITOR INFORMATION The **Office de Tourisme** is at 2 av. de Résistance (☎ **02-54-00-04-42**).

Where to Stay & Dine

Hôtel Le Relais du Moulin The town's best overnight choice is a 5-minute walk from the entrance to the château. It's also immediately adjacent to a stream and the now-disabled water wheel of an 18th-century textile mill that, during the age of Talleyrand and Napoleon, produced fabrics for curtains, clothing, and upholsteries. The hotel has a cream-colored facade, bedrooms outfitted with contemporary-looking furniture and tones of pale yellow and soft red, and views that overlook the château, the river, vineyards, and/or the park surrounding the hotel and the château. Fixed-price menus in the dining room cost from 18€ to 38€, and focus on traditional and well-prepared French food.

94 rue Nationale, Valençay 36600. ☎ **02-54-00-38-00.** Fax 02-54-00-38-79. www.hotel-lerelaisdu moulin.com. 54 units. 65€–69€ double. AE, DC, MC, V. Closed Nov–Mar. **Amenities:** Restaurant; bar; exercise room; indoor pool; room service; sauna. *In room:* TV, minibar (in some), Wi-Fi (free).

CHAUMONT-SUR-LOIRE

200km (124 miles) SW of Paris; 40km (25 miles) E of Tours

On the morning when Diane de Poitiers first crossed the drawbridge, the **Château de Chaumont** ★★ (☎ **02-54-51-26-26;** www.chaumont-jardin.com) looked grim. Henri II, her lover, had recently died. The king had given her Chenonceau, but his angry widow, Catherine de Médicis, forced her to trade her favorite château for Chaumont, with its battlements and pepper-pot turrets. Inside, portraits reveal that Diane deserved her reputation as forever beautiful. Another portrait—of Catherine looking like a devout nun—invites unfavorable comparisons.

Charles d'Amboise built Chaumont (Burning Mount) during the reign of Louis XII. Overlooking the Loire, it's approached by a long walk up from the village through a tree-studded park. The castle spans the period between the Middle Ages and the Renaissance, and its prize exhibit is a collection of medallions by the Italian artist Nini. A guest of the château, he made medallion portraits of kings, queens, nobles, and dignitaries—including Benjamin Franklin, who once visited. In the bedroom occupied by Catherine de Médicis, you can see a portrait of the Italian-born queen.

The superstitious Catherine housed her astrologer, Cosimo Ruggieri, in one of the tower rooms (a portrait of him remains). He reportedly foretold the disasters awaiting her sons. In Ruggieri's room, a tapestry depicts Medusa with a flying horse escaping from her head.

The château is open daily (except Jan 1, May 1, Nov 1 and 11, and Dec 25): November 3 to March 31 10am to 5pm, April 1 to June 30 10am to 6:30pm, July 1 to August 31 10am to 7pm, September 10am to 6:30pm, and October 10am to 6pm. Admission is 8€ for adults, 5.50€ for students and children 18 and under. Allow 2 hours to see Chaumont.

Essentials

GETTING THERE   Seventeen **trains** per day travel to Chaumont from Blois (trip time: 15 min.) and Tours (about 45 min.). The one-way fare is 3.10€ from Blois, 7.30€ from Tours. The railway station serving Chaumont is in Onzain, a nice 1½-mile walk north of the château. For transportation information, call ℂ **36-35** or 08-92-35-35-35.

VISITOR INFORMATION   The **Office de Tourisme** is on rue du 24 Maréchal-Leclerc (ℂ **02-54-20-91-73;** www.chaumont-sur-loire.eu).

Where to Stay & Dine

Hostellerie du Château 🍴   Most visitors to the château who want to stay close to the castle have to go to hotels nearby. This completely renovated half-timbered inn offers lodgings directly in front of the gateway to the château. Accommodations open onto the riverbank of the Loire; ask for a room with a view. The rooms are modestly yet comfortably furnished, and each has a small bathroom with shower. In the summer you can enjoy regional specialties in the restaurant and swim in the terrace-flanked pool.

2 rue Maréchal de-Lattre-de-Tassigny, Chaumont-sur-Loire 41150. ℂ **02-54-20-98-04.** Fax 02-54-20-97-98. www.hostellerie-du-chateau.com. 15 units. 64€–80€ double. MC, V. **Amenities:** Restaurant; bar; babysitting; outdoor pool; room service. *In room:* TV, hair dryer, Wi-Fi (free).

Le Domaine des Hauts de Loire ★★   Less than 3km (1¾ miles) from the Château de Chaumont, this Relais & Châteaux property sits on the opposite side of the Loire. The manor house was built by the owner of a Paris-based newspaper in 1840 and called, rather coyly, a "hunting lodge." It's the most appealing stopover in the neighborhood, with rooms decorated in Louis Philippe or Empire style. More than half of the rooms are in the slightly less desirable half-timbered annex that was originally the stables.

The stately dining room is open to nonguests who phone in advance. Its well-prepared food is a local favorite. The menu includes a salad of marinated eel with shallot-flavored vinaigrette, scampi served in celery-based consommé with roasted chestnuts and fried ham, carpaccio of scallops with Iberian ham, roasted pikeperch with parsley sauce and coconut, and pigeon roasted with rutabaga and served with the oil from smoked nuts. Main courses range from 49€ to 69€, with fixed-price menus offered at 49€ to 75€, 90€, and 150€.

Rte. d'Herbault, Onzain 41150. ℂ **02-54-20-72-57.** Fax 02-54-20-77-32. www.domainehautsloire.com. 32 units. 130€–290€ double; 320€–550€ suite. AE, DC, MC, V. Closed Dec–Feb. **Amenities:** Restaurant; bar; outdoor pool; room service. *In room:* TV, hair dryer, minibar, Wi-Fi (10€ per hr.).

AMBOISE ★★

219km (136 miles) SW of Paris; 35km (22 miles) E of Tours

Amboise is on the banks of the Loire in the center of vineyards known as Touraine-Amboise. The good news: This is a real Renaissance town. The bad news: Because it is so beautiful, tour buses overrun it, especially in summer. Many townspeople still talk about Mick Jagger's purchase of a nearby château. An earlier resident of the town was Leonardo da Vinci, who spent his last years here.

Essentials

8

GETTING THERE Amboise is on the Paris-Blois-Tours rail line, with about a dozen **trains** per day from both Tours and Blois. The trip from Tours takes 20 minutes and costs 4.80€ one-way; from Blois, it takes 20 minutes and costs 6€ one-way. About five conventional trains a day leave from Paris's Gare d'Austerlitz (trip time: 3 hr.), and several TGVs (trip time: 2 hr., 15 min.) depart from the Gare Montparnasse for St-Pierre-des-Corps, less than a kilometer (½ mile) from Tours. From St-Pierre-des-Corps, you can transfer to a conventional train to Amboise. Fares from Paris to Amboise start at 27€. For information, call ☎ **36-35** or 08-92-35-35-35.

If you prefer to travel by bus, **Fil Vert Buses** (www.touraine-filvert.com), which operates out of the Gare Routière in Tours, just across from the railway station, runs about 8 to 11 **buses** every day between Tours and Amboise. The one-way trip takes about 35 minutes and costs 3.20€.

If you're **driving** from Tours, take N152 east to D32 and then turn south, following signs to Amboise.

VISITOR INFORMATION The **Office de Tourisme** is on quai du Général-de-Gaulle (☎ **02-47-57-09-28;** www.amboise-valdeloire.com).

Exploring the Town

Château d'Amboise ★★

This 15th-century château, which dominates the town, was the first in France to reflect the Italian Renaissance. A combination of Gothic and Renaissance styles, it is associated with Charles VIII, who built it on a rocky spur separating the valleys of the Loire and the Amasse.

You enter on a ramp that opens onto a panoramic terrace fronting the river. At one time, buildings surrounded this terrace, and fetes took place in the enclosed courtyard. The castle fell into decline during the Revolution, and today only about a quarter of the once-sprawling edifice remains. You first come to the Flamboyant Gothic **Chapelle de St-Hubert,** distinguished by its lacelike tracery. Today, tapestries cover the walls of the château's grandly furnished rooms. The **Logis du Roi (King's Apartment)** is open to visitors. It was built against the **Tour des Minimes** (also known as the Tour des Cavaliers), which was noteworthy for its ramp up which horsemen could ride. The other notable tower is the Heurtault, which is broader than the Minimes, with thicker walls.

☎ **02-47-57-00-98.** www.chateau-amboise.com. Admission 9.70€ adults, 8.30€ students, 6.30€ ages 7–14, free for children 7 and under. Daily as follows: Jan 2–31 9am–12:30pm and 2–4:45pm; Feb 9am–12:30pm and 1:30–5pm; Mar 9am–5:30pm; Apr–June 9am–6:30pm; July–Aug 9am–7pm; Sept–Nov 15 9am–5:30pm; Nov 16–Dec 31 9am–12:30pm and 2–4:45pm.

THE LOIRE VALLEY | Amboise

Château du Clos-Lucé ★ Within 3km (1¼ miles) of the base of Amboise's château, this brick-and-stone building was constructed in the 1400s. It later served as a retreat for Anne de Bretagne, who, according to legend, spent a lot of time praying and meditating. Later, François I installed "the great master in all forms of art and science," Leonardo himself. Da Vinci lived here for 3 years, until his death in 1519. (The paintings of Leonardo dying in François's arms are probably symbolic; the king was supposedly out of town at the time.) Today, the site functions as a small museum, offering insights into Leonardo's life and a sense of the decorative arts of the era. The manor contains furniture from his era; examples of his sketches; models for his flying machines, bridges, and cannon; and even a primitive example of a machine gun.

2 rue de Clos-Lucé. ✆ **02-47-57-00-73.** www.vinci-closluce.com. May–Oct admission 13€ adults, 9.50€ students and seniors, 7€ children 6–15, 32€ family ticket (2 adults, 2 children), free for children 5 and under; Nov–Mar admission 9.50€ adults, 6€ students and seniors, 6€ children 6–15, 25€ family ticket (2 adults, 2 children), free for children 5 and under. Jan daily 10am–6pm; Feb–June daily 9am–7pm; July–Aug daily 9am–8pm; Sept–Oct daily 9am–7pm; Nov–Dec daily 9am–6pm. Closed Jan 1 and Dec 25.

Nearby Attractions

The region around Amboise has attractions that resemble a mix of Disney's Magic Kingdom and the court of the Renaissance kings. The most frequently visited attraction, the **Aquarium du Val de Loire,** Parc des Mini-Châteaux (✆ **02-47-23-44-57**), lies 9.5km (6 miles) west of Amboise. It has more than 10,000 freshwater and saltwater fish, including about a half-dozen sharks. Admission is 14€ for adults and 9.50€ for children 4 to 14; it's open daily 10am to 8pm June to August; off-season hours are daily 10:30am to 6pm.

At the same address (same phone) is the **Parc des Mini-Châteaux,** which holds replicas of France's most famous castles built at ⅟₂₅ the size of the originals. Chambord, for example, is less than 3.5m (11 ft.) tall. It's all very patriotic—a sort of learning game that teaches French schoolchildren the glories of their *patrimoine* (heritage) and collects some of the most celebrated architecture in Europe. Admission is 14€ for adults, 9.50€ for students and children 4 to 16, and free for children 3 and under. The Parc des Mini-Châteaux is open daily 10am to 8pm April to mid-November.

To get here from Amboise, follow signs to Tours and take RD751 along the southern bank of the Loire. The aquarium is 1km (⅔ mile) beyond the village of Lussault-sur-Loire (it's clearly marked).

Where to Stay

Belle-Vue Although its rooms aren't particularly plush, this modest, old-fashioned inn gives a sense of the basic conservatism of the Loire Valley of 25 years ago. Built of stone nearly 250 years ago, it sits in the shadow of the château. The clientele is mostly interested in touring the châteaux. Guest rooms are small, nostalgically furnished, and comfortable. Breakfast is the only meal served.

12 quai Charles-Guinot, Amboise 37400. ✆ **02-47-57-02-26.** Fax 02-47-30-51-23. 32 units. 65€–72€ double. MC, V. Closed Nov 1–Mar 15. **Amenities:** Bar; room service. *In room:* TV.

Best Western Le Vinci Loire Valley This modern design boutique hotel stands only a 3-minute ride from the historical center of Amboise. Everything is bright and airy here, from the lounges to the cozy, well-furnished bedrooms. A sleek contemporary look prevails, enlivened by some modern statuary. In the restoration, all the latest safety standards were adhered to and a private enclosed car park created. The hotel staff serves a substantial buffet breakfast in a brightly decorated modern room.

12 av. Emile Gounin, Amboise 37400. ℭ **02-47-57-10-90.** Fax 02-47-57-17-52. www.vinciloirevalley. com. 26 units. 61€–95€ double. AE, DC, MC, V. Free parking. **Amenities:** Breakfast room. *In room:* A/C, TV, Internet (free), minibar.

Le Château-de-Pray ★ This 1224 château 1.6km (1 mile) west of the town center resembles a tower-flanked castle on the Rhine. You'll find antlers, hunting trophies, and a paneled drawing room with a fireplace and a collection of antique oils. Rooms in the main building are conservative and comfortable. The more spacious guest rooms are near the ground floor. Small but well-organized bathrooms contain tubs and showers. Try to avoid the four rooms in the 1990s annex; they're impersonally furnished and lack character. The restaurant, open to nonguests, offers fixed-price menus (30€–60€) of excellent Loire cuisine; reservations are required.

Rue de Cédre, Chargé 37530. ℭ **02-47-57-23-67.** Fax 02-47-57-32-50. http://praycastel.online.fr. 20 units. 120€–195€ double; 225€–245€ suite. AE, DC, MC, V. Free parking. Closed Nov and Jan. **Amenities:** Restaurant; babysitting. *In room:* TV, hair dryer, Internet (free).

Le Choiseul ★★★ This 18th-century hotel, in the valley between a hillside and the Loire, is the best address in Amboise and serves the best cuisine. Guest rooms, 25 of which are air-conditioned, are luxurious; though modernized, they retain their old-world charm. The small bathrooms contain combination tub/showers. The formal dining room has a view of the Loire and welcomes nonguests who phone ahead. The cuisine is better than that in Tours or the surrounding area: deluxe, international, classic French, and regional, utilizing the freshest ingredients. Lunch ranges from 27€ to 41€, with dinner going for 45€ to 80€. The grounds showcase a garden with flowering terraces.

36 quai Charles-Guinot, Amboise 37400. ℭ **02-47-30-45-45.** Fax 02-47-30-46-10. www.le-choiseul. com. 32 units. 152€–295€ double; 355€ suite. AE, DC, MC, V. **Amenities:** Restaurant; bar; babysitting; bicycles; outdoor pool; room service. *In room:* A/C, TV, hair dryer, minibar, Wi-Fi (free).

Le Fleuray ★ 🏠 One of the most appealing hotels in the region is this well-maintained pink stucco manor house. Managed by English expatriates Peter and Hazel Newington, with their children Jordan and Cassie, it was built in the mid-1800s as the centerpiece of a farm. It's a marvel of country-living grandeur, partly because of the masses of geraniums, marigolds, and flowering vines that adorn the masonry in warm weather. Mick Jagger has discovered the place; he probably stays here whenever he feels his 19th nervous breakdown coming on. Guest rooms are cozy and homelike, dotted with antique accessories evoking an elegant but not terribly formal English country house, though you shouldn't expect a lot of modern amenities. Bathrooms are compact and well organized with showers.

Don't miss the restaurant; locals flock here. Items on the fixed-price menus (29€ to 49€) include dates stuffed with warm Roquefort cheese, pork pâté with onions and chutney, and Creole-style chicken in curry-flavored cream sauce garnished with pineapples.

Rte. Dame Marie, Cangey 37530, near Amboise. ℭ **02-47-56-09-25.** Fax 02-47-56-93-97. www.lefleuray hotel.com. 20 units. 78€–130€ double; 140€–226€ suite. MC, V. Free parking. From Amboise, take N152 northeast of town, following signs to Blois; 12km (7½ miles) from Amboise, turn onto D74, in the direction of Cangey. **Amenities:** Restaurant; bar; outdoor pool; room service. *In room:* TV, hair dryer, Wi-Fi (free).

Le Manoir Les Minimes ★★ This restored 18th-century mansion is a welcoming, cozy hotel built on the foundation of an ancient convent. On the river's edge, in the shadow of the château, it is surrounded by acres of gardens. Inside, furnishings are elegant in both the public and private rooms, with much use made of antiques. You can dine in the garden if weather permits. The most desirable rooms are in the main building; a comfortable, well-furnished trio of units is in an annex, although these lack character. Our favorite unit is no. 10, a corner suite with panoramic views. Many of the second-floor bedrooms open onto views of the Loire. The best-value rooms are smaller and on the third floor. Each room has its individual decor and comes with an elegant bathroom with tub.

34 quai Charles Guinot, Amboise 37400. ☏ **02-47-30-40-40.** Fax 02-47-30-40-77. www.manoirles minimes.com. 15 units. 122€–195€ double; 270€–465€ suite. V. Closed Nov 15–Dec 15. **Amenities:** Breakfast room; garden; room service. *In room:* A/C, TV, minibar, Wi-Fi (free).

Le Manoir Saint Thomas ★ 🎁 Antonella and Bertrand Pautout have installed a government-rated four-star hotel in a manor that dates originally from the 12th century. The living conditions have never been better around here; there's even a heated swimming pool in the garden. Rooms are spacious with luxury bathrooms and are completely modernized, although the antique character has been retained. Parquet floors, period fireplaces, and stained-glass windows evoke the past. The hotel is only a 2-minute walk from the royal château and is close to the former home of Leonardo da Vinci.

1 mail Saint Thomas, Amboise 37400. ☏ **02-47-23-21-82.** Fax 02-47-23-24-96. www.manoir-saint-thomas. com. 10 units. 90€–180€ double; 170€–340€ suite. Off-season reductions Nov–Mar. AE, MC, V. **Amenities:** Outdoor pool; room service. *In room:* A/C, TV, hair dryer, minibar, Wi-Fi (free).

Le Vieux Manoir ★★ 🎁 Americans Gloria and Bob Belknap fell in love with France and this 18th-century manor, which they restored and turned into an elegant B&B. They accommodate guests in beautifully furnished rooms with country antiques, exposed oak beams, stone walls, and tile floors. Accommodations are named after various legends, from George Sand and Colette to Joséphine and Mme. du Barry. A 17th-century structure with old oak beams and exposed stone walls also houses guests; with a fully equipped kitchen, it's ideal for families. A glass conservatory overlooks a manicured garden. Bathrooms, lined with locally made tiles, are the finest in Amboise; they have period mirrors and washstands and heavy German fixtures with tub/shower combinations.

13 rue Rabelais, Amboise 37400. ☏ **02-47-30-41-27.** Fax 02-47-30-41-27. www.le-vieux-manoir.com. 6 units, 2-bedroom cottage. 145€–190€ double; 260€–290€ cottage for 4. Rates include breakfast. MC, V. **Amenities:** Wi-Fi (free). *In room:* A/C, TV.

Where to Dine

The finest dining choice is in **Le Choiseul;** the restaurant at **Le Fleuray** is also excellent (for reviews of both hotels, see "Where to Stay," above).

Brasserie de l'Hôtel de Ville ☺ FRENCH In the town's historic core, a short walk from the château, this bustling Paris-style brasserie has enjoyed a solid reputation since the early 1990s. It attracts local office workers and art lovers visiting the historic sites during the day, and boisterous groups of friends at night. Expect a noisy environment focused on rows of banquettes, hassled waiters, and steaming platters that emerge relatively quickly from the overworked kitchen. Menu items include a full range of old-fashioned cuisine that many locals remember from their childhoods. Examples include such mainstream staples as sole meunière, grilled beefsteak with french fries, *pot-au-feu*, calves' liver, and dishes from France's southwest, including a savory version of cassoulet.

3 rue François 1er. (📞 **02-47-57-26-30.** Reservations recommended. Main courses 7€–18€; fixed-price menu 15€–25 €; children's menu 6.90€. AE, DC, MC, V. Daily noon–2:30pm and 7–9:30pm.

CHENONCEAUX

224km (139 miles) SW of Paris; 26km (16 miles) E of Tours

A Renaissance masterpiece, the **Château de Chenonceau ★★★** (📞 **02-47-23-90-07;** www.chenonceau.com) is best known for the dames de Chenonceau, who once occupied it. (The village, whose year-round population is less than 300, is spelled with a final "x," but the château isn't.)

In 1547, Henri II gave Chenonceau to his mistress, Diane de Poitiers. For a time this remarkable woman was virtually queen of France, infuriating Henri's dour wife, Catherine de Médicis. Diane's critics accused her of using magic to preserve her celebrated beauty and to keep Henri's attentions from waning. Apparently Henri's love for Diane continued unabated, and she was in her 60s when he died in a jousting tournament in 1559.

When Henri died, Catherine became regent (her eldest son was still a child) and forced Diane to return the jewelry Henri had given her and to abandon her beloved home. Catherine added her own touches, building a two-story gallery across the bridge—obviously inspired by her native Florence.

Chenonceau is one of the most remarkable castles in France because it spans an entire river. The way the waters of the Cher surge and foam beneath its vaulted medieval foundations has been described as mystical. Many visitors consider this their favorite château in all of France.

Gobelin tapestries, including one depicting a woman pouring water over the back of an angry dragon, cover many of the château's walls. The chapel contains a marble *Virgin and Child* by Murillo as well as portraits of Catherine de Médicis in black and white. There's even a portrait of the stern Catherine in the former bedroom of her rival, Diane de Poitiers. In François I's Renaissance bedchamber, the most interesting portrait is that of Diane as the huntress Diana.

The history of Chenonceau is related in 15 tableaux in the **Musée de Cire (Wax Museum),** located in a Renaissance-era annex a few steps from the château. Open the same hours as the château, it charges admission of 13€ for adults, 10€ ages 7 to 18, free for 6 and under. Diane de Poitiers, who, among other accomplishments, introduced the artichoke to France, is depicted in three tableaux. One portrays Catherine de Medicis tossing out her husband's mistress.

The chateau is open daily 9am to 8pm July and August; 9am to 7pm mid-March to June; 9am to 6:30pm September and October; 9am to 5pm the rest of the year. Admission is 11€ for adults, and 8€ for students and children 7 to 15. A *son-et-lumière* show, "The Era of the Ladies of Chenonceau," starts at 10:15pm daily in July and August; admission is 6€ and free for children 6 and under. Allow 2 hours to see this château.

Essentials

GETTING THERE   Four daily **trains** run from Tours to Chenonceaux (trip time: 30 min.), costing 5.80€ one-way. The train deposits you at the base of the château; from there, you can walk or take a taxi. If you're **driving,** from the center of Tours, follow the directions east until you reach the N76, which will take you to the sign-posted turnoff for Chenonceaux.

VISITOR INFORMATION   The **Syndicat d'Initiative** (tourist office), 1 rue du Dr. Bretonneau (📞 **02-47-23-94-45**), is open year-round.

Where to Stay

Auberge du Bon-Laboureur ★★   This inn, within walking distance of the château, is your best bet for a comfortable night's sleep and some of the best cuisine in the Loire Valley. Founded in 1786, the hotel maintains the flavor of that era, thanks to thick walls, solid masonry, and a scattering of antiques. The author Henry James stopped here in 1882, and the inn won his praise. Most guest rooms are small, especially on the upper floors; each comes with a private bathroom with shower or tub. The rear garden has a guesthouse and formally planted roses. The place is noted for its restaurant. In fair weather, tables are set up in the courtyard, amid trees and flowering shrubs.

6 rue du Dr. Bretonneau, Chenonceaux, Bléré 37150. 📞 **02-47-23-90-02.** Fax 02-47-23-82-01. www.amboise.com/laboureur. 25 units. 120€–155€ double; 190€–260€ suite. AE, DC, MC, V. Closed Nov 11–Dec 20 and Jan 7–Feb 14. **Amenities:** Restaurant; bar; babysitting; outdoor pool; room service. *In room:* A/C, TV, hair dryer, Wi-Fi (free).

Hostellerie de la Renaudière ☺   This welcoming family-run hotel is in a converted 18th-century private residence. The convenient location in the middle of town is 8 minutes on foot from the château. The front rooms open onto rail tracks; if you're a light sleeper, request a room in the rear. Each of the intimate, cozily furnished guest rooms has a little bathroom with shower. Kid-friendly innkeepers Isabella and Joel Camus provide toys in the garden. The restaurant serves excellent regional dishes, many based on ancient Loire recipes.

24 rue du Dr. Bretonneau, Chenonceaux, Bléré 37150. 📞 **02-47-23-90-04.** Fax 02-47-23-90-51. www.chenonceaux-renaudiere.com. 12 units. 60€–71€ double; 125€ family room. AE, DC, MC, V. Closed mid-Nov to mid-Feb. **Amenities:** Restaurant; exercise room; outdoor heated pool; room service. *In room:* TV, fridge, hair dryer, Wi-Fi (free).

La Roseraie ★ 🍴   La Roseraie is the most charming hotel in Chenonceaux, with individually decorated rooms and well-kept gardens. Each unit contains a small bathroom with shower. During World War II, the innkeeper gained fame with the Allies because of his role in smuggling Churchill's nephew out of Vichy-occupied France. The English-speaking innkeepers are the exceptionally charming Laurent and Sophie Fiorito. Their restaurant is open to the public for lunch and dinner. Our favorite dishes include house-style foie gras, *magret* of duckling with pears and cherries, and an unusual and delicious invention—*emincée* (a dish made with braised meat) of rump steak with wine-marinated pears.

7 rue du Dr. Bretonneau, Chenonceaux, Bléré 37150. 📞 **02-47-23-90-09.** Fax 02-47-23-91-59. 18 units. 65€–129€ double; 80€–112€ quad. AE, DC, MC, V. Closed mid-Nov to late Mar. Free parking. **Amenities:** Restaurant; bar; outdoor pool. *In room:* A/C, TV, Wi-Fi (free).

Le Relais Chenonceaux 🔑 This is a typical French country inn with a dormer roof and an inviting courtyard filled with flowers in summer. Inside, exposed beams and an old fireplace decorate the dining room, which is open to all visitors, serving a traditional Loire Valley cuisine. The on-site crêperie is the best in town. The rustic bedrooms are personalized and comfortable, and also tidily maintained. The location is only 500m (1,640 ft.) from the château, and the inn is classified as a Logis de France.

10 rue du Docteur Brettoneau, Chenonceaux, Bléré 37150. ℭ **02-47-23-98-11.** Fax 02-47-23-84-07. www.chenonceaux.com. 24 units. 50€–68€ double. MC, V. Closed Nov 15–Feb 1. **Amenities:** Restaurant; bar. *In room:* TV, Wi-Fi (free).

Where to Dine

Hostellerie de la Renaudière and **La Roseraie** (see above) have very good restaurants.

Au Gâteau Breton TRADITIONAL FRENCH The sun terrace in back of this 2-century-old Breton-type inn, a short walk from the château, is a refreshing place for dinner or tea. Gravel paths run among beds of pink geraniums and lilacs, and bright umbrellas adorn the red tables. In cool months, meals are served in the rustic dining rooms. Make a meal of the home cooking and cherry liqueur, a specialty of the region. Worthwhile dishes include small chitterling sausages of Tours, *poulet Tourangelle* (fried chicken with a mushroom-flavored cream sauce), chicken with Armagnac sauce, and coq au vin. Medallions of veal with mushroom-cream sauce are excellent. Tasty pastries are sold in the front room.

16 rue du Dr. Bretonneau. ℭ **02-47-23-90-14.** Fax 02-47-23-92-57. www.restaurant-gateau-breton. com. Reservations required July–Aug. Main courses 14€–21€; fixed-price menus 15€–26€. MC, V. Apr–Sept daily noon–2:30pm, daily 7–10pm; Nov–Mar daily noon–2:30pm.

TOURS ★

232km (144 miles) SW of Paris; 113km (70 miles) SW of Orléans

Though it doesn't have a major château, Tours (pop. 138,000) at the junction of the Loire and Cher rivers, is known for its food and wine. Many of its buildings were bombed in World War II, and 20th-century apartment towers have taken the place of châteaux. However, because Tours is at the doorstep of some of the most magnificent châteaux in France, it makes a good base from which to explore. Pilgrims en route to Santiago de Compostela in northwest Spain once stopped here to pay homage at the tomb of St-Martin, the "Apostle of Gaul," who was bishop of Tours in the 4th century. One of the most significant conflicts in world history, the 732 Battle of Tours, checked the Arab advance into Gaul.

Most Loire Valley towns are rather sleepy, and Tours is where the action is, with busy streets and cafes. A quarter of the residents are students, who add a vibrant touch to a soulless commercial enclave. Allow a morning or an afternoon to see Tours.

Essentials

GETTING THERE Most of the trains bound for Tours, including all TGVs (as many as 14 per day), depart from Paris's Gare Montparnasse, although a very limited

FUN-FILLED WAYS TO GET around

For a commentary-filled English-language overview of Tours, its monuments, and its layout, ride through the streets of the city aboard a simulated train with rubber wheels. It operates from Easter to mid-October, daily at 10am, 11am, 2pm, 3pm, 4pm, 5pm, and 6pm. Tickets, available at the tourist office or onboard, cost 5€ for adults and 3€ for children 11 and under. Rides (about 50 min.) begin and end in front of the tourist office, 78–82 rue Bernard-Palissy (✆ **02-47-70-37-37**).

An old-fashioned alternative is a ride on one of the horse-drawn carriages (les calèches) operated by **Fil Bleu** (✆ **02-47-66-70-70**). A pair of slow-moving workhorses pull the wagonlike conveyances, which hold up to 10 passengers, through the city's medieval neighborhoods. There's no commentary. Tickets cost 1.20€ per person. May through September, rides are given Tuesday to Saturday at 10am, 11am, 3pm, 4pm, and 5pm; and on Sunday at 3, 4, and 5pm.

Daily in July and August, the tourist office (✆ **02-47-70-37-34**) leads guided old-town walking tours in a mixture of French and English. The 2-hour excursions depart from the tourist office, usually at 10am or 2:30pm. April to June and September and October tours are conducted only on Saturday, Sunday, and holidays. Reservations are required. The cost is 5.60€ for adults and 4.60€ for children 6 to 12.

number of trains, including some of the slow and conventional commuter trains, depart from Gare d'Austerlitz. One-way fares range from 29€ to 49€. Many, but not all, of the conventional (non-TGV) trains pull into the center of Tours, at the **Gare Tours Centre Ville,** place du Maréchal-Leclerc, 3 rue Edouard-Vaillant. Some conventional trains and virtually all the TGV trains, however, arrive at the isolated railway station of **Tours/St-Pierre-des-Corps,** about 6km (3¾ miles) east of the center of Tours. If your train drops you off here, know in advance that at least one (and during peak hours, several) *navette* (bus) awaits every TGV train for free ongoing transport to the center of Tours.

If you're **driving,** take highway A10 to Tours.

GETTING AROUND   It's easy to walk from one end of central Tours to the other, and most of the good hotels are near the train station. For taxi service, call **Taxi Radio** (✆ **02-47-20-30-40**). Car-rental offices in or near the train station include **Avis,** inside the station (✆ **02-47-20-53-27**), open Monday to Friday 8am to 12:30pm and 1:30 to 6pm, and Saturday 8am to noon and 2 to 6pm; and **Europcar,** 194 av. Maginot (✆ **02-47-85-85-85**), open Monday to Saturday 8am to noon and 2 to 6:30pm. You can rent a bike at **Detours de Loire,** 35 rue Charles Gilles (✆ **02-47-61-22-23;** www.locationdevelos.com), at a cost of 14€ per day. A passport deposit is required. It's open Monday to Saturday 9am to 1pm and 2 to 7pm, and Sunday 9:30am to 12:30pm and 6 to 7pm.

VISITOR INFORMATION   The **Office de Tourisme** is at 78–82 rue Bernard-Palissy (✆ **02-47-70-37-37;** www.ligeris.com).

Exploring the City

The heart of town is **place Jean-Jaurès.** The principal street is **rue Nationale,** running north to the Loire River. Head west along rue du Commerce and rue du Grand-Marché to Vieux Tours/Vieille Ville (old town).

Cathédrale St-Gatien   This cathedral honors a 3rd-century evangelist and has a Flamboyant Gothic facade flanked by towers with bases from the 12th century. The lanterns date from the Renaissance. The choir is from the 13th century, with new additions built in each century through the 16th. Sheltered inside is the handsome 16th-century tomb of Charles VIII and Anne de Bretagne's two children. Some of the glorious stained-glass windows are from the 13th century.

5 place de la Cathédrale. ℰ **02-47-70-21-00.** Free admission. Daily 9am–7pm (until 8pm July–Aug).

Musée des Beaux-Arts   This fine provincial museum in the Palais des Archevêques is worth a visit just to see its lovely rooms and gardens. There are old masters here as well, including works by Degas, Delacroix, Rembrandt, and Boucher.

The sculpture collection includes works by Houdon and Bourdelle. You can tour the gardens for free, daily from 7am to 8:30pm.

18 place François-Sicard. ✆ **02-47-05-68-73.** Admission 4€ adults, 2€ seniors and students, free for children 12 and under. Wed–Mon 9am–12:45pm and 2–6pm. Bus: 3.

Shopping: To the Market we Go

In the pedestrian area of rue de Bordeaux, from the magnificent train station to rue Nationale, you'll find dozens of mall-type shops and department stores selling clothes, shoes, jewelry, leather goods, and the like. Up rue Nationale toward the river are more shops and upscale boutiques, and a small mall with chain stores. Rue Nationale continues across the river, but turn left on rue du Commerce toward the old town center. You'll want to explore the streets and courtyards for regional specialties, books, toys, and crafts. A hotbed for antiques is east of rue Nationale (toward the cathedral), along rue de la Scellerie.

Of the more than 30 markets here, the most animated are the **gourmet market (Marché Gourmand),** the first and third Friday of each summer month, 4 to 10pm, place de la Résistance; the **antiques market,** the first and third Friday of the month in the pedestrian zone on rue de Bordeaux, and on the fourth Sunday of the month, a larger version of the event with more *brocante* than genuine antiques; the **flower market,** Wednesday and Saturday 8am to 6pm, boulevard Béranger; and the **craft market (Marché Artisanal),** Saturday 9am to 1pm, place des Halles. **Traditional food markets** take place Tuesday to Sunday mornings at various locations; ask at the tourist office. The covered market, **Les Halles et Grand Marché,** with a huge selection of fresh local meat, cheese, and produce, is at place Gaston-Pailhou Monday through Saturday 6am to 7pm and Sunday 6am to 1pm.

Where to Stay

Best Western Le Central Off the main boulevard, this old-fashioned hotel is within walking distance of the river and cathedral, surrounded by gardens, lawns, and trees. Built in 1850, it is a more modest and economical choice than others in town. The Tremouilles family provides comfortable rooms at reasonable rates. Accommodations come in a variety of shapes and sizes. Half of the guest rooms have tub/shower combos, the others only showers.

21 rue Berthelot, Tours 37000. ✆ **800/528-1234** in the U.S. and Canada, or 02-47-05-46-44. Fax 02-47-66-10-26. www.bestwestern.com. 37 units. 92€–152€ double; 173€–250€ suite. AE, DC, MC, V. Parking 10€. Bus: 1, 4, or 5. **Amenities:** Bar; babysitting; room service. *In room:* A/C, TV, hair dryer, minibar, Wi-Fi (free).

Hôtel de l'Univers This hotel was erected in 1853, making it the oldest in town. Upgraded to government-rated four-star status, it's the best in the town center. Its midsize rooms, outfitted in a conservative contemporary style, have monochromatic and tasteful soft-color schemes. The bathrooms, with shower and tub, have also been renewed. On weekdays, the hotel fills with business travelers; on weekends, it hosts many area brides and grooms.

5 bd. Heurteloup, Tours 37000. ✆ **02-47-05-37-12.** Fax 02-47-61-51-80. www.hotel-univers.fr. 85 units. 125€–270€ double; 344€–398€ suite. AE, DC, MC, V. Parking 15€. Bus: 1, 4, or 5. **Amenities:** Room service. *In room:* A/C, TV, hair dryer, minibar, Wi-Fi (free).

Hôtel du Manoir   On a quiet street near the train station, this 19th-century residence is a comfortable place to stay. The cheerful reception area reflects the quality of the rooms. Though small to average in size, all units have windows that let in lots of light and afford views of the neighborhood or the hotel courtyard. Most have simple furnishings. About half the rooms have tub/shower combos; the other half have only showers.

2 rue Traversière, Tours 37000. ℂ **02-47-05-37-37.** Fax 02-47-05-16-00. www.hotel-manoir-tours. federal-hotel.com. 20 units. 56€–70€ double. AE, DC, MC, V. Parking 6€. Bus: 3 or 70. *In room:* A/C, TV, Wi-Fi (free).

Where to Dine

Restaurants can be pricey, but you can keep costs low at **La Souris Gourmande,** 100 rue Colbert (ℂ **02-47-47-04-80**), where the chef is respected for the diversity of his cheese selection. Try it in half a dozen fondues. You may be asked to join a communal table. Main courses cost 13€ to 15€. At the raffish but cheerful bistro **Le Lapin qui Fume,** 90 rue Colbert (ℂ **02-47-66-95-49**), a fixed-price menu costs 19€ to 23€.

EXPENSIVE

La Roche le Roy ★★ MODERN FRENCH   Alain Couturier, one of the hottest chefs in town, blends new and old techniques in a gabled 15th-century manor south of the town center. Couturier's repertoire includes scalloped foie gras with lentils, cod with saffron cream sauce, pan-fried scallops with truffle vinaigrette, and *matelote* (stew) of eel with Chinon or Bourgueil wine. His masterpiece is suprême of pigeon with "roughly textured" sauce. For dessert, try a slice of warm orange-flavored chocolate served with coffee-flavored sherbet.

55 rte. St-Avertin. ℂ **02-47-27-22-00.** Reservations recommended. Main courses 28€–32€. AE, MC, V. Tues–Sat noon–1:30pm and 7:30–9:30pm. Closed 1 week in Feb and 3 weeks in Aug. From the center of town, take av. Grammont south (follow signs to St-Avertin–Vierzon). The road crosses a bridge but doesn't change names. The restaurant is beside that road, on the southern periphery of Tours.

MODERATE

Les Tuffeaux ✒ TRADITIONAL FRENCH   This restaurant in an 18th-century house is one of the best in Tours. Menu items change three times a year, depending on the inspiration of chef Gildas Marsollier. He prepares classics but also experiments, with offerings such as noisettes of roasted rabbit with bacon and almonds, crisp grilled crayfish with partridge-stuffed ravioli, and braised turbot with gratinéed *viennoise* of Comté cheese. Roasted filet of pigeon with pink grapefruit is an enduring favorite.

19 rue Lavoisier. ℂ **02-47-47-19-89.** Reservations required. Main courses 20€–26€. AE, DC, MC, V. Mon–Tues and Thurs–Sat noon–1:30pm; Mon–Sat 7:30–9:30pm. Bus: 1, 4, or 5.

Rive Gauche TRADITIONAL FRENCH   Under another name, this has been a local favorite since shortly after World War II. In the commercial heart of Tours, it has two dining rooms and an outdoor terrace for warm-weather dining. The everchanging menu may include homemade foie gras and whitefish caught in the Loire and served with beurre blanc. Regional ingredients mix well with the local wines, as exemplified by pikeperch with sabayon; a *beuchelle Tourangelle,* a ragout composed of local red wine from the Loire Valley mixed with veal sweetbreads and kidneys; and *magret de canard* (duckling) served with a "jam" of red Chinon wine. In summer, strawberry parfait with raspberry coulis is a perfect finish.

23 rue du Commerce. © **02-47-05-71-21.** Reservations required. Main courses 30€–50€; fixed-price menu 30€–70€. MC, V. Daily 10:30am–4pm and 7:30pm–1am. Bus: 1, 4, or 5.

INEXPENSIVE

La Brasserie Buré TRADITIONAL FRENCH   A 5-minute walk east of the center of Tours, this somewhat unimaginative brasserie specializes in shellfish and regional recipes. It has a busy bar and a front terrace, with tables inside on the street level and mezzanine. Menu items include six well-flavored versions of sauerkraut; a wide choice of grilled meats, including steak au poivre; foie gras and smoked salmon; and a tempting array of desserts.

1 place de la Résistance. © **02-47-05-67-74.** Main courses 15€–23€; fixed-price menu 20€–30€. AE, DC, MC, V. Daily noon–3pm and 7pm–midnight. Bus: 1 or 5.

Le Petit Patrimoine TRADITIONAL FRENCH   Despite the proliferation of newer, trend-conscious restaurants along rue Colbert, this pocket-size, long-established restaurant exudes a powerful, albeit quirky and idiosyncratic, appeal. Outfitted in a rustic and old-fashioned style that might have been inspired by someone's early-20th-century grandmother, it has ceiling beams, old masonry walls, and a sense of respect for old-fashioned French aesthetics and values. Your hosts, each a distinct personality known by clients as either independent-minded or curmudgeonly, depending on their mood of the moment, will propose dishes that include a savory *matelote* of veal with baby vegetables, a salad of *rillons* (a meat byproduct made from bacon), grilled beefsteaks with goat cheese, and a *torte Tourangelle* composed of pastry casing filled with goat cheese and the above-mentioned *rillons*.

58 rue Colbert. © **02-47-66-05-81.** Reservations recommended. Main courses 12€–17€; fixed-price menu 13€ lunch, 17€–24€ dinner. AE, DC, MC, V. Tues–Sat noon–2pm and 7–10pm.

Where to Stay & Dine Nearby

Château d'Artigny ★★★   This is the grandest address in the Loire Valley. About 1.5km (1 mile) west of the hamlet of Montbazon, the château was built between 1912 and 1920 for perfume and cosmetics king François Coty, who lived and entertained lavishly. Set in a forest, overlooking formal gardens, in an obscure villa near Paris, the Château de Champlatreux, the château combines Jazz Age ostentation and 18th-century French aesthetics. The drawing room and corridors are furnished with fine antiques, Louis XV–style chairs, and bronze statuary. The grounds contain acres of parks and a large garden with a reflecting pool. Guest rooms are outfitted in period style, with many antiques, comfortable mattresses, and all the perks of upscale country living. Only 31 units are in the main building; the others are in four annexes—a former chapel, gatehouse, mill, and staff dormitory.

Rte. d'Azay-le-Rideau (D17), Montbazon 37250. © **02-47-34-30-30.** Fax 02-47-34-30-39. www.artigny. com. 60 units. 225€–375€ double; 485€ junior suite. Half board 85€ per person. AE, DC, MC, V. From Tours, take N10 south for 11km (6¾ miles) to Montbazon, and then take D17 1.5km (1 mile) southeast. **Amenities:** Restaurant; bar; babysitting; exercise room; outdoor pool; room service; sauna; spa; 2 tennis courts. *In room:* TV, hair dryer, minibar, Wi-Fi (in some, free).

Château de Beaulieu ★★   At this 17th-century estate, you can experience the lifestyle of another era. Beyond the entrance, a double curving stairway leads to the

Château Hopping Made Easy

Several tour companies in Tours arrange visits to four or five castles per day, departing daily at 9am. Costs range from 40€ to 50€, depending on the company. The best tours are offered by **Saint-Eloi Excursions** (☎ **02-47-37-08-04**) and by **Quart de Tours** (☎ **06-30-65-52-01**). The price does not include admission to the châteaux, but participation in the tour qualifies you for reduced group rates. Some visitors combine two half-day tours into a full day of château hopping. Because trains from Paris take only 55 minutes each way, this makes a worthwhile side trip.

reception hall. Guest rooms have mahogany and chestnut furniture, decorative fireplaces, and good plumbing. Nine are in the château (we recommend these); the others, a bit more sterile, are in a turn-of-the-20th-century pavilion a stone's throw away. All have elegant beds outfitted with comfortable mattresses.

67 rue de Beaulieu, Joué-les-Tours 37300. ☎ **02-47-53-20-26.** Fax 02-47-53-84-20. www.chateaude beaulieu37.com. 19 units. 105€–170€ double. Half board 190€–255€ for 2. AE, MC, V. Take D86 from Tours, and then D207 toward Beaulieu, 7km (4⅓ miles) southwest of Tours. **Amenities:** Restaurant; bar; 3 tennis courts (across road). In room: A/C, TV, hair dryer, minibar, Wi-Fi (free).

Tours After Dark

Long a student town, Tours has a lively young population. Even during summer, when most students have left, a youthful crowd rules the hot spots. **Place Plumereau** (often shortened to "place Plume"), a square of medieval buildings, houses a riot of restaurants and bars. In the warmer months, the square explodes with tables, which fill with people who like to people-watch (and be watched themselves). In addition to the bars and clubs around the place Plumereau, an even trendier street, **rue Colbert,** has emerged as a hip and fashionable street. Rue Colbert lies in the heart of Tours, midway between the place Plumereau and the cathedral.

A popular site is **Le Louis XIV,** 37 rue Briçonnet (☎ **02-47-05-77-17**), a stylish bar where meeting new friends and companions is not out of the question. The hottest place in town is **L'Excalibur,** 35 rue Briçonnet (☎ **02-47-64-76-78**), with a disco beat and video system. A clientele of all ages, many from the surrounding countryside, heads to **Le Pyms,** 170 av. de Grammont (☎ **02-47-66-22-22**), an alternative disco open Wednesday to Sunday 11pm to at least 5am.

And if you're gay, relatively energetic, and like to dance, check out the town's most popular gay bar and disco, **Le G.I.,** 13 rue Lavoisier (☎ **02-47-66-29-96**). Positioned on a dark street in a safe but somewhat run-down neighborhood, it attracts a local, mostly male crowd that packs the place on weekends.

LOCHES ★★

258km (160 miles) SW of Paris; 40km (25 miles) SE of Tours

Forever linked to legendary beauty Agnès Sorel, Loches is the *cité médiévale* of the valley, situated in the hills on the banks of the Indre. Known as the acropolis of the

Loire, the château and its satellite buildings form a complex called the **Cité Royale ★**. The House of Anjou, from which the Plantagenets descended, owned the castle from 886 to 1205. The kings of France occupied it from the mid–13th century until Charles IX became king in 1560.

Château de Loches ★★, 5 place Charles-VII (_𝒞_ **02-47-59-01-32**), is remembered for the _belle des belles_ (beauty of beauties) Agnès Sorel. Inside is her tomb, where two angels guard her velvet cushion. In 1777, the tomb was opened, but all that remained of the 15th-century beauty were a set of dentures and some locks of hair. Maid of honor to Isabelle de Lorraine, she was singled out by Charles VII to be his mistress and had great influence on the king until her mysterious death. Afterward, Fouquet painted her as a practically topless Virgin Mary, with a disgruntled Charles VII looking on. (The original is in Antwerp; the château has a copy.) The château also contains the oratory of Anne de Bretagne, decorated with ermine tails. One of its outstanding treasures is a triptych of _The Passion_ (1485) from the Fouquet school.

You can visit the château without a guide daily. It's open April to September from 9am to 7pm, and October to March 9:30am to 5pm.

The ancient keep, or _donjon,_ of the comtes d'Anjou (_𝒞_ **02-47-59-07-86**) is open the same hours as the château. The Round Tower of Louis XI contains rooms used for torture; a favorite method involved suspending the victim in an iron cage. In the 15th century, the duke of Milan, Ludovico Sforza, was imprisoned in the Martelet and painted frescoes on the walls to pass the time; he died here in 1508.

Tickets to the château or the dungeon cost 7€ for adults, 4.50€ for students, and 4.50€ for children 12 to 18. A combination ticket to both costs 7€ for adults, 4.50€ for students, and 3.50€ for children ages 12 to 18. Children 11 and under enter free.

Nearby, the Romanesque **Collégiale St-Ours (Collegiate Church of St-Ours),** 1 rue Thomas-Pactius (_𝒞_ **02-47-59-02-36**), spans the 10th to 15th centuries. Sculpted figures, damaged but still attractive, decorate the portal. Stone pyramids (_dubes_) surmount the nave; the carving on the west door is exceptional. The church is open daily from 9am to 7pm, except during class; admission is free.

Finally, you may want to walk the ramparts and enjoy the view of the town, including a 15th-century gate and Renaissance inns.

Allow 3 hours to see Loches.

Essentials

GETTING THERE Six to 10 **buses** run daily from Tours; the 45-minute trip costs 8€ one-way. The one-way **train** fare from Tours is also 7.80€. For bus information, call _𝒞_ **02-47-05-30-49;** for train schedules, call _𝒞_ **36-35** or 08-91-35-35-35. If you're **driving** from Tours, take N143 southeast to Loches.

VISITOR INFORMATION The **Office de Tourisme** is near the bus station on place de la Marne (_𝒞_ **02-47-91-82-82;** www.loches-tourainecotesud.com).

Where to Stay & Dine

Loches is short on inns and good restaurants. If you're here for lunch, we recommend the 18th-century **Hôtel George-Sand,** 39 rue Quintefol (_𝒞_ **02-47-59-39-74;** fax 02-47-91-55-75; www.hotelrestaurant-georgesand.com), for its Touraine cuisine, including filet of pikeperch from the Loire. It also rents 19 rooms; doubles go for 60€ to 115€.

Grand Hotel de France ★   This charming hotel was a postal relay station until the mid–19th century. In 1932, it gained three floors and became an inn. Before the turn of the 21st century, management upgraded and redecorated the guest rooms, added new beds, and restored the small bathrooms. The most tranquil rooms overlook the courtyard. You can dine in the wood-paneled dining room or under the parasols in the courtyard.

6 rue Picois, Loches 37600. ✆ **02-47-59-00-32.** Fax 02-47-59-28-66. http://h.france.loches.free.fr. 17 units. 62€–90€ double. AE, DC, MC, V. Parking 5€. Closed Jan 5 to early Feb and mid-Nov to mid-Dec. **Amenities:** Restaurant; bar; room service. *In room:* TV, Internet (free).

Le Château de Reignac ★★ 🎁   The former château of the Marquis de la Fayette has been entirely renovated and is today one of the most luxurious châteaux in the Loire. You can explore the landscaped grounds with their ancient trees, have a drink in a plush 18th-century living room, or relax in the book-lined library as you listen to your favorite opera. The antique-filled bedrooms, each sumptuously furnished, were named for famous people in French history, each a guest who had stayed here with the marquis. Gourmet-level food is served in the evening along with wine from the Touraine. A stay here is like wandering back to a more elegant age.

Reignac-sur-Indre 37310. ✆ **02-47-94-14-10.** Fax 02-47-94-12-67. www.lechateaudereignac.com. 12 units. 170€–200€ double; 250€ junior suite; 320€–350€ family suite for 4. AE, MC, V. Lies 10km (6¼ miles) north of Loches. **Amenities:** Restaurant for guests; room service. *In room:* A/C, TV, hair dryer, Wi-Fi (free).

VILLANDRY

253km (157 miles) SW of Paris; 32km (20 miles) NE of Chinon; 18km (11 miles) W of Tours; 8km (5 miles) E of Azay-le-Rideau

The 16th-century-style gardens of the Renaissance **Château de Villandry** ★★★, 3 rue Principale, 37510 Villandry (✆ **02-47-50-02-09;** www.chateauvillandry. com), are celebrated throughout the Touraine. A trio of superimposed cloisters with a water garden on the highest level, they were restored by the Spanish doctor and scientist Joachim Carvallo, grandfather of the present owner.

The grounds contain 17km (11 miles) of boxwood sculpture, which the gardeners cut to style in only 2 weeks each September. Every square of the gardens is like a geometric mosaic. The borders symbolize the faces of love: tender, tragic (represented by daggers), and crazy (with a labyrinth that doesn't get you anywhere). Pink tulips and dahlias suggest sweet love; red, tragic; and yellow, unfaithful. All colors signify crazy love. The vine arbors, citrus hedges, and walks keep six men busy fulltime. One garden contains all the French vegetables except the potato, which wasn't known in France in the 16th century.

A feudal castle once stood at Villandry. In 1536, Jean Lebreton, François I's chancellor, built the present château, whose buildings form a U and are surrounded by a moat. Near the gardens is a terrace from which you can see the small village and its 12th-century church. A tearoom on-site, **La Doulce Terrasse** (✆ **02-47-50-02-10;** www.chateauvillandry.com), serves traditional Loire cooking, including hot dishes, freshly baked bread, homemade ice cream, and cocktails made from fresh fruit.

Admission to the gardens, including a guided tour of the château, costs 9€ for adults, 5€ for children 8 to 18, and is free for children 7 and under. Visiting the gardens separately, without a guide, costs 6€ for adults and 3.50€ for children 8 to 18. The gardens are open daily 9am to between 5 and 7:30pm, depending on the hour of sunset; the château is open daily from 9am to between 4:30 and 6:30pm, depending on a complicated seasonal schedule. Tours are conducted in French; leaflets are available in English.

Villandry has no train service. The nearest connection from Tours is at the town of Savonnières. From Savonnières, you can walk along the Loire for 4km (2½ miles) to reach Villandry, rent a **bike** at the station, or take a **taxi.** You can also **drive,** following D7 from Tours. Allow 1½ hours to see Villandry.

Where to Stay & Dine

Le Cheval Rouge MODERN FRENCH   The well-known dining stopover near the château extends a congenial welcome. The conservatively decorated dining room lies about 91m (300 ft.) from the banks of the Cher. Specialties include Quiche Tourangel (made with pork byproducts including chitterling sausages), a flavorful version of eel stew, medallions of veal with morels, and turbot with hollandaise sauce. The inn also rents 41 rooms, all with private bathroom and free in room Wi-Fi. A double is 58€ to 62€.

9 rue Principale, Villandry 37510. ✆ **02-47-50-02-07.** Fax 02-47-50-08-77. www.lecheval-rouge.com. Reservations recommended. Main courses 15€–17€; fixed-price menu 20€–39€. AE, DC, MC, V. Daily noon–2:30pm and 7–9pm.

LANGEAIS

259km (161 miles) SW of Paris; 26km (16 miles) W of Tours

On December 6, 1491, Anne de Bretagne arrived at Langeais on a cloud of gold and sable. Her marriage to Charles VIII was Langeais's golden hour.

Château de Langeais ★★   This is a medieval fortress, a formidable gray pile that dominates the town. It's one of the few châteaux actually on the Loire. The facade is forbidding, but once you cross the drawbridge, you'll find the apartments so richly decorated that they soften the effect. The castle dates from the 9th century. Fulk III (972–1040), Count of Anjou, sometimes called The Black Falcon, erected the first dungeon in Europe here, the ruins of which can still be seen. The present structure was built in 1465. The interior is well preserved and furnished thanks to Jacques Siegfried, who not only restored it over 20 years but also bequeathed it to the Institut de France in 1904.

Anne de Bretagne and Charles VIII's symbols—scallops, fleurs-de-lis, and ermine—set the motif for the Guard Room, and seven tapestries known as the Valiant Knights cover the walls of the Wedding Chamber.

In a bedchamber known as the Crucifixion, the 15th-century black-oak four-poster bed is reputed to be one of the earliest known. The room takes its name from a tapestry of the Virgin and St. John on flower-bedecked ground. A rare Flemish tapestry hangs in the Monsieur's Room. The Chapel Hall was built by joining two stories under a ceiling of Gothic arches. In the Luini Room is a large 1522 fresco by that artist, removed from a chapel on Lake Maggiore, Italy. It depicts Saint Francis of Assisi and Saint Elizabeth of Hungary with Mary and Joseph. The Byzantine Virgin in the drawing room is thought to be an early work of Cimabue, the Florentine artist. Finally, the tapestry of the *Thousand Flowers* is a celebration of spring, a joyous riot of growth and symbol of life's renewal. Allow 1½ hours to go through the château.

Langeais 37130. ℭ **02-47-96-72-60.** www.chateau-de-langeais.com. Admission 8.50€ adults, 7.20€ students and ages 18–25, 5€ for children 10–17, free for 9 and under. Visits daily: Oct 16–Jan 10am–5pm; Feb–Mar 9:30am–5:30pm; Apr–July 13 and Aug 21–Oct 15 9:30am–6:30pm; July 14–Aug 20 9am–7pm.

Essentials

GETTING THERE Seven **trains** per day stop here en route from Tours or Saumur. The one-way fare from Saumur is 6.90€, the one-way fare from Tours 4.80€. Transit time from Tours is 20 minutes. For schedules and information, call ℭ **36-35** or 08-92-35-35-39. If you're **driving** from Tours, take N152 southwest to Langeais.

VISITOR INFORMATION The **Office de Tourisme** is at place du 14-Juillet (ℭ **02-47-96-58-22;** www.tourisme-langeais.com).

Where to Stay & Dine

Hotel Hosten et Restaurant Errard ★ This ivy-draped country inn in the center of town was built in 1853. In 2002, it added a neighboring house, creating a hotel-restaurant complex. The restaurant, which has received many honors, is elegant and formal, the hotel that houses it a bit more relaxed. Guest rooms are rustic and comfortable, and some (particularly the suites in the annex) are surprisingly large. Most of the well-maintained tiled bathrooms have tub/shower combinations. Guests dine indoors or at tables in the open courtyard under umbrellas and flowering trees. The *menu de prestige* includes *matelote* of eel with Bourgueil red wine, and stuffed venison. Dessert may be pear mousse with Jamaican pepper ice cream.

2 rue Gambetta, Langeais 37130. ℭ **02-47-96-82-12.** Fax 02-47-96-56-72. www.errard.com. 10 units. 69€–79€ double; 95€–112€ apt. AE, MC, V. Parking 5€. Closed Dec–Jan. **Amenities:** Restaurant; bar. *In room:* TV, Internet (free).

La Duchesse Anne On the eastern outskirts of town, this hotel opened in the 18th century as a coaching inn, providing food and shelter for people and horses. Guest rooms are decorated with flowered wallpaper and filled with comfortable, traditional furniture. Units vary in size and shape, and most of the tiled bathrooms have tubs and showers. Garden tables are set out for dining. The cuisine reflects the traditions of the Loire Valley. It includes flavorful but not experimental dishes such as fresh salmon with beurre blanc, and guinea fowl with Bourgueil wine sauce. From April to October, the restaurant is open for lunch and dinner daily; the rest of the year, it's closed Monday and Friday for lunch.

10 rue de Tours, Langeais 37130. ℭ **02-47-96-82-03.** Fax 02-47-96-68-60. 15 units. 50€–60€ double. AE, MC, V. **Amenities:** Restaurant; bar; room service. *In room:* TV.

AZAY-LE-RIDEAU

261km (162 miles) SW of Paris; 21km (13 miles) SW of Tours

Its machicolated towers and blue-slate roof pierced with dormers shimmer in the moat, creating a reflection like a Monet painting. The defensive medieval look is all for show: the Renaissance **Château d'Azay-le-Rideau** ★★, 19 rue Balzac, Azay-le-Rideau 37190 (ℭ **02-47-45-42-04;** www.monum.fr), was created as a residence

For Literary Fans: An Ode to Balzac

Four kilometers (3 miles) east of Azay-le-Rideau (take D17), you can visit **Saché**, the hometown of Honoré de Balzac. Here he wrote *The Lily of the Valley* and declared that his affection for the Touraine was like "the love of the artist for his art." Of interest to fans is the **Musée Balzac,** in the 19th-century Château de Saché, Saché 37190 (*©* **02-47-26-86-50;** www.musee-balzac.fr). The small château contains the writer's bedrooms, preserved as they were when he lived here. A collection of Balzac's notes, first editions, etchings, letters, and cartoons are on display, as is a copy of Rodin's sculpture of the writer. The castle and museum are open daily April to June (and Sept) 10am to 6pm, July and August 10am to 7pm; and October to March 10am to 12:30pm and 2 to 5pm. Admission is 4.50€ for adults, 3€ for seniors and students, and free for children 6 and under.

at an idyllic spot on the Indre River. Gilles Berthelot, François I's finance minister, commissioned the castle, and his spendthrift wife, Philippa, supervised its construction. So elegant was the creation that the Chevalier King grew jealous. Berthelot was accused of misappropriation of funds and forced to flee, and the château reverted to the king. He didn't live here, but granted it to "friends of the Crown." It became the property of the state in 1905.

Before you enter, circle the château and note the perfect proportions of the crowning achievement of the Renaissance in the Touraine. Check out its most fancifully ornate feature, the bay enclosing a grand stairway with a straight flight of steps. The Renaissance interior is a virtual museum.

From the second-floor Royal Chamber, look out at the gardens. This bedroom, also known as the Green Room, is believed to have housed Louis XIII. The adjoining Red Chamber contains a portrait gallery that includes *Lady in Red* and Diane de Poitiers (Henri II's favorite) in her bath.

The château is open daily in July and August 9:30am to 7pm; April to June and September, 9:30am to 6pm; and October to March 10am to 12:30pm and 2 to 5:30pm. Admission is 8€ for adults, 5€ for ages 18 to 25, and free for children 17 and under. Allow 2 hours for a visit.

In warm weather, *son-et-lumière* performances feature recorded music and lights beaming on the exterior of the château. The shows, which last about 1½ hours, begin at 10:30pm from May to July, at 10:30pm in August, and at 10:30pm in September. Tickets are 9€ for adults, 5€ for ages 12 to 25, and free for children 11 and under.

Essentials

GETTING THERE To reach Azay-le-Rideau, take the **train** from Tours or Chinon. From either starting point, the trip time is about 30 minutes and the one-way fare is 4.40€ from Chinon, 4.90€ from Tours. Both Tours and Chinon have express service to Paris. For SNCF bus and rail schedules to Azay-le-Rideau, call *©* **36-35** or 08-91-35-35-35. If you're **driving** from Tours, take D759 southwest to Azay-le-Rideau.

Because trains arrive at Azay-le-Rideau's railway station in relatively small numbers, some visitors prefer to travel to the railway station at nearby Tours, switching to any of the frequent buses between Tours's railway station and Azay. TER, a subsidiary of the SNCF, operates the route and charges 4.50€ each way. For more information, call ✆ **08-92-35-35-35.**

VISITOR INFORMATION The **Office de Tourisme** is on place de L'Europe (✆ **02-47-45-44-40;** www.ot-paysazaylerideau.com).

Where to Stay & Dine

L'Aigle d'Or ★ TRADITIONAL FRENCH Owners Jean-Luc and Ghislaine Fèvre work in the kitchens and dining room of this century-old house, which has been the best restaurant in town for nearly 2 decades. The restaurant is in the village center, about .3km (¼ mile) from the château. The service is professional, the welcome charming, and the food the best in Azay. In a dining room accented with ceiling beams, a fireplace, and pastel colors, you can savor dishes including crayfish with foie gras and blanquette (stew) of Loire Valley whitefish prepared with one of the region's white wines. Desserts are made fresh daily. In summer, the party expands onto an outdoor terrace.

10 av. Adélaïde-Riché. ✆ **02-47-45-24-58.** Reservations recommended. Main courses 16€–28€. V. Wed–Mon noon–1:30pm; Thurs–Mon 7:30–9pm.

Le Grand Monarque The ivy that covers the exterior of this hotel—less than 150m (492 ft.) from the château—seems to protect it from the modern world. As you enter the manor house, with its dark ceiling beams, you'll be transported to a different era. The large guest rooms are outfitted with antiques. Units in the annex aren't as well decorated but are more tranquil. Half the well-maintained bathrooms hold tub/shower combinations. You can enjoy a casual evening in the lounge area or in the dining room.

The superb restaurant features such dishes as brochette of crayfish with sesame sauce, suprême of *sandre* in shallot-flavored broth, and galette of pig's feet *en confit*. Look for specialties that include a terrine of stingray with celery, steak of mullet prepared with the local wine of Azay, and a kettle of crayfish with a bouillon of mushrooms. Fixed-price menus range from 28€ to 55€. During warmer months, you can dine out on the courtyard terrace. In February, March, October, and November, the restaurant closes on Sunday night, all day Monday, and at lunchtime Tuesday and Friday.

3 place de la République, Azay-le-Rideau 37190. ✆ **02-47-45-40-08.** Fax 02-47-45-46-25. www.le grandmonarque.com. 24 units. 60€–140€ double. AE, MC, V. Parking 10€. Closed Dec to mid-Jan. **Amenities:** Restaurant; bar; babysitting; room service. *In room:* TV, hair dryer, Wi-Fi (free).

CHINON ★★

283km (176 miles) SW of Paris; 48km (30 miles) SW of Tours; 31km (19 miles) SW of Langeais

In the film *Joan of Arc*, Ingrid Bergman sought out the dauphin as he tried to conceal himself among his courtiers. This took place in real life at the Château de Chinon, one of the oldest fortress-châteaux in France. Charles VII centered his government at Chinon from 1429 to 1450. In 1429, with the English besieging Orléans, the Maid of Orléans prevailed upon the dauphin to give her an army. The rest is history. The seat of French power stayed at Chinon until the end of the Hundred Years' War.

Today, Chinon remains a tranquil village known mainly for its delightful red wines. After you visit the attractions, we recommend taking a walk along the Vienne

IN PURSUIT OF grape

Chinon is famous for its wines, which crop up on prestigious lists around the world. Supermarkets and wine shops throughout the region sell them; families that have been in the business longer than anyone can remember maintain the two most interesting stores. At **Caves Plouzeau,** 94 rue Haute-St-Maurice (*C* **02-47-93-32-11;** www.plouzeau. com), the 12th-century cellars were dug to provide building blocks for the foundations of the château. The present management dates from 1929; bottles of red or white wine cost from 6€ to 11€. You're welcome to climb down to the cellars. They are open for wine sales and

visits April to September Tuesday to Saturday 11am to 1pm and 3 to 7pm.

The cellars at **Couly-Dutheil,** 12 rue Diderot (*C* **02-47-97-20-20;** www. coulydutheil-chinon.com), are suitably medieval; many were carved from rock. This company produces largely Chinon wines (mostly reds), and it's proud of the Bourgueil and St-Nicolas de Bourgueil, whose popularity in North America has grown in recent years. Tours of the caves and a *dégustation des vins* (wine tasting) require an advance call and cost 4€ to 6€ per person. Visits are conducted April to September Monday to Friday 8am to noon and 1:45 to 5:45pm.

River; definitely stop to taste the wine at one of Chinon's terraced cafes. Allow 3 hours to see Chinon.

Essentials

GETTING THERE   The SNCF runs about 7 **trains** and four **buses** every day to Chinon from Tours (trip time: about 1 hr.). Call *C* **36-35** or 08-92-35-35-35 for information and schedules. Both buses and trains arrive at the train station, which lies at the edge of the very small town. If you're **driving** from Tours, take D759 southwest through Azay-le-Rideau to Chinon.

VISITOR INFORMATION   The **Office de Tourisme** is at place Hofheim (*C* **02-47-93-17-85;** www.chinon.com).

Exploring the Town & the Château

On the banks of the Vienne, the town of Chinon consists of winding streets and turreted houses, many built in the 15th and 16th centuries in the heyday of the court. For the best view, drive across the river and turn right onto quai Danton. From this vantage point, you'll be able to see the castle in relation to the village and the river. The most typical street is rue Voltaire, lined with 15th- and 16th-century town houses. At no. 44, Richard the Lion-Hearted died on April 6, 1199, from a wound suffered during the siege of Chalus in Limousin. The Grand Carroi, in the heart of Chinon, served as the crossroads of the Middle Ages.

Château de Chinon ★★   The château consists of three buildings, two of which have been partially restored (they're still missing roofs). One of the restored buildings, Château du Milieu, dates from the 11th to the 15th centuries and contains the keep and clock tower, which houses a museum of Joan of Arc. A moat separates Château du Milieu from the other, Château du Coudray, which contains the Tour du Coudray, where Joan of Arc once stayed. In the 14th century, the Knights Templar were imprisoned here (they're responsible for the graffiti) before meeting violent deaths. Some of the grim walls from other dilapidated edifices remain, although many buildings—including the Great Hall where Joan of Arc sought out the dauphin—have been torn down.

Btw. rue St-Maurice and av. Francois Mitterrand. ℭ **02-47-93-13-45.** Admission 7€ adults, free for children 12 and under. Apr–Sept daily 9am–7pm; Oct–Mar daily 9:30am–5pm. Closed Jan 1 and Dec 25.

Musée de la Devinière   The most famous son of Chinon, François Rabelais, the earthy and often bawdy Renaissance writer, lived on rue de la Lamproie. (A plaque marks the spot where his father practiced law and maintained a home and office.) This site, in the suburb of La Devinière, 5.5km (3½ miles) west of Chinon, was an isolated cottage at the time of his birth. It was maintained, because of local superstition and custom, for the sole purpose of delivering the children of the Rabelais clan into the world.

The museum has three floors of exhibition space, each focusing on an aspect of Rabelais, his times, and his role in Chinon. In two neighboring buildings, you'll find exhibits on aspects of life during the Middle Ages, including an unusual display on medicinal plants. Regrettably, the theater presentations that showcased some of Rabelais's literary achievements are no longer presented.

La Devinière, on D117 near N751. ℭ **02-47-95-91-18.** www.monuments-touraine.fr. Admission 4.50€ adults, 3€ students, free for children 12 and under. Apr–June Wed–Sun 10am–12:30pm and 2–6pm; July–Aug daily 10am–7pm; Sept Wed–Sun 10am–12:30pm and 2–6pm; Oct–Mar Wed–Sun 10am–12:30pm and 2–5pm. From Chinon, follow the road signs pointing to Saumur and the D117.

Where to Stay

Hostellerie Gargantua ★   This 15th-century mansion has a terrace with a château view. The grand building was once a courthouse where the father of François Rabelais worked as a lawyer in the 15th century. Art historians admire the building's early Renaissance staircase and its chiseled-stone details. The traditional guest rooms have been renovated and are comfortably furnished and well kept. Half of the old-fashioned bathrooms contain tubs. Try to stop here for a meal, served in a medieval hall. You can sample Loire *sandre* prepared with Chinon wine or duckling with dried pears and smoked lard, followed by a medley of seasonal red fruits in puff pastry.

73 rue Haute St. Maurice, Chinon 37500. ℭ **02-47-93-04-71.** Fax 02-47-93-08-02. www.hotel-gargantua. com. 7 units. 53€–79€ double. AE, DC, MC, V. **Amenities:** Restaurant; bar; babysitting; room service. *In room:* TV, Wi-Fi (free).

Hôtel Diderot ★ 💼   Within a 5-minute walk of the town's historic core, this is a comfortable hotel with strands of ivy climbing romantically up its stone front. Although the foundations date from the 14th century, the building was radically altered in the 1700s; today, you'll see remnants of thick wall and ceiling beams throughout the public rooms and in some of the guest rooms. Rooms are midsize to spacious, outfitted in Henry II or Napoleon III style, usually with big windows letting in maximum sunlight. One of the architectural highlights is a magnificent 15th-century fireplace in the breakfast room, where you'll enjoy as many as 52 kinds of jams and jellies as part of your morning ritual. Françoise and Laurent are the congenial hosts. The hotel's name derives not from the philosopher but from the rue Diderot, a few steps away.

4 rue du Buffon, Chinon 37500. ℭ **02-47-93-18-87.** Fax 02-47-93-37-10. www.hoteldiderot.com. 27 units. 55€–79€ double. AE, DC, MC, V. Parking 6€. **Amenities:** Bar; babysitting. *In room:* TV, hair dryer, Wi-Fi (free).

Hôtel Le Plantagenet This 19th-century mansion in the center of town has been transformed into a well-run hotel. The hotel opens onto views of the river Vienne and lies close to the medieval heart of Chinon. Rooms are midsize and filled with character, each tastefully and comfortably furnished, and each with a private bathroom with tub or shower. The grace note of the hotel is its private garden and terrace, where you can enjoy a drink. Some rooms, just as good as those in the main building, are in an annex manor house, the Maison Bourgeoise.

12 place Jeanne d'Arc, Chinon 37500. (✆) **02-47-93-36-92.** Fax 02-47-98-48-92. www.hotel-plantagenet. com. 32 units. 65€–80€ double. AE, DC, MC, V. Parking 7€. **Amenities:** Bar. *In room:* A/C (in 6 units), TV, hair dryer, Wi-Fi (free).

Where to Dine

Au Plaisir Gourmand ★★ TRADITIONAL FRENCH This is the premier restaurant in the area. Owner Jean-Claude Rigollet used to direct the chefs at the fabled Les Templiers in Les Bézards. The 18th-century building contains an intimate dining room. Menu items are likely to include roasted duck with foie gras sauce, oxtail in Chinon red-wine sauce, and sautéed crayfish with a spicy salad. For dessert, try prunes stuffed in puff pastry.

2 rue Parmentier. (✆) **02-47-93-20-48.** Reservations required. Main courses 18€–42€; tasting menu 28€–59€. AE, V. Wed–Sun noon–1:30pm; Tues–Sat 7:30–9pm. Closed mid-Feb to mid-Mar.

L'Oceanic SEAFOOD/FRENCH As its name implies, this restaurant specializes in fresh seafood, even though Chinon is inland. Marie-Paule and Patrick Descoubes change the specialties daily based on what's fresh and good at the marketplace. Locals as well as visitors appreciate the value and the reliable cooking techniques. A particularly delicious meal may include cassoulet of lobster and scallops with vanilla-flavored butter, carpaccio of sea scallops with fried leeks and herb-flavored vinaigrette, stingray with Camembert sauce, and roasted filets of codfish with Münster cheese cream sauce. If you don't like fish, the owners prepare delicious steak.

13 rue Rabelais. (✆) **02-47-93-44-55.** Reservations required. Main courses 18€–32€; fixed-price menu 24€–35€. MC, V. Tues–Sun noon–1:30pm; Tues–Sat 7:30–9:30pm.

Where to Stay & Dine Nearby

Château de Marçay ★★★ This Relais & Châteaux property began in the 1100s as a fortress and changed to its present form during the Renaissance. It remained untouched during the region's civil wars. The centerpiece of the wine-producing hamlet of Marçay, it's sumptuously decorated. The main building houses the more opulent lodgings; a handful of less expensive, less dramatic rooms are in an annex a short walk away. About half of the units come with tub and shower; more-modern rooms have only a shower. Menu specialties change with the season, and the chef works hard to maintain high standards. The garden terrace and elegantly rustic dining room afford a panoramic view.

Marçay, Chinon 37500 (✆) **02-47-93-03-47.** Fax 02-47-93-45-33. www.chateaudemarcay.com. 33 units. 120€–215€ double; 250€–285€ suite. AE, DC, MC, V. Closed Jan 15–Mar 15. Take D116 for 7km (4¼ miles) southwest of Chinon. **Amenities:** Restaurant; bar; outdoor pool; room service; tennis court. *In room:* TV, Wi-Fi, hair dryer, minibar.

Manoir de la Giraudière Built during the mid-1600s, this elegant manor house resembles a small château because of its use of *tuffeau* (the beige stone used in residences of many of the French monarchs). In a 2.4-hectare (6-acre) park surrounded by hundreds of acres of fields and forests, this government-rated two-star establishment offers classic decor and modern comforts. Each good-size room comes with a fine bed and quality linen. Air-conditioning isn't necessary because the thick walls act as natural insulation against heat and cold.

Beaumont-en-Veron, Avoine 37420. (✆ **02-47-58-40-36.** Fax 02-47-58-46-06. www.giraudiere.com. 24 units. 67€–135€ double; 95€–110€ suite. AE, DC, MC, V. Head 5km (3 miles) west of Chinon along D749 toward Bourgueil. **Amenities:** Restaurant; bar; babysitting. *In room:* TV, hair dryer, Wi-Fi (free).

Chinon After Dark

A charming bar and nighttime hangout is **Le Café Français,** 37 place du Général-de-Gaulle (✆ **02-47-93-32-78**). Behind the Hotel de Ville (town hall), it attracts many good-looking singles. There's a modest admission charge for occasional concerts.

USSE

295km (183 miles) SW of Paris; 14km (8⅔ miles) NE of Chinon

At the edge of the dark forest of Chinon in Rigny-Ussé, **Château d'Ussé ★** (✆ **02-47-95-54-05;** www.chateaudusse.fr) was the inspiration for Perrault's legend of *The Sleeping Beauty (La Belle au bois dormant).* Conceived as a fortress, the complex of steeples, turrets, towers, and dormers was erected at the dawn of the Renaissance on a hill overlooking the Indre River. The terraces, laden with orange trees, were laid out in the 18th century. When the need for a fortified château passed, the north wing was demolished to open up a greater view.

The château was later owned by the duc de Duras and then by Mme. de la Rochejacquelin; its present owner, the marquis de Blacas, has opened many rooms to the public. The guided tour begins in the Renaissance chapel, with its sculptured portal and handsome stalls. You then proceed to the royal apartments, furnished with tapestries and antiques. One gallery displays an extensive collection of swords and rifles. A spiral stairway leads to a tower with a panoramic view of the river and a waxwork Sleeping Beauty waiting for her prince to come.

The château is open daily February 18 to March 10am to 6pm; April to August 10am to 7pm, and September to November 10am to 6pm; closed otherwise. Entrance costs 13€ for adults, 4€ for students and children 8 to 16, and is free for children 7 and under. Allow 1½ hours for the tour. The château is best visited by car or on an organized bus tour from Tours. If you're driving from Tours or Villandry, follow D7 to Ussé.

Where to Stay

Le Clos d'Ussé ★ 🎁 Although most visitors make Ussé a day trip, this little B&B across the street from the castle makes a good overnight stop. The Duchemin family offers well-maintained rooms that are midsize and comfortably furnished; bathrooms have showers. The friendly owners are experts on the lore of the castle.

7 rue Principale, on D7, Rigny-Ussé 37130. (✆ **02-47-95-55-47.** Fax 02-47-95-55-47. 7 units. 62€–70€ double. DC, MC, V. Closed Nov–Feb. **Amenities:** Restaurant, Wi-Fi (free). *In room:* TV, hair dryer, no phone.

FONTEVRAUD-L'ABBAYE ★★

304km (189 miles) SW of Paris; 16km (10 miles) SE of Saumur

You'll find the Plantagenet dynasty buried in the **Abbaye Royale de Fontevraud** (© **02-41-51-87-97;** www.abbaye-fontevraud.com). The kings, whose male line ended in 1485, were also the comtes d'Anjou, and they wanted to be buried in their native soil.

In the 12th-century Romanesque church—with four Byzantine domes—are the remains of two English kings or princes, including Henry II of England, the first Plantagenet king, and his wife, Eleanor of Aquitaine, the most famous woman of the Middle Ages. Her crusading son, Richard the Lion-Hearted, was also entombed here. The Plantagenet line ended with the death of Richard III at the 1485 Battle of Bosworth. The tombs fared badly during the Revolution, when mobs desecrated the sarcophagi and scattered their contents on the floor.

More intriguing than the tombs is the octagonal **Tour d'Evraud,** the last remaining Romanesque kitchen in France. Dating from the 12th century, it contains five of its original eight *apsides* (half-rounded indentations originally conceived as chapels), each crowned with a conically roofed turret. A pyramid tops the conglomeration, capped by an open-air lantern tower pierced with lancets.

Robert d'Arbrissel, who spent much of his life as a recluse, founded the abbey in 1099. Aristocratic ladies occupied one part; many, including discarded mistresses of kings, had been banished from court. The four youngest daughters of Louis XV were educated here.

Admission is 8.40€ in summer for adults or 7€ in winter. Free for ages 25 and under. Hours are daily: April to June and September to October 9:30am to 6pm; July and August 9:30am to 7pm, and November to March 10am to 5pm. Allow ½ hour for the abbey.

Essentials

GETTING THERE   If you're **driving,** take N147 about 4km (2½ miles) from the village of Montsoreau. About five **buses** run daily from Saumur; the one-way fare for the 30-minute trip is 3€.

VISITOR INFORMATION   The **Office de Tourisme,** allée Ste-Catherine (© **02-41-51-79-45**), within the compound of the medieval abbey, is open only from May 15 to September 30.

Where to Stay

Hostellerie du Prieuré St-Lazare ★ 📖   This is one of the most unusual hotels in Europe, set on 11th-century foundations within the perimeter of the legendary Abbaye Royale in one-time monks' cells. It became a hotel in 1990. The guest rooms are well maintained and monastically simple, with white walls, modern furniture, and exposed sections of cream-colored *tuffeau,* the easy-to-carve rock used to build the abbey during the early Middle Ages. A third of the units come with tub/shower combinations.

Rue St-Jean de lHabit, Fontevraud-l'Abbaye 49590. © **02-41-51-73-16.** Fax 02-41-51-75-50. www. hotelfp-fontevraud.com. 52 units. 63€–122€ double. AE, MC, V. Closed Nov 16–Mar 15. **Amenities:** Restaurant; bar; babysitting; Wi-Fi (free). *In room:* TV, minibar.

Where to Dine

The **Hostellerie du Prieuré St-Lazare** (see above) has a good restaurant.

La Licorne ★ MODERN FRENCH   For the perfect combination of medieval history and culinary sensuality, visit the abbey and then dine at this 35-seat restaurant on a linden-lined walkway between the abbey and a nearby parish church. Its symmetrical proportions and neoclassical pilasters, built in the 1700s just before what the owners refer to as "La Révolution," evoke the *ancien régime* at its most graceful and opulent. In summer, guests sit in the garden or the elegantly rustic dining room. Chef Jean-Michel Bézille, aided by Fabrice Bretel, has created a menu that almost always includes filet of beef flavored with smoked pork and shallots, roasted *sandre* with Szechuan peppers, crayfish-stuffed ravioli with basil-flavored morel sauce, variations on many of the freshwater fish of the Loire Valley, and luscious desserts such as a warm chocolate tart with pears and lemon-butter sauce.

Allée Ste-Catherine. ✆ **02-41-51-72-49.** www.la-licorne-restaurant.com. Reservations required. Main courses 16€–32€; fixed-price menu 25€–55€. AE, DC, MC, V. Nov–Apr Tues–Sun noon–2pm, Tues and Thurs–Sat 7–9pm; May–Oct daily noon–2pm and 7–9pm. Closed 1 week in Dec.

SAUMUR

299km (186 miles) SW of Paris; 53km (33 miles) SE of Angers

Saumur is in a region of vineyards, where the Loire separates to encircle an island; it makes one of the best bases for exploring the western Loire Valley. A small but thriving town, it doesn't entirely live off its past: Saumur produces some 100,000 tons per year of the mushrooms the French adore. Balzac left us this advice: "Taste a mushroom and delight in the essential strangeness of the place." The cool tunnels for the *champignons* also provide the ideal resting place for the celebrated sparkling wines of the region. Enjoy both of these local favorites at a neighborhood cafe.

Essentials

GETTING THERE   **Trains** run frequently between Tours and Nantes, stopping at Saumur. Some 20 trains per day arrive from Tours (trip time: 45 min.); the one-way fare is 11€. Fifteen trains per day pull in from Angers (trip time: 21 min.), costing 7.60€ one-way. The train station is on the north side of town. Most major points of interest, including the château, are on the south bank. From the station, take bus A into town. If you're **driving** from Tours, follow N152 southwest to Saumur.

VISITOR INFORMATION   The **Office de Tourisme** is on place de la Bilange (✆ **02-41-40-20-60**).

Exploring the Area

Of all the Loire cities, Saumur remains the most bourgeois; perhaps that's why Balzac used it for his classic characterization of a smug little town in *Eugénie Grandet*. Saumur is also famous as the birthplace of the *couturière* Coco Chanel.

The men of Saumur are among the best equestrians in the world. Founded in 1768, the city's riding school, **Cadre Noir de Saumur** ★, rue de l'Abbaye (✆ **02-41-53-50-60**), is one of the grandest in Europe, rivaling Vienna's. The stables house some 350 horses. April to mid-October, tours (7€ adult, 5€ child) begin at 9:30 to 11am and 2 to 4pm Tuesday to Sunday. Tours depart about every 20 minutes. Morning tours last about 1½ hours and the afternoon tour lasts 1 hour. Some 48km (30 miles) of specialty tracks wind around the town—to see a rider carry out a curvet is a thrill. The performances peak during the **Carrousel de Saumur ★★** on the last two Saturdays and Sundays in July.

The area surrounding the town has become famous for its delicate sparkling wines. In the center of Saumur, you can wander the many aisles of **La Maison du Vin,** quai Lucien Gauthier (© **02-41-38-45-83**), and choose from a large stock direct from the many surrounding vineyards.

An alternative is to travel east of Saumur to the village of St-Hilaire, where you'll find a host of vineyards. One of the better ones is **Veuve Amiot,** 21 rue Jean-Ackerman (© **02-41-83-14-14;** www.veuveamiot.fr), where you can tour the wine cellars, taste different vintages, and buy bottles and gift boxes right in the showroom.

Regrettably, **Château de Saumur,** the main reason for visiting the town, is closed with no announced opening date.

Where to Stay

Hotel Adagio Best Western   Erected around 1900 and bombed into rubble during World War II, this riverfront hotel was rebuilt in the 1950s using the same honey-colored stone as in its original construction. The large, conservative, comfortably furnished rooms have double-paned windows and high ceilings; some units have air-conditioning. Renovations have destroyed any vestige of old-fashioned France. The staff is hardworking and thoughtful.

94 av. du Général-de-Gaulle, Saumur 49400. © **02-41-67-45-30.** Fax 02-41-67-74-59. www.hoteladagio. com. 38 units. 93€–120€ double; 105€–160€ suite. AE, DC, MC, V. Parking 7€. **Amenities:** Bar; room service. *In room:* A/C, TV, hair dryer, minibar, Wi-Fi (free).

Hôtel Anne d'Anjou ★   This 18th-century building was constructed as a family home; its magnificent stairwell below a *trompe l'oeil* ceiling has been designated a historic monument. The rooms in the back overlook the château, and the front faces the Loire. Five units still have their original decor, ranging from Louis XVI to Empire. Accommodations are renovated room by room "as they begin to look a bit tired."

The hotel operates Les Menestrels, one of the most prestigious restaurants in Saumur. Open Monday through Saturday for lunch and dinner, it offers creative fixed-price menus for 35€ to 65€. The restaurant is in a 16th-century structure with a vaulted cellar, opening onto landscaped gardens.

32–33 quai Mayaud, Saumur 49400. © **02-41-67-30-30.** Fax 02-41-67-51-00. www.hotel-anneanjou. com. 43 units. 100€–155€ double; 155€–210€ suite. AE, DC, MC, V. Parking 10€. **Amenities:** Restaurant; bar; babysitting; room service. *In room:* TV, hair dryer, minibar, Wi-Fi (free).

Hôtel St-Pierre ★   Nestled among tiny winding roads and built against the Eglise St-Pierre, this hotel overflows with character. Appointments include finely upholstered antiques, half-timbered walls, beamed ceilings, stained-glass windows, massive stone fireplaces, and spiral staircases. Guest rooms are individually decorated in the same rich style; even the bathroom walls showcase custom tile designs. Overall, the hotel is an appealing middle-bracket choice in a historic location. The intimate breakfast room opens onto a small garden terrace.

Rue Haute-Saint-Pierre, Saumur 49400. © **02-41-50-33-00.** Fax 02-41-50-38-68. www.saintpierresaumur. com. 14 units. 100€–160€ double. AE, DC, DISC, MC, V. Free parking. **Amenities:** Room service; babysitting. *In room:* A/C, TV, hair dryer, minibar, Wi-Fi (free).

Le Prieuré ★★★ This is the grandest address in the region, a bastion of comfort, charm, and grace. The 12th-century priory is in a 24-hectare (59-acre) park 8km (5 miles) from town. The hotel has a steep roof, dormer windows, and a large peaked tower. It provides gracious, comfortable rooms; two of the most beautiful are in a 10th-century chapel. The least expensive (and less desirable) rooms are in an outlying pavilion. No matter where, each room comes with fine linen and quality furnishings. The Grand Salon features an ornately carved stone fireplace, crystal chandeliers, oak furniture, and a bar with a fleur-de-lis motif.

From the dining room you'll get one of the finest views of the Loire, spanning 64km (40 miles)—it's truly beautiful at sunset. The chef wisely recommends filet of beef in wine sauce. Other specialties include grilled filet of Loire salmon and filet of rabbit with goat cheese and fresh herbs. Even if you're not a guest, consider dining here. Fixed-price menus cost 33€ to 99€.

Chênehutte-les-Tuffeaux 49350. ℂ **02-41-67-90-14.** Fax 02-41-67-92-24. www.grandesetapes.fr. 36 units. 130€–299€ double; 349€ suite. AE, DC, MC, V. **Amenities:** Restaurant; bar; babysitting; outdoor pool; room service; tennis court. *In room:* TV, hair dryer, minibar, Wi-Fi (free).

Les Terrasses de Saumur Although it was built relatively recently, this hotel has many of the architectural details (a steep slate roof, a U-shaped design ringing a formal courtyard) of a much older building. Rooms are pleasantly furnished, with comfortable beds and modern-looking furniture. There's also a large outdoor swimming pool, rambling green lawns, and plenty of parkland dotted with benches, tables, and chairs. The medium-size guest rooms are standard, with contemporary built-in furniture; the best have private balconies overlooking the Loire Valley.

2 rue des Lilas, St-Hilaire-St-Florent, Saumur 49400. ℂ **02-41-67-28-48.** Fax 02-41-67-13-71. www.les terrassesdesaumur.fr. 20 units. 70€–120€ double; 120€–160€ suite. AE, MC, V. **Amenities:** 2 restaurants; bar; babysitting; gym; 2 outdoor pools; room service; sauna; rooms for those w/limited mobility; smoke-free rooms. *In room:* A/C (in some), TV, hair dryer, minibar, Wi-Fi (free).

Where to Dine

Le Prieuré and Hôtel Anne d'Anjou's **Les Menestrels** (see above) serve some of the finest cuisine in town.

Gambetta ★ TRADITIONAL FRENCH This is not the least expensive restaurant in Saumur but if you want tasty seasonal dishes with market-fresh ingredients, it's the place to go. Locals will often direct you here for the creative and absolutely delicious cuisine—such dishes as tomato basil toasts topped with fresh fish, or grilled trout in butter. A puff pastry filled with Camembert cheese and drizzled with honey is a delight. Try the foie gras or the smoked salmon. Some of the best lamb and veal dishes in town, in various combinations, are served here, as is wild sea bass that is delectable. For a spectacular dessert, try, if featured, a pineapple sorbet with crème fraîche and raspberries.

12 rue Gambetta. ℂ **02-41-67-66-66.** Reservations recommended. Main courses 19€–30€; fixed-price menus 20€–82€. Tues and Thurs–Sat noon–2pm; Tues and Thurs–Sat 7–9pm. Closed 2 weeks in Jan, 3 weeks in Aug.

ANGERS ★★★

288km (179 miles) SW of Paris; 89km (55 miles) E of Nantes

Once the capital of Anjou, Angers straddles the Maine River at the western end of the Loire Valley. Though it suffered extensive damage in World War II, it has been restored, blending provincial charm with a suggestion of sophistication. The bustling regional center is often used as a base for exploring the château district to the west. Young people, including some 30,000 college students, keep this vital city of 260,000 jumping until late at night. Allow 3 hours to see the attractions at Angers.

Essentials

GETTING THERE Fifteen **trains** per day make the 1- to 2-hour trip from Paris's Gare de Montparnasse; the cost is 40€ to 59€ one-way. From Tours, 10 trains per day make the 1-hour trip; a one-way ticket is 20€. The Angers train station, at place de la Gare, is a convenient walk from the château. For train information, call ℂ **08-92-35-35-35.** From Saumur, there are three **bus** connections a day Monday to Saturday (1½ hr.). Buses arrive at place de la République. If you're **driving** from Tours, take N152 southwest to Saumur, turning west on D952.

VISITOR INFORMATION The **Office de Tourisme,** 7 place du Président-Kennedy (ℂ **02-41-23-50-00;** www.angers-tourisme.com), is opposite the entrance to the château.

Exploring the Town

If you have time for shopping, wander to the pedestrian zone in the center of town. Its boutiques and small shops sell everything from clothes and shoes to jewelry and books. For regional specialties, head to **Maison du Vin de l'Anjou,** 5 bis place du Président-Kennedy (ℂ **02-41-88-81-13**), where you can learn about the area's vineyards and buy a bottle or two for gifts or a picnic.

Cathédrale St-Maurice ★★ The cathedral dates mostly from the 12th and 13th centuries; the main tower is from the 16th century. The statues on the portal represent everybody from the Queen of Sheba to David at the harp. The tympanum depicts Christ Enthroned. The stained-glass windows from the 12th through the 16th centuries have made the cathedral famous. The oldest one illustrates the martyrdom of St. Vincent; the most unusual is of St. Christopher with the head of a dog. The Apocalypse Tapestries were once here; now only a few remain, with the majority on display in the nearby château (see below). The 12th-century nave, a landmark in cathedral architecture, is a work of harmonious beauty. If you're interested in a guided tour, call the church's presbytery at the number below. Tours are conducted erratically, often by an associate of the church, and usually with much charm and humor. The tours are available in French, English (offered July–Aug), and Italian.

Place Freppel. ℂ **02-41-87-58-45.** Free admission; donations appreciated. Daily 9am–7pm.

Château d'Angers ★★★ The moated château, dating from the 9th century, was the home of the comtes d'Anjou. The notorious Black Falcon lived here, and in time, the Plantagenets took up residence. From 1230 to 1238, the outer walls and 17 towers were built, creating a fortress. King René favored the château, and during his reign a brilliant court life flourished until he was forced to surrender to Louis XI. Louis XIV turned the château into a prison. In World War II, the Nazis used it as a munitions depot, and the Allies bombed it in 1944.

Visit the castle to see the **Apocalypse Tapestries ★★★**. They weren't always so highly regarded—they once served as a canopy to protect orange trees and were also used to cover the damaged walls of a church. Woven in Paris by Nicolas Bataille from cartoons by Jean de Bruges around 1375 for Louis I of Anjou, they were purchased for a nominal sum in the 19th century. The series of 77 pieces, illustrating the Book of St. John, stretch 100m (328 ft.).

After seeing the tapestries, you can tour the fortress, including the courtyard, prison, ramparts, windmill tower, 15th-century chapel, and royal apartments. Once you've paid the entrance fee, you can take a guided tour focusing on the architecture and history of the château. Throughout most of the year, guided tours depart daily at 10am, 11:30am, 1:15pm, 2:30pm, and 3:30pm, but between September and April, departures are usually (depending on business) at 10:15am and 2:15pm. Each tour lasts 90 minutes, and it can be conducted in four different languages—French, English, German, and Italian.

2 promenade du Bout-du-Monde. © **02-41-86-48-77.** Fax 02-41-87-17-50. www.monum.fr. Admission 6€ adults, 5€ seniors and students 18–25, free for children 16 and under. Sept–Apr daily 10am–5:30pm; May–Aug daily 9:30am–6:30pm.

Musée Jean Lurçat ★★   The town's most intriguing museum is in the Ancien Hôpital St-Jean, founded in 1174 to care for the sick. The museum is known for its famous tapestry, *Le Chant du Monde (The Song of the World)*, designed by Jean Lurçat and executed in 10 panels between 1957 and 1966. It depicts an abstract conglomeration of beneficent suns, popping champagne bottles, and life cycles of birth and death. You can visit a 17th-century dispensary, with earthenware jars and trivets still on its wooden shelves, and see everything from a Romanesque cloister with a secret garden to a pewter vessel from 1720 that once contained an antidote for snakebites.

4 bd. Arago. © **02-41-24-18-45.** Admission 4€ adults, free for children 16 and under. June–Sept daily 10am–6:30pm, Oct–May Tues–Sun 10am–noon and 2–6pm.

Where to Stay

Hôtel d'Anjou   Beside a park, this hotel, built in 1846, is the best choice for overnighting in the area. Although comparable in price to the quality Hôtel de France, it has more upscale appointments and amenities, along with a better restaurant, La Salamandre (see "Where to Dine," below). The guest rooms closer to the ground have higher ceilings and are more spacious.

1 bd. Foch, Angers 49100. © **800/528-1234** in the U.S. and Canada, or 02-41-21-12-11. Fax 02-41-87-22-21. www.hoteldanjou.fr. 53 units. 121€–176€ double; extra bed 30€. AE, DC, MC, V. Parking 8.50€. **Amenities:** Restaurant; bar. *In room:* TV, minibar, Wi-Fi (free).

L'Hôtel de France   This 19th-century hotel, one of the most respected in town, has been run by the Bouyers since 1893. It's the best choice near the railway station. Rooms are soundproof; each is comfortably furnished and well maintained. Bathrooms are very small and hold tubs.

8 place de la Gare, Angers 49100. © **02-41-88-49-42.** Fax 02-41-87-19-50. www.destination-anjou.com/hoteldefrance. 55 units. 100€–140€ double. AE, DC, MC, V. Parking 7€. **Amenities:** 2 restaurants; bar; room service. *In room:* A/C, TV, hair dryer, minibar, Wi-Fi (free).

Where to Dine

Le Crémet d'Anjou TRADITIONAL FRENCH   Located midway between the château and the railway station, this restaurant serves a tried-and-true French menu. Examples include filet of *sandre* cooked in butter sauce, filet of beef marinated in red Bourgueil wine, and succulent roasted duckling stuffed with homemade foie

A Toast with the Home-Brew—Cointreau

Another libation unique to Angers is Cointreau. **La Distillerie Cointreau**, 2 bd. des Bretonnières (℃ **02-41-31-50-50**; www.cointreau.fr), is in the suburb of St-Barthèlemy, a 10-minute drive east of the town center. It has a showroom where you can sample and stock up on the fruity liqueur.

Two brothers in Angers were confectioners who set out to create a drink of "crystal-clear purity." Today, some 13 million bottles of Cointreau are consumed annually. Packaged in a square bottle with rounded corners, Cointreau is made from twice-distilled alcohol from the peels of two types of oranges, bitter and sweet. The factory has turned out the drink since 1849. Cointreau flavors such drinks as the cosmopolitan and the sidecar.

gras. The salmon-and-gray-colored dining room is formal, with Louis XVI furniture and glittering chandeliers.

21 rue Delâge. ℃ **02-41-88-38-38.** Reservations recommended. Fixed-price menus 24€–28€. MC, V. Mon–Fri noon–1:30pm and 7–10pm.

La Salamandre ★ CLASSIC FRENCH   The salamander was the symbol of Renaissance king François I. In this formal, elegant restaurant, you'll see portraits of and references to that cunning strategist everywhere. Beneath massive sculpted ceiling beams, beside a large wooden fireplace, you'll enjoy the most impeccable service and best food in town. Shining examples include filet of red snapper in lime-flavored cream sauce, crayfish in various presentations, scallops in mushroom cream sauce, roasted turbot with Béarnaise sauce, and squid stuffed with crayfish and served with shellfish-flavored cream sauce. The restaurant is in a hotel but not owned by the hostelry.

In the Hotel d'Anjou, 1 bd. Foch. ℃ **02-41-88-99-55.** www.restaurant-lasalamandre.fr. Reservations recommended. Main courses 21€–38€; fixed-price menu 28€–75€. AE, DC, MC, V. Mon–Sat noon–2pm and 7:30–9pm and Sun 11:30am–2pm.

Provence Caffè PROVENÇAL   This restaurant celebrates the herbs, spices, and seafood of Provence. The bright decor includes bundles of herbs and souvenirs of the Mediterranean. The chef delights diners with such dishes as risotto served with rabbit and basil or grilled salmon with Provençal herbs.

9 place du Ralliement. ℃ **02-41-87-44-15.** Reservations recommended. Main courses 15€; fixed-price menu 18€–32€. MC, V. Tues–Sat noon–2pm and 7–10pm.

Angers After Dark

If you head to **place du Ralliement** or **rue St-Laud,** with its many bars and cafes, you'll find yourself in the center of Angers's nightlife. For a great night of beer drinking with friends, go to **Le Kent,** 7 place Ste-Croix (℃ **02-41-87-88-55**). The Irish pub serves some 50 beers and 70 brands of whiskey. If a night of dancing seems the perfect antidote to a day of château gazing, consider **Disco Le Boléro,** 38 rue St-Laud, adjacent to the place de Ralliement (℃ **02-41-88-61-19**). From June to September, it's open Tuesday through Friday 11:30pm to 3am, Saturday 11:30pm to 4am. There's no cover, but beer costs around 8€. The club attracts a lot of singles, ranging in age from 18 to 45. At the disco **Studio 49,** 8 place Vigan (℃ **02-41-48-15-28**), patrons range in age from 20 to 50, and the entrance fee is 10€, including a beverage.

NORMANDY & MONT-ST-MICHEL

Ten centuries have passed since the Vikings invaded Normandy. The early Scandinavians came to seize the land, but they stayed to cultivate it. The Normans produced great soldiers, none more famous than William the Conqueror, who defeated King Harold at the Battle of Hastings in 1066. The English and the French continued to battle for centuries.

The invasion of June 6, 1944, ravaged much of Normandy. The largest armada ever assembled was responsible for regaining control of Europe from the Nazis. Today, many visitors come to Normandy to see the D-day beachheads.

Some of this province may remind you of a Millet landscape, with cattle grazing in fields and wood-framed houses alongside modern buildings. Not far from the Seine is the hamlet where Monet painted his waterlilies. Here and there are stained-glass windows and Gothic architecture that survived the bombardments; however, many great buildings were leveled. Normandy's wide beaches attract families, and in August, the Deauville sands draw the chicest of the chic from Europe and North America. The resort towns of Deauville and Trouville are part of the region known as La Côte Fleurie (the Flower Coast), so called because of the profusion of flowers that grow there in the summer.

A 4-Day Normandy Itinerary

On your first day, head for Rouen and explore its old town and cathedral. On your second day, go to Caen, William the Conqueror's seat of government. Stay in Caen or in Bayeux, where you can see the local cathedral and the Bayeux tapestry. On your third day (from Caen or Bayeux), explore the D-day beaches. On your fourth day, continue west toward the ancient island-abbey of Mont-St-Michel.

ROUEN ★★★

135km (84 miles) NW of Paris; 89km (55 miles) E of Le Havre

The capital of Normandy and the fifth-largest port in France, Rouen is a hub of commerce. It's a bustling, vibrant place, bursting with activity generated by the industries connected to the port and the students at nearby universities and art schools. Former occupants include the writers Pierre Corneille and Gustave Flaubert, Claude Monet (who endlessly painted Rouen's Cathédrale de Notre-Dame), and Joan of Arc ("Oh, Rouen, art thou then my final resting place?"). Today, it's a city of half a million people.

Victor Hugo called Rouen "the city of a hundred spires." Half of it was destroyed during World War II, mostly by Allied bombers, and many Rouennais were killed. During the reconstruction of the old quarters, some of the almost-forgotten crafts of the Middle Ages were revived. The city on the Seine is rich in historical associations: William the Conqueror died here in 1087, and Joan of Arc was burned at the stake on place du Vieux-Marché in 1431.

As in Paris, the Seine splits Rouen into a **Rive Gauche (Left Bank)** and **Rive Droite (Right Bank).** The old city is on the right bank.

Essentials

GETTING THERE From Paris's Gare St-Lazare, **trains** leave for Rouen about once an hour (trip time: 1½ hr.). The one-way fare is 20€. The station is at the corner of rue Jeanne d'Arc and rue Verte. For information, call ✆ **36-35** or 08-92-35-35-35, or visit www.voyages-sncf.com. To **drive** from Paris, take A13 northwest to Rouen (trip time: 1½ hr.).

GETTING AROUND The **Métro** is part of the city's MétroBus system (✆ **02-35-52-52-52**). It has one north-south line. The most central stations in Old Rouen are Palais de Justice and Gare (Rue Verte). Tickets cost 1.40€ per ride and are good for bus transfers within 1 hour of entering the Métro. Buy tickets from kiosks or automated machines.

VISITOR INFORMATION The **Office de Tourisme** is at 25 place de la Cathédrale (✆ **02-32-08-32-40;** www.rouentourisme.com).

Seeing the Sights

Cathédrale Notre-Dame de Rouen ★★★ Monet immortalized Rouen's cathedral (particularly the facade, with its galaxy of statues) in his paintings. The main door, **Porte Central,** is embellished with sculptures (some decapitated) depicting the Tree of Jesus. The 12th-century Porte St-Jean and Porte St-Etienne flank it. Consecrated in 1063, the cathedral, a symphony of lacy stonework, was reconstructed after suffering damage in World War II. Two towers distinguish it: **Tour de Beurre** was financed by the faithful who were willing to pay for the privilege of eating butter during Lent. Containing a carillon of 56 bells, the **Tour Lanterne (Lantern Tower)**—built in 1877 and using 740 tons of iron and bronze—rises to almost 150m (492 ft.).

The cathedral's interior is fairly uniform. The choir is a masterpiece, with 14 soaring pillars. The Booksellers' Stairway, in the north wing of the transept, is adorned with a stained-glass rose window that dates, in part, from the 1500s. The 13th-century chancel is beautiful, with simple lines. Especially interesting is the **Chapelle de la Vierge,** adorned with Renaissance tombs of the cardinals d'Amboise. Also entombed is the heart of Richard the Lion-Hearted, a token of his affection for the people of Rouen.

Behind the cathedral is the **Palais de l'Archevêché (Archbishop's Palace),** which was bombed in the war. Now it stands naked against the sky. The broken arches and rosette windows witnessed the trial of Joan of Arc in 1431, and her rehabilitation was proclaimed here in 1456.

Place de la Cathédrale. © **02-35-71-71-60.** www.cathedrale-rouen.net. Free admission. Mon 2-6pm; Tues-Sat 7:30am-noon and 2-6pm; Sun 8am-6pm. Closed during Mass and on bank holidays.

Eglise St-Maclou ★★   St-Maclou was built in the Flamboyant Gothic style, with a step-gabled porch and cloisters, and is known for the 16th-century panels on its doors. Our favorite (to the left) is the Portail des Fontaines (Portal of the Fonts). The church was built in 1200, rebuilt in 1432, and consecrated in 1521; its lantern tower is from the 19th century. It sits on a square full of old Norman crooked-timbered buildings. Inside, pictures dating from June 4, 1944, document St-Maclou's destruction and its subsequent restoration.

3 place Barthélémy, behind the cathedral. ✆ **02-35-71-28-09.** Free admission. Apr-Oct daily 10am-noon and 2-6pm; Nov-Mar daily 10am-noon and 2-5:30pm.

Eglise St-Ouen ★★   This church is the outgrowth of a 7th-century Benedictine abbey. Flanked by four turrets, its 115m (377-ft.) octagonal lantern tower is called "the ducal crown of Normandy." The church represents the work of 5 centuries. Its nave is from the 15th century, its choir from the 14th (with 18th-c. railings), and its stained glass from the 14th to the 16th. On May 23, 1431, Joan of Arc was taken to the cemetery here, and officials sentenced her to be burned at the stake unless she recanted. She signed an abjuration, condemning herself to life imprisonment, but that sentence was later revoked.

Place du Général-de-Gaulle. ✆ **02-32-08-31-01.** Free admission. Mar-Oct Tues-Sun 10am-noon and 2-6pm; Nov-Feb Tues-Sun 10am-noon and 2-5:30pm.

Musée de la Céramique ★★   One of the great treasures here is the collection of 17th- and 18th-century Rouen faïence (opaquely glazed earthenware), which has a distinctive red hue because of the color of the local clay. The exhibits provide a showcase for Masseot Abaquesne, the premier French artist in faïence. An exceptional display is devoted to chinoiserie from 1699 to 1745.

94 rue Jeanne d'Arc. ✆ **02-35-07-31-74.** Admission 2.30€ adults, 1.55€ students, free for children 17 and under. Wed-Mon 10am-1pm and 2-6pm.

Musée des Beaux-Arts ★★★   This is one of France's most important provincial museums, with more than 65 rooms of art that ranges from medieval primitives to contemporary paintings. You'll find portraits by David and works by Delacroix and Ingres (seek out his *La Belle Zélie*). A Gérard David retable (altarpiece), *La Vierge et les saints (The Virgin and the Saints),* is a masterpiece. One salon is devoted to Géricault, including his portrait of Delacroix. Other works here are by Veronese, Velázquez, Caravaggio, Rubens, Poussin, Fragonard, and Corot, and by Impressionists such as Monet, including several paintings of the Rouen cathedral.

Esplanade de Marcel Duchamp. ✆ **02-35-71-28-40.** Admission 4€ adults, 2.50€ students, free for children 17 and under. Mon and Wed-Sun 10am-6pm.

Musée Flaubert et d'Histoire de la Médécine   Gustave Flaubert, author of *Madame Bovary,* was born in the director's quarters of Rouen's public hospital (his father was the director) in 1821. The room in which he was born is intact. You'll see the glass door that separated the Flauberts from the ward and its patients. Family furniture and medical paraphernalia are also displayed.

51 rue de Lecat. ✆ **02-35-15-59-95.** Admission 3€ adults, 1.50€ for students and ages 18-25, free for children 17 and under. Tues 10am-6pm; Wed-Sat 10am-noon and 2-6pm.

Musée Jeanne-d'Arc   The life and the martyrdom of Joan of Arc, France's national heroine, are the focus here. In a vaulted cellar, dioramas, waxworks, and commentary

Rouen

Cathédrale Notre-Dame de Rouen **7**		Musée Flaubert et d'Histoire de la Médécine **4**
Eglise St-Maclou **8**		Musée Jeanne-d'Arc **5**
Eglise St-Ouen **9**		Musée Le Secq des Tournelles (Wrought Ironworks Museum) **3**
Hôtel de Bourgtheroulde **6**		
Musée de la Céramique **1**		
Musée des Beaux-Arts **2**		

in four languages tell the story of her life—from Domrémy, where she was born, to Rouen, where she was burned at the stake. The museum also contains a research library that concentrates on her life and the politics of her era. Visitors can hear, without charge, recorded narration on hand-held devices.

33 place du Vieux-Marché. ℂ **02-35-88-02-70.** www.jeanne-darc.com. Admission 4€ adults, 2.50€ students and children 17 and under. Apr–Sept daily 9:30am–7pm; Oct–Mar daily 10am–noon and 2–6:30pm.

Musée Le Secq des Tournelles (Wrought Ironworks Museum) ★   Housed in the 15th-century Eglise St-Laurent, this museum showcases ironwork, a Norman art form. Its collection ranges from what a critic once called "forthright masculine forging to lacy feminine filigree, from Roman keys to the needlepoint balustrade that graced Mme. de Pompadour's country mansion." The collection displays some 14,000 pieces.

2 rue Jacques-Villon. ℂ **02-35-88-42-92.** Admission 2.30€ adults, 1.55€ students, free for children 17 and under. Wed–Mon 10am–1pm and 2–6pm.

The rubber-wheeled **Petit Train** (📞 02-32-18-40-23) is the most fun way to see this ancient city. The 40-minute tours leave from the front of the tourist office, 25 place de la Cathédrale (📞 02-32-08-32-40). Departures are daily at 10, 11am, 2, 4, and 5pm. Tickets cost 6.50€ for adults and 4.50€ for children 12 and under. The train operates from April 1 to October 15, with limited service over the Christmas holidays.

Place du Vieux-Marché ★   Joan of Arc was executed for heresy at the Old Marketplace. Tied to a stake, she was burned on May 30, 1431. Her ashes were gathered and tossed into the Seine. A modern church with stained-glass windows from St-Vincent sits in the center of a monumental complex in the square; beside it a bronze cross marks the position of St. Joan's stake.

Rue du Gros-Horloge ★★   The "Street of the Great Clock" runs between the cathedral and place du Vieux-Marché. Now a pedestrian mall, it's named for an ornate gilt Renaissance clock mounted on an arch, Rouen's most popular monument. The arch bridges the street and connects to a Louis XV fountain with a bevy of cherubs and a bell tower. At night the bells still toll a curfew.

Shopping

Rouen was once one of France's major producers of the fine decorative ceramic ware known as *faïence de Rouen.* Examples of both antique and contemporary faïence abound, and it's worth picking up one or two pieces. For contemporary faïence, your best bet is **Faïencerie Carpentier Augy,** 26 rue St-Romain (📞 02-35-88-77-47). The well-known studio sells reproductions of historical styles in an array of colors.

Another Rouen specialty is *les coffret de Rouen.* The little hand-painted wooden boxes were all the rage during the 18th and 19th centuries. The original versions continue to be popular, but watch out for modern forgeries.

Rouen is also an antiques capital, with more than 80 vendors in the Old Town. The best hunting ground is in Vieux Rouen (the Old Town), along **rue Eau-de-Robec, place Barthélémy, rue Damiette,** and **rue St-Romain.** The city has two **flea markets,** on Saturday and Sunday at place St-Mare, and on Thursday at place des Emmurés. Medium- and large-scale auctions take place year-round at **Les Salles des Ventes** and 20 rue de la Croix-de-Fer (📞 02-35-71-54-48).

Other antiques shops worth visiting are **Michel Bertran,** 108 rue Molière (📞 02-35-98-24-06), with a good selection of 18th- and 19th-century paintings, especially by School of Rouen Impressionists; **Etienne Bertran,** 110 rue Molière (📞 02-35-70-79-96), with its collection of antique books dating to the 16th century; and **Patrick Chasset,** 12 rue de la Croix-de-Fer (📞 02-35-70-59-97), for toys and cards from the 1700s and 1800s as well as bottles and glassware. You'll find watercolors by local artists, as well as antique Norman and English engravings.

Lovers of chocolate will discover a veritable paradise at **La Chocolatière,** 18 rue Guillaume-le-Conquérant (📞 02-35-71-00-79). The specialty that has attracted local gourmets for as long as anyone can remember is a praline-layered *paillardises,* rich in velvety chocolate that many readers describe as sinful.

Where to Stay

MODERATE

Hôtel de Dieppe   The Gueret family has run this Best Western property, across from the train station, since 1880. Although it has been modernized, it's still a traditional French inn. The only problem might be noise, but double-glazed windows help, and the area quiets down after the last train from Paris arrives around 10:30pm. Rooms are compact, with comfortable beds. Half the guest rooms have a full bathroom, the rest just a shower. In **Le Quatre Saisons,** the adjoining rotisserie, you can enjoy dishes such as duckling *à la presse* (pressed duck) and sole poached in red wine.

Place Bernard-Tissot, Rouen 76000. ℭ **800/528-1234** in the U.S. and Canada, or 02-35-71-96-00. Fax 02-35-89-65-21. www.hotel-dieppe.fr. 41 units. 99€–120€ double. AE, DC, MC, V. Parking 5€. **Amenities:** Restaurant; bar; room service. *In room:* TV, hair dryer, Wi-Fi (free).

Mercure Centre ★   In a town of lackluster hotels, the Mercure, close to the cathedral, is a fine choice for an overnight stay. The functionally designed rooms are almost identical to hundreds of other Mercure accommodations across Europe and are a tad small. Breakfast is the only meal served.

7 rue de la Croix-de-Fer, Rouen 76000. ℭ **02-35-52-69-52.** Fax 02-35-89-41-46. 125 units. 169€–185€ double; 270€–280€ suite. AE, DC, MC, V. Parking 12€. **Amenities:** Bar; room service. *In room:* A/C, TV, hair dryer, minibar, Wi-Fi (free).

INEXPENSIVE

Alive Hôtel De Québec 🍴   In the historic core, this budget hotel stands close to the cathedral and its surrounding antiques shops. It is a very typical Norman city hotel, without any grand design, but offering affordable comfortable rooms. Bedrooms are generally small, but each is well kept and many open onto a view of a garden. Suitable for families, some units have both a double bed and a single bed.

18–24 rue Québec, Rouen 76000. ℭ **02-35-70-09-38.** Fax 02-35-15-80-15. www.hotel-rouen.com. 38 units. 55€–60€ double; 66€–73€ triple. AE, MC, V. **Amenities:** Breakfast room. *In room:* TV, hair dryer, Wi-Fi (free).

Hôtel Cardinal 🍴   Not only is this hotel ideally located, it's also affordable. It's across from the cathedral (imagine waking up to a view of the majestic structure and the surrounding half-timbered buildings), in the middle of a neighborhood known for antiques, art galleries, and fine dining. With so much to do in the area, you won't mind the hotel's simplicity. Rooms are business-class plain with built-in furnishings and a small bathroom with tub or shower.

1 place de la Cathédrale, Rouen 76000. ℭ **02-35-70-24-42.** Fax 02-35-89-75-14. www.cardinal-hotel. fr. 18 units. 66€–86€ double; 86€–116€ triple or family room. MC, V. Parking 6€ nearby. Closed mid-Dec to mid-Jan. **Amenities:** Room service. *In room:* TV, hair dryer, Wi-Fi (free).

Hôtel de Bordeaux   Practically on the banks of the Seine, this hotel offers medium-size and renovated rooms with standard furnishings. They're acceptably comfortable, if a bit sterile-looking. All have views of either the town's medieval rooftops or the cathedral. Rooms on the upper floors afford river views. About half the guest rooms have bathrooms with tubs; the others have showers.

9 place de la République, Rouen 76000. ℭ **02-35-71-93-58.** Fax 02-35-71-92-15. www.book-your-hotel. com. 48 units. 76€–82€ double. AE, DC, MC, V. Parking 7€. **Amenities:** Bar. *In room:* TV, Wi-Fi (free).

Hôtel de la Cathédrale   Built around a timbered and cobble-covered courtyard, this hotel is on a pedestrian street midway between the cathedral and the Eglise St-Maclou, opposite the Archbishop's Palace where Joan of Arc was tried. The remodeled rooms are well maintained and tastefully furnished, accessible by both stairs and an elevator. Breakfast is the only meal served.

12 rue St-Romain, Rouen 76000. ℂ **02-35-71-57-95.** Fax 02-35-70-15-54. www.hotel-de-la-cathedrale.fr. 26 units. 69€–96€ double. AE, MC, V. Parking 10€ nearby. **Amenities:** Tea lounge; babysitting; room service. *In room:* TV, hair dryer, Wi-Fi (free).

Hôtel du Vieux Carré ★ 📖   In a restored half-timbered 18th-century house, this is one of the most charming and tranquil lodgings in Rouen. After inspecting too many impersonally furnished hotels, we found this one a surprise and a delight. Patrick Beaumont, the enthusiastic and much-traveled owner, has tastefully decorated the midsize guest rooms in comfortable rustic fashion. Unusual for central Rouen, its restaurant opens onto a flower-filled courtyard.

34 rue Ganterie, Rouen 76000. ℂ **02-35-71-67-70.** Fax 02-35-71-19-17. www.vieux-carre.fr. 13 units. 58€–65€ double. AE, MC, V. **Amenities:** Restaurant (lunch only); tearoom/cafe. *In room:* TV, Wi-Fi (free).

Where to Dine

Gill ★★★ MODERN FRENCH   The best restaurant in town sits beside the traffic of the Seine's quays. The minimalist decor, with high-tech lighting and accessories, is an appropriate backdrop for the sophisticated cuisine of Gilles Tournadre. Who can resist ravioli stuffed with foie gras and served in a bouillon sprinkled with fresh truffles? How about terrine of artichoke with fresh truffles or roasted white turbot with fresh asparagus flavored with Parmesan? The best items on the menu are pan-fried foie gras of duckling served with caramelized turnips and a turnip-green salad; a salad of crayfish tails with tomato-and-black-pepper chutney; and the most famous and popular specialty, Rouen-style pigeon with vegetables floating in densely concentrated consommé.

9 quai de la Bourse. ℂ **02-35-71-16-14.** www.gill.fr. Reservations required far in advance. Main courses 30€–57€; business lunch 35€; fixed-price dinner 92€. AE, DC, MC, V. Tues–Sat noon–1:45pm and 7:30–9:30pm. Closed Aug and 2 weeks in Apr.

Les Nymphéas ★★★ MODERN FRENCH   One of the most appealing restaurants in Rouen bears the name of a painting by Monet *(Water Lilies)*. The setting is a 16th-century half-timbered house that fits gracefully into the centrally located neighborhood (place du Vieux-Marché). The restaurant features sophisticated, savory cuisine. It's celebrated for its warm foie gras with cider sauce; wild duckling Rouennais style, served with wild mushrooms and caramelized onions; and *civet* (stew) of lobster with Sauternes. An award-winning dessert that evokes the Norman countryside is a warm soufflé flavored with apples and Calvados.

7 rue de la Pie. ℂ **02-35-89-26-69.** www.lesnympheas-rouen.com. Reservations required. Main courses 24€–55€; fixed-price menu 40€–70€. AE, MC, V. Tues–Sat 12:15–2pm and 7:30–9:45pm. Closed late Aug to mid-Sept.

Pascaline 🍴 TRADITIONAL FRENCH   This informal bistro is often filled with regulars and has been a favorite since its opening in 1880. The decor hasn't changed much since. The cheapest fixed-price menus are among the best bargains in town.

Menu items include seafood dishes such as pavé of monkfish with roughly textured mustard sauce, breast of duck cooked in beer, and savory *pot-au-feu maison* (house stew). Don't come for refined cuisine—you should expect hearty, time-tested favorites.

5 rue de la Poterne. ℂ **02-35-89-67-44.** www.pascaline.fr. Reservations recommended. Main courses 10€–20€; fixed-price menu 13€–28€. AE, MC, V. Daily noon–2:30pm and 7–11pm.

Rouen After Dark

Cette Semaine à Rouen, a pamphlet that details the week's entertainment offerings and events, is available free at the tourist office and most hotels.

For highbrow entertainment, **Théâtre des Arts,** 7 rue du Dr.-Rambert (ℂ **02-35-71-41-36**), presents ballet, opera, and classical music. **Théâtre des Deux Rives,** 48 rue Louis-Ricard (ℂ **02-35-89-63-41**), presents plays in French. **Théâtre des Arts/Opéra Léonard de Vinci,** 7 rue du Dr.-Rambert (ℂ **02-35-71-41-36**), has a busy schedule of classical and contemporary opera. A variety of concerts takes place at **Eglise St-Ouen,** place du Général-de-Gaulle. For information about who's playing, contact the tourist office.

Much of the nightlife, especially pubs, centers on place du Vieux-Marché. **La Bohème,** 18 rue St-Amand (ℂ **02-35-71-53-99;** www.laboheme-discotheque.com), is a small discothèque with a cozy, publike ambience. Many students meet at the **Underground Pub,** 26 rue des Champs-Maillets (ℂ **02-35-98-44-84**), which has a street-level bar and an underground bar fitted with wood and British bric-a-brac.

WINE BAR   **Le P'tit Zinc,** 20 place du Vieux-Marché (ℂ **02-35-89-39-69**), is a bistro-style wine bar with early-1900s decor and one of the best wine selections in town. Of course, you can order Norman cider as well.

DISCOS   At **Le Kiosque,** 43 bd. de Verdun (ℂ **02-35-88-54-50**), 20-some-things rule the dance floor. You'll pay a cover of 15€ to enjoy hard-edged techno music and psychedelic light action. A disco that appeals to a somewhat mature (22–40) crowd is **l'Ibiza,** 29 bd. Des Belges (ℂ **02-35-07-76-20**). Located near place du Vieux-Marché, it has modern decor, a crowded dance floor, occasional karaoke, and a cover charge of 8€ to 12€, which includes one drink.

GAY & LESBIAN BARS   The modern **Le Chakra,** 4 bis bd. Ferdinand-de-Lesseps (ℂ **02-32-10-12-02**), attracts its share of young, well-connected gays and lesbians. It's known for light shows and techno music. A wild crowd parties here until the wee hours, especially on weekends. You'll pay an 8€ to 10€ cover, which includes one drink.

 Finding Old Normandy in Calvados Country

For a taste of old Normandy, motorists heading from Rouen to Deauville should stop in Pont-Audemer, 50km (31 miles) west of Rouen. On the banks of the River Risle, Pont-Audemer is in the heart of Calvados country. In spite of war damage, Pont-Audemer retains much of its old look, especially if you wander its historic streets, rue de la Licorne (unicorn) and rue de la République. Along rue de la République, look for Eglise St-Ouen, dating from the 11th century.

HONFLEUR ★★

201km (125 miles) NW of Paris; 63km (39 miles) NE of Caen

At the mouth of the Seine opposite Le Havre, Honfleur is one of Normandy's most charming fishing ports. Having escaped major damage in World War II, the working port looks like an antique. Thanks to the pont de Normande, the bridge that links Honfleur to Le Havre, visitors flock here. Honfleur is 500 years older than Le Havre, dating from the 11th century. Artists, including Daubigny, Corot, and Monet, have long favored this township.

Essentials

GETTING THERE If you're **driving** from Pont l'Evêque or other points south (including Paris), D579 leads to the major boulevard, rue de la République. Follow it to the town center. Driving time from Paris is 2 to 2½ hours.

There's no direct **train** service into Honfleur. From Paris, take one of the dozen or so daily trains from Gare St-Lazare to Deauville for 30€ one-way. From there, bus no. 20 makes the 25-minute ride to Honfleur; the one-way fare is about 2.15€. From Rouen, take the train to Le Havre and transfer to bus no. 50, which costs 4.10€ each way, for the 30-minute ride to Honfleur. Several **buses** run daily between Caen and Honfleur (trip time: 2 hr.); the one-way fare is 7.20€. For information, call **Bus Verts du Calvados** (✆ **08-10-21-42-14**).

VISITOR INFORMATION The **Office de Tourisme** is on quai Lepaulmier (✆ **02-31-89-23-30**; www.ot-honfleur.fr).

Seeing the Town

Begin your tour, which should take about an hour, at place de la Porte-de-Rouen. Stroll along the **Vieux Bassin,** the old harbor, taking in the fishing boats and narrow, slate-roofed houses. On the north side of the basin, the former governor's house, **Lieutenance,** dates from the 16th century. Nearby is the **Eglise Ste-Catherine,** place Ste-Catherine (✆ **02-31-89-11-83**), constructed of timber by 15th-century shipbuilders. The church's wooden belfry is on the other side of the street. The church is open July and August daily from 8am to 8pm, September through June daily 8:30am to noon and 2 to 6pm.

Maisons Satie Opened in 1998, this high-tech museum honors Honfleur's native son Erik Satie in the house where he was born in 1866. Satie was a "complete artist": He became most famous for his music, but he was also a painter and acted as a muse and inspiration to Picasso, Braque, Cocteau, Debussy, Ravel, and Stravinsky. This is not a traditional museum. The walk-through exhibitions incorporate sound, light, and recordings of Satie's compositions. Visitors wear high-tech helmets that transmit sound, which allows for a degree of play and experimentation in some of the exhibits.

67 bd. Charles V. ✆ **02-31-89-11-11.** Admission 5.10€ adults, 3.60€ ages 10–17, free for children 9 and under. May–Sept Wed–Mon 10am–7pm; Oct–Apr Wed–Mon 11am–6pm. Closed Jan–Feb 15.

Musée d'Ethnographie et d'Art Populaire This place celebrates the unique cultural and aesthetic contributions of Normandy to the rest of Europe. You'll find old furniture, lace headdresses, embroidery, candle-making equipment, and farm implements, as well as several rooms outfitted with period art and antiques.

Quai St-Etienne. 📞 **02-31-89-14-12.** Admission 3.50€ adults, 2.10€ students and children 10–18, free for children 9 and under. July–Aug daily 10am–noon and 2–6:30pm; Apr–June and Sept Tues–Fri 10am–noon and 2–6pm; Oct to mid-Nov and mid-Feb to Mar Tues–Fri 2–5:30pm, Sat–Sun 10am–noon and 2:30–5:30pm.

Musée Eugène-Boudin This museum showcases a good collection of works by the painters who flocked to this port when Impressionism was new. The largest assortment is of the pastels and paintings of Boudin.

Place Erik-Satie. 📞 **02-31-89-54-00.** Admission 5.30€ adults, 3.80€ students and children 10 and over. Mar 15–Sept Wed–Mon 10am–noon and 2–6pm; Oct–Mar 14 Wed–Mon 2:30–5:30pm, Sat–Sun 10am–noon and 2:30–5:30pm. Closed Jan to mid-Feb, July 14, and Dec 25.

NaturoSpace Inaugurated in 1999 on the western outskirts of town, adjacent to the seacoast, Honfleur's modern attraction displays the flora and butterfly life of some of the most exotic climates on earth. Designed like an enormous greenhouse bursting with tropical plants and butterflies, it contains a labyrinth of walkways that cut through Normandy's approximation of a tropical rainforest. Most visitors spend about an hour in this environment, which is in distinct contrast to the old Norman ethnicity that's otherwise associated with Honfleur.

Bd. Charles V. 📞 **02-31-81-77-00.** www.naturospace.com. Admission 7.80€ adults, 6€ students and children 13 and under, family package 30€. Apr–June and Sept daily 10am–1pm and 2–7pm; Feb–Nov 10am–1pm and 2–5:30pm; July–Aug daily 10am–7pm.

Where to Stay

Restaurant/Hôtel L'Absinthe (see "Where to Dine," below) also rents rooms.

Castel Albertine ★ 📖 Management takes great care to maintain the character of this home of Albert Sorel, a 19th-century historian and scholar. The impressive house, of red-brick and rose-hued stone, is a 3-minute walk from the port. It is a handsome, welcoming hotel. All of the individually decorated rooms have floor-to-ceiling windows that open onto views of gardens and trees. Each room was renovated in 2002 or 2003, and many have king-size beds. Bathrooms are small but tidily kept, with either a tub or a shower.

19 cours Albert-Manuel, Honfleur 14600. 📞 **02-31-98-85-56.** Fax 02-31-98-83-18. www.honfleurhotels. com. 27 units. 80€–150€ double. MC, V. Parking 10€. Closed Jan. **Amenities:** Bar; babysitting; room service; sauna. *In room:* TV, hair dryer, Wi-Fi (free).

La Ferme St-Siméon ★★★ An old farmhouse is the focal point of this 17th-century half-timbered slate hotel, one of Normandy's most elegant and prestigious inns. It's in the hills above Honfleur, about 1.5km (1 mile) from the old port. The shimmering water of the English Channel draws artists to the hilltop inn, said to be where Impressionism was born in the 19th century. Much of the hotel has terracotta floors, carved wood, and copper and faïence touches. Guest rooms, which are formal and comfortable, have fabric-covered walls. Some rooms contain exposed half-timbering or ceiling beams; others hold canopy-covered beds. Most have antique or heirloom furnishings. Bathrooms are beautifully maintained; about half have tub/shower combinations.

20 rue Adolphe-Marais, Honfleur 14600. 📞 **02-31-81-78-00.** Fax 02-31-89-48-48. www.fermesaint simeon.fr. 34 units. 220€–450€ double; 550€–850€ suite. AE, MC, V. **Amenities:** Restaurant; bar; babysitting; indoor pool; room service; sauna; spa. *In room:* TV, hair dryer, minibar, Wi-Fi (free).

Le Manoir de Butin ★   Surrounded by well-landscaped grounds, this villa châ-teau evokes a more gracious era at the turn of the 20th century. The villa's half-timbered and dormers–styled structure suggest the frivolity of late-19th-century seaside architecture in Normandy. The bedrooms are some of the most intimate and cozy in the area, each with beautiful furnishings, often with a poster bed along with marble-clad bathrooms. *Fin de siècle* architectural details include a grand staircase, bay or bow windows, and wooden balconies.

Phare du Butin, 14600 Honfleur. ✆ **02-31-81-63-00.** Fax 02-31-89-59-23. www.hotel-lemanoir.fr. 10 units. 120€–350€ double. AE, MC, V. Closed Nov and mid-Dec to Jan. **Amenities:** Restaurant; room service. *In room:* TV, minibar, Wi-Fi (free).

Les Maisons de Léa ★★   A sense of old-fashioned coziness abounds here. In 1900, the hotel owners enclosed a 16th-century fish market and added plumbing and partitions between what are now comfortable, warmly decorated guest rooms. The renovated rooms have individual color schemes and canopy-covered beds. The accommodations, though modest, are perfect for an overnight stop. All bathrooms contain showers, but only about a third have tubs.

Place Ste-Catherine, Honfleur 14600. ✆ **02-31-14-49-49.** Fax 02-31-89-28-61. www.lesmaisonsdelea.com. 30 units. 145€–200€ double; 180€–285€ suite. AE, MC, V. Bus: 20 or 50. **Amenities:** Snack bar; babysitting; room service (breakfast only). *In room:* TV, hair dryer, Wi-Fi (free).

Where to Dine

La Terrasse et l'Assiette ★★ TRADITIONAL FRENCH   Outfitted "in the Norman style" with heavy beams and lots of exposed brick, the gourmet citadel of Honfleur attracts an upscale international clientele. Owner Gérard Bonnefoy churns out dishes that include crayfish with sautéed vermicelli and truffles, an omelet studded with chunks of lobster, unctuous fried foie gras served with lentils, and braised scallops with a purée of Brussels sprouts and smoked-ham sauce. Leave room for *petit gateau moelleux au chocolat* (very moist chocolate-fudge cake). In summer, if the weather is clement, ask for a table on the terrace, overlooking the historic Eglise Ste-Catherine.

8 place Ste-Catherine. ✆ **02-31-89-31-33.** www.laterrasseetlassiette.com. Reservations recommended. Main courses 26€–40€; fixed-price menu 32€–54€. AE, MC, V. Wed–Sun noon–2pm and 7:30–9pm. Closed in Jan.

Restaurant/Hôtel L'Absinthe ★★ TRADITIONAL FRENCH   This tavern, named for the drink preferred by many 19th-century writers, is known for its beautiful decor, extravagant portions, and well-prepared cuisine. Rooms in the 16th-century building have beamed ceilings, parquet floors, and furniture that matches the architectural grandeur. The restaurant consists of two dining rooms (one from the 15th c. with exposed beams and exposed stone, and one from the 17th c. with a stately fireplace). The menu changes frequently. The best menu items include foie gras with caramelized ginger and apples, and sea bass roasted with laurel leaves and red wine.

If you're taken with the place, you can rent a room or the suite. A double runs 115€ to 185€, and the suite goes for 250€. Parking costs 12€.

10 quai de la Quarantaine, Honfleur 14600. ✆ **02-31-89-39-00.** Fax 02-31-89-53-60. www.absinthe.fr. Reservations required. Main courses 26€–48€; fixed-price menu 33€–62€. AE, DC, MC, V. Daily 12:15–3pm and 7:15–10pm. Closed Nov 15–Dec 17.

DEAUVILLE ★★★

206km (128 miles) NW of Paris; 47km (29 miles) NE of Caen

Deauville has been associated with the rich and famous since the duc de Morny, Napoleon III's half-brother, founded it as an upscale resort in 1859. In 1913, it entered sartorial history when Coco Chanel launched her career here, opening a boutique selling tiny hats that challenged the fashion of huge-brimmed hats loaded with flowers and fruit. (Coco's point of view: "How can the mind breathe under those things?")

Essentials

GETTING THERE   There are 6 to 10 daily **rail** connections from Paris's Gare St-Lazare (trip time: 2 hr., 15 min.); prices start at 30€ one-way. The rail depot lies between Trouville and Deauville, south of town. Take a taxi from the station. **Bus Verts du Calvados** (*©* **08-10-21-42-14;** www.busverts.fr) serves the Normandy coast from Caen to Le Havre. To **drive** from Paris (trip time: 2½ hr.), take A13 west to Pont L'Evêque, and then follow N177 east to Deauville.

VISITOR INFORMATION   The **Office de Tourisme** is on place de la Mairie (*©* **02-31-14-40-00;** www.deauville.org).

SPECIAL EVENTS   For a week in September, the **Deauville Festival of American Film** (*©* **02-31-14-40-00;** www.festival-deauville.com) honors movies made in the United States. Actors, producers, directors, and writers flock here and briefly eclipse the high rollers at the casinos and the horse-racing and polo crowd.

Exploring the Resort

Coco Chanel cultivated a tradition of elegance that survives in Deauville and in its smaller and less prestigious neighbor Trouville, on the opposite bank of the Toques (see the next section). Don't expect flash; in its way, restrained and ever-so-polite Deauville is the most British seaside resort in France.

However, in its heart, Deauville is less English than French. It has even been dubbed "Paris's 21st arrondissement." The crowds here tend to be urban and hip. Deauville is stylish and not (by anyone's definition) inexpensive.

With its golf courses, casinos, deluxe hotels, La Touques and Clairefontaine race-tracks, regattas, a yachting harbor, polo grounds, and tennis courts, Deauville is a formidable contender for the business of the upper class. Looking for a charming place to stroll? Head for boutique-lined **rue Eugène-Colas, place Morny** (named for the resort's founder), and **place du Casino.**

BEACHES   Expect to spend time on Deauville's boardwalk, **Les Planches,** a promenade running parallel to the beach. Beaux Arts and half-timbered Norman-inspired buildings line its edges. In summer, especially August, parasols dot the beach and oiled bodies cover seemingly every inch of sand. The resort's only beach is **Plage de Deauville,** a strip that's part of La Côte Fleurie.

If you're looking for a gay and nude beach, you'll have to go to **Merville-France-Ville,** 39km (24 miles) from Deauville toward Caen. But considering how permissive most Deauville fans are, many gay travelers feel perfectly comfortable here.

Access to every beach in Normandy is free; in Deauville, you'll pay from 2€ per hour for parking in any of the many public lots beside the sea.

The **Piscine Municipale,** boulevard de la Mer (✆ **02-31-14-02-17**), is a large indoor seawater pool. Depending on the season, bathers pay 4€ to 5€ per person. Hours are July and August daily 9:30am to 7:30pm, June and September daily 10am to 7pm, and October to December and February to May daily 10:30am to 7pm.

HORSE RACES/POLO You can watch horses every day from late June to early October. There's either a race at 2pm or a polo match at 3pm. The venues are the **Hippodrome de Deauville La Touques,** boulevard Mauger (✆ **02-31-14-20-00**), in the heart of town near the Mairie de Deauville (town hall); and the **Hippodrome de Deauville Clairefontaine,** route de Clairefontaine (✆ **02-31-14-69-00**), within the city limits, 2km (1¼ miles) west of the center.

Shopping

This seaside town has a pedestrian shopping area between the polo field and the port; the main drags are **rue Mirabeau, rue Albert-Fracasse,** and the west end of **avenue de la République.** The leading shops, selling some of the world's most elegant merchandise (with prices to match), cluster on **rue Eugène-Colas, place Morny,** and **place du Casino.** At **La Cave de Deauville,** 48 rue Mirabeau (✆ **02-31-87-35-36;** www.cave-de-deauville.com), you'll find a wide selection of apple ciders, Calvados, and the apple aperitif known as *pommeau.*

For an overview of the bounty of the fertile Norman soil, head for the **Marché Publique** (open-air market) in the place du Marché, adjacent to place Morny. From July to mid-September, it's open daily 8am to 1pm. The rest of the year, market days are Tuesday, Friday, Saturday, and occasionally Sunday. In addition to fruits, vegetables, poultry, cider, wine, and cheese, you'll find cookware, porcelain tableware, and cutlery.

Where to Stay
EXPENSIVE

Hôtel du Golf Barrière ★★★ ☺ Golfers gravitate to this half-timbered hotel created by the Lucien Barrière chain in the late 1980s. The location, in the hills above Deauville, about 3km (1¾ miles) from the center of town, creates an aura of country-club tranquillity. Outfitted in English country-house style, it's one of the few hotels in Normandy with its own golf course. If the links aren't your thing, you might consider the Normandy or Royal hotels (reviewed below, and all three Lucien Barrière properties). The children's center and activities program are the best in Deauville. Rooms come in a wide range of sizes; those in back open onto the links, those in front have better views of the Channel. The best rooms, called "prestige luxe," feature antique-style furnishings, French windows, and spacious bathrooms and balconies.

At New-Golf Club, Mont Canisy, St-Arnoult Deauville 14800. ✆ **02-31-14-24-00.** Fax 02-31-14-24-01. www.lucienbarriere.com. 178 units. 239€–610€ double; 395€–649€ junior suite. AE, DC, MC, V. Closed mid-Nov to mid-Mar. From Deauville, take D278 south for 2.5km (1½ miles). **Amenities:** 2 restaurants; bar; babysitting; children's center; exercise room; 27-hole golf course; massage; heated outdoor pool; room service; rooms for those w/limited mobility; sauna; smoke-free rooms; 3 tennis courts. *In room:* TV, hair dryer, minibar, Wi-Fi.

Normandy Barrière ★★★ ☺ This is the most famous hotel in Deauville, with a legendary chic that dates back to the Edwardian age. The Anglo-Norman design includes half-timbering, dovecotes, turrets, and gables; the 1912 building resembles a cozy but stately English country house. A renovation updated all the rooms, public areas, and security systems. Because of its extensive facilities for children, including a nursery and babysitting, it attracts upscale families with children—although that doesn't interfere with the hotel's image as a chic nest for Francophone celebrities. During the Deauville Festival of American Film, it attracts French stars, the press, and jury members. Originally built to house well-heeled gamblers from the nearby casino, it continues to draw the gambling crowd today.

38 rue Jean-Mermoz, Deauville 14800. ☎ **02-31-98-66-22.** Fax 02-31-98-66-23. www.lucienbarriere. com. 298 units. 319€–719€ double; 670€–1,020€ suite. AE, DC, MC, V. Parking 30€ in garage. **Amenities:** Restaurant; children's dining room; bar; babysitting; exercise room; heated outdoor pool; room service; steam room; 2 tennis courts. In room: TV, hair dryer, minibar, Wi-Fi (8€ per hour).

Royal-Barrière ★★★   The Royal adjoins the casino and fronts a park near the Channel. It rises like a palace, with columns and exposed timbers. Although it doesn't have the insider cachet of the Normandy Barrière (see above), it is a grander and more opulent hotel. It's a member of Leading Hotels of the World, and its architecture evokes an Edwardian-era grand palace hotel. The hotel was built in 1913 on architectural principles conceived by Gustav Eiffel (an iron skeleton supports walls and ceilings). Post-millennium the hotel concluded a 5-year renovation program that included virtually every aspect of the establishment, including elegant bathrooms with tubs and showers. The decor of the guest rooms, conceived by megadesigner Jacques Garcia, is a reinterpretation of Directoire and Napoleon III styles. During the Deauville Festival of American Film, the U.S. stars stay here.

Bd. Eugène-Cornuché, Deauville 14800. ☎ **02-31-98-66-33.** Fax 02-31-98-66-34. www.lucienbarriere. com. 290 units. 329€–750€ double; 645€–1,065€ suite. AE, DC, MC, V. Closed Nov to early Mar. **Amenities:** 2 restaurants; bar; health club; heated outdoor pool; room service; sauna. In room: TV, hair dryer, minibar, Wi-Fi (8€ per hour).

INEXPENSIVE

Hôtel Ibis ✔   Built in the 1980s as part of the nationwide chain, the Ibis is on the periphery of Deauville about 1km (½ mile) from the casino. The modern building, overlooking the harbor, is one of the best bargains in town. Rooms are comfortable and tidy, but decorated in dull chain style. The small tiled bathrooms contain showers and the restaurant offers a traditional French menu.

9–10 quai de la Marine, Deauville 14800. ☎ **02-31-14-50-00.** Fax 02-31-14-50-05. www.hotelibis.com. 95 units. 76€–175€ double; 100€–185€ duplex suite for 2–6 people. AE, DC, MC, V. Parking 10€. **Amenities:** Restaurant; bar; babysitting. In room: A/C, TV, Wi-Fi (free).

Hôtel Le Trophée   This modern replica of a half-timbered medieval building is in the middle of Deauville, 150m (492 ft.) from the beach. The small rooms have contemporary furniture and private balconies overlooking the shopping streets. Bathrooms are also small. A sun terrace on the roof provides a bird's-eye view of the town and a more private tanning area than the beach. If you plan to eat here, enjoy at least one meal under the stars in the patio courtyard garden. The hotel has also transformed what was a private house, immediately across the street, into an annex, creating an additional 15 suites.

81 rue du Général-Leclerc, Deauville 14800. ☎ **02-31-88-45-86.** Fax 02-31-88-07-94. www.letrophee. com. 35 units. 59€–159€ double; 129€–219€ suite. AE, DC, MC, V. Parking 10€. **Amenities:** Restaurant; babysitting; exercise room; heated outdoor pool; sauna; steam bath. In room: TV, hair dryer, minibar, Wi-Fi (20€ per day).

L'Augeval ★   Across from the racetrack and just blocks from the beach and casino, this hotel mixes city flair and country charm. The former private villa was built in the early 1900s and sits amid well-kept lawns and gardens. The cozy rooms range from medium to spacious, and each has at least one high-quality antique. Some units have Jacuzzis.

15 av. Hocquart-de-Turtot, Deauville 14800. ℭ **02-31-81-13-18.** Fax 02-31-81-00-40. www.augeval.com. 52 units. 95€–110€ double; 222€–333€ suite. AE, DC, MC, V. Parking 8€. **Amenities:** Bar; babysitting; exercise room; small heated outdoor pool; room service. *In room:* TV, hair dryer, minibar, Wi-Fi (free).

Where to Dine

Chez Miocque TRADITIONAL FRENCH   This hip cafe near the casino and the boutiques does a bustling business at its sidewalk tables. The place serves hearty brasserie-style food, including succulent lamb stew with spring vegetables, filet of skate with cream-based caper sauce, mussels in white-wine sauce, and steaks. Portions are filling, and the atmosphere can be lively. The dish of the day is always from the sea.

81 rue Eugène-Colas. ℭ **02-31-88-09-52.** Reservations recommended. Main courses 19€–43€. AE, MC, V. July–Sept daily 9am–midnight; mid-Feb to June and Oct–Dec Fri–Mon noon–4pm and 7–11:30pm.

Le Ciro's Barrière ★★★ FRENCH/SEAFOOD   Hot on the resort's social scene, Le Ciro's serves Deauville's best seafood. It's expensive but worth it. If you want a bit of everything, ask for the *plateau de fruits de mer,* brimming with lobster and shellfish. For an elaborate appetizer, we recommend lobster salad with truffles. Marmite of scallops with sweet sauterne wine and saffron makes a superb main course. The collection of Bordeaux wine is exceptional. The ambience is airy, stylish, and evocative of the Belle Epoque heyday of Deauville.

Promenade des Planches. ℭ **02-31-14-31-31.** Fax 02-31-88-32-02. Reservations required. Main courses 23€–54€; fixed-price menu 29€. AE, DC, MC, V. Thurs–Mon 12:30–2:30pm and 7:30–9:30pm. Closed 2 weeks in Jan.

Le Spinnaker ★ NORMAN   Owner-chef Pascal Angenard's charming yellow-and-blue restaurant features regional cuisine. The satisfying specialties include terrine of foie gras with four spices, roast lobster with cider vinegar and cream-enriched potatoes, slow-cooked veal flank, and hot apple tart. Pascal recommends roast turbot flavored with shallots *en confit.* A fine array of wines can accompany your meal. On some nights a dish here or there might not be sublime, but most are excellent.

52 rue Mirabeau. ℭ **02-31-88-24-40.** www.spinnakerdeauville.com. Reservations required. Main courses 20€–50€; fixed-price menu 38€–52€. AE, DC, MC, V. Wed–Sun 12:30–1:30pm and 7:30–10pm. Closed June 21–28, Nov 15–30, and Jan 2–31.

Deauville After Dark

Opened in 1912, the **Casino de Deauville,** rue Edmond-Blanc (ℭ **02-31-14-31-14;** www.lucienbarriere.com), is one of France's premier casinos. Its original Belle Epoque core has been expanded with a theater, a nightclub, three restaurants, and an extensive collection of slot machines (*machines à sous*). The casino distinguishes areas for slot machines from more formal locales containing such games as roulette, baccarat, blackjack, and poker. The slots are open daily from 11am to 2am (to 3am Fri and 4am Sat) and have no dress code; access to this area is free. The areas containing *les jeux traditionnels* (traditional games) are open daily at 4pm and close between 3 and 4am, depending on business and the day of the week. Entrance is free, and you must present a passport or identity card to gain admission. The most interesting nights are Friday and Saturday, when the cabaret theater and all the restaurants are open. The theater presents glittering, moderately titillating shows at 10:30pm on Friday and Saturday. Admission is 25€ Friday, rising to 29€ on Saturday. Dinner and the show costs 55€ to 59€.

If it's a dance club you're looking for, head to the high-energy **Y Club,** 14 bis rue Désiré-le-Hoc (✆ **02-31-88-30-91**), which charges a cover of 15€. For salsa, merengue, and reggae, visit **Brok Café,** 14 av. du Général-de-Gaulle (✆ **02-31-81-30-81**). If you want to re-create the restrained but decadent ambience of the 1970s, consider **Le Régine's,** inside Deauville's casino, rue Edmond-Blanc (✆ **02-31-14-31-96**).

Dancing Les Planches, Le Bois Lauret, Blonville (✆ **02-31-87-58-09**), 4km (2½ miles) from Deauville, is a club where you'll find up-to-date music, a dance floor, and even an indoor swimming pool near an indoor/outdoor bar. It's open from 11pm until dawn every Friday and Saturday night.

TROUVILLE ★★

206km (128 miles) NW of Paris; 43km (27 miles) NE of Caen

Across the Touques River from the fashionable (and expensive) Deauville, Trouville feels more like a fishing port. The town is like Honfleur, but with fewer boutiques and art galleries. Don't expect the grand atmosphere of Deauville; Trouville is more low-key. It's also less dependent on resort euros; when the bathers leave its splendid sands, Trouville continues to thrive—its resident population of fishermen sees to that.

Essentials

GETTING THERE There are **rail** connections from Gare St-Lazare in Paris to Trouville (see the "Deauville" section, earlier in this chapter). **Bus Verts du Calvados** (www.busverts.fr) links Trouville, Deauville, and the surrounding region with the rest of Normandy. For bus information, call the **Gare Routière** (✆ **08-10-21-42-14**). If you're traveling by **car** from Deauville, drive west along D180.

VISITOR INFORMATION The **Office de Tourisme** is at 32 quai Fernand-Moureaux (✆ **02-31-14-60-70;** www.trouvillesurmer.org).

Exploring the Town

In the heyday of Napoleon III, during the 1860s, *boulevardiers* (men about town) used to bring their wives and families to Trouville and stash their mistresses in Deauville. Deauville was just coming into existence; it's a planned city, with straight avenues and a sense of industrial-age orderliness. By contrast, the narrow, labyrinthine alleyways of Trouville hint at its origins as a medieval fishing port.

Our recommendation? Explore Trouville, enjoying its low-key charm, and when you tire of it, join the caravan of traffic that heads across the river to the bright lights and glamour of Deauville.

Les Planches is a stretch of seafront boardwalk dotted with concessions on one side and overlooking the sea on the other. In midsummer, expect lots of flesh sprawled on the sands in various states of undress. There's only one beach, **Plage de Trouville** (though when you've tired of it, you only have to cross the river to reach the Plage de Deauville). On Trouville's seafront is the **Piscine de Trouville,** promenade des Planches (✆ **02-31-14-48-10**), an indoor freshwater pool that gets very crowded in summer. Depending on the season, bathers pay 6€ to 7€ per person.

Hours are July and August daily 9:30am to 7:30pm, June and September daily 10am to 7pm, and October to May daily 10:30am to 7pm.

Shopping

Trouville's main shopping streets are **quai Fernand-Moureaux** and **rue des Bains** (some sections of which are off-limits to conventional traffic). The **rue du Général-de-Gaulle** has a greater concentration of everyday shops such as food outlets and hardware stores. The rue des Bains has its share of boutiques and clothing stores, but stylish shops are more numerous in neighboring Deauville.

Where to Stay

Best Western Hostellerie du Vallon ★   The best place to stay in town is this modern hotel constructed in a traditional Norman style. Lying a short walk from the beach, the hotel is far more affordable than so many of the properties at neighboring Deauville. Well run and spacious, it boasts a modern interior with such facilities as an indoor swimming pool, which makes it a good year-round choice. Many of the attractively and comfortably furnished bedrooms open onto private balconies with a view. There are several public lounges but no restaurant. However, many good bistros lie nearby, specializing in seafood.

12 rue Sylvestre Lassere, 14360 Trouville. ✆ **02-31-98-35-00.** www.hostellerie-du-vallon.com. 62 units. 120€–180€ double; 200€–260€ junior suite. AE, DC, MC, V. **Amenities:** Bar; exercise room; indoor pool; Jacuzzi; sauna; steam room. *In room:* TV, hair dryer, minibar.

Le Beach Hotel   Although a poor relation to the palaces of Deauville, Le Beach Hotel provides comfort at more affordable prices. The seven-story hotel, constructed in 1984, emerges from a lackluster lot only 45m (148 ft.) from the beach. Its average-size rooms have modern furniture and comfortable beds, plus views of Trouville harbor; most bathrooms have showers only.

1 quai Albert-1er, Trouville 14360. ✆ **02-31-98-12-00.** Fax 02-31-87-30-29. 110 units. 99€–220€ double. AE, DC, MC, V. Parking 8.50€. **Amenities:** Restaurant; bar; babysitting; indoor pool; room service. *In room:* TV, minibar, Wi-Fi (free).

Where to Dine

La Petite Auberge NORMAN   For a quality meal, head to this Norman bistro a block from the casino. Try cream of cauliflower soup with scallops or a *pot-au-feu Dieppoise* featuring filet of sole, scallops, monkfish, and salmon beautifully simmered together. You can also order grilled beef and chicken thighs braised in cider. Because the bistro seats only 30, reservations are vital in summer.

7 rue Carnot. ✆ **02-31-88-11-07.** Reservations required. Main courses 22€–29€; fixed-price menu 33€–52€. MC, V. Thurs-Mon noon-2:30pm and 7:15-9:30pm.

Les Vapeurs ★★ FRENCH/SEAFOOD   This Art Deco brasserie, one of the most popular on the Norman coast, is frequented by stylish Parisians on *le weekend*. Established in 1926, it has been called the Brasserie Lipp of Normandy. The windows face the port, and in warm weather you can dine at sidewalk tables. Seafood—a wide range of shrimp, mussels laced with cream, crinkle-shelled oysters, and fish—is the specialty. Sauerkraut is also popular.

162 bd. Fernand-Moureaux. ✆ **02-31-88-15-24.** www.lesvapeurs.fr. Reservations recommended. Main courses 14€–33€. AE, MC, V. Mon-Fri noon-10:30pm; Sat-Sun noon-12:30am.

Trouville After Dark

If the casino in Deauville is too stuffy for you, you'll feel more comfortable in its smaller, less architecturally distinctive sibling in Trouville, **Casino Barrière de Trouville,** place du Maréchal-Foch (© **02-31-87-75-00;** www.lucienbarriere.com). It has more of a New Orleans–style environment, with a blues and jazz bar that schedules live music Friday and Saturday night, and a small-scale replica of Bourbon Street. Entrance to the slot machines is free. Entrance to the more formal area—with roulette, black-jack, and craps—costs 14€ per person. You must present a passport or identity card to gain admission. The formal area is open Sunday through Thursday 8pm to 2am, Friday 8pm to 3am, and Saturday 8pm to 4am. The rest of the casino is open daily from 10am. Men aren't required to wear jackets and ties, but tennis shoes are not allowed.

CAEN ★★★

238km (148 miles) NW of Paris; 119km (74 miles) SE of Cherbourg

Situated on the banks of the Orne, the port of Caen suffered great damage in the 1944 invasion of Normandy. Nearly three-quarters of its buildings, 10,000 in all, were destroyed, though the twin abbeys founded by William the Conqueror and his wife, Mathilda, were spared. The city today is essentially modern and has many broad avenues and new apartment buildings. Completely different from Deauville and Trouville, the capital of Lower Normandy is bustling, congested, and commercial; it's a major rail and ferry junction. The student population of 30,000 and the hordes of travelers have made Caen more cosmopolitan than ever.

Essentials

GETTING THERE　From Paris's Gare St-Lazare, 12 **trains** per day arrive in Caen (trip time: 1 hr., 50 min.–2½ hr.). One-way fares start at 32€ to 47€. One-way fares from Rouen (trip time: 1 hr., 45 min.) start at 23€. To **drive** from Paris, travel west along A13 to Caen (driving time: 2½–3 hr.).

VISITOR INFORMATION　The **Office de Tourisme** is on place St-Pierre in the 16th-century Hôtel d'Escoville (© **02-31-27-14-14;** www.tourisme.caen.fr).

Exploring the City

Abbaye aux Dames　Founded by Mathilda, wife of William the Conqueror, this abbey embraces Eglise de la Trinité, which is flanked by Romanesque towers. Its spires were destroyed in the Hundred Years' War. The 12th-century choir houses the tomb of Queen Mathilda; note the ribbed vaulting.

Place de la Reine-Mathilde. © **02-31-06-98-98.** Free admission. Daily 2–5:30pm. Free guided 1-hr. tour of choir, transept, and crypt (in French) daily 2:30 and 4pm.

Abbaye aux Hommes ★★　Founded by William and Mathilda, this abbey is adjacent to the Eglise St-Etienne, which you enter on place Monseigneur-des-Hameaux. During the height of the Allied invasion, residents of Caen flocked to St-Etienne for protection. Twin Romanesque towers 84m (276 ft.) tall dominate the church; they helped earn Caen the appellation "city of spires." A marble slab inside the high altar marks the site of William's tomb. The Huguenots destroyed the tomb in 1562—only a hipbone was recovered. During the French Revolution, the last of

William's dust was scattered to the wind. The hand-carved wooden doors and elaborate wrought-iron staircase are exceptional. From the cloisters you get a good view of the two towers of St-Etienne.

Esplanade Jean-Marie-Louvel. © **02-31-30-42-81.** Obligatory tours (in French, accompanied by broken-English translation) 2.40€ adults, 1.20€ students, free for children 17 and under. Daily 8:30am–12:30pm and 1:30–7:30pm (2:30–7:30pm Sun). Tours daily 9:30am, 11am, 2:30pm, and 4pm. Ticket office for tours daily 8am–4pm.

Le Château de Caen   This complex was built on the ruins of a fortress erected by William the Conqueror in 1060. Enter the grounds at esplanade de la Paix. The gardens are ideal for strolling and, from the ramparts, a panoramic view of Caen unfolds. Within the compound are two museums. The **Musée de Normandie** (© 02-31-30-47-60; www.musee-de-normandie.caen.fr) displays artifacts from Normandy, including archaeological finds, along with a collection of regional sculpture, paintings, and ceramics. Admission is free, and it's open Wednesday to Monday 9:30am to 6pm. Also within the walls is the **Musée des Beaux-Arts** (© 02-31-30-47-70; www.ville-caen.fr/mba), with a collection of works—though not their finest—by old masters including Veronese and Rubens. Admission is free except for temporary exhibits costing 3€ to 5€. It's open Wednesday through Monday from 9:30am to 6pm.

Le Mémorial de Caen (Caen Memorial)   The memorial is a 15-minute drive away from the Pegasus Bridge and 15 minutes from the landing beaches. The museum presents a journey through history from 1918 to the present. It's an ideal place to relax. You can walk through International Park, have a meal or drink at the restaurant, or browse through the boutique. Expect to spend at least 2½ hours at this site—anyone intrigued by 20th-century European history will be fascinated. One wing is dedicated to a depiction of the American and global role after World War II. Its photo documentaries and exhibits illustrate the Cold War, the construction and collapse of the Berlin Wall, and the assault of military weapons (especially nuclear testing) on the environment.

 AN excursion TO THE FORBES CHÂTEAU

Built by François Mansart between 1626 and 1636, the **Château de Balleroy ★**, between Bayeux and Caen, has been owned by the Forbes family for more than 3 decades. The late Malcolm Forbes was an internationally known balloonist, and his dream of opening the world's first balloon museum has been fulfilled at the château. Today it is the venue for the biannual international ballooning festival.

The museum, in a converted stable, is filled with artifacts related to the history of ballooning. The château also contains many period rooms that abound with elegant art and antiques. Admission to the museum and castle is 8€ for adults or 6€ for students and children 7 to 18, and free for those 6 and under; entrance to just the grounds costs 3€ for everyone. Visiting times are from mid-March to mid-October Wednesday to Monday 10am to noon and 2 to 6pm (July–August hours are 10am–6pm).

The museum (© **02-31-21-60-61;** www.chateau-balleroy.com) lies at F-14490 Balleroy outside the village of Balleroy. To reach it from Caen (40km/25 miles), head west along N13, cutting south at the junction with D572, and follow the road to Balleroy, where the château is signposted.

Esplanade Général Dwight-Eisenhower. ℂ **02-31-06-06-45.** www.memorial-caen.fr. Admission Apr–Sept 18€ adults, 15€ students and children 10–18; Oct–Mar 17€ adults, 14€ students and children 10–18; free to World War II veterans, those with war disabilities, war widows, and children 9 and under. Daily 9am–7pm (until 8pm mid-July to mid-Aug). Closed Jan 4–26.

Shopping

Caen has some good boutique-lined shopping streets, including **boulevard du Maréchal-Leclerc, rue St-Pierre,** and **rue de Strasbourg. Antiques** hunters should check out the shops along rue Ecuyère and rue Commerçantes, and the antiques show at the **Parc des Expositions,** rue Joseph-Philippon (ℂ **02-31-29-99-99**), in early May. The **markets** at place St-Sauveur on Friday morning and place Courtonne on Sunday morning also sell secondhand articles.

For custom-built reproduction antique furniture, visit **La Reine Matilde,** 47 rue St-Jean (ℂ **02-31-85-45-52**); it also sells decorative items, including a selection of bed linens and curtains. **Le Chocolaterie Hotot,** 13 rue St-Pierre (ℂ **02-31-86-31-90**), has a cornucopia of chocolate products as well as local jams and jellies. At **Le Comptoir Normand,** 7 rue de Geôle (ℂ **02-31-86-34-13**), you'll find many regional items, including Calvados and various charcuterie products such as tripe in the style of Caen.

For objets d'art and paintings, check out **L'Atelier,** 33 rue Montoir-Poissonnerie (ℂ **02-31-44-49-38**), which showcases the work of local painters. To browse through inventories of wine and *eaux-de-vie* from throughout France, head for **Nicolas,** 10 rue Bellivet (ℂ **02-31-85-24-19**).

Where to Stay

Le Manoir d'Hastings (see p. 308) also rents rooms.

Holiday Inn Caen City Centre ★ This is the best hotel in town, with a flavor that's both French and international. Across from the racecourse, the hotel predates World War II. It was enlarged and modernized in 2008. Rooms are predictable, comfortable, and well maintained. Americans visiting the D-day beaches favor the cozy bar.

Place du Maréchal-Foch, Caen 14000. ℂ **800/465-4329** in the U.S., or 02-31-27-57-57. Fax 02-31-27-57-58. www.holiday-inn.com. 88 units. 115€–165€ double. AE, DC, MC, V. **Amenities:** Restaurant; bar; babysitting; room service. *In room:* A/C (in some), TV, hair dryer, minibar, Wi-Fi (free).

Hôtel de France The exterior of this 1950s brick building is plain, but windows that open to flower boxes add a bit of charm. Rooms are functional, with modern furnishings; each has a small bathroom with shower or tub. The public areas have a provincial charm. This hotel is a favorite with tour groups.

10 rue de la Gare, Caen 14000. ℂ **02-31-52-16-99.** Fax 02-31-83-23-16. 47 units. 64€–83€ double. AE, MC, V. Free parking. *In room:* A/C, TV, Wi-Fi (free).

Hôtel des Quatrans 🍴 This agreeable, unpretentious hotel was rebuilt after World War II, and thanks to continual renovations, it's one of Caen's best bargains. Don't expect luxury: The hotel has four floors of old-fashioned rooms that offer basic amenities, including small, shower-only bathrooms. A buffet breakfast, available in the breakfast room or delivered to your room, is the only meal served.

17 rue Gémare, Caen 14300. ℂ **02-31-86-25-57.** Fax 02-31-85-27-80. www.hotel-des-quatrans.com. 47 units. 65€ double; 75€ triple. MC, V. Parking free. **Amenities:** Restaurant; bar. *In room:* TV, hair dryer, Wi-Fi (free).

Hôtel Kyriad This hotel is a reliable bargain. The original was destroyed during a World War II bombing raid. Rebuilt several years later, it's surrounded by a commercial area of shops and restaurants as well as more tranquil pedestrian streets. Massively renovated after it joined the Kyriad chain, the hotel provides bedrooms in attractive color schemes such as soft yellows and reds. There's no restaurant, but an independent grill-style restaurant across the street offers inexpensive breakfast plans for hotel guests.

1 place de la République, Caen 14000. (✆) **02-31-86-55-33.** Fax 02-31-79-89-44. 47 units. 57€–90€ double. AE, MC, V. Parking 7€. **Amenities:** Bar. *In room:* A/C, TV, hair dryer, Wi-Fi (free).

A NEARBY LODGING CHOICE

Château d'Audrieu ★★ This château in a park offers the most luxurious accommodations near Caen. It was built of local stone (*pierre de Caen*) at the beginning of the 18th century. During the invasion, some of the fiercest fighting took place around it. Notice the gashes in the trees in the park. The château functioned as a private home until 1976, when it became a hotel. Rooms are lovely and well appointed with antiques. Beds have tasteful linens.

Audrieu 14250. (✆) **02-31-80-21-52.** Fax 02-31-80-24-73. www.chateaudaudrieu.com. 29 units. 155€– 454€ double; 380€–491€ suite. AE, DC, MC, V. Closed Dec 7–Feb 7. From Caen, take N13 west for 18km (11 miles), and then D158 for 3km (1¾ miles) to Audrieu. **Amenities:** Restaurant; bar; babysitting; Internet; outdoor heated pool; room service. *In room:* TV, hair dryer, minibar, Wi-Fi (free).

Where to Dine

Le Carlotta FRENCH/SEAFOOD This is a well-established brasserie, one of the best known in town, with a high-volume turnover and a penchant for seafood. Within a decor inspired by the Art Deco movement of the 1920s, you'll find yourself in a bustling, sometimes animated venue where tried-and-true menu items include platters of shellfish, especially oysters; snails in garlic-flavored butter sauce; filets of cod with stewed hearts of artichokes; strips of duck breast with parsley sauce; braised oxtail with truffles and mashed potatoes; filet of haddock with lemon-flavored butter sauce; and roasted shoulder of lamb *en confit*, served with Middle Eastern spices and mashed potatoes. Desserts usually include a homemade version of tiramisu and a gratin of seasonal berries.

16 quai Vendeuvre. (✆) **02-31-86-68-99.** www.lecarlotta.fr. Reservations recommended. Main courses 18€–28€; set menus 23€–36€. AE, MC, V. Mon–Sat noon–2pm and 6–10:30pm.

Le p'tit B 🍴 FRENCH/NORMAN A growing number of local diners are enthusiastic about this place, which is set in a 17th-century house in the center of town. Its fixed-price menu, with loads of good choices, is a great deal. You might begin with *terrine maison* or a slice of Norman-style Camembert tart, followed by a seafood brochette, and ending with chocolate mousse.

15 rue de Vaugueux. (✆) **02-31-93-50-76.** Reservations recommended. Main courses 14€–18€; fixed-price lunch 15€; fixed-price dinner 28€. AE, DC, MC, V. Daily noon–2:30pm and 7pm–midnight.

A NEARBY DINING CHOICE

Le Manoir d'Hastings ★★ FRENCH/NORMAN This restaurant, 6.5km (4 miles) north of Caen, occupies a 17th-century monastery with an enclosed Norman garden. It's one of Normandy's most famous and charming inns, and a magnet for Parisians seeking a rustically elegant getaway. Many dishes are twists on Norman

A Proustian Remembrance of "Balbec"

Torn from the pages of Marcel Proust's *Remembrance of Things Past*, the resort of "Balbec" was really Cabourg, 24km (15 miles) northeast of Caen. Fans still come to this Second Empire resort, much of which looks as it did in the Belle Epoque. Guests can check into the 1907 **Grand Hotel,** promenade Marcel Proust, 14390 Cabourg (℡ 02-31- 91-01-79; fax 02-31-24-03-20; www. mercure.com), a holdover from the opulent days of the 19th century and now part of the Mercure chain. One room, La Chambre Marcel Proust, has been restored from a description in *Remembrance.* A double costs from 158€ to 360€, with a suite going for 425€ to 625€.

favorites, such as cider-cooked lobster with Nantua sauce, delicately flavored sea bass, and filet of monkfish poached in port. Beef filets are stuffed with foie gras, scallops are braised in the local apple-based liqueur *pommeau,* and filets of turbot and sea bass are served on the same platter and drenched in champagne sauce. For dessert, try *tarte Normande* flambéed with Calvados.

The manor also offers 15 rooms in a stone-sided annex. Each has a garden view, bathroom with tub, TV, minibar, and phone. A double goes for 90€ to 115€. The hotel lies very close to Pegasus Bridge, one of the first strategic targets liberated by Allied soldiers after the invasion of Normandy in 1944.

Av. Côte-de-Nacre, Bénouville 14970. ℡ **02-31-44-62-43.** Fax 02-31-44-76-18. www.manoirhastings. com. Reservations required. Main courses 25€–35€; fixed-price lunch (Tues–Fri only) 23€–35€; fixed- price dinner 48€. AE, DC, MC, V. Tues–Sun noon–2pm; Tues–Sat 7–9:30pm. From Caen, follow signs north for Ouistreham and turn onto RD35. Stay on this road for 10km (6¼ miles), following signs to Bayeux and Bénouville; the manor is next to the village church.

Caen After Dark

Take a walk down rue de Bras, rue St-Pierre, and the north end of rue Vaugueux to size up the action. If you want to connect with the hip 18-to-35 crowd, go to **Le Chic,** rue des Prairies St-Gilles (℡ **02-31-94-48-72**), where disco music begins at 10:30pm. **Le Carré,** 32 quai Vendeuvre (℡ **02-31-38-90-90**), is a disco that caters to patrons over 27 with rock 'n' roll, cutting-edge techno, and a goodly assortment of music from the '70s and '80s. Upstairs, there's the hip and often charming Bar de Nuit.

Intensely connected to the hip and trendy night-soul of Caen is an Irish-style pub, **O'Donnell's,** 20 quai Vendeuvre (℡ **02-31-85-51-50**). It's the site of televised European soccer matches and live Irish rock-'n'-roll shows. The live music is every Friday night; otherwise, a DJ rules the night. It's open Monday through Wednesday 4:30pm to 2:30am, Thursday through Saturday 4:30pm to 4am, and Sunday 4:30pm to midnight.

BAYEUX ★★

267km (166 miles) NW of Paris; 25km (16 miles) NW of Caen

The *ducs de Normandie* sent their sons to this Viking settlement to learn the Norse language. Bayeux has changed a lot since then, but was spared from bombardment in 1944. This was the first French town liberated, and the citizens gave de Gaulle an enthusiastic welcome when he arrived on June 14. The town is filled with timbered houses, stone mansions, and cobblestone streets.

Visitors wanting to explore sites associated with "the Longest Day" flood the town, because many memorials (not to mention the beaches) are only 9.5 to 19km (6–12 miles) away. Shops line the cozy little streets. Many sell World War II memorabilia, and more postcards and T-shirts than you'll ever need.

Essentials

GETTING THERE Twelve **trains** depart daily from Paris's Gare St-Lazare. The 2½-hour trip to Bayeux costs 35€. Most trains stop in Caen. Travel time between Caen and Bayeux is about 20 minutes and costs 5.80€. To **drive** to Bayeux from Paris (trip time: 3 hr.), take A13 to Caen and E46 west to Bayeux.

VISITOR INFORMATION The **Office de Tourisme** is at pont St-Jean (✆ 02-31-51-28-28; www.bayeux-bessin-tourism.com).

SPECIAL EVENTS The town goes wild on the first weekend in July during **Fêtes Médiévales;** the streets fill with wine and song during 2 days of medieval revelry. For information, call ✆ 02-31-92-03-30.

Seeing the Sights

Musée de la Tapisserie de Bayeux ★★★ The most famous tapestry in the world is actually an embroidery on linen, 69m (226 ft.) long and .5m (20 in.) wide, depicting 58 scenes in eight colors. Contrary to legend, it wasn't made by Queen Mathilda, the wife of William the Conqueror, but was probably commissioned in Kent and created by unknown embroiderers between 1066 and 1077. The first mention of the embroidery was in 1476, when it decorated the nave of the Cathédrale Notre-Dame de Bayeux.

Housed in a Plexiglas case, the embroidery tells the story of the conquest of England by William the Conqueror, including such scenes as the coronation of Harold as the Saxon king of England, Harold returning from his journey to Normandy, the surrender of Dinan, Harold being told of the apparition of a comet (a portent of misfortune), William dressed for war, and the death of Harold. The decorative borders include scenes from *Aesop's Fables*.

Admission to the museum includes access to an annex whose collections are not as spectacular. The **Collections Baron Gérard** is housed in **Le Musée de l'Hôtel du Doyen,** 6 rue Lambert le Forestier (✆ 02-31-92-14-21). Exhibitions feature examples of regional lacework, porcelain, and religious and secular paintings, many of them created within this region.

Centre Guillaume-le-Conquérant, 13 rue de Nesmond. ✆ **02-31-51-25-50.** www.tapisserie-bayeux.fr. Admission 7.80€ adults, 3.80€ students, free for children 9 and under. Mar 15–Nov 15 daily 9am–6:30pm; off season daily 9:30am–12:30pm and 2–6pm.

Musée Memorial de la Bataille de Normandie This museum deals with the military and human history of the Battle of Normandy (June 6–Aug 22, 1944). In a low-slung building designed like a bunker are 132m (433 ft.) of window and film displays, plus a diorama. Wax soldiers in uniform, along with the tanks and guns used to win the battle, are on exhibit. Across from the museum, the **Commonwealth Cemetery** (✆ 03-21-21-77-00) lies on the northwestern perimeter of

Bayeux, containing 4,144 graves of soldiers from throughout the British Commonwealth, all of them killed during the Battle of Normandy.

Bd. Fabian Ware. ✆ **02-31-51-46-90.** Admission 6.50€ adults, 3.80€ students and children, free for children 9 and under. May–Sept 15 daily 9:30am–6:30pm; Sept 16–Apr daily 10am–12:30pm and 2–6pm.

Notre-Dame de Bayeux ★★   This cathedral was consecrated in 1077 and partially destroyed in 1105. Romanesque towers from the original church rise on the western side. The central tower is from the 15th century. The nave is a fine example of Norman Romanesque style. The 13th-century choir, a perfect example of Norman Gothic style, is rich in sculpture and has Renaissance stalls. The crypt was built in the 11th century and then sealed, its existence unknown until 1412.

Rue du Bienvenu. ✆ **02-31-92-14-21.** Admission 4€, free ages 14 and under. Daily 8:30am–6pm (to 7pm July–Aug).

Where to Stay

Best Western Grand Hôtel de Luxembourg ★   After Le Lion d'Or (see below), this Best Western is the area's finest hotel. The restored interior has terrazzo floors; the decor combines neoclassical and Art Deco design. Rooms range in size from small to medium and have been overhauled with an eye to modern comfort, including fine bed linens. All units come with small bathrooms with showers, and more than half also have tubs.

25 rue des Bouchers, Bayeux 14400. ✆ **800/528-1234** in the U.S. and Canada, or 02-31-92-00-04. Fax 02-31-92-54-26. www.hotel-luxembourg-bayeux.com. 27 units. 80€–125€ double; 115€–180€ suite. AE, MC, V. Parking 9€. **Amenities:** Restaurant; bar; room service. *In room:* TV, Wi-Fi (free).

Churchill ★ ✦   Open from March to November, this renovated hotel lies in the heart of the medieval town, close to the famous tapestry and the cathedral. Excursions for the D-day beaches leave from the square behind the hotel, and a shuttle to Mont-St-Michel can also be arranged. The staff, headed by Rima and François Hebert, are among the most accommodating in town. Their midsize bedrooms are personalized, each comfortably furnished on an individual basis. Of course, their deluxe rooms are the way to go, unless you're economizing, in which case you'll find their standard units most adequate.

14 rue St-Jean, 14400 Bayeux. ✆ **02-31-21-31-80.** www.hotel-churchill.fr. 32 units. 100€–110€ standard double, 150€–160€ deluxe double. MC, V. **Amenities:** Deli; Internet (free). *In room:* TV, hair dryer.

Hôtel d'Argouges   This much-improved hotel underwent major renovations in 2007. Now a government-rated three-star hotel, it's even more comfortable than it was before. It consists of a pair of 18th-century town houses, set across a garden from one another, with exposed beams, thick walls, and sloping ceilings. Rooms are comfortable, intimate, and cozy, with old-fashioned furniture and modern conveniences. Breakfast is the only meal served, but at least three restaurants are within a 2-minute walk. In good weather, you can wander in the garden.

21 rue St-Patrice, Bayeux 14402. ✆ **02-31-92-88-86.** Fax 02-31-92-69-16. www.hotel-dargouges.com. 28 units. 70€–121€ double; 150€–285€ suite. MC, V. Parking 5€. **Amenities:** Babysitting; room service; bar. *In room:* TV, hair dryer, Internet (free).

Le Lion d'Or ★★★   This old-world hotel, originally built in 1734, is the oldest and most nostalgic in town, dating from 1928. It has an open courtyard with lush flower boxes decorating the facade. As befits an old inn, rooms come in various shapes and sizes. The midsize bathrooms are well equipped; each has a shower and more than half have tubs. Guests are required to take at least one meal here, but that shouldn't be a problem—the traditional cuisine is delicious. The restaurant serves lots of reasonably priced wines.

71 rue St-Jean, Bayeux 14400. ℰ **02-31-92-06-90.** Fax 02-31-22-15-64. www.liondor-bayeux.fr. 28 units. 115€–185€ double. AE, DC, MC, V. Parking 8€. **Amenities:** Restaurant; bar; babysitting; exercise room. *In room:* TV, minibar, Wi-Fi (free).

Where to Dine

Le Pommier ★ 🍴 NORMAN   One of the most appealing restaurants in Bayeux's historic zone occupies an 18th-century building. Ceiling beams, stone ceiling vaults, and exposed masonry enhance the trio of dining rooms. The establishment is devotedly Norman, with cuisine that reflects the region's long tradition of baking with apples (the name translates as "the apple tree") and cream (though its use is limited to make the food a bit healthier). The health-conscious staff is proud that the dishes "aren't drowned in gravies and sauces." Menu items evolve with the seasons. You can usually expect dishes such as foie gras of duckling; rabbit stew braised in cider; and a platter that contains two kinds of fish served with chitterling sausage and a sauce of cream and chitterling drippings.

38 rue des Cuisiniers. ℰ **02-31-21-52-10.** Fax 02-31-21-06-01. www.restaurantlepommier.com. Reservations recommended. Main courses 16€–22€; fixed-price menus 23€–36€. AE, MC, V. Apr–Sept daily noon–2:30pm and 7–9:30pm; Oct–Mar Mon–Sat noon–2pm and 7–9:30pm. Closed mid-Dec to mid-Jan.

THE D-DAY BEACHES ★★

Arromanches-les-Bains: 272km (169 miles) NW of Paris, 11km (6¾ miles) NW of Bayeux; Grandcamp-Maisy (near Omaha Beach): 299km (186 miles) NW of Paris, 56km (35 miles) NW of Caen

During a rainy week in June 1944, the greatest armada ever—soldiers and sailors, warships, landing craft, tugboats, jeeps—assembled along the southern coast of England. At 9:15pm on June 5, the BBC announced to the French Resistance that the invasion was imminent, signaling the underground to start dynamiting the railways. Before midnight, Allied planes began bombing the Norman coast. By 1:30am on June 6 ("the Longest Day"), members of the 101st Airborne were parachuting to the ground on German-occupied French soil. At 6:30am, the Americans began landing on the beaches, code-named Utah and Omaha. An hour later, British and Canadian forces made beachheads at Juno, Gold, and Sword.

The Nazis had mocked Churchill's promise in 1943 to liberate France "before the fall of the autumn leaves." When the invasion did come, it was swift, sudden, and a surprise to the formidable "Atlantic wall." Today, veterans walk with their children and grandchildren across the beaches where "Czech hedgehogs," "Belgian grills," pillboxes, and "Rommel asparagus" (all military barriers or structures) once stood.

Essentials

GETTING THERE   The best way to get to the D-day beaches is to **drive.** Public transportation is unreliable. The trip takes about 3 hours from Paris. Take A13 west to Caen, and continue west along A13 to Bayeux. From Bayeux, travel north along D6 until you reach the coast at Port-en-Bessin. From here, D514 runs along the coastline; most D-day sites are west of Port-en-Bessin. Parking is not a problem, and most of the designated areas along the roadway are free. It's best to visit on a weekday, because weekends (especially in summer) can be crowded with tourists and sunbathers.

Bus service from Bayeux is uneven and usually involves long delays. **Bus Verts** (© 08-10-21-42-14; www.busverts.fr) runs to Port-en-Bessin and points west, and bus no. 75 offers service year-round to Arromanches and other points in the east. Bus no. 70 travels west (June–Sept only) from Bayeux toward Omaha Beach and the American cemetery.

If you don't have a car, the best way to see the D-day beaches is on a **tour. Normandy Tours,** Hotel de la Gare, Bayeux (© 02-31-92-10-70; www.normandy-landing-tours.com), runs a 4- to 5-hour tour (in English) to Arromanches, Omaha Beach, the American Military Cemetery, and Pointe du Hoc for 48€ adults and 40€ students and seniors. **D-Day Tours,** 52 rte. de Porte en Bessin, Bayeux (© 02-31-51-70-52; www.normandywebguide.com), conducts tours with a bit more pizazz and guides who speak better English. A half-day trip costs 45€ for adults and 40€ for students; a full-day trip is 75€ for adults and 65€ for students. The company picks you up at your hotel in Bayeux. A final option, **Battlebus** (© 02-31-22-28-82; www.battlebus.fr), leads a full-day tour encompassing all sites and beaches that were pivotal during the D-day landing and Battle of Normandy; cost is 85€ per person. Most participants have found this latter option the best tour of all—simultaneously riveting, exhausting, and stimulating.

VISITOR INFORMATION The **Office de Tourisme,** 4 rue du Maréchal-Joffre, Arromanches-les-Bains (© 02-31-21-47-56), is open year-round.

Reliving the Longest Day

Start your exploration at the seaside resort of **Arromanches-les-Bains.** In June 1944, this was a fishing port until the 50th British Division took it. A mammoth prefabricated port known as Winston was towed across the Channel and installed to supply the Allied forces. "Victory could not have been achieved without it," Eisenhower said. The wreckage of that artificial harbor is just off the beach, **Plage du Débarquement. Musée du Débarquement,** place du 6-Juin (© 02-31-22-34-31; www.normandy1944.com), in Arromanches, features maps, models, a cinema, photographs, and a diorama of the landing, all with English commentary. Admission is 6.50€ for adults and 4.50€ for students and children. From June to August, hours are daily 9am to 7pm; September Monday to Saturday 9am to 6pm, Sunday 10am to 6pm; October and March daily 9:30am to 12:30pm and 1:30 to 5:30pm; November

---

Americans Return to Normandy

Sixty-three years after the D-day landings, in 2007 the **Normandy American Visitor Center** opened at 14710 Colleville-sur-Mer (© 02-31-51-62-00; www.abmc.gov), in the vicinity of Caen. The center, dedicated to those heroes of World War II who liberated mainland France from the Nazis, tells the story of the 9,387 Americans buried on French soil. The center relates that dramatic story through narrative text, photos, films, interactive displays, and artifacts. Admission is free. The center is open April 15 through September 15 daily 9am to 6pm, and off season daily 9am to 5pm.

to December and February daily 10am to 12:30pm and 1:30 to 5pm; April Monday to Saturday 9am to 12:30pm and 1:30 to 6pm, Sunday 10am to 12:30pm and 1:30 to 6pm; and May Monday to Saturday 9am to 7pm, Sunday 10am to 7pm. It's closed December 24 to December 26, December 31, and the month of January.

Moving along the coast, you'll arrive at **Omaha Beach,** where you can still see the war wreckage. "Hanging on by their toenails," the men of the 1st and 29th American Divisions occupied the beach that June day. The code name Omaha became famous; until then the beaches had been called St-Laurent, Vierville-sur-Mer, and Colleville. A monument commemorates the heroism of the invaders. Covering some 70 hectares (173 acres) at Omaha Beach, the **Normandy American Cemetery** (✆ 02-31-51-62-00; www.abmc.gov) is filled with crosses and Stars of David in Lasa marble. The remains of 9,387 American military were buried here on territory now owned by the United States, a gift from the French nation. Admission is free. The cemetery is open daily 9am to 5pm, the visitor center until 6pm (both are closed Dec 25 and Jan 1).

Farther along the coast you'll see the jagged lime cliffs of the **Pointe du Hoc.** A cross honors a group of American Rangers, led by Lt. Col. James Rudder, who scaled the cliffs using hooks to get at the pillboxes (gun emplacements). The scars of war are more visible here than at any other point along the beach. Farther along the Cotentin Peninsula is **Utah Beach,** where the 4th U.S. Infantry Division landed at 6:30am. The landing force was nearly 3km (1¾ miles) south of its intended destination, but Nazi defenses were weak. By midday the infantry had completely cleared the beach. A U.S. monument commemorates their heroism.

Nearby, you can visit the hamlet of **Ste-Mère-Eglise,** which was virtually unknown outside of France before paratroopers dropped from the sky. In Ste-Mère-Eglise is Kilometer "0" on the Liberty Highway, marking the first of the milestones the American armies reached on their way to Metz and Bastogne.

reliving THE ALLIED INVASION OF NORMANDY

One of the most evocative ways to re-create the sensations that the combat troops felt just prior to their invasion of Normandy involves signing up for a waterborne tour. Maintained by **Les Vedettes de Normandie,** and entitled "Balades sur les plages du Débarquement," the tour offers prerecorded English-language commentary on a cassette player, live commentary from a French-language guide, and boats with a capacity of 200 sightseers at a time. Commentary focuses on the physicality of the Norman coastline; the region's construction, shipping, and fishing industries; and the historic events associated with the invasion of Normandy by Allied troops in 1944.

Between mid-April and mid-October, boats depart between one and three times a day, with a schedule that varies with the tides, the season, the day of the week, and French national holidays. All tours depart from the harborfront quays of the hamlet of Port-en-Bessin. Tours lasting 90 minutes each, and which cost 15€ per participant, focus on either Arromanches or Omaha beaches. Lasting 3 hours, tours at 23€ focus on Omaha Beach and the Pointe du Hoc. There's no discount for children. For information about departure times and reservations, contact *Les Vedettes de Normandie,* Ste. H.C., bd. De Général de Gaulle Point de Cabourg, 14160 Dives-sur-Mer (✆ **02-31-43-86-12**).

Where To Stay & Dine at Grandcamp-Maisy

Hôtel Duguesclin TRADITIONAL FRENCH We recommend this Norman inn for lunch or even an overnight stay. The fish soup, grilled scallops, Norman sole (when it's available), and grilled turbot with white butter are excellent. Everything tastes better with the dining room's country bread and Norman butter.

The hotel rents 23 simple, comfortable rooms, all with bathroom, phone, and TV. Accommodations have a shower or tub (sometimes both). A double costs 45€ to 66€.

4 quai Crampon, Grandcamp-Maisy 14450. (✆) **02-31-22-64-22.** Fax 02-31-22-34-79. Reservations recommended. Main courses 12€–32€; fixed-price menu 13€–32€. AE, MC, V. Daily noon–2pm and 7–9pm.

La Marée NORMAN Set beside the port, this small, nautically decorated restaurant serves mostly fish and only fish caught in the English Channel or within a reasonable distance out in the Atlantic, guaranteeing a local culinary experience. During nice weather, the dining room expands onto a terrace.

5 quai Henri Chéron. (✆) **02-31-21-41-00.** Reservations required. Main courses 18€–22€; fixed-price menus 14€–25€. AE, MC, V. Daily 12:30–2:30pm and 7–9:30pm. Closed Jan 1–Feb 7.

Where to Stay at Arromanches

Hôtel de la Marine A hotel has stood on this spot since 1837, although the one you see today wins over any of its earlier incarnations when it comes to comfort and style. The hotel directly faces the beach that played a keynote role during the U.S. invasion of Normandy and offers many of the charming details of a Norman private country estate. Bedrooms are rustically outfitted with colorful fabrics and solid, traditional furnishings. The restaurant appeals even to nonguests. It's open daily noon to 2pm and 7 to 9:30pm, and serves set price, thoroughly French meals priced at 22€ to 35€ each.

1 quai du Canada, Arromanches les Bains 14117. (✆) **02-31-22-34-19.** Fax 02-31-22-98-80. www.hotel-de-la-marine.fr. 33 units. 72€–172€ double. Rates include breakfast and dinner. AE, MC, V. Free parking. **Amenities:** Restaurant; bar. *In room:* A/C, TV, hair dryer, Wi-Fi (free).

MONT-ST-MICHEL ★★★

324km (201 miles) W of Paris; 129km (80 miles) SW of Caen; 76km (47 miles) E of Dinan; 48km (30 miles) E of St-Malo

Massive walls measuring more than half a mile in circumference surround one of Europe's great attractions, the island of Mont-St-Michel. Connected to the shore by a causeway, it crowns a rocky islet at the border between Normandy and Brittany. The rock is 78m (256 ft.) high.

Essentials

GETTING THERE The most efficient way to reach Mont-St-Michel is to **drive.** From Caen, follow A84 southwest to Pontorson, continuing a few more kilometers to Avranches; from there, merge onto D43, following signs to its end at Mont-St-Michel. Total driving time from Paris is about 4½ hours.

There are no direct trains between Paris and Mont-St-Michel. We suggest taking the high-speed **TGV train** from Paris's Gare Montparnasse to Rennes, where you can transfer to the **bus** run by the **SNCF** (℃ **36-35** or 08-92-35-35-35; www.voyages-sncf.com) for the 75-minute trip to Mont-St-Michel. Depending on the season, two to five buses a day run to Rennes for 12€ per person. Another company, **Les Courriers Bretons** (℃ **02-99-19-70-70;** www.lescourriersbretons.fr), also operates buses that make the 75-minute ride to Mont-St-Michel from St-Malo two to five times a day for 13€ per person.

VISITOR INFORMATION   The **Office de Tourisme** is in the Corps de Garde des Bourgeois (the Old Guard Room of the Bourgeois), at the left of the town gates (℃ **02-33-60-14-30;** www.ot-montsaintmichel.com). The tourist office is open daily year-round except Christmas and New Year's.

Exploring Mont-St-Michel

You'll have a steep climb up Grande Rue, lined with 15th- and 16th-century houses, to reach the **abbey** (℃ **02-33-89-80-00;** www.monuments-nationaux.fr). Those who make it to the top can begin their exploration of the Marvel of the West. In the 8th century, St. Aubert, the bishop of Avranches, founded an oratory on this spot. A Benedictine monastery, founded in 966 by Richard I, replaced it. That burned in 1203. Philip Augustus financed the building of an abbey in the 13th century.

Ramparts encircle the church and a three-tiered ensemble of 13th-century buildings called **La Merveille** that rise to the pointed spire of the abbey church. This terraced complex is one of Europe's most important Gothic monuments, a citadel in which the concept of an independent France was nurtured during the darkest years of the English occupation of Aquitaine.

On the second terrace of La Merveille is one of Mont-St-Michel's largest and most beautiful rooms, a 13th-century hall known as the **Salle des Chevaliers.**

Crowning the mountain's summit is the **Eglise Abbatiale** (not to be confused with the parish church, Eglise St-Pierre, lower on the mountain). Begun in the 11th century, the abbey church consists of a Romanesque nave and transept, plus a choir in Flamboyant Gothic style. The rectangular refectory dates from 1212, and the cloisters with their columns of pink granite are from 1225.

The abbey is open daily May through September 9am to 7pm, and October to April 9:30am to 6pm. From June to September, it's also open Monday to Saturday 9pm to 1am (last entrance at midnight). Mass begins at 12:15pm Tuesday through Sunday. Entrance during daytime or nighttime tours includes a guided group tour, but you can also wander around on your own. Year-round, day or night visits, with or without the tour, cost 8.50€ for adults, 5€ for students and ages 18 to 25, and free for children 17 and under.

Guided tours in French depart at intervals of 30 to 45 minutes, depending on the season. There are usually two to four English-language tours per day. Everything is closed January 1, May 1, and December 25.

Archeoscope, chemin de la Ronde (℃ **02-33-89-01-85**), is a small theater that presents *L'Eau et La Lumière* (Water and Light), celebrating the legend and lore of Mont-St-Michel and its role as a preserver of French medieval nationalism. The 30-minute shows begin every 30 to 60 minutes between 9:30am and 5:30pm. An unusual diversion is the adjacent **Musée de la Mer,** Grande Rue (℃ **02-33-89-02-02**). It showcases marine crafts throughout history; the ecology of the local tidal flats; and illustrations of the French government's ongoing project intended to reactivate

Mont-St-Michel

Fontaine St-Aubert

Chapelle St-Aubert

Bois de l'Abbaye

Tour du Nord

La Merveille

Cloître *Réfectoire*

Logis Tiphaine

Eglise Abbatiale →

Tour Gabriel

Tour Boucle

Eglise St-Pierre

Musée Grevin

Tour Cholet

Archéoscope

Porte Echaugette

Grande Rue

Tour Basse

Porte de l'Avancée

Tour du Roi

Tour de l'Arcade

Tour de la Liberté

0   1/8 mile

0   100 meters

the tidal cleansing of the nearby marshes. **Musée Grevin (Musée Historique de Mont-St-Michel),** chemin de la Ronde (*©* **02-33-89-02-02**), traces the history of the abbey.

A museum that's worth a visit is the **Logis Tiphaine,** Grande Rue (*©* **02-33-89-02-02**), a 15th-century home originally under the control of the Duguesclin family, noted defenders of the fortress from English intrigue. In the building, next to the Eglise St-Pierre, you'll find furniture and accessories from that era, and a sense of pride at the fortress's durability as a bastion of all things French.

A combined ticket for all four of these attractions costs 16€ for adults and 13€ for students, 9€ ages 10 to 18. Free 9 and under. Other than the Archeoscope, whose hours are noted above, the museums are open daily from 9am to 5pm.

Where to Stay & Dine

Hôtel du Mouton-Blanc   Occupying a pair of buildings, parts of which date from the 14th century, this inn stands between the sea and the basilica and has accepted guests since the 1700s. Rooms are small but cozy. Eight are in a comfortable annex, where all units have small bathrooms with showers. The seven better-equipped units in the main building have bathrooms with both tubs and showers. A rustic Norman-style dining room sits on a terrace overlooking the sea. Popular dishes include succulent omelets with seafood, delectable mussels in white wine and garlic, and two marvelous versions of lamb—one roasted in its own juice, the other on a skewer.

Grande Rue, Mont-St-Michel 50116. © **02-33-60-14-08.** Fax 02-33-60-05-62. 15 units. 90€ double; 110€ suite. AE, MC, V. **Amenities:** Restaurant; bar. *In room:* TV.

La Mère Poulard NORMAN   This country inn is a shrine to those who revere the omelet that Annette Poulard created in 1888, when the hotel was founded. It's under the same ownership as the more rustic Les Terrasses Poulard (see below). Annette Poulard's secret has been passed on to the inn's operators: The beaten eggs are cooked over an oak fire in a long-handled copper skillet. The frothy mixture creates more of an open-fire soufflé than an omelet. Other specialties are *agneau du pré salé* (lamb raised on the saltwater marshes near the foundations of the abbey) and an array of fish, including lobster.

Grande Rue, Mont-St-Michel 50116. © **02-33-89-68-68.** Fax 02-33-89-68-69. www.mere-poulard.fr. Reservations recommended. Main courses 34€–42€; fixed-price lunch 55€–75€; fixed-price dinner 39€–85€. AE, DC, MC, V. Daily noon–10pm.

Les Terrasses Poulard   This inn consists of two village houses, one medieval, the other built in the 1800s. It's one of the best in town, with an English-speaking staff, cozy rooms, comfortable beds, and neatly maintained, shower-only bathrooms. The rates depend on the view: the main street, the village, or the medieval ramparts. The largest and most expensive rooms have fireplaces. The restaurant offers a sweeping view over the bay to accompany its seafood and regional Norman specialties.

Grande Rue, Mont-St-Michel 50116. © **02-33-89-02-02.** Fax 02-33-60-37-31. www.terrasses-poulard.com. 29 units. 125€–200€ double. AE, DC, MC, V. **Amenities:** Restaurant. *In room:* TV, minibar, Wi-Fi (free).

BRITTANY

In this ancient northwestern province, Bretons cling to their traditions. Deep in *l'Argoat* (the interior), many older folks live in stone farmhouses, as their grandparents did, and on special occasions the women wear starched-lace headdresses. The Breton language is spoken, but the Welsh and Cornish understand it better than the French. Sadly, it may die out altogether.

Nearly every village and hamlet has its own *pardon,* a religious festival that can attract thousands of pilgrims in traditional dress. The best known are on May 19 at Treguier (honoring St-Yves); on the second Sunday in July at Locronan (honoring St-Ronan); on July 26 at St-Anne-d'Auray (honoring the "mothers of Bretons"); and on September 8 at Le Folgoet (honoring *ar foll coat*—"idiot of the forest").

Like the prow of a ship, Brittany juts into the sea. Traditionally, the province is divided into Haute-Bretagne and Basse-Bretagne. Promontories, coves, and beaches stud the rocky coastline, some 1,207km (750 miles) long. The interior is a land of hamlets, farmhouses, and moors covered with yellow broom and purple heather.

Brittany is a resort region. Many families visit for the beaches. British tourists frequent Dinard, although the water can be choppy and cold, with high waves. La Baule in the south is warmer, with a great beach, restaurants, and the best hotels in the region.

We suggest first-time visitors stick to the coast, where you can see salt-meadow sheep grazing. If you're coming from Mont-St-Michel, you can use St-Malo, Dinan, or Dinard as a base. Visitors from the château country of the Loire can explore the coastline of southern Brittany.

ST-MALO ★★★

414km (257 miles) W of Paris; 69km (43 miles) N of Rennes; 13km (8 miles) E of Dinard

Built on a granite rock in the Channel, St-Malo is joined to the mainland by a causeway. It's popular with the English, especially Channel Islanders, and its warm brown sands give it a modest claim to being a beach resort. The peninsula curves around a natural harbor that comprises several smaller basins. The walled city radiates outward from the town's château and its spiritual centerpiece, the Cathédrale St-Vincent, both of which lie near the peninsula's tip. The curse of St-Malo is the swarm of tour buses and their passengers engulfing the narrow streets. But there's charm here, though it's "merely the mock," having been virtually rebuilt after damage during World War II. The challenge is to appreciate that charm while contending with so many other travelers on the same pursuit.

Essentials

GETTING THERE   From Paris's Gare Montparnasse, about 14 TGV **trains** per day make the journey; a one-way ticket costs around 61€ to 77€. Two of these trains are nonstop, making the journey in 2¾ hours; other less direct trains take 4 hours. For information, call ✆ **36-35** or 08-92-35-35-35. If you're **driving** from Paris, take A13 west to Caen and continue southwest along N175 to the town of Miniac Morvan. From there, travel north on N137 directly to St-Malo. Driving time is 5 to 6 hours from Paris.

VISITOR INFORMATION   The **Office de Tourisme** is on esplanade St-Vincent (✆ **08-25-13-52-00;** www.saint-malo-tourisme.com). You must show a passport to take the car-ferry trips and tours to the Channel Islands or Les Iles Anglo-Normandes.

SPECIAL EVENTS   One of the most important Breton *pardons* is at St-Malo, usually the third weekend in January: the **Pardon of the Newfoundland Fishing Fleet (Pardon de St-Ouen).** The town's **Festival de la Musique Sacrée,** from mid-July to mid-August, stages evening concerts twice a week presented in the cathedral. Call ✆ **02-99-56-05-38** for more information.

Exploring the City

Walk along the **ramparts ★★★** for the best view of the bay and the islets at the mouth of the Rance. These walls were built over several centuries; some date from the 14th century. They were reconstructed in the 17th century and restored in the 19th. You can begin at the 15th-century **Porte St-Vincent.**

At the harbor, you can book tours of the **Channel Islands.** Car ferries, leaving for the English island of Jersey from March to October are operated by **Condor** (✆ **08-25-13-51-35;** www.condorferries.com). The round-trip fare for a pedestrian without a car from St-Malo is 55€.

At low tide, a 15-minute stroll leads to the **Ile du Grand-Bé ★★**, the site of the tomb of Chateaubriand, who was born in St-Malo, "deserted by others and completely surrounded by storms." The tomb, marked by a cross, is simple, unlike the man it honors, but the view of the Emerald Coast makes up for it.

The "Bastille of the West," the **Château de St-Malo ★★**, Porte St-Vincent (✆ **02-99-40-71-57**), and its towers shelter the **Musée de l'Histoire de St-Malo** (✆ **02-99-40-71-57**). It abounds with insights into the role of St-Malo, as well as souvenirs of the pirates Duguay-Trouin and Surcouf, the most famous of the privateers. Admission costs 5.20€ for adults and 2.60€ for students and children 17 and under. It's open April through October daily 10am to noon and 2 to 6pm, November through March Tuesday to Sunday 10am to noon and 2 to 6pm.

After you visit the château, try to carve out some time for wandering through the narrow streets and alleyways of St-Malo's historic core. Memories of the town's origins as a medieval fishing village confront you at nearly every turn.

St-Malo's **Cathédrale St-Vincent,** 12 rue St-Benoît (✆ **02-99-40-82-31**), is known for its nave vault dating from 1160. It's of the Angevin or Plantagenet style, elegantly marking the transition between Romanesque and Gothic. The cathedral also has a Renaissance facade (the west), with additions from the 18th century and a 15th-century tower. The 14th-century choir is surmounted by a triforium with trefoiled arches and flanked by chapels. Admission is free, and it's open June through August Monday to Saturday 9:45am to 7pm, Sunday 9:30am to 6pm (Sept–May closed noon–2pm).

BEACHES   Along the coast, long stretches of sand intersperse with rocky outcroppings that suggest fortresses protecting Brittany from Atlantic storms. You can swim wherever you like, but beware of the very strong undertow. If you're staying in St-Malo, the two best beaches are **Plage de Bon Secours,** near the northern tip of the Vieille Ville (old town), and **La Grande Plage du Sillon,** a longer stretch of sand at the eastern perimeter of the Vieille Ville.

SHOPPING If you're in St-Malo on Tuesday or Friday between 8am and 1pm and want to experience a great Breton **market,** head for the place de la Poissonerie and the Halles au Blé, in the heart of the old city. You can't miss the activity, the bustle, and the hawking of country-fresh produce, cheese, fish, and dozens of household items, including dishware, cooking utensils, and handicrafts.

For **boutique shopping,** head to rue St-Vincent, rue Porcon, rue Broussais, rue Georges Clemenceau, rue des Merciers, rue Ste. Barbe, rue Ville Pépin, and rue de Dinan. You'll find everything from the trendy to the trashy. Check out **Marin-Marine,** 5 Grande Rue (② 02-99-40-90-32), for quality men's and women's fashions that include great Breton wool sweaters, one of the town's best buys. Rue Clemenceau and rue Ville Pépin lie within the 19th-century neighborhood known as **St-Servan,** less than 1km (⅔ mile) southwest from the medieval core of St-Malo. To reach that district, take bus no. 2 from the center of St-Malo.

For last-minute souvenirs, stop by **Aux Délices Malouins,** 12 rue St-Vincent (② 02-99-40-55-22). This shop also specializes in pastries, cookies, and chocolates in the regional style.

For Breton handicrafts, try **Le Comptoir des Cotonniers,** 6 rue Broussais (② 02-99-40-57-01). In addition to hand-painted stoneware, books, and Gaelic CDs, you'll find Breton lace, Celtic souvenirs, and food items such as almond-flavored pastries and sugarcoated galettes. Other shops offering crafts such as Breton pottery include **La Palette Bretonne,** 4 rue de Dinan (② 02-99-40-05-41), and **La Manne Bretonne,** 2 place Guy la Chambre (② 02-23-18-28-20).

Where to Stay

Hotel Alba ★ ☺ For those who want to stay outside the walls near the beach, this boutique hotel is a winning choice, its rooms opening onto panoramic views of the English Channel. Guest rooms are small but attractively decorated in earthy tones with contemporary furnishings; some are large enough for families. In fair weather guests gather on the sunny terrace, or else enjoy a drink at night from the scenic bar. The best rooms have an ocean view and a private balcony.

17 rue des dune Dunes, St-Malo 35400. ② **02-99-40-37-18.** Fax 02-99-40-96-40. www.hotelalba.com. 22 units. 79€–171€ double; 130€–200€ family room. AE, MC, V. Free parking. **Amenities:** Bar; room service; Wi-Fi. *In room:* A/C, TV, Wi-Fi (free).

Hôtel de la Cité You'd never guess that this inn is new. It was built in 18th-century style following the plan of a building that once stood here. The contemporary interior, however, is no match for the richly embellished facade. Like most modern chain hotels, it offers solid comfort but is short on style. The rooms range from cramped to spacious; most bathrooms come with tub/shower combinations. Those on the top floor break away from the norm with angled ceilings. As a saving grace, many units open onto views of the oft-turbulent sea.

Place Vauban, St-Malo 35412. ② **02-99-40-55-40.** Fax 02-99-40-10-04. www.hotelcite.com. 41 units. 69€–133€ double. AE, DC, MC, V. Parking 12€. **Amenities:** Bar; babysitting; room service; rooms for those w/limited mobility. *In room:* A/C, TV, hair dryer, minibar, Wi-Fi (free)

Hôtel Elizabeth ★ Adjacent to the medieval ramparts of the old town, this stone-sided hotel was built in the 17th century as a baronial private home. Traditional artifacts and antiques evoke old-time Brittany at its most authentic. The cozy, renovated guest rooms have mellow-grained paneling and comfortable but unpretentious period-reproduction furniture. Breakfast (the only meal available) is served in a cellar under stout antique ceiling beams.

2 rue des Cordiers, St-Malo 35400. ☎ **02-99-56-24-98.** Fax 02-99-56-39-24. www.hotel-elizabeth.fr. 17 units. 80€–145€ double. Rates include breakfast. AE, DC, V. Parking 12€–15€. **Amenities:** Room service. *In room:* TV, hair dryer, minibar, Wi-Fi (free).

Hôtel France et Chateaubriand   This hotel, inside the walls of old St-Malo, is a good example of Napoleon III architecture. Guest rooms range from cozy to spacious and feature such details as cove moldings, plaster ceiling reliefs, and chandeliers. All contain period reproductions, and 20 have panoramic ocean views. In the chic bar with gold-trimmed Corinthian columns, you can chat over drinks and listen occasionally to the pianist on the baby grand.

Place Chateaubriand, St-Malo 35412. ☎ **02-99-56-66-52.** Fax 02-99-40-10-04. www.hotel-chateau briand-st-malo.com. 80 units. 69€–185€ double. AE, DC, MC, V. Parking 12€. **Amenities:** Restaurant; cafe; bar; babysitting; room service. *In room:* TV, hair dryer, Wi-Fi (free).

Where to Dine

Hôtel France et Chateaubriand (see above) has one of the finest dining rooms in town.

A la Duchesse Anne ★★★ TRADITIONAL FRENCH   Year after year, this restaurant delivers the finest food in town. Built into the ramparts, it offers summer dining under a canopy amid hydrangeas. Main courses include fish soup with chunks of fresh seafood, spiced and cooked in an iron pot; Cancale oysters; grilled turbot with beurre blanc; and a superb version of grilled lobster. The tempting desserts may include *fantaisie du chocolat*—several chocolate-based desserts artfully arranged on a platter.

5 place Guy-La-Chambre. ☎ **02-99-40-85-33.** Reservations required. Main courses 21€–32€; fixed-price menu 78€. MC, V. May–Nov Thurs–Sat and Tues 12:15–1:30pm and Thurs–Tues 7:15–9:30pm. Closed Dec–Jan.

Le Chalut ★★ SEAFOOD/FRENCH   This restaurant is *the* place to go for fresh fish. Chef Jean-Philippe Foucat's flavorful cuisine, based on fresh ingredients, includes a tart with layers of salmon and scallops, sprinkled with lime juice; John Dory with wild mushrooms, essence of lobster, and fresh coriander; and succulent line-caught sea bass with sherry sauce and braised endive. For dessert, try gateau of bitter chocolate with almond paste, or homemade ice cream flavored with malt whiskey.

8 rue de la Corne-de-Cerf. ☎ **02-99-56-71-58.** Reservations required. Main courses 23€–29€; fixed-price menu Mon–Fri 25€; fixed-price dinner 40€–50€. AE, MC, V. Wed–Sun noon–1:30pm and 7–9:30pm.

Where to Stay & Dine On the Outskirts

Le Relais Gourmand Olivier Roellinger ★★★ BRETON/SEAFOOD   After cooking with some of France's grandest chefs, including Guy Savoy and Gérard Vié, Olivier Roellinger struck out on his own. His restaurant in the town of Cancale attracts serious foodies from all over; many Parisians even travel 400km (250 miles) to enjoy the remarkable chef's work. His restaurant lies on the western flank of the Bay of Mont-St-Michel (see chapter 9), 16km (10 miles) west of St-Malo.

In a former family home, the restaurant stands behind a wall in the upper town. A domed conservatory opens onto a garden with a duck pond. Roellinger accurately calls his cuisine *marine, potagère, et épicée*—of the sea, the kitchen garden, and the spice cabinet. Start, perhaps, with a light cream-of-coconut soup studded with crayfish and garnished with exotic spices; and follow with brochettes of sweetbreads with laurel, grilled over charcoal and drizzled with essence of quince.

The restaurant is the centerpiece of a sprawling compound of at least seven historic buildings, some of them dating from the 1760s, and each scattered within the village of Cancale and along its nearby coastline. Collectively known as Les Maisons de Bricourt, they include two separate hotels (Le Château Richeux and the Hotel les Rimains), which jointly contain 17 comfortable and expensively decorated accommodations. The separate parts of the hotel lie 5km (3 miles) apart but a shuttle van hauls guests back and forth between the two. Accommodations range from 190€ to 290€ in a double, 330€ in a suite.

1 rue Duguesclin, Cancale. ✆ **02-99-89-64-76.** www.maisons-de-bricourt.com. Reservations required. Main courses 21€–163€; fixed-price menus 41€–110€. AE, DC, MC, V. Fri–Tues noon–1:30pm and 7:30–9pm. Closed Oct to mid-Dec and mid-Mar to late Apr. From St-Malo, take av. Pasteur along the seafront and continue west toward D201, following signposts toward Cancale.

St-Malo After Dark

For an evening of gambling, head to **Le Casino Barrière,** 2 chaussée du Sillon (✆ **02-99-40-64-00**). You can also order dinner, sometimes accompanied by live music. Presentation of a passport is required.

For dancing, consider **L'Escalier,** La Buzardière (✆ **02-99-81-65-56**), open Thursday to Saturday midnight to 5am. The cover doesn't exceed 13€. You'll need a car or taxi—the club is in the countryside, 5km (3 miles) east of town. A disco, **Le 109,** 3 rue des Cordiers (✆ **02-99-56-81-09**), is in a vaulted cellar that's at least 300 years old. It isn't as fashionable as L'Escalier, but it's accessible without a car. It's open Tuesday to Sunday 8pm to 3am, charging a cover of 10€ after midnight, including a first drink.

On weekends, and in search of nightlife, many young Bretons head for Rennes, but if you're interested in seeing the town's biggest disco, check out **Le Klub,** at L'Etanchet, just outside the hamlet of Pleurtuit (✆ **02-99-88-81-17**). Housed in an isolated farmhouse on the outskirts of St-Malo, it contains a bar, a dance floor, and a revolving series of lights that evoke a 1980s disco. It's open Thursday, Friday, and Saturday nights, and on the evening before national holidays. Cover is 11€ and includes the first drink.

Popular bars include **L'Aviso,** 12 rue du Point du Jour (✆ **02-99-40-99-08**), which specializes in beers from everywhere. **Pub Saint Patrick,** 24 rue Sainte-Barbe (✆ **02-99-56-66-90**), serves 50 different Irish whiskeys along with brew from Brittany. It regularly schedules concerts. Also appealing is **La Caravelle,** 95 bd. De Rochebonne (✆ **02-99-56-39-83**), a piano bar, 2km (1¼ miles) east of St-Malo, with a fine view of the sea.

DINARD ★★★

417km (259 miles) W of Paris; 23km (14 miles) N of Dinan

Dinard (not to be confused with its inland neighbor Dinan) sits on a rocky promontory at the top of the Rance River, opposite St-Malo. Ferries ply the waters between the two resorts. Victorian Gothic villas, many now hotels, overlook the sea, and gardens and parks abound. The old is still best; for a look at what the Edwardians admired, go down the pointe de la Vicomte at the resort's southern tip or stroll along the promenade.

One of France's best-known resorts, Dinard offers well-sheltered bathing and healthful sea air in La Manche ("the Sleeve," as the French call the English Channel). During the Victorian era, Dinard, once a fishing port, became popular with the English, who wanted a Continental holiday that was "not too foreign."

Essentials

GETTING THERE   If you're **driving,** take D186 west from St-Malo to Dinard. SNCF **trains** go only as far as St-Malo; from there, take bus no. 10, which departs from the St-Malo rail station daily for the 20-minute ride to Dinard. The one-way fare is 1.50€. **Buses** arrive from many large cities in Brittany, including Rennes. For information, call **Compagnie T.I.V.** (✆ **08-10-35-10-35**). Between April and November, **Compagnie Corsaire,** Gare Maritime de la Bourse, St. Malo (✆ **02-23-18-15-15**), operates ferryboats from St-Malo to Dinard. The trip takes 10 minutes and costs 4€ one-way. During the same months, the company operates a **ferry** from Dinan to Dinard. The trip takes 90 minutes and costs 20€ one-way. A **taxi** to Dinard from St-Malo is another option; it costs 22€ during the day and 30€ after 7pm and on holidays. For information, call ✆ **02-99-46-75-75.**

VISITOR INFORMATION   The **Office de Tourisme** is at 2 bd. Féart (✆ **02-99-46-94-12;** fax 02-99-88-21-07; www.ot-dinard.com).

SPECIAL EVENTS   From early June to mid-September, *musique-et-lumière* adds the drama of floodlights and recorded jazz, pop, or classical music to walks along the city's flowered seafront promenade du Clair-de-Lune.

Enjoying the Resort

A 10-minute walk from the town's historic core to the Pointe du Moulinet encircles most of the old town and encompasses views as far away as St-Malo.

BEACHES & SWIMMING   Dinard's main beach is **Plage de l'Ecluse** or **La Grande Plage,** the strip of sand between the peninsulas that defines the edges of the old town. Favored by families and vacationers, it's crowded on hot days. Smaller and more isolated is **Plage de St-Enogat** (you pass through the village of St-Enogat on the 20-min. hike east from Dinard). **Plage du Prieuré,** a 10-minute walk from the center, has many trees that shade the sand. Because there's such a difference between high and low tides, the municipality has built swimming pool–style basins along the Plage de L'Ecluse and the Plage du Prieuré beaches to catch seawater during high tide. Most people trek along the salt flats at low tide to bathe in the sea.

Looking for a pool that's covered, heated, filled with seawater, and open year-round? Head for the **Piscine Olympique,** boulevard du Président-Wilson (✆ **02-99-46-22-77**), next to the casino. Entrance is 4.30€ for adults, 3.35€ for children 5 to 16, and free for children 4 and under. From July to mid-September, it's open Monday to Saturday 10am to 12:30pm and 3 to 7:30pm, Sunday 10am to 12:30pm and 3 to 6:30pm. The rest of the year, it runs on a varying schedule according to the needs of school groups and swim teams.

SHOPPING   For shops and boutiques, concentrate on rue du Maréchal-Leclerc, rue Levavasseur, and boulevard Féart. In the 15th-century house containing **Atelier du Prince Noir,** 70 av. George-V (✆ **02-99-46-29-99**), you'll find paintings and sculptures by some of the most talented artists in France. The gallery is closed from October to April. Another worthwhile destination is **Marinette,** 29 rue Jacques-Cartier (☏ **02-99-46-82-88**), in a former Protestant church. The high-ceilinged showrooms feature upscale porcelain, stoneware, kitchen utensils, gift items, and fresh flowers.

Where to Stay

Didier Méril (see "Where to Dine," below) also rents rooms.

Grand Hôtel Barrière de Dinard ★★   Dinard's largest hotel, a member of the Lucien Barrière chain, dates from 1859. Its location, a 2-minute walk from the town center, commands an excellent view of the harbor. It rises in two wings, separated by a heated outdoor pool. Most rooms have balconies and are equipped with traditional furnishings and combination tub/showers. The inviting bar is a popular spot before and after dinner.

46 av. George-V, Dinard 35801. ☏ **02-99-88-26-26.** Fax 02-99-88-26-27. www.lucienbarriere.com. 90 units. 130€–230€ double; from 380€ junior suite. AE, DC, MC, V. Closed mid-Nov to Mar. **Amenities:** Restaurant; bar; babysitting; fitness center; 2 pools (indoor and outdoor); room service; rooms for those w/limited mobility; sauna; smoke-free rooms. *In room:* TV, hair dryer, minibar, Wi-Fi (free).

Hôtel Printania   Originally built in 1920, and a longtime favorite of nostalgia buffs, writers, and artists, the Printania lies a 2-minute walk from the beaches. On August 15, 1944, a bombing raid damaged the hotel. Terraces and a glassed-in veranda with potted palms highlight the main villa. The guest rooms contain antiques and Breton decorations. Some have *des lits Bretons* (Brittany-style beds), which surround the occupant with either curtains or paneled doors.

5 av. George-V, Dinard 35800. ☏ **02-99-46-13-07.** Fax 02-99-46-26-32. www.printaniahotel.com. 55 units. 73€–130€ double; 185€–220€ suite. Half board 60€–90€ per person. MC, V. Closed mid-Nov to mid-Mar. **Amenities:** 3 restaurants; bar. *In room:* TV, hair dryer, Wi-Fi (free).

Villa Reine-Hortense ★★   Though not as grand as the Grand, this is our second choice in Dinard. The hotel on the beach was built in 1860 as a retreat for one of the Russian-born courtiers of Queen Hortense de Beauharnais, daughter of Joséphine de Beauharnais (who married Napoleon) and mother of Napoleon III. It offers glamorously outfitted public salons and guest rooms decorated in either Louis XV or Napoleon III style. Most units have private balconies. One high-ceilinged room (no. 4) has Hortense's silver-plated bathtub, dating from the early 1800s. Breakfast is the only meal served.

19 rue de la Malouine, Dinard 35800. ☏ **02-99-46-54-31.** Fax 02-99-88-15-88. www.villa-reine-hortense.com. 8 units. 160€–255€ double; 320€–395€ suite. AE, DC, MC, V. Closed Oct–Apr. **Amenities:** Bar. *In room:* TV, hair dryer.

Where to Dine

Another choice is the restaurant at the **Grand Hôtel Barrière de Dinard** (see above).

Didier Méril ★ FRENCH/BRETON   The finest dining room in town offers tables opening onto the panoramic view of the Bay of Prieuré. Filled with designer furniture, it offers traditional fare in spite of its contemporary look. Located in the historic center of Dinard, the restaurant edges close to the beach. The chef, Didier Méril, takes full advantage of the local seafood and vegetables from neighboring farmland. He also offers the finest and most varied wine *carte* in the area. In good

AN idyll ON AN ILE

Ile de Bréhat is home to some 350 hearty folk who live most of the year in isolation—until the summer crowds arrive. The tiny island (actually two islands, Ile Nord and Ile Sud, linked by a bridge, Le Pont Vauban) is in the Golfe de St-Malo, north of Paimpol. A visit to Bréhat is an adventure, even to the French. The only settlement on the islands is Le Bourg, in the south. The only bona fide beach is a strip of sand at Guerzido.

Walking is the primary activity, and it's possible to stroll the footpaths around the island in a day. Cars other than police and fire vehicles aren't allowed. Tractor-driven carts carry visitors on an 8km (5-mile) circuit of Bréhat's two islands, charging 13€ for the 45-minute jaunt. A number of places rent bikes, but they aren't necessary.

The rich flora here astonishes many visitors, who get off the ferry expecting a wind-swept island, only to discover a more Mediterranean clime. Flower gardens are in full summer bloom, though both the gardens and houses appear tiny because of the scarcity of land. At the highest point, Chapelle St-Michel, you'll be rewarded with a panoramic view.

The tourist office, place du Bourg, Le Bourg (② **02-96-20-83-16**), is open Monday to Saturday mid-June to mid-September.

To reach Paimpol, **drive** west on D768 from Dinard to Lamballe, then take E50 west to Plérin, and D786 north to Paimpol. To reach the island, take D789 4km (2½ miles) north of Paimpol, where the peninsula ends at the Pointe de l'Arcouest. From Paimpol, 5 to 10 **CAT buses** make the 10-minute run to the point for a one-way fare of 3€. Then catch one of the **ferries** operated by **Les Vedettes de Bréhat** (② **02-96-55-79-50;** www.vedettesdebrehat.com). Ferries depart about every 30 minutes in summer, two or three times per day in the off season; the round-trip costs 9.50€. Visitors in April, May, June, and September will find the island much less crowded than in July and August. Cars are not allowed on the ferry.

weather, tables are placed on a sea-bordering terrace. Try such tasty specialties as sweetbreads in a truffle sauce, foie gras with caramelized apples, roast pigeon with cabbage, and lobster flavored with cognac. John Dory, sea bass, and turbot, depending on the catch of the day, are regularly featured.

The restaurant also rents six stylish bedrooms, the simplest renting for 85€, the best for 220€.

1 place du Gen. de Gaulle. ② **02-99-46-95-74.** Reservations required. Fixed-price menus 22€–65€. Main courses 20€–45€. AE, DC, MC, V. Daily noon–2:30pm and 7–9:30pm.

Dinard After Dark

Like many of Brittany's seaside towns, Dinard has a casino, **Le Casino Barrière,** 4 bd. Du Président-Wilson (② **02-99-16-30-30**). It's liveliest from Easter to late October, when all its facilities, including a room for roulette and blackjack, are open. The rest of the year, only the slot machines operate. Hours for the slots are Sunday through Thursday from 10am to 3am, Friday and Saturday from 10am to 4am. Admission to the slot machines is free. Also on the premises is **La Brasserie,** a bar and bistro that's open year-round except for 2 weeks in February and 2 weeks in October. An alternative (not within the casino) is **Le Metro-Dôme,** Le Haut-Chemin

(☎ 02-99-46-46-46), a nightclub and disco that has earned the loyalty of many residents thanks to a good selection of wine and an amiable ambience. It lies on the outskirts of town on the road to St-Malo.

In the evenings from June to September, the **promenade du Clair-de-Lune** attracts a huge crowd of strollers for the *musique-et-lumière,* when the buildings and flowers along the promenade are illuminated and musical groups of just about every ilk—from rock to blues to jazz—perform.

DINAN ★★

396km (246 miles) W of Paris; 52km (32 miles) NW of Rennes

Once a stronghold of the ducs de Bretagne, Dinan is one of the best-preserved towns in Brittany. It's noted for houses built on stilts over the sidewalks. The 18th-century granite dwellings provide a sharp contrast to the medieval timbered houses in this walled town with a once-fortified château. Dinan (pop. 14,000) is one of Brittany's prettiest towns—it's not overrun like St-Malo.

Essentials

GETTING THERE   Dinan has a railway station, but few SNCF **trains** stop here. Railway passengers usually travel to Rennes or St-Malo, and then transfer to one of the **buses** (about five a day from each) that line up in front of the railway stations. The one-way train fare from Rennes is 13€, from St-Malo 2.50€. For information about bus service to Dinan, call the town's Gare Routière, adjacent to the railway station, about 1km (⅔ mile) west of the center (☎ 08-10-22-22-22). If you're **driving** from Dinard, take highway D166 south to Dinan.

VISITOR INFORMATION   The **Office de Tourisme** is at 9 rue du Château (☎ 02-96-87-69-76; fax 02-96-87-69-77; www.dinan-tourisme.com).

SPECIAL EVENTS   The most activity occurs on the third weekend of July, during the **Fêtes des Remparts,** held in even-numbered years (2012 is the next one). Duels from the age of chivalry are staged, and locals don medieval apparel for carousing in the streets of the city's historic core.

Exploring the Town

For a panoramic view of the valley, head for the **Jardin Anglais (English Garden),** a terraced garden that huddles up to the ramparts. A Gothic-style bridge spans the Rance River; damaged in World War II, it has since been restored. Dinan's most typical and one of its most appealing streets is the sloping **rue du Jerzual,** flanked with some buildings dating from the 15th century. The street ends at **Porte du Jerzual,** a 13th- and 14th-century gate. **Rue du Petit-Fort** and place des Merciers contain a number of 15th-century *maisons.*

Dominating the city's ramparts, **Château Musée de Dinan,** rue du Château (☎ 02-96-39-45-20), contains a 14th-century keep and a 15th-century tower, built to withstand sieges. In the stones, you'll see the space for the portcullis and the drawbridge. Inside, you can view an exhibition on the architecture and art of the city, including sculpture from the 12th to the 15th centuries. Admission is 4.40€ for adults, 1.75€ for children 12 to 18, and free for children 11 and under. It's open June to September daily 10am to 6:30pm, October to May daily 1:30 to 5:30pm (closed Jan).

Tour de l'Horloge (Clock Tower), on rue de l'Horloge (© 02-96-87-02-26), boasts a clock made in 1498 and a bell donated by Anne de Bretagne in 1507. You'll have a view of Dinan from the 23m (75-ft.) belfry. Admission is 2.95€ for adults, 1.90€ for children 12 to 18, and free for children 11 and under. The tower is open daily July to September 10am to 6:30pm, and mid-May to June and October daily 2 to 6:30pm.

The heart of Bertrand du Guesclin, who defended the town when the duke of Lancaster threatened it in 1359, is entombed in a place of honor in the **Basilique St-Sauveur,** place St-Sauveur (© 02-96-39-06-67). Note the basilica's Romanesque portals and ornamented chapels. It's open daily from 9am to 6pm.

REGIONAL CRAFTS Dinan has attracted craftspeople and artists for at least 20 years. The densest concentration of studios is along the **rue du Jerzual,** rue de la Chaux, and the **rue l'Apport,** where art objects are crafted from glass, wood, silk, leather, and clay. Our favorite shopping street is Jerzual. Other good streets include **place des Merciers** and **place des Cordeliers.** You may be able to buy an item directly from the artisan, but it's more efficient to visit galleries that sell objects by an assortment of the artisans. One of the best is **Galerie St-Sauveur,** 12 rue de l'Apport (© 02-96-85-26-62) where wide cross sections of paintings and crafts help provide perspective on the arts in Dinan. St-Sauveur specializes in avant-garde paintings and sculptures by living artists.

Where to Stay

Hôtel Arvor 🗝 This is a comfortable, relatively inexpensive hotel in a 14th-century Jacobin convent. During renovation in the 1990s, most of the building's interior was demolished and rebuilt. The result is comfortable, contemporary-looking guest rooms with small bathrooms. They retain none of their original medieval characteristics, but provide a cozy haven in one of Dinan's oldest neighborhoods. Breakfast is the only meal served, but many inviting restaurants lie within a short walk.

5 rue Pavie, Dinan 22100. © **02-96-39-21-22.** Fax 02-96-39-83-09. www.hotelarvordinan.com. 23 units. 49€–64€ double. MC, V. Closed Jan. *In room:* TV, hair dryer, Wi-Fi (free).

Hôtel d'Avaugour ★★ Set on the town ramparts, this is one of the town's best hotels. It's hard to believe that a pair of gutted stone-fronted buildings has been transformed into an up-to-date hotel. Guest rooms are decorated in a style that reflects the historical charm of the area. The rooms contain fabrics inspired by 18th-century design, furniture reflecting the heritage of Dinan, canopied beds, and mid-size bathrooms (most with tubs and showers). Half the units overlook the square; the others face the garden.

1 place du Champs-Clos, Dinan 22100. © **02-96-39-07-49.** Fax 02-96-85-43-04. www.avaugourhotel. com. 24 units. 87€–182€ double; 220€–278€ suite. MC, V. Closed Nov 10 to mid-Feb. *In room:* TV, hair dryer, Wi-Fi (free).

Where to Dine

L'Auberge de Pélican ★ FRENCH/BRETON This traditional restaurant's decor is contemporary but the food is often based on time-honored recipes, all of which are homemade, even the bread. Our favorite dish is the casserole of fresh fish served daily with beurre blanc, or "white butter." Fat, succulent scallops from the bay are also a worthy choice for seafood lovers. But the chef prepares meat and poultry dishes equally well, particularly the *magret de canard* (duckling) with figs and a tender, well-flavored filet of beef with truffles.

3 rue Haute Voie. ☎ **02-96-39-47-05.** Reservations recommended. Main courses 16€–23€; fixed-price menus 18€–37€. AE, MC, V. July–Aug Tues–Fri and Sun noon–2pm, daily 7–10pm; Sept–June Tues–Sun noon–2pm, Tues–Wed and Fri–Sun 7–10pm. Closed Jan–Feb 4.

ON THE OUTSKIRTS

Jean-Pierre Crousil ★★ 🏠 BRETON/NORMAN   Those who think there's nothing left to discover on the Breton coast can drive to this restaurant tucked away in the hamlet of Plancoët, 28km (17 miles) from St-Malo and 17km (11 miles) from Dinan. A smooth beginning is foie gras en terrine in sauterne wine jelly. The most lavish dish is lobster roasted in Calvados, which imparts a wonderfully rich, aromatic flavor. We are fond of the duck served in thick, rosy slices; farmhouse quail; and *pigoneaux de nid au Port* (pigeons in potato baskets with port-wine sauce). The chef also prepares turbot with beurre blanc, and scallops in dishes that change depending on his inspiration for the evening.

20 Les Quais, Plancoët. ☎ **02-96-84-10-24.** Reservations required. Fixed-price menu 40€. AE, MC, V. Wed–Sun noon–1:30pm; Wed–Sat 7:30–9:15pm. Closed 3 weeks in Jan. From Dinan, take rue des Rouairies west, and follow signs to Plancoët.

Dinan After Dark

The densest concentration of cafes and bars in Dinan lines the **rue de la Cordon-nerie,** nicknamed *la rue de la soif* ("the street where you go when you're thirsty") by long-ago sailors.

QUIMPER ★★

570km (354 miles) W of Paris; 205km (127 miles) NW of Rennes

The town that pottery built, Quimper, at the meeting of the Odet and Steir rivers, is the historic capital of Brittany's most traditional region, La Cornouaille. Today, its faïence decorates tables from Europe to the United States. Skilled artisans have been turning out Quimperware since the 17th century, using bold provincial designs. You can tour one of the ateliers; inquire at the tourist office (see below). Today Quimper is rather smug and bourgeois, home to some 65,000 Quimperois, who walk narrow streets spared from World War II damage.

Essentials

GETTING THERE   Slow **trains** (Les Corails) from Paris's Montparnasse station take 6 hours. Speedy TGVs take only 4½ hours from Paris. By all means, skip the slow train and opt for the TGV; the one-way fare is 75€. For information, call ☎ **36-35** or 08-92-35-35-35. If you're **driving,** the best route is from Rennes: Take E50/N12 west to just outside the town of Montauban, continue west along N164 to Châteaulin, and head south along N165 to Quimper.

VISITOR INFORMATION   The **Office de Tourisme** is on place de la Résis-tance (☎ **02-98-53-04-05;** www.quimper-tourisme.com).

SPECIAL EVENTS   For 8 days in mid- to late July, the **Festival de Cornouaille** adds a traditional flavor to the nightlife scene with Celtic and Breton concerts throughout the city. For information, contact the Office de Tourisme.

Exploring the Town

In the summer, the tourist office organizes a 90-minute walking tour of the city (*des circuits de ville*). It costs 5.20€. Tours in French depart daily at 10:30am from in front of the tourist office; tours in English start at 2pm on Tuesday and Friday only.

In some quarters, Quimper maintains its old-world atmosphere, with footbridges spanning the rivers. At place St-Corentin is the **Cathédrale St-Corentin ★★** (© **02-98-95-06-19**), characterized by two towers that climb 75m (246 ft.). The cathedral was built from the 13th to the 15th century; the spires were added in the 19th. Inside, note the 15th-century stained glass. It's open May to October daily 9:30am to 1:30pm and 2 to 6:30pm, November to April Monday to Saturday 9am to noon and daily 1:30 to 6:30pm.

Also on the square is the **Musée des Beaux-Arts ★★**, 40 place St-Corentin (© **02-98-95-45-20**). The collection includes work by Rubens, Boucher, Fragonard, and Corot, plus an exceptional exhibit from the Pont-Aven school (Bernard, Sérusier, Lacombe, Maufra, Denis). Admission is 4.50€ for adults, 2.50€ for ages 12 to 26, and free for children 11 and under. The museum is open July and August daily from 10am to 7pm; April to June and September and October, Monday and Wednesday to Sunday 10am to noon and 2 to 6pm; and November to March, Monday and Wednesday to Saturday 10am to noon and 2 to 6pm, Sunday 2 to 6pm.

Musée Departemental Breton, 1–3 rue Roi Gradlon (© **02-98-95-21-60**), is in the medieval Palais des Eveques de Cornouailles (Palace of the Bishops of Cornwall), adjacent to the cathedral. The museum showcases the evolution of Breton costumes, with examples of local handicrafts, archaeology, and furniture. It is open June through September daily 9am to 6pm, November through May Tuesday to Saturday 9am to noon and daily 2 to 5pm. Admission is 4€ for adults, 2.50€ for ages 18 to 25, and free for children 17 and under.

Shopping

When artisans from Rouen settled in Quimper, the city became forever associated with ceramics. It produces the most recognized and the most popular French porcelain. Typical are chunky white pieces painted with blue-and-yellow Breton figures, fruits, and flowers. The most popular feature a male *Breton* or a female *Bretonne,* both in profile and in traditional Breton costume. Today, that 19th-century design is copyrighted and fiercely protected.

The best shopping streets are **rue Kéréon** and **rue du Parc,** where you'll find Breton products including pottery, dolls and puppets, clothing made from regional cloth and wool, jewelry, lace, and beautiful Breton costumes.

One of three sites that produce stoneware is open for tours. Monday to Friday 9am to 4:30pm, five to seven tours a day depart from the visitor information center of **HB-Henriot Faïenceries de Quimper,** rue Haute, Quartier Locmaria (© **02-98-90-09-36**; www.hb-henriot.com). Tours, in English or French or both, last 40 to 45 minutes and cost 5€ for adults, 2.50€ for children 8 to 14, and free for children 7 and under. On-site, a store sells the most complete inventory of Quimper porcelain in the world. You can invest in first-run (nearly perfect) pieces or slightly discounted "seconds," with nearly imperceptible flaws. Anything you buy can be shipped.

For other Breton pottery and pieces of the faïence once heavily produced in this area, visit **François le Villec,** 4 rue Roi-Gradlon (© **02-98-95-31-54**). Here you'll find quality tablecloths, linens, and other household linens.

Another good choice for Breton items is **La Galerie le Cornet à Dés,** 1 rue Ste-Thérêse (✆ **02-98-53-37-51**). It stocks hand-painted porcelain and antique and contemporary paintings, mostly of Quimper landscapes.

Where to Stay

Hôtel Gradlon ★ ✒ The town's most consistently reliable hotel is this 19th-century landmark. The frequently renovated hotel has a simple modern annex a few steps away. The decor is simple, angular, and solid, with framed posters of Breton landscapes and monuments, and lots of varnished-wood trim. Guest rooms are simple and comfortable.

30 rue de Brest, Quimper 29000. ✆ **02-98-95-04-39.** Fax 02-98-95-61-25. www.hotel-gradlon.com. 22 units. 82€–155€ double; 130€–175€ suite. AE, DC, MC, V. Parking 8€. Closed late Dec to mid-Jan. **Amenities:** Bar. *In room:* TV, hair dryer, minibar, Wi-Fi (free).

Hôtel Océania ☺ In a garden 1.5km (1 mile) southwest of the town center, the Océania, despite its blandness, is the best choice for families. Built in the 1980s with comfortable, standardized rooms, its Breton-style slate roof would be the envy of any homeowner. It's ideal for motoring families (the pool is a magnet in summer) and is the best business-oriented hotel in the region. Each unit has lots of space, a writing desk, and a midsize bathroom with tub and shower.

2 rue du Poher, Quimper 29000. ✆ **02-98-90-46-26.** Fax 02-98-53-01-96. www.oceaniahotels.com. 92 units. 65€–140€ double; 115€–165€ suite. Up to 2 children 15 or under stay free in parent's room. AE, DC, MC, V. From town center, follow signs to rte. Pont-l'Abbé. Free parking. **Amenities:** Restaurant; bar; babysitting; heated outdoor pool; room service. *In room:* TV, hair dryer, Wi-Fi (free).

Where to Dine

Ambroise ★ ☺ BRETON/FRENCH Although it's surpassed by Acacias, this restaurant remains one of the most respected and sought-after in Quimper. A 5-minute walk north of the cathedral, the airy ocher-and-gold dining room has contemporary furniture and large paintings in a style inspired by the English neosurrealist Francis Bacon. Menu items incorporate Breton traditions, with an occasional contemporary twist. The finest examples include a crusty buckwheat galette stuffed with spiced crabmeat, braised scallops with asparagus and citrus sauce, and filet of John Dory on an artfully contrived bed of vegetable ragout.

49 rue Elie Fréron. ✆ **02-98-95-00-02.** Reservations recommended. Main courses 30€ each; fixed-price menu 21€–53€; children's menu 15€. MC, V. Tues–Sun noon–1:30pm; Tues–Sat 7:30–9:15pm.

Les Acacias ★ ☺ BRETON/SEAFOOD This is Quimper's leading restaurant, serving lunch only. In a contemporary-looking dining room, it focuses on seafood and very fresh fish, but offers a scattering of meat dishes. Your meal may include roasted crayfish with sweet spices, delectable smoked John Dory perfumed with algae, fondant of pigs' foot with exotic mushrooms, and roasted pigeon with baby vegetables. Customers rave about the dessert specialty of local strawberries marinated in spiced wine. The wine list features 150 to 200 mostly French vintages.

88 bd. Creac'h Gwen. ✆ **02-98-52-15-20.** Reservations recommended. Main courses 27€–60€; fixed-price menu 29€–49€; children's menu 12€. MC, V. Sun–Fri 12:30–2:30pm. Closed May 1–7. From Quimper, drive 2km (1¼ miles), following signs to Benodet.

Where to Stay & Dine Nearby

In an orchard district 13km (8 miles) from Quimper, the sleepy village of **La Forêt-Fouesnant** produces the best cider in the province and is home to one of Brittany's finest manor houses.

Manoir du Stang ★★★ To get to this 16th-century ivy-covered manor, you travel down a tree-lined avenue, through a stone gate, and into a courtyard. On your right is a formal garden; stone terraces lead to 10 hectares (25 acres) of woodland. M. and Mme. Hubert provide gracious lodging in period rooms. Guests stay in the main building or in the even older but less desirable annex, which has a circular stone staircase. Your room is likely to be furnished with silk and fine antiques; each midsize bathroom comes with a combination tub/shower. One luxury is that a maid brings you breakfast on a tray each morning.

La Forêt-Fouesnant 29940. ℂ **02-98-56-96-38.** Fax 02-98-56-97-37. www.manoirdustang.com. 24 units. 65€–142€ double. AE, MC, V. Free parking. Closed mid-Sept to mid-May. Drive 1.5km (1 mile) north of the village center and follow signs from N783; access is by private road. **Amenities:** Bar. *In room:* Hair dryer, Wi-Fi (free).

Quimper After Dark

The steadfastly Celtic bar **Céili Pub,** 4 rue Aristide-Briand (ℂ **02-98-95-17-61**), has lots of polished wood, regional music, and happy people—join in a game of darts with one of the regulars. Two animated pubs with state-of-the-art recorded music and a lot of innate Breton/Celtic pride are **Le Limerick,** 15 bd. De Kerguelen (ℂ **02-98-95-28-05**), and **O Patchwork,** Place Pierre de Ronsard (ℂ **02-98-95-05-72**). Both are favorites of the young, the restless, and the *Vive La Bretagne* fervor, especially during soccer matches.

The young and stylish flock to **Les Naïades Discothèque,** boulevard Creac'h Gwen (ℂ **02-98-53-32-30**), where you can dance to the latest tunes. It sometimes charges a cover.

CONCARNEAU ★★

539km (335 miles) W of Paris; 93km (58 miles) SE of Brest

This port is a favorite of painters, who never tire of capturing the subtleties of the fishing fleet. It's also our favorite of the coast communities—primarily because it doesn't depend on tourists. Its canneries produce most of the tuna in France. Walk along the quays, especially in the evening, and watch the Breton fishers unload their catch; later, join them for a pint of cider in the taverns.

Essentials

GETTING THERE There's no **rail** service to Concarneau. If you're **driving,** the town is 21km (13 miles) southeast of Quimper along D783. A **bus** (ℂ **02-98-56-96-72**) runs from Quimper to Concarneau (trip time: 30 min.); the one-way fare is 2€. The bus from Resporden, site of another SNCF railway station, runs 8 to 10 times per day (trip time: 20 min.) for a fare of 2€.

VISITOR INFORMATION The **Office de Tourisme** is on quai d'Aiguillon (ℂ **02-98-97-01-44;** www.tourismeconcarneau.fr).

Exploring the Area

The town is built on three sides of a natural harbor whose innermost sheltered section is the **Nouveau Port.** In the center of the harbor is the heavily fortified **Ville-Close,** an ancient hamlet surrounded by ramparts, some from the 14th century. From the quay, cross the bridge and descend into the town. Souvenir shops have taken over, but don't let that spoil it for you. You can spend an hour wandering the alleys, gazing up at the towers, peering at the stone houses, and stopping in secluded squares.

For a splendid view of the port, walk the **ramparts.** They're open to pedestrians mid-April to mid-September daily 10am to 9:30pm. Access to the ramparts is closed the rest of the year whenever icy rain makes them slippery. The cost is .80€ per adult and .40€ for children 12 and under.

Also in the old town is a fishing museum, **Musée de la Pêche,** 3 rue Vauban (ℂ **02-98-97-10-20**). The 17th-century building has ship models and exhibits tracing the development of the fishing industry; you can also view the ship *Hemerica.* Admission is 6€ for adults and 4€ for students and children 14 and under. It's open April through October daily 10am to 6pm (July–Aug until 8pm).

BEACHES   Concarneau's largest, most beautiful beach, popular with families, is **Plage des Sables Blancs,** near the historic core. Within a 10-minute walk are **Plage de Cornouaille** and two small beaches, **Plage des Dames** and **Plage de Rodel,** where you'll find fewer families with children. The wide-open **Plage du Cabellou,** 5km (3 miles) west of town, is less crowded than the others.

SEA EXCURSIONS   Boat rides are usually fine between June and September, but they're treacherous the rest of the year. During midsummer, you can arrange deep-sea fishing with the captain of the *Santa Maria* (ℂ **06-62-88-00-87**). For excursions along the coastline of southern Brittany, contact **Vedettes Glenn** (ℂ **02-98-97-10-31**) or **Vedettes de l'Odet** (ℂ **02-98-57-00-58**).

Where to Stay

Hôtel des Halles 🎏   The tourist board gives only two stars to this cement-sided 1960s-era hotel, which is short on historical charm. Yet it's affordable and warm, with guest rooms that are cozier than you may expect. The frequently upgraded rooms have white ceiling beams and wood paneling, plus small shower-only bathrooms. The location, a short distance from the fortifications encircling the town's historic core, is convenient. The city's covered food market, Les Halles (daily 8am–1pm), is a short walk away. Breakfast is the only meal served.

Place de l'Hôtel de Ville, Concarneau 29900. ℂ **02-98-97-11-41.** Fax 02-98-50-58-54. www.hotel deshalles.com. 25 units. 63€–84€ double. AE, MC, V. Parking 6€. **Amenities:** Internet (free). *In room:* TV, hair dryer.

Where to Dine

La Coquille ★ SEAFOOD/TRADITIONAL FRENCH   This 4-decade-old restaurant occupies one end of a stone-sided harborfront building; guests dine in a trio of rooms with stone walls, ceiling beams, and century-old oil paintings from the School of Pont-Aven. Seafood is the focus at La Coquille, and much of what is on the menu is offered simply because the fish is so fresh and succulent. A particularly excellent dish is a scallop tart with shellfish and cream sauce. The service is bistro style, with a cheerful, old-fashioned panache enhanced by the harbor view.

1 rue du Moros, at Nouveau Port.© **02-98-97-08-52.** www.lacoquille-concarneau.com. Reservations required Sat–Sun and in summer. Main courses 15€–45€; fixed-price menu 13€–45€. AE, DC, MC, V. Tues–Sun noon–1:30pm; Tues–Sat 7:30–9:30pm.

L'Ancre 🍴 FRENCH/SEAFOOD/INTERNATIONAL   A cost-conscious choice that's a magnet for local residents, this cozy restaurant lies just outside the fortified central core of historic Concarneau, a few steps from the exterior fortifications of the *centre ville*. About half of the interior is outfitted in the Breton style, the other half reflects the owners' frequent travels to the French Antilles or French-speaking Africa, outfitted with tribal and carnival masks. Two specialties that always seem appreciated are a platter with four kinds of barbecued fish (swordfish, tuna, sardines, and shrimp) and another with four skewers of barbecued meat (ostrich, kangaroo, turkey, and a half quail). Accompaniments in both cases include a baked potato and salad.

22 rue Dumont d'Urvilles.© **02-98-50-56-58.** Reservations recommended. Main courses 9.90€–24€; set-price menus 16€–19€. MC, V. Wed–Sun noon–2pm and 7–9:30pm. Closed mid-Jan to mid-Feb.

Where to Stay & Dine Nearby

On the outskirts of the once-fortified town of **Hennebont,** 56km (35 miles) southeast of Concarneau, is the most delightful hotel in all of southern Brittany.

Château de Locguénolé ★★★   This country estate is owned by the same family that ran it some 5 centuries ago. Following a devastating fire, the 15th-century château was rebuilt in its present form in 1805. A Relais & Châteaux member since 1970, with views over coastline and an inlet, it's filled with antiques, tapestries, and paintings. Guest rooms vary in size and style, but each has a harmonious color scheme and, season permitting, sprays of flowers. The converted maids' rooms are smaller, yet still charming; some units are in a converted 1720 Breton cottage.

Rte. De Port-Louis en Kervignac, Hennebont 56700.© **02-97-76-76-76.** Fax 02-97-76-82-35. www. chateau-de-locguenole.com. 22 units. 112€–240€ double; 250€–410€ suite. AE, DC, MC, V. Closed Jan 2 to mid-Feb. From Hennebont, follow signs to château, 4km (2½ miles) south. **Amenities:** Restaurant; babysitting; outdoor pool; room service; 2 saunas. *In room:* TV, hair dryer, minibar, Wi-Fi (free).

PONT-AVEN ★

522km (324 miles) W of Paris; 32km (20 miles) SE of Quimper; 16km (10 miles) S of Concarneau

Paul Gauguin loved this village, with its white houses along the gently flowing Aven River. In the late 19th century, many painters followed him here, including Maurice Denis, Paul Sérusier, and Emile Bernard. The theories and techniques developed at the time have been known ever since as the School of Pont-Aven.

Essentials

GETTING THERE   If you're **driving** from Quimper, go southeast on N165 and follow signs into Pont-Aven. From Quimperlé, head west along D783. SNCF **trains** stop at Quimperlé, where you can transfer to between four and six daily **buses** for the 30-minute ride to Pont-Aven. The one-way fare is 2.50€. For train information, call the Pont-Aven tourist office (see below) or © **08-92-35-35-35,** or visit www. voyages-sncf.com.

VISITOR INFORMATION   The **Office de Tourisme** is at 5 place de l'Hôtel-de-Ville (© **02-98-06-04-70;** www.pontaven.com).

In 1886, Paul Gauguin blazed the trail to the Breton village of Pont-Aven, and in time lesser artists followed. One of Gauguin's most memorable works, *The Yellow Christ,* exemplified the credo of the School of Pont-Aven. Breaking from mainstream Impressionism, Pont-Aven artists emphasized purer colors ("as true as nature itself"). They shunned perspective and simplified human figures.

The tourist office sells a walking-tour guide (.50€) that directs you on a trail once trod by the artists who drew inspiration from the sea and landscapes of this region.

Musée Municipal de Pont-Aven, place de l'Hôtel de Ville (✆ 02-98-06-14-43), provides one of the best overviews of the 19th-century painters. Expect muted greens and blues and lots of Breton patriotism as interpreted through the most famous artistic movement to emerge from Brittany. Admission is 6€ for adults, 4€ for people under 25, and free for children 17 and under. The museum is open in July and August daily 10am to 7pm, September to March daily 10am to noon and 2 to 6pm, and April to June daily 10am to 12:30pm and 2 to 6:30pm.

Exploring the Area

The 16th-century **Chapelle de Trémalo,** lieu-dit Trémalo (✆ 02-98-06-01-68), lies 1.2km (¾ mile) north of the town center. Severely dignified and set on private lands, which still belong to descendants of the Plessis-Nizon family that originally built and consecrated the chapel in 1532, it contains a wooden crucifix that inspired two of Gauguin's best-known paintings, *The Yellow Christ* (displayed today in a museum in Buffalo, New York) and his *Self-Portrait with the Yellow Christ* (displayed today in the Musée d'Orsay in Paris). The elderly caretakers of this place unlock it every morning at 10am and close it at 5pm (at 6pm July–Aug). The location is signposted, and entrance is free. The chapel, incidentally, still defines itself as a place of worship, and occasionally Masses are conducted from time to time. Plunk a coin or two into a machine to briefly illuminate the interior—otherwise midday sunlight from the windows is sufficient.

Where to Stay & Dine

Le Moulin de Rosmadec ★★★ 🏠TRADITIONAL FRENCH   For a charming setting, nothing in Brittany compares to this 15th-century stone mill. Meals are served in a bi-level dining room with antique furnishings or, in good weather, on a flower-filled "island" terrace. The owners, M. and Mme. Sébilleau, serve carefully prepared specialties such as ragout of freshwater crayfish. Among the proficiently prepared dishes are *croustillant de pigeon* (crisply baked pigeon in puff pastry) and grilled lobster. Well worth ordering is stir-fried crayfish in its natural juices or a tart layered with red snapper and a confit of tomatoes. A traditional and tasty favorite is grilled John Dory with fresh artichokes.

The Moulin rents four comfortable double rooms for 90€ to 120€. Each has a TV and a tidy bathroom with tub and shower. Because of the location at the end of a cul-de-sac, the accommodations are quiet and calm.

Pont-Aven 29123. ✆ **02-98-06-00-22.** www.moulinderosmadec.com. Reservations recommended. Main courses 50€–70€; fixed-price menu 35€–76€; *menu tradition* (with oysters and lobster) 76€. MC, V. Fri–Wed 12:30–2pm and 7:30–9pm. Closed Feb and 2 weeks in Oct.

CARNAC ★

486km (302 miles) W of Paris; 37km (23 miles) SE of Lorient; 100km (62 miles) SE of Quimper

Aside from being a seaside resort, Carnac is home to the hundreds of huge stones in the **Field of Megaliths ("Les Alignements")** that date from Neolithic times. Scholars have debated their purpose for centuries, although most suggest they had astronomical or religious significance to the people of the area. One theory is that some of the stones marked burial sites. In all, the town contains 2,732 menhirs (monumental stones), some of them rising to heights of 20m (66 ft.). They stand in 11 more or less straight lines in at least three separate fields.

Even if Carnac didn't possess these monuments, its pine-studded sand dunes would be worth the trip. Protected by the Quiberon Peninsula, **Carnac-Plage** is a family resort beside the ocean and along the waterfront boulevard de la Plage. And in May and June, the fields—especially around the megaliths—are resplendent with golden broom.

Essentials

GETTING THERE   Driving is the most convenient way to get to Carnac. From Pont-Aven, travel east along N165, passing through Hennebont. At the intersection with D768, continue south along the signposted road to Carnac. From Lorient, take N165 east to Auray, and turn south on D768 to Carnac.

Links to Carnac by public transport are inconvenient, as there's no SNCF railway station in town. Instead, travelers, depending on the origin of their train and the season, get off the SNCF network at either Quiberon or Auray, two nearby towns, both of which lie on the SNCF lines. An additional option, available only between June and August, involves getting off in the hamlet of Plouharnel-Carnac, 3km (2 miles) from Carnac.

From any of the above-mentioned towns, **buses** make between two and seven departures per day for the center of Carnac. One-way transit into Carnac by bus from any of the above-mentioned hamlets ranges from 4.30€ to 5.90€ per person, depending on the point of origin. Know in advance that the SNCF itself will usually advise you, when you buy your ticket to Carnac from other points throughout France, which of the above-mentioned hamlets is the most convenient for your descent.

For information about rail transits throughout the region, call ✆ **08-92-35-35-35.** For more information about bus transit from any of the above-mentioned hamlets into Carnac, call ✆ **02-97-47-29-64.**

VISITOR INFORMATION   The Office de Tourisme, 74 av. Des Druides in Carnac-Plage (✆ **02-97-52-13-52;** www.carnac.fr), is open year-round.

Exploring the Area

Out of fear of vandalism, the local tourist authorities have fenced in the **megaliths,** and now allow visitors to wander freely among the menhirs *only* between October and March, when the park is open daily from 10am to 5pm, and when entrance is free. From April to September, the park can be visited only as part of a rigidly controlled 1-hour guided tour, priced at 4€ per person (3€ for students or anyone 24 and under).

Tours are usually in French but, depending on the perceived need, may include some additional commentary in English; or, during high season, there may even be an all-English-language tour offered, but nothing is guaranteed. The only way to be sure involves calling the Parc's Visitor Center (*Maison des Mégalithes*) for a rundown on the tours that will be arranged on the day of your intended visit.

At Carnac Ville, **Musée de Préhistoire**, 10 place de la Chapelle (✆ **02-97-52-22-04**), displays collections from 450,000 B.C. to the 8th century. Admission is 5€ for adults, 2.50€ for children 6 to 18, and free for children 5 and under. Hours are as follows: July and August daily 10am to 6pm; October to March Wednesday to Monday 10am to 12:30pm and 2 to 5pm; April, May, June, and September Wednesday to Monday 10am to 12:30pm and 2 to 6pm.

The center of Carnac is about .8km (½ mile) from the sea. From the main square, rue du Tumulus leads north from the center of town to the **Tumulus St-Michel,** a Celtic burial chamber 1.2km (¾ mile) from the center (it is closed to the public).

Shopping

Carnac has two shopping areas: one along the beachfront called Carnac-Plage, and the other about 2.5km (1½ miles) inland in Carnac proper. Along the beach you'll find souvenir shops; venture down avenue des Druids and avenue de l'Atlantique for more specialized galleries and antiques stores. Other good areas are rue St-Cornély and place de l'Eglise, with a host of clothing and shoe stores, antiques dealers, and jewelers.

Opale, 10 rue St-Cornély (✆ **02-97-52-28-31**), sells unique creations of jewelry combining silver and semiprecious and precious stones, as well as mother-of-pearl. Go to **Clémentine,** avenue de l'Atlantique (✆ **02-97-52-96-34**), if you're in the market for quality household linens, porcelain, Breton fabric, and dishware.

Where to Stay & Dine

Auberge le Ratelier ★ 👔 BRETON   A short walk from the center of Carnac Ville, this vine-covered, time-mellowed inn is one of our favorite dining stops in the area. It highlights local seafood, often using recipes handed down from generation to generation. Other dishes have been modernized: gazpacho with fresh prawns, seasoned with basil from the garden; and sea bream, flavored with lemon grass and served with potatoes. The owners are proud of their dessert specialty, a candied fruit ice cream with strawberries and honey.

The inn offers eight small, simple guest rooms, comfortably furnished and quite affordable. Doubles cost 46€ to 60€.

4 chemin du Douët. ✆ **02-97-52-05-04.** www.le-ratelier.com. Reservations required. Main courses 13€–34€; fixed-price menu 23€–45€. MC, V. Thurs–Mon noon–2:30pm and 7:30–9:30pm.

Hôtel Lann-Roz   Within walking distance of the water, this oasis for the budget-minded is surrounded by a garden and lawns. The midsize guest rooms are modest yet comfortably furnished; the small bathrooms have tub/shower combinations. The dining room, which is open to the public, serves generous portions of regional food. Examples include fresh Breton tuna with basil and fresh noodles, a rillette (chunky terrine) of fish with shrimp and beurre blanc, and house-smoked salmon with creamy chive sauce. Dessert may be an apple-and–caramelized rhubarb tart.

36 av. De la Poste, Carnac 56340. ✆ **02-97-52-10-48.** Fax 02-97-52-24-36. www.lannroz.com. 20 units. 55€–85€ double. MC, V. Restaurant closed Jan 1 to mid-Mar. **Amenities:** Restaurant; bar. *In room:* TV.

THE WILD, WILD coast

If you take D768 south from Carnac and follow it onto the peninsula (formerly an island) connected to the mainland by a narrow strip of alluvial deposits, you'll come to the port of **Quiberon,** with its white-sand beach. You'll probably see the rugged Breton fishers hauling in their sardine catch.

This entire coast—the **Côte Sauvage,** or Wild Coast—is dramatic and rugged; the ocean breaks with fury against the reefs. Winds, especially in winter, lash across the dunes, shaving the short pines that grow here. On the landward side, the beach is calm and relatively protected.

Sixteen kilometers (10 miles) west of Brittany's shoreline is **Belle-Ile-en-Mer,** an outpost of sand, rock, and vegetation the French love for summer holidays. For information, contact the **Office de Tourisme,** Quai Bonnelle Le Palais (© **02-97-31-81-93**). Depending on the season, 4 to 12 ferries depart daily from Port Maria in Quiberon (© **08-20-05-61-56**). The trip takes 45 minutes; a round-trip ticket costs 26€ for adults and 15€ for those 24 and under. In summer, you must reserve space for your car, as well as for passengers.

The ferry docks at **Le Palais,** a fortified 16th-century port that is the island's window to the rest of France. Storm-wracked and eerie, the topography consists of rocky cliffs, a reef-fringed west coast, and the Grotte de l'Apothicairerie, a cave (closed to visitors) whose name derives from stalactites shaped like apothecary jars. Despite a scattering of hotels and seasonal restaurants, the island feels isolated. A drive around the periphery is about 56km (35 miles).

You'll find excellent accommodations in **Port de Goulphar,** on the southern shore on an inlet framed by cliffs. The standout is the 39-unit Relais & Châteaux property **Castel Clara,** Port de Goulphar, 56360 Bangor (© **02-97-31-84-21;** fax 02-97-31-51-69; www.castel-clara.com). Ideal service and first-class cuisine add to the sense of peace. The rooms are comfortable, with TVs and balconies facing the sea. The hotel also has a terrace with a solarium around a heated seawater pool. Depending on the season, rates range from 155€ to 380€ in a double, 290€ to 590€ in a suite. The hotel is closed from mid-December to mid-February.

10

BRITTANY | Carnac

Carnac After Dark

Carnac doesn't stay up very late, but a few places are worth checking out. The **Whisky Club,** 8 av. Des Druides (© 02-97-52-10-52), operates in an old stone house with two floors devoted to entertainment. The first offers an atmosphere conducive to conversation over drinks; the second is home to dancing and music. **Les Chandelles,** avenue de l'Atlantique (© 02-97-52-90-98), pulls in a young, flashy crowd. The club plays mainly disco and charges an 11€ cover. As at most discos in France, no jeans or sneakers are allowed. The professional crowd gathers at **Petit Bedon,** 106 av. Des Druides (© 02-97-52-11-62). With its mixture of African and Mexican decor, this is the place to dance to '60s rock. There's no cover, but a beer will set you back 7€.

LA BAULE ★★★

452km (281 miles) W of Paris; 79km (49 miles) NW of Nantes

Founded during the Victorian seaside craze, La Baule remains as inviting as the Gulf Stream that warms the waters of its 8km (5-mile) crescent of white-sand beach. Occupying the Côte d'Amour (Coast of Love), it competes with Biarritz as the Atlantic coast's most fashionable resort. La Baule is essentially French, drawing only a small number of foreigners.

Gambler François André founded the casino and major resort hotels here. Pines grow on the dunes, and villas on the outskirts draw a chic crowd from late June to mid-September; if you arrive at any other time, you may have La Baule all to yourself. While the movie stars and flashy rich go to Deauville or Cannes, La Baule draws a more middle-class crowd, but the more reserved wealthy also come here—as the yachts in the harbor testify.

The town is north of a popular stretch of beachfront. The two main boulevards run parallel through the long, narrow town; the one closer to the ocean changes its name six times—at its most famous point, it's called boulevard de l'Océan.

Other than a rock outcropping much weathered by Atlantic storms, the beaches here are clean and sandy-bottomed, providing safe swimming and lots of options for admiring flesh in all states of fitness.

Avenue du Général-de-Gaulle and **avenue Louis-Lajarrige** have the best shops and boutiques. Next to the casino on esplanade de François-André, you'll find a minimall with 40 or so French chain stores and boutiques.

Essentials

GETTING THERE If you're **driving** from Nantes, take N165 northwest to Savenay and continue west along D773 to La Baule. The **train** trip from Nantes takes about an hour and costs 13€ one-way. The town's most convenient railway station is La Baule–Escoublac, in the heart of town. Try to avoid getting off at La Baule–Les Pins, which is 4km (2½ miles) northeast of the commercial center. For train information, call ✆ **36-35** or 08-92-35-35-35.

VISITOR INFORMATION The **Office de Tourisme** is at 8 place de la Victoire (✆ **02-40-24-34-44;** www.labaule.fr).

Where to Stay

Castel Marie-Louise ★★★ This turn-of-the-20th-century Breton manor offers grand lodgings in an oceanfront park. The public rooms are furnished in French Provincial style, with tapestries of animals. Most upper-floor units come with balconies; two are in a tower, each with a private terrace. Each sumptuous bathroom holds a tub and shower. Furnishings reflect several styles: Louis XV, Directoire, and rustic. The excellent chef is reason enough to stay here, and even if you aren't a guest, you may want to stop in for a meal of regional fare that dares to be different. Specialties are lobster, home-smoked salmon, and half-baked chocolate cake.

1 av. Andrieu, La Baule 44504. ✆ **02-40-11-48-38.** Fax 02-40-11-48-35. www.castel-marie-louise.com. 31 units. 170€–400€ double; from 375€ suite. AE, DC, MC, V. Parking 12€ July–Aug. Closed mid-Jan to mid-Feb. **Amenities:** Restaurant; bar; babysitting; nearby golf; room service. *In room:* TV, hair dryer, minibar, Wi-Fi (free).

Hôtel Bellevue-Plage This sea-fronting hotel is reliable, if not exciting, with a tranquil position in the center of the shoreline around the bay. Built around 1937, it has lost many of its original Art Deco features to renovation. The current modern, durable decor, often in tones of pale blue, is appropriate for a beach hotel. The comfortable rooms have small bathrooms with tub/shower combinations. Guests gravitate to the rooftop solarium and the ground-floor restaurant, which has a sweeping view. You'll also find a beach, sailboats for rent, and access to spa facilities.

27 bd. De l'Océan, La Baule 44500. ℂ **02-40-60-28-55.** Fax 02-40-60-10-18. www.hotel-bellevue-plage.fr. 35 units. 110€–190€ double; 115€–195€ suite. AE, DC, MC, V. Closed Jan. **Amenities:** Restaurant; bar; babysitting; exercise room; room service; sauna. *In room:* TV, minibar, Wi-Fi (free).

Hôtel La Palmeraie ★ 🛅 In high-priced La Baule, this is a reasonably priced charmer. Built in the 1930s and renovated in 2008, it's named after eight large palms that thrive in the garden, thanks to the mild climate. Decorated in festive pink and white, La Palmeraie is near a beach and luxuriant with flowers in summer. The rooms are attractively decorated, often with English-style pieces. Each has high ceilings and dignified (sometimes antique) furniture. The only drawback: The soundproof rooms aren't all that soundproof. Half board is obligatory in July and August; the food, however, is hardly in the league of that at the first-class hotels. The management and staff are helpful and even friendly.

7 allée des Cormorans, La Baule 44500. ℂ **02-40-60-24-41.** Fax 02-40-42-73-71. www.hotel-lapalmeraie-labaule.com. 24 units. 68€–107€ double. Half board (required July-Aug) 68€–95€ per person. AE, DC, MC, V. Closed Oct 1-Feb 1. **Amenities:** Restaurant; bar; babysitting. *In room:* TV, hair dryer, Wi-Fi (free).

Where to Dine

Castel Marie-Louise (see "Where to Stay," above) has an elegant restaurant known for its haute cuisine.

Barbade 🍴 CLASSIC FRENCH With its verdant plants and big windows, Barbade looks like an oversize greenhouse. It creates competent, well-flavored cuisine that's fairly priced, particularly compared to many of the more expensive establishments nearby. Menu items include sole meunière, grilled dorado, stuffed oysters, a hefty chunk of baked goat cheese with a crisp outer skin, and the chef's pride, freshwater crayfish in puff pastry.

31 Bd. René Dubois (at the corner of av. Ramblais). ℂ **02-40-42-01-01.** Reservations recommended. Main courses 14€–38€; fixed-price menus 16€ lunch, 26€–30€ dinner. MC, V. Daily noon–3pm; Mon-Sat 8–11pm. Closed Jan.

La Baule After Dark

The most visible nighttime venue is the **Casino Barrière de La Baule,** 24 esplanade de Lucien Barrière (ℂ **02-40-11-48-28**). Some areas are stylish, but it can't compete with the glamour of Deauville. Entrance to the slot machine area is open daily 9pm to 4am. The casino has a brasserie that serves lunch and dinner daily, as well as a sometimes-crowded disco, **L'Indiana** (ℂ **02-40-11-48-28**), open year-round Tuesday through Saturday midnight to 6am. The cover is 12€ and includes a drink.

   Le Théâtre, 10 av. Pavie (ℂ **02-40-60-41-00**), is the biggest, splashiest disco in town, noteworthy for the phallic-looking pillar rising from the big dance floor. It's close to the casino, in the heart of La Baule's resort neighborhood. From June to

September it's open nightly from 11pm to 4am. The rest of the year, it's open only Thursday to Sunday (same hours).

A stroll down avenue du Général-de-Gaulle or avenue Maréchale-de-Lattre-de-Tassigny will uncover any number of interesting bars and pubs. Newcomers feel welcome at **Le Bax,** 12 av. De Pavie (✆ **02-40-60-90-00**), a cozy environment that survives despite the seasonal clientele. Other choices include **Klimt Café,** 157 av. Du Général-de-Gaulle (✆ **02-40-24-14-46**), and **Le Sailor,** 305 av. Maréchale-de-Lattre-de-Tassigny (✆ **02-40-60-24-49**). **Antidote,** 104 av. Du Général-de-Gaulle (✆ **02-40-11-04-03**), is open only June to September.

NANTES ★★★

385km (239 miles) W of Paris; 325km (202 miles) N of Bordeaux

Nantes is Brittany's largest town, although in spirit it seems closer to the Loire Valley's château country. The mouth of the Loire is 48km (30 miles) away, and here it divides into several branches. Nantes is a busy port that suffered great damage in World War II. It's best known for the Edict of Nantes, issued by Henri IV in 1598, which guaranteed religious freedom to Protestants (it was later revoked). Many famous people, from Molière to Stendhal, have lived here. But Nantes hardly rests on its illustrious past. Now home to high-tech industries, it has some 30,000 college students and a population of half a million.

Built on the largest of three islands in the Loire, the city expanded in the Middle Ages to the northern edge of the river, where its center lies today. The most prominent building, the **Château des Ducs de Bretagne,** rises high above the wide boulevard quai de la Fosse.

Believe it or not, staid old Nantes is taking on a kind of Atlantic Coast chic. Impressive revitalization is changing the city, as once dreary industrial suburbs are being transformed into places you'd actually like to visit.

The most outstanding example of that is the compound, **Le Lieu Unique,** 2 rue de la Biscuiterie, a former biscuit factory converted into a venue for art exhibitions, a restaurant, a bar/cafe, and fashionable shops. For the restaurant, see **Du Lieu Unique,** below. At one end of this boulevard is the train station; at the other are the promenades beside the Loire.

Essentials

GETTING THERE The **TGV** (fast train) from Paris's Gare Montparnasse takes about 2 to 2½ hours to get to Nantes and costs 55€. Beware of slower trains, which can take up to 5½ hours. For information, call ✆ **36-35** or 08-92-35-35-35. Nantes's **Gare SNCF,** 27 bd. de Stalingrad, is a 5-minute walk from the town center. If you're **driving,** take A11 for 385km (239 miles) west of Paris. The trip takes about 3 hours. **Aéroport Nantes-Atlantique** (✆ **02-40-84-80-00**) is 12km (7½ miles) southeast of town. **Air France** (✆ **3654**) offers daily flights from Paris. A shuttle bus between the airport and the Nantes train station takes 25 minutes and costs 6.20€. A taxi from the airport costs 25€ and takes about 15 minutes.

VISITOR INFORMATION The **Office de Tourisme** is at 3 cours Olivier de Clisson (✆ **08-92-46-40-44;** fax 02-40-89-11-99; www.nantes-tourisme.com).

Nantes

Cathédrale St-Pierre **4**
Château des Ducs de Bretagne **3**
Musée des Beaux-Arts de Nantes **5**
Musée Jules Verne de Nantes **1**
Musée Thomas-Dobrée **2**

Church ✝
Information ⓘ
Post Office ✉

Exploring the City

At the tourist office, you can buy a **Pass Nantes,** which allows you to enter museums and ride any of the city's public conveyances, including buses, trains, and some of the boats (summer only) that cruise along the river Erdre through the town. The pass costs 16€ for 1 day, 28€ for 2 days, and 36€ for 3 days.

Cathédrale St-Pierre ★★ Begun in 1434, this cathedral wasn't finished until the end of the 19th century, but it remained architecturally harmonious—a rare feat. Two square towers dominate the facade; more impressive is the 100m-long (328-ft.) interior. Its *pièce de résistance* is Michel Colomb's Renaissance tomb of François II, duc de Bretagne, and his second wife, Marguerite de Foix. Also noteworthy is the tomb of Gen. Juchault de Lamoricière, a Nantes native and a great African campaigner; sculptor Paul Dubois completed the tomb in 1879. After a 1972 fire destroyed the roof, the interior was restored. The white walls and pillars contrast with the rich colors of the stained-glass windows. The crypt is from the 11th century. It is open only Saturday and Sunday 3 to 6pm.

Place St-Pierre. ⓒ **02-40-47-84-64.** Free admission. Daily 8:30am–6:15pm.

343

Château des Ducs de Bretagne ★★   Between the cathedral and the Loire is Nantes's second major sight, where the Edict of Nantes was signed. The castle was constructed in the 9th or 10th century, enlarged in the 13th century, destroyed, and rebuilt into its present shape by François II in 1466. His daughter, Anne de Bretagne, continued the work. Large towers and a bastion flank the castle, which contains a symmetrical section (the Grand Gouvernement) built during the 17th and 18th centuries. The duchesse du Berry, royal courtesan, was imprisoned here, as was Gilles de Retz ("Bluebeard"), one of France's most notorious mass murderers. The castle's rich collections were shaped into a museum of the history of Nantes from the 17th century to the present. About 30 rooms are devoted to a depiction of the history of one of France's most important ports. Included are many evocative objects, including scaled-down models of the city during different eras. The museum charges admission, but you can visit the courtyard of the château and parade along the ramparts for free.

4 place Marc-Elder. ℂ **02-51-17-49-48.** www.chateau-nantes.fr. Ramparts free daily 9:30am–6pm (until 7pm July–Aug). Museum 5€ adults, 3€ students 25 and under, free for children 17 and under. Daily 10am–6pm.

Musée des Beaux-Arts de Nantes ★   In one of western France's most interesting provincial galleries, you'll find an unusually fine collection of sculptures and paintings from the 12th to the late 19th centuries. The street level is devoted to mostly French modern or contemporary art created since 1900, with special emphasis on painters from the 1950s and 1960s.

10 rue Georges-Clemenceau. ℂ **02-51-17-45-00.** Admission 3.50€ adults, 2€ students 19–26, free for children 18 and under; free to all 1st Sun of every month. Wed–Mon 10am–6pm.

Musée Jules Verne de Nantes   The novelist Jules Verne (*Journey to the Center of the Earth, Around the World in Eighty Days*) was born in Nantes in 1828. This museum is filled with memorabilia and objects inspired by his writings, from ink spots to a "magic" lantern with glass slides. Fans also seek out Verne's house at 4 rue de Clisson in the Ile-Feydeau, which is privately owned and not open to the public. In a historic, mostly 18th-century neighborhood in the heart of the town, the house was named after an island (l'Ile Feydeau) that became part of "mainland" Nantes after the river was diverted into a series of canals during the 18th century.

3 rue de l'Hermitage. ℂ **02-40-69-72-52.** Admission 3€ adults, 1.50€ for students, free for children 6 and under. Wed–Mon 10am–noon and 2–6pm.

Musée Thomas-Dobrée   This 19th-century neo-Romanesque mansion was built by Thomas Dobrée, an important collector and traveler. It stands in the town center, adjacent to the 15th-century manor of Jean V, where the bishops of Nantes

---

  The Secret Garden of Nantes

Two blocks east of the cathedral, you can visit one of France's most beautiful gardens, the **Jardin des Plantes**, boulevard Stalingrad, adjacent to Gare SNCF (ℂ **02-40-41-90-09**). The northern entrance is close to the Musée des Beaux-Arts, the southern border across from the train station. Admission is free. It is open March through October daily 8:30am to 8pm. In winter it is open only in November and December 8:30am to 5:30pm.

occasionally lived. You'll see Dobrée's eclectic collection, gathered during the height of France's Gilded Age, including prehistoric and medieval antiquities, Flemish paintings from the 15th century, ecclesiastical relics, paintings by masters such as Dürer, art objects from India, and the Dobrée family jewels. The collection and building were deeded to the Département de Loire-Atlantique after the death of M. Dobrée in 1894.

18 rue Voltaire. © **02-40-71-03-50.** Admission 3€ adults; 1.50€ seniors, students, and children. Tues–Fri 1:30–5:30pm; Sat–Sun 2:30–5:30pm.

Shopping

Nantes overflows with shops and boutiques. The principal shopping streets are rue du Calvaire, rue Crébillon, rue Boileau, rue d'Orléans, rue de la Marne, rue de Verdun, and passage Pommeraye. Most of these encompass the shopping districts around place Graslin, place Royale, the château, and the cathedral. One of the prime areas for antiques is around place Aristide-Briand and rue Mercoeur.

Interesting antiques dealers include **Ecritoire Antiquités Poidras,** 12 rue Jean-Jaurès (© **02-40-47-78-18**), offering 18th- and 19th-century furniture and decorative pieces such as historic mantels.

For unusual gifts, check out the stores of two master artisans: **Maison Devineau,** 4 rue Belle (© **02-40-47-19-59**), which brings the art of waxworking to a new level, "growing" bushels of fruits, flowers, and vegetables from liquid wax; and **Gautier de Botte,** 9 rue de la Fosse (© **02-40-48-23-19**), a historic boutique established in 1823 with the town's best chocolates.

Where to Stay

Hôtel de France ★ 🏨 Classified by the government as a historic monument, this well-run, beautifully maintained hotel dates from the 1700s. Many of the accommodations are decorated with reproductions of Louis XV– or Louis XVI–style furnishings. The comfortable midsize guest rooms have small bathrooms with a tub and shower. A few of the guest rooms are quite spacious, with high ceilings. The hotel is a 3-minute walk from the pedestrian zone.

24 rue Crébillon, Nantes 44000. © **02-40-73-57-91.** Fax 02-40-69-75-75. www.oceaniahotels.com. 74 units. 98€–145€ double; 190€ suite. AE, MC, V. Free parking. **Amenities:** Restaurant; bar; room service. *In room:* TV, Wi-Fi (free).

Hôtel Graslin In 1944, the pilot of an American bomber misjudged the wind factor while trying to bomb a German ship in the port of Nantes, and to everyone's horror, a then-antique hotel was blasted and virtually incinerated. In its place, built shortly after the war, came this five-story, beige-fronted structure. Its interior was completely renovated, based on the conservative modern taste of its owner, M. LeMoine. The comfortable, midsize rooms are well furnished and tidily maintained. There's no restaurant on-site, but thanks to its location in the heart of Nantes's historic core, there are "at least 50" restaurants within a relatively short walking distance.

1 rue Piron, Nantes 44000. © **02-40-69-72-91.** Fax 02-40-69-04-44. www.hotel-graslin.com. 47 units. 74€–102€ double. AE, DC, MC, V. Parking 2.40€. *In room:* TV, hair dryer, Wi-Fi (free).

L'Hôtel Within sight of the château and the cathedral, this hotel is, for the price, a perfect base in Nantes. Built in the 1980s, the place is neat and modern but maintains an inviting atmosphere. Firm beds, rich colors, and contemporary furnishings fill the hotel. Some units have private balconies overlooking the château, while others open onto a garden and terrace. Each neatly tiled bathroom has a tub or shower. You'll find a paneled sitting area with couches and chairs next to the reception desk, as well as a softly lit breakfast room with terrace views.

6 rue Henri-IV, Nantes 44000. ℭ **02-40-29-30-31.** Fax 02-40-29-00-95. www.nanteshotel.com. 31 units. 90€–160€ double. AE, MC, V. Parking 9€. **Amenities:** Room service. *In room:* A/C, TV, hair dryer, minibar, Wi-Fi (free).

Where to Dine

Du Lieu Unique FRENCH/BRETON   The chief attraction of this restored old biscuit factory, Le Lieu Unique, is this restaurant and bar, which has become a major nighttime rendezvous for the young people of Nantes. In an atmospheric setting, diners can order from a market-fresh menu. Begin perhaps with a homemade terrine or else a "duet" of smoked salmon and rillettes. At least three fish dishes are featuring nightly, including, perhaps, sander in a white butter sauce or grilled dorado with lentils. Filet of bar also appears regularly on the menu with wild rice. Other dishes are likely to include a honey-flavored *magret* of duckling or roast lamb flavored with thyme juice. For dessert you might order roast pineapple with vanilla ice cream or else a crème brûlée.

Le Lieu Unique, 2 rue de la biscuterie. ℭ **02-51-72-05-55.** Reservations recommended. Main courses 10€–17€; fixed-price lunch 12€; fixed-price dinners 12€–25€. MC, V. Mon–Sat noon-2:30pm; Tues–Sat 7pm–midnight.

La Cigale FRENCH/SEAFOOD   This is Nantes's most historic and charming brasserie, decorated in a Belle Epoque style that has changed little since the place opened in 1895 across from the landmark Théâtre Graslin. Menu items may include platters of fresh shellfish, *confit des cuisses de canard* (duckling), and fresh scallops with green peppers and emulsified butter. The sprawling restaurant is usually quite loud, and the staff members tend to be overworked.

4 place Graslin. ℭ **02-51-84-94-94.** Reservations recommended. Main courses 16€–23€; fixed-price menu 14€–28€. MC, V. Daily 7:30am-12:30am. Bus: 11 or 34.

L'Atlantide ★★★ MODERN FRENCH   On the fourth floor of the complex that houses the city's chamber of commerce, this panoramic restaurant, with views over the semi-industrial landscape, serves the finest cuisine in the area. The world-renowned designer Jean-Pierre Wilmotte created the nautical-looking enclave with lots of mirrors, but Jean-Yves Gueho's innovative cooking is what draws patrons. Menu items, steeped in the traditions of both the Loire Valley and the Breton coast, may include lobster salad with yellow-wine sauce; potato-and-herb tart capped with foie gras; Breton turbot with Cantonese spices; and braised sweetbreads with Anjou wine. An excellent dessert is bananas braised in local beer. The cellar is known for some of the finest vintages of Loire Valley wine anywhere, with an emphasis on Anjous and Muscadets.

Centre des Salorges, 16 quai Ernest-Renaud. ℭ **02-40-73-23-23.** www.restaurant-atlantide.net. Reservations required. Main courses 23€–58€; fixed-price lunch 30€–75€, dinner 40€–95€. AE, V. Mon–Fri noon-2pm; Mon–Sat 8-9:45pm. Closed 1st 3 weeks of Aug and Dec 23-Jan 3.

Les Oubliettes ⚓ FRENCH   As part of the restoration of the château at Nantes, a luncheon restaurant was installed with an ancient atmosphere with a large fireplace and an outdoor terrace. The walls are made from *tuffaud*, the local stone. Affordable fixed-price menus are offered, with good-tasting, classic French dishes served, including such appetizers as a terrine of duckling foie gras or a salad of tomatoes, mozzarella, and anchovies with fresh basil. A fish of the day is usually served with *beurre blanc* (white butter) from Nantes. Also veal piccata appears regularly on the menu as does a pâté of beef. For dessert you might opt for strawberries with sabayon, chocolate mousse, or a soufflé Grand Marnier.

Château des Ducs de Bretagne, Place Marc-Elder. ℂ **02-51-82-67-04.** http://lesoubliettes.fr. Reservations recommended. Fixed-price menus 14€–21€. MC, V. Thurs–Sat and Mon 10am–5pm; Sun 10am–5pm.

Villa Mon Rêve MODERN FRENCH This restaurant, in a stone-sided 19th-century villa built by a prosperous producer of fruits and vegetables, is in a .4-hectare (1-acre) garden awash with roses in summer. Chef Gérard Ryngel's repertoire includes regional specialties and his own creations: wild duck with Bourgueil wine sauce, *sandre* (fish) from the Loire with beurre blanc, frogs' legs sautéed in white wine, and gazpacho studded with chunks of lobster. An unusual dish is roasted duckling with caramelized Muscadet wine. The wine list features more than 40 local choices.

Porte du Vignoble, rte. des Bords-de-Loire, Basse-Goulaine. ℂ **02-40-03-55-50.** www.villa-mon-reve. com. Reservations recommended. Main courses 18€–29€; fixed-price menu 32€. AE, DC, MC, V. Daily noon–1:30pm and 7–9:30pm. Closed 2 weeks in Feb and 2 weeks in Nov. Take D751 8km (5 miles) south of Nantes.

Nantes After Dark

When the sun goes down, the town turns into one big party. On **place du Bouffay, place du Pilori,** and **rue Kervégan,** you'll find lots of cafes and pubs, many with live music and fun people. A younger crowd rules **rue Scribe.**

The hippest location in Nantes, and the town's leading cultural center, is **Le Lieu Unique,** 2 rue de la Biscuiterie (ℂ **02-51-82-15-00**). Converted from a 19th-century biscuit factory, the venue's presentations range from plays (in French) to art exhibitions. Admission is free to the dimly lit, concrete-floored bar at ground level, which is frequented by students and artists. A packed floor of young people dance to the sounds of DJs playing everything from love songs to "hate songs." Beer is cheap, only 2.50€ a mug. The bar is open Monday 11am to 8pm, Tuesday through Thursday 11am to 2am, Friday and Saturday 11am to 3am, and Sunday 3 to 8pm.

Catch some live blues, jazz, or rock at **L'Univers Café,** 16 rue Jean-Jacques-Rousseau (ℂ **02-40-73-49-55**), or techno and disco at **L.C. Club,** 3 quai François-Mitterrand (ℂ **02-40-47-68-45**), open all night. A great piano bar with a dance floor and occasional jazz concerts is **Le Tie Break,** 1 rue des Petites-Ecuries (ℂ **02-40-47-77-00**).

The pump-it-up dance scene has a huge following of everyone from students to seniors. The over-30 crowd heads to the vintage 1970s disco **L'Evasion,** 3 rue de l'Emery (ℂ **02-40-47-99-84**). Other discos include **Le Royal Club Privé,** 7 rue des Salorges (ℂ **02-40-69-11-10**). Don't wear jeans to any of these places, and be prepared to pay 15€ to 20€ to get in.

The favorite with gays and lesbians is **Le Petit Marais,** 15 rue Kervégan (ℂ **02-40-20-15-25**), where people meet and talk in a friendly atmosphere that welcomes everything from leather to lace. **Le Temps d'Aimer,** 14 rue Alexandre-Fourny (ℂ **02-40-89-48-60**), is mixed and gay-friendly. This disco with its small dance floor attracts a sophisticated crowd. The most you'll pay to get in is 15€.

THE CHAMPAGNE COUNTRY

I n about 3 days, you can take the Autoroute de l'Est (N3) from Paris and explore a region of cathedrals, historic battlefields, great food, and vineyards, topping your tour with a glass or two of bubbly. On the Routes du Champagne, you can drive to the wine-producing center of Epernay, and on to Reims, 145km (90 miles) northeast of Paris. After visiting Reims and its cathedral, you can head toward Verdun, of World War I fame.

LA FERTE-SOUS-JOUARRE

66km (41 miles) E of Paris; 82km (51 miles) SW of Reims

The little town of La Ferté-sous-Jouarre and the village of Jouarre are twin communities—you can't tell where one ends and the other begins. Although La Ferté-sous-Jouarre, which took its name from a now-gone 10th-century fortress, played a role in French history, it is of little interest today and is worth a visit chiefly for the lodging at Château des Bondons (see below).

In the village of Jouarre, 3km (1¾ miles) south of La Ferté-sous-Jouarre, you can visit a 12th-century Benedictine abbey and explore one of the oldest crypts in France. At the **Tour et Crypt de l'Abbaye de Jouarre,** 6 rue Montmorin (☎ 01-60-22-64-54), those interested in medieval history will appreciate the documents referring to the Royal Abbey of Jouarre as well as the stones in the Merovingian crypt, which evoke the 7th century. There's also a collection of prehistoric artifacts, remnants of the Roman occupation, and sculptural fragments. Each of these monuments is a medieval treasure. Entrance to the crypt costs 4.50€ for adults and 4€ for students and children 17 and under. Entrance to the tower is included. One floor above the crypt, a small-scale museum, **Musée Briard,** showcases the medieval history of the region of Brie. Entrance to the museum costs 2.50€ for adults and 2€ for children.

The crypt is the star of the three attractions, the tower somewhat less famous and evocative. All three sites are open Wednesday to Monday but

To Laon & Amiens

Soissons

Villers-Cotterêts

Fisme

Fère-en-Tardenois

Reims

Montagne de Reims

Château-Thierry

Meaux

Condé-en-Brie

Épernay

La Ferté-sous-Jouarre

Châlons-en-Champagne

Coulommiers

Montmirail

Fère-Champenoise

Sézanne

Vitry-le-François

Provins

Lhuître

Noget-sur-Seine

Romilly

Troyes

Sens

Aix-en-Othe

Bar-sur-Seine

Paris

CHAMPAGNE

FRANCE

Mountain

To Paris

can only be visited on guided tours, lasting 30 to 45 minutes. From April to October tours leave every hour on the hour from 10:15am to 5:15pm.

Essentials

GETTING THERE If you're **driving,** take N3 along the Marne. About 10 **trains** per day make the 55-minute run from Paris's Gare de l'Est, stopping at La Ferté-sous-Jouarre. From there, take a taxi 3km (1¾ miles) south to Jouarre and its abbey. For train reservations and schedules, call ✆ **36-35** or 08-92-35-35-35, or visit www.voyages-sncf.com.

VISITOR INFORMATION The **Office de Tourisme** in Jouarre is on rue de la Tour, adjacent to the tower and the abbey (✆ **01-60-22-64-54;** fax 01-60-22-65-15; www.tourisme-jouarre.com).

Where to Stay

Château des Bondons ★★ Surrounded by a 7-hectare (17-acre) park and forest, this château dates from the French Revolution. The doomed Louis XVI and

Marie-Antoinette were brought here following their arrest at Varennes in June 1791. They were then taken to Paris and executed. Not much of the furniture is original to the building; a country aesthetic, complete with chintz upholstery and antiques, characterizes the public areas. As befits a château, guest rooms come in a variety of shapes, but they are all comfortable, filled with old and new furnishings.

47-49 rue des Bondons, La Ferté-sous-Jouarre 77260. ⓒ **01-60-22-00-98.** Fax 01-60-22-97-01. www. chateaudesbondons.com. 14 units. 120€-160€ double; 160€-240€ suite. AE, DC, MC, V. Follow signs to Montménard; take D70 for 2.5km (1½ miles) east of the town center. **Amenities:** Restaurant; bar; room service. *In room:* TV, hair dryer, Jacuzzi (in some suites), minibar, Wi-Fi (free).

Where to Dine

Château des Bondons (see above) has a restaurant.

Le Plat d'Etain TRADITIONAL FRENCH   This homelike, conservative restaurant caters to the gastronomic needs of art-history lovers who make the pilgrimage to see the famous Merovingian crypt, which is nearby. It has exposed ceiling beams, lacy curtains, and tokens of old-fashioned France. The food might remind locals of the style of cuisine once prepared by their grandmothers. The best examples include *blanquette de veau* (veal stew), boeuf bourguignon, and whatever is seasonal and appeals to the whims of the chef. The restaurant also rents 18 simply furnished bedrooms, costing 62€ to 68€ for a double.

6 place Auguste-Tinchant, Jouarre. ⓒ **01-60-22-06-07.** Reservations recommended. Main courses 18€-27€; fixed-price menus 19€-48€. MC, V. Daily noon-2pm; Mon-Thurs and Sat 7:30-9pm.

CHATEAU-THIERRY

90km (56 miles) E of Paris; 9.5km (6 miles) SW of Reims

An industrial town on the Marne's right bank, Château-Thierry contains the ruins of a castle believed to have been constructed for the Frankish king Thierry IV. Château-Thierry gained fame for being the farthest point the German offensive reached in 1918. Under heavy bombardment, the Second and Third Divisions of the U.S. Expeditionary Force aided French troops. The battlefields of the Marne are just west of town; thousands of Allied soldiers who died in World War I are buried here. Atop Hill 204 is a monument honoring American troops.

The poet and fable writer Jean de la Fontaine (1621-95) was born here, in a stone-sided house built in 1452. Today, it contains one of France's most visited literary shrines, the **Musée Jean-de-la-Fontaine,** 12 rue Jean de la Fontaine (ⓒ **03-23-69-05-60;** www.musee-jean-de-la-fontaine.fr). Located a few steps from place de l'Hôtel-de-Ville, it contains a collection of his mementos, editions of his works published over many centuries, and a trio of rooms outfitted with furniture from the 17th through 19th centuries. Each room centers on some aspect of the effect of de la Fontaine on those centuries. Copies of his fables (allegorical barnyard stories depicting the foibles of humans) and *contes* (short stories a lot racier than the fables) are for sale in the bookshop. The museum is open Tuesday to Sunday 9:30am to noon and 2 to 5:30pm. Admission is 3.60€ for adults, 2.20€ students, and 1.80€ for children 17 and under; it's free to everyone on Wednesday.

If you're interested in World War I, head 8km (5 miles) northwest of Château-Thierry to the **Bois de Belleau (Belleau Wood).** The Battle of Belleau Wood marked the second clash between American and German troops in World War I and demonstrated the bravery of the U.S. soldiers. After a 2-week struggle, the Second Division of the U.S. Expeditionary Force under Maj. Gen. Omar Bundy took the woods. Though the Germans suffered many losses and some 1,650 prisoners were taken, U.S. casualties were appalling—more than 8,000 American troops were wounded, killed, or missing. In 1923, the battleground was dedicated as a memorial to the men who gave their lives here. The **American cemetery,** also known as Le Cimetière de Belleau (✆ **03-23-70-70-90**), contains 2,288 graves. You'll also see a chapel that was damaged in World War II. Entrance is free; it's open daily 9am to 5pm.

Essentials

GETTING THERE   If you're **driving,** take A4 southwest from Reims or northeast from La Ferté-sous-Jouarre. There are **trains** from Paris's Gare de l'Est (16€ one-way) and Reims (12€ one-way); each trip takes 1 hour. For information, call ✆ **36-35** or 08-92-35-35-35.

VISITOR INFORMATION   The **Office de Tourisme** is at 11 rue Vallée (✆ **03-23-83-10-14;** fax 03-23-83-14-74; www.otsichateau-thierry.com).

Where to Stay

Ile-de-France   This modern hotel is the leading choice in an area of not-so-hot options. After renovations the hotel shrank from 50 units to just 32, making all the accommodations larger and more comfortable. In a park overlooking the Marne Valley, near the ruins of the town's château, the four-story structure boasts balconies and dormers, a view of the town, and well-maintained guest rooms.

Rte. de Soissons, Château-Thierry 02400. ✆ **03-23-69-10-12.** Fax 03-23-83-49-70. www.hotel-iledefrance.fr. 32 units. 90€ double; 140€–180€ suite. AE, DC, MC, V. **Amenities:** Restaurant; bar; baby-sitting; fitness center; indoor pool; room service; rooms for those w/limited mobility; smoke-free rooms; spa. *In room:* TV, hair dryer, Wi-Fi (free).

Where to Dine

Les Fabliaux TRADITIONAL FRENCH   Outfitted in a conservatively modern and cozy style, and accented with framed illustrations based on the short fables of La Fontaine, this restaurant is widely respected in the district for its well-prepared, traditional French food. Outfitted in pastel colors, it offers a menu that includes snails poached in garlic butter; curried rack of lamb with almond butter, and sea bass with asparagus-studded risotto. The restaurant also rents simply furnished bedrooms that nonetheless are equipped with TVs, minibars, and Wi-Fi, costing 58€ to 64€ for a double. Technically, it lies in the suburb of Brasles, about 45m (150 ft.) northwest of the boundary of Chateau-Thierry, very close to that city's historic core.

3 av. de Château-Thierry, Brasles. ✆ **03-23-83-23-14.** www.les-fabliaux.com. Main courses 15€–17€; set-price menus 20€–47€. AE, MC, V. Sun–Fri noon–2pm; Mon–Sat 7:30–9pm.

CONDE-EN-BRIE ★

89km (55 miles) E of Paris; 24km (15 miles) W of Epernay

West of Epernay, **Château de Condé ★**, rue du Château, Condé-en-Brie 02330 (✆ **03-23-82-42-25;** www.chateaudeconde.com), was bequeathed to the comte de Sade in 1814 and remained in his family until 1983. The name gained notoriety from the works of the marquis, an innovative writer (*Justine, Juliette, The 120 Days of Sodom*) whose sexual practices as described in his works gave us the word "sadism."

Enguerrand of Coucy built the castle in the late 12th century. A part of the old keep—two big rooms with great chimneys and thick walls—survives. Cardinal de Bourbon, a member of the royal family, reconstructed the castle in the Renaissance style early in the 16th century. His nephew, Louis de Bourbon, called himself the prince de Condé, most likely because he had many fond childhood memories of the place. After sustaining damage in the 18th century, the château was rebuilt for the marquis de La Faye. The Italian architect Servandoni invited artists Boucher and Watteau to do frescoes and paintings, which you can see today. Servandoni decorated the largest room, making it a theater for music and entertainment. The present castle is exceptional, with its paintings, woodwork, chimneys, and so-called Versailles floor.

In 1994, the new owners, the de Rocheforts, discovered several Watteau frescoes behind mirrors installed during the 18th century. Now, at the push of a button, the mirrors open to reveal the previously hidden treasures.

Admission is 9.50€ for adults, 4.50€ for children 6 to 12, and free for children 5 and under. The castle is open only during the afternoon, and only between mid-April and mid-October, Tuesday to Sunday from 2:30 to 5:30pm. Visits are self-guided, conducted with the help of a free leaflet outlining the history of the building and some of its most important features. Families with children sometimes opt to collectively follow a self-guided treasure hunt, whereby the gift at the end of the hunt is a key that opens a treasure chest loaded with candy and simple toys.

If you're **driving** between Château-Thierry and Epernay on N3, head south at Dormans, and follow the signs to Condé-en-Brie.

REIMS ★★★

143km (89 miles) E of Paris; 45km (28 miles) NW of Châlons-en-Champagne

Reims (pronounced "rahns"), an ancient Roman city, was important when Caesar conquered Gaul. French kings came here to be crowned, and it's said that the French nation was born here in A.D. 498. Joan of Arc escorted Charles VII here in 1429, kissing the silly man's feet. But don't let its ancient background mislead you: As you approach Reims, you'll pass through prefabricated suburbs that look like eastern European apartment-house blocks. There are gems in Reims, including the cathedral, but you must seek them out.

Most visitors come to Reims because it's the center of a winegrowing district; its bubbly is present at celebrations all over the world. The city (pop. 200,000) is filled with swank restaurants, ritzy champagne houses, large squares, and long, tree-lined avenues. The champagne bottled here has the lightest and most subtle flavor in the world. Make an effort to linger, and explore the vineyards and wine cellars, the Gothic monuments, and the battlefields.

Essentials

GETTING THERE   If you're **driving** from Paris, take A4 east. **Trains** depart from Paris's Gare de l'Est every 1½ hours (trip time: 45 min.); the one-way fare is 30€ to 38€. Five trains per day arrive from Strasbourg (trip time: 2 hr.; one-way fare is 48€). For information, call ⓒ **08-36-35-35-35**, or visit www.voyages-sncf.com.

To Laon

rue du Mont-d'Arène

rue F. Roosevelt

de - Mars

Champs

1

2

place de la République

rue du

To Rethel

bd. Jamin

Information ⓘ
Post Office ✉
Railway ┄┄┄

Port de Mars ✉

bd. Joffre

bd. Foch

Lundy

Jean-Jaurès

av.

bd.

Cernay

Gare Centrale

place A. Briand

rue

de

Carteret

place du Forum

rue Cérès

Roederer

bd. L.

rue Général-Leclerc

Buirette

place Royale

ⓘ

rue Voltaire

rue G. Laurent

St-Marceaux

rue Clovis

de Vesle

Musée St-Denis

4 **3**

Palais du Tau place Carnégie

de

la

Paix

av. G. Clemenceau

To Epernay

rue

5

rue Chanzy

To Soissons

rue Libergier

rue Clovis

rue des

Jard

rue Gambetta

rue Barbâtre

rue

de

Sillery

bd. P. Doumer

Halen Canal

rue du Capucines

Venise

bd. Pommery

chaussée

rue de

rue des Moulins

rue

St-

bd. H. Vasnier

place du Général-Gouraud

To Paris

rue de Courlancy

av. P. Marchandeau

Bocquaine

N. Dr. Henrot

Vesle

A4

Simon

6

place St-Nicaise

8

7

bd. Diancourt

9

To Verdun

place des Droits-de-l'Homme

Paris ★ ● Reims

FRANCE

Basilique St-Rémi **8**	Salle de Reddition **1**
Cathédrale Notre-Dame de Reims **4**	Maison de Pommery **7**
	Mumm **2**
Musée des Beaux-Arts **5**	Taittinger **6**
Palais du Tau **3**	Veuve Clicquot Ponsardin **9**

VISITOR INFORMATION The **Office de Tourisme** is at 2 rue Guillaume-de-Machault (ⓒ **03-26-77-45-00;** fax 03-26-77-45-19; www.reims-tourisme.com).

Exploring the City

Basilique St-Rémi ★★ This church dates from 1007, making it the oldest in Reims. Though an example of classic medieval French masonry, it's often unfavorably compared to the more spectacular cathedral. Within the complex is the former royal abbey of St-Rémi, who as the guardian of the holy ampula used to anoint the kings of France. The abbey now functions as a museum, with an extensive collection covering the history of Reims, regional archaeology, and military history. Architect Louis Duroché designed the majestic ornamental front of the main quadrangle and the Grand Staircase (1778), where you can admire a portrait of the young Louis XV in his coronation robes. The church also contains a Romanesque nave leading to a magnificent choir crowned with pointed arches. The nave, the transepts, one of the towers, and the aisles date from the 11th century; the portal of the south transept is in early-16th-century Flamboyant Gothic style. Some of the stained glass in the apse is from the 13th century. The tomb of St. Rémi is elaborately carved with Renaissance figures and columns.

Place Chanoine Ladame, Basilique. ℂ **03-26-85-31-20.** Free admission. Daily 8am–7pm. Musée: ℂ **03-26-85-23-36.** Admission 3€ adults, free for children 16 and under. Mon–Fri 2–6:30pm; Sat–Sun 2–7pm.

Cathédrale Notre-Dame de Reims ★★★   One of the world's most famous cathedrals was restored after World War I, funded largely by contributions from John D. Rockefeller; it escaped World War II relatively unharmed. Built on the site of a church that burned in 1211, it was intended as a sanctuary where French kings would be anointed. St-Rémi, the bishop of Reims, baptized Clovis, the king of the Franks, here in A.D. 496. All the kings of France from Louis the Pious in 815 to Charles X in 1825 were crowned here.

Laden with statuettes, its three western facade portals are spectacular. A rose window above the central portal is dedicated to the Virgin. The right portal portrays the Apocalypse and the Last Judgment; the left, martyrs and saints. At the western facade's northern door is a smiling angel. Lit by lancet windows, the immense nave has many bays.

Place du Cardinal-Luçon. ℂ **03-26-35-36-00.** Free admission. Daily 7:30am–7:30pm.

Musée des Beaux-Arts   Housed in the 18th-century buildings belonging to the old Abbaye St-Denis, this fine provincial gallery contains more than a dozen portraits of German princes by both "the Elder" and "the Younger" Cranach; the museum has owned this collection since it opened in 1795. You can see the *toiles peintes* (light painting on rough linen) that date from the 15th and 16th centuries and depict the *Passion du Christ* and *Vengeance du Christ*. Paintings and furniture from the 17th and 18th centuries are in the salles Diancourt and Jamot-Neveux. There's an excellent series of 27 of Corot's tree-shaded walks.

8 rue Chanzy. ℂ **03-26-47-28-44.** Admission 3€ adults, free for students and children 17 and under; free to all 1st Sun of every month. Wed–Mon 10am–noon and 2–6pm. Closed Jan 1, May 1, July 14, Nov 1 and 11, and Dec 25.

Palais du Tau ★★   Built in 1690 as the residence of the bishops of Reims, this stone mansion beside the cathedral contains many statues that, until recently, decorated the cathedral facade. (The ones there now are mostly copies.) Also on display are holy relics associated with Reims, including a 12th-century chalice for the communion of French monarchs and a talisman supposedly containing a relic of the True Cross that Charlemagne is said to have worn.

Place du Cardinal-Luçon. ℂ **03-26-47-81-79.** Admission 6.10€ adults, 4.50€ students and ages 18–25, free for children 17 and under. May–Sept Tues–Sun 9:30am–6:30pm; Oct–Apr Tues–Sun 9:30am–12:30pm and 2–5:30pm.

Salle de Reddition On May 7, 1945, the Germans surrendered to General Eisenhower in this structure, which was once a schoolhouse near the railroad tracks. Maps of the rail routes line the walls of the rooms, exactly as they did on the day of surrender.

12 rue Franklin-D-Roosevelt. ✆ **03-26-47-84-19.** Admission 3€ adults, free for children 17 and under. Wed–Mon 10am–noon and 2–6pm. Closed May 1 and July 14.

Exploring the Champagne Cellars ★★

Many of the champagne cellars of Reims extend for miles through chalky deposits. During the German siege of 1914 and throughout the war, people lived and even published a daily paper in them. The cellars are open year-round, but are most interesting during the fall grape harvest. After that, the wine is fermented in vats in the caves and then bottled with a small amount of sugar and natural yeast. The yeast feeds on the sugar and causes a second fermentation that produces those fabulous bubbles. The winegrowers wait until the sparkle has "taken" before they move the bottles to racks or pulpits. For about 3 months, *remueurs* (migrant workers) turn them every day, which brings the impurities (dead yeast cells and other matter) toward the cork. Eventually the sediments are removed and the wine is given its proper dosage (sugar dissolved in wine), depending on the desired sweetness. The process takes 4 or 5 years and takes place in caves that are 30m (98 ft.) deep, where the temperature is a constant 50°F (10°C).

Maison de Pommery Among the most visited cellars are those under the Gothic-style buildings and gardens of the Maison de Pommery. A magnificent 116-step stairway leads to a maze of galleries dug into the chalk; the complex is more than 18km (11 miles) long and about 30m (98 ft.) below ground. Various stages of champagne making are shown, and the end product is for sale in the gift shop.

Place du Général-Gouraud. ✆ **03-26-61-62-55.** www.pommery.com. Reservations required. Admission 10€, free for children 11 and under. Daily 9:30am–7pm.

Mumm Founded in 1827, Mumm welcomes visitors with a video that explains how champagne is made. An in-house museum exhibits casks and illustrates the ancient role of the vintner. On a 1-hour tour, a guide will lead visitors into a labyrinth of tunnels and storage cellars in the chalky bedrock; they contain a vast inventory—almost 25 million bottles—of slowly fermenting champagne.

34 rue du Champ-de-Mars. ✆ **03-26-49-59-70.** www.mumm.com. Reservations required. Tours (in English) 8€–20€ adults, free for children 15 and under. Mar–Oct daily 9–11am and 2–5pm.

Taittinger Taittinger is a grand *marque* of French champagne, one of the few still controlled by members of the family that founded it (in 1930). It's one of the most visitor-friendly champagne houses. The Romanesque cellars were dug from the site of Gallo-Roman chalk mines in use from the 4th to the 13th century. Tours—including a film, a guided cellar visit, and anecdotes about Reims, the champagne-making process, and Taittinger family lore—last about an hour.

9 place St-Nicaise. ✆ **03-26-85-84-35.** www.taittinger.com. Admission 10€ adults, free for children 11 and under. Mid-Mar to mid-Nov daily 9:30am–1pm and 2–5:30pm; mid-Nov to mid-Mar Mon–Fri 9:30am–1pm and 2–5:30pm.

Veuve Clicquot–Ponsardin One of the most memorable and successful logos in France shows a 19th-century matriarch, Nicole Ponsardin, outfitted in dowdy but expensive finery. She remained firmly in control of the *maison de champagne* that bears her name from 1866 (when her husband died) to 1895. You can visit some of the 26km (16 miles) of underground galleries as part of guided tours that last 75 to 90 minutes.

1 place des Droits-de-l'Homme. © **03-26-89-53-90.** www.veuve-clicquot.com. Reservations required. Admission 13€, free for 15 and under. Apr–Oct Mon–Sat 10am–6pm; Nov 2–Dec 22 and Jan 12–Mar Mon–Fri 10am–6pm.

Shopping

The main shopping district is around the cathedral. Nearby streets to browse are the long **rue de Vesle,** the **cours Langlet,** and **place Drouet d'Erlon.**

You'll want to include champagne on your shopping list. Many people opt to visit one of the major houses in town; others drive along the **Routes du Champagne.** This is where you'll find the smaller champagne makers. When you're making the rounds, know that most houses prefer that you take the tour and not just stop in the shop. If you do take the tour, you'll at least get a glass of bubbly at the end. Bottles are priced individually, but you can get discounts if you buy three or six bottles. If you're looking for a good deal, you may want to buy at a store in town, such as **a Grande Boutique du Vin,** 3 place Léon-Bourgeois (© **03-26-40-12-12**). It stocks one of the most comprehensive inventories of champagne in Reims, with 150 types of bubbly from more than 100 companies. They include many superb brands for 15€ to 38€ per bottle, which are virtually never advertised in North America. Excellent, lesser known brands include Deutz, Billecart Salmon, Henriot, Guy Charlemagne, and Erick de Sousa. Staff members speak English.

Another specialty is the light, delicious little pink cookie known as *biscuit de Reims.* The best place to find this treat is **La Maison Fossier/Biscuits Fossier,** 25 cours Langlet (© **03-26-47-59-84**). For chocolate and candied specialties, try **La Petite Friande,** 15 cours Langlet (© **03-26-47-50-44**), where you can purchase liqueur-filled chocolate champagne bubbles and corks.

Parc des Expositions (© **03-26-84-69-69**), route de Châlons-en-Champagne (4km/2½ miles east of Reims), plays host to a flea market the first Sunday of every month except July and August. On the first weekend of April, there's a huge "Euro" flea market, with more than 500 vendors, in the same location. The organization responsible for these events is **Artcom/Puces de Reims,** 82 rue Jacquart (© **03-26-02-04-06**).

Where to Stay

EXPENSIVE

Grand Hôtel des Templiers ★★   This chic hotel a short walk from the cathedral is small, but it's your best inner-city bet. In a restored 1800s mock-Gothic house, antiques, ornate ceilings, and hand-carved woodwork create an inviting ambience. The guest rooms maintain the 19th-century atmosphere, with color-coordinated fabrics and bold-print wall coverings. Each comes with a quality bed and well-maintained bathroom, most often with both tub and shower.

22 rue des Templiers, Reims 51100. © **03-26-88-55-08.** Fax 03-26-47-80-60. 17 units. 190€–280€ double; 350€ suite. AE, DC, MC, V. Bus: H. **Amenities:** Bar; indoor heated pool; sauna. *In room:* A/C, TV, hair dryer, minibar, Wi-Fi (free).

Les Crayères ★★★ In Reims, there's no better place to stay or dine than here, one of the finest châteaux in eastern France. Located in a 7-hectare (17-acre) park, it has 5.5m (18-ft.) ceilings, paneling, and luxurious furnishings. The guest rooms, with terraces and all the amenities, are individually decorated in a country-manor style and usually available when a champagne mogul isn't in residence. The bathrooms hold deluxe toiletries and tub/shower combinations. The restaurant is the greatest in the region (p. 358).

64 bd. Henri-Vasnier, Reims 51685. ✆ **03-26-82-80-80.** Fax 03-26-82-65-52. www.lescrayeres.com. 20 units. 325€–660€. AE, DC, MC, V. Closed Jan. **Amenities:** Restaurant; bar; babysitting; room service; tennis court. *In room:* A/C, hair dryer, minibar, Wi-Fi (free).

MODERATE

L'Assiette Champenoise ★★ 🏨 About 3km (1¾ miles) southwest from Reims in the suburb of Tinqueux, this is the second-best hotel and restaurant in the area. Built in the 1970s among century-old trees, it occupies part of a former Norman estate, standing in a 1.6-hectare (4-acre) park. The well-maintained rooms are attractively furnished in a mix of French traditional and modern style. Many visitors come here just for the rustic dining room. Chef Arnaud Lallement's cuisine covers a medley of classics, some with an innovative twist. Try John Dory with ragout of vegetables, suckling veal with seven vegetables, or grilled duck liver with fondue of tomatoes. Homemade foie gras is always a reliable starter.

40 av. Paul-Vaillant-Couturier, Tinqueux 51430. ✆ **03-26-84-64-64.** Fax 03-26-04-15-69. www.assiette champenoise.com. 55 units. 160€–240€ double; 310€ suite. AE, DC, MC, V. Free parking. From Reims, take A4 west toward Paris and exit at SORTIE 22–TINQUEUX; av. Paul-Vaillant-Couturier will lead you directly to Tinqueux. **Amenities:** Restaurant; bar; indoor pool; sauna. *In room:* TV (in some), hair dryer, minibar, Wi-Fi (free).

INEXPENSIVE

Best Western Hôtel de la Paix Located between the train station and the cathedral, this is the only modern hotel in France with a medieval chapel (built for Benedictine nuns in the 1200s) overlooking its garden and pool. Constructed in 1946, it has been enlarged since then. The rooms in this pleasant chain hotel are contemporary and well maintained, and many are air-conditioned. Furnishings are a bit sterile, but the beds are comfortable and most bathrooms have tub/shower combinations. The hotel's restaurant (✆ **03-26-47-00-45**) serves excellent meals daily at lunch and dinner. The cuisine may include sauerkrauts, fish, grills, oysters, and casseroles.

9 rue Buirette, Reims 51100. ✆ **800/528-1234** in the U.S. and Canada, or 03-26-40-04-08. Fax 03-26-47-75-04. www.hotel-lapaix.fr. 169 units. 155€–205€ double; 350€ suite. AE, DC, MC, V. Parking 10€. Bus: G or H. **Amenities:** Restaurant; bar; exercise room; indoor pool; room service; sauna. *In room:* A/C, TV, hair dryer, minibar, Wi-Fi (free).

Grand Hôtel de l'Univers In the heart of Reims, across from the train station, this five-story hotel offers small- to average-size guest rooms outfitted in a basic manner. The hotel is affiliated with the Grand Hôtel du Nord (see below). This area can get noisy, but rooms have double-paned windows. You can have breakfast in the American-style piano bar, where an automated piano plays melodies whenever you press a button, or dinner in the small but well-managed restaurant, which specializes in traditional French cuisine and offers fixed-price menus.

41 bd. Foch, Reims 51100. ✆ **03-26-88-68-08.** Fax 03-26-40-95-61. www.hotel-univers-reims.com. 42 units. 88€–122€ double. AE, DC, MC, V. **Amenities:** Restaurant; bar; Wi-Fi (free). *In room:* TV, hair dryer, minibar.

Grand Hôtel du Nord This 1920s hotel is a former relay station for the postal service. The high-ceilinged guest rooms are renovated and decorated in comfortable contemporary style. The hotel lies in a pedestrian-only zone in Reims's historic core, a 10-minute walk from the cathedral and just steps from the rail station. Two steps from the entrance, lively place Drouet-d'Erlon has many boutiques, cafes, and cinemas. The hotel is also near the cathedral, the basilica, and various museums.

75 place Drouet-d'Erlon, Reims 51100. (℃ **03-26-47-39-03.** Fax 03-26-40-92-26. www.hotel-nord-reims.com. 50 units. 65€–79€ double. AE, DC, MC, V. Take A4 (A26) to Reims-Centre. Bus: G or H. **Amenities:** Smoke-free rooms. *In room:* TV, hair dryer.

Mercure Reims Cathédrale ★ 🏷 This chain hotel from the 1970s sits on the banks of the Marne Canal, a 5-minute walk from the town center and the cathedral. It's near the entrance to the highway A4, so it's easy to find. The good-size rooms have all the modern conveniences, including bathrooms with tubs and showers; some have views of a waterway. Furnishings are standard motel style.

31 bd. Paul-Doumer, Reims 51100. (℃ **03-26-04-78-23.** Fax 03-26-84-49-84. www.mercure.com. 126 units. 124€–179€ double; 162€–209€ suite. AE, DC, MC, V. Parking 11€. **Amenities:** Restaurant; bar; babysitting; room service. *In room:* A/C, TV, hair dryer, minibar, Wi-Fi (free).

Where to Dine

L'Assiette Champenoise (see "Where to Stay," above) has an excellent restaurant.

Le Jamin ★ FRENCH Airy, clean, well respected, and outfitted in a pleasantly contemporary, noncontroversial style, and a fixture in Reims for more than a decade, this restaurant describes itself as "semi-gastronomique," and as such, offers reasonable prices for some remarkably stylish food. The best examples include a salad composed of scallops, crayfish, and sweetbreads; St-Marcellin cheese, fried and served with pine nuts as a salad; and a "*declinaison* of duckling" whereby at least four different preparations (*rillettes, magret* both smoked and unsmoked, and terrine of duck liver) are assembled onto a single flavorful platter. Delectable main courses include roasted turbot in champagne sauce, stingray with garlic butter, and English-style calves' liver.

18 bd. Jamin. (℃ **03-26-07-37-30.** www.lejamin.com. Reservations recommended. Main courses 12€–19€; set menus 20€–31€. AE, MC, V. Tues–Sun noon–2:30pm; Tues–Sat 7:30–9:30pm. Closed last 2 weeks in Aug and last 2 weeks in Jan.

Le Millénaire ★★★ FRENCH Competing for supremacy in a town where the culinary competition is severe, Le Millénaire emerges near the very top. Set near the place Royale, it offers a contemporary setting with frequently changing art exhibitions. Its market-fresh cuisine is sublime, with the finest ingredients deftly handled by a skilled staff. Many gourmets begin with the foie gras or a plate of fresh crayfish, perhaps a tartare of scallops with a truffle tapenade. A risotto is made with black truffles and shavings of parmesan, or else you can opt for the turbot in a champagne sauce with leeks. Sweetbreads are served with a foie gras ravioli, and yet another specialty is the roast lamb in a rosemary sauce.

4 rue Bertin. (℃ **02-26-08-26-62.** Reservations required. Main courses 32€–42€; fixed-price menus 30€–47€. AE, DC, MC, V. Mon–Fri noon–2pm and Mon–Sat 7-10pm.

Les Crayères ★★★ MODERN FRENCH There is no restaurant to equal this one in the entire champagne country—and the setting is elegant, too (p. 357). The restaurant installed in the château originated as a hyper-upscale *maison bourgeoise* (actually a mini-château) back in 1903. The cuisine here has always been a magnet for the champagne barons of the area, and the restaurant is the number-one choice for wine buyers from around the world. Under the superb direction of the talented culinary artist, Didier Elena, the cuisine is as sublime as ever. Launch your meal with ravioli stuffed with escargots or sample another appetizer that is celestial in its taste—three different preparations of foie gras, including one presented au naturel. The wild turbot and the grilled lobster are ineffably delicate, and the roast duck with honey-vinegar sauce is earthy, regional, and a delight.

64 bd. Henri-Vasnier. ✆ **03-26-82-80-80.** Fax 03-26-82-65-52. Reservations required a few days in advance for weekday dinners, at least a month in advance for weekend dinners. Main courses 50€– 140€; fixed-price menus (including red bordeaux and champagne) 185€–305€; fixed-price lunch 70€. AE, DC, MC, V. Wed–Sun noon–1:30pm and 7–9:30pm.

Where to Stay & Dine Nearby

Château de Fère ★★ MODERN FRENCH   This fabulous restaurant occupies a turreted 16th-century château in a park. The only restaurant in Champagne with superior cuisine is Les Crayères (see above). Begin in the garden, sipping an aperitif or a glass of champagne with juice from freshly crushed raspberries. Your meal may consist of specialties such as foie gras of duckling with confit of ginger and a sauce made from the dessert wine Muscats de Venise, nuggets of suckling lamb cooked in a truffle-and-parsley-flavored crust, and deliberately undercooked Scottish salmon in lemon-flavored sweet-and-sour sauce. The desserts are mouthwatering, but we prefer the *boulette d'Avesnes,* a cone of cheese flecked with herbs and crushed peppercorns, coated with paprika.

Also available are 26 guest rooms with minibars and TVs. Doubles are 150€ to 360€, suites 300€ to 410€.

Rte. de Fismes (D967), Fère-en-Tardenois 02130. ✆ **03-23-82-21-13.** Fax 03-23-82-37-81. www.chateau defere.com. Reservations required. Main courses 34€–65€; fixed-price menu 36€–90€. AE, DC, MC, V. Wed–Sun 12:30–2pm; Tues–Sun 7:30–9:30pm. Closed Jan–Feb 15. From Reims (35 min.), take E46 northwest toward Soissons. At Fismes, take D367 toward Fère-en-Tardenois and follow signs to Château de Fère. About 2.5km (1½ miles) north of the restaurant, you'll see the ruins of a 12th-century castle, also called the Château de Fère.

Reims After Dark

Reims has the most vibrant nightlife in the region. The best place to start is **place Drouet-d'Erlon,** home to the city's premier clubs. This is a university town—for the most part, students rule the night. Just follow them to the best venues.

For a beer and a heavy dose of noise and rowdy students, head to the **Glue Pot,** 49 place Drouet-d'Erlon (✆ **03-26-47-36-46**). At **James Joyce Pub,** 80 place Drouet-d'Erlon (✆ **03-26-40-33-06**), a mixed-age crowd congregates in an Irish-style pub that has more than 120 types of beer. In the exotic **Au Lion de Belfort,** 37 place Drouet-d'Erlon (✆ **03-26-47-48-17**), stuffed heads of hippos, elephants, and the like keep watch. For a more sedate experience, try **L'Escale,** 132 rue Vesle (✆ **03-26-88-17-85**), where the atmosphere is more conducive to conversation with locals and other tourists.

The best dance floors in town are at **Le Vogue,** 93 bd. Général-Leclerc (✆ **03-26-47-34-29**), which attracts a mixed-age crowd (25–40); and **Le Soft,** 2 bis av. Georges-Clemenceau (✆ **03-26-35-78-19**), with its decor of old French cars placed like artwork against the brick walls and mirrors. Young gays and lesbians go

The Route de Champagne

Whether for hiking or for biking, the Montagne de Reims or Route de Champagne is the best place to experience the beauty of this vineyard-studded region. Montagne de Reims is a forested plateau south of Reims, where the slopes produce the grapes used to make bubbly.

Armed with a map from the tourist office in Reims or Epernay, you can explore this area along trails called *sentiers de Grandes Randonnées,* along the top of the northern plateau of Montagne de Reims.

These trails are called GRs. Because you're not likely to have time to visit all of them, we recommend routes GR14 and GR141. They form a loop of some 50km (31 miles) around the plateau's eastern section, taking in such towns as Verzy. Several train stations along the way, including a convenient one at Verzy, offer opportunities to take you back to Reims or Epernay should you tire before finishing the full loop.

to **Bar Lilas,** 75 rue des Courcelles (✆ **03-26-47-02-81**). Everybody wears jeans; the cover at any of these clubs ranges from free to 11€.

Comédie de Reims, chaussée Bocquaine (✆ **03-26-48-49-10**), has a varied schedule; tickets cost 12€ to 19€ for adults and 6€ to 8€ for children.

SIDE TRIPS FROM REIMS: LAON ★★ & AMIENS ★★★

Laon: 45km (28 miles) NW of Reims; 119km (74 miles) SE of Amiens; 138km (86 miles) NE of Paris
Amiens: 109km (68 miles) NW of Reims; 121km (75 miles) N of Paris; 114km (71 miles) SW of Lille

Savvy travelers know that this pristine area offers restful alternatives to the tourist meccas of Paris and the Riviera. The landscape of the low-lying region adjacent to Belgium's border will be familiar to admirers of Matisse, who found much inspiration here. Laon and Amiens are the area's major draws.

From Reims, **Laon** is a logical first stop, particularly for those traveling by rail who must transfer en route to Amiens. This site is the north's most intriguing for its history and setting on a ridge above the plain and the Ardon River. Over the years, it has witnessed much turbulence.

Amiens, on the Somme River, has been a textile center since medieval days. Its old town is a warren of jumbled streets and canals. Amiens is renowned for its Gothic cathedral, one of the finest in France.

Beyond Amiens and Laon, the heavily forested **Ardennes** attracts lovers of nature and French poetry alike. Rimbaud lived and wrote here; writers such as Victor Hugo, George Sand, and Alexandre Dumas expounded upon its beauty in their writings. The sandy beaches of **Le Touquet-Paris-Plage** are the most fashionable and best equipped of the many resorts along the Channel. A mini–Monte Carlo, it was dubbed the "playground of kings" in the days before World War II. Many other stops merit a look if you have the time.

Laon

Arguably the most intriguing town in the north of France, Laon perches on a ridge that rises 98m (322 ft.) above the plain and the Ardon River. The capital of the *département* (ministate) of Aisne, Laon has a long, turbulent history, attributable in large part to its remarkable location.

ESSENTIALS

GETTING THERE If you're **driving** from Reims, go 45km (28 miles) north on A26. **Trains** arrive from Paris's Gare du Nord at least 15 times a day (trip time: 1½–2 hr.). Others arrive from Reims seven times a day (trip time: 30–45 min.). For information and schedules, call ℭ **08-92-35-35-85.**

VISITOR INFORMATION The **Office de Tourisme** is on place Gautier de Montagne (ℭ **03-23-20-28-62;** fax 03-23-20-68-11; www.tourisme-paysdelaon. com).

EXPLORING THE TOWN

The Romans, recognizing Laon's strategic value, had it fortified. Vandals, Burgundians, Franks, and many others later besieged it. German troops entered in 1870 and in the summer of 1914, holding it until the end of World War I. Medieval ramparts still surround the town. They appear to have survived intact from the Middle Ages and provide a ready-made itinerary for touring Laon. They aren't sound enough to be climbed on and must be admired from below.

You don't have to huff and puff as you head from Laon's **Basse Ville** to its **Haute Ville,** thanks to a cable-operated tram, **Poma** (ℭ **03-23-79-07-59**), that shuttles passengers up and down the hill at 2½-minute intervals. It departs from the rail station on place de la Gare and ascends to the Hôtel-de-Ville on place du Général-Leclerc. It operates Monday to Saturday 7am to 8pm. The cost is 1.10€ one-way. After visiting the cathedral, stroll down pedestrian-only **rue Châtelaine,** Laon's major shopping street.

Cathédrale Notre-Dame de Laon ★★ Most visitors head to this cathedral with the carved oxen on its facade. Having escaped World War I unharmed, it inhabits the spot where an ancient basilica stood until it burned in 1111. The structure has six towers, four of which are complete. Inside are stained-glass panels dating from the 13th century, and an 18th-century choir grille. Tours (available in French only) are conducted from Easter to October on Saturday and Sunday at 3pm (arrange through the tourist office).

8 rue du Cloître, off place Aubry. ℭ **03-23-20-28-62.** Free admission to cathedral; tours 4€ adults, 3.60€ students and children. Daily 8:30am–7pm.

Musée Archéologique Municipal ★ This museum was founded in 1861 and remained rather sleepy until 1937, when it gained a collection of 1,700 artifacts (mainly from Greece, Rome, Egypt, Cyprus, and Asia Minor) as well as a collection of French painting and sculpture. The latest attraction is an annex in the courtyard of the museum, where you can visit the restored Chapelle Romaine des Templiers (Chapel of the Templars), originally associated with the Crusades of the Knights Templar. The chapel is noteworthy for its medieval stonework.

32 rue Georges-Ermant. ℭ **03-23-20-19-87.** Admission 3.60€ adults, free for children 17 and under. Tues–Sun 2–6pm.

WHERE TO STAY

Hostellerie St-Vincent   At the edge of the city, near the point where the road from Reims (A26) enters the Basse Ville, this simple government-rated two-star hotel is the most modern and best in town. It offers basic but comfortable guest rooms and has a good restaurant on premises, serving Alsatian specialties.

111 av. Charles-de-Gaulle, Laon 02000. ✆ **03-23-23-42-43.** Fax 03-23-79-22-55. www.stvincent-laon. com. 47 units. 60€–68€ double. AE, MC, V. Free parking. **Amenities:** Restaurant; bar; room service. *In room:* TV, Wi-Fi (free).

Hôtel de la Bannière de France   This revered hotel, built in 1685, is in the most historic part of Laon, Haute Ville. Behind its antique-looking facade, it has a modernized interior and the ambience of a traditional French hotel. The rooms are small but cozy and comfortably furnished. The personality of the owner, Mme. Lefevre, is apparent in the traditional style of the restaurant.

11 rue Franklin-D-Roosevelt, Laon 02000. ✆ **03-23-23-21-44.** Fax 03-23-23-31-56. www.hoteldela banneredefrance.com. 18 units. 68€–80€ double. AE, DC, MC, V. Parking 7€. Closed July. **Amenities:** Restaurant; bar; smoke-free rooms. *In room:* TV, hair dryer, Wi-Fi (free).

WHERE TO DINE

Hostellerie St-Vincent and **Hôtel de la Bannière de France** (see above) contain good restaurants.

Brasserie du Parvis PICARD/FRENCH   The allure here is the location opposite the main facade of the cathedral. In warm weather, the outdoor tables facing the church are hard to snag. Inside, the owners redecorate frequently, focusing on whatever festival or event happens to be on the minds of local residents—eclipses of the sun or moon, medieval festivals, and the like. Menu items include *ficelle Picard,* a kind of crepe made with ham and mushrooms; a pungent tart of local maroilles cheese; and a very ethnic version of chitterling sausages, *les andouillettes de Troyes,* with mustard sauce. More appetizing, at least to North American palates, is chicken cutlet with mushroom cream sauce. A well-known specialty, beloved by locals, is *pella Theirachienne,* made from boiled potatoes, a local cheese that's a lot like Münster, and lardoons—it's much like a tartifle Savoyard.

Place du Parvis Laon. ✆ **03-23-20-27-27.** Reservations recommended. Main courses 8€–27€; fixed-price menu 17€–26€. MC, V. Mar to mid-Oct daily 11:30am–10pm; mid-Oct to Feb daily 11:30am–3pm, Fri-Sat 6-10pm.

Estaminet Saint-Jean ★ PICARD/FLEMISH   Many of the dishes featured at this antique-studded restaurant are remembered since the days of their childhood by the many local residents who appreciate this place. That sense of nostalgia, coupled with its low prices, make it a winning and relatively new choice for dining in Laon. Within either of two amicably cramped dining rooms, you'll be offered dishes such as a cheese tart draped with melted cheese from the nearby hamlet of Maroilles, a beef-soaked-in-beer *carbonnade flamande,* and pork chops marinated and braised in cider and honey. What, you might ask, is an *estaminet?* In the old days here in Picardy, it was an all-purpose rendezvous combining functions of a bar, hardware store, druggist, post office, and perhaps a feed store for animals, all congenially clustered under one roof.

23 rue St-Jean. ✆ **03-23-23-04-89.** www.estaminetsaintjean.com. Reservations recommended. Main courses 12€–14€; set-price lunch 13€. MC, V. Tues–Sun noon–2pm; Tues-Sat 7-9:30pm.

Amiens

A textile center since medieval times, Amiens was the ancient capital of Picardy. It sits on the south bank of the Somme, where it is divided into a series of canals and irrigation networks. The old town, a jumble of narrow streets crisscrossed by canals, is run-down and seedy but still worth exploring. The city's focal point is its world-famous Gothic cathedral, one of France's finest.

ESSENTIALS

GETTING THERE If you're **driving** from Reims, take A26 north 45km (28 miles) to Laon, and then head west on N44 to N32, which becomes D934 to Amiens. The distance is 109km (68 miles); however, the trek may take you more than 1½ hours because of the country roads you'll be on after you exit A26. Amiens is adjacent to the main autoroute (A1) connecting Paris with Lille. Driving time from Paris is about 90 minutes. Those coming from the northern suburbs of Paris prefer A16, which passes near Amiens on its way to Calais.

Reaching Amiens by **train** from Reims requires a transfer in Laon or Tergnier. There are only three trains a day, which take 80 minutes to 3 hours, depending on the schedule.

Many visitors arrive straight from Paris—Amiens is on the main line connecting Paris's Gare du Nord with Lille. Depending on the season, four or five trains a day make the 70-minute trip (each way); the fare is 19€ one-way. The rail station in Amiens is at place Alphonse-Fiquet, a 10-minute walk from the old town. For information and schedules, call ✆ **08-92-35-35-35.**

VISITOR INFORMATION The **Office de Tourisme** is at 40 place Notre-Dame (✆ **03-22-71-60-50;** fax 03-22-71-60-51; www.amiens.com/tourisme).

EXPLORING THE TOWN

Julius Caesar praised the fertility of the fields around Amiens. During the Middle Ages, **Les Hortillonages ★**, an expanse of almost 242 hectares (598 acres) at the eastern edge of the core, was set aside for the cultivation of all kinds of herbs, fruits, and vegetables. Irrigated by a web of canals fed by the Somme, the district is still producing foodstuffs. Not long ago, the harvest was floated on barges and in shallow-bottomed boats to be sold on the Quai Bélu, near the cathedral. Although today the produce comes from the fields into the town center by truck, the ritual retains its medieval name, the **Marché sur l'Eau** (though locals increasingly refer to it as **Marché St-Leu**). The tradition continues every Saturday from 8:30am to 1pm, when the river's quays are transformed into a huge outdoor vegetable market.

A boat excursion April to October through the swamplands and tributaries of La Somme gives visitors a firsthand view of this archaic time-tested agrarian hideaway. Maintained and organized by the Association des sauvegardes des Hortillonages (✆ **03-22-92-12-18** for information), it conducts boat tours of 40 minutes each, priced at 5.30€ per adult or 4.55€ for children 11 to 16, 3.65€ 10 and under. Boats contain no more than 12 passengers at a time, with recorded French commentary. Boats depart by reservations, and whenever they are full following a very flexible timetable based on advance reservations and bookings.

A few paces north of the cathedral, straddling both banks of the Somme, is a cluster of carefully restored 13th- and 14th-century houses in a labyrinth of narrow cobblestone streets. Known as the **Quartier St-Leu,** this is a neighborhood of gift shops, antiques shops, art galleries, boutiques, and cafes.

Jules Verne, author of *20,000 Leagues Under the Sea* and *Journey to the Center of the Earth,* is buried in Amiens at the **Cimetière de la Madeleine,** rue St-Maurice, northwest of the town center. The representation of Verne on the Beaux Arts tomb appears to be physically rising from the dead. The cemetery is open April to October daily 8am to 6pm. From November to March it is open daily 8am to 5pm. Verne's home is at 2 rue Charles-Dubois (© **03-22-45-45-75;** www.jules-verne.net). It's now a research center documenting his life and literary achievements. It is open April 15 to October 15 Monday, Wednesday, Thursday, and Friday 10am to 12:30pm and 2 to 6pm, Tuesday 2 to 6:30pm, and Saturday and Sunday 2 to 6pm. Off-season hours are Monday and Wednesday to Friday 10am to 12:30pm and 2 to 6pm, Saturday and Sunday 2 to 6pm. Admission is 7€ adults, 5€ students, and 3.50€ kids 11 and under.

Cathédrale Notre-Dame d'Amiens ★★★ At 141m (463 ft.) long, this cathedral is the largest church in France. It was begun in 1220 by Robert de Luzarches and completed around 1270. Its original purpose was to house the head of St. John the Baptist, brought back from the Crusades in 1206. Two unequal towers were added later—the south one in 1366, the north one in 1402. The renowned architect Viollet-le-Duc restored the cathedral in the 1850s.

The cathedral is the crowning example of French Gothic architecture. In John Ruskin's *Bible of Amiens* (1884), which Proust translated into French, he extolled the door arches. The portals of the west front are lavishly decorated, important examples of Gothic cathedral sculpture. Two galleries surmount the portals; the upper has 22 statues of kings. The large rose window is from the 16th century.

Inside are carved stalls and a Flamboyant Gothic choir screen. Local artisans made these stalls, with some 3,500 figures, in the early 16th century. Slender pillars—126 of them—hold up the interior of the church, the zenith of the High Gothic in the north of France. The cathedral escaped destruction in World War II. In 1996, the Portail de la Mère-Dieu (Portal of the Mother of God), to the right of the cathedral's main entrance as you look over the facade, was restored at enormous expense.

Place Notre-Dame. © **03-22-71-60-50.** Free admission. Guided tours 5.50€, free for children 18 and under at 10:45am and 4:30pm. Apr–Sept Wed–Mon 7:30am–noon and 2–7pm; Oct–Mar daily 7:30am–noon and 2–5pm. Audio-guided tours are available in English for 3€.

Musée de Picardie ★★ This museum occupies a building constructed from 1855 to 1867. The palace of the Napoleonic dynasty, inaugurated by Napoleon III, consists of three sections, including one devoted to archaeology. Other sections include exhibits on the Roman occupation of Gaul, the Merovingian era, ancient Greece, and Egypt. One collection documents the Middle Ages with ivories, enamels, objets d'art, and sculpture. The sculpture and painting collection traces the European schools from the 16th to the 20th centuries, with works by El Greco, Maurice Quentin de La Tour, Guardi, and Tiepolo. Fragonard's *Les Lavandières* is his most beautiful work here.

48 rue de la République. © **03-22-97-14-00.** Admission 3.50€ adults, 2.50€ students, free for children 15 and under; 4€–6€ surcharge may apply for temporary exhibitions. Tues–Sun 10am–12:30pm and 2–6pm.

WHERE TO STAY

Le Carlton ★   From a glance at this hotel's Napoleon III architecture, you'll see that it's the stellar choice in Amiens. Though geared toward business travelers, its guest rooms are luxurious, with rich furniture and hand-painted frescoes depicting nostalgic scenes within Amiens's antique medieval St-Leu district. Appointments include fine linens and bathrooms with tub/shower combinations. The public areas, all featuring polished dark wood, range from an English bar to a brasserie-style restaurant.

42 rue de Noyon, Amiens 80000. ℂ **03-22-97-72-22.** Fax 03-22-97-72-00. www.lecarlton.fr. 24 units. 75€–105€ double; 130€ suite. AE, DC, MC, V. Parking 3.50€. **Amenities:** Restaurant; bar; room service. *In room:* A/C, TV, hair dryer, Wi-Fi (free).

Mercure Amiens Cathedrale 🐟   Overall, this hotel provides good value, unbeatable location, and the cost-consciousness of the Accor group. It sits opposite the main facade of the cathedral right in the center of town. In 2008 the hotel moved into a larger building where the rooms are more spacious and better equipped. Bedrooms are soundproof and comfortable and well maintained by a hardworking staff. The interior has a sleek modern look and the hotel is popular with both vacationers and business clients.

21-23 rue Flatters, Amiens 80000. ℂ **03-22-80-60-81.** www.mercure.com. 102 units. 155€–175€ double; 200€–290€ suite. AE, MC, V. Free parking overnight, 1€ during the day. **Amenities:** Restaurant; bar. *In room:* A/C, TV, hair dryer, Wi-Fi (free).

WHERE TO DINE

Les Marissons ★ PICARD/FRENCH   Two or three places around town match the quality of the food here, but none offers such a charming setting. The restaurant sits in a 15th-century building adjacent to one of the city's oldest bridges, pont de la Dodane. The cuisine is elegantly presented. Chef Antoine Benoit's specialties include a unique terrine *(pâté d'estran)* made from chunks of locally raised lamb mixed with sheep's cheese and wrapped in puff pastry, sea bass with apricots, roast lamb *pré salé* (salt from the marshes), scallops baked in their shells, and veal kidneys with rosemary sauce. In summer, you can dine in the garden.

68 rue les Marissons. ℂ **03-22-92-96-66.** www.les-marissons.fr. Reservations recommended. Main courses 28€–30€; fixed-price menu 19€–46€. AE, DC, MC, V. Mon–Tues and Thurs–Fri noon–1:45pm; Mon–Sat 7:30–9:30pm. Closed 1 week in Nov.

AMIENS AFTER DARK

You'll find the largest number of nightspots around quai Bélu in the St-Leu district. Try **Disco Le Millenium,** 87 rue Gutenberg (ℂ **03-22-43-36-42**), the largest and best in town. It's filled with the young people of Amiens Thursday to Saturday nights.

If you're big on musical events, head for the 1950 Picard-style house next to the train station, **Le Grand Wazoo,** 5 rue Vulfran-Warmé (ℂ **03-22-91-64-91**). Named in honor of a Frank Zappa album, this club draws a mixed crowd intent on listening to local musicians as well as more famous groups. It's open Monday to Saturday 6pm until 1am. Concerts (usually heavy metal, acid rock, and techno) take place about three times a week, usually on Friday and Saturday. When there's live music, cover ranges from 2€ to 5€; otherwise, admission is free.

While you're checking out the scene along the canal area, stop in the old medieval house that's home to the restaurant/wine bar **La Queue de Vache (the Cow's Tail),** 51 quai Bélu (ℂ **03-22-91-38-91**). Containing no more than 30 seats on two different levels, the restaurant and wine bar serves snacks and full-fledged meals, with main courses priced at 7€ to 18€. It pours about 30 wines, many sold by the glass. Platters of sausage, terrines, and cheeses go well with the wine, but if you want a full platter, consider a hearty portion of roasted *magret de canard* (duck). Every first Tuesday of the month, there's live New Orleans–style jazz.

Nelson's Pub, 5 quai Bélu (© **03-22-91-56-00**), and its next-door neighbor, **Le Newport,** 3 quai Bélu (© **03-22-91-01-55**), play recorded rock 'n' roll in environments favored by thirsty conversationalists. A short walk away is **Le Squale,** 18 rue de Dodane (© **03-22-72-20-46**), a pub with pinewood planks and a decor that reminds some Francophiles of the interior of a wine barrel.

If you're gay and on the loose in Amiens, **Red and White,** rue de la Dodane, in the Quartier St-Leu (© **03-22-72-34-00**), offers the chance to meet and talk with like-minded folks who might have dropped in for an after-dinner drink or to hear some music. Its opening and closing times tend to be erratic.

EPERNAY

140km (87 miles) E of Paris; 26km (16 miles) S of Reims

On the left bank of the Marne, Epernay rivals Reims as a center for champagne. Although it only has one-sixth Reims's population, Epernay produces nearly as much champagne, with an estimated 322km (200 miles) or more of cellars and tunnels. These caves are vast vaults cut into the chalk rock on which the town is built. Represented in Epernay are such champagne companies as Moët et Chandon (the largest), Pol Roger, Mercier, and de Castellane.

Epernay's main boulevards are the elegant residential avenue de Champagne, rue Mercier, and rue de Reims, all radiating from place de la République. Two important squares in the narrow streets of the commercial district are place Hughes-Plomb and place des Arcades.

Invading armies have destroyed or burned Epernay nearly two dozen times. Few of its buildings have survived. However, check out the neoclassical villas and Victorian town houses on avenue de Champagne.

Essentials

GETTING THERE If you're **driving** to Epernay from Reims, head south on E51. Eighteen **trains** per day arrive from Paris's Gare de l'Est (trip time: 1 hr., 15 min.); the one-way fare is 20€. From Reims, there are 16 trains per day (trip time: 25 min.; 5.60€ one-way). For information, call © **08-92-35-35-35,** or visit www.voyages-sncf.com. The major **bus** link is SDM Trans-Champagne (© **03-26-65-17-07** in Epernay), operating four buses per day Monday to Saturday between Châlons-en-Champagne and Epernay (trip time: 45 min.).

VISITOR INFORMATION The **Office de Tourisme** is at 7 av. de Champagne (© **03-26-53-33-00;** fax 03-26-51-95-22; www.ot-epernay.fr).

Exploring the Town

Boutiques and shops abound in the pedestrian district of **place des Arcades, rue du Général-Leclerc, rue St-Thibault, rue St-Martin,** and **rue Porte Lucas.** You'll find stores selling gifts, clothes, antiques, books, and regional food items.

For champagne, you can go to the individual houses along avenue de Champagne (see below) or try one of the stores that represent a variety of houses. Two of the best are **La Cave Salvatori,** 11 rue Flodoard (✆ **03-26-55-32-32**), and **Le Domaine des Crus,** 2 rue Henri Dunant (✆ **03-26-54-18-60**), known for a staggering array of champagnes.

For regional antiques from the 18th and 19th centuries, try **Antiquités Jocelyne Huzette,** 35 rue Blandin (✆ **03-26-54-58-52**).

For champagne gift items such as flutes and corks, as well as table decorations and linens, visit **De-ci-de-ca,** 34 rue du Général-Leclerc (✆ **03-26-55-67-68**). **Fromm Jacques,** 33 rue St-Thibault (✆ **03-26-55-25-64**), and **Camaieu,** 12 rue de Professeur Langevin (✆ **03-26-51-83-83**), sell garden ornaments, souvenirs, and art objects commemorating the historic medievalism of Amiens.

Champagne de Castellane   Across from Mercier (see below), this champagne house, unlike the two recommended below, gives you a closer view of how champagne is actually produced. You see workers doing it all—corking, labeling, even removing sediment. The museum on-site may be a bit dull, but the climb to the tower (237 steps) for a panoramic view of the area is not. The tower is from 1904 and has become the symbol of Epernay. A tasting of the house Brut Croix Rouge is included after the tours, some of which are conducted in English (depending on demand).

63 av. de Champagne. ✆ **03-26-51-19-19.** www.castellane.com. Admission 2.50€, free for ages 16 and under. Apr–Dec daily 10am–noon and 2–6pm. Closed Jan–Mar.

Mercier   Mercier is near Moët et Chandon, and you can visit them both on the same day. Mercier conducts tours in English of its 18km (11 miles) of tunnels from laser-guided trains. The caves contain one of the world's largest wooden barrels, with a capacity of more than 200,000 bottles. No reservation is necessary if there are fewer than 10 in your group.

70 av. de Champagne. ✆ **03-26-51-22-22.** www.champagnemercier.fr. Admission 8€. Mid-Feb to mid-Nov Thurs–Mon 9:30–11:30am and 2–4:30pm.

Moët et Chandon Champagne Cellars   A staff member gives guided tours in English, describing the champagne-making process and filling you in on champagne lore: Napoleon, a friend of Jean-Rémy Moët, used to stop by for thousands of bottles on his way to battle. The only time he didn't take a supply was at Waterloo—and look what happened there. At the end of the tour, you're given a glass of bubbly. No reservations are necessary, except for large groups.

20 av. de Champagne. ✆ **03-26-51-20-20.** www.moet.com. Admission 14€–28€. Early May to early Nov daily 9:30–11:30am and 2–4:30pm; early Nov to Apr Mon–Fri 9:30–11:30am and 2–4:30pm. Closed Jan.

Where to Stay

Les Berceaux (see "Where to Dine," below) also rents rooms.

Best Western Hôtel de Champagne   This simple 1970s inn lies about 180m (591 ft.) from the Moët et Chandon showroom, near place de la République. Some rooms are outfitted in modern style; others look vaguely inspired by Louis XV. A buffet breakfast is served every morning.

30 rue Eugène-Mercier, Epernay 51200. ✆ **800/528-1234** in the U.S. and Canada, or 03-26-53-10-60. Fax 03-26-51-94-63. www.bw-hotel-champagne.com. 30 units. 105€–130€ double. AE, DC, MC, V. Free parking. Closed Dec to mid-Jan. **Amenities:** Bar; exercise room; sauna. *In room:* A/C, TV, hair dryer, minibar, Wi-Fi (free).

Royal Champagne ★★★ Constructed around an 18th-century relay station for the postal system, this hotel is a member of the Relais & Châteaux group. The establishment's historic core contains the reception area, bar, and dining facilities; guest rooms are in town house–style accommodations overlooking the nearby vineyards. The units are rustic and very comfortable, exemplifying the coziness of wine-country living. Each comes with a sumptuous bed with fine linen, plus a combination tub/shower.

The chef is known for classic dishes with an innovative twist. The food is exceptional, with specialties such as lobster ragout, John Dory with a purée of celery and truffle-flavored cream sauce, and roast lamb with garlic.

Champillon Bellevue 51160. (© **03-26-52-87-11.** Fax 03-26-52-89-69. www.royalchampagne.com. 25 units. 240€–375€ double; 355€–400€ suite. AE, DC, MC, V. Closed Dec 2–Feb 15. Drive 8km (5 miles) north from Epernay toward Reims on the rte. du Vignoble (N2051) to Champillon. **Amenities:** Restaurant; bar; babysitting; room service. *In room:* A/C, TV, hair dryer, minibar, Wi-Fi (free).

Where to Dine

The food at **Royal Champagne** (see above) is excellent.

Les Berceaux ★★★ CHAMPENOISE Chef-owner Patrick Michelon serves generous portions of flavorful, conservative regional cuisine. The menu changes seasonally and always features fresh produce and superior cuts of fish, meat, and game. Particularly scrumptious are such dishes as Pyrénéan suckling lamb roasted on a spit; snails in champagne sauce; roast filet of John Dory; and galette of roasted and minced pigs' feet in puff pastry, served with potatoes. At an on-site wine bar, Bistrot le 7, you can sample an assortment of vintages by the glass. It showcases local wines, especially champagne. If Les Berceaux errs at all, it tends to be a bit pretentious, a flaw that you may be able to overcome with a touch of humor.

Available upstairs are 28 comfortable guest rooms, each with TV. A double with a tub/shower combination rents for 95€ or else 130€ in a junior suite.

13 rue des Berceaux, Epernay 51200. (© **03-26-55-28-84.** Fax 03-26-55-10-36. www.lesberceaux.com. Reservations recommended. Main courses 34€–70€; fixed-price menu 58€–69€. AE, DC, MC, V. Wed-Sun noon-2pm and 7–9pm. Closed Feb 11–Mar 4.

Epernay After Dark

Start out at the chic cafe and bar **Le Progrès,** 5 place de la République (© **03-26-55-22-72**). For a glass of wine or even Scotch (something you don't see enough of in this wine-crazed region), consider a visit to **Le Chriss Bar,** a nightclub at 40 rue de Sézanne (© **03-26-57-87-18**).

ALSACE-LORRAINE

The provinces of Alsace and Lorraine, with ancient capitals at Strasbourg and Nancy, have been the object of many disputes between Germany and France. Alsace has been called "the least French of French provinces," more reminiscent of the Black Forest across the Rhine. In fact, it became German from 1870 until after World War I and was ruled by Hitler from 1940 to 1944. These days, both provinces are back under French control, though they remain somewhat independent.

In the Vosges Mountains you can follow **La Route des Crêtes (Crest Road)** or skirt the foothills, visiting the wine towns of Alsace. In its cities and cathedrals, the castle-dotted landscape evokes a past filled with military glory or defeat. Lorraine is Joan of Arc country, and many of its towns still suggest their medieval heritage.

No clear-cut line delineates Alsace from Lorraine. Alsace is more German. Lorraine, with its rolling landscape, appears more French in character.

STRASBOURG ★★★

488km (303 miles) SE of Paris; 217km (135 miles) SW of Frankfurt

The capital of Alsace, Strasbourg is one of France's greatest cities and the birthplace of *pâté de foie gras.* Here Rouget de Lisle first sang "La Marseillaise," the French national anthem. Strasbourg is one of France's major ports, only 3km (1¾ miles) west of the Rhine. In addition to being the site of the Council of Europe, Strasbourg is home to the European Parliament, which convenes at the Palais de l'Europe.

In 1871, Strasbourg was absorbed by Germany and made the capital of the territory of Alsace-Lorraine. It reverted to France in 1918. One street is a perfect illustration of the city's identity crisis: More than a century ago it was avenue Napoleon. In 1871, it became Kaiser-Wilhelmstrasse, and then boulevard de la République in 1918. In 1940, it became Adolf-Hitler-Strasse, and it ended up as avenue du Général-de-Gaulle in 1945.

Now one of the most happening cities in France, Strasbourg is home to the University of Strasbourg, once attended by the likes of Goethe, Napoleon, and Pasteur. Today, some 40,000 students follow in their footsteps.

Essentials

GETTING THERE   The **Strasbourg-Entzheim Airport** (Aéroport International Strasbourg; © **03-88-64-67-67;** www.strasbourg.aeroport.fr), 15km (9⅓ miles) southwest of the city center, receives daily flights from many European cities, including Paris, London, Rome, Vienna, and Moscow. You can get from the airport to the town center by using **shuttle buses** and **city trams.** They run at 40-minute intervals all day long. The one-way cost is 3.60€. Take a shuttle bus to the south side of Strasbourg, to a junction point known as Baggersee. From there, you'll continue to the town center on tram line A. Combined travel time is between 35 and 40 minutes each way. For information, call © **03-88-77-70-70.**

The superfast TGV train now makes round-trips from Paris to Strasbourg, cutting travel time nearly in half to 2 hours, 20 minutes. At least 20 **trains** a day arrive from Paris's Gare de l'Est (trip time: 4 hr.); the one-way fare is 70€. For information and schedules, call © **36-35** or 08-92-35-35-35.

By **car,** the giant A35 crosses the plain of Alsace, with occasional references to its original name, the N83. It links Strasbourg with Colmar and Mulhouse.

VISITOR INFORMATION   The **Office de Tourisme** is on 17 place de la Cathédrale (© **03-88-52-28-28;** fax 03-88-52-28-29; www.otstrasbourg.fr).

SPECIAL EVENTS   **Wolf Music,** 24 rue de la Mésange (© **03-88-32-43-10;** http://wolf-musique.musicunivers.com), arranges ticket sales for two festivals: the **Festival of Classical Music** (© **03-88-15-29-29**), for 2 weeks in June, and the **Festival de Jazz** (© **03-88-15-29-29**), July 1 to July 3. Both feature international artists and draw large crowds. Ticket prices range from 19€ to 70€ and go on sale in mid-April. The Association Musica (© **03-88-23-46-46;** www.festival-musica.org) organizes the **Festival International des Musiques d'Aujourd'hui.** It takes place from the end of September to the first week of October and combines contemporary music concerts with movies and modern opera performances. Tickets are 6€ to 19€ and go on sale at the end of June.

Exploring Strasbourg

Despite war damage, much remains of Old Strasbourg, including covered bridges and towers from its former fortifications, plus many 15th- and 17th-century dwellings with painted wooden fronts and carved beams.

The city's traffic hub is **place Kléber ★**, dating from the 15th century. Sit here with a tankard of Alsatian beer and get to know Strasbourg. The bronze statue in the center is of J. B. Kléber, born in Strasbourg in 1753; he became one of Napoleon's most noted generals and was buried under the monument. Apparently his presence offended the Nazis, who removed the statue in 1940. This Alsatian bronze was restored to its proper place in 1945.

From here, take rue des Grandes-Arcades southeast to **place Gutenberg,** one of the city's oldest squares. The central statue (1840) by David d'Angers is of Gutenberg, who perfected his printing press in Strasbourg in the winter of 1436 and 1437. The former town hall, now the **Hôtel du Commerce,** was built in 1582 and is one of the most significant Renaissance buildings in Alsace. The neighborhoods within a few blocks of the city's **cathedral** are loaded with medieval references and historical charm.

La Petite France ★★ is the most interesting quarter of Strasbourg. A virtual island, it's surrounded by scenic canals on four sides, and its 16th-century houses reflect in the waters of the Ill River. In "Little France," old roofs with gray tiles have sheltered families for ages, and the cross-beamed facades with roughly carved rafters are in typical Alsatian style. For a good view, walk along rue des Moulins, branching off from rue du Bain-aux-Plantes.

Cathédrale Notre-Dame de Strasbourg ★★★   The city's crowning glory is an outstanding example of Gothic architecture, representing a transition from the Romanesque. Construction began in 1176. The pyramidal tower in rose-colored stone was completed in 1439; at 141m (463 ft.), it's the tallest one from medieval times. This cathedral is still in use. Religious ceremonies, particularly on feast days, meld perfectly with the architectural majesty. Individual tourists can visit the tower only in the summer (you may have to wait to climb it). The Office de Tourisme (see above) organizes tours for groups; call for the schedule.

Exploring Strasbourg by Boat

One of the most romantic ways to spend time in Strasbourg is to take an excursion on the **Ill River** from the Palais de Rohan. The 75-minute cruises cost 8€ for adults and 4€ for children. They include recorded commentary in six languages. From mid-March to early November, rides depart at 30-minute intervals daily between 9:30am and 9pm, and with hours extended to 10pm May to September. In November departures are at 10:30am, 1pm, 2:30pm, and 4pm; in December rides depart every half-hour from 9:30am to 5pm. For information, call **Batorama,** 9 rue de Nantes (✆ **03-88-84-13-13; www.batorama.fr**).

Four large counterforts divide the **main facade ★★★** into three vertical parts and two horizontal galleries. Note the **rose window,** which looks like stone lace. The facade is rich in decoration: On the portal of the south transept, the *Coronation and Death of the Virgin* in one of the two tympanums is the finest such medieval work. In the north transept, see also the facade of the **Chapelle St-Laurence,** a stunning achievement of the late Gothic German style.

A Romanesque **crypt** lies under the chancel, which is covered with square stonework. The stained-glass window is the work of Max Ingrand. The **nave** is majestic, with windows depicting emperors and kings on the north Strasbourg aisle. Five chapels cluster around the transept, including one built in 1500 in the Flamboyant Gothic style. In the south transept stands the **Angel Pillar ★★**, illustrating the Last Judgment, with angels lowering their trumpets.

The **astronomical clock ★** was built between 1547 and 1574. It stopped during the Revolution, and from 1838 to 1842 the mechanism was replaced. Each day at 12:30pm, crowds gather to see its show of allegorical figures. On Sunday, Apollo drives his sun horses; on Thursday, you see Jupiter and his eagle. The body of the clock has a planetarium based on the theories of Copernicus. Close-up views of the clock are available Monday to Saturday noon to 12:30pm; tickets (2€ adults, 1.50€ ages 5–18 and students) go on sale in the south portal at 11:45am.

Place de la Cathédrale. ✆ **03-88-32-75-78** for times of services. Cathedral: Daily 7–11:20am and 12:35-7pm. Tower: ✆ **03-88-43-60-40.** Apr–Sept daily 9am-7:15pm; Oct–Mar daily 10am-5:15pm. Tower admission 4.60€ adults, 2.30€ children 17 and under and students.

Eglise St-Thomas   Built between 1230 and 1330, this Protestant church houses five naves. It contains the **mausoleum ★★** of Maréchal de Saxe, a masterpiece of French art by Pigalle (1777).

Rue Martin-Luther (along rue St-Thomas, near pont St-Thomas). ✆ **03-88-32-14-46.** Free admission. Apr–Oct daily 10am-6pm; Nov–Dec and daily 10am-5pm; Feb–Mar daily 2-5pm. Closed Jan and Mar daily 10am-5pm.

Musée Alsacien ★   This museum occupies three mansions from the 16th and 17th centuries. It's like a living textbook of the folklore and customs of Alsace, containing arts, crafts, and tools of the old province.

23 quai St-Nicolas. ✆ **03-88-52-50-01.** Admission 5€ adults, 2.50€ students, free for children 17 and under. Wed–Fri and Mon noon-6pm; Sat–Sun 10am-6pm.

Musée d'Art Moderne   In the heart of La Petite France, this is Strasbourg's showcase of modern European art. Don't take the word "modern" too literally—the collection dates from 1870 to the present. The layout of the museum starts with a historical section tracing the emergence of modern art and going forward to the 21st century. Other facilities include a graphic art and photography room, an art library, a museum shop, and a cafe-restaurant on the terrace.

1 place Jean-Hans Arp. ☎ **03-88-23-31-31.** Admission 6€ adults, 3€ students 24 and under and seniors, free for children 17 and under. Tues–Wed and Fri noon–7pm; Thurs noon–9pm; Sat–Sun 10am–6pm.

Musée de l'Oeuvre Notre-Dame ★★★   This museum illustrates the art of the Middle Ages and Renaissance in Strasbourg and Alsace. Some pieces were displayed in the cathedral, where copies have been substituted. The most celebrated is a stained-glass head of Christ from about the 11th century. There's also a window depicting an emperor from around 1200. The sculpture is of great interest, as are the works of Strasbourg goldsmiths from the 16th and 17th centuries. The winding staircase and interior are in the Renaissance style. The 13th-century hall contains sculptures from the cathedral, including the wise and foolish virgins from 1280.

3 place du Château. ☎ **03-88-52-50-00.** Admission 5€ adults, 2.50€ students, free for children 17 and under. Tues–Fri noon–6pm; Sat–Sun 10am–6pm.

Palais de Rohan ★★   This palace south of the cathedral was built from 1732 to 1742. It's an example of supreme elegance and proportion. Noted for its facades and rococo interior, it's one of the crowning design achievements in eastern France. On the first floor is a fine-arts museum (Musée des Beaux-Arts) with works by Rubens, Rembrandt, Van Dyck, El Greco, Goya, Watteau, Renoir, and Monet. On the street level is a decorative-arts museum that exhibits ceramics and the original machinery of the cathedral's first astronomical clock. Also on the premises are collections of artifacts excavated from nearby digs, focusing especially on art and utilitarian objects from the Roman and early medieval (Merovingian) eras.

2 place du Château. ☎ **03-88-52-50-00.** Admission for 1 museum 5€ adults, 2.50€ students, free for children 17 and under; combo ticket 6€ adults, 3€ students, free for children 17 and under. Wed–Mon noon–6pm.

Shopping

Strasbourg overflows with antiques shops, artisans, craftspeople, and beer makers. Every well-accessorized home in Alsace owns some of the napkins, aprons, tablecloths, and tea and bath towels of the Beauvillé textile mills. **Nappes d'Alsace,** 6 rue Mercière, near the cathedral (☎ **03-88-22-69-29**), has one of the widest selections of textiles in town.

Bastian, 22–24 place de la Cathédrale (☎ **03-88-32-45-93**), specializes in 18th- and 19th-century ceramic tureens that Alsace produced in abundance. Look for ragout pots in the forms of a cabbage, a trout, a boar's head, or a turkey, painted in bright colors. There's also a selection of Louis XV and Louis XVI furniture, crafted in the region during the 18th and 19th centuries following Parisian models from the same era.

Bastian's main competitor is **Ville et Campagne,** 23 quai des Bateliers (☎ **03-88-36-96-84**), housed in a Renaissance-style 17th-century building across from the Palais de Rohan. Standout items are polychromed Alsatian antiques (especially 18th- and 19th-c. armoires and chests), Louis- and Directoire-style furnishings, statues, and antique paintings.

One of the most appealing shops in Strasbourg is **Arts et Collections d'Alsace,** 4 place du Marché aux Poissons (© **03-88-14-03-77**), which sells copies of art objects and utilitarian ware from museums and private collections through Alsace. You'll see upscale gift items for the home and kitchen, made from pottery, stone, wrought iron, glass, copper, and carved wood. The shop also sells fabric by the yard.

A name in pottery that you're likely to encounter is **Soufflenheim,** a provincial rococo pattern—usually in blues and reds—named after the Alsatian village north of Strasbourg where the style originated. To get there, take N63 north of the center of Strasbourg for 24km (15 miles). In the village, ceramics and pottery have been made since the Bronze Age. Soufflenheim is home to at least a dozen outlets selling cake molds, tureens, saucers and cups, dinnerware, and more, usually in rustic patterns. One of the most prominent retailers is **Gérard Wehrling,** 64 rue de Haguenau (© **03-88-86-65-25**), known for pottery that can withstand the rigors of modern ovens, microwaves, and refrigerators.

If you're driving, you may want to check out the villages of Obernai, Illhaeusern, Ribeauvillé, and Schiltigheim. The last is beer-drinking territory; the others offer country wares and antiques.

Where to Stay
EXPENSIVE
Hilton International Strasbourg ★★★
The luxurious, seven-story steel-and-glass Hilton—the best hotel in the city—stands over a university complex opposite the Palais de la Musique et des Congrès. The decor incorporates five kinds of Iberian marble, much of it chosen to resemble the ruddy sandstone of the famous cathedral, which is visible from the hotel. The midsize guest rooms are decorated in standard international chain style—comfortable but not outstanding. They contain tasteful artwork and have spacious marble-trimmed bathrooms.

Av. Herrenschmidt, Strasbourg 67000. © **800/445-8667** in the U.S. and Canada, or 03-88-37-10-10. Fax 03-88-25-55-03. www.hilton-strasbourg.com. 243 units. 165€–360€ double; from 465€ suite. AE, DC, MC, V. Parking 19€. Take the Strasbourg-Centre exit from the autoroute and follow signs to the Wacken, Palais des Congrès, and Palais de l'Europe. **Amenities:** 2 restaurants; 2 bars; babysitting; exercise room; room service. *In room:* A/C, TV, hair dryer, minibar, Wi-Fi (free).

Le Régent Petite France ★★
This well-run hotel gives serious competition to the Hilton. Many guests choose it for its more comfortable rooms and atmosphere. This site was once an ice factory, and many of the old steam machines remain. The marble lobby sets the tone, with ice-cream colors and potted palms. Guest rooms come in various sizes, the best of which are quite spacious and open onto river views. The luxurious beds are among the city's finest, and the bathrooms are state of the art. The staff is one of the most professional in Strasbourg.

5 rue des Moulins, Strasbourg 67000. © **800/223-5652** in the U.S. and Canada, or 03-88-76-43-43. Fax 03-88-76-43-76. www.regent-petite-france.com. 72 units. 176€–386€ double; 260€–786€ suite. AE, DC, MC, V. Parking 22€. **Amenities:** Restaurant; bar; babysitting; exercise room; room service; sauna. *In room:* A/C, TV, hair dryer, Jacuzzi (in suites), minibar, Wi-Fi (free).

MODERATE
Hôtel Beaucour ★★
This hotel is geared toward business travelers, but anyone will find it ideal—it's the city's most tranquil lodging. At the end of a private street a few blocks east of the cathedral, within what used to be an umbrella factory, it occupies a

17th-century building with timbered ceilings. Every guest room contains a whirlpool tub and a fax hookup. Furnishings are of standard international style, but comfortable. The hotel maintains an affiliation with at least two restaurants a short walk away. The concierge, who seems to know all the city's secrets, will make reservations for you.

5 rue des Bouchers, Strasbourg 67000. ✆ **03-88-76-72-00.** Fax 03-88-76-72-60. www.hotel-beaucour.com. 49 units. 116€–165€ double; 113€–220€ suite. AE, DC, MC, V. Parking 9€. **Amenities:** Babysitting. *In room:* TV, hair dryer, minibar, Wi-Fi (free).

Hôtel Best Western Monopole–Métropole

This hotel is on a quiet street near the train station. Its lobby features a scattering of antiques, among them a 17th-century armoire and a statue of a night watchman. An extension of the salon displays oil portraits of 18th-century Alsatian personalities and glass cases with pewter tankards and candlesticks. Breakfast (the only meal available) is served in the high-ceilinged Alsatian-style dining room. The guest rooms are comfortable, with crisp white linens and (in most) air-conditioning. Each unit is unique; some have Alsatian-style antiques.

16 rue Kuhn, Strasbourg 67000. ✆ **800/528-1234** in the U.S. and Canada, or 03-88-14-39-14. Fax 03-88-32-82-55. www.bw-monopole.com. 86 units. 100€–200€ double; 200€ suite. Rates include breakfast. AE, DC, MC, V. Parking 12€. **Amenities:** Bar; babysitting. *In room:* TV, hair dryer, minibar, Wi-Fi (free).

Hôtel Cardinal de Rohan ★ 🍴

In the pedestrian zone steps from the cathedral, this five-story hotel is one of the city's best values and within walking distance of the Palais de Rohan. The 17th-century building was rebuilt shortly after World War II. It offers a choice of elegantly furnished rooms, the cheapest of which are small and have a French bed called a *matrimonial* (a standard double bed). Guest-room decor ranges from Louis XV to a regional Alsatian look with lots of wood paneling.

17–19 rue du Maroquin, Strasbourg 67060. ✆ **03-88-32-85-11.** Fax 03-88-75-65-37. www.hotel-rohan. com. 36 units. 75€–159€ double. AE, DC, MC, V. Parking 17€. **Amenities:** Babysitting. *In room:* A/C, TV, hair dryer, minibar, Wi-Fi (free).

Hôtel de l'Europe

Behind a half-timbered facade a 3-minute walk west of the cathedral, this is one of the best-located government-rated three-star hotels in town. Its roots go back to the 15th century, when it functioned as a coaching inn; it was enlarged with the annexation of an 18th-century house next door. Frequently renovated, it's comfortable and unpretentious, with all the electronic gadgets you may want. Units run the gamut from modern to a half-timbered fantasy directly under the roof (room no. 404), where angled beams evoke the original construction. Each of the accommodations has a tiled and tidily maintained bathroom.

38–40 rue du Fossé-des-Tanneurs, Strasbourg 67000. ✆ **03-88-32-17-88.** Fax 03-88-75-65-45. www. hotel-europe.com. 60 units. 75€–205€ double. AE, DC, MC, V. Parking 14€. **Amenities:** Babysitting; room service. *In room:* A/C, TV, hair dryer, minibar (in some), Wi-Fi (free).

Hôtel des Princes 🍴

A 15-minute walk from the center of town, the Hôtel des Princes enjoys a three-star government rating and is one of the best bargains in the city. The management is helpful; the renovated rooms are furnished comfortably but simply. Continental breakfast is the only meal served.

33 rue Geiler, Quartier du Conseil de l'Europe, Strasbourg 67000. ✆ **03-88-61-55-19.** Fax 03-88-41-10-92. www.hotel-princes.com. 43 units. 110€–135€ double. AE, MC, V. Closed in Aug. **Amenities:** Babysitting; Wi-Fi (free). *In room:* TV, minibar.

Le Régent Contades ★★ 🛍

Our favorite moderately priced choice is this glorified B&B, in a five-story structure with dormers, close to the cathedral. Diplomats may consider it a secret, but word is out. The stylish hostelry has an intelligent, helpful staff. The guest rooms are furnished in a romantic style with a variety of monochromatic colors that include pink, blue, or soft browns or reds. The most spacious units are in a new wing. Breakfast is the only meal served.

8 av. de la Liberté, Strasbourg 67000. © **03-88-15-05-05.** Fax 03-88-15-05-15. www.regent-contades. com. 47 units. 105€–325€ double; 170€–560€ suite. AE, DC, MC, V. Parking 20€. **Amenities:** Bar; room service. *In room:* A/C, TV, hair dryer, minibar, Wi-Fi (free).

INEXPENSIVE

Hôtel de l'Ill 🎗 A 5-minute walk from the cathedral, this government-rated two-star hotel is a good deal. The former restaurant added rooms in the 1920s. In the 1990s, the property became a hotel and gained a modern wing. An inviting, unpretentious place, it houses quiet, comfortably furnished rooms decorated in either modern or Alsatian traditional style. Two rooms at the rear have a private terrace or balcony opening onto a view of neighboring gardens. Each room comes with a tidily kept, shower-only bathroom, but no amenities other than a phone (some have a TV). The breakfast room is decorated Laura Ashley–style—well, except for the cuckoo clock.

8 quai des Bateliers, Strasbourg 67000. © **03-88-36-20-01.** Fax 03-88-35-30-03. www.hotel-ill.com. 27 units. 60€–79€ double. AE, MC, V. Parking 9€. **Amenities:** Wi-Fi (free). *In room:* A/C (in some), TV.

Hôtel Gutenberg ★ 🏨 Just off place Gutenberg, this many-windowed hotel is both a bargain and a discovery. The renovated mansion exudes old-fashioned charm—the sculptured walls date to 1745—yet is completely modern (with soundproofing). Many of the guest rooms, with flowery draperies and upholstered furniture, have wooden beams. The most romantic accommodations, evoking old France, are on the fifth floor under timbers.

31 rue des Serruriers, Strasbourg 67000. © **03-88-32-17-15.** Fax 03-88-75-76-67. www.hotel-gutenberg. com. 42 units. 75€–135€ double. AE, MC, V. **Amenities:** Internet (free). *In room:* A/C (in some), TV.

Where to Dine
VERY EXPENSIVE

Au Crocodile ★★★ ALSATIAN A beautiful sky-lit restaurant, Au Crocodile serves the most inventive food in Strasbourg. Only two restaurants in this region equal it: Le Buerehiesel (see below) and the Auberge de l'Ill (p. 392). An especially appealing feature is the fixed-price menus that revolve around creative themes, which have included Egypt and Victor Hugo. Chef Emile Jung offers a wide array of inventive dishes. Some of the best include strips of duckling cooked in a sauce of red wine and a reduction of the bird's blood; sautéed scallops with purée of celery and Indian-style (Marsala-style) spiced butter sauce; delicate local freshwater whitefish *(sandre)* served in sauerkraut; and duck liver cooked in a salt crust. Our major problem comes only when the bill *(la note,* as the French say) arrives—especially when we indulge in the high-priced wines.

10 rue de l'Outre. © **03-88-32-13-02.** www.au-crocodile.com. Reservations required. Main courses 39€–78€; fixed-price lunch 49€–108€; dinner 89€–132€. AE, DC, MC, V. Tues–Sat noon–1:30pm and 7:30–9:30pm. Closed last 3 weeks of July and Dec 24–28.

Le Buerehiesel ★★★ MODERN FRENCH Also known as Le Restaurant Westermann, Buerehiesel is famous for its *cuisine moderne* and for its prime location in l'Orangerie, a park at the end of the allée de la Robertsau planned by the landscape artist Le Nôtre, who gave the park to Joséphine during her marriage to Napoleon. The decor includes richly grained wooden ceilings and a conservatively modern design. The kitchen recycles heirloom recipes in innovative and exciting ways. Of special merit are foie gras of goose with truffles; frogs' legs fried with local herbs; ravioli stuffed with confit of onions; and steamed sea bass with a marinade of crisp, al dente vegetables and aromatic herbs. Appealingly old-fashioned, and prepared for only two diners at a time, is one of the Alsace's most classic recipes, *poularde baeckoffe*: Consisting of a top-quality Bresse hen that's slow-cooked in a covered ceramic dish, it comes in versions appropriate to both summer (with potatoes, artichoke hearts, and a confit of lemons) and winter (with leeks, potatoes, and truffles).

4 parc de l'Orangerie. ℂ **03-88-45-56-65.** www.buerehiesel.fr. Reservations required. Main courses 21€–39€; fixed-price menu 65€–86€. AE, DC, MC, V. Tues–Sat noon–2pm and 7–9:45pm. Closed 1st 3 weeks of Jan and 1st 3 weeks of Aug.

MODERATE

Chez Yvonne ★ FRENCH/ALSATIAN Journalists and other political dignitaries frequent this traditional Alsatian *winstub*, which has operated here since 1873. It's located near the cathedral in the middle of the historic core. The backdrop is in the traditional bistro style, with lots of wood and red-checked curtains. Steaming platters of well-prepared food emerge from the kitchen, including such appetizers as snails Alsatian or foie gras of the house. For a main course, opt for such temptations as hen cooked in Riesling and served with spaëtzle or choucroute (sauerkraut) with pork products. Suckling pig is another one of the specialties.

10 rue du Sanglier. ℂ **03-88-32-84-15.** www.chez-yvonne.net. Reservations required. Main courses 13€–26€. AE, DC, MC, V. Daily noon–2:15pm and 6pm–midnight.

Maison des Tanneurs ★ ALSATIAN This longtime favorite, housed in a building from 1572, opened in 1949. The restaurant abounds with flowers and antiques that create a warm atmosphere, and has a terrace that opens onto the canal. The restaurant has been called "La Maison de la Choucroute," because its sauerkraut-and-pork platter is the finest in the area. But the chef prepares many other tasty dishes, including snails cooked Alsatian style with local white wine, a traditional version of Strasbourg foie gras, and guinea fowl stuffed with green peppers. We recommend crayfish tails in court bouillon and *coq au Riesling* (chicken cooked in white wine, with noodles).

42 rue du Bain-aux-Plantes. ℂ **03-88-32-79-70.** www.maison-des-tanneurs.com. Reservations required. Main courses 21€–24€; fixed-price lunch 20€–26€. AE, DC, MC, V. Tues–Sat noon–1:45pm and 7–10pm (also Sun noon–2pm in Dec). Closed 3 weeks in Jan.

Maison Kammerzell ★ ☺ ALSATIAN The gingerbread Maison Kammerzell is an attraction as well as a fantastic restaurant. The carved-wood framework was constructed during the Renaissance, the overhanging stories in 1589. We suggest *la choucroute formidable,* the Alsatian specialty prepared with goose fat, Riesling wine, and Strasbourg sausages. The owner, Guy-Pierre Baumann, also prepares homemade foie gras, guinea hen with mushrooms, medallion of young wild boar, and other regional dishes. A concession to modern cuisine is the chef's version of sauerkraut with fish. Families will want to take advantage of the free meals for children 9 and under at lunch, which makes the place popular with big broods. If you'd rather eat your sauerkraut in relative peace, come for dinner.

16 place de la Cathédrale. ℂ **03-88-32-42-14.** www.maison-kammerzell.com. Reservations required. Main courses 17€–26€; fixed-price menu 31€–46€. AE, DC, MC, V. Daily noon–2:30pm and 7–11pm.

INEXPENSIVE

Brasserie de l'Ancienne Douane ★★ 🔪 ALSATIAN   This is the largest and most colorful dining spot in Strasbourg. Established in the oldest part of town as part of a historical renovation, it offers 600 seats indoors and 200 seats on a terrace. The high-ceilinged rooms are somewhat formal, with Teutonic chairs and heavily timbered ceilings. Among the Alsatian specialties are the well-known "sauerkraut of the Customs officers" and the foie gras of Strasbourg. Onion pie and ham knuckle with potato salad and horseradish are also popular.

6 rue de la Douane. ✆ **03-88-15-78-78.** www.anciennedouane.fr. Reservations recommended. Main courses 16€–24€; fixed-price menu 25€–32€. AE, DC, MC, V. Daily 11:30am–2:30pm and 6:30–11pm.

Where to Stay & Dine Nearby

Many visitors head north 12km (7½ miles) to La Wantzenau, which has very good restaurants. From Strasbourg, take D468 along the west bank of the Rhine.

Relais de la Poste ★★★ FRENCH/ALSATIAN   The leading restaurant in this citadel of fine dining is a cozy half-timbered 18th-century house in the heart of the little Alsatian village. The chefs depend on the changing seasons for their inspiration. They prepare traditional dishes with a modern twist, lighter versions of old favorites. Their succulent concoctions include boned and stuffed quail with a sauce of morels, and fried turbot *osso buco* with Szechuan peppercorn sauce. Two superb appetizers are fresh gooseliver and game terrine. Other memorable dishes include pikeperch in lobster sauce with basil noodles, and salmon tournedos with white beans.

The inn also rents 18 comfortably furnished guest rooms, each in a rustic style, for a double rate of 80€ to 150€.

21 rue du Général-de-Gaulle, La Wantzenau 67610. ✆ **03-88-59-24-80.** Fax 03-88-59-24-89. www.relais-poste.com. Main courses 26€–89€; fixed-price menu 50€–90€. AE, DC, MC, V. Tues–Fri and Sun noon–2pm; Tues–Sat 7-10pm. Closed first 2 weeks of Jan.

Strasbourg After Dark

A bastion of outdoor entertainment is **place de la Cathédrale,** where you can find an assortment of performers and artists. Dancers perform spontaneously against the illumination of the cathedral. From mid-July to early August, additional folk dances take place in La Petite France on Monday night in the places des Tripiers, Tuesday in the place Benjamin Zix, and Wednesday in the place du Marché aux Cochons de Lait. Performance dates vary; check with the Office de Tourisme (✆ **03-88-52-28-29;** www.otstrasbourg.fr) for a schedule.

THE PERFORMING ARTS   For opera and ballet, seek out the **Opéra du Rhin,** 19 place Broglie (✆ **03-88-75-48-23;** www.operanationaldurhin.fr); tickets cost 12€ to 78€. The **Orchestre Philharmonique de Strasbourg** performs at the Palais de la Musique et des Congrès, place de Bordeaux (✆ **03-69-06-37-00;** www.philharmonique-strasbourg.com). Tickets cost 20€ to 55€. The **Théâtre National de Strasbourg** plays a busy schedule at 1 av. de la Marseillaise (✆ **03-88-24-88-00;** www.tns.fr). Tickets cost 5.50€ to 25€.

CLUBS   Head to the streets surrounding place de la Cathédrale: rue des Frères, rue des Soeurs, and rue de la Croix. **Jeannette et les Cycleux,** 3 rue des Tonneliers (✆ **03-88-23-02-71;** www.lenetdejeannette.com), is a wine bar with a jukebox playing rock 'n' roll and other hits from America in the 1950s. Entrance is free.

Le Seven, 25 rue des Tonneliers (☎ **03-88-32-77-77**), has a below-street-level dance floor that features all types of music except disco. The place packs in a stylish crowd ages 20 to 35.

One of the biggest and most visible discos in the region, **Le Chalet,** 376 rte. de Wantzenau (☎ **03-88-31-18-31**), lies 8km (5 miles) north of Strasbourg. The 8€ cover on Friday and 10€ cover on Saturday buys the first drink and access to two huge and distinctly different sections. One is designed for techno fans, another for less harsh dance music, with a good mix of disco classics. It's open 10pm to 4am Friday and Saturday. To get here, follow signs to Wantzenau.

LA ROUTE DU VIN (WINE ROAD) ★★★

The fastest route between Strasbourg and Colmar, 68km (42 miles) south, is N83. But if you have time, the famous Route du Vin makes a rewarding experience. It rolls through 60 charming villages. Along the way are inns where you can sample wine, take a leisurely meal, or spend the night.

The Wine Road runs along the Vosges foothills, with medieval towers and feudal ruins evoking faded pageantry. The vine-covered slopes sometimes reach a height of 435m (1,427 ft.), and an estimated 20,000 hectares (50,000 acres) of vineyards line the road. Some 30,000 families earn their living tending the grapes. The best time to go is for the harvest in September and October. The well-marked route starts at Marlenheim.

Marlenheim

This agreeable town, noted for its Vorlauf red wine, is 21km (13 miles) west of Strasbourg on N4. Even if you can't drive the full length of the Wine Road, you may want to visit for the excellent inn.

WHERE TO STAY & DINE

Le Cerf ★★★   In the heart of this medieval village, occupying a half-timbered building at least 300 years old, this hotel offers pleasantly furnished rooms adjoining

---

 Biking the Wine Road

To rent bikes, visit **Association Velo Emploi (Velocation),** 10 rue des Bouchers (☎ **03-88-24-05-61;** www.velo cation.net). Subsidized by the city of Strasbourg, this place offers among the cheapest rentals anywhere. Half-day rentals cost 5€, full-day rentals 8€. It's open April to September daily 9:30am to 12:30pm and 1:30 to 7pm, and October through March Monday to Friday 10am to 12:30pm and 1 to 5pm. A security deposit of 200€ is required.

The Strasbourg tourist office provides maps showing bike routes that fan out from the city into the countryside, with emphasis on cycle lanes (*les pistes cyclables* in French) that prohibit cars. One of these is a 27km (17-mile) stretch that runs southwest from Strasbourg to the wine hamlet of Molsheim. It has a forest on one side, the banks of the Brûche River (a tributary of the Rhine) on the other, and little car traffic.

an excellent restaurant. Michel Husser and his wife, Cathyok, will feed you elegant, esoteric, and upscale menu items that include, depending on the mood of the chef, such dishes as a fricassee of crayfish and wild mushrooms, a gratin of mushrooms with Riesling, an exotic version of sauerkraut that supplements the normal roster of pork and sausage with smoked foie gras, and a roulade of lobster with spinach and a broth that's brewed from the lobster shells. Fixed-price menus range from 39€ to 125€. The restaurant (but not the hotel) is closed on Tuesday and Wednesday year-round.

30 rue du Général-de-Gaulle, Marlenheim 67520. ✆ **03-88-87-73-73.** Fax 03-88-87-68-08. www. lecerf.com. 14 units. 187€–237€ double; 297€–347€ suite. AE, DC, MC, V. Parking 14€. **Amenities:** Restaurant; Wi-Fi (free). In room: A/C, TV, hair dryer.

Wangen

One of the jewels of the route, Wangen (30km/19 miles from Strasbourg) has a city gate crowned by a tower and twisting, narrow streets—one of the most typical of the wine towns. The road from Wangen winds down to Molsheim.

Molsheim ★

Molsheim (32km/20 miles from Strasbourg) retains its ramparts and a Gothic-Renaissance church built from 1614 to 1619. The Guild of Butchers erected its *Alte Metzig* (town hall), which has a turret, gargoyles, and a loggia. The belfry houses a clock with allegorical figures striking the hour. The local **Office de Tourisme** is at 19 place de l'Hôtel de Ville (✆ **03-88-38-11-61;** fax 03-88-49-80-40; www. ot-molsheim-mutzig.com).

Rosheim ★

Nestled behind medieval fortifications, this town (31km/19 miles from Strasbourg) has a 12th-century Romanesque house and the Eglise St-Pierre et St-Paul, also Romanesque, from 2 centuries later; it's dominated by an octagonal tower. Medieval walls and gate towers evoke Rosheim's past. The **Office de Tourisme** is at 94 rue du Général de Gaulle (✆ **03-88-50-75-38;** fax 03-88-50-45-49; www.rosheim.com).

Obernai ★★

The patron saint of Alsace, Obernai, was born here, 32km (20 miles) from Strasbourg. With its timbered houses and colorful marketplace, **place du Marché,** this town is one of the most interesting stops on the Wine Road. There's a **market** on Thursday 8am to noon; go early. **Place de l'Etoile** abounds with flowers, and the **Hôtel de Ville** has a delightful loggia. An old watchtower, the **Tour de la Chapelle,** is from the 13th and 16th centuries. The town's six-pail **fountain** is one of the most spectacular in Alsace. The **Office de Tourisme** is at place du Beffroi (✆ **03-88-95-64-13;** fax 03-88-49-90-84; www.obernai.fr).

WHERE TO STAY & DINE

Le Parc ★★   This contemporary hotel offers fine dining and many facilities you'd find in a spa, with a traditional Alsatian motif and architectural style. City dwellers seeking R & R appreciate the well-furnished, spacious guest rooms. The well-managed restaurant serves dishes that vary depending on what's in the local markets. That may include monkfish with mushrooms, duckling with apples and cèpes (flap mushrooms), crayfish salad, salmon in red-wine sauce, and rich fruit desserts.

169 rte. d'Ottrott, Obernai 67210. ☏ **03-88-95-50-08.** Fax 03-88-95-37-29. www.hotel-du-parc.com. 62 units. 120€–240€ double; 275€–340€ suite. AE, MC, V. Closed 2 weeks in late June to mid-July and mid-Dec to mid-Jan. **Amenities:** 2 restaurants; 3 bars; cigar bar; Jacuzzi; indoor and outdoor pools; room service; sauna; solarium; spa; steam room. *In room:* A/C, TV, hair dryer, Wi-Fi (free).

Barr

The grapes for some of the finest Alsatian wines, Sylvaner and Gewürztraminer, are harvested here. The castles of Landsberg and Andlau stand high above the town. Barr (37km/23 miles from Strasbourg) has many pleasant old-timbered houses. The charming **place de l'Hôtel-de-Ville** has a town hall from 1640. Call ☏ **03-88-08-66-65** for tourist information at 1 rue des Bouchers.

Mittelbergheim

Mittelbergheim, 43km (27 miles) from Strasbourg, is a special village. Houses in the Renaissance style border its **place de l'Hôtel-de-Ville.**

WHERE TO STAY & DINE

Winstub Gilg ★ This is an excellent inn. Though parts of the building date from 1614, its showpiece is a two-story stone staircase, classified as a historic monument. Medieval stonemasons who worked on the cathedral at Strasbourg carved it. Each attractively furnished guest room has a combination tub/shower. Chef Vincent Reuschlé attracts a loyal following with regional specialties such as onion tart, sauerkraut, and foie gras in brioche. Main courses include stewed kidneys and sweetbreads, rack of lamb cooked pink, duck with oranges, and, in season, roast pheasant with grapes. The hotel and restaurant close in January and from June 21 to July 8. The rest of the year, the restaurant closes on Tuesday and Wednesday.

1 rte. du Vin, Mittelbergheim, Barr 67140. ☏ **03-88-08-91-37.** Fax 03-88-08-45-17. www.hotel-gilg.com. 15 units. 57€–87€ double. AE, DC, MC, V. **Amenities:** Restaurant; Wi-Fi in lobby. *In room:* TV.

Andlau

This gardenlike resort, 42km (26 miles) from Strasbourg, was the site of an abbey founded in 887 by the disgraced wife of Emperor Charles the Fat. It has now faded into history, but a church remains that dates from the 12th century. In the tympanum are noteworthy Romanesque carvings. The **Office de Tourisme,** 5 rue du Général-de-Gaulle (☏ **03-88-08-22-57;** www.pays-de-barr.com), is open Monday through Friday 9am to noon.

WHERE TO DINE

Au Boeuf Rouge TRADITIONAL FRENCH This bustling, unpretentious bistro has a busy bar and a comfortably battered dining room. Its menu of time-tested specialties includes homemade terrines, gamecock, fresh fish, and a tempting dessert cart. Noted chef Pierre Kieffer prepares a fabulous quenelle of brochet, a local whitefish, according to his grandmother's recipe. Although the fare is reliable and consistent, it isn't the most innovative cookery on the wine trail, excepting his seasonal version of wild boar with cassis sauce and spaëtzle. For dessert, try a slice of Baettelman, an Alsatian cake baked with apples and cherries. There's also a wine *stube* (tavern) on-site to the right as you enter. From March to October, you can sit on the terrace in front.

6 rue du Dr.-Stoltz. ☏ **03-88-08-96-26.** Reservations recommended. Main courses 17€–37€; fixed-price menu 15€–24€. AE, DC, MC, V. Oct–July 12 Fri–Wed 11:30am–2:30pm, Fri–Tues 6–9:30pm; July 15–Sept daily 11:30am–2:30pm and 6–9:30pm. Closed 10 days in Feb and 3 weeks June–July.

Dambach

In the midst of its vineyards, Dambach (48km/30 miles from Strasbourg) is one of the delights of the Wine Road. The town, formally Dambach-la-Ville, has ramparts and three fortified gates. Its timbered houses are gabled with galleries, and many contain oriels. Wrought-iron signs still tell you if a place is a bakery or a butcher shop. A short drive from the town is the **Chapelle St-Sebastian,** with a 15th-century ossuary. The **Office de Tourisme** (℃ **03-88-92-61-00;** fax 03-88-92-47-11; www.dambach-la-ville.fr) is in La Mairie (town hall), place du Marché.

Sélestat ★

Sélestat lies 52km (32 miles) from Strasbourg. It was once a free city, a center of the Renaissance, and the seat of a great school. Towered battlements enclose the town. The **Bibliothèque Humaniste,** 1 rue de la Bibliothèque (℃ **03-88-58-07-20**), houses a collection of manuscripts, including Sainte-Foy's *Book of Miracles.* It's open Monday and Wednesday through Friday from 9am to noon and 2 to 6pm, Saturday from 9am to noon (July–Aug also Sat–Sun 2–5pm). Admission is 3.80€ for adults, 2.30€ for students, and free for children 11 and under.

The Gothic **Eglise St-George** has some fine stained glass and a gilded and painted stone pulpit. Also try to visit the 12th-century **Eglise Ste-Foy,** built of red sandstone in the Romanesque style. One of the town's most noteworthy Renaissance buildings is the **Maison de Stephan Ziegler** on rue de Verdun.

The **Office de Tourisme** is in La Commanderie St-Jean, boulevard du Général-Leclerc (℃ **03-88-58-87-20;** fax 03-88-92-88-63; www.selestat-tourisme.com).

From Sélestat, you can detour about 750m (2,460 ft.) up an isolated peak to **Château Haut-Koenigsbourg** (℃ **03-88-82-50-60;** www.haut-koenigsbourg.net), a 15th-century castle. It's the largest in Alsace and affords an eagle's-nest view. It once belonged to the Hohenstaufens. During the Thirty Years' War, the Swedes dismantled it. In 1901, the then-ruined pile was offered as a gift by the city of Sélestat to the German kaiser, Wilhelm II, who rebuilt it at massive personal expense. At the end of World War I, it was ceded back to the French nation as part of the Treaty of Versailles. Admission is 7.50€ for adults, 4.80€ for students 18 to 25, and free for children 17 and under. During April, May, and September, it's open daily 9:30am to 5pm; during June to August, it's open daily 9:30am to 6pm; during October and March, it's open daily 9:45am to 4:30pm; from November to February, it's open daily 9:45am to noon and 1 to 4:30pm.

WHERE TO DINE NEARBY

La Couronne ★★★ ALSATIAN   This charming family-run place serves deftly prepared dishes reflecting the bounty of Alsace. A flower-filled vestibule leads to a trio of dining rooms. The chefs know the classics but give a personal twist to most dishes, using market-fresh ingredients in skillful concoctions that look as delectable as they taste. They prepare light, modern interpretations of Alsatian dishes without heavy sauces and fats. The restaurant has a fine cellar of Alsatian wines. Menu choices may include noisettes of roebuck (from midsummer to Christmas), ragout of fish, foie gras, *omble chevalier* (whitefish from Lake Geneva) with sauerkraut and cumin-laced potatoes, and frogs' legs served with freshwater-shrimp flan.

45 rue de Sélestat-Baldenheim. ✆ **03-88-85-32-22.** Reservations required. Main courses 17€–26€; fixed-price menu 32€–62€. MC, V. Tues–Sun noon–2:30pm; Tues–Wed and Fri–Sat 7–9:30pm. Closed 1st week of Jan and mid-July to Aug. From Sélestat, go 9km (5⅗ miles) east on D21; when the road forks, bear right and take D209 to the village of Baldenheim.

12 Bergheim

Renowned for its wines, this town (85km/53 miles from Strasbourg) has kept part of its 15th-century fortifications. You can see timbered Alsatian houses and a Gothic church.

Ribeauville ★

At the foot of vine-clad hills, Ribeauvillé (87km/54 miles from Strasbourg) is picturesque, with old shop signs, pierced balconies, turrets, and flower-decorated houses. The town is noted for its Riesling and Gewürztraminer wines. See its Renaissance fountain and **Hôtel de Ville,** place de la Mairie, which has a collection of silver-gilt medieval and Renaissance tankards known as *hanaps.* For information, go to the tourist office at 1 Grand'rue (✆ **03-89-73-23-23;** www.ribeauville-riquewihr.com).

Guided tours showcase the *hanaps,* the building's architecture, and the history of the town. The free 90-minute tours run from May to September, on Sunday and Tuesday through Friday at 10am, 11am, and 2pm. On tour days at 3pm, the same guide leads a 90-minute walking tour of the town. Tours are in French, German, or halting English.

Also of interest in Ribeauvillé is the **Tour des Bouchers** ("butcher's tower"), built in stages from the 13th to the 16th century.

Every year on the first Sunday in September, visitors fill the town for its **Jour des Menetriers (Day of the Minstrels).** Beginning at 3pm and lasting almost 2½ hours, it features a parade of flute players from Alsace, the rest of France, Switzerland, and Germany, and as many as 600 parade participants. You can stand anywhere to watch the spectacle, but seats on the medieval stone benches line either side of the parade route.

WHERE TO STAY & DINE

Clos St-Vincent ★★★   This is one of the most elegant choices along Route du Vin. Most of the individually decorated guest rooms have a balcony or terrace, but you get much more than a view of the Haut-Rhin vineyards and summer roses. The rooms, ranging from medium to large, are furnished with grand comfort; each has a bed covered in fine linen and a bathroom with state-of-the-art plumbing and combination tub/shower. Some have air-conditioning. The Chapotin family's cuisine is exceptional: hot duck liver with nuts, turbot with sorrel, roebuck (in season) in hot sauce, and veal kidneys in pinot noir. The wines are smooth, especially the popular Riesling and Gewürztraminer.

Rte. de Bergheim, Ribeauvillé 68150. ✆ **03-89-73-67-65.** Fax 03-89-73-32-20. www.leclossaint vincent.com. 24 units. 135€–220€ double; 200€–250€ suite. AE, MC, V. Closed Dec 15–Mar 15. **Amenities:** Restaurant (dinner only Wed–Mon); bar; babysitting; Jacuzzi; indoor pool; room service; sauna. *In room:* TV, hair dryer, minibar, Wi-Fi (free).

Riquewihr ★★★

Surrounded by some of the finest vineyards in Alsace, this town (89km/55 miles from Strasbourg) appears much as it did in the 16th century. With well-preserved walls and towers and wine presses, it's one of the most rewarding destinations along the route.

You can see Gothic and Renaissance houses, with balconies, gables, and carved doors and windows. The most interesting are **Maison Liebrich** (1535), **Maison Preiss-Zimmer** (1686), and **Maison Kiener** (1574). Try to peer into some of the courtyards, where time seems frozen. **Tour de Dolder (Dolder Belfry Tower)** is from 1291. Riquewihr contains at least four minor museums, plus a handful of other quasi-museums that the average short-term visitor may, without missing a lot, opt to skip. Two of the most important, however—and even these are worth only a very brief visit—are the pentagonal **Musée de la Tour des Voleurs,** in the rue des Juifs, which is the site of a medieval torture chamber, and the **Musée Dolder,** which showcases a handful of civic exhibits from the earliest days of the city's medieval history. A combined ticket to both museums costs 3€ for adults and 2€ for students and children 17 and under. Both monuments are open April through October Wednesday to Monday 10:15am to 12:30pm and 2 to 6:30pm, and for 2 weeks in December. For more information about either of these very minor museums, contact the local **Office de Tourisme,** 1 Grand'rue in nearby Ribeauvillé (© **03-89-73-23-23;** fax 03-89-73-23-29; www.ribeauville-riquewihr.com). Another minor museum within Riquewihr is the **Musée de la Communication,** a site also known as the **Alsace Postal History Museum** (© **03-89-47-93-80**). Set within the thick stone walls of the Château de Riquewihr, which was originally built in 1539 by the Duke of Wurttemberg, it costs 4€ for adults, 3.50€ for students, and 2.50€ for children 17 and under. Hours are the same, with the same annual closing, as the two other museums noted immediately above.

WHERE TO STAY & DINE

Auberge du Schoenenbourg ★★★ FRENCH We highly recommend the food here. You'll dine in a garden surrounded by vineyards at the edge of the village. The chef offers a delectable array of tantalizing fare. *Foie gras maison* is de rigueur, but salmon soufflé with sabayon truffles is an elegant surprise. Try panache of fish with sorrel, ravioli of snails with poppy seeds, or tournedos in puff pastry with mushrooms and foie gras. Especially flavorful is a platter of both smoked and fresh salmon, served with creamy horseradish sauce and herb-flavored sauerkraut.

Although the restaurant does not rent rooms, the 58-room **Hôtel Le Schoenenbourg** is next door on rue du Schoenenbourg (© **03-89-49-01-11;** fax 03-89-47-95-88; www.auberge-schoenenbourg.fr). It offers comfortably furnished guest rooms for 97€ to 123€ for a double, 176€ to 232€ for a suite.

2 rue de la Piscine. © **03-89-47-92-28.** Reservations required. Main courses 18€–32€; fixed-price menu 29€ Mon–Fri and for lunch only, and 39€–81€ dinner. AE, MC, V. Year-round Sun–Mon noon–2pm; Mar–Oct daily 7–10pm; Nov–Mar Thurs–Tues 7–10pm. Closed Jan.

Kientzheim

Kientzheim (90km/56 miles from Strasbourg) is known for its wine, two castles, timber-framed houses, and walls from the Middle Ages. From here, it's just a short drive to Kaysersberg, also known for its vineyards. Tourist info can be found in Kaysersberg.

Kaysersberg ★★

Once a free city of the empire, Kaysersberg (93km/58 miles from Strasbourg) lies at the mouth of the Weiss Valley, between two vine-covered slopes; it's crowned by a castle ruined in the Thirty Years' War. From one of the many ornately carved bridges, you can see the city's medieval fortifications along the top of one of the nearby hills.

Many of the houses are Gothic and Renaissance, and most have half-timbering, wrought-iron accents, leaded windows, and multiple designs carved into reddish sandstone.

In the cafes, you'll hear a combination of French and Alsatian. The age of the speaker usually determines the language—the older ones remain faithful to the dialect of their grandparents.

Dr. Albert Schweitzer was born here in 1875; his house is near the bridge over the Weiss. You can visit the **Musée du Docteur Schweitzer,** 126 rue du Général de Gaulle (℃ **03-89-47-36-55**), from April to November daily from 9am to noon and 2 to 6pm. Admission is 2€ adults and 1€ for students and children 11 and under.

The **Office de Tourisme** is at 39 rue du Général-de-Gaulle (℃ **03-89-78-22-78;** fax 03-89-71-34-11; www.kaysersberg.com).

WHERE TO STAY & DINE

Au Lion d'Or FRENCH/ALSATIAN   This 1521 building boasts an exceptionally beautiful decor. A carved lion's head adorns the oak door leading into the restaurant, which has a beamed ceiling, stone detailing, brass chandeliers, and a massive fireplace. If you eat at an outdoor table, you'll have a view of one of Alsace's prettiest streets. The classic Alsatian dishes include wild game, foie gras (which Alsatians claim to have invented), and yummy pork dishes, often with hams and sausage. Sauerkraut, served in its traditional meat-and-potato form or with fish, is an enduring specialty and a favorite with the loyal clientele.

66 rue du Général-de-Gaulle. ℃ **03-89-47-11-16.** www.auliondor.fr. Reservations required. Main courses 13€–19€; fixed-price menu 20€–29€. AE, MC, V. Thurs–Mon noon–2:30pm and 6:30–9:30pm.

Le Chambard ★★★ FRENCH/ALSATIAN   The regional cuisine here is so good, it's worth planning a stop. You'll recognize the restaurant by the gilded wrought-iron sign above the cobblestones. Exposed stone and polished wood accent the rustic interior. Regional specialties with Mediterranean influences attest to the mastery of the kitchen. The imaginative chef, Olivier Nasti, presents impeccably flavored and sophisticated cuisine. The restaurant is known for sauerkraut served with a host of (mostly smoked) pork specialties, as well as foie gras and pungent Münster cheese. Other choices include a "cake" of eggplant with goose foie gras, an upscale version of traditional Alsatian stew made with foie gras, and traditional Alsatian cake (*kugelhof*) with cinnamon-flavored ice cream. The cellar stocks the best local vintages.

A 20-room hotel annex, built in 1981 to match the other structures on the street, has a massive Renaissance fireplace that was transported from another building. A double goes for 140€ to 190€, a suite from 240€. An elegant spa was added in 2008.

9-13 rue du Général-de-Gaulle, Kaysersberg 68240. ℃ **03-89-47-10-17.** Fax 03-89-47-35-03. www.lechambard.com. Reservations required. Main courses 26€–39€; fixed-price menu 18€–85€. AE, MC, V. Thurs–Sun noon–2pm; Tues–Sun 7–9pm.

Ammerschwihr

Ammerschwihr, 9km (5⅗ miles) north of Colmar (79km/49 miles from Strasbourg), is a good stop to cap off your Wine Road tour. Once a free city of the empire, the town was almost destroyed in 1944 and has been reconstructed in the traditional style. More and more travelers visit to sample the wine, especially Käferkopf. Check out the town's gate towers, 16th-century parish church, and remains of early fortifications.

WHERE TO STAY & DINE

A l'Arbre Vert ★ ✷   At least part of this hotel's charm derives from the close supervision of Joël and Evelyne Tournier, chef and *maître d'hôtel,* respectively, who represent at least three generations of attentive, family-managed service. Public rooms are delightful, loaded with regional artifacts and coziness. Guest rooms were renovated several years ago, and each is clean, well maintained, and comfortable, with a shower-only bathroom. The restaurant, which is closed every Tuesday, is open to nonresidents and serves very good Alsatian specialties, including savory scallop of gooseliver with pinot noir, cassoulet of snails with mushrooms, and crisp-baked salmon with leeks. Some of the best warm dessert soufflés in the region emerge steaming from the kitchens, many laden with whatever fresh fruit happens to be in season at the time. (In midwinter, look for a superb version with oranges, clementines, or lemons.)

7 rue des Cigognes, Ammerschwihr 68770. ✆ **03-89-47-12-23.** Fax 03-89-78-27-21. www.arbre-vert. net. 19 units. 53€–74€ double. Half board 59€–69€ per person double occupancy. AE, DC, MC, V. Closed mid-Feb to mid-Mar and 2 weeks in Nov. **Amenities:** Restaurant; bar. *In room:* TV.

Aux Armes de France ★★★ FRENCH/ALSATIAN   This is the best restaurant along the Wine Road. Although you can rent one of 10 rooms here (doubles go for 69€–84€), the real reason to come is the cuisine. In a flower-filled setting, Philippe Gaertner and his staff attract many French and German gourmets. A specialty is fresh foie gras served in its own golden aspic. Main courses include classics with imaginative variations, such as roebuck (in season) in hot sauce, and lobster fricassee with cream and truffles. Spicy duckling is savory, as is filet of sole with fresh noodles. Terrine of lobster and calf's head in aspic *(presskopf),* which we've never seen in any other restaurant in France, is a particular enticement for adventurous gastronomes.

1 Grand' Rue, Ammerschwihr 68770. ✆ **03-89-47-10-12.** Fax 03-89-47-38-12. www.aux-armes-de-france.com. Reservations required. Main courses 16€–66€; fixed-price menu 27€–48€. AE, DC, MC, V. Fri–Tues noon–2pm and 7:30–9pm.

Rouffach

Rouffach is south of Colmar. One of the highest of the Vosges Mountains, Grand-Ballon shelters the town from the winds that bring rain, which makes for a dry climate and a special grape. We include it here because of the excellent vineyard **Clos St-Landelin** (✆ **03-89-78-58-00;** www.mure.com), on the Route du Vin, at the intersection of RN83 and route de Soultzmatt. A clerical estate from the 6th century until the Revolution, it has been celebrated over the centuries for the quality of its wine. Clos St-Landelin covers 21 hectares (52 acres) at the southern end of the Vorbourg Grand Cru area. Its steep slopes call for terrace cultivation.

The soil that produces these wines is anything but fertile. Loaded with pebbles, sand, and limestone, the high-alkaline earth produces low-yield, scraggly vines whose fruit goes into superb Rieslings, Gewürztraminers, and pinot noirs. Members of the Muré family have owned these vineyards since 1648. In their cellar is a 13th-century wine press, the oldest in Alsace, and one of only three like it in France. (The other two are in Burgundy.) The family welcomes visitors who want to tour the cellars and ask about the wine, which is for sale. It's open Monday to Friday 8am to 6:30pm, and Saturday 10am to 1pm and 2 to 6pm.

COLMAR ★★★

440km (273 miles) SE of Paris; 140km (87 miles) SE of Nancy; 71km (44 miles) SW of Strasbourg

One of the most attractive towns in Alsace, Colmar abounds with medieval and early Renaissance buildings, half-timbered structures, gables, and gracious loggias. Tiny gardens and wash houses surround many of the homes. Its old quarter looks more German than French, filled with streets of unexpected twists and turns. As a gateway to the Rhine country, Colmar is a major destination for travelers heading south from Strasbourg. Near the vine-covered slopes of the southern Vosges, it's the third-largest town in Alsace.

Colmar has been so well restored that it's Alsace's most beautiful city, far more pleasing than Strasbourg. It's hard to tell that Colmar was hard hit in two world wars.

Essentials

GETTING THERE   If you're **driving,** take N83 from Strasbourg; trip time is 1 hour. Because of the narrow streets, we suggest that you park and walk. Leave the car in the Champ-de-Mars, or in the underground Place Rapp for a fee of around 1.20€ per hour, northeast of the railway station, and then walk a few blocks east to the old city; or park in the lot designated PARKING VIEILLE VILLE, accessible from rue de l'Est at the edge of the Petite Venise neighborhood, and walk a few blocks southeast to reach the old city. **Trains** link Colmar to Nancy, Strasbourg, and Mulhouse, as well as to Germany via Strasbourg, across the Rhine. Twenty-one trains per day arrive from Paris's Gare de l'Est (trip time: 4–6 hr.); the one-way fare is 68€. For information, call ✆ **36-35,** or 08-92-35-35-35 from outside France.

VISITOR INFORMATION   The **Office de Tourisme** is at 4 rue Unterlinden (✆ **03-89-20-68-92;** fax 03-89-41-34-13; www.ot-colmar.fr).

For information on wines, vintages, and winery visits, contact the **CIVA** (Alsace Wine Committee), Maison du Vin d'Alsace, 12 av. de la Foire-aux-Vins (✆ **03-89-20-16-20**). It's usually open Monday to Friday 8am to noon and 2 to 5pm. Make arrangements far in advance.

SPECIAL EVENTS   Alsatian **folk dances** on place de l'Ancienne-Douane begin at 8:30pm on Tuesday from mid-May to mid-September. If you want to listen to classical music, visit during the first 2 weeks in July for the **Festival International de Musique de Colmar** (✆ **03-89-20-68-97;** www.festival-colmar.com), which schedules 24 concerts in venues around the city, such as churches and public monuments. **Les Mardis de la Collégiale,** at place de la Cathédrale (✆ **06-71-06-50-18**), stages concerts every Tuesday at 8:45pm from the end of July to mid-September. Tickets for these events cost 10€ to 15€. You can get complete information on any of the events in town at the Office de Tourisme.

Exploring Colmar

Colmar is rich with historic houses, many half-timbered and, in summer, accented with geranium-draped window boxes. One of the most beautiful is the **Maison Pfister,** 11 rue des Marchands, at the corner of rue Mercière, a 1537 building with wooden balconies. On the ground floor is a wine boutique owned by a major Alsace winegrower, **Muré,** proprietor of the vineyard Clos St-Landelin (✆ **03-89-41-33-61**).

If you take pont St-Pierre over the Lauch River, you'll have an excellent view of Old Colmar and can explore **Petite Venise,** which is filled with canals.

SHOPPING   Head for the old town of Colmar, particularly ·rue de Clefs, Grand'rue, rue des Têtes, and rue des Marchands.

Antiques abound, and you'll find a large grouping of stores in the old town, especially along rue des Marchands. Shops that deserve particular attention include **Geismar Dany,** 32 rue des Marchands (✆/fax **03-89-23-30-41**), specializing in antique painted furniture, and **Antiquités Guy Caffard,** 56 rue des Marchands (✆ **03-89-41-31-78;** www.caffard-antiquites.com), with its mishmash of furniture, postcards, books, toys, bibelots, and the like. Also worth noting are **Lire & Chiner,** 36 rue des Marchands (✆ **03-89-24-16-78;** www.lire-et-chiner.fr), and **Antiquité Arcana,** 13 place l'Ancienne Douane (✆ **03-89-41-59-81**).

One of the most appealing stores is **Arts et Collections d'Alsace,** 1 rue des Tanneurs (✆ **03-89-24-09-78**), which stocks copies of art objects and utilitarian wares of yesteryear. There are items for the home and kitchen, made from wrought iron, pottery, glass, copper, carved wood, and fabric.

WINERIES   Because Colmar is one of the gateways to the wine-producing Rhine country, local wine is one of the best purchases you can make. If you don't have time to visit the vineyards along the Wine Road, stop in at **Cave du Musée,** 11 rue Kléber (✆ **03-89-23-85-29**), for one of the largest selections of wines and liqueurs from the region and the rest of France.

You can drive to one of the most historic vineyards in Alsace-Lorraine. **Domaines Schlumberger** (✆ **03-89-74-27-00;** www.domaines-schlumberger.com) lies 26km (16 miles) southwest of Colmar in Guebwiller. The cellars, established by the Schlumberger family in 1810, are an unusual combination of early-19th-century brickwork and modern stainless steel. These grapes become such famous wines as Rieslings, Gewürztraminers, muscats, sylvaners, and pinots (blanc, gris, and noir). Views of the vineyards and tasting rooms are available without an appointment, but group tours of the cellars are conducted only when a staff member is available. Call before you go to find out when that might be. The vineyard is closed 2 weeks in August and December 22 to January 2.

Eglise des Dominicains   This church contains one of Colmar's most famous treasures: Martin Schongauer's painting *Virgin of the Rosebush,* or *Vierge au buisson de rose* (1473), all gold, red, and white, with fluttering birds. Look for it in the choir.

Place des Dominicains. ✆ **03-89-24-46-57.** Admission 1.50€ adults, 1€ students, .50€ ages 12–16, free for children 11 and under. Apr–Dec daily 10am–1pm and 3–6pm.

Eglise St-Martin ★   In the heart of Old Colmar is a collegiate church begun in 1230 on the site of a Romanesque church. It has a choir erected by William of Marburg in 1350 and a steeple that rises to 70m (230 ft.).

Place de la Cathédrale. ✆ **03-89-41-27-20.** Free admission. Daily 8am–7pm. Closed to casual visitors during Mass.

Musée Bartholdi   Statue of Liberty sculptor Frédéric-Auguste Bartholdi was born in Colmar in 1834. This small, memento-filled museum is in the house where he was born. It has Statue of Liberty rooms containing plans and scale models, and documents related to its construction and other works regarding U.S. history. Bartholdi's Paris apartment, with furniture and memorabilia, has been reconstructed here. The museum supplements its exhibits with paintings of Egyptian scenes that Bartholdi collected during his travels in 1856.

30 rue des Marchands. (©) **03-89-41-90-60.** www.musee-bartholdi.com. Admission 5€ adults, 2.50€ students and children 12-18, free for children 11 and under. Wed-Mon 10am-noon and 2-6pm. Closed Jan-Feb, May 1, Nov 1, and Dec 25.

Musée d'Unterlinden (Under the Linden Trees) ★★ This former Dominican convent (1232), the chief seat of Rhenish mysticism in the 14th and 15th centuries, became a museum around 1850, and it's been a treasure house of the art and history of Alsace ever since.

The jewel of its collection is the **Issenheim Altarpiece (Le Retable d'Issenheim)** ★★★, created by Würzburg-born Matthias Grünewald, "the most furious of realists," around 1515. His colors glow, and his fantasy will overwhelm you. One of the most exciting works in German art, it's an immense altar screen with two-sided folding wing pieces—designed to show the Crucifixion, then the Incarnation, framed by the Annunciation and the Resurrection. The carved altar screen depicts St. Anthony visiting the hermit St. Paul; it also shows the Temptation of St. Anthony, the most beguiling part of a work that contains some ghastly birds, weird monsters, and loathsome animals. The demon of the plague is depicted with a swollen belly and purple skin, his body blotched with boils; a diabolical grin appears on his horrible face.

Other attractions include the magnificent altarpiece (dating from 1470) of Jean d'Orlier by Martin Schongauer, a large collection of religious woodcarvings and stained glass from the 14th to the 18th centuries, and Gallo-Roman lapidary collections, including funeral slabs. The armory collection contains ancient arms from the Romanesque to the Renaissance, featuring halberds and crossbows.

1 rue d'Unterlinden. (©) **03-89-20-15-58.** www.musee-unterlinden.com. Admission 7€ adults, 5€ students and children 12-17, free for children 11 and under. May-Oct daily 9am-6pm; Nov-Apr Wed-Mon 9am-noon and 2-5pm. Closed national holidays.

Where to Stay

Rooms are also available in **La Maison des Têtes** (see "Where to Dine," below).

Grand Hôtel Bristol This 1926 red sandstone "grand hotel" has been totally renovated. Right at the train station, it provides well-maintained rooms with both modern and provincial decor. Accommodations are rather standardized and not quite as grand as the name of the hotel suggests. Most of the tidy, midsize bathrooms have tub/shower combinations.

7 place de la Gare, Colmar 68000. (©) **03-89-23-59-59.** Fax 03-89-23-92-26. www.grand-hotel-bristol. com. 91 units. 96€-165€ double. AE, DC, MC, V. **Amenities:** 2 restaurants; bar; babysitting; room service; rooms for those w/limited mobility; smoke-free rooms. *In room:* A/C (in some), TV, hair dryer, minibar, Wi-Fi (free).

Hostellerie Le Maréchal ★★ Three 16th-century houses make up this hotel, the most tranquil in town. You climb a wide staircase to reach the guest rooms, most of which are air-conditioned. In the east wing is a small, partially timbered room with a sloping ceiling. Accommodations are small but neatly organized, each with a tiled bathroom, most with tub/shower combinations. The restaurant has a fireplace in winter; in summer, seating moves to the terrace, where you can enjoy a water view. Feast on stuffed quail, good beef and veal dishes, and lamb Provençal, all accompanied by Tokay and Alsatian wines.

4-6 place des Six-Montagnes-Noires, Colmar 68000. ☎ **03-89-41-60-32.** Fax 03-89-24-59-40. www.hotel-le-marechal.com. 30 units. 105€–225€ double; 255€ suite. AE, DC, MC, V. Parking 15€. **Amenities:** Restaurant; room service; smoke-free rooms. *In room:* TV, hair dryer, minibar, Wi-Fi (free).

Le Colombier ★   Originally built as a half-timbered house in the 14th century, this building is among the town's finest hotels. Very old beams and masonry contrast pleasantly with contemporary lighting and furniture. The staff is engaging and helpful. If the government-rated three-star hotel had a restaurant (breakfast is the only meal served), it would surely earn four-star status. With the exception of the cozy unit beneath the steeply pitched pinnacle of the roof, all of the guest rooms have high ceilings; they vary in size and shape. Each contains comfortable appointments and fine linen, plus a small but tidy shower-only bathroom. Some rooms overlook the canals of Petite Venise; others open onto a half-timbered courtyard.

7 rue Turenne, Colmar 68000. ☎ **03-89-23-96-00.** Fax 03-89-23-97-27. www.hotel-le-colombier.fr. 28 units. 95€–182€ double; 205€–255€ suite. AE, DC, MC, V. Parking 10€. **Amenities:** Bar; room service. *In room:* A/C, TV, hair dryer, minibar, Wi-Fi (3.50€ per day).

Where to Dine

Chez Hansi 🍴 ALSATIAN   Set within two rooms of a half-timbered house dating from 1532, this is the most historic and most folklorically charming restaurant in a town that's loaded with worthy competitors. Even its name is a reference to the pen name (Hansi) of Jean-Jacques Waltz, a 19th-century illustrator, who in his artwork elevated Alsatian kitsch to an art form rivaled in America by Norman Rockwell. You'll find this hypertraditional place in the Vieille Ville, beneath massively beamed ceilings and a staff whose women are clad in dirndls. Come here for steaming and heaping platters of choucroute (sauerkraut garnished with pork products), foie gras, onion tarte, *pot au feu* that's redolent with gravy and chunks of beef, and, for the ultra-adventurous, calf-head (*tete de veau*) garnished with an apple in its mouth.

23 rue des Marchands. ☎ **03-89-41-37-84.** Reservations recommended. Main courses 17€–28€; set-price menus 18€–46€. MC, V. Fri–Tues 11:45am–1:45pm and 6:45–9:30pm. Closed Jan.

La Maison des Têtes ★★★ TRADITIONAL FRENCH   This Colmar monument, named for the sculptured heads on its stone facade, is the town's leading hotel and one of its top restaurants. It opens off a covered cobblestone drive and courtyard. The 17th-century house lies in the center of town, near the Unterlinden Museum. The dining rooms are decorated with aged-wood beams and paneling, Art Nouveau lighting fixtures, and stained glass and leaded windows. The excellent food includes foie gras with truffles, choucroute, seasonal roebuck with morels and dried fruits, roasted duck with two spices, and fresh trout or Rhine salmon braised in Riesling. The Alsatian wines are sublime. There are also 21 nicely furnished rooms with minibars, safes, air-conditioning, and TVs; some have Jacuzzis. Rates are 91€ to 235€ for a double, 205€ to 269€ for a suite.

In the Hôtel des Têtes, 19 rue des Têtes, Colmar 68000. ☎ **03-89-24-43-43.** Fax 03-89-24-58-34. www.la-maison-des-tetes.com. Reservations required. Main courses 10€–28€; fixed-price menu 33€–72€; menu dégustation 65€. AE, DC, MC, V. Wed–Sun noon–2pm; Tues–Sat 7–9:30pm. Closed Feb.

Where to Stay & Dine Nearby

Gourmets flock to **Illhaeusern,** 18km (11 miles) from Colmar, east of the N83 highway, to dine at the Auberge de l'Ill, one of France's great restaurants. The signs for the restaurant, beside the main highway, are difficult to miss.

Auberge de l'Ill ★★★ MODERN FRENCH   This is the greatest restaurant in eastern France. Run by the Haeberlin family in their 19th-century farmhouse, Auberge de l'Ill combines the finest Alsatian specialties with *cuisine moderne* and classic offerings. You can enjoy your aperitif or coffee under the weeping willows in a beautiful garden with a river view. Chef Marc Haeberlin takes dishes of Alsatian origin and makes them into *grande cuisine*—freshwater eel stewed in Riesling, *matelotes* (small glazed onions) in Riesling, and an inventive foie gras. His partridge, pheasant, and duckling are among the best in Europe. Two unsurpassed choices are braised slices of pheasant and partridge served with winey game sauce, chestnuts, wild mushrooms, and Breton cornmeal; and salmon soufflé. A divine starter is mousseline of frogs' legs with white-wine and chive sauce; you may follow that with mallard duckling lacquered with spices and served with a confit of red cabbage and figs. Some dishes require 24 hours' notice, so inquire when you make reservations.

You can spend the night in one of 13 rooms at the **Hôtel des Berges,** in a delightfully furnished, air-conditioned room overlooking the Ill River. The rates are 262€ to 300€ for a double, 350€ to 520€ for a suite, and 465€ for a decade-old cottage on the grounds.

Rue de Collonges, Illhaeusern 68970. ✆ **03-89-71-89-00.** Fax 03-89-71-82-83. www.auberge-de-l-ill. com. Reservations required (1 week in advance for summer weekends). Main courses 46€–140€; fixed-price menu 117€–148€. AE, DC, MC, V. Wed–Sun noon–2pm and 7–9pm. Closed early Feb to mid-Mar.

Colmar After Dark

Head for the seductive **La Fiesta/Le Cotton Club,** place de la Gare (✆ **03-89-23-43-04**). Popular and busy, this nightclub consists of two strikingly different venues: On street level, La Fiesta is a bar with lots of suds, margaritas, and a busy after-work scene. Upstairs, there's a cocktail lounge with a dance floor and a calmer, more urban (think Paris or Berlin) ambience. For a mellow atmosphere, try the piano bar **Louisiana Club,** 3A rue Berthe-Molly (✆ **03-89-24-94-18**), where you can groove to authentic blues and jazz.

LA ROUTE DES CRETES ★★★

From Basel, Switzerland, to Mainz, Germany, a distance of some 242km (150 miles), the Vosges Mountains stretch along the west side of the Rhine Valley, bearing a similarity to the Black Forest of Germany. Many German and French families spend their summer vacation exploring the Vosges. Travelers with less time may want to settle for a quick look at the ancient mountains that once formed the boundary between France and Germany. They are filled with tall hardwood and fir trees, and a network of twisting roads with hairpin curves traverses them. The depths of the mountain forests are the closest France comes to wilderness.

Exploring the Area

You can explore the mountains by heading west from Strasbourg, but there's a more interesting route from Colmar. La Route des Crêtes (Crest Road) begins at **Col du Bonhomme,** west of Colmar. The French High Command created it during World War I to carry supplies over the mountains. From Col du Bonhomme, you can strike out on this magnificent road, once the object of bitter fighting but today a series of panoramic vistas, including one of the Black Forest.

By **Col de la Schlucht,** 62km (39 miles) west of Colmar, you'll have climbed 1,472m (4,829 ft.). Schlucht is a summer and winter resort, one of the most beautiful spots in the Vosges, with a panoramic view of the Valley of Münster and the slopes of Hohneck. As you skirt the edge of this glacier-carved valley, you'll be in the midst of a land of pine groves with a necklace of lakes. You may want to turn off the main road and go exploring in several directions; the scenery is that tempting. But if you're still on the Crest Road, you can circle **Hohneck,** one of the highest peaks at 1,590m (5,217 ft.), dominating the Wildenstein Dam of the Bresse winter-sports station.

At **Markstein,** you'll come to another resort. From here, take N430 and then D10 to **Münster,** where the savory cheese is made. You'll go via the Petit-Ballon, a landscape of forest and mountain meadows with grazing cows. Finally, **Grand-Ballon,** at 1,400m (4,593 ft.), is the highest point you can reach by car in the Vosges. Get out of your car and go for a walk; if it's a clear day, you'll be able to see the Jura, with the French Alps beyond.

Where to Stay & Dine in Munster

Au Chêne Voltaire This chalet-style inn, built in 1939 and renovated many times, lies in an isolated section of the forest. Most of the modern, no-frills rooms are in a building separate from the rustic core that contains the popular restaurant, which is open to the public (closed Wed–Thurs). The hotel isn't a destination; it's just good to keep in mind if you need to rest for the night before pressing on in the morning. Each unit comes with a small, shower-only bathroom, a balcony, and clean, comfortable, no-nonsense furniture. Set-price menus in the dining room go for 10€ to 25€.

Rte. du Chêne-Voltaire, Luttenbach, Münster 68140. ℂ **03-89-77-31-74.** Fax 03-89-77-45-71. http://au-chene-voltaire.fr. 20 units. 37€–63€ double. AE, MC, V. Take D10 less than 2.5km (1½ miles) southwest from the center of Münster. **Amenities:** Internet (free); outdoor pool; sauna. *In room:* TV.

NANCY ★★★

370km (230 miles) E of Paris; 148km (92 miles) W of Strasbourg

Nancy, in France's northeast corner, was the capital of old Lorraine. The city was built around a fortified castle on a rock in the swampland near the Meurthe River. A canal a few blocks east of the historic center connects the Marne to the Rhine.

The city is serenely beautiful, with a history, cuisine, and architecture all its own. It once rivaled Paris as the center for the design and production of Art Nouveau. Nancy has three faces: the medieval alleys and towers around the old Palais Ducal where Charles II received Joan of Arc, the rococo golden gates and fountains, and the dull modern sections.

With a population of more than 100,000, Nancy remains the hub of commerce and politics in Lorraine. Home to a large university, it's a center of mining, engineering, metallurgy, and finance. Its 30,000 students, who have a passion for *le cool jazz,* keep Nancy jumping at night.

Essentials

GETTING THERE The fast **TGV train** from Paris's Gare de l'Est arrives in Nancy after just 90 minutes, making the city a virtual commute from Paris. Many Parisians now visit for *le weekend.* The one-way fare ranges between 50€ and 55€. Trains from Strasbourg arrive in Nancy every hour, a one-way fare costing 20€ to

27€. For information and schedules, call ℭ **36-35,** or 08-92-35-35-35 from outside France. If you're **driving** to Nancy from Paris, follow N4 east (trip time: 4 hr.).

VISITOR INFORMATION The **Office de Tourisme** is at place Stanislas (ℭ **03-83-35-22-41;** fax 03-83-35-90-10; www.ot-nancy.fr).

SPECIAL EVENTS Serious jazz lovers come to town for 2 weeks in October to attend **Jazz Pulsations** (ℭ **03-83-35-40-86;** www.nancyjazzpulsations.com). Some kind of performance takes place every night around sundown in a tent in the Parc de la Pépinière, a very short walk from the place Stanislas. Tickets cost 10€ to 30€.

Exploring Nancy

A **Passe-Musée** is a combination ticket that allows entrance to three of the town's most visited attractions, all for a net price of 10€ per person (another 14€ pass gives access to six museums in town), with no discounts for students or children. Included in the pass is access to the Musée de l'Ecole de Nancy, the Musée des Beaux-Arts, and the Musée Historique Lorraine (which is also known as the Musée des Arts et Traditions Populaires). Ask about the ticket at the tourist office.

The most monumental square in eastern France, and the heart of Nancy, is **place Stanislas ★★★**, named for Stanislas Leszczynski, the last of the ducs de Lorraine, ex-king of Poland, and father-in-law of Louis XV. His 18th-century building programs transformed Nancy into one of Europe's most palatial cities. The square stands between Nancy's two most notable neighborhoods: the **Ville Vieille** (old town), in the medieval core in the northwest, centered on the cathedral, Grande-Rue, and the labyrinth of narrow, meandering streets that funnel into it; and the **Ville Neuve,** in the southwest. Built in the 16th and 17th centuries, when streets were laid out in straight lines, Ville Neuve centers on rue St-Jean.

Place Stanislas was laid out from 1752 to 1760 according to the designs of Emmanuel Héré. Its ironwork gates are magnificent. The square is fabled for the brilliant and fanciful railings, the work of Jean Lamour. His gilded railings with flowery decorations and crests evoke Versailles. In 2005 cars were banished from the plaza, making it an all-pedestrian zone.

The **Arc de Triomphe,** constructed by Stanislas from 1754 to 1756 to honor Louis XV, adjoins the place de la Carrière, a tree-lined promenade leading to the 1760 **Palais du Gouvernement.** This governmental palace adjoins the **Palais Ducal,** built in 1502 in the Gothic style with Flamboyant Gothic balconies.

Musée de l'Ecole de Nancy ★ In a turn-of-the-20th-century building is a museum displaying the works of Emile Gallé, the greatest artist of the Nancy style. See Gallé's celebrated "Dawn and Dusk" bed and our favorite, the "Mushroom Lamp." Works by Eugène Vallin, another outstanding artist, are also on display.

36–38 rue Sergent-Blandan. ℭ **03-83-40-14-86.** www.ecole-de-nancy.com. Admission 4€ adults, 2.50€ students, free for children 17 and under. Free for students on Wed. Wed–Sun 10am–6pm.

Musée des Beaux-Arts ★★ Built in the 1700s, this is an outstanding regional museum, encompassing the Collection Galilée, works displayed in Paris between 1919 and 1930. It houses a rare Manet portrait of the wife of Napoleon III's dentist—remarkable because of its brilliance and intensity. There are also works by Delacroix, Utrillo, Modigliani, Boucher, and Rubens. Italians such as Perugino, Caravaggio, Ribera, and Tintoretto are represented as well.

3 place Stanislas. ℰ **03-83-85-30-72.** www.iac-nancy.com. Admission 6€ adults, 4€ students and children. Free for students on Wed. Wed–Mon 10am–6pm.

Musée Historique Lorrain ★★★   This is one of France's great museums, covering the art and history of the Lorraine region from ancient times. The first floor devotes an entire room to Jacques Callot, an engraver born in Nancy in 1592. Galerie des Cerfs displays tapestries. You'll see a collection of 17th-century masterpieces by Jacques Bellange, Jacques Callot, Georges de la Tour, and Claude Deruet, dating from when the duchy was known as a cultural center.

Until the Revolution this was a Franciscan convent. Franciscans were known as Cordeliers—hence the name of the church that adjoins the museum. The Flamboyant Gothic **Eglise des Cordeliers ★** is the burial site of the dukes of Lorraine. The most notable of the burial monuments are those of René II (1509; attributed to the sculptor Mansuy Gauvain) and a reclining statue of his second wife, Philippa of Gueldres, by Ligier Richier. The limestone rendering of Philippa is one of Nancy's most stunning examples of Renaissance portraiture. The octagonal Chapel of the Dukes (1607) holds the baroque sarcophagi.

In the Palais Ducal, 64 Grande-Rue. © **03-83-32-18-74.** Admission 6€ adults, 4€ students and children 12–18, free for children 11 and under (combo ticket for Palais Ducal and Eglise des Cordeliers). Free for students 1st Sun of each month. Tues–Sun 10am–12:30pm and 2–6pm.

Shopping

For glitz and glamour, your first stops should be **rue Gambetta** and **rue des Dominicains,** where boutiques carry the best names in fashion and perfume. Along **rue St-Dizier,** you'll run across shops selling clothes, shoes, jewelry, and leather goods at more affordable prices. Two additional shopping streets—each running perpendicular to those noted above, and each with what's usually viewed as cheaper and less glamorous merchandise—are the **rue St-Jean** and **rue St-Georges.** The Old Town is home to boutiques that carry antiques, arts and crafts, and bric-a-brac, as well as clothing and jewelry.

For chic women's clothing, accessories, and shoes, try **Vanessa,** 14 rue Gambetta (© **03-83-32-85-88;** www.vanessa-nancy.com). From the sophisticated to the trendy, men seek out **Alto Stratus,** 34 rue des Dominicains (© **03-83-30-17-33**), and **Tolub,** 9 rue Gambetta (© **03-83-32-98-14**).

Many of Nancy's antiques shops specialize in Art Nouveau. Visit **Denis Rugat,** 13 rue Stanislas (© **03-83-35-20-79**), for the best pieces. Another good outlet is **Galerie d'Art International,** 17 rue Amerval (© **03-83-35-06-83;** www.galerie-art-international.com). Both stock inventories of Lalique crystal, brightly colored vases, and enameled boxes made with a technique known locally as *les émaux de Longwy,* plus an assortment of glass-shaded lamps. And if you're a longtime fan of the glassmaking techniques of the late 19th century, you'll find more glass and crystal by Daum, at more reasonable prices, than virtually anywhere else in France. The company's premier outlet is **Boutique Daum,** 14 place Stanislas (© **03-83-32-21-65;** www.daum.fr), where the most perfect specimens from the Daum factory are sold at prices that are usually about 30% less than what you'd pay in other glass galleries in France. Each piece, a work of art in its own right, is signed "Daum." In contrast, and for prices that are about 30% to 40% less than what's sold in the above-mentioned boutique, you can head to Daum's factory outlet, **Magasin d'Usine Daum,** 17 rue Cristallerie (© **03-83-30-80-24**), a 5-minute walk from the place Stanislas. Their "slightly flawed" factory seconds are gift-wrapped and sold, each signed with the more enigmatic (and less prestigious) "Nancy."

Where to Stay

All Seasons Nancy Centre Gare   Near the back of the railway station, this hotel was built after World War II and has an annex just around the corner. Guests select this efficiently operated, government-rated two-star hotel for its reasonable prices and central location. It provides comfortable but not particularly plush guest rooms, outfitted in contemporary style with a monochromatic color scheme. The hotel has a pleasant garden. Breakfast is the only meal served.

3 rue de l'Armée-Patton, Nancy 54000. © **03-83-40-31-24.** Fax 03-83-28-47-78. www.all-seasons-hotels.com. 85 units. 72€–98€ double. AE, MC, V. Parking 6.50€. **Amenities:** Bar. *In room:* A/C, TV, hair dryer, Wi-Fi (free).

Grand Hôtel de la Reine ★★★   This is the grandest hotel in Nancy. The 18th-century mansion was built simultaneously with the monumental square that contains it. The hotel is one of the showplaces of the Concorde chain, which operates such bastions of luxury as Paris's Hôtel de Crillon. The Louis XV–style guest rooms are appointed with draped testers over comfortable beds, Venetian-style chandeliers, and gilt-framed mirrors. All accommodations contain roomy bathrooms with tub/shower combos. Units overlooking place Stanislas are expensive. If you can live without a view, some suites (those overlooking the hotel's back and sides) are cheaper than the most expensive double. The elegant and very grand Stanislas restaurant serves classic and modern dishes.

2 place Stanislas, Nancy 54000. © **800/777-4182** in the U.S. and Canada, or 03-83-35-03-01. Fax 03-83-32-86-04. www.hoteldelareine.com. 42 units. 120€–250€ double; 300€ suite. AE, DC, MC, V. Parking 16€. **Amenities:** Restaurant; bar; babysitting; room service. *In room:* A/C, TV, hair dryer, minibar, Wi-Fi (free).

Hotel D'Haussonville ★★   This grand town house originally dating from the 1500s has been magnificently restored and is today the finest B&B in Nancy. Standing in the town's medieval heart, the hotel is an elegant, tranquil choice. Of course, it's a bit old-fashioned, but its antique charm is appreciated by many discerning guests, seeking an old Lorraine ambience. The midsize-to-spacious bedrooms are a bit plush, with parquet flooring, antiques, and fireplaces. Bathrooms are thoroughly modernized and clad in marble. Each room has a special name, ranging from "Ming" to "Nairobi."

9 rue Mgr. Trouillet, Nancy 54000. © **03-83-35-85-84.** Fax 03-83-32-78-96. 7 units. 140€–230€ double. AE, DC, MC, V. Closed Aug 3–25 and Jan 1–18. **Amenities:** Breakfast room. *In room:* TV.

Mercure Centre Stanislas ★   Right in the town center, close to the best shopping, this chain-run hotel hardly competes with the Grand, but it's admirable in many ways. Rated three stars by the government, it lies just a short walk from place Stanislas and a 10-minute hike over to the rail station. Bedrooms are midsize and comfortably furnished with many pieces in the Art Nouveau style. It's the thoughtful extras that make this hotel special, including everything from magnifying mirrors and radios in the bathrooms to the tasty Lorraine specialties served in the bar.

5 rue des Carmes, Nancy 54000. © **03-83-30-92-60.** Fax 03-83-30-92-92. 80 units. 120€–180€ double. AE, DC, MC, V. Parking 12€. **Amenities:** Bar; room service. *In room:* A/C, TV, minibar, Wi-Fi (free).

Park Inn ★★   Rising above every other building in Nancy, this 1970s seven-story hotel opposite the train station caters to business and leisure travelers. Functional and efficient, with a hardworking staff, it's a top choice for Nancy but lacks the style of the Grand Hôtel de la Reine. The chain style of the guest rooms offers comfort, predictability, and warmth, with firm beds and serviceable bathrooms that hold tub/shower combinations.

11 rue Raymond-Poincaré, Nancy 54000. © **03-83-39-75-75.** Fax 03-83-32-78-17. www.parkinn.com. 192 units. 89€–159€ double; 159€ suite. AE, DC, MC, V. Parking 9€. **Amenities:** Restaurant; bar; room service. *In room:* A/C, TV, hair dryer, minibar, Wi-Fi (10€ per day).

Where to Dine

The **Park Inn** hotel and **Grand Hôtel de la Reine** (see above) have decent restaurants.

While exploring the city, you can stop for food and wine at the minuscule **Le V'Four,** 10 rue St-Michel (© **03-83-32-49-48**), where set menus are priced from 26€ to 39€. A special fixed-price lunch is 18€. The best version of the celebrated quiche Lorraine (the egg, ham, and cheese tart) is sold at **Nathalie Lalonde,** 3 rue Stanislas (© **03-83-51-67-08**), a tradition since 1901.

The macaroon, that almond cookie so beloved by foodies, was said to have been invented in Nancy by Benedictine nuns. Their original recipe is followed at **Soeurs Macarons,** 21 rue Gambetta (✆ **03-83-32-24-25**). You might end your sightseeing day by calling at the century-old brasserie, **L'Excelsior,** 50 rue Henri Poincare (✆ **03-83-35-24-57**), a period piece from 1911 with stained-glass windows and polished brass chandeliers. Just a block from the rail station, it serves Lorraine specialties with fresh oysters, a delight in season.

Le Capucin Gourmand ★★ TRADITIONAL FRENCH This is the leading grand restaurant of Nancy, within a 5-minute walk of place Stanislaus, and offers diners a warm, cozy decor with tones of gray and wood paneling. On our last visit we savored such creations as minced scallops and truffles pressed into patties and served with a walnut-oil vinaigrette; a "marble" of foie gras with exotic mushrooms; and a turbot steak that was "clothed" in baby vegetables. A signature dish is a civet of rabbit *à la royale*—in a sauce of its own blood mixed with red wine and just a hint of bitter chocolate. Another equally commendable dish is a noisette of venison Grand Veneur. For dessert, a "passion of chocolate" came with baked fresh figs marinated in honey and served with a yogurt-flavored ice cream.

31 rue Gambetta. ✆ **03-83-35-26-98.** www.lecapu.com. Reservations required. Main courses 28€–36€; fixed-price menu 29€–76€. AE, MC, V. Tues–Fri and Sun noon–2pm; Tues–Sat 7:30–10pm.

Le Grand Café Foy TRADITIONAL FRENCH This restaurant occupies the second floor of a building that borders place Stanislas. Outfitted with exposed timbers and Louis XIII furnishings, it is independent of a simple street-level brasserie (Café Foy) that serves less appealing food. The menu is a stylish roster of dishes such as roasted rabbit with violet-flavored mustard sauce, foie gras (a specialty of the house), braised lobster with a compote of fennel and veal juices, and local freshwater fish baked in a potato crust. Try a dessert that's unusual and heavenly: honey mousse cake prepared with brandy.

1 place Stanislas. ✆ **03-83-32-15-97.** www.grandcafefoy.com. Reservations recommended. Main courses 13€–23€; fixed-price menu 25€–35€. MC, V. Daily noon–2pm and 7–11pm.

Les Pissenlits (The Dandelions) 🍖 TRADITIONAL FRENCH At this cost-conscious brasserie, the food is simple but flavorful and artfully prepared. Chef Jean-Luc Mengin's specialties are likely to include *matelote* of freshwater zander with shallots, dandelion salad with bacon and creamy vinaigrette, and aiguillettes of duckling with spice-flavored honey sauce. The chef's wife, Danièle, is one of the few accredited female wine stewards in France. Art Nouveau antiques, many of them crafted in Nancy, fill the dining room.

27 bis rue des Ponts. ✆ **03-83-37-43-97.** www.les-pissenlits.com. Reservations recommended. Main courses 13€–16€; fixed-price menu 17€–38€. MC, V. Tues–Sat 11:45am–2:30pm and 7:15–10:30pm.

Nancy After Dark

As night approaches, most of the student population heads to the Old Town. **Le Blue Note III,** 3 rue des Michottes (✆ **03-83-30-31-18**), has a room for rock performances, a piano bar, a lounge with a fireplace and comfy armchairs, and a rowdy beer hall. It's open Wednesday through Sunday. Entrance is free except on Friday and Saturday night, when there's a 12€ cover. Women enter free on those nights before 12:30am.

Nancy's most popular dance club is **Les Caves du Roy,** 9 place Stanislas (© **03-83-35-24-14**), where a techno crowd flails around in a chrome-and-metallic space. It's open Tuesday to Thursday 11pm to 4am, Friday 11pm to 5am, Saturday midnight to 6:15am.

The hottest nightclub in the region is a converted warehouse in the suburb of Vandoeuvre, 4km (2½ miles) south of the center of town. **Le Circus,** 42 rue Jean-Mermoz (© **03-83-57-53-85;** www.circusmedia.fr; for many events you can print out a "pass" from their website that gives free or discounted access), sits near the town's wholesale food market (le Marché en Gros). It features fire-eaters, jugglers, and techno music. Expect up to 2,000 revelers on a Friday or Saturday night, when the cover is 11€ and includes the first drink; it's open from 11pm to 5am.

DOMREMY-LA-PUCELLE

443km (275 miles) SE of Paris; 10km (6¼ miles) NW of Neufchâteau

Most often visited on a day trip, Domrémy is a plain village that would have slumbered in obscurity but for the fact that Joan of Arc was born here in 1412. Today, it's a pilgrimage center attracting tourists from all over the world.

A residence traditionally considered her family's house is known as **Maison Natale de Jeanne d'Arc,** 2 rue de la Basilique (© **03-29-06-95-86**). Here you can see the chamber where she was born. A museum beside the house shows a film depicting St. Joan's life. The house is open April to September Wednesday to Monday 10am to 6pm, and October to March Wednesday to Monday 10am to noon and 2 to 5pm. Admission is 3€ for adults, free for children 9 and under. The house is closed in January.

Adjacent to the museum, on rue Principale, is **Eglise St-Rémi;** repairs and partial reconstructions have masked its 12th-century origins. All that remains from the age of Joan of Arc are a baptismal font and some stonework. On a slope of the Bois-Chenu 1.5km (1 mile) uphill from the village is a monument steeped in French nationalism, the **Basilique du Bois-Chenu.** It was begun in 1881 and consecrated in 1926. To reach it, follow signs from the center and along rue de la Basilique.

Essentials

GETTING THERE If you're **driving,** take N4 southeast of Paris to Toul, and then A31 south toward Neufchâteau/Charmes. Then take N74 southwest (signposted in the direction of Neufchâteau). At Neufchâteau, follow D164 northwest to Coussey. From there, take D53 into Domrémy.

There is no railway station in Domrémy—you must take one of four **trains** daily going to either Nancy or Toul, where you can make bus and rail connections to Neufchâteau, 9.5km (6 miles) away. You can also take a **taxi,** MBM Assistance 88 (© **03-29-06-12-13**), for about 100€ each way.

VERDUN ★★

261km (162 miles) E of Paris; 66km (41 miles) W of Metz

Built on both banks of the Meuse and intersected by a series of canals, Verdun has an old section, the Ville Haute, on the east bank, which includes the cathedral and Episcopal palace. Today, stone houses on narrow cobblestone streets give Verdun a medieval appearance. However, most visitors come to see the famous World War I battlefields, 3km (1¾ miles) east of the town, off N3 toward Metz.

Essentials

GETTING THERE Two **trains** arrive daily from Paris's Gare de l'Est; you'll have to change at Châlons-en-Champagne. Several daily trains also arrive from Metz, after a change at Conflans. The one-way fare from Paris is 33€ to 40€; from Metz, it's 13€. For train information and schedules, call ✆ **36-35** or 08-92-35-35-35. Driving is easy; Verdun is several miles north of the Paris-Strasbourg autoroute (A4).

VISITOR INFORMATION The **Office de Tourisme** is on place de la Nation (✆ **03-29-84-18-85;** fax 03-29-83-99-93; www.verdun-tourisme.com). It's closed on bank holidays.

Touring the Battlefields

At this garrison town in eastern France, Maréchal Pétain said, "They shall not pass!" And they didn't. Verdun is where the Allies held out against a massive assault by the German army in World War I. Near the end of the war, 600,000 to 800,000 French and German soldiers died battling over a few miles along the muddy Meuse between Paris and the Rhine. Two monuments commemorate these tragic events: Rodin's *Defense* and Boucher's *To Victory and the Dead.*

The local tourist office provides maps and advice on two carefully delineated, and separate, tours of the brutal and bloody battlefields that helped define World War I. They include the "Circuit Champs de Bataille Rive Droite," which encompasses the better-known battlegrounds on the River Meuse's right bank. They also have maps for two self-guided tours. The first, whose estimated length is about 4 hours, will include, on the Meuse's right bank, a 32km (20-mile) run, taking in **Fort Vaux,** where Raynal staged a heroic defense after sending his last message by carrier pigeon. After passing a **French cemetery** of 16,000 graves—an endless field of crosses—you arrive at the **Ossuaire de Douaumont,** where the bones of those blown to bits were embedded. Nearby, at the **Fort de Douaumont,** the "hell of Verdun" was unleashed. From the roof you can look out at a vast field of corroded tops of "pillboxes." Then you proceed to the **Tranchée des Baïonettes (Trench of Bayonets).** Bayonets of French soldiers entombed by a shell burst form this unique memorial.

Within a few paces of the Tranchée des Baïonettes, you'll see the premises of the **Mémorial de Verdun** (built around 1967), Fleury Devant Douaumont (✆ **03-29-84-35-34;** www.memorial-de-verdun.fr), a museum that commemorates the weapons, uniforms, photographs, and geography of one of the bloodiest battles of World War I. From February to mid-December, it's open daily 9am to noon and 2 to 6pm. Entrance is 7€ for adults and students, 3.50€ for children 8 to 16, free for children 7 and under.

The second self-guided tour, known as **"Circuit Champs de Bataille Rive Gauche"** (or "Circuit de l'Argonne"), also requires about 4 hours, and during its 97km (60 miles), it focuses on mostly outdoor sites, as opposed to the monuments and museums that are included in the tour's first 2 hours. It takes in the **Butte de Montfaucon,** a hill on which Americans erected a memorial tower, and the **Cimetière Américain at Romagne,** with some 15,000 graves.

Because public transportation is inadequate, only visitors with cars should attempt to make these circuits.

Where to Stay & Dine

Château des Monthairons ★★   This hotel, operated by the Thouvenin family, occupies an 1857 château crafted of blocks of pale stone. Guest rooms vary in shape and size, most with locally made furniture. All have luxury beds and quality linens. Generous shelf space and tub/shower combinations enhance the bathrooms. On the property are a pair of 15th-century chapels, a nesting ground for herons, and opportunities for canoeing and fishing.

Rte. D34, Dieue-sur-Meuse 55320. ☏ **03-29-87-78-55.** Fax 03-29-87-73-49. www.chateaudes monthairons.fr. 25 units. 98€–190€ double; 236€–315€ suite. AE, DC, MC, V. Closed Jan to mid-Feb. Drive 12km (7½ miles) south of Verdun on D334. **Amenities:** Restaurant; bar; spa; children's play area. *In room:* TV, hair dryer, minibar, Wi-Fi (free).

Hostellerie du Coq Hardi ★★   This is our favorite hotel in town, composed of four connected 18th-century houses near the Meuse. It contains church pews, antiques, and a Renaissance fireplace. Most of the well-maintained guest rooms have been decorated in regional style. Each has a comfortable bed and an efficient but small bathroom, mainly with tub and shower. The dining room serves the best food in town. It has a painted ceiling, Louis XIII chairs, and two deactivated World War I bombshells at its entrance. Fixed-price menus cost 46€ to 97€.

8 av. de la Victoire, Verdun 55100. ☏ **03-29-86-36-36.** Fax 03-29-86-09-21. www.coq-hardi.com. 35 units. 99€–132€ double; 250€ suite. AE, MC, V. Parking 14€. **Amenities:** 2 restaurants; bar; room service. *In room:* TV, hair dryer, minibar, Wi-Fi (free).

BURGUNDY

Castles rising from vineyards and medieval churches mark the landscape of Burgundy, the land of the good life for those who savor fine cuisine and wine in historic settings. Burgundy was once an independent province; its Valois dukes spread their might across Europe from 1363 to 1477. In preserving its independence, Burgundy weathered many struggles, notably under Charles the Bold, always in conflict with Louis XI. When Charles died in 1477, Louis annexed the duchy. Burgundy later suffered more upheaval, including much damage to its cities during the Franco-Spanish wars that began in 1636. Peace finally held in 1678.

At the time of the Revolution, Burgundy had disappeared as a political entity and was divided into the *départements* (ministates) of Yonne, Saône-et-Loire, and Côte-d'Or. The ducs de Bourgogne are but a memory, but they left a legacy of vintage red and white wines to please and excite the palate. The major winegrowing regions of Burgundy are Chablis, Côte de Nuits, Côte de Beaune, Côte de Chalon, Mâconnais, and Nivernais.

AUXERRE ★★

154km (96 miles) SE of Paris; 148km (92 miles) NW of Dijon

Auxerre was founded by the Gauls and enlarged by the Romans. On a hill overlooking the Yonne River, it's the capital of Lower Burgundy and home to many vineyards, some of which produce Chablis. Joan of Arc spent several days here in 1429. Napoleon met Maréchal Ney here in 1815, on the former emperor's return from Elba. Louis XVIII had sent Ney to stop Napoleon, but Ney embraced him and turned his army against the king. For that, Ney was later shot.

This city is a sleepy place. Its 42,000 residents will admit that not a lot happens around here—and that's how they like it.

Essentials

GETTING THERE Visitors often **drive** here because Auxerre is near A6/E1 (Autoroute du Soleil). Many **trains** between Paris (Gare de Lyon) and Lyon stop at Auxerre. There are 12 trains per day from Paris (the fare is 24€ one-way) and from Lyon via Dijon (41€ one-way); trip time from either city is 3 to 5 hours. For train information, call ℂ **08-92-35-35-35.**

VISITOR INFORMATION The **Office de Tourisme** is at 1–2 quai de la République (ℂ **03-86-51-03-26;** www.ot-auxerre.fr).

Exploring Auxerre

The railway station is at the eastern edge of town, about 1.5km (1 mile) from the historic center. Most of Auxerre is on the western bank of the Yonne. Its heart is between place du Maréchal-Leclerc (where you'll find the Hôtel de Ville [city hall]) and the Cathédrale St-Etienne.

Cathédrale St-Etienne ★★ Pay a visit to the Flamboyant Gothic Cathédrale St-Etienne, begun in the 13th century but not completed until the 16th. The front facade is remarkable, with sculptured portals. The stained glass, some of it original, is famous. In the crypt, which is all that remains of the Romanesque church that stood on this site, you can see 11th-century frescoes.

Every Sunday in July and August, organ concerts run from 5 to 6pm; admission is free. Daily from June to August at 10pm and in September at 9:30pm, a 70-minute sound-and-light show relates the history of the church. It's presented in English, French, and German and costs 5€ for adults and is free for children 13 and under.

Place St-Etienne. ✆ **03-86-52-23-29.** Free admission to church. Admission 1.90€ to treasury, 3€ to crypt. Cathedral daily 9am–6pm (till 5pm Nov–Mar); crypt and treasury Easter to Nov daily 9am–6pm, Nov–Mar Mon–Sat 10am–5pm.

Where to Stay

Hôtel Le Maxime   Attractive, high-ceilinged rooms, many with views of the river or the old city, highlight this family-run hotel. Most units retain their original wall and ceiling beams. Built as a private villa in 1855, the gracious, old-fashioned inn has been a hotel since 1900. A thorough renovation has upgraded the accommodations. You can take breakfast in your room or in the quiet salon, amid Oriental rugs, polished paneling, and a sense of the gentility of an earlier era.

2 quai de la Marine, Auxerre 89000. ✆ **03-86-52-14-19.** Fax 03-86-52-21-70. www.lemaxime.com. 25 units. 82€–118€ double; 135€–220€ suite. AE, DC, MC, V. Parking 7€. **Amenities:** Bar. *In room:* A/C, TV, hair dryer, minibar, Wi-Fi (free).

Hôtel Normandie   Inside this centrally located three-story hotel, antique furnishings complement modern amenities. The tranquil, comfortably furnished rooms open onto garden views; each unit is different. Most bathrooms come with multijet showers only, but some have tubs.

41 bd. Vauban, Auxerre 89000. ✆ **03-86-52-57-80.** Fax 03-86-51-54-33. www.hotelnormandie.fr. 47 units. 63€–96€ double; 76€–125€ family room. AE, DC, MC, V. Parking 6.80€. **Amenities:** Bar; exercise room; room service; sauna. *In room:* A/C, TV, minibar, hair dryer, Wi-Fi (free).

Le Parc des Maréchaux ★★   A gem that outshines the competition, this was a Napoleon III–style private residence in the 19th century, set in its own .4-hectare (1-acre) park. The most secluded choice in the area, it's on the western outskirts of town, surrounded by century-old trees. The decor in the public areas and the lounge is French Empire; the style of the guest rooms is less consistent—a mixture of contemporary and Empire. The only available meal is breakfast, but the staff will serve hot food, on special request, in your room or in one of the salons.

6 av. Foch, Auxerre 89000. ✆ **03-86-51-43-77.** Fax 03-86-51-31-72. www.hotel-parcmarechaux.com. 25 units. 90€–134€ double; 126€–155€ triple or quad. AE, DC, MC, V. **Amenities:** Heated outdoor pool; room service. *In room:* A/C, TV, minibar, Wi-Fi (free).

Where to Dine

Le Jardin Gourmand ★★ FRENCH   The most sophisticated restaurant in town specializes in *cuisine moderne du marché* (modern market cuisine), employing the freshest ingredients to create artfully presented menus that change, often radically, eight times a year. The setting is an 1870 house a 10-minute walk from the cathedral. In summer, an awning shades a pleasant terrace. Pierre Boussereau and Olivier Laplaine are devoted to cultivating fresh salad greens and herbs in their garden, and use them to garnish such platters as carpaccio of duck liver. Other tasty dishes include grilled scallops with bacon, or duckling confit with a fresh carrot salad. Smoked lamb is served straight from the grill with a pepperoni-studded salsa, or else you can order John Dory in an oyster sauce.

56 bd. Vauban. ✆ **03-86-51-53-52.** www.lejardingourmand.com. Reservations required. Main courses 32€–40€; fixed-price menus 46€–68€ and 58€–92€. AE, MC, V. Thurs–Mon noon–1:45pm and 7:30–9:15pm. Closed Nov 11–Dec 2.

Where to Stay & Dine Nearby

A la Côte St-Jacques ★★★ FRENCH/BURGUNDIAN   This is one of the top Relais & Châteaux members in France, with a 300-year-old foundation, a clientele that has included Catherine Deneuve and several French presidents, and a well-engrained sense of comfort and culinary style. Specialties include sea scallops roasted with caramelized spices, braised endive, and zabaglione; exotic mushrooms, foie gras, terrine of Brittany oysters; and smoked sea bass served with Sevruga caviar.

The restaurant and 32 opulent rooms—air-conditioned, contemporary, very comfortable, and decorated with individual color schemes and parquet floors—lie in modern quarters adjacent to the Yonne River. Ten less expensive, non-air-conditioned rooms lie on an older site. An underground tunnel, fashioned from rocks salvaged from old buildings, connects the two sections. Rates run 185€ to 420€ for a double and 495€ to 620€ for a suite.

14 Faubourg de Paris (N6), Joigny 89300. ✆ **03-86-62-09-70.** Fax 03-86-91-49-70. www.cotesaint jacques.com. Reservations required. Main courses 46€–90€; fixed-price lunch 42€–125€, dinner 140€–220€. AE, DC, MC, V. Daily 12:15–2pm and 7:30–9:45pm. Hotel and restaurant closed Jan 5–29. From Auxerre, head north on N6 (toward Sens) for 27km (17 miles). **Amenities:** Restaurant; indoor pool; sauna. *In room:* TV; minibar; Wi-Fi (first hour free, 5€/hour thereafter).

La Lucarne aux Chouettes ★★ 🎁   Remember Leslie Caron, at least on the late show? She was that French gamin who won our hearts by sexily pirouetting with Gene Kelly in *An American in Paris* in 1951 and later in 1958 portraying a Parisian courtesan-in-training in *Gigi*. She was more recently seen playing a widow who found passion in *Chocolat* (2000). In this village 46km (29 miles) north of Auxerre, she has taken some 17th-century buildings and turned them into a small inn. She also renovated an annex near the inn, which she designed herself, including her own stencil work. You dine festively in summer under the trees and in the midst of flowers lining the terrace, right on the river. That is followed with a good night's sleep under a canopy of one of the beds collected by Leslie herself, who has a passion for antiques.

Quai Bretoche, Villeneuve-sur-Yonne 89500. ✆ **03-86-87-18-26.** Fax 03-86-87-22-63. www.lesliecaron-auberge.com. 4 units. 50€–120€ double; 120€ triple; 120€ duplex. MC, V. **Amenities:** Restaurant. *In room:* No phone.

VEZELAY ★★

217km (135 miles) SE of Paris; 52km (32 miles) S of Auxerre

Vézelay, a living museum of French antiquity, stands frozen in time. For many, the town is the high point of a trip through Burgundy. Because it contained what was believed to be the tomb of St. Mary Magdalene, that "beloved and pardoned sinner," it was one of the great pilgrimage sites of the Christian world.

Today, the medieval charm of Vézelay is widely known throughout France, and visitors virtually overrun the town in summer. The hordes are especially thick on July 22, the official day of homage to La Madeleine.

Essentials

GETTING THERE   If you're **driving** from Paris, take A6 south to Auxerre, then continue south along N151 to Clamecy and turn east on D951 to Vézelay. Four **trains** a day travel from Paris Gare de Lyon via Auxerre to Sermizelles, taking 2½ hours and costing 28€ one-way.

VISITOR INFORMATION   The **Office de Tourisme** is at 12 rue St-Etienne (© **03-86-33-23-69;** fax 03-86-33-34-00; www.vezelaytourisme.com).

Exploring the Town

On a hill 108m (354 ft.) above the countryside, Vézelay is known for its ramparts and houses with sculptured doorways, corbeled staircases, and mullioned windows. The site of the town was an abbey founded by Girart de Roussillon, *comte* de Bourgogne. Pope John VIII consecrated the abbey in 878.

On March 31, 1146, St. Bernard preached the Second Crusade here; in 1190, the town was the rendezvous point for the Third Crusade, drawing such personages as Richard the Lion-Hearted and King Philippe-Auguste of France. Later, St. Louis of France came here several times on pilgrimages.

Park outside the town hall and walk through the medieval streets lined with 15th-, 16th-, and 18th-century houses and flower-filled gardens.

If you're in the mood to shop, head for rue St-Etienne and rue St-Pierre. You'll find an assortment of stores selling religious books and statuary, including **La Pierre d'angle,** place de la Basilique (© **03-86-33-29-14**). **Galerie Lieber,** 14 rue St-Etienne (© **03-86-33-33-90**), specializes in handmade jewelry, using semiprecious and precious stones in both heavy and delicate settings of silver and gold, including some African and Asian items. You may also want to pick up a bottle or two of Vézelay wine at **La Cave Henry de Vézelay,** route de Nanchèvres, St-Père-sous-Vézelay (© **03-86-33-29-62**).

Basilique Ste-Madeleine ★★   Built in the 12th century, France's largest and most famous Romanesque church is only 9m (30 ft.) shorter than Notre-Dame de Paris. When you enter the narthex, a vestibule of about 370 sq. m (4,000 sq. ft.), raise your eyes to the doorway depicting Christ giving the apostles the Holy Spirit. From the Romanesque nave, with its traverse arches in white-and-gray stone, you'll see the light Gothic chancel. You can visit the Carolingian crypt, where the tomb of Mary Magdalene formerly rested (today the crypt contains some of her relics). There's a panoramic view from the back terrace.

Place de la Basilique, Vézelay 89450. © **03-86-33-39-50.** Free admission. Daily 8am–7pm.

Where to Stay

L'Espérance (see "Where to Dine," below) also rents luxurious rooms.

Le Compostelle   This pleasant hotel is the best of Vézelay's more affordable inns. It's in the center of town, up the hill leading to the basilica, in a late-19th-century building that was transformed into this hotel in 1991. It's reminiscent of an English country house. Guest rooms are midsize and comfortably furnished, with small, shower-only bathrooms. Breakfast is the only meal served.

Place du Champ-de-Foire, Vézelay 89450. © **03-86-33-28-63.** Fax 03-86-33-34-34. www.lecompostelle levezelay.com. 18 units. 50€–63€ double. AE, MC, V. Closed Nov 29–Dec 4, Dec 20–26, and Jan 15 to mid-Feb. **Amenities:** Bar. *In room:* TV, Wi-Fi (free).

Poste et Lion d'Or ★ 🦃 This local favorite is filled with character and tradition. On the main square, at the bottom of the hill that rises to the basilica, this hotel was built in the 17th century as a postal station. With a terrace and small garden, the Poste et Lion d'Or is a first-class lodging with surprisingly reasonable rates. The functional guest rooms are conservatively outfitted in some cases in a vaguely Louis XVI style. Other than L'Espérance (see below), it's the finest address in town.

Place du Champ-de-Foire, Vézelay 89450. ℂ **03-86-33-21-23.** Fax 03-86-32-30-92. www.laposte-liondor.com. 38 units. 37€–75€ double; 135€–180€ suite. AE, DC, MC, V. Parking 6€. Closed Jan–Feb. **Amenities:** Bar. *In room:* A/C, TV, Wi-Fi (free).

Where to Dine

La Bougainville ★ BURGUNDIAN Not all of us can afford to dine at L'Espérance (see below), so La Bougainville is a more affordable alternative. This elegantly decorated antique house, complete with fireplace, serves as a backdrop for such regional specialties as *oeufs en meurette* (eggs poached in red wine and served with red-wine sauce) or a platter of oysters. After that, you can plunge into *filet de boeuf bourguignon* (beef cooked in burgundy with crème fraîche and escargots). The restaurant is also adept at concocting game dishes, such as venison with chestnuts or a delightful hare stew. For dessert, the specialty is *success aux noisettes avec nectarines rôti pralinée* (hazelnut cakes with roasted nectarines and praline ice cream).

28 rue St-Etienne. ℂ **03-86-33-27-57.** Reservations required. Main courses 10€–30€; fixed-price menus 12€–32€. MC, V. Thurs–Mon noon–2pm and 7–9pm. Closed mid-Nov to mid-Feb.

L'Espérance ★★★ MODERN FRENCH No other restaurant in Burgundy is as frequently assessed and gossiped about as this one, directed by Marc and Françoise Meneau. The restaurant has the feel of an old-fashioned farm and bakery, with Napoleon III decor. Located in a fertile valley, it emanates Burgundian wholesomeness as well as Parisian chic. Flagstone floors and big windows overlooking a garden complement the superb cuisine. Menu items change frequently but are likely to include *cromesquis de foie gras* (in the form of a cube that melts in your mouth), potato galette with caviar, turbot en croûte, and roasted and caramelized filet of veal. The overworked staff struggles valiantly with the traffic generated by the place's fame.

On the premises are 31 well-maintained and comfortable guest rooms in three historic buildings. The accommodations epitomize French country living at its best. Doubles cost 150€ to 300€, suites 390€ to 470€.

St-Père-sous-Vézelay, Vézelay 89450. ℂ **03-86-33-39-10.** Fax 03-86-33-26-15. www.marc-meneau-esperance.com. Reservations recommended. Main courses 52€–110€; fixed-price lunch 57€–210€, dinner 140€–210€. AE, DC, MC, V. Thurs–Sun noon–2pm; Wed–Mon 7:30–9:30pm. Closed mid-Jan to Mar.

AVALLON ★

214km (133 miles) SE of Paris; 52km (32 miles) SE of Auxerre; 96km (60 miles) NW of Dijon

This fortified town sits behind ancient ramparts, upon which you can stroll. A medieval atmosphere permeates Avallon, where you'll find many 15th- and 16th-century houses. At the town gate on Grande Rue Aristide-Briand is a clock tower from 1460. The Romanesque **Eglise St-Lazare** dates from the 12th century and has two interesting doorways. The church, open daily from 8am to 7pm, is said to have received the head of St. Lazarus in 1000, thus turning Avallon into a pilgrimage site. Today, Avallon is a destination mainly for its fabulous food.

Essentials

GETTING THERE   If you're **driving,** travel south from Paris along A6 to Auxerre; from Auxerre, take N6 south to Avallon. Four **trains** arrive daily from Paris Gare de Lyon (trip time: 2½ hr.; one-way fare 29€–52€). For train information, call ✆ **08-92-35-35-35.** Bus service from Dijon takes 2 hours and costs 17€ one-way; purchase tickets on the bus. For bus information, contact the railway station in Avallon (✆ **03-80-42-11-00**).

VISITOR INFORMATION   The **Office de Tourisme** is at 6 rue Bocquillot (✆ **03-86-34-14-19;** www.avallonnais-tourisme.com).

Where to Stay

Château de Vault-de-Lugny ★★★   Between Avallon and Vézelay is this 16th-century moat-encircled château, with a fortress tower and peacocks on the grounds. It emphasizes service, with two staff members to every guest. The accommodations are sumptuous, with canopy beds, antique furnishings, and fireplaces. Luxurious bathrooms hold tub/shower combinations. You can order cocktails in the salon, and then eat dinner by candlelight. Fresh ingredients are the hallmark of the cuisine here. A special bourguignon meal of typical regional dishes is offered nightly.

11 rue du Chateau, A Vault-de-Lugny, Avallon 89200. ✆ **03-86-34-07-86.** Fax 03-86-34-16-36. www.lugny.fr. 16 units. 185€–620€ (king's bedroom); 460€–530€ suite. AE, DC, MC, V. Closed mid-Nov to mid-Apr. Take D957 from Avallon, turn right in Pontaubert (after the church) and follow signs; Vault-de-Lugny is about 3km (1¾ miles) away. **Amenities:** Restaurant; bar; babysitting; indoor pool; room service. *In room:* TV, hair dryer, minibar, Wi-Fi (10€ daily).

Moulin des Ruats ★ 🎁   This enchanting country inn sits on the banks of the Cousin. Constructed as a flour mill in the 17th century, it has been a family hotel since 1924. Some guest rooms have exposed beams and intimate alcoves. Each contains a small bathroom with a shower, and some have tubs as well. Try for a room with a balcony overlooking the river. The elegant dining room serves a menu of freshwater fish, complemented by a fine wine list and a terrace. The restaurant and the accommodations are equally atmospheric and impressive.

9, rue des Isles Labaumes, Avallon 89200. ✆ **03-86-34-97-00.** Fax 03-86-31-65-47. www.moulin-des-ruats.com. 25 units. 82€–159€ double. AE, DC, MC, V. Closed mid-Nov to mid-Feb. Take D427 3km (1¾ miles) outside town. **Amenities:** Restaurant; bar; babysitting; room service. *In room:* TV, Wi-Fi (10€ per day).

Where to Dine

Les Capucins ★★ BURGUNDIAN   Warm colors and fresh flowers brighten the rustic decor and country furnishings. The restaurant is on a sleepy square just a 12-minute stroll from the heart of town. It's on the ground floor of a little hotel that rents 16 guest rooms for 40€ to 130€ double, 14 containing air-conditioning. Free Wi-Fi is offered in every room. The chef fashions such dishes as tender veal shanks with morels. Two typical Burgundian dishes are beef Charolais and classic *oeufs en meurette.* Foie gras is also roasted with potatoes charlotte. For dessert, lemon- and anise-flavored madeleines are served with ice cream.

6 av. Paul-Doumer, Avallon 89200. ✆ **03-86-34-06-52.** Fax 03-86-34-58-47. www.avallonlescapucins.com. Main courses 12€–24€; fixed-price menu 18€–36€. AE, MC, V. Daily noon–2pm and 7–9:30pm.

AUTUN ★★

293km (182 miles) SE of Paris; 85km (53 miles) SW of Dijon; 48km (30 miles) W of Beaune; 60km (37 miles) SE of Auxerre

Deep in Burgundy, Autun is one of the oldest towns in France. In the days of the Roman Empire, it was called "the other Rome." Some relics still stand, including the remains of the largest theater in Gaul, the Théâtre Romain. It was nearly 150m (492 ft.) in diameter and could hold some 15,000 people. Outside the town, you can see the tower of the 24m-high (79-ft.) Temple de Janus.

Autun is a thriving provincial town of 20,000. Because it's off the beaten track, the hordes go elsewhere. Still, it has its historical associations—Napoleon studied here in 1779 at the military academy (today the Lycée Bonaparte).

Essentials

GETTING THERE If you're **driving,** take D944 south from Avallon to Château-Chinon. Follow D978 east into Autun. Rail links to Autun are awkward. Five trains a day from Paris's Gare de Lyon run to Montchanin–Le Creusot, 40km (25 miles) south of Autun (one-way fare: 50€–67€). From there, take a 45-minute bus connection to Autun. In Autun, **buses** arrive at a parking lot by the railway station on avenue de la République. For bus information, call ✆ **03-85-86-92-55.** For railway information, call the station in Autun (✆ **03-85-52-73-65**) or SNCF (✆ **03-80-42-11-00**).

VISITOR INFORMATION The **Office de Tourisme** is at 2 av. Charles-de-Gaulle (✆ **03-85-86-80-38;** fax 03-85-86-80-49; www.autun-tourisme.com).

Seeing the Sights

Autun was once an important link on the road from Lyon to Boulogne. A legacy of that period is the 17m-high (56-ft.) **Porte d'Arroux,** once the city gate, which has two archways now used for cars and smaller ones used for pedestrians. Also exceptional is the **Porte St-André (St. Andrew's Gate),** northwest of the Roman theater. Rising 20m (66 ft.), it has four doorways and is surmounted by a gallery of 10 arcades.

Cathédrale St-Lazare ★★ On the highest point in Autun, the cathedral was built in 1120 to house the relics of St. Lazarus. On the facade, the tympanum in the central portal depicts the Last Judgment—a triumph of Romanesque sculpture. Inside, a painting by Ingres depicts the martyrdom of St. Symphorien, who was killed in Autun. In the 1860s, Viollet-le-Duc, the architect who restored many monuments of France, had to double the size of some of the columns supporting the roof to avoid a collapse. New capitals matching the Romanesque style of the originals were crafted to top the new columns. The original capitals are on display, more or less at eye level, in the Salle Capitulaire, one flight above street level; especially noteworthy are *La Reveil des Mages (The Awakening of the Magi)* and *La Fuite en Egypte (The Flight into Egypt).*

Place St-Louis. ✆ **03-85-52-12-37.** Free admission. Daily 9am–7pm.

Musée Rolin ★ This 15th-century mansion was built for a famous lawyer, Nicolas Rolin (b. 1380). An easy walk from the cathedral, the museum displays a collection of

Burgundian Romanesque sculpture, as well as paintings and archaeological mementos. From the original Rolin collection are *Nativity* by the Maître de Moulins, and a statue that's a 15th-century masterpiece, *Our Lady of Autun* (*La Vierge d'Autun*, also known as *La Vierge Bulliot* after the benefactor who returned the original statue to the cathedral in 1948).

5 rue des Bancs. © **03-85-52-09-76.** Admission 3.50€ adults, 1.85€ students and children. Apr–Sept Mon and Wed–Sun 9:30am–noon and 1:30–6pm; Oct–Mar Wed–Mon 10am–noon and 2–5pm.

Nearby Attractions

After visiting Autun (if you have a car), you can tour one of Burgundy's finest wineries: **Domaine Maurice Protheau,** Château d'Etroyes, in Mercurey, 40km (25 miles) southeast along D978 (© **03-85-45-10-84**). Among the selections are at least two *appellations contrôlées* (a regulation system that ensures a wine has been produced where the bottles says), so you'll have a chance to immerse yourself in the subtle differences between reds (both pinot noirs and burgundies), whites, and rosés produced under the auspices of Rully and Mercurey. The headquarters of the winery, founded in the 1740s, is a château built in the 1700s and early 1800s. Free tours of the cellars are offered, in French and halting English, daily from 10am to noon and 2 to 7pm (call ahead to confirm). A *dégustation des vins* (wine tasting) and the opportunity to haul a bottle or two away costs 4€.

Three kilometers (1¾ miles) away, you can visit the **Château de Rully,** site of the **Domaine de la Bressande** (© **03-85-87-20-89**), a well-respected producer of white and some red burgundies. Originally built in the 12th century as a stronghold for the *comte* de Ternay, it offers tours to the public. The owner prefers that you visit the château as part of a group. Individuals can visit in July and August Wednesday to Sunday at 2, 4, and 5pm, but this offering is more limited than the group tour. The cost ranges from 4€ to 8€.

Where to Stay & Dine

Hostellerie du Vieux Moulin ★★   This fine hotel, a 10-minute walk north of the town center, also contains Autun's best restaurant. It's at the edge of the Arroux River, in a stone-walled former grain mill built in the 1870s. The hotel is appointed with a scattering of 19th-century regional antiques and houses simple but comfortable guest rooms. Reminders of the winemaking trade accent the rooms.

In summer, you can dine at a table overlooking the garden and a stream. Menu items include filet of sea bass, scallop with mango sauce; Charolais beef simmered in red wine; and tournedos Talleyrand, flavored with shallots and red wine (the dish is named for a local bishop, not the politician). Any of dozens of red burgundies can accompany your meal. Fixed-price menus cost 17€ to 37€ at lunch, 27€ to 37€ at dinner.

Porte d'Arroux, Autun 71403. © **03-85-52-10-90.** Fax 03-85-86-32-15. 16 units. 63€–85€ double. AE, MC, V. **Amenities:** Restaurant; bar. *In room:* A/C (in some), TV, Wi-Fi (free).

Hôtel les Ursulines ★   The best hotel in Autun, the Ursulines offers attractive rooms with views of the countryside and the Morvan mountains. Built in the 1600s as a convent, it gained a comfortable annex in 2000 that holds about half the rooms. Accommodations vary in shape and size, but each comes with a fine bed, quality linens, and antique furniture. Units under the mansard eaves of the old building are the cheapest, smallest, and coziest. The hotel is known for its cuisine, with fixed-price menus costing from 39€ to 89€.

14 rue Rivault, Autun 71400. ✆ **03-85-86-58-58.** Fax 03-85-86-23-07. www.hotelursulines.fr. 43 units. 71€–123€ double; 139€–154€ suite. AE, DC, MC, V. Parking 7€. **Amenities:** Restaurant; bar; babysitting. *In room:* A/C (in some), TV, hair dryer, minibar, Wi-Fi (in some; free).

BEAUNE ★★

316km (196 miles) SE of Paris; 39km (24 miles) SW of Dijon

This is the capital of the Burgundy wine country and one of the best-preserved medieval cities in the district, with a girdle of ramparts. Its history spans over 2,000 years. Beaune was a Gallic sanctuary, then a Roman town. Until the 14th century, it was the residence of the ducs de Bourgogne. When the last duke, Charles the Bold, died in 1477, Louis XI annexed Beaune.

Essentials

GETTING THERE   If you're **driving,** note that Beaune is a few miles from the junction of four highways—A6, A31, A36, and N6. Beaune has good railway connections with Dijon, Lyon, and Paris. From Paris's Gare de Lyon, there are 14 TGV **trains** per day (trip time: 2 hr.; one-way fare 46€–70€); from Lyon, 10 trains per day (trip time: 1½ hr.; 22€ one-way); and from Dijon, 26 trains per day (trip time: 35 min.; 6.70€). For train information and schedules, call ✆ **08-92-35-35-35.**

VISITOR INFORMATION   The **Office de Tourisme** is at 6 blvd. Perpreuil (✆ **03-80-26-21-30;** fax 03-80-26-21-39; www.ot-beaune.fr).

SPECIAL EVENTS   The town comes to life during the third weekend in November, when wine buyers and oenophiles from the world over descend on the old town for a 3-day festival and wine auction called **Les Trois Glorieuses.** The town is packed with wineries offering dégustations priced from 20€ to 35€ for "several" glasses each of a different vintage—and with tourists visiting the labyrinth of caves and wine cellars. With all the free spirits (both kinds), visitors crowding the streets can be more than a bit tipsy.

Exploring the Town

North of the Hôtel-Dieu, the **Collégiale Notre-Dame,** place du Général Leclerc (✆ **03-80-26-22-70**), is an 1120 Burgundian Romanesque church. Some remarkable tapestries illustrating scenes from the life of the Virgin Mary are on display in the sanctuary. You can view them from Easter to mid-November.

The best **shopping** streets are rue de Lorraine, rue d'Alsace, rue Maufoux, and place de la Madeleine. For smaller boutiques, stroll down the pedestrian rue Carnot

---

 Burgundy by Bike

The best way to see this golden land is by bike. Near the Beaune Rail Station, **Bourgogne Randonnées,** 7 av. du 8 Septembre (✆ **03-80-22-06-03;** www.bourgogne-randonnees.com), rents bikes for 17€ per day.

and rue Monge. For antiques, concentrate your efforts around **Quartier du Camp Americain,** 3km (1¾ miles) northeast of the center of Beaune.

Beaune is one of the best towns in the region for sampling and buying Burgundy wines. You can tour, taste, and buy at **Marché aux Vins,** rue Nicolas-Rolin (✆ 03-80-25-08-20), housed in a 14th-century church. Entrance is 10€. Its cellars are in and among the ancient tombs, under the floor of the church. A well-stocked competitor, stocking most of the vintages of Burgundy, is **Cordelier,** 6 rue de l'Hôtel-Dieu (✆ 03-80-25-08-20). Another cellar, **Caves Patriarche Père et Fils,** 7 rue du Collège (✆ 03-80-24-53-78), is under the former Convent of the Visitandines, with cellars from the 13th, 16th, and 17th centuries.

Musée de l'Hôtel-Dieu ★★   One of the town's most visible antique buildings is the Hôtel-Dieu. It thrived during the Middle Ages under an order of nuns associated with the famous vineyards of Aloxe-Corton and Meursault. It functioned as a hospital until 1970, and some sections still hold a retirement home. The Musée de l'Hôtel-Dieu displays Flemish-Burgundian art such as Rogier van der Weyden's 1443 polyptych *The Last Judgment* ★★★. In the Salle des Pauvres (Room of the Poor), you'll find painted, broken-barrel, timbered vaulting and mostly authentic furnishings.

Rue de l'Hôtel-Dieu. ✆ **03-80-24-47-00.** Admission 6.50€ adults, 2.80€ ages 10–18, free for children 9 and under. Apr–Nov 19 daily 9am–6:30pm; Nov 20–Mar daily 9–11:30am and 2–5:30pm.

Musée des Beaux-Arts   Along with a rich Gallo-Roman archaeological section, this museum has paintings from the 16th to the 19th centuries, including Flemish primitives, and pieces by Felix Ziem, a precursor of the Impressionists. Sculptures from the Middle Ages and the Renaissance are also on display.

6 bd. Perpreuil (Porte Marie de Bourgogne). ✆ **03-80-24-56-78.** Admission (includes Musée du Vin de Bourgogne) 5.50€ adults, 3.50€ students and children, free for children 11 and under. Apr–Oct daily 2–6pm; Nov–Mar Wed–Mon 2–6pm.

Musée du Vin de Bourgogne ★   Housed in the former mansion of the ducs de Bourgogne, the Musée du Vin de Bourgogne traces the evolution of the region's winemaking. The collection of tools, objets d'art, and documents is contained in 15th- and 16th-century rooms. On display in the 14th-century press house is a collection of wine presses.

Rue d'Enfer. ✆ **03-80-22-08-19.** Admission 5.50€ adults, 3.50€ students and children, free for children 11 and under. Apr–Nov daily 9:30am–6pm; Dec–Mar Wed–Mon 9:30am–5pm.

Where to Stay

Hôtel de la Poste ★   Outside the town fortifications, this traditional hotel rivals but does not surpass the more elegant Hôtel Le Cep (see below). Its origins as an inn go back to 1660; it was radically restored in the 1990s and has been upgraded every year since. The rooms overlook the ramparts or the vineyards, and some have brass beds. Specialties at the restaurant range from chicken fricassee with tarragon to sole in court bouillon with white butter.

1-5 bd. Georges-Clemenceau, Beaune 21200. ✆ **03-80-22-08-11.** Fax 03-80-24-19-71. www.hoteldela postebeaune.com. 36 units. 160€–220€ double; 290€–550€ suite. AE, DC, MC, V. Parking 10€. **Amenities:** 2 restaurants; bar; room service. *In room:* A/C, TV, hair dryer, minibar, Wi-Fi (free).

Hôtel Le Cep ★★★   The chic spot for oenophiles is this former residential mansion in the town center, fit for the ducs de Bourgogne. Each antiques-filled guest room is individually decorated and named after a Grand Cru wine of the Côte-d'Or vineyards; our favorites are the Chambre Montrachet and the Chambre Meloisey. On the grounds are two of the loveliest arcaded courtyards in Beaune, one from the 16th century, another from the 14th century. A tower housing one of the city's most beautiful stone staircases rises from here. A former wine cellar is the breakfast room. One of Beaune's finest restaurants is inside the hotel.

27 rue Maufoux, Beaune 21200. ✆ **03-80-22-35-48.** Fax 03-80-22-76-80. www.hotel-cep-beaune. com. 64 units. 168€–208€ double; from 298€–348€ suite. AE, DC, MC, V. Parking 15€. **Amenities:** Restaurant; room service. *In room:* A/C, TV, hair dryer, minibar, Wi-Fi (free).

L'Hostellerie de Bretonnière ✦ This is the best bargain in town. It's well run, with quiet rooms, and 5 minutes on foot from the center of town. The inn was built as a postal relay station around 1900 and became a hotel in 1950. In 2004, management enlarged the hotel with the addition of a seven-unit annex in the garden, containing only duplex suites, each rustically outfitted in a style that evokes the traditions of rural Burgundy. The accommodations in the rear are the most tranquil, though most visitors prefer those overlooking the garden. Rooms are small, but adequate for an overnight; each has a shower-only bathroom. Continental breakfast is available.

43 rue de Faubourg Bretonnière, Beaune 21200. ✆ **03-80-22-15-77.** Fax 03-80-22-72-54. www.hotel bretonniere.com. 32 units. 55€–80€ double; 100€–110€ duplex suite. AE, DC, MC, V. Free parking. **Amenities:** Bar. *In room:* A/C (in some), TV, hair dryer, Wi-Fi (5€ for 2 days).

L'Hôtel de Beaune ★★ Although Le Cep is more tranquil and luxurious, L'Hôtel (which opened in 2002) is the second-most desirable hotel in town. Marble, mahogany, teak, and Italian stucco abound. Behind the 19th-century exterior, its guest rooms are tastefully furnished and comfortable, though lacking some of Le Cep's glamour. Each of the accommodations here is individually decorated, with lustrous yellow-and-orange quilts on mahogany beds of royal size. The hotel maintains an extraordinarily comprehensive wine cellar that, on advance notice, visitors can examine. Wines inside are for sale, either for consumption within the hotel's bar or for take-away.

3–5 rue Samuel Legay, Beaune 21200. ✆ **03-80-25-94-14.** Fax 03-80-25-94-13. www.lhoteldebeaune. com. 7 units. 270€–370€ double. AE, DC, MC, V. **Amenities:** Restaurant; bar; babysitting; room service. *In room:* A/C, TV, hair dryer, Internet (10€ per day).

Where to Dine

Hôtel de la Poste (see "Where to Stay," above) has a good restaurant.

Bistro de L'Hotel ★ FRENCH/BURGUNDIAN   A lot of the movers and shakers of the wine industry patronize this elegant bistro, where summer diners enjoy a terrace. The chef and owner, Johan Björklund, is from Sweden, but he invites favorable comparison to some of the finest chefs of Burgundy. He is known for taking advantage of the best of regional produce, including a divine Bresse chicken carved tableside. His fixed-price menu is always a good recommendation, or else you can order a la carte, beginning with such appetizers as a terrine of duckling foie gras or else tuna carpaccio with Asian spices. Ravioli is stuffed with frogs' legs appearing in a bouillon, or else you can order the town's finest sole meunière, served for two. Finish perhaps with the caramelized Tarte Tatin.

In L'Hotel de Beaune, 3–5 rue Samuel Legay. ✆ **03-80-25-94-10.** Reservations required. Main courses 35€–65€; fixed-price menu 80€. AE, DC, MC, V. Dec 8–Jan 4 daily 12:30–2pm and 7–10pm.

Jardin des Remparts ★★★ MODERN FRENCH   This is the finest restaurant in Beaune, topping even Bernard Morillon. Just outside the city's medieval wall, it's in a 1930s-era Art Deco *maison bourgeoise*. Two pale-yellow-and-green dining rooms open onto a terrace overlooking the garden. Happily, prices for the well-regarded cuisine are a bit lower than you may expect. Menu items are adventurous and creative, and include tartare of beef and minced oysters, whitefish baked in a mushroom crust, and pigeon roasted with licorice and softened caramel.

10 rue de l'Hôtel-Dieu ✆ **03-80-24-79-41.** Reservations recommended. Main courses 31€–37€; fixed-price menu 35€–90€. MC, V. Tues–Sat noon–1:30pm and 7–9pm. Closed Dec 1–Jan 15.

Ma Cuisine ★ 🍴 BURGUNDIAN   Open only 4 days a week, Ma Cuisine enjoys a reputation for well-prepared regional food and an impressively varied wine cellar. Fabienne Escoffier presides over the kitchen, and her husband, Pierre, maintains the dining room. The restaurant attracts local residents, many of them wine producers. Your old-fashioned meal may begin with a platter of thin-sliced cured ham with parsley, or compote of rabbit with fresh tarragon. Main courses include spit-roasted and deboned pigeon and beef bourguignon with garlic. Desserts are 19th-century French brasserie favorites: thin-sliced apple or pear tart, crème brûlée, almond cake. The setting, a much-renovated 15th-century stable, is appropriately historic.

Passage Ste-Hélène. ✆ **03-80-22-30-22.** Reservations recommended. Main courses 15€–35€; fixed-price menu 24€. MC, V. Mon–Tues and Thurs–Fri noon–1:30pm and 7–9:30pm.

Relais des Saulx ★ FRENCH   In a 200-year-old stone-trimmed building named after one of the region's ancient and noble families, Relais de Saulx is decorated with heavy timbers, and all the accouterments you'd expect from one of the region's most respected restaurants. The kitchen prepares traditional Bourguignon cuisine and up-to-date adaptations. Staples are Bresse chicken with morel sauce, scallops with truffle sauce, sea bass with fresh morel, and roast duck with sauces and garnishes that vary according to the season.

6 rue Louis-Very. ✆ **03-80-22-01-35.** Reservations required for large groups. Main courses 24€–20€; fixed-price menu 18€–33€. AE, DC, MC, V. Tues and Thurs–Sat noon–2pm; Mon–Sat 7–10pm. Closed 1 week in Feb, 2 weeks in Aug, and 2 weeks in early Dec.

Where to Stay & Dine Nearby

Hostellerie de Levernois ★ FRENCH   Under Jean Croet and his sons, this became one of the most celebrated restaurants of regional France. New owners are now in charge, and the restaurant is still trying to find its way. It creates grand cuisine in a stone-sided 17th-century *maison bourgeoise* in a 3.2-hectare (8-acre) park. The kitchen doesn't emphasize virtuoso techniques, but it knows what to do with first-class ingredients. The snails in risotto are a pure delight, as is a brochette of crayfish tails with spicy sauce. Chickens for roasting come from Bresse and are acclaimed as the best in France.

The inn rents 26 carefully decorated rooms in a well-designed modern annex. They have TV, air-conditioning, and (in most) tub/shower combos. Doubles cost 130€ to 265€; the suites go for 245€ to 350€. Free Wi-Fi is offered in the lobby.

Rue du Golf, Levernois 21200. ✆ **03-80-24-73-58.** Fax 03-80-22-78-00. www.levernois.com. Reservations required. Main courses 41€–48€; fixed-price dinner 65€–98€. AE, DC, MC, V. Mon–Sat 7–9:30pm; Sun noon–2pm and 7–9:30pm. Nov–Apr: closed Wed. Take D970 south of Beaune for 3km (1¾ miles), following signs for LONS LE SAUNIER.

Beaune After Dark

To hear jazz and rock music and flirt with the locals, head to **Le Raisin de Bourgogne,** 164 rte. de Dijon (✆ **03-80-24-69-48**), which fills up early with a 30-plus crowd. If you're in the mood for an ale or two, try the English-style **Pickwick's Pub,** 2 rue Notre-Dame (✆ **03-80-22-55-92**). **Opéra-Night,** rue du Beaumarché (✆ **03-80-24-10-11**), plays booming house music and has a huge dance floor, strobe lights, and mirrors revealing every angle imaginable.

DIJON ★★★

312km (194 miles) SE of Paris; 320km (199 miles) NE of Lyon

Dijon is known overseas mainly for its mustard. Located in the center of the Côte d'Or, it's the ancient capital of Burgundy. Here, great wine accompanies good food. Between meals, you can enjoy the art and architecture.

Your first impression, especially if you arrive at the rail station, can be misleading. You may think Dijon is a dreary modern city, but press on to its medieval core and discover old streets and buildings that have been restored. The mayor, François Rebsamen, was elected on a platform that mixed aspects of socialist, communist, and Greenpeace rhetoric. He is committed to the verdancy of Dijon.

Essentials

GETTING THERE The best way to reach Dijon is by **driving.** From Paris, follow A6 southeast to Pouilly-en-Auxois, and then go east along A38 into Dijon. Dijon also has excellent rail and bus connections to the rest of Europe. A total of four TGV **trains** arrive from Paris's Gare de Lyon each day (trip time: 1 hr., 45 min.); the one-way fare is 42€ to 53€. Trains arrive from Lyon every hour (trip time: 2 hr.; 26€–30€ one-way). For information, call ✆ **08-92-35-35-35.**

VISITOR INFORMATION The **Office de Tourisme** is at Place Darcy (✆ **08-92-70-05-58;** www.dijon-tourism.com).

SPECIAL EVENTS Between the end of June and the beginning of August, the streets of Dijon experience a lively renaissance when **Estivade** (✆ **03-80-74-51-51**) comes to town. The festival uses the city's streets as a stage for folk dances, music, and theater. It's always a big hit. You can get a schedule of events from the city tourist office (see above) or La Mairie (the town hall; ✆ **03-80-74-51-51**).

Seeing the Sights

One of the most historic buildings in this ancient province is the **Palais des Ducs et des Etats de Bourgogne,** which symbolizes the independent (or semi-independent, depending on the era) status of this fertile region. Capped with an elaborate tile roof, the complex is arranged around a trio of courtyards. The oldest section, only part of which you can visit, is the **Ancien Palais des Ducs de Bourgogne,** erected in the 12th century and rebuilt in the 14th. The newer section is the **Palais des Etats de Bourgogne,** constructed in the 17th and 18th centuries for the Burgundian parliament. Today, the palace is La Mairie; all of its newer section and much of its older section are reserved for the municipal government and not open to the public. However, there's a fine museum, the **Musée des Beaux-Arts** (see below).

On N5, 1.5km (1 mile) west from the center of town, stands the **Chartreuse de Champmol,** the Carthusian monastery built by Philip the Bold as a burial place; it's now a psychiatric hospital. Much of it was destroyed during the Revolution. You may not be permitted to enter the building, but you can see the Moses Fountain in the gardens designed by Sluter at the end of the 14th century. The Gothic entrance is superb.

The **Musée Archéologique,** 5 rue du Dr-Maret (✆ **03-80-48-83-70;** www.musees-bourgogne.org), contains findings unearthed from Dijon's archaeological digs. A medieval nunnery, **L'Ancien Couvent des Bernardines,** 17 rue Ste-Anne (✆ **03-80-44-12-69**), is home to two museums. The chapel holds the Musée d'Arts Sacrés, devoted to art from regional churches, and the cloister contains the **Musée de la Vie Bourguignonne** (also known as the Musée Perrin de Puy-cousin), which exhibits folkloric costumes, farm implements, and some 19th- and early-20th-century storefronts from Dijon's center. Admission is free to all three of these museums. Hours are Wednesday to Monday 10am to noon and 2 to 6pm.

Musée des Beaux-Arts ★★ The part of the old palace that you can visit contains one of France's oldest and richest museums. It showcases exceptional sculpture, ducal kitchens from the mid-1400s (with great chimney pieces), a collection of European paintings from the 14th to the 19th centuries, and modern French paintings and sculptures. Take special note of the Salle des Gardes, the banquet hall of the old palace built by Philip the Good (Philippe le Hardi). The tomb of Philip the Bold was created between 1385 and 1411 and is one of the best in France: A reclining figure rests on a slab of black marble, surrounded by 41 mourners.

In the Palais des Ducs et des Etats de Bourgogne, cour de Bar. ✆ **03-80-74-52-09.** Free admission. Temporary expositions cost 2€ each (free Sun). May–Oct Wed–Mon 10am–6pm; Nov–Apr Wed–Mon 10am–5pm.

Musée Magnin This museum was built in the 19th century as the home of an arts-conscious member of the *grande bourgeoisie.* The city of Dijon inherited the building and its contents following the death of the family's last descendant. It contains an eclectic display of 19th-century antiques and art objects, as well as a collection of paintings accumulated or painted by the former owners.

4 rue des Bons-Enfants. ✆ **03-80-67-11-10.** www.musee-magnin.fr. Admission 3.50€ adults, 2.50€, free for ages 25 and under. Tues–Sun 10am–noon and 2–6pm.

Shopping

Your shopping list may include robust regional wines, Dijon mustard, antiques, and the black-currant cordial cassis (try a splash in champagne to make a kir royale). The best shopping streets are rue de la Liberté, rue du Bourg, rue Bossuet, and (for antiques) rue Verrerie.

The market at **Les Halles Centrales,** rue Odebert, sells fruits, vegetables, and foodstuffs on Tuesday, Thursday, and Friday from 8am to noon, and Saturday from 8am to around 5pm. A separate endeavor that specializes in used clothing, kitchen utensils, housewares, and flea-market castoffs, **Les Marchés autour des Halles** operates along the market's periphery Tuesday, Thursday, and Friday 8am to noon, and Saturday 8am to around 5pm.

For the ideal picnic lunch, begin at **La Boutique Maille,** 32 rue de la Liberté (✆ **03-80-30-41-02**), where you can purchase many varieties of the world-famous

Dijon

Ancien Palais des Ducs de Bourgogne **2**
L'Ancien Couvent de Bernardines **5**
Musée Archéologique **1**
Musée des Beaux-Arts **3**
Musée Magnin **4**
Palais des Etats de Bourgogne **2**

Church ✝
Information (i)

mustard. Follow with a visit to the **Crémerie Porcheret,** 18 rue Bannelier (℡ **03-80-30-21-05**), to pick up several varieties of regional cheese, including *citeaux,* made by the brothers at a nearby monastery. Finish your journey at one of the three locations of **Mulot et Petitjean,** 1 place Notre-Dame, 16 rue de la Liberté, or 13 place Bossuet (℡ **03-80-30-07-10**), where you can pick up a pastry (especially gingerbread) for dessert.

For antiques, try **Monique Buisson,** 21 rue Verrerie (℡ **03-80-30-31-19**), which offers a good collection of regional furniture from the 1700s, or **Dubard,** 25 bis rue Verrerie (℡ **03-80-30-50-81**), for 19th-century garden ornaments and contemporary upholstery fabric. Other choice stops include **Aux Occasions,** 11 rue Auguste-Comte (℡ **03-80-73-55-13**), where you can browse through a multitude of mainly English antiques from the 1800s, as well as old and new Oriental rugs. Also appealing is **Antiquaires Golmard,** 3 rue Auguste-Comte (℡ **03-80-67-14-15**), which specializes in objects originating on private estates in the region. This store is flexible about trading antiques with individuals and other dealers, making it something of a clearinghouse for unusual antiques from throughout Europe. **Le**

Consortium, 16 rue Quentin (📞 **03-80-68-45-55**), is one of Dijon's most interesting modern-art galleries.

Where to Stay

Hostellerie du Chapeau-Rouge ★

This Dijon landmark, which has an acclaimed restaurant, is the town's best address. The hotel is filled with 19th-century antiques, and its rooms have modern conveniences and comfortable furnishings. Most of the bathrooms have Jacuzzis. Because no other hotel restaurant in town serves comparable food, you may want to visit here even if you're not a guest. The chef creates Burgundian favorites and more innovative fare. Specialties depend on what's good in any given season.

5 rue Michelet, Dijon 21000. 📞 **03-80-50-88-88.** Fax 03-80-50-88-89. www.chapeau-rouge.fr. 30 units. 147€–169€ double; 229€ suite. AE, DC, MC, V. Parking 13€. **Amenities:** Restaurant; bar; room service. *In room:* A/C, TV, hair dryer, minibar, Wi-Fi (free).

Hôtel de La Cloche ★

Legends associated with this site date from the 15th century, but the building evokes a late-19th-century grand hotel, complete with high ceilings and the modernized decor favored by Napoleon III. Located in the center of town, it features pink-and-gray marble floors, Oriental carpets, comfortable and conservative guest rooms with tub/shower combinations, and a lobby bar that's one of the most elegant places of its kind in town, with a view of the garden.

14 place Darcy, Dijon 21000. 📞 **03-80-30-12-32.** Fax 03-80-30-04-15. www.hotel-lacloche.com. 68 units. 200€–220€ double; 270€–800€ suite. AE, DC, MC, V. **Amenities:** Restaurant; bar; babysitting; exercise room; room service; sauna. *In room:* A/C, TV, hair dryer, minibar, Wi-Fi (9.90€ per day).

Hôtel Wilson ★ 🛍

Our favorite nest in Dijon, opening onto a pleasant square, this *ancien relais de poste* (coaching inn) dates from the 17th century and has been tastefully restored. Although it has been modernized and decorated with Burgundian wood furniture, many of the old wood ceiling beams have been exposed, adding authentic charm. All units have small bathrooms, each with a shower and some with tubs.

1 rue de Longvic, Dijon 21000. 📞 **03-80-66-82-50.** Fax 03-80-36-41-54. www.wilson-hotel.com. 27 units. 78€–96€ double. AE, MC, V. Parking 9€. **Amenities:** Bar. *In room:* A/C, TV, Wi-Fi (free).

Le Jacquemart 🗝

In the center of Old Dijon is one of the town's most affordable hotels. A building from the 1900s was completely restored, yet retains its steep stairwell and high ceilings. It's furnished in a comfortable yet provincial style, with immaculate bathrooms and crisp bed linens. There is no elevator or air conditioning, but the welcome is genuine. Some of the accommodations are large enough to house three or four guests. The car park is within a minute's walk.

32 rue Verrerie, 21000 Dijon. 📞 **03-80-60-09-60.** www.hotel-lejacquemart.fr. 31 units. 65€ double, 73€ triple; 80€ quad. AE, MC, V. Parking 5€. **Amenities:** Breakfast room. *In room:* TV, hair dryer, Wi-Fi (free).

Where to Dine

Hostellerie du Chapeau-Rouge (see "Where to Stay," above) has a marvelous restaurant.

Le Pré aux Clercs ★★★ BURGUNDIAN/FRENCH

In an 18th-century house across from the Palais des Ducs, this is one of Burgundy's finest restaurants, with a reputation that dates to 1833. Chef-owner Jean-Pierre Billoux, assisted by his wife,

Marie Françoise, prepares meals that have won acclaim. Menu items, served beneath an intricately beamed ceiling, may include such dishes as a terrine of pigeon with a confit of garlic, crayfish prepared with aged sherry vinegar, and roasted duckling with gingerbread stuffing. The array of wines will delight any connoisseur.

13 place de la Libération. ℰ **03-80-38-05-05.** www.bourgogne-restaurants.com/lepreauxclercs. Reservations required. Main courses 25€–45€; fixed-price lunch 35€, dinner 49€ and 95€. AE, DC, MC, V. Tues–Sun noon–1:45pm; Tues–Sat 7:30–9:30pm. Closed 10 days in Aug.

Les Oenophiles ★ FRENCH   You enter this elegant, grand restaurant through an antique courtyard. Stone walls surround a dining room decorated with Oriental carpets and Louis XII chairs. It serves traditional food that's hearty and satisfying, in a style somewhere between old-fashioned and conservatively modern. Specialties include foie gras of duckling in puff pastry, served with fruited wine; marinated scallops and shrimp prepared tempura-style; and scallops in a medley of spring vegetables and ginger. On the premises is a modern 32-room hotel, Hotel Philippe-le-Bon. Rooms have minibars, air-conditioning, and TVs. Rates for a double are 97€ to 125€, or 163€ to 208€ for a suite.

18 rue Ste-Anne, Dijon 21000. ℰ **03-80-30-73-52.** Fax 03-80-30-95-51. Reservations required. Main courses 18€–50€; fixed-price dinner 39€–59€. AE, MC, V. Mon–Sat noon–1:30pm and 7–9:30pm.

Stéphane Derbord ★★★ FRENCH   Given the prices and acclaim of this restaurant, customers have a right to expect perfection—and they get it. Prominently positioned a few steps from the Hôtel Wilson, Stéphane Derbord is the most sought-after restaurant in Dijon. Isabelle Derbord, Stéphane's charming wife, presides over the cozy dining room. Many menu items are accurately called "delectables," including duck liver in a terrine and fresh scallops in lemon oil. Saône River *sandre* (a local whitefish) is steamed and served with crayfish and pike dumplings; and chicken is roasted to perfection and served with spicy gravy. And if it's on the menu, try the pheasant pie with fresh duck liver.

10 place Wilson. ℰ **03-80-67-74-64.** www.restaurantstephanederbord.fr. Reservations required. Main courses 30€–46€; fixed-price menu 25€–88€. AE, DC, MC, V. Wed–Sat noon–1:45pm; Mon–Sat 7:30–9:45pm. Closed 1 week in Jan and 2 weeks in Aug.

Where to Dine Nearby

Restaurant des Gourmets ★★ FRENCH   This restaurant is reason enough to journey outside Dijon to a charming medieval village 6km (3¾ miles) south of Dijon. In a modern room overlooking a garden, you can enjoy a seasonal menu that may include such tantalizing appetizers as foie gras with a fig marmalade or lobster from Brittany. Main course delights might feature a John Dory with orange flavoring. Turbot is made all the tastier with a subtle flavoring of vanilla. The cellar contains more than 600 wines; many are burgundies from lesser known, small-scale wineries.

8 rue Puits-de-Têt, Marsannay-la-Côte 21160. ℰ **03-80-52-16-32.** www.les-gourmets.com. Reservations required. Main courses 28€–34€; fixed-price menu 25€ and 59€; *ménu surprise* 95€. AE, DC, MC, V. Wed–Sun noon–1:30pm and 7–9:30pm. Closed 3 weeks in Aug. Drive 9.5km (6 miles) south of Dijon on N74, following the signs for Beaune and then Marsannay-la-Côte.

Dijon After Dark

Begin your evening at one of the cafes or brasseries lining place Zola, rue des Godrans, place du Théâtre, or place Darcy, such as the **Concorde,** 2 place Darcy

Leave Dijon on A38 heading northwest on a good road in the Vallée de l'Ouche, alongside the Burgundy Canal. At pont de Pany, on the outskirts of Sombernon, exit onto a local highway (D905) and continue northwest. On your left lies the lake of Grosbois. The scenery is typical of agricultural France, with isolated farms, woods, and pastures.

Pass through Vitteaux; just before the next village, Posanges, stands a feudal château. You can't visit it, but it's worth a picture. Continue on D905 until you come to a railroad crossing. On your left is another old castle, now part of a private farm. The next village you reach along D905 is Pouillenay. Follow the signs for a short detour to the hamlet of **Flavigny-sur-Ozerain.** Park your car outside the walls and walk through the old streets.

Leave Flavigny and follow signs for a few miles on country roads to **Alise-Ste-Reine,** the site of what was once Alésia, the camp of the Gallic chieftain Vercingetorix. Alise-Ste-Reine was named after a local Christian who was decapitated for refusing to marry a Roman governor. In the town center stands a statue of Vercingetorix crafted by Millet. You can explore the ruins of a Roman-Gallic town, **Les Fouilles d'Alésia,** and **Le Musée d'Alésia.**

After Alise-Ste-Reine, you can head back to the village of Les Laumes, a railroad center. Before entering the village, make a U-turn to the right and take N454 to Baigneux-les-Juifs. After the village of Grésigny, you'll see a farm-fortress surrounded by water on your left.

Go 1.5km (1 mile) farther and turn right toward the **Château de Bussy-Rabutin** (✆ **03-80-96-00-03**). Roger de Rabutin ridiculed Louis XIV's court, for which he spent 6 years in the Bastille. The château, with two towers, has survived mostly intact. The gardens and park are attributed to Le Nôtre. It's open Tuesday to Sunday from 9:15am to noon and 2 to 5pm. Admission is 7€ for adults, 4.50€ for students 18 to 25, and free for those 17 and under.

Return to Grésigny, turn right before the farm-fortress, and then go left. Outside the village, turn right toward Menetreux Le Pitois. You're off the main road and into the real countryside. Back on D905, head to **Montbard,** hometown of George-Louis Leclerc, *comte* de Buffon, one of the 18th century's great naturalists and author of *L'Histoire Naturelle,* a 44-volume encyclopedia. The scientist's home is open to visitors, and a mini-museum, **Musée Buffon** (✆ **03-80-92-50-42**), is dedicated to his life and work. It's open only from April to October Wednesday through Sunday from 10am to noon and 2 to 5pm. The **Hôtel de l'Ecu,** 7 rue Auguste-Carré (✆ **03-80-92-11-66**), serves moderately priced meals in an 18th-century postal relay station; menus cost 21€ to 30€. The inn also rents 23 simply furnished yet comfortable bedrooms, costing 78€ to 90€ a night in a double. Closed February 20 to March 9.

Continue east 9.5km (6 miles) to Marmagne, then turn left on D32 and head toward the **Abbaye de Fontenay** (✆ **03-80-92-15-00;** www.abbayede fontenay.com). Isolated in a valley, Fontenay is one of Europe's most unspoiled 12th-century Cistercian abbeys. It is open mid-November to March daily 10am to noon and 2 to 5pm; April to mid-November daily 10am to 6pm (until 7pm in July and Aug). Admission is 9€ for adults, 4.20€ for children and students, and free for children 6 and under.

(✆ 03-80-30-69-43); **Jardin Théâtre,** 1 bis place du Théâtre (✆ 03-80-67-13-59); or **La Comédie,** 3 place du Théâtre (✆ 03-80-67-11-62). These spots fill up with young people who start the night with a drink and a look around.

If you prefer a 30s-to-40s crowd that likes to mingle in the low-key atmosphere of a piano bar, try **Hunky Dory,** 5 av. Foch (✆ 03-80-53-17-24); **Le Messire,** 3 rue Jules-Mercier (✆ 03-80-30-16-40); or **Le Cintra,** 13 av. Foch (✆ 03-80-53-19-53), which also has a little disco. For the boisterous (and often sloshed) atmosphere of an Irish pub, head over to **Le Kilkenny,** 1 rue Auguste-Perdrix (✆ 03-80-30-02-48).

Appealing to a more sedate crowd is **Le Chat Noir,** 20 av. Garibaldi (✆ 03-80-73-39-57), which emphasizes slower, more romantic music.

The opera season in Dijon stretches from the middle of October to May. The city's premier venue is the **Grand Théâtre de Dijon,** 2 rue Longepierre (✆ 03-80-60-44-00); call ahead for information on operas, operettas, dance recitals, and concerts. The city's second-most visible cultural venue is the **Théâtre National Dijon-Bourgogne,** rue Danton (✆ 03-80-68-47-47). Tickets for performances at either theater range from 15€ to 40€.

SAULIEU ★

250km (155 miles) SE of Paris; 76km (47 miles) NW of Beaune

Saulieu is interesting, but its food put it on the international map. The town (pop. 3,000) has enjoyed a reputation for cooking since the 17th century. Even Mme. de Sévigné praised it in her letters. So did Rabelais.

The main sight is the **Basilique St-Andoche,** place de la Fontaine (✆ 03-80-64-07-03), which has some interesting decorated capitals. Next door, in the **Musée François-Pompon,** place du Docteur, at rue Sallier (✆ 03-80-64-19-51), you can see works by François Pompon (d. 1930), the sculptor of animals whose works are featured in Paris's Musée d'Orsay. Pompon's large statue of a bull stands on a plaza off N6 at the entrance to Saulieu. Also in the museum are archaeological remnants from the Gallo-Roman era, sacred medieval art, and old tools illustrating aspects of life in Burgundy several centuries ago. Admission is 4€ for adults and 2.50€ for children 12 to 16. It's closed in January and February.

Essentials

GETTING THERE If you're **driving,** head along N80 from Montbard or N6 from Paris or Lyon. The **train** station is northeast of the town center. Passengers coming from Paris sometimes opt to take the TGV from the Gare de Lyon, getting off in Montbard, 48km (30 miles) to the north. From Montbard, a series of **buses** carry passengers on to Saulieu about three times a day for a one-way fare of 7.65€. For bus and rail information, call ✆ **36-35.**

VISITOR INFORMATION The **Office de Tourisme** is at 24 rue d'Argentine (✆ 03-80-64-00-21; www.saulieu.fr).

Where to Stay & Dine

Château Les Roches ★★ Right to the east of Saulieu, reached along A38, stands this imposing country residence in a medieval hilltop village, with panoramic views of the countryside. This magnificent house, decorated in exquisite taste, was built by a judge at the turn of the 20th century as an abode for his mistress. The face of that long-ago mistress can be found on the hand-painted ceiling panels in the dining room. The architect borrowed freely from styles in Austria, Switzerland, and Germany. Public rooms are adorned with original wood paneling, high ceilings, and intricate plasterwork. Bedrooms are spacious and furnished with a mix of antique and contemporary furnishings, but don't expect many in-room amenities except ultimate comfort.

Rue de Glanot, Mont Saint-Jean 21320. ℃ **03-80-84-32-71.** www.lesroches-burgundy.com. 6 units. 125€–165€ double. Rates include breakfast. MC, V. **Amenities:** Bistro (Mon only); dinner Thurs and Sat; room service (breakfast only). *In room:* Wi-Fi (free).

Le Relais Bernard Loiseau ★★ This former stagecoach stop with one of the best-known restaurants in France is an excellent choice. If you want to stay overnight, you'll find guest rooms with everything from Empire to Louis XV decor. You'll sleep on a comfortable mattress, on a bed that's likely to be 200 years old.

The 2003 suicide of its famous chef, Bernard Loiseau (rumored to be despondent at the thought of losing a Michelin star), shocked the culinary world and made international headlines. Loiseau's wife, Dominique, and staff are carrying on admirably under Patrick Bertron, who was culinary disciple of Loiseau for 20 years. The cooking remains in his style: less traditional, leaning away from heavy sauces. The emphasis is on bringing out maximum taste with no excess fat or sugar. All the great burgundies are on the wine list. A fixed-price lunch costs 66€ to 185€, with a fixed-price dinner going for 120€ to 185€.

2 rue Argentine, Saulieu 21210. ℃ **03-80-90-53-53.** Fax 03-80-64-08-92. www.bernard-loiseau.com. 32 units. 175€–345€ double; 375€–450€ suite. AE, MC, V. Closed Jan 4–Feb 15. **Amenities:** Restaurant; bar; exercise room; indoor and outdoor pools; room service; sauna; spa; Wi-Fi (free). *In room:* A/C (in some), TV, hair dryer, minibar.

THE RHONE VALLEY

The Rhône is as mighty as the Saône is peaceful, and these rivers form a part of the countryside that most travelers experience only briefly as they rush to the Riviera on the Mediterranean Express. This land of mountains and rivers is Beaujolais country, filled with Roman ruins, castles, and the Grand Canyon of France. It's also home to Lyon, a fabulous stop for gourmets.

The district brims with time-mellowed inns and stylish restaurants serving cuisine that's among the finest in the world.

LYON ★★★

431km (268 miles) SE of Paris; 311km (193 miles) N of Marseille

At the junction of the turbulent Rhône and the tranquil Saône, Lyon is the third-largest city in France. The city has a population of 472,000, with more than 2.9 million people spread across the large urban area that surrounds it. Lyon is the center of an industrial region—textile manufacturing is especially important. It's a leader in publishing and banking, and it's one of the world's silk capitals. Some of the country's best restaurants, including Paul Bocuse, are in and around Lyon. Such dishes as Lyon sausage, quenelles, and tripe Lyonnais are world famous. The region's succulent Bresse poultry is the best in France.

Lyon has urban sprawl, and some of the most humid summers in France. Still, it's much more relaxed and friendlier than Paris. Parks in full bloom, skyscrapers and sidewalk cafes, a great transport system, and a nightlife fueled by student energy invigorate Lyon, along with talented chefs, both young and old.

Lyon is the best base for exploring the Rhône region. It has the finest food in France and a historic core unequaled in the region.

Essentials

GETTING THERE If you're arriving from the north by **train,** don't get off at the first station, Gare La Part-Dieu; continue to Gare de Perrache, where you can begin sightseeing. The high-speed TGV takes only 2 hours from Paris; the one-way fare is 60€ to 80€. Lyon makes a good stopover en route to the Alps or the Riviera. For information, call ℂ **08-92-35-35-35,** or visit www.voyages-sncf.com.

By **plane,** it's a 45-minute flight from Paris to Aéroport Saint-Exupéry (ℂ **08-26-80-08-26**), 25km (16 miles) east of the city. **Satobuses** (ℂ **04-72-68-72-17**) run from the airport into the center of Lyon every 20 minutes during the day. The 40-minute bus trip costs 8.90€ each way.

If you're **driving** from Paris, head southeast on A8/E1 into Lyon. From Nice, head west on E1/A7 toward Aix-en-Provence, continuing northwest toward Avignon. Bypass the city and continue north along the same route into Lyon. From Grenoble or the French Alps, head northwest on A48 to A43, which will take you northwest into Lyon.

GETTING AROUND A network of Métro lines, trams, and buses branch out to serve the city. A *plan de poche* (pocket map) is available at any office of **TCL** (ℂ **08-20-42-70-00;** www.tcl.fr), which handles all forms of mass transport. Tickets are valid on all forms of public transport, costing 1.60€ for the average ride or else 13€ for a *carnet* of 10 tickets. Most short-time visitors may want to purchase a **Ticket Liberté** day pass for 4.40€. For a cab, call **Taxi Radio de Lyon** at ℂ **08-72-10-86-86**.

VISITOR INFORMATION The **Office de Tourisme** is on place Bellecour (ℂ **04-72-77-69-69;** fax 04-78-42-04-32; www.lyon-france.com).

SPECIAL EVENTS Festivals take place practically every day, especially in summer. Music festivals reign supreme, with the most popular occurring on France's National Day of Music, around June 21. The **Fête de la Musique** turns the streets of Lyon into performance spaces for local bands. From late November to late December, the **Festival de Musique du Vieux-Lyon,** 5 place du Petit-Collège (ℂ **04-78-38-09-09**), takes place in churches around the city. Tickets range from 14€ to 30€.

Exploring the City

The city sprawls over many miles, divided, like Paris, into *arrondissements.* Its heart straddles the Saône, around the east bank's place Bellecour and the west bank's Primatiale St-Jean. Begin your tour of Lyon at **place Bellecour,** one of France's largest and most charming squares. A statue of Louis XIV looks out on the encircling 18th-century buildings. Urban sociologists are proud of Lyon's efforts to decorate some of its drab facades with *trompe l'oeil* murals. Among the most frequently cited works are the facade of the Musée Tony Garnier, 4 rue des Serpollières, 8e, and the fresco "des Lyonnais célèbres" in the 2e.

IN VIEUX LYON ★★★

From place Bellecour, walk across pont Bonaparte to the right bank of the Saône River and **Vieux Lyon.** (From elsewhere in the city, you can take bus no. 28, or Métro: Vieux Lyon.) Covering about a square mile, Old Lyon contains an amazing collection of medieval and Renaissance buildings. After years of existence as a slum, the area is now fashionable, attracting antiques dealers, artisans, weavers, sculptors, and painters who depict scenes along the **rue du Boeuf,** one of the most interesting streets for exploring.

Your first stop should be the cathedral, **Primatiale St-Jean** (see later in this chapter). North of the cathedral is the most historically and architecturally evocative neighborhood of Old Lyon, with narrow streets, spiral stairs, hanging gardens, soaring

The Rhône Valley

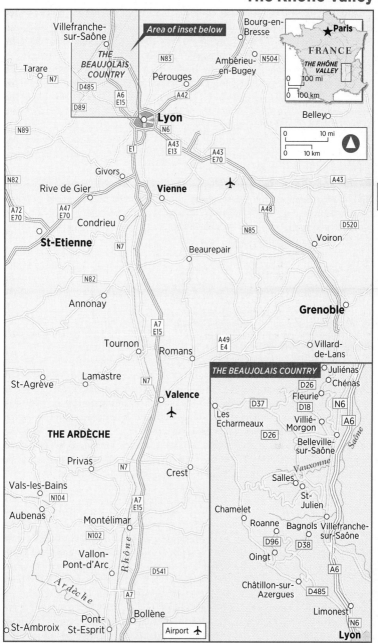

towers, and unusual courtyards whose balconies seem to perch precariously atop medieval pilings or columns.

One architectural aspect that's unique to Lyon is its *traboules,* a series of short covered passageways that connect longer avenues running parallel to one another. Scattered throughout Vieux Lyon, they're capped with vaulted masonry ceilings. They often open unexpectedly into flower-ringed courtyards.

Try to see the Gothic arcades of the 16th-century **Maison Thomassin,** place du Change, and the 16th-century **Hôtel du Chamarier,** 37 rue St-Jean, where Mme. de Sévigné lived. You can admire these buildings from the outside, but you are not allowed to enter. The neighborhood also contains the **Eglise St-Paul,** 3 place Gerson (✆ **04-78-28-34-45**), consecrated in A.D. 549. Rebuilding began in 1084 after its destruction by the Saracens. Its octagonal lantern tower was completed in the 1100s, the rest of the premises in the 13th century. You can visit Monday to Saturday noon to 6pm (Sun 2–6pm), and admission is free.

Musée Historique de Lyon (Musée Gadagne) ★   This museum is in the Hôtel de Gadagne, an early-16th-century residence. You'll find interesting Romanesque sculptures on the ground floor. Other exhibits include 18th-century Lyonnais furniture and pottery, antique ceramics from the town of Nevers, a pewter collection, and numerous paintings and engravings of Lyon.

In the same building is the **Musée de la Marionette** (same phone and hours), which has three puppets by Laurent Mourguet, creator of Guignol, the best-known French marionette character. The museum also displays marionettes from other parts of France (Amiens, Lille, and Aix-en-Provence) and from around the world.

1 place du Petit-Collège. ✆ **04-78-42-03-61.** Admission (including Musée de la Marionette) 6€ adults, free students and children 17 and under. Wed–Sun 11am–6:30pm.

Primatiale St-Jean ★   This cathedral was built between the 12th and the 15th centuries, and its exceptional stained-glass windows date from the same era. Its apse is a masterpiece of Lyonnais Romanesque architecture. A highlight is the Flamboyant Gothic chapel of the Bourbons. On the front portals are medallions depicting the signs of the zodiac, the Creation, and the life of St. John. The cathedral's 16th-century clock is intricate and beautiful. It announces the hour daily at noon, 2pm, 3pm, and 4pm in grand style: A rooster crows, and angels herald the event. The treasury is in a wing called **La Manécanterie.** Entrance is free, and hours are Tuesday to Saturday 10am to noon and 2 to 6pm. The wing of the cathedral that houses the treasury is noted for the beauty and severe dignity of its 12th-century Romanesque facade. Its origins date to the 11th century, when it was established as a music school.

Place St-Jean. ✆ **04-78-92-82-29.** Free admission. Tues–Sun 9:30am–noon and 2–6pm.

IN FOURVIERE HILL ★

Rising to the west of Vieux Lyon is **Colline de Fourvière** (**Fourvière Hill;** www.fourviere.org). The wooded hill—home to numerous convents, colleges, and hospitals; two Roman theaters; and a superb Gallo-Roman museum—affords a panoramic vista of Lyon. You can see the city's many bridges across the two rivers, and the rooftops of the medieval town. In clear weather, you can even view the countryside extending to the snowcapped Alps.

Enthroned on the hill's summit is the 19th-century **Basilique Notre-Dame de Fourvière,** 8 place de Fourvière (✆ **04-78-25-13-01**), rising fortresslike with four

Lyon

Abbaye Romane de St-Martin-d-Ainay **12**
Basilique Notre-Dame Fourvière **7**
Eglise St-Paul **3**
Hôtel de Ville **1**
Hôtel du Chamarier **8**
Maison Thomassin **4**
Musée de la Civilisation Gallo-Romaine **10**
Musée de l'Imprimerie de Lyon **6**

Musée des Arts-Décoratifs **13**
Musée des Beaux-Arts **2**
Musée des Tissus **14**
Musée Historique de Lyon
  (Musée Gadagne) **5**
Primatiale St-Jean **9**
Théâtres Romains **11**

octagonal towers and crenelated walls. Colored mosaics cover its interior, and an ancient chapel adjoins the church. A gilded statue of the Virgin surmounts the belfry. Admission is free; it's open daily 8am to 7pm.

Jardin du Rosaire extends along the hillside between the basilica and the 13th-century Primatiale St-Jean. It's open daily 6:30am to 9:30pm and promises a scenic walk. You'll see a vast shelter for up to 200 pilgrims. Additional mobility is provided by a pair of cable-driven funiculars that make runs every 10 minutes from a point immediately adjacent to the Métro station in Vieux Lyon to the top of Fourvière Hill. Priced at 2.20€ each way, they run daily between 5am and midnight.

Théâtres Romains, 7 rue du Cirque 1, Montée de Fourvière (© 04-74-85-39-23), a Roman theater-odeum complex, is in a park south of the basilica. The theater is the most ancient in France, built by order of Augustus from 17 to 15 B.C. and expanded during the reign of Hadrian. The odeum, reserved for musical performances, was once sumptuously decorated; its orchestra floor still contains mosaics of marble and porphyry. The third building was dedicated in A.D. 160 to the goddess Cybele, or Sibella. Only the building's foundations remain. The archaeological site is open April to September 15 daily 9:30am to 1pm and 2 to 6pm; off season Tuesday to Friday 9:30am to 12:30pm or Saturday and Sunday 1:30 to 5:30pm. Admission is 2.50€ for adults, 1.70€ students, or free for children 17 and under. Performances are given at both theaters in June and July during Les Nuits de Fourvière, when dance recitals, concerts, and plays are staged atop Fourvière Hill; make reservations at © 04-72-32-00-00.

An altar dedicated to a bull cult and a marble statue of a goddess are on display in the **Musée de la Civilisation Gallo-Romaine,** 17 rue Cléberg (© 04-72-38-81-90), near the archaeological site. The museum's collection of Gallo-Roman artifacts is the finest in France outside Paris. The site is open Tuesday through Sunday 10am to 6pm. Admission is 4€ adults, 2.50€ students, free for ages 17 and under. Entrance is free on Thursday. Guides are available on Sundays and holidays at 3pm.

ELSEWHERE AROUND THE CITY

In addition to the sites below, you can also visit Lyon's oldest church, the 1107 **Abbaye Romaine de St-Martin-d'Ainay,** 11 rue Bourgelat (© 04-72-40-02-50), south of place Bellecour, near place Ampère. Admission is free; hours are daily 8:30am to noon and 2:30 to 6:30pm. The rue de l'Hôtel-de-Ville extends north from place Bellecour to **place des Terreaux,** dominated by one of the most beautiful of Europe's city halls, the 1746 **Hôtel de Ville.** Its outside is dark and severe; the brilliant interior is closed to the public.

L'Institut & Musée Lumière   Film buffs from all over the world come here. The famous Lumière family, including Antoine (1840–1911), Auguste (1862–1954), and Louis (1864–1948), once lived in Lyon. The brothers were chemists, industrialists, and motion-picture pioneers. In Lyon, they founded a factory for producing photographic plates, paper, and chemicals. They invented the Lumière process of color photography and the Cinématographe, an early motion picture camera, in 1895. They produced films, including *La Sortie des Usines Lumière,* released in 1895 and considered the first movie. The complex is dedicated to the memory of the innovators and is a living museum of cinema. Early films are shown, and books, photos, posters, and pre-cinematographic and cinematographic equipment are on display.

25 rue du Premier Film. ☎ **04-78-78-18-95.** www.institut-lumiere.org. Admission 6€ adults, 5€ students and children 7–18, free for children 6 and under. Tues–Sun 11am–6:30pm. Métro: Montplaisir-Lumière.

Musée de l'Imprimerie de Lyon   Occupying a 15th-century mansion, this museum is devoted to Lyon's role in the world of printing. Exhibits include a page from a Gutenberg Bible, 17th- to 20th-century presses, 16th- to 19th-century wood-cuts, and engravings. This is one of the most important printing museums in Europe, along with those at Mainz and Antwerp. It has a collection of books from "all epochs," including *incunabula,* books printed before Easter 1500.

13 rue de la Poulaillerie. ☎ **04-78-37-65-98.** Admission 3.80€ adults, 2€ students, free for children 17 and under. Wed–Sun 9:30am–noon and 2–6pm.

Musée des Arts-Décoratifs ★★   In the 1739 Lacroix-Laval mansion by Souf-flot (architect of the Panthéon in Paris), the Musée des Arts-Décoratifs contains furniture and objets d'art from the 17th and 18th centuries. The medieval and Renaissance periods are also represented. Look for a five-octave clavecin by Donz-elague, the 18th-century creator of musical instruments.

34 rue de la Charité. ☎ **04-78-38-42-00.** Admission (includes Musée des Tissus; see below) 4.60€ adults, 2.30€ students, free for children 17 and under. Tues–Sun 10am–noon and 2–5:30pm. Métro: Ampère.

Musée des Beaux-Arts ★★   On the south side of the place des Terreaux stands the Palais des Arts (also called the Musée de St-Pierre). The former Benedictine abbey was built between 1659 and 1685 in the Italian baroque style. Today, it is home to the Musée des Beaux-Arts, which has an outstanding collection of paintings and sculpture. You enter through a courtyard graced with statuary and shade trees. The ground floor showcases an array of 14th-century paintings. The collection also includes Etruscan, Egyptian, Phoenician, Sumerian, and Persian art. Of special note is Perugino's altarpiece. The top floor holds one of France's richest 19th-century collections, with works by artists from Veronese, Tintoretto, and Rubens to Braque, Bonnard, and Picasso. Be sure to see Joseph Chinard's bust of Mme. Récamier, the Lyon beauty who charmed Napoleonic Paris by merely reclining, and the Fantin-Latour masterpiece *Reading.*

20 place des Terreaux. ☎ **04-72-10-17-40.** Admission 6€ adults, 4€ for students and children. Wed–Thurs and Sat–Mon 10am–6pm; Fri 10:30am–6pm.

Musée des Tissus ★★★   Next door to the Musée des Arts-Décoratifs (see above), in the 1730 Palais de Villeroy, is an even more interesting collection. On view are priceless fabrics from all over the world, spanning 2,000 years. Some of the fin-est fabrics made in Lyon from the 18th century to the present are displayed. The 15th- and 16th-century textiles embroidered with religious motifs are noteworthy, as are the 17th-century Persian carpets. Look for the partridge-motif brocade from Marie Antoinette's bedchamber at Versailles, as well as a 150-color brocaded satin woven for Queen Victoria, which is decorated with birds of paradise and orchids.

34 rue de la Charité. ☎ **04-78-38-42-00.** Admission (includes Musée des Arts-Décoratifs) 6€ adults, 3.50€ students, free for children 16 and under. Tues–Sun 10am–5:30pm.

OUTSIDE THE HEART OF THE CITY

One of Lyon's grandest archaeological sites is **Amphithéâtre des Trois-Gauls,** rue du Jardin-des-Plantes, Croix-Rousse (no phone), near the city's northern perimeter. You can view the site only from the outside. At the time of its construction, it was the centerpiece of Condate, a Gallic village that predated the arrival of the Romans by centuries. Various accounts have members of Gallic tribes meeting here in the earliest example of a parliamentary system. Based on that information, France's 2,000th anniversary was celebrated in Lyon in 1989.

On the opposite side of the Rhône, you can explore Lyon's largest public park and garden, the 105-hectare (259-acre) **Parc de la Tête d'Or** (© **04-78-89-02-03**). Its largest entrance is on boulevard des Belges. It opened in 1857 and has all the fountains, pedestrian walkways, and statues you'd expect. Surrounded by wealthy neighborhoods, the park has a lake, a zoo, a botanic garden with greenhouses, and a rose garden with some 100,000 plants. It's open daily 6:30am to 10pm (until 8:30pm Oct–Apr). Entrance is free.

At Rochetaillée-sur-Saône, 11km (6¾ miles) north of Lyon on D433, the **Musée Français de l'Automobile "Henri Malartre"** is in the Château de Rochetaillée, 645 rue du Musée (© **04-78-22-18-80**). The château was built in 1131 on even older foundations and rebuilt in the 1400s. The curators are proud of the majestic 15th-century staircase, the Romanesque gateway that's part of the original 12th-century design, and a policy that permits photography, smoking, and any motorcycle-fetish garb you care to wear while admiring the collection of vehicles. The collection includes 100 cars dating to 1890, 65 motorcycles from 1903 and after, and 40 bicycles from 1818 and later. Admission to the museum and château is 6€ adults, and free for ages 25 and under. It is open Tuesday through Sunday 9am to 6pm (until 7pm July to August). From Lyon, take bus no. 40 or 70.

Shopping

The third-largest city in France offers an array of retail outlets. For boutiques, art galleries, and artists' studios, head to Vieux Lyon and the area around rue de la République, rue Victor Hugo, rue Mercière, and quai St-Antoine. Antiques dealers concentrate around rue Auguste-Comte as it approaches place Bellecour. Also consider venturing to the **Cité des Antiquaires,** 117 bd. Stalingrad (© **04-72-69-00-00**), with more than 100 dealers spread over two floors, and merchandise from the 18th century to the 1950s. It's open Thursday through Sunday from 10am to 7pm.

Lyon is a bastion of fashion. The densest concentrations of retail shops are along rue Emile Zola, rue de Président-Herriot, and place Kléber. For chic women's couture that rivals anything you'll find in Paris, try **George Rech,** 59 rue du Président-Herriot (© **04-78-37-82-90**). More than 235 shops and boutiques fill the largest shopping center in Lyon, the **Centre Commercial de la Part-Dieu,** 17 rue du Dr. Bouchut (© **04-72-60-60-62**). Although Lyon is not the major silk center that it used to be, it is home to several silk manufacturers. You'll see a good selection of silk scarves, ties, sashes, and squares at **Hermès,** 96 rue du Président-Herriot (© **04-78-42-25-14**).

Bernachon, 42 cours Franklin-Roosevelt (© **04-78-24-37-98**), is home to Lyon's best chocolates and pastries. Here you'll find 30 varieties of bite-size pastries known as mini-gâteaux, 30 varieties of petits fours, and even dark, rich chocolates lightly dusted with 24-karat gold. The Bernachon store houses a small restaurant and tearoom, **Bernachon Passion** (© **04-78-52-23-65**).

Where to Stay

Alain Chapel (p. 433) rents rooms.

EXPENSIVE

Hôtel la Cour des Loges ★★★   This luxury hotel in Old Lyon occupies four connected houses dating from the 15th and 16th centuries. Among its allures are a rooftop bar and garden, an indoor pool, and a magnificent loggia-ringed courtyard. Most of its beautifully furnished rooms and suites face gardens, the square, or a large, sunny lobby. The size and configuration of the rooms vary, but all are lavishly decorated. Most of the immaculate tiled bathrooms have both tub and shower. The savviest staff in Lyon is usually courteous and efficient.

2-8 rue du Boeuf, Vieux Lyon 69005. ✆ **04-72-77-44-44.** Fax 04-72-40-93-61. www.courdesloges. com. 62 units. 240€–618€ double; 505€ suite. AE, DC, MC, V. Parking 35€. Métro: St-Jean. **Amenities:** 2 restaurants; bar; indoor pool; room service; sauna. *In room:* A/C, TV, hair dryer, minibar, Wi-Fi (free).

Villa Florentine ★★★   Conveniently located in Vieux Lyon, this Relais & Châteaux hotel is an even more stunning choice than Cour des Loges (see above). One of the great city hotels along the Rhône, it is a bastion of taste and luxury. The views from the lounges, terraces, and guest rooms are the most panoramic in town. Converted from a 17th-century convent, the building retains many of its original Italianate architectural details. The accommodations are spacious and comfortable, decorated in a style that blends modern Italian design with Renaissance reproductions. A nine-unit annex, just across the street, features rooms and suites that are a bit larger and more modern than those within the hotel's original core.

25 montée Saint-Barthélemy, Lyon 69005. ✆ **04-72-56-56-56.** Fax 04-72-40-90-56. www.villaflorentine. com. 28 units. 230€–385€ double; 445€–470€ junior suite; 550€–950€ suite. AE, DC, MC, V. Parking 18€. **Amenities:** Restaurant; bar; babysitting; exercise room; outdoor pool; room service; sauna; minispa. *In room:* A/C, TV, hair dryer, minibar, Wi-Fi (free).

MODERATE

Grand Hôtel Mercure Château Perrache ★   This hotel near the Perrache train station houses Lyon's most traditional rooms. The style is polarizing: You will either love or hate this monument to Art Nouveau. Admittedly, the old dame has seen better times. Originally built in 1906 and classified as a national monument, the hotel is one of the genuinely fine examples of Art Nouveau in Lyon. Renovated units contain contemporary furnishings, while the older units retain more of their original antique styling. Romantics and nostalgia buffs love the creaky furnishings, the antiques, and the winter garden. The restaurant, Les Belles Saisons, does more than just cater to the tired business traveler; its finely honed Continental and regional dishes are often innovative.

12 cours de Verdon Rambaud, Lyon 69002. ✆ **800/MERCURE** (637-2873) in the U.S., or 04-72-77-15-00. Fax 04-78-37-06-56. www.mercure.com. 111 units. 90€–250€ double; 270€ suite. AE, DC, MC, V. Parking 14€. Métro: Perrache. **Amenities:** Restaurant; bar; babysitting; room service. *In room:* A/C, TV, hair dryer, minibar, Wi-Fi (4.50€ per hr.).

Hôtel Globe et Cécil   Near place Bellecour, this hotel is a good deal because of its location and attentive staff. Built as a private mansion during France's 19th-century Gilded Age, it became a hotel in 1892. Today the six-story property (with elevator) is a government-rated three-star staple. Some of the individually decorated rooms are old-fashioned and charmingly dowdy; others are more modern and efficient. Many restaurants are nearby.

21 rue Gasparin, Lyon 69002. ✆ **04-78-42-58-95.** Fax 04-72-41-99-06. www.globeetcecilhotel.com. 60 units. 170€ double. Rates include breakfast. AE, DC, MC, V. Métro: Bellecour. *In room:* A/C, TV, hair dryer, Wi-Fi (free).

Le Phénix Hotel ★★ ✦   Overlooking the Soane in Vieux Lyon, this hotel dates in part from the 16th century when it was a meeting place for theatrical troupes. Today, the old structure has been joined with other buildings to create this atmospheric choice with its original Florentine architectural design. Tradition has been respected but modern touches added in all the bedrooms. Rooms are intimate and decorated in warm colors with stylish furnishings and all the latest gadgets such as smoke detectors. The bar is known for its private jazz concerts.

7 quai de Bondy, 69005 Lyon. ✆ **04-78-28-24-24.** Fax 04-78-28-62-86. 36 units. 135€–191€ double. AE, DC, MC, V. **Amenities:** Restaurant; bar; room service. *In room:* TV, minibar, Wi-Fi (free).

Mercure Lyon Beaux-Arts   In the center of Lyon, this is one of the city's best moderately priced hotel choices. The lobby evokes the 1930s. The guest rooms, though comfortable, are outfitted in businesslike modern style. Because this is a noisy part of the city, double-glazing on the windows helps shut out traffic sounds; the quieter rooms are in the rear. Breakfast is the only meal served, though you may prefer croissants and coffee at one of the cafes on place Bellecour.

73–75 rue du Président-Herriot, Lyon 69002. ✆ **800/MERCURE** (637-2873) in the U.S., or 04-78-38-09-50. Fax 04-78-42-19-19. www.mercure.com. 75 units. 154€–184€ double; from 210€ suite. AE, DC, MC, V. Métro: Cordelier. **Amenities:** Bar; babysitting; room service. *In room:* A/C, TV, hair dryer, minibar, Wi-Fi (4.50€ per hr.).

INEXPENSIVE

Collège Hôtel ✦   Accommodations, which adopt a tongue-in-cheek theme of a university dorm, are not the spartan affair you might expect; in fact, they are comfortable and include a number of attractive features. Located on the right bank of the Saône within the heart of Vieux Lyon, Collège Hôtel offers 39 small but well-furnished bedrooms with immaculate linens and a choice of modern bathrooms (the best ones are the corner units with hand-held showers). Many of the bedrooms open onto private terraces or balconies. Each floor has a 1960s vintage refrigerator from which "boarders" can help themselves to free nonalcoholic drinks. Best of all is the roof garden terrace with its gym. As soon as night falls, the hotel's 130 windows light up as part of a unique light show, enhancing the magnificent 1930s facade.

5 place Saint-Paul, Lyon 69005. ✆ **04-72-10-05-05.** Fax 04-78-27-98-84. www.college-hotel.com. 39 units. 115€–145€ double. AE, MC, V. Parking 15€. **Amenities:** Roof garden; gym; library. *In room:* A/C, TV, Wi-Fi (free).

Hôtel Bayard   The foundations of this dignified town house date from the 16th century. Some guest rooms were decorated in romantic French style, with draped canopies or four-poster beds. Each room is outfitted in a style inspired by a period of French history. Most of the compact bathrooms have showers and tubs. You enter the hotel through a narrow hallway and climb one flight of stairs to the reception area. Don't be put off by the staff members, who may appear detached.

23 place Bellecour, Lyon 69002. ✆ **04-78-37-39-64.** Fax 04-72-40-95-51. www.hotelbayard.fr. 22 units. 89€–179€ double. AE, DC, MC, V. Parking 14€–20€. Métro: Bellecour. *In room:* TV, Wi-Fi (free).

Hôtel Bellecordière   The small, neatly kept accommodations at this nondescript hotel are no-frills and, at their worst, a bit drab. Each unit has a compact shower-only bathroom. Breakfast is the only available meal, but many worthwhile restaurants are within a short walk.

18 rue Bellecordière, Lyon 69002. ☏ **04-78-42-27-78.** Fax 04-72-40-92-27. www.hotel-bellecordiere. com. 44 units. 70€ double; 80€ triple. Rates include breakfast. AE, MC, V. Métro: Bellecour. **Amenities:** Wi-Fi (free). *In room:* TV, hair dryer.

La Résidence ✦ Long a favorite with budget travelers, this hotel is in a pedestrian zone in the center of Lyon. Beyond an ornate 19th-century facade, the guest rooms are comfortably though not spectacularly furnished. Half come with tub/ shower combinations. For the price, the place offers one of the best bargains in this rather overpriced city. Breakfast is the only meal served, but many restaurants are literally outside the door, as is some of the finest shopping.

18 rue Victor-Hugo, Lyon 69002. ☏ **04-78-42-63-28.** Fax 04-78-42-85-76. www.hotel-la-residence. com. 67 units. 81€ double; 96€ triple. AE, DC, MC, V. Métro: Bellecour. **Amenities:** Restaurant. *In room:* A/C, TV, hair dryer, minibar, Wi-Fi (free).

Where to Dine

The food in Lyon is among the finest in the world—with prices to match. However, we've found that a person of moderate means can often afford the most reasonable fixed-price menu even in the priciest establishments.

VERY EXPENSIVE

Alain Chapel ★★ MODERN FRENCH This Relais Gourmand property occupies a 19th-century postal station that has evolved into a comfortable, stylish restaurant and lodging. Alain Chapel was one of the world's premier chefs, and after his death, many claimed that the reputation of his restaurant would falter. That hasn't been the case. Chef Philippe Jousse, who trained under Chapel, helps maintain Lyon's status as a gastronomic capital. Menu items served within a rustically antique-looking setting change with the seasons, but are likely to include lobster salad with pigeon necks and black truffles; Bresse chicken cooked in a pig's bladder, stuffed with foie gras, and drizzled with foie gras sauce; puff pastry with apples and vanilla-flavored bourbon sauce and champagne-flavored sorbet; and a particularly appealing assortment of unusual local cheeses, charmingly presented.

Alain Chapel also has 12 beautiful guest rooms; a double runs 130€ to 150€.

60 route de Bourg, St-André-de-Corcy 01390. ☏ **04-78-91-82-02.** Fax 04-78-91-82-37. www.alainchapel. fr. Reservations required. Main courses 42€–60€; fixed-price lunch Wed–Thurs 70€; fixed-price dinner 112€–155€. AE, DC, MC, V. Wed–Thurs and Sat–Sun noon–1pm; Wed–Sun 7:30–10pm. Closed Jan and 1 week in Aug. Take N83 20km (12 miles) north of Lyon.

Les Loges ★ FRENCH This hotel restaurant originated with lofty ambitions, a celebrity chef, and a flurry of promotion. In 2003 it dropped the pretense and gradually evolved into a desirable—albeit not particularly cutting-edge—dining room. The flavorful food is beautifully prepared and served in generous portions— well-executed fare that you'd expect from a top-notch steakhouse or hotel dining room. Surrounded by Renaissance-era stone walls, wrought iron, and ornate crystal chandeliers, you may begin with foie gras, marinated salmon, or crabmeat cocktail with guacamole. Continue with grilled lamb, beef, veal, or pork, served with virtually any sauce you specify, or roasted quail in a succulent mixture of herbs and its own juices.

In the Hôtel la Cour des Loges, 6 rue du Boeuf. ☏ **04-72-77-44-44.** Reservations recommended. Main courses 35€–39€; fixed-price menu 58€–85€; Sun brunch 49€. AE, DC, MC, V. Tues–Sat 7:30–9:30pm, Sun 12:30–2pm.

M Restaurant ★★★ FRENCH   Hot new chef Julien Gautier is the darling of Lyon food critics, the most hard-to-please in France, teasing new tastes and savors out of the pungent foodstuffs in the Rhône region. The chef continues to extend his repertoire and tantalize palates in his ultramodern dining room with colorful chairs and parquet flooring set off by a candelabrum created by the famed Lyon designer, Alain Vavry. Each plate that emerges from the kitchen seems to burst with flavor. Try the melon soup with Iberian ham or his rabbit with foie gras. Gautier also makes smooth risotto with flap mushrooms and offers such main dishes as shrimp with cocoa milk or *omble chevalier* (that gourmet fish from Lake Geneva). Veal comes in a piquant sauce, and the lamb curry with ravioli is a surprising delicacy.

47 av. Foch. ☎ **04-78-89-55-19.** Reservations required. Main courses 18€–25€; fixed-price menu 18€–35€. AE, DC, MC, V. Mon–Fri noon–2pm and 7:30–10pm. Closed weekends and Aug 2–31 and Feb 14–22.

Paul Bocuse ★★★ LYONNAIS   Whether the namesake chef is on site or not, the standards of this restaurant continue to reach for the skies. Serious Parisian foodies take the TGV from Paris just to dine at this remarkable citadel of haute cuisine. Paul Bocuse is one of the world's most famous chefs. He specializes in regional cuisine, though long ago he was the leading exponent of nouvelle cuisine (which he later called "a joke"). Because Bocuse, who is now in his 70s, is gone at least part of the time, other chefs carry on with the mass production (for up to 180 diners) of the signature dishes that the master created. There isn't a lot of room for variation. Tired of the conventional facades of most French restaurants, Bocuse commissioned a local artist to paint the history of French cuisine. The tale begins in the 1700s and proceeds through the years to its "defining moment"—a depiction of Bocuse himself.

You can begin your meal with the famous black-truffle soup, and then try one of the most enduring dishes in the Bocuse repertoire: Bresse chicken cooked in a pig's bladder. Other options include roast pigeon in puff pastry with baby cabbage leaves, and red snapper served in a potato casing. A boutique sells Bocuse's preferred wine, cognac, jams and jellies, coffees and teas, and cookbooks.

40 quai de la Plage, Pont de Collonges, Collonges-au-Mont-d'Or. ☎ **04-72-42-90-90.** www.bocuse.fr. Reservations required as far in advance as possible. Main courses 48€–84€; fixed-price menu 130€–210€. AE, DC, MC, V. Daily noon–1:30pm and 8–9:30pm. Closed Dec 25 and Jan 1. Take N433 9km (5⅔ miles) north of Lyon.

MODERATE

La Tassée 🍴 FRENCH   The chef here believes in serving good food at prices most people can afford, rather than dazzling with frills. La Tassée serves huge portions of anything from strips of tripe to game. Favorites include quenelles of *brochet* (pike) with lobster sauce, and sautéed chicken with drizzles of vinegar, served with freshly made pasta. The dining room is appointed with noteworthy frescoes painted in 1951, when the restaurant opened.

20 rue de la Charité. ☎ **04-72-77-79-00.** www.latassee.fr. Main courses 16€–30€; fixed-price menus 28€–78€. AE, MC, V. Sept–June Mon–Sat noon–2pm and 7–10pm; July–Aug Mon–Fri noon–2pm and 7–10pm. Métro: Bellecour.

Le Bistrot de Lyon TRADITIONAL LYONNAIS   One of the largest and busiest restaurants in town was established in 1974. It incorporates at least four dining rooms, velvet banquettes, mirrors, and mosaics. The harried staff rushes amiably through the place, hauling giant platters. The kitchen showcases the recipes that

BEAUCOUP BOCUSE

A resurgence of interest in chef Paul Bocuse swept across Lyon when Bocuse bought **Brasserie le Nord ★**, 18 rue Neuve, de Mon Plaisir (℃ **04-78-27-29-34**), where he had worked as a teenager. Its prices (20€–30€ for a main course) signaled that the last of the great chefs had finally decided to go for the mass market. It's one of the most popular places in Lyon for traditional Lyonnais cuisine. A short while later, Bocuse opened a clone of Le Nord, **Brasserie le Sud,** 11 place Antonin Poncet (℃ **04-78-42-82-41**), where the culinary venue celebrates all points south (including Provence and, to a lesser degree, French-speaking North Africa) with a Mediterranean-inspired diet that includes tagines and couscous, and a color scheme of vivid blues and yellows. In 1998, he endorsed the opening of **Brasserie de l'Est,** 14 place Jules-Ferry (℃ **04-37-24-25-26**), a large,

bustling place offering Pan-French cuisine and a noisy and animated ambience that evokes the *brasseries de gare* of faraway Paris. And, finally, the Bocuse empire rounded out the four directions of the compass with the establishment of its final bistro, **La Brasserie de l'Ouest,** 1 Quai du Commerce (℃ **04-72-29-12-82**). Actually, its venue is more like the wild, wild American West (that is, California) than you may have expected. There's a hint of Pacific Rim cuisine here, and its layout is described as "American style" with an open kitchen, wide-open vistas, and a bustling kind of theatricality. Each of the five is open for lunch and dinner daily. The latest to open is **La Brasserie d'Argençon,** 40 allée Pierre de Coubertin (℃ **04-72-73-72-73**), adjacent to the town's biggest soccer stadium, La Stade Gerland.

made Lyon famous, with "soul food" dishes that include *salade Lyonnais, pot-au-feu,* crispy pigs' trotters, snails in puff pastry, fried steaks with garlic sauce, and a succulent and spicy version of steak tartare.

64 rue Mercière. ℃ **04-78-38-47-47.** www.bistrot-de-lyon.com. Main courses each 16€; fixed-price lunch 17€, dinner 27€. AE, MC, V. Daily noon–2:30pm and 7pm–midnight. Métro: Cordelier.

INEXPENSIVE

Brasserie Georges ★ 🍴 FRENCH/LYONNAIS   With prices that are reasonable, a historic core that, for a restaurant, is almost unbeatable, and a list of Lyonnais classics that residents travel in from the suburbs for, this is one of the must-visit restaurants of Lyon. It's the oldest in Lyon (founded in 1836), and probably the largest in Europe (with 450 seats). Turn-of-the-20th-century French poet Lamartine still owes the restaurant 40 francs for a meal he consumed 100 years ago. If you thrill to nest where the proud and mighty have already nested, you can ask specifically for a table that is identified with a plaque as having hosted Ernest Hemingway, the Lumière brothers, Edith Piaf, Rodin, Jean-Paul Sartre, or Jules Verne. Other more recent guests have included the Dalai Lama and former president Jacques Chirac. Specialties include standing roast beef, prepared for two diners at a time; snails in garlic butter; heaping platters of smoked salmon; hearty stews whose ingredients (veal, game, fish, shellfish) tend to change with the seasons; and pepper steaks.

30 cours Verdun, Perrache. ✆ **04-72-56-54-54.** www.brasseriegeorges.com. Main courses 13€–27€; fixed-price menus 19€–24€. AE, DC, MC, V. Daily 11:30am–11:15pm (until 12:15am Fri–Sat). Closed May 1. Métro: Perrache.

Café des Fédérations 🍴 TRADITIONAL FRENCH   This is one of the busiest bistros in Lyon, and sometimes the most amusingly raucous. Catering to the office-worker crowd, it's operated with panache by a team of hardworking employees who would probably perform beautifully in the trenches of a war zone. The fixed-price menus offer a selection of appetizers, main courses, and desserts. Each evokes old-time Lyonnais cuisine at its least pretentious, with such options as a green salad with bacon and croutons; eggs *en meurette* (poached in red wine); pork chops; *andouillettes* (chitterling sausages) served with *gratin dauphinois* (potato croquettes); and several other kinds of sausage, usually with *pommes de terre* (a potato gratin dish with cream and garlic).

8 rue Major-Martin. ✆ **04-78-28-26-00.** Reservations recommended. Fixed-price lunch 19€, dinner 24€. V. Mon–Sat noon–2pm and 8–9:30pm. Closed 1 week in Jan. Métro: Hôtel-de-Ville.

Lyon After Dark

This cosmopolitan hub offers many entertainment and culture options. At any newsstand, pick up a copy of the weekly guide *Lyon-Poche,* which lists happenings and venues around town, from bars to classical concerts.

For the theater or opera buff, Lyon's **Théâtre des Célestins,** place Célestins (✆ **04-72-77-40-00**), is the premier venue for comedy and drama; and the **Opéra,** place de la Comédie (✆ **08-26-30-53-25**), always has a lively and diverse season. **Halle Tony Garnier,** 20 place Antonin Perrin (✆ **04-72-76-85-85**), originated as a 19th-century food market. The immense space with excellent acoustics is known for concerts, trade fairs, and temporary art exhibitions.

The best pub in town is the **Smoking Dog,** 16 rue Lainerie (✆ **04-78-28-38-27**), a happy neighborhood bar with a mixed-age crowd.

The best of the former cargo boats parked on the Rhône is **Le Sirius,** Berges du Rhône, 4 quai Augagneur (✆ **04-78-71-78-71;** www.lesirius.com; Métro: Buillotière). A hot crowd under 35 packs the ship for dancing to the sounds of Lyon's best DJs on the lower-level floor. There's also an outdoor deck for fair weather. Sometimes big musical acts are booked here, at which time various cover charges will be imposed. It's open Tuesday through Saturday from 6pm to 3am.

As you may have expected in a city the size of Lyon, there are a scattering of busy and popular gay bars. Popular spots for men include **La Ruche,** 22 rue Gentil, 2e (✆ **04-78-37-42-26;** Métro: Cordelier), and **Le Forum,** 15 rue des Quatres Chapeaux, 2e (✆ **04-78-37-19-74;** Métro: Cordelier), in the city's historic core.

One gay bar enjoying a certain vogue is **Le Domaine,** 9 rue du Jardin des Plantes (✆ **04-72-98-85-33;** www.ledomainebar.fr). Attracting a young, vibrant crowd, it's open daily 6pm to 3am.

THE BEAUJOLAIS COUNTRY ★★

The vineyards of Beaujolais start about 40km (25 miles) north of Lyon. This wine-producing region is small—64km (40 miles) long and less than 16km (10 miles) wide—yet it's one of the most famous in France. It's known throughout the world because of the Beaujolais wine craze that began in Paris some 30 years ago. In an average year, this region produces more than 190 million bottles of wine. Some 180 châteaux are scattered throughout this part of France. At many of them, you can sample and buy bottles of Beaujolais.

This region is a colorful and prosperous rural area, with vineyards on hillsides, cottages where the growers live, and historic houses and castles. It has been called the "Land of the Golden Stones," but don't expect architectural monuments.

Unlike Alsace, with its Route du Vin, the Beaujolais country doesn't have a defined route. You can branch off in any direction, stopping at whatever point or wine cellar intrigues you. Don't be worried about losing your way after meandering off the A6 superhighway. This is one of the easiest parts of eastern France to negotiate, with clear road signs. If you're in doubt, simply follow the signs to the region's capital and commercial center, Villefranche-sur-Saône.

If you're pressed for time, you can tie the highlights together in a one-way drive, beginning at the region's southern terminus, Villefranche-sur-Saône, known as **Villefranche,** which you can reach from A6 between Mâcon and Lyon. (If you're heading north to south, follow the drive in reverse order, beginning in Juliénas, also off A6.)

Start in Villefranche. After an excursion west on D38 to **Bagnols-en-Beaujolais,** return to Villefranche. From here, take the meandering D504 and D20, which make sharp bends toward the east en route to **St-Julien-sous-Montmelas.** From St-Julien, take D19 to **Salles-en-Beaujolais.** From Salles, take D62 and D19 to **Belleville-sur-Saône.** Then follow D37 and D68 to **Villié-Morgon.** From Villié-Morgon, take D68 and D266 to **Juliénas.**

Villefranche-Sur-Saone: Capital Of Beaujolais

Go to the **Office du Tourisme,** 96 rue de la Sous-Préfecture, not far from the marketplace (© **04-74-07-27-50;** www.villefranche-beaujolais.fr), for a booklet on the Beaujolais country. It includes a map and itineraries and lists the wine-tasting cellars open to the public. It also lists and details some 30 villages.

Bagnols-En-Beaujolais

To reach Bagnols from Villefranche, head west on D38.

WHERE TO STAY & DINE

Château de Bagnols-en-Beaujolais ★★★   This is lordly living on a grand scale. France's premier château hotel, this one-time Renaissance ruin has been restored by 400 artisans. It has been taken over by a British chain that owns such hotels as Lady Astor's former home, Cliveden, in England. As such, it attracts large numbers of British oenophiles. Antiques, paintings, and art, much from the 17th century, fill the mansion. The individually decorated guest rooms are sumptuous, with antique beds, period velvets, embroidered linen sheets, and down pillows; one unit is named for Mme. de Sévigné, who spent a restless night here in 1673. The bathrooms have tiled floors, brass fittings, and luxurious tubs. Although this place does have a pool, it's not for the young and restless—you won't find a gym or tennis courts. La Salle des Gardes serves elegant Continental fare.

Place du Chateau, Bagnols 69620. © **04-74-71-40-00.** Fax 04-74-71-40-49. www.chateaudebagnols. fr. 21 units. 460€–655€ double; from 655€–760€ suite. AE, DC, MC, V. **Amenities:** Restaurant; lounge; outdoor pool; room service. *In room:* TV, hair dryer, Wi-Fi (15€ per day).

St-Julien-Sous-Montmelas

This charming village is 11km (6¾ miles) northwest of Villefranche (take D504, then D20). Claude Bernard, the father of physiology, was born here in 1813. His small stone house—now the **Musée Claude-Bernard** (© **04-74-67-51-44**)—exhibits the scholar's mementos, instruments, and books. Except for March, the museum is open year round Wednesday to Saturday 2 to 6pm, Sunday 10am to noon and 2 to 6pm. Admission is 50€ for adults, 4€ for students, and 3€ for ages 10 to 16 (free 9 and under).

Salles-En-Beaujolais

Eglise de Salles Arbuissonnas ★ (© **04-74-03-40-88**) was begun in A.D. 1090 and completed in the 1700s. The religious hideaway is mostly Romanesque, with an occasional Gothic overlay, especially in its doorways. Connoisseurs of Romanesque architecture will love the golden ocher color of the limestone. Notice the Salle Capitulaire, where the capitals of columns from throughout the building's history are on display. The church is open May to September daily 9am to 6pm, and October to April daily 9am to 5pm. Admission is free. From St-Julien, take D19 a short distance to Salles.

Belleville-Sur-Saone

For an excellent dining experience, drive north from Salles on D19 and D62 to Belleville-sur-Saône.

WHERE TO DINE

Le Rhône au Rhin ★ MODERN FRENCH   This out-of-the-way restaurant lies (1km/⅔ mile north of the village of Belleville-sur-Saône) in a converted antique house as a refuge from the more congested regions. As you try the flavorful cuisine, you may surrender to the chef's escapist dream. The decor is contemporary and comfortable, outfitted in warm tones of brown and soft orange. Menu items change with the seasons, but may include terrine of foie gras, scallops, or farmer chicken with wild mushrooms. Salmon and crayfish also appear regularly on the menu.

10 av. du Port. © **04-74-66-16-23.** Reservations required. Main courses 18€–27€; fixed-price dinner 23€–40€; fixed-price lunch 17€. MC, V. Tues–Sun noon–2pm; Tues and Thurs–Sat 7–9pm.

Villie-Morgon

For another wine tour in the Beaujolais country, we suggest driving west from Belleville-sur-Saône on D37, and then north on D18 to Villié-Morgon. The village and the surrounding region contain around 250 wine producers. Their product, at its best, is usually judged among the best Beaujolais wines in France.

In the basement of the **Château de Fontcrenne,** immediately adjacent to the Hôtel de Ville, is the **Caveau de Morgon** (© **04-74-04-20-99;** www.morgon.fr). It assembles and "marries" a selection of the Villié-Morgon region's best wines into a well-respected brand name (Caveau de Morgon) whose savvy marketing benefits winegrowers and consumers alike. Whatever you do, don't use the word "blend" to describe this company's product; the word is usually received with something akin to horror. The cellar is open for tours and sales daily 10am to noon and 2 to 6:15pm (winter), 10am to 12:15pm and 2 to 7:15pm (summer). Admission is free. You'll pay a nominal charge—1€ per glass, 7€ per bottle—for wine you consume.

Julienas

Wines are also a reason to travel north on D266 and D68 to Juliénas. This village produces a full-bodied, robust wine. Go to the **Cellier de la Vieille Eglise** (*© 04-04-42-98*), an old church cellar, to sip the wine. A statue of Bacchus with some tipsy, scantily clad girlfriends looks on from what used to be the altar. It's open from Wednesday to Monday from 9:45am to noon and 2:30 to 6:30pm. The local farmers' and winegrowers' cooperative helps support this wine outlet. Admission is free, but expect to pay 6.50€ to 10€ per bottle, depending on the vintage.

ROANNE

390km (242 miles) SE of Paris; 87km (54 miles) NW of Lyon

This industrial town on the left bank of the Loire is a popular excursion from Lyon and Vichy because it's home to one of France's greatest three-star restaurants, the La Maison Troisgros (see "Where to Stay & Dine," below).

In a neoclassical mansion built at the end of the 18th century, **Musée Joseph-Déchelette,** 22 rue Anatole-France (*© 04-77-23-68-77*), showcases an exceptional collection of Italian and French earthenware from the 16th though 20th centuries, as well as Roanne earthenware. Hours are Wednesday to Monday 10am to noon and 2 to 6pm. On Sunday, the museum is open only in the afternoon, and on Saturday there is no noontime break. Admission is 4.50€ for adults, 2.50€ for students, free for ages 25 and under, and free for everyone on Wednesday afternoon.

Essentials

GETTING THERE Trains and some **buses** serve Roanne from nearby cities, notably Lyon; the train is a lot more convenient. By train, Roanne lies 3 hours from Paris and 1 hour and 10 minutes from Lyon; for information, call *© 08-92-35-35-35,* or visit www.voyages-sncf.com. If you're **driving,** follow N7 northwest from Lyon to Roanne. From Paris, follow A6 south to Nemours and continue southwest on N7.

VISITOR INFORMATION The **Office de Tourisme** is at Place Maréchal de Lattre-de-Tassigny (*© 04-77-71-51-77*; www.leroannais.com).

Where to Stay & Dine

La Maison Troisgros ★★★ FRENCH/LYONNAIS This Relais & Châteaux property is one of the top 10 restaurants in France. It attained that reputation in the 1950s and has since factored into the itineraries of globe-trotting foodies, visiting heads of state, and wealthy people touring the region. Come here with respect for the French *grande bourgeoisie* and the appeal of French culinary finesse. The place is too conservative and devoted to impeccably tailored service for anything radical or provocative.

Decorated in neutral colors and lined with contemporary artwork, the restaurant features superb cuisine at astronomical prices. The current keepers of the flame celebrate the bounty of the Lyonnais countryside. Some of the best dishes are sautéed foie gras served with marinated eggplant; oysters in turnips; sautéed frog legs with Satay; king prawns with truffles; and boned monkfish with herbs and butter. To finish the meal, ask for one of the region's best assortments of cheese or perhaps a praline soufflé.

The hotel also rents 16 traditionally furnished rooms; a double costs 195€ to 570€, each with free Wi-Fi.

Place Jean Troisgros, Roanne 42300. ✆ **04-77-71-66-97.** Fax 04-77-70-39-77. www.troisgros.com. Reservations required. Main courses 65€–150€; fixed-price menu 155€–195€; 90€ lunch. AE, DC, MC, V. Thurs–Mon noon–1:30pm and 7:30–9pm. Closed 2 weeks in Feb and 2 weeks in Aug.

Where to Stay & Dine Nearby

In the nearby village of **Le Coteau,** you'll find several worthy restaurants. These two are our favorites. To get there, take N7 3km (1¾ miles) south from the center of Roanne.

Auberge Costelloise ★★ FRENCH   This is the place to head when you can't afford the dazzling but expensive food at Troisgros. Chef Christophe Suchon provides what this region needs: an attractive restaurant with fine cuisine and reasonable prices. The restaurant is adjacent to the banks of the headwaters of the Loire, in a dining room ringed with paintings and wood paneling. Choose one of the fixed-price menus, which change weekly. The well-planned menu focuses on fish. *Daurade* (bream) comes in garlic-flavored cream sauce, crayfish is served with saffron-flavored potatoes and a Thai-inspired lemon grass, and red snapper is enhanced by Provençal pistou. You can order fine vintages of Burgundian wines by the pitcher.

2 av. de la Libération. ✆ **04-77-68-12-71.** Reservations required. Main courses 11€–32€; fixed-price lunch 19€–26€; fixed-price dinner 27€–53€. AE, MC, V. Wed–Sun noon–1:30pm and 7:45–9:30pm. Closed mid-July to mid-Aug.

Hôtel-Restaurant de Lys TRADITIONAL FRENCH   This *restaurant avec chambres* dates from around 1900, with many renovations and reconstructions since the turn of the millennium. Bedrooms are uncomplicated, contemporary, and well maintained, each with private bathroom, TV, and phone—a kind of afterthought for the well-prepared but reasonably priced cuisine that emerges steaming from the kitchens. Doubles, with breakfast included, cost from 78€ to 98€, including free Wi-Fi. Menu items focus on the tried-and-true repertoire of French classics, including baked goat's cheese on a base of braised leeks, smoked salmon, filet of sea wolf, and a confit of duckling with red berries.

133 av. de la Libération, Le Coteau 42120. ✆ **04-77-68-46-44.** Fax 04-77-72-23-50. www.hotel-des-lys. com. Reservations recommended. Main courses 12€–18€; set-price menus 17€–27€. AE, DC, MC, V. Mon–Fri noon–2pm; Mon–Sat 7–9:30pm. Closed 3 weeks in Aug.

PEROUGES ★★

464km (288 miles) SE of Paris; 35km (22 miles) NE of Lyon

Saved from demolition by a courageous mayor in 1909 and preserved by the government, this village of craftspeople (pop. 1,119) often attracts movie crews: *The Three Musketeers* (1973) and *Monsieur Vincent* (1948) were filmed here. However, films have not been made here since the 1970s, since French film production moved primarily to eastern Europe. The town sits on what has been called an "isolated throne," atop a hill northeast of Lyon.

Follow rue du Prince, once the main business street, to place des Tilleuls, at the center of which is the **Arbre de la Liberté (Tree of Liberty),** planted in 1792 to commemorate the Revolution. Nearby, in a 14th-century building, is the **Musée du Vieux-Pérouges,** place de la Halle (📞 **04-74-61-00-88**), displaying such artifacts as hand looms. It's open Easter to October daily 10am to noon and 2 to 6pm; off season, Saturday and Sunday 10am to noon and 2 to 6pm. Admission is 4€; free ages 11 and under. The price includes access to the museum and, through adjoining doors, to one of the finest houses in the village, the **Maison des Princes de Savoie,** with a watchtower (**La Tour de Guet**) and a replica of a 13th-century garden, the **Jardin de Hortulus.**

Wander through town, soaking in the atmosphere of a stone village that's remained virtually unchanged.

Essentials

GETTING THERE   It's easiest to **drive** to Pérouges, though the signs for the town, especially at night, are confusing. From Lyon, take route 84 northeast and exit near Meximieux.

VISITOR INFORMATION   The **Tourist Office** (**Syndicat d'Initiative,** Cité de Pérouges; 📞 **04-74-46-70-84;** www.perouges.org) lies adjacent to the entrance of this very small village.

Where to Stay & Dine

Ostellerie du Vieux-Pérouges ★★ 🏠   This is a treasure in a restored group of 13th-century timbered buildings. The Thibaut family runs a museum-caliber inn furnished with cupboards housing pewter plates, iron lanterns hanging from medieval beams, refectory dining tables, and stone fireplaces. The midsize to spacious guest rooms are completely up-to-date, with modern amenities, yet they have an old-fashioned atmosphere and style that recall medieval France.

The restaurant's food is exceptional, especially when accompanied by the local sparkling wine, Montagnieu, which has been compared to Asti Spumante. Specialties include Bresse chicken in morel-studded cream sauce, filet of carp stuffed *à l'ancienne* with pikeperch, and *panache Pérougien* (an omelet stuffed with creamed morels and served with shrimp and crayfish cream sauce). By far the best-selling dessert is a crepe known as a *galette pérougienne à la crème,* from a century-old secret recipe. After dinner, ask for a glass of Ypocras, a unique liqueur made from a recipe dating from the Middle Ages. Fixed-price menus range from 35€ to 62€.

Place des Tilleuls, Pérouges 01800. 📞 **04-74-61-00-88.** Fax 04-74-34-77-90. www.hostelleriedeperouges. com. 28 units. 124€–240€ double; 190€–290€ triple or quad. AE, MC, V. **Amenities:** Restaurant; bar; room service. *In room:* TV, hair dryer, Wi-Fi (in some; free).

BOURG-EN-BRESSE

425km (264 miles) SE of Paris; 61km (38 miles) NE of Lyon

The ancient capital of Bresse, this farming and business center on the border between Burgundy and the Jura offers fabulous food.

Essentials

GETTING THERE   Bourg-en-Bresse is accessible by **train** from Paris, Lyon, and Dijon. Fifteen TGV (fast) trains arrive from Paris's Gare de Lyon daily (trip time: 2

hr.). From Lyon (45–60 min.), 10 trains arrive per day. From Dijon (2 hr.), five trains arrive daily. For information, call ✆ **08-92-35-35-35,** or visit www.voyages-sncf. com. If **driving** from Lyon, take A42 or N83 for the 40-minute trip; from Dijon (2 hr.), follow A31 to Mâcon and take A40 to Bourg-en-Bresse.

VISITOR INFORMATION   The **Office de Tourisme** is at 6 av. Alsace-Lorraine (✆ **04-74-22-49-40;** www.bourg-en-bresse.fr).

Seeing the Sights

If you have time, visit the **Eglise Notre-Dame,** rue Notre-Dame, off place Carriat. Begun in 1505, it contains some finely carved 16th-century stalls. If you'd like to wander around town, check out the 15th-century houses on rue du Palais and rue Gambetta.

Monastère Royal de Brou ★   Art lovers will want to stop at the Eglise de Brou to see its magnificent royal tombs. One of the great artistic treasures of France, this Flamboyant Gothic monastery was built between 1506 and 1532 (the three cloisters btw. 1506 and 1512, the church btw. 1513 and 1532) for Margaret of Austria, the ill-fated daughter of Emperor Maximilian. Over the ornate Renaissance doorway, the tympanum depicts Margaret and her "handsome duke," Philibert, who died after he caught a cold on a hunting expedition. The nave and its double aisles are admirable. Look for the ornate rood screen, decorated with basket-handle arching. Ask a guide for a tour of the choir, which is rich in decorative detail; Flemish sculptors and local craftsmen made the 74 choir stalls of oak in just 2 years.

The tombs are the church's treasure. The Carrara marble statues are of Philibert and Margaret. Another tomb is that of Marguerite de Bourbon, mother of Philibert and grandmother of François I, who died in 1483. See also the stained-glass windows inspired by a Dürer engraving and an alabaster retable (altarpiece) depicting *The Seven Joys of the Madonna.* The monastery sometimes mounts expositions of modern art.

63 bd. de Brou. ✆ **04-74-22-83-83.** Admission to church, cloisters, and museum 7€ adults, 4.50€ students, free for children 17 and under. Mid-June to mid-Sept daily 9am–6pm; Apr to mid-June daily 9am–12:30pm and 2–6pm; Mid-Sept to Mar daily 9am–noon and 2–5pm. Closed Jan 1, May 1, Nov 1 and 11, and Dec 25.

Where to Stay

Hôtel du Prieuré ★   Erected in 1982, this is the town's most gracious hotel. The angular structure sits on .4 hectare (1 acre) of gardens surrounded by 500-year-old stone walls. This place is especially alluring in spring, when forsythia, lilacs, roses, and Japanese cherries fill the air with their perfume. Most guest rooms are large and tranquil, outfitted in Louis XV, Louis XVI, or French country style.

49–51 bd. de Brou, Bourg-en-Bresse 01000. ✆ **04-74-22-44-60.** Fax 04-74-22-71-07. www.hoteldu prieure.com. 14 units. 85€–105€ double. AE, MC, V. Free parking. **Amenities:** Room service. *In room:* TV, hair dryer, Wi-Fi (free).

Le Logis de Brou   This four-story property has landscaped grounds and is near the road fronting the church. Each comfortable guest room has reproductions of antique furniture, plus a small shower-only bathroom. Jacqueline and Gérard Roger run a fine inn and employ an especially helpful staff.

132 bd. de Brou, Bourg-en-Bresse 01000. ✆ **04-74-22-11-55.** Fax 04-74-22-37-30. www.logisdebrou.com. 30 units. 68€–78€ double. AE, MC, V. Free parking. **Amenities:** Bar. *In room:* TV, hair dryer, Wi-Fi (free).

Where to Dine

Auberge Bressane ★★ TRADITIONAL FRENCH   Bresse poultry is the best in France, and chef Jean-Pierre Vullin specializes in succulent *volaille de Bresse,* served five ways, including a delectable version in cream sauce with morels. You also may enjoy gâteau of chicken liver, fried frogs' legs with garlic and wild mushrooms, quenelles of pikeperch with shrimp, or sea bass with fresh basil, accompanied by regional wines such as Seyssel and Montagnieu.

166 bd. de Brou. ℂ **04-74-22-22-68.** Reservations recommended. Main courses 23€–48€; fixed-price menus 29€–52€. AE, DC, MC, V. Wed–Mon noon–2pm and 7:15–9:30pm.

Au Chalet de Brou ★★ TRADITIONAL FRENCH   You'll find flavorful and relatively inexpensive food at this unpretentious restaurant across from the village's most famous church. Specialties include a "cake" of chicken livers served with essence of tomato; quenelle of pikeperch with lobster sauce; frogs' legs in parsley sauce; and at least a half-dozen kinds of Bresse chicken, served with your choice of morel-flavored cream sauce, raspberry vinegar, or chardonnay sauce. Some purists (including us) opt for it simply grilled in order to appreciate the unadorned flavor of the bird in its own drippings. Dessert may be an apple tart presented, according to your choice, hot or semifrozen.

168 bd. de Brou. ℂ **04-74-22-26-28.** Reservations recommended. Main courses 17€–28€; fixed-price menu 21€–44€. AE, MC, V. Tues–Wed and Sat–Sun 7–10pm. Closed Mon, Thurs, Dec 20–Jan 15, and July 2–10.

VIENNE ★★

489km (304 miles) SE of Paris; 31km (19 miles) S of Lyon

Gastronomes know Vienne because it's the home of one of France's leading restaurants, La Pyramide. Even if you can't afford the haute cuisine, you may want to visit. It's a wine center and the southernmost Burgundian town.

Essentials

GETTING THERE   **Trains** connect Vienne with the rest of France. Some trips require a transfer in Lyon, 20 minutes away. For information, call ℂ **08-92-35-35-35,** or visit www.voyages-sncf.com. **Buses** from Lyon arrive about eight times a day, making many stops and taking about an hour; for information, contact Vienne's Gare Routière (ℂ **04-74-85-18-51**), adjacent to the railway station. The one-way bus or train fare from Lyon is 6€. If you're **driving** from Lyon, take N7 (which is more direct) or A7, an expressway that meanders along the banks of the Rhône.

VISITOR INFORMATION   The **Office de Tourisme** is at cours Brillier (ℂ **04-74-53-80-30;** fax 04-74-53-80-31; www.vienne-tourisme.com).

SPECIAL EVENTS   In the first 2 weeks of July, Vienne attracts some of the biggest names in jazz for the annual **Festival du Jazz à Vienne.** Tickets range from 29€ to 35€. You can get tickets and information from the **Théâtre Antique de Vienne,** 4 rue du Cirque (ℂ **04-74-78-87-87;** www.jazzavienne.com).

Seeing the Sights

Vienne contains many antique buildings, making it a *ville romaine et médiévale.* Near the center of town on place du Palais is the **Temple d'Auguste et de Livie,** built on the orders of the Roman emperor Claudius and turned into a "temple of reason" during the French Revolution. Another outstanding monument is the **Pyramide du Cirque Romain,** part of the Roman circus. Rising 16m (52 ft.), it rests on a portico with four arches and is sometimes called the tomb of Pilate.

Take rue Clémentine to the **Cathédrale St-Maurice ★★**, place St-Maurice (© 04-74-85-60-28), which dates from the 12th century and wasn't completed until the 15th. It has three aisles but no transepts. Its west front is built in the Flamboyant Gothic style, and inside are many fine Romanesque sculptures. The cathedral is open daily 8am to 5pm; admission is free.

In the south part of town is the **Eglise St-Pierre ★**, place St-Pierre (© 04-74-85-20-35). A landmark with origins in the 5th century, it's one of the oldest medieval churches in France. Inside, the **Musée Lapidaire** (© 04-74-85-20-35) displays architectural fragments and sculptures from excavations. The museum is open April to October Tuesday to Sunday 9:30am to 1pm and 2 to 6pm; January to March and November and December Tuesday to Friday 9:30am to 12:30pm and 2 to 5pm, Saturday and Sunday 1:30 to 5:30pm. Admission is 2.70€ for adults, 1.90€ for students, and free for children 17 and under. The museum is closed January 1, May 1, November 1, November 11, and December 25.

A **Roman Theater (Théâtre Romain) ★**, 7 rue du Cirque (© 04-74-85-39-23), has been excavated east of town at the foot of Mont Pipet. Theatrical spectacles were staged here for an audience of thousands. You can visit September and October Tuesday to Sunday 9:30am to 1pm and 2 to 6pm; January to March and November and December Tuesday to Friday 9:30am to 12:30pm and 2 to 5:30pm, Saturday and Sunday 1:30 to 5:30pm; and April to August daily 9:30am to 1pm and 2 to 6pm. Admission is 6€ for a day pass.

If you have about an hour for a side trip, in Hauterives, south of Vienne, you'll find one of the world's strangest pieces of architecture. The **Palais du Facteur Cheval,** or **Palace of the Mailman Cheval** (© 04-75-68-81-19; www.facteur cheval.com), the lifelong work of French postman Ferdinand Cheval, is built of stone and concrete and elaborately decorated, often with clamshells. It's an eccentric palace of fantasy and a tribute to the aesthetic value, or mania, of the individual. The work was finished in 1912, when Cheval was 76. Admission is 5.40€ for adults, 4.40€ students, and 3.90€ for children 6 to 16. The palace is open in July and August daily 9:30am to 12:30pm and 1:30 to 7pm; April, May, June, and September daily 9:30am to 12:30pm and 1:30 to 6:30pm; February, March, October, and November daily 9:30am to 12:30pm and 1:30 to 5:30pm; and December and January 1 to January 14 daily 9:30am to 12:30pm and 1:30 to 4:30pm.

Where to Stay

La Pyramide (see below) also offers rooms.

Hostellerie Beau-Rivage   A Relais du Silence property, this place originated around 1900 as a simple inn that served food and wine to fishermen who traveled from Lyon to the well-stocked waters of this section of the Rhône. It has evolved into a stylish, nostalgic enclave. The rooms are well furnished; some are larger than you may expect. Most come with a tub/shower combination.

The Rhône passes by the dining terrace. The traditional cuisine is exceptional. Try quenelles of pike; stuffed brochet with new potatoes; and delicious suprême of pigeon on a platter with confit of pigeon, roasted foie gras, and turnips. The Côtes du Rhône wines complement the food well. Fixed-price menus range from 38€ to 82€.

2 rue du Beau-Rivage, Condrieu 69420. ℘ **04-74-56-82-82.** Fax 04-74-59-59-36. www.hotel-beau rivage.com. 30 units. 135€–160€ double; 230€–250€ suite. DC, MC, V. From Vienne, cross the Rhône on N86 and head south 12km (7½ miles); pass through Condrieu and, on the southern outskirts, look for signs on the left. **Amenities:** Restaurant. *In room:* A/C, TV, hair dryer, minibar, Wi-Fi (free).

Where to Dine

La Pyramide ★★★ MODERN FRENCH   This is the area's premier place to stay or dine, and for many it's the preferred stopover between Paris and the Riviera. The restaurant perpetuates the memory of a superb chef, Fernand Point, who died in 1955. Through the continuing efforts of Patrick Henriroux, many of Point's secrets, especially his sauces, have been preserved. Menus change seasonally, but the cuisine is always imaginative. Examples include watercress and zander soup garnished with braised endive; roast duck, wild mushrooms, and liqueur-soaked grapes; and John Dory wrapped in Parma ham, with soya-flavored endive and Tabasco-flavored sabayon. The cheese platter is wonderful, and desserts are as artfully caloric, and as stylish, as anything else in the Rhône Valley.

The hotel offers 25 charming, air-conditioned guest rooms, each with minibar, TV, and dataport. Doubles go for 200€ to 240€, suites for 390€ to 420€. Free Wi-Fi is included in all accommodations.

14 bd. Fernand-Point, Vienne 38200. ℘ **04-74-53-01-96.** Fax 04-74-85-69-73. www.lapyramide.com. Reservations required. Main courses 48€–80€; fixed-price menu 158€–195€. AE, DC, MC, V. Thurs–Mon 12:30–1:30pm and 7:30–9:30pm. Closed Feb and 1 week in mid-Aug.

Les Saveurs du Marché FRENCH   This bustling, high-turnover, and slightly rowdy restaurant is known to many of the hardworking laborers of Vienne, who come here for inexpensive lunchtime meals, and for slightly more leisurely and more intricate food at night. Within a 10-minute walk south of the town center, the blue-and-white dining room reflects, so its owners say, the colors of southern France. Along one wall is a massively paneled bar. Menu items change with the seasons and the availability of raw ingredients, but may include a delectable soufflé of pikeperch with fresh mussels, a salad of warm goat cheese, pheasant stew with wild mushrooms, and a savory casserole of spicy scallops and crayfish. Expect good value and a sense of cheerful informality.

34 cours de Verdun. ℘ **04-74-31-65-65.** Reservations recommended. Main courses 16€–20€. Fixed-price lunch 14€; fixed-price dinner 18€–37€. DC, MC, V. Mon–Fri noon–1:45pm and 7:30–9:30pm. Closed mid-July to mid-Aug.

VALENCE ★

671km (417 miles) SE of Paris; 100km (62 miles) S of Lyon

Valence stands on the left bank of the Rhône between Lyon and Avignon. A former Roman colony, it later became the capital of the Duchy of Valentinois, set up by Louis XII in 1493 for Cesare Borgia. Today, Valence is a market town and distribution point for Rhône Valley fruit and vegetable producers. It's fitting that François Rabelais, who wrote of gargantuan appetites, spent time here as a student.

Visitors can climb the ruined château atop the white stone **Mont Crussol.** The ruins date from the 12th century. Valence is still the home of the Arsenal, one of France's oldest gunpowder factories.

The major sight is the **Cathédrale St-Apollinaire,** place de Ormeaux (© **04-75-43-13-32**), consecrated by Urban II in 1095 and much restored since. Built in the Auvergnat-Romanesque style, the cathedral is on place des Clercs in the center of town. The choir contains the tomb of Pope Pius VI, who died a prisoner here in the 18th century. It's open daily from 8am to 7pm.

Adjoining the cathedral is the **Musée Municipal,** 4 place des Ormeaux (© **04-75-79-20-80**), noted for its nearly 100 red-chalk drawings by Hubert Robert done in the 18th century. It's open June to September Tuesday to Saturday 10am to noon and 2 to 6:45pm, and Sunday 2 to 6:45pm; and October to May Tuesday to Sunday 2 to 5:45pm. Admission is 4.60€ adults, 2.30€ students, and free for children 15 and under. The museum is currently closed but will reopen sometime in 2012.

Essentials

GETTING THERE **Trains** run from Lyon, Grenoble, and Marseille. For information, call © **08-92-35-35-35.** If you're **driving** from Lyon, take A7 south. From Grenoble, follow E711 to outside the town of Voreppe, go southwest along E713, and follow W532 into Valence. From Marseille, follow A7 north.

VISITOR INFORMATION The **Office de Tourisme** is at 11 bd. Bancel (© **08-92-70-70-99;** fax 04-75-44-90-41; www.tourisme-valence.com).

Where to Stay & Dine

Hôtel-Restaurant Pic ★★★ FRENCH   This is the least known of France's great restaurants, although it ranks among the top 10. The cooking and the wine list (featuring regional selections such as Hermitage, St-Péray, and Côtes du Rhône) are exceptional. The villa has a courtyard and a dining room with big tables and ample chairs. Chef Anne-Sophie Pic has been called a fireball in the kitchen, bringing modern (often Asian) touches to classical dishes. Her appetizers, such as chicken skewered on twigs of aromatic rosemary, are a delight. For a main dish you may select such dishes as sea bass with caviar; delightful scallops imported from Brittany; duck liver from Landes with black truffles; or a classic tournedos of beef Charolais. Pic pays special attention to fresh vegetables, including fava beans and baby spinach. The desserts are rapturous, from grapefruit sorbet to cold orange soufflé. Menu items change every 3 weeks.

The on-site brasserie, **Le 7** (© **04-75-44-53-86**), serves more affordable regional food without a lot of culinary fuss. Pic also rents 15 individually decorated guest rooms. They cost 250€ to 400€ for a double, 440€ to 890€ for a suite.

285 av. Victor-Hugo. © **04-75-44-15-32.** Fax 04-75-40-96-03. www.pic-valence.com. Reservations required in restaurant. Restaurant: set lunch 110€–320€; set dinner 195€–320€. MC, V. Tues–Sat noon–1:30pm and 7:30–9:30pm. Brasserie: set lunch Mon–Fri 28€, set dinner 30€; main courses 10€–22€. Daily 12:30–2:30pm and 8–10pm. Closed: Jan.

THE ARDECHE ★★★

The Ardèche occupies the eastern flank of the Massif Central (see chapter 22), a landscape of jagged, much-eroded granite-and-limestone highlands. Although it

THE GRAND CANYON OF FRANCE

The ebbs and flows of the Ardèche, France's fastest-flowing river, have created the Grand Canyon of France. Littered with alluvial deposits, strewn in ravines whose depth can exceed 285m (935 ft.), the river's final 58km (36 miles), before the waters dump into the Rhône, is one of the country's most unusual geological areas. A **panoramic road (D290)** runs along a rim of these canyons, providing views over an arid landscape of grasses, trees, hardy shrubs, and some of the most distinctive deposits of granite, limestone, and basalt in Europe.

The beautiful driving route, which you can traverse in a few hours even if you stop for sightseeing (follow signs directing you along well-marked footpaths), stretches north to south between the towns of Vallon-Pont-d'Arc and Pont St-Esprit. The meandering corniche roads are a challenge. Beware of other vehicles weaving frighteningly as drivers and passengers admire the scenery and snap photos.

defines itself as Le Midi—its southern border lies less than 40km (25 miles) from Avignon and 48km (30 miles) from Nîmes—its culture and landscape are more rooted in the rugged uplands of France's central highlands.

Through its territory flow the streams and rivers that drain the snow and rain of the Massif Central. They include rivers such as the Ligne, Fontolière, Lignon, Tanargue, and, most important, Ardèche. They flow beside, around, and through rocky ravines, feudal ruins, and stone-sided villages perched in high-altitude sites originally chosen for ease of defense in medieval times.

The most famous and visited section of the Ardèche is its southern extremity, with granite-sided ravines 300m (984 ft.) deep, gouged by millions of springtime floodings of the Ardèche River—no wonder it's called the Grand Canyon of France. This area draws thousands of tourists, often with their children, who take driving tours along the highways flanking the ravines.

We recommend that you stop in the southern Ardèche to admire the gorges only briefly. It's better to spend the night in the less touristy northern reaches. The northern Ardèche, in the 45km (28 miles) of hills and valleys separating the hamlets of Vals-les-Bains and Lamastre, is a soft and civilized wilderness, with landscapes devoted to grape growing, shepherding, and hill trekking. One writer described **Vallon-Pont-d'Arc,** the gateway to the gorges, as a Gallic version of Gatlinburg, Tennessee. For your overnight stop, we suggest you continue north to the more picturesque towns of Vals-les-Bains or Lamastre.

If you want to kayak in the gorges, go between early April and late November, when the waters are green and sluggish and safer than they are during the winter and spring floods. In Vallon-Pont-d'Arc, you'll find at least three dozen rental agencies for everything from plastic kayaks to horses. One of the best, **Aventure Canoës,** place du Marché (B.P. 27), Vallon-Pont-d'Arc 07150 (© **04-75-37-18-14;** www.aventure-canoes.fr), rents canoes and kayaks. A 3-hour *mini-descente* costs around 14€ per person for use of a canoe or kayak. The ride will take you along a 6.5km (4-mile) route from Vallon-Pont-d'Arc to the downstream hamlet of Chames.

A full-day *grande descente* along the 31km (19-mile) downstream route from Vallon-Pont-d'Arc to St-Martin d'Ardèche costs around 20€ per person. A 2-day trip by canoe or kayak costs 30€ per person. Prices include transport by minivan back to Vallon-Pont-d'Arc at the end of the ride. Lunch is not included, so bring your own. Picnic fixings are available at dozens of bakeries and delicatessens near each point of origin.

Despite the appeal of kayaking, most travelers stick with driving along the upper summits of the gorges.

Vals-Les-Bains

43km (27 miles) W of Montélimar; 138km (86 miles) SW of Lyon

In a depression of the valley of the Volane River, Vals-les-Bains is surrounded by about 150 springs whose existence was discovered around 1600. Scientists have never understood why each spring contains a different percentage of minerals: Most contain bicarbonate of soda, some are almost tasteless, and one—La Source Dominique—has such a high percentage of iron and arsenic that it's poisonous. Waters from Dominique are piped away from the town; others are funneled into a Station Thermale adjacent to the town's casino.

In the park outside the Station Thermale, a *source intermittante* erupts, Old Faithful style, to a height of around 7.5m (25 ft.) every 6 hours or so. Small crowds gather for eruptions usually at 5:30, 11:30am, 5:30, and 11:30pm.

The Belle Epoque **Casino de Vals-Les-Bains** (☎ **04-75-88-77-77**), avenue Expilly, is open Friday and Saturday noon to 3am; admission is free. The only casino between Lyon and Aigues-Mortes, it's mobbed on weekends by locals playing roulette or the slot machines, the only options offered. The bistro-style theme restaurant, **Le Venetian,** is open Wednesday to Saturday 7:30 to 11pm and Sunday noon to 3pm.

Other than the scenery, the town's most unusual site is about 23km (14 miles) south, beside the highway to Privas. The 16th-century entrance gate of a ruined feudal château stands here. The views over the confluence of two ravines and the valley are worth the detour.

WHERE TO STAY

Grand Hôtel des Bains This is the largest and best hotel in town. The central wing was built in 1870 in anticipation of a visit from Empress Eugénie. Alas, Eugénie, finding she was comfortable in the nearby resort of Vichy, canceled her visit. The hotel has a cordial staff and well-maintained, conservatively furnished rooms, most with both tub and shower.

3 montée de l'Hôtel-des-Bains, Vals-les-Bains 07600. ☎ **04-75-37-42-13.** Fax 04-75-37-67-02. www. hotel-des-bains.com. 65 units. 73€–110€ double; 134€–160€ suite. AE, DC, MC, V. **Amenities:** Restaurant; bar; outdoor pools; room service; Wi-Fi (free). *In room:* TV, hair dryer.

WHERE TO DINE

Restaurant Mireille TRADITIONAL FRENCH This tiny (26-seat) restaurant occupies a space below vaulted stone ceilings that for centuries sheltered a herd of goats. Known for its earthy warmth, Mireille serves an ambitious menu of carefully crafted cuisine. Choices range from local mousse of flap mushrooms with scallops to filet of turbot with white butter. The chef also smokes his own salmon and makes his own foie gras.

3 rue Jean-Jaurès. ⓒ **04-75-37-49-06.** Reservations recommended. Main courses 12€–18€; fixed-price menus 15€–31€. AE, MC, V. Sept–June Thurs-Tues noon–2pm; Thurs–Sat and Mon 7–9pm; July–Aug daily noon–2pm and 7–9:30pm. Closed 1 week in Feb and 1 week in Nov.

Lamastre

42km (26 miles) N of Vals-les-Bains; 30km (19 miles) W of Valence

Many connoisseurs of Ardèche architecture view Lamastre as the most unaltered and evocative village in the district. Its most important site is its church, in Macheville, the upper part of the village. Built of pink Romanesque stone, it encompasses portions that date from the 12th century, and it's a frequent site of weddings. Most visitors use the town as a base for nature walks and hikes through the surrounding hills and valleys. A series of brown-and-white signs marks each trail.

WHERE TO STAY & DINE

Château d'Urbilhac ★ Its history is rich and illustrious, and if you ask them, the congenial owners (Sylvie and Claude Aillaud) of this massive stone palace will recite dates, names, and conflicts that date from France's wars of religion during the 16th century. For nearly 30 years, this high-altitude château and its 30 hectares (74 acres) of forest functioned as an upscale hotel with an equally upscale restaurant, but today, things have been scaled back to family-friendly proportions, and meals are available only to residents and their invited guests. One of the high points is the pool, a 24m-long (80-ft.) watery rectangle that overlooks the valley of the River Doux, far below. Bedrooms are high ceilinged, rather formal, and furnished with 19th- and early-20th-century antiques. The Aillaud family also rents two houses, one with one bedroom, the other with four, as part of long-term rentals for families and groups of friends who want to spend a significant block of time within the region.

Rue de Vernoux, Lamastre 07270. ⓒ **04-75-06-42-11.** Fax 04-75-06-52-75. www.chateaudurbilhac.fr. 10 units. 130€–200€ double. Rates include breakfast. Dinner 38€ extra per person. MC, V. From the center of Lamastre, drive for 2km (1¼ miles) southeast along Rte. de Vernoux-en-Vivarois. **Amenities:** Restaurant; bar; bicycle rental; outdoor pool; sauna; tennis court. *In room:* A/C, TV, Wi-Fi (in some; free).

THE FRENCH ALPS

No part of France has more dramatic scenery than the Alps; the western ramparts of the mountains and their foothills are truly majestic. From the Mediterranean to the Rhine, they stretch along the southeastern flank of France. The skiing here is the best in Europe. Some resorts are legendary, such as Chamonix–Mont Blanc, the capital of Alpine skiing, with its 19km (12-mile) Vallée Blanche run. Mont Blanc, at 4,810m (15,780 ft.), is the highest mountain in western Europe.

Most of this chapter covers the area known as the Savoy (Savoie), taking in the French lake district and the largest Alpine lake, Lac Léman (Lake Geneva).

From January to March, skiers flock to Chamonix–Mont Blanc, Megève, Val d'Isère, and Courchevel 1850; from July to September, spa fans head to Evian-les-Bains and Aix-les-Bains. Grenoble, the capital of the French Alps, is the gateway. Grenoble lies 30 minutes by car from the Grenoble–St-Geoirs airport, 40 minutes from the Lyon-Satolas international airport, and 90 minutes from Geneva's Cointrin airport. The city is connected to the Paris-Lyon-Marseille motorway on the west and to the Chambéry-Geneva motorway on the east.

EVIAN-LES-BAINS ★★★

576km (358 miles) SW of Paris; 42km (26 miles) NE of Geneva

On the château-dotted southern shore of Lac Léman (Lake Geneva), Evian-les-Bains is one of the leading spa resorts in France. Its lakeside promenade, lined with trees and lawns, has been fashionable since the 19th century. Evian's waters became famous in the 18th century, and the first spa buildings were built in 1839. Bottled Evian is considered useful in everything from baby formula to salt-free diets and is seen as a treatment for gout and arthritis.

In the days when Marcel Proust came to enjoy the Belle Epoque grandeur, Evian was the haunt of the very rich. Proust modeled his "Balbec baths" on Evian's. Today, the spa, with its promenade and elegant casino, attracts a broader range of guests—it's not just for the rich anymore.

The French Alps

In addition to its **spa buildings,** Evian holds an imposing **Ville des Congrès (Convention Hall)** that has earned the resort the title of "City of Conventions." From late April to September, the **Nautical Center** (✆ **04-50-75-02-69**) on the lake is a popular attraction; it has a 115m (377-ft.) pool with a diving stage, solarium, restaurant, bar, and children's paddling pool.

The major excursion from Evian is a boat trip on Lake Geneva offered by the **Compagnie Générale de Navigation (CGN),** a Swiss outfit whose agent is in Evian. Call the port office directly at ✆ **04-50-70-73-20.** A round-trip ticket from Evian to Lausanne in Switzerland costs 23€, 12€ for children. Contact the company or head for the Office de Tourisme (see "Visitor Information," below) for other prices

Driving the Route des Grandes Alpes

Evian can be a starting point for the 741km (460-mile) drive to Nice along the **Route des Grandes Alpes ★★★**. One of Europe's great drives, it links Lake Geneva with the Riviera, crossing 35 passes along the way. Leaping from valley to valley, it's open from end to end only in summer (many passes are closed in winter).

You can make the drive in 2 days, but why hurry? The charm of this journey involves stopping at scenic highlights along the way, including Chamonix, Megève, and Val d'Isère. The most dramatic pass is the **Galibier Pass (Col du Galibier)**, at 2,645m (8,678 ft.), which marks the dividing line between the northern and southern parts of the French Alps.

En route to Nice, you'll pass to such towns as St-Veran (1,959m/6,427 ft.), the highest community in Europe; Entrevaux, once a fortress town marking the border between Upper Provence and the Alps; and Touet-sur-Var, a village filled with tall, narrow houses constructed directly against the towering rocky slope.

and hours. If you want to see it all, you can tour both the Haut-Lac and the Grand-Lac. The most popular trip is the crossing from Evian to Ouchy-Lausanne, Switzerland (the port for Lausanne), on the north side.

Crescent-shaped **Lake Geneva (Lac Léman)** is the largest lake in central Europe. Covering about 362 sq. km (140 sq. miles), the lake is formed by the Rhône River and is noted for its exceptional blue color.

Essentials

GETTING THERE   The best way to approach Evian-les-Bains by **train** from the French Alps is to the gateway city of Annecy. (Many trains from other parts of France and Switzerland require transfers to the railway junction of Bellegarde.) The one-way fare from Annecy is 15€. For train information and schedules, call ✆ **36-35** or 08-92-35-35-35.

Popular **ferries (CGN)** leave Geneva from quai du Mont-Blanc, at the foot of the rue des Alpes, or from Le Jardin Anglais. From May 28 to September 21, one ferry a day departs Geneva at 9am, arriving in Evian at 11:45am. The return trip leaves Evian at 5:50pm daily and reaches Geneva at 8:45pm. A first-class, one-way ticket costs 49€, a second-class ticket 36€. For ferry information and schedules, call ✆ **0848/811-848** or 04-50-70-73-20, or visit www.cgn.ch.

If you're **driving** from Geneva (trip time: 50 min.), take N5 east along the southern rim of the lake. From Paris, take A6 south. Before Mâcon, you'll see signs pointing to the turnoff for Thonon-Evian. From Thonon, N5 leads to Evian. Trip time is about 5½ hours, which can vary depending on traffic.

VISITOR INFORMATION   The **Office de Tourisme** is on place d'Allinges (✆ **04-50-75-04-26;** fax 04-50-75-61-08; www.eviantourism.com).

Taking the Waters at Evian

The clear, cold waters at Evian, legendary for their health and beauty benefits, attract a clientele that possesses both the time and the money to appreciate them.

The most luxurious way to immerse yourself in the resort's hydro-rituals is to check into either of these hotels, both of which maintain private spa facilities open only to well-heeled guests: **Hôtel Royal,** boulevard de Royal, or **Hôtel Ermitage,** avenue du Léman (contact for both ✆ **04-50-26-85-00;** www.royalparcevian. com). They offer the most expensive packages and are adept at pampering patrons' bodies, souls, and egos.

More reasonably priced are the spa facilities at **Les Thermes Evian,** place de la Libération (✆ **04-50-75-02-30;** www.lesthermesevian.com). This public spa is adjacent to Débarcadère (the dock), just uphill from the edge of the lake. The hotel spas are more likely to emphasize beauty regimes and stress therapies; the public facility offers a broader range of services, including tanning, massage, and skin and beauty care (but no facilities for overnight guests).

You can indulge yourself with a daylong *thermale,* which provides access to exercise rooms and classes, saunas, steam baths, water from the Evian springs, and two massage sessions. Depending on the program you select, you will spend 55€ to 165€. You can also spend up to 130€ extra per day on additional massage, health, and beauty regimes. The spa is open Monday to Saturday, usually from 9am to 7pm.

Where to Stay

The **Hôtel-Restaurant Le Bourgogne** (see below) also rents rooms.

Hôtel de la Verniaz et ses Chalets ★★★   This glamorous country house, owned by the Verdier family, stands on a hillside with a view of woods, water (Lac Léman), and the Alps. The antique-filled rooms are in either the main house or one of the separate chalets; the chalets have their own gardens and more privacy but cost a small fortune. Throughout the hotel, you'll find comfortable, even plush, accommodations. Main courses in the hotel restaurant run from 25€ to 30€; fixed-price menus, 25€ to 75€.

Avenue D'Abondance, à Neuvecelle Eglise, Evian-les-Bains 74500. ✆ **800/735-2478** in the U.S. and Canada, or 04-50-75-04-90. Fax 04-50-70-78-92. www.verniaz.com. 36 units. 107€–292€ double; 269€–370€ suite; 285€–610€ chalet. AE, DC, MC, V. Closed mid-Nov to mid-Feb. **Amenities:** Restaurant; bar; babysitting; outdoor pool; room service; 2 tennis courts. *In room:* TV, hair dryer, minibar, Wi-Fi (free).

Where to Dine

Hôtel-Restaurant Le Bourgogne ★ TRADITIONAL FRENCH   Come here for a delectable meal, impeccable service, an attractive setting, and excellent wine. Featured regional wines are Crépy and Rousette. Menu choices in the restaurant are likely to include the house version of foie gras, beef served with morels or a peppercorn sauce, and a poached version of *omble chevalier* (tiny local whitefish) with whiskey sauce. You'll also find robust portions of cassoulet, terrine of oxtail or salmon, *magret* of duckling with orange, and steak.

The inn also offers 30 comfortable rooms with TVs for 71€ to 98€ double.

73 rue Nationale, Evian-les-Bains 74500. ✆ **04-50-75-01-05.** www.hotel-evian-bourgogne.com. Reservations required. Main courses 19€–25€; fixed-price menu 12€–46€. AE, DC, MC, V. Tues–Sun noon–2pm; Tues–Sat 7-10pm. Closed Jan.

Evian-Les-Bains After Dark

In the town center on the south bank of Lake Geneva is the **Casino Royal Evian,** domaine du Royal Club Evian (✆ **04-50-26-87-87;** www.casino-evian.fr). It's popular with the Swiss from across the lake. It offers blackjack, baccarat, and roulette and has more than 250 slot, roller, and video-poker machines. Jackets for men are preferred. The Jackpot Restaurant and Bar is open until the casino closes. Hours Monday to Friday are 10am to 2am (until 3am Sat–Sun).

ANNECY ★★★

538km (334 miles) SE of Paris; 56km (35 miles) SE of Geneva; 140km (87 miles) E of Lyon

Lac d'Annecy is the jewel of the Savoy Alps. The resort of Annecy, which is the region's capital, makes the best base for touring the Haute-Savoie. Once a Gallo-Roman town, the seat of the *comtes* de Genève, Annecy opens onto one of the best views of lakes and mountains in the French Alps. Since the 1980s, Annecy has become a booming urban center that has managed to preserve its natural setting. In summer, its lakefront promenade is crowded and active.

Essentials

GETTING THERE If you're **driving,** Annecy is near several highways: From Paris, take A6 southeast to Beaune and connect with A6/N6 south to Mâcon-Nord. Then follow A40 southeast to Seyssel, connecting with N508 going southeast to Annecy. Allow at least 5 hours. From Geneva, follow A40W to St. Julien and take RN201 south toward Annecy. Trip time is 30 minutes.

A car is useful but not essential in the Alps. Annecy has rail links with Paris and Lyon. Nine **trains** arrive daily from Lyon (trip time: 5 hr.), a one-way fare costing 22€ to 40€. About six trains daily arrive from Paris's Gare de Lyon (trip time: around 5 hr., transfer at Lyon or Bellegarde); the fare is 77€ to 96€ one-way. For information, call © **36-35** or 08-92-35-35-35.

There's also a nearby **airport** (© **04-50-27-30-06**) in the hamlet of Meythet (Aéroport Annecy-Haute-Savoie-Mont-Blanc), with service on Air France from Paris's Orly airport.

VISITOR INFORMATION The **Office de Tourisme** is at 1 rue Jean-Jaurès (© **04-50-45-00-33;** fax 04-50-51-87-20; www.lac-annecy.com).

Seeing the Sights

Built around the river Thiou, Annecy has been called the Venice of the Alps because of the canals that cut to the old part of town, **Vieil Annecy.** You can explore the arcaded streets where Jean-Jacques Rousseau arrived in 1728.

After seeing Annecy, consider a trek to the **Gorges du Fier ★★** (© **04-50-46-23-07;** www.gorgesdufier.com), a dramatic river gorge 9.5km (6 miles) to the west. To reach it, take a train or bus from Annecy's rail station to Poisy. From the station, go about 1.5km (1 mile), following the clearly marked signs. This striking gorge is one of the most interesting sights in the French Alps. A gangway takes you to a gully 3 to 10m (10–33 ft.) wide, cut through the rock by torrents of water; you'll hear the roar of the river at the bottom. Emerging from this labyrinth, you'll be greeted by a huge expanse of boulders. You can visit the gorge from June 15 to September 10 daily 9:30am to 7:15pm (last trip at 6:25pm), and from March 15 to June 14 and September 11 to October 15 daily 9:30am to 6:15pm (last trip at 5:25pm). The site is closed to the public October 16 to March 14. A hike to its well-signposted depths

The Office de Tourisme (see above) distributes free pamphlets that describe about a dozen easy, family-oriented hiking and biking excursions in the forests around Annecy. More experienced hikers may wish to pick up a free map with a detailed set of challenging walks.

Walks in both categories last 2 to 6 hours. Some begin in the center of Annecy; others require a trip by car or bus from one of several towns in the area—such as Saint-Jorioz or Sevrier, to the west, or Talloires, to the east—to the excursion's origination point. A travel agency in Annecy, **Agence Crolard,** place de la Gare (✆ **04-50-51-74-62**), sells bus tickets to the destinations around Annecy and Lac d'Annecy and Lac Léman. It also arranges excursions by minibus to sites of panoramic interest in July and August (✆ **04-50-45-00-56** for information about these excursions).

takes less than an hour and costs 4.90€ for adults, 2.70€ for children 7 to 15; it's free for kids 6 and under.

You can also take a cruise on the ice-blue lake for which the town is famous. Tours of **Lac d'Annecy,** conducted from February to December, last an hour and cost 12€. An English-speaking guide points out the sights. Tours depart between one and six times a day, depending on the season. Inquire at the Office de Tourisme (see above), or call the **Compagnie des Bateaux du Lac d'Annecy** (✆ **04-50-51-08-40;** www.annecy-croisieres.com).

Château de Montrottier Within walking distance of the gorges, in the hamlet of Montrottier, is the 13th- and 14th-century Château de Montrottier. A one-time feudal citadel partially protected by the rugged geology around it, the château's tower offers a panoramic view of Mont Blanc. A small museum features items collected by a local dilettante, showcasing pottery, Asian and African costumes, armor, tapestries, and lace antiques, as well as some bronze bas-reliefs from the 16th century.

Lovagny 74330. ✆ **04-50-46-23-02.** www.chateaudemontrottier.com. Admission 7€ adults, 6.20€ students, 4.50€ children 7-15, free for children 6 and under. Mar 15-May 31 Wed-Mon 2-6pm; June-Aug daily 2-7pm; Sept Wed-Mon 2-6pm; Oct daily 2-6pm.

Le Palais de l'Ile This is the town's most potent and most frequently photographed visual symbol. Built before the 18th century and connected to the "mainland" of Annecy via a bridge, it resembles a miniature château, surrounded by water, despite its long-term use as a prison (and certainly a very cold one) for local malefactors.

3 passage de l'Ile. ✆ **04-50-33-87-30.** Admission 3.50€ adults, 1.20€ students and persons 12-25, free for children 11 and under. June-Sept daily 10:30am-6pm; Oct-May Wed-Mon 10am-noon and 2-5pm.

Musée Château d'Annecy This forbidding gray-stone monument, whose 12th-century pinnacle is known as the Queen's Tower, dominates the resort. The château contains a museum of regional artifacts that include Alpine furniture, religious art, oil paintings, and modern works. One section is devoted to the geology and marine life of the region's deep, cold lakes.

Place du Château. ✆ **04-50-33-87-30.** Admission 4.80€ adults, 2.20€ ages 12-25, free for children 11 and under. June-Sept daily 10:30am-6pm; Oct-May Wed-Mon 10am-noon and 2-5pm.

Where to Stay

La Maison de Marc Veyrat (see "Where to Dine," below) also rents rooms.

Au Faisan Doré ☺ Near the casino at the end of a tree-lined lakefront boulevard, this government-rated three-star hotel is 2 minutes on foot from the lake and Imperial Park. Owned by the Clavel family since 1919, it's a member of the Logis de France chain, which caters to families. The public and private rooms are decorated in the style of the Haute-Savoie region—wooden overhead beams, rustic country furniture, and unpainted wood walls. Each guest room is cozy and comfortable but not extravagant. The chef serves four different fixed-price menus in the adjacent restaurant, costing from 20€ to 48€.

34 av. d'Albigny, Annecy 74000. ② **04-50-23-02-46.** Fax 04-50-23-11-10. www.hotel-aufaisandore. com. 40 units. 72€–88€ double. AE, DC, MC, V. Parking 10€. Closed Dec 20–Feb 1. **Amenities:** Restaurant; bar. *In room:* TV.

Hôtel du Nord ⚓ A government-rated two-star hotel in the center of Annecy, minutes from the train station and Lac d'Annecy, the continually renovated du Nord is one of the town's better bargains. Guests appreciate the modernity of the soundproof rooms; 20 come with showers only, others with tub and shower. The helpful staff speaks English and can direct you to reasonably priced restaurants nearby. Breakfast is the only meal served.

24 rue Sommeiller, Annecy 74000. ② **04-50-45-08-78.** Fax 04-50-51-22-04. www.annecy-hotel-du-nord.com. 30 units. 68€–89€ double. MC, V. *In room:* A/C (in some), TV, dataport.

Hôtel La Demeure de Chavoire ★★ One of the most charming accommodations in the area is at Chavoires, about 3km (1¾ miles) east of Annecy. It's intimate and cozy, decorated with well-chosen Savoy antiques. Large doors lead to the gardens overlooking the lake. The guest rooms have names rather than numbers, and each is uniquely decorated with wood beams. Thoughtful service makes this a deserving selection, and it's more tranquil than the hotels in the center of Annecy. The staff will direct you to nearby restaurants.

71 rte. d'Annecy, Veyrier-du-Lac 74290. ② **04-50-60-04-38.** Fax 04-50-60-05-36. www.demeure dechavoire.com. 13 units. 126€–195€ double; 225€–275€ suite. AE, DC, MC, V. Parking 10€. From Annecy, follow signs to Chavoires and Talloires. **Amenities:** Bar; tearoom; babysitting; room service; spa. *In room:* TV, hair dryer, minibar, Wi-Fi (free).

Where to Dine

La Maison de Marc Veyrat ★★★ MODERN FRENCH Famous throughout France for owner Marc Veyrat-Durebex's excellent and unusual cuisine, this world-class and horrendously priced restaurant occupies a romanticized version of a Savoyard château at the edge of a lake in the village of Veyrier-du-Lac, 1.5km (1 mile) south of Annecy. Guests dine in a posh room with ceiling frescoes.

The chef has been dubbed *l'enfant terrible* of upscale Alpine cuisine. He offers a unique dining experience, marked by an almost ritualistic etiquette. Fortunately, the waitstaff advises you on the order in which the meal and its components are designed to be eaten. For example, a "declination of local cheeses," consisting of three large ravioli, each stuffed with a different cheese—a mild cow cheese, a pungent goat cheese, and a very strong blue—is eaten in ascending order of strength. Other choices include ravioli of vegetables, flavored with rare mountain herbs gathered by

M. Veyrat-Durebex and his team; pikeperch sausage; crayfish poached with bitter almonds; and poached sea bass with caviar. Desserts include a miniature chestnut cake served with essence of truffles. The wine list is excellent.

The *auberge* rents 11 expensive and beautifully furnished rooms. Rates are 260€ to 670€ for a double; a suite costs from 695€ to 880€.

13 vieille rte. des Pensières, Veyrier-du-Lac 74290. © **04-50-60-24-00.** Fax 04-50-60-23-63. www. marcveyrat.fr. Reservations required. Main courses 75€–134€; fixed-price dinner 475€. AE, DC, MC, V. Sat–Sun noon–1:30pm; Wed–Sun 7:30–9pm. Closed Nov to mid-June. From Annecy's lakefront boulevard, follow signs to Veyrier-du-Lac, Chavoires, and Talloires.

Le Belvédère FRENCH/SEAFOOD   This is one of the most appealing reasonably priced restaurants in town. On a belvedere above Annecy, about 1.5km (1 mile) west of the town center, it provides views that extend up to 8km (5 miles) over mountains and lakes. Menu items include a salad of Breton lobster with freshwater crayfish and strips of foie gras; a platter containing scallops and red mullet with shellfish-flavored butter sauce; and an unusual pairing of foie gras with a purée of figs and vanilla-flavored bourbon sauce. Dessert may be a selection of tropical-flavored sorbets.

The 10 simple guest rooms are much less opulent than the restaurant. Rooms go for 110€ to 145€ double.

7 chemin du Belvédère, Annecy 7400. © **04-50-45-04-90.** www.belvedere-annecy.com. Reservations recommended. Main courses 16€–40€; fixed-price menus 28€ (lunch only) and 42€–85€ dinner. AE, MC, V. Thurs–Tues 12:15–1:30pm; Mon and Thurs–Sat 7:30–9:30pm. Closed Jan. From downtown Annecy, follow signs leading uphill to Le Semnoz.

Le Clos des Sens ★★ FRENCH/SAVOYARD   The charm of this restaurant derives from its inspired cuisine, based on local ingredients, and its decor, salvaged from several Savoyard chalets. At street level is a contemporary bar; in the upstairs dining room, the food is elaborate, savory, and geared to the cold climate. The best examples include consommé of shrimp studded with chunks of firm crayfish meat; filets of fera (a Lac d'Annecy fish) that are partially smoked, partially marinated; spit-roasted suckling pig served with polenta; and a dessert specialty of caramelized fennel served with tarragon-flavored ice cream. The establishment maintains comfortable, cozy bedrooms, each with cable TV and minibar (but oddly, no phone), priced from 180€ to 230€.

13 rue Jean-Mermoz, Annecy-le-Vieux. © **04-50-23-07-90.** www.closdessens.com. Reservations recommended. Main courses 25€–40€; fixed-price lunch Wed–Fri 33€, dinner 48€–100€. AE, DC, MC, V. Wed–Sat noon–1:30pm; Tues–Sat 7:30–9:30pm. Closed Jan 1–15, May 1–8, and Sept 1–15.

Annecy After Dark

In the old town, you'll find bars, cafes, pubs, and (in warmer months) street dances, fairs, and even carnivals. A calmer alternative is an evening of theater or dance at the **Théâtre d'Annecy,** 1 rue Jean-Jaurès (© **04-50-33-44-00;** www.bonlieu-annecy. com); tickets cost 15€ to 50€.

If a long day has left you thirsty, try the traditional Irish pub, **Le Captain Pub,** 11 rue Pont-Morens (© **04-50-45-79-80**), with hearty ales on tap. **Le Vieux Necy,** 3 rue Filaterie (© **04-50-45-01-57**), attracts a younger, more boisterous crowd.

The best piano bar in town is **Le Duo,** 104 av. de Genève (© **04-50-57-01-46**). It's ideal for quiet conversation. Annecy's most visible and popular gay bar is the

Happy People Disco, 48 rue Carnot (✆ **04-50-51-08-66**), where both locals and visitors dance the night away.

For the most elegant evening on the town, head to the **Casino de l'Impérial,** 33 av. d'Albigny (✆ **04-50-09-30-00**), part of the Belle Epoque–style Impérial Palace hotel on a peninsula jutting into Lac d'Annecy. Entrance to the gaming rooms is free; you must present a passport. The casino is open Sunday to Thursday noon to 2am, and Friday and Saturday noon to 4am.

TALLOIRES ★★

551km (342 miles) SE of Paris; 32km (20 miles) N of Albertville; 13km (8 miles) S of Annecy

The charming village of Talloires, which dates from 866, is old enough to appear on lists of territories once controlled by Lothar II, great-grandson of Charlemagne. Chalk cliffs surround a bay, and at the lower end a promontory encloses a port. An 18-hole golf course, **Golf Club du Lac d'Annecy** (✆ **04-50-60-12-89;** www. golf-lacannecy.com), and watersports such as boating, swimming, water-skiing, and fishing make this a favorite vacation spot. Talloires also has one of France's great restaurants, Auberge du Père-Bise, and a Benedictine abbey founded in the 11th century, now the deluxe Hôtel de l'Abbaye.

Essentials

GETTING THERE From Annecy, you can reach Talloires by **driving** south along N508 for 13km (8 miles). There are about eight daily **buses** from Annecy to Talloires, which take 35 minutes. In Talloires, buses stop in front of the post office. For bus information, call Autocars Frossard in Annecy (✆ **04-50-45-73-90**).

VISITOR INFORMATION The **Office de Tourisme** is on rue André-Theuriet (✆ **04-50-60-70-64;** fax 04-50-60-76-59; www.talloires.fr).

Where to Stay

Auberge du Père-Bise and **La Villa des Fleurs** (see below) also rent rooms.

Hôtel de l'Abbaye ★★ This 16th-century Benedictine monastery has been a hotel since the French Revolution. It's one of the grand inns of the Alps. With close-up views of the lake, it makes for a memorable stop. It doesn't equal the cuisine or the luxury of the Auberge du Père-Bise (see below), but then again, it's a lot more affordable. The hotel is rich with beamed ceilings, antique portraits, leather chairs, gardens, and carved balustrades. The great corridors lead to converted guest rooms, of which no two are alike. The furnishings include all the Louis periods as well as Directoire and Empire. In summer, the restaurant expands onto a shaded lakefront terrace. Overall, this is an extremely pleasant escape from urban life.

Chemin des Moines, Talloires 74290. ✆ **04-50-60-77-33.** Fax 04-50-60-78-81. www.abbaye-talloires. com. 33 units. 150€–320€ double; 345€–620€ suite. AE, DC, MC, V. Closed Nov 17 to mid-Feb. **Amenities:** Restaurant; bar; babysitting; room service; sauna; spa. *In room:* TV, minibar, Wi-Fi (free).

Where to Dine

Auberge du Père-Bise ★★★ FRENCH Since the 1950s, when it attracted starlets and millionaires (when being a millionaire actually meant something), Auberge du Père-Bise has radiated style and charm. A chalet built in 1901 and renovated many times since, it's one of France's most acclaimed—and expensive—restaurants. In fair weather you can dine under a vine-covered pergola and enjoy the view of mountains and the lake. The kitchen excels at dishes such as mousse of foie gras, layered potatoes with truffles and foie gras, delicate young lamb, and gratin of crayfish tails.

The inn also offers 34 air-conditioned guest rooms with minibars, TV, and free Wi-Fi (free). Rates are 240€ to 400€ for a double and 580€ to 680€ for a suite. Reserve at least 2 months in advance, especially in summer.

Rte. du Port, bord du Lac, Talloires 74290. © **04-50-60-72-01.** Fax 04-50-60-73-05. www.perebise. com. Reservations required. Main courses 38€–100€; fixed-price menu 76€–175€. AE, DC, MC, V. Daily noon–2pm and 7–9pm. Closed mid-Nov to mid-Feb.

La Villa des Fleurs ⚓ TRADITIONAL FRENCH This *restaurant avec chambres* should be better known, because it's the best place in Talloires for the price. Proprietors Marie-France and Charles Jaegler serve wonderful meals, which often include *salade landaise* with foie gras, and filet of fera (a Lac d'Annecy fish) with sage sauce. The dining room overlooks the water.

Eight simply furnished rooms with minibars and Victorian-era decor are at the top of a winding staircase—there's no elevator. Doubles cost 98€ to 135€.

779 rte. du Port, Talloires 74290. © **04-50-60-71-14.** Fax 04-50-60-74-06. www.la-villa-talloires.com. Reservations required. Main courses 22€–54€. AE, MC, V. Tues–Sun noon–2pm; Tues–Sat 7–9pm.

AIX-LES-BAINS ★★★

535km (332 miles) SE of Paris; 34km (21 miles) SW of Annecy; 16km (10 miles) N of Chambéry

On the eastern edge of Lac du Bourget, modern Aix-les-Bains is the most fashionable (and largest) spa in eastern France. The hot springs, which provided comfort to the Romans, are said to be useful for treating rheumatism.

Essentials

GETTING THERE Some 20 **trains** per day arrive from Paris (trip time: 4 or 5 hr.); the one-way fare is 74€ to 90€. Ten daily trains pull in from Annecy (trip time: 30 min.; one-way fare: 7.10€–10€). For information and schedules, call © **36-35** or 08-92-35-35-35. For information on **bus** routes in and around the French Alps, including the status of service from Nice to Aix, call the Gare Routière in Chambéry (© **04-79-69-11-88**). If you're **driving** to Aix-les-Bains from Annecy, follow RN 201 south.

VISITOR INFORMATION The **Office de Tourisme** is on place Maurice-Mollard (© **04-79-88-68-00;** fax 04-79-88-68-01; www.aixlesbains.com).

Seeing the Sights

Aix is well equipped for visitors, with flower gardens, a casino (the Palais de Savoie), a racecourse, a golf course, and Lac du Bourget, which has a beach. **Thermes d'Aix-les-Bains** (© **04-79-35-38-50;** www.thermaix.com) lies in the center of town, near the casino, the Temple of Diana, and the Hôtel de Ville (town hall). Closer to the lake, a string of flower beds and ornamental shrubs border the town's waterside promenades, where you can take a lovely stroll.

Steamboats take visitors on a beautiful 4-hour **boat ride** on Lac du Bourget. The trip travels most of the length of the Canal de Savière (which links the lake with the Rhône) between early February and mid-December, daily or four times a week, depending on the season. Prices for boat rides range from 14€ to 15€. For departure times, which change almost weekly throughout the season, contact the ferry operator, **Les Bateaux d'Aix** (☎ **04-79-63-45-00**). Boats depart from the piers of Grand Port, 3km (1¾ miles) northwest of the center. You can also take a bus ride from Aix to the town of **Revard,** at 1,524m (5,000 ft.), which affords a panoramic view of Mont Blanc. For information, contact **Trans Savoie** (☎ **04-79-68-32-90**).

Abbaye d'Hautecombe ★★   This is the spiritual centerpiece of the French Alps and the mausoleum of many princes of the House of Savoy. It was built by a succession of monks, beginning in the 1100s, from the Cîteaux, Cistercian, and Benedictine orders. The abbey stands on a promontory over the western edge of Lac du Bourget, almost directly across the water from Aix-les-Bains. Before the 1500s, at least 40 members of the royal family of the Savoy were buried here.

After years of neglect, the church was reconstructed and embellished during the 19th century by Charles-Felix, king of Sardinia, in the Troubadour Gothic style. The fervently religious ecumenical community (Communaute du Chemin Neuf) occupying the abbey organizes seminars, welcomes short- and medium-term devotees, and perpetuates the site's tradition of worship. Pilgrims are welcome to attend daily Mass at noon.

Self-guided half-hour tours with recorded narration, in English and French, depart at 6-minute intervals during open hours. You can drive to the abbey or take a 30-minute boat ride. Four steamers per day leave the landing stage at Aix-les-Bains; the round-trip fare is 13€ for adults and 8€ for children 11 and under.

St-Pierre de Curtille 73310. ☎ **04-79-54-58-80.** Tours 3€, free for ages 17 and under. Wed–Mon 10am–noon and 2–5pm.

Musée Faure   This is the town's most interesting museum, with a modern-art collection that includes sculptures by Rodin and works by Degas, Corot, and Cézanne. It's on a hill overlooking the lake and the town.

10 bd. des Côtes. ☎ **04-79-61-06-57.** Admission 4.60€ adults, 2.30€ students, free for children 15 and under. Wed–Mon 10am–noon and 1:30–6pm (Nov–Feb Wed–Sun).

Where to Stay

Hostellerie Le Manoir ★   This architecturally interesting site—a 19th-century stable until the present owners transformed it into a hotel—includes paths weaving to turn-of-the-20th-century gardens with outdoor furniture under shade trees. The decor in the midsize-to-spacious guest rooms is old-fashioned—with antique and provincial furniture—yet up-to-date, each different from its neighbors. The government rates the Ariana (see below) higher because of its superior facilities, but the Manoir has more French charm and personality. You can order breakfast or dinner on a terrace bordering the garden. Most of the public and guest rooms open onto terraces.

37 rue Georges-1er, Aix-les-Bains 73105. ☎ **04-79-61-44-00.** Fax 04-79-35-67-67. www.hotel-lemanoir. com. 73 units. 99€–169€ double; 179€ suite. AE, DC, MC, V. Parking 8.50€. **Amenities:** Restaurant; bar; exercise room; hammam; Jacuzzi; indoor pool; room service; sauna. *In room:* TV, hair dryer, Wi-Fi (free).

Hôtel Mercure Ariana ★★   The Ariana caters to a spa-oriented crowd that enjoys quiet walks in the surrounding park. The loggia-dotted glass exterior opens into an Art Deco interior highlighted by metal, wood, and fabrics; plenty of white marble; and antique reproductions. Tunnel-like glass walkways connect the hotel's sports facilities to its main core. The guest rooms come in a range of sizes and styles, each comfortable and well appointed. Café Adelaïde is both a cafe and a restaurant.

111 av. de Marlioz, à Marlioz, Aix-les-Bains 73101. © **04-79-61-79-79.** Fax 04-79-61-79-00. www. mercure.com. 60 units. 100€–144€ double. AE, DC, MC, V. **Amenities:** Restaurant; bar; babysitting; bike rentals; health club; indoor pool; room service; sauna; 2 nearby tennis courts. *In room:* A/C, TV, hair dryer, minibar, Wi-Fi (free).

Where to Dine

Brasserie de la Poste FRENCH   Since the mid-1960s, from a position in the heart of town, immediately across from the railway station and the post office, this cozy brasserie has served bountiful, cost-conscious meals to office workers, day laborers, and commuters. The interior is outfitted in tones of dark bordeaux and hardwood paneling, waiters are attentive and hardworking, and food is doled out in generous portions. Long-standing specialties include choucroute, slabs of buttery foie gras, cheese-laden *fondues Savoyardes,* frogs' legs in garlic butter, pepper steaks with french fries, and sautéed crayfish.

32 av. Victoria. © **04-79-35-00-65.** Main courses 9€–21€; fixed-price menus 12€–31€. AE, DC, MC, V. Tues–Sun noon–2:30pm; Tues–Sat 7–10pm.

Restaurant du Casino Grand Cercle (Koupol') FRENCH   No other setting in Aix-les-Bains provides as rich an environment as this Beaux Arts restaurant in the town casino. For a taste of glamour and glitter in a beautiful place, it's one of the most enjoyable experiences in town. The restaurant occupies a corner of the area reserved for blackjack and roulette, giving diners a close-up view of the gamblers testing their luck. The food is not elaborate; the menu offers conservative but flavorful dishes of veal, beef, and chicken, with a scattering of terrines, soups, and salads. A passport is required for visitors to enter the casino. The slots are open Sunday to Thursday 11am to 3am, and Friday and Saturday 11am to 4am; the gaming rooms are open Tuesday to Thursday 8pm to 3am, and Friday and Saturday 8pm to 4am. This site can also be your after-dark choice, as the compound includes a nightclub, Club Casino; a pub, Murphy's; and a piano bar, Le Colisée.

Rue du Casino. © **04-79-35-16-16.** Reservations recommended. Fixed-price menu 12€–21€. AE, DC, MC, V. Daily noon–2pm and 7–11pm.

GRENOBLE ★★★

567km (352 miles) SE of Paris; 55km (34 miles) S of Chambéry; 103km (64 miles) SE of Lyon

The ancient capital of the Dauphine, Grenoble is the commercial, intellectual, and tourist center of the Alps. It's a major stop for travelers, including those driving between the Riviera and Geneva.

A sports capital in winter (it hosted the 1968 Winter Olympic Games) and summer, it attracts many foreign students; its university has the largest summer-session program in Europe. Founded in 1339, the University of Grenoble has a student body of some 50,000. The city (pop. 405,000) is also home to four other universities with a large contingent of English and American students, giving the city a cosmopolitan air.

Essentials

GETTING THERE   An important rail and bus junction, Grenoble is easily accessible from Paris and all the cities in this chapter. About 11 **trains** per day arrive from Paris Gare de Lyon (trip time: 3½ hr.); the one-way fare is 74€ to 97€. Trains arrive almost every hour from Chambéry (trip time: 30 min.; one-way fare is 10€). For information, call ☎ **36-35** or 08-92-35-35-35.

Until 2004, Grenoble's airport accepted Air France flights from Paris and the rest of Europe. But when Air France transferred all of its inbound flights to nearby Lyon, air traffic to the airport in Grenoble virtually dried up. Flights arrive to Grenoble from London and Bristol (England). **EasyJet** and **British Airways** fly in only September to April, but **Ryanair** also flies in summer. For more information contact Grenoble's **Aéroport Grenoble-Isère** (☎ **04-76-65-48-48**), 41km (25 miles) northwest of the city center. A shuttle bus meets every flight and takes passengers to and from Grenoble's center; the cost is 4.10€ each way. A taxi (☎ **04-76-65-46-18**) to the town center costs 70€ to 100€.

For information on flying into Lyon, see chapter 14. **Satobus** (☎ **04-72-68-72-17** or 04-76-27-89-29) meets most flights at the Lyon airport and takes passengers to Grenoble. Travel time is an hour; the fare is 20€ each way, 15€ students, and 10€ ages 4 to 12.

If you're **driving,** take A6 from Paris to Lyon, and then continue on A48 into Grenoble. Depending on conditions, the drive should take 6 to 7 hours.

VISITOR INFORMATION   The **Office de Tourisme** is at 14 rue de la République (☎ **04-76-42-41-41;** fax 04-76-00-18-98; www.grenoble-isere-tourisme.com). For information about public transportation in Grenoble, call ☎ **04-76-20-66-66.**

Seeing the Sights

Grenoble lies near the junction of the Isère and Drac rivers. Most of the city is on the south bank of the Isère, though its most impressive monument, the **Fort de la Bastille,** stands on a rocky hilltop on the north bank. A cable car will carry you from the south bank across the river to the top of the fort. The center of Grenoble's historic section is the **Palais de Justice** and **place St-André.** The more modern part of town is southeast, centered on the contemporary **Hôtel de Ville** (town hall) and the nearby **Tour Perret.**

Begin at **place Grenette,** where you can enjoy a drink or an espresso at a cafe. Don't miss the **place aux Herbes** and the **place St-André,** in the very heart of the *centre ville.* Place St-André, dating from the Middle Ages, is the most evocative square in old Grenoble, with the Palais de Justice on one side and the Eglise St-André on the other. The Palace of Justice was built in many stages. The brick church went up in the 13th century. Two great streets for strolling and browsing are rue de la Poste, in the medieval core, and rue J.-J.-Rousseau, a 5-minute walk southwest of the city.

Enjoy a ride on the **Téléphérique-Grenoble-Bastille** (☎ **04-76-44-33-65;** www.bastille-grenoble.fr), cable cars that take you over the banks of the Isère River and its valley. Check the website for the cable car's operating hours, which vary by day and month. A round-trip ticket costs 6.50€ for adults, 5€ for students, and 4€ for ages 5 to 18. It's closed for a period during the month of January (btw. 4 days and 2 weeks). At the belvedere where you land, you'll have a view of the city, the mountains, and the remains of the Fort de la Bastille. Come for the view, not the fort. You can walk up in an hour or so if you're an Olympic athlete; the beginning of the route is signposted to the west of place St-André. We suggest you take the *téléphérique* to the top, and then stroll down along the footpath, Montée de Chalmont, that winds to Alpine gardens and past old ruins before reaching a cobblestone walk that leads to the old town.

Musée Dauphinois ★ Housed in the 17th-century convent Ste-Marie-d'en-Haut and enhanced by the convent's cloister, gardens, and baroque chapel, this museum lies across the Isère in the Ste-Marie-d'en-Haut section of town. A collection of ethnographic and historical mementos of the Dauphine region is on exhibit, along with folk arts and crafts. This place is a quick course on life in the Alps: No other museum gives such a detailed view of the people. Furnishings, tools, artifacts, and replicas of Alpine settings are on display. Check out the special exhibition on skiing, tracing the development of the sport from its origins to the 21st century's high-tech innovations.

30 rue Maurice-Gignoux. ℂ **04-57-58-89-01.** www.musee-dauphinois.fr. Free admission. June–Sept Wed–Mon 10am–7pm; Oct–May Wed–Mon 10am–6pm. Closed Jan 1, May 1, and Dec 25.

Musée de Grenoble ★★★ Founded in 1796, this is one of the country's oldest art museums. It was the first French museum outside of Paris to focus on modern art, a fact appreciated by Picasso, who donated his *Femme Lisant* in 1921. The collection includes Flemish and Italian Renaissance works, but the Impressionist paintings generate the most interest. Note Matisse's *Intérieur aux aubergines* and Léger's *Le Remorqueur*. Ernst, Corot, Klee, Bonnard, Gauguin, Monet—they're all here. On display are a number of older paintings and sculptures, along with artifacts and relics from Greek, Egyptian, and Roman times, including a well-preserved mosaic. The artistic highlight is a sculpted door panel from the 1400s, depicting Jacob and his sons. A collection of 20th-century sculptures occupies the François Mitterrand Esplanade and the Albert Michallon Park surrounding the museum.

5 place de Lavalete. ℂ **04-76-63-44-44.** www.museedegrenoble.fr. Admission 5€ adults, 3€ seniors and students, free for children 17 and under. Free for everyone on 1st Sun of each month. Wed–Mon 10am–6:30pm.

Where to Stay

Hôtel d'Angleterre Tulip Inn Grenoble In the center of town, this hotel features tall windows and wrought-iron balconies, and opens onto a pleasant square with huge chestnut trees. The stylish salons boast wood-grained walls and ceilings and tropical plants. Some guest rooms look out on the Vercors Massif. Most of the small to midsize units are comfortably furnished and come with shower-only bathrooms; some have Jacuzzi tubs. Breakfast is the only meal served.

5 place Victor-Hugo, Grenoble 38000. ℂ **04-76-87-37-21.** Fax 04-76-50-94-10. www.hotel-angleterre-grenoble.com. 62 units. 110€–185€ double. AE, DC, MC, V. Free parking. **Amenities:** Room service. *In room:* A/C, TV, hair dryer, minibar, Wi-Fi (free).

Hôtel Trianon Few other hotels in town have masked a banal 1950s design so effectively. Here, historical decorative styles do the trick. The rooms are cramped but cozy, furnished in just about every Louis style; in a handful, the decor evokes a folkloric grange in the Alps. The midsize bathrooms are equipped with showers, and some have tubs as well. A comfortable, well-managed hotel, Trianon caters to business travelers during the week, so rates drop on weekends. You'll find this hotel a short walk south of the pedestrian-only district in the town center, near a well-known school, the Lycée Champollion.

3 rue Pierre-Arthaud, Grenoble 38000. ℂ **04-76-46-21-62.** Fax 04-76-46-37-56. www.hotel-trianon. com. 38 units. 59€–82€ double. AE, MC, V. Parking 7€. **Amenities:** Bar; room service. *In room:* TV, Wi-Fi (free).

Park Hôtel Concorde ★★ This is the most opulent and prestigious hotel in Grenoble, a government-rated four-star legend that welcomes most of the important politicians and entertainment-industry moguls who visit the region. On the lower four floors of a mid-1960s tower mostly devoted to private condominiums, it's a short drive south of Grenoble's commercial center and close to City Hall. Each guest room is decorated differently, with a blend of dignified (sometimes antique) furniture, state-of-the-art lighting, and modern upholstery.

10 place Paul-Mistral, Grenoble 38027. © **04-76-85-81-23.** Fax 04-76-46-49-88. www.park-hotel-grenoble.fr. 50 units. 245€–360€ double; from 450€ suite. AE, DC, MC, V. Parking 16€. Tram: A to Chavant. **Amenities:** Restaurant; bar; babysitting; room service. *In room:* A/C, TV, hair dryer, minibar, Wi-Fi (free).

Where to Dine

Auberge Napoleon ★★★ FRENCH No other restaurant in France boasts as intense an association with Napoleon Bonaparte, but that's less important to diners than the fact that the restaurant is the finest in the Grenoble area. In 1815, Napoleon spent the night here at the beginning of a 100-day reign that ended with his defeat by Wellington at the Battle of Waterloo. You'll find enough subtle references to the history of France, from the Revolution to around 1820, to keep a student of French history busy throughout the superb meal. The restaurant seats only 23, in a plush, manicured dining room with upholstered walls and about 20 contemporary floral still lifes by renowned Grenoblois artist Martine Poller. Your host is Avignon-born Frederic Caby, an expert in the history of French cuisine, the exploits of Napoleon, and the nuances of Grenoble. We'd vote the bouillabaisse the best in the Alps. Cuisine is by resident chef Agnès Chotin. Try velvety-smooth crayfish-and-shrimp cream soup, or duck foie gras terrine. The chef makes a superb filet of beef in game sauce.

7 rue de Montorge. © **04-76-87-53-64.** www.auberge-napoleon.fr. Reservations recommended. Main courses 22€–36€; fixed-price menu 35€–69€. AE, DC, MC, V. Mon–Sat 7:30–10pm. Closed May 1-15, July 13-14, and Aug 10-25.

Café de la Table Ronde FRENCH This is the second-oldest cafe in France, after the more famous Procope in Paris. It is still going strong and still serving good, affordable cuisine. Founded in 1739, the cafe has attracted such luminaries as Stendhal and Sarah Bernhardt. It is said to be the spot where Pierre Choderlos de Laclos conceived the plot for his 1784 novel *Les Liaisons Dangereuses*. The menu offers both regional and national cuisine—the ingredients always fresh. We gravitate to *le poisson du jour* (fresh fish of the day), although the *fondue Savoyarde* with char-cuterie is a winter delight as is the Alpine ham. The cafe conducts concerts and poetry readings.

7 place St-André. © **04-76-44-51-41.** www.restaurant-tableronde-grenoble.com. Main courses 9€–23€; fixed-price menus 22€–30€. AE, DC, MC, V. Apr–Oct daily 8am–11pm; off season Mon–Sat 8am–11pm, Sun 1–3pm.

ON THE OUTSKIRTS

Restaurant Alain Pic ★★ FRENCH/SAVOYARD The creative statement of a legendary chef, this restaurant occupies a substantial Savoyard house originally built in 1905 in the quiet hamlet of Montbonnot (7km/4⅓ miles north of Grenoble). Three peaks of the Chartreuse mountain group surround the hamlet. In a comfortable dining room outfitted in richly textured Savoyard style, famed chef Alain Pic prepares sublime dishes that include carpaccio of tuna with baby vegetables, fresh foie gras of duckling served with liqueur-marinated grapes, beef layered with foie gras in a sauce of Syrah red wine, sea scallops in champagne sauce, and tuna steaks with sesame seeds and red wine.

876 rue du Général-de-Gaulle (RN90), Lieu-dit Les Mésanges, Montbonnot-Saint-Martin. © **04-76-90-21-57.** www.restaurant-alain-pic.com. Reservations recommended. Main courses 15€–49€; fixed-price menu 17€ Tues–Fri only, 26€–58€ all other times. AE, MC, V. Tues–Fri and Sun noon–2pm; Tues–Sat 7:30–9pm. Closed 2 weeks in late Aug. Bus: 602 from Grenoble.

Grenoble After Dark

To get things started, walk to **place St-André, place aux Herbes,** or **place de Gordes.** On a good night, these squares overflow with young people, and the energy level builds in anticipation of an explosion of dancing and partying.

Join fun-loving crowds of students at **Le Couche Tard,** 1 rue Palais (© **04-76-44-18-79**), and the **London Pub,** 11 rue Brochene (© **04-76-44-41-90**).

For a great outdoor party, check out **Le Saxo,** 5 place d'Agier (© **04-38-37-07-49**). Its patio, with speakers blasting techno and rock into the wee hours, has the feeling of a college party. If you're pumped up and need to cut loose on the dance floor, bop on over to **Coco-Loco-Nae-Vas,** 1 rue Lamartine (© **04-76-87-23-48**), where the young rule. A cover of 12€ is charged Thursday to Saturday including a first drink.

Le Styx, 6 place Claveyson (© **04-76-44-09-99**), is attuned to cutting-edge music from such centers as London and Los Angeles. Expect a mix of hip-hop, R&B, soul, and techno, but be prepared for anything. The dance floor is too small, but it's popular anyway. Young office workers head here after 5pm to sample some of the 70 different cocktails, but beer and pastis are the drinks of choice.

The town's most animated gay disco is **Le Georges V,** 124 cour Berriat (© **04-76-84-16-20**), which is open Wednesday from 9pm, Thursday to Sunday from 11:30pm (closing times vary).

COURCHEVEL 1850 ★★

633km (393 miles) SE of Paris; 52km (32 miles) SE of Albertville; 97km (60 miles) SE of Chambéry

Courchevel has been called a resort of "high taste, high fashion, and high profile," a chic spot where multimillion-dollar chalets sit on pristine pine-covered slopes. Skiers and geographers know it as part of Les Trois Vallées, sometimes called "the skiing supermarket of France." The resort, with 150km (93 miles) of ski runs in Courchevel and 604km (375 miles) of ski runs in the Trois Vallées around it, employs as many workers in winter as in summer, many of whom do nothing more than manicure and maintain the slopes. Courchevel 1850 has excellent resorts and hotels—with price tags to match—so it draws the super-rich. Travelers on average budgets should avoid it and head for more reasonably priced resorts, especially Chamonix (see "Chamonix–Mont Blanc," later in this chapter).

Courchevel consists of four planned ski towns, each designated by its elevation in meters. They are the less fashionable Courchevel 1300 (Le Prez), Courchevel 1550, Courchevel 1650, and, crowning them all, Courchevel 1850. Courchevel maintains three ski schools with a staff of 700 instructors, a labyrinth of chairlifts, and more than 200 ski runs, which are excellent in the intermediate and advanced categories. Also in Les Trois Vallées are the less well-known resorts of **Méribel, Les Menuires, La**

Snowboarding is indulged and accepted at even the grandest resorts. For safety reasons, the pistes for snowboards are designated areas segregated from conventional ski runs. In Courchevel, the site is Le Snowpark. Peppered with all the moguls and hillocks a snowboarder would expect, it straddles the side of La Piste des Chenus, running parallel to conventional ski runs and accessible by way of la Telecabine des Chenus. Check with the tourist office for more details.

Tania, and **Val Thorens,** which you should avoid unless you direly need to save money.

Courchevel 1850 is the most attractive ski mecca in the French Alps. It's also the focal point of a chair-hoist network crisscrossing the Les Trois Vallées region. At the center of one of the largest ski areas in the world, Courchevel sits at the base of a soaring amphitheater whose deep snowfalls last longer than those at most other resorts because it faces north. Expect reliable snow conditions, perfectly groomed runs, vertical cliffs, and enough wide runs to appease the intermediate skier. The glacier skiing draws experts from around the world.

SKI PASSES A 1-day pass (lift ticket) for Courchevel costs 39€, and a 1-day pass to Les Trois Vallées goes for 47€. A 3-day pass costs 115€ for Courchevel, 137€ for Les Trois Vallées.

Essentials

GETTING THERE If you're **driving** from Paris, take A6 to Lyon, then A42 to Chambéry, and then A430 to Albertville. At Albertville, take N90 to Moutiers, and then follow the narrow roads 915 and 75 into Courchevel. Courchevel 1850 is the last stop on a steep Alpine road that dead-ends at the village center. Roads are open year-round, but driving can be treacherous during snowstorms. To go any higher, you'll have to take a cable car from the center of town. Most visitors drive here (you'll need snow tires and chains), but some buses link the city to railway junctions farther down the mountain.

The nearest **train** station is in Moutiers Salins. From Paris's Gare de Lyon, five trains per day leave for Moutiers. The high-speed TGV covers the distance from Paris to Chambéry in about 3 hours. In Chambéry, transfer for Moutiers. From the station in Moutiers, a 1-hour **bus** trip completes the journey to Courchevel. There are five buses per day Monday to Friday and 15 per day on Saturday and Sunday costing from 10€ to 14€.

The nearest international **airport** is at Geneva. From there, you can catch a bus to Courchevel. There are three buses per day Monday to Friday and eight on Saturday and Sunday. The 4-hour ride costs 70€ one-way. From the airport at Lyon, there are three to five buses a day to Courchevel; the 4-hour trip costs 65€ one-way.

VISITOR INFORMATION The **Office de Tourisme,** at La Croisette in the heart of town (© **04-79-08-00-29;** fax 04-79-08-15-63; www.courchevel.com), provides information on skiing and each of the four Courchevel ski towns.

Where to Stay

VERY EXPENSIVE

Hôtel Bellecôte ★★   This seven-story chalet, with direct access to the slopes, is known for its collection of unusual antiques. Bored with traditional Alpine motifs, the founder scoured the bazaars of Afghanistan and the Himalayas for objects that lend exotic warmth to the wood-sheathed walls and ceilings. Guest rooms are outfitted with lots of varnished paneling, plush accessories, and carved wooden objects from the Far or Middle East. The hotel has its own ski-rental shop.

Full meals in the elegant dining room include cassoulet of sweetbreads with flap mushrooms, frogs' legs Provençal, and chicken with morels. The impressive luncheon buffet has a dazzling array of seafood, such as crayfish and urchins, followed by sauerkraut with pork.

Rue de Bellecôte, Courchevel 1850 73120. ✆**04-79-08-10-19.** Fax 04-79-08-17-16. www.hotels-restaurants-courchevel.com. 54 units. 265€–370€ double; 490€–565€ suite for 2. Rates include half board. AE, DC, MC, V. Closed mid-Apr to Dec 20. **Amenities:** Restaurant; bar; babysitting; exercise room; Jacuzzi; indoor pool; room service; sauna; Wi-Fi (free) in lobby. *In room:* TV, hair dryer, minibar.

EXPENSIVE

Courcheneige ☺   This hotel is at the heart of the slopes—you can practically ski from your doorstep. Built like a chalet, with balconies, the hotel has its own ski shop. Guest rooms mostly open onto views of the mountain ranges, including l'Aiguille du Fruit. Most of the midsize bathrooms have tub/shower combinations. Some rooms are large enough for a family of five. Courcheneige is always warm and cozy, especially in the art-filled, elegantly decorated public rooms. The Alpine and international cooking is excellent; meals are sometimes served on the terrace.

Rue Nogentil, Courchevel 1850 73120. ✆ **04-79-08-02-59.** Fax 04-79-08-11-79. www.courcheneige. com. 85 units. 175€–309€ double; 210€–568€ suite for 2. Rates include half board. AE, MC, V. Parking 11€. **Amenities:** Restaurant; 2 bars; babysitting; exercise room; Jacuzzi; sauna; free shuttle bus to ski lifts. *In room:* TV, hair dryer, Wi-Fi (in some; free).

La Sivolière ★★   The secret of La Sivolière's success is its owner, Madeleine Cattelin, who has a rich knowledge of and appreciation for her native Savoy. The hotel was constructed in the 1970s, with lots of pinewood boards and artfully rustic lichen-covered boulders, but was since radically upgraded to a four-star hotel. It's near a small forest in a sunny spot near the ski slopes. Each guest room contains tasteful furnishings.

Rue des Chenus, Courchevel 1850 73120. ✆ **04-79-08-08-33.** Fax 04-79-08-15-73. www.hotel-la-sivoliere.com. 44 units. 400€–840€ double; from 840€ suite. AE, MC, V. Parking 20€. Closed late Apr to early Dec. **Amenities:** Restaurant; bar; babysitting; indoor pool; room service; sauna. *In room:* TV, hair dryer, Wi-Fi (free).

Le Chabichou ★★   This is one of the town's finest hotels, within easy walking distance of many bars and clubs and boasting a superb restaurant of the same name (later in this chapter). Most of the guest rooms in the gingerbread-trimmed chalet are large and well furnished; their daring modern design may not appeal to everyone, however. Beds offer grand Alpine comfort, with quality mattresses and fine linens.

Rue des Chenus, Courchevel 1850 73120. ✆**04-79-08-00-55.** Fax 04-79-08-33-58. www.chabichou-courchevel.com. 42 units. 470€–830€ double; from 600€ suite for 2. Rates include half board. AE, DC, MC, V. Parking 30€. Closed May–June and Sept to mid-Dec. **Amenities:** Restaurant; bar; babysitting; exercise room; room service; sauna; spa. *In room:* TV, hair dryer, minibar, Wi-Fi (free).

Les Ducs de Savoie ★   This hotel, one of the largest in Courchevel, has elaborately scrolled pinewood and rows of picturesque icicles hanging from the protruding eaves. Each spacious, pleasant guest room has a balcony or terrace. Decorated in Alpine style, the modern rooms have comfortable beds and combination tub/showers. The property is a few feet from the Téléski (ski lift) of the Jardin Alpin, and you can ski directly to the hotel's vestibule.

Le Jardin Alpin, Courchevel 1850 73120. ✆ **04-79-08-03-00.** Fax 04-79-08-16-30. www.lesducsde savoie.com. 71 units. 210€–315€ double. Rates include half board. AE, DC, MC, V. Parking 18€. Closed Apr 16–Dec 15. **Amenities:** Restaurant; bar; babysitting; exercise room; Jacuzzi; massage; indoor pool; ski shop; Wi-Fi (free) in lobby. *In room:* TV, hair dryer.

Where to Dine

Chalet des Pierres FRENCH/SAVOYARD   This is the best of the lunch restaurants scattered across the slopes. Accented with weathered planking and warmed by open hearths, it sits in the middle of the Des Verdons ski slope, a few paces from the path of whizzing skiers. Lunch can be served on a terrace, but most visitors gravitate to the two-story interior, where blazing fireplaces, hunting trophies, and a hip international crowd contribute to the place's charm. Items include air-dried Alpine meat and sausages, the best french fries in Courchevel, pepper steak, and *fondue Savoyarde.* Two appealing dishes are the Beaufort cheese tart and a leg of lamb that's suspended, the traditional way, from a string in the chimney and left to slowly cook in the smoke from the smoldering fire.

Au Jardin Alpin. ✆ **04-79-08-18-61.** www.chaletdepierres.com. Reservations required. Main courses 35€–48€. AE, MC, V. Daily noon–4:30pm. Closed late Apr to mid-July and mid-Aug to early Dec.

La Bergerie TRADITIONAL FRENCH   Its uneven flagstone steps, stacks of firewood, and weathered pine logs and planks testify to La Bergerie's origins as an 1830s shepherd's hut. The ambience is sports-oriented and outdoorsy. Well-prepared menu items include scallops in shallot butter, fondue bourguignon, raclette made with cheese from small-scale producers in Switzerland, and cheesy Savoyard pasta with ham. An especially refined platter that usually meets with success is pâté of salmon smoked, poached, grilled, and served with lemon-and-caviar crème fraîche.

Rte. de Nogentile. ✆ **04-79-08-24-70.** Reservations required. Main courses lunch 17€–31€; fixed-price menu dinner 35€–45€. AE, MC, V. Restaurant daily noon–3pm; Tues–Sat 8–10pm. Bar and cafe daily 10am–midnight. Closed late Apr to mid-Dec.

Le Bateau Ivre ★★★ MODERN FRENCH   This restaurant, one of the greatest in the French Alps, occupies two floors of a hotel in the upper reaches of the resort. The paneled room has parquet floors and big windows that afford a view over the town and its slopes. Enjoyable dishes include *les oeufs cassées* (literally, "broken eggs"), an elegant house specialty accented with roasted crayfish tails and truffles. Also look for frogs' legs in garlic-flavored cream sauce, grilled red snapper with balsamic vinegar and fresh vegetables, polenta with escalopes of foie gras in vinaigrette, and succulent rack of lamb with olives and artichoke hearts. Scallops may be scented with gentian, an Alpine wildflower.

In the Hôtel Pomme-de-Pin, quartier Les Chenus. ✆ **04-79-00-11-71.** Reservations required. Main courses 35€–110€; fixed-price menu 90€–190€. AE, DC, MC, V. Sat–Sun 12:30–2:15pm; daily 7:30–10pm. Closed Easter to mid-Dec.

EN ROUTE TO GENEVA

If you're leaving France and headed toward western Switzerland, specifically Geneva, consider a final R & R stopover at **Jiva Hill Park Hotel** ★, Route d'Harée, Crozet 01170 (℗ **04-50-28-48-48;** fax 04-50-28-48-49; www.jivahill.com). Set on 28 hectares (70 acres) of parkland, it's within France, but only a 10-minute drive from the Geneva airport. This frontier region of the Alpine foothills, where Voltaire was exiled by the French monarchs, seems more closely tuned to Switzerland (especially Geneva) than to the rest of France. Isolated and peaceful, with only 34 rooms, the hotel bills itself as "a boutique resort."

Angular and avant-garde, it has interiors by Jean-Philippe Nuel, the famous French hotel designer. Each unit is accented with exposed wood and touches of wrought iron, and manages to be minimalist, stylish, and ultracomfortable at the same time. On the premises is a highly rated deluxe spa, the Carita, decorated like the rest of the hotel with a spectacular collection of contemporary art, and with state-of-the-art equipment. Other amenities include a gourmet restaurant, bar, heated indoor pool, two tennis courts, and a nearby golf course. Rates, requiring a 3-night minimum stay, range from 320€ to 420€ for a double to 515€ to 615€ for a junior suite.

Le Chabichou ★★★ MODERN FRENCH   This is the second-best restaurant in town (only Le Bateau Ivre, above, is better). Le Chabichou is on the second floor of the hotel of the same name; big windows showcase a view of the slopes. The cuisine includes a number of superlative dishes, such as soup made from "fish from the lake," *magret* of duckling with honey sauce, divine lobster salad, red mullet with vinaigrette sauce, and velvety risotto with giant prawns.

In Le Chabichou hotel, quartier Les Chenus. ℗ **04-79-08-00-55.** Reservations required. Main courses 42€–60€; fixed-price lunch 35€, dinner 70€–160€. AE, DC, MC, V. Daily 12:30–2pm and 7:15–9:30pm. Closed May–June and Sept–Nov.

Courchevel After Dark

A chic but seasonal resort, Courchevel offers nightlife that roars into the wee hours in midwinter but melts away with the snow. You'll never have to walk far from the center to sample the fun, because the area around **La Croisette** (the departure point for most of the lifts) contains lots of restaurants, bars, and clubs that come and go.

Les Caves de Courchevel, Porte de Courchevel (℗ **04-79-08-12-74**), attracts an upscale crowd. A mock Tyrolean facade of weathered wood hides a club evoking a medieval cloister, with stone arches and columns. From December to April, Les Caves is open nightly for drinks from 11pm to 5am. Also appealing is **Piggy's Pub,** rue de la Croisette (℗ **04-79-08-00-71**), where stiff drinks and recorded music contribute to the sensation that you're far, far away from the French Alps. **Rhumerie Le Kalico,** Au Forum (℗ **04-79-08-20-28;** www.lekalico.com), is the closest thing in town to a British pub; it's open from December to April only.

MEGEVE ★★★

599km (372 miles) SE of Paris; 72km (45 miles) SE of Geneva

Megève is a summer resort set amid forests, foothills, and mountain streams. But it's better known as a cosmopolitan ski resort, with more than 290km (190 miles) of downhill runs plus nearly 81km (50 miles) of cross-country trails.

The village, with its turreted houses around a 17th-century church, suggests that Megève looks much the same as it did at the turn of the 20th century. Hubert de Givenchy claims that the big draw of Megève is its *"parfum d'authenticité,"* from its scent of wood smoke to the sounds of hooves clopping on cobblestones. From 11am to 6am, the center of the old village closes to traffic, except for pedestrians and sledges. You can shop at your leisure, stopping everywhere from the cobbler to the antiques dealer to the many boutiques. The town center contains **place de l'Eglise** and the famous **Hôtel du Mont-Blanc**, south of the main arteries that cut to the valley.

Some of the resort's hotels and one of its most important cable-car depots are in the village of **Mont d'Arbois**, about 1.5km (1 mile) east of the center of Megève, at the end of a steep, narrow, winding road. (In winter, it's unwise to drive up this road without chains and snow tires.)

Tennis, horseback riding, and cable railways add to the attractions, with views of the Mont Blanc area from the top of the chairlifts. Amusement includes a casino, clubs, and shows. Megève has more diversions than most other French winter resorts and is a social center of international status.

Essentials

GETTING THERE Air France serves Geneva's **Cointrin Airport** (⌀ 022/717-71-11). There's bus service four times a day directly to Megève, 69km (43 miles) southeast of the airport. The 90-minute ride costs 44€. For information, contact Megève's tourist office (see below) or **Borini & Cie** (⌀ 04-50-21-18-24).

Many visitors come by **train.** Get off at Sallanches, 13km (8 miles) away. From Sallanches, three to six buses a day make the trip to Megève at a cost of 7€. For schedules, call ⌀ **04-50-21-25-18,** or visit www.sat-montblanc.com. The train journey from Paris (one-way fare: 75€–83€) to Megève is faster on weekends, when the TGV travels directly to Sallanches, taking about 5½ hours. Monday to Friday, the TGV goes only as far as Annecy, after which travelers transfer onto slower trains to Sallanches. Total trip time is around 7½ hours. For train information, contact Megève's tourist office (see below) or the SNCF at ⌀ **36-35** or 08-92-35-35-35.

Buses serve the Autogare SNCF (also known as the Gare Routière de Megève), beside the highway running to the town center.

If you're **driving** to Megève from Paris, take A6 southeast to Mâcon, connect to A40 east to St-Gervais, and follow N212 south straight into Megève.

Warning: Winter driving conditions can be perilous. Make sure your car has snow tires and chains.

VISITOR INFORMATION The **Office de Tourisme** is at 70 rue Monseigneur-Conseil (⌀ **04-50-21-27-28;** fax 04-50-93-03-09; www.megeve.com).

Outdoor Pursuits on the Slopes & Beyond

You can take a chair hoist to **Mont d'Arbois,** at 1,800m (5,900 ft.), where a panorama unfolds of Mont Blanc as well as the Fis and Aravis massifs. Cable service

Two Megève Highlights

If you have the stamina, take the 15km (9½-mile) footpath called the **Route de la Croix (Way of the Cross)** from the edge of town; it links more than a dozen country chapels. Nothing in Megève is more memorable than the annual **Foire de la Croix,** on the last Sunday of September. It marks the return of the herds from the high Alpine pastures. You can taste the farmers' bounty at dozens of stands at the fair, a tradition here since 1282.

operates from June 17 to September 5, every half-hour daily from 9am to 6pm, and costs 11€ round-trip. To reach the station, take route Edmond-de-Rothschild from the resort's center, past the golf course. Mont d'Arbois is a pocket of greater luxury in an already-posh resort. For information, call ✆ **04-50-21-22-07.**

The **French Ski School,** 176 rue de la Poste (✆ **04-50-21-00-97**), is one of Europe's foremost, with 300 instructors for adults and 32 for children. Classes include the complete French skiing method, modern ski techniques, acrobatic skiing, cross-country skiing, and ski touring. The school is open December 20 to April daily 9am to 6:30pm.

A similar option is the **Ecole de Ski Internationale,** 273 rue de la Poste (✆ **04-50-58-78-88;** www.esimegeve.com). Facilities include a Chamois gondola, which takes skiers to the mountain from the center of town; the Rocharbois cable car, linking the ski areas of Mont d'Arbois and Rochebrune; and a gondola and chairlift at the Rochebrune Massif. Skiing here appeals to both intermediates and experts. A 1-day ski pass (lift ticket) costs 34€. Prices for a 3-day pass start at 97€.

Megève Palais des Sports et des Congrès (Sports Palace and Assembly Hall), route du Jaillet (✆ **04-50-21-15-71**), has two pools, saunas, an outdoor Olympic-size skating rink open year-round, a curling track, a body-building room, a bar, a gymnasium, indoor tennis courts, an auditorium, conference rooms, and a gallery. Hours change with the seasons and event schedule; it's usually open daily 9am to 11pm (closed May–June).

Where to Stay

VERY EXPENSIVE

Chalet du Mont d'Arbois ★★★   Built in 1928 in a design emulating Switzerland's chalets, this is the most opulent and stylish small resort on the mountain. Guest rooms are spacious, sunny, and sumptuous. The public rooms are the grandest in Megève, with fireplaces, beamed ceilings, and antiques. The restaurant, Le 1920, (p. 473) serves modern French cuisine.

447 chemin de la Rocaille, Megève 74120. ✆ **04-50-21-25-03.** Fax 04-50-21-24-79. www.domainedu montdarbois.com. 41 units. Winter 610€–1,080€ double, from 2,526€ apt; off season 385€–830€ double, from 1,956€ apt. Rates include breakfast. Half board 65€ per person. AE, DC, MC, V. Closed Apr to mid-June and Oct to mid-Dec. **Amenities:** Restaurant; bar; babysitting; Jacuzzi; massage; indoor and outdoor pools; room service; sauna. *In room:* TV, hair dryer, minibar, Wi-Fi (free).

Les Fermes de Marie ★★★   This unique inn offers the grandest comfort at the resort. It consists of remnants of at least 20 antique barns and crumbling chalets that were assembled and discreetly modernized in a desirable location at the eastern edge of the resort. The result is a compound of appealing, comfortable buildings loaded with atmosphere and eccentricities. The folkloric theme extends to the guest rooms, which look like attractive Alpine cabins and have deluxe beds.

Chemin de Riante Colline, Megève 74120. © **04-50-93-03-10.** Fax 04-50-93-09-84. www.fermesde marie.com. 71 units. Winter 475€–830€ double, from 890€ suite; off season 325€–480€ double, from 565€ suite. Rates include half board. AE, DC, MC, V. Closed mid-Apr to early June and mid-Sept to early Dec. **Amenities:** 2 restaurants; bar; bar lounge; babysitting; health club; Jacuzzi; indoor pool; room service; sauna; spa. *In room:* TV, hair dryer, minibar, Wi-Fi (free).

EXPENSIVE

Au Coin du Feu ★   Modern, spacious, and comfortable, this is one of the best of Megève's middle-bracket (middle for Megève, anyway) hotels. It's under the same management as the more glamorous Les Fermes de Marie (see above). It originated in the mid-1980s, when its owners maneuvered 23 guest rooms into an older chalet. Rooms are cozy and medium-size. Public areas contain fireplaces (one of them monumental) and lots of exposed stone. You'll find the place within a 10-minute uphill walk of Megève's center, beside the path leading to the Rochebrune cable car.

Rte. du Téléphérique de Rochebrune, Megève 74120. © **04-50-21-04-94.** Fax 04-50-21-20-15. www. coindufeu.com. 23 units. Winter 315€–470€ double. Rates include half board. AE, DC, MC, V. Closed early Apr to late Dec. **Amenities:** Restaurant; bar w/outdoor terrace; babysitting; hammam; massage room; room service; sauna; Wi-Fi (free) in public rooms. *In room:* TV, hair dryer.

MODERATE

Le Fer à Cheval ★★   This is the finest hotel in the center of the village. Its rivals are the pricier Chalet du Mont d'Arbois and Les Fermes de Marie, both outside the town center. This hotel was built in 1960 and has been renovated frequently. Designed like an enlarged chalet, it incorporates many square yards of recycled weathered planking and paneling, all salvaged from antique buildings throughout the region. Genuine Savoyard antiques fill the beautifully maintained guest rooms. The rooms are traditional in style, with quality beds and linens. Most are spacious and sunny, opening onto a view.

36 rte. du Crêt-d'Arbois, Megève 74120. © **04-50-21-30-39.** Fax 04-50-93-07-60. www.feracheval-megeve.com. 56 units. 324€–564€ double; from 527€ suite. Rates include half board. AE, MC, V. Closed Apr 8–June 7 and mid-Sept to mid-Dec. **Amenities:** 2 restaurants; bar; babysitting; exercise room; Jacuzzi; outdoor pool; room service; sauna; spa. *In room:* TV, hair dryer, minibar, Wi-Fi (free).

INEXPENSIVE

Hôtel Gai Soleil   At the base of hills at the southeast edge of town, between Megève's center and the Rochebrune slopes, this hotel was built in 1929 and has been much renovated since. The broad staircase that sweeps down to the front contrasts with the Swiss chalet–inspired design of the rest of the property. Inside, it's warm and colorful, with lots of exposed wood and well-upholstered comfort. Varnished pine highlights the small, cozy rooms. It also has a heated outdoor pool.

343 rue Crêt-du-Midi, Megève 74120. © **04-50-21-00-70.** Fax 04-50-21-57-63. www.le-gai-soleil.fr. 21 units. 81€–140€ double. Rates include breakfast. Half board 69€–102€ per person. 20%–50% discount for children 3–12. AE, MC, V. Parking 6€. Closed Sept 14–Dec 14 and Apr 18–June 15. **Amenities:** Restaurant; bar; exercise room; Jacuzzi; movie theater; outdoor pool; room service. *In room:* TV, hair dryer, minibar, Wi-Fi (free).

Where to Dine

Also try the deluxe restaurant at **Le Fer à Cheval** (see above), one of the finest in the area, serving haute alpine cuisine.

L'Alpette SAVOYARD   This is the oldest mountain restaurant in the French Alps, opening onto panoramic views of Megève. It's also one of the best choices for Savoyard staples such as Alpine ham, steak, and grilled meats (the Savoy lamb is especially delectable). The fine cuisine has a loyal following of both residents and skiers who flock here on a yearly basis. While many patrons prefer to end their meal with one of the regional cheeses, dessert lovers should try a tarte tatin (thin-crusted apple tart) or a succulent "chocolate pot" made with two kinds of chocolate, orange zest, and Kahlúa.

222 rte. du Téléphérique de Rochebrune. ☏ **04-50-21-03-69.** www.restaurant-alpette.com. Reservations recommended. Main courses 12€–30€. AE, MC, V. Daily 9am–5pm. Closed Apr 30–July 1 and Aug 30 to mid-Dec.

Le Chamoix SAVOYARD   This is a typical mountain restaurant with hardwood floors and visible beams. It serves "the food of the people," dishes for which the Savoy region of France is known, including fondues, raclettes, and other regional products. You can devour all these cheesy specialties, including "Le Berthoud," which is about 200 grams of melted cheese flavored with Madeira, garlic, and spices. All the food, including the meats, focuses on regional produce. Come here for hearty rib-sticking fare such as strips of air-dried beef and meats from the grill. Don't expect haute cuisine or anything particularly innovative. What you get is Alpine charm and plenty of authentic cooking.

21 rue Monseigneur Conseil. ☏ **04-50-21-25-01.** Reservations not accepted. Main courses 18€–30€. V. Winter daily noon–10pm; off season daily noon–2pm and 7–9:30pm. Closed 3 weeks in May and 3 weeks in Nov.

Le 1920 ★ MODERN FRENCH   Often cited in French fashion magazines as one of the most elegant places in Megève, this restaurant is known for its spit-roasted meats. The flavors and spices of the cuisine suit the bracing climate. Scattered throughout are mementos of the owners, the Rothschilds, and of their association with some of the greatest vineyards in the world. Savory items include foie gras of duckling, *omble chevalier* (local freshwater fish) meunière, spit-roasted turbot served with shellfish-studded risotto, and a dish that never fails to please: spit-roasted Bresse chicken in its own drippings. Part of the menu is devoted to low-fat, low-sodium choices.

In Chalet du Mont d'Arbois resort, 447 chemin de la Rocaille. ☏ **04-50-21-25-03.** Reservations required. Main courses 26€–65€; fixed-price menu 60€–110€. AE, MC, V. Daily noon–2pm and 7:30–10pm (closed Mon off season). Closed Apr to mid-June and Oct to mid-Dec.

Le Prieuré TRADITIONAL FRENCH   The name "priory" dates from A.D. 746, when this place was used as a dining hall for monks. Over the centuries, the building was rebuilt and restored with stones from the local hillside. Today it is one of the best dining choices outside of the hotels. Specialties include *foie gras de canard* and salad made from crab, mussels, and lake fish; and excellent versions of beef stew (*pot-au-feu*), which is simmered for up to 8 hours. An excellent appetizer is melon with locally cured ham, perhaps followed by grilled bass with fennel or *magret* of duckling flavored with peaches. For dessert, try half-baked chocolate cake.

116 Place de l'Eglise. ☏ **04-50-21-01-79.** www.leprieure-megeve.com. Reservations required. Main courses 12€–34€; fixed-price menu 26€–40€ (lunch only). AE, DC, MC, V. Daily noon–2:30pm and 7:30–10pm. Closed June 2–30, Nov 6–Dec 19, and Sun night and all day Mon–Tues in low season.

Les Enfants Terribles TRADITIONAL FRENCH Since the 1950s, this acclaimed restaurant has been a fun and irreverent place to dine. The decor emulates that of an upscale brasserie, thanks to bordeaux-colored banquettes, well-maintained wooden paneling, and a skylight-style ceiling that floods the interior with natural light. On the main square of Megève, the restaurant is warmly outfitted with wood panels and rustic artifacts. The extensive menu encompasses pizzas, pastas, grills, Savoyard raclettes and fondues, veal kidneys, and filets of beef layered with foie gras.

In the Hôtel du Mont-Blanc, place de l'Eglise. ℂ **04-50-58-76-69.** Reservations required. Main courses 30€–54€. AE, DC, MC, V. Winter daily noon–midnight; off season Thurs–Mon noon–3pm and 7–11pm. Closed 3 weeks Apr–May and 3 weeks in Oct.

Megève After Dark

This town is a hotbed of clubs and bars for après-ski fun. The ultimate is **Club de Jazz des 5 Rues,** 19 passage de Cinq Rues (ℂ **04-50-91-90-69**), a rendezvous for such jazz notables as Claude Luter and Claude Bolling; it's open only during the peak winter season. **Le Casino,** 115 av. Charles-Feige (ℂ **04-50-93-01-83;** www. casino-megeve.com), is a small, sedate casino—although you can still lose lots of money here. Most vacationers bypass the gaming tables and head for the disco immediately across the street, **Palo Alto** (ℂ **04-50-91-82-58;** www.palo-alto.fr). On the street level, you'll find a restaurant and music that management loosely advises is for persons ages 25 and older; upstairs, the louder and more frenetic scene is recommended for 18- to 25-year-olds. There's no cover charge in either room, but a beer will cost 15€.

The underground **Les Caves de Megève,** rue Amboise Martin (ℂ **04-50-21-30-11**), located at the end of an impossibly narrow staircase, is small and cozy, with a small dance floor. A French celebrity might make a highly theatrical appearance at any minute. There's no cover, but drinks cost 13€ to 21€.

CHAMONIX–MONT BLANC ★★★

613km (381 miles) SE of Paris; 82km (51 miles) E of Annecy

At an altitude of 1,027m (3,369 ft.), Chamonix is the historic capital of Alpine skiing. This is the resort to choose if you're not a millionaire. Site of the first Winter Olympic Games, in 1924, Chamonix is in a valley almost at the junction of France, Italy, and Switzerland. Skiers the world over know its 20km (12-mile) **Vallée Blanche run,** one of the most rugged, and the longest, in Europe. With exceptional equipment—gondolas, cable cars, and chairlifts—Chamonix is among Europe's major sports resorts, attracting an international crowd with lots of English and Swedish skiers. Thrill seekers also flock here for mountain climbing and hang gliding. An old-fashioned mountain town, Chamonix has a breathtaking backdrop, **Mont Blanc ★★★**, western Europe's highest mountain at 4,734m (15,531 ft.).

The 11km (6¾-mile) **Mont Blanc Tunnel** (ℂ **04-50-55-39-36**) has made Chamonix a major stop along one of Europe's busiest highways. The tunnel is the easiest way to the mountains to Italy; motorists stop here even if they aren't interested in skiing or mountain climbing. For vehicles originating in France, the round-trip toll for a car and its passengers is 33€ one-way, 41€ round-trip. The return half of the round-trip ticket must be used within 7 days of issue. For information, call ℂ **04-50-55-55-00.**

Chamonix sprawls in a narrow strip along both banks of the Arve River. Its casino, rail and bus stations, and most restaurants and nightlife are in the town center. Cable cars reach into the mountains from the town's edge. Locals refer to Les Praz, Les Bossons, Les Moussoux, Argentière, and Les Pélérins as satellite villages within greater Chamonix, though technically Chamonix refers to only a section around place de l'Eglise.

Essentials

GETTING THERE   Most (but not all) **trains** coming from other parts of France or Switzerland require a transfer in such nearby villages as St-Gervais (in France) or Martigny (in Switzerland). Passengers change trains in either of these villages before continuing on by train to Chamonix. Passengers from Aix-les-Bains, Annecy, Lyon, Chambéry, Paris, and Geneva pass to those villages. There are six daily connections from Paris (trip time: 7 hr.); the one-way fare is 84€ to 102€. From Lyon, there are six relatively complicated rail links per day (trip time: 4 hr.). A one-way fare costs 36€ with transfers at Bellegarde and St-Gervais. For more information and schedules for trains throughout France, call ✆ **36-35** or 08-92-35-35-35.

Year-round, two to six buses a day run from the Geneva airport; the one-way fare is 37€. Buses arrive and depart from a spot adjacent to the railway station. For information, call **Cie S.A.T.** (✆ **04-50-53-01-15;** www.sat-montblanc.com).

If you're **driving,** you probably won't have to worry about road conditions: Because Chamonix lies on a main road between Italy and the Mont Blanc Tunnel, conditions are excellent year-round. Even after a storm, roads are quickly cleared. From Paris, follow A6 toward Lyon, and then take A40 toward Geneva. Before Geneva, turn south along A40, which runs to Chamonix.

GETTING AROUND   Within Chamonix, a local network of small buses (*navettes*, usually painted yellow and blue) make frequent runs from points in town to many of the *téléphériques* (cable cars) and villages up and down the valley. The price of a lift ticket usually includes the fare. Daily ski passes cost 37€ to 47€, depending on the areas you specify. For information, contact **Chambus** (✆ **04-50-53-05-55;** www. chamonix-bus.com).

VISITOR INFORMATION   Chamonix's **Office de Tourisme** is on place du Triangle-de-l'Amitié (✆ **04-50-53-00-24;** fax 04-50-53-58-90; www.chamonix.com).

Skiing

With the highest mountain in western Europe, this is an area for the skilled skier. Regrettably, the five main ski areas are not connected by lifts (you must return to the resort and take a different lift to ski a different area), and lines at the most popular areas are the longest in the Alpine world. Weather and snow conditions create crevasses and avalanches that may close sections for days and even threaten parts of the resort.

Skiing is not actually on Mont Blanc, but on the shoulders and slopes across the valley facing the giant. Vertical drops can be spectacular, with lift-serviced hills rising to as high as 3,150m (10,335 ft.). Glacier skiing begins at 3,740m (12,270 ft.). This is not for beginners or timid intermediate skiers, who should head for Les Houches or Le Tour. World-class skiers come here to face the challenges of the high snows of Brévent, La Flégère, and especially Les Grands Montets, a fierce north-facing wall of snow about 3 city blocks wide.

Seeing the Area by Cable Car

The belvederes accessible from Chamonix by cable car or mountain railway are famous. For information, contact the **Compagnie du Mont-Blanc,** 35 place de la Mer de Glace (© **04-50-53-22-75**).

In town, you can board a cable car for the **Aiguille du Midi ★★★** and on to Italy—a harrowing full-day journey. The first stage, a 9-minute run to the Plan des Aiguilles at an altitude of 2,263m (7,425 ft.), isn't so alarming. But the second stage, to the Aiguille du Midi station at 3,781m (12,405 ft.), may make your heart leap, especially when the car rises 600m (1,970 ft.) between towers. At the summit, you'll be about 100m (328 ft.) from Mont Blanc's peak. You'll have a commanding view of the aiguilles of Chamonix and Vallée Blanche, the largest glacier in Europe (15km/9⅓ miles long and 6km/3¾ miles wide), and of the Jura and the French, Swiss, and Italian Alps.

You leave the tram station along a chasm-spanning narrow bridge leading to the third cable car and the glacial fields beyond. Or you can end your journey at Aiguille du Midi and return to Chamonix; this excursion takes half a day. Generally, the cable cars operate year-round: in summer daily 7am to 5pm, leaving at least every 10 minutes, and in winter daily 8:30am to 3:30pm, leaving every 10 minutes. The first stage, to Plan de L'Aiguille, costs 13€ round-trip. The complete round-trip from Chamonix to Aiguille du Midi goes for 40€.

You can also cross over high mountains and pass jagged needles of rock and ice bathed in dazzling light. The final trip to **Pointe Helbronner,** Italy—at 3,407m (11,178 ft.)—does not require a passport if you want to leave the station and descend on two more cable cars to the village of Courmayeur. From there, you can go to nearby Entrèves to dine at **La Maison de Filippo** (© **01-65-86-97-97;** www.lamaison.com), a "chalet of gluttony." The round-trip from Chamonix to Pointe Helbronner is 60€; the cable car operates from mid-May to mid-October only.

Another cableway takes you up to **Le Brévent ★★★,** at 2,485m (8,153 ft.). From here, you'll have a first-rate view of Mont Blanc and the Aiguilles de Chamonix. The round-trip excursion takes about 1½ hours. Cable cars operate year-round from 8am to 5pm. Summer departures are at least every 15 minutes. A round-trip costs 23€.

Another journey takes you to **Le Montenvers ★★★** (© **04-50-53-12-54**), at 1,883m (6,178 ft.). Access is not by cable car but on a **cog railway** known as the **Train Montenvers–Mer de Glace.** It departs from the Gare Montenvers–Mer de Glace, behind Chamonix's Gare SNCF, near the center of town. At the end of the run, you'll have a view of the 6.5km-long (4-mile) *mer de glace* ("sea of ice," or glacier). Immediately east of the glacier, Aiguille du Dru is a rock climb notorious for its difficulty. The trip takes 1½ hours, including a return by rail. Departures are 8am to 6pm in summer, until 4:30pm in the off season; service usually operates year-round. The round-trip fare is 23€.

You can also visit a cave, **La Grotte de Glace,** hollowed out of the *mer de glace;* a cable car connects it with the resort of Montenvers, and the trip takes 3 minutes. The train, cable car, and visit to the cave cost 23€.

Where to Stay

Chalet Hôtel Le Chantel   A 30-minute walk west of the city hall, this white-stucco B&B evokes a Swiss chalet, with dark-stained wood, balconies, and mountain panoramas. It benefits from the care and attention of its owners, who have added touches you'd expect in a private home. The cozy, knotty-pine-paneled rooms are small but homey, without many amenities; each has a comfortable bed and a compact shower-only bathroom.

391 rte. des Pecles, Chamonix 74400. ☎ **04-50-53-06-69.** Fax 04-50-55-52-42. www.skiambiance. co.uk. 8 units. 96€–124€ double. Rates include breakfast. MC, V. Free parking. **Amenities:** Breakfast lounge. *In room:* No phone, Wi-Fi (free).

Hôtel de l'Arve   Originally a cafe around the turn of the 20th century, this place is now a comfortable hotel. Most of its stucco facade dates from the 1960s. The interior is simple, with childproof, much-used furniture and accessories. Furnishings in the small to medium guest rooms are functional, and the compact bathrooms contain shower stalls. This is a simple place that offers a friendly welcome, an appreciation for the outdoors, and views of the Arve River from many rooms. The setting is convenient, a 5-minute walk from the town hall.

60 impasse des Anémones, Chamonix 74400. ☎ **04-50-53-02-31.** Fax 04-50-53-56-92. www.hotel arve-chamonix.com. 37 units. 61€–118€ double. AE, DC, MC, V. Closed mid-Oct to Dec 17. **Amenities:** Restaurant; exercise room; sauna. *In room:* TV, Wi-Fi (in some; free).

Where to Dine

Bartavel ITALIAN   The place is a sporty, informal pizzeria and brasserie. Service is a bit rough, but that's part of its style. Decorated much like a tavern in Italy, this restaurant serves a range of pastas, salads, soups, and rib-sticking platters designed to go well with cold air and high altitudes. Beer and wine flow liberally. Bartavel attracts many outdoor enthusiasts who appreciate its copious portions and reasonable prices.

26 cours du Bartavel. ☎ **04-50-53-97-19.** Main courses 14€–30€; pasta and pizzas 8.50€–12€. MC, V. Daily 11:30am–11:30pm.

La Casa Valerio ITALIAN   This good-natured restaurant is the domain of long-time Chamonix resident Valerio Comazetto, whose customers have followed him from restaurant to restaurant for 2 decades. You may enjoy a drink at the cozy bar, filled with chianti bottles and Alpine souvenirs, before proceeding upstairs to the dining room, where red-and-white-checked tablecloths set the trattoria mood. You'll find the best pizzas in the region, many redolent of Mediterranean herbs. The restaurant serves up to 25 kinds of fresh-made pasta, including succulent versions with salmon and thin-sliced *jambon de Parme*. More substantial dishes include grilled calamari and mussels in white-wine sauce.

88 rue du Lyret. ☎ **04-50-55-93-40.** Main courses 11€–33€. AE, DC, MC, V. Daily noon–2am (restaurant until midnight).

Le Chaudron ★ 🍷 TRADITIONAL FRENCH   You'll find fancier places in town, but for good value, honest cooking, and fine mountain ingredients, Le Chaudron is near the top of our list. Chef Stephan Osterberger cooks in front of you, and you're sure to appreciate his specialties, which include house-style sweetbreads, rabbit stew with juniper berries, several robust beef dishes, and fondues, as well as many salads and desserts. The cellar is filled with well-chosen wines, including Château Mouton-Rothschild and Château Latour.

79 rue des Moulins. ☎ **04-50-53-40-34.** Reservations recommended. Main courses 15€–35€; fixed-price menu 20€–35€. MC, V. Daily 7–10:30pm. Closed May–June and Oct–Nov.

Restaurant Albert 1er ★★★ MODERN FRENCH   Although the hotel complex that contains this establishment features other, newer eateries, this is the star. You'll dine in one of a trio of cozily decorated dining rooms, with bay windows opening onto views of Mont Blanc and walls accented by rustic artifacts and antique farm implements. Begin with chef Pierre Carrier's broth (*fumet*) of wild mushrooms garnished with ravioli stuffed with foie gras. Main courses include bison steak with green-peppercorn sauce; superb pan-fried scallops with risotto and lobster sauce; locally smoked salmon with caviar-flavored cream sauce; and foie gras of duck with truffled chicken rillettes. Try the honey ice cream with raspberry coulis for dessert. In summer, dine alfresco in the garden.

In the Hameau Albert 1er hotel, 38 rte. du Bouchet. ✆ **04-50-53-05-09.** Reservations recommended. Main courses 43€–160€; fixed-price menus 76€–156€; fixed-price lunch 56€. AE, DC, MC, V. Fri-Mon 12:30–2pm; Thurs-Tues 7:30–9:30pm. Closed mid-May to June 5 and early Nov to early Dec.

Restaurant Les Jardins du Mont-Blanc ★ FRENCH   This stellar restaurant centers on a pentagonal fireplace. Specialties change seasonally but may include *omble chevalier* (lake fish) meunière, medallions of veal in white-truffle sauce, rack of lamb roasted with herbs (for two), and sinful desserts such as a mousse of apples and white chocolate. The excellent cellar contains more than 500 wines, many reasonably priced. In summer, you can lunch next to the pool in the garden. There's music in the adjacent piano bar every night.

In the Hôtel Mont-Blanc, 62 allée du Majéstic. ✆ **04-50-53-05-64.** Reservations required. Main courses 25€–30€; fixed-price menu 36€–79€. AE, MC, V. Summer daily noon–2:30pm and 7–10pm. Closed for lunch in winter. Closed Oct–Nov.

Chamonix After Dark

Nightlife in Chamonix runs the gamut from the classical to riotous. You'll find the most bars and pubs along rue des Moulins and rue Paccard. Chamonix's most popular disco is **Le Garage,** Avenue de l'Aiguille du Midi (✆ **06-33-76-86-00;** www.nightclubgarage.com). Open nightly during the height of winter and summer high seasons, but only Thursday to Sunday during rainy months, it's outfitted with a modern format, very artfully "designed" with lots of chrome, steel, and glass. Clientele here could include just about anyone, reflecting the changing hordes of skiers and mountaineers who swarm to Chamonix at regular intervals. Entrance ranges from 5€ to 15€. The **casino,** 12 place H.-B.-de-Saussure (✆ **04-50-53-07-65**), has slot machines and roulette and blackjack tables.

VAL D'ISERE ★★

665km (413 miles) SE of Paris; 118km (73 miles) E of Albertville; 130km (81 miles) E of Chambéry

In an open valley, Val d'Isère (1,820m/5,971 ft. above sea level) was originally a hunting station for the ducs de Savoie. It's now a center of some of Europe's most spectacular skiing. Less snobbish than Courchevel and less old-fashioned than Megève, it's a youthful, rather brash resort where virtually everyone comes to enjoy outdoor pursuits. Its fans compare it favorably to Chamonix, which—despite the allure of nearby Mont Blanc and superb skiing—seems to be burdened with longer lift lines and a less accessible layout of ski lifts and slopes.

Essentials

GETTING THERE & GETTING AROUND   **Driving** is the preferred way to get to Val d'Isère. Most motorists come from Albertville, accessible by superhighway from Paris. From Albertville, follow signs to Moutiers, then take RN202 to Bourg-St-Maurice (58km/36 miles) and continue another 31km (19 miles) to Val d'Isère. The meandering RN202 is panoramic and breathtaking—for its views and its lack of guardrails along some sections. During snowfalls, chains on tires are required. When you get to the resort, we strongly advise you to park your car and not use it again until you leave. Parking problems are legendary, and without chains, you'll risk getting stuck during snowfalls. You can walk virtually anywhere in town faster than you can drive.

Two dozen red-and-white Train Rouge free **shuttle buses,** each with a capacity of 100 people and their equipment, connect the hamlets at either end of the valley (La Daille and Le Fornet) to the center. The central terminus is the Rond-Point des Pistes. In summer, service is available only in July and August.

Parking lots and garages scattered around the valley are clearly marked. Each charges 14€ per day, 81€ per week, depending on the season and the size of your car.

Nearby **airports** include Cointrin, outside Geneva (✆ **04122/717-7111** or 04122/717-7105); Lyon-St-Exupéry (✆ **08-26-80-08-26**); Grenoble (✆ **04-76-65-48-48**); and Chambéry (✆ **04-79-54-49-54**). Bus and limo service is available from these airports; contact Cars Martin (✆ **04-79-06-00-42**).

The nearest **train** station is at Bourg-St-Maurice (✆ **36-35**), an Alpine village 31km (19 miles) west of Val d'Isère. For train information, also call ✆ **36-35.** From there, Cars Martin (✆ **04-79-68-32-96;** www.altibus.com) **buses** depart 4 to 10 times a day, depending on the season. The one-way fare is 13€. Or you can take a **taxi** from Bourg-St-Maurice that costs about 80€ for up to four passengers. Call **Altitude Taxis** (✆ **06-07-41-11-53;** www.altitude-espace-taxi.com), or arrange pickup in advance with your hotel.

VISITOR INFORMATION   The resort's **Office de Tourisme,** rue Principale, Val Village (✆ **04-79-06-06-60;** fax 04-79-06-04-56; www.valdisere.com), is a font of information on outdoor activities. The widest spectrum of information on sports is available from the **Club des Sports (Sports Department),** route de la Balme, Quartier Balme B.P. 61, 73152 Val d'Isère (✆ **04-79-06-03-49;** www.valsport.org).

Outdoor Pursuits On & Off the Slopes

Don't expect a pristine Alpine village. In Val d'Isère, traffic roars to the town center. Clusters of cheap restaurants, crêperies, and more than 125 stores and outlets line the road. Since 1983, some of the worst of the town's architectural sins have been corrected, thanks to tighter building codes and greater emphasis on traditional chalet-style architecture.

Access to Val d'Isère, less than 9.5km (6 miles) from the Italian border, is inconvenient and time-consuming, and parking is a nightmare during busy seasons. But despite the commercialism, the town hums with the sense that its visitors are here to enjoy skiing. And few other European resorts can boast as logical a layout for a far-flung collection of ski slopes.

Val d'Isère is the focal point for a network of satellite resorts scattered around the nearby valleys, including the architecturally uninspired **Tignes** (2,066m/6,778 ft. above sea level), whose layout is divided into four resort-style villages. The most stylish and prosperous of the villages is **Val Claret;** less fortunate and successful are **Tignes le Lac, Tignes les Boisses,** and **Tignes les Brévières.**

Guarding one entrance to Val d'Isère is **La Daille,** a resort of mostly high-rise condominiums and timeshares. At the other end of town is the medieval hamlet of **Le Fornet,** the departure point for gondolas crossing a mountain ridge to the Pissaillas Glacier and another network of ski trails, the Système de Solaise.

All of these satellites lack the cachet and diversity of Val d'Isère's nightlife and dining. Public transport (the Train Rouge; see "Getting There & Getting Around," above) can pick you up and deposit you at the departure point to the terminus of virtually any ski lift or trail in the region.

Val d'Isère is legendary for its "death-defying" chutes and its off-piste walls. These slopes are for experts, but the intermediate skier will also find open snowfields. The best place for intermediates is Tignes, with its wide variety of runs, including the Grande Motte (3,345m/10,974 ft.). Skiers find enough variety here to stay 2 weeks and never revisit the slopes that stretch from the Pissaillas Glacier far above Val d'Isère to Tignes Les Brévières four valleys away.

There are only a few marked expert runs; the more accessible off-piste areas lure experts from all over Europe and the United States. Most of these runs can be reached after short traverses from the Bellevarde, Solaise, and Fornet cable cars in Val d'Isère and the Grande Motte cable car in Val Claret.

In winter, half-day, full-day, and 2-day **ski passes** (lift tickets) sell for 32€, 44€, and 76€, respectively.

At least a dozen **ski schools** flourish in winter. One of the largest and busiest is the **Ecole de Ski Français,** or French National Ski School (© 04-79-06-35-76; www.esf.net), with 250 guides and teachers. Somewhat more personal is **Snow Fun** (© 04-79-06-16-79; www.snowfun.com), with 60 guides. Purists usually gravitate to **Top Ski,** galerie des Cimes (© 04-79-06-14-80; www.topskival.com), a small but choice outfit with 24 extremely well-trained guides catering exclusively to Alpine connoisseurs who want to ski off-piste (away from the officially recognized and maintained trails).

Officially, the resort's sports activities slow down or stop altogether between early May and late June, and from early September to mid-November.

Where to Stay

The staff at **Val Hôtel** (© 04-79-06-18-90; fax 04-79-06-11-88), the resort's central reservations network, can book accommodations for you.

Hôtel Altitude   This oft-modernized chalet dates from the 1970s, when it was built in Savoyard style. The Altitude is comfortable and cozy, a short walk south of the town center, so you'll be able to escape the crowds. Many guests return each year, occupying elegantly appointed guest rooms with quality beds and fine linens.

Rte. de la Balme, Val d'Isère 73150. © **04-79-06-12-55.** Fax 04-79-41-11-09. www.hotelaltitude.com. 40 units. Winter 145€–170€ double; off season 103€–108€ double. Rates include half board. AE, DC, MC, V. Closed May 5–June 30 and late Aug to Dec 1. **Amenities:** Restaurant; bar; babysitting; health club; hammam; outdoor pool; room service; sauna. *In room:* TV, hair dryer, Wi-Fi (free).

Hôtel Christiania ★★   This is the best hotel in a town of worthy contenders, and the only government-rated four-star hotel in Val d'Isère. The stylishly designed 1949 lodging was almost completely rebuilt in 1991. However, reminders of its original design appear, most obviously in the *Sputnik*-style furniture in a sunken lobby ringed with exposed stone, varnished pine, and blazing fireplaces. Ski buffs are willing to pay the high prices because of the location, although the hotel doesn't measure up to similarly priced, more atmospheric resorts in Megève and Chamonix. The guest rooms range from midsize to spacious, with pine trim and Alpine touches. Some accommodations contain sleeping lofts or bunk beds. The restaurant offers international and French—especially Savoyard—specialties.

B.P. 48, Val d'Isère 73152. ☎ **04-79-06-08-25.** Fax 04-79-41-11-10. www.hotel-christiania.com. 69 units. 319€–358€ double; from 478€ suite. Rates include half board. AE, DC, MC, V. Closed late Apr to Dec 5. **Amenities:** Restaurant; bar; babysitting; exercise room; massage; indoor pool; room service; sauna; spa. *In room:* TV, hair dryer, Wi-Fi (free).

Where to Dine

La Grande Ourse FRENCH   Although it's open for lunch, this restaurant doesn't exhibit its trademark coziness until after dark, when flickering candles and a blazing fireplace generate lots of Savoyard charm. In a small, charming wooden house built in 1937, La Grande Ourse has the resort's most intriguing mural, a depiction of the zodiac on the ceiling of its richly paneled main dining room. Menu items at lunch include grilled meats, pastas, salads, and simple but fortifying dishes of the day. Evening menus offer more sophisticated fare, such as fricassee of guinea fowl with fondant of foie gras, warm foie gras with apples and cider sauce, roast rack of lamb with herbs, large pockets of lobster-stuffed ravioli with lobster sauce, and Savoyard fondue with three cheeses.

B.P. 57, Val d'Isère 73150, Sur le Front de Neige, adjacent to the church. ☎ **04-79-06-00-19.** www. grande-ourse.com. Reservations recommended at dinner. Main courses lunch 13€–26€, dinner 22€–32€; fixed-price menu 25€ at lunch, 49€ at dinner. AE, DC, MC, V. Daily noon–3pm; Wed–Mon 7:30–9:30pm. Closed mid-May to Nov.

La Vieille Maison ★ 🏠 SAVOYARD   Amid relatively new buildings in the hamlet of La Daille, this former farmhouse is one of the valley's oldest chalets. Constructed in 1780, it has lots of exposed stone and old-fashioned style. Menu items are based on Savoyard themes, with hearty cold-weather dishes such as fondues and raclettes, many of which are prepared only for two to four diners. Menu items include *tartiflette*, a succulent dish made from Reblochon cheese, potatoes, onions, butter, and lardons; game dishes, including wild boar steak; such local freshwater fish as *omble chevalier* in white-wine sauce; and raclette garnished with a green salad and a small platter of charcuterie. Hands-on diners sometimes opt for "La Viande à l'Auze"—a superhot slab of rock is placed on your table so you can sizzle your beef strips yourself.

Vieux Village de la Daille. ☎ **04-79-06-11-76.** www.resto-lavieillemaison.fr. Reservations recommended. Main courses 20€–24€; fixed-price menu 31€. MC, V. Mon–Sat 7–9:30pm. Closed May–June and Oct–Nov.

Val d'Isère After Dark

Most bars are in the town's pedestrian zone or adjacent to rue Principale. **Café Face,** rue Principale (☎ **04-79-06-29-80**), draws an attractive crowd and plays the best music. Its most fun alternative, **Dick's Tea Bar** (☎ **04-79-06-14-87;** www. dicksteabar.com), just off the rue Principale and opposite the Hôtel Christiania, is the wildest après-ski joint in Val d'Isère. Inside you'll find a rustic and cozily appointed timber-and-stone interior (including an Internet cafe) where you can drink as merrily and as uninhibitedly as you want, and—after around 9pm—dance, dance, dance. Although a cover charge of 10€ is imposed after midnight, the bar is open every day during winter from 9am (for breakfast) to 4am. Hours vary during off season, but even during the slowest period, the place is usually open on Friday and Saturday nights. Smaller and more intimate, without dancing, is a bar that has a neighborhood feel, two pool tables, and lots of English-speaking patrons: **Le Petit Danois,** behind the bus station, off rue Principale (✆ **04-79-06-27-97;** www.le petitdanois.com).

A Side Trip to Albertville

The rail and highway junction of Albertville lies in **La Vallée de la Tarantaise,** a sinuous valley that climbs 85km (53 miles) along Route 90. Route 90 extends from low-lying Albertville and branches into **La Vallée d'Isère,** whose focal point is the resort of Val d'Isère. Most visitors travel between the two by car, although about five trains a day connect Albertville and Bourg-St-Maurice. From Bourg-St-Maurice, a bus continues for another 30km (19 miles) up to Val d'Isère, leaving at times that coincide with train arrivals. Train passengers should expect a total transit time of 60 to 90 minutes, depending on the day of the week. The one-way fare is around 14€.

WHERE TO STAY & DINE

Hôtel Million ★★★ TRADITIONAL FRENCH   This is the area's finest choice, attracting gastronomes and sports enthusiasts. Set back from the main road, the Hôtel Million was established in 1770 by Jean-Pierre Million (who named it Etoile du Nord). It's a white building with strong horizontal lines and gables on a flagstone-covered square; the anterooms have authentic 19th-century decor, while the dining room has high ceilings and classic furnishings. Some of chef/owner Jose de Anacleto and his wife, Su-Chen's, traditional dishes derive from popular Savoy tastes of the 19th century, in particular frogs' legs, freshwater fish from Lake Annecy, and freshwater crayfish. Other choices include fera (an Alpine whitefish) served with wild celery and herb-flavored butter; *foie gras maison;* and filet of John Dory with artichokes and snails.

Twenty-six spacious, attractive guest rooms are available. Outfitted in rustic Alpine style, each contains a TV. Year-round, doubles cost 137€ to 165€.

8 place de la Liberté, Albertville 73200. ✆ **04-79-32-25-15.** Fax 04-79-32-25-36. www.hotelmillion. com. Reservations recommended. Main courses 32€–38€; fixed-price menu 28€–80€. AE, DC, MC, V. Tues–Fri and Sun noon–2pm; Tues–Sat 7–10pm.

PROVENCE: IN THE FOOTSTEPS OF CEZANNE & VAN GOGH

Provence has been called a bridge between the past and the present, which blend in a quiet, often melancholy way. Peter Mayle's *A Year in Provence* and its sequels have played a large role in the popularity of this sunny corner of southern France.

The Greeks and Romans filled the landscape with cities boasting baths, theaters, and arches. Romanesque fortresses and Gothic cathedrals followed. In the 19th century, the light and landscapes attracted painters such as Cézanne and van Gogh.

Provence has its own language and its own customs. The region is bounded on the north by the Dauphiné, on the west by the Rhône, on the east by the Alps, and on the south by the Mediterranean. In chapter 17, we focus on the part of Provence known as the Côte d'Azur, or the French Riviera.

For more coverage of the region, see *Frommer's Provence & the Riviera*.

ORANGE ★★

659km (409 miles) S of Paris; 55km (34 miles) NE of Nîmes; 121km (75 miles) NW of Marseille; 26km (16 miles) S of Avignon

Orange gets its name from when it was a dependency of the Dutch House of Orange-Nassau. The last orange grove disappeared 2,000 years ago. The juice that flows in Orange today comes from its vineyards, which turn out a Côtes-du-Rhône vintage. Many wine caves, some of which offer dégustations to paying customers, thrive throughout the district. (The tourist office can provide a list.)

Overlooking the Valley of the Rhône, today's Orange (pop. 30,000) has Europe's third-largest extant triumphal arch and best-preserved Roman theater. Louis XIV, who toyed with the idea of moving the theater to Versailles, said, "It is the finest wall in my kingdom."

Essentials

GETTING THERE   Orange sits on major rail and highway arteries. Some 20 **trains** per day arrive from Avignon (trip time: 20 min.); the one-way fare is around 7€. From Marseille, there are 11 trains per day (trip time: 1 hr., 15 min.), for 21€ one-way. From Paris, you can catch a TGV train to Orange; the one-way fare is 76€, and the trip takes 3 hours. For rail information, call © **36-35;** www.voyages-sncf. com. For information on bus routes, contact the **Gare Routière,** place Pourtoules, behind the Théâtre Antique (© **04-90-34-15-59**). If you're **driving** from Paris, take A6 south to Lyon, and then A7 to Orange. The 684km (425-mile) drive takes 5½ to 6½ hours.

VISITOR INFORMATION   The **Office de Tourisme** is at 5 cours Aristide-Briand (© **04-90-34-70-88;** fax 04-90-34-99-62; www.otorange.fr).

SPECIAL EVENTS   From July 11 to August 4, a drama, dance, and music festival called **Les Chorégies d'Orange** takes place at the Théâtre Antique, one of the most evocative ancient theaters in Europe. For information or tickets, visit or contact the office, 18 place Sylvain, adjacent to the theater (© **04-90-34-24-24;** fax 04-90-11-04-04; www.choregies.asso.fr).

Exploring the Town

In the southern part of town, the carefully restored **Théâtre Antique ★★★**, place des Frères-Mounet (© **04-90-51-17-60;** www.theatre-antique.com), dates from the days of Augustus. Built into the side of a hill, it once held 8,000 spectators in tiered seats. The theater is nearly 105m (345 ft.) long, 38m (125 ft.) high, and noted for its acoustics. It's open daily November to February 9:30am to 4:30pm, March and October 9:30am to 5:30pm, April to May and September 9am to 6pm, and June to August 9am to 7pm. Admission is 7.90€ for adults and 5.90€ for students and children 17 and under.

West of the theater stood a huge temple that, along with a gymnasium, formed one of the greatest buildings in the empire. Across the street, the **Musée Municipal d'Orange,** place du Théâtre-Antique (© **04-90-51-17-60**), displays fragments of the temple. Your ticket to the theater also admits you to the museum. Hours are November to February daily 9:30am to 12:30pm and 1:30 to 4:30pm; March and October daily 9:30am to 12:30pm and 1:30 to 5:30pm; April to May and September daily 9am to 6pm; and June to August daily 9am to 7pm.

Even older than the theater is the **Arc de Triomphe ★★**, on avenue de l'Arc-de-Triomphe. It's decayed, but its decorations and other elements are fairly well preserved. Built to honor the conquering legions of Caesar, it rises 22m (72 ft.) and is nearly 21m (69 ft.) wide. Composed of a trio of arches held up by Corinthian columns, it was used as a dungeon in the Middle Ages.

Before leaving Orange, head for the park **Colline St-Eutrope,** adjacent to the Théâtre Antique, for a view of the valley and its mulberry plantations.

After exploring the town, drive south for 13km (8 miles) along A9 to **Châteauneuf-du-Pape,** where you can have lunch at the **Hostellerie du Château des Fines-Roches,** route d'Avignon (© **04-90-83-70-23;** www.chateaufinesroches.com).

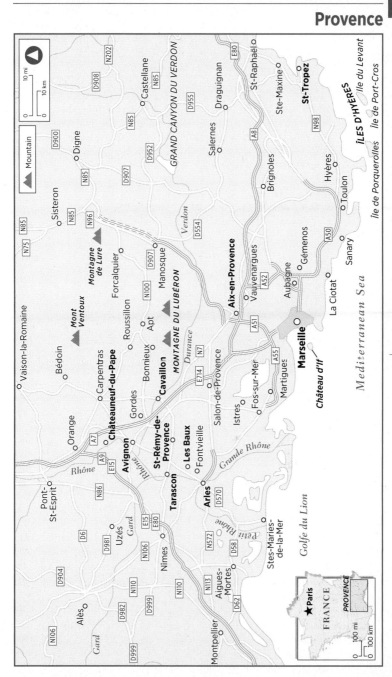

Although the *hostellerie* was built in the 19th century, its medieval features make it look feudal. Fixed-price lunches cost from 19€ to 24€, with set dinners going for 36€ to 85€. The restaurant is open daily in summer, but from November to April it's closed Sunday night and Monday. If you're pressing on to Avignon, it's only another 13km (8 miles) south along any of three highways (each marked AVIGNON).

Where to Stay

Hôtel Arène ★ 🎁 On a pedestrian street in the shade of century-old plane trees, this hotel sits in the center of the historic district. The bull's-eye location is a compelling reason to stay here. Try to get a room with a balcony opening onto the old square in front; it's more nostalgic. The complex consists of a series of four antique town houses woven into a seamless whole. Guest rooms are traditionally furnished with French decor. About half the rooms were renovated in 2010. Amenities are up-to-date, and the staff is among the more courteous and helpful in town.

Place de Langes, Orange 84100. © **04-90-11-40-40.** Fax 04-90-11-40-45. www.hotel-arene.fr. 35 units. 78€–145€ double; 180€ junior suite. AE, DC, MC, V. Parking 9€. **Amenities:** 2 restaurants; room service; rooms for those w/limited mobility; smoke-free rooms. *In room:* TV, hair dryer, minibar, Wi-Fi (free).

Park Inn This is one of your best bets for general overnight comfort far from the crowds. Wings curve around a landscaped courtyard at this well-managed hotel in a 1980s building. Its well-furnished rooms are arranged around a series of gardens, the largest of which contains a pool. Rooms have compact modern bathrooms (most with tub/shower combos). The poolside restaurant serves fixed-price menus.

80 rte. de Caderousse, Orange 84100. © **04-90-34-24-10.** Fax 04-90-34-85-48. www.parkinn.com. 99 units. 89€–140€ double. AE, DC, MC, V. Free parking. Drive .8km (½ mile) west of the city center, following directions to Caderousse. **Amenities:** Restaurant; bar; outdoor pool; room service. *In room:* A/C, TV, hair dryer, minibar, Wi-Fi (free).

Where to Dine

Le Parvis ☺ TRADITIONAL FRENCH Jean-Michel Berengier sets the best table in Orange, albeit in a rather austere dining room. He bases his cuisine on prime vegetables and the best ingredients from mountain or sea. Try escalope of braised sea bass with fennel or asparagus, or lamb with garlic-cream sauce. A can't-miss dish is foie gras. Fresh and flavorful seafood is prepared in different ways according to the season, and the staff prides itself on its dozens of preparations. The service is efficient and polite, and there's a children's menu.

55 cours Pourtoules. © **04-90-34-82-00.** Reservations required. Main courses 17€–26€; fixed-price menu 26€–44€; children's menu 8.50€. MC, V. Tues–Sun noon–1:45pm; Tues–Sat 7:30–9:15pm. Closed mid-Nov to Dec 3 and Jan 16–Feb 3.

Where to Stay & Dine Nearby

Château de Rochegude ★★ This Relais & Châteaux member stands on 10 hectares (25 acres) of parkland. The castle is at the edge of a hill, surrounded by vineyards. The 12th-century turreted residence has been renovated by a series of distinguished owners, ranging from a pope to a dauphin. Each room is done in Provençal style, with fabrics and furniture influenced by the region's 18th- and 19th-century traditions. As befits a château, rooms come in many shapes and sizes, and some are quite spacious. All have bathrooms with tub/shower combinations. At the château's restaurant, both the food and the service are exceptional. You can enjoy

SHOPPING FOR BROCANTE IN PROVENCE

In France, there's a big difference between antiques and fun old junk. They even have different names. For serious purchases, you may want to stick to well-established antiques stores, found in great abundance all over France. But if you prefer something more affordable and your idea of fun is a flea market, then what you really want is *brocante*. Your best bet is to head to a town's regular market on a specific day (the markets in Cannes are a good example; see chapter 17).

If you find yourself in Provence on Sunday, head out early (around 9am) for **Isle-sur-la-Sorgue,** a village that specializes in *brocante.* The town is 23km (14 miles) east of Avignon, 11km (6¾ miles) north of Cavaillon, and 42km (26 miles) south of Orange. The *brocante* market, **Foire à la Brocante** (no phone), is on Saturday, Sunday, and Monday; Sunday is most fun because there's also a food market. Everything is over by 6pm. If you're driving, try for a parking space in the free outdoor lot, Parking Portalet, adjacent to the fairgrounds. The *brocante* is on the near side of the river, a little farther downstream. Every building on the side of the street facing the river is a warehouse filled with dealers and loot.

Surprisingly for such a small place, Isle-sur-la-Sorgue has a Michelin-starred restaurant: **La Prévôté,** 4 rue J.-J.-Rousseau (*℃* **04-90-38-57-29;** www.la-prevote.fr). Technically, this restaurant lies 4km (2½ miles) outside of town, in the hamlet of Lagnes. To get here from Isle-sur-la-Sorgue, follow the signs pointing to Gordes for 4km (2½ miles). It's widely signposted. You should make your lunch reservation before arriving in town. In the rear of a flower-filled courtyard, the chef wows shoppers and locals with sublime cuisine. The *pièce de résistance* is a hot chocolate tart. Fixed-price menus cost 26€ to 68€ at lunch, 43€ to 68€ at dinner. It's closed 3 weeks in February, Tuesday and Wednesday October through June, and all of November.

Isle-sur-la-Sorgue's Office de Tourisme is at place de la Liberté (*℃* **04-90-38-04-78**).

meals in the stately dining room, barbecue by the pool, and refreshments on sunny terraces. Fixed-price lunches cost 16€ to 31€, fixed-price dinners 35€ to 85€.

26790 Rochegude. *℃* **04-75-97-21-10.** Fax 04-75-04-89-87. www.chateauderochegude.com. 25 units. 195€–355€ double; 350€–555€ suite. AE, DC, MC, V. Parking 7€. Closed Nov. Take D976 13km (8 miles) north of Orange, following signs toward Gap and Rochegude. **Amenities:** Restaurant; bar; outdoor pool; room service; tennis court. *In room:* A/C, TV, minibar, Wi-Fi (free).

AVIGNON ★★★

684km (425 miles) S of Paris; 81km (50 miles) NW of Aix-en-Provence; 106km (66 miles) NW of Marseille

In the 14th century, Avignon was the capital of Christendom. The pope lived here during what the Romans called the Babylonian Captivity. The legacy left by that court makes Avignon one of the most beautiful of Europe's medieval cities.

Today, this walled city of some 85,000 residents is a major stop on the route from Paris to the Mediterranean. It is increasingly known as a cultural center. Artists and painters have been moving here, especially to rue des Teinturiers. Experimental theaters, galleries, and cinemas have brought diversity to the inner city. The popes are long gone, but life goes on exceedingly well.

Essentials

GETTING THERE   The fastest and easiest way to get here is to **fly** from Paris's Orly Airport to **Aéroport Avignon-Caumont** (© **04-90-81-51-51**), 8km (5 miles) southeast of Avignon (trip time: 1 hr.). Taxis from the airport to the center cost 21€. Call © **04-90-82-20-20.** From Paris, TGV **trains** from Gare de Lyon take 3 hours and 30 minutes. The one-way fare is 78€. Trains arrive frequently from Marseille (70 min.; 23€) and from Arles (20 min.; 6€). For train information, call © **36-35** or visit www.voyages-sncf.com. The main **bus** routes connect Avignon to Arles (trip time: 1½ hr.), costing 6.60€ one-way, and Marseille (trip time: 2 hr.), costing 19€ one-way. The bus station at Avignon is Gare Routière, 5 av. Monclar (© **04-90-82-07-35**).

If you're **driving** from Paris, take A6 south to Lyon, and then A7 south to Avignon. If you'd like to explore the area by **bike,** go to **Provence Bike,** 52 bd. St-Roch (© **04-90-27-92-61;** www.provence-bike.com), which rents all sorts of bikes, including 10-speed road bikes and mountain bikes, for around 15€ to 25€ per day. A deposit of 150€ to 450€, in cash or a credit card imprint, is required.

VISITOR INFORMATION   The **Office de Tourisme** is at 41 cours Jean-Jaurès (© **04-32-74-32-74;** fax 04-90-82-95-03; www.ot-avignon.fr).

SPECIAL EVENTS   The biggest celebration is the **Festival d'Avignon,** held July 7 to July 27. The international festival focuses on avant-garde theater, dance, and music. Part of the fun is the bacchanalia nightly in the streets. Tickets cost 5€ to 40€. Prices for rooms and meals skyrocket, so make reservations far in advance. For information, contact the **Bureaux du Festival,** Espace Saint-Louis, 20 rue du Portail Boquier, Avignon 84000 (© **04-90-27-66-50;** www.festival-avignon.com).

Seeing the Sights

Even more famous than the papal residency is the ditty *"Sur le pont d'Avignon, l'on y danse, l'on y danse"* ("On the bridge of Avignon, we dance, we dance"). **Pont St-Bénézet ★★** (© **04-90-27-51-16**) was far too narrow for the *danse* of the rhyme, however. Spanning the Rhône and connecting Avignon with Villeneuve-lèz-Avignon, the bridge is now a ruin, with only 4 of its original 22 arches. According to legend, it was inspired by a vision that a shepherd named Bénézet had while tending his flock. The bridge was built between 1177 and 1185 and suffered various disasters. (In 1669, half of it fell into the river.) On one of the piers is the two-story **Chapelle St-Nicolas**—one story in Romanesque style, the other in Gothic. The remains of the bridge are open November through March daily 9:30am to 5:45pm, April to June and October daily 9am to 7pm, July and September daily 9am to 8pm, and August daily 9am to 9pm. Admission is 4.50€ for adults, 3.50€ for seniors and students, and free for children 7 and under. Once you pay to walk on the bridge, the small chapel on the bridge can be visited as part of the overall admission fee.

Cathédrale Notre-Dame des Doms   Near the Palais des Papes is the 12th-century Cathédrale Notre-Dame des Doms, containing the Flamboyant Gothic tomb of some of the apostate popes. Crowning the top is a statue of the Virgin from the 19th century. From the cathedral, enter the **promenade du Rocher-des-Doms** (© **04-90-82-27-96**) to stroll its garden and enjoy the view across the Rhône to Villeneuve-lèz-Avignon.

Place du Palais. © **04-90-86-81-01.** Free admission. Daily 8am–6pm. Hours may vary according to religious ceremonies.

La Fondation Angladon-Dubrujeaud ★★   The magnificent art collection of Jacques Doucet (1853–1929), the Belle Epoque dandy, dilettante, and designer of Parisian haute couture, is on view here. When not designing, Doucet collected the early works of a number of artists, among them Picasso, Max Jacob, and van Gogh. You can wander through Doucet's former abode viewing rare antiques; 16th-century Buddhas; Louis XVI chairs designed by Jacob; and canvases by Cézanne, Sisley, Degas, and Modigliani. At Doucet's death, his fortune was so diminished that his nephew paid for his funeral—but his rich legacy lives on here.

5 rue Laboureur. © **04-90-82-29-03.** www.angladon.com. Admission 6€ adults, 3€ students and children 15–18, 1.50€ children 7–14. Tues–Sun 1–6pm. Closed Tues in winter.

Musée Calvet ★   In an 18th-century mansion, this museum holds a fine- and decorative-art collection that features the works of Vernet, David, Corot, Manet, and Soutine, plus a collection of ancient silverware. Our favorite oil is Bruegel the Younger's *Le Cortège Nuptial (The Bridal Procession)*. Look for a copy of Bosch's *Adoration of the Magi,* plus sculptures by Camille Claudel.

65 rue Joseph-Vernet. (C) **04-90-86-33-84.** www.musee-calvet.org. Admission 6€ adults, 3€ students, free for children 12 and under. Wed–Mon 10am–1pm and 2–6pm.

Musée du Petit-Palais   The museum contains an important collection of paintings from the Italian schools of the 13th to 16th centuries, with works from Florence, Venice, Siena, and Lombardy. Salons display 15th-century paintings done in Avignon, and several galleries contain Roman and Gothic sculptures.

Place du Palais des Papes. (C) **04-90-86-44-58.** www.petit-palais.org. Admission 6€ adults, 2€ students, free for children 12 and under. Wed–Mon 10am–1pm and 2–6pm.

Musée Lapidaire   A 17th-century Jesuit church houses this collection of Gallo-Roman sculptures. This museum has been called a junkyard of antiquity: Gargoyles, Gallic and Roman statues, and broken pillars confront you at every turn. Most of the pieces have known greater glory and placement (often in temples); use your imagination to conjure up their lost splendor.

27 rue de la République. (C) **04-90-85-75-38.** www.musee-lapidaire.org. Admission 2€ adults, 2€ students 13–18, free for children 12 and under. Wed–Mon 10am–noon and 2–6pm.

Palais des Papes ★★★   Dominating Avignon from a hilltop is one of the most famous, or notorious, palaces in the Christian world. Headquarters of a schismatic group of cardinals who came close to destroying the authority of the popes in Rome, this fortress-showplace is the monument most frequently associated with Avignon. The guided tour (usually lasting 50 min.) can be monotonous, because most of the rooms have been stripped of their finery. The exception is the **Chapelle St-Jean,** known for its frescoes, which are attributed to the school of Matteo Giovanetti and were painted between 1345 and 1348. These frescoes present scenes from the life of John the Baptist and John the Evangelist. More Giovanetti frescoes are in the Chapelle St-Martial. They depict the miracles of St. Martial, the patron saint of Limousin.

The **Grand Tinel (Banquet Hall)** is about 41m (135 ft.) long and 9m (30 ft.) wide; the pope's table stood on the south side. The **Pope's Bedroom** is on the first floor of the Tour des Anges. Its walls are decorated in tempera foliage on which birds and squirrels perch. Bird cages are painted in the recesses of the windows. In a secular vein, the **Studium (Stag Room)**—the study of Clement VI—was frescoed in 1343 with hunting scenes. Added under the same Clement, who had a taste for grandeur, the **Grande Audience (Great Audience Hall)** contains frescoes of the prophets, also attributed to Giovanetti and painted in 1352. If you have time, consider a visit to the Musée du Petit-Palais (see above).

Place du Palais des Papes. (C) **04-90-27-50-00.** www.palais-des-papes.com. Admission (including tour with guide or recording) 11€ adults, 8.50€ seniors and students, free for children 7 and under. July daily 9am–8pm; Apr–June and Aug–Oct daily 9am–7pm; Nov–Mar daily 9:30am–5:45pm.

**1er étage
(First Floor)**

**Rez-de-chaussée
(Ground Floor)**

Palais Vieux   Palais Neuf

Stepping Back in Time in Villeneuve-Lez-Avignon ★

The modern world is impinging on Avignon, but across the Rhône, the Middle Ages slumber on. When the popes lived in exile at Avignon, cardinals built palaces (*livrées*) across the river. Many visitors prefer to stay or dine here rather than in Avignon. Villeneuve-lez-Avignon lies just across the Rhône from Avignon and is easiest to reach on bus no. 11, which crosses the larger of the two relatively modern bridges, the **pont Daladier.**

For information about the town, contact the **Office de Tourisme,** place Charles David (*✆* **04-90-25-61-33;** fax 04-90-25-91-55; www.villeneuvelesavignon.fr/tourisme).

Cardinal Arnaud de Via founded the **Eglise Notre-Dame,** place du Chapître (*✆* **04-90-25-46-24**), in 1333. Other than its architecture, the church's most popular attraction is an antique copy (by an unknown sculptor) of Enguerrand Charonton's *Pietà,* the original of which is in the Louvre. The church is open April to September daily 10am to 12:30pm and 2 to 6:30pm, and October to March daily 10am to noon and 2 to 5pm. Admission is free.

Chartreuse du Val-de-Bénédiction
Inside France's largest Carthusian monastery, built in 1352, you'll find a church, three cloisters, rows of cells that housed the medieval monks, and rooms depicting aspects of their daily lives. Part of the complex is devoted to a workshop (the Centre National d'Ecritures et du Spectacle) for painters and writers, who live in the cells rent-free for up to a year to pursue their craft. Photo and art exhibits take place throughout the year.

Pope Innocent VI (whose tomb you can view) founded this charterhouse, which became the country's most powerful. The 12th-century graveyard cloister is lined with cells where the fathers prayed and meditated.

Rue de la République. *✆* **04-90-15-24-24.** www.chartreuse.org. Admission 7€ adults, 4.50€ students, free for children 17 and under. Mon-Fri 9:30am-5pm; Sat-Sun 10am-5pm.

Fort St-André ★
Crowning the town is Fort St-André, founded in 1360 by Jean-le-Bon to serve as a symbol of might to the pontifical powers across the river. Inside the fort is the Abbaye St-André, opened in the 18th century but now privately owned. Also within the fort you can visit a formal garden, a tranquil setting with a rose-trellis colonnade, fountains, and flowers.

Mont Andaon. *✆* **04-90-25-45-35.** Admission 5€ adults, 3.50€ students and ages 17-25, free for children 16 and under. Mid-June to Sept daily 10am-1pm and 2-6pm; Oct-Mar daily 10am-1pm and 2-5pm; Apr to mid-June daily 10am-1pm and 2-5:30pm.

Musée Pierre de Luxembourg (Musée de Villeneuve-lez-Avignon) ★
Villeneuve's most important museum occupies a 14th-century home constructed for a local cardinal. The building was enlarged with a second story in the 1600s. Since its designation as a museum in 1996, it's been the richest repository of medieval painting and sculpture in the region. Its most treasured possessions include a remarkable *Coronation of the Virgin* by Enguerrand Charonton. Painted in 1453, it contains scenes that are Bosch-like in their horror, representing the denizens of hell supplicating the eternally calm mother of Christ. Equally important is a rare 14th-century ivory statue of the Virgin, by an unknown sculptor; it's one of the finest of its type anywhere.

Rue de la République. ☏ **04-90-27-49-66.** Admission 3.10€ adults, 2.10€ students and ages 18–25, free for children 17 and under. Apr–Sept Tues–Sun 10am–12:30pm and 2–6:30pm; Mar and Oct–Jan Tues–Sun 10am–noon and 2–5pm.

Tour Philippe le Bel   Philippe the Fair constructed this tower in the 13th century, when Villeneuve became a French possession; it served as a gateway to the kingdom. If you have the stamina, you can climb to the top for a view of Avignon and the Rhône Valley.

Rue Montée-de-la-Tour. ☏ **04-32-70-08-57.** Admission 2.10€ adults, 1.60€ students and children 12–17, free for children 11 and under. Apr–Sept daily 10am–12:30pm and 2–6pm; Mar and Oct–Nov Tues–Sun 10am–noon and 2–5pm.

Shopping

The idea behind **Souleiado,** 19 rue Joseph-Vernet (☏ **04-90-86-32-05**), is to duplicate 18th- and 19th-century Provençal fabric patterns. Fabrics are available by the meter and in the form of clothing for men, women, and children. In addition, you can buy kitchenware and furniture inspired by Provence and the steamy wetlands west of Marseille.

Hervé Baume, 19 rue Petite Fusterie (☏ **04-90-86-37-66**), is for those who yearn to set a Provençal table. The place is piled high with a little bit of everything—from Directoire dinner services to handblown crystal hurricane lamps. **Jaffier-Parsi,** 42 rue des Fourbisseurs (☏ **04-90-86-08-85**), is known for its copper saucepans from the Norman town of Villedieu-les-Poêles, which has been making them since the Middle Ages.

Most markets in Avignon are open 6am to 1pm. The biggest covered market with 40 different merchants is **Les Halles,** place Pie, open Tuesday through Sunday. Other smaller **food markets** are on place Parking des Italiens on Sunday, and on place St-Chamand also on Sunday. The **flower market** is on place des Carmes on Saturday, and the **flea market** is in the same place on Sunday.

Where to Stay

EXPENSIVE

Hôtel d'Europe ★★★   This deluxe hostelry, in operation since 1799, is almost the equal of La Mirande (see below), though slightly cheaper. You enter the vine-covered hotel through a courtyard, which holds tables in the warmer months. The grand hall and salons contain antiques, and the good-size guest rooms have handsome decor and period furnishings. Two suites are on the roof, with views of the Palais des Papes. In some twin-bedded rooms, the beds are a bit narrow. Overall, accommodations are comfortable, with touches of Gallic charm. The spacious bathrooms are handsomely equipped, and each has a combination tub/shower. The restaurant, which specializes in traditional French and Provençal cuisine, is one of the best in Avignon.

12 place Crillon, Avignon 84000. ☏ **04-90-14-76-76.** Fax 04-90-14-76-71. www.heurope.com. 44 units. 175€–480€ double; 655€–820€ suite. AE, DC, MC, V. Parking 16€. **Amenities:** Restaurant; bar; babysitting; room service. *In room:* A/C, TV, hair dryer, minibar, Wi-Fi (free).

La Mirande ★★★   In the heart of Avignon behind the Palais des Papes, this 700-year-old town house is one of France's grand little luxuries. In 1987, Achim and Hannelore Stein transformed it into a citadel of opulence. The hotel displays 2 centuries of decorative art, from the 1700s Salon Chinois to the Salon Rouge, with striped walls in Rothschild red. Room no. 20 is the most sought after—its lavish premises open onto the garden. All rooms are stunning, with exquisite decor, hand-printed fabrics on the walls, antiques, bedside controls, and huge bathtubs. The restaurant, among the finest in Avignon, deserves its one Michelin star.

4 place de la Mirande, Avignon 84000. ℂ **04-90-85-93-93.** Fax 04-90-86-26-85. www.la-mirande.fr. 19 units. 390€–540€ double; 660€–850€ suite. AE, DC, MC, V. Parking 25€. **Amenities:** Restaurant; bar; babysitting; room service. *In room:* A/C, TV, hair dryer, minibar, Wi-Fi (free).

MODERATE

Hôtel Clarion Cloître St-Louis ★   This hotel is in a former Jesuit school built in the 1580s. Much of the original premises remain, including the baroque facade, the wraparound arcades, and the soaring ceiling vaults. Guest rooms are more functional; in fact, they're rather dull as a result of renovations. Rooms range from medium-size to spacious, and some have sliding glass doors overlooking the patio. Each unit has modern decor without a lot of extras.

20 rue du Portail Boquier, Avignon 84000. ℂ **800/CLARION** (252-7466) in the U.S., or 04-90-27-55-55. Fax 04-90-82-24-01. www.cloitre-saint-louis.com. 80 units. 100€–210€ double; 250€–350€ suite. AE, DC, MC, V. Parking 12€–15€. **Amenities:** Restaurant; bar; outdoor pool; room service. *In room:* A/C, TV, hair dryer, minibar, Wi-Fi (free).

La Banasterie ★ 🏨   Just a short walk from the papal palace, this is one of the finer B&Bs of Avignon. It is especially recommended to lovers of chocolate. Hosts Françoise and Jean-Michel left Paris to open this place and share their passion of *chocolat* with visitors. The warmly elegant bedrooms, beautifully furnished, are named for varieties of chocolate and also for the Aztec god who gave his name to this "divine" beverage. Each guest will find chocolate on their night table upon arrival. You're also offered a decadently rich cup of cocoa before retiring.

11 rue de la Banasterie, 84000 Avignon. ℂ **04-32-76-30-78.** www.labanasterie.com. 5 units. 100€ double; 170€ suite. Rates include continental breakfast. MC, V. **Amenities:** Breakfast room; Wi-Fi (free). *In room:* Fridge.

Mercure Pont d'Avignon 🗡   This chain hotel is one of the best in Avignon, and it's a good deal for what it offers. It lies within the city walls, at the foot of the Palais des Papes. Rooms are well furnished yet functional; what they lack in style they make up for in comfort. Bathrooms are small, but most contain tub/shower combinations. Breakfast is the only meal served.

Quartier de la Balance, rue Ferruce, Avignon 84000. ℂ **04-90-80-93-93.** Fax 04-90-80-93-94. www.mercure.com. 88 units. 125€–170€ double; 250€ suite. Children 15 and under stay free in parent's room. AE, DC, MC, V. Parking 5.80€. **Amenities:** Bar. *In room:* A/C, TV, hair dryer, minibar, Wi-Fi (free).

INEXPENSIVE

Hôtel d'Angleterre   This three-story Art Deco structure in the heart of Avignon is the city's best budget hotel, with the advantage of being located inside the city ramparts. It was built in 1929 of gray stone, emulating the style that local builders imagined was characteristic of English houses. The rooms are on the small side, but they are comfortably furnished; and most have compact shower-only bathrooms. Breakfast is the only meal served.

29 bd. Raspail, Avignon 84000. ℂ **04-90-86-34-31.** Fax 04-90-86-86-74. www.hoteldangleterre.fr. 39 units. 60€–85€ double. AE, MC, V. Free parking. Closed Dec 19–Jan 19. *In room:* A/C, TV, Wi-Fi (free).

Hôtel de l'Atelier   The name of this 16th-century house (which translates as "the workshop") derives from the weaving machines that produced fabrics here during the 1950s. Since 2003, it has been the domain of Gérard and Annick Burret, who outfit their rooms in as romantic and nostalgic a style as possible. Each of the accommodations, some with high beamed ceilings, comes with a neatly tiled bathroom with shower or bathtub. You'll find the hotel in the heart of Villeneuve-lèz-Avignon, a 2-minute walk from the Pierre de Luxembourg museum. A rear garden with potted orange and fig trees provides fruit for breakfast. A stone fireplace in the duplex lounge blazes on cold winter nights. Continental breakfast is the only meal served.

5 rue de la Foire, Villeneuve-lez-Avignon 30400. ℂ **04-90-25-01-84.** Fax 04-90-25-80-06. www. hoteldelatelier.com. 23 units. 59€–115€ double; 107€–135€ triple. AE, MC, V. Parking 9€ in nearby garage. **Amenities:** Room service. *In room:* TV, hair dryer, Wi-Fi (free).

Hôtel le Médiéval   About 3 blocks south of the Palais des Papes, this three-story town house from the late 1600s is well maintained and uncomplicated. Under beamed ceilings, the comfortable guest rooms are medium-size to spacious. Most peaceful are the units that overlook the inner courtyard, with its pots of flowers and shrubs. Those that overlook a congested medieval street corner might be noisier, but they have a rough-and-ready charm of their own. Most of the small bathrooms have tub/shower combinations.

15 rue Petite Saunerie, Avignon 84000. ℂ **04-90-86-11-06.** Fax 04-90-82-08-64. www.hotelmedieval. com. 35 units. 66€–73€ double; extra bed 8€. MC, V. Closed Dec 22–Feb 3. **Amenities:** Room service. *In room:* TV, hair dryer, Wi-Fi (free).

Where to Dine

Hôtel d'Europe and **La Mirande** (see "Where to Stay," above) have excellent restaurants.

Brunel PROVENÇAL   This flower-filled restaurant is in the heart of Avignon. Managed by the Brunel family, it serves such superb dishes as monkfish with anise-flavored butter, confit of lamb couscous, and tuna steak with coulis of capers and onions. Artichoke hearts accompany grilled John Dory, and even pigs' feet are sublime. The desserts are prepared fresh daily. You can order house wines by the carafe.

46 rue de La Balance. ℂ **04-90-85-24-83.** Reservations required. Main courses 10€–20€ lunch; fixed-price menu 33€. AE, MC, V. Tues–Sat noon–1:30pm and 7:30–9:30pm (Mon–Sat in July). Closed last 2 weeks Dec.

Christian Etienne ★★★ PROVENÇAL   The stone house containing this restaurant was built in 1180, around the same time as the Palais des Papes (next door). Owner Christian Etienne reaches new culinary heights. His dining room contains early-16th-century frescoes honoring the marriage of Anne de Bretagne to the French king in 1491. Several of the fixed-price menus feature themes: Two present seasonal tomatoes, mushrooms, or other vegetables; one offers preparations of lobster; and the priciest relies on the chef's imagination (*menu confiance*) for unique combinations. In summer, look for the vegetable menu entirely based on ripe tomatoes; the main course is a mousse of lamb, eggplants, tomatoes, and herbs. The vegetable menus aren't completely vegetarian; they're flavored with meat, fish, or meat drippings. A la carte specialties include filet of perch with Châteauneuf-du-Pape, rack of lamb with fresh thyme-and-garlic essence, filet of venison with foie gras, and a dessert of fennel sorbet with saffron-flavored English cream sauce.

10 rue Mons. ℂ **04-90-86-16-50.** www.christian-etienne.fr. Reservations required. Main courses 28€–45€; fixed-price lunch 32€–120€, dinner 65€–120€. AE, DC, MC, V. Tues–Sat noon–1:15pm and 7:30–9:15pm.

Hiély-Lucullus ★★ FRENCH   Before the arrival of Christian Etienne (see above), this Relais Gourmand property reigned supreme in Avignon. Today it is still a formidable competitor. The Belle Epoque decor enhances the grand cuisine. Market-fresh products go into innovative dishes such as crayfish-stuffed ravioli flavored with fresh sage and served with pumpkin sauce, filet of female venison with tangy honey sauce, and escalope of sautéed foie gras on toasted rye bread. Lots of fresh fish is imported daily and cooked to perfection. The *pièce de résistance* is *agneau des Alpilles grillé* (grilled Alpine lamb). Dessert may be vanilla-bourbon cream in puff pastry. Carafe wines include Tavel Rosé and Châteauneuf-du-Pape.

5 rue de la République. ✆ **04-90-86-17-07.** Reservations required. Main courses 25€–40€; fixed-price menu 35€–60€. AE, MC, V. Thurs–Tues noon–2pm and 7–10pm.

La Compagnie ★ MEDITERRANEAN   Part of the charm of this place derives from the contrast between its contemporary cuisine and the grandeur of its medieval setting, a 10-minute walk from the Palais des Papes. The menu celebrates France's many colonial influences—spices and techniques from North Africa, Egypt, India, Canada, Louisiana, and parts of Africa. Menu items may include a tart with comfit of onions, thin-sliced smoked swordfish, and orange-flavored vinaigrette; giant prawns slowly cooked with comfit of lemons, coriander, cucumbers, and onions; roasted flank of Provençal bull with anchovy sauce, potato purée, and olive oil; and chicken breasts dredged in pulverized hazelnuts, served with prunes and exotic mushrooms.

The long, narrow, high-ceilinged dining rooms—originally the hallways and courtyards of a 1363 Benedictine convent that was dissolved during the French Revolution—have been meticulously restored. The restaurant is also a nightclub and bar, and the action spills into the gracefully proportioned interior courtyard. Music derives from a changing series of DJs who spin tunes Thursday to Saturday in the bar-lounge from 6pm to 1am.

83 rue Joseph-Vernet. ✆ **04-90-85-99-04.** www.lacompagniedescomptoirs.com. Reservations recommended. Main courses 11€–28€ and fixed-price menu 22€ for dinner. AE, DC, MC, V. Mon–Sat noon–2pm and 7:30–11pm.

La Fourchette 🍴 FRENCH   This bistro creates innovative cuisine at a moderate price, although it shuts down on the weekends. Its two airy dining rooms have large bay windows that flood the inside with light. You may begin with fresh sardines flavored with citrus, ravioli filled with haddock, or parfait of chicken livers with spinach flan and comfit of onions. For a main course, we recommend monkfish stew with endive, or daube of beef with gratin of macaroni.

17 rue Racine. ✆ **04-90-85-20-93.** Fixed-price lunch 25€–31€; fixed-price dinner 31€. MC, V. Mon–Fri 12:15–1:45pm and 7:15–9:45pm. Closed 3 weeks in Aug. Bus: 11.

Avignon After Dark

Near the Palais des Papes is **Le Grand Café,** La Manutention (✆ **04-90-86-86-77**), a restaurant-bar-cafe that just may become your favorite watering hole. Behind the Palais des Papes, it's in an entertainment complex in a former military supply warehouse. The dance-club standby is **Les Ambassadeurs,** 27 rue Bancasse (✆ **04-90-86-31-55**); it's more animated than its competitor, **Piano Bar Le Blues,** 25 rue Carnot (✆ **04-90-85-79-71**). Nearby is a restaurant, **Red Zone,** 27 rue Carnot (✆ **04-90-27-02-44;** www.redzonebar.com), that books live performances in the bar area by whatever band happens to be in town. There's also music and dancing at **La Compagnie** (see above).

An alternative is **Bokao's Café,** 9 quai St-Lazare (✆ **04-90-82-47-95;** www. bokaos.fr), a restaurant and disco. The most viable option for lesbians and gays is **L'Esclave,** 12 rue de Limas (✆ **04-90-85-14-91**), a bar and disco that are the focal point of the city's gay community.

ST-REMY-DE-PROVENCE ★

705km (438 miles) S of Paris; 26km (16 miles) NE of Arles; 19km (12 miles) S of Avignon; 13km (8 miles) N of Les Baux

Nostradamus, the physician and astrologer, was born here in 1503. However, St-Rémy is more closely associated with van Gogh. He committed himself to an asylum here in 1889 after cutting off his left ear. Between moods of despair, he painted such works as *Olive Trees* and *Cypresses.*

Come to sleepy St-Rémy not only for its memories and sights but also for a glimpse of small-town Provençal life. It's a market town of considerable charm that draws the occasional visiting celebrity trying to escape the spotlight.

Essentials

GETTING THERE Local **buses** from Avignon (four to nine per day) take 40 minutes and cost around 4€ one-way. In St-Rémy, buses pull into the place de la République, in the town center. For bus information, call ✆ **04-90-82-07-35.** If you're **driving,** head south from Avignon along D571.

VISITOR INFORMATION The **Office de Tourisme** is on place Jean-Jaurès (✆ **04-90-92-05-22;** fax 04-90-92-38-52; www.saintremy-de-provence.com).

Seeing the Sights

Monastère St-Paul-de-Mausolée ★★ Visitors can see the 12th-century cloisters of the asylum that van Gogh made famous in his paintings. Now a psychiatric hospital for women, the former monastery is east of D5, a short drive north of Glanum (see below). You can't visit the cell where the artist was confined from 1889 to 1890, but it's worth visiting to explore the Romanesque chapel and cloisters. The circular arches and columns have beautifully carved capitals. On your way to the church, you'll see a bust of van Gogh.

Av. Edgar-le-Roy. ✆ **04-90-92-77-00.** Admission 4€ adults, 3€ students and children 12–16, free for children 11 and under. Apr–Sept daily 9:30am–7pm; Oct–Dec and Feb–Mar daily 10:15am–5pm.

Ruines de Glanum ★ A Gallo-Roman settlement thrived here during the final days of the Roman Empire. Its monuments include a triumphal arch from the time of Julius Caesar, along with a cenotaph called the Mausolée des Jules. Garlanded with sculptured fruits and flowers, the arch dates from 20 B.C. and is the oldest in Provence. The mausoleum was raised to honor the grandsons of Augustus and is the only extant monument of its type. In the area are entire streets and foundations of private residences from the 1st-century town, plus some remains from a Gallo-Greek town of the 2nd century B.C.

Av. Vincent-van-Gogh. ✆ **04-90-92-23-79.** Admission 7€ adults, 5.50€ students and ages 18–25, free for children 17 and under. Apr–Aug daily 10am–6:30pm; Sept–Mar Tues–Sun 10:30am–5pm. From St-Rémy, take D5 1.5km (1 mile) south, following signs to LES ANTIQUES.

Shopping

St-Rémy is a center for home decorating, with many antiques shops and fabric stores on the narrow streets of the old town and the boulevards surrounding it. **Portes Anciennes,** route d'Avignon (✆ **04-90-92-13-13;** www.portesanciennes.com), sells a good selection of antiques and flea-market finds. St-Rémy is known for its great **markets.** On Wednesday morning on the streets of the old town, vendors spread out their wares, including spices, olives, fabrics, and crafts. On Saturday morning, a small vegetable market is held near the Eglise St-Martin on boulevard Marceau.

Where to Stay

Château des Alpilles ★★★   For luxury and refinement, this is the only château in the area that can equal Vallon de Valrugues (see below). It sits in the center of a tree-studded park 2km (1¼ miles) from the center of St-Rémy. The Pichot family built it in 1827, and it housed Chateaubriand and other luminaries. When Françoise Bon converted the mansion in 1980, she wanted to create a "house for paying friends." The rooms combine an antique setting with plush upholstery, rich carpeting, and vibrant colors with a garden graced with majestic magnolias. Each guest room is appointed with whimsical accessories, like a pair of porcelain panthers flanking one of the mantels, and travertine-trimmed bathtubs. Units in the 19th-century annex are as comfortable as those in the main house. The midsize bathrooms have tub/showers.

Ancienne Route du Grès, St-Rémy-de-Provence 13210. ✆ **04-90-92-03-33.** Fax 04-90-92-45-17. www. chateaudesalpilles.com. 21 units. 180€–320€ double; 260€–337€ suite. AE, DC, MC, V. Closed early Jan to mid-Mar. **Amenities:** Restaurant; bar; outdoor pool; room service; sauna; 2 tennis courts. *In room:* A/C, TV, hair dryer, minibar, Wi-Fi (free).

Hostellerie du Vallon de Valrugues ★★★   Surrounded by a park, this hotel has the best accommodations and restaurant in town. Constructed in the 1970s, it resembles a fantasy version of an ancient Roman villa. Owner Jean-Michel Gallon offers beautiful rooms and suites. They have marble bathrooms, all with tub/showers. The property has a putting green, and guests have access to horseback riding. The restaurant's terrace is as appealing as its cuisine, which is winning praise for innovative light dishes, such as John Dory with truffles, and frozen nougat with comfit of fruits. Fixed-price menus are 58€ to 85€; a children's menu is 20€.

Chemin Canto-Cigalo, St-Rémy-de-Provence 13210. ✆ **04-90-92-04-40.** Fax 04-90-92-44-01. www. vallondevalrugues.com. 52 units. 190€–310€ double; 310€–1,310€ suite. AE, MC, V. Closed mid-Jan to mid-Feb. **Amenities:** Restaurant; bar; babysitting; exercise room; outdoor pool; room service; sauna; tennis court. *In room:* A/C, TV, hair dryer, minibar, Wi-Fi (free).

Hôtel du Soleil   In 1965, a private home was converted into this amiable, unpretentious hotel, a 4-minute walk south of the town center. The hotel is set in a garden with grand trees and a wrought-iron gazebo. Inside, the assortment of ceiling beams and Provençal accessories evoke the region around you. Guest rooms are simple but convenient, with tasteful furnishings and small, tiled bathrooms (some with both tub and shower). You'll want to spend part of your time beside the pool, ringed by chaise longues.

35 av. Pasteur, St-Rémy-de-Provence 13210. ✆ **04-90-92-00-63.** Fax 04-90-92-61-07. www.hotel soleil.com. 24 units. 64€–80€ double; 110€ suite. AE, DC, MC, V. Closed mid-Nov to early Mar. **Amenities:** Bar; outdoor pool; room service. *In room:* TV, hair dryer, Wi-Fi (free).

Hôtel les Ateliers de l'Image   Fans refer to this place as "trendy but not posh." It's one of the most unusual hotels in the region, nestled in a 1-hectare (2½-acre) park studded with olive trees and cypresses. The bar and the less expensive guest rooms are in a simple, boxy building that was originally a movie theater. The more luxurious rooms and the restaurant fill the radically restored premises of a 19th-century building that was the town's first bona fide hotel. In both buildings, rooms are comfortable, stylish, and airy, outfitted with minimalist wood and metallic furniture. Many look out on the park and the faraway foothills. Four units are duplex suites, each with a private steam room, and one suite is a "treehouse," supported by the majestic branches of a century-old plane tree and accessible from an upper floor of the main building by a catwalk. Its restaurant, **Le Provence,** fuses French and Asian flavors, and its unique Le Bar (see "St-Rémy After Dark," below) is a nighttime draw.

36 bd. Victor Hugo, St-Rémy-de-Provence 13210. ℂ **04-90-92-51-50.** Fax 04-90-92-43-52. www. hotelphoto.com. 32 units. 165€–400€ double; 400€–600€ duplex suite. AE, DC, MC, V. Closed end Oct to early Mar. **Amenities:** 2 restaurants; bar; babysitting; 2 outdoor pools; room service. *In room:* A/C, TV, hair dryer, Wi-Fi (free).

La Maison du Village ★★ 🎁   Our favorite nest in this über-Provençal town is this meticulously restored 18th-century town house in the center of St-Rémy. Warm and welcoming, each unit is a suite with a big sitting area and a luxurious bathroom. They're decorated in soft colors, with tasteful fabrics and wrought-iron beds. The old-fashioned, free-standing bathtubs are large enough for a romantic duo. On request, the innkeepers serve organic meals in the family-style dining room or the little "secret garden" out back. Drinks are served and soft music plays in the communal lounge.

10 rue du 8 Mai 1945, St-Rémy-de-Provence 13210. ℂ **04-32-60-68-20.** Fax 04-32-60-68-21. www. lamaisonduvillage.com. 5 units. 150€–190€ double. MC, V. **Amenities:** Lounge; room service. *In room:* A/C, TV, Wi-Fi (free).

Where to Dine

Another great choice is the restaurant at the **Hostellerie du Vallon de Valrugues** (see "Where to Stay," above).

La Gousse d'Ail PROVENÇAL   A small, family-run place, La Gousse d'Ail serves good food at reasonable prices. Specialties include *escargot à la Provençal* (snails with garlic and regional herbs) and vegetarian dishes featuring colorful produce from the market, prepared with light sauces and local herbs. At least 1 day a week the chef prepares the restaurant's famous bouillabaisse. The waitstaff speaks English.

6 bd. Marceau. ℂ **04-90-92-16-87.** www.la-goussedail.com. Reservations recommended. Main courses 19€–28€; dinner 27€–34€. AE, MC, V. Fri–Wed noon–2pm and 7–10pm. Closed mid-Jan to early Feb.

La Maison Jaune ★★ FRENCH/PROVENÇAL   One of the most enduringly popular restaurants in St-Rémy is in the former residence of an 18th-century merchant. Today, in a pair of dining rooms occupying two floors, you'll appreciate cuisine prepared and served with flair by François and Catherine Perraud. In nice weather, additional seats are on a terrace overlooking the Hôtel de Sade. Menu items include pigeon roasted in wine from Les Baux; grilled sardines served with candied lemon and raw fennel; artichoke hearts marinated in white wine and served with tomatoes; and succulent roasted rack of lamb served with tapenade of black olives and anchovies.

15 rue Carnot. ℂ **04-90-92-56-14.** www.franceweb.org/lamaisonjaune. Reservations required. Fixed-price menu 36€–66€. MC, V. Tues–Sun noon–1:30pm; Tues–Sat 7:30–9pm. Closed Dec–Jan.

St-Rémy After Dark

Le Bar, in the Hôtel les Ateliers de l'Image, 36 bd. Victor Hugo (✆ **04-90-92-51-50**), is an unusual destination in this laid-back town. In a former Art Deco movie theater, it is open June to September daily 5pm to 7am.

ARLES ★★★

725km (450 miles) S of Paris; 35km (22 miles) SW of Avignon; 89km (55 miles) NW of Marseille

Often called the soul of Provence, this town on the Rhône attracts art lovers, archaeologists, and historians. To the delight of visitors, many of the vistas van Gogh painted so luminously remain. The painter left Paris for Arles in 1888, the same year he cut off part of his left ear. He painted some of his most celebrated works here, including *The Starry Night, The Bridge at Arles, Sunflowers,* and *L'Arlésienne.*

The Greeks are said to have founded Arles in the 6th century B.C. Julius Caesar established a Roman colony here. Constantine the Great named it the second capital of his empire in A.D. 306, when it was known as "the little Rome of the Gauls." Arles was incorporated into France in 1481.

Though Arles doesn't possess as much charm as Aix-en-Provence, it's still rewarding to visit, with first-rate museums, excellent restaurants, and summer festivals. The city today, with a population of 55,000, isn't quite as lovely as it was, but it has enough of the antique charm of Provence to keep its appeal alive.

Essentials

GETTING THERE   There are hourly rail connections between Arles and Avignon (20 min.; 6€–8€), Marseille (50 min.; 13€), and Nîmes (20 min.; 7.30€). For rail schedules and information, call ✆ **36-35.** There are about four **buses** per day from Aix-en-Provence (trip time: 1 hr., 45 min.). For bus information, call ✆ **08-10-00-08-16.** If **driving,** head south along D570 from Avignon.

If you'd like to get around by bicycle, head for **Cycles Peugeot,** 15 rue du Pont (✆ **04-90-96-03-77**), which rents bikes at 15€ per day.

VISITOR INFORMATION   The **Office de Tourisme** is on esplanade Charles-de-Gaulle (✆ **04-90-18-41-20;** fax 04-90-18-41-29; www.arlestourisme.com).

Exploring the Town

Arles is full of Roman monuments. **Place du Forum,** shaded by plane trees, is around the old Roman forum. The Café de Nuit, immortalized by van Gogh, once

---

Van Gogh's "Different Light"

What strikes me here is the transparency of the air.

— Vincent van Gogh

Dutch-born Vincent van Gogh (1853–90) moved to Arles in 1888 and spent 2 years in the historic towns of Les Baux, St-Rémy, and Stes-Maries, recording, through the filter of his neuroses, dozens of Impressionistic scenes now prized by museums. His search, he said, was for "a different light." When he found it, he created masterpieces such as *The Starry Night, Cypresses, Olive Trees,* and *Boats Along the Beach.*

ACCOMMODATIONS ■
Grand Hotel Nord Pinus **4**
Hôtel Calendal **6**
Hôtel d'Arlatan **1**
Hôtel de l'Amphithéatre **5**
Hôtel Jules César **7**
L'Hôtel Particulier **8**
Hôtel Le Cloître **2**

DINING ◆
La Gueule du Loup **3**
Restaurant Lou Marquês **7**

stood on this square. You can see two Corinthian columns and fragments from a temple at the corner of the Hôtel Nord-Pinus. Three blocks south of here is **place de la République,** dominated by a 15m-tall (49-ft.) blue porphyry obelisk. On the north is the **Hôtel de Ville** (town hall) from 1673, built to Mansart's plans and surmounted by a Renaissance belfry.

One of the city's great classical monuments is the Roman **Théâtre Antique ★★**, rue du Cloître (*✆* **04-90-49-38-20**). Augustus began the theater in the 1st century; only two Corinthian columns remain. The *Venus of Arles* was discovered here in 1651. Take rue de la Calade from city hall. The theater is open May to September daily 9am to 6:30pm; March, April, and October daily 9 to 11:30am and 2 to 6pm; and November to February daily 10 to 11:30am and 2 to 4:30pm. Admission is 3€ for adults, 2.20€ for students and children 12 to 18, and free for children 11 and under. Nearby is the **Amphitheater (Les Arènes) ★★**, rond-point des Arènes (*✆* **04-90-49-36-86**), also built in the 1st century. Sometimes called Le Cirque Romain, it seats almost 25,000 and still hosts bullfights in summer. Visit at your own risk: The stone steps are uneven, and much of the masonry is worn. For a good view, you can climb the three towers that remain from medieval times, when the amphitheater was

Le Olé

Bullfights, or corridas, are held about 5 weekends a year, between Easter and late September. The bull is killed only during the Easter corridas (perhaps a reference to the death of Christ?); otherwise, the bull is not killed, making the ritual less bloody than the Spanish version. The Easter event begins at 11am, the others around 5pm. A seat on the stone benches of the Roman amphitheater costs 16€ to 90€. Tickets are usually available at the amphitheater a few hours beforehand. For advance ticket sales, call ℭ **04-90-96-03-70.**

turned into a fortress. Hours are May through September daily 9am to 6pm; March, April, and October daily 9am to 6pm; and November to February daily 10am to 5pm. Admission costs 6€ for adults, 4.50€ for students and children 18 and under.

Eglise St-Trophime ★   This church is noted for its 12th-century portal, one of the finest achievements of the southern Romanesque style. Frederick Barbarossa was crowned king of Arles here in 1178. In the pediment, Christ is surrounded by the symbols of the Evangelists. The cloister, in Gothic and Romanesque styles, is noted for its medieval carvings.

East side of place de la République. ℭ **04-90-96-07-38.** Free admission to church; cloister 3.50€ adults, 2.60€ students and children 12–18, free for children 11 and under. Church daily 8:30am–6:30pm. Cloister Nov–Feb daily 10am–5pm; Mar–Apr and Oct daily 9am–6pm; May–Sept daily 9am–6:30pm. Closed Jan 1, May 1, Nov 1, and Dec 25.

Les Alyscamps ★   Perhaps the most memorable sight in Arles, this Christian graveyard was once a Roman necropolis. After being converted into a Christian burial ground in the 4th century, it became a setting for legends and was even mentioned in Dante's *Inferno*. Today, it's lined with poplars and studded with ancient sarcophagi. Arlesiens escape here to enjoy a respite from the heat.

Rue Pierre-Renaudel. ℭ **04-90-49-36-87.** Admission 3.50€ adults, 2.60€ children 12–18, free for children 11 and under. Nov–Feb daily 10am–noon and 2–4:30pm; Mar–Apr and Oct daily 9:30am–noon and 2–5:30pm; May–Sept daily 9am–6:30pm. Closed Jan 1, May 1, Nov 1, and Dec 25.

Musée de l'Arles et de la Provence Antiques ★★   About 1km (½ mile) south of the town center within a hypermodern setting built in 1995, you'll find one of the world's most famous collections of Roman Christian sarcophagi, plus a rich ensemble of sculptures, mosaics, and inscriptions from the Augustinian period to the 6th century A.D. Eleven detailed models show ancient monuments of the region as they existed in the past.

Presqu'île du Cirque Romain. ℭ **04-90-18-88-88.** Admission 6€ adults, 4.50€ students and children 17 and under. Apr–Oct daily 9am–7pm; Nov–Mar daily 10am–5pm. Closed Jan 1, May 1, Nov 1, and Dec 25.

Musée Réattu ★   This collection, which belonged to the local painter Jacques Réattu, has been updated recently with works including etchings and drawings by Picasso. Other pieces are by Alechinsky, Dufy, and Zadkine. Note the Arras tapestries from the 16th century.

10 rue du Grand-Prieuré. ✆ **04-90-49-37-58.** Admission 7€ adults, 5€ students and children 12-18, free for children 11 and under. May–Sept daily 10am–noon and 2–6:30pm; Mar–Apr and Oct daily 10am–noon and 2–5pm; Nov–Feb daily 1–5:30pm.

Where to Stay

Grand Hôtel Nord-Pinus ★ Few other hotels in town evoke Provence's charm as well as this one, which originated as a bakery at the turn of the 20th century. Occupying a town house on a tree-lined square in the heart of Arles, it has public rooms filled with antiques, an ornate staircase with wrought-iron balustrades, and many of the trappings you'd expect in an upscale private home. Guest rooms are glamorous, even theatrical; they come in a range of shapes, sizes, and decors, and are filled with rich upholsteries and draperies arranged artfully beside oversize French doors. Many bullfighters and artists have stayed here; their photographs, as well as a collection of safari photos by Peter Beard, decorate the public areas.

14 place du Forum, Arles 13200. ✆ **04-90-93-44-44.** Fax 04-90-93-34-00. www.nord-pinus.com. 26 units. 160€–310€ double; 570€ suite. AE, DC, MC, V. Parking 17€. **Amenities:** Restaurant; bar; room service. *In room:* TV.

Hôtel Calendal ★ ✿ Because of its reasonable rates, the Calendal is a bargain hunter's favorite. On a quiet square near the arena, it provides high-ceilinged accommodations decorated in bright colors. Most rooms have views of the hotel's garden, filled with palms and palmettos. Each unit comes with a compact shower-only bathroom.

5 rue Porte de Laure, Arles 13200. ✆ **04-90-96-11-89.** Fax 04-90-96-05-84. www.lecalendal.com. 38 units. 79€–109€ double; 159€ suite. AE, DC, MC, V. Parking 8€. Bus: 4. **Amenities:** Restaurant; bar; room service; spa. *In room:* A/C, TV, hair dryer, Wi-Fi (free).

Hôtel d'Arlatan ★ In the former residence of the *comtes* d'Arlatan de Beaumont, this hotel has been managed by the same family since 1920. It was built in the 15th century on ancient Roman foundations. Rooms are furnished with authentic Provençal antiques and have tapestry-covered walls. Try to get a room overlooking the garden. Those on the ground floor are largest. About two-thirds of the guest rooms have tub/shower combos, and the rest have showers.

26 rue du Sauvage, Arles 13100. ✆ **04-90-93-56-66.** Fax 04-90-49-68-45. www.hotel-arlatan.fr. 47 units. 85€–157€ double; 175€–247€ suite. AE, MC, V. Parking 13€–14€. Closed Jan. **Amenities:** Bar; rooms for those w/limited mobility. *In room:* A/C, TV, minibar, Wi-Fi (free).

 A Shopping Expedition

In an isolated spot 12km (7½ miles) north of Arles, **Magasin d'Usine Les Olivades,** chemin des Indienneurs, St-Etienne-du-Grès (✆ **04-90-49-18-04**), sits by the road leading to Tarascon. A trek here is worth your while for the wide array of art objects and fabrics inspired by Provence. The inexpensive prices here result from small flaws, most of them not noticeable, in some of the fabric or color runs. Some of the patterns may be from previous outdated seasons, but no one back home will know the difference. Dresses, shirts for men and women, table linens, and fabric are available at Olivades retail outlets throughout Provence, but the selection here is better and cheaper.

An Homage to Mistral

If you're interested in Frédéric Mistral and how he revitalized the Provençal language, opt for a pilgrimage to the village of Maillane, 15km (9⅓ miles) north of Arles. To get there, follow the signs to Avignon and turn off at the clearly signposted routes to Maillane and the **Musée de Frédéric Mistral**, avenue Lamartine, Maillane (✆ **04-90-95-74-06**). Here, within Mistral's childhood home, you'll find his daily writing implements; evidence of his devotion to his early widowed mother; insights into some of his romantic dalliances with local damsels; a writing desk that had belonged to his close friend, 19th-century novelist and poet Lamartine; and a letter, in French, from then–U.S. president Theodore Roosevelt, bearing the letterhead of the White House in Washington. From October to March, the museum is open Tuesday to Sunday 10 to 11:30am and 2 to 4:30pm; from April to September, hours are Tuesday to Sunday 9:30 to 11:30am and 2:30 to 6:30pm. Entrance is 4€ for adults, 3€ for ages 12 to 18, and free for children 11 and under.

Hôtel de l'Amphitheatre   Originally built in the 1600s, this hotel is ideally situated midway between the ancient Roman amphitheater and the Roman theater. Today, it's on the short list of the city's centrally located and particularly charming hotels. The antique atmosphere is filled with hand-hewn wood ceiling beams, bright fabrics, soft lighting, reproductions of Provençal or rococo furniture, and a layout of bedrooms that in some cases feature sweeping views out over the terra-cotta roofs of historic Arles. Our preferred nest here is the Belvedere Suite, whose windows offer 360-degree views over the town. No meals are served other than breakfast, but many dining options lie within a short walk.

5–7 rue Diderot, Arles 13200. ✆ **04-90-96-10-30.** Fax 04-90-93-98-69. www.hotelamphitheatre.fr. 28 units. 55€–95€ double; 125€–155€ suite. AE, MC, V. Parking 5.50€. **Amenities:** Breakfast room. *In room:* A/C, TV, fridge, hair dryer, Wi-Fi (free).

Hôtel Jules César ★★★   This 17th-century Carmelite convent is now a stately country hotel with one of the best restaurants in town. Although it's in a noisy neighborhood, most rooms face the unspoiled cloister. You'll wake to the scent of roses and the sounds of birds singing. Throughout, you'll find a blend of neoclassical architecture and modern amenities. The decor is luxurious, with antique Provençal furnishings found at auctions in the countryside. The interior rooms are the most tranquil and the darkest, though enlivened by bright fabrics. Most of the downstairs units are spacious; the upstairs rooms are small but have a certain old-world charm. The rooms in the modern extensions are comfortable but lack character. Each bathroom comes with a combination tub/shower.

9 bd. des Lices, Arles Cedex 13631. ✆ **04-90-52-52-52.** Fax 04-90-52-52-53. www.hotel-julescesar.fr. 58 units. 160€–250€ double; 300€–385€ suite. AE, DC, MC, V. Parking 13€. Closed Nov–Mar. **Amenities:** Restaurant (see Lou Marquès, below); bar; babysitting; room service. *In room:* TV, hair dryer, minibar, Wi-Fi (10€ per hr.).

L'Hôtel Particulier ★★   Occupying an 18th-century pavilion, this was the last of the grand private town houses built in the center of Arles. It may not be as grand as the Jules César, but it has become a formidable challenger to the Nord

Pinus even though Particulier is very small. Behind its monumental gate, you'll encounter ancient yew trees and a courtyard with teak lounges and a limestone-built *bassin* which contains a lap pool. Imagine fresh rose petals scattered on your breakfast table. Each bedroom is decorated individually and elegantly, some with four-poster beds and draped canopies. The furnishings are Provençal antiques or tasteful reproductions.

4 rue de la Monnaie, 13200 Arles. ✆ **04-90-52-51-40.** Fax 04-90-96-16-70. www.hotel-particulier. com. 15 units. 209€–259€ double; 259€–389€ suite. AE, DC, MC, V. Parking 19€. **Amenities:** Restaurant; outdoor pool; room service; small spa. *In room:* A/C, TV, minibar, Wi-Fi (free).

Muette ★ 🏠 In the heart of Arles, this hotel was created from a historic building with roots going back to the 12th and 15th centuries. Of course, it's been much altered and changed over the years, and today is equipped with up-to-date amenities. The bedrooms are large for the most part and still have their original stone walls. Modern bathrooms have been discreetly installed. The hotel lies only a short walk from the Arena.

15 res des Suisses, 13200 Arles. ✆ **94-90-96-15-39.** www.hotel-muette.com. 18 units. 54€–74€ double; 79€–90€ quad. AE, MC, V. Closed: Jan. **Amenities:** Breakfast room. *In room:* TV, minibar, Wi-Fi (free).

Where to Dine

La Gueule du Loup FRENCH/PROVENÇAL   Named for its founder, who, according to local legend, grew to resemble a wolf as he aged, this cozy, well-managed restaurant occupies a stone-fronted antique house in the historic core of Arles, near the ancient Roman arena. Today it's owned by members of the Allard family, who prepare serious gourmet-style French food that's more elaborate than the cuisine at many competitors. The best examples include hearty filet of bull braised in red wine, monkfish in saffron sauce, roasted cod with green and sweet red peppers in saffron sauce, and superb duckling cooked in duck fat and served with flap mushrooms. Reservations are important: The room seats only 30.

39 rue des Arènes. ✆ **04-90-96-96-69.** Reservations recommended. Main courses 24€–30€; fixed-price lunch 12€–17€, dinner 23€–30€. MC, V. Tues–Sun noon–2pm and 7–9:30pm. Closed mid-Jan to early Feb.

Restaurant Lou Marquès ★★ PROVENÇAL   Lou Marquès, at the Hôtel Jules-César, has the best reputation in town. Seating is in the formal dining room or on the terrace. The cuisine features creative twists on Provençal specialties. A first course could be *queues de langoustine en salade vinaigrette d'agrumes et basilic* (crustaceans and salad with citrus-and-basil vinaigrette) or *risotto de homard aux truffes* (lobster risotto with truffles). As a main course, try *pavé de loup en barigoule d'artichaut et à la sauge* (a thick slice of wolf fish with sage-stuffed artichokes) or *filet mignon de veau et ragoût fin de cèpes et salsifis* (veal with a stew of mushrooms and salsify, a long-forgotten oyster-flavored vegetable). For a light dessert, there's *biscuit glacé au miel de lavande* (a small cake glazed with lavender honey).

At the Hôtel Jules César, 9 bd. des Lices. ✆ **04-90-52-52-52.** Reservations recommended. Main courses 26€–34€; fixed-price lunch 21€–28€, dinner 28€–60€. AE, DC, MC, V. Mon–Fri and Sun noon–1:30pm; Mon–Sat 7–9:30pm.

Arles After Dark

Because of its relatively small population (around 50,000), Arles doesn't offer as many nightlife options as Aix-en-Provence, Avignon, Nice, or Marseille. The town's most appealing choice is the bar-cafe–music hall **Le Cargo de Nuit,** 7 av.

Sadi-Carnot (© **04-90-49-55-99;** www.cargodenuit.com). Open Wednesday to Saturday night, it's a club that later has live music—salsa, jazz, rock 'n' roll—and then disco dancing until 3am. Cover ranges from 8€ to 25€.

The town's most animated cafe, where most singles go, is **Le Café van Gogh,** 11 place du Forum (© **04-90-96-44-56**). Overlooking an attractive plaza, it features live music and an ambience that the almost young and the restless refer to as *super-chouette,* or "supercool."

LES BAUX ★★★

715km (444 miles) S of Paris; 19km (12 miles) NE of Arles; 81km (50 miles) N of Marseille

Cardinal Richelieu called Les Baux "a nesting place for eagles." On a wind-swept plateau overlooking the southern Alpilles, Les Baux is a ghost of its former self, though still very dramatic. It was once the citadel of seigneurs who ruled with an iron fist and sent their armies as far as Albania. In medieval times, troubadours from all over the Continent came to this "court of love," where they recited western Europe's earliest-known vernacular poetry. Eventually, Alix of Baux, the "Scourge of Provence," ruled Les Baux, sending his men throughout the land to kidnap people. If no one was willing to pay ransom for one of his victims, the poor wretch was forced to walk a gangplank over the cliff's edge.

Fed up with the rebellions against Louis XIII in 1632, Richelieu commanded his armies to destroy Les Baux. Today, the castle and ramparts are mere shells, though you can see remains of Renaissance mansions. The dry, foreboding countryside around Les Baux, which nestles in a valley surrounded by shadowy rock formations, offers its own fascination. Vertical ravines lie on either side of the town. Vineyards—officially classified as Coteaux d'Aix-en-Provence—surround Les Baux, facing the Alpilles. If you follow the signposted *route des vin,* you can motor through the vineyards in an afternoon, perhaps stopping off at growers' estates.

Now the bad news: Because of the beauty and drama of the area, Les Baux is virtually overrun with visitors; it's not unlike Mont-St-Michel in that respect.

Essentials

GETTING THERE　　Les Baux is best reached by car; there is no rail service. From Arles, take the express highway N570 northeast until you reach the turnoff for a secondary road (D17), which will lead you northeast to Fontvieille. From here, just follow the signs east into Les Baux. By **train,** most passengers get off at Arles. Bus service has been discontinued. Taxis in Arles (© **06-80-27-60-92**) will take you to Les Baux for around 30€ to 40€; be sure to agree upon the fare in advance.

VISITOR INFORMATION　　The **Office de Tourisme** (© **04-90-54-34-39;** fax 04-90-54-51-15; www.lesbauxdeprovence.com) is on Maison du Roy, near the northern entrance to the old city.

Exploring the Area

Les Baux is one of the most dramatic towns in Provence. You can wander through feudal ruins, called **La Ville Morte (Ghost Village) ★★★**, at the northern end of town. The site of this citadel covers an area at least five times that of Les Baux itself. As you stand at the ruins, you can look out over the Val d'Enfer (Valley of Hell) and even see the Mediterranean in the distance.

You can reach **La Citadelle ★★**, the castle ruins at the bottom of the town, by walking up rue du Château, which leads into the **Château des Baux** (✆ 04-90-54-55-56). Allow at least an hour to explore. You enter the citadel by going through the **Hôtel de la Tour du Brau,** which houses the Musée du Château. The building was the residence of the powerful Tour de Brau family. The museum has exhibits related to the history of Les Baux, which will help you understand the ruins in the compound. Models of the fortress in medieval times explain how the site has evolved architecturally.

After leaving the Hôtel de la Tour du Brau, you're free to wander through the ruins. You'll take in such sites as the ruined chapel of St-Blaise (now home to a little museum devoted to the olive), replicas of medieval siege engines, grottoes used for storage or lodgings in the Middle Ages, the skeleton of a hospital built in the 16th century, and a cemetery. Finally, from the **Tour Sarrazin (Saracen Tower)** you get a view of the village and the citadel compound. Admission to the castle, including the museum and access to the ruins, is 7.80€ for adults, 5.80€ for students, and free for children 17 and under. The site is open in July and August daily 9am to 7:30pm, March to June and in September and October daily 9am to 6:30pm, and November to February daily 9:30am to 5pm.

In the village, you can visit the **Yves Brayer Museum,** at the intersection of rue de la Calade and rue de l'Eglise (✆ 04-90-54-36-99; www.yvesbrayer.com). In a 16th-century house (Hôtel de Porcelet), the museum is devoted to the works of Yves Brayer (1907–90), a figurative painter and a famous native son (he's buried in the village cemetery). His works depict Italy, Morocco, and Spain, along with bullfighting scenes. The museum is open April to September daily 10am to 12:30pm and 2 to 6:30pm; off-season hours are Wednesday to Monday 10am to 12:30pm and 2 to 5:30pm (closed January to mid-February). Admission is 4€ for adults, 2.50€ for students and children 12 and under.

Cathédrale d'Images ★ (✆ 04-90-54-38-65) is one of the most remarkable cathedrals in Provence. It lies in a limestone quarry a quarter-mile north of the village; take route du Val d'Enfer. Outside, you can marvel at the fact that the cathedral is carved out of the stone mountain. It's just as amazing inside, where the limestone surfaces of the large rooms and pillars become three-dimensional screens for a bizarre audiovisual show. Hundreds of projectors splash images from all directions according to themes that change throughout the season. In the past, shows have celebrated the triumphs of the Italian Renaissance, medieval pilgrimages, the works of van Gogh, and Romanesque sculpture and architecture. Photographer Albert Plecy created the site in 1977. It's open daily 10am to 6pm (closed January 2 to February 8). Admission is 7.50€ for adults and 3.50€ for children 17 and under.

Musée des Santons is in the town's **Ancien Hôtel de Ville,** place Louis Jou (✆ 04-90-54-34-39). Built in the 16th century as a chapel, La Chapelle des Pénitents Blancs, the museum displays antique and idiosyncratic woodcarvings, each representing a different saint or legend. It's open April to October daily 9am to 7pm, and November to March daily 9am to 5pm. Admission is free.

Climb to the much-praised **place St-Vincent** for a sweeping view over the Vallon de la Fontaine. This is also the site of the much-respected **Eglise St-Vincent** (no phone), which is open April to October daily 9am to 7pm, November to March daily 9am to 5:30pm. Its campanile is called La Lanterne des Morts (Lantern of the Dead). The modern windows were a gift from Rainier of Monaco, when he was the marquis des Baux during the 1980s. Today, Albert of Monaco fulfills the honorary/ceremonial duties associated with that role. If anything, you're more likely to see Caroline of Monaco, thanks to her residency within a private home in nearby St-Rémy-de-Provence, a few miles downhill from here.

The Renaissance-era **Hôtel de Manville,** rue Frédéric Mistral, was built in the 16th century as a private mansion. Today, it is the **Mairie** (town hall) of Les Baux. You can visit its courtyard. It's open the same hours as Musée des Santons (see above). **Fondation Louis Jou** lies in the Renaissance-era **Hôtel Jean-de-Brion,** rue Frédéric Mistral (⏍ **04-90-54-34-17**). It can be visited only by appointment and does not maintain regular hours, even during the times when they're "officially posted" as being open. Those official hours are defined as April through December, every Thursday to Monday from 11am to 1pm and 2 to 6pm. In reality they are less frequent than that, so be sure to call before your arrival. Inside are engravings and serigraphs by the Barcelona-born artist Louis Jou (1882–1968), as well as a few small-scale works by Rembrandt, Dürer, and Goya. Jou frequently visited Paris but considered Les Baux his home from 1917 until his death. He is considered the most important contemporary artist to come out of Les Baux. Admission is 3€ for adults, 1.50€ for children.

Where to Stay

La Riboto de Taven (see "Where to Dine," below) rents rooms.

Auberge de la Benvengudo ★   In a quiet location about 1.5km (1 mile) south of town, this *auberge* is a 19th-century farmhouse surrounded by sculptured shrubbery, towering trees, and parasol pines. The property has an outdoor pool, a tennis court, and a terrace filled with the scent of lavender and thyme. About half the rooms are in the original building, above the restaurant, and the rest in an attractive stone-sided annex. All are sunny and well maintained. Each has a private terrace or balcony, and some have antique four-poster beds. Five units come with shower only; the others have a combination tub/shower.

Vallon de l'Arcoule, rte. d'Arles, Les Baux 13520. ⏍ **04-90-54-32-54.** Fax 04-90-54-42-58. www.benvengudo.com. 26 units. 105€–200€ double; 155€–370€ suite. AE, MC, V. Parking free. Closed Nov 1–Mar 15. Take RD78 for 1.5km (1 mile) southwest of Les Baux, following signs to Arles. **Amenities:** Restaurant; babysitting; outdoor pool; room service; tennis court. *In room:* A/C, TV, hair dryer, Wi-Fi (4€ per day).

Hostellerie de la Reine-Jeanne ✇   In the heart of the village, this warm, well-scrubbed inn is the best bargain in Les Baux. You enter through a typical provincial French bistro. All the guest rooms are spartan but comfortable, and three have terraces. Bathrooms are cramped and relatively modest, with a shower stall only.

Grand Rue, Les Baux 13520. ⏍ **04-90-54-32-06.** Fax 04-90-54-32-33. www.la-reinejeanne.com. 10 units. 50€–70€ double; 100€ apt for 4. AE, MC, V. Closed Jan 5–31. **Amenities:** Restaurant; bar; room service. *In room:* A/C, TV, Wi-Fi (free).

La Cabro d'Or ★★★   This is the less famous, less celebrated sibling of the nearby Oustau de Baumanière (see below). You'll find some of the most comfortable accommodations in the region in these five low-slung stone buildings. The original building, a farmhouse, dates from the 18th century. The guest room decor evokes old-time Provence with art and antiques. Some rooms have sweeping views over the countryside. The dining room sits in a much-altered agrarian building from the 1800s. The massive ceiling beams are works of art in their own right.

The restaurant is flanked by a vine-covered terrace with views of a pond, a garden, and a rocky and barren landscape that has been compared to the surface of the moon. The cuisine, although not on the level of Oustau de Baumanière's, is sublime: light and flavorful, with a special emphasis on fresh produce. Specialties include a thick roasted slice of foie gras of duckling served with lemon-flavored quince sauce and red port wine, carpaccio of red mullet flavored with olive oil and sea salt, and a lasagna of scallops served with strips of Serrano ham. Main courses range from 45€ to 47€; the restaurant also features a fixed-price menu for 110€.

Les Baux de Provence 13520. ⓒ **04-90-54-33-21.** Fax 04-90-54-45-98. www.lacabrodor.com. 31 units. 160€–300€ double; 430€–610€ suite. AE, DC, MC, V. Closed mid-Nov to Dec 18. **Amenities:** Restaurant; babysitting; outdoor pool; 2 tennis courts. In room: A/C, TV, hair dryer, minibar, Wi-Fi (free).

Oustau de Baumanière ★★★ This Relais & Châteaux member is one of southern France's legendary hotels. Raymond Thuilier bought the 14th-century farmhouse in 1945, and by the 1950s, it was a rendezvous for the glitterati. Today, managed by its founder's grandson, it's not as glitzy, but the three stone houses draped in flowering vines are still charming. The plush rooms evoke the 16th and 17th centuries. All units contain large sitting areas, and no two are alike. If there's no vacancy in the main building, the hotel will assign you to one of the annexes. Request Le Manoir, the most appealing. The spacious bathrooms contain tub/shower combinations.

In the stone-vaulted dining room, the chef serves specialties such as ravioli of truffles with leeks, *rossini* (stuffed with foie gras) of veal with fresh truffles, and roast duckling with olives. The award-winning *gigot d'agneau* (lamb) *en croûte* has become this place's trademark. Fixed-price menus cost 120€ to 175€.

Les Baux, Maussane-les-Alpilles 13520. ⓒ **04-90-54-33-07.** Fax 04-90-54-40-46. www.oustaudebaumaniere. com. 30 units. 230€–410€ double; 380€–555€ suite. AE, DC, MC, V. Closed Jan 4–Feb 5. Restaurant closed Wed all day and Thurs at lunch Oct–Mar. **Amenities:** Restaurant; babysitting; outdoor pool; room service. In room: A/C, TV, hair dryer, minibar, Wi-Fi (free).

Where to Dine

La Cabro d'Or and **Oustau de Baumanière** (see above) offer excellent dining.

La Riboto de Taven ★★★ PROVENÇAL Known for its flawless cuisine and market-fresh ingredients, this is one of the great restaurants of the area, a rival of La Cabro d'Or. The 1835 farmhouse outside the medieval section of town has been owned by two generations of the Novi family. In summer, you can sit outdoors. Brawny flavors and the heady perfumes of Provençal herbs characterize chef Jean-Pierre Novi's cuisine. Menu items may include sea bass in olive oil; fricassee of mussels flavored with basil; lamb en croûte with olives; or perhaps, in late autumn and winter, medallions of roebuck served with caramelized root vegetables; plus homemade desserts. The menu changes virtually every day and always features an intelligent and tasteful use of local ingredients and produce.

Accommodations include four rooms within the thick walls of the main *mas* (Provençal farmhouse) costing 180€ to 290€, and two "cave-dweller junior suites" that have been shoehorned into the grottoes at the far end of the establishment's garden, and which look out across the ravine toward the once-fortified citadel of Les Baux. These go for 280€. Each of the accommodations is gracefully accessorized with Provençal-style furniture, and each contains a minibar, phone, TV, hair dryer, and full bathroom. The property has a swimming pool. Wi-Fi in the room is free.

Le Val d'Enfer, Les Baux 13520. ℗ **04-90-54-34-23.** Fax 04-90-54-38-88. www.riboto-de-taven.fr. Reservations required. Fixed-price menu 56€. AE, MC, V. Thurs–Tues 7:30–9:30pm. Closed Jan–Mar.

AIX-EN-PROVENCE ★★

755km (469 miles) S of Paris; 81km (50 miles) SE of Avignon; 32km (20 miles) N of Marseille; 306km (190 miles) W of Nice

This faded university town is the most charming center in Provence. Founded in 122 B.C. by Roman general Caius Sextius Calvinus, who named the town Aquae Sextiae after himself, Aix (pronounced *ex*) originated as a military outpost. It became a civilian colony, the administrative capital of a province of the late Roman Empire, the seat of an archbishop, and official residence of the medieval *comtes* de Provence. After the union of Provence with France, Aix remained a judicial and administrative center until the Revolution.

Paul Cézanne, the celebrated son of this old capital of Provence, immortalized the countryside in his paintings. Just as he saw it, Montagne Ste-Victoire looms over the town today, though a string of high-rises now interrupts the landscape.

Today, this city of 160,000 is quiet in winter but active and bustling when the summer hordes pour in. Many local residents are international students. (The Université d'Aix dates from 1413.) Summer is lively, with frequent cultural events, ranging from opera to jazz, from June to August. Aix is an increasingly popular bedroom community for urbanites fleeing Marseille after 5pm.

Essentials

GETTING THERE   The city is easily accessible. Twenty-seven **trains** arrive daily from Marseille; the trip takes 45 minutes and costs 7€ one-way. Twenty-five trains arrive from Nice; the trip takes 3 to 4 hours and costs 36€ one-way. There are also 25 trains per day from Cannes (3½ hr.), costing 35€ one-way. High-speed TGV trains arrive at Vitroll, 5.5km (3⅓ miles) west of Aix. Bus links to the center of Aix cost 4.10€ one-way. For more information, call ℗ **36-35. Buses** from Marseille arrive every 10 minutes; from Avignon, five times a day; and twice a day from Nice. For more information, call ℗ **08-91-02-40-25.** If you're **driving** to Aix from Avignon or other points north, take A7 south to RN7 and follow it into town. From Marseille or other points south, take A51 north into town.

 Aix Through the Eyes of Cézanne

One of the best experiences in Aix is a walk along the well-marked *route de Cézanne* (D17), which winds eastward through the countryside toward Ste-Victoire. From the east end of cours Mirabeau, take rue du Maréchal-Joffre across boulevard Carnot to boulevard des Poilus, which becomes avenue des Ecoles-Militaires and finally D17. The

stretch between Aix and the hamlet of Le Tholonet is full of twists and turns where Cézanne often set up his easel. The entire route makes a lovely 5.5km (3½-mile) stroll. Le Tholonet has a cafe or two where you can refresh yourself while waiting for one of the frequent buses back to Aix.

510

To explore the region by bike, head for **La Rotondo,** 2 av. Des Belges (© **04-42-26-78-92**), a short walk northeast of the cours Mirabeau. Here you can rent 10-speed racing bikes or more durable mountain bikes for 20€ per day. You must leave a deposit—your passport or driver's license, or cash or monetary objects worth the value of the bike, usually 250€.

VISITOR INFORMATION The **Office de Tourisme** is at 2 place du Général-de-Gaulle (© **04-42-16-11-61;** fax 04-42-16-11-62; www.aixenprovencetourism.com).

SPECIAL EVENTS Aix celebrates the performing arts, particularly music, more than any other city in the south of France. **Festival International d'Art Lyrique & de Musique** (© **04-42-17-34-34;** www.festival-aix.com) in late July, attracts musicians from all over the world.

Exploring the Area

Aix's main street, **cours Mirabeau ★**, is one of Europe's most beautiful. Plane trees stretch across the street like umbrellas, shading it from the hot Provençal sun and filtering the light into shadows that play on the rococo fountains below. Shops and sidewalk cafes line one side of the street; sandstone *hôtels particuliers* (mansions) from the 17th and 18th centuries fill the other. The street begins at the 1860 fountain on place de la Libération, which honors Mirabeau, the revolutionary and statesman. A ring of streets, including boulevard Carnot and cours Sextius, circles the heart of the old quarter (Vieille Ville, or old town). Inside this périphérique is the pedestrian zone.

After touring Aix, you may consider a side trip on D10 15km (9⅓ miles) east to the **Château de Vauvenarges,** the privately owned site of Pablo Picasso's last home. You can't visit the château's interior, but Picasso and one of his wives, Jacqueline Roche, are buried nearby. Stop for a meal at **Au Moulin de Provence,** 33 rue des Maquisards (© **04-42-66-02-22**), across the road from the château.

Atelier de Cézanne   Cézanne was the major forerunner of cubism. This house, surrounded by a wall and restored by American admirers, is where he worked. Repaired in 1970, it remains much as Cézanne left it in 1906, "his coat hanging on the wall, his easel with an unfinished picture waiting for a touch of the master's brush," as Thomas R. Parker wrote.

9 av. Paul-Cézanne (outside town). © **04-42-21-06-53.** Admission 5.50€ adults, 2€ students and children 12 and under. Apr–June and Sept daily 10am–noon and 2–6pm; July–Aug daily 10am–6pm; Oct–Mar daily 10am–noon and 2–5pm. Closed Jan 1, May 1, and Dec 25.

Cathédrale St-Sauveur ★   The cathedral of Aix is dedicated to Christ under the title St-Sauveur (Holy Savior or Redeemer). Its baptistery dates from the 4th and 5th centuries, and the complex as a whole has seen many additions. It contains a 15th-century Nicolas Froment triptych, *The Burning Bush.* One side depicts the Virgin and Child; the other, Good King René and his second wife, Jeanne de Laval.

Place des Martyrs de la Résistance. © **04-42-23-45-65.** Free admission. Daily 8am–noon and 2–6pm. Mass Sun 10:30am and 7pm.

Chapelle Penitents-gris (Chapelle des Bourras)   This 16th-century chapel honoring St. Joseph was built on the ancient Roman Aurelian road linking Rome and Spain. Herbert Maza, founder and former president of the Institute for American Universities, restored the chapel. M. Borricand, rector of a group of local ecclesiastics, arranges visits.

15 rue Lieutaud. © **04-42-26-60-99.** Free admission; donations welcome. Visits by reservation only.

Musée des Tapisseries ★   Three series of tapestries from the 17th and 18th centuries line the gilded walls of this former archbishop's palace. The prelates decorated the palace with *The History of Don Quixote,* by Natoire; *The Russian Games,* by Leprince; and *The Grotesques,* by Monnoyer. The museum also exhibits rare furnishings from the 17th and 18th centuries.

28 place des Martyrs de la Résistance. © **04-42-23-09-91.** Admission 3€ adults, free for ages 24 and under. Mid-Oct to mid-Apr Wed–Mon 1:30–5pm; mid-Apr to mid-Oct Wed–Mon 10am–6pm. Closed Jan, May 1, and Dec 25–26.

Shopping

Opened more than a century ago, **Bechard,** 12 cours Mirabeau (© **04-42-26-06-78**), is the most famous bakery in town. It takes its work so seriously that it refers to its underground kitchens as a *laboratoire* (laboratory). Most of the delectable pastries are made fresh every day.

To the Markets We Will Go

Aix offers the best markets in the region. Place Richelme holds a **fruit-and-vegetable market** every morning. Come here to buy the exquisite products of Provence, such as olives, lavender, local cheeses, and fresh produce. There's a **flower market** Tuesday, Thursday, and Saturday morning on place des Prêcheurs. The **fish market** is daily in the morning on place Richelme.

Founded in 1934 on a busy boulevard just east of the center of town, **Santons Fouque,** 65 cours Gambetta, route de Nice (☎ **04-42-26-33-38**), stocks the largest assortment of *santons* (wooden figurines of saints) in Aix. More than 1,900 figurines are cast in terra cotta, finished by hand, and painted according to 18th-century models. Each of the trades practiced in medieval Provence is represented, including shoemakers, barrel makers, coppersmiths, and ironsmiths, poised to welcome the newborn Jesus.

Where to Stay
EXPENSIVE

Hôtel Cézanne ★★ Named in honor of the painter, this is the first boutique hotel to open in Aix-en-Provence. Bathed in light, the rooms and suites pay homage to Provence and the paintings of Cézanne. The bedrooms are spacious and modern, from the "tropical" showers to free cold drinks in the minibar. Breakfast, served until noon, might include smoked salmon and champagne. The hotel is not only up-to-date, but innovative and colorful with a strong sense of design. What we like most is how the sunlight seems to caress the mother-of-pearl inlaid walls, on which the light almost dances, as in a Cézanne painting.

40 av. Victor Hugo, Aix-en-Provence 13100. ☎ **04-42-91-11-11.** Fax 04-42-91-11-10. www.hotelaix.com/cezanne. 55 units. 179€ double; 249€ junior suite; 310€ suite. AE, MC, V. **Amenities:** Bar; room service. *In room:* A/C, TV, hair dryer, minibar, Wi-Fi (free).

Hôtel des Augustins ★ Converted from the 12th-century Grands Augustins Convent, this hotel is beautifully restored, with ribbed-vault ceilings, stained glass, stone walls, terra-cotta floors, and an entry hall loaded with Louis XIII furnishings. The reception desk is in a chapel, and paintings and watercolors decorate the public rooms. This place won a spot in history by sheltering an excommunicated Martin Luther on his return from Rome. The rooms are outfitted in a restrained contemporary style, with dark-wood furniture and high ceilings. Breakfast is the only meal served.

3 rue de la Masse, Aix-en-Provence 13100. ☎ **04-42-27-28-59.** Fax 04-42-26-74-87. www.hotel-augustins.com. 29 units. 99€–250€ double. AE, MC, V. *In room:* A/C, TV, minibar, Wi-Fi (free).

La Villa Gallici ★★★ This elegant, relentlessly chic inn, which originated in the 18th century as a private home, is the most stylish hotel in town. The rooms, richly infused with the decorative traditions of Aix, are subtle and charming. Some rooms have a private terrace or garden, and each comes with a combination tub/shower. The villa sits in a large enclosed garden in the heart of Aix, close to one of the best restaurants, Le Clos de la Violette (see "Where to Dine," below). It's a 5-minute walk to the town center.

Av. de la Violette, Aix-en-Provence 13100. ℂ **04-42-23-29-23.** Fax 04-42-96-30-45. www.villagallici. com. 22 units. 230€–780€ double; 440€–945€ suite. AE, DC, MC, V. Closed Jan. **Amenities:** Restaurant; bar; babysitting; outdoor pool; room service. *In room:* A/C, TV, hair dryer, minibar, Wi-Fi (free).

28 à Aix ★★★ 🏠 This *hotel particulier* is as good as it gets if you want to live in a small, sumptuously decorated town house created from a restored 17th-century mansion. With its voluptuous little garden out back, it's like living in a jewel box, complete with a rococo-esque salon for afternoon tea. Its sophisticated owners have created this oasis of charm, tranquillity, style, and comfort, only steps away from cours Mirabeau. You're able to enjoy light lunches and pastries near the fireplace, or outside in the sunny garden. Perfection rules: Even the air is scented.

28 rue du 4 Septembre, Aix-en-Provence 13100. ℂ **04-42-54-82-01.** Fax 04-42-53-10-13. www.28aix. com. 4 units. 250€–500€ double. Rates include breakfast. MC, V. Parking 20€. **Amenities:** Breakfast lounge; room service. *In room:* A/C, TV, hair dryer, minibar, Wi-Fi (free).

MODERATE

Grand Hôtel Nègre Coste   This hotel, an 18th-century former town house, is so popular with the musicians who flock to Aix for the summer festivals that it's difficult to get a room at any price. Such popularity is understandable. Flowers cascade from jardinières, and 18th-century carvings surround the windows. Inside, there's a wide staircase, marble portrait busts, and a Provençal armoire. The medium-size soundproof rooms contain interesting antiques. The higher floors overlook cours Mirabeau or the old city. Each unit comes with a compact bathroom with shower; some have tubs as well.

33 cours Mirabeau, Aix-en-Provence 13100. ℂ **04-42-27-74-22.** Fax 04-42-26-80-93. www.hotel negrecoste.com. 37 units. 90€–145€ double. AE, DC, MC, V. Parking 10€. **Amenities:** Room service; smoke-free rooms. *In room:* A/C, TV, hair dryer, minibar, Wi-Fi (free).

INEXPENSIVE

Hôtel Cardinal 🗝   Not everything in this hotel is state-of-the-art, but because of the old-fashioned setting (an 18th-c. town house loaded with personalized quirks), a collection of 18th- and 19th-century antiques, and upscale and historically appropriate upholsteries, many clients don't seem to mind. Located in the Mazarin quarter, on the side of the cours Mirabeau that's less frequently visited by foreign visitors, it has touches of nostalgia that many locals associate with old-time Provence. The annex, which lies about 7.5m (25 ft.) away, near an antique church, holds most of the suites, each of which has a simple kitchenette.

24 rue Cardinale, Aix-en-Provence 13100. ℂ **04-42-38-32-30.** Fax 04-42-26-39-05. www.hotel-cardinal-aix.com. 29 units. 70€ double; 110€ suite. MC, V. **Amenities:** Room service. *In room:* TV, hair dryer.

Hôtel des Quatre Dauphins   This 18th-century town house is a short walk from place des Quatre Dauphins and the cours Mirabeau. Some original motifs have survived through frequent modernizations. The medium-size guest rooms were refurbished in simplified Provençal style, some with painted ceiling beams and casement windows that overlook the street. Five units come with a compact bathroom with tub/shower, the rest with shower only. You can have breakfast in your room or in a small salon.

54 rue Roux-Alphéran, Aix-en-Provence 13100. ℂ **04-42-38-16-39.** Fax 04-42-38-60-19. 13 units. 65€–100€ double. AE, MC, V. **Amenities:** Room service. *In room:* A/C, TV, Wi-Fi (5€ per day).

Hôtel La Caravelle 🏊 This conservatively furnished hotel, with a bas-relief of a three-masted caravel on its stucco facade, is a 3-minute walk from the center of town. It offers warm hospitality. One nice touch is the breakfast served in the stone-floored lobby. The rooms have double-glazed windows to help muffle the noise. Most bathrooms contain showers only.

29 bd. du Roi-René (at cours Mirabeau), Aix-en-Provence 13100. ℂ **04-42-21-53-05.** Fax 04-42-96-55-46. www.lacaravelle-hotel.com. 30 units. 65€–70€ double. AE, DC, MC, V. Parking free. **Amenities:** Room service. *In room:* A/C, TV, Wi-Fi (free).

Where to Dine
VERY EXPENSIVE

Le Clos de la Violette ★★★ MODERN FRENCH This innovative restaurant is a few steps from La Villa Gallici (see "Where to Stay," above) in an elegant neighborhood that most visitors reach by taxi. The Provençal villa has an octagonal reception area and several dining rooms. The stylish, seasonal dishes highlight the flavors of Provence. A stellar example of the innovative cuisine is an appetizer of mousseline of potatoes with sea urchins and fish roe. An elegant dish is braised sea wolf with crisp fried shallots and spicy Spanish sausages. Delightful rack of suckling lamb is stuffed with carrots and chickpeas and served under an herb-flavored pastry crust. For dessert, try multilayered sugar cookies with hazelnut- and vanilla-flavored cream sauce and thin slices of white chocolate, or a "celebration" of Provençal figs—an artfully arranged platter containing a galette, tart, parfait, and sorbet.

10 av. de la Violette. ℂ **04-42-23-30-71.** www.closdelaviolette.fr. Reservations required. Main courses 46€–49€; fixed-price lunch 50€; tasting menu 130€. AE, MC, V. Tues–Sat noon–1:30pm and 7:30–9:30pm.

MODERATE

Brasserie Les Deux Garçons PROVENÇAL No patron necessarily comes here for the food, although it's not bad, just standard fare. You come here for the memories and the atmosphere of a brasserie founded in 1792. Emile Zola and Cézanne used to dine here, as has everybody from Picasso to Sir Winston Churchill. On a winter's night the piano bar upstairs is the coziest rendezvous in Aix, attracting jazz lovers. In summer linen-draped sidewalk tables open onto cours Mirabeau. You dine on Provençale fare, including *daube de boeuf à la provençale* (stewed beef marinated in a garlic purée); roast goose, wild rabbit, and the fresh fruits and vegetables of the season.

53 cours Mirabeau. ℂ **04-42-26-00-51.** www.les2garcons.com. Reservations recommended. Main courses 16€–36€; fixed-price menu 25€. AE, MC, V. Daily 11am–3pm and 7pm–2am.

Chez Maxime GRILLS/PROVENÇAL Set in the heart of Aix's pedestrian shopping zone, this likeable restaurant offers an all-Provençal ambience of bordeaux-colored banquettes, salmon-colored walls, and tables, each shaded by an enormous linden tree, that spill out onto the pavement during clement weather. There's a succulent array of a dozen grills, beefsteaks, and fresh fish, as well as a main course laced with saffron and the flavors of the sea, a *marmite* (stewpot) *de la mer.* Also appealing is house-made foie gras of duckling, a kind of pâté made from beef and Provençal herbs known as *caillette de province,* and such desserts as a *fondant au chocolat.* The wine list features dozens of vintages, many of them esoteric bottles from the region.

12 place Ramus. ℂ **04-42-26-28-51.** www.restaurant-chezmaxime.com. Reservations recommended. Main courses 12€–20€; fixed-price lunch 12€, dinner 25€–30€. MC, V. Tues–Sat noon–2pm; Mon–Sat 7–10pm (Oct–Mar closed Sun–Mon).

Le Bistro Latin ★★ 🍴 PROVENÇAL This is the best little bistro in Aix-en-Provence for the price. Guests dine in two intimate rooms: a street-level space and a cellar decorated in Greco-Latin style. The staff is young and enthusiastic, taking special pride in their fixed-price menus. Try chartreuse of mussels, a meat dish with spinach-and-saffron cream sauce, scampi risotto, or rack of lamb in an herbed crust.

18 rue de la Couronne. ⓒ **04-42-38-22-88.** Reservations recommended. Main courses 16€–20€; fixed-price lunch 23€, dinner 23€–45€. MC, V. Thurs–Tues noon–2pm and 7–10:30pm.

Aix After Dark

An easy-to-reach bar that manages to be convenient and hip at the same time lies almost directly across from the city's tourist office. Open daily 8am until at least 2am, **La Rotonde,** place Jeanne d'Arc (ⓒ **04-42-91-61-70**), functions as a bar, a cafe, and a rendezvous point for friends and business associates throughout the day and evening.

People between the ages of 20 and 30 who like animated bar scenes and loud electronic music head for **Le Mistral,** 3 rue Frédéric-Mistral (ⓒ **04-42-38-16-49**), where techno and house music blares long and loud, all for a cover charge of around 16€ to 20€—unless you happen to be gorgeous and female, in which case you'll get in free and, depending on the mood of the staff, you may even receive a free glass or two of champagne.

For jazz that's produced by a changing roster of visiting musicians, head for the **Scat Club,** 11 rue de la Verrerie (ⓒ **04-42-23-00-23**), a smoky jazz den that's the preferred venue for patrons in their late 30s and 40s. Open Tuesday through Sunday, it maintains notoriously late hours, with live music often not beginning until around midnight. And last but certainly not least is Aix's body-shop bar, **La Joia** (ⓒ **06-80-35-92-94;** www.joia-club.com), route de l'Enfant, in the hamlet of Les Milles, 8km (5 miles) south of Aix (to get there, follow the signs to Marseille). On-site you'll find a restaurant, several bars, an outdoor swimming pool (the kind where you may opt to jump in topless), a dance floor with both indoor and outdoor sections, and a venue that's more hip than it is chic. Know in advance that long lines await on Fridays and Saturdays. Entrance usually costs 12€ to 18€, unless you're a star or self-enchanted enough to convince the doorman that you are.

MARSEILLE ★★★

771km (479 miles) S of Paris; 187km (116 miles) SW of Nice; 31km (19 miles) S of Aix-en-Provence

Bustling Marseille, with more than a million inhabitants, is the second-largest city in France and the country's premier port. It's been called France's New Orleans and (by Dumas) "the meeting place of the entire world." The city is ancient, founded by Greeks in the 6th century B.C. Marseille is a place of unique sounds, smells, and sights. It has seen wars and destruction, but trade has always been its raison d'être.

Perhaps its most common association is with the national anthem of France, "La Marseillaise." During the French Revolution, 500 volunteers marched to Paris, singing this rousing song along the way. The rest is history.

Although Marseille is sprawling, dirty, and slumlike in many respects, it also exhibits much elegance and charm. The **Vieux-Port,** the colorful old harbor, compensates for the dreary industrial dockland nearby. Marseille is also the home of

Basilique Notre-Dame-de-la-Garde **4**
Basilique St-Victor **3**
Cathédrale de la Major **1**
Musée Cantini **5**
Musée d'Histoire de Marseille **7**
Musée Grobet-Labadié **8**
Parc du Pharo **2**
RTM (Transit Office) **6**

many North and sub-Saharan Africans, creating a lively medley of races and creeds. A quarter of the population is of North African descent.

Marseille is twice the size of Paris, and its age-old problems include a drug industry, smuggling, corruption, the Mafia, and racial tension. Unemployment is on the rise. Nevertheless, it's always fascinating and unlike any other city in France. A city official proclaimed: "Marseille is the unbeloved child of France. It's attached to France, but has the collective consciousness of an Italian city-state, like Genoa or Venice." A renaissance of sorts is underway. Tourism has risen, and some cruise ships are again including Marseille as a port of call. Scaffolding and grand construction projects are everywhere—and it's about time.

To the astonishment of much of the country, a 2007 poll of French people under 25 years cited Marseille as the number-one French city in which they'd like to live, with Montpellier second. Paris tied for third place with Bordeaux.

Essentials

GETTING THERE   **Marseille Airport** (✆ 04-42-14-14-14), 27km (17 miles) northwest of the city center, receives international flights from all over Europe. From the airport, blue-and-white minivans (*navettes*) make the trip to Marseille's St-Charles rail station, near the Vieux-Port, for 8.50€. The minivans run daily every 20 minutes from 6am (hourly) until the arrival of the last flight.

Marseille has **train** connections from all over Europe, with especially good connections to and from Italy. The city is the terminus for the TGV bullet train, which departs daily from Paris's Gare de Lyon (trip time: 3 hr., 15 min.; one-way fare 50€–95€). Some Parisians plan a day trip to the Mediterranean beaches at Marseille, returning to the City of Light for dinner. Local trains leave Paris almost every hour, making a number of stops before reaching Marseille. For information, call ✆ **36-35. Buses** serve the Gare Routière, place Victor Hugo (✆ 04-91-08-16-40), adjacent to the St-Charles railway station. Five buses arrive daily from Aix-en-Provence every 20 minutes, a one-way ticket costing 4.90€. The trip time is 35 minutes.

If you're **driving** from Paris, follow A6 south to Lyon, and then continue south along A7 to Marseille. The drive takes about 7 hours. From Provence, take A7 south to Marseille.

GETTING AROUND   Parking and car safety are so problematic that your best bet is to park your car in a garage and rely on public transportation.

Métro lines 1 and 2 both stop at the main train station, Gare St-Charles, place Victor Hugo. Individual tickets are for sale at Métro and bus stops for 1.50€ each; they're valid on Métro and bus lines for up to 60 minutes after purchase. If you plan to take public transport several times during your stay, you get a discount if you buy a **Carte Liberté,** valid for either 5 rides for 6.30€ or 10 rides for 13€. They're available at any Métro station or **Espace Info** booth. The kiosks provide information about Marseille's public transport system at strategic points throughout the city, usually in or near Métro stations. Information and public-transit maps are available at the main office, **Espace Info,** 6 rue des Fabres (✆ 04-91-91-92-10).

The major arteries divide Marseille into 16 *quartiers*. Unlike Paris's *arrondissements,* the designations rarely appear in addresses.

Call ✆ 04-91-02-20-20 for a **taxi.**

VISITOR INFORMATION   The **Office de Tourisme** is at 4 la Canebière (✆ 04-91-13-89-00; fax 04-91-13-89-20; www.marseille-tourisme.com; Métro: Vieux-Port).

Seeing the Sights

Many travelers never visit the museums, preferring to absorb the life of the city on its busy streets and at its cafes, particularly those along the main street, **La Canebière.** Known as "can of beer" to World War II GIs, it's the heart and soul of Marseille—and the seediest main street in France. Lined with hotels, shops, and restaurants, it fills with sailors from every nation and people of every nationality, including many Algerians. (Some 100,000 North Africans live in the city and its tenement suburbs, often in communities that resemble *souks.*)

La Canebière winds down to the **Vieux-Port ★★**, dominated by the massive neoclassical forts of St-Jean and St-Nicholas. The port is filled with fishing craft and yachts and ringed with seafood restaurants. For a panoramic view, head to the **Parc du Pharo,** a promontory facing the entrance to the Vieux-Port. From a terrace overlooking the Château du Pharo, built by Napoleon III for his Eugénie, you can clearly see Fort St-Jean and the old and new cathedrals.

One of the most efficient, and easiest, ways to see Marseille's centrally located monuments is aboard the hop-on, hop-off fleet of **Le Grand Tour Buses** (© 04-91-91-05-82; www.marseillelegrandtour.com). Each bus is painted in highly recognizable shades of white, blue, and yellow, and each sports an open-air deck that you'll either appreciate for its unobstructed view or avoid because of its exposure to the blasting heat of the midsummer sun. The buses run year-round, although more buses run between March and mid-November (about eight per day, usually from 10am–5pm) than during other times of the year (about four per day, usually every other hour from 10:30am–4:15pm). There's a one-time fee of 18€ for adults and 15€ for seniors and students with proper ID; children ages 4 to 11 pay 8€. Participants can get off at any of 16 different stops en route, and then climb back onto the next bus in the day's sequence, usually arriving between 1 and 2 hours later, depending on the season. For additional details, contact the tourist office at © 04-91-13-89-00.

A tourist train, the **Petit Train de la Bonne Mère** (© 04-91-25-24-69; Métro: Vieux-Port), makes two circuits around town. Year-round, train no. 1 makes a 50-minute round-trip to Basilique Notre-Dame-de-la-Garde and Basilique St-Victor. From Easter to October, train no. 2 makes a 40-minute round-trip of old Marseille by way of the cathedral, Vieille Charité, and the Quartier du Panier. The trains depart from quai des Belges at the Vieux-Port. Each trip costs 6€ for adults and 3€ for children.

From quai des Belges at the Vieux-Port, you can take a 25-minute motorboat ride to **Château d'If** for 10€ round-trip. Boats leave every 60 to 90 minutes, depending on the season. For information, contact the **Frioul If Express** (© 04-91-46-54-65; Métro: Vieux-Port), daily 9am to 6:30pm. On the sparsely vegetated island of Château d'If (© 04-91-59-02-30 for information), François I built a fortress to defend Marseille. The site later housed a prison, where carvings by Huguenot prisoners can still be seen. Alexandre Dumas used the château as a setting for the fictional adventures of *The Count of Monte Cristo.* The château's most famous association—with the legendary Man in the Iron Mask—is also apocryphal. The château is open Tuesday to Sunday 9am to 5:30pm (until 6:30pm Apr–Sept). Entrance to the island is 5€ adults, 3.50€ ages 18 to 25, and free for those 17 and under.

If you're driving, continue from the old port to the **corniche Président-J.-F.-Kennedy,** a 4km (2½-mile) promenade. You'll pass villas and gardens and have a good view of the Mediterranean. To the north is the **Port Moderne,** the "gateway to the East." Its construction began in 1844, and a century later the Germans destroyed it. Motorboat trips are conducted along the docks.

Basilique Notre-Dame-de-la-Garde   This landmark church crowns a limestone rock overlooking the southern side of the Vieux-Port. It was built in the Romanesque-Byzantine style popular in the 19th century and topped by a 9m (30-ft.) gilded statue of the Virgin. Visitors come for the view—best at sunset—from its terrace. Spread out before you are the city, the islands, and the sea.

Rue Fort-du-Sanctuaire. ℭ **04-91-13-40-80.** www.notredamedelagarde.com. Free admission. Daily 7am–7pm. Métro: Vieux-Port. Bus: 60.

Basilique St-Victor ★   This semifortified basilica was built above a crypt from the 5th century, when St. Cassianus founded the church and abbey. You can visit the crypt, which also reflects work done in the 10th and 11th centuries.

Place St-Victor. ℭ **04-96-11-22-60.** Admission to crypt 2€. Church and crypt daily 9am–7pm. Head west along quai de Rive-Neuve (near the Gare du Vieux-Port). Métro: Vieux-Port.

Cathédrale de la Major   This was one of the largest cathedrals (some 135m/443 ft. long) built in Europe in the 19th century. It has mosaic floors and red-and-white marble banners, and the exterior is in a bastardized Romanesque-Byzantine style. The domes and cupolas may remind you of Istanbul. This vast pile has almost swallowed its 12th-century Romanesque predecessor, built on the ruins of a temple of Diana.

Place de la Major. ℭ **04-91-90-53-57.** Free admission. Hours vary. Métro: Vieux-Port.

Musée Cantini   The temporary exhibitions of contemporary art here are often as good as the permanent collection. This museum is devoted to modern art, with masterpieces by Derain, Marquet, Ernst, Masson, Balthus, and others. It also owns a selection of works by important young international artists.

19 rue Grignan. ℭ **04-91-54-77-75.** Admission 3€ adults, 1.50€ students, free for seniors and children 9 and under. Oct–May Tues–Sun 10am–5pm; June–Sept Tues–Sun 11am–6pm. Métro: Vieux-Port.

Musée d'Histoire de Marseille   Visitors may wander through an archaeological garden where excavations are going on, as scholars learn more about the ancient town of Massalia, founded by Greek sailors. To help you more fully realize the era, audiovisual exhibits and a free exhibition room set the scene. A medieval quarter of potters has been discovered and is open to the public. You can also see what's left of a Roman shipwreck excavated from the site.

Centre Bourse, Square Belsunce. ℭ **04-91-14-59-62.** Admission 2€ adults, 1.50€ students and children 11–18, free for children 10 and under. Mon–Sat noon–7pm. Métro: Vieux-Port.

Musée Grobet-Labadié ★   This collection, bequeathed to the city in 1919, includes Louis XV and Louis XVI furniture, as well as an outstanding collection of medieval Burgundian and Provençal sculpture. Other exhibits showcase 17th-century Gobelin tapestries; 15th- to 19th-century German, Italian, French, and Flemish paintings; and 16th- and 17th-century Italian and French faïence.

140 bd. Longchamp. ℭ **04-91-62-21-82.** Admission 2€. June–Sept Tues–Sun 11am–6pm; Oct–May Tues–Sun 10am–5pm. Closed public holidays. Métro: Cinq av. Longchamp.

Shopping

Only Paris and Lyon can compete with Marseille for its breadth and diversity of merchandise. Your best bet is a trip to the **Vieux-Port** and the streets surrounding it, where folkloric objects cram the boutiques. Many shops are loaded with souvenirs such as crèche-style *santons*. The best place to buy these is above the Vieux-Port, behind the Théâtre National de la Criée. At **Ateliers Marcel Carbonel,** 47 rue Neuve-Ste-Catherine (© **04-91-13-61-36**), more than 600 Nativity-related figures, in half a dozen sizes, sell for 10€ and up.

Bring a photo to the artists at **Amandine,** 69 bd. Eugène-Pierre (© **04-91-47-00-83**), and they'll frost a cake with an amazing likeness. If you don't have a snapshot with you, choose from their images, which include scenes of the Vieux-Port. More traditional pastries and chocolates are at **Puyricard,** 25 rue Francis-Davso (© **04-91-54-26-25**), or 30 bd. Georges Clemenceau (© **04-91-85-19-87**). The treats include chocolates stuffed with *pâté d'amande* (almond paste) and *confits de fruits* (candied fruit).

Since medieval times, Marseille has thrived on the legend of Les Trois Maries—three saints named Mary, including everyone's favorite ex-sinner, Mary Magdalene. Assisted by awakened-from-the-dead St. Lazarus, they reportedly came ashore near Marseille to Christianize ancient Provence. In commemoration of their voyage, small boat-shaped cookies *(les navettes)*, flavored with secret ingredients that include tons of orange zest, orange-flower water, and sugar, are forever associated with Marseille. They're sold throughout the city, most notably at **Le Four des Navettes,** 136 rue Sainte (© **04-91-33-32-12;** www.fourdesnavettes.com). Opened in 1791, it sells the cookies for 15€ per dozen and does very little else besides perpetuate the city's most cherished (and dubious) medieval myth.

Antiques from around Provence are for sale along cours Julien and in La Préfecture neighborhood. One of the best stores is **Antiquités François-Décamp,** 302 rue Paradis (© **04-91-81-18-00**). At **Felio,** 4 place Gabriel-Péri (© **04-91-90-32-67**), you'll find large-brimmed hats that would have thrilled ladies of the Belle Epoque, as well as berets and other styles of chapeaus.

Looking for something that approximates a sun-flooded mall in California, with a Provençal accent? Head for the most talked about real-estate development in the city's recent history, **L'Escale Borély,** avenue Mendès-France. A 25-minute trip south of Marseille (take the Métro to Rond-Point du Prado, and then transfer to bus no. 19; or from the center of Marseille, take bus no. 83, and then walk about a quarter-mile), it incorporates shops, cafes, bars, and restaurants. For more on L'Escale Borély, see "Marseille After Dark," later in this chapter.

You may not think of Marseille as a place to shop for fashion, but the local industry is booming. Its center is along **cours Julien** and **rue de la Tour,** where you'll find many boutiques and ateliers. Much of the clothing reflects North African influences. Many items are rich, brocaded, and ethnic, cut chic and close to the body.

Here's a sampling of the best markets in Marseille: The **Capucins Market** (daily 8am–7pm), place des Capucins, has fruit, herbs, fish, and food products; **Quai du Port** (daily 8am–1pm) is a fish market on the old port; **Allées de Meilhan,** on La Canebière (Tues and Sat 8am–1pm), sells flowers year-round, and from the last Sunday in November to December, vendors sell *santons* here daily 8am to 7pm. On **cours Julien** near Notre-Dame du Mont, you'll find a market with fruits, vegetables, and other foods (Tues, Thurs, Sat 8am–1pm). At the same location, vendors sell stamps (Sunday 8am–1pm) and secondhand goods (every other Sun 8am–1pm). Also on cours Julien, there are old-book vendors every other Saturday (8am–3pm), organic products (Friday 8am–1pm), and a flower market (Sat and Wed 8am–1pm).

Where to Stay
VERY EXPENSIVE
Le Petit Nice ★★★   This is the best hotel in Marseille. It opened in 1917, when the Passédat family joined two villas in a secluded area below the street paralleling the beach. The spacious Marina Wing across from the main building offers rooms individually decorated in an antique style, opening onto sea views. The rooms in the main house are more modern and avant-garde. Four units were inspired by the cubist movement, with posh geometric appointments and bright colors. Each unit comes with a luxurious bathroom with tub/shower. The hotel restaurant is beautiful, with a view of the shore and the rocky islands off its coast. In summer, dinner is served in the garden facing the sea.

Corniche Président-J.-F.-Kennedy/Anse-de-Maldormé, Marseille 13007. ☎ **04-91-59-25-92.** Fax 04-91-59-28-08. www.petitnice-passedat.com. 16 units. 195€–640€ double; 500€–1,090€ suite. AE, DC, MC, V. Free parking. Métro: Vieux-Port. **Amenities:** Restaurant; bar; babysitting; free use of bikes; outdoor pool; room service. In room: A/C, TV, hair dryer, minibar, Wi-Fi (free).

Sofitel Marseille Vieux Port ★★★   This government-rated four-star hotel lacks the glamour and style of Le Petit Nice, but it is the highest-rated lodging in the city center. A glistening modern palace, it stands above the embankments of the old port. Some guest rooms have panoramic views of the Vieux-Port; others look out on the boulevard. Rooms are modern, comfortable, and furnished in Provençal style, with a combination tub/shower. All are fairly generous in size. This hotel and its corporate sibling, the Novotel Vieux Port (see later in this chapter), are in the same building and share a staff and dining facilities.

36 bd. Charles-Livon, Marseille 13007. ☎ **04-91-15-59-00.** Fax 04-91-15-59-50. www.accorhotels.com. 134 units. 265€–500€ double; 800€–1,500€ suite. AE, DC, MC, V. Parking 16€. Métro: Vieux-Port. **Amenities:** Restaurant; bar; babysitting; room service. In room: A/C, TV, hair dryer, minibar, Wi-Fi (4.50€ per hr.).

EXPENSIVE
Mercure Beauvau Vieux Port ★★   Although completely restored and up-to-date, this is the oldest hotel in Marseille, having hosted such artsy types as Chopin and George Sand in the 19th century. It is decorated in the various epoch styles of France, including Louis XIII, Napoleon III, and Empire. In the public rooms antique Provençal furnishings are used as accents, whereas the bedrooms, for the most part, have contemporary furnishings that are both tasteful and comfortable. There is no restaurant on-site, but many are available nearby; and the bar, one of the most attractive places in Marseille for a rendezvous, overlooks the port.

4 rue Beauvau, Marseille 13001. ☎ **04-91-54-91-00.** Fax 04-91-54-15-76. www.mercure.com. 73 units. 149€–209€ double; 260€–479€ suite. AE, DC, MC, V. Parking 20€. **Amenities:** Bar; breakfast room; room service. In room: A/C, TV, hair dryer, minibar, Wi-Fi (10€ per day).

Villa Massalia Concorde Marseille ★   Near the Borély racetrack and Parc Chanot, this hotel lies in an upmarket residential district of the city. With a stunning modern design, it showcases such materials as real oak, feather bedding, and leather.

It is close to several sandy beaches, and is ideal for both the business traveler and the vacationer. The hotel is elegantly and warmly decorated with fine natural materials. Bedrooms are sleek and modern, with all the latest gadgets.

17 place Louis Bonnefon, Marseille 13008. ℂ **04-91-72-90-00.** Fax 04-91-72-90-01. www.concorde-hotels.com. 140 units. 164€–325€ double; 305€–690€ suite. AE, DC, MC, V. **Amenities:** Restaurant; bar; exercise room; outdoor pool; room service. *In room:* A/C, TV, hair dryer, minibar, Wi-Fi (free).

MODERATE

Hôtel le Corbusier ★   The radical designs of Swiss-born architect Le Corbusier (aka Charles-Edouard Jeanneret, 1887–1965) have long been associated with Marseille. In 1952, in a location 2km (1¼ miles) south of Marseille's Vieux Port, he designed l'Unité d'Habitation (it's also known as La Cité Radieuse), a multi-functional, nine-story building that combines shops and apartments for 1,500 residents. Within his original plan, he even included a provision for the inclusion of a hotel, which, beginning in 1959, opened its doors for business to the general public from premises on the building's third and fourth floors. At the time, horrified neighbors referred to the place as *La maison du fada* (House of the Crazy) because it was so ugly.

The husband-and-wife team of Alban and Dominique Gérardin spent a ton of money stripping the hotel back to the original combination of expressionism and functionalism for which Le Corbusier is known. They've zealously retained a handful of their studios' original kitchens, each designed by Le Corbusier's now-celebrated collaborator Charlotte Perriand (none of them actually work, but they're highly prized as minimalist statements nonetheless), and outfitted the hotel with the kind of spartan, functional, and often metallic furniture, lighting fixtures, and accessories of which the great designer would have approved.

On the 3rd and 4th floors of La Cité Radieuse, 280 bd. Michelet, Marseille 13008. ℂ **04-91-16-78-00.** www.hotellecorbusier.com. 21 units. 94€–114€ double; 120€ suite. DC, MC, V. Bus: 21. **Amenities:** Restaurant; bar; exercise room; wading pool. *In room:* A/C, TV, crib 10€, fridge, Wi-Fi (4€ per hr.).

Novotel Vieux Port ✒   In the same building as the Sofitel (see earlier in this chapter), the Novotel broke off from its more upscale affiliate in 1987. Services are less extensive, amenities less plush, and spaces a bit more cramped than at the Sofitel, but because this is one of the most reasonably priced hotels in town, no one seems to mind. The few rooms overlooking the old port tend to fill up first. Each unit is outfitted in chain-hotel style and comes with a small, well-equipped bathroom.

36 bd. Charles-Livon, Marseille 13007. ℂ **04-96-11-42-11.** Fax 04-96-11-42-20. www.accorhotels.com. 110 units. 115€–210€ double. AE, DC, MC, V. Parking 16€. Métro: Vieux-Port. **Amenities:** Restaurant; bar; exercise room; outdoor pool; room service; spa. *In room:* A/C, TV, hair dryer, minibar, Wi-Fi (4.50€ per hr.).

Résidence du Vieux Port   Although this hotel may have seen better days, we enjoy it for its location, opening onto a panoramic view of the old port and Notre-Dame de la Garde. It also lies within walking distance of many of the major attractions of the city. Most of the midsize guest rooms have loggia-style terraces opening onto the port. Rooms blend traditional furnishings with modern amenities, and windows are soundproof.

18 quai du Port, Marseille 13002. ℂ **04-91-91-91-22.** Fax 04-91-56-60-88. www.hotelmarseille.com. 50 units. 180€–200€ double; 260€–290€ suite. AE, DC, MC, V. Parking 10€. Métro: Vieux-Port. **Amenities:** Cafe; bar; room service. *In room:* A/C, TV, hair dryer, minibar, Wi-Fi (free).

INEXPENSIVE

Hôtel Escale Oceania   This hotel evokes the grandeur of 19th-century life in Marseille. It's less than 2 blocks from the Vieux-Port, in the heart of town. The sun and mistrals of many seasons have battered the Beaux Arts facade, decorated with ornate corbels and cornices. Renovations have stripped the guest rooms of some of their old-fashioned charm, but have left efficient, soundproof spaces. Each unit has a compact bathroom with a shower and tub. Breakfast is the only meal served, but the neighborhood abounds with dining options.

5 la Canebière, Marseille 13001. © **04-91-90-61-61.** Fax 04-91-90-95-61. 45 units. 140€–160€ double; 200€ suite. AE, DC, MC, V. Parking in nearby public lot 16€. **Amenities:** Room service. *In room:* A/C, TV, hair dryer, Wi-Fi (free).

New Hôtel Bompard   This tranquil retreat, built after World War II, lies atop a cliff along the corniche, about 3km (1¾ miles) east of the Vieux-Port. Partly because of its garden, it may remind you of a well-appointed private home. A Provençal *mas* (farmhouse) in the garden holds four large rooms that are more luxurious and atmospheric than those in the main building. Some of the beds are baldachin-style (canopied); floors have Provençal tiles; bathrooms are relatively large, with tub/shower combos; and furnishings are romantic. Rooms in the main building are cheap, modern, and streamlined, with tub/shower combos, and not terribly romantic.

2 rue des Flots Bleus, Marseille 13007. © **04-91-99-22-22.** Fax 04-91-31-02-14. www.new-hotel.com. 49 units. 95€–149€ standard double; 145€–215€ Provençal *mas* double. AE, DC, MC, V. Free parking. Bus: 61 or 83. **Amenities:** Restaurant; bar; outdoor pool; room service. *In room:* A/C, TV, hair dryer, minibar, Wi-Fi (8€ per hr.).

Where to Dine
EXPENSIVE

Le Petit Nice (see "Where to Stay," earlier in this chapter) has a lovely restaurant.

Le Miramar ★★★ SEAFOOD   Except for Le Petit Nice (see above), Le Miramar offers the grandest dining in Marseille. Bouillabaisse aficionados flock here to savor a version that will surely be a culinary highlight of your trip. It's hard to imagine that this was once a rough-and-tumble recipe favored by local fishermen, a way of using the least desirable portion of their catch. Actually, it's traditionally two dishes, a saffron-tinted soup followed by the fish poached in the soup. It's eaten with *une rouille,* a sauce of red chilies, garlic, olive oil, egg yolk, and cayenne. The version served here involves lots of labor and just as much costly seafood. The setting is a room with frescoes of underwater life and big windows that open onto the Vieux-Port. It's linked to a terrace that overlooks Marseille's most famous church, Notre-Dame-de-la-Garde.

12 quai du Port. © **04-91-91-10-40.** Reservations recommended. Main courses 31€–45€; bouillabaisse from 58€ per person (minimum 2). AE, DC, MC, V. Tues–Sat noon–2:30pm and 7–9:30pm. Métro: Vieux-Port.

Une Table au Sud ★★ MODERN PROVENÇAL   One floor above street level, in a modern dining room with views of the Vieux-Port, this restaurant serves some of the most creative cuisine in Marseille. The historically important 19th-century building has sculpted lion heads embellishing its facade. Chef de cuisine Lionel Levy and his wife, Florence, the *maître d'hôtel,* are the creative forces here. Their cuisine changes daily according to the ingredients available at local markets. Menu items include a creamy soup made from chestnuts and sea urchins, and a thick slice of a local saltwater fish known as *denti,* which local gastronomes compare to a *daurade royale* (sea bream) served with flap mushrooms and chicken stock; mullet served with saffron and herb risotto; and roasted squab with Arabica coffee-flavored juices. Depending on the mood of the chef, desserts may include pineapple *dacquoise* (stacked meringue dessert) served with vanilla-flavor whipped cream.

2 quai du Port. ✆ **04-91-90-63-53.** Reservations recommended. Fixed-price lunch 33€, dinner 68€-110€. AE, MC, V. Tues–Thurs noon–2pm and 7:30–10pm; Fri–Sat noon–2pm and 7:30pm–midnight. Métro: Vieux-Port.

MODERATE

Le Comptoir des Favouilles PROVENÇAL/SOUTHWESERN FRENCH On the opposite side of the building from Les Arcenaulx (see below), this restaurant occupies a former dorm for prisoners who were forced to row the ornamental barges of Louis XIV during his inspections of Marseille's harbor. You'll get a lot for your money: Prices are relatively reasonable and ingredients very fresh. Provençal dishes include succulent baked sea wolf prepared as simply as possible—with herbs and olive oil. Particularly noteworthy is bouillabaisse (which, at 45€ per person, is the most expensive main course on the menu) and a delectable combination of saltwater crayfish with foie gras. Desserts usually include roasted figs served with sweet dessert wine.

44 rue Sainte. ✆ **04-96-11-03-11.** Reservations recommended. Main courses 12€-18€. AE, DC, MC, V. Mon–Fri noon–2:30pm; Mon–Sat 7:30–10:30pm. Métro: Vieux-Port.

Le Ventre de l'Architect FRENCH With a westward-facing view of the sea and the setting sun, this is the restaurant that's associated with the hotel that occupies a building that, when designed by Le Corbusier between 1952 and 1954, was considered one of the most revolutionary designs in Europe. You'll benefit from both an architecturally historic setting and menu items that are creative, imaginative, and—if you understand a bit of French—described in ways that would have pleased a 19th-century Impressionistic poet. Examples include cream of pumpkin soup; a "pillow" of foie gras "draped" with slices of Serrano ham; a "waltz" of jumbo shrimp with scallops, served with pink risotto; beef medallions "rolled together" with cured ham and served with "herbs from the chef's garden"; and veal chops with braised endives and a purée of violets.

In the Hotel le Corbusier, on the 3rd floor of La Cité Radieuse, 280 bd. Michelet. ✆ **04-91-16-78-23.** Main courses 24€-60€; fixed-price lunch 28€; fixed-price dinner 60€. DC, MC, V. Tues–Sat noon–2pm and 8–11pm.

Les Arcenaulx ★ 🍽 PROVENÇAL This is an architectural oddity that serves memorable cuisine. The navies of Louis XIV built these stone warehouses near the Vieux-Port; they now contain this restaurant and two bookstores, run by the charming sisters Simone and Jeanne Laffitte. Look for Provençal cuisine with a Marseillais accent in such dishes as roasted pigeon or duckling with caramelized quince; roasted scallops with hearts of violet artichokes; *daurade* (bream) roasted whole "on its skin"; and filet of beef *rossini,* layered with foie gras. Equally tempting are artichokes *barigoule* (loaded with aromatic spices and olive oil) and a worthy assortment of *petites légumes farcies* (Provençal vegetables stuffed with chopped meat and herbs).

25 cours d'Estienne d'Orves. ✆ **04-91-59-80-30.** www.les-arcenaulx.com. Reservations recommended. Main courses 18€-34€; fixed-price menu 27€-57€. AE, DC, MC, V. Mon–Sat noon–2pm and 8–11pm. Métro: Vieux-Port.

Toinou SEAFOOD   In a massive building that overshadows every other structure nearby, this landmark restaurant serves more shellfish than any other restaurant in Marseille. Inside, a display of more than 40 species of shellfish is laid out for inspection by some of the canniest judges of seafood in France: Toinou's customers. Dining rooms are on three floors, served by a waitstaff who are very entrenched in their *Marseillais* accents and demeanors. Don't come here unless you're really fond of shellfish, any species of which can be served raw or cooked. The wine list is extensive, with attractively priced whites from such regions as the Loire Valley.

3 cours St-Louis, 1e. ✆ **04-91-33-14-94.** www.toinou.com. Reservations recommended. Main courses 15€–35€; fixed-price shellfish platter for 2 42€ or 72€ with lobster. DC, MC, V. Daily 11:30am–11:30pm. Métro: Vieux-Port.

INEXPENSIVE

La Kahena TUNISIAN   This is one of the busiest and most-respected Tunisian restaurants in a city that's loaded with worthy competitors. Established in 1976 and set close to the Vieux-Port, it's a two-room enclave of savory North African aromas: minced or grilled lamb, tomatoes, eggplant, herbs, and couscous, so beloved by Tunisian expatriates. The menu lists 10 varieties of couscous, including versions with lamb, chicken, fish, the savory sausages known as *merguez,* and a "complete" version that includes a little bit of each of those ingredients. Also look for *méchouia,* a succulent version of roasted lamb. The restaurant's name, incidentally, derives from a 6th-century-B.C. Tunisian princess who was legendary for uniting all the Berber tribes of North Africa.

2 rue de la République. ✆ **04-91-90-61-93.** Reservations recommended. Main courses 9€–16€. MC, V. Daily noon–2:30pm and 7:30–11pm. Métro: Vieux-Port.

Marseille After Dark

For an amusing and relatively harmless exposure to the town's saltiness, walk around the **Vieux-Port,** where cafes and restaurants angle their sightlines for the best view of the harbor.

L'Escale Borély, avenue Mendès-France, is a modern-day equivalent of the Vieux-Port. It's a waterfront development south of the town center, only 20 minutes away (take bus no. 83 or 19). About a dozen cafes, as well as restaurants of every possible ilk, serve many cuisines. They offer views of in-line skaters on the promenade in front and the potential for conversation with friendly strangers, with less likelihood of street crime.

Unless the air-conditioning is powerful, Marseille's dance clubs produce a lot of sweat. Close to Vieux-Port, you can dance and drink at the **Metal Café,** 20 rue Fortia (✆ **04-91-54-03-03**), where 20- to 50-year-olds listen to R&B, house, and techno music recently released in London and Los Angeles. Or try the nearby **Trolley Bus,** 24 quai de Rive-Neuve (✆ **04-91-54-30-45;** www.letrolley.com), best known for its techno, house, hip-hop, jazz, and salsa.

If you miss free-form modern jazz and don't mind taking your chances in the less-than-savory neighborhood adjacent to the city's rail station (La Gare St-Charles—take a taxi there and back), consider dropping into **La Cité de la Musique** (also known as **La Cave à Jazz**), 4 rue Bernard-du-Bois (✆ **04-91-39-28-28**). Other nightlife venues in Marseille evoke Paris, but with lots of extra *méridional* (southern) spice thrown in for extra flavor. Three Marseillais bars that we found particularly intriguing include **Le Pharaon,** Place de l'Opéra (✆ **04-91-54-09-89;** Métro:

Vieux-Port), a cozy enclave of deep sofas and armchairs, soft lighting, and—usually—a sense of well-being.

Somewhat more bustling and animated is **l'Exit,** 12 quai de Riveneuve (ⓒ **04-91-54-29-43;** Métro: Vieux-Port), a bar with a terrace that profits from Marseille's sultry nights, and two floors of seething nocturnal energy. And for a bar that prides itself on its wide array of complicated cocktails and tapas, as well as a lot of attractive 30-somethings, consider **l'Interdit,** 9 rue Molière (ⓒ **06-23-22-74-71;** Métro: Vieux-Port). A place that's loaded with razzmatazz, and appealing for both its dance floor and its cabaret acts, is **Le Circus,** 5 rue du Chantier (ⓒ **04-91-33-77-22;** Métro: Vieux-Port). A fee of 15€ gets you entrance into the overall compound, after which you can visit any aspect of the place (cabaret vs. dance floor) that appeals to you at the time.

The gay scene in Marseille isn't as crowded, or as intriguing, as the one in Nice, but its premier gay bar, the **Get Bar-MP Bar,** 10 rue Beauvau (ⓒ **04-91-33-64-79**), benefits from a long history of being the town's gay bar of record. It's open Tuesday through Sunday from 7pm to 3am. An equally valid, and equally gay, option is **New Can Can,** 3–5 rue Sénac (ⓒ **04-91-48-59-76;** www.newcancan.com), a broad and sprawling bar-and-disco venue that, at least in Marseille, seems to be everybody's favorite dance-club venue. Technically, the place identifies as a mostly gay venue, but frankly, it gets so many heterosexuals that the gender-specific definitions that dominate many of the town's other nightclubs are—at least here—practically moot. One or another of its subdivisions tends to open nightly at around 8:30pm, and by the weekend, it blossoms into full electronic bloom. It is open Thursday through Sunday from 11pm until dawn. There is no cover except on Friday and Saturday nights, when a 17€ admission fee is levied.

TOULON

836km (519 miles) S of Paris; 127km (80 miles) SW of Cannes; 68km (42 miles) E of Marseille

This fortress and town is France's principal naval base, the headquarters of the Mediterranean fleet, with hundreds of sailors wandering the streets. It's not as seedy, but also not as intriguing, as Marseille. The beautiful harbor is surrounded by hills and crowned by forts, protected on the east by a breakwater and on the west by the great peninsula of Cap Sicié. The outer roads are known as the Grande Rade and the inner roads as the Petite Rade. A winter resort colony lies on the outskirts. Like Marseille, Toulon has a large Arab population. There's racial tension here, worsened by the closing of the shipyards.

Park your car underground at place de la Liberté, and then walk along boulevard des Strasbourg, turning right onto rue Berthelot. This will take you into the pedestrian-only area in the core of the old city. It's filled with shops, hotels, restaurants, and cobblestone streets—but it can be dangerous at night. The best beach, **Plage du Mourillon,** is 2km (1¼ miles) east of the heart of town.

Essentials

GETTING THERE & GETTING AROUND   **Trains** arrive from Marseille about every 5 to 30 minutes (trip time: 1 hr.); the one-way fare is 13€. If you're on the Riviera, trains arrive frequently from Nice (trip time: 1 hr., 45 min.) and Cannes (trip time: 80 min.). For information, call ⓒ **36-35.**

Three **buses** per day arrive from Aix-en-Provence (trip time: 1 hr., 15 min.); the fare is about 15€ one-way. For information, call **Sodetrav** (© **08-25-00-06-50**). If you're **driving** from Marseille, take A50 east to Toulon. When you arrive, park your car and get around on foot; the Vieille Ville (old town) and most attractions are easy to reach. A municipal **bus** system serves the town as well. A bus map is available at the tourist office. For information, call **Le Réseau Mistral** at © **04-94-03-87-03.**

VISITOR INFORMATION The **Office de Tourisme** is at 334 avenue de la République (© **04-94-18-53-00;** fax 04-94-18-53-09; www.toulontourisme.com).

Exploring the Town

In **Vieux Toulon,** between the harbor and boulevard de Strasbourg (the main axis of town), are many remains of the port's former days. A colorful food market, conducted Tuesday through Sunday from 8am to 1pm, **Le Marché du cours Lafayette,** spills onto the streets around cours Lafayette. Also in old Toulon is the **Cathédrale Ste-Marie-Majeure** (© **04-94-92-28-91**), built in the Romanesque style in the 11th and 12th centuries, and expanded in the 17th. Its badly lit nave is Gothic; the belfry and facade are from the 18th century. It's open daily from 7:30am to noon and 2:30 to 7pm.

In contrast to the cathedral, tall modern buildings line quai Stalingrad, opening onto **Vieille d'Arse.** On place Puget, look for the *atlantes* **(caryatids),** figures of men used as columns. These figures support a balcony at the **Hôtel de Ville (City Hall)** and are also included in the facade of the naval museum.

Musée de la Marine, place du Ingénieur-Général-Monsenergue (© **04-94-02-02-01;** www.musee-marine.fr), contains figureheads and ship models. Year-round, it's open daily from 10am to 6pm; closed Tuesday September to June. Admission is 5€ for adults, 3.50€ for students, free for ages 17 and under.

Musée de Toulon, 113 bd. du Maréchal-Leclerc (© **04-94-36-81-00**), displays works from the 16th century to the present. There's a good collection of Provençal and Italian paintings and religious works. The latest acquisitions include New Realism pieces and minimalist art. It's open Tuesday to Sunday from noon to 6pm; admission is free.

After you've covered the top attractions, we suggest taking a drive, an hour or two before sunset, along the **corniche du Mont-Faron.** It's a scenic boulevard along the lower slopes of Mont Faron, providing views of the busy port, the town, the cliffs, and, in the distance, the Mediterranean.

Memorial du Débarquement en Provence, Mont Faron (© **04-94-88-08-09**), documents the Allied landings in Provence in 1944, among other events. It's open October to April Tuesday to Sunday 10am to 1pm and 2 to 5:30pm; May and June Tuesday to Sunday 10am to 1pm and 2 to 6:30pm; and July to September daily 10am to 1pm and 2 to 6:30pm. Admission is 3.80€ for adults and 1.55€ for children 8 to 18.

Where to Stay

Grand Hotel de La Gare Lying in front of the SNCF railway and bus stations in the town center, this hotel also is close to the Parc des Lices and the harbor. The hotel is better than ever now that it's been given a wholesale facelift. The bedrooms have been revitalized and are midsize and tastefully decorated, with much use made of wooden furnishings. All the bathrooms have also been renewed. Because the hotel lies in a busy section of Toulon, all the windows have been soundproofed.

14 blvd. Tesse, 83000 Toulon. © **04-94-24-10-00.** Fax 04-94-22-34-82. www.grandhotelgare.com. 38 units. 57€–83€ double; 110€ triple or quad. AE, DC, MC, V. **Amenities:** Breakfast room. *In room:* TV, hair dryer, Wi-Fi (free).

Where to Dine

Au Sourd ★ SEAFOOD   This restaurant dates from 1862, and it's still going strong after all these years. The original owner, a former soldier, was nicknamed "Le Sourd," or the deaf one, because his ear had been badly injured during the Crimean War. The interior is a replica of an old Provençal house. There's nothing old about the cuisine: It's among the freshest in the area, especially if you stick to the fish and seafood dishes. The present chefs make the finest bouillabaisse in the area. Equally good is the savory kettle of *bourride,* which is various small fish cooked with onions, tomatoes, and garlic, and flavored with saffron and olive oil. We are also fond of the various fish of the day, which are grilled to perfection. Two other commendable dishes are the sautéed calamari and the fricassee of scallops.

10 rue Molière. © **04-94-92-28-52.** www.ausourd.com. Reservations recommended. Main courses 12€–55€; fixed-price lunch 27€; fixed-price dinner 27€. AE, MC, V. Tues–Sat noon–2pm and 7:15–10pm.

Le Jardin du Sommelier ★ FRENCH/PROVENÇAL   This is a wine restaurant with some of the finest vintages in the area, but it also turns out a savory cuisine of well-prepared dishes with market-fresh produce. Since 1992, it's been recognized as the leading restaurant of this port city. Much of the chef's repertoire is based on the sea, including a medley of scallops and shrimp au gratin. Meat and poultry dishes are also respected, the best, in our view, being the *magret* of roast duckling with a Thai preparation. The atmosphere is that of an old Provençal home, and your host is Christian Scalisi, the leading food and wine expert in the area.

20 allées Courbet. © **04-94-62-03-27.** www.le-jardin-du-sommelier.com. Reservations required. Fixed-price menus 38€–65€. AE, MC, V. Mon–Fri noon–1:15pm; Mon–Tues and Thurs–Sat 8–9:30pm.

Toulon After Dark

The temporary home of thousands of sailors is bound to have a nightlife scene that's earthier, and a bit raunchier, than those of equivalent-size towns elsewhere. A rough-and-ready bar that offers stiff drinks, live music, and a complete lack of pretension is **Le Bar 113,** 113 av. de Infanterie de la Marine (© **04-94-03-42-41**). At **Bar à Thym,** 32 bd. Cuneo (© **04-94-41-90-10**), everybody seems to drink beer, gossip, and listen to live music.

Toulon is also home to one of the region's best-known gay discos, **Boy's Paradise,** 1 bd. Pierre-Toesca (© **04-94-09-35-90**), near the train station. Adjacent to the port is the gay **Bar La Lampa,** Port de Toulon (© **04-94-03-06-09**), where tapas and live music accompany lots of beer and wine or whiskey.

ILES D'HYERES ★

39km (24 miles) SE of Toulon; 119km (74 miles) SW of Cannes

Off the Riviera in the Mediterranean, a little group of islands encloses the southern boundary of the Hyères anchorage. During the Renaissance they were called the Iles d'Or, named for the golden glow the rocks sometimes give off in sunlight. Nothing in the islands today will remind you of the turbulent times when they were attacked by pirates and Turkish galleys, or even of the Allied landings in World War II.

Mass tourism has arrived on these sun-baked islands, with some of the tackiness that accompanies it. Cars are forbidden on all three major islands, and the ferryboats cannot transport them. Expect a Gallic version of Nantucket, with thousands of midsummer day-trippers arriving, often with children, for a day of sun, sand, and people-watching.

Which island is the most appealing? Ile des Porquerolles is the most beautiful. Thinking of heading to Le Levant? You may want to steer clear: Only 25% of the island is accessible to visitors. The remainder belongs to the French army and is used frequently for testing missiles.

Essentials

GETTING TO ILE DE PORQUEROLLES   Ferryboats leave from several points along the Côte d'Azur. The most frequent, most convenient, and shortest trip is from the harbor of La Tour Fondue on the peninsula of Giens, a 32km (20-mile) drive east of Toulon. Depending on the season, there are 4 to 20 departures a day. The round-trip fare for the 15-minute crossing is 16€ for adults, 14€ ages 4 to 10. For information, call the **Transports Maritimes et Terrestres du Littoral Varois,** La Tour Fondue, Giens 83400 (© **04-94-58-21-81**). The next-best option is the ferryboat from Toulon, but only between June and September. Other options, each of them available only between June and September, involve taking one of the ferryboats maintained by the **Compagnie Maritime des Vedettes Ile d'Or & Le Corsaire** (© **04-94-71-01-02**). Their ferryboats offer crossings from either of *Les Gares Maritimes* in Le Lavandou and Cavalaire.

On any of the venues noted above, round-trip fares to the Ile de Porquerolles cost 32€ from Lavandou, 37€ from Cavalaire. Children ages 4 to 11 pay 25€ to 30€, respectively.

GETTING TO ILE DE PORT-CROS   The most popular ferry route to the island is the 35-minute crossing that departs between four and seven times daily, depending on the season. (From Oct–Mar, there are only three crossings per week.) For information, contact the **Compagnie Maritime des Vedettes** (© **04-94-71-01-02**). Round-trip fares cost 25€ from Lavandou or 30€ from Cavalaire. Children 4 to 11 pay 21€ to 25€, respectively. The same company, for approximately the same price, also offers crossings to Port-Cros from Cavalaire, but only between April and September. For no additional fee, vessels will drop passengers at the military installations at Le Levant.

VISITOR INFORMATION   Other than temporary, summer-only kiosks without phones that distribute brochures and advice near the ferry docks in Porquerolles and Port-Cros, there are no tourist bureaus on the islands. The offices in Hyères and Toulon try to fill in the gaps. Contact the **Office de Tourisme,** 3 av. Ambroise Thomas, Hyères (© **04-94-01-84-50**), or the **Office de Tourisme,** 334 avenue de la République, Toulon (© **04-94-18-53-00**).

Ile de Porquerolles ★

This is the largest and westernmost of the Iles d'Hyères. It has a rugged south coast, but the north strand, facing the mainland, has sandy beaches bordered by heather, scented myrtles, and pine trees. The island is about 8km (5 miles) long and 2km (1¼ miles) wide, and is 4.8km (3 miles) from the mainland.

The population is only 400. The island is said to receive 275 days of sunshine annually. It's a land of rocky capes, pine forests twisted by the mistral, sun-drenched vineyards, and pale ocher houses. The "hot spots," if there are any, are the cafes around **place d'Armes,** where everybody gathers.

The island has a violent history of raids, attacks, and occupation by everybody from the Dutch and the English to the Turks and the Spaniards. Ten forts, some in ruins, testify to its fierce past. The most ancient is **Fort Ste-Agathe,** built in 1531 by François I. In time it was a penal colony and a retirement center for soldiers of the colonial wars.

The French government purchased the largest hunk of the island in 1971 and turned it into a national park and botanical garden.

WHERE TO STAY & DINE

Hotel et Residence Les Medes ★
In the center of the village is this tranquil choice set in a large private garden with a sun deck. Well-furnished rooms, studios, and apartments are rented. Even the least expensive units are suitable for two to four guests, each provided with a kitchenette. Many of the accommodations contain bunk beds for children. The more desirable units open onto private terraces with a view. The location is 400m (1,312 ft.) from Courtade Beach and only a short walk from the wharf. Guests gather in the lounge with its bar, fireplace, library, and public Internet. Main courses in the restaurant range from 16€ to 23€ and include Provençal food, even international specialties such as rabbit with chocolate, various fresh fish, and a spicy tagine Moroccan style. The chefs even serve kangaroo meat from Australia.

2 rue de la Douane, Porquerolles 83400. ✆ **04-94-12-41-24.** Fax 04-94-58-32-49. www.hotel-les-medes.fr. 93€–379€ double. MC, V. Closed Nov 8–Dec 26. **Amenities:** Restaurant; bar. *In room:* A/C, TV, Wi-Fi (free).

Mas du Langoustier ★★
In a large park on the island's western tip, this tranquil resort hotel is an old *mas* with a view of a lovely pine-ringed bay. Employees greet guests in a covered wagon by the jetty. Guest rooms, in antique Provençal style, are the most elegantly decorated on the island. Bathrooms are roomy, and most have tub/shower combinations. Should you visit for a meal, the menu is the finest in the Hyère islands, offering mainly seafood in a light nouvelle style. Try *loup* (wolf fish) with Noilly Prat in puff pastry, or tender kid with dried tomatoes roasted in casserole. You can drink and dine on the terraces.

Porquerolles 83400. ✆ **04-94-58-30-09.** Fax 04-94-58-36-02. www.langoustier.com. 50 units. 190€–275€ double; from 290€ suite. Rates include half board. MC, V. Closed late Sept to late Apr. **Amenities:** 2 restaurants; bar; babysitting; outdoor pool; room service. *In room:* A/C, TV, minibar.

Ile de Port-Cros ★

Lush subtropical vegetation reminiscent of a Caribbean island makes this a green paradise, 5km (3 miles) long and 2km (1¼ miles) wide. The most mountainous island of the archipelago, Port-Cros has been a French national park since 1963. A fire in 1892 devastated the island, which now abounds with pine forests and ilexes. Birders flock here to observe nearly 100 different species. There are many marked trails, mainly for day-trippers. The most popular and scenic is *sentier botanique;* the more adventurous and athletic take the 10km (6¼-mile) *circuit historique* (you'll need a packed lunch for this one). Divers follow a 274m (899-ft.) trail from Plage de la Palud to the islet of Rascas, where a plastic guide sheet identifies the underwater flora. Thousands of pleasure crafts call here annually, which does little to help the island's fragile environment.

WHERE TO STAY & DINE

Le Manoir ★   This is the only bona fide hotel on the island, but despite lack of competition, its owners work hard to make their guests as comfortable as possible. Originally, it functioned as the grandiose home of the family that owned the entire island. Today, the hotel consists of an 18th-century architectural core, plus an annex that contains most of the guest accommodations. Accommodations are simple, and bathrooms come equipped with tub/shower combinations. The restaurant serves lobster-and-fish terrine, several seasoned meats, and fresh local fish with baby vegetables, as well as regional goat cheese and velvety mousses. A fixed-price menu costs 58€.

Ile de Port-Cros 83400. ℂ **04-94-05-90-52.** Fax 04-94-05-90-89. lemanoir.portcros@wanadoo.fr. 22 units. 170€–210€ double; 200€–235€ suite. MC, V. Closed Oct–Apr. **Amenities:** Restaurant; bar; outdoor pool; room service. *In room:* A/C, hair dryer.

THE FRENCH RIVIERA

Each resort on the Riviera, known as the Côte d'Azur (Azure Coast), offers its own unique flavor and charms. This narrow strip of fabled real estate, less than 201km (125 miles) long and located between the Mediterranean and a trio of mountain ranges, has always attracted the jet set with its clear skies, blue waters, and orange groves.

A trail of modern artists captivated by the light and setting has left a rich heritage: Matisse at Vence, Cocteau at Menton and Villefranche, Picasso at Antibes and seemingly everywhere else, Léger at Biot, Renoir at Cagnes, and Bonnard at Le Cannet. The best collection is at the Foundation Maeght in St-Paul-de-Vence.

The Riviera's high season used to be winter and spring only. In recent years, July and August have become the most crowded, and reservations are imperative. The average summer temperature is 75°F (24°C); in winter it's 49°F (9°C).

The corniches of the Riviera, depicted in countless films, stretch from Nice to Menton. The Alps drop into the Mediterranean here, and roads were carved along the way. The lower road, 32km (20 miles) long, is the Corniche Inférieure. Along this road are the ports of Villefranche, Cap-Ferrat, Beaulieu, and Cap-Martin. The 31km (19-mile) Moyenne Corniche (Middle Road), built between World War I and World War II, runs from Nice to Menton, winding in and out of tunnels and through mountains. The highlight is at Eze. Napoleon built the Grande Corniche—the most panoramic—in 1806. La Turbie and Le Vistaero are the principal towns along the 32km (20-mile) stretch, which reaches more than 480m (1,575 ft.) high at Col d'Eze.

Note: For more extensive coverage of this region, check out *Frommer's Provence & the Riviera.*

ST-TROPEZ ★★

874km (543 miles) S of Paris; 76km (47 miles) SW of Cannes

An air of hedonism runs rampant in this sun-kissed town, but the true Tropezian resents the fact that the port has such a bad reputation. "We can be classy, too," one native insisted. Creative people along with ordinary folk create a varied atmosphere. St-Tropez attracts artists, composers, novelists, and the film colony in the summer. Trailing behind is a flamboyant parade of humanity. Some of the most fashionable yachts, bearing some of the most chic people, anchor here in summer.

The Brigitte Bardot vehicle, *And God Created Woman,* put St-Tropez on the tourist map, but it has more history. Colette lived here for years, and the diarist Anaïs Nin, confidante of Henry Miller, posed for a little cheesecake on the beach in 1939 in a Dorothy Lamour–style bathing suit. In 1995, Bardot pronounced St-Tropez dead, "squatted by a lot of no-goods, drugheads, and villains." But 1997 saw her return, and headlines in France announced that St-Tropez was "hot once again." (Today she owns two houses in St-Tropez and is occasionally spotted among groups of her friends.) Other celebrities have been showing up, including Oprah, Barbra Streisand, Jack Nicholson, Robert De Niro, Jay-Z and Beyoncé, and Elton John.

Essentials

GETTING THERE The nearest rail station is in St-Raphaël, a neighboring resort. At St-Raphaël's Vieux Port, **boats** leave the Gare Maritime de St-Raphaël, rue Pierre-Auble (© **04-94-95-17-46**), for St-Tropez (trip time: 50 min.). Sailings are Tuesday and Saturday. The one-way fare is 14€. Year-round, 10 to 15 Sodetrav **buses** per day leave from the Gare Routière in St-Raphaël (© **04-94-97-88-51**) for St-Tropez. The trip takes 1½ to 2½ hours, depending on the bus and the traffic, which during midsummer is usually horrendous. A one-way ticket costs 12€. Buses run directly to St-Tropez from Toulon and Hyères and from the nearest airport, at Toulon-Hyères, 56km (35 miles) away.

If you **drive,** note that parking in St-Tropez is very difficult, especially in summer. You can park in the **Parking des Lices** (© **04-94-97-34-46**), beneath place des Lices; enter on avenue Paul-Roussel. Designed for 300 cars, this lot charges 2.20€ per hour. Many visitors with expensive cars prefer this lot because it's more secure than any other. Charging the same rates, a new garage, **Parking du Nouveau Port,** avenue Charles de Gaulle (© **04-94-97-74-99**), stands at the waterfront. Every municipal engineer in St-Tropez has worked hard to funnel incoming traffic toward either of these two underground garages. Drivers can't enter the resort without seeing prominent signs funneling traffic to either location. To get here from **Cannes,** drive southwest along the coastal highway (RD98), turning east when you see signs pointing to St-Tropez.

VISITOR INFORMATION The **Office de Tourisme** is on quai Jean-Jaurès (© **04-94-97-45-21;** fax 04-94-97-82-66; www.ot-saint-tropez.com).

A Day at the Beach

The hottest Riviera beaches are at St-Tropez. The best for families are closest to the center, including the **Plage de la Bouillabaisse** and **Plage des Graniers.** More daring are the 9.5km (6-mile) crescents at **Plage des Salins** and **Plage de Pampelonne,** some 3km (1¾ miles) from the town center. At Pampelonne about 35 businesses line a 4.8km (3-mile) stretch, located about 10km (6¼ miles) from St-Tropez. The concessionaire that's noted as an all-gay venue is the **Aqua Club,** Plage de Pampelonne in Ramatuelle (© **04-94-79-84-35**). You'll need a car, bike, or scooter to get from town to the beach. Parking is 6€ for the day. Famous hedonistic

The French Riviera

Beach

10 mi

10 km

ITALY

Ventimiglia

Menton

Cap-Martin

Roquebrune

Monte
Carlo

MONACO

Corniche
de la Riviera

Cap d'Ail

St-Jean-
Cap-Ferrat

Beaulieu

Èze

La Turbie

Èze-
sur-Mer

Villefranche-
sur-Mer

Cap-Ferrat

Peille

Peillon

L'Escarène

Contes

Sospel

PARC NATIONAL
DU MERCANTOUR

St-Martin-
Vésubie

Les Granges

La-Rivière

Plan-du-Var

Thiéry

Touët

ALPES MARITIMES

Aéroport de Nice–
Côte d'Azur

Nice

Ste-Hélène

Californie

Plage la Plage

Baie
des Anges

Plage de la Garoupe

Cap d'Antibes

Antibes

Juan-les-Pins

Plage d'Antibes

Golfe-Juan

Vallauris

Biot

Villeneuve-Loubet

Cagnes-
sur-Mer

Vence

St-Paul-de-Vence

Tourettes-
sur-Loup

Gréolières

Gourdon

Cabris

St-Cézaire-
sur-Siagne

Escragnolles

Théniers

Grasse

Mougins

Cannes

Falm-
Beach

Île Ste-Marguerite

Île St-Honorat

ILES DE LÉRINS

Mediterranean Sea

La Napoule-Plage

Mandelieu-
la-Napoule

Théoule-sur-Mer

Miramar

Le Trayas

Anthéor-
Cap-Roux

Corniche de l'Estérel

MASSIF DE L'ESTÉREL

Fayence

Bargemon

Agay

St-Raphaël

Fréjus-Plage

Fréjus

Golfe
de Fréjus

St-Aygulf

Le Muy

Draguignan

MASSIF DES MAURES

Ste-Maxime

Les Issambres

St-Tropez

Golfe de St-Tropez

Plage de Graniers

Plage des Salins

Pampelonne

Ramatuelle

Plage de Tahiti

Plage de Pampelonne

Plage de l'Escalet

Paris

FRANCE

The French
Riviera

N202

N85

N98

N7

N85

E80

E80

E80

N8E

2565

2566

2565

2205

2085

562

955

25

535

spots along Pampelonne include the cash-only club **La Voile Rouge** (© **04-94-79-84-34**), which features bawdy spring break–style entertainment. This is the most outrageous, the sexiest, and the most exhibitionist (not for children) of the beaches of St-Tropez. Also thriving are **Club 55,** 55 bd. Patch, Plage de Pampelonne (© **04-94-55-55-55**), and **Nikki Beach,** Plage de Pampelonne (© **04-94-79-82-04;** www.nikkibeach.com). Maintained by an American from Miami, Nikki Beach is wild, frenetic, uninhibited, and about as Floridian a venue as you're likely to find in the south of France. **Plage des Jumeaux** (© **04-94-55-21-80**) is another active beach; it draws many families with young kids because it has playground equipment. **Marine Air Sport** (© **04-94-97-89-19;** www.marine-air-sport. com) rents boats costing from 280€ a day. **Sun Force** (© **04-94-79-90-11**) rents jet skis, scooters, water-skiing equipment, and boats.

Notoriously decadent **Plage de Tahiti** occupies the north end of the 5.5km-long (3½-mile) Pampelonne, lined with concessions, cafes, and restaurants. It's a strip of golden sand long favored by exhibitionists wearing next to nothing (or nothing) and cruising shamelessly. If you ever wanted to go topless, this is the place to do it. Gay men tend to gravitate to **Coco Beach** in Ramatuelle, about 6.5km (4 miles) from the center of St-Tropez.

Outdoor Pursuits

BOATING The highly recommended **Suncap Company,** 15 quai de Suffren (© **04-94-97-11-23**), rents boats 5.4 to 12m (18–39 ft.) long. Larger ones come with a captain at the helm. Prices begin at 1,500€ per day.

TENNIS Anyone who phones in advance can use the eight courts (artificial grass or "Quick," a form of concrete) at the **Tennis-Club de St-Tropez,** route des Plages, St-Claude (© **04-94-97-15-52**), about 1km (½ mile) from the resort's center. Open year-round, the courts rent for 20€ per hour for green set, 25€ per hour for clay set, from 9am to 8pm. there's an extra charge of 4€ for nighttime lighting.

Shopping

St-Tropez is dense with stylish shops, but has no specific shopping street. Most shops are tucked in out-of-the-way corners of the old town. Big names include Hermès, Sonia Rykiel, and Dior. **Galeries Tropéziennes,** 56 rue Gambetta (© **04-94-97-02-21**), crowds hundreds of gift items—some worthwhile, some silly—into its showrooms near place des Lices. The merchandise is Mediterranean, breezy, and sophisticated.

And even chic St-Tropez has **Le Dépot,** boulevard Louis-Blanc (© **04-94-97-80-10**), which sells secondhand designer clothes by the likes of Hermès, Moschino, Gaultier, and Chanel. Some of the merchandise even has its original tags.

On Tuesday and Saturday mornings on place des Lices, there's an **outdoor market,** Marché Provençal, with food, clothes, and *brocante.* This is one of the best Provençal markets in the south of France, with more than 100 vendors selling everything from tableware to homemade bread. The fish, vegetable, and flower market is down a tiled alley (place aux Herbes) behind the tourist office. It operates daily 8am to noon in summer and Tuesday to Sunday 8am to noon in winter.

St-Tropez

ACCOMMODATIONS ■
Hôtel Byblos **12**
Hôtel La Ponche **1**
Hôtel La Tartane **11**
Hôtel Le Yaca **4**
Hotel Les Palmiers **10**
Hôtel Sube **5**
Pastis Hotel-St-Tropez **7**

DINING ◆
Auberge des Maures **6**
Chez Joseph/
  Le Petit Joseph **2**
Colors **9**
Le Girelier **3**
Spoon Byblos **12**
Villa Romana **8**

Exploring the City

Château Suffren is east of the port at the top end of quai Jean-Jaurès. It was built in A.D. 980 by Comte Guillame I of Provence, but can be viewed only from the outside.

Near the junction of quai Suffren and quai Jean-Jaurès stands the bronze **Statue de Suffren,** paying tribute to Vice-Admiral Pierre André de Suffren. Though largely forgotten today, the St-Tropez native was one of the greatest sailors of 18th-century France. In the Vieille Ville (old town), one of the most interesting streets is **rue de la Miséricorde.** It's lined with stone houses that hold boutiques. This street evokes medieval St-Tropez better than any other in town. At the corner of rue Gambetta is the **Chapelle de la Miséricorde,** with a blue, green, and gold tile roof.

Port Grimaud ★ makes an interesting outing. From St-Tropez, drive 4km (2¾ miles) west on A98 to Route 98, and then 1.5km (1 mile) north to the Port Grimaud exit. If you approach the village at dusk, when it's bathed in Riviera pastels, it looks like a 16th-century hamlet. This is a mirage: Port Grimaud is the dream of its promoter, François Spoerry, who carved it out of marshland and dug canals. Flanking the canals, fingers of land extend from the square to the sea. The homes are Provençal-style,

537

many with Italianate window arches. Boat owners can anchor at their doorsteps. One newspaper called the port "the most magnificent fake since Disneyland." Most shops and restaurants in Port Grimaud close from October to March.

Musée de l'Annonciade (Musée St-Tropez) ★★ Near the harbor, this museum occupies the former chapel of the Annonciade. It showcases one of the Riviera's finest modern-art collections of post-Impressionist masters. Many of the artists, including Paul Signac, depicted the port of St-Tropez. The collection includes such works as Van Dongen's *Women of the Balustrade* and paintings and sculpture by Bonnard, Matisse, Braque, Dufy, Utrillo, Seurat, Derain, and Maillol.

Quai de l'Epi le Port. © **04-94-17-84-10.** Admission 6€ adults, 4€ children 11 and under. June-Sept Wed-Mon 10am-noon and 3-7pm. Closed Nov.

Where to Stay

VERY EXPENSIVE

Hôtel Byblos ★★★ The builder said he created "an anti-hotel, a place like home." That's true if your home resembles a palace in Beirut and has salons decorated with Phoenician gold statues from 3000 B.C. On a hill above the harbor, this complex encompasses intimate patios and courtyards. It's filled with antiques and rare objects such as polychrome carved woodwork, marquetry floors, and a Persian-rug ceiling. Every room is unique, and all have elegant beds. Unusual features might include a fireplace on a raised hearth or a bed recessed on a dais. The rooms range in size from medium to spacious, often with high ceilings and antiques or reproductions. Some units have such special features as four-posters with furry spreads or sunken whirlpool tubs. Le Hameau, a stylish annex, contains 10 duplex suites built around a small courtyard with an outdoor spa. Some rooms have balconies overlooking an inner courtyard; others open onto a flowery terrace. Deluxe bathrooms hold tub/shower combinations.

Av. Paul Signac, St-Tropez 83990. © **04-94-56-68-00.** Fax 04-94-56-68-01. www.byblos.com. 94 units. 360€-900€ double; from 640€ suite. AE, DC, MC, V. Parking 30€. Closed Nov-Mar. **Amenities:** 2 restaurants; 2 bars; nightclub; babysitting; exercise room; massage; outdoor pool; room service; sauna; spa. *In room:* A/C, TV, hair dryer, minibar, Wi-Fi (free).

Hôtel La Tartane ★ This small hotel lies between the center of St-Tropez and the Plage des Salins, about a 3-minute drive from each. After a comprehensive upgrade, its government rating jumped from three stars to four. It has a heated stone-rimmed pool in the garden, attractively furnished public rooms with terra-cotta floors, and attentive, hardworking management. The midsize guest rooms are bungalows surrounding the pool. Each holds a small tiled bathroom with a shower stall or tub/shower combo. Breakfasts are elaborate.

Rte. des Salins, St-Tropez 83990. © **04-94-97-21-23.** Fax 04-94-97-09-16. www.latartane.fr. 28 units. 290€-895€ double; 600€-935€ suite. AE, DC, V. Closed mid-Oct to mid-Apr. **Amenities:** 2 restaurants; bar; massage; outdoor pool; spa; steam bath; free shuttle to beach. *In room:* A/C, TV, hair dryer, minibar, Wi-Fi (free).

Hôtel Le Yaca ★ Life here is *la dolce vita*. Built in 1722 off a narrow street in the old part of town, this was the first hotel in St-Tropez. The high-ceilinged reception area overlooks an inner courtyard filled with flowers. Many rooms also have views of this courtyard; all were renovated in the early part of the millennium. Some are on the upper level, with terra-cotta floor tiles and massive ceiling timbers. Each has a comfortable bed, utilitarian furniture, and high ceilings, and most have a roomy bathroom with tub and shower (otherwise only a shower).

1 bd. d'Aumale, St-Tropez 83900. ✆ 04-94-55-81-00. Fax 04-94-97-58-50. www.hotel-le-yaca.fr. 28 units. 270€–650€ double; 790€–1,350€ suite. AE, DC, MC, V. Parking 25€. Closed mid-Oct to mid-Apr. **Amenities:** Restaurant; bar; babysitting; massage; outdoor pool; room service. *In room:* A/C, TV, hair dryer, minibar, Wi-Fi (free).

Pastis Hôtel-St-Tropez ★★ 🎁 Best-selling author Peter Mayle, whose writings have drawn thousands to visit Provence, occasionally drops by this boutique hotel. Here he is welcomed by two expat Brits, John and Pauline Larkin, who took a portside Provençal house and transformed it into a chic little inn. They have decorated it in a sophisticated eclectic style, even featuring their collection of framed albums including the Sex Pistols and the Rolling Stones. Guests intermingle as they sip an aperitif by the pool in the courtyard. You get the feeling that you're staying in a private home when you lodge here, one discreetly decorated with art. Like the public lounges, the rooms are also furnished in an eclectic mix, and each unit comes with a spacious bathroom as well as a balcony or breakfast terrace. Some accommodations are large enough for extra beds or cots. Indian rugs, Chinese armoires, and beds adorned with Provençal *boutis* spreads enhance the warm, intimate ambience.

61 av. du Général Leclerc, St-Tropez 83990. ✆ 04-98-12-56-50. Fax 04-94-96-99-82. www.pastis-st-tropez. com. 9 units. 175€–600€ double. AE, MC, V. Free parking. **Amenities:** Outdoor pool. *In room:* A/C, TV, Wi-Fi (free).

EXPENSIVE

Hôtel La Ponche ★★ The same family has run this hotel overlooking the port for more than half a century. The cozy nest has long been a favorite of ours, as it's the most discreet, most charming, and least celebrity flashy establishment in town, making Byblos (see above) look nouveau riche and a bit strident. It's filled with the original airy paintings of Jacques Cordier, who died in 1978, which add to the atmosphere. The redecorated rooms are well equipped and open onto sea views. Each floor holds two or three rooms. Sun-colored walls with subtle lighting lend a homey feeling. The beds are elegantly appointed with linen and quality mattresses, and the midsize to large bathrooms have tub/shower combinations or a shower only.

Port des Pêcheurs, St-Tropez 83990. ✆ 04-94-97-02-53. Fax 04-94-97-78-61. www.laponche.com. 18 units. 195€–460€ double; 225€–630€ suite. AE, MC, V. Parking 21€. Closed Nov–Mar. **Amenities:** Restaurant; bar; babysitting; room service. *In room:* A/C, TV, hair dryer, minibar, Wi-Fi (free).

MODERATE

Hôtel Les Palmiers Accompanied by a verdant garden, this pleasant and practical government-rated three-star hotel was created in 1955 with the union of two once-separate houses, the older of which dates from the late 18th century. One of the best things about it is its location directly astride place des Lices in the center of St-Tropez. Bedrooms are simple and compact, and outfitted in a modernized Provençal theme highlighted with blue, soft orange, and ocher. Christian Guerin is the extroverted owner. There's a bar on the premises, but no restaurant.

24–26 bd. Vasserot (place des Lices), St-Tropez 83991. ✆ 04-94-97-01-61. Fax 04-94-97-10-02. www. hotel-les-palmiers.com. 25 units. 70€–230€ double. AE, MC, V. **Amenities:** Room service. *In room:* A/C, TV, hair dryer, minibar, Wi-Fi (free).

Hôtel Sube If you want to be right on the port, in a location that's perfect for ship- and celebrity-watching, this might be your first choice. It's directly over the

Café de Paris bar, in the center of a shopping arcade. The two-story lounge has a beamed ceiling and a glass front, allowing a great view of the harbor. The rooms aren't large but are comfortable and decorated in French Provincial style. The more expensive units have scenic views of the port. Each comes with a private bathroom with a shower and tub.

15 quai Suffren, 83900 St-Tropez. ☏ **04-94-97-30-04.** Fax 04-94-54-89-08. 25 units. 140€–290€ double. AE, MC, V. Closed Oct–May. **Amenities:** Cafe; bar; Wi-Fi (free). *In room:* A/C, TV.

Where to Dine

Auberge des Maures ★ PROVENÇAL   One of our favorite cost-conscious restaurants in an otherwise very expensive town lies close to one end of the all-pedestrian rue Allard. The stone-sided building, highlighted with Provence-specific murals, has a rollaway roof and garden seating (both experienced during nice weather). The open kitchen affords views of the staff preparing items such as grilled versions of many kinds of fresh fish and meat; *panache Provençal,* on which are piled deep-fried zucchini blossoms; hearts of artichoke *barigoule;* and a medley of *petits farcis* (stuffed vegetables). The Salinesi family (Evelyn and Philippe) takes pride in using seasonal, all-fresh ingredients.

4 rue du Docteur Boutin. ☏ **04-94-97-01-50.** www.aubergedesmaures.com. Reservations recommended. Main courses 40€–60€; fixed-price menu 47€. AE, DC, MC, V. Daily 7:30pm–1am. Closed Nov–Mar.

Chez Joseph/Le Petit Joseph ★ PROVENÇAL   These side-by-side restaurants are serviced by the same kitchen, and the menus are quite similar. Le Petit Joseph is quieter and more romantic, with low-beamed ceilings, an Asian decor, and cozy banquettes. Chez Joseph, where you sit with other patrons at long tables, tends to be completely booked and packed at 10pm. Both restaurants offer outdoor seating, but Le Petit has just a few tables; Chez features a large terrace. The traditional yet creatively presented cuisine emphasizes fish, and the menu changes often. For dessert, the *parfait léger* is a treat—vanilla custard with chocolate powder on a cherry crumble with a scoop of cherry-vanilla ice cream and fresh fruit.

1 place de l'Hôtel-de-Ville. ☏ **04-94-97-01-66.** www.joseph-saint-tropez.com. Reservations recommended at Chez Joseph. Main courses 29€–155€; fixed-price lunch 39€. AE, MC, V. Daily noon–2pm and 7:30pm–midnight.

Colors ★ GRILL/SUSHI   Relatively new on the St-Tropez dining scene, this restaurant offers a verdant garden setting and one of the town's very few wood-burning ovens, on which a succulent array of fresh meat and fish is slowly cooked. Here, amid a décor of—you guessed it—strong colors, you can enjoy grilled filet steaks, rib-eyes, and such fresh fish as sea bass. Most are accompanied with creamy house-style mashed potatoes and fresh vegetables.

3 rue du Temple. ☏ **04-94-97-00-15.** Reservations required July–Aug. Main courses 25€–30€; sushi assortment 29€. AE, MC, V. Daily 7:30pm–1am. Closed mid-Oct to mid-Mar.

Le Girelier PROVENÇAL   The Rouets own this portside restaurant, whose blue-and-white color scheme has become a trademark. They serve grilled fish in many versions, as well as bouillabaisse (only for two). Also on the menu are brochette of monkfish, a kettle of spicy mussels, and *pipérade* (a Basque omelet with pimientos, garlic, and tomatoes). Most dishes are moderately priced.

Quai Jean-Jaurès. ☏ **04-94-97-03-87.** www.legirelier.fr. Main courses 21€–50€; fixed-price menu 39€. AE, DC, MC, V. Daily noon–6pm and 7–11pm. Closed Nov 1–Mar 30.

Spoon Byblos ★★ FRENCH/INTERNATIONAL Originally launched in Paris, Spoon has traveled everywhere from London to the Riviera. Here it serves the cuisines of many cultures with produce mainly from the Mediterranean. It draws special inspiration from the food of Catalonia, Andalusia, and Morocco, and offers more than 300 wines from around the world. Background music ranges from hip-hop to the hits of the '70s. It's terribly fashionable, although you may grow a bit weary of its self-conscious sense of chic after an hour or two within its ultradesigned premises.

The restaurant opens onto a circular bar made of blue-tinted glass and polished stainless steel. Dig into shrimp and squid consommé with a hint of jasmine and orange; spicy king prawns on a skewer; delectable lamb couscous; or spit-roasted John Dory. You may top off a meal with the chef's favorite cheesecake or a slice of Neapolitan with the taste of strawberry, vanilla, and pistachio.

In the Hôtel Byblos, av. Paul-Signac. ℂ **04-94-56-68-20.** Reservations required. Main courses 32€– 49€; fixed-price menu 89€. AE, DC, MC, V. Mid-Apr to Oct daily 8–11pm.

Villa Romana ★ ITALIAN This is where the St-Tropez party scene breaks for dinner; it's behind place des Lices, close to the nightclub Les Caves du Roy. The Italian cuisine here hardly ranks with the best you've ever had, but watching the (often scantily clad) patrons makes for the most amusing dinner in town. The place looks like Hugh Hefner designed it for his Playboy Mansion. Tycoons, wannabes, tabloid celebrities, and yachties look up as each new diner enters. When we went, it seemed a particular Italophile celebrity enjoyed the grilled calamari and the beef filet with summer truffles more than we did. We think your best bet is one of the homemade pastas or the catch of the day. In summer wear your skimpiest attire (that goes for men and women alike).

Impasse des Conquetes (near the corner of av. Paul Roussel, a short walk southwest of Place des Lices). ℂ **04-94-97-15-50.** Reservations required. Main courses 24€–75€; pizzas 20€–35€. MC, V. Easter to early Oct Thurs–Sun 8–11:30pm.

St-Tropez After Dark

On the lobby level of the Hôtel Byblos, **Les Caves du Roy,** avenue Paul-Signac (ℂ **04-94-97-16-02**), is the most self-consciously chic nightclub in St-Tropez and the most famous in France. Entrance is free, but drink prices begin at a whopping 18€. It's open nightly from May to late September from 11:30pm until dawn. **Le Papagayo,** in the Résidence du Nouveau-Port, rue Gambetta (ℂ **04-94-97-95-95**), is one of the largest nightclubs in town. The decor was inspired by the psychedelic 1960s. Entrance is between 15€ and 18€, and includes one drink.

Adjacent to Le Papagayo is **Le VIP Room,** in the Résidence du Nouveau-Port (ℂ **04-94-97-14-70**), whose upscale male and female patrons may be equally at home in Les Caves du Roy. Cocktails run between 14€ and 15€. The club is all steel, chrome, mirrors, and glass. Expect an active bar area, dance floor, and the kind of social posturing and preening that can be amusing—or not.

Le Pigeonnier, 13 rue de la Ponche (ℂ **04-94-97-84-26**), rocks, rolls, and welcomes a crowd that's mostly gay or lesbian and between 20 and 50. Most of the socializing revolves around the long, narrow bar, where patrons from all over Europe enjoy chitchat. There's also a dance floor.

Below the Hôtel Sube, the **Café de Paris,** sur le Port (ℂ **04-94-97-00-56**), is one of the most popular hangouts. The utilitarian room has early-1900s globe lights, an occasional 19th-century bronze artifact, masses of artificial flowers, and a long zinc bar. The crowd is irreverent and animated. **Café Sénéquier,** sur le Port (© **04-94-97-20-20**), is historic, venerable, snobbish, and, at its worst, off-puttingly stylish.

Le Bar du Port, quai Suffren, adjacent to the Café de Paris (© **04-94-97-00-54**), is breezy, airy, and almost obsessively hip and self-consciously trendy. This cafe-bar attracts a consistently young clientele. Expect lots of table-hopping, stylishly skimpy clothing, recorded music that may want to make you get up and dance, and insights into what's really going on in the minds of French 20-somethings.

If your idea of a night out is sitting in a cafe drinking wine, you can "hang out" at such joints as **Kelly's Irish Pub,** quai F. Mistral, at the bottom end of the Vieux Port (© **04-94-54-89-11**), which draws a mostly foreign crowd. The tavern is casual, not chic. If you're nostalgic for St-Germain-des-Prés, head for the old-fashioned **Le Café,** place des Lices (© **04-94-97-44-69**), with its famous zinc bar. Its glory lies in its location and not because of any innate value as a warm and cozy cafe (it's both a bistro/restaurant and cafe).

LA NAPOULE–PLAGE ★

901km (560 miles) S of Paris; 8km (5 miles) W of Cannes

This secluded resort is on the sandy beaches of the Golfe de la Napoule. In 1919, the fishing village was a paradise for the sculptor Henry Clews and his wife, Marie, an architect. Fleeing America's "charlatans," whom he believed had profited from World War I, the New York banker's son emphasized the fairy-tale qualities of his new home. An inscription over the entrance to his house—now the **Musée Henry-Clews**—reads ONCE UPON A TIME.

The museum is in the **Château de la Napoule ★**, boulevard Henry-Clews (© **04-93-49-95-05**; www.chateau-lanapoule.com), which was rebuilt from the ruins of a medieval château. Clews covered the capitals and lintels with a grotesque menagerie—scorpions, pelicans, gnomes, monkeys, and lizards. Women, feminism, and old age are recurring themes in the sculptor's work, as exemplified by the distorted suffragette depicted in his *Cat Woman*. The artist admired chivalry and dignity as represented by *Don Quixote*—to whom he likened himself. Clews died in Switzerland in 1937, and his body was returned to La Napoule for burial. Marie Clews later opened the château to the public. To visit the castle and gardens costs 6€ for adults, 4€ for those 16 and under. Open February 7 to November 7 daily 10am to 6pm; and November 8 to February 6 Monday to Friday 2 to 6pm, and Saturday and Sunday 10am to 6pm.

Essentials

GETTING THERE   The waterside community of La Napoule–Plage is part of La Mandelieu–La Napoule, which lies on the **bus** and **train** routes between Cannes and St-Raphaël. The one-way fare, for the bus or train, from Cannes to La Mandelieu–La Napoule is 2€. For information and schedules, call © **08-92-35-35-35.** If you're **driving,** take A8 west from Cannes.

VISITOR INFORMATION   The **Office de Tourisme** is on avenue Henry-Clews (© **04-92-97-99-27**; fax 04-93-93-64-66; www.ot-mandelieu.fr).

Where to Stay

La Calanque   The foundations of this well-positioned government-rated two-star hotel date from the Roman Empire, when it was an aristocrat's villa. The present hotel, run by the same family since 1942, looks like a chalet, with stucco walls. Guest rooms are small to medium in size, and each has a comfortable bed and bathroom with a tub or shower. The hotel's restaurant spills onto a terrace and serves some of the cheapest fixed-price meals around. Nonguests are welcome.

Av. Henry-Clews, La Napoule 06210. © **04-93-49-95-11.** Fax 04-93-49-67-44. 17 units. 47€–81€ double. MC, V. Closed mid-Oct to Feb. **Amenities:** Restaurant; bar (guests only), Wi-Fi (free). *In room:* A/C (in some), TV.

L'Ermitage du Riou ★★ 📖   This old Provençal house, the most tranquil choice at the resort, is a seaside government-rated four-star hotel bordering the Riou River and the Cannes-Mandelieu golf club. The rooms are furnished in regional style, with authentic furniture and ancient paintings. The rooms range in size from medium to spacious, and each has an elegant bed and fine linen. Views are of the sea or the golf course.

Av. Henry-Clews, La Napoule 06210. © **04-93-49-95-56.** Fax 04-92-97-69-05. www.ermitage-du-riou.fr. 41 units. 126€–192€ double; 375€–529€ suite. AE, DC, MC, V. **Amenities:** Restaurant; bar; outdoor pool; sauna. *In room:* A/C, TV, hair dryer, minibar, Wi-Fi (free).

Pullman Royal Casino ★★   This Las Vegas–style hotel is on the beach near a man-made harbor, about 8km (5 miles) from Cannes. It was the first French hotel with a casino and the last (before building codes changed) to have a casino directly on the beach. The hotel has one of the most contemporary designs on the Côte d'Azur. Most of the good-size rooms angle toward a sea view; those facing the street are likely to be noisy, despite soundproofing.

605 av. du Général-de-Gaulle, La Mandelieu–La Napoule 06212. © **800/221-4542** in the U.S. and Canada, or 04-92-97-70-00. Fax 04-93-49-51-50. www.pullman.com. 213 units. 285€–745€ double; from 1,350€ suite. AE, DC, MC, V. Parking 12€. **Amenities:** 2 restaurants; 2 bars; nightclub; babysitting; exercise room; room service; spa; 2 tennis courts. *In room:* A/C, TV, hair dryer, minibar, Wi-Fi (4.50€ per hr.).

Where to Dine

La Calanque's restaurant (see "Where to Stay," above) is open to nonguests.

Le Féréol ★ FRENCH   This well-designed restaurant serves most of the culinary needs of the largest hotel (and only casino) in town. Outfitted in nautical style, it prepares impressive lunch buffets. At night the room is candlelit and more elegant, and the view through bay windows is soothing. Menu items include Breton artichokes with a stuffing that's composed of minced cured ham, cheese, and herbs; a "frivolity" of mushrooms composed of two kinds of exotic mushrooms plus a confit of quail all served atop a warm brioche; filet of John Dory with artichoke hearts, lavender, and scampi; and a succulent version of roasted veal with baby Provençal vegetables and herbs.

In the Pullman Royal Casino, 605 av. du Général-de-Gaulle. © **04-92-97-70-20.** Reservations recommended. Main courses 16€–30€. AE, DC, MC, V. Sept–June daily 12:30–2:30pm and 7:30–9:30pm; July–Aug daily 12:30–3pm and 7–10:30pm.

L'Oasis ★★★ MODERN FRENCH   Here you'll find the most wonderful cuisine on the western Riviera. At the entrance to the harbor of La Napoule, in a mid-20th-century house with a lovely garden and a re-creation of a medieval cloister, this restaurant became world famous under now-retired Louis Outhier. Today, his protégé, Stéphane Raimbault, prepares sophisticated cuisine. Because Raimbault cooked in Japan for 9 years, many of his dishes are of the "East meets West" variety, with dishes such as crayfish cooked "in the fires of hell" and served with wok-fried baby vegetables; perfectly grilled Mediterranean fish; or a masterful saddle of venison with hazelnuts, pepper sauce, and caramelized pears. The cellar houses one of the finest collections of Provençal wines anywhere. In summer, meals are served under the plane trees in the garden.

Rue Jean-Honoré-Carle. © **04-93-49-95-52.** www.oasis-raimbault.com. Reservations required. Main courses 24€–115€; fixed-price lunch 58€–89€, dinner 96€–190€. AE, DC, MC, V. Daily noon–2pm; Mon-Sat 7:30–10pm. Closed Mon Nov–Mar; closed mid-Dec to mid-Jan.

CANNES ★★★

905km (562 miles) S of Paris; 163km (101 miles) E of Marseille; 26km (16 miles) SW of Nice

When Coco Chanel came here and got a suntan, returning to Paris bronzed, she startled the milk-white society ladies, who quickly began copying her. Today the bronzed bodies—clad in nearly nonexistent swimsuits—that line the beaches of this chic resort continue the late fashion designer's example.

Essentials

GETTING THERE   **Trains** from the other Mediterranean resorts, Paris, and the rest of France arrive frequently throughout the day. By train, Cannes is 15 minutes from Antibes and 35 minutes from Nice. The TGV from Paris via Marseille reaches Cannes in about 5 breathless hours. The one-way fare from Paris is 50€ to 95€. For rail information and schedules, call © **08-92-35-35-35,** or visit www.voyages-sncf. com. **Rapide Côte d'Azur,** place de l'Hôtel de Ville, Cannes (© **04-93-85-64-44**), provides bus service to Nice and back every 20 minutes during the day (trip time: 1½ hr.). The one-way fare is 1€.

The Nice **international airport** (© **08-20-42-33-33;** www.rca.tm.fr) is a 30-minute drive northeast. **Buses** pick up passengers at the airport every 40 minutes during the day and drop them at the Gare Routière, place de l'Hôtel de Ville (© **04-93-45-20-08**). Bus service from Antibes operates every half-hour.

By **car** from Marseille, take A51 north to Aix-en-Provence, continuing along A8 east to Cannes. From Nice, follow A8 southwest to Cannes.

VISITOR INFORMATION   The **Office de Tourisme** is at 1 bd. de la Croisette (© **04-92-99-84-22;** fax 04-92-99-84-23; www.cannes.travel).

SPECIAL EVENTS   Cannes is at its most frenzied at the end of May, during the **International Film Festival** at the Palais des Festivals on promenade de la Croisette. It attracts not only film stars but also seemingly every photographer in the world. You have a better chance of being named prime minister of France than you do of attending one of the major screenings. (Hotel rooms and tables at restaurants are equally scarce during the festival.) But the people-watching is fabulous. If you find yourself here at the right time, you can join the thousands who line up in front of the Palais des Festivals, where the premières are held. With paparazzi shouting and gendarmes holding back fans, the guests parade along the red carpet, stopping for a moment to strike a pose. *C'est Cannes!*

You may be able to get tickets for some of the lesser films, which play 24 hours. For information, see "France Calendar of Events," in chapter 3, or visit **www.festival-cannes.org**.

From international regattas and galas to *concours d'élégance* (an extravagant car show) and even a Mimosa Festival (focusing on local handicrafts) in February, something's always happening at Cannes, except in November, which is traditionally a dead month.

A Day at the Beach

Beachgoing in Cannes has more to do with exhibitionism and voyeurism than with actual swimming.

Plage de la Croisette extends between the Vieux Port and the Port Canto. Though the beaches along this billion-dollar stretch of sand aren't in the strictest sense private, they're *payante,* meaning entrance costs 15€ to 22€. You don't need to be a guest of the Noga Hilton, Martinez, Carlton, or Majestic to use the beaches associated with those hotels, though if you are you'll usually get a 50% discount. A wooden barricade that stops close to the sea separates each beach from its neighbors, making it easy for you to stroll from one to another.

Why should you pay a fee at all? Well, it includes a full day's use of a mattress, a chaise longue (the seafront isn't sandy or even soft, but covered with pebbles and dark-gray shingles), and a parasol, as well as easy access to freshwater showers and kiosks selling beverages. There are also outdoor restaurants where no one minds if you appear in your swimsuit.

For nostalgia's sake, our favorite beach is the one associated with the **Carlton** (p. 550)—it was the first beach we went to, as teenagers, in Cannes. The merits of each of the 20 or so beaches vary daily depending on the crowd, and because every beach allows topless bathing (keep your bottom covered), you're likely to find the same forms of décolletage along the entire strip.

Looking for a free public beach where you'll have to survive without renting chaises or parasols? Head for **Plage du Midi,** sometimes called Midi Plage, just west of the Vieux Port (no phone), or **Plage Gazagnaire,** just east of the Port Canto (no phone). Here you'll find families with children and lots of caravan-type vehicles parked nearby.

Outdoor Pursuits

BICYCLING & MOTOR SCOOTERING   Despite the roaring traffic, the flat landscapes between Cannes and satellite resorts such as La Napoule are well suited for riding a bike or motor scooter. At **Daniel Location,** 7 rue Suffern (℃ **04-93-99-90-30**), *vélos tout terrain* (mountain bikes) cost 16€ a day. Motorized bikes and scooters cost 36€ per day; renters must be at least 14 years old. For larger scooters, you must present a valid driver's license. Another purveyor of bikes is **Mistral Location,** 4 rue Georges Clemenceau (℃ **04-93-39-08-53**), which charges 14€ per day.

BOATING   Several companies rent boats of any size, with or without a crew, for a day, a week, or a month. An outfit known for short-term rentals of small craft, including motorboats, sailboats, and canoes, is **Elco Marine,** 110 bd. du Midi (℃ **04-93-47-12-62;** www.elcomarine.fr).

SWIMMING   Cannes probably has more privately owned swimming pools, per capita, than anywhere else in France. If your hotel doesn't have one, consider an

Cannes

excursion to the **Piscine Pierre de Coubertin,** avenue P. de Coubertin (© **04-93-47-12-94**). Its length of almost 23m (75 ft.) makes this outdoor pool ideal for swimming laps. Because it's used for a variety of civic functions, including practices for local swim teams, hours are limited, so call ahead. Entrance costs 3€ for adults, 1.50€ for children 3 to 15.

TENNIS   Some resorts have their own courts. The city of Cannes also maintains a half-dozen courts (one made from synthetic resins, five clay-topped); you'll pay 12€ to 15€ per hour, depending on the court and the time you want to play, plus 3.25€ per hour for lighting. They're at **Garden Tennis Club,** 99 av. Maurice Chevalier (© **04-93-47-29-33**). If those courts are already taken, **ASLM Tennis Munici-pal Aérodrome,** Aérodrome de Cannes Mandelieu (© **04-93-47-29-33**), also maintained by the municipality, charges the same rates for its five clay-topped courts.

ACCOMMODATIONS ■
Hôtel de Provence **10**
Hôtel Gray-d'Albion **6**
Hôtel Le Florian **7**
Hôtel le Fouquet's **12**
Hôtel Martinez **17**
Hôtel Splendid **5**
Hôtel Victoria **11**
Hôtel Villa de l'Olivier **3**
InterContinental Carlton
  Cannes **15**
Palais Stephanie **13**

DINING ◆
Côte Jardin **1**
Gaston et Gastounette **4**
La Brouette de
  Grand-Mère **9**
La Canna Suisse **2**
La Mère Besson **8**
La Palme d'Or **16**
Le Festival **14**

★ Paris

FRANCE

Cannes

Shopping

Cannes achieves a blend of resort-style leisure, glamour, and media glitz more successfully than many of its neighbors. So you're likely to find branch outlets of virtually every stylish Paris retailer.

You'll see every big-name designer you can think of (Saint-Laurent, Rykiel, and Hermès) and designers you've never heard of (Claude Bonucci, Basile, and Durrani). There are also real-people shops; resale shops for star-studded castoffs; flea markets for fun junk; and a fruit, flower, and vegetable market.

ANTIQUES   One of the city's most noteworthy antiques dealers is **Hubert Herpin,** 20 rue Macé (✆ **04-93-39-56-18**). This store carries a wide selection of marble statues, marquetry, and 18th- and 19th-century furniture.

BOOKS   Ciné-Folie, 14 rue des Frères-Pradignac (✆ **04-93-39-22-99**), is devoted entirely to film. Called *La Boutique du Cinema,* it is the finest film bookstore in the south of France; vintage film stills and movie posters are also for sale.

SEEING CANNES FROM A PETIT TRAIN

One of the best ways to get your bearings in Cannes (and to get an idea of the difference between the city's new and old neighborhoods) is to climb aboard a white-sided Petit Train touristique de Cannes. The diesel-powered vehicles roll through the streets on rubber tires. They operate every day from 10am to between 7 and 11:30pm, depending on the season. Two itineraries are offered: For views of glittery modern Cannes, board the train at a designated spot in front of either of the town's two casinos for a ride along La Croisette and its side streets. For a ride through the narrow streets of Vieux Cannes (Le Suquet), board the train at a clearly designated site on the seaward side of La Croisette, opposite the Hôtel Majestic. Both tours depart every 30 to 60 minutes. They last around 45 minutes, depending on traffic, and cost 7€ for adults and 3€ for children 9 and younger, depending on the tour. (The tour of the old town is the less expensive.) A combination ticket to both tours (good on separate days, if you prefer) costs 10€ for adults and 5€ for children 9 and under. For details, call © **04-93-38-39-18;** www.cannes-petit-train.com.

CHOCOLATE & JELLIED FRUITS   Cannes is home to several famous chocolatiers. Try **Chez Bruno,** 50 rue d'Antibes (© **04-93-39-26-63**). Opened in 1929 and maintained by a descendant of its founder, the shop is famous for fruit confits as well as marrons glacés (glazed chestnuts), made fresh daily.

DEPARTMENT STORES   Near the train station in the heart of Cannes, **Galeries Lafayette** has a small branch at 6 rue du Maréchal-Foch (© **04-97-06-25-00**). It's noted for the upscale fashion in its carefully arranged interiors.

DESIGNER SHOPS   Most of the big names in fashion, for both men and women, line **promenade de la Croisette,** known as **La Croisette,** the main drag facing the sea. Among the most prestigious is **Dior,** 38 La Croisette (© **04-92-98-98-00**). The stores are in a row, stretching from the Hôtel Carlton almost to the Palais des Festivals, with the best names closest to the **Gray-d'Albion,** 38 rue des Ferbes (© **04-92-99-79-79**), which is both a mall and a hotel (how convenient). The stores in the Gray-d'Albion mall include **Hermès.** The two-section mall serves as a cut-through from the primary expensive shopping street, La Croisette, to the less expensive shopping street, **rue d'Antibes.**

FLEA MARKETS   Cannes has two regular flea markets. Casual, dusty, and increasingly filled with castaways from estate sales, the **Marché Forville,** conducted in the neighborhood of the same name, near the Palais des Festivals, is a stucco structure with a roof and a few arches but no sides. From Tuesday to Sunday, it's the fruit, vegetable, and flower market that supplies dozens of grand restaurants. Monday is *brocante* day, when the market fills with dealers selling everything from Grandmère's dishes to bone-handled carving knives.

On Saturdays, from 8am to 12:30pm, a somewhat disorganized and busy **Marché aux Fleurs** takes place outdoors along the edges of the allée de la Liberté, across from the Palais des Festivals. Hours depend on the whims of whatever dealer happens to haul in a cache of merchandise, but it usually begins around 8am and runs out of steam by around 4:30pm. *Note:* Vendors at the two flea markets may or may not be the same.

FOOD The street with the greatest density of emporiums selling wine, olives, herbs, cheese, bread, and oils is the appealing **rue Meynadier.**

A charming old-fashioned shop, **Cannolive,** 16–20 rue Vénizelos (✆ **04-93-39-08-19**), is owned by members of the Raynaud family, which founded the place in 1880. It sells Provençal olives and their byproducts—tapenades that connoisseurs refer to as "Provençal caviar," black "olives de Nice," and green "olives de Provence," as well as three grades of olive oil from regional producers. Oils and food products are at no. 16; gift items (fabrics, porcelain, and Provençal souvenirs) are sold next door.

PERFUME The best and most expensive shop is **Bouteille,** 59 rue d'Antibes (✆ **04-93-39-05-16**). Its prices are higher than its competitors' because it stocks more brands, has a wider selection, and gives away occasional samples. Other shops dot rue d'Antibes. Any may feature your favorite fragrance in a promotional deal. For reasonably priced perfumes, head to the boutiques associated with the Hôtel Gray-d'Albion.

Seeing the Sights

For many visitors, Cannes might as well consist of only one street, the **promenade de la Croisette**—or just La Croisette—curving along the coast and split by islands of palms and flowers.

A port of call for cruise liners, Cannes is sheltered by hills. Hotels, apartment houses, and boutiques line the seafront. Many of the bigger hotels, some dating from the 19th century, claim part of the beaches for their guests; there are also public areas. Above the harbor, the old town of Cannes sits on Suquet Hill, where you'll see the 14th-century **Tour de Suquet,** which the English dubbed the Lord's Tower.

Nearby is the **Musée de la Castre** ★, in the Château de la Castre, Le Suquet (✆ **04-93-38-55-26**). It displays paintings, sculpture, and works of decorative art. The ethnography section includes objects from all over, including Peruvian and Mayan pottery. There's also a gallery devoted to relics of Mediterranean civilizations, from the Greeks to the Romans, from the Cypriots to the Egyptians. Five rooms hold 19th-century paintings. The museum is open daily in July and August 10am to 7pm; September to March Tuesday to Sunday 10am to 1pm and 2 to 5pm; April to June Tuesday to Sunday 10am to 1pm and 2 to 6pm. Admission is 3.20€ adults, 2€ ages 18 to 25, free 17 and under.

Ferrying to the Iles de Lérins ★★

Across the bay from Cannes, the Lérins Islands are the major excursion from the port. Ferries depart every half-hour from 7:30am to 30 minutes before sundown. For access to Ile Ste-Marguerite, head for the quai Laubeuf, opposite the Hotel Sofitel, in Cannes where ferryboats operated by **Trans-Côte d'Azur** (✆ **04-92-98-71-30**), haul passengers back and forth, year-round, at intervals of between every 15 and 75 minutes, depending on the season. For access to Ile St-Honorat, head for the same quai (quai Laubeuf), for the ferryboats operated by **Cie Transports Planaria** (✆ **04-92-98-71-38**). Boats depart daily year-round at intervals of between 30 and 90 minutes, depending on the season. Round-trip transport to both venues costs 11€ per adult, 5.50€ for children 5 to 10, and free for children 4 and under. Ferryboats operated by both of the above-noted companies have a capacity of around 220 passengers.

ILE STE-MARGUERITE

This island was named after St-Honorat's sister, Ste-Marguerite, who lived here with a group of nuns in the 5th century. Today it is a youth center whose members are dedicated to the restoration of the fort—when they aren't sailing and diving. From the dock, you can stroll along the island (signs point the way) to the Fort de l'Ile, built by Spanish troops from 1635 to 1637. Below is the 1st-century-B.C. Roman town where the "Man in the Iron Mask" was imprisoned. You can visit his cell at Ste-Marguerite. As you listen to the sound of the sea, you realize what a forlorn outpost this was.

Musée de la Mer, Fort Royal (© **04-93-43-18-17**), traces the history of the island, displaying artifacts of Ligurian, Roman, and Arab civilizations, plus the remains discovered by excavations, including paintings, mosaics, and ceramics. The museum is open April to September Tuesday to Sunday 10:30am to 5:45pm (closing at 4:45pm Oct–Mar). Admission is 3.20€ for adults, free for students and children 17 and under.

ILE ST-HONORAT ★★

Only 1.6km (1 mile) long, but richer in history than its sibling islands, the Ile St-Honorat is the site of a monastery whose origins date from the 5th century. The **Abbaye de St-Honorat ★**, Les Iles de Lérins, Cannes 06400 (© **04-92-99-54-00**), boasts a combination of medieval ruins and early-20th-century ecclesiastical buildings, and is home to a community of about 30 Cistercian monks. Under controlled circumstances, if space is available, well-intentioned outsiders can visit and spend the night, but only for prayer and meditation. Most visitors opt to wander through the pine forests on the island's western side and sunbathe on its beaches.

Where to Stay

VERY EXPENSIVE

Hôtel Martinez ★★   Although it's a bit less appealing than the Carlton, this is a popular convention hotel and a desirable property for the individual. When the Art Deco hotel was built in the 1930s, it rivaled any other lodging along the coast in sheer size. Over the years, however, it fell into disrepair. But in 1982, the hotel and its restaurants were returned to their former luster. The aim of the decor was a Roaring '20s style, and all units have full marble bathrooms, wood furnishings, tasteful carpets, quality mattresses, and pastel fabrics. Called a hotel within a hotel, the penthouse floor has become the chicest place to stay in Cannes, featuring 11 suites, the most sought-after in town following a massive restyling. It has a private beach, one of the finest restaurants in Cannes (La Palme d'Or, p. 553), and a water-skiing school.

73 bd. de la Croisette, Cannes 06406. © **04-92-98-73-00.** Fax 04-93-39-67-82. www.hotel-martinez. com. 412 units. 545€–1,000€ double; from 2,900€ suite. AE, DC, MC, V. Parking 35€. **Amenities:** 3 summer restaurants, 2 winter restaurants; bar; babysitting; private beach; exercise room; outdoor pool; room service; sauna; spa; 7 tennis courts nearby. *In room:* A/C, TV, hair dryer, minibar, Wi-Fi (free).

InterContinental Carlton Cannes ★★★   Here you'll see vehicles of every description dropping off huge amounts of baggage and numbers of fashionable (and sometimes not-so-fashionable) guests. The twin gray domes at either end of the facade are often the first things recognized by starlets planning their grand entrances, grand exits, and grand scenes in the hotel's public and private rooms.

Built in 1912, the Carlton once attracted the most prominent members of Europe's *haut monde*. Today the hotel is more democratic, booking lots of conventions and motorcoach tour groups; however, in summer (especially during the film festival) the public rooms still fill with all the voyeuristic and exhibitionistic fervor that seems so much a part of the Riviera. Guest rooms are plush; the most spacious are in the west wing; and many upper-floor rooms open onto waterfront balconies.

58 bd. de la Croisette, Cannes 06400. © **04-93-06-40-06.** Fax 04-93-06-40-25. www.intercontinental. com. 343 units. 250€–1,050€ double; from 615€ suite. AE, DC, MC, V. Parking 37€. **Amenities:** 3 summer restaurants; 1 winter restaurant; 2 bars; health club; room service. *In room:* A/C, TV, hair dryer, Internet (24€ per day), minibar.

Palais Stéphanie ★   This hotel results from a name change in 2007 that was wrought upon a six-story contemporary hotel previously known as Cannes's Noga Hilton. Built upon the site of the old Palais des Festivals, and well known as one of Cannes's most visible modern palace hotels, it has massive amounts of glass, steel, and marble, whose gleaming gray-white sheen is especially visible within the atrium-style lobby. That lobby is dotted with sofas and chairs upholstered in red leather and illuminated from a skylight six stories above, and festooned with verdant plants. Guest rooms are carefully soundproofed, each with a balcony, a fresh coat of paint, and angular, contemporary-looking furniture from the mid-1990s that was not changed during the name change. The in-house restaurant, Le Grand Bleu, is stylish, glossy, and upscale.

50 bd. De la Croisette, Cannes 06414. © **04-92-99-70-00.** Fax 04-92-99-70-11. www.hotel-palaise-stephanie-cannes.com. 232 units. 210€–1,100€ double; from 450€ suite. AE, DC, MC, V. **Amenities:** Restaurant; bar; casino; babysitting; outdoor pool; room service. *In room:* A/C, TV, minibar, hair dryer, Wi-Fi (free).

EXPENSIVE

Hôtel Gray-d'Albion ★★   The smallest of the major hotels isn't on La Croisette. It occupies mostly contemporary, not particularly historic premises and enjoys a four-star rating from the French government. Although it cannot compete on many levels with the larger, better-accessorized palace hotels (such as the Carlton) with which it is often compared, it maintains a conservative, somewhat staid image as solid, dependable, and reliable. Now part of the Lucien Barrière chain, it's uncontroversial, but nonetheless completely respectable. Groups form a large part of its clientele, but it also caters to the individual. The medium-size rooms blend contemporary and traditional furnishings. Each unit has a balcony, but the views aren't notable, except from the eighth and ninth floors.

38 rue des Serbes, Cannes 06400. © **04-92-99-79-79.** Fax 04-93-99-26-10. www.lucienbarriere.com. 198 units. 199€–549€ double; from 419€ suite. AE, DC, MC, V. **Amenities:** Restaurant; bar; babysitting; 24-hr. room service in summer (limited in winter). *In room:* A/C, TV, hair dryer, minibar, Wi-Fi (15€ per day).

MODERATE

Château de la Tour ★ 🎁   Enveloped by its fine garden, this hotel was created from a former private estate. Lying 252m (825 ft.) from the beaches, the hotel has been elegantly restored and turned into a beautiful gem of accommodations. Guest rooms look out to the sea and lush gardens below. The small standard rooms are cozy yet comfortable, while superior units get the panoramic views, are more spacious, and are usually accompanied by a balcony or terrace. There is a Provençal elegance and charm found here that's rarely achieved by more modern, impersonal hotels.

10 av. Font de Veyre, Cannes 06150. © **04-93-90-52-52.** Fax 04-93-47-86-61. www.hotelchateaudela tour.com. 34 units. 125€–295€ double. Rates include continental breakfast. AE, MC, V. Parking: 10€. **Amenities:** Restaurant; bar; Jacuzzi; outdoor pool; Wi-Fi (free). *In room:* A/C, TV, hair dryer, minibar.

Hôtel Le Fouquet's ★ 🏠 This intimate lodging draws a discreet clientele, often from Paris, who'd never think of patronizing the grand hotels. Riviera French in design and decor, the hotel is several blocks from the beach. Each of the cozy guest rooms is outfitted just a bit differently from its neighbor. They're decorated in bold Provençal colors of ocher and blue, and have contemporary, vaguely regional furniture. The owner is often on-site, making the hotel feel like an intimate B&B.

2 rond-point Duboys-d'Angers, Cannes 06400. © **04-92-59-25-00.** Fax 04-92-98-03-39. www.le-fouquets.com. 12 units. 110€–280€ double; 280€–320€ suite. AE, DC, MC, V. Closed Nov 1–Apr 12. Bus: 1. **Amenities:** Babysitting; room service. *In room:* A/C, TV, hair dryer, minibar, Wi-Fi (free).

Hôtel Splendid ★ 🗡 Opened in 1871, and widely renovated, this is a favorite of scholars, politicians, actors, and musicians. The ornate white building with wrought-iron accents looks out onto the sea, the old port, and a park. The rooms are appointed with antique furniture and paintings; about 15 have kitchenettes. Each comes with a good bed and a small but efficient bathroom. The more expensive rooms have sea views.

4–6 Rue Félix-Faure, Cannes 06400. © **04-97-06-22-22.** Fax 04-93-99-55-02. www.splendid-hotel-cannes.fr. 62 units. 131€–264€ double. Rates include breakfast. AE, MC, V. **Amenities:** Babysitting; room service. *In room:* A/C, TV, hair dryer, Internet (free).

Hôtel Victoria ★ The Victoria, a stylish modern hotel offers accommodations with period reproductions and refrigerators. Nearly half the rooms have balconies overlooking a small park and the hotel pool. The accommodations facing the park cost a little more but are worth it. In all units, silk bedspreads, padded headboards, and quality mattresses create a boudoir feel. After a day on the beach, guests congregate in the paneled bar and sink comfortably into couches and armchairs.

Rond-point Duboys-d'Angers, Cannes 06400. © **04-92-59-40-00.** Fax 04-93-38-03-91. www.hotel-victoria-cannes.com. 25 units. 110€–305€ double; 250€–435€ suite. AE, DC, MC, V. Parking 17€. Closed 2 weeks Dec, 3 weeks Feb. **Amenities:** Bar; babysitting; outdoor pool. *In room:* A/C, TV, hair dryer, minibar, Wi-Fi (4.50€ per hr.).

Hôtel Villa de l'Olivier 🏠 Charming and personal, this is a hideaway with a low-key management style. In the 1930s, it was a private villa; in 1963 it became a hotel, with a wing extending deep into its garden. Today, you'll find buildings with lots of glass overlooking a kidney-shaped pool, and decor combining the French colonial tropics with the romantic late 19th century and Provence. Rooms have upholstered walls, each in a different color and pattern, and lots of Provençal accessories.

5 rue des Tambourinaires, Cannes 06400. © **04-93-39-53-28.** Fax 04-93-39-55-85. www.hotelolivier. com. 24 units. 95€–145€ double; 145€–170€ triple; 260€–360€ suite. AE, DC, MC, V. Parking 10€. Closed Nov 21–Dec 27. **Amenities:** Bar; outdoor pool; room service. *In room:* A/C, TV, hair dryer, Wi-Fi (free).

INEXPENSIVE
Hôtel de Provence 🗡 Built in the 1930s, this hotel is small and unpretentious—a contrast to the intensely stylish, larger hotels with which it competes. Most of the rooms have private balconies, and many overlook the shrubs and palms of the hotel's walled garden. Guest rooms are showing their age but are still comfortable, and for Cannes this is a remarkable bargain. In warm weather, breakfast is served under the flowers of an arbor.

9 rue Molière, Cannes 06400. ✆ **04-93-38-44-35.** Fax 04-93-39-63-14. www.hotel-de-provence.com. 30 units. 92€–122€ double; 122€–152€ suite. AE, MC, V. Closed Dec. Parking: 13€. **Amenities:** Bar; room service. *In room:* A/C, TV, hair dryer, minibar, Wi-Fi (10€ for 3 hr.).

Hôtel Le Florian   This hotel is on a busy but narrow, densely commercial street that leads directly into La Croisette, near the beach. Three generations of the Giordano family have maintained it since the 1950s. The hotel is basic but comfortable, and most rooms are rather small, Provençal in their styling, with decor that dates from 2004. Breakfast is the only meal available.

8 rue Commandant-André, Cannes 06400. ✆ **04-93-39-24-82.** Fax 04-92-99-18-30. www.hotel-leflorian.com. 35 units. 60€–80€ double. AE, MC, V. Parking 12€ nearby. Closed Dec to mid-Jan. Bus: 1. *In room:* A/C, TV, hair dryer, Wi-Fi (free).

Where to Dine
VERY EXPENSIVE
La Palme d'Or ★★★ MODERN FRENCH   Movie stars on the see-and-be-seen circuit head here during the film festival. It's a sophisticated rendezvous that serves some of the Riviera's finest hotel cuisine. The decor is a tawny-colored Art Deco marvel with bay windows, a winter-garden theme, and outdoor and enclosed terraces overlooking the pool, the sea, and La Croisette. Menu items change with the seasons but are likely to include warm foie gras with fondue of rhubarb; filets of fried red mullet with a beignet of potatoes, zucchini, and olive-cream sauce; or crayfish, clams, and squid marinated in peppered citrus sauce. A modernized version of a Niçoise staple includes three parts of a rabbit with rosemary sauce, fresh vegetables, and chickpea rosettes. The most appealing dessert is wild strawberries from Carros with Grand Marnier–flavored *nage* and "cream sauce of frozen milk." The service is worldly without being stiff.

In the Hôtel Martinez, 73 bd. de la Croisette. ✆ **04-92-98-74-14.** www.hotel-martinez.com. Reservations required. Main courses 65€–180€; fixed-price lunch 64€–155€, dinner 79€–180€. AE, DC, MC, V. Wed–Sat 12:30–2pm and 8–10pm. Closed Jan–Feb.

EXPENSIVE
Gaston et Gastounette ★ TRADITIONAL FRENCH   For views of the marina, this is your best bet. Located in the old port, it has a stucco exterior with oak moldings and big windows, and a sidewalk terrace surrounded by flowers. It serves two different bouillabaisses—a full-blown authentic stewpot prepared only for two diners at a time and a less daunting individualized version designed as an appetizer. Other choices include baby turbot with hollandaise sauce; John Dory filets with wild mushrooms; and an unusual Japanese-style broth flavored with monkfish, saltwater salmon, and chives. Profiteroles with hot chocolate sauce make a memorable dessert.

7 quai St-Pierre. ✆ **04-93-39-49-44.** Reservations required. Main courses 28€–50€; fixed-price menus 34€. AE, DC, MC, V. Daily noon–2pm and 7–10:30pm.

La Mère Besson ★ TRADITIONAL FRENCH   The culinary traditions of the late Mère Besson, who opened her restaurant in the 1930s, endure in one of Cannes's favorite places. The specialties are prepared with respect for Provençal traditions. Most delectable is *estouffade Provençal* (beef braised with red wine and rich stock flavored with garlic, onions, herbs, and mushrooms). Every Friday, you can sample a platter with codfish, fresh vegetables, and dollops of the famous garlic mayonnaise (aioli) of Provence. Other specialties are fish soup and roasted rack of lamb with mint.

13 rue des Frères-Pradignac. ⓒ **04-93-39-59-24.** Reservations required. Main courses 25€–29€; fixed-price dinner 22€–34€. AE, MC, V. Mon–Sat 7–10:30pm. Bus: 1.

Le Festival ★ TRADITIONAL FRENCH   Screen idols and sex symbols flood the front terrace during the film festival. Almost every chair is emblazoned with the names of movie stars (who may or may not have occupied it), and tables are among the most sought-after in town. You can choose from the restaurant or the less formal grill room. Meals in the restaurant may include rack of lamb, *soupe des poissons* (fish soup) with rouille, simply grilled fresh fish (perhaps with aioli), bouillabaisse with lobster, pepper steak, and sea bass flambéed with fennel. Items in the grill are more in the style of an elegant brasserie, served a bit more rapidly and without as much fuss but at more or less the same prices. An appropriate finish in either section may be smooth peach melba.

52 bd. de la Croisette. ⓒ **04-93-38-04-81.** Reservations required. Main courses 20€–30€; fixed-price menu 43€. AE, DC, MC, V. July–Aug daily 9am–midnight; Sept–June daily 9am–1am. Closed Nov 19–Dec 25.

MODERATE

La Canna Suisse ★ 🍴 SWISS   Two sisters own this small 30-year-old restaurant in Vieux-Cannes. Decked out like a Swiss chalet, it specializes in the cheese-based cuisine of Switzerland's high Alps. Because its cuisine is so suitable to cold-weather dining, the restaurant wisely opts to close during the crush of Cannes's midsummer tourist season. It does great business the rest of the year. The menu features two kinds of fondue—a traditional version concocted from six kinds of cheese and served in a bubbling pot with chunks of bread on skewers, and another that adds mushrooms (morels or cèpes) to the blend. The only other dining options here include raclette and equally savory *tartiflette* (an age-old recipe that combines boiled potatoes with fatback, onions, cream, herbs, and Reblochon cheese). There's a long list of (mostly white) French and Swiss wines, wonderful with these ultratraditional dishes.

23 rue Forville, Le Suquet. ⓒ **04-93-99-01-27.** www.cannasuisse.com. Reservations recommended. Main courses 17€–26€; fixed-price menu 26€–27€. AE, MC, V. Mon–Sat 7:30–10:30pm. Closed May 20 to late Aug.

INEXPENSIVE

Côté Jardin ★ 🍴 FRENCH/PROVENÇAL   Set near the courthouse (Palais de Justice) in the heart of commercial Cannes, this restaurant attracts loyal locals because of its unpretentious ambience and its reasonably priced and generous portions. You're offered three different choices as seating options: on the street-level glassed-in veranda; at a table amid the flowering shrubs of the garden terrace; or upstairs within the cozy Provençal dining room. The best menu items include open-faced ravioli filled with minced beef jowls, filets of red mullet with butter-flavored parsley sauce, a range of grilled and roasted meats and fish, and a dessert of praline-and-pineapple tart with vanilla-flavored cream sauce.

12 av. St-Louis. ⓒ **04-93-38-60-28.** Reservations required, especially in summer. Fixed-price menus 22€–38€. AE, DC, MC, V. Tues–Sat noon–2pm and 7:30–10pm. Closed 1 week in Oct.

La Brouette de Grand-Mère 🍴 TRADITIONAL FRENCH   Few other restaurants in Cannes work so successfully at establishing a cozy testimonial to the culinary skills of old-fashioned French cooking. The owner has revitalized the recipes that many of the chic and trendy residents of Cannes remember from their child-hoods (or from an idealized version of their childhoods). Memories are evoked, in a way that Proust might have appreciated, through dishes that include a savory meat-and-potato stew known as *pot-au-feu,* roasted quail served with cream sauce, and chicken casserole cooked with beer. Traditional starters may include sausage links, terrines, and baked potatoes stuffed with smoked fish roe and served with a small glass of vodka. Set in the heart of town just behind the Palais Stephanie and the InterContinental Carlton, the place offers two dining rooms, each outfitted in Art Deco style in tones of deep red and soft violet and an outdoor terrace.

9 bis rue d'Oran. (✆ **04-93-39-12-10.** Reservations recommended. Fixed-price menu, including aperitif with half bottle of wine, 35€. AE, MC, V. Daily 7–10pm, Sun noon–2pm. Closed Feb.

Cannes After Dark

Cannes is invariably associated with permissiveness, filmmakers celebrating film-making, and gambling. If gambling is your thing, Cannes has some world-class casinos, each loaded with addicts, voyeurs, and everyone in between. The better established is the **Casino Croisette,** in the Palais des Festivals, Esplanade Lucien Barrière (✆ **04-92-98-78-00**). Run by the Lucien Barrière group, and a well-respected fixture in town since the 1950s, it's a competitor of the newer **Palm Beach Casino,** place F-D-Roosevelt, Pointe de la Croisette (✆ **04-97-06-36-90**), on the southeast edge of La Croisette. Inaugurated in 1933 and rebuilt in 2002, it features three restaurants and Art Deco decor. It's glossier, newer, and a bit hungrier for new business. Both casinos maintain slot machines that operate daily 10am to 5am. Suites of rooms devoted to *les grands jeux* (blackjack, roulette, and chemin de fer) open nightly 8pm to 4am.

Yet a third gambling den, **Casino des Princes,** is more intimate than either of its more flamboyant competitors, occupying the subterranean levels of Palais Stephanie, 50 bd. de la Croisette (✆ **04-97-06-18-50**). Outfitted in tones of gold and ocher, it is open nightly 8pm to 3am. A government-issued photo ID is necessary, and jackets for men are requested. Adjoining the casino is the hotel's most upscale restaurant, Restaurant/Bar des Princes, open for dinner nightly from 8pm to 1am.

After-dark diversions continue to grow, including **Morrison's Irish Pub,** 10 rue Teisseire (✆ **04-92-98-16-17**), which has become the meeting place for the expat community. The mix of French with foreign languages creates a wonderful ambi-ence. Staff members are native English speakers. There's a live DJ every night. The **Quays Pub,** 17 quai St-Pierre (✆ **04-93-39-27-84**), is the most popular joint at the old port, especially among yachties. Live music and sports broadcasts fill the night.

The aptly named **Bar des Stars,** in the Restaurant Fouquet's in the Hôtel Majes-tic Barrière, 14 La Croisette (✆ **04-92-98-77-00**), is where deals go down during the film festival. Directors, producers, stars, press agents, screenwriters, and wan-nabes crowd in here at festival time. Even when there's no festival, it's a lively place for a drink; its scarlet decor evokes an Art Deco Asian fantasy.

Gays and lesbians will feel comfortable at **Le Vogue,** 20 rue du Suquet (✆ **04-93-39-99-18**), a mixed bar open Tuesday to Sunday from 7pm until 2:30am. Another gay option is **Disco Le Sept,** 7 rue Rouguière (✆ **04-93-39-10-36**), where drag shows appear nightly at 1:30am. Entrance is free, except on weekends, when it's 16€ (includes a drink). A lot of straights go here, too.

The most visible gay clientele in Cannes tends to gravitate toward **Le Nightlife,** 52 rue Jean-Jaurès (✆ **04-93-39-20-50**), which was reoutfitted late in 2008 with white walls, a busy bar, occasional fashion shows, and lots of randomly scheduled and somewhat flippant theme parties. Open for drinks and dining daily 6pm to 2:30am, with fixed-price meals priced from 32€, it's a popular and convivial spot for same-sex socializing. A lot rougher, darker, and more shadowy is the gay male disco, **Le Divan,** 3 rue Rouguière (✆ **04-93-68-73-70**), located within a vaulted cellar that's designed to look a lot older than it really is. This place is not for the timid: If you opt for a visit, leave your valuables in your hotel safe and remain alert. It's open Tuesday to Sunday 6pm until around 4am, depending on the crowds.

A discreet ambience prevails at **Zanzibar,** 85 rue Félix-Faure (✆ **04-93-39-30-75**). A bartender confided to us, "If a gay man wants to meet a French version of Brad Pitt, especially at festival time, this is the place." The bar is open all night and caters to people of all sexual persuasions. At dawn the doors open, and the last of the drag queens stagger out.

MOUGINS

903km (561 miles) S of Paris; 11km (6¾ miles) S of Grasse; 8km (5 miles) N of Cannes

This former fortified town on the crest of a hill provides an alternative for those who want to be near the excitement of Cannes but not in the midst of it. Picasso and other artists appreciated the sun-drenched hills covered with gnarled olive trees. The artist arrived in 1936; in time, Jean Cocteau, Paul Eluard, and Man Ray followed. Picasso later decided to move here permanently. He spent the latter part of his life here with his wife Jacqueline. Fernand Léger, René Clair, Isadora Duncan, and even Christian Dior have lived at Mougins.

Mougins is a haven for those who feel that the Riviera is overrun, spoiled, and overbuilt. It preserves the quiet life even though it's a stone's throw from Cannes. Though Mougins looks serene and tranquil, it's actually part of the industrial park of Sophia Antipolis, a center where more than 1,000 companies have offices. Many visitors on a gastronomic tour of the Riviera spend the night here because of the celebrated inn Le Moulin de Mougins (p. 558).

Essentials

GETTING THERE The best way to get to Mougins is to **drive.** From Nice, follow E80/A8 west, and then cut north on Route 85 into Mougins. From Cannes, head north of the city along N85. From La Napoule–Plage, head east toward Cannes on N7, and then north at the turnoff to Mougins up in the hills.

In 2005, the French railways, **SNCF,** reactivated an antique rail line stretching between Grasse (the perfume capital) and Cannes, linking the hamlet of Mouans-Sartoux en route. The village of Mouans-Sartoux lies only 457m (1,500 ft.) from the center of Mougins. Rail service costs 2.60€ one-way from either Cannes or Grasse to Mouans-Sartoux. There are several **trains** per day. Among buses, **Société Tam** (✆ **08-00-06-01-06**) runs **buses** between Cannes and Grasse. Bus no. 600 stops in Val-de-Mougins, a 10-minute walk from the center of Mougins. One-way fares from either Cannes or Grasse cost 1.25€. Given the complexities of a bus transfer from Cannes, it's a lot easier just to pay 25€ to 35€ for a **taxi** to haul you and your possessions northward from Cannes.

VISITOR INFORMATION   The **Office de Tourisme** is at 15 av. Jean-Charles-Mallet (© **04-93-75-87-67;** fax 04-92-92-04-03; www.mougins-coteazur.org).

Seeing the Sights

For a look at the history of the area, visit the **Espace Culturel,** place du Commandant-Lamy (© **04-92-92-50-42**), in the St. Bernardin Chapel. It was built in 1618 and traces area history from 1553 to the 1950s. It's open December to October Monday to Friday from 9am to 5pm, and Saturday and Sunday from 11am to 6pm. Admission is free.

You can also visit the **Chapelle Notre-Dame de Vie,** chemin de la Chapelle, 1.5km (1 mile) southeast of Mougins. The chapel, once painted by Churchill, is best known for the priory next door, where Picasso spent his last 12 years. It was built in the 12th century and reconstructed in 1646; it was an old custom to bring stillborn babies to the chapel to have them baptized. The priory is still a private home occupied intermittently by the Picasso heirs. Alas, because of a series of break-ins and ongoing renovations, the chapel is open only during Sunday Mass from 9 to 10am.

Where to Stay

Le Moulin de Mougins (see "Where to Dine," below) offers rooms and suites.

Le Manoir de l'Etang ★★   You'll get a strong sense of life in rural Provence within the thick, ivy-covered stone walls of this artfully renovated 19th-century manor house, located within a verdant 4-hectare (10-acre) park a short drive east from the center of Mougins. A mass of nearby olive trees and cypresses seem to showcase a small pond covered with lotuses and waterlilies. The interior, including the bedrooms, is bright and modern, the perfect place for a hideaway, off-the-record weekend. The in-house restaurant serves artfully conceived food, some platters arranged in ways that qualify them as sculptural statements in their own right. Despite its modernity and its airy and contemporary decorative style, the place still captivates the romance of the old, romantic Riviera of long ago.

Aux Bois de Font-Merle, 66 allée du Manoir, Mougins 06250. © **04-92-28-36-00.** Fax 04-92-28-36-10. www.manoir-de-letang.com. 20 units. 125€–275€ double; 300€–500€ suite. AE, MC, V. Closed Oct 13–Mar. **Amenities:** Restaurant; bar; outdoor pool; room service. *In room:* A/C, TV, minibar, Wi-Fi (free).

Le Mas Candille ★★   With a staff that at times might be just a bit too easygoing, this 200-year-old Provençal *mas* (farmhouse) was renovated in 2005 after gaining a well-designed annex in 2001. The public rooms contain many 19th-century furnishings, and some open onto the gardens. Rooms are individually decorated in different styles, including Japanese, medieval, French colonial (Indochina), and Provençal regional. Bathrooms are of good size, with tub/shower combinations. The dining room, with stone detailing and a massive fireplace with a timbered mantel, serves exceptional food. Fresh salads and light meals are available throughout the day. In clement weather, lunch is served on the terrace; dinner is served on the terrace in summer only.

Bd. Clément Rebuffel, Mougins 06250 © **04-92-28-43-43.** Fax 04-92-28-43-40. www.lemascandille.com. 46 units. 300€–395€ double; from 750€ suite. AE, DC, MC, V. **Amenities:** 2 restaurants; bar; exercise room; 3 outdoor pools; room service; spa. *In room:* A/C, TV, hair dryer, minibar, Wi-Fi (free).

Where to Dine

Le Mas Candille is noted for its sublime cuisine; you may want to call to reserve a table. **Le Manoir de l'Etang** also earns praise for its Provençal cuisine. See above for more information about both.

L'Amandier de Mougins Restaurant ★ 🍴 NIÇOISE/PROVENÇAL   This relatively inexpensive bistro was founded about a decade ago by the world-famous chef Roger Vergé. Today the restaurant carries on admirably under new owners. A mass-market cousin to its exclusive neighbor, this restaurant serves simple platters in an airy stone house. The specialties, based on traditional recipes, may include sea bream with zucchini flower fritters, tartare of fresh salmon, and ceviche of tuna with hot spices; or *magret* of duckling with honey sauce and lemons, served with deliberately undercooked polenta.

48 av. Jean-Charles Mallet. 📞 **04-93-90-00-91.** Reservations recommended. Main courses 30€–45€; fixed-price lunch 25€–44€, dinner 29€–44€. AE, DC, MC, V. Thurs–Tues noon–2pm and 7–10:30pm.

Le Moulin de Mougins ★★ FRENCH   Once this address was arguably the most celebrated dining spot on the Riviera when it was the domain of Roger Vergé, one of France's top three chefs. The years have come and gone, and other chefs have tried to fill Vergé's very large shoes. The current chef Sebastien Chambreu does an admirable job, without all the publicity hype. Like Vergé, he too employs market-fresh ingredients in his "cuisine of the sun," a reference to Provence's sun-drenched countryside. Cuisine is earthy but upscale, often with modern twists on culinary traditions both from France and other regions of the country. Some of the chef's best-known dishes include pan-fried duck foie gras, carpaccio of scallops, and a truly delectable filet of sole stuffed with prawns.

The inn also rents 11 accommodations with air-conditioning, minibars, and TVs. Double rooms cost 160€ to 290€, suites 300€ to 390€.

Notre-Dame de Vie, Mougins 06250. 📞 **04-93-75-78-24.** Fax 04-93-90-18-55. www.moulindemougins. com. Reservations required. Main courses 41€–59€; fixed-price menu 49€–160€ lunch, 90€–160€ dinner. AE, DC, MC, V. Wed–Mon noon–2pm and 7:30–10pm.

GRASSE ★★

906km (563 miles) S of Paris; 18km (11 miles) N of Cannes; 9.5km (6 miles) N of Mougins; 23km (14 miles) NW of Antibes

Grasse, a 20-minute drive from Cannes, is the most fragrant town on the Riviera. Surrounded by jasmine and roses, it has been the capital of the perfume industry since the Renaissance. It was once a famous resort, attracting such royals as Queen Victoria and Princess Pauline Borghese, Napoleon's lascivious sister.

Today some three-quarters of the world's essences are produced here from foliage that includes violets, daffodils, wild lavender, and jasmine. It takes 10,000 flowers to produce just more than 1 kilogram of jasmine petals. Almost a ton of petals is needed to distill 1 liter of essence. These figures are important to remember when looking at that high price tag on a bottle of perfume.

Essentials

GETTING THERE   Trains now run to Grasse from Nice, Cannes, or Antibes. One-way tickets cost 5.80€ from Cannes, 5.40€ from Antibes, and 8.40€ from Nice.

For train schedules and more information, call ✆ **08-91-70-30-00,** or visit www.voyages-sncf.com. **Buses** pull into town every 30 to 60 minutes daily from Cannes (trip time: 50 min.). The one-way fare is 1€. There are also about 14 buses every day from Nice (1 hr.). The one-way fare is around 1€. They arrive at the Gare Routière, place Notre Dame des Fleurs (✆ **04-93-36-37-37**), a 10-minute walk north of the town center. Visitors arriving by **car** take A8, which funnels in traffic from Monaco, Aix-en-Provence, and Marseille.

VISITOR INFORMATION The **Office de Tourisme** is at Place du cours Honoré Cresp (✆ **04-93-36-03-56;** fax 04-93-36-03-56; www.grasse.fr).

Seeing the Sights

Musée d'Art et d'Histoire de Provence ★ This museum is in the Hôtel de Clapiers-Cabris, built in 1771 by Louise de Mirabeau, the marquise de Cabris and sister of Mirabeau. Its collections include paintings, four-poster beds, marquetry, ceramics, brasses, kitchenware, pottery, urns, and archaeological finds.

2 rue Mirabeau. ✆ **04-93-36-80-20.** Free admission. June–Sept daily 10am–12:30pm and 1:30–6:30pm; Oct–May Wed–Mon 10am–12:30pm and 2–5:30pm. Closed Nov 6–Dec 5.

Parfumerie Fragonard ★ One of the best-known perfume factories is named after an 18th-century French painter. This factory has the best villa, the best museum, and the best tour. An English-speaking guide will show you how "the soul of the flower" is extracted. After the tour, you can explore the museum, which displays bottles and vases that trace the industry back to ancient times. If you're shopping for perfume and want to skip the tour, that's okay.

20 bd. Fragonard. ✆ **04-93-36-44-65.** www.fragonard.com. Mar–Oct daily 9am–6:30pm; Nov–Feb daily 9am–12:30pm and 2–6pm

Parfumerie Molinard This firm is well known in the United States, where its products are sold at Saks, Neiman Marcus, and Bloomingdale's. In the factory you can witness the extraction of the essence of the flowers. You'll also learn all the details of the process of converting flowers into essential oils. You can admire a collection of antique perfume-bottle labels and see a rare collection of perfume *flacons* by Baccarat and Lalique.

60 bd. Victor-Hugo. ✆ **04-93-36-01-62.** www.molinard.com. Free admission. Apr–Sept daily 9am–6:30pm; Oct–Mar Mon–Sat 9am–12:30pm and 2–6:30pm.

Villa Musée Fragonard The setting is an 18th-century aristocrat's town house with a magnificent garden in back. The collection displayed here includes the paintings of Jean-Honoré Fragonard, who was born in Grasse in 1732; his sister-in-law, Marguerite Gérard; his son, Alexandre; and his grandson, Théophile. Alexandre decorated the grand staircase.

23 bd. Fragonard. ✆ **04-97-05-58-00.** Free admission. June–Sept daily 10am–6:30pm; Oct–May Wed–Mon 10am–12:30pm and 2–5:30pm.

Where to Stay

Hôtel La Bellaudière 🥄 Part of the respected Logis de France chain, this unpretentious family-run hotel is 3km (1¾ miles) east of the town center in the hills above Grasse. The stone-sided farmhouse was built in stages beginning 400 years ago, with most of what you see today built in the 1700s. Guest rooms are simple but dignified and outfitted with Provençal motifs, and many boast views of the sea. A garden terrace is lined with flowering shrubs, and guests get a sense of friendly cooperation from the hosts. Fixed-price meals in the dining room cost 20€ to 25€ each.

78 av. Pierre Ziller. ©︎ **04-93-36-02-57.** Fax 04-93-36-40-03. 17 units. 69€–145€ double. AE, DC, MC, V. Free parking. **Amenities:** Restaurant; Internet; room service. *In room:* TV, Wi-Fi (free).

Where to Dine

For inexpensive dining, you can head for **Hôtel La Bellaudière** (see above).

La Bastide St-Antoine (Restaurant Chibois) ★★★ FRENCH/PROVENÇAL
La Bastide St-Antoine offers one of the grandest culinary experiences along the Riviera. Jacques Chibois and his restaurant have attracted national attention since 1996. In a 200-year-old Provençal farmhouse surrounded by 2.8 hectares (7 acres) of trees and shrubbery, the restaurant serves a sophisticated array of dishes. The best examples are oysters flavored with yucca leaves, a terrine of foie gras with celery, roasted suckling lamb with a fricassee of fresh vegetables and basil, and fresh crayfish with sautéed flap mushrooms. Desserts may include strawberry soup with spice wine or ice cream made with olives and a hint of olive oil. The chef also does wonders with wild duck.

You can stay in one of nine rooms and seven suites, decorated in Provençal style with upscale furnishings and comfortable beds. They have air-conditioning, free Wi-Fi, hair dryers, minibars, and TVs. Doubles cost 230€ to 395€, suites 440€ to 910€.

48 av. Henri-Dunant. ©︎ **04-93-70-94-94.** Fax 04-93-70-94-95. www.jacques-chibois.com. Reservations required. Main courses 39€–75€; fixed-price lunch Mon–Sat 59€–190€; fixed-price dinner 145€–190€. AE, DC, MC, V. Daily noon–2pm and 8–9:30pm.

BIOT ★

918km (570 miles) S of Paris; 9.5km (6 miles) E of Cagnes-sur-Mer; 6.5km (4 miles) NW of Antibes

Biot has been famous for its pottery since merchants began to ship earthenware jars to Phoenicia and throughout the Mediterranean. Settled by Gallo-Romans, Biot has a long, war-torn history. Somehow the potters persevered at their ancient craft. Biot is also where Fernand Léger painted until the day he died. A magnificent collection of his work is on display at a museum here.

Essentials

GETTING THERE Biot's **train** station is 3km (1¾ miles) east of the town center. There's frequent service from Nice and Antibes. For rail information and schedules, call ©︎ **08-92-35-35-35,** or visit www.voyages-sncf.com. The **bus** from Antibes is even more convenient than the train. To **drive** to Biot from Nice, take N7 west. From Antibes, follow N7 east.

VISITOR INFORMATION The **Office de Tourisme** is at 46 rue St-Sébastien (©︎ **04-93-65-78-00;** fax 04-93-65-78-04; www.biot.fr).

Exploring the Town

If you have time, explore the village. Begin at the **place des Arcades,** where you can see the 16th-century gates and the remains of the town's ramparts. Biot is known for its carnations and roses, which are sold on this lovely square. The **Eglise de Biot,** place des Arcades (©︎ **04-93-65-00-85**), dates from the 15th century. It's the work of Italian immigrants who resettled the town after the Black Death. The church is known for two stunning 15th-century retables (altarpieces): the red-and-gold *Retable du Rosaire* by Ludovico Bréa, and the recently restored *Christ aux Plaies* by Canavesio.

Musée d'Histoire Locale et de Céramique Biotoise, 9 rue St-Sebastien (✆ **04-93-65-54-54**), has assembled the best work of local artists, potters, ceramists, painters, and silver- and goldsmiths. Hours are Wednesday to Sunday 2 to 6pm. Admission is 2€; free ages 16 and under.

In the late 1940s, glassmakers created a bubble-flecked glass known as *verre rustique.* It comes in brilliant colors such as cobalt and emerald, and is displayed in many store windows on the main shopping street, **rue St-Sebastien.** The best place to watch the glass blowers and to buy glass, aside from the shops along rue St-Sebastien, is **Verrerie de Biot,** 5 chemin des Combes (✆ **04-93-65-03-00**), at the bottom of town. Tours, costing 6€, are conducted daily from June to August at 9:30am to 8pm; September to May daily at 4:30pm. While you're here, you can call at **Galerie International du Verre** (✆ **04-93-65-03-00**; www.verreriebiot. com), where beautifully displayed glassworks are for sale, often at exorbitant prices. Hours are June to September Monday to Saturday 10am to 8pm, Sunday 10am to 1pm and 3 to 7:30pm; and October to May Monday to Saturday 9:30am to 6:30pm, Sunday 10am to 1pm and 2:30 to 6:30pm.

The namesake of the **Galerie Jean-Claude Novaro** (also known as Galerie de la Patrimoine), place des Arcades (✆ **04-93-65-60-23**), is known as the Picasso of glass artists. His works are pretty and colorful, though they sometimes lack the diversity and flair of the creations displayed at the Galerie International du Verre. Most of his glass art is for sale. You may also want to shop at **La Poterie Provençale,** 1689 rte. de la Mer (✆ **04-93-65-63-30**; www.poterie-provencale.com), adjacent to the Musée Fernand-Léger, about 3km (1¾ miles) southeast of town. It's one of the last potteries in Provence to specialize in the amphora-like containers known as *jarres.*

Bonzaï Arboretum de la Côte d'Azur   Privately owned and maintained by members of the Okonek family, this arboretum and showroom contains the largest collection of bonsai in France. Most of the potted trees sell for between 30€ and 200€, and most were crafted from artfully tormented-looking versions of local fig, almond, or olive trees. Especially noteworthy are some bonsai versions of rare tropical cypresses and tropical figs, some as tall as 2m (6½ ft.), loaded with aerial root systems and miniaturized trunks and branches that many botanists find fascinating.

299 Chemin de Val de Pôme, Biot 06410. 3km (1¾ miles) south of Biot. ✆ **04-93-65-63-99.** Admission 4€ for adults, 2€ for students. Mar–Dec Wed–Mon 10am–noon and 2–6pm; Jan–Feb Sun 10am–5pm.

Musée National Fernand-Léger ★★   The artist's widow, Nadia Léger, assembled this collection and donated it to the French government after the artist's death in 1955. Léger's mosaic-and-ceramic mural enhances the stone-and-marble facade. On the grounds is a polychrome ceramic sculpture, *Le Jardin d'enfant;* inside are two floors of geometrical forms in pure, flat colors. The collection includes paintings, ceramics, tapestries, and sculptures showing the artist's development from 1905 until his death. His paintings abound with cranes, acrobats, scaffolding, railroad signals, buxom nudes, casings, and crankshafts. The most unusual work depicts a Léger Mona Lisa (*La Giaconde aux Clés*) contemplating a set of keys, a wide-mouthed fish dangling over her head.

Chemin du Val-de-Pôme (on the eastern edge of town, beside the road to the rail station). ✆ **04-92-91-50-30.** www.musee-fernandleger.fr. Admission 7.50€ adults, 6€ ages 12–18, free 17 and under. Wed–Mon 10am–6pm.

Where to Dine

Le Jarrier ★ PROVENÇAL   One of the most enduringly excellent restaurants in Biot was built 300 years ago as a pottery for the *jarres* used to transport and store olive oil and wine. One of its two dining rooms has its walls removed every summer and becomes an open-air terrace with views over the valley. The cuisine is "personalized"—an idiosyncratic and modernized interpretation of Provençal staples. Examples include stuffed zucchini blossoms; several versions of risotto, many of them vegetarian; *daurade* (bream) served with herb-laden vinaigrette; and Challons duckling with lavender-honey sauce and either figs or braised leeks. Even if you don't usually order dessert, consider the comfit of oranges in puff pastry.

30 passage de la Bourgade. ✆ **04-93-65-11-68.** www.lejarrierrestaurant.com. Reservations recommended. Main courses 19€–40€; fixed-price lunch 19€–29€; fixed-price dinner 34€–84€. AE, MC, V. Wed–Sun 12:30–2:30pm and 7:30–10pm.

Les Terraillers ★★★ MEDITERRANEAN   This stone-sided restaurant is .8km (about ½ mile) south of Biot, in a 16th-century studio for the production of clay pots and ceramics. The cuisine of the chef changes with the seasons and is more sophisticated and appetizing than that at many competitors. Examples are a platter containing two preparations of pigeon (thigh and breast cooked in different ways), served with a corn galette and the pigeon's own drippings; "fish of the day" in saffron sauce; roasted scallops with saffron and mussel-flavored cream sauce and leek comfit; a tart with artichoke hearts and tomatoes en comfit with lobster salad; braised John Dory Provençal style, with olive oil and a fricassee of zucchini, artichokes, tomatoes, and olives; and ravioli filled with pan-fried foie gras and served with essence of morels and mushroom duxelles.

11 rte. du Chemin-Neuf. ✆ **04-93-65-01-59.** www.lesterraillers.com. Reservations required as far in advance as possible. Main courses 32€–49€; fixed-price lunch 39€–55€, dinner 65€–110€. AE, MC, V. June–Sept Fri-Tues noon–2pm and 7–10pm. Closed Jan 24–Feb 10. Take rte. du Chemin-Neuf, following signs to Antibes.

GOLFE-JUAN & VALLAURIS ★

Golfe-Juan: 913km (567 miles) S of Paris, 6.5km (4 miles) E of Cannes; Vallauris: 910km (565 miles) S of Paris, 6.5km (4 miles) E of Cannes

Napoleon and 800 men landed at Golfe-Juan in 1815 to begin his Hundred Days. Protected by hills, this spot beside the coast was also a favored port for the American navy. Today it's a family resort known for its beaches and a noteworthy restaurant (see "Where to Dine," below).

The 2km-long (1¼-mile) RN135 leads inland from Golfe-Juan to Vallauris. Once just a stopover along the Riviera, Vallauris (noted for its pottery) owes its reputation to Picasso. The master "discovered" Vallauris after World War II and occupied a villa known as "The Woman from Wales."

Essentials

GETTING THERE   You can **drive** to Golfe-Juan or Vallauris on any of the Riviera's three east-west highways. Although route numbers are not always indicated, city names are clear once you're on the highway. From Cannes or Antibes, N7 east is the fastest route. From Nice or Biot, take A8/E80 west.

There's a sleepy-looking rail station in Golfe-Juan, on avenue de la Gare. To get here, you'll have to transfer from a **train** in Cannes. The train from Cannes costs 1.80€ each way. For railway information, call ℂ **08-92-35-35-35,** or visit www.voyages-sncf.com. A flotilla of **buses** operated by Envibus (ℂ **04-93-64-18-37)** makes frequent trips from Cannes; the 20-minute trip costs 1€ each way; from Nice, the 90-minute trip costs 1.30€ each way.

VISITOR INFORMATION There's an **Office de Tourisme** (www.vallauris-golfe-juan.fr) on boulevard des Frères-Roustan, Golfe-Juan (ℂ **04-93-63-73-12;** fax 04-93-63-21-07), and another on square du 8-Mai, 1945 Vallauris (ℂ **04-93-63-82-58;** fax 04-93-63-13-66).

A Day at the Beach

Because of its position beside the sea, Golfe-Juan long ago developed into a warm-weather resort. The town's twin strips of beach are **Plage du Soleil** (east of the Vieux Port and the newer Port Camille-Rayon) and **Plage du Midi** (west of those two). Each stretches 1km (⅔ mile) and charges no entry fee, with the exception of small areas administered by concessions that rent mattresses and chaises and have snack kiosks. Regardless of which concession you select (on Plage du Midi they sport names like Au Vieux Rocher, Palma Beach, and Corail Plage; on Plage du Soleil, Plage Nounou and Plage Tétou), you'll pay 12€ to 38€ for a day's use of a mattress. Plage Tétou is associated with the upscale Chez Tétou (p. 564). If you don't want to rent a mattress, you can cavort unhindered anywhere along the sands, moving freely from one area to another. Golfe-Juan indulges bathers who remove their bikini tops, but in theory it forbids nude sunbathing.

Seeing the Sights

Picasso's *l' Homme au Mouton* (*Man and Sheep*) is the outdoor statue at place Isnard in front of which Prince Aly Kahn and screen goddess Rita Hayworth were married. The council of Vallauris had intended to enclose this statue in a museum, but Picasso insisted that it remain on the square, "where the children could climb over it and the dogs water it unhindered."

L'Espace Jean Marais If you're a fan of early movies, you'll remember the robust, macho French actor who symbolized for many of us the bonhomie of France's working-class heroes before World War II. Jean Marais (1913–98) spent the final 18 years of his life based in Vallauris, painting and sculpting. After his death, the city assembled his paintings and sculptures into this masonry-sided space. Come here for a nostalgic homage to one of France's memorable actors, star of such films as *La Belle et la Bête*, and for an insight into the fact that, indeed, life still continues after an actor's cinematic star has faded.

Av. des Martyrs de la Résistance. ℂ **04-93-63-46-11.** Free admission. Sept–June Tues–Sat 10am–12:30pm and 2–6pm; July–Aug daily 10am–1pm and 3–7pm.

Musée Magnelli, Musée de la Céramique, & Musée National Picasso La Guerre et La Paix ★ A chapel of rough stone shaped like a Quonset hut is the focal point of a three-in-one sightseeing highlight. The museum grew from the site of a chapel that Picasso decorated with two paintings: *La Paix (Peace)* and *La Guerre*

(*War*). The paintings offer contrasting images of love and peace on the one hand, and violence and conflict on the other. In 1970, a house painter illegally gained entrance to the museum and substituted one of his designs after whitewashing a portion of the original. When the aging master inspected the damage, he said, "Not bad at all." In 1996, the site added a permanent exposition devoted to the works of the Florentine-born Alberto Magnelli, a pioneer of abstract art. A third section showcases ceramics, both traditional and innovative, from potters throughout the region.

Place de la Libération. © **04-93-64-71-83.** Admission 3.25€ adults, 1.70€ seniors and students, free for children 15 and under. June–Aug daily 10am–7pm; Sept–May Wed–Mon 10am–noon and 2–6pm.

Shopping

A gallery to seek out is the **Galerie Sassi-Milici,** 65 bis av. Georges-Clemenceau (© **04-93-64-65-71**), which displays works by contemporary artists.

Market days in Vallauris are Tuesday to Sunday 7am to 12:30pm, at **place de l'Homme au Mouton,** with its flower stalls and local produce. For a souvenir, you may want to visit a farming cooperative, the **Cooperative Nérolium,** 12 av. Georges-Clemenceau (© **04-93-64-27-54**). It produces such foods as bitter-orange marmalade and quince jam, olive oils, and scented products such as orange-flower water. Another unusual outlet for local products is the **Parfumerie Bouis,** 50 av. Georges-Clemenceau (© **04-93-64-38-27**).

La Boutique de l'Olivier, 46 av. Georges-Clemenceau (© **04-93-64-16-63**), specializes in olive-wood objects. They include pepper mills, salad servers, cheese boards, free-form bowls, and bread-slicing boxes. **Terres à Terre,** 58 av. Georges-Clemenceau (© **04-93-63-16-80**), is known for its culinary pottery, made of local clay. This is an excellent outlet for terra-cotta pottery. Gratin dishes and casseroles have long been big sellers.

Where to Dine

Chez Tétou ★★★ SEAFOOD   In its own amusing way, this is one of the Côte d'Azur's most famous restaurants, capitalizing on the beau monde that came here in the 1950s and 1960s. Retaining its Provençal earthiness despite its high prices, it has thrived in a white-sided beach cottage for more than 65 years. Appetizers are limited to platters of charcuterie or several almost-perfect slices of fresh melon. Most diners order the house specialty, bouillabaisse. Also on the limited menu are grilled sea bass with tomatoes Provençal, sole meunière, and several preparations of lobster—the most famous is grilled and served with lemon-butter sauce, fresh parsley, and basmati rice. Dessert may be a powdered croissant with grandmother's jams (winter) or a raspberry-and-strawberry tart (summer).

Av. des Frères-Roustan, sur la Plage, Golfe-Juan. © **04-93-63-71-16.** Reservations required. Main courses 77€; bouillabaisse 97€–124€. No credit cards. Thurs–Sun noon–2:30pm; Thurs–Tues 8–10:30pm. Closed Nov to early Mar.

JUAN-LES-PINS ★★

913km (567 miles) S of Paris; 9.5km (6 miles) S of Cannes

This suburb of Antibes is a resort developed in the 1920s by Frank Jay Gould. People flocked to "John of the Pines" to escape the crassness of Cannes. In the 1930s Juan-les-Pins drew a chic winter crowd. Today it attracts young Europeans from many economic backgrounds in pursuit of sex, sun, and sea, in that order. F. Scott Fitzgerald decried Juan-les-Pins as a "constant carnival." If he could see it now, he'd know he was a prophet.

Essentials

GETTING THERE   Juan-les-Pins is connected by **rail** and bus to most other Mediterranean coastal resorts, especially Nice (trip time: 30 min.; one-way fare: 4.80€). For rail information and schedules, call ℭ **08-92-35-35-35,** or visit www.voyages-sncf.com. **Buses** arrive from Nice and its airport at 40-minute intervals throughout the day. A bus leaves for Juan-les-Pins from Antibes at place Guynemer (ℭ **04-93-34-37-60**) daily every 20 minutes and costs 1.45€ one-way (trip time: 10–15 min.). To **drive** to Juan-les-Pins from Nice, travel along N7 south; from Cannes, follow the signposted roads. Juan-les-Pins is just outside of Cannes.

VISITOR INFORMATION   The **Office de Tourisme** is at 51 bd. Charles-Guillaumont (ℭ **04-92-90-53-05;** fax 04-93-61-55-13; www.antibesjuanlespins.com).

SPECIAL EVENTS   The town offers some of the best nightlife on the Riviera, and the action reaches its height during the annual jazz festival. The 10- to 12-day **Festival International de Jazz,** in mid-July, attracts jazz masters and their fans. Concerts are in a temporary stadium, custom-built for the event in Le Parc de la Pinède. Tickets cost 20€ to 65€ and can be purchased at the Office de Tourisme in both Antibes and Juan-les-Pins.

A Day at the Beach

Part of the reason people flock here is that the town's beaches have sand, unlike many of the other resorts along this coast, which have pebbly beaches. **Plage de Juan-les-Pins** is the most central beach. Its subdivisions, all public, include **Plage de la Salis** and **Plage de la Garoupe.** If you don't have a beach chair, go to the concessions operated by each of the major beachfront hotels. Even if you're not a guest, you can rent a chaise and mattress for around 17€ to 21€. The most chic is the area maintained by the Hôtel des Belles-Rives. Competitors more or less in the same category are La Jetée and La Voile Blanche, both opposite the tourist information office. Topless sunbathing is permitted, but total nudity isn't.

Watersports

If you're interested in scuba diving, check with your hotel staff, **Easy Dive,** Port Gallice (ℭ **04-93-61-41-49;** www.easydrive.fr), or **EPAJ,** embarcadère Courbet (ℭ **04-93-67-52-59**). A one-tank dive costs 30€ to 50€, including all equipment. **Water-skiing** is available at virtually every beach in Juan-les-Pins. Concessionaires include one outfit that's more or less permanently located on the beach of the Hôtel des Belles-Rives. Ask any beach attendant or bartender, and he or she will guide you to the water-skiing representatives who station themselves on the sands. A 10-minute session costs around 30€, 1 hour goes for 110€.

Where to Stay
VERY EXPENSIVE

Hôtel Belles-Rives ★★★   This is one of the Riviera's fabled addresses, on par with the equally famous Juana (see below), though the Juana serves superior cuisine.

It was once a holiday villa occupied by Zelda and F. Scott Fitzgerald, and the scene of many a drunken brawl. It later played host to the illustrious, such as the duke and duchess of Windsor, Josephine Baker, and Edith Piaf. A 1930s aura lingers through recent renovations. As befits a hotel of this age, rooms come in a variety of shapes and sizes, from small to spacious; each has a luxurious bathroom with a combination tub/shower. The lower terraces hold garden dining rooms, a waterside aquatic club with a snack bar and lounge, as well as a jetty. There are also a private beach and a dock.

33 bd. Edouard Baudoin, Juan-les-Pins 06160. © **04-93-61-02-79.** Fax 04-93-67-43-51. www.belles rives.com. 43 units. 150€–750€ double. AE, DC, MC, V. Free parking. Closed Jan–Mar 11. **Amenities:** 2 summer restaurants, 1 winter restaurant; 2 bars; room service. *In room:* A/C, TV, hair dryer, minibar, Wi-Fi (20€ per day).

Hôtel Juana ★★★   This balconied Art Deco hotel, beloved by F. Scott Fitzgerald, is separated from the sea by the park of pines that gave Juan-les-Pins its name. The hotel is constantly being refurbished, as reflected in the attractive rooms with mahogany pieces, well-chosen fabrics, tasteful carpets, and large bathrooms (tub and shower) in marble or tile. The rooms often have such extras as balconies. The hotel has a private swimming club where you can rent a "parasol and pad" on the sandy beach at reduced rates. Nearby is a park with umbrella-shaded tables and palms.

La Pinède, av. Gallice, Juan-les-Pins 06160. © **04-93-61-08-70.** Fax 04-93-61-76-60. www.hotel-juana. com. 40 units. 160€–260€ double; from 365€ suite. AE, MC, V. Parking 25€. Closed Nov–Dec. **Amenities:** Restaurant; bar; bike rentals; gym; heated outdoor pool; room service; sauna. *In room:* A/C, TV, minibar, hair dryer, Wi-Fi.

MODERATE

Hôtel des Mimosas   This elegant 1870s-style villa sprawls in a subtropical garden on a hilltop, a 10-minute walk to a good beach. The decor is a mix of high-tech and Italian-style comfort, with antique and modern furniture. Guest rooms come in a variety of shapes and sizes—some quite small. Try for one of the four rooms with a balcony or the nine rooms with a terrace. A pool sits amid huge palm trees. The hotel is fully booked in summer, so reserve far in advance.

Rue Pauline, Juan-les-Pins 06160. © **04-93-61-04-16.** Fax 04-92-93-06-46. www.hotelmimosas.com. 34 units. 95€–140€ double. AE, MC, V. Free parking. Closed Oct–May. From the town center, drive .4km (¼ mile) west, following N7 toward Cannes. **Amenities:** Bar; outdoor pool; room service; Wi-Fi (free). *In room:* A/C, TV, hair dryer, minibar.

Hôtel Le Pré Catelan   In a residential area near the town park, 200m (656 ft.) from a sandy beach, this year-round Provençal villa (built ca. 1900) features a garden with rock terraces, towering palms, lemon and orange trees, large pots of pink geraniums, and outdoor furniture. The atmosphere is casual, the setting uncomplicated and unstuffy. Furnishings are durable and basic. As is typical of such old villas, guest rooms come in a variety of shapes and sizes. Some have kitchenettes, and more expensive units have terraces. Despite the setting in the heart of town, the garden lends a sense of isolation. Breakfast is the only meal served.

27 av. des Palmiers, Juan-les-Pins 06160. © **04-93-61-05-11.** Fax 04-93-67-83-11. www.precatelan. com. 24 units. 108€–154€ double; 236€–328€ suite. AE, MC, V. Parking 8€–10€. **Amenities:** Bar; babysitting; outdoor pool. *In room:* TV, hair dryer, minibar, Wi-Fi (free).

INEXPENSIVE

Hôtel Cecil 🏅 A stone's throw from the beach, this small, well-kept hotel is one of the best bargains in Juan-les-Pins. It originated in 1929 when a 19th-century villa was radically enlarged with another story and transformed into a hotel. The traditionally furnished rooms are worn yet well kept, ranging from small to midsize, each with a compact tiled bathroom with shower only. The owners provide a courteous welcome and a good meal.

Rue Jonnard, Juan-les-Pins 06160. ✆ **04-93-61-05-12.** Fax 04-93-67-09-14. www.hotelcecilfrance. com. 21 units. 55€–100€ double. AE, DC, MC, V. Parking 15€. Closed Nov 7–Jan 14. **Amenities:** Restaurant; babysitting; room service. *In room:* A/C, TV (in some), hair dryer, Wi-Fi (free).

Where to Dine

Le Bijou Plage 🏅 FRENCH/PROVENÇAL   This upscale brasserie has flourished beside the seafront promenade since 1923. The marine-style decor includes lots of varnished wood and bouquets of flowers. Windows overlook a private beach that's much less crowded than the public beaches nearby. Menu items are sophisticated and less expensive than you'd expect. Examples include excellent bouillabaisse, grilled sardines, risotto with John Dory and truffled butter, steamed mussels with *sauce poulette* (frothy cream sauce with herbs and butter), grilled John Dory with a vinaigrette enriched by a tapenade of olives and fresh basil, and a supersize *plateau des coquillages et fruits de mer* (shellfish and seafood). Don't confuse this informally elegant place with its beachfront terrace, open year round daily noon to 2:30pm.

Bd. du Littoral. ✆ **04-93-61-39-07.** Reservations recommended. Main courses 19€–40€; fixed-price menu 22€–50€. AE, DC, MC, V. Daily noon–2:30pm and 7–10:30pm.

Le Perroquet PROVENÇAL   The cuisine is well presented and prepared, and the restaurant's ambience is carefully synchronized to the resort's casual and carnival-like summer aura. It's across from the Parc de la Pinède, and it's decorated with depictions of every imaginable form of parakeet, the restaurant's namesake. Look for savory versions of fish, at its best when grilled simply with olive oil and basil, and served with lemons. A worthwhile appetizer is the *assortiment Provençale,* which includes tapenade of olives, marinated peppers, grilled sardines, and stuffed and grilled vegetables. Steaks may be served with green peppercorns or Béarnaise sauce, and desserts include three types of pastries on the same platter.

Av. Georges-Gallice. ✆ **04-93-61-02-20.** Reservations recommended. Main courses 20€–30€; fixed-price menu 29€–36€. MC, V. Daily noon–2pm and 7–10:30pm. Closed early Nov to Dec 26.

Juan-les-Pins After Dark

For starters, visit the **Eden Casino,** boulevard Baudoin in the heart of Juan-les-Pins (✆ **04-92-93-71-71**), and try your luck at the roulette wheel or at one of the slot machines. The area containing slot machines is open every day 4pm to 5am. The area containing *les grands jeux* is open daily 10am to 5am. A photo ID is required, preferably in the form of a passport.

For a faux-tropical experience, head to **Le Pam Pam,** route Wilson (✆ **04-93-61-11-05**), where you can sip rum drinks in an atmosphere that celebrates reggae and Brazilian and African music and dance performances.

If you prefer high-energy reveling, check out the town's many discos. **Whisky à Gogo,** boulevard de la Pinède (✆ **04-93-61-26-40**), attracts young trendsetters with its rock beats. In summer it fills up with the young, restless, and horny; between October and Easter, it's closed. **Le Village,** 1 bd. de la Pinède (© **04-92-93-90-00**), boasts an action-packed dance floor and DJs spinning the latest sounds from the international music scene. The cover charge is a stiff 20€, but it's free for women before 1am on Friday.

ANTIBES & CAP D'ANTIBES ★★

913km (567 miles) S of Paris; 21km (13 miles) SW of Nice; 11km (6¾ miles) NE of Cannes

On the other side of the Baie des Anges (Bay of Angels) from Nice is the port of Antibes. The town has a quiet charm unique on the Côte d'Azur. Its harbor is filled with fishing boats and yachts, and in recent years it has emerged as a hot spot. The marketplaces are full of flowers. If you're in Antibes in the evening, you can watch fishermen playing the popular Riviera game of *boule* (similar to boccie).

Spiritually, Antibes is totally divorced from Cap d'Antibes, a peninsula studded with the villas of the super-rich. In *Tender Is the Night,* Fitzgerald described it as a place where "old villas rotted like water lilies among the massed pines."

Essentials

GETTING THERE   **Trains** from Cannes arrive at the rail station, place Pierre-Semard, every 20 minutes (trip time: 15 min.); the one-way fare is 2.50€. Trains from Nice arrive at the rate of 25 per day (trip time: 18 min.); the one-way fare is 4.40€. For rail information, call © **36-35,** or visit www.voyages-sncf.com. The **bus** station, La Gare Routière, place Guynemer (© **04-93-34-37-60**), receives buses from throughout Provence. Partially subsidized by the government, bus fares between Nice and Antibes or Cannes and Antibes cost only 1€ one-way.

If you're **driving,** follow E1 east from Cannes and take the turnoff to the south for Antibes, which will lead to the historic core of the old city. From Nice, take E1 west until you come to the turnoff for Antibes. From the center of Antibes, follow the coastal road, boulevard Leclerc, south to Cap d'Antibes.

VISITOR INFORMATION   The **Office de Tourisme** is at 11 place du Général-de-Gaulle (© **04-97-23-11-11;** fax 04-97-23-11-12; www.antibesjuanlespins.com).

Seeing the Sights

Musée Napoleonien ☺   In this stone-sided fort and tower, built in stages in the 17th and 18th centuries, you'll find an interesting collection of Napoleonic memorabilia, naval models, and paintings, many of which were donated by at least two world-class collectors. A toy-soldier collection depicts various uniforms, including one used by Napoleon in the Marengo campaign. A wall painting on wood shows Napoleon's entrance into Grenoble; another shows him disembarking at Golfe-Juan on March 1, 1815. In contrast to Canova's Greek-god image of Napoleon, a miniature pendant by Barrault reveals the general as he really looked, with pudgy cheeks and a receding hairline. In the rear rotunda is one of the many hats worn by the emperor. You can climb to the top of the tower for a view of the coast that's worth the admission price.

Batterie du Graillon, bd. J.-F.-Kennedy. © **04-93-61-45-32.** Admission 4.50€ adults; 1.50€ seniors, students, and ages 19–25; free for children 18 and under. June–Sept Tues–Sat 10am–6pm; Oct–May Tues–Sat 10am–4:30pm.

Musée Picasso ★★　On the ramparts above the port is the Château Grimaldi, once the home of the princes of Antibes of the Grimaldi family, who ruled the city from 1385 to 1608. Today it houses one of the world's great Picasso collections. Picasso came to town after the war and stayed in a small hotel at Golfe-Juan until the museum director at Antibes invited him to work and live at the museum. Picasso spent 1946 painting here. When he departed, he gave the museum all the work he'd done: 23 paintings, 80 pieces of ceramics, 44 drawings, 32 lithographs, 11 oils on paper, 2 sculptures, and 5 tapestries. In addition, a gallery of contemporary art exhibits Léger, Miró, Ernst, and Calder, among others.

Place du Mariejol. ✆ **04-92-90-54-20.** Admission 6€ adults, 3€ students and seniors; free for ages 18 and under. June–Sept Tues–Sun 10am–6pm; Oct–May Tues–Sun 10am–noon and 2–6pm.

Where to Stay
VERY EXPENSIVE
Hôtel du Cap–Eden Roc ★★★　Legendary for the glamour of its setting and its clientele, this Second Empire hotel, opened in 1870, is surrounded by masses of gardens. It's like a country estate, with spacious public rooms, marble fireplaces, paneling, chandeliers, and upholstered armchairs. The guest rooms are among the most sumptuous on the Riviera, with deluxe beds. Bathrooms are spacious, with brass fittings and tub/shower combinations. Even though the guests snoozing by the pool—blasted out of the cliff-side at enormous expense—appear artfully undraped during the day, evenings are upscale, with lots of emphasis on clothing and style. The world-famous Pavillon Eden Roc, near a rock garden apart from the hotel, has a panoramic sea view. Venetian chandeliers, Louis XV chairs, and elegant draperies add to the drama. Lunch is served on a terrace, under umbrellas and an arbor.

Bd. J.-F.-Kennedy, Cap d'Antibes 06600. ✆ **04-93-61-39-01.** Fax 04-93-67-13-83. www.edenroc-hotel. fr. 130 units. 460€–880€ double; 970€–1,600€ suite. No credit cards. Closed mid-Oct to mid-Apr. Bus: A2. **Amenities:** 2 restaurants; bar; babysitting; exercise room; massage; outdoor pool; room service; sauna. *In room:* A/C, TV (on request), hair dryer, Wi-Fi (free).

Hôtel Impérial Garoupe ★★　Within steps of the beach, this hotel is the centerpiece of a small park with rows of pines that block some of the sea views. The heiress to the Moulinex housewares fortune built it in 1993. Gilbert Irondelle, son of the director of Antibes' Grand Hôtel du Cap-Ferrat, has transformed it into a pocket of posh that's less intimidating than his father's more monumental hotel. The luxurious rooms contain contemporary furnishings, luxury beds, and deluxe bathrooms with tub/shower combinations. The in-house restaurant serves French and international cuisine.

60–74 chemin de la Garoupe, Cap d'Antibes 06600. ✆ **800/525-4800** in the U.S., or 04-92-93-31-61. Fax 04-92-93-31-62. www.imperial-garoupe.com. 34 units. 295€–620€ double; 560€–890€ suite. AE, DC, MC, V. Bus: A2. **Amenities:** Restaurant; bar; babysitting; heated outdoor pool; room service. *In room:* A/C, TV, hair dryer, minibar, Wi-Fi (free).

MODERATE
Castel Garoupe ✦　We highly recommend this Mediterranean villa, which was built in 1968 on a private lane in the center of the cape. It offers tastefully furnished, spacious rooms with fine beds and compact bathrooms with showers and tubs. Many rooms have private balconies, and each has shuttered windows. Some units have air-conditioning, whereas others have TVs. There's a tranquil garden on the premises.

959 bd. de la Garoupe, Cap d'Antibes 06160. (✆) **04-93-61-36-51.** Fax 04-93-67-74-88. www.castel-garoupe.com. 28 units. 128€–168€ double; 147€–235€ studio apt with kitchenette. AE, MC, V. Closed Nov to mid-Mar. Bus: A2. **Amenities:** 2 bars; babysitting; exercise room; outdoor pool; room service; tennis court. *In room:* Hair dryer, kitchenette, minibar, Wi-Fi (free).

Villa Val des Roses ★ 🏠 Two Flemish brothers, Frederik and Filip Vanderho-even, have created a relaxed place to stay only a minute's walk from the sea with a sandy beach, and just a 10-minute trek from the historic old town. The whitewashed Art Deco villa, a boutique alternative to the larger, grander hotels in the area, is built in the colonial style with such extras as an outdoor pool with a large terrace set against a backdrop of century-old palm trees. The decor is light and contemporary; each of the accommodations is individually decorated, often in soft, creamy tones. Rooms also come with a private terrace or balcony, and there are often marble pillars and views from the modern bathrooms. The hotel opens onto a small alleyway, away from the noise of the boulevards of Antibes. Fish barbecue is served at the hotel's restaurant.

6 chemin des Lauriers, Cap d'Antibes 06160. (✆) **06-85-06-06-29.** Fax 04-92-93-97-24. www.val-des-roses.com. 4 units. 150€–290€ double. MC, V. Free parking. Closed: Nov–Dec. **Amenities:** Restaurant; outdoor pool; tennis court. *In room:* A/C, TV, fridge, Wi-Fi.

INEXPENSIVE

Hôtel Beau Site This white stucco villa with a tile roof and heavy shutters is surrounded by eucalyptus trees, pines, and palms. Located off the main road, a 7-minute walk from the beach, it has a low wall of flower turns and wrought-iron gates. The interior is like a country inn, with oak beams and antiques. Guest rooms are comfortable and well maintained, and bathrooms are small.

141 bd. J.-F.-Kennedy, Cap d'Antibes 06150. (✆) **04-93-61-53-43.** Fax 04-93-67-78-16. www.hotel beausite.net. 31 units. 90€–155€ double; 160€–225€ suite. AE, DC, MC, V. Bus: A2. Closed Oct 21–Mar 10. **Amenities:** Bar; babysitting; pool; room service. *In room:* A/C, TV, hair dryer, Wi-Fi (free).

La Jabotte ★ 🛏 Only 54m (180 ft.) from the beach, this one-story villa with a trio of bungalows is built around a citrus garden. Yves, Claude, and Tommy are gracious hosts, welcoming you into their homelike environment where they serve breakfast on the terrace, with homemade jams, freshly squeezed orange juice, and "the surprise of the morning." Each day the bar proposes a different aperitif. Bedrooms are small but rather elegantly decorated, with rich colors, original paintings, and an intriguing hodge-podge of furnishings. Accommodations often have themes, ranging from birds to angels. Many of the paintings and ceramics on display are also for sale.

13 av. Max Maurey, Cap d'Antibes 06160. (✆) **04-93-61-45-89.** www.jabotte.com. 10 units. 75€–95€ double. MC, V. Closed Nov–Feb. **Amenities:** Garden; room service (breakfast only). *In room:* TV (in some), Wi-Fi (free).

Where to Dine

The Zelda and Scott Fitzgerald of today head for the **Eden Roc Restaurant** at the Hôtel du Cap–Eden Roc for grand service and grand cuisine. The dining room at the **Hôtel Impérial Garoupe** (see "Where to Stay," above) is also open to the public.

La Taverne du Saffranier 🛏 PROVENÇAL Earthy and irreverent, this bras-serie in a century-old building serves a changing roster of savory local specialties. Portions are generous. Examples are a platter of *petits farcis* (stuffed vegetables); a mini-bouillabaisse for single diners; savory fish soup; and an assortment of grilled fish (including sardines) that's served only with a dash of fresh lemon.

Place du Saffranier. ☏ **04-93-34-80-50.** Reservations recommended. Main courses 18€–26€; fixed-price menu 25€. MC, V. Tues–Sun noon–2pm; Tues–Sat 7–10:30pm. Closed mid-Nov to early Feb.

Les Vieux Murs FRENCH/SEAFOOD   This charming Provençal tavern is inside the 17th-century ramparts that used to fortify the old seaport, not far from the Musée Picasso. White paint complements soaring stone vaults, and a glassed-in front terrace overlooks the water. The chef uses market-fresh ingredients, especially seafood, which is prepared with flavor and served with style. Daily offerings depend on what's best at the market. Lusty Provençal meat and poultry dishes are menu staples.

Promenade de l'Amiral-de-Grasse. ☏ **04-93-34-06-73.** Reservations recommended. Main courses 25€–33€; fixed-price menu 44€–60€. AE, DC, MC, V. Tues–Sun noon–2:30pm; Tues–Sun 7:30–10:30pm. Closed 3 weeks in Nov.

Restaurant de Bacon ★★★ SEAFOOD   The Eden Roc restaurant at the Hôtel du Cap is more elegant, but Bacon serves the best seafood around. Surrounded by ultraexpensive residences, this restaurant on a rocky peninsula offers a panoramic coast view. Bouillabaisse aficionados claim that Bacon offers the best in France. In its deluxe version, saltwater crayfish float atop the savory brew; we prefer the simple version—a waiter adds the finishing touches at your table. If bouillabaisse isn't to your liking, try fish soup with garlic-laden rouille sauce; fish terrine; sea bass; John Dory; or something from a collection of fish unknown in North America—for example, sar, pageot, or denti.

Bd. de Bacon. ☏ **04-93-61-50-02.** www.restaurantdebacon.com. Reservations required. Main courses 40€–145€; fixed-price lunch 49€–79€; fixed-price dinner 79€. AE, DC, MC, V. Tues–Sun noon–2pm; Tues–Sun 8–10pm. Closed Nov–Mar.

CAGNES-SUR-MER ★

918km (570 miles) S of Paris; 21km (13 miles) NE of Cannes

Cagnes-sur-Mer, like the Roman god Janus, has two faces. Perched on a hill in the "hinterlands" of Nice, **Haut-de-Cagnes** is one of the most charming spots on the Riviera. At the foot of the hill is an old fishing port and rapidly developing beach resort, **Cros-de-Cagnes,** which lies between Nice and Antibes.

For years Haut-de-Cagnes attracted the French literati, including Simone de Beauvoir, who wrote *Les Mandarins* here. A colony of painters also settled here; Renoir said the village was "the place where I want to paint until the last day of my life." The racecourse is one of the finest in France.

Essentials

GETTING THERE   The **train** depot, Gare SNCF, lies in Cagnes-Ville (the more commercial part of town) at avenue de la Gare. It serves trains that run along the Mediterranean coast, with arrivals every hour from both Nice (trip time: 13 min.; one-way fare 3€) and Cannes (trip time: 23 min.; 3.90€). For rail information, call ☏ **36-35,** or visit www.voyages-sncf.com. **Buses,** costing 2€ from Nice and Cannes, stop at Cagnes-Ville and at Béal/Les Collettes, within walking distance of Cros-de-Cagnes. For information, call **Ligne d'Azur** (☏ **08-10-06-10-06**). The climb from Cagnes-Ville to Haut-de-Cagnes is strenuous; a free minibus runs daily about every 15 minutes year-round from place du Général-de-Gaulle in the center of Cagnes-Ville to Haut-de-Cagnes. By **car** from any of the coastal cities of

Provence, follow the A8 coastal highway, exiting at CAGNES-SUR-MER/CROS-DE-CAGNES.

VISITOR INFORMATION   The **Office de Tourisme** is at 6 bd. Maréchal-Juin, Cagnes-Ville (☏ **04-93-20-61-64;** fax 04-93-20-52-63; www.cagnes-tourisme.com).

SPECIAL EVENTS   Cagnes is the site, for 2 days every August, of a **Medieval Festival (La Fête Médiévale de Cagnes)** that dominates the medieval core of Haut-de-Cagnes. Highlights include equestrian tournaments, jousting exhibitions, and knights, knaves, and damsels in medieval costumes. Tickets to the individual festival events sell for 5€ to 10€ each, and, along with festival information, are available at the local tourist office.

Exploring the Town

Cros-de-Cagnes, a part of Cagnes-Sur-Mer, is known for its 4km (2½ miles) of seafront, covered with light-gray pebbles smoothed by centuries of wave action. These beaches are **Plages de Cros-de-Cagnes.** As usual, toplessness is accepted but full nudity isn't.

At least five concessions along this expanse rent beach mattresses and chaises for 15€. The most centrally located are **Tiercé Plage** (☏ **04-93-20-13-89**), **Le Cigalon** (☏ **04-93-07-74-82**), **La Gougouline** (☏ **04-93-31-08-72**), and **Le Neptune** (☏ **04-93-22-02-85**).

The orange groves and fields of carnations of the upper village provide a beautiful setting for the narrow cobblestone streets and 17th- and 18th-century homes. Drive to the top, where you can enjoy the view from **place du Château** and have lunch or a drink at a sidewalk cafe.

Château-Musée Grimaldi (Musée de l'Olivier & Musée d'Art Moderne Méditerranéen) ★   The Château-Musée was a fortress built in 1301 by Rainier Grimaldi I, a lord of Monaco and a French admiral (his portrait is in the museum). Charts illustrate how the defenses were organized. In the early 17th century, the castle was converted into a gracious Louis XIII château, which now contains two museums. The Museum of the Olive Tree shows the steps involved in cultivating and processing the olive. The Museum of Mediterranean Modern Art displays works by Kisling, Carzou, Dufy, Cocteau, and Seyssaud, among others, and temporary exhibits. In one salon is an interesting *trompe l'oeil* fresco, *La Chute de Phaeton*. The tower affords a view of the Côte d'Azur.

7 place Grimaldi. ☏ **04-92-02-47-30.** Admission to both museums 4€ adults, 2€ students, free for children 17 and under. May–Sept Wed–Mon 10am–noon and 2–6pm; Oct–Apr Wed–Mon 10am–noon and 2–5pm.

Musée Renoir & Les Collettes ★   Les Collettes has been restored to its appearance when Renoir lived here, from 1908 until his death in 1919. He continued to sculpt here, even though he was crippled by arthritis. He also continued to paint, with a brush tied to his hand and the help of assistants.

The house was built in 1907 in an olive and orange grove. There's a bust of Mme. Renoir in the entrance room. You can explore the drawing room and dining room on your own before going up to the artist's bedroom. In his atelier are his wheelchair, easel, and brushes. The terrace of Mme. Renoir's bedroom faces a stunning view of Cap d'Antibes and Haut-de-Cagnes. On a wall hangs a photograph of one of Renoir's sons, Pierre, as he appeared in the 1932 film *Madame Bovary.* Although Renoir is best remembered for his paintings, in Cagnes he began experimenting with sculpture. The museum has 20 portrait busts and portrait medallions, most of which depict his wife and children. The curators say they represent the largest collection of Renoir sculpture in the world.

19 chemin des Collettes. © **04-93-20-61-07.** Admission 4€ adults, 2€ students, free for ages 18 and under. May–Sept Wed–Mon 10am–noon and 2–6pm; Oct–Nov 23 and Dec 2–Apr Wed–Mon 10am–noon and 2–5pm. Ticket sales end 30 min. before lunch and evening closing hours.

Shopping

Terraïo, 12 place du Dr.-Maurel, Haut-de-Cagnes (© **04-93-20-86-83**), is a tiny gem. Art critics claim the stoneware in this shop captures the celadon and turquoise tones of the nearby Mediterranean. Artist, owner, and native son Claude Barnoin has spent nearly 25 years perfecting the mixture of copper-based glazes that produce these tones. The ashtrays, dinner services, and showcase pieces produced in the artist's studio (which you cannot visit) are the pride of many French and U.S. collections. Prices run from around 12€ for a simple ashtray to as much as 600€ for something spectacular. The shop, which lies just across the square from the Château-Musée Grimaldi, is open daily from 2 to around 6pm, except in midsummer, when it may close for an occasional day.

Where to Stay
IN CAGNES-SUR-MER

Hôtel Le Chantilly 🏷 This is the best bargain for those who prefer to stay near the beach. Built in a boxy and angular style in 1960, the hotel's landscaping and homey interior, with Oriental rugs and potted plants, make this place as inviting as possible. Most rooms are small but cozily furnished and well kept, often opening onto balconies; each has a compact tiled bathroom with shower. In fair weather you can enjoy breakfast, the only meal served, on the terrace.

31 chemin de la Minoterie, Cagnes-sur-Mer 06800. © **04-93-20-25-50.** Fax 04-92-02-82-63. www.hotel-lechantilly.fr. 17 units. 68€–77€ double; 71€–92€ triple. AE, DC, MC, V. Free parking. **Amenities:** Babysitting; room service. *In room:* TV, minibar, Wi-Fi (free).

IN HAUT-DE-CAGNES

Le Cagnard ★★★ Several 13th-century houses were joined in the 1960s to form this glamorous Relais & Châteaux property. The dining room is covered with frescoes, and there's a vine-draped terrace. The rooms and salons are furnished with antiques such as provincial chests, armoires, and Louis XV chairs. Each room has its own style: Some are duplexes, others have terraces and views of the countryside. The luxurious bathrooms are spacious, with tub/shower combinations.

The cuisine of the chef has been awarded a Michelin star and is reason enough to make the trip. Fresh ingredients go into delectable dishes. Fixed-price menus cost 50€ to 85€ at lunch and 75€ to 110€ at dinner. The hotel is open year-round; the restaurant closes from November to April 15 and on Monday, Tuesday, and Thursday at lunch.

Rue du Pontis-Long, Le Haut-de-Cagnes, Cagnes-sur-Mer 06800. © **04-93-20-73-21.** Fax 04-93-22-06-39. www.le-cagnard.com. 23 units. 100€–255€ double; 180€–385€ suite. AE, DC, MC, V. Free parking. **Amenities:** Restaurant; bar; babysitting; room service. *In room:* A/C, TV, hair dryer, minibar, Wi-Fi (in some; free).

Where to Dine

In Haut-de-Cagnes, the hotel **Le Cagnard** (see above) has a remarkable restaurant.

IN HAUT-DE-CAGNES

Fleur de Sel FRENCH/PROVENÇAL   Energetic owners Philippe and Pascale Loose run this charming restaurant in a 200-year-old stone-sided house in the center of the village. In two ocher-toned dining rooms outfitted with Provençal furniture and oil paintings, you'll enjoy the kind of cuisine that Philippe learned during stints at some of the grandest restaurants of France, including a brief time with Marc Meneau at L'Espérance in Vézelay. Tasty recommendations include foie gras with artichoke hearts in puff pastry, cappuccino of crayfish with paprika and pistachios, scallops braised with spinach, and filet of beef braised in a hearty local red wine, Bellet.

85 Montée de la Bourgade. (℃) **04-93-20-33-33.** www.restaurant-fleur-desel.com. Reservations recommended. Main courses 18€–36€; fixed-price menus 32€–55€. MC, V. Fri–Tues noon–2pm; Thurs–Tues 7:30–10pm. Closed 10 days in Nov.

Josy-Jo ★★ TRADITIONAL FRENCH   Le Cagnard (see above) has a more elegant setting, but the food here is comparable. Behind a 200-year-old facade covered with vines and flowers, this Michelin star–rated restaurant was the home and studio of Modigliani and Soutine during their hungriest years. Paintings cover the walls, and the Bandecchi family runs everything smoothly. The menu features grilled meats and a variety of fish. You can enjoy brochette of gigot of lamb with kidneys, calves' liver, homemade terrine of foie gras of duckling, stuffed Provençal vegetables, and an array of salads.

2 rue Planastel. (℃) **04-93-20-68-76.** www.restaurant-josyjo.com. Reservations required. Main courses 22€–45€; fixed-price lunch 29€–40€. AE, MC, V. Mon–Fri 12:30–1:30pm; Mon–Sat 7:30–9:30pm. Closed Nov 19–Dec 26.

IN CROS-DE-CAGNES

Loulou (La Réserve) ★★ FRENCH   This restaurant, which like Josy-Jo and Cagnard has a Michelin star, makes the Cagnes area a gourmet enclave. It's across the boulevard from the sea and named for a famous long-departed chef. Brothers Eric and Joseph Campo prepare spectacular versions of fish soup; shrimp steamed and served with fresh ginger and cinnamon; and grilled versions of the catch of the day. These dishes are served as simply as possible, usually with just a drizzling of olive oil and balsamic vinegar. Meat dishes include flavorful veal kidneys with port sauce, and delectable grilled steaks, chops, and cutlets. Dessert may include caramelized-apple tart. The glassed-in veranda in front is a prime people-watching spot.

91 bd. de la Plage. (℃) **04-93-31-00-17.** www.louloureserve.com. Reservations recommended. Main courses 30€–103€; fixed-price menus 42€–49€. AE, MC, V. Mon–Fri noon–1:30pm and 7:30–9:30pm; Sat 7–9:30pm.

ST-PAUL-DE-VENCE ★★

926km (575 miles) S of Paris; 23km (14 miles) E of Grasse; 28km (17 miles) E of Cannes; 31km (19 miles) N of Nice

Of all the cliff-side villages of the Riviera, St-Paul-de-Vence is the best known. It gained popularity in the 1920s, when many artists lived here, occupying the 16th-century houses that flank the cobblestone streets. Its ramparts (allow about 30 min.

to circle them) overlook flowers and olive and orange trees. They haven't changed much since they were constructed from 1537 to 1547 by order of François I. From the north ramparts you can look out on Baou de St-Jeannet, a sphinx-shaped rock that was painted into the landscape of Poussin's *Polyphème*.

Essentials

GETTING THERE   The nearest **rail** station is in Cagnes-sur-Mer. Some 20 **buses** per day leave from Nice's Gare Routière, dropping passengers off in St-Paul-de-Vence (one-way fare: 1€), then in Vence. For information, call the **Compagnie SAP** (*©* **04-93-58-37-60**). If you're **driving** from Nice, take the coastal A8 highway east, turn inland at Cagnes-sur-Mer, and follow signs north to St-Paul-de-Vence.

VISITOR INFORMATION   The **Office de Tourisme** is at 2 rue Grande (*©* **04-93-32-86-95;** fax 04-93-32-60-27; www.saint-pauldevence.com).

Exploring the Town

Note: Driving a car in St-Paul's old town is prohibited, except to drop off luggage at your hotel.

The local tourist office, if you phone at least a day (and sometimes a few hours) in advance, can arrange any of several distinctly themed walking tours of the town's historic core, as well as to some of the town's outskirts. Most tours last for about an hour and are priced at 5€ each; all of them depart from the tourist office. Depending on your interests, tours may highlight the city's history and architecture, the artists who lived here and the works they created, even the lessons and lore of the French pastime of *pétanques* (also known as *boules*), wherein a practice session with seasoned locals is included as part of the experience. We advise you to approach the experience with an open mind, and to accept substitute tours if the one stressing your particular area of interest is not available during your time in St-Paul. For more information and reservations, contact the local tourist office (see "Visitor Information," above).

The pedestrian-only **rue Grande** is the most evocative street, running the length of St-Paul. Most of the stone houses along it are from the 16th and 17th centuries, and many still bear the coats of arms placed there by the original builders. Today, most of the houses are antiques shops, arts-and-crafts galleries, and souvenir and gift shops; some are still artists' studios.

The village's chief sight is the **Collégiale de la Conversion de St-Paul ★**, constructed in the 12th and 13th centuries and much altered over the years. The Romanesque choir is the oldest part, containing some remarkable stalls carved in walnut in the 17th century. The bell tower was built in 1740. Look to the left as you enter: You'll see the painting *Ste-Cathérine d'Alexandrie,* which has been attributed to Tintoretto. The **Trésor de l'Eglise** is one of the most beautiful in the Alpes-Maritimes, with a spectacular ciborium. Look also for a low relief of the *Martyrdom of St-Clément* on the last altar on the right. In the baptismal chapter is a 15th-century alabaster Madonna. It's open daily 9am to 6pm (to 7pm July–Aug). Admission is free.

Near the church is the **Musée d'Histoire de St-Paul,** place de l'Eglise (*©* **04-93-32-41-13**), a museum in a village house that dates to the 1500s. It was restored and refurnished in 16th-century style, with artifacts illustrating the history of the village. It's open daily 10am to noon and 2 to 5pm. Admission is 3€ adults, 2€ students and children 5 to 18, and free for children 4 and under.

Foundation Maeght ★★★   This avant-garde building houses one of the most modern art museums in Europe. On a hill in pine-studded woods, the Foundation Maeght is like Shangri-La. Nature and the creations of men and women blend harmoniously in this unique achievement of the architect José Luis Sert. Its white concrete arcs give the impression of a giant pagoda.

A stark Calder rises like some futuristic monster on the lawn. In a courtyard, the bronze works of Giacometti, marble statues by Miró, and mosaics by Chagall form a surrealistic garden. Sculpture is displayed inside, but the museum is at its best in a natural setting of terraces and gardens. It's built on several levels, its many glass walls providing an indoor-outdoor vista. The foundation, a gift "to the people" from Aimé and Marguerite Maeght, also provides a showcase for new talent. On the property are a library, a cinema, and a cafeteria. In one showroom you can buy original lithographs by artists such as Chagall and Giacometti, and limited-edition prints.

Outside the town walls. ⓒ **04-93-32-81-63.** www.maeght.com. Admission 11€ adults, 9€ students and ages 10–18, free for children 9 and under. July–Sept daily 10am–7pm; Oct–June daily 10am–6pm.

Where to Stay

La Colombe d'Or rents deluxe rooms (p. 577).

EXPENSIVE

Hôtel Le St-Paul ★★★   Converted from a 16th-century Renaissance residence and retaining many original features, this Relais & Châteaux member is in the heart of the village. The guest rooms, decorated in sophisticated Provençal style, have sumptuous beds and midsize bathrooms with tub/shower combinations. Sitting on the balcony of room no. 30 will help you understand why Renoir, Léger, Matisse, and Picasso were inspired by Provence. Many rooms enjoy a view of the valley with the Mediterranean in the distance. The restaurant has a flower-bedecked terrace sheltered by 16th-century ramparts and a superb dining room with vaulted ceilings.

86 rue Grande, St-Paul-de-Vence 06570. ⓒ **04-93-32-65-25.** Fax 04-93-32-52-94. www.lesaintpaul. com. 16 units. 250€–330€ double; 320€–750€ suite. AE, DC, MC, V. Closed mid-Dec to Jan 25. Free parking. **Amenities:** Restaurant; bar; babysitting; room service; 3 tennis courts; Wi-Fi (free). *In room:* A/C, TV, hair dryer, minibar.

MODERATE

Auberge Les Orangers ★ 🎁   M. Franklin has created a "living oasis" in his villa, which is configured like a highly personalized bed-and-breakfast. The scents of rose, orange, and lemon waft through the air. The main lounge is decorated with original oils and furnished in a provincial style. Expect to be treated like a guest in a private home. The rooms, with antiques and Oriental carpets, have panoramic views; the small bathrooms have tub/shower combinations. Banana trees and climbing geraniums surround the sun terrace.

Quartier les Fumerates, rte. de la Colle (D107), St-Paul-de-Vence 06570. ⓒ **04-93-32-80-95.** Fax 04-93-32-00-32. www.lesorangers.fr. 5 units. 104€–185€ double; 170€ suite. Rates include breakfast. MC, V. Free parking. From the town center, follow the signs to Cagnes-sur-Mer for 1km (⅔ mile) south. **Amenities:** Babysitting; room service; Wi-Fi (free). *In room:* Hair dryer.

Hostellerie des Messugues ★ 🎁   Those wishing to escape the hordes of this overrun hill town head to this idyllic retreat set in a flowery park with a sizeable swimming pool. Only a few steps from the Maeght Foundation, the hotel offers a countrylike environment, though close to the action, only 1km (½ mile) from the village center. Bedrooms are small to midsize but attractively furnished and most comfortable.

Domaine des Gardettes, St-Paul-de-Vence 06570. ✆ **04-93-32-53-32.** Fax 04-93-32-94-15. 15 units. 95€–160€ double. AE, DC, MC, V. Free parking. Closed Nov–Apr 1. **Amenities:** Breakfast room; outdoor pool; room service. *In room:* A/C, TV, hair dryer, Wi-Fi (free).

Hôtel Le Hameau ★ ✔   This romantic Mediterranean villa is on a hilltop on the outskirts of St-Paul-de-Vence, on the road to Colle at Hauts-de-St-Paul. Built as a farmhouse in the 1920s and enlarged and transformed into a hotel in 1967, it contains high-ceilinged rooms, each with a compact tub/shower bathroom. You'll have a remarkable view of the surrounding hills and valleys. There is also a vineyard and a sunny terrace with fruit trees, flowers, and a pool.

528 rte. de la Colle (D107), St-Paul-de-Vence 06570. ✆ **04-93-32-80-24.** Fax 04-93-32-55-75. www.le-hameau.com. 17 units. 105€–170€ double; 190€–270€ suite. MC, V. Closed Nov 15–Feb 15. From the town, take D107 about 1km (⅔ mile), following the signs south of town toward Colle. **Amenities:** Bar; outdoor pool; Wi-Fi (free). *In room:* A/C, TV, hair dryer.

La Grande Bastide ★   Between the sea and the hills, this 18th-century villa and estate has been transformed into a little inn of charm and grace. The owners welcome you as if inviting you into their private home, which this is, of course. The inn opens onto two panoramic terraces with views of the village (breakfast is served here). The pool house is one of the best in the area, with sofas placed in front of an open fire on nippy nights. The bedrooms are furnished with taste and sophistication, with your comfort in mind.

1350 rte. de la Colle, St-Paul-de-Vence 06570. ✆ **04-93-32-50-30.** 14 units. 145€–240€ double; 210€–335€ suite. AE, DC, MC, V. Free parking. Closed Nov 20–Dec 20. **Amenities:** Bar; outdoor pool; spa. *In room:* A/C, TV, hair dryer, Wi-Fi (free).

INEXPENSIVE

Les Bastides St-Paul   This hotel is in the hills outside town, 1.5km (1 mile) south of St-Paul and 4km (2½ miles) south of Vence. Spread over two buildings, it provides comfortable carpeted rooms, each accented with regional artifacts and opening onto a terrace and garden. The compact bathrooms hold tub/shower combinations. On the premises is a cloverleaf-shaped pool. Longtime hoteliers Marie José and Maurice Giraudet head the responsive management staff. Breakfast is served anytime you want it.

880 rte. des Blaquières (rte. Cagnes-Vence), St-Paul-de-Vence 06570. ✆ **04-92-02-08-07.** Fax 04-93-20-50-41. 20 units. 85€–140€ double. AE, DC, MC, V. From the town center, follow signs toward Cagnes-sur-Mer for 1.5km (1 mile) south. **Amenities:** Babysitting; outdoor pool; room service; Wi-Fi (free). *In room:* A/C, TV, minibar.

Where to Dine

The dining room at the **Hôtel Le St-Paul** (p. 576) features exceptional cuisine based on market-fresh ingredients.

La Colombe d'Or ★ PROVENÇAL   For more than a decade, "The Golden Dove" has been St-Paul's most celebrated restaurant—not for cutting-edge cuisine or exotic experiments, but for its remarkable art collection. You can dine amid Mirós, Picassos, Klees, Dufys, Utrillos, and Calders. In fair weather everyone tries for a seat on the terrace. You may begin with smoked salmon or foie gras from Landes if you've recently won at the casino. If not, you can count on a soup made with fresh seasonal vegetables. The best fish dishes are poached sea bass with mousseline sauce, and sea wolf baked with fennel. Tender beef comes with *gratin dauphinois* (potatoes), or you may prefer lamb from Sisteron. A classic finish to any meal is a *soufflé flambé au Grand-Marnier.*

The guest rooms (16 doubles, 10 suites) contain French antiques and Provençal accessories. They're in the original 16th-century stone house and in two wings added in the 1950s, one of which stretches into the garden next to the pool. Some units have exposed stone and ceiling beams; all are comfortable, with air-conditioning, minibars, and TVs. Prices are 290€ for a double, 390€ for a suite, including free Wi-Fi.

1 place du Général-de-Gaulle, St-Paul-de-Vence 06570. ℂ **04-93-32-80-02.** Fax 04-93-32-77-78. www.la-colombe-dor.com. Reservations required. Main courses 17€–35€. AE, DC, MC, V. Daily noon– 2pm and 7:30–10pm. Closed Nov–Dec and Jan 10–20.

VENCE ★

926km (575 miles) S of Paris; 31km (19 miles) N of Cannes; 24km (15 miles) NW of Nice

Travel into the hills northwest of Nice—across country studded with cypresses, olive trees, and pines, where carnations, roses, oleanders, and other flowers grow in profusion—and Vence comes into view. Outside the town, along boulevard Paul-André, two olive presses carry on their age-old duties. The attraction here is the **Vieille Ville (Old Town).** Visitors pose for photographs on place du Peyra in front of the **Vieille Fontaine (Old Fountain),** a feature in several films. The 15th-century square tower is also a curiosity.

If you're wearing sturdy shoes, the narrow, steep streets of the old town are worth exploring. Dating from the 10th century, the cathedral on place Godeau is unremarkable except for some 15th-century Gothic choir stalls. But if it's the right day of the week, most visitors quickly pass through the narrow gates of this once-fortified walled town to see one of Matisse's most remarkable achievements, the Chapelle du Rosaire.

Essentials

GETTING THERE   Frequent **buses** (no. 94 or 200) originating in Nice take 45 minutes to reach Vence; the one-way fare is 1€. For information, contact the **Compagnie SAP** (ℂ **04-93-58-37-60**). The nearest **rail** station is in Cagnes-sur-Mer, about 10km (6¼ miles) southwest from Vence. From there, about 20 buses per day priced at 1.50€ make the trip to Vence. For train information, call ℂ **36-35,** or visit www.voyages-sncf.com. To **drive** to Vence from Nice, take N7 west to Cagnes-sur-Mer, and then D236 north to Vence.

VISITOR INFORMATION   The **Office de Tourisme** is on place Grand-Jardin (ℂ **04-93-58-06-38;** www.vence.fr).

A Matisse Masterpiece

Chapelle du Rosaire ★★   It was a beautiful golden autumn along the Côte d'Azur. The great Henri Matisse was 77, and after a turbulent time he set out to design and decorate his masterpiece. Outside Vence, Matisse created the Chapelle du Rosaire for the Dominican nuns of Monteils. (Sister Jacques-Marie, a member of the order, had nursed him back to health after a serious illness.) From the front

A Goat of Note

Le Château du Domaine St-Martin stands on the site of an ancient fortress belonging to the Knights Templar. Local legend has it that this is where the	knights buried a store of treasure, including *la chèvre d'or*—a large goat made of solid gold.

you might find it unremarkable and pass it by—until you spot a 12m (39-ft.) crescent-adorned cross rising from a blue-tile roof.

Matisse wrote: "What I have done in the chapel is to create a religious space . . . in an enclosed area of very reduced proportions and to give it, solely by the play of colors and lines, the dimensions of infinity." The light picks up the subtle coloring in the simply rendered leaf forms and abstract patterns: sapphire blue, aquamarine, and lemon yellow. In black-and-white ceramics, St. Dominic is depicted in only a few lines. The most remarkable design is in the black-and-white-tile Stations of the Cross, with Matisse's self-styled "tormented and passionate" figures. The bishop of Nice came to bless the chapel in the late spring of 1951 when the artist's work was completed. Matisse died 3 years later.

Av. Henri-Matisse. ☏ **04-93-58-03-26.** Admission 3€ adults, 1.50€ for children 16 and under; contributions to maintain the chapel are welcome. Mon, Wed, Sat 2–5:30pm; Tues and Thurs 10–11:30am, 2–5:30pm.

Where to Stay
VERY EXPENSIVE
Le Château du Domaine St-Martin ★★★   If you're heading into the hill towns above Nice and you seek luxury and refinement, this is your address. The château, in a 14-hectare (36-acre) park with terraced gardens, was built in 1936 on the grounds where the "Golden Goat" treasure was reputedly buried. The main building holds the standard units; suites are in the tile-roofed villas. You can walk through the gardens on winding paths lined with tall cypresses, past the chapel ruins and olive trees. The spacious rooms are distinctively decorated, and the large rose-colored bathrooms have tub/shower combinations. The luxurious restaurant has a view of the coast and serves superb French cuisine. In summer, many guests prefer the poolside grill.

Av. des Templiers B.P. 102, Vence 06140. ☏ **04-93-58-02-02.** Fax 04-93-24-08-91. www.chateau-st-martin.com. 39 units, 6 villas. 290€–500€ double; 600€–1,500€ suite. AE, DC, MC, V. Closed Dec–Feb. From the town center, follow signs toward Coursegoules and Col-de-Vence for 1.5km (1 mile) north. **Amenities:** Restaurant; bar; babysitting; outdoor pool; room service; spa; 2 tennis courts. *In room:* A/C, TV, hair dryer, Wi-Fi (free).

EXPENSIVE
Hôtel Cantemerle ★   One of the most appealing places in Vence is this artfully designed cluster that resembles an old-fashioned compound of Provençal buildings. Capped with rounded terra-cotta roof tiles, they stand on a lawn dotted with old trees, surrounding a pool. Public areas, stylishly outfitted with Art Deco furniture and accessories, include a paneled bar and a sun-flooded flagstone terrace where meals are served. Rooms aren't overly large but contain unusual reproductions of overscale Art Deco armchairs, louvered wooden closet doors, and balcony-style

sleeping lofts with comfortable beds. The restaurant serves worthwhile regional and mainstream French cuisine.

258 chemin Cantemerle, Vence 06140. ℭ **04-93-58-08-18.** Fax 04-93-58-32-89. www.hotelcantemerle. com. 27 units. 200€–230€ double; 460€–510€ suite. AE, MC, V. Closed late Oct to Apr. **Amenities:** Restaurant; bar; babysitting; gym; 2 pools (indoor and outdoor); room service; sauna; spa. *In room:* A/C, TV, hair dryer, minibar, Wi-Fi (free).

MODERATE

La Maison du Frêne ★ 🏠   In the heart of Vence, this Provençal guesthouse, now an elegant retreat, was once a private home in the 18th century. Vence has far more lavish and luxurious retreats, but none with this snug, cozy comfort—and at an affordable price. It is an inn aficionado's gem. Guest rooms are midsize to spacious, and both beautifully and comfortably furnished. An old ash tree planted in front of the house during the reign of François I and the manse itself have been the subject of countless paintings. The original architecture has been preserved, although all the modern comforts have been added. The reception area contains original sculptures and modern paintings, and it's linked to the country kitchen, where delicious home-made breakfasts are prepared. Of all the rooms, we prefer the junior suite on the highest level with its sloping ceiling.

1 place du Frêne, Vence 06140. ℭ **04-93-24-37-80.** www.lamaisondufrene.com. 4 units. 140€–180€. MC, V. Parking 13€. **Amenities:** Dinner upon request in winter. *In room:* A/C, TV on request, Wi-Fi (free).

INEXPENSIVE

Auberge des Seigneurs ★   This 400-year-old stone hotel gives you a taste of old Provence. Decorative objects and antiques are everywhere. The guest rooms are well maintained, but the management dedicates its energy to the restaurant. Nevertheless, the Provençal-style rooms are comfortable, with lots of exposed paneling and beams. Two have decorative fireplaces. The small, tiled bathrooms contain showers. The restaurant is in a stone building that used to be the kitchen of the Château de Villeneuve, where François I spent part of his youth. The specialty is grills prepared on an open spit in view of the dining room, which holds a long wooden table and an open fireplace with a row of hanging copper pots and pans.

1 rue de Docteur Biret, Vence 06140. ℭ **04-93-58-04-24.** 5 units. 85€–95€ double. DC, MC, V. Closed mid-Dec to mid-Jan. **Amenities:** Restaurant; bar; room service. *In room:* Hair dryer, Wi-Fi (free).

Le Floréal   On the road to Grasse is this pleasant, comfortable hotel with a view of the mountains and a refreshing lack of pretension. Many of the well-furnished rooms look out into the garden, where orange trees and mimosa add fragrance to the breezes. Most accommodations are medium-size, and each is comfortable, with quality mattresses and fine linen. Bathrooms are compact and tiled.

440 av. Rhin-et-Danube, Vence 06140. ℭ **04-93-58-64-40.** Fax 04-93-58-79-69. www.bestwestern. fr. 41 units. 78€–137€ double. AE, DC, MC, V. Free parking. **Amenities:** Restaurant; bar; babysitting; pool; room service; sauna. *In room:* A/C, TV, hair dryer, Wi-Fi (free).

Where to Dine

Auberge des Seigneurs, Hôtel Cantemerle, and **Le Château du Domaine St-Martin** (see reviews for all in "Where to Stay," above) offer excellent dining.

La Farigoule PROVENÇAL   In a century-old house that opens onto a rose garden, this restaurant specializes in Provençal cuisine. Menu items are conservative but flavorful: They include *bourride Provençale* (bouillabaisse with a dollop of cream and lots of garlic); shoulder of roasted lamb with a ragout of fresh vegetables, served with fresh thyme; and such fish dishes as dorado with comfit of lemons and fresh, aromatic coriander. In the summer, you can dine in the rose garden.

15 av. Henri-Isnard. © **04-93-58-01-27.** Reservations recommended. Main courses 25€–29€; fixed-price menus 30€–40€. MC, V. Wed-Mon noon–2pm and 7:30–10pm. Closed Nov 15–Dec 15.

NICE ★★★

929km (577 miles) S of Paris; 32km (20 miles) NE of Cannes

Nice is the capital of the Riviera, the largest city between Genoa and Marseille. It's also one of the most ancient, founded by the Greeks, who called it Nike (Victory). By the 19th century, the Victorian upper class and tsarist aristocrats were flocking here. But these days it's not as chichi and expensive, especially compared to Cannes. In fact, of all the major French resorts, from Deauville to Biarritz to Cannes, Nice is the most affordable. It's also the best place to base yourself on the Riviera, especially if you're dependent on public transportation. You can go to San Remo, "the queen of the Italian Riviera," and return to Nice by nightfall. From the Nice airport, the second largest in France, you can travel by train or bus along the entire coast to resorts such as Juan-les-Pins and Cannes.

Because of its brilliant sunshine and relaxed living, Nice has long attracted artists and writers, among them Dumas, Nietzsche, Flaubert, Hugo, Sand, and Stendhal. Henri Matisse, who made his home in Nice, said, "Though the light is intense, it's also soft and tender." The city averages 300 days of sunshine a year.

Essentials

GETTING THERE **Trains** arrive at Gare Nice-Ville, avenue Thiers (© 08-92-35-35-35; www.voyages-sncf.com). From there you can take trains to Cannes for 5.80€, Monaco 2.80€, and Antibes 3.90€, with easy connections to anywhere else along the Mediterranean coast. There's a small tourist center at the train station, open Monday to Saturday 8am to 7pm and Sunday 9am to 6pm. If you face a long delay, you can eat at the cafeteria and even shower at the station.

Buses to and from Monaco, Cannes, St-Tropez, and other parts of France and Europe serve the main bus station, or **Gare Routière,** 5 bd. Jean-Jaurès (© 08-92-70-12-06).

Transatlantic and intercontinental flights land at **Aéroport Nice–Côte d'Azur** (© 08-20-42-33-33). From there, municipal bus no. 98 departs at 30-minute intervals for the Gare Routière (see above); the one-way fare is 4€. Bus nos. 23 and 99 go to Gare SNCF. A **taxi** from the airport into the city center will cost at least 30€ to 40€ each way. Trip time is about 30 minutes.

VISITOR INFORMATION Nice maintains three **tourist offices,** the largest and most central of which is at 5 promenade des Anglais, near place Masséna (© 08-92-70-74-07; fax 04-92-14-46-49; www.nicetourisme.com). Additional offices are in the arrivals hall of the Aéroport Nice–Côte d'Azur and the railway station on avenue Thiers. Any office can make a hotel reservation (but only for the night of the day you show up) for a modest fee that varies according to the classification of the hotel.

GETTING AROUND   Most local buses serve the **Station Central SNCF,** 10 av. Félix-Faure (☎ **04-93-13-53-13;** www.voyages-sncf.com), a very short walk from the place Masséna. Municipal buses charge 1€ for a ride within Greater Nice. Bus nos. 2 and 12 make frequent trips to the beach.

No point within downtown Nice is more than about a 10-minute walk from the seafronting promenade, site of such well-known quays as the promenade des Anglais and the promenade des Etats-Unis. Bus nos. 2 and 12 run along its length, dropping passengers off at any of the beaches and concessions that front the edge of the sea.

The best place to rent bikes and mopeds is **Energy Scoot,** Promenade des Anglais (☎ **04-97-07-12-64**), just behind the place Grimaldi. Open Monday to Saturday 9am to noon and 2 to 7pm, it charges 15€ per day for a bike or moped and requires a deposit of at least 55€, depending on the value of the machine you rent. Scooter rental is 39€ per day. Somewhat less appealing, but useful when Energy Scoot is closed, is **Nicea Rent,** 12 rue de Belgique (☎ **04-93-82-42-71**). It charges about the same rates, but the staff isn't always on the premises.

SPECIAL EVENTS   The **Nice Carnaval** draws visitors from all over Europe and North America. The "Mardi Gras of the Riviera" begins sometime in February, usually 12 days before Shrove Tuesday, celebrating the return of spring with 3 weeks of parades, *corsi* (floats), *veglioni* (masked balls), confetti, and battles in which young women toss flowers (some throw rotten eggs instead of carnations). The climax, a fireworks display on Shrove Tuesday, lights up the Baie des Anges (Bay of Angels). King Carnival goes up in flames on his pyre, but rises from the ashes the following spring. For information, contact the tourist office (see above).

The **Nice Festival du Jazz** (☎ **01-47-23-07-58;** www.nicejazzfest.com) runs for a week in mid-July, when jazz artists perform in the ancient Arène de Cimiez.

Exploring the City

One of the most efficient ways to quickly gain an overview of the layout and architecture of Nice involves boarding one of the double-decker buses associated with **Nice–Le Grand Tour** (☎ **04-92-29-17-00**). Every day of the year, between 9:30am and 6:50pm, one of a flotilla of this company's buses departs from a position adjacent to the Jardins Albert I, on the quai des Etats-Unis, for a panoramic 90-minute tour of Nice and its outlying historic suburb of Cimiez. Per-person rates for the experience are 20€ for adults, 18€ for students, and 5€ children 4 to 11. Participants can get off at any of 11 stops en route, opting to reboard any other buses, which follow at 40-minute intervals, after they've explored the neighborhood. Advance reservations aren't necessary.

Nice

ACCOMMODATIONS ■

Folts d'Azur **16**
Four Points by Sheraton
Elysée Palace **16**
Hôtel Aria **5**
Hôtel de la Buffa **9**
Hôtel de la Mer **10**
Hôtel du Petit Palais **1**
Hôtel Excelsior **2**
Hôtel Gounod **4**
Hôtel Hi **6**
Hôtel Magnan **16**
Hôtel Négresco **14**
Hôtel Windsor **8**
La Pérouse **12**
Palais de la
Méditerranée **13**

ATTRACTIONS ●

Cathédrale Orthodoxe
Russe St-Nicolas à Nice **3**
Musée des Arts
Asiatiques **15**
Musée des Beau-Arts **7**
Musée International d'Art
Naïf Anatole-Jakovsky
(Museum of Naïve Art) **15**
Palais Lascaris **11**

583

In 1822, the orange crop at Nice was bad. The workers faced a lean time, so the English residents put them to work building the **promenade des Anglais ★★**, a wide boulevard fronting the bay, split by "islands" of palms and flowers and stretching for about 7km (4⅓ miles). Along the beach are rows of grand cafes, the Musée Masséna, villas, and hotels—some good, others decaying.

Crossing this boulevard in the tiniest bikinis or thongs are some of the world's most attractive bronzed bodies. They're heading for the **beach**—"on the rocks," as it's called here. Tough on tender feet, the beach is made not of sand but of pebbles (and not small ones, either). It's one of the least attractive aspects of the cosmopolitan resort city. Many bathhouses provide mattresses for a fee.

In the east, the promenade becomes **quai des Etats-Unis,** the original boulevard. It's lined with some of the best restaurants in Nice, most offering their own versions of bouillabaisse. Rising sharply on a rock is the site known as **Le Château,** where the ducs de Savoie built their castle, which was torn down in 1706. Even the foundations have disappeared in the wake of Louis XIV's destruction of what was viewed as a bulwark of Provençal resistance to his regime; all that remains are two or three stones. The hill has been turned into a garden of pines and exotic flowers. To reach the site and take in the view, board an elevator; many people take the elevator up, and then walk down. The park is open daily from 8am to dusk.

At the north end of Le Château is the famous old **graveyard** of Nice, known primarily for lavish monuments that form their own enduring art statement. It's the largest one in France. To reach it, you can take a small, canopied **Train Touristique de Nice** (✆ **06-16-39-53-51;** fax 04-93-62-85-48), which departs from the Jardin Albert-1er. The 40-minute ride passes many of Nice's most heralded sites, including place Masséna, promenade des Anglais, and quai des Etats-Unis. Departing every 30 to 60 minutes, the train operates daily 10am to 5pm (until 6pm April to May and September; until 7pm June to August). There's no service between mid-November and mid-December and during most of January. The round-trip price is 7€ for adults and 4€ for children 9 and under.

Continuing east from "the Rock" (the site of Le Château), you reach the **harbor,** where the restaurants are even cheaper and the bouillabaisse is just as good. While lingering over a drink at a sidewalk cafe, you can watch the boats depart for Corsica. The port was excavated between 1750 and 1830. Since then the port has gained an outer harbor, protected by two jetties.

The "authentic" Niçoise live in **Vieille Ville ★**, the old town, beginning at the foot of the Rock and stretching to place Masséna. Sheltered by sienna-tiled roofs, many of the Italianate facades suggest 17th-century Genoese palaces. The old town is a maze of narrow streets, teeming with local life and studded with the least expensive restaurants in Nice. Buy an onion pizza *(la pissaladière)* from a vendor. Many of the buildings are painted a faded Roman gold, and their banners are laundry flapping in the sea breezes.

While here, try to visit the **Marché aux Fleurs,** the flower market at cours Saleya. A flamboyant array of carnations, violets, jonquils, roses, and birds of paradise, it operates Tuesday to Sunday 8am to 6pm in summer, and 8am until between 2 and 4pm in winter, depending on the vendors' remaining inventory and energy level.

Nice's commercial centerpiece is **place Masséna,** with pink buildings in the 17th-century Genoese style and fountains with water jets. Stretching from the main square to the promenade is the **Jardin Albert-1er,** with an open-air terrace and a Triton Fountain. With palms and exotic flowers, it's the most relaxing oasis in town.

Cathédrale Orthodoxe Russe St-Nicolas à Nice ★ Ordered and built by none other than Tsar Nicholas II, this is the most beautiful religious edifice of the Orthodoxy outside Russia, and a perfect expression of Russian religious art abroad. It dates from the Belle Epoque, when some of the Romanovs and their entourage turned the Riviera into a stamping ground (everyone from grand dukes to ballerinas walked the promenade). The cathedral is richly ornamented and decorated with icons. You'll spot the building from afar because of its collection of ornate onion-shaped domes. During church services on Sunday morning, the building closes to tourist visits.

Av. Nicolas-II (off bd. du Tzaréwitch). ℂ **04-93-96-88-02.** Admission 3€ adults, 2€ students, free for children 12 and under. May–Sept daily 9am–noon and 2:30–6pm; Oct–Apr daily 9:30am–noon and 2:30–5pm. From the central rail station, head west along av. Thiers to bd. Gambetta, and then go north to av. Nicolas-II.

Musée des Arts Asiatiques A tribute to the sculpture and paintings of Cambodia, China, India, Tibet, and Japan, this museum opened near the airport in 1998. Inside are some of the best ceramics and devotional carvings ever found; colonials brought many of them back to France during the 19th and early 20th centuries. Of special interest are the accouterments associated with Japan's tea-drinking ceremony and several monumental representations of Buddha.

405 promenade des Anglais. ℂ **04-92-29-37-00.** Free admission. Wed–Mon 10am–5pm. Bus: 9, 10, or 23.

Musée des Beaux-Arts ★★ The collection is in the former residence of the Ukrainian Princess Kotchubey. It has an important gallery devoted to the masters of the Second Empire and the Belle Epoque, with an extensive collection of 19th-century French experts. The gallery of sculptures includes works by J. B. Carpeaux, Rude, and Rodin. Note the important collection by a dynasty of painters, the Dutch Vanloo family. One of its best-known members, Carle Vanloo, born in Nice in 1705, was Louis XV's premier *peintre.* A fine collection of 19th- and 20th-century art includes works by Ziem, Raffaelli, Boudin, Monet, Guillaumin, and Sisley.

33 av. des Baumettes. ℂ **04-92-15-28-28.** www.musee-beaux-arts-nice.org. Free admission. Tues–Sun 10am–6pm. Bus: 3, 9, 12, 22, 24, 38, 60, or 62.

Musée International d'Art Naïf Anatole-Jakovsky (Museum of Naive Art) ★ This museum is in the beautifully restored Château Ste-Hélène in the Fabron district. The museum's namesake, for years one of the world's leading art critics, once owned the collection. His 600 drawings and canvases were turned over to the institution and opened to the public. Artists from more than two dozen countries are represented by everything from primitive painting to 20th-century works.

Château St-Hélène, av. de Fabron. ℂ **04-93-71-78-33.** Free admission. Wed–Mon 10am–6pm. Bus: 9, 10, or 23; 10-min. walk. Closed Dec 25, Jan 1, and May 1.

Palais Lascaris ☺ The baroque Palais Lascaris in the city's historic core is associated with the Lascaris-Vintimille family, whose recorded history predates the year 1261. Built in the 17th century, it contains elaborately detailed ornaments. An intensive restoration by the city of Nice in 1946 brought back its original beauty, and the palace is now classified as a historic monument. The most elaborate floor, the *étage noble,* retains many of its 18th-century panels and plaster embellishments. A pharmacy, built around 1738 and complete with many of the original delftware accessories, is on the premises.

15 rue Droite. ℂ **04-93-62-72-40.** Free admission. Wed–Mon 10am–6pm. Bus: 1, 2, 3, 5, 6, 14, 16, or 17.

Nearby Attractions in Cimiez ★★

In the once-aristocratic hilltop quarter of Cimiez, 5km (3 miles) north of Nice, Queen Victoria wintered at the Hôtel Excelsior and brought half the English court with her. Founded by the Romans, who called it Cemenelum, Cimiez was the capital of the Maritime Alps province. Excavations have uncovered the ruins of a Roman town, and you can wander the dig sites. The arena was big enough to hold at least 5,000 spectators, who watched contests between gladiators and wild beasts. To reach this suburb and its attractions, take bus no. 15 or 17 from place Masséna.

Monastère de Cimiez (Cimiez Convent) ★   The convent embraces a church that owns three of the most important works by the locally prominent Bréa brothers, who painted in the late 15th century. See the carved and gilded wooden main altar-piece. In a restored part of the convent where some Franciscan friars still live, the Musée Franciscain is decorated with 17th-century frescoes. Some 350 documents and works of art from the 15th to the 18th centuries are on display, and a monk's cell has been re-created in all its severe simplicity. Also visit the 17th-century chapel. From the magnificent gardens, you'll have a panoramic view of Nice and the Baie des Anges. Matisse and Dufy are buried in the cemetery.

Place du Monastère. ✆ **04-93-81-00-04.** Free admission. Museum Mon–Fri 10am–noon and 3–6pm. Church daily 9am–6pm.

Musée Matisse ★   This museum honors the artist, who died in Nice in 1954. Seeing his nude sketches today, you'll wonder how early critics could have denounced them as "the female animal in all her shame and horror." Most of the pieces in the museum's permanent collection were painted in Nice, and many were donated by Matisse and his heirs. These include *Nude in an Armchair with a Green Plant* (1937), *Nymph in the Forest* (1935–42), and a chronologically arranged series of paintings from 1890 to 1919. The most famous of these is *Portrait of Madame Matisse* (1905), usually displayed near a portrait of the artist's wife by Marquet, painted in 1900. There's also an assemblage of designs he prepared as practice sketches for the Matisse Chapel at Vence. Also here are *The Créole Dancer* (1951), *Blue Nude IV* (1952), and around 50 dance-related sketches he did between 1930 and 1931. The artist's last work, *Flowers and Fruit* (1953), is made of cut-out gouache.

In the Villa des Arènes-de-Cimiez, 164 av. des Arènes-de-Cimiez. ✆ **04-93-81-08-08.** www.musee-matisse.nice.org. Free admission. Wed–Mon 10am–6pm. Closed Jan 1, May 1, and Dec 25.

Musée National Message Biblique Marc Chagall ★★   In the hills of Cimiez, this handsome museum, surrounded by pools and a garden, is devoted to Marc Chagall's treatment of biblical themes. Born in Russia in 1887, Chagall became a French citizen in 1937. The artist and his wife donated the works—the most important Chagall collection ever assembled—to France in 1966 and 1972. On display are 450 of his oils, gouaches, drawings, pastels, lithographs, sculptures, and ceramics; a mosaic; three stained-glass windows; and a tapestry. Chagall decorated a concert room with brilliantly hued stained-glass windows. Temporary exhibits each summer feature great periods and artists of all times.

Av. du Dr.-Ménard. ✆ **04-93-53-87-20.** Admission 9.50€ adults, 7.50€ students, free for children 17 and under. May–Oct Wed–Mon 10am–6pm; Nov–June Wed–Mon 10am–5pm.

Outdoor Pursuits

BEACHES   Along Nice's seafront, beaches extend uninterrupted for more than 7km (4⅓ miles), going from the edge of Vieux-Port (the old port) to the international airport, with most of the best bathing spots subdivided into public beaches and private concessionaires. None has sand; they're covered with gravel (often the size of golf balls). The rocks are smooth but can be mettlesome to people with poor balance or tender feet. Tucked between the seven public beaches are the private beaches of hotels such as the Beau Rivage. Most of the public beaches consist of two sections: a free area and one where you can rent chaise longues, mattresses, and parasols, use changing rooms, and take freshwater showers. For that, you'll pay 10€ to 12€ for a half-day, 12€ to 20€ for a full day. Nude sunbathing is prohibited, but toplessness is common. Take bus no. 9, 10, 12, or 23 to get to the beach.

SCUBA DIVING   The best outfit is the **Centre International de Plongée (CIP) de Nice,** 14 quai des Dock (© **04-93-89-42-44**). A *baptême* (dive for first-timers) costs 45€. A two-tank dive for experienced divers, equipment included, is 140€; appropriate diver's certification is required.

SPA   Billing itself as the first holistic spa in France, **Hip** at 2 rue de Longchamp (© **04-93-16-00-20**), is a sight both for the eye and the body, with its egg-shaped treatment beds upholstered in a wet-look vinyl. Its haircutting salons are constructed around sculpted cement boulders. After a day spent here, one woman customer claimed, "I emerged a new person." We can't guarantee that, however.

Shopping

You may want to begin with a stroll through the streets and alleys of Nice's historic core. The densest concentrations of boutiques are along **rue Masséna, place Magenta, avenue Jean-Médecin, rue de Verdun, rue Paradis,** and on the streets around them. A shop of note is **Gigi,** 10 rue de la Liberté (© **04-93-87-81-78**), which sells sophisticated clothing for women.

Opened in 1949 by Joseph Fuchs, the grandfather of the present English-speaking owners, the **Confiserie Florian du Vieux-Nice,** 14 quai Papacino (© **04-93-55-43-50**), is near the Old Port. The specialty is glazed fruit crystallized in sugar or artfully arranged into chocolates. Look for exotic jams (rose-petal preserves, mandarin marmalade) and the free recipe leaflet, as well as candied violets, verbena leaves, and rosebuds. One of the oldest chocolatiers in Nice, **Confiserie Auer,** 7 rue St-François-de-Paule, near the opera house (© **04-93-85-77-98**), was established in 1820. Since then, few of the original decorative accessories have changed. The shop specializes in chocolates, candies, and fruits confits, the signature Provençal goodies.

Façonnable, 7–9 rue Paradis (© **04-93-87-88-80**), is the original site of a chain with several hundred branches around the world. This is one of the largest, with a wide range of men's suits, raincoats, overcoats, sportswear, and jeans. The look is youthful and conservatively stylish, for relatively slim French bodies. An outlet for women's clothing and sportswear (Façonnable Sport) and the main line of Façonnable women's wear (Façonnable Femmes) lies immediately across the street at 10 rue Paradis (© **04-93-88-06-97**).

If you're thinking of indulging in a Provençale *pique-nique,* **Nicola Alziari,** 318 bd. Madeleine (© **04-93-44-45-12**), will provide everything from olives, anchovies, and pistous to aiolis and tapenades. It's one of Nice's oldest purveyors of olive oil, with a house brand that comes in two strengths: a light version that aficionados claim is vaguely perfumed with Provence, and a stronger version suited to the earthy flavors and robust ingredients of a Provençal winter. Also for sale are objects crafted from olive wood.

For arts and crafts, head to the **Atelier Contre-Jour,** 3 rue du Pont Vieux (© **04-93-80-20-50**). It carries painted-wood handicrafts, including picture frames; painted furniture; and silk lampshades, as well as decorative posters showing the best of their painted work of the past 25 years. **Plat Jérôme,** 34 rue Centrale (© **04-93-62-17-09**), stocks varnished pottery. Many artists' studios and galleries are on side streets near the cathedral in the old town.

La Couqueto, 8 rue St-François-de-Paule (© **04-93-80-90-30**), sells *santons,* the traditional Provençal figurines. The best selection of Provençal fabrics is at **Le Chandelier,** 7 rue de la Boucherie (© **04-93-85-85-19**), where you'll see designs by two of the region's best-known producers of cloth, Les Olivades and Valdrôme.

Nice is also known for its **street markets.** In addition to the flower market, **Marché aux Fleurs** (see "Exploring the City," above), the main flea market, **Marché à la Brocante,** also at cours Saleya, takes place Monday 8am to 5pm. Another flea market on the port, **Les Puces de Nice,** place Robilante, is open Tuesday to Saturday 9am to 6pm.

Where to Stay
VERY EXPENSIVE

Hôtel Negresco ★★★   The Negresco, on the seafront in the heart of Nice, is one of the Riviera's superglamorous hotels. The Victorian wedding-cake hotel is named after its founder, Henry Negresco, a Romanian who died a pauper in Paris in 1920. The country's châteaux inspired both the interior and the exterior, with its mansard roof and domed tower. The hotel's decorators scoured Europe to gather antiques, tapestries, and art. Some of the accommodations, such as the Coco Chanel room, are outfitted in homage to the personalities who stayed here. Others are modeled on literary or musical themes, such as *La Traviata*. Suites and public areas include the Louis XIV salon, reminiscent of the Sun King, and the Napoleon III suite. The most expensive rooms with balconies face the Mediterranean and the private beach. The staff wears 18th-century costumes.

37 promenade des Anglais, Nice Cedex 06007. © **04-93-16-64-00.** Fax 04-93-88-35-68. www.hotel-negresco-nice.com. 146 units. 290€–590€ double; from 680€ suite. AE, DC, MC, V. Free parking. **Amenities:** 2 restaurants; bar; babysitting; exercise room; massage; room service. *In room:* A/C, TV, hair dryer, Internet (free), minibar.

Palais de la Méditerranée ★★★   Long hailed as a "Queen of the Nice Riviera," this glittering seaside palace on the promenade des Anglais reigned from 1929 to 1978 and then was shuttered. In its heyday, the hotel's theater stage hosted everyone from Maurice Chevalier to American chanteuse Josephine Baker. Its Art Deco facade was left intact after a restoration, but the interior of this place was gutted and turned into a marble pile with glamorous touches such as plush hallways and such modern amenities as a heated outdoor swimming pool. Monumental chandeliers and stained-glass windows, among other architectural features, were spared in the renovations. Bedrooms, midsize to grandly spacious, are outfitted in a tasteful modern decor. Ninety of the bedrooms also open onto sea views. Behind the facade, the hotel's casino has been restored to its Art Deco glamour.

13–15 promenade des Anglais, Nice 06011. ✆ **04-92-14-77-00.** Fax 04-92-14-77-14. www.lepalaisdela
mediterranee.com. 188 units. 285€–570€ double; from 665€–1,840€ suite. AE, DC, MC, V. **Amenities:**
Restaurant; bar; casino; exercise room; 2 pools (indoor and outdoor); room service; solarium; Turkish
bath; watersports equipment/rentals. *In room:* A/C, TV, hair dryer, minibar, Wi-Fi (free).

EXPENSIVE

Four Points by Sheraton Elysée Palace ★★   Views sweep out over the sea

from most of the rooms of this hotel. Decor is conservative and contemporary, and the
in-room amenities are typical. The seafront rooms, of course, are the more desirable.
Rooms on the fifth, sixth, and seventh floors overlook the Mediterranean. Bathrooms
are clad in marble with bidets, but you have to request robes and hair dryers from
reception. The hotel has its own private beach a short walk from its premises.

59 promenade des Anglais, 06005 Nice. ✆ **04-93-97-90-90.** Fax 04-93-44-50-40. www.elyseepalace.
com. 143 units. 125€–285€ double; 265€–405€ suite. AE, DC, MC, V. Parking 17€. Bus: 9, 10, or 12. **Amenities:** Restaurant; bar; babysitting; pool; room service. *In room:* A/C, TV, hair dryer, minibar, Wi-Fi (free).

Hôtel Hi ★ 👔👔   An architectural and decorative "statement," this hotel occupies a

former boardinghouse that dates to the 1930s. Spearheaded by Matali Crasset, a
one-time colleague of Philippe Starck, a team of architects and engineers created
one of the most aggressively avant-garde hotels in the south of France. The angular
seven-story hotel opened in 2003. Each of the nine high-tech room "concepts" is
different. They range from white-on-white to birch-wood veneer and acid green to
cool violet and gray. The unconventional layouts may include a bathtub tucked
behind a screen of potted plants or elevated to a position of theatrical prominence.
Electronic gizmos include state-of-the-art CD systems. The Japanese word *hi*
describes the black mottling on the back of an ornamental carp, which has traditionally been associated with good luck.

3 av. des Fleurs, Nice 06000. ✆ **04-97-07-26-26.** Fax 04-97-07-26-27. www.hi-hotel.net. 38 units.
209€–369€ double; from 440€ suite. AE, DC, MC, V. Parking 24€. Bus: 23. **Amenities:** Organic restaurant; 24-hr. bar and snack bar; rooftop swimming pool; Turkish bath. *In room:* A/C, TV, Wi-Fi (free).

La Pérouse ★★ 👔   Once a prison, La Pérouse has been reconstructed and is

now a unique Riviera hotel. Set on a cliff, it's built right in the gardens of an ancient
château-fort. No hotel affords a better view over both the old city and the Baie des
Anges. In fact, many people stay here just for the view. The hotel resembles an old
Provençal home, with low ceilings, white walls, and antique furnishings. The lovely,
spacious rooms are beautifully furnished, often with Provençal fabrics. Most have
loggias overlooking the bay. The bathrooms are large, clad in Boticino marble, and
hold tubs and showers.

11 quai Rauba-Capéu, Nice 06300. ✆ **04-93-62-34-63.** Fax 04-93-62-59-41. www.hotel-la-perouse.
com. 65 units. 270€–750€ double; 650€–1,500€ suite. AE, DC, MC, V. Parking 19€. **Amenities:** Restaurant (mid-May to mid-Sept); bar; babysitting; exercise room; Jacuzzi; outdoor pool; room service;
sauna. *In room:* A/C, TV, hair dryer, minibar, Wi-Fi (free).

MODERATE

Hôtel du Petit Palais   This whimsical hotel occupies a mansion built around
1890; in the 1970s it was the home of the actor and writer Sacha Guitry (a name
that's instantly recognized in millions of French households). It lies about a 10-min-
ute drive from the city center in the Carabacel district near the Musée Chagall.
Many of the Art Deco and Italianate furnishings and Florentine moldings and friezes
remain intact. The preferred rooms, and the most expensive, have balconies that

afford sea views during the day and sunset views at dusk. Bathrooms are small but efficient, and each has a shower and tub. Breakfast is served in a small but pretty salon.

17 av. Emile-Bieckert, Nice 06000. © **04-93-62-19-11.** Fax 04-93-62-53-60. www.petitpalaisnice.com. 25 units. 90€–170€ double. AE, DC, MC, V. Parking 10€. **Amenities:** Bar; babysitting; room service. *In room:* A/C, hair dryer, minibar, Wi-Fi (free).

Hôtel Gounod ★ A winning choice in the city center, this hotel is a 5-minute walk from the sea. It was built around 1910 in a neighborhood where the street names honor composers. Ornate balconies, a domed roof, and an elaborate canopy of wrought iron and glass embellish the Gounod. The attractive lobby and adjoining lounge are festive and stylish, with old prints, copper flowerpots, and antiques. The high-ceilinged guest rooms are quiet; most overlook the gardens of private homes. The tiled bathrooms are small but efficiently organized, mainly with shower units. Suites have safes. Guests have free unlimited use of the pool and Jacuzzi at the Hôtel Splendid, next door.

3 rue Gounod, Nice 06000. © **04-93-16-42-00.** Fax 04-93-88-23-84. www.gounod-nice.com. 45 units. 110€–160€ double; 150€–260€ suite. AE, DC, MC, V. Parking 17€. Closed Nov 20–Dec 20. Bus: 98. **Amenities:** Babysitting; Internet (free); Jacuzzi; outdoor pool; room service; spa. *In room:* A/C, TV, hair dryer, minibar.

Hôtel Windsor 🍴 One of the most arts-conscious hotels in Provence is in a *maison bourgeoise* built by disciples of Gustav Eiffel in 1895. It's near the Negresco and the promenade des Anglais. Each unit is a unique decorative statement by a different artist. The heir and scion of the longtime owners, the Redolfi family, commissioned manifestations of his mystical and mythical visions after years of traveling through Asia, Africa, and South America. In the "Ben" room, for example, a Provençal artist of the same name painted verses of his own poetry, in tones of blue, orange, yellow, and green, on a white background. You can take your chances or select a room based on the photos on the hotel website. Most units have a combination tub/shower. The fifth floor holds the health club, steam room, and sauna. The garden contains scores of tropical and exotic plants and the recorded sounds of birds singing in the jungles of the Amazon.

11 rue Dalpozzo, Nice 06000. © **04-93-88-59-35.** Fax 04-93-88-94-57. www.hotelwindsornice.com. 54 units. 90€–175€ double. MC, V. Parking 10€. Bus: 9, 10, or 22. **Amenities:** Restaurant; bar; babysitting; health club; outdoor pool; room service; sauna; smoke-free rooms. *In room:* A/C, TV, hair dryer, minibar.

INEXPENSIVE

Flots d'Azur This three-story 19th-century villa is next to the sea and a short walk from the more elaborate and costlier promenade hotels. The rooms vary in size and decor; all have good views and sea breezes. Each unit comes with a tiled and immaculately kept bathroom. Double-glazed windows cut down on noise. There's a small sitting room and sun terrace in front, where a continental breakfast is served.

101 promenade des Anglais, Nice 06000. © **04-93-86-51-25.** Fax 04-93-97-22-07. www.flotsdazur.com. 20 units. 57€–117€ double. MC, V. Free parking. Bus: 23. Closed 10 days in Dec. **Amenities:** Wi-Fi (free). *In room:* A/C, TV, hair dryer, minibar.

Hôtel Aria The grandiose facade of this stately hotel contrasts distinctly with the simple interior. A 5-minute walk from the railway station, it's unpretentious and charges relatively reasonable rates. Guest rooms are outfitted in cozy Provençal style, with wrought iron and wooden furniture. After a radical restoration, it earned an upgrade to government-rated three-star status. It stands in a small park near the place Mozart, in a neighborhood known as the musicians' quarter (Berlioz, Wagner, Paganini, and Verdi once lived nearby).

15 av. Auber. © **04-93-88-30-69.** Fax 04-93-88-11-35. www.aria-nice.com. 30 units. 59€–124€ double; 69€–150€ suite. AE, DC, MC, V. Parking 13€ in lot across street. Bus: 23. **Amenities:** Breakfast room. *In room:* A/C, TV, hair dryer, minibar, Wi-Fi (2€ per 30 min.).

Hôtel de la Buffa ★ 🍴 Lying only a few steps from the promenade des Anglais and the pebbly beaches, this centrally located hotel combines charm with value. Decorated with a certain flair and style, it offers a prevailing family atmosphere. Rooms are tastefully and comfortably furnished, with the larger accommodations suitable for a family of up to four persons. If you wish, a safe and a refrigerator can be installed in your room. All the midsize bathrooms contain showers. Those units facing the streets have double-glazing on their windows. If you wish to partake of discounted meals, an arrangement can be made for you to take half or full board at the adjoining restaurant, which is under different management.

56 rue de la Buffa, Nice 06000. © **04-93-88-77-35.** Fax 04-93-88-83-39. www.hotel-buffa.com. 13 units. 58€–73€ double; 76€–103€ quad. AE, DC, V. Bus: 23. Closed Nov. **Amenities:** Wi-Fi (free). *In room:* A/C, TV, fridge in some, hair dryer in some.

Hôtel de la Mer 🍴 In the center of Old Nice, this ocher-colored government-rated two-star hotel was built around 1910 and transformed into a hotel in 1947. Pierre Da Cruz, the owner, welcomes guests with personal charm. Most rooms are of good size, and all have small bathrooms with showers. Some contain minibars. It's a 2-minute walk to the promenade des Anglais and the seafront. Breakfast is served in one of the public salons or in your room.

4 place Masséna, Nice 06000. © **04-93-92-09-10.** Fax 04-93-85-00-64. www.hoteldelamernice.com. 12 units. 65€–95€ double. AE, MC, V. Parking 15€ in nearby lot. Bus: 3, 9, 10, or 12. **Amenities:** Room service. *In room:* A/C, TV, Wi-Fi (free).

Hôtel Excelsior The Excelsior's ornate corbels and stone pediments rise grandly a few steps from the railway station. This much-renovated 19th-century hotel has modern decor, most of it from the mid-1990s, and rooms outfitted in tones of Provençal ocher, blue, and brown that have seen a lot of wear but are still comfortable. They have small, shower-only bathrooms. Furnishings, for the most part, are functional and conservative. There's a garden, and the beach is a 20-minute walk through the residential and commercial heart of Nice.

19 av. Durante, Nice 06000. © **04-93-88-18-05.** Fax 04-93-88-38-69. www.excelsiornice.com. 42 units. 60€–200€ double. AE, DC, MC, V. Bus: 99. *In room:* A/C, TV, hair dryer, Wi-Fi (4€ per hr.).

Hôtel Magnan This well-run hotel was built around 1945 and has been renovated frequently. It's a 10-minute bus ride from the heart of town but only a minute or so from the promenade des Anglais and the bay. Many of the simply furnished rooms have balconies facing the sea. The look is a bit functional, but for Nice this is a good price, especially considering the comfortable beds. The bathrooms are small, each with a shower stall. Breakfast can be served in your room.

1 av. de la Californie, Nice 06200. © **04-93-86-76-00.** Fax 04-93-44-48-31. www.hotelmagnan-nice.com. 25 units. 48€–90€ double. AE, MC, V. Bus: 23. *In room:* TV, minibar, Wi-Fi (free).

Villa Saint-Exupéry 🍴 This former Carmelite monastery has been completely renovated and turned into a first-rate youth hostel. In winter it's a student residence, but in the busy summer months it turns into a hotel catering to backpackers, sea-soned travelers on a budget, artists, musicians, and, of course, students. The restored and comfort-filled villa offers good though very standard hotel rooms (some with kitchenette), as well as some dormitory accommodations at youth hostel-level tariffs. Furnishings are modern and selected more for comfort than style. Echoing its past life, the former chapel preserved its open stage and stained-glass windows. Guests are also welcome to use a fully equipped kitchen.

22 av. Gravier, Nice 06100. (℃) **04-93-84-42-83.** Fax 04-92-09-82-94. www.vsaint.com. 60 units. 35€–45€ per person in a single or twin-bedded room; 16€–30€ per person for dormitory bed. Rates include continental breakfast. MC, V. Free parking. **Amenities:** Bar; cooking facilities; free Internet access in lounge-area computers. *In room:* Kitchenettes (in some).

Where to Dine
VERY EXPENSIVE
Le Chantecler ★★★ TRADITIONAL/MODERN FRENCH   This is Nice's most prestigious and best restaurant. In 1989, a redecoration sheathed its walls with panels removed from a château in Pouilly-Fuissé; a Regency-style salon was installed for before- or after-dinner drinks; and a collection of 16th-century paintings, exe-cuted on leather backgrounds in the Belgian town of Malines, was imported. A much-respected chef, Jean-Denis Rieubland, revised the menu to include the most sophisticated and creative dishes in Nice. They change almost weekly but may include turbot filet served with purée of broad beans, sun-dried tomatoes, and asparagus; roasted suckling lamb served with beignets of fresh vegetables and ricotta-stuffed ravioli; and a melt-in-your-mouth fantasy of marbled hot chocolate drenched in almond-flavored cream sauce.

In the Hôtel Negresco, 37 promenade des Anglais. (℃) **04-93-16-64-00.** Reservations required. Main courses 48€–80€; fixed-price lunch 50€–130€, dinner 90€–130€. AE, MC, V. Wed–Sun 12:30–1:45pm and 7:30–10pm. Closed Jan–Feb 7. Bus: 8, 9, 10, or 11.

EXPENSIVE
La Merenda ★★ 🍴 NIÇOISE   Because there's no phone, you have to go by this place twice—once to make a reservation and once to dine—but it's worth the effort. Forsaking his chef's crown at Le Chantecler (see above), Dominique Le Stanc opened this tiny bistro serving sublime cuisine. Though he was born in Alsace, his heart and soul belong to the Mediterranean, the land of black truffles, wild morels, sea bass, and asparagus. His food is a lullaby of gastronomic unity, with texture, crunch, richness, and balance. Le Stanc never knows what he's going to serve until he goes to the market. Look for specials on a chalkboard. Perhaps you'll find stuffed cabbage, fried zucchini flowers, or oxtail flavored with fresh oranges. Lamb from the Sisteron is cooked until it practically falls from the bone. Raw artichokes are paired with a salad of mâche. Service is discreet and personable.

4 rue Raoul Bosio. No phone. Reservations required. Main courses 38€–55€. No credit cards. Mon–Fri seatings at 7:15 and 9:15pm. Closed Feb 5–13 and Aug 1–15. Bus: 8.

MODERATE
Brasserie Flo TRADITIONAL FRENCH   This is the town's most bustling bras-serie. In 1991, the Jean-Paul Bucher group, a French chain noted for its skill at restoring historic brasseries, bought the premises of a faded early-1900s restaurant near place Masséna and injected it with new life. The original frescoes cover the

high ceilings. The place (which is affiliated with Brasserie Flo in Paris) is brisk, stylish, reasonably priced, and fun. Menu items include an array of grilled fish, Alsatian-style choucroute, steak with brandied pepper sauce, and fresh oysters and shellfish.

2-4 rue Sacha-Guitry. © **04-93-13-38-38.** Reservations recommended. Main courses 18€–40€; fixed-price menu 23€–38€. AE, DC, MC, V. Daily noon–2:30pm and 7–11pm. Bus: 1, 2, or 5.

L'Ane Rouge ★★ PROVENÇAL   Facing the old port and occupying an antique building whose owners have carefully retained its ceiling beams and stone walls, this is one of the city's best-known seafood restaurants. In the two modern yet cozy dining rooms, you can enjoy traditional specialties such as bouillabaisse, *bourride* (stew), filet of John Dory with roulades of stuffed lettuce leaves, mussels stuffed with bread crumbs and herbs, and salmon in wine sauce with spinach. Service is commendable.

7 quai des Deux-Emmanuels. © **04-93-89-49-63.** www.anerougenice.com. Reservations required. Main courses 26€–78€; fixed-price dinner 35€–78€. AE, DC, MC, V. Fri–Tues noon–2pm and Thurs–Tues 7–10:30pm. Closed Feb. Bus: 30.

Le Safari ★ PROVENÇAL/NIÇOISE   The decor couldn't be simpler: a black ceiling, white walls, and an old-fashioned terra-cotta floor. The youthful staff is relaxed, sometimes in jeans, and always alert to the latest fashion. Many diners prefer the terrace overlooking the Marché aux Fleurs, but all appreciate the reasonably priced meals that appear in generous portions. Menu items include a pungent *bagna cauda,* which calls for diners to immerse vegetables in a sizzling brew of hot oil and anchovy paste; grilled peppers bathed in olive oil; daube (stew) of beef; fresh pasta with basil; and an omelet with *blettes* (tough but flavorful greens). The unfortunately named *merda de can* (dog poop) is gnocchi stuffed with spinach and is a lot more appetizing than it sounds.

1 cours Saleya. © **04-93-80-18-44.** Reservations recommended. Main courses 18€–30€. AE, DC, MC, V. Daily noon–11pm. Bus: 1.

INEXPENSIVE

La Petite Maison ★★ 📖 FRENCH/PROVENÇAL   This bustling and noisy tavern in the heart of the old town resides in a 19th-century grocery store. Locals guard the address, hoping it won't be mobbed by tourists. Regulars include Elton John and his longtime companion, who live in a villa a few miles away. It's usually packed with diners wanting to taste the array of Niçoise cuisine, the authenticity of which is virtually unequaled in the city. Try the town's finest zucchini blossom fritters and finish with homemade ice cream flavored with pine nuts and candied orange blossoms. In between, you may enjoy a succulent array of grilled fish, pastas, and steaks, all prepared with the right Mediterranean touches and just enough garlic.

11 rue St.-Francoise de Paule. © **04-93-92-59-59.** www.lapetitemaison-nice.com. Reservations recommended. Main courses 12€–35€. AE, V. Mon–Sat noon–2:30pm and 7:30pm–midnight.

La Zucca Magica ★ 📖 VEGETARIAN/ITALIAN   The chef at this popular harborside restaurant has been named the best Italian chef in Nice. That this honor should go to a vegetarian restaurant was the most startling part of the news. Chef Marco, who opened his restaurant in 1997 after cooking for many years in Rome, certainly has a fine pedigree—he's a relative of Luciano Pavarotti. He serves refined cuisine at reasonable prices, using recipes from Italy's Piedmont region and updating them with no meat or fish. The red-and-green decor (the colors of Italy) will put you in the mood for the creative cuisine. You'll have to trust Marco, though, because everyone is served the same meal. You can count on savory cuisine using lots of herbs, Italian cheeses, beans, and pasta. Lasagna is a specialty.

4 bis quai Papacino. © **04-93-56-25-27.** Reservations recommended. Fixed-price lunch 17€, dinner 29€. No credit cards. Tues–Sat 12:30–2pm and 7–9:30pm.

Nice After Dark

Nice has some of the most active nightlife along the Riviera. Evenings usually begin at a cafe. At kiosks around town you can pick up a copy of *La Semaine des Spectacles,* which outlines the week's diversions.

The major cultural center on the Riviera is the **Opéra de Nice,** 4 rue St-François-de-Paule (© **04-92-17-40-00**), built in 1885 by Charles Garnier, fabled architect of the Paris Opéra. It presents a full repertoire, with emphasis on serious, often large-scale operas. In one season you might see *Tosca, Les Contes de Hoffmann,* Verdi's *Macbeth,* Beethoven's *Fidelio,* and *Carmen,* as well as a *saison symphonique,* dominated by the Orchestre Philharmonique de Nice. The opera hall is also the major venue for concerts and recitals. Tickets are available (to concerts, recitals, and full-blown operas) a day or two before any performance. You can show up at the box office (Mon–Sat 10am–5:30pm; Sun 10am–6pm), or buy tickets in advance with a major credit card by phoning © **04-92-17-40-47.** Tickets run from 10€ for nose-bleed seats (and we mean it) to 100€ for front-and-center seats on opening night.

Cabaret du Casino Ruhl, in the Casino Ruhl, 1 promenade des Anglais (© **04-97-03-12-22**), is Nice's answer to the more ostentatious glitter of Monte Carlo and Las Vegas. It includes just enough flesh to titillate; lots of spangles, feathers, and sequins; a medley of cross-cultural jokes and nostalgia for the old days of French *chanson;* and an acrobat or juggler. The 22€ cover includes one drink; dinner and the show, complete with a bottle of wine per person, costs 62€. Shows begin only Friday and Saturday at 10:15pm. No jeans or sneakers.

The casino contains an area exclusively for slot machines, open daily from noon to 4am; entrance is free. A more formal gaming room (jacket required, but not a tie) offers blackjack, baccarat, and chemin de fer. Presentation of a government-issued photo ID, preferably a passport, is required. It's open Sunday to Thursday 10pm to 4am, or Friday and Saturday 5pm to 5am.

Le Relais, in the Hôtel Negresco, 37 promenade des Anglais (© **04-93-16-64-00**), is the most beautiful museum-quality bar in Nice, with an oxblood-red ceiling, Oriental carpets, English paneling, Italianate chairs, and tapestries. It was once a haunt of the actress Lillie Langtry. With its piano music and white-jacketed waiters, the bar still attracts a chic crowd.

At many bars in the old town, Americans will feel right at home. They include **Chez Wayne's,** 15 rue de la Préfecture (© **04-93-13-46-99**). Another adjacent sports bar with roughly equivalent decor, clientele, and sports priorities is **Le Master Home Bar,** 11 rue de la Prefecture (© **04-95-85-51-64**). Both occasionally sponsor live bands and offer the option of a rollicking good time. When live music is presented at either of these bars, it tends to begin around 9pm. **La Bodeguita,** 14 rue Chavin (© **04-93-92-67-24**), serves tapas, wine by the glass, and lots of beer, and both re-create some of the sun-and-salsa motifs of nightlife at its best in the Caribbean and South America.

Devoted to contemporary electronic jazz, **Smarties,** 10 rue Defly (© **04-93-62-30-75**), is a cool lounge with the hottest DJs in town on Tuesday nights, when the club is the place to be in Nice. It is closed on Saturday and during all of August. **Perle,** 16 quai Lunel (© **04-93-26-54-79**), draws a choice set of fashionistas mostly in their 20s to its elegant pink-and-white precincts. It doesn't get going until after midnight. One of the latest clubs to open is **Guest,** 5 quai des Deux Emmanuel (© **04-93-56-83-83**), attracting a crowd in their early 20s to late 30s to its setting of romantic lighting and deep banquettes.

GAY NIGHTLIFE

A trend-conscious gay bar in Nice is **Le Klub,** 6 rue Halevy (© **04-95-16-27-56;** www.leklub.net), near the Casino Ruhl. Entrance costs 10€ and includes one drink. Expect a hard-dancing, high-energy crowd of mostly gay men, many of them under 35, as well as lots of straight people who come for the nonstop barrage of house music and the focus on dancing.

VILLEFRANCHE-SUR-MER ★

935km (581 miles) S of Paris; 6.5km (4 miles) E of Nice

According to legend, Hercules opened his arms, and Villefranche was born. It sits on a big blue bay that looks like a gigantic bowl, large enough to attract U.S. Sixth Fleet cruisers and destroyers. Quietly slumbering otherwise, Villefranche transforms into an exciting Mediterranean port when the fleet is in. About 7km (4⅓ miles) east of Nice, it's the first town you reach along the Lower Corniche.

Essentials

GETTING THERE   **Trains** arrive from most towns on the Côte d'Azur, especially Nice (every 45 min.), but most visitors **drive** via the Corniche Inférieure (Lower Corniche). For rail information and schedules, call © **36-35,** or visit www.voyages-sncf.com. Ligne d'Azur (© **08-10-06-10-06**) maintains service at 15-minute intervals aboard line no. 100 from Nice and from Monte Carlo into Villefranche. One-way bus transit from Nice costs 1€; from Monaco the cost is also 1€. Buses deposit their passengers in the heart of town, directly opposite the tourist information office.

VISITOR INFORMATION   The **Office de Tourisme** is on Jardin François-Binon (© **04-93-01-73-68;** fax 04-93-76-63-65; www.villefranche-sur-mer.com).

Exploring the Town

The vaulted **rue Obscure** is one of the strangest streets in France. In spirit it belongs more to a North African casbah than to a European port. People live in tiny houses, and occasionally there's an open space, allowing for a courtyard. To get there, take rue de l'Eglise.

Once popular with such writers as Katherine Mansfield and Aldous Huxley, the town is still a haven for artists, many of whom take over the little houses that climb the hillside. More recent arrivals who've bought homes in the area are Tina Turner and U2's Bono.

One artist who came to Villefranche left a memorial: Jean Cocteau, the painter, writer, filmmaker, and well-respected dilettante, spent a year (1956–57) painting frescoes on the 14th-century walls of the Romanesque **Chapelle St-Pierre,** quai

Courbet (☎ **04-93-76-90-70**). He presented it to "the fishermen of Villefranche in homage to the Prince of Apostles, the patron of fishermen." One panel pays tribute to the Gypsies of the Stes-Maries-de-la-Mer. In the apse is a depiction of the miracle of St. Peter walking on the water, not knowing that an angel supports him. Villefranche's women, in their regional costumes, are honored on the left side of the narthex. Admission is 2.50€, but free for ages 15 and under. In summer the attraction is open daily 10am to noon and 3 to 7pm; off season hours are daily 10am to noon and 2 to 6pm.

Where to Stay

Hôtel Welcome ★   This is as good as it gets in Villefranche. The Welcome was a favorite of author and filmmaker Jean Cocteau. In the six-story villa hotel, with shutters and balconies, everything has been modernized and extensively renovated. Try for a fifth-floor room overlooking the water. All the midsize to spacious rooms are comfortably furnished, each with a small bathroom, and most with a combination tub/shower. The sidewalk cafe is the focal point of town life. The on-site wine bar and the restaurant, St-Pierre, have open fireplaces and fruitwood furniture.

1 quai Amiral-Courbet, Villefranche-sur-Mer 06231. ☎ **04-93-76-27-62.** Fax 04-93-76-27-66. www. welcomehotel.com. 36 units. 98€–228€ double; 214€–380€ suite. AE, DC, MC, V. Parking 25€. **Amenities:** Bar; babysitting; room service. In room: A/C, TV, hair dryer, minibar, Wi-Fi (free).

Where to Dine

La Mère Germaine FRENCH/SEAFOOD   This is the best of the string of restaurants on the port. Plan to relax over lunch while watching fishermen repair their nets. Mère Germaine opened the place in the 1930s, and these days a descendant, Remy Blouin, handles the cuisine, producing bouillabaisse celebrated across the Riviera. We recommend grilled sea bass with fennel, sole Tante Marie (stuffed with mushroom purée), lobster ravioli with shellfish sauce, and beef filet with garlic and seasonal vegetables. Perfectly roasted *carré d'agneau* (lamb) is prepared for two.

Quai Courbet. ☎ **04-93-01-71-39.** Reservations recommended. Main courses 35€–48€; fixed-price menu 41€. AE, DC, MC, V. Daily noon–2:30pm and 7–10:30pm. Closed mid-Nov to Christmas.

ST-JEAN-CAP-FERRAT ★★

939km (583 miles) S of Paris; 9.5km (6 miles) E of Nice

Of all the oases along the Côte d'Azur, no other place has the snob appeal of Cap-Ferrat. It's a 15km (9⅓-mile) promontory sprinkled with luxurious villas and outlined by sheltered bays, beaches, and coves. The vegetation is lush. In the port of St-Jean, the harbor accommodates yachts and fishing boats.

Essentials

GETTING THERE   Most visitors drive or take a **bus** or **taxi** from the rail station at nearby Beaulieu. Buses from the station at Beaulieu depart hourly for Cap-Ferrat; the one-way fare is 1€. There's also bus service from Nice. For bus information and schedules, call ☎ **08-10-06-10-06.** By **car** from Nice, take N7 east.

VISITOR INFORMATION   The **Office de Tourisme** is on 59 av. Denis-Séméria (☎ **04-93-76-08-90;** fax 04-93-76-16-67; www.ville-saint-jean-cap-ferrat.fr).

Seeing the Sights

One way to enjoy the scenery here is to wander on some of the public paths. The most scenic goes from **Plage de Paloma** to **Pointe St-Hospice,** where a panoramic view of the Riviera landscape unfolds. You can also wander around the hamlet **St-Jean,** a colorful fishing village with bars, bistros, and inns.

Everyone tries to visit the **Villa Mauresque,** avenue Somerset-Maugham, but it's closed to the public. Near the cape, it's where Maugham spent his final years. When tourists tried to visit him, he proclaimed that he wasn't one of the local sights.

Villa Ephrussi de Rothschild ★★ Built by Baronne Ephrussi de Rothschild, this is one of the Côte d'Azur's legendary villas. Born a Rothschild, the baronne married a Hungarian banker and friend of her father, about whom even the museum's curator knows little. She died in 1934, leaving the Italianate building and its gardens to the Institut de France on behalf of the Académie des Beaux-Arts. The museum preserves the wealth of her collection: 18th-century furniture; Tiepolo ceilings; Savonnerie carpets; screens and panels from the Far East; tapestries from Gobelin, Aubusson, and Beauvais; Fragonard drawings; canvases by Boucher; Sèvres porcelain; and more. The sprawling gardens contain fragments of statuary from churches, monasteries, and palaces. An entire section is planted with cacti.

1 av. de Rothschild. ✆ **04-93-01-45-90.** www.villa-ephrussi.com. Admission 10€ adults, 7.50€ students and children 7–18. Feb–June and Sept–Oct daily 10am–6pm; July–Aug daily 10am–7pm; Nov–Jan Mon–Fri 2–6pm, Sat–Sun 10am–6pm.

Hitting the Beach

The town's most visible and popular beaches are **Plage Passable,** on the northeastern "neck" of the Cap-Ferrat peninsula, close to where it connects to the French mainland; and **Plage de Paloma,** near the peninsula's southernmost tip, overlooked by the Chapelle St-Hospice. Neither is sandy (the beaches are made of pebbles and gravel), but they do have snack bars, souvenir stands, and restaurants. Most hotel guests opt to remain around their pools, and indeed, many hotels don't have beaches. A noteworthy exception is the Grand Hôtel du Cap-Ferrat (see below), which acquired a rocky beach in the early 1900s.

Where to Stay

EXPENSIVE

Grand Hôtel du Cap-Ferrat ★★★ One of the best features of this early-1900s palace is its location: at the tip of the peninsula in the midst of a 5.6-hectare (14-acre) garden of semitropical trees and manicured lawns. It has been the retreat of the international elite since 1908 and occupies the same celestial status as La Réserve de Beaulieu (p. 600). Parts of the exterior have open loggias and big arched windows; you can also enjoy the views from the elaborately flowering terrace over the sea. Accommodations look as if the late Princess Grace might settle in comfortably at any minute. They're generally spacious and open to sea views. Rates include admission to the pool, Club Dauphin. The pool is accessible by funicular from the main building.

71 bd. du Général-de-Gaulle, St-Jean-Cap-Ferrat 06230. ✆ **04-93-76-50-50.** Fax 04-93-76-04-52. www.grand-hotel-cap-ferrat.com. 73 units. 250€–560€ double; 530€–4,200€ suite. AE, DC, MC, V. Parking 35€. **Amenities:** 2 restaurants; bar; babysitting; use of bicycles; Olympic-size heated outdoor pool; room service; spa; 2 tennis courts. *In room:* A/C, TV, hair dryer, minibar, Wi-Fi (free).

La Voile d'Or ★★   Established in 1966, the "Golden Sail" is a tour de force. It provides intimate luxury in a converted 19th-century villa at the edge of the little fishing port and yacht harbor, with a panoramic coast view. It's equal to the Grand Hôtel in every feature except cuisine, which is just a notch lower. The guest rooms, lounges, and restaurant open onto terraces. Accommodations are individually decorated, with hand-painted reproductions, carved gilt headboards, baroque paneled doors, parquet floors, antique clocks, and paintings. The luxurious bathrooms have tub/shower combinations. Guests gather on the canopied terrace for lunch, and in a stately room with Spanish armchairs and white wrought-iron chandeliers for dinner.

31 av. Jean-Mermoz, St-Jean-Cap-Ferrat 06230. ℰ **04-93-01-13-13.** Fax 04-93-76-11-17. www.lavoiledor. fr. 45 units. 270€–456€ double; 583€–890€ suite. Rates include continental breakfast. AE, MC, V. Parking 25€. Closed Oct to mid-Apr. **Amenities:** 2 restaurants; bar; babysitting; exercise room; 2 saltwater outdoor pools; room service; sauna. *In room:* A/C, TV, hair dryer, Internet (free), minibar.

MODERATE

Hôtel Brise Marine   Built around 1878, this villa with front and rear terraces sits on a hillside. A long rose arbor, beds of subtropical flowers, palms, and pines provide an attractive setting. The atmosphere is casual and informal, and the rooms are comfortably but simply furnished. They have small, tiled bathrooms with shower and tub. You can have breakfast in the beamed lounge or under the rose trellis. The little corner bar serves afternoon drinks.

58 av. Jean-Mermoz, St-Jean-Cap-Ferrat 06230. ℰ **04-93-76-04-36.** Fax 04-93-76-11-49. www.hotel-brisemarine.com. 16 units. 155€–178€ double. AE, DC, MC, V. Parking 14€. Closed Nov–Jan. **Amenities:** Bar; room service. *In room:* A/C, TV, hair dryer, minibar, Wi-Fi (free).

Hotel Oursin 🐟   Finding a reasonably priced hotel in this expensive stretch of Riviera real estate is a daunting challenge, but Oursin fits the bill. The bedrooms are simply but comfortably furnished, and the welcome from the staff is most cordial. The location is only 50m (164 ft.) from the beach. The hotel serves a first-rate breakfast.

1 av. Denis Semeria, St-Jean-Cap-Ferrat 06230. ℰ **04-93-76-04-65.** Fax 04-93-76-12-55. www.hotel oursin.com. 55€–120€ double. MC, V. **Amenities:** Breakfast room. *In room:* TV, hair dryer, minibar, Wi-Fi (free).

Where to Dine

Capitaine Cook ★ PROVENÇAL/SEAFOOD   Next door to the fancy La Voile d'Or hotel (see "Where to Stay," above), a few blocks uphill from the center of the village, this restaurant specializes in seafood served in hearty portions. You'll have a panoramic view of the coast from the terrace; inside, the decor is maritime and rugged. Oysters, served simply on the half shell or in several creative ways with sauces and herbs, are a specialty. Roasted catch of the day is the mainstay, but filet mignon is also popular. The staff speaks English.

11 av. Jean-Mermoz. ℰ **04-93-76-02-66.** Main courses 17€–30€; fixed-price menu 26€–31€. MC, V. Fri–Tues noon–2pm; Thurs–Tues 7:15–10pm. Closed mid-Nov to Dec.

La Luna Rossa ★ ITALIAN   With the Italian border so close at hand, it's only natural that an Italian restaurant would open at this resort. Many different types of savory pastas are offered, along with the catch of the day which can be grilled if you wish. A wide selection of meats, freshly made salads, and other regional dishes, such as pan-fried squid, are a regular feature.

2 av. Denis-Séméria. © **04-93-76-03-97.** Reservations required. Main courses 18€–26€. MC, V. Wed-Sun noon–3pm; Tues–Sun 7:30–10:30pm.

Le Sloop FRENCH/PROVENÇAL   Le Sloop is the most popular and most reasonably priced bistro in this expensive area. Outfitted in blue and white inside and out, it sits at the edge of the port, overlooking the yachts in the harbor. A meal may begin with a salad of flap mushrooms steeped *en cappuccino* with liquefied foie gras, or perhaps tartare of salmon with aioli and lemon crepes. You may follow with a filet of sea bass served with red-wine sauce, or a mixed fish fry of three kinds of Mediterranean fish, bound together with olive oil and truffles. Dessert may include strawberry soup with sweet white wine and apricot ice cream, or any of about seven other choices, each based on "the red fruits of the region." The regional wines are reasonably priced.

Au Nouveau Port. © **04-93-01-48-63.** www.restaurantsloop.com. Reservations recommended. Main courses 22€–26€; fixed-price menu 30€. AE, MC, V. Thurs–Tues noon–2pm; Thurs–Mon 7–10pm. Closed mid-Nov to mid-Dec.

BEAULIEU-SUR-MER ★★

939km (583 miles) S of Paris; 9.5km (6 miles) E of Nice; 11km (6¾ miles) W of Monte Carlo

Protected from the north winds blowing down from the Alps, Beaulieu-sur-Mer is often referred to as "La Petite Afrique" (Little Africa). Like Menton, it has the mildest climate along the Côte d'Azur and is popular with the wintering wealthy. English visitors originally staked it out after an English industrialist founded a hotel here between the rock-studded slopes and the sea. Beaulieu is rich with lush vegetation, with palms as well as oranges, lemons, and bananas.

Essentials

GETTING THERE   Most visitors **drive** from Nice on the Moyenne Corniche or the coastal highway. **Trains** connect Beaulieu with Nice, Monaco, and the rest of the Côte d'Azur. For rail information, call © **08-92-35-35-35,** or visit www.voyages-sncf.com.

VISITOR INFORMATION   The **Office de Tourisme** is on place Georges Clemenceau (© **04-93-01-02-21;** fax 04-93-01-44-04).

Fun on & off the Beach

Beaulieu does have a beach scene, but don't expect soft sand. The beaches aren't as rocky as those in Nice or other nearby resorts, but they're still closer to gravel than to sand. The longer of the town's two free public beaches is **Petite Afrique,** adjacent to the yacht basin; the shorter is **Baie des Fourmis,** beneath the casino. **Plage de la Calanque** (© **04-93-01-45-00**) rents mattresses for 8€ per half-day and sells snacks and drinks.

The town is home to an important church, the late-19th-century **Eglise de Sacré-Coeur,** a quasi-Byzantine, quasi-Gothic mishmash at 13 bd. du Maréchal-Leclerc (© **04-93-35-70-45**). It's open daily 8am to 7pm. At the same address (same phone) is the 12th-century Romanesque chapel of Santa Maria de Olivo, used mostly for temporary exhibits of painting, sculpture, and civic memorabilia. Unlike the Eglise de Sacré-Coeur, the chapel is not an active house of worship and is open only for special exhibitions.

As you walk along the seafront promenade, you can see many stately Belle Epoque villas that evoke the days when Beaulieu was the height of fashion. Although you can't go inside, you'll see signs for **Villa Namouna,** which once belonged to Gordon Bennett, the owner of the *New York Herald,* and **Villa Léonine,** former home of the marquess of Salisbury.

For a memorable 90-minute walk, start north of boulevard Edouard-VII, where a path leads up the Riviera escarpment to **Sentier du Plateau St-Michel.** A belvedere here offers panoramic views from Cap d'Ail to the Estérel. A 1-hour alternative is the stroll along **promenade Maurice-Rouvier.** The promenade runs parallel to the water, stretching from Beaulieu to St-Jean. On one side you'll see the most elegant mansions in well-landscaped gardens; on the other, views of the Riviera landscape and the peninsular point of St-Hospice.

Casino de Beaulieu, avenue Fernand-Dunan (© **04-93-76-48-00**), was built in the Art Nouveau style in 1903. The slot machines are open daily, without charge, 11am to 4am. The *salles des grands jeux* are open daily 9pm to 4am. Management strongly recommends that men wear jackets, or at least appropriate clothing. Patrons must present a photo ID.

Villa Kérylos ★★   This is a replica of an ancient Greek residence, painstakingly designed and built by the archaeologist Theodore Reinach. A collection of Greek figurines and ceramics fills the cabinets. Most interesting is the reconstructed Greek furniture, much of which would be fashionable today. One curious mosaic depicts the slaying of the Minotaur and provides its own labyrinth. (If you try to trace the path, expect to stay for weeks.)

Rue Gustave-Eiffel. © **04-93-01-01-44.** www.villa-kerylos.com. Admission 6.50€ adults, 6.20€ seniors and children 7–18, free for children 6 and under. Feb 15–Nov 1 daily 10am–6pm (until 7pm July–Aug); Nov 2–Feb 14 Sun 2–6pm.

Where to Stay

EXPENSIVE

La Réserve de Beaulieu ★★★   This pink-and-white *fin de siècle* palace is one of the Riviera's most famous hotels. Here you can sit, have an aperitif, and watch the sunset while a pianist plays Mozart. A number of the lounges open onto a courtyard with bamboo chairs, grass borders, and urns of flowers. The social life revolves around the main drawing room. The individually decorated guest rooms range widely in size and design; most overlook the Mediterranean, and some have a view of the mountains. They come with deluxe beds and luxurious bathrooms. Some have private balconies.

5 bd. du Maréchal-Leclerc, Beaulieu-sur-Mer 06310. © **04-93-01-00-01.** Fax 04-93-01-28-99. www. reservebeaulieu.com. 39 units. 160€–1,700€ double; 545€–3,320€ suite. AE, DC, MC, V. Parking 36€. Closed mid-Oct to mid-Dec. **Amenities:** Restaurant; bar; babysitting; exercise room; massage; outdoor pool; room service. *In room:* A/C, TV, hair dryer, minibar, Wi-Fi (free).

INEXPENSIVE

Hôtel Le Havre Bleu 🦋   This is a great bargain if you don't require a lot of services and amenities. Le Havre Bleu has one of the prettiest facades of any inexpensive hotel in town. In a former Victorian villa, the hotel has arched ornate windows and a front garden dotted with flowering urns. The impeccable guest rooms are comfortable and functional. Breakfast is the only meal served.

29 bd. du Maréchal-Joffre, Beaulieu-sur-Mer 06310. ℂ **04-93-01-01-40.** Fax 04-93-01-29-92. 20 units. 63€–78€ double; 78€–88€ triple. AE, MC, V. Free parking. **Amenities:** Babysitting; room service. *In room:* A/C, TV, Wi-Fi (free).

Inter-Hôtel Frisia Most of the Frisia's rooms, decorated in a modern style, open onto views of the harbor. The water-view units are the most expensive. All rooms have small bathrooms, with a combination tub/shower. Two spacious suites with kitchenettes are in free-standing villas near the hotel's main building. Public areas include a sunny garden and inviting lounges. English is widely spoken here, and the management makes foreign guests feel especially welcome. Breakfast is the only meal served, but many reasonably priced restaurants are nearby.

2 bd. Eugène-Gauthier, Beaulieu-sur-Mer 06310. ℂ **04-93-01-01-04.** Fax 04-93-01-31-92. www.frisia-beaulieu.com. 33 units. 70€–135€ double; 110€–195€ suite. AE, MC, V. Parking 9€. Closed Nov 13–Dec 17. **Amenities:** Bar; babysitting; room service; Wi-Fi (free). *In room:* A/C, TV, hair dryer, minibar.

Where to Dine

La Pignatelle 🍴 FRENCH/PROVENÇAL Even in this expensive town, you can find an excellent, affordable Provençal bistro. Despite its relatively low prices, La Pignatelle prides itself on the fresh ingredients in its robust cuisine. Specialties include mushroom-stuffed ravioli with truffled cream sauce, succulent *soupe de poissons* from which the kitchen has labored to remove the bones, cassoulet of mussels, monkfish steak garnished with olive oil and herbs, fricassee of sea bass with shrimp, and *petite friture du pays*, which incorporates small fish using old Provençal traditions.

10 rue de Quincenet. ℂ **04-93-01-03-37.** Reservations recommended. Main courses 9€–27€; fixed-price lunch 15€–32€, dinner 22€–32€. MC, V. Fri–Tues noon–2pm and 7–9:30pm. Closed Nov 15–Dec 15.

Le Catalan 🍴 FRENCH/CATALAN/INTERNATIONAL This place is endlessly popular, and endlessly busy, thanks to relatively low prices and succulent food. You'll dine within any of three separate dining rooms or on a terrace overlooking the sea. The pizza comes in at least a dozen varieties and is baked to bubbling perfection in a wood-burning beehive oven. More substantial fare includes paella and zarzuela, pasta with shellfish, and a full roster of grilled meats and fish. Everybody from dockworkers in grimy clothes to plump society matrons from Paris dines here virtually elbow to elbow in an establishment that's acclaimed for its *égalité*.

52 bd. Général Leclerc. ℂ **04-93-01-02-78.** Reservations recommended. Pizzas 7€–12€; main courses 8€–20€. MC, V. Mon–Sat noon–2:30pm and 7–11pm.

Les Agaves ★★ MODERN FRENCH One of the most stylish restaurants in Beaulieu is in an early-1900s villa across the street from the railway station. U.S.-based publications such as *Bon Appétit* have praised the cuisine. Of note are curry-enhanced scallops with garlic-flavored tomatoes and parsley, terrine of pork with comfit of onions, lobster salad with mango, ravioli with flap mushrooms, rockfish soup, chopped shrimp with Provençal herbs, and several preparations of foie gras. Filet of sea bass with truffles and champagne sauce is delectable.

4 av. Maréchal Foch. ℂ **04-93-01-13-12.** Reservations recommended. Main courses 24€–40€; fixed-price menu 38€. AE, MC, V. Daily 7–10pm. Closed Nov 15–Dec 20.

Beaulieu After Dark

The Art Deco–style **Grand Casino de Beaulieu,** 4 av. Fernand-Dunan (ℂ **04-93-76-48-00**), encourages jackets for men in its fancier areas, and absolutely forbids tennis shoes. It requires that patrons show a passport. The slot-machine section, where dress is more casual, is free to enter and doesn't require a passport.

EZE & LA TURBIE ★★

942km (585 miles) S of Paris; 11km (6¾ miles) NE of Nice

The hamlets of Eze and La Turbie, though 6.5km (4 miles) apart, are so similar that most tourism officials speak of them as if they're one entity. Both boast fortified feudal cores in the hills overlooking the coast, and both were built during the early Middle Ages to stave off raids from corsairs who wanted to capture harem slaves and laborers. Clinging to the hillsides around these hamlets are upscale villas, many of which have been built since the 1950s by retirees from colder climes. Closely linked, culturally and fiscally, to nearby Monaco, Eze and La Turbie have full-time populations of less than 3,000. The medieval cores of both contain galleries, boutiques, and artisans' shops that have been restored.

Eze is accessible on the Moyenne (Middle) Corniche; La Turbie, by way of the Grande (Upper) Corniche. Signs along the coastal road indicate the direction motorists should take to reach either of the hamlets.

The leading attraction in Eze is the **Jardin d'Eze ★**, boulevard du Jardin-Exotique (*Ⓒ 04-93-41-10-30*), a showcase of exotic plants in Eze-Village, at the pinnacle of the town's highest hill. Admission is 5€ for adults, 2.50€ for students and ages 12 to 25, and free for children 11 and under. In July and August, it's open daily 9am to 8pm; the rest of the year, it opens daily at 9am and closes between 5 and 7pm, depending on the time of sunset.

La Turbie boasts a ruined monument erected by Roman emperor Augustus in 6 B.C., the **Trophée des Alps (Trophy of the Alps) ★**. It's near a rock formation known as La Tête de Chien, at the highest point along the Grand Corniche, 450m (1,476 ft.) above sea level. The Roman Senate ordered the creation of the monument, which many locals call La Trophée d'Auguste, to celebrate the subjugation of the people of the French Alps by the Roman armies.

A short distance from the monument is the **Musée du Trophée d'Auguste,** rue Albert-1er, La Turbie (*Ⓒ 04-93-41-20-84*), a minimuseum containing finds from digs nearby and information about the monument's restoration. It's open daily: April to June 9:30am to 6pm; July to September 9:30am to 7pm, and October to March 10am to 5pm. Admission is 5€ for adults and free for children 17 and under. It's closed January 1, May 1, November, and December 25.

The **Office de Tourisme** is on place du Général-de-Gaulle, Eze-Village (*Ⓒ 04-93-41-26-00;* fax 04-93-41-04-80; www.eze-riviera.com).

Where to Stay

Hostellerie du Château de la Chèvre d'Or ★★★ This is one of the grandest resort hotels along the eastern Riviera. The miniature-village retreat was built in the 1920s in neo-Gothic style. It's a Relais & Châteaux property in a complex of village houses, all with views of the coastline. But unlike most villages in the area, this one doesn't have a beach. The decor of the "Golden Goat" maintains its character while adding modern comfort. The spacious guest rooms are filled with quality furnishings. Even if you don't spend the night, try to visit for a drink in the lounge, which has a panoramic view.

Rue du Barri, Eze-Village 06360. ☎ **04-92-10-66-66.** Fax 04-93-41-06-72. www.chevredor.com. 36 units. 290€–760€ double; 870€–2,900€ suite. AE, DC, MC, V. Closed mid-Nov to mid-Mar. **Amenities:** 3 restaurants; bar; babysitting; exercise room; outdoor pool; room service; sauna. *In room:* A/C, TV, hair dryer, minibar, Wi-Fi (free).

Where to Dine

Le Troubadour FRENCH/PROVENÇAL   The stone-fronted medieval house that contains this well-known restaurant has, since World War I, housed businesses that have included a bar, a delicatessen, and the local post office. Today, within three dining rooms, each accented with thick ceiling beams, you can order succulent and flavorful dishes that include braised rabbit in aspic, served with warm hearts of artichoke, foie gras, and carrots; a delightful filet of John Dory with stuffed and deep-fried zucchini blossoms; roasted rack of lamb with parsley sauce; and other dishes that each manage to showcase some aspect of the Mediterranean diet. You'll find the place close to the village church, in the upper heights of Eze Village.

4 rue du Brec, Eze Village. ☎ **04-93-41-19-03.** Reservations recommended. Main courses 22€–38€; fixed-price menus 39€–52€. MC, V. Tues–Sat 12:30–2pm and 7:30–9:30pm. Closed Nov 15–Dec 20, first week of June, first week of Mar.

MONACO ★★★

939km (583 miles) S of Paris; 18km (11 miles) E of Nice

Monaco, according to Somerset Maugham, is defined as "370 sunny acres peopled with shady characters." Katharine Hepburn once called it "a pimple on the chin of the south of France." She wasn't referring to the principality's lack of beauty but rather to the preposterous idea of a little country, a feudal anomaly, taking up some of the choicest Riviera coastline. Monaco became the property of the Grimaldi clan as early as 1297. It has maintained something resembling independence since. In a fit of impatience, the French annexed it in 1793, but the ruling family recovered it in 1814.

Hemmed in by France on three sides and the Mediterranean on the fourth, tiny Monaco maintains its independence. And as almost everybody knows, the Monégasques do not pay taxes. Nearly all their country's revenue comes from tourism and gambling.

Monaco, or more precisely its capital of Monte Carlo, has for a century been a symbol of glamour. The 1956 marriage of Prince Rainier III to American actress Grace Kelly enhanced its status. She had met the prince when she was in Cannes to promote *To Catch a Thief.* Their daughter Caroline was born in 1957; a son, Albert, in 1958; and a second daughter, Stephanie, in 1965. The Monégasques welcomed the birth of Caroline but went wild for Albert, a male heir. According to a 1918 treaty, Monaco would become an autonomous state under French protection should the ruling dynasty become extinct. Though not always happy in her role, Princess Grace won the respect and admiration of her people. The Monégasques still mourn her death in a 1982 car accident.

In April 2005, Prince Rainier died after suffering ailing health for many years. Upon his father's death, the unmarried Prince Albert became the reigning prince. Unlike his father's storybook marriage to Grace Kelly, Albert remains not only unmarried but also without an heir, even though he's admitted to having a son out

Reach Out & Touch Someone in Monaco

To call Monaco from within France, dial 00 (the access code for all international long-distance calls from France), followed by the **country code, 377,** and then the eight-digit local phone number. (Don't dial the 33 code; that's the country code for France.)

To call Monaco from North America, dial the international access code, 011, the country code, 377, and then the eight-digit Monaco number.

To call any other country from within Monaco, dial 00 (the international access code), then the applicable country code, and the number. For example, to call Cannes, you would dial 00, 33 (France's country code), 4 (the city code, without the zero), and the eight-digit number.

of wedlock. (His illegitimate son cannot ascend to the throne.) So concerned was Prince Rainier with this situation that he changed the Monaco constitution in 2002, allowing the crown to pass to one of the princesses or their children if Albert abdicated or died without a child. Currently, Princess Caroline is in line to succeed Albert.

The second-smallest state in Europe (Vatican City is the tiniest), Monaco consists of four parts. The old town, **Monaco-Ville,** on a promontory, "the Rock," 60m (197 ft.) high, is the seat of the royal palace and the government building, as well as the Oceanographic Museum. To the west, **La Condamine,** the home of the Monégasques, is at the foot of the old town, forming its harbor and port sector. Up from the port (Monaco is steep) is **Monte Carlo,** once the playground of royalty and still the center for the wintering wealthy, the setting for the casino and its gardens and the deluxe hotels. The fourth part, **Fontvieille,** is a neat industrial suburb. **Monte-Carlo Beach,** at the far frontier, is on French soil. It attracts a chic crowd, including movie stars in the skimpiest bikinis and thongs.

Monaco used to be slow in summer, but now July and August tend to be so crowded that it's hard to get a room. The Monégasques court an affluent crowd. But with the decline of royalty, Monaco has had to develop a broader tourism base. You can now stay here moderately, though still not cheaply. As always, you can lose your shirt at the casinos. "Suicide Terrace" at the casino, though not used as frequently as in the old days, is still a real temptation to many.

Even when family fortunes aren't slipping through the fingers of gamblers, the casino has been the subject of legends and the setting for many films. Richard Burton presented Elizabeth Taylor with the huge Kohinoor diamond here. Because Monaco is a tax haven, many celebrities have become residents, including Plácido Domingo, Claudia Schiffer, Boris Becker, and Ringo Starr.

Essentials

GETTING THERE Monaco has rail, bus, and highway connections from other coastal cities, especially Nice. **Trains** arrive every 30 minutes from Cannes, Nice, Menton, and Antibes. For more rail information, call © **36-35,** or visit www.voyages-sncf.com. Monaco's underground railway station (Gare SNCF) is on place St. Devote. It's a long walk uphill from the train station to Monte Carlo. If you'd rather take a **taxi** but can't find one at the station, call © **08-20-20-98-98.** There are no border formalities when entering Monaco from mainland France. Monaco is a

Monaco

**Map labels:**

To Grande Corniche

BEAUSOLEIL

To Menton

FRANCE

av. de Villain

av. P. Doumer

bd. des Moulins

MONTE CARLO

bd. Princesse-Charlotte

bd. Larvotto

av. Princesse-Grâce

MONEGHETTI

MONACO

pl. du Casino 6

7 Plage de Larvotto

To Nice

av. de

av. d'Ostende

Costa

la

bd. du Jardin-Exotique

bd. de Belgique

Rainier-III

Grimaldi

bd. Albert-Ier

quai des Etats-Unis

Stade Nautique Rainier-III

Port de Monaco

PARC PRINCESSE ANTOINETTE

rue

LA CONDAMINE

JARDIN EXOTIQUE

Station

pl. du Canton

Charles-III

quai Antoine-Ier

bd.

av. de la Porte-Neuve

pl. du Palais

MONACO-VILLE

Information (i)
Post Office ✉

Heliport

FONTVIEILLE

av. St-Martin

JARDINS ST-MARTIN

0   1/5 mile
0   200 meters

★ Paris

FRANCE

MONACO ■

0   100 mi
0   100 km

Collection des Voitures Anciennes de S.A.S. 1ᵉ Prince de Monaco **4**

Jardin Exotique **1**

Monte-Carlo Casino **6**

Musée d'Anthropologie Préhistorique **2**

Musée National de Monaco **8**

Musée Océanographique de Monaco **5**

Musée du Palais du Prince/
  Les Grands Appartements du Palais **3**

Sun Casino **7**

lengthy **drive** from Paris. Take A6 south to Lyon. At Lyon, connect with A7 south to Aix-en-Provence and take A6 south directly to Monaco. If you're already on the Riviera, drive from Nice along N7 northeast. It's only 19km (12 miles), but with traffic, the drive can take 30 minutes.

VISITOR INFORMATION   The **Direction du Tourisme et des Congrés** office is at 2A bd. des Moulins (© **92-16-61-16;** fax 92-16-60-00; www.visitmonaco.com).

SPECIAL EVENTS   Two of the most-watched **car-racing events** in Europe are in January (Le Rallye) and May (the Grand Prix). For more information, call © **93-15-26-00.** In June, Monte Carlo is home to a weeklong convention that attracts media moguls from virtually everywhere, **Le Festival International de la Télévision,** Grimaldi Forum, avenue Princess Grace (© **99-99-30-00**). Shows from all over the world are broadcast and judged on their merits.

Fun on & off the Beach

BEACHES   Just outside the border, on French soil, the **Monte-Carlo Beach Club** adjoins the Monte-Carlo Beach Hotel, 22 av. Princesse-Grace (© **98-06-50-00**). The beach club has thrived for years; it's an integral part of Monaco's social life. Princess Grace used to come here in flowery swimsuits, greeting her friends and subjects with humor and style. The sand is replenished at regular intervals. You'll find two large pools (one for children), cabanas, a restaurant, a cafe, and a bar. As the temperature drops in late August, the beach closes for the winter. The admission charge of 50€ to 90€, depending on the season, grants you access to the changing rooms, toilets, restaurants, and bar, and use of a mattress for sunbathing. A day's use of a cubicle, where you can lock up your street clothes, costs an extra 20€ to 27€. A fee of 35€ to 90€ will get you a day's use of a private cabana. Most socializing occurs around the pool's edges. As usual, topless is de rigueur, but bottomless isn't.

Monaco, the quintessential kingdom by the sea, offers swimming and sunbathing at the **Plage du Larvotto,** off avenue Princesse-Grace (© **93-30-63-84**). There's a charge of 2.20€ to enter this strip of beach, whose surface is frequently replenished with sand hauled in by barge. Part of it is open; other sections are private.

SPA TREATMENTS   In 1908, the Société des Bains de Mer launched a seawater (thalassotherapy) spa in Monte Carlo, inaugurated by Prince Albert I. It was bombed during World War II and didn't reopen until 1996. **Les Thermes Marins de Monte-Carlo,** 2 av. de Monte-Carlo (© **98-06-69-00**), is one of the largest spas in Europe. Spread over four floors are a pool, a Turkish hammam (steam bath), a healthy restaurant, a juice bar, two tanning booths, a fitness center, a beauty center, and private treatment rooms. A day pass, giving access to the sauna, steam rooms, fitness facilities, and pools, costs 85€. Massages cost 75€ for a 30-minute session, 125€ for a 60-minute session.

SWIMMING   Overlooking the yacht-clogged harbor, the **Stade Nautique Rainier-III,** quai Albert-1er, at La Condamine (© **93-30-64-83**), a pool frequented by the Monégasques, was a gift from Prince Rainier to his subjects. It's open May to October daily 9am to 6pm (until midnight July–Aug). Admission for a one-time visit costs 4.70€ per person; discounts are available if you plan to visit 10 times or more. Between November and April, it's an ice-skating rink. If you want to swim in winter, try the indoor **Piscine du Prince Héréditaire Albert,** in the Stade Louis II, 7 av. de Castellane (© **92-05-42-13**). It's open Monday, Tuesday, Thursday, and Friday 7:30am to 2:30pm; Saturday 1 to 6pm; and Sunday 8am to 1pm. Admission is 2.30€.

TENNIS & SQUASH   The **Monte Carlo Country Club,** 155 av. Princesse-Grace, Roquebrune-Cap Martin, France (© **04-93-41-30-15;** www.mccc.mc), has 21 clay and 2 concrete tennis courts. The 41€ fee provides access to a restaurant, health club with Jacuzzi and sauna, putting green, beach, squash courts, and the well-maintained tennis courts. Guests of the hotels administered by the Société des Bains de Mer (Hôtel de Paris, Hermitage, Mirabeau, and Monte Carlo Beach Club) pay half-price. Plan to spend at least half a day, ending a round of tennis with use of any of the other facilities. It's open daily 8am to 8 or 9pm, depending on the season.

Shopping

Bijoux Marlene, Les Galeries du Métropole, 207 av. des Spélugues (✆ 93-50-17-57), sells only imitation gemstones. They're shamelessly copied from the real McCoys sold by Cartier and Van Cleef & Arpels. Made in Italy of gold-plated silver, the jewelry (the staff refers to it as Les Bijoux Fantaisies) costs 10€ to 1,000€ per piece.

Boutique du Rocher, 1 av. de la Madone (✆ 93-30-91-17), is the larger of two boutiques Princess Grace opened in 1966 as the official retail outlets of her charitable foundation. The organization merchandises Monégasque and Provençal handicrafts. A short walk from place du Casino, the shop sells carved frames for pictures or mirrors; housewares; gift items crafted from porcelain, textiles, and wood; toys; and dolls. On the premises are workshops where artisans produce the goods. The second branch is at 25 rue Emile de Loth, Monaco-Ville (✆ 93-30-33-99).

If you insist on ultrafancy stores, you'll find them cheek by jowl with the Hôtel de Paris and the casino, lining the streets leading to the Hôtel Hermitage, and across from the gardens at the minimall Park Palace. **Allée Serge-Diaghilev** is just that, an alley, but a very tiny one filled with designer shops.

You don't have to be Princess Caroline to shop in Monaco, especially now that **FNAC** (✆ 93-10-81-81) has opened in the heart of town. A branch of the big French chain that sells CDs, tapes, and books is at the **Galeries du Métropole,** 17 av. des Spélugues, in the Jardins du Casino, next to the Hôtel Métropole and across from the casino.

The Galeries du Métropole also has a few specialty shops worth visiting. Check out **Manufacture de Monaco** (✆ 93-50-64-63) for glorious bone china and elegant tabletop items. Two doors away is a branch of the chic but often affordable French linen house **Yves Delorme** (✆ 93-50-08-70). **Royal Food** (✆ 93-15-05-04) is a gourmet grocery store, which you'll find down a set of curving stairs hidden in the side entrance of the mall; here you can buy food from France, Lebanon, and the United States, or stock up for *le pique-nique* or for day trips. This market is open Monday to Saturday 10am to 7:30pm.

For real-people shopping, stroll **rue Grimaldi,** the principality's most commercial street, near the fruit, flower, and food market (see below), and **boulevard des Moulins,** closer to the casino, where you'll see glamorous boutiques. There's also a pedestrian thoroughfare with shops less forbiddingly chic than those along boulevard des Moulins: **Rue Princesse-Caroline** is loaded with bakeries, flower shops, and the closest thing you'll find to funkiness in Monaco. Also check out the **Formule 1** shop, 15 rue Grimaldi (✆ 93-15-92-44), where everything from racing helmets to specialty key chains and T-shirts celebrates the roaring, high-octane racing machines.

No one comes to the Riviera for bargain shopping but, even in chic Monte Carlo, there is **Stock Griffe,** 5 bis av. St-Michel (✆ 93-50-86-06). It slashes prices on Prada, Pucci, Escada, and the like. A tremendous amount of merchandise is packed into these tiny precincts. The place may be small, but not the discounts, some of which add up to an astonishing 90%. Greater reductions are for older garments that didn't move, but you can also snap up some newer fashions.

MARKETS For a look at the heart and soul of the real Monaco, head to place des Armes for the **fruit, flower, and food market,** which starts daily at 7:30am. The indoor and outdoor market has a fountain, cafes, and hand-painted vegetable tiles beneath your feet. The outdoor market packs up at noon, and some dealers at the indoor market stay open to 2pm. If you prefer bric-a-brac, there's a small but funky (especially for Monaco) flea market, **Les Puces de Fontvieille,** on Saturday 9:30am to 5:30pm on the quai Jean-Charles Rey, immediately adjacent to Port de Fontvieille.

Seeing the Sights

Collection des Voitures Anciennes de S.A.S. le Prince de Monaco ☺

Prince Rainier III opened a showcase of his private collection of more than 100 vintage autos, including the 1956 Rolls-Royce Silver Cloud that carried the prince and princess on their wedding day. Monaco shopkeepers gave it to the royal couple as a wedding present. A 1952 Austin Taxi on display was once used as the royal "family car." Other exhibits are a "woodie" (a 1937 Ford station wagon Prince Louis II used on hunting trips); a 1925 Bugatti 35B, winner of the Monaco Grand Prix in 1929; a 1903 De Dion Bouton; and a 1986 Lamborghini Countach.

Les Terrasses de Fontvieille. ✆ **92-05-28-56.** www.palais.mc. Admission 6€ adults, 3€ students and children 8-14, free for children 7 and under. Daily 10am–6pm. Closed Dec 25.

Jardin Exotique ★★

Built on the side of a rock, the gardens are known for their cactus collection. They were begun by Prince Albert I, who was a naturalist and scientist. He spotted some succulents growing in the palace gardens and created this garden from them. You can also explore the grottoes here, as well as the **Musée d'Anthropologie Préhistorique** (✆ **93-15-29-80**). The view of the principality is splendid.

Bd. du Jardin-Exotique. ✆ **93-15-29-80.** www.jardineexotique.mc. Admission (includes museum) 6.90€ adults, 3.60€ children 6-18, free for children 5 and under. Mid-May to mid-Sept daily 9am–7pm; mid-Sept to mid-May daily 9am–6pm. Closed Nov 19–Dec 25.

Les Grands Appartements du Palais ★

Most summer day-trippers from Nice want to see the home of Monaco's royal family, the Palais du Prince, which dominates the principality from the Rock. A tour of the Grands Appartements allows you a glimpse of the Throne Room and some of the art, including works by Bruegel and Holbein, as well as Princess Grace's state portrait. The palace was built in the 13th century, and part dates from the Renaissance. The ideal time to arrive is 11:55am, to watch the 10-minute **Relève de la Garde (Changing of the Guard).**

In a wing of the palace, the **Musée du Palais du Prince (Souvenirs Napoleoniens et Collection d'Archives)** holds a collection of mementos of Napoleon and Monaco. When the royal residence is closed, this museum is the only part of the palace the public can visit.

Place du Palais. ✆ **93-25-18-31.** www.palais.mc. Combination ticket 4€ adults, 2€ children 8-14, free for children 7 and under. Palace and museum daily: Jan-Mar 10:30am–5pm; Apr 10:30am–6pm; May-Sept 9:30am–6:30pm; Oct 10am–5:30pm; Dec 10:30am–5pm. Closed in Nov.

Musée National de Monaco ★ ☺

In a villa designed in a style similar to that of Charles Garnier (architect of Paris's Opéra Garnier), this museum houses a magnificent collection of antique mechanical toys and dolls. See the 18th-century Neapolitan crib, which contains some 200 figures. This collection, assembled by Mme. de Galea, was presented to the principality in 1972; it originated with the 18th- and 19th-century practice of displaying new fashions on doll models.

17 av. Princesse-Grace. ✆ **98-98-91-26.** www.monte-carlo.mc/musee-national. Admission 6€ adults, 3.50€ students and children 6-14, free for children 5 and under. Daily 10am–6pm. Closed Jan 1, May 1, Nov 19, Dec 25, and 4 days during Grand Prix.

Musée Océanographique de Monaco ★★ ☺   Albert I, great-grandfather of the present prince, founded this museum in 1910. In the main rotunda is a statue of Albert in his favorite costume: that of a sea captain. Displayed are specimens he collected during 30 years of expeditions. The aquarium, one of the finest in Europe, contains more than 90 tanks.

The collection is exhibited in the zoology room. Some of the exotic creatures were unknown before he captured them. You'll see models of the ships aboard which he directed his scientific cruises from 1885 to 1914. The most important part of the laboratory has been preserved and re-created as closely as possible. Skeletons of specimens, including a whale that drifted ashore at Pietra Ligure in 1896, are on the main floor. The whale skeleton is remarkable for its healed fractures sustained when a vessel struck the animal as it was drifting on the surface. An exhibition devoted to the discovery of the ocean is in the physical-oceanography room on the first floor. Underwater movies are shown in the lecture room. There is also a shark lagoon.

Av. St-Martin. ℂ **93-15-36-00.** www.oceano.mc. Admission 13€ adults, 6€ children 6–18, free for children 5 and under. Apr–June and Sept daily 9:30am–7pm; July–Aug daily 9:30am–7:30pm; Oct–Mar daily 10am–6pm.

Where to Stay
VERY EXPENSIVE
Hôtel de Paris ★★★   On the resort's main plaza, opposite the casino, this is one of the world's most famous hotels. The ornate facade has marble pillars, and the lounge has an Art Nouveau rose window at the peak of the dome. The decor includes marble pillars, statues, crystal chandeliers, sumptuous carpets, Louis XVI chairs, and a wall-size mural. Elegant fabrics, rich carpeting, classic accessories, and an excellent restaurant make this hotel a favorite of the world's most discerning travelers. The guest rooms come in a variety of styles, with period or contemporary furnishings. Some units are enormous. Bathrooms are large, with marble and elegant brass fittings. *Note:* The rooms opening onto the sea aren't as spacious as those in the rear.

Place du Casino, Monaco 98007. ℂ **98-06-30-16.** Fax 98-06-59-13. www.montecarloresort.com. 182 units. 420€–960€ double; from 760€ suite. AE, DC, MC, V. Valet parking 32€. **Amenities:** 3 restaurants (see "Where to Dine," below); bar; babysitting; concierge; exercise room; large indoor pool; room service; 2 saunas; smoke-free rooms; Thermes Marins spa offering thalassotherapy under medical supervision. *In room:* A/C, TV, hair dryer, minibar, Wi-Fi (25€ per day).

Hôtel Hermitage ★★   Picture yourself sitting in a wicker armchair, enjoying a drink under an ornate stained-glass dome with an encircling wrought-iron balcony. You can do this at the cliff-top Hermitage. The "palace," with its wedding-cake facade, was the creation of Jean Marquet (who also created marquetry). Most rooms have large brass beds and decoratively framed doors that open onto balconies. Even the smallest rooms are medium-size, and the largest one is fit for the biggest movie star with the most trunks. Large mirrors, elegant fabrics and upholstery, and sumptuous beds make living here idyllic. In 2003, the hotel added two floors to its century-old main building. Guest rooms are modern and sleek in the styling.

Square Beaumarchais, Monaco Cedex 98005. ℂ **98-06-48-12.** Fax 98-06-48-23. www.montecarlo resort.com. 280 units. 370€–940€ double; from 605€ junior suite; from 1,520€ suite. AE, DISC, MC, V. Parking 34€. **Amenities:** Restaurant; bar; health club; indoor pool; room service; sauna. *In room:* A/C, TV, hair dryer, minibar, Wi-Fi (20€ per day).

EXPENSIVE

Columbus Monaco Hotel ★★ ✦ In the modern Fontvieille section of Monaco, this stylish, contemporary hotel faces Princess Grace's rose garden and the sea. Guest rooms are appointed in what owner Ken McCulloch calls "hybrid hip," a style that evokes both Miami and London. Elegant touches include Lartigue photos of the Riviera, high-tech cabinets filled with video games, and chocolate-leather furnishings; deluxe linens and Frette bathrobes round out the comforts. There are some disadvantages: For example, the hotel is in a condo complex whose residents share the pool. However, a boat carries guests to a tranquil sandy beach nearby.

23 av. des Papalins, Monaco 98000. ✆ **92-05-90-00.** Fax 92-05-23-86. www.columbushotels.com. 181 units. 310€–345€ double; 610€–920€ suite. AE, MC, V. Parking 23€. **Amenities:** Restaurant (brasserie w/antipasto buffet); bar; babysitting; exercise room; outdoor pool; room service; Wi-Fi (12€–48€ per day). In room: A/C, TV, hair dryer, minibar, iron.

Fairmont Monte Carlo ★ Although a bit down the scale from the two previous choices, this is also a deluxe palace, built by the Loews Corporation but bought in 1998 by a consortium of local investors and renamed the Monte Carlo Grand Hôtel. Fairmont Hotels & Resorts took over the property in early 2005. It hugs the coast below the terraces that support the famous casino, on one of the most valuable pieces of real estate along the Côte d'Azur. Architecturally daring when built (some of its foundations were sunk into the seabed, and some of the principality's busiest highways roar beneath it), the resort is viewed as an integral enhancement of Monégasque life. It contains Monaco's highest concentration of restaurants, bars, and nightclubs—think of it as Las Vegas with a Gallic accent. The guest rooms are conservatively furnished. Each has a pastel decor that's flooded with light from big windows and views over the town or the sea.

12 av. des Spélugues, Monaco 98007. ✆ **93-50-65-00.** Fax 93-15-48-93. www.fairmont.com/monte carlo. 616 units. 389€–869€ double; from 1,500€ suite. AE, DC, MC, V. Parking 38€. **Amenities:** 2 restaurants; 2 bars; babysitting; health club; outdoor pool; room service; sauna. In room: A/C, TV, hair dryer, Internet (20€ per day), minibar.

Monte Carlo Bay Hotel & Resort ★★★ Occupying a 4-hectare (10-acre) Mediterranean garden, this is a plush garden of Eden for the principality. It doesn't have the age or tradition of other Societé des Bains de Mer properties, such as the Paris and the Hermitage, but it seemingly offers everything else.

Built on the seashore, this is the first time in 75 years the society has launched a new hotel. Its aim is to recapture some of the chic and splendor of the 1920s. Its neoclassical architecture, with arcades and colonnades, has created a new landmark in Monaco. The sumptuous nature of the resort is reflected in its waterfalls, terraces, spacious bedrooms, exotic woods, lavish marble, and even an indoor pool covered with a monumental glass dome. Of the beautifully furnished bedrooms, more than three-quarters of them open onto sea views. Rooms are decorated with white-oak furnishings, often sandstone floors, and soft Mediterranean pastels.

40 av. Princesse Grace, Monaco 98000. ✆ **98-06-02-00.** Fax 98-06-00-03. www.montecarlobay.com. 334 units. 270€–800€ double; 750€–2,300€ suite. AE, DC, MC, V. Parking 15€. **Amenities:** 4 restaurants; 2 bars; nightclub; casino; disco; babysitting; concierge; exercise rooms; 3 pools (indoor, outdoor, and children's); spa. In room: A/C, TV, hair dryer, minibar, Wi-Fi (20€ per day).

INEXPENSIVE

Hôtel de France Not all Monégasques are rich, as a stroll along rue de la Turbie will convince you. Here you'll find some of the cheapest accommodations and eateries in the high-priced principality. This 19th-century hotel, 3 minutes from the rail station, has modest furnishings but is well kept and comfortable. The guest rooms and bathrooms are small, and each unit has a shower.

6 rue de la Turbie, Monaco 98000. ✆ **93-30-24-64.** Fax 92-16-13-34. www.monte-carlo.mc/france. 27 units. 94€–112€ double. Rates include breakfast. MC, V. Parking 7.50€. **Amenities:** Bar; room service. *In room:* TV, hair dryer, Wi-Fi (free).

Where to Dine
VERY EXPENSIVE

Le Louis XV ★★★ MEDITERRANEAN In the Hôtel de Paris, the Louis XV offers what one critic called "down-home Riviera cooking within a Fabergé egg." Star chef Alain Ducasse creates refined but not overly adorned cuisine, served by the finest staff in Monaco. Everything is light and attuned to the seasons, with intelligent, modern interpretations of Provençal and northern Italian dishes. You'll find chargrilled breast of baby pigeon with sautéed duck liver, an ongoing specialty known as "Provençal vegetables with crushed truffles," and everything from truffles and caviar to the best stewed salt cod on the coast. Ducasse divides his time between this enclave and his restaurants in Paris and New York. The hotel keeps its collection of rare fine wines in a dungeon chiseled out of the rocks.

In the Hôtel de Paris, place du Casino. ✆ **98-06-88-64.** Reservations recommended. Jacket and tie required for men. Main courses 80€–120€; fixed-price lunch 140€, dinner 210€–280€. AE, MC, V. Thurs–Mon 12:15–1:45pm and 8–9:45pm; also June–Sept Wed 12:15–1:45pm. Closed Feb 9–24.

EXPENSIVE

Bar et Boeuf ★★ INTERNATIONAL This restaurant is one of the many jewels in the crown of superchef Alain Ducasse, who is, according to many critics, both a culinary genius and the orchestrator of an upscale international assembly line. Acclaimed restaurant critic Gael Greene has referred to him as "Robo-Chef," and a small number of increasingly vocal critics complain about "franchise sprawl." You can still get a genuinely good meal here, even if none of it is prepared or even supervised by Ducasse. Bar et Boeuf is an upscale Gallic reinvention of a surf-and-turf restaurant. The only fish here is sea bass (*bar*), and the beef is perhaps the most cosseted and fussed-over meat in France. Examples include filets of sea bass with citrus marmalade and an assortment of species of braised celery; filet steak with Sicilian herbs; beef Wellington; and beef with a sauté of *taggiasche* (Italian) olives and wine glaze, served with fried spiny artichokes. The most lavish dish is *tournedos rossini* layered with foie gras and truffles, served with a tartare of truffled foie gras and pan-fried exotic mushrooms.

In the Sporting d'Eté Monte Carlo, av. Princesse-Grace. ✆ **98-06-71-71.** Reservations recommended. Main courses 32€–68€. AE, DC, MC, V. Late May to mid-Sept daily 8pm–1am.

Beefbar ★ STEAKS/FRENCH One patron said that this restaurant buzzes with a "polyglot crowd of dealmakers, socialites, and pre-club beauties," and so it does. A chic crowd comes to this elegant salon overlooking the Mediterranean to feast on everything from Argentine steaks to raw fish specials, the menu backed up by the best collection of Bordeaux in Monaco. Most guests prefer their meats grilled a bit crunchy on the outside and tender and juicy inside. The chef claims he selects only "the most noble pieces" from the slaughterhouses of the world, mostly from the United States, Argentina, and the Netherlands. The chef's Black Angus beef from Kansas is some of the best you are likely to find in the south of France. For the noncarnivore, there are many other choices such as tagliolini with flap mushrooms. You can also order lighter fare such as chicken Caesar salad.

42 quai Jean-Charles Rey. ✆ **97-77-09-29.** www.beefbar.com. Reservations required. Main courses 23€–79€; fixed-price menu 39€–90€. AE, MC, V. Daily noon–2:30pm and 8–11pm.

La Mandarine ★★ FRENCH/MEDITERRANEAN   In the chic Port Palace Hotel, this restaurant lies on the sixth floor, opening onto a panoramic and glittering vista of Monte Carlo's harbor and the sea. The cuisine is created from fresh, natural ingredients, mostly fashioned into dishes familiar along the Mediterranean. You can feast on such expensive produce as lobster, tender veal, or a risotto studded with truffles. Two other superbly crafted specialties are sautéed foie gras in a chutney-mango-coriander reduction and green curry with lacquered duck. The ever-changing menu features both classic and traditional dishes, and is backed up by one of the best wine cellars in Monaco, with some 20,000 bottles awaiting your selection.

7 av. President J. F. Kennedy. ✆ **97-97-90-00.** Main courses 30€–40€; fixed-price lunch 32€–43€. AE, MC, V. Daily noon–2pm and 7:30–10:30pm. Closed Nov 1–Dec 15.

Le Café de Paris ★ TRADITIONAL FRENCH   Its *plats du jour* are well pre-pared, and its location, the plaza adjacent to the casino and the Hôtel de Paris, allows a front-row view of the comings and goings of the nerve center of Monte Carlo. We find this 1985 re-creation of old-time Monaco a bit too enraptured with the devil-may-care glamour of early-1900s Monte Carlo. Despite that, the Café de Paris continues to draw patrons who appreciate the razzmatazz and all the glass and chrome. Menu items change frequently. Local office workers appreciate the platters, especially at lunchtime, because they can be served and consumed quickly. They range from fresh grilled sea bass to steak tartare with matchstick frites. Adjacent to the restaurant, you'll find (and hear) a jangling collection of slot machines and a predictable cluster of boutiques.

Place du Casino. ✆ **92-16-20-20.** Reservations recommended. Main courses 30€–50€; fixed-price menu 35€. AE, DC, MC, V. Daily 8am–3am.

Maya Bay ★ ASIAN   One of the most coveted dinner reservations is this chic restaurant with an Asian-inspired cuisine. Some of the tastiest dishes in the princi-pality are served here as stone Buddhas look down on you. The menu changes fre-quently to take advantage of the best produce in any given month. Try some of the chef's specialties, including stir-fried lobster with Chinese noodles or miso-glazed black cod. Some of the dishes are most imaginative, including duck consommé with Thai basil served with coriander and egg yolk ravioli with a side of fried duck liver and shiitake mushrooms. A medley of lemon thyme–sweetened giant prawns comes with a creamy mango sauce and a banana-and-avocado mousse with a sprinkling of pomegranate seeds.

24 av. Princesse Grace. ✆ **97-70-74-67.** Reservations required. Main courses 30€–70€; fixed-price lunch 18€–35€. AE, DC, MC, V. Tues–Sat noon–2pm and 7:30–11pm. Closed Nov.

INEXPENSIVE

Stars 'n' Bars ☺ AMERICAN/PACIFIC RIM   Modeled on the sports bars popular in the U.S., this place features two dining and drinking areas devoted to American-style food, as well as a bar decorated with memorabilia of notable athletes. No one will mind if you drop in just for a drink, but if you're hungry, menu items read like an homage to the American experience. Try an Indy 500, a Triathlon salad, or the Breakfast of Champions (eggs and bacon with all the fixings). For kids under 12, order the Little Leaguer's Platter or pizza.

The owners also operate **Fusion Cuisine** (same address, phone, and hours), in a space upstairs from the main dining room. Here, platters inspired by the cuisines of the Pacific Rim are featured, each within the same price range as the food served on the restaurant's street level. Examples include sushi, tempuras, rice-based dishes, and fast-wok-fried dishes of meats and seafood.

6 quai Antoine-1er. ⓒ **97-97-95-95.** Reservations recommended. Dinner salads and platters 10€–28€; sandwiches 11€–15€; pizzas 10€–15€. AE, DC, MC, V. June–Sept daily 11am–midnight; Oct–May Tues–Sun 11am–1am. Bar open until 3am.

Monaco After Dark

CASINOS   **Sun Casino,** in the Fairmont Monte Carlo, 12 av. des Spélugues (ⓒ **98-06-12-12**), is a huge room filled with one-armed bandits. It also features blackjack, craps, and American roulette. Additional slot machines are on the roof, with a wide view of the sea. Slot machines operate daily 11am to 4am, and gaming tables are open daily 10am to 4am. Admission is free.

François Blanc developed the **Monte-Carlo Casino,** place du Casino (ⓒ **98-06-20-00**), into the most famous in the world, attracting the exiled aristocracy of Russia, Sarah Bernhardt, Mata Hari, King Farouk, and Aly Khan. The architect of Paris's Opéra Garnier, Charles Garnier, built the oldest part of the casino, and it remains an example of the 19th century's most opulent architecture. The building encompasses the casino and other areas for different kinds of entertainment, including a theater (Opéra de Monte-Carlo; see below) presenting opera and ballet. Baccarat, roulette, and chemin de fer are the most popular games, though you can play *le craps* and blackjack as well.

The casino's **Salle Américaine,** containing only slot machines, opens at 2pm Monday to Friday, noon on weekends. Doors for roulette and *trente et quarante* open at the same time. A section for roulette and chemin de fer opens at 3pm. Additional rooms open at 4pm with more roulette, craps, and blackjack. The gambling continues until very late or early, depending on the crowd. The casino classifies its "private rooms" as the more demure, nonelectronic areas without slots. To enter the casino, you must show a passport or other photo ID, and be at least 18. After 9pm, the staff will insist that men wear jackets and neckties for entrance to the private rooms.

The **Opéra de Monte-Carlo** is headquartered in the lavish, recently renovated Belle Epoque **Salle Garnier** of the casino. Tickets to the operas and other events scheduled inside range from 35€ to 120€. Tickets to events within the Salle Garnier are available from a kiosk in the Atrium du Casino (ⓒ **98-06-28-28**), located within the casino; tickets can be purchased Tuesday to Saturday from 10am to 5:30pm.

Salle du Canton, Les Terrasses, avenue de Fontvieille (ⓒ **93-10-12-00** for tickets and information), which filled in for the Salle Garnier during renovations, now hosts smaller concerts, chamber music concerts, and some ballet. At the

Grimaldi Forum, 10 av. Princesse-Grace (✆ **99-99-20-00** for tickets and information), chamber music and smaller orchestral pieces are usually performed. At both the Salle du Canton and the Grimaldi Forum, ballet tickets cost 8€ to 26€; concert tickets cost 15€ to 30€; and opera tickets cost 40€ to 150€. If tickets are hard to come by, your best bet is to ask your hotel concierge for assistance.

DANCING & DRINKING The **Legend,** 3 av. des Spélugues (✆ **93-50-53-13**), is a favorite of the 25- to 30-year-old crowd that likes a glamorous modern setting. It's open Thursday to Sunday 11:30pm to dawn. Entrance is free. The wildest night is Saturday, when it's mobbed. At **Le Living Room** (✆ **93-50-80-31**), 7 av. des Spélugues, crowds are international and dance-oriented. It's open every night from 10:30pm until dawn. Cozy and comfortable, it's a bit more formal and sedate than the Legend, attracting patrons over 35. There's no cover. Two nearly neighboring piano bars are **Le Sass-Café,** 5 av. des Spélugues (✆ **93-25-52-00**), and the **Zelos Café,** 10 av. des Spélugues (✆ **99-99-25-50**). Drink prices start at around 8€. Toniest of all, and under the same management as the Hôtel de Paris, is **Jimmy's,** in the Sporting d'Eté, avenue Princesse-Grace (✆ **92-16-22-77**), open nightly 11pm to 5am. The hot spot along the eastern Riviera is **Point Rouge,** 11 rue du Portier (✆ **97-77-03-04**), the brainstorm of two local entrepreneurs who have created this chic enclave, a disco-cum-nightclub. You can dance the night away here and also enjoy a light, highly flavorful Mediterranean cuisine such as a clay pot bubbling with lobster stew with fresh vegetables and Moroccan couscous.

Le Karement, in the Grimaldi Forum (✆ **99-99-20-20**), is sprawling, ultracontemporary, and bigger than any nightlife venue ever before seen in Monte Carlo. It boasts two bars inside, a third bar on a terrace, a sprawling bay window that encompasses a view of the sea, and the kind of house and garage music that the young and young-at-heart clientele can really dance to. Open Thursday to Saturday year-round 10pm to 4am (often later, if business allows), its cover is 20€ and includes your first drink.

ROQUEBRUNE & CAP-MARTIN ★★

Roquebrune: 953km (592 miles) S of Paris, 7km (4½ miles) W of Menton, 58km (36 miles) NE of Cannes, 3km (1¾ miles) E of Monaco; Cap-Martin: 4km (2½ miles) W of Menton, 2.5km (1½ miles) W of Roquebrune

Roquebrune, along the Grande Corniche, is a charming mountain village with vaulted streets. It has been restored, though some critics find the restoration artificial. Artists' workshops and boutiques, with merchandise at inflated prices, line rue Moncollet.

Down the hill from Roquebrune, Cap-Martin is a satellite of the larger resort and technically part of the same town. It has been associated with the rich and famous since the empress Eugénie wintered here in the 19th century. In time, the resort was honored by the presence of Sir Winston Churchill, who came here often in his final years. Don't expect to find a wide sandy beach—you'll encounter plenty of rocks against a backdrop of pine and olive trees.

Essentials

GETTING THERE To **drive** to Roquebrune and Cap-Martin from Nice, follow N7 east for 26km (16 miles). Cap-Martin has **train** and bus connections from the other cities on the coast, including Nice and Menton. For **railway** information and schedules, call ✆ **36-35,** or visit www.voyages-sncf.com. To reach Roquebrune, you'll have to take a **taxi.** There's no formal station in Roquebrune; you get off on the side of the highway. For bus information, contact the Gare Routière in Menton (✆ **04-93-35-93-60**).

VISITOR INFORMATION The **Office de Tourisme** is at 218 av. Aristide-Briand, Roquebrune (✆ **04-93-35-62-87;** fax 04-93-28-57-00; www.roquebrune-cap-martin.com).

More than any other municipality in the region, Roquebrune and Cap Martin have at least three guided walking tours of its attractions. The most popular of the three is a 90- to 120-minute guided tour of the old town, priced at 5€ for adults and 2€ for students. Tours depart whenever there are enough (at least four) participants to justify it. More esoteric tours, conducted for the most part exclusively in French, are tours of the municipality's wealth of public buildings, one of them a rather humble campsite, designed by native son and world-famous architect Le Corbusier. It's conducted every Tuesday and Friday at 10am. For history buffs, there is a tour of the municipality's role as France's most southeasterly bulwark of the fabled (and doomed) Maginot Line. Visits to its remaining traces, with historical commentary, are conducted every Saturday at 3pm for 3.50€ for adults, 2.50€ for students. Participation in any of the tours is free for children 11 and under; advance reservations, through the tourist office (see above) are recommended.

Seeing the Sights
IN ROQUEBRUNE

Exploring Roquebrune will take about an hour. You can stroll through its colorful covered streets, which retain their authentic look even though the buildings are now devoted to handicrafts, gift and souvenir shops, and art galleries. From the parking lot at place de la République, head for place des Deux-Frères, turning left into rue Grimaldi. Then head left to **rue Moncollet.** This long, narrow street is covered with stepped passageways and filled with houses that date from the Middle Ages, most often with barred windows. Rue Moncollet leads into **rue du Château,** where you may want to explore the château.

Château de Roquebrune (✆ **04-93-35-07-22**) was originally a 10th-century Carolingian castle; the present structure dates in part from the 13th century. Dominated by two square towers, it houses a museum. From the towers there's a panoramic view along the coast. The interior is open in July and August daily 10am to 12:30pm and 3 to 7:30pm; April to June and September daily 10am to 12:30pm and 2 to 6:30pm; February, March, and October daily 10am to 12:30pm and 2 to 6pm; and November to January daily 10am to 12:30pm and 2 to 5pm. Admission is 3.70€ for adults, 2.70€ for seniors, 1.60€ students and children 7 to 11, and free for children 6 and under.

Rue du Château leads to place William-Ingram. Cross this square to rue de la Fontaine, and take a left. This leads you to the **Olivier millénaire** (millenary olive tree), one of the oldest in the world—it's at least 1,000 years old.

On rue du Grimaldi is **Eglise Ste-Marguerite,** which hides behind a relatively common baroque facade that masks the 12th-century church. It's not entirely from that time, however, having undergone many alterations over the years. The interior is of polychrome plaster. Look for two paintings by a 17th-century local artist, Marc-Antoine Otto, who painted a Crucifixion (in the second altar) and a Pietà (above the entrance door). It's open Monday to Saturday 3 to 5pm, Sunday 10am to 5pm.

IN CAP-MARTIN

Cap-Martin is a rich town. At the center of the cape is a feudal tower that's now a telecommunications relay station. At its base you can see the ruins of the **Basilique St-Martin,** a ruined priory constructed by the monks of the Lérins Islands in the 11th century. Privately owned, it is not open to visitors. After pirate raids in later centuries, notably around the 15th century, it was destroyed and abandoned. If you follow the road (by car) along the eastern shoreline of the cape, you'll be rewarded with a view of Menton against a backdrop of mountains. In the far distance looms the Italian Riviera, and you can see as far as the resort of Bordighera.

You can take one of the most scenic walks along the Riviera here, lasting about 2 hours. The coastal path, **Sentier Le Corbusier ★**, extends between the "Pointe du Cap-Martin" to the eastern (meaning, the closest) frontier of Monaco. If you have a car, you can park it in the lot at avenue Winston-Churchill and begin your stroll. A sign labeled PROMENADE LE CORBUSIER marks the path. As you go along, you'll take in a view of Monaco set in a natural amphitheater. In the distance you'll see Cap-Ferrat and even Roquebrune. The scenic path ends at Monte-Carlo Beach and takes about 2 hours.

If you have a car, you can take a **scenic 9.5km (6-mile) drive ★**. Leave the town on D23, following signs to Gorbio, a village on a hill reached by this winding road. Along the way you'll pass homes of the wealthy and view a verdant setting with pines and silvery olives. The site is wild and rocky, and the buildings were constructed to withstand pirate attacks. The most scenic street is **rue Garibaldi,** which leads past an old church to a panoramic belvedere.

LANGUEDOC-ROUSSILLON

anguedoc is a loosely defined area encompassing the cities of Nîmes, Toulouse, and Carcassonne. It's one of the leading wine-producing areas of the world, and it's fabled for its art treasures.

The coast of Languedoc, from Montpellier to the Spanish frontier, might be called France's "second Riviera" (after the Côte d'Azur). This land of ancient cities has an almost continuous strip of sand stretching west from the Rhône toward the Pyrénées. In the days of Charles de Gaulle, the government began a project to develop the coastline, and in July and August, the miles of sun-baking bodies along the coast attest to its success.

Ancient Roussillon is a small region of Languedoc, forming the Pyrénées Orientales *département* (ministate). This is French Catalonia, inspired more by Barcelona than by Paris. Over its long history, it has known many rulers. Part of the French kingdom until 1258, it was surrendered to James I of Aragón. Until 1344, it was part of the kingdom of Majorca. By 1463, Roussillon had been annexed to France again. Then Ferdinand of Aragón won it back, but by 1659, France had it again. Despite local sentiment favoring reunion with Spain, France firmly controls the land.

The Camargue is a marshy delta between two arms of the Rhône. South of Arles is cattle country. Black bulls are bred here for the bullfighting arenas of Arles and Nîmes. The cattle are herded by *Gardians* (French cowboys), who ride white horses said to have been brought here by the Saracens. The whitewashed houses, plaited-straw roofs, plains, sandbars, and pink flamingos in the marshes make this area exotic.

As for wine, Hérault, Aude, and Garde rank first, second, and third, respectively, in total wine production in France. Most of this is ordinary table wine. A few, however, have been granted an Appellation d'Origine Contrôlée. Some of the best are Fitou, produced in the Hautes-Corbières district near Narbonne, and Minervois, from west and northwest of Narbonne.

NIMES ★★★

721km (448 miles) S of Paris; 43km (27 miles) W of Avignon

Nîmes, the ancient Nemausus, is one of the finest places in the world for wandering among Roman relics. The city grew to prominence during the reign of Caesar Augustus (27 B.C.–A.D. 14). It possesses one of the best-preserved Roman amphitheaters in the world and a near-perfect Roman temple. The city is more like Provence than Languedoc, in which it lies. And there's a touch of Pamplona, Spain, in the festivals of the *corridas* (bullfights) at the arena. The Spanish influence is even more apparent at night, when the bodegas fill, usually with students drinking sangria and listening to flamenco.

By 1860, the togas of Nîmes's citizenry had long given way to denim, the cloth *de Nîmes*. An Austrian immigrant to Nîmes, Levi Strauss, exported the heavy fabric to California to make into work pants for gold-rush prospectors. The rest, as they say, is history.

Essentials

GETTING THERE   The entire town center is now free of vehicular traffic. Nîmes has bus and train service from the rest of France and is near several autoroutes. It lies on the main **rail** line between Marseille and Bordeaux. Thirteen TGV trains arrive daily from Paris's Gare de Lyon; the one-way fare is 92€. For train information and schedules, call ℂ **36-35** or 08-92-35-35-35. If you're **driving,** take A7 south from Lyon to the town of Orange and connect to A9 into Nîmes.

VISITOR INFORMATION   The **Office de Tourisme** is at 6 rue Auguste (ℂ **04-66-58-38-00;** fax 04-66-58-38-01; www.ot-nimes.fr).

SPECIAL EVENTS   Festivals, parties, and cultural events rule the summer nights. Once warm weather hits, all sorts of activities take place at the arena, including concerts and theater performances. Contact the Office de Tourisme for information.

Every Thursday night during July and August, many of Nîmes's squares burst with music, crowds of pedestrians, and rich troves of paintings, crafts, used objects, and sculpture. Artists, musicians, and local residents gather in observance of the city's **Les Jeudis de Nîmes.** Of special interest are place d'Assas, place de l'Horloge, place du Marché, place aux Herbes, and place de la Maison Carrée.

Exploring the City

If you want to see all of the city's monuments and museums, consider buying a *billet global* (Forfait Monuments), sold at the ticket counter of any of the local attractions. It provides access for a 3-day period to Maison Carrée, les Arènes de Nîmes, and Tour Magne. For more information call **Culturespace** (ℂ **04-66-21-82-56**). The fee is 9.80€ for adults, 7.50€ for students and children 10 to 15, and free for children 9 and under.

The pride of Nîmes is the **Maison Carrée ★★★**, place de la Maison Carrée (ℂ **04-66-21-82-56**), built during the reign of Caesar Augustus. Consisting of a raised platform with tall Corinthian columns, it's one of Europe's most beautiful, best-preserved Roman temples. It inspired the builders of La Madeleine in Paris as well as Thomas Jefferson. It schedules cultural and art exhibits, presented beneath an authentically preserved roof. Admission is 4.50€ for adults or 3.70€ for students and children (free ages 9 and under). Hours from October to February are daily 10am to 5pm; March 10am to 1pm and 2 to 6pm; April, May and September daily 10am to 7pm, and June to August daily 10am to 7:30pm.

Across the square stands its modern-day twin, the **Carré d'Art** (with one *e*), a research center and exhibition space that contains a library, newspaper kiosk, and art museum. Its understated design was inspired by (but doesn't overpower) the

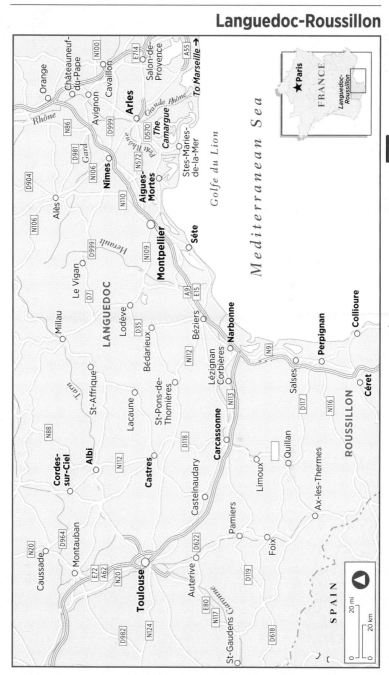

ancient monument. The most visible component is the **Musée d'Art Contempo-rain,** place de la Maison Carrée (✆ **04-66-76-35-35**), which often supplements its exhibitions with displays of contemporary art. It's open Tuesday through Sunday 10am to 6pm. It charges 5€ for adults and 3.70€ for students and children 14 and under. Entrance is free the first Sunday of each month.

Note: This building's terrace provides a panorama of most of the ancient monuments and medieval churches of Nîmes.

Scholars call it **Amphithéâtre Romain de Nîmes ★★★**, and locals refer to it as **Les Arènes de Nîmes.** The monument at place des Arènes (✆ **04-66-76-72-77**) is a better-preserved twin of the one at Arles, and far more complete than Rome's Colosseum. It's two stories high—each floor has 60 arches—and was built of huge stones painstakingly fitted together without mortar. It once held more than 20,000 spectators who came to see gladiatorial combat and wolf or boar hunts. Today it's used for everything from ballet recitals to bullfights. Admission is 7.70€ for adults and 5.90€ for students and children 9 and under. Open January, February, November, and December daily 9:30am to 5pm; March and October daily 9am to 6pm; April, May, and September daily 9am to 6:30pm, and June to August daily 9am to 7pm.

One of the most beautiful gardens in France, **Jardins de la Fontaine ★★**, at the end of quai de la Fontaine, was laid out in the 18th century using the ruins of a Roman shrine as a centerpiece. It was planted with rows of chestnuts and elms, adorned with statuary and urns, and intersected by grottoes and canals. The garden is open from April to mid-September daily 7:30am to 10pm, and from mid-September to March daily 7:30am to 6:30pm. Within the garden are the ruined **Le Temple de Diane ★** and the remains of some Roman baths. Over the park, within a 10-minute walk north of the town center, is **Mont Cavalier,** a low, rocky hill on top of which rises the sturdy bulk of the **Tour Magne ★**, the city's oldest Roman monument. You can climb it for 2.70€ for adults and 2.30€ for students and children 9 and under. It provides a panoramic view over Nîmes and its environs. For more information, call ✆ **04-66-67-65-56.**

Nîmes is home to many museums. The largest and most respected, the **Musée des Beaux-Arts,** rue Cité-Foulc (✆ **04-66-67-38-21**), contains French paintings and sculptures from the 17th to the 20th centuries as well as Flemish, Dutch, and Italian works from the 15th to the 18th centuries. Seek out one of G. B. Moroni's masterpieces, *La Calomnie d'Apelle,* and a well-preserved Gallo-Roman mosaic. The museum is open Tuesday to Sunday 10am to 6pm and until 9pm on the first Thursday of each month. Admission is 5.23€ for adults and 3.79€ for students and children 10 to 16. Free for ages 9 and under.

If time allows, visit the **Musée du Vieux-Nîmes,** place aux Herbes (✆ **04-66-76-73-70**), housed in an Episcopal palace from the 1700s. It's rich in antiques, antique porcelain, and workday objects from the 18th and 19th centuries. Admission is free; hours are Tuesday to Sunday 10am to 6pm.

One of the city's busiest thoroughfares, **boulevard de l'Amiral-Courbet,** leads to the **Porte d'Auguste (Porte d'Arles)**—the remains of a gate built by the Romans during the reign of Augustus. About 45m (148 ft.) to the south are the **Musée de Préhistoire et d'Histoire Naturelle** (✆ **04-66-76-73-45**) and the **Musée Archéologique ★** (✆ **04-66-76-74-80**), in the same building at 13 bis bd. l'Amiral-Courbet. Admission is free; hours are Tuesday to Sunday 10am to 6pm.

Outside the city, 23km (14 miles) northeast, the **pont du Gard ★** spans the Gard River; its huge stones, fitted together without mortar, stand as one of the

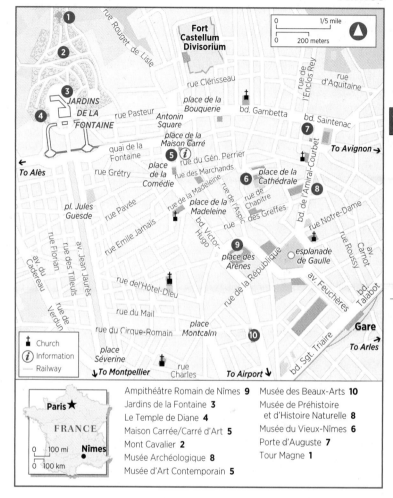

Nîmes

Fort Castellum Divisorium

rue Clérisseau

JARDINS DE LA FONTAINE

rue Pasteur

Antonin Square

place de la Bouquerie

bd. Gambetta

bd. Saintenac

To Avignon →

quai de la Fontaine

place de la Maison Carré

rue du Gén. Perrier

place de la Cathédrale

To Alès ←

rue Grétry

place de la Comédie

rue des Marchands

rue de la Madeleine

place de la Madeleine

rue de l'Aspic

rue de Chapitre

rue des Greffes

rue Notre-Dame

pl. Jules Guesde

rue Pavée

rue Emile Jamais

bd. Victor-Hugo

esplanade de Gaulle

av. Jean Jaurès

rue des Tilleuls

place des Arènes

rue de la République

av. Feuchères

Gare

av. du Cadereau

av. Florian

rue de Verdun

rue del'Hôtel-Dieu

rue du Mail

rue du Cirque-Romain

place Montcalm

To Arles →

Church
Information
Railway

place Séverine

↓ To Montpellier

rue Charles

To Airport ↓

bd. Sgt. Triaire

Paris ★

FRANCE

Nîmes

0   100 mi
0   100 km

Ampithéâtre Romain de Nîmes **9**
Jardins de la Fontaine **3**
Le Temple de Diane **4**
Maison Carrée/Carré d'Art **5**
Mont Cavalier **2**
Musée Archéologique **8**
Musée d'Art Contemporain **5**

Musée des Beaux-Arts **10**
Musée de Préhistoire et d'Histoire Naturelle **8**
Musée du Vieux-Nîmes **6**
Porte d'Auguste **7**
Tour Magne **1**

region's most vivid reminders of the ancient glory. Consisting of three tiers of arches arranged into gracefully symmetrical patterns, it dates from about 19 B.C. Frédéric Mistral, national poet of Provence and Languedoc, recorded a legend alleging that the devil constructed the bridge with the promise that he could claim the soul of the first person to cross it. To visit it, take highway N86 from Nîmes to a point 3km (1¾ miles) from the village of Remoulins, where signs are posted.

The pont du Gard has a museum, **La Grande Expo du Pont du Gard** (© 04-66-37-50-99). Four exhibits detail the bridge's construction, its function throughout the Middle Ages, and insights into its role as a symbol of the architectural savvy of ancient Rome. There's also a restaurant, cafe, and gift shop. It's open daily from

May to August 9am to 8pm, February to April and September to October 9am to 7pm; it is closed otherwise. Admission is 12€ for adults and 9€ for students and children 10 to 16. Free 9 and under.

Shopping

Head to the center of town and **rue du Général-Perrier, rue des Marchands, rue du Chapître,** and the pedestrian **rue de l'Aspic** and **rue de la Madeleine.** A Sunday flea market runs from 8am to around 1pm in the parking lot of the **Stade des Costières,** site of most of the town's football (soccer) matches, adjacent to the southern edge of the boulevard *périphérique* that encircles Nîmes.

To appease your sweet tooth, go to just about any pastry shop in town and ask for the regional almond-based cookies called *croquants villaret* and *caladons.* They're great for a burst of energy or for souvenirs. One of the best purchases you can make, especially if you're not continuing east into Provence, is a *santon.* These wood or clay figurines are sculpted into characters from Provençal country life and can be collected to create a country-French nativity scene. For a selection of *santons* in various sizes, visit the **Boutique Provençale,** 10 place de la Maison Carré (© **04-66-67-81-71**).

Where to Stay

Hôtel l'Amphithéâtre 🏷 The core of this hotel dates from the 18th century, when it was built as a private home. A stay here involves trekking to your room up steep flights of creaking stairs and navigating a labyrinth of corridors. The small rooms are deliberately old-fashioned, usually containing antiques or antique reproductions and creaky, albeit comfortable, beds. The staff long ago grew jaded about the fact that the hotel is less than perfect, but at these prices, who's complaining?

4 rue des Arènes, Nîmes 30000. © **04-66-67-28-51.** Fax 04-66-67-07-79. 15 units. 53€–65€ double. MC, V. Closed mid-Dec to mid-Jan. **Amenities:** Internet (free). *In room:* A/C (in some), TV.

Hôtel Vatel ★ Built around 1990, this hotel lies 3km (1¾ miles) north of the town center, in a cluster of buildings that includes a university and a hospital. It's efficiently staffed with students from the local hotel school, who work here as part of their on-the-job training. The rooms are streamlined, tasteful, and contemporary, with terraces. The modern establishment provides a level of comfort that older hotels, in more historic but limited settings, can't provide.

140 rue Vatel, B.P. 7128, Nîmes 30913. © **04-66-62-57-57.** Fax 04-66-62-57-50. www.hotelvatel.com. 46 units. 145€ double; 200€ suite. AE, DC, MC, V. Free parking. From the A4 autoroute, exit at NIMES OUEST. **Amenities:** 2 restaurants; bar; indoor pool; room service; sauna; spa. *In room:* A/C, TV, hair dryer, minibar, Wi-Fi (free).

Imperator Concorde ★★ This hotel, part of the Concorde chain, is the largest and finest in town, and is adjacent to Les Jardins de la Fontaine—it's the one with the pale pink Italianate facade. In 2005, it underwent a major renovation that left it much improved. The artful and cozy good-size rooms have traditional or French furniture, with fluted or cabriole legs in one or another of the Louis styles. You can order a meal in the hotel's verdant rear gardens or in the high-ceilinged dining room, L'Enclos de la Fontaine.

15 rue Gaston Boissier, Nîmes 30900. © **04-66-21-90-30.** Fax 04-66-67-70-25. www.hotel-imperator. com. 60 units. 153€–250€ double; 250€ suite. AE, DC, MC, V. Parking 13€. **Amenities:** Restaurant; bar; babysitting; room service. *In room:* A/C, TV, hair dryer, minibar, Wi-Fi (free).

New Hôtel La Baume ★ 🏨 One of our favorite nests in Nîmes bears the name of the Marquis de la Baume, whose family built this 17th-century mansion. Its best features are the magnificent staircase that ornaments the interior courtyard and the overall sense of grandeur. During the hotel conversion, the designers carefully preserved the original architecture, and the result is a winning combination of modern and traditional. In contrast to the stately exterior, the guest rooms are hypercontemporary, usually in tones of soft red, orange, and ocher, and the tiled bathrooms are in a postmodern style evocative of Philippe Starck's work.

21 rue Nationale, Nîmes 30000. © **04-66-76-28-42.** Fax 04-66-76-28-45. www.new-hotel.com. 34 units. 140€ double; 170€ junior suite. AE, DC, MC, V. **Amenities:** Bar; room service. *In room:* A/C, TV, hair dryer, minibar, Wi-Fi (8€ per day).

Where to Dine

The dining rooms at the **New Hôtel La Baume** and the **Imperator Concorde** (see above) are good choices.

Alexandre (Michel Kayser) ★★★ TRADITIONAL FRENCH The most charming restaurant around is on the outskirts of Nîmes, 8km (5 miles) south of the center. It's the elegantly rustic domain of Michel Kayser, who adheres to classic tradition, with subtle improvements. His wife, Monique, assists him in the ultramodern dining room, which is outfitted in tones of soft red and ocher with gilded highlights. Menu items are designed to amuse as well as delight the palate: *île flottante,* a playful update of old-fashioned floating island, with truffles and velouté of cèpe mushrooms; roasted pigeon stuffed with vegetable purée and foie gras; tartare of oysters and shellfish with cardamom seeds; *brandade de Nîmes,* a regional version of *brandade* of codfish, elevated here to gourmet standards; and filet of bull from the Camargue in red-wine sauce with Camarguais herbs.

Rte. de l'Aéroport de Garons. © **04-66-70-08-99.** www.michelkayser.com. Reservations recommended. Main courses 40€–72€; fixed-price menus 46€–134€. AE, DC, MC, V. July–Aug Tues–Sat noon–1:30pm and 8–9:30pm; Sept–June Wed–Sun noon–1:30pm, Wed–Sat 8–9:30pm. Closed 2 weeks in Feb–Mar. From town center, take rue de la République southwest to av. Jean-Jaurès; then head south and follow signs to the airport (toward Garons). Closed 2 weeks end of Aug into Sept and first week of Jan.

Restaurant au Chapon Fin ALSATIAN/LANGUEDOCIENNE This tavern-restaurant stands on a little square behind St. Paul's. It has beamed ceilings, small lamps, and a black-and-white stone floor. You'll have a choice of Alsatian and Languedocienne specialties. From the a la carte menu you can order foie gras with truffles, casserole of roasted lamb and eggplant, beefsteak *péllardon* (with goat-cheese sauce), and *brandade* of codfish. Other menu items include several kinds of Charolais beefsteak, a platter piled high with grilled sweetbreads and grilled veal kidneys, and several variations of savory sauerkraut.

3 rue du Château-Fadaise. © **04-66-67-34-73.** www.chaponfin-restaurant-nimes.com. Reservations required. All main courses 16€; fixed-price lunch 13€, dinner 25€. MC, V. Mon–Sat noon–2pm and 7:30–10pm.

Wine Bar le Cheval Blanc 🍴 TRADITIONAL FRENCH This mahogany-paneled place has leather banquettes evocative of an early-1900s California saloon. Choices include an array of salads and platters. At lunch you can order a quick menu, including an appetizer, a garnished main course, and two glasses of wine. Typical dishes are *magret* of duckling, top-notch beefsteaks, and fresh (usually grilled) fish. You can also enjoy lunch on the terrace in the courtyard. A restaurateur extraordinaire, Michel Hermet makes his own wine at vineyards that have been associated with his family for many generations. More than 300 other varieties of wine are in stock, 15 of which are available by the glass or by the pitcher.

1, place des Arènes. (✆ **04-66-76-19-59.** Main courses 9€–24€; fixed-price lunch 13€–24€, dinner 16€–24€. AE, MC, V. Mon–Sat noon–2pm; Mon–Thurs 7–11pm, Fri–Sat 7pm–midnight.

Nîmes After Dark

Once warm weather hits, all sorts of activities take place at the arena, including open-air concerts and theater. The Office de Tourisme has a complete listing. For popular events such as football (soccer), bullfights, and rock concerts, you can contact the **Bureau de Location des Arènes,** 4 rue de la Violette (✆ **04-66-02-80-80**). Tickets for higher-brow events, such as symphonic or chamber-music concerts, theater, and opera performances, are sold through **Le Théâtre Municipal (Le Théâtre de Nîmes),** 1 place de la Calade (✆ **04-66-36-65-10;** www.theatredenimes.com).

If you like hanging out with students and soldiers, head to **Café Le Napoleon,** 46 bd. Victor-Hugo (✆ **04-66-67-20-23**). Popular with the intelligentsia is the **Haddock Cafe,** 13 rue de l'Agau (✆ **04-66-67-86-57**), which books occasional rock concerts.

Sexy, hip **La Comédie,** 28 rue Jean-Reboul (✆ **04-66-76-13-66**), is hands-down the best for dancing and attracts a pretty crowd of youthful danceaholics. A little less flashy but a lot more fun, **Lulu Club,** 10 impasse de la Curaterie (✆ **04-66-36-28-20**), is the gay and lesbian stronghold in Nîmes. Open Thursday to Saturday, it's a magnet for hip and straight folk as well. A youth-oriented contender is **Le C-Cafe,** 20 rue de l'Etoile (✆ **04-66-21-59-22**); open Thursday to Saturday at 11pm, it rocks 'n' rolls to music from L.A. to London.

Streets to explore on virtually any night of the week include **place de la Maison Carrée** and **boulevard Victor-Hugo.**

AIGUES-MORTES ★★

750km (466 miles) SW of Paris; 63km (39 miles) NE of Séte; 40km (25 miles) E of Nîmes; 48km (30 miles) SW of Arles

South of Nîmes, you can explore much of the Camargue by car. The most rewarding place to focus on is Aigues-Mortes, the city of the "dead waters." In the middle of swamps and lagoons, Aigues-Mortes is France's most perfectly preserved walled town. Louis IX and his crusaders once set forth from Aigues-Mortes, which was then a thriving port, the first in France on the Mediterranean. Now 6.5km (4 miles) inland from the sea, it stands on four canals. The **ramparts ★★,** which still enclose the town, were constructed between 1272 and 1300. The **Tour de Constance ★★** (✆ **04-66-53-61-55**) is a model castle of the Middle Ages. At the top, which you can reach by elevator, a panoramic view of the marshes unfolds. Admission is 6.50€ for adults, 4.50€ for ages 18 to 25, and free for children 17 and under. The monument is open May to August daily 10am to 7pm, and September to April daily 10am to 5pm.

Aigues-Mortes's main appeal is the medieval feeling that permeates virtually every building, rampart, and cobble-covered street. The city's religious centerpiece is the **Eglise Notre-Dame des Sablons,** rue Jean-Jaurès (no phone). Constructed of wood in 1183, it was rebuilt in stone in 1246 in the ogival style. Its modern stained-glass windows were installed in 1980 as replacements for the badly damaged originals.

FRANCE'S COWBOY COUNTRY: THE CAMARGUE

The Camargue, where the cowboys of France ride the range, is an alluvial plain inhabited by wild horses, fighting black bulls, roaming Gypsies, pink flamingos, lagoons, salt marshes, wetlands, and gluttonous mosquitoes. Explore the rugged terrain by boat, bike, horse, or jeep.

With the most fragile ecosystem in France, the Camargue has been a national park since 1970. It's known for its small white horses, whose ancestors were brought here by the Arabs long ago. They roam wild in the national park, guarded by cowboys, or *Gardians,* who wear large felt hats and carry long three-pronged sticks to prod the cattle. The cowboys live in thatched huts called *cabanes.* Ancestors of the *Gardians* may have been the first American cowboys, who sailed on French ships to the port of New Orleans, where they rode the bayous of Louisiana and east Texas, rounding up cattle—in French, no less.

There's no more evocative sight than the proud snow-white horses running at liberty through the marshlands, with hoofs so tough that they don't need shoes. It is said that their long manes and bushy tails evolved over the centuries to slap those pesky mosquitoes.

Exotic flora and fauna abound where the delta of the Rhône River empties into the Mediterranean. The bird life is the most luxuriant in Europe. The area, which resembles the Florida Everglades, is known for its colonies of pink flamingos *(Flamants roses).* They share living quarters with some 400 other bird species, including ibises, egrets, kingfishers, owls, wild ducks, swans, and ferocious birds of prey. The best place to see flamingo colonies is the area around Ginès, a hamlet on N570, 5km (3 miles) north of Camargue's capital, Stes-Maries-de-la-Mer.

Exploring the Camargue is best undertaken on the back of a Camarguais horse. The steeds can take you into the interior, which you couldn't see otherwise, fording waters to places where the black bulls graze and wild birds nest. You'll find two to three dozen stables (depending on the time of year) along the highway from Arles to Stes-Maries. Virtually all of them charge the same rate, 17€ per hour. The rides are aimed at the neophyte, not the champion equestrian. They're so easy that they're recommended even for those who have never been on a horse before.

The church is open May to September daily 8:30am to 6pm, and October to April daily 10am to 5pm.

Essentials

GETTING THERE Five **trains** and four **buses** per day connect Aigues-Mortes and Nîmes. Trip time is about an hour. For information and schedules, call ✆ **36-35** or 08-92-35-35-35 from outside France. If you're **driving** to Aigues-Mortes, take D979 south from Gallargues, or A9 from Montpellier or Nîmes.

VISITOR INFORMATION The **Office de Tourisme** is at place St. Louis (✆ **04-66-53-73-00;** fax 04-66-53-65-94; www.ot-aiguesmortes.fr).

Where to Stay

The **Restaurant Les Arcades** (see "Where to Dine," below) also rents rooms.

Hostellerie des Remparts Opened about 300 years ago, this weather-worn inn lies at the foot of the Tour de Constance, adjacent to the medieval fortifications. Popular and often fully booked (especially in summer), it evokes the defensive atmosphere of the Middle Ages, albeit with charm and a sense of nostalgia. Narrow stone staircases lead to the small, simply furnished rooms. Breakfast is the only meal served.

6 place Anatole-France, Aigues-Mortes 30220. ℰ **04-66-53-82-77.** Fax 04-66-53-73-77. 12 units. 60€–110€ double. AE, MC, V. **Amenities:** Restaurant; bar; room service. *In room:* A/C, TV.

Hôtel Les Templiers ★ The leading inn in town is a gem of peace and tranquility. Protected by the ramparts built by St. Louis, king of France, this 17th-century residence has small to medium-size rooms decorated in Provençal style, with just enough decorative objects to lend a homelike aura. You can relax in the courtyard, where you can also enjoy breakfast. The establishment contains two restaurants, each featuring competent and traditional, if not terribly experimental, food. The less formal option is open for both lunch and dinner Wednesday through Monday; the somewhat more formal restaurant is open only for dinner Thursday through Sunday, or Tuesday through Sunday in July and August.

23 rue de la République, Aigues-Mortes 30220. ℰ **04-66-53-66-56.** Fax 04-66-53-69-61. www.hotel lestempliers.fr. 14 units. 125€–190€ double. MC, V. **Amenities:** 2 restaurants; bar; outdoor pool; room service. *In room:* A/C, TV, hair dryer, Wi-Fi (free).

Hôtel St-Louis Even though it's not grand in any way, this is the town's second-best lodging choice. Located near place St-Louis, the inn is not as fine as the Templiers (see above) but does offer comfortably furnished rooms. They're small, with compact, shower-only bathrooms.

10 rue de l'Amiral-Courbet, Aigues-Mortes 30220. ℰ **04-66-53-72-68.** Fax 04-66-53-75-92. www. lesaintlouis.fr. 22 units. 79€–102€ double. AE, MC, V. Parking 12€. Closed mid-Nov to mid-Mar. **Amenities:** Bar; room service. *In room:* A/C, TV, minibar, Wi-Fi (free).

Where to Dine

Hôtel Les Templiers and **Hôtel St-Louis** (see above) are also good choices for dining.

Restaurant Les Arcades ★★ TRADITIONAL FRENCH There's no contest: This is the area's finest dining choice. This restaurant has several formal sections with beamed ceilings or stone vaults. Almost as old as the nearby fortifications, the place is especially charming on sultry days, when the thick masonry keeps the interior cool. The good, reasonably priced food is likely to include warm oysters, fish soup, fried stuffed zucchini flowers, grilled beefsteak from the Camargue, roasted monkfish in red-wine sauce, and grilled duckling. A typical local dish is minced bull steak from the local salt marshes, served with regional herb sauce.

The owner also rents nine large, comfortable rooms with air-conditioning and TVs. The double rate of 108€ to 144€ includes breakfast.

23 bd. Gambetta, Aigues-Mortes 30220. ℰ **04-66-53-81-13.** www.les-arcades.fr. Reservations recommended. Main courses 20€–30€; fixed-price lunch 25€, dinner 34€–44€; children's menu 12€. AE, DC, MC, V. Wed and Fri–Sun noon–2pm; Tues–Sun 7:30–10pm; daily July–Aug noon–2pm, 7:30–10pm. Closed 3 weeks in Mar and 2 weeks in Oct.

MONTPELLIER ★★

758km (471 miles) SW of Paris; 161km (100 miles) NW of Marseille; 50km (31 miles) SW of Nîmes

The capital of Mediterranean (or Lower) Languedoc, the ancient university city of Montpellier is renowned for its medical school, founded in the 13th century. Nostradamus qualified as a doctor here, and Rabelais studied at the school. Petrarch came to Montpellier in 1317 and stayed for 7 years.

Today Montpellier is a bustling metropolis with a population of 380,000, one of southern France's fastest-growing cities, thanks to an influx of new immigrants. Although some suburbs are dreary, the city has a handsome core, with tree-flanked promenades, broad avenues, and historic monuments. Students make up a quarter of the population, giving the city a lively feel. In recent years, many high-tech corporations, including IBM, have opened offices in Montpellier.

Essentials

GETTING THERE Some 12 **trains** per day arrive from Avignon (trip time: 1 hr.); 12 from Marseille (trip time: 1¾ hr.); one every 2 hours from Toulouse (trip time: 2 hr.); and 17 per day from Perpignan (trip time: 1½ hr.). Trains arriving hourly from Paris's Gare de Lyon take 8 to 10 hours, depending on the train, and usually require a change of equipment in Lyon. One TGV (very fast) train arrives daily from Paris, taking less than 3½ hours. The one-way fare starts from 77€. For rail information, call ✆ **36-35** or 08-92-35-35-35.

If you're **driving,** Montpellier lies off A9.

VISITOR INFORMATION The **Office de Tourisme** is at 30 allée Jean de L. de Tassigny (✆ **04-67-60-60-60;** fax 04-67-60-60-61; www.ot-montpellier.fr).

SPECIAL EVENTS From June 24 to July 7 (approximately), classical and modern dancers leap into town for the **Festival International Montpellier Danse.** Tickets for performances cost 6€ to 30€ and can be purchased through the box office, **Montpellierdanse,** 18 rue Ste-Ursule (✆ **08-00-60-07-40** or 04-67-60-83-60; www.montpellierdanse.com). During the last 3 weeks of July, the **Festival de Radio France et de Montpellier** presents orchestral music, jazz, and opera. Tickets run from free to 48€; call ✆ **04-67-61-66-81** for more information or contact the **Cité des Congrés Le Corum,** esplanade Charles de Gaulle (✆ **04-67-61-67-61**; www.festivalradiofrancemontpellier.com).

Exploring the Town

Called the Oxford of France because of its academic community, Montpellier is a city of young people. The **place de la Comédie** is the living room of Montpellier, where you can admire the theater, the 18th-century "Fountain of the Three Graces," or whatever else amuses you.

Before leaving town, stroll along the 17th-century **promenade du Peyrou ★★,** a terraced park with views of the Cévennes and the Mediterranean. The broad esplanade sits at the loftiest point in Montpellier. Opposite its entrance at the end of rue Foch is the **Arc de Triomphe,** erected in 1691 to celebrate the victories of Louis XIV. In the center of the promenade is an equestrian statue of the Sun King, and at the end is the **Château d'Eau,** a pavilion with Corinthian columns that is a monument to 18th-century classicism. Water travels here along a 15km-long (9⅓-mile) conduit and an aqueduct.

Cathédrale St-Pierre The town's spiritual centerpiece was founded in 1364. Once associated with a Benedictine monastery, the cathedral suffered badly during the religious wars of the 16th and 17th centuries. (After 1795, the medical school occupied the monastery.) Today it has a somewhat bleak western front with two towers and a canopied porch.

Place St-Pierre. © **04-67-66-04-12.** Free admission. Mon–Sat 9am–noon and 2:30–7pm; Sun 9am–1pm.

Jardin des Plantes Paul Valéry met André Gide in the Jardin des Plantes, the oldest such garden in France. The botanical garden, filled with exotic plants and a handful of greenhouses, opened in 1593. Check with the tourist office before visiting to make sure it's open.

163 rue Auguste-Broussonnet (enter from bd. Henri-IV). © **04-67-63-43-22.** Free admission. Apr–Sept Tues–Sun noon–8pm; Oct–Mar Tues–Sun noon–6pm.

Musée Fabre ★★★ One of France's great provincial art galleries occupies the former Hôtel de Massilian, where Molière once played for a season. The collection originated when Napoleon sent Montpellier an exhibition of the Royal Academy in 1803. François Fabre, a Montpellier painter, contributed its most important works in 1825. After Fabre's death, other paintings from his collection were donated to the gallery. Several were his own creations, but the more significant works were ones he had acquired—including Poussin's *Venus and Adonis* and Italian paintings such as *The Mystical Marriage of Saint Catherine*. The museum grew through other donations, notably from Valedau, who in 1836 left his collection of Rubens, Gérard Dou, and Téniers. After 2 years of renovations, the museum reopened in 2007 with expanded exhibition space so that more than 300 new works can now be displayed.

2 rue Montpellieret. © **04-67-14-83-00.** Admission 6€ adults, 4€ students and ages 6-26, free for children 6 and under. Tues–Fri and Sun 10am–6pm; Wed 1–9pm; Sat 11am–6pm.

Where to Stay

Le Jardin des Sens (p. 630) also rents rooms.

Hôtel des Arceaux It's basic but still acceptable, and the price is right. A hotel has stood at this prime location, right off the promenade du Peyrou, since the late 1800s. The small rooms are simply but pleasantly furnished, each in a different color and each with a compact bathroom with shower. At the on-site bar, which overflows into a summer garden, simple platters are served. This is not a full-fledged restaurant; what you get is a "bar-bistro platter," a daily special including fish, meat, or poultry with vegetables.

33–35 bd. des Arceaux, Montpellier 34000. © **04-67-92-03-03.** Fax 04-67-92-05-09. www.hoteldes arceaux.com. 18 units. 63€–100€ double; 75€–110€ triple. AE, MC, V. Parking 6€ in nearby lot. **Amenities:** Bar; room service; smoke-free rooms. *In room:* A/C in some, TV, minibar, Wi-Fi (free).

Hôtel du Palais ★ This hotel in the heart of a neighborhood loaded with antiques dealers is one of the best bargains in town. Built in the late 18th century, Hôtel du Palais is in the center of Montpellier, amid a labyrinth of narrow streets and monumental plazas and parks. Much of the decor dates from around 1983, when the hotel was richly restored in a style that uses lots of fabrics, big curtains, and faux marble finishes on walls of public areas. Subsequent renovations have kept the property up-to-date. The guest rooms are relatively large and appealing, thanks to thoughtful placement of antique reproductions and good maintenance. Breakfast is the only meal served.

3 rue du Palais, Montpellier 34000. ✆ **04-67-60-47-38.** Fax 04-67-60-40-23. 26 units. 72€–85€ double. MC, V. Parking 6.50€. **Amenities:** Room service. *In room:* A/C, TV, hair dryer, minibar, Wi-Fi (free).

Hôtel Le Guilhem ★ 🏨 Two 16th-century houses make up this oasis, located on a back street. In its transformation to a hotel, the connected buildings gained all the modern conveniences, including an elevator. Each room is furnished and decorated in individual style, with more than a hint of Laura Ashley design in the striped wallpaper and flowery spreads. Although the accommodations are small, they are tastefully furnished and comfortable. The day begins with a breakfast of freshly baked *pain au chocolat* and croissants served on a terrace overlooking the garden and the cathedral. The location is in the old town, an ideal base from which to explore the sights.

18 rue Jean-Jacques-Rousseau, Montpellier 34000. ✆ **800/528-1234** or 04-67-52-90-90. Fax 04-67-60-67-67. www.leguilhem.com. 35 units. 105€–172€ double. AE, DC, MC, V. Parking 6.50€ in nearby garage. **Amenities:** Room service. *In room:* A/C, TV, hair dryer, minibar, Wi-Fi (free).

Hôtel Ulysse ★ 🍴 One of the city's better bargains, built in 1993, Ulysse delivers a lot of bang for your euro. The owners have worked hard to make the simple hotel as stylish as possible. Each room is uniquely decorated. The furnishings are in an original wrought-iron design, functional but with flair. The hotel lies within a 15-minute walk south of Montpellier's center.

338 av. de St-Maur, Montpellier 34000. ✆ **04-67-02-02-30.** Fax 04-67-02-16-50. www.hotel-ulysse.fr. 24 units. 60€–80€ double. AE, DC, MC, V. Parking 5€. Tram: 1 (Le Mosson line). Bus: 8. From bd. d'Antigone, go north on av. Jean-Mermoz to rue de la Pépinière; continue right and make a left at the 1st intersection, which leads to av. de St-Maur. **Amenities:** Room service. *In room:* A/C, TV, hair dryer, minibar, Wi-Fi (free).

La Maison Blanche ★★ Few other hotels in the south of France work so hard to emulate the gingerbread and French Creole ambience of old New Orleans. Suites are stylishly furnished in rattan and wicker with plenty of wood paneling, whereas standard guest rooms are outfitted with oak. Bathrooms are midsize to roomy. Parts of the interior, especially the dining room, may remind you of Louis XIII's France more than Louisiana, but overall the setting in a verdant park (a 10-min. drive northeast of Montpellier's center) is as charming and unusual as anything else in town.

1796 av. de la Pompignane, Montpellier 34000. ✆ **04-99-58-20-70.** Fax 04-67-79-53-39. www.hotel-maison-blanche.com. 35 units. 79€–116€ double; 160€–180€ suite. AE, DC, MC, V. Free parking. Take bd. d'Antigone east until you reach the intersection with av. de la Pompignane and head north until you see the hotel on your right (trip time: 5 min.). **Amenities:** Restaurant; bar; outdoor pool; room service. *In room:* A/C, TV, hair dryer, minibar, Wi-Fi (free).

Pullman Montpellier Antigone ★ In the heart of Montpellier, this angular, modern, glass-sheathed hotel is the city's top hotel for comfort and first-class amenities. In summer, it does quite a trade with visitors. A particularly appealing feature is the pool, which, along with a bar and breakfast room, occupies most of the top floor. The rooms are chain format but first class. The Antigone is a winning choice, with the most efficient staff in the city, and its bar is one of the coziest hideaways in town.

1 rue des Pertuisanes, Montpellier 34000. ✆ **04-67-99-72-72.** Fax 04-67-65-17-50. www.pullmanhotels.com. 89 units. 220€–260€ double; 480€ suite. AE, DC, MC, V. Parking 3€–10€. **Amenities:** Restaurant; bar; exercise room; Jacuzzi; outdoor pool; room service. *In room:* A/C, TV, hair dryer, Wi-Fi (9.90€ per day).

Where to Dine

La Compagnie des Comptoirs INTERNATIONAL   Just a 5-minute walk east of the town center, lodged behind a set of massive doors that were intricately sculpted by artisans in Morocco, this restaurant manages to evoke the aesthetic and sense of internationalism of the late-19th-century French colonies in, say, India, North Africa, or Indochina. There's room inside for about 130 diners; a big terrace with flowering shrubs and a splashing fountain; and an ongoing emphasis on the kind of sunny, flavorful, and pungent cuisine you're likely to find around the edges of the Mediterranean. The best examples include a succulent version of tempura of crayfish; *accras* (beignets) of crab; grilled calamari with a confit of lemon; grilled steak from bulls from the Camargue, served with red-wine sauce; and a winning collection of desserts.

51 rue François Delmas. ℂ **04-99-58-39-29.** Reservations recommended. Fixed-price menus 28€. AE, DC, MC, V. Tues–Sun noon–2:30pm; Tues–Sun 8–11:30pm.

Le Jardin des Sens ★★★ FRENCH   This is one of the great restaurants of southern France, with two Michelin stars. The chefs, twins Laurent and Jacques Pourcel, have taken Montpellier by storm, and their cuisine could involve almost anything, depending on where their imaginations roam. The rich bounty of Languedoc goes through a process designed to enhance its natural flavor. A starter may be ravioli stuffed with foie gras of duckling and flap mushrooms, floating in chicken bouillon fortified with truffles, broad beans, and crispy potatoes. Main courses of note are shelled lobster, pressed flat and served with duck meat and vanilla oil; and filet of pigeon stuffed with pistachios. A dessert specialty is gratin of limes with slices of pineapple *en confit.*

Le Jardin des Sens also rents 13 guest rooms, plus two suites, each designed in cutting-edge style by Bruno Borrione, a colleague of Philippe Starck. They cost 170€ to 280€ for a double and 310€ to 480€ for a suite.

11 av. St-Lazare. ℂ **04-99-58-38-38.** Fax 04-99-58-38-39. www.jardindessens.com. Reservations required. Main courses 45€–85€; fixed-price lunch Tues–Fri 45€; fixed-price dinner and Sat lunch 80€–170€. AE, MC, V. Mon–Sat noon–2pm and 8–10pm.

Les Vignes ★ PROVENÇAL/LANGUEDOCIENNE   This small restaurant near the Préfecture building serves one of the finest regional cuisines in Montpellier. Walk down the stairs into a spectacular 13th-century arched dining room. Once here, you can enjoy the products of the land, including fresh thyme, olives, and other herbs. Bull from the Camargue is served, along with Provence lamb as well as fish caught in the Mediterranean. Specialties include braised turbot with baby vegetables or wild shrimp cooked in pastis, perhaps a mousselline of scallops with crayfish and red pepper. A selection from Languedoc vineyards accompanies most dishes.

2 rue Bonnier d'Alco. ℂ **04-67-60-48-42.** www.lesvignesrestaurant.com. Reservations recommended. Fixed-price lunch menus 14€–22€; fixed-price dinner menus 33€–52€; main courses 22€–16€. AE, MC, V. Mon–Sat noon–1:30pm and 7:45–9:30pm.

L'Olivier ★★ 🍴 MODERN FRENCH   This charming restaurant's cuisine is so satisfying that we consider it the finest in Montpellier outside the luxe Jardin des Sens. Chef Michel Breton, assisted by his charming wife, Yvette, cooks to perfection. The establishment seats only 22, in a subdued and rather bland modern space accented only by contemporary paintings. But you don't come to L'Olivier to look at the walls. You come for Breton's salmon with a tartare of oysters, warm monkfish terrine, roasted filet of lamb with sweetbread-studded macaroni, and haunch of rabbit stuffed with wild mushrooms. The welcome is warm and sincere.

12 rue Aristide-Olivier. (©) **04-67-92-86-28.** Reservations required. Main courses 21€–27€; fixed-price lunch 21€; fixed-price dinner 38€–48€. AE, MC, V. Tues–Sat noon–1:30pm and 7:30–10pm. Closed Aug and holidays.

Montpellier After Dark

After the sun sets, head for **place Jean-Jaurès, rue de Verdun,** and **rue des Ecoles Laïques,** or walk down **rue de la Loge** and soak up its carnival atmosphere, watching talented jugglers, mimes, and musicians.

Rockstore, 20 rue de Verdun ((©) **04-67-06-80-00**), draws lots of students with 1950s rock memorabilia and live concerts. Up a flight of stairs is its disco, which pounds out techno and rock. There is no cover, except on concert nights. For the best jazz and blues in town, check out **JAM,** 100 rue Ferdinand-de-Lesseps ((©) **04-67-58-30-30;** www.lejam.com). In a noisy, smoky, and even gritty space, its regular concerts attract jazz enthusiasts from miles around. Concert tickets average 10€ to 25€.

A modern, noisy, convivial disco, known throughout the region, is **Le Pacha,** route des Plages, in the hamlet of Lattes ((©) **04-99-52-97-06**), 4km (2½ miles) south of Montpellier. It attracts drinkers and dancers ages 23 to 40. Le Pacha is open Thursday through Saturday beginning around 11pm; on Friday and Saturday it charges a 10€ to 15€ cover, which includes one drink. Gays and lesbians gather at the town's most animated bar and disco, **La Villa Rouge,** route de Palavas ((©) **04-67-06-50-54**), also in Lattes. Both clubs lie about 5km (3 miles) south of the town center.

Le Corum ((©) **04-67-61-67-61**), the most up-to-date theater in town, books many plays, dance recitals, operas, and symphonic presentations. It's in the Palais des Congrès, esplanade Charles-de-Gaulle. For ticket information and schedules, contact the Corum or the **Opéra Comédie,** place de la Comédie ((©) **04-67-60-19-99**).

NARBONNE ★

845km (525 miles) SW of Paris; 61km (38 miles) E of Carcassonne; 93km (58 miles) S of Montpellier

Medieval Narbonne was a port to rival the Marseille of Roman times, its "galleys laden with riches." At the time, Narbonne's size, population, and wealth were greater than those of Rome, London, and Prague. An important Jewish community existed here starting in the 6th century, and Narbonne was also the seat of an important archbishopric from the 11th century. Since then, the Mediterranean has receded from Narbonne, and the town is now 8km (5 miles) inland.

Narbonne was the first town outside Italy to be colonized by the Romans, which makes it an intriguing place. After Lyon, Narbonne was the largest town in Gaul, and even today you can see evidence of the town's former wealth. Too far from the sea to be a beach town, it attracts history buffs and others drawn to memories of its glorious past.

Some 50,000 Narbonnais live in this sleepy backwater. However, many locals are trying to raise the profile of their vineyards. Caves are open to visitors in the surrounding area (the tourist office will advise you). If you want to go to the beach, head to the nearby village of **Gruissan** and its adjoining beach, Gruisson-Plage, or to the suburb of **St-Pierre la Mer** and its adjoining beach, Narbonne-Plage. Both are

15km (9⅓ miles) south of Narbonne. Buses from the town are frequent, each marked with its destination.

Essentials

GETTING THERE   Narbonne has rail, bus, and highway connections with other cities on the Mediterranean coast and with Toulouse. Rail travel is the most popular way to get here, with 14 **trains** per day arriving from Perpignan (trip time: 50 min.), 13 per day from Toulouse (trip time: 1½ hr.), and 12 per day from Montpellier (trip time: 1 hr.). Most rail passengers arriving from Paris take the TGV directly to Narbonne (trip time: 4 hr.). The one-way fare from Paris starts from 85€; from Montpellier, 14€ to 18€. For rail information, call ℂ **36-35,** or 08-92-35-35-35 from outside France. If you're **driving,** Narbonne is at the junction of A61 and A9, easily accessible from either Toulouse or the Riviera.

VISITOR INFORMATION   The **Office de Tourisme** is on 31 rue Jean Jaurès (ℂ **04-68-65-15-60;** fax 04-68-65-59-12; www.mairie-narbonne.fr).

Exploring the town

Few other cities in France contain such a massive medieval architectural block in their centers. Foremost among Narbonne's religious and civic buildings is the **Cathédrale St-Just ★★**, place de l'Hôtel-de-Ville, entrance on rue Gauthier (no phone). The cathedral replaced three primitive churches, the earliest of which dated from A.D. 313. Its construction began in 1272 but was never finished. Only the transept and a choir were completed; the choir is 39m (128 ft.) high, built in the bold Gothic style of northern France. At each end of the transept are 58m (190-ft.) towers from 1480. Pope Clement IV, a former archbishop of Narbonne, sent the cornerstone of the church from Rome. Inside is an impressive collection of Flemish tapestries. In 2000, the grand retable (altarpiece) of the cathedral was restored and reinaugurated with pomp and circumstance. Originally painted by unknown craftsmen in 1381, it graced a side chapel ("Axial Chapel") in the cathedral. In 1732, it was judged old-fashioned and concealed by alterations. In 1847, Viollet-le-Duc ripped out some of the 18th-century changes but never got a full understanding of the extent of the 14th-century murals in the Axial Chapel. In 1981, during the removal of a statue for an art exhibit in Paris, a glimpse of the original altarpiece emerged. A corps of volunteers, all experts in restoration, began the task of piecing together artwork that was broken into as many as 1,500 pieces. The result of their efforts is a polychromed sculpture that's celebrated in art circles throughout France. The cloisters, from the 14th and 15th centuries, connect the cathedral with the Archbishops' Palace (see below). The cathedral is open June to September daily 9am to noon, 2 to 6pm, and October to May daily 9am to noon and 2 to 6pm. Entrance is free.

The cathedral is attached to the **Palais des Archevêques (Archbishops' Palace,** sometimes referred to as the Palais-Vieux), place de l'Hôtel-de-Ville (ℂ **04-68-90-30-66**). It was conceived as part fortress, part palace, with three military-style towers from the 13th and 14th centuries. The Old Palace on the right is from the 12th century, the so-called New Palace on the left from the 14th. It's said that the old, arthritic, and sometimes overweight archbishops were hauled up the interior's Louis XIII–style stairs on mules. Part of the complex is devoted to the neo-Gothic **Hôtel de Ville** (town hall), which was reconstructed between 1845 and 1850 by

Viollet-le-Duc, a 19th-century architect involved with the refurbishment of such sites as the cathedral at Paris.

The Archbishops' Palace is the site of the Musée Archéologique, the Musée d'Art, and the Donjon Gilles-Aycelin, all previewed below.

Musée Archéologique ★ contains prehistoric artifacts, Bronze Age tools, 14th-century frescoes, and Greco-Roman amphorae. Several of the sarcophagi date from the 3rd century, and some of the mosaics are of pagan origin. The **Musée d'Art et d'histoire** is three floors above street level in the former private apartments of the archbishops, the rooms in which Louis XII stayed during his siege of Perpignan. Panels depicting the nine Muses enhance their coffered ceilings. A Roman mosaic floor is on display, as is a collection of antique porcelain, enamels, and a portrait bust of Louis XIV. The museum exhibits a wealth of French paintings from the 17th century. Part of the collection depicts *Arabian Nights*–style scenes with camels, palm trees, sex slaves, and lusty Saracens. In the **Horreum Romain,** 7 rue Rouget-de-l'Isle (② **04-68-32-45-30**), you'll find a labyrinth of underground passages dug by the Gallo-Romans and their successors for storage of food and supplies during times of siege. At this same site in front of the Archbishops' Palace, you can view the remains of a road constructed in 120 B.C. and not discovered until 1997.

A combination ticket (5.20€ adults, 3.70€ students and children 10 to 17, free for 9 and under) admits you to all of these attractions for 6 days. If you don't visit the palace, you can pay for those attractions separately. The palace is open April to September daily 9:30am to 12:15pm and 2 to 6pm, and October to March Tuesday to Sunday 10am to noon and 2 to 5pm.

If you visit between July and September, you may want to participate in one of the occasional hikes up the steep steps of the **Donjon Gilles-Aycelin,** place de l'Hôtel-de-Ville (② **04-68-90-30-30**). A watchtower and prison in the late 13th century, it has an observation platform with a view of the cathedral, the plain, and the Pyrénées. Entrance costs 2.20€; there's no extra charge for the hikes. The watchtower is open May to September daily 9:30am to 12:15pm and 2 to 6pm, October to March Tuesday to Sunday 10am to noon and 2 to 5pm.

A final site worth visiting is the Gothic **Basilique St-Paul-Serge,** rue de l'Hôtel-Dieu (② **04-68-42-28-61**), built on the site of a 4th-century necropolis. It has an elegant choir with fine Renaissance woodcarvings and some ancient Christian sarcophagi. The chancel, from 1229, is admirable. The north door leads to the Paleo-Christian Cemetery, part of an early Christian burial ground. The basilica is open Monday to Saturday 2 to 6pm, Sunday 2 to 5pm.

Where to Stay

Hôtel du Languedoc   Despite frequent modernizations, the grand stone structure of this Belle Epoque hotel still stands out from the cityscape around it. Beside the canal du Rhône, it's the site of municipal meetings and social events, with high-ceilinged public rooms and a mishmash of decors. The rooms come in a variety of shapes and sizes, usually with some of the hotel's original wood furniture and pastel color schemes.

22 bd. Gambetta, Narbonne 11100. ② **04-68-65-14-74.** Fax 04-68-65-81-48. www.hoteldulanguedoc. com. 40 units. 62€–77€ double; 92€ suite. AE, DC, MC, V. Parking 9€. **Amenities:** Bar/Breton-style crêperie; room service. *In room:* TV, hair dryer, Wi-Fi (free).

La Résidence ★ Our favorite hotel in Narbonne is near the Cathédrale St-Just. The 19th-century La Résidence, converted from a stately villa, is comfortable and decorated with antiques. The rooms are midsize to spacious, tastefully furnished, and very well maintained. Most of the good-size bathrooms have tub/shower combinations. The hotel doesn't have a restaurant but serves breakfast.

6 rue du 1er-Mai, Narbonne 11100. © **04-68-32-19-41.** Fax 04-68-65-51-82. www.hotelresidence.fr. 26 units. 76€–125€ double. AE, DC, MC, V. Parking 7.50€. Closed Jan 20–Feb 20. **Amenities:** Smoke-free rooms. *In room:* A/C, TV, hair dryer, minibar, Wi-Fi (free).

Where to Dine

La Table St-Crescent ★★★ FRENCH/LANGUEDOCIENNE This is one of the region's best-respected restaurants. It's just east of town, beside the road leading to Perpignan, in a complex of wine-tasting boutiques established by a local syndicate of growers. The foundations date from the 8th century when it functioned as an oratory (small chapel) and prayer site. Today it's outfitted with modern furniture that's little more than a foil for the cuisine. The chef delivers refined, brilliantly realized dishes, with sublime sauces and sophisticated herbs and seasonings. Menu items change four times a year based on the availability of seasonal ingredients and the inspiration of the owners. Some of the best main courses include sea bass marinated with olives; fresh scallops with artichokes; tuna tartare with roasted almonds; or chicken served with a truffle sauce.

In the Palais des Vins, 68 av. Général Leclerc, rte. de Perpignan. © **04-68-41-37-37.** www.la-table-saint-crescent.com. Reservations recommended. Main courses 26€–41€; fixed-price lunch Tues–Fri 25€; fixed-price dinner and Sun lunch 42€–80€. AE, DC, MC, V. Tues–Fri and Sun noon–1:30pm; Tues–Sat 8–9:30pm.

COLLIOURE ★★

929km (577 miles) SW of Paris; 28km (17 miles) SE of Perpignan

This port was established by the Greeks in 6000 B.C. and renamed "Cauco Illiberis" by the Romans. Destroyed several times by the Arabs, it was rebuilt in the 900s by the counts of Barcelona. The port later belonged to the kings of Majorca, who established a community of Knights Templar in 1344. Still later, it passed to the kings of Aragón. Ownership passed back and forth between the kings of Spain and France before General Dugommier seized it for France in 1794. In modern times, it sheltered a colony of painters including Derain, Dufy, Picasso, and Juan Gris.

You may recognize this port and its sailboats from the fauvist paintings of Lhote and Derain. It's said to resemble St-Tropez before it was overrun; in days past, Collioure attracted Matisse, Picasso, and Dalí. It is the most alluring port of Roussillon, a gem with a vivid Spanish and Catalan flavor. Some visitors believe it's the most charming village on the Côte Vermeille (Vermilion Coast, a nickname for this area). The town's sloping narrow streets, semifortified church, lighthouse, and rich artistic culture make it worth an afternoon's stopover. While this is the ideal small-town antidote to the condominium-choked Riviera (in winter, its pop. is only 3,000), its population swells during the summer months to 15,000.

Essentials

GETTING THERE Collioure has frequent **train** and bus service, especially from Perpignan (trip time: 20 min.). For train information and schedules, call © **36-35**

or 08-92-35-35-35. Many visitors **drive** along the coastal road (RN114) leading to the Spanish border.

VISITOR INFORMATION   The **Office de Tourisme** is on place du 18-Juin (© **04-68-82-15-47;** fax 04-68-82-46-29; www.collioure.com).

Exploring the town

The two curving ports sit on either side of the heavy masonry of the 13th-century **Château Royal,** place de 8-Mai-1945 (© **04-68-82-06-43**). It's of interest in its own right for its medieval fortifications and overall bulk, but between the months of May and September, it's also the home to a changing series of special (temporary) exhibitions, each of which comes and goes at regular intervals. The château assesses the same entrance charge regardless of whether there's a temporary exhibition inside on the day of your visit: 4€ for adults, 2€ students and children ages 12 to 18, and free for children 11 and under. In July and August hours are daily 10am to 6:15pm; June and September daily 10am to 5:15pm; October to May daily 9am to 4:15pm.

Also try to visit the **Musée Jean-Peské,** route de Port-Vendres (© **04-68-82-10-19**), home to a collection of works by artists who painted here. It's open in July and August daily 10am to noon and 2 to 6pm, and September to June Wednesday to Monday 10am to noon and 2 to 6pm. Admission is 2€ for adults, 1.50€ for children 12 to 16 and students, and free for children 11 and under.

Where to Stay

Casa Pairal ★   This pleasant family-operated hotel is in a 150-year-old house a very short walk from the port and beach. In the guest rooms, charming antiques blend with more modern pieces. The best doubles have *petit salons* plus small balconies. Breakfast is the only meal served, but there are many restaurants nearby. On sunny days, guests can take a dip in the pool, which sits in the shadow of century-old trees.

Impasse des Palmiers, Collioure 66190. © **04-68-82-05-81.** Fax 04-68-82-52-10. www.hotel-casa-pairal.com. 27 units. 89€–187€ double; 184€–233€ suite. AE, DC, MC, V. Parking 14€. Closed Nov–Mar. **Amenities:** Outdoor pool; room service. *In room:* A/C, TV, hair dryer, minibar, Wi-Fi (free).

Les Caranques 🦑   Constructed around the core of a private villa built after World War II and enlarged twice since then, this comfortably furnished hotel is one of the best bargains in town. The rooms are a bit small but neatly maintained. On the perimeter of Collioure, away from the crush (and the charm) of the center, the hotel features a terrace that opens onto a view of the old port. The terrace stretches from the hotel to the sea, where guests can swim directly from the rocks.

Rte. de Port-Vendres, Collioure 66190. © **04-68-82-06-68.** Fax 04-68-82-00-92. www.les-caranques.com. 22 units. 85€–125€ double. AE, MC, V. Parking: 10€ (Apr–Sept; otherwise free). Closed in Jan. **Amenities:** Room service. *In room:* TV, minibar.

Relais des 3 Mas et Restaurant La Balette ★★   This is the town's premier hotel and the restaurant of choice; the hotel was established more than 20 years ago by connecting a trio of older Provençal farmhouses. In the decor of its beautiful rooms, the hotel honors the famous artists who lived at Collioure. The rooms, which have spacious bathrooms with Jacuzzis, open onto water views. Even if you aren't a guest, you may want to have a meal in the dining room and take in its vistas of the harbor. Frederic Bacquié is the best chef in town. His cooking is inventive—often simple but always refined. Fixed-price menus cost 37€ to 85€ and are served Wednesday to Sunday at lunch and dinner.

Rte. de Port-Vendres, Collioure 66190. © **04-68-82-05-07.** Fax 04-68-82-38-08. www.relaisdes3mas. com. 23 units. 100€–465€ double; 190€–425€ suite. Half board 75€ per person. AE, MC, V. Free parking. Closed Dec–Feb. **Amenities:** Restaurant; babysitting; outdoor pool; room service; sauna; Wi-Fi (free). *In room:* A/C, TV, hair dryer, minibar.

Where to Dine

Restaurant La Balette at the Relais des 3 Mas (see above) is the best hotel dining room in town.

Neptune ★★★ FRENCH/CATALAN   This is the best restaurant in Collioure, but much to the credit of its owners and staff, it's easygoing and remarkably unpretentious. You'll find it on the southeastern edge of town in a salmon-toned Provençal *mas* (farmhouse). The establishment has for many years been the domain of the talented, hardworking Mourlane family. Menu items are noteworthy for their top-quality ingredients and the respect and care with which they're handled. Our favorite starter is a platter of local anchovies marinated in herbs; you may opt for a salad of fresh wild greens garnished with chunks of lobster. Main courses change with the seasons but may include grilled Mediterranean sea wolf; several versions of lobster; or rack of suckling lamb from the nearby salt marshes, served in orange sauce or an herb-flavored pastry crust. Equally appealing are lightly braised scallops in delicate butter, herb, and garlic sauce, and simple but succulent sole meunière.

9 rte. de Porte-Vendres. © **04-68-82-02-27.** Reservations recommended. Main courses 22€–56€; fixed-price menus 32€–70€. AE, MC, V. Wed–Mon noon–2pm and 7:30–9pm.

PERPIGNAN ★★

905km (562 miles) SW of Paris; 369km (229 miles) NW of Marseille; 64km (40 miles) S of Narbonne

At Perpignan you may think you've crossed into Spain; this was once Catalonia's second city, after Barcelona. Earlier, it was the capital of the kingdom of Majorca. But when Roussillon—the French part of Catalonia—was partitioned off, Perpignan became French forever, under the terms of the 1659 Treaty of the Pyrénées. Catalan is still spoken here, especially among country folk.

Today Perpignan is content to rest on its former glory. Its 120,000 residents enjoy the closeness of the Côte Catalane (the coastline of Catalonia, in neighboring Spain) and the mountains to the north. The pace is relaxed. You'll have time to smell the flowers that grow here in great abundance.

This is one of the sunniest places in France, but during summer afternoons in July and August, it's a cauldron. That's when many locals catch the 9.5km (6-mile) ride to the beach resort of Canet. Bus no. 1 runs from the center of Perpignan every 15 minutes in the summer and costs 4€. A young scene brings energy to Perpignan, especially along the quays of the Basse River, site of impromptu nighttime concerts, beer drinking, and the devouring of tapas, a tradition adopted from nearby Barcelona.

Essentials

GETTING THERE   Four **trains** per day arrive from Paris from both the Gare St. Lazare and the Gare de Nord (trip time: 6–10 hr.) after stopping at Montpellier; the one-way fare is 91€. There are also three conventional trains from Marseille via

Narbonne (trip time: 4½ hr.; one-way fare: 40€). For rail information and schedules, call ✆ **36-35** or 08-92-35-35-35. If you're **driving** from the French Riviera, drive west along A9 to Perpignan.

VISITOR INFORMATION The **Office Municipal du Tourisme** is in the Palais des Congrès, place Armand-Lanoux (✆ **04-68-66-30-30;** fax 04-68-66-30-26; www.perpignantourisme.com).

SPECIAL EVENTS In the heat of July, **Les Estivales** (✆ **04-68-35-01-77;** www.estivales.com) causes the city to go on a 4-week cultural binge, with music, expositions, and theater. Our favorite time to visit this area is during September. If you visit then, you may want to drive through vineyards of the Rivesaltes district bordering the city to the west and north. Temperatures have usually dropped by then.

Perpignan is host to one of the most widely discussed celebrations of photojournalism in the industry, the **Festival International du Photojournalisme** (✆ **04-68-62-38-00;** www.visapourlimage.com). Established in the late 1980s, it's also called **Le Visa pour l'Image.** From September 2 to September 17, at least 10 sites of historical (usually medieval) interest are devoted to photojournalistic expositions from around the world. Entrance to the shows is free and an international committee awards prizes.

Exploring the city

With its inviting pedestrian streets, Perpignan is a good town for shopping. Catalan is the style indigenous to the area, and its influence is evident in the textiles, pottery, and furniture. For one of the best selections of Catalan pieces, including pottery, furniture, carpets, and antiques, visit the **Centre Sant-Vicens,** rue Sant-Vicens (✆ **04-68-50-02-18),** where about a dozen merchants sell ceramics, pottery, and art. You'll find it 4km (2½ miles) south of the town center; follow signs pointing to Enne and Collioure. A competitor selling Catalan-inspired home-decorating items is **La Maison Quinta,** 3 rue des Grands-des-Fabriques (✆ **04-68-34-41-62;** www.maison-quinta.com), in the town center.

A 3-hour guided **walking tour** is a good way to see the attractions in the town's historic core. On Fridays, some tour leaders even lace their commentary with English. Tours begin at 5pm daily from mid-June to mid-September. The rest of the year, they start at 2:30pm on Wednesday and 10:30am on Saturday only. They depart from in front of the tourist office and cost 5€ per person. For more details, contact the tourist office (see above).

Cathédrale St-Jean ★ The cathedral dates from the 14th and 15th centuries and has an admirable nave and interesting 17th-century retables (altarpieces). Leaving through the south door, you'll find on the left a chapel with the *Devost-Christ* (Devout Christ), a magnificent woodcarving depicting Jesus contorted with pain and suffering, his head, crowned with thorns, drooping on his chest. Sightseeing visits are discouraged during Sunday Mass. On Good Friday, the statue is promenaded through the streets of the town center.

Place Gambetta/rue de l'Horloge. ✆ **04-68-51-33-72.** Free admission. Daily 7:30am–6:30pm. Closes 5:30pm Dec–Feb.

Château de Salses Since the days of the Romans a fort of some sort has guarded the main road linking Spain and France. In 1497 Ferdinand of Aragón erected the most elaborate fort, hoping to protect his northern frontier. Even today, the town of Salses marks the language-barrier point between Catalonia in Spain and Languedoc in France. This Spanish-style fort designed by Ferdinand is a curious example of an Iberian structure in France, but in the 17th century it was modified to look more like a château. Salses fell to Louis XIII in September 1642, and its Spanish garrison left forever. Some 2 decades later, Roussillon was incorporated into France.

Salses, 16km (10 miles) north of the center of Perpignan. ✆ **04-68-38-60-13.** Admission 7€ adults, free for ages 25 and under. Oct–May daily 10am–noon and 2–5pm; June–Sept daily 9:30am–7pm. From Perpignan, follow signs to Narbonne and RN9.

Le Castillet ★   This crenelated red-brick building is a combination gateway and fortress from the 14th century. You can climb its bulky tower for a view of the town. Also here is the **Musée des Arts et Traditions Populaires Catalans** (also known as La Casa Païral), with exhibitions of Catalan regional artifacts and folkloric items, including typical dress.

Place de Verdun. ✆ **04-68-35-42-05.** Admission 4€ adults, 2€ students, and free 18 and under. May–Sept Wed–Mon 10am–6:30pm; Oct–Apr Wed–Mon 11am–5:30pm.

Palais des Rois de Majorque (Palace of the Kings of Majorca) ★   At the top of the town, the Spanish citadel encloses the Palace of the Kings of Majorca. The government has restored this structure, built in the 13th and 14th centuries, around a court encircled by arcades. You can see the old throne room, with its large fireplaces, and a square tower with a double gallery; from the tower there's a fine view of the Pyrénées. A free guided tour, in French only, departs four times a day if demand warrants it.

Rue des Archers. ✆ **04-68-34-48-29.** Admission 4€ adults, 2€ students, free for children 11 and under. June–Sept daily 10am–6pm; Oct–May daily 9am–5pm.

Where to Stay

La Villa Duflot ★★★   This is the area's greatest hotel, yet its prices are reasonable for the luxury it offers. Tranquillity, style, and refinement reign supreme. Located in a suburb 4km (2½ miles) from Perpignan, La Villa Duflot is a Mediterranean-style dwelling surrounded by a park of pine, palm, and eucalyptus. You can sunbathe in the gardens surrounding the pool and order drinks from the outside bar. The good-size Art Deco guest rooms surround a patio planted with century-old olive trees. All are spacious and soundproof, with Art Deco interiors. The restaurant (reviewed below) is reason enough to stay.

Rond-Point Albert Donnezan, Perpignan 66000. ✆ **04-68-56-67-67.** Fax 04-68-56-54-05. www.villa-duflot.com. 24 units. 150€–250€ double. Half board 117€–163€ per person double occupancy. AE, DC, MC, V. From the center of Perpignan, follow signs to Perthus-Le Belou and A9, and travel 3km (1¾ miles) south. Just before you reach A9, you'll see the hotel. **Amenities:** Restaurant; 2 bars; babysitting; outdoor pool; room service. *In room:* A/C, TV, hair dryer, minibar, Wi-Fi (free).

Park Hotel ★   This five-story, mid-'60s hotel, facing the Jardins de la Ville, provides well-furnished, soundproof rooms. Although the Park is solid and reliable, it's the town's second choice, with none of the glamour of the Duflot. The midsize to spacious rooms are comfortably furnished with taste but not much flair; each comes with an average-size bathroom, and most have tub/shower combinations. The restaurant serves first-class Mediterranean cuisine. Post-nouvelle choices include roast sea scallops flavored with succulent sea urchin velouté, various lobster dishes, and penne with truffles. As an accompaniment, try one of the local wines—perhaps a Collioure or Côtes du Roussillon.

18 bd. Jean-Bourrat, Perpignan 66000. © **04-68-35-14-14.** Fax 04-68-35-48-18. www.parkhotel-fr. com. 69 units. 80€–110€ double; 180€–280€ suite. AE, DC, MC, V. Parking 10€. **Amenities:** Restaurant; bar; room service. *In room:* A/C, TV, hair dryer, minibar, Wi-Fi (free).

Where to Dine

The **Park Hotel** (see above) has a well-recommended restaurant, serving fixed-price menus from 28€ to 50€.

L'Assiette Catalane ♦ FRENCH/SPANISH/CATALAN   Known to virtually every resident of Perpignan for its well-prepared cuisine, this restaurant resembles something you'd expect across the Pyrénées in Spain. Hand-painted ceramic plates, rugby and flamenco posters, and antique farm implements cover the thick stone walls. Even the long, lively bar is inlaid with Iberian mosaics, and copies of works by Dalí and Picasso seem to stare back at you as you dine. Menu items include four kinds of *parrilladas* (mixed grills)—one of the most appealing consists entirely of fish served on a hot slab of iron that's brought directly to your table—and zarzuelas, paella, and tapas, prepared in the Spanish style, but served as an appetizer. Chicken with crayfish is another regional specialty. It seems appropriate to follow up with a portion of flan.

9 rue de la République. © **04-68-34-77-62.** www.assiettecatalane.com. Reservations recommended. Main courses 12€–18€; fixed-price lunch 8€–11€, dinner 16€–27€. MC, V. Mon–Sat noon–2pm; Tues–Sat 7:15–10:30pm.

La Villa Duflot ★ FRENCH   Slightly removed from the city center, this *restaurant avec chambres* (see "Where to Stay," above) is the most tranquil oasis in the area. Owner André Duflot employs top-notch chefs who turn out dish after dish with remarkable skill and professionalism. Try, for example, a salad of warm squid, a platter of fresh anchovies marinated in vinegar, excellent foie gras of duckling, or lasagna of foie gras with asparagus points. A wonderful dessert is chocolate cake with saffron-flavored cream sauce. On the premises is an American-style bar.

Rond-Point Albert Donnezan, Perpignan 66000. © **04-68-56-67-67.** Fax 04-68-56-54-05. Reservations required. Main courses 19€–25€; Mon–Fri fixed-price menu 23€. AE, DC, MC, V. Daily noon–2pm and 8–11pm. From the center of Perpignan, follow signs to Perthus–Le Belou and A9, and travel 3km (1¾ miles) south. Just before you reach A9, you'll see the hotel.

Le Clos des Lys ★ ♦ FRENCH/CATALAN   This well-recommended restaurant, in a stately building that sits apart from its neighbors, has an outdoor terrace overlooking a copse of cypresses and bubbling fountains. It's supervised by Jean-Claude Vila and Frank Seguret, respected chefs who have been finalists in several culinary competitions. The fixed-price menus vary widely in selection and cost. Dishes may include goat cheese in puff pastry, garnished with sesame seeds and a reduction of banyuls dessert wine; terrine of three kinds of liver accompanied with a salad of wild greens and walnuts; foie gras of duck with passion fruit–and–mango chutney sauce; filets of sea wolf fried with sesame seeds and served with eggplant mousse and tomato-flavored risotto; and tournedos of beef with a layer of foie gras, creamed morels, and soufflé potatoes. The restaurant incorporates a thriving catering business that books conventions and weddings.

660 chemin de la Fauceille. © **04-68-56-79-00.** www.closdeslys.com. Reservations recommended. Fixed-price lunch 20€–79€, dinner 26€–79€. AE, DC, MC, V. Tues–Sun noon–2pm; Tues and Thurs–Sat

7pm–midnight. Closed 2 weeks in Feb. From the center of Perpignan, drive 2.5km (1½ miles) west, following the rte. d'Espagne.

Perpignan After Dark

Perpignan shows its Spanish and Catalan side at night, when a round of tapas and late-night promenades are among the activities. The streets radiating from **place de la Loge** offer a higher concentration of bars and clubs than any other part of town.

Hot and sometimes overheated Perpignan offers lots of diversions to amuse visitors during the cool of the night. An evening on the town involves a drink and a chat in one of the *bars de nuit,* followed by a visit to a disco. You may begin at **Le Habana Bodegita-Club,** 5 rue Grande-des-Fabriques (✆ **04-68-34-11-00**), where salsa and merengue play and sunset-colored cocktails flow. Suds with an Irish accent are the attraction at **Le O'Shannon Bar,** 3 rue de l'Incendie (✆ **04-68-35-12-48**), where a small community of Irish expats (and Celtic wannabes) wax nostalgic.

Discos in Perpignan open around 11pm. **Le Napoli,** 3 rue place de Catalogne (✆ **04-68-51-25-02**), a modern, mirror-sheathed space, may remind you of an airport waiting area without the chairs. (Yes, you'll have to stand up and mingle or dance, because there's almost nowhere to sit.) Another option for dancing is the **Uba-Club,** 5 bd. Mercader (✆ **04-68-34-06-70**), which has a smallish dance floor and, thankfully, some sofas and chairs.

During summer, the beachfront strip at the nearby resort of **Canet-Plage,** 12km (7½ miles) east of Perpignan's historic core, abounds with seasonal bars and dance clubs that come and go with the tourist tides.

CARCASSONNE ★★★

797km (495 miles) SW of Paris; 92km (57 miles) SE of Toulouse; 105km (65 miles) S of Albi

Evoking bold knights, fair damsels, and troubadours, the greatest fortress city of Europe rises against a background of the Pyrénées. Floodlit at night, it suggests fairy-tale magic, but in its heyday in the Middle Ages, it wasn't so romantic. Shattering the peace and quiet were battering rams, grapnels, a mobile tower (inspired by the Trojan horse), catapults, flaming arrows, and the mangonel (a type of catapult).

Today the city that once served as a backdrop for the 1991 movie *Robin Hood, Prince of Thieves* is overrun with visitors and tacky gift shops. But the elusive charm of Carcassonne emerges in the evening, when thousands of day-trippers have departed and floodlights bathe the ancient monuments.

Essentials

GETTING THERE Carcassonne is a major stop for **trains** between Toulouse and destinations south and east. There are five trains per day from Toulouse (trip time: 1 hr.; one-way fare: 15€), nine per day from Montpellier (trip time: 1½ hr.; 23€ one-way), and three per day from Marseille (trip time: 4 hr.; 43€ one-way). For rail information, call ✆ **36-35** or 08-92-35-35-35. If you're **driving,** Carcassonne is on A61 south of Toulouse.

VISITOR INFORMATION The **Office de Tourisme** has locations at 28 rue de Verdun (✆ **04-68-10-24-30;** fax 04-68-10-24-38; www.carcassonne-tourisme. com) and in the medieval town at Porte Narbonnaise (✆ **04-68-10-24-36**).

SPECIAL EVENTS The town's nightlife sparkles during its summer festivals. During the **Festival de Carcassonne** (www.festivaldecarcassonne.com) in July, concerts, modern and classical dance, operas, and theater fill the city. Tickets run 25€ to 65€ and can be purchased by calling ✆ **04-68-11-59-15** or 04-68-77-74-31. On July 14, **Bastille Day,** one of the best fireworks spectacles in France lights up the skies at 10:30pm. Over 6 weeks in July and August, the merriment and raucousness of the Middle Ages overtake the city during the **Spectacles Medievaux,** in the form of jousts, food fairs, and street festivals. For information, contact the **Office de Tourisme** (✆ **04-68-10-24-30**).

Exploring the town

Carcassonne consists of two towns: the **Bastide St-Louis** (also known as the Ville Basse or Lower City) and the medieval **Cité.** The former has little of interest, but the latter is among the major attractions in France. The fortifications consist of the inner and outer walls, a double line of ramparts. The Visigoths built the inner rampart in the 5th century. Clovis, king of the Franks, attacked it in 506 but failed to breach the fortifications. The Saracens overcame the city in 728, but Pepin the Short (father of Charlemagne) drove them out in 752.

The epic medieval poems *Chansons de Geste* tell the tale of the origin of the town's name. During a siege by Charlemagne, the populace of the city was starving and near surrender until a local noblewoman, Dame Carcas, reputedly gathered up the last of their grain, fed it to a sow, and then tossed the pig over the ramparts. The pig burst, scattering the grain. Dame Carcas then ordered the trumpets sounded for a parley and cried, *"Carcas te sonne!"* ("Carcas is calling you!"). The Franks concluded that Carcassonne must have unlimited food supplies and ended their siege.

Carcassonne's walls were further fortified by the *vicomtes* de Trencavel in the 12th century and by Louis IX and Philip the Bold during the following century. By the mid–17th century the city had lost its position as a strategic frontier, and the ramparts were left to decay. In the 19th century, the builders of the Lower Town began to remove the stone for use in new construction. But interest in the Middle Ages revived, and the government ordered Viollet-le-Duc (who restored Notre-Dame in Paris) to repair and, where necessary, rebuild the walls. Reconstruction continued until very recently. A small population lives inside the walls.

In the highest elevation of the Cité, at the uppermost terminus of rue Principale (rue Cros Mayrevielle), you'll find the **Château Comtal,** place du Château (✆ **04-68-11-70-70**), a restored 12th-century fortress that's open April through September daily 10am to 6:30pm, October through March daily 9:30am to 5pm. Entrance includes an obligatory 40-minute guided tour, in French and broken English. It's also the only way to climb onto the city's inner ramparts. The cost is 8€ for adults, and free for ages 26 and under. The tour includes access to expositions that display the archaeological remnants discovered on-site, plus an explanation of the 19th-century restorations.

Another major monument in the fortifications is the **Basilique St-Nazaire ★**, La Cité (✆ **04-68-25-27-65**), dating from the 11th to the 14th centuries and containing some beautiful stained-glass windows and a pair of rose medallions. The nave is in the Romanesque style, and the choir and transept are Gothic. The 16th-century organ is one of the oldest in southwestern France. The 1266 tomb of Bishop Radulphe is well preserved. The cathedral is open in July and August daily 9am to

6pm, September through June daily 9am to noon and 1 to 5pm. Mass is celebrated on Sunday at 11am. Admission is free.

Shopping

Carcassonne has two distinct shopping areas. In the modern lower city, the major streets for shopping, particularly if you're in the market for clothing, are **rue Clemenceau** and **rue de Verdun.** In the walled medieval city, the streets are chock-full of tiny stores and boutiques; most sell gift items such as antiques and local arts and crafts.

Stores worth visiting, all in the Cité, include **Comptoir des Vins,** rue du Conte Roger (𝓒 **04-68-26-44-76**), where you'll find a wide selection of regional wines ranging from simple table wines to those awarded the distinction of Appellation d'Origine Contrôlée. Some antiques stores of merit are **Mme. Faye-Nunez,** 4 place du Château (𝓒 **04-68-47-09-45**), for antique furniture; **Antiquités Safi,** 26 rue Trivalle (𝓒 **04-68-25-60-51**), for paintings and art objects; and **Maison du Sud,** 13 porte d'Aude (𝓒 **04-68-47-10-06**), for home decoration.

Where to Stay

IN THE CITE

Hôtel de la Cité ★★★ Originally a palace for whatever bishop or prelate happened to be in power at the time, this has been the most desirable hotel in town since 1909. It's in the actual walls of the city, adjoining the cathedral. The Orient-Express Hotel group acquired the hotel in the '90s and fluffed it up to the tune of $3 million. You enter a long Gothic corridor-gallery leading to the lounge. Many rooms open onto the ramparts and a garden, and feature antiques or reproductions. A few accommodations contain wood headboards and four-poster beds. The ideal unit is no. 308, which opens onto the most panoramic view of the city. The hotel is renowned for its restaurant.

Place Auguste Pierre Pont, Carcassonne 11000. 𝓒 **04-68-71-98-71.** Fax 04-68-71-50-15. www.hotelde lacite.com. 61 units. 425€–525€ double; 725€–1,325€ suite. AE, DC, MC, V. Parking 21€. Closed Feb to early Mar. **Amenities:** 3 restaurants (including La Barbacane, p. 643); bar; babysitting; outdoor pool; room service. *In room:* A/C, TV, hair dryer, minibar, Wi-Fi (free).

AT THE ENTRANCE TO THE CITE

Best Western Le Donjon et Les Remparts ★★ 🖋 This little hotel is big on charm and is the best value in the moderate price range. Built in the style of the old Cité, it has a honey-colored stone exterior with iron bars on the windows. The interior is a jewel. Elaborate Louis XIII–style furniture graces the reception lounges. A newer wing contains additional rooms in medieval architectural style. Their furnishings are in a severe style that's consistent with the medieval look of the nearby ramparts. The hotel also runs the nearby Brasserie Le Donjon. In summer, the garden is the perfect breakfast spot.

2 rue du Comte-Roger, Carcassonne 11000. 𝓒 **04-68-11-23-00.** Fax 04-68-25-06-60. www.hotel-donjon.fr. 62 units. 105€–197€ double; 200€–300€ suite. AE, DC, MC, V. Parking 10€. **Amenities:** Restaurant; bar; room service. *In room:* A/C, TV, hair dryer, minibar, Wi-Fi (free).

IN VILLE-BASSE

Hôtel Montségur ★ 🖋 This stately town house with a mansard roof and dormers was built in 1887. Trees and a high wrought-iron fence screen the front garden from the street. Didier and Isabelle Faugeras have furnished the hotel with antiques, lending it a residential feel. Guest rooms vary in size, from small to spacious. Continental breakfast is available on-site, but for dinner you may wish to visit their highly recommended restaurant across the street, Le Languedoc, where Didier is the chef.

27 allée d'Iéna, Carcassonne 11000. ⓒ **04-68-25-31-41.** Fax 04-68-47-13-22. www.hotelmontsegur. com. 21 units. 65€–108€ double. AE, DC, MC, V. Free parking. **Amenities:** Restaurant; bar; room service. *In room:* A/C, TV, hair dryer, Wi-Fi (free).

Trois Couronnes ★★   Reliable and dependable, though not exciting, this serviceable favorite is the best choice in Ville-Basse. It lies south of the landmark Square Gambetta, immediately west of the bridge, pont Vieux. Built in 1992, the hotel rises five stories. Rooms open onto views of the Aude River and the ramparts of the old city. A government-rated three-star hotel, "Three Crowns" has some of the best facilities in town, including an indoor pool. The rooms are functionally comfortable with tasteful furnishings. Service is top rate, and maintenance is good. A good regional cuisine is served in the on-site restaurant.

2 rue des Trois Couronnes, Carcassonne 11000. ⓒ **04-68-25-36-10.** Fax 04-68-25-92-92. www.hotel-destroiscouronnes.com. 69 units. 100€–120€ double. AE, DC, MC, V. Parking 6€–9€. **Amenities:** Restaurant; bar; indoor pool; room service. *In room:* A/C, TV, hair dryer, minibar, Wi-Fi (free).

Where to Dine

Brasserie Donjon, run by Le Donjon et Les Remparts hotel, is a good, affordable choice for meals, especially if you're visiting the Cité at lunchtime. In Ville-Basse, the moderately priced restaurant at **Trois Couronnes** (see above) serves well-prepared regional cuisine.

Au Jardin de la Tour INTERNATIONAL   This restaurant and its verdant garden introduce greenery and charm into the city's medieval core. Rustic finds from local antiques fairs decorate the early-19th-century building. You can order from a large selection of salads, beef filet with morels, sushi, cassoulet, terrines of foie gras, and all kinds of grilled fish. The consistently good cooking relies on fresh ingredients deftly handled by a talented kitchen staff.

11, Porte-d'Aude. ⓒ **04-68-25-71-24.** Reservations recommended in summer. Main courses 15€–25€; fixed-price menu 30€. MC, V. Tues–Sat noon–2pm and 7:30–10pm. Closed Nov 1–Dec 15.

La Barbacane ★ FRENCH   Named after its medieval neighborhood, this restaurant enjoys equal billing with the celebrated hotel that contains it. Its soothing-looking dining room, with green walls and lots of paneling, features the cuisine of noted chef Jérome Ryon and pastry chef Régis Chanel. Menu items are based on seasonal ingredients, with just enough zest. Examples are green ravioli perfumed with seiche (a species of octopus) and its own ink, crisp-fried cod with black olives, saltwater crayfish with strips of Bayonne ham, Breton lobster with artichoke hearts and caviar, and organically fed free-range guinea fowl rubbed with vanilla and stuffed with truffles. A star dessert is the warm soufflé flavored with coffee from Ecuador and chocolate, served with peppermint sherbet.

In the Hôtel de la Cité, place de l'Eglise. ⓒ **04-68-71-98-71.** www.hoteldelacite.com. Reservations recommended. Main courses 40€–60€; fixed-price menu 70€–160€. AE, DC, MC, V. Thurs–Mon 7:30–10pm. Closed Feb–Mar.

Le Languedoc ★★ TRADITIONAL FRENCH   Acclaimed chef Didier Faugeras is the creative force behind the inspired cuisine here. The high-ceilinged century-old dining room is filled with antiques; a brick fireplace contributes to the warm atmo-sphere. The specialty is *cassoulet au confit de canard* (the famous stew made with duck cooked in its own fat). It has been celebrated here since the early 1960s. A smooth dessert is flambéed crepes Languedoc. In summer you can dine on a patio or in the air-conditioned restaurant. Faugeras and his wife, Isabelle, own the worthy Hôtel Montségur, across the street (see "Where to Stay," above).

32 allée d'Iéna. © **04-68-25-22-17.** Reservations recommended. Main courses 18€–28€; fixed-price menu 22€–45€. AE, DC, MC, V. Tues–Sun noon–1:30pm; Tues–Sat 7:30–9:30pm. Closed Dec 20–Jan 20.

Where to Stay & Dine Nearby

Château St-Martin ★ FRENCH   One of Languedoc's most successful chefs operates out of this 16th-century château at Montredon, 4km (2½ miles) northeast of Carcassonne. Ringed by a wooded park, the restaurant serves the superb cuisine of co-owners Jean-Claude and Jacqueline Rodriguez. Dine inside or on the terrace. Recommended dishes are fish (according to the daily catch) with fondue of baby vegetables, sea bass with scallop mousseline, sole in tarragon, and *confit de canard carcassonnaise* (duck meat cooked in its own fat and kept in earthenware pots). Two other specialties are *cassoulet languedocienne* (made with pork, mutton, and goose or duck) and *boullinade nouvelloise* (made with an assortment of seafood that includes scallops, monkfish, sole, and turbot). On the premises are 15 simple, but comfort-able, hotel rooms; doubles rent for 80€ to 100€. The hotel is closed November 15 to March 11. Call © **04-68-47-44-41;** www.chateausaintmartin.net for informa-tion on rooms.

Montredon, Carcassonne 11090. © **04-68-71-09-53.** Fax 04-68-25-46-55. www.chateausaintmartin. net. Reservations required. Main courses 18€–28€; fixed-price menu 32€–56€. AE, DC, MC, V. Thurs–Tues noon–1:30pm; Thurs–Sat and Mon–Tues 7:45–9:15pm. From La Cité, follow signs pointing to Stade Albert Domec 4km (2½ miles) northeast.

Domaine d'Auriac ★★★   The Carcassonne area's premier address for food and lodging is this moss-covered 19th-century manor house about 2.5km (1½ miles) west of the Cité. It was built around 1880 on the ruins of a medieval monastery; some of the monastery's ceiling vaults are still visible in the cellars. The cube-shaped building, a Relais & Châteaux member, has six stone-sided annexes, which hold many of the accommodations. Each guest room has a photo-magazine aura, with lots of flowered fabrics, a range of decorative styles, and, in many, massive sculpted ceil-ing beams. Anne-Marie Rigaudis is the experienced owner, assisted by her grown children, Marie-Hélène and Pierre. The hotel is one of the few in the area with its own 18-hole golf course, which affords gorgeous panoramas over the countryside (ask about combination golf/stay packages).

Part of the property's allure is the well-crafted and well-conceived meals. Fixed-price menus, costing 70€ to 150€, change several times each season, but always demonstrate a sophisticated twist that makes local recipes more glamorous and inter-esting. During warmer weather, there's seating beside the pool on flowery terraces.

Rte. de Saint-Hilaire, Carcassonne 11000. © **04-68-25-72-22.** Fax 04-68-47-35-54. www.domaine-d-auriac.com. 24 units. 152€–390€ double; 400€–450€ suite. AE, DC, MC, V. Free parking. Closed Jan 3–Feb 8. Take D104 west 2.5km (1½ miles) from Carcassonne. **Amenities:** Restaurant; bar; babysitting; 18-hole golf course; outdoor pool; room service; tennis court. *In room:* A/C, TV, hair dryer, minibar, Wi-Fi (10€ for 3 hr.).

Carcassone After Dark

Carcassonne nightlife centers on **rue Omer-Sarraut** in La Bastide and **place Marcou** in La Cité. **La Bulle,** 115 rue Barbacane (✆ **04-68-72-47-70**), explodes with techno and rock dance tunes for an under-30 crowd that keeps the place hopping until 5am Wednesday to Sunday. The cover charge begins at 10€ per person. Another enduringly popular disco, 4km (2½ miles) southwest of town, is **Le Black Bottom,** route de Limoux (✆ **04-68-47-37-11**), which plays every conceivable kind of dance music Thursday through Sunday beginning at 11pm. Entrance costs 10€ on Saturday only.

CASTRES ★

728km (452 miles) SW of Paris; 42km (26 miles) S of Albi

On the bank of the Agout River, Castres is the gateway for trips to the Sidobre, the mountains of Lacaune, and the Black Mountains. Castres is one of France's most important wool-producing areas; the industry's origins in the region date to the 14th century. The town, with a current population of 50,000, was once a Roman military installation. A Benedictine monastery was founded here in the 9th century, and the town fell under the *comtes* d'Albi in the 10th century. During the wars of religion, it was Protestant.

Essentials

GETTING THERE   From Toulouse, there are seven **trains** per day (trip time: 1 hr., 15 min.); the one-way fare from Toulouse is 13€. For information, call ✆ **36-35** or 08-92-35-35-35. If you're **driving,** Castres is on N126 east of Toulouse and N112 south of Albi.

VISITOR INFORMATION   The **Office de Tourisme** is at 2 place de la République (✆ **05-63-62-63-62;** fax 05-63-62-63-60; www.tourisme-castres.fr).

Exploring the town

Eglise St-Benoît   The town's most prominent church is an outstanding example of French baroque architecture. The architect Caillau began construction in 1677 on the site of a 9th-century Benedictine abbey, but the structure was never completed according to its original plans. Gabriel Briard executed the painting above the altar in the 18th century.

Place du 8-Mai-1945. ✆ **05-63-59-05-19.** Free admission. Mon–Sat 9am–noon and 2–6pm; Sun 8:30am–noon. Closed to casual visitors Sun Oct–May, except for religious services.

Musée Goya ★   The museum is in the town hall, an archbishop's palace designed by Mansart in 1669. Some of the spacious public rooms have ceilings supported by a frieze of the archbishop's coats of arms. The collection includes 16th-century tapestries and the works of Spanish painters from the 15th to the 20th centuries. Most notable are the paintings of Francisco Goya y Lucientes, all donated to the town in 1894 by Pierre Briguiboul, son of the Castres-born artist Marcel Briguiboul. *Les Caprices* is a study of figures created in 1799 after the illness that left Goya deaf. Filling much of an entire room, the work consists of symbolic images of demons and monsters, a satire of Spanish society.

In the Jardin de l'Evêché. ✆ **05-63-71-59-30.** Admission 2.30€ adults, 1.15€ for students, free for children 18 and under. July–Aug daily 10am–6pm; Apr–June and Sept daily 9am–noon and 2–6pm; Oct–Mar Tues–Sat 9am–noon and 2–5pm.

Where to Stay

Hôtel Renaissance ★   The Renaissance is the best hotel in Castres. It was built in the 17th century as a courthouse and had become a colorful but run-down hotel when it was restored in 1993. Today you'll see a dignified building with *colombages*-style half-timbering and a mixture of stone blocks and bricks. Some of the comfortable rooms have exposed timbers. Some rooms are in the style of Napoleon III, some are 18th-century Asiatic, and some are country-comfortable with safari-themed fabrics.

17 rue Victor-Hugo, Castres 81100. ✆ **05-63-59-30-42.** Fax 05-63-59-21-38. www.hotel-renaissance.fr. 22 units. 65€ double; 92€ suite. AE, DC, MC, V. Parking 6€. **Amenities:** Restaurant; bar; room service. *In room:* A/C, TV, hair dryer, minibar, Wi-Fi (free).

Where to Dine

Brasserie de l'Europe ✦ FRENCH/PROVENÇAL   This modern brasserie is a good bet for solid cuisine. The rustic decor features English-inspired furnishings with lots of well-oiled wood paneling. The expanded menu includes a selection of regional platters as well as pizzas. There are also regional sausages served with purée of apples and cheese from the foothills of the Pyrénées. Other menu items include cassoulets and roasted Camembert cheese with Provençal herbs. The service is polite, but pressed for time. Many visitors find it suitable for a simple noontime meal.

1 place Jean-Jaurès. ✆ **05-63-59-01-44.** Reservations recommended. Main courses 15€–19€; fixed-price lunch 14€–21€, dinner 22€. MC, V. Mon–Sat noon–2:30pm and 7–10:30pm.

La Mandragore ★ LANGUEDOCIENNE   On an easily overlooked narrow street, this restaurant, named for a legendary plant with magic powers, occupies a small section of one of the many wings of the medieval château-fort of Castres. The decor is simple, with stone walls and tones of autumn colors. The regional cuisine is among the best in town, and it's served with a smile. Among the best dishes are ravioli stuffed with truffles, snails, and pink garlic and flavored with basil, rack of suckling veal with exotic mushrooms, and *magret* of duckling with natural Canadian maple syrup. The owners are French citizens who lived in Montreal for 15 years and worked at a restaurant there.

1 rue Malpas. ✆ **05-63-59-51-27.** Reservations recommended. Main courses 12€–18€; fixed-price menu 13€ at lunch, 18€–26€ at dinner. DC, MC, V. Tues–Sat noon–2pm and 7–9pm. Closed 2 weeks in Sept and 2 weeks in Mar.

ALBI ★★★

697km (433 miles) SW of Paris; 76km (47 miles) NE of Toulouse

The "red city" (for the color of its bricks) of Albi straddles both banks of the Tarn River and is dominated by its 13th-century cathedral. Toulouse-Lautrec was born in the Hôtel Bosc in Albi; it's still a private home and not open to visitors, but there's a plaque on the wall of the building, on rue Toulouse-Lautrec in the town center. The town's major attraction is a museum with a world-class collection of the artist's work.

Essentials

GETTING THERE   Fifteen **trains** per day link Toulouse with Albi (trip time: 1 hr.); the one-way fare is 12€. There's also a Paris-Albi night train. For rail information, call ✆ **36-35** or 08-92-35-35-35. If you're **driving** from Toulouse, take N88 northeast.

The **Office de Tourisme** is in the Palais de la Berbie, place Ste-Cécile (☎ **05-63-49-48-80;** fax 05-63-49-48-98; www.albi-tourisme.fr).

Exploring the town

Cathédrale Ste-Cécile ★★★
Fortified with ramparts and parapets and containing frescoes and paintings, this 13th-century cathedral was built by a local lord-bishop after a religious struggle with the *comte* de Toulouse (the crusade against the Cathars). Note the exceptional 16th-century rood screen with a unique suit of polychromatic statues from the Old and New Testaments. Free classical concerts take place in July and August on Wednesday at 5pm and Sunday at 4pm.

Near place du Vigan, in the medieval center of town. ☎ **05-63-43-23-43.** Cathédrale: Free admission. Treasury: 2€ adults, free for children 14 and under. June–Sept daily 9:30am–6pm; Oct–May daily 9:30am–noon and 2–6pm.

Musée de Lapérouse
Set on the opposite bank of the Tarn from the bulk of Albi's medieval core (take the Pont-Vieux to reach it), within what was originally built in the 18th century as a factory for pasta, this museum honors the achievements of Albi's native son, Jean-François de la Pérouse. Commissioned as an explorer by Louis XVI in the late 1600s, he mapped and charted the coastlines of Alaska, California, and China, bringing the French up to speed against England in its rush for colonies outside of Europe. The museum contains maps, charts, navigational instructions, and memorabilia that illustrate the progress and achievements of not only the explorer himself, but France's self-image during a period of some of its greatest glory.

Square Botany Bay. ☎ **05-63-46-01-87.** Admission 3€ adults, 2€ students and ages 13–25, free for children 12 and under. Mar–June and Sept–Oct Tues–Sun 9am–noon and 2–6pm; July–Aug Mon–Fri 9am–noon and 2–6pm, Sat–Sun 10am–noon and 2–7pm; Nov–Feb Tues–Sun 10am–noon and 2–5pm.

Musée Toulouse-Lautrec ★★
The Palais de la Berbie (Archbishop's Palace) is a fortified structure dating from the 13th century. This museum contains the world's most important collection of the artist's paintings, more than 600 in all. His family bequeathed the works remaining in his studio. The museum also owns paintings by Degas, Bonnard, Matisse, Utrillo, and Rouault. Late in 2005, the museum enlarged its premises with three additional display rooms, each of them a brick-lined refuge within the premises of a neighboring historic building. Within, you'll see, gathered together, some of Toulouse-Lautrec's earliest works, formulated during his earliest creative years.

Opposite the north side of the cathedral. ☎ **05-63-49-48-78.** Admission 5.50€ adults, 2.50€ students, free for children 13 and under. July–Aug daily 9am–6pm; June and Sept daily 9am–noon and 2–6pm; Apr–May daily 10am–noon and 2–6pm; Mar and Oct Wed–Mon 10am–noon and 2–5:30pm; Nov–Feb Wed–Mon 10am–noon and 2–5pm. Closed Jan 1, May 1, Nov 1, and Dec 25.

Where to Stay

Hostellerie St-Antoine ★★
Some historians say this is one of the oldest continuously operated hotels in France. Originally a monastery, then a medieval hospital, the property became an inn in 1734 (when the present building was constructed). The same family has owned it for five generations; today the father-son team of Jacques and Jean-François Rieux manages it. Jacques's mother focused on Toulouse-Lautrec when designing the hotel, because her grandfather was a friend of the

painter and was given a few of his paintings, sketches, and prints. Several are in the lounge, which opens onto a rear garden. The rooms have been delightfully decorated, with a sophisticated use of color, reproductions, and occasional antiques. They're generally spacious, furnished with French Provincial pieces. Even if you're not staying, visit the dining room. The Rieux culinary tradition is revealed in their traditional yet creative cuisine.

17 rue St-Antoine, Albi 81000. ☎ **05-63-54-04-04.** Fax 05-63-47-10-47. www.saint-antoine-albi.com. 44 units. 125€–185€ double; 185€–245€ suite. AE, DC, MC, V. Parking 7€. **Amenities:** Restaurant (open only to groups); bar; babysitting; room service. *In room:* A/C, TV, hair dryer, minibar, Wi-Fi (free).

Hôtel Chiffre 🖉 This hotel in the city center was built as a lodging for passengers on the mail coaches that hauled letters and people across France. The renovated building retains the original porch that sheltered carriages from the rain and sun. The rooms are artfully cozy, with upholstered walls in floral patterns; some have views of the inner courtyard. The midsize bathrooms come with tub/shower combinations or showers only. The hotel restaurant is popular among locals because of its good-value fixed-price menus. The menu priced at 20€ to 27€ per person consists of choices that were compiled after Toulouse-Lautrec's death by his friends. They remembered the way he'd often prepare the dishes himself during his dinner parties. Some of his favorite dishes included radishes stuffed with braised liver, suprême of *sandre* (fish), and duckling roasted with garlic.

50 rue Séré-de-Rivières, Albi 81000. ☎ **05-63-48-58-48.** Fax 05-63-38-11-15. www.hotelchiffre.com. 39 units. 88€–112€ double; 200€ suite. AE, MC, V. Parking 9€. **Amenities:** Restaurant; bar; room service; Wi-Fi (free). *In room:* A/C, TV, hair dryer.

La Réserve ★★★ The queen of England slept here. This country-club villa in a 1.6-hectare (4-acre) park on the northern outskirts of Albi is managed by the Rieux family, who also run the Hostellerie St-Antoine. A Relais & Châteaux member, La Réserve is a Mediterranean-style villa with a pool and a fine garden in which you can dine. The rooms, well furnished and color coordinated, contain imaginative decorations (but avoid the rooms over the kitchen, which are noisy at mealtimes). The upper-story rooms have sun terraces and French doors. The modern tiled bathrooms come with deluxe toiletries and showers.

Rte. de Cordes à Fonvialane, Albi 81000. ☎ **05-63-60-80-80.** Fax 05-63-47-63-60. www.relaischateaux. fr/reservealbi. 23 units. 158€–398€ double; 398€–498€ suite. AE, DC, MC, V. Closed Nov–Apr. From the center of town, follow signs to Carmaux-Rodez until you cross the Tarn; then follow signs to Cordes. The hotel is adjacent to the main road leading to Cordes, 2km (1¼ miles) from Albi. **Amenities:** Restaurant; bar; babysitting; outdoor pool; room service; rooms for those w/limited mobility; smoke-free rooms. *In room:* A/C, TV, hair dryer, minibar, Wi-Fi (free).

Where to Dine

La Réserve has a wonderful restaurant, as does **Hostellerie St-Antoine.** Bateau Ivre at the **Hôtel Chiffre** is another worthy choice. See "Where to Stay," above.

Jardin des Quatre Saisons ★★ MODERN FRENCH The best food in Albi is served by Georges Muriel Bermond, who believes that menus, like life, should change with the seasons, which is how the restaurant got its name. In his two simple dining rooms, the service is always competent and polite. Fine-tuned menu items include delicious fricassee of snails garnished with strips of the famous hams produced in the nearby hamlet of Lacaune, and ravioli stuffed with pulverized shrimp and served with truffled cream sauce. Most delectable of all—an excuse for returning—is *pot-au-feu* of the sea, with three or four species of fish garnished with crayfish-cream sauce. The wine list is the finest in Albi.

19 bd. de Strasbourg. ☏ **05-63-60-77-76.** www.lejardindes4saisons.chez-alice.fr. Reservations recommended. Fixed-price menu 24€–35€. AE, DC, MC, V. Tues–Sun noon–2:30pm; Tues–Sat 7:30–10pm.

Le Lautrec TRADITIONAL FRENCH   Part of its charm derives from its associations with Toulouse-Lautrec—the restaurant lies across the street from his birthplace and is decorated with paintings by local artists. Also appealing is the rich patina of its interior brickwork. The skillfully prepared food items include scallops that come with rose oil and essence of shrimp, sweetbreads with morels, and roasted rack of lamb marinated in a brewed infusion of Provençal thyme. Hearty regional dishes—beloved by local diners—are a cassoulet of codfish, savory sweetbreads (an acquired taste for some), duckling *en confit,* and rabbit stew with vegetables.

13-15 rue Toulouse-Lautrec. ☏ **05-63-54-86-55.** www.restaurant-le-lautrec.com. Reservations recommended. Main courses 18€–38€; fixed-price lunch Tues–Fri 15€–38€; other fixed-price meals 18€–50€. AE, MC, V. Tues–Sun noon–2pm; Tues–Sat 7–9:30pm. Closed 1 week in Jan; 1 week in Aug; and 2 weeks in Nov.

CORDES-SUR-CIEL ★★

678km (421 miles) SW of Paris; 25km (16 miles) NW of Albi

This remarkable site is like an eagle's nest on a hilltop, opening onto the Cérou valley. In days gone by, celebrities such as Jean-Paul Sartre and Albert Camus considered this town a favorite hideaway. In low season, the population is only 1,050, but swells to 10,000 in midsummer.

Through the centuries, Cordes has been known for its textile, leather, and silk industries. Even today, it's an arts-and-crafts city, and in many of the old houses on the narrow streets, artisans—blacksmiths, enamelers, graphic artists, weavers, engravers, sculptors, and painters—ply their trades. Park outside and then pass under an arch leading to the old town.

Essentials

GETTING THERE   If you're **driving,** take N88 northwest from Toulouse to Gaillac, turning north on D922 into Cordes-sur-Ciel. If you're coming by **train,** get off in Cordes-Vindrac and walk, rent a bicycle, or take a taxi the remaining 3km (1¾ miles) west of Cordes. For train information, call ☏ **36-35** or 08-92-35-35-35. For a **minibus,** call Taxi Barrois (☏ **05-63-56-14-80**). The one-way fare is 4.15€ Monday through Saturday, rising to 6.65€ after 7pm and on Sunday. There's no regular bus service.

VISITOR INFORMATION   The **Office de Tourisme** is at 8 place Jeanne Ramel-Cals (☏ **05-63-56-00-52;** fax 05-63-56-19-52; www.cordessurciel.eu).

Exploring the town

Often called "the city of a hundred Gothic arches," Cordes contains numerous *maisons gothiques* ★★ of pink sandstone. Many of the doors and windows are fashioned of pointed (broken) arches that retain their 13th- and 14th-century grace. Some of the best-preserved ones line **Grande Rue Raymond VII,** also called **rue Droite.**

Eglise St-Michel   The church, the most important historic building in town, dates from the late 13th century and has undergone many alterations. Most of the lateral design of the side chapels probably comes from the cathedral at Albi. Before being shipped here, the organ (dating from 1830) was in Notre-Dame in Paris.

Rue St-Michel. ℂ **05-63-56-00-15** (tourist office). Free admission. Summer tours daily 10:30am–12:30pm and 3–6:30pm.

Musée Charles-Portal   Small, quirky, and relatively unvisited even by residents of Cordes, this somewhat sleepy museum is named after a nearby pass-through (the Painted Gate) that pierces the fortifications surrounding the city's medieval center. It's also named for Charles-Portal (d. 1936), a 1920s-era archivist of the Tarn region and a local historian. In a medieval house whose foundations date from the Gallo-Roman era, it contains artifacts of the textile industry, farming implements, samples of local embroidery, a reconstruction of an old peasant home, and a scattering of medieval pieces.

Porte des Ormeaux. ℂ **05-63-53-44-41.** Admission 2.50€ adults, 1.50€ students and ages 12–25, free for children 11 and under. July–Aug Wed–Mon 2–6pm; Apr–June and Sept–Oct only Sat–Sun 2–5pm. Closed otherwise.

Where to Stay & Dine

Hostellerie du Parc 🍴 TRADITIONAL FRENCH   This inn originated in the 18th century as a landowner's thick-walled home. Today, in a verdant park, the stone house holds this charming getaway *restaurant avec chambres.* It serves generous meals in a garden or paneled dining room. Specialties include homemade foie gras, duckling, *poularde* (chicken) *occitaine,* rabbit with cabbage leaves, *ballotine* of duck with foie gras, and confit of roasted rabbit with pink garlic from the nearby town of Lautrec.

The hotel offers 13 comfortable and well-furnished rooms; a double costs 65€ to 110€. Each accommodation comes with free Wi-Fi.

Les Cabannes, Cordes 81170. ℂ **05-63-56-02-59.** Fax 05-63-56-18-03. www.hostellerie-du-parc.com. Reservations recommended. Main courses 14€–32€; fixed-price menu 28€–65€. AE, DC, MC, V. June–Oct daily noon–2pm and 7–9:30pm; off season Fri–Sun noon–2pm, Fri–Sat 7–10pm. Closed 3 weeks in Jan. From the town center, take rte. de St-Antonin (D600) for about 1km (⅔ mile) west.

Le Grand Ecuyer ★★★ MODERN FRENCH   The medieval monument that contains this restaurant (the 15th-c. hunting lodge of Raymond VII, *comte* de Toulouse) is a national historic treasure. Despite its glamour and undeniable charm, the restaurant remains intimate and unstuffy, although guests in recent years have included King Juan Carlos of Spain, the emperor of Japan, and even Queen Elizabeth. Chef Yves Thuriès's platters have made his dining room an almost mandatory stop for the rich and famous. Specialties include three confits of lobster, red mullet salad with fondue of vegetables, confit of pigeon with olive oil and rosemary, and noisette of lamb in chicory sauce. The dessert selection is nearly overwhelming.

The hotel contains 12 rooms and one suite, all with antiques and modern comforts. Doubles cost 115€ to 165€; the suite is 265€. The most popular room, honoring former guest Albert Camus, has a four-poster bed and a fireplace. During its annual closing, a nearby twin hotel, the **Hostellerie du Vieux Cordes,** 21 rue St-Michel (ℂ **05-63-53-79-20**), is an alternative. This hotel is also very old (13th c.) and loaded with elegant architectural touches (marble and granite bathrooms, antiques, and high ceilings), and is under the management of Thuriès, the region's grandest and most entrepreneurial chef. Here a double ranges from 52€ to 120€, with a suite costing 162€. Wi-Fi is free. On the premises is a terrace shaded with an arbor and a 300-year-old wisteria vine. The house that contains this immediately abuts the Eglise St-Michel.

Grand-Rue Raymond VIII, Haute de la Cite, Cordes 81170. © **05-63-53-79-50.** Fax 05-63-53-79-51. www.thuries.fr. Reservations required. Main courses 28€–38€; fixed-price menu 43€–93€. AE, DC, MC, V. July–Aug Thurs–Sun noon–1:30pm, daily 7–9:30pm; Apr–June and Sept to mid-Oct Tues–Sun 7–9:30pm. Closed mid-Oct–Mar.

TOULOUSE ★★★

705km (438 miles) SW of Paris; 245km (152 miles) SE of Bordeaux; 97km (60 miles) W of Carcassonne

The old capital of Languedoc and France's fourth-largest city, Toulouse (known as La Ville Rose) has a cosmopolitan flavor. The major city of the southwest, filled with gardens and squares, it's the gateway to the Pyrénées. Most of Toulouse's fine old mansions date from the Renaissance, when this was one of the richest cities in Europe. Today Toulouse is an artistic and cultural hub and a high-tech center, home to two huge aircraft makers—Airbus and Aerospatiale. Also making the city tick is its great number of students: some 110,000 out of a total population of 800,000.

A city with a distinguished past, Toulouse is also a city of the future. The National Center for Space Research has been headquartered here for more than 3 decades. The first regularly scheduled airline flights from France took off from the local airport in the 1920s. Today, Airbus planes are assembled in a gargantuan hangar in the suburb of Colombiers.

Essentials

GETTING THERE   The Toulouse-Blagnac international **airport** lies in the city's northwestern suburbs, 11km (6¾ miles) from the center; for flight information, call © **08-25-38-00-00. Air France** (© **08-20-80-28-02**) has about 25 flights a day from Paris and flies to Toulouse from London twice a day.

Some four high-speed TGV **trains** per day arrive from Paris (trip time: 6 hr.; one-way fare: 85€), 14 from Bordeaux (trip time: 2–3 hr.; one-way fare: 35€), and eight from Marseille (trip time: 4½ hr.; one-way fare: 52€). For information, call © **36-35** or 08-92-35-35-35. The **drive** from Paris takes 6 to 7 hours. Take A10 south to Bordeaux, connecting to A62 to Toulouse. The Canal du Midi links many of the region's cities with Toulouse by waterway.

VISITOR INFORMATION   The **Office de Tourisme** is in the Donjon du Capitole in the Square de Gaulle (© **05-61-11-02-22;** fax 05-61-23-74-97; www.ot-toulouse.fr).

Exploring the city

In addition to the sights listed below, architectural highlights include the Gothic brick **Eglise des Jacobins ★★**, parvis des Jacobins (© **05-61-22-21-92**), in Old Toulouse, west of place du Capitole along rue Lakanal. The church and the restored convent, daring in its architecture and its use of "palm tree"–shaped vaults, form the largest extant monastery complex in France. It's open daily 9am to 7pm. Admission to most of the complex is free, but a visit to the cloisters costs 3€, free for 17 and under.

Small, charming, and dating mostly from the 18th century, the **Notre-Dame La Daurade,** 1 place de la Daurade (*℃* **05-61-21-38-32**), gets its name from the gilding that covers its partially baroque exterior. Its prize possession is a statue of the Black Virgin, about 1m (3¼ ft.) tall, to which some locals attribute quasi-mystical powers. The one you'll see today was crafted in 1807 as a replacement for a much older statue that was burned during the French Revolution. Admission is free, and the Basilique Notre-Dame is open daily 8:30am to 6:30pm.

In civic architecture, **Le Capitole ★**, place du Capitole (*℃* **05-61-22-34-12**), is an outstanding achievement and one of the most potent symbols of Toulouse. Built in a baroque style in 1753, it houses the **Hôtel de Ville** (city hall) as well as the **Théâtre National du Capitole** (*℃* **05-61-63-13-13**), which presents concerts, ballets, and operas. It's outfitted in an Italian-inspired 18th-century style with shades of scarlet and gold. Admission, which usually includes a view of the theater, is free. The Capitole complex is open Monday through Saturday 9am to 5pm, and until 7pm during holidays.

After all that sightseeing, head for **place Wilson,** a showcase 19th-century square (actually an oval) lined with fashionable cafes.

Basilique St-Sernin ★★★ Consecrated in 1096, this is the largest, finest, and most pure Romanesque church in Europe. One of its most outstanding features is the Porte Miègeville, opening onto the south aisle and decorated with 12th-century sculptures. The door into the south transept is the Porte des Comtes; its capitals depict the story of Lazarus. Nearby are the tombs of the *comtes* de Toulouse. Entering by the main west door, you can see the double side aisles that give the church five naves, an unusual feature in Romanesque architecture. An upper cloister forms a passageway around the interior. Look for the Romanesque capitals surmounting the columns.

In the axis of the basilica, in the ambulatory, 11th-century bas-reliefs depict *Christ in His Majesty.* The ambulatory leads to the crypt (ask the custodian for permission to enter), which contains the relics of 128 saints, plus a thorn said to be from the Crown of Thorns. The old baroque retables (altarpieces) and shrine in the ambulatory have been reset; the relics here are those of the apostles and the first bishops of Toulouse.

Place St-Sernin. *℃* **05-61-21-70-18.** Free admission to church; combined admission to the crypt and ambulatory 2€. Church Mon–Sat 10:30am–6:30pm; Sun noon–6:30pm; off season Mon–Sat 10am–noon and 2–6pm; Sun 2–6:30pm. Crypt and ambulatory summer Mon–Sat noon–6:30pm; off season Mon–Sat 10am–noon and 2–6pm.

Cathédrale St-Etienne ★ Because it took so long to build (it was designed and constructed from the 11th–17th c.), some critics scorn this cathedral for its mishmash of styles. The rectangular bell tower is from the 16th century. A Gothic choir has been added to its unique ogival nave.

Place St-Etienne, at the eastern end of rue de Metz. *℃* **05-61-52-03-82.** Mon–Sat 8am–7pm; Sun 9am–7pm.

Fondation Bemberg Opened in 1995, this quickly became one of the city's most important museums. Housed in the magnificent Hôtel Assézat (built in 1555), the museum provides an overview of 5 centuries of European art, showcasing world-class paintings from the Renaissance to the late 19th century. The nucleus of the collection represents the lifelong work of German-French collector extraordinaire Georges Bemberg, who donated 331 works. The largest bequest was 28 paintings by

Toulouse

To Montauban
place St-Sernin 1

To Albi
place Jeanne-d'Arc

To Bus Station

place de Belfort

To Gare Matabiau

Information (i)
Post Office ✉

Université

rue Valade
rue des Lois
rue du Taur
rue de Rémusat
bd. de Strasbourg
rue D. Rochereau
allées Jean – Jaurès
rue des Sept-Troubadours
rue Gabriel Péri

rue Deville

rue Pargaminières

To Airport

✉ rue Lafayette
place du Capitole 3
(i)
CAPITOLE M
rue Gambetta

JEAN-JAURÈS M

place Wilson

bd. Lazare Carnot

rue de la Colombette

rue M. Fonvielle

rue St-Antoine du Toulouse
rue St-Jérôme

rue d'Aubuisson

To St-Aubin

2 Eglise des Jacobins

rue Gambetta

place de la Daurade

rue Cujas

7

6

ESQUIROL M
place Esquirol

4

place St-Georges

rue des Arts

rue du Remp. St-Etienne

rue Riquet

8 →

pont Neuf

rue de Metz

rue des Filatiers

rue St-Rome

rue d'Alsace-Lorraine

rue de Metz

place St-Etienne

rue Croix-Baragnon

5

allées Fr. Verdier

Garonne

quai de Tounis

rue des Couteliers

rue de la Dalbade

rue du Pharaon

place des Carmes

rue du Languedoc

rue Ozenne

rue Fermat

rue Merlane

rue Perchepinte

rue E. Montgaillard

JARDIN ROYAL

GRAND ROND

rue des Potiers

allées F. Mistral

place du Salin

place du Salin

JARDIN DES PLANTES

pont St-Michel

BASSO CAMBO M

allées P. Feuga

allées Jules-Guesde

To Carcassonne

| 0 | 1/5 mile |
| 0 | 200 meters |

FRANCE
★ Paris

Toulouse

Basilique Notre-Dame la Daurade **7**
Basilique St-Sernin **1**
Cathédrale St-Etienne **5**
Eglise des Jacobins **2**

Fondation Bemberg **6**
La Cité de l'espace **8**
Le Capitole **3**
Musée des Augustins **4**

Pierre Bonnard, including his *Moulin Rouge*. Bemberg also donated works by Pissarro, Matisse *(Vue d'Antibes),* and Monet, plus the fauves. The foundation also owns Canaletto's much-reproduced *Vue de Mestre.* The mansion houses the **Académie des Jeux-Floraux,** which since 1323 has presented literary awards in the form of wrought-metal flowers to poets.

Place d'Assézat, rue de Metz. ✆ **05-61-12-06-89.** www.fondation-bemberg.fr. Admission 5€ adults, 3€ students and children 8-18, free for children 7 and under. Tues–Wed and Fri–Sun 10am–12:30pm and 1:30–6pm; Thurs 10am–9pm.

La Cité de l'Espace ★ ☺ Some half a million visitors a year come here to learn what it's like to program the launch of a satellite or how to maneuver one in space. You learn, for example, how easy it is to lose a satellite by putting on a burst of speed at the wrong point during a launch. Life-size structural models abound, including a model of an astronaut riding an exercise bike in zero gravity. On the grounds you can walk through a replica of Russia's Mir space station. The place is both a teaching tool and a lot of fun to visit. The top floor focuses on exploration of the universe, with close-ups from flybys of the moons of Jupiter.

Av. Jean Gonord. ✆ **08-20-37-72-23.** www.cite-espace.com. Admission 22€ adults, 15€ ages 5–15, free for children 4 and under. July–Aug daily 9:30am–7pm; Sept–June Tues–Fri 9:30am–5pm, Sat–Sun 9:30am–6pm. Closed Jan. Bus: 37 (Sat–Sun only). Follow N126 from the center of town to the E. Peripheral route and take exit 17.

Musée des Augustins ★★ The museum was established in this convent in 1793, shortly after the French Revolution, when revolutionary acts closed the institution—then one of the city's most important monasteries—and adapted it for public use. In addition to the fabulous paintings, a stroll through this place gives you the chance to view a 14th-century monastery in all its mystical splendor. This museum's 14th-century cloisters contain the world's largest and most valuable collection of Romanesque capitals. The sculptures and carvings are magnificent, and there are some fine examples of early Christian sarcophagi. On the upper floors is a large painting collection, with works by Toulouse-Lautrec, Gérard, Delacroix, and Ingres. The museum also contains several portraits by Antoine Rivalz, a local artist and major talent.

21 rue de Metz. ✆ **05-61-22-21-82.** www.augustins.org. Admission 3€, free for children 18 and under. Wed 10am–9pm; Thurs–Tues 10am–6pm. Closed Jan 1, May 1, and Dec 25.

Shopping

Head for **rue d'Alsace-Lorraine,** which is rich in clothing and housewares. At the well-stocked shopping mall, the **Centre Commercial St-Georges,** rue du Rempart St-Etienne, you can fill your suitcases with all kinds of glittery loot. For upscale boutiques, head to **rue Croix-Baragnon, rue des Arts,** and **rue St-Antoine du T.** The pearly gates of antiques heaven are on **rue Fermat.** More down-market antiques spread out each Saturday and Sunday 6am to 1pm during the weekly **flea market** adjacent to the Basilique St-Sernin. In addition to that, in the same spot, a *brocante* sale takes place on the first weekend (Fri–Sun) of each month from 8am to 1pm.

Violets grow in abundance in meadows on the outskirts of Toulouse. Two shops that sell everything related to violets include **Violettes & Pastels,** 10 rue St-Pantaléon (✆ **05-61-22-14-22**), and **Péniche Maison de la Violette,** 4 bd. Bonrepos

(© **05-61-99-01-30**). Inventories include violet-scented perfume, and clothing—especially scarves—patterned with the dainty purple flower.

Where to Stay

EXPENSIVE

Grand Hôtel de l'Opéra ★★★   This is the most elegant oasis in Toulouse, and the owners have won several prestigious awards for transforming a 17th-century convent into a sophisticated hotel. The public rooms contain early-19th-century antiques and Napoleonic-inspired tenting over the bars. Some of the spacious and stylish guest rooms have urn-shaped balustrades overlooking formal squares, and all have high ceilings and modern amenities. The beds are elegantly attired in tasteful fabrics and soft pillows. The hotel restaurant, Les Jardins de l'Opéra (p. 657), is the town's most prestigious.

1 place du Capitole, Toulouse 31000. © **05-61-21-82-66.** Fax 05-61-23-41-04. www.grand-hotel-opera.com. 57 units. 190€–490€ double; 390€–490€ suite. AE, DC, MC, V. Parking 17€. Métro: Capitole. **Amenities:** Restaurant; brasserie; bar; room service; sauna. *In room:* A/C, TV, hair dryer, minibar, Wi-Fi (12€ per day).

MODERATE

Les Bains-Douches ★★   Small and intimate, Toulouse's best boutique hotel is the latest word in modernity. It is so sleek it's almost self-consciously so, and its cocktail lounge has become a chic rendezvous. All the bedrooms are tasteful and stylish, the beds comfortable with fine linens, and the bathrooms reflect a designer's touch. A terrace opens up during the summer months.

4 and 4 bis rue du Point Guilheméry, Toulouse 31000. © **05-62-77-52-52.** Fax 05-34-42-09-98. www. hotel-bainsdouches.com. 22 units. 140€–210€ double; 280€–330€ suite. AE, MC, V. Parking 12€. **Amenities:** Breakfast room; room service. *In room:* A/C, TV, hair dryer, minibar, Wi-Fi (free).

Mercure Wilson ★   Set behind a rather formal stone facade, this historic building operates a government-rated three-star hotel in the heart of Toulouse's historic core, a 5-minute walk southwest of the heartbeat place Wilson. Inside, some of the rooms radiate off of a glassed-over interior courtyard that contains touches of wrought-iron filigree similar to what you'll find in Spain. Bedrooms are high-ceilinged and, despite the prevalence of angular, not particularly distinctive furniture, still retain the relatively large proportions of the building's role as a well-heeled private home. Staff here isn't as helpful or well informed as that within this hotel's nearby competitor, the St-Claire Hôtel (see below), but it's nonetheless a worthy and cost-effective choice.

6 rue Labéda, Toulouse 31000. © **05-34-45-40-60.** Fax 05-34-45-40-61. www.mercure.com. 95 units. 125€–195€ double; 225€ family room for 2 adults and up to 2 children. AE, MC, V. Parking 11€. Métro: Place Jean-Jaurès or Capitole. **Amenities:** Restaurant; bar. *In room:* A/C, TV, hair dryer, Wi-Fi (10€ per 3 hr.).

Pullman Toulouse Centre ★★ ☺   Business travelers deem this hotel, built in 1989, as the best in town (though we prefer the Grand Hôtel de l'Opéra as the most tranquil retreat). Adjacent to place Wilson, this Sofitel employs a charming bilingual staff and offers suites big enough to fit an entire family or serve as an office away from the office. The rooms are furnished in chain format.

84 allée Jean-Jaurès, Toulouse 31000. © **05-61-10-23-10.** Fax 05-61-10-23-20. www.sofitel.com. 125 units. 130€–350€ double; 145€–400€ suite. AE, DC, MC, V. Parking 17€. Métro: Jean-Jaurès. **Amenities:** Restaurant; bar; babysitting; health club. *In room:* A/C, TV, hair dryer, minibar, Wi-Fi (free).

INEXPENSIVE

Grand Hôtel Raymond-IV   On a quiet street close to the town center and the train station, this 19th-century red-brick building contains pleasant rooms with bland but comfortable furniture and restful beds. All of the individually decorated accommodations are different—some small, others rather grand—with a vaguely Art Deco motif. Some rooms have air-conditioning. Although breakfast is the only meal served, the English-speaking staff will direct you to nearby restaurants.

16 rue Raymond-IV, Toulouse 31000. ☎ **05-61-62-89-41.** Fax 05-61-62-38-01. www.grandhotel-raymond4. com. 38 units. 70€–145€ double; 135€–200€ triple. AE, MC, V. Parking 10€. Métro: Jean-Jaurès or Capitole. **Amenities:** Bar; room service. *In room:* A/C, TV, hair dryer, minibar, Wi-Fi (free).

Hotel de France ★   In the heart of Toulouse, this hotel in a restored historic monument from 1890 stands near the landmark squares, Wilson and Capitole. Restaurants, cafes, cinemas, markets, and shops lie just a few feet from the hotel's doorstep. The midsize bedrooms combine charm, convenience, and comfort, and each is tastefully decorated, with a travertine-tiled bathroom. The facade may suggest the halcyon days of Belle Epoque, but the interior is sleekly modern with splashes of sophistication in the decor.

5 rue Austerlitz, 31000 Toulouse. ☎ **05-61-21-88-24.** Fax 05-61-21-99-77. www.hotel-france-toulouse. com. 63 units. 63€–66€ double; 86€ quad. AE, MC, V. **Amenities:** Breakfast room; room service. *In room:* A/C, TV, Wi-Fi (free).

St-Claire Hôtel   Set in the heart of Toulouse's historic core, within a narrow, five-story town house whose foundations go back to the 15th century, this is a government-rated two-star hotel with few frills but a good location and a solid and comfortable presence. It was radically upgraded when its owners brought in a simple collection of furniture, most of it painted in tones of cream and white, and positioned it according to the Chinese principles of harmony and feng shui. There's no restaurant on-site, but many bars and dining outlets lie within a short walk. The staff is well equipped to offer advice about attractions and diversions within the neighborhood.

29 place Nicolas Bachelier, Toulouse 31000. ☎ **05-34-40-58-88.** Fax 05-61-57-85-89. www.stclaire hotel.fr. 16 units. 85€–109€ double. AE, MC, V. Parking 5.50€. Métro: Place Jean-Jaurès. **Amenities:** Room service. *In room:* A/C, TV, fax, hair dryer, Wi-Fi (free).

Where to Dine

EXPENSIVE

Chez Michel Sarran ★★★ MODERN FRENCH   At the most stylish restaurant in Toulouse, you can enjoy the cuisine of master chef Michel Sarran. Sarran's wife, Françoise, oversees the three red, green, or violet dining rooms, in a building in the heart of town near the Novotel Centre. The food brings out the flavors of southern and southwestern France. Start with a warm soup of foie gras and oysters. Move on to a succulent version of poached sea bass served with a creamy polenta and lobster sauce; or perhaps a portion of roasted pigeon from the underpopulated Bigorre region of France, served in a stewpot with thyme and wine-roasted potatoes.

21 bd. Armand Duportal. ☎ **05-61-12-32-32.** www.michel-sarran.com. Reservations recommended. Main courses 36€–68€; fixed-price lunch 44€–165€, dinner 98€–165€. AE, DC, MC, V. Mon–Fri noon–1:45pm and 8–9:45pm (closed Wed for lunch). Closed Aug and 1 week around Christmas. Métro: Capitole.

Le 19 ★ MODERN FRENCH   This high-profile cellar restaurant is one of the city's finest. It's 19 steps down from the street, in the high-ceilinged cellar of a medieval building once used for the storage of fish and the salts to preserve them. Inside, wood panels and carpeting contrast with its terra-cotta bricks. The delicate, creative menu items change with the seasons. Among delectable dishes are a terrine of deliberately undercooked foie gras, served with figs; cream of watercress soup with warm oysters; *magret* of duckling served with apples; roasted shoulder of rabbit served in a stewpot with polenta and baby vegetables; filet of baked red snapper with spider-crab sauce; and filet of curried duck breast with Asian-style vegetables. To end your meal, try a stir-fry of mandarin oranges flavored with balsamic vinegar, or saffron-flavored sabayon with ice cream made from unpasteurized milk.

19 descente de la Halle aux Poissons. ℰ **05-34-31-94-84.** www.restaurantle19.com. Reservations recommended. Main courses 20€–27€; fixed-price lunch 13€–20€, dinner 37€. AE, DC, MC, V. Tues–Fri noon–2pm; Mon–Sat 8-10:30pm. Métro: Esquirol.

Les Jardins de l'Opéra ★★★ FRENCH   The entrance to the city's best restaurant is in the 18th-century Florentine courtyard of the Grand Hôtel de l'Opéra (p. 655). The dining area is a series of salons, several of which face a winter garden and a reflecting pool. A long-standing staple, praised by gastronomes, is ravioli stuffed with foie gras of duckling and served with essence of truffles. Equally appealing are carpaccio of lobster served with foie gras; tartare of sturgeon, mushrooms, and oysters; and spicy breast of pigeon with a "surprise" preparation of the bird's organs decorated with rosettes of zucchini. One of the most appealing desserts is figs poached in red banyuls wine, stuffed with homemade vanilla ice cream.

In the Grand Hôtel de l'Opéra, 1 place du Capitole. ℰ **05-61-23-07-76.** www.lesjardinsdelopera.com. Reservations required. All main courses 25€–42€; fixed-price lunch 29€–99€, dinner 29€–99€. AE, DC, MC, V. Tues–Sat noon–2pm and 8-10pm. Closed Jan 1-17 and July 28–Aug 29. Métro: Capitole.

Metropolitan ★★★ FRENCH   This is a bright, modern restaurant, which is a showcase for one of Toulouse's most celebrated chefs, Jeremy Morin. Trained at the Hotel Meurice in Paris, Morin offers sublime dishes that are not only creative but prepared with well-chosen ingredients. Try his scallops roasted with herb-studded ravioli and served with candied carrots or else his lean, roast filet of beef with pressed artichokes, foie gras, and a truffle vinaigrette. Another delight is saddle of rabbit flavored with grape juice. His roasted veal sweetbreads with truffles and Roman hazelnuts have won him deserved praise. The designer dining room contains a chic bar, and there's a small terrace draped with vines.

2 place Auguste Albert. ℰ **05-61-34-63-11.** www.metropolitan-restaurant.fr. Fixed-price lunch 23€–30€; fixed-price dinner 39€–85€. Main courses 24€–50€. AE, MC, V. Tues–Fri noon–2pm and Tues–Sat 8-10pm.

MODERATE

Emile ★ TOULOUSIAN   In an old-fashioned house on one of Toulouse's most beautiful squares, this restaurant prepares the specialties of chef Christophe Fasan. In winter, meals are served upstairs overlooking the square; in summer, seating moves to the street-level dining room and flower-filled terrace. Menu choices include cassoulet Toulousian (cooked in goose fat), *magret* of duckling in traditional style, a medley of Catalonian fish, and a very fresh *parillade* (mixed grill) of fish with a pungently aromatic cold sauce of sweet peppers and olive oil. The wine list is filled with intriguing surprises.

13 place St-Georges. ℰ **05-61-21-05-56.** www.restaurant-emile.com. Reservations recommended. Main courses 20€–35€; fixed-price lunch 20€–30€, dinner 36€–55€. AE, DC, MC, V. Oct to mid-May

Inexpensive

Brasserie les Beaux-Arts/La Brasserie Flo TRADITIONAL FRENCH   This early-1900s brasserie has an authentic Art Nouveau interior that's been enhanced because of its connection with the Jean Bucher chain (the most successful director of Art Nouveau French brasseries in the world, some of which are classified as national historic monuments). The carefully restored decor features walnut paneling and mirrors. The cuisine emphasizes well-prepared seafood and all the typical local dishes, including cassoulet, *magret* of duckling, lightly smoked salmon, and confit of duckling. Try foie gras or country-style sauerkraut, accompanied by the house Riesling, served in an earthenware pitcher. During warm weather, eat on the terrace. The staff is likely to be hysterical and less than suave during peak times.

In the Hôtel des Beaux-Arts, 1 quai de la Daurade. © **05-61-21-12-12.** www.flobrasseries.com. Reservations recommended. Main courses 12€–29€; fixed-price menu 23€–38€. AE, DC, MC, V. Daily noon–2:30pm and 7–11:30pm. Métro: Esquirol.

Eau de Folles TRADITIONAL FRENCH   Low prices and the variety of the menu keep patrons coming back to this place. In a room filled with mirrors, you can choose from 10 starters, 10 main courses, and 10 desserts on the fixed-price menu. Choices vary according to the inspiration of the chef and the availability of fresh ingredients. A typical meal may include a marinade of fish, followed by strips of duck meat with green-pepper sauce, and a homemade pastry such as a tarte tatin. Everything is very simple, served in a cramped but convivial setting.

14 allée du President Roosevelt. © **05-61-23-45-50.** Reservations recommended. Fixed-price lunch 18€, dinner 28€. MC, V. Tues–Sat noon–2pm and Mon–Sat 7–11pm. Closed Dec 24–Jan 3. Métro: Wilson.

Le Bon Vivre ★ SOUTHWESERN FRENCH   One of downtown Toulouse's most appealing bistros occupies the street level of a historic 18th-century mansion immediately adjacent to the Hôtel de Ville (town hall). Established in 2004, it provides cost-conscious dining within an environment surrounded by the pink-colored bricks of antique Toulouse. Menu items feature contemporary twists upon time-tested French specialties, many of them heralded by workaday diners who appreciate the attractive ratios of value to quality. The best examples include an unusual version of macaroni studded with flap mushrooms, truffles, and foie gras; and a version of cassoulet (the specialty of France's southwest) that's made with both duck and pork.

15 bis place Wilson. © **05-61-23-07-17.** www.lebonvivre.com. Reservations recommended. Main courses 17€–28€; fixed-price menus lunch 26€–40€. AE, DC, MC, V. Daily 7am–midnight.

Le Colombier ★ TOULOUSIAN   Don't tell your cardiologist and slip away to this bastion of regional cookery. Alain Lacoste arguably serves the best cassoulet in Toulouse, and also lures with white beans in pork fat, red sausage, white sausage, and, of course, goose confit. His duck foie gras comes with figs and, of all things, gingerbread. Calves' sweetbreads are delectable with morels, and scallops are served in the Provençal style. Nearly all locals order the cassoulet; it's slow cooked to perfection. The restaurant itself is a simple stone-and-brick dining room. With all this fat, you can cut it with the acidity of strawberry soup with lime sorbet. If not that, then opt for the apple "croustade."

14 rue Bayard. ✆ **05-61-62-40-05.** www.restaurant-lecolombier.com. Reservations recommended. Main courses 18€–30€; fixed-price menus 21€–49€. MC, V. Tues–Fri noon–2pm and Mon–Fri 7:15–10pm; Sat 7:15–10:30pm.

Where to Stay & Dine Nearby

La Flanerie   Within a large garden that slopes down to the edge of the Garonne, about 8km (5 miles) south of Toulouse, stands this dignified-looking manor house, originally built in 1799 for a local landowner. Part of its allure derives from the early 1970s, when it was the site of a hotel favored by French celebrities and international rock stars, whose names fill the guest book that the Irish-born owners, the Moloney family, have presented since their acquisition of the place in 2004. You might be happiest interpreting this place as an informal bed-and-breakfast, where the rooms just happen to be country elegant and the welcome particularly warm. An oddity associated with the place involves the fact that there's a free-standing garage for each of the establishment's 12 bedrooms, a quirk deriving from one of the auto-obsessed former owners. Accommodations are stylish and midsize, and although there's no restaurant on-site, the owners are well informed about dining options nearby.

7 chemin des Etroits, Vieille-Toulouse 31320. ✆ **05-61-73-39-12.** Fax 05-61-73-18-56. www.hotellaflanerie. com. 12 units. 86€–110€ double. AE, MC, V. Free parking. Bus: R. Take D4 south of Toulouse for 8km (5 miles). **Amenities:** Bar; outdoor pool. *In room:* A/C, TV, hair dryer, minibar, Wi-Fi (free).

Toulouse After Dark

Toulouse's theater, dance, and opera are often on a par with those found in Paris. To stay on top of the arts scene, pick up a copy of the free monthly magazine *Toulouse Culture* from the Office de Tourisme.

PERFORMING ARTS

The city's most notable theaters are the **Théâtre du Capitole,** place du Capitole (✆ **05-61-63-13-13**), which specializes in operas, operettas, and often works from the classical French repertoire; the **Théâtre de la Digue,** 3 rue de la Digue (✆ **05-61-42-97-79**), for ballets and works by local theater companies; and the **Halle aux Grains,** place Dupuy (✆ **05-61-63-13-13**). The home of the Orchestre du Capitole, the Halle aux Grains is the venue for mostly classical concerts. The **Théâtre Garonne,** 1 av. du Château d'Eau (✆ **05-62-48-56-56**), stages everything from works by Molière to current dramas. Another important venue is the **Théâtre Zenith,** 11 av. Raymond-Badiou (✆ **05-62-74-49-49**), which has a large stage and seating capacity. It usually schedules rock concerts, variety acts, and musical comedies from other European cities. A smaller competitor, with a roughly equivalent mix of music, theater, and entertainment, is the **Théâtre de la Cité,** 1 rue Pierre Baudis (✆ **05-34-45-05-05**).

BARS & CLUBS

The liveliest squares to wander after dark are **place du Capitole, place St-Georges, place St-Pierre,** and **place Wilson.**

For bars and pubs, **La Tantina de Bourgos,** 27 rue de la Garonette (✆ **05-61-55-59-29**), has a Latin flair that's popular with students, and the rowdier **Chez Tonton,** 16 place St-Pierre (✆ **05-61-21-89-54**), has an *après-match* atmosphere, complete with the winning teams boozing it up. A popular bar that schedules both live and recorded music is **Monsieur Carnaval,** 34 rue Bayard (✆ **05-61-99-14-**

56), where there's lots of rocking and rolling *à la française* for the under-35 crowd. The busiest English-style pub in town, **Le Frog & Le Roast Beef,** 14 rue de l'Industrie (☎ **05-61-99-28-57**), is woodsy and Celtic looking, and often very crowded with the city's English-speaking community. **La Pelouse Interdite,** 72 av. des Etats-Unis (☎ **05-61-47-30-40**), offers a charming restaurant and bar behind a simple, discreetly marked green door within a venue that incorporates a garden, a restaurant, a bar, and lots of charm.

The town's trendiest and most widely sought-after disco for persons younger than 35 is **Le Purple,** 2 rue Castellane (☎ **05-62-73-04-67**). Set close to the Pullman, it's the disco that has the longest lines, generates the most interest within the counterculture press, and elicits the highest level of passion within the city's A-list wannabe junkies.

Mostly heterosexuals migrate to **Disco Le Maximo,** 3 rue Gabrielle-Peri (☎ **05-61-62-08-07**), which starts hopping Tuesday to Saturday after 11pm, and serves a distinctly French-inspired list of tapas (foie gras on toast, perhaps). There's also a vaguely Iberian-looking establishment, **Bar La Bodega,** rue Gabriel-Peri (☎ **05-61-63-03-63**), that's about as beer-soaked and raucous as anything else in town. It's particularly interesting in the wake of one of the region's football (soccer) games, especially if the home team has won.

The oldest and most deeply entrenched gay bar in Toulouse is **Shanghai Express,** 12 rue de la Pomme (☎ **05-61-23-37-80**), a man's dance domain playing the latest in techno. Farther inside, it gives way to a darker and, at its best, sexy cruise-bar environment with lots of hot men on the prowl. Entrance is free and it's open every night.

THE BASQUE COUNTRY

The chief area of interest in the Basque country, a land rich in folklore, is a corner of southwest France, near the Spanish border, where you can visit the Basque capital, Bayonne, and explore the resorts, Biarritz and St-Jean-de-Luz. In Bayonne's Roman arena, you can see a bullfight.

19

The vast Pyrénéan region is a land of glaciers, summits, thermal baths, subterranean grottoes and caverns, winter-sports centers, and trout-filled mountain streams. **Pau** is a good base for excursions to the western Pyrénées. **Lourdes** is the major religious pilgrimage center in France.

LOURDES ★
800km (497 miles) SW of Paris; 40km (25 miles) SE of Pau

Muslims turn to Mecca and Hindus to the Ganges, but for Catholics, Lourdes is the world's most evocative shrine. Nestled in a valley in the southwestern part of the Hautes-Pyrénées, it draws pilgrims from all over the world. If you're coming in August, the shrine's high season, book your hotel as early as possible.

Many Roman Catholics believe that on February 11, 1858, the Virgin revealed herself to a shepherd girl, Bernadette Soubirous. Eighteen such apparitions were reported. Bernadette, subject of the film *Song of Bernadette*, died in a convent in 1879. She was beatified in 1925 and canonized in 1933.

Her apparitions put Lourdes on the map. The town has attracted millions of visitors, from the illustrious to the poverty stricken. The devout are often disappointed by the commercialism of Lourdes today. And some vacationers are disturbed by the human desperation of victims of various afflictions spending their hard-earned savings seeking a "miracle," then having to return home without a cure. However, the church has recognized many "cures" that took place after patients bathed in the springs, labeling them "true miracles."

Essentials

GETTING THERE   Sixteen **trains** run from Pau (see section 2 in this chapter) daily (trip time: 30 min.; one-way fare 8€); there are also five trains from Bayonne (trip time: 2 hr.; one-way fare: 20€) and Paris (trip time: 7 hr.; 94€ one-way). For train information and schedules, call ✆ **36-35.**

If you're **driving** from Toulouse, take N117 west until you reach Tarbes, and then take N21 south to Lourdes. From Paris, follow A10 south to Vierzon, take N20 south to Limoges, and continue on N21 south to Lourdes.

VISITOR INFORMATION The **Office de Tourisme,** place Peyramale (✆ **05-62-42-77-40;** fax 05-62-94-60-95; www.lourdes-infotourisme.com), fields questions about Lourdes. But for questions regarding the religious landscape of the city, including its shrines, grottoes, Masses, cults, ecstatic visions, and snake charmers, seek out the *Le Centre Information des Sanctuaires,* avenue Monseigneur Théas (✆ **05-62-42-78-78**). Staffed by members of the clergy and religious volunteers, it's the coordinator of everything to do with Catholicism in Lourdes.

SPECIAL EVENTS From Easter to mid-October, tourists and pilgrims can join the **Day Pilgrims,** or Pélerin d'un Jour (✆ **05-62-42-78-78;** www.lourdes-fr.com), a pilgrimage in English that begins daily at 8:30am at the statue of the Crowned Virgin with a prayer meeting in the meadow facing the grotto. The services include the Stations of the Cross (8:30am) and an 11:15am Mass. At 2:30pm, assembling at the same spot, pilgrims take a guided visit to the sanctuaries, or places associated with Bernadette. In the sanctuaries, you'll hear the story of Lourdes and Bernadette, complete with a free 30-minute slide show (also in English). At 5pm, a Procession of the Blessed Eucharist starts from the grotto. The 9pm Marian celebration, rosary, and torchlight procession all start from the grotto as well.

Exploring the Town & Its Environs

At the **Grotto of Massabielle,** the Virgin is said to have appeared to Bernadette 18 times in 1858. The site is accessible to pilgrims both day and night, and Mass is celebrated every day. The Statue of Our Lady depicts the Virgin in the posture she is said to have taken in the place she reputedly appeared, saying to Bernadette in Pyrénéan dialect, "I am the Immaculate Conception."

At the back of the Grotto, on the left of the altar, is the **Miraculous Spring (La Source)** that reportedly spouted on February 25, 1858, during the ninth apparition, when Bernadette scraped the earth. The Virgin is said to have commanded her, "Go and drink at the spring and wash there." The water from this spring is collected in several reservoirs, from which you can drink.

The **Upper Basilica (La Basilique Supérieure),** place du Rosaire, was built in the ogival style typical of the 13th century, but wasn't consecrated until 1876. It contains one nave split into five equal bays. Votive tablets line its interior. On the west side of the square is the Rosary Basilica, with two small towers. It was built in 1889 in the Roman-Byzantine style and holds up to 4,000 people. Inside, 15 chapels are dedicated to the mysteries of the rosary.

The oval **Basilica of Pius X,** 1 av. Monseigneur Théas, was consecrated in 1958. An enormous underground chamber covered by a concrete roof, it's 198m (650 ft.) long and 81m (266 ft.) wide, and holds as many as 20,000 people. It's one of the world's largest churches. It's open daily 7am to 6pm. International Masses are conducted in six languages, including English, every Wednesday and Sunday at 9:30am from April to October.

Nearby, the **Musée Ste-Bernadette** (*©* **05-62-42-78-78**) contains scenes from the life of the saint; it's open daily 9am to noon and 2 to 7pm (closed during winter). Admission is free.

The privately owned and overly commercial wax museum, **Musée Grévin,** 87 rue de la Grotte (*©* **05-62-94-33-74**), displays depictions of Bernadette's life and the life of Christ, along with a bad reproduction of Leonardo da Vinci's *Last Supper.* From mid-March to October, it's open daily 9am to noon and 1:45 to 6:30pm. During July and August, it's open 9am to 6:30pm. It's closed November to mid-March. Admission is 6.50€ for adults, 5.20€ for students, and 3.30€ for ages 6 to 9 (free 5 and under).

If you want a panoramic view, take an elevator to the terrace of the **Château-Fort de Lourdes,** an example of medieval military architecture. The castle contains the **Musée Pyrénéen,** 25 rue du Fort (✆ 05-62-42-37-37), with regional handicrafts and costumes, including a collection of dolls in nuns' habits. In the courtyard are scale models of different styles of regional architecture. Admission is 5€ adults, 3€ students and children 6 to 18, and free for children 5 and under. From April to mid-July and mid-August to September, the château and museum are open daily 9am to noon and 1:30 to 6:30pm, mid-July to mid-August daily 9am to 6:30pm and from October to March daily 9am to noon and 2 to 6pm.

OUTDOOR ACTIVITIES   Lourdes is a good base for exploring the Pyrénées. You can take tours into the snowcapped mountains across the border to Spain or go horseback riding near **Lac de Lourdes,** 3km (1¾ miles) northwest of town. Among the outstanding sites is **Bagnères-de-Bigorre,** a renowned thermal spa 23km (14 miles) east of Lourdes on D935.

Visit **Pic du Jer,** a rocky peak 933m (3,061 ft.) above sea level, high over the surrounding land formations, for a view of the countryside. To reach its summit, board the Pic de Jer funicular, which departs from the south side of esplanade des Proceswinos in the center of Lourdes. Round-trip fares are 9€ for adults and 6.50€ for students and children ages 6 to 14. At the summit, you'll see the entrance to some caves, **Les Grottes de Jer** (✆ 05-62-94-00-41 for both the funicular and the grottoes), a sightseeing attraction. Entrance to the grottoes costs 3.50€ adults and 2.50€ children 6 to 12. In July and August hours are daily 10am to 7pm; otherwise daily 9:30am to 6pm.

Farther afield, 23km (14 miles) southeast of Lourdes in the hamlet of Aste, you'll find even bigger and much more dramatic caves, **Les Grottes de Médous** (✆ 05-62-91-78-46). An underground river formed them, along with numerous stalactites and stalagmites. Reach them by following signs to les Grottes de Médous along D26. During July and August, they're open daily 9am to noon and 2 to 6pm; otherwise daily 9 to 11:30am and 2 to 5pm. Admission is 8€ for adults and 4€ for ages 5 to 10 (4 and under free).

If you're in the mood for a full-fledged outing from Lourdes into the Pyrénées, drive south along D921 to a mountainous national park, **Cirque de Gavarnie (Heights of Gavarnie),** whose summits reach 1,350m (4,429 ft.). The distance from Lourdes to the center of the region is 52km (32 miles).

Where to Stay

Grand Hôtel de la Grotte ★   The Grand Hôtel is an old favorite, having catered to pilgrims (and, to an increasing degree, tourists) since 1872, although it is equipped with modern amenities. It remains the best lodging choice in Lourdes. It's furnished with comfortable upper-bourgeois French decor in the style of Napoleon III. Some rooms on the upper floor open onto one of the most panoramic views in town, taking in the mountains as well as the sanctuaries and the river. Rooms on the basilica side tend to be noisy. The garden sits beside the banks of the river Gave de Pau.

66 rue de la Grotte, Lourdes 65100. ✆ **05-62-94-58-87.** Fax 05-62-94-20-50. www.hotel-grotte.com. 83 units. Summer 104€–181€ double, 279€ junior suite; low season 94€–166€ double, 259€ junior suite. AE, DC, MC, V. Free parking. Closed late Oct to mid-Apr. Bus: 2. **Amenities:** 2 restaurants; bar; room service. *In room:* A/C, TV, hair dryer, minibar, Wi-Fi (free).

Hôtel Galilée et Windsor This government-rated three-star hotel, often confused with the more comfortable, more expensive Gallia et Londres (below), has been a favorite since it was built after the war. Rooms are pleasant, if dull and anonymous. It is located near the grotto and is close to the railway station. Each room has a small shower-only bathroom. Because this is one of the largest hotels in Lourdes, it's a magnet for religious groups.

10–12 av. Peyramale, Lourdes 65100. ℭ **05-62-94-21-55.** Fax 05-62-94-53-66. www.galilee-windsor.fr. 158 units. 104€ double. AE, DC, MC, V. Closed Nov–Mar. Bus: 2. **Amenities:** Restaurant; bar. *In room:* TV, hair dryer, minibar, Wi-Fi.

Hôtel Gallia et Londres This old-fashioned choice, dating from 1880, has been completely improved and renovated with Louis XVI furnishings. The complete overhaul of the guest rooms included an upgrade in the quality of the beds. All rooms contain midsize bathrooms, and most have tubs and showers. Most guests here are parts of religious groups that tend to book en masse.

26 av. Bernadette-Soubirous, Lourdes 65100. ℭ **05-62-94-35-44.** Fax 05-62-42-24-64. www.hotel gallialondres.com. 93 units. 120€–150€ double; 210€–240€ suite. AE, MC, V. Parking 12€. Closed Nov–Mar. Bus: 2. **Amenities:** Restaurant; bar; free use of indoor pool next door; Wi-Fi (free). *In room:* A/C, TV, minibar.

Hôtel Notre-Dame de France Located next to the Galilée et Windsor, this hotel is steps from the main monument (the sanctuaries associated with the visions of Bernadette). Originally built around 1928, it underwent radical rebuilding in the late 1980s that eliminated virtually every vestige of its Art Deco detailing. The owners, M. and Mme. Imbert, offer simple, no-frills rooms with almost monastic furnishings, plus small bathrooms—some with shower only, some with combination tub/showers. Some bedrooms have a view of the fortress of Lourdes and the nearest Pyrénées summits. Pilgrims appreciate the emphasis here on religious activities. Overall, it's a worthy budget choice.

8 av. Peyramale, Lourdes 65100. ℭ **05-62-94-91-45.** Fax 05-62-94-57-21. www.hotelnd-france.fr. 75 units. 75€–80€ double. Half board 60€–80€ per person. MC, V. Parking 10€. Closed Nov to mid-Mar. Bus: 2. **Amenities:** Restaurant; bar. *In room:* A/C, TV, Wi-Fi (free).

Where to Dine

Les Arcades 🍴 FRENCH Some of the best and most affordable dining is found at this restaurant that features both fixed-price menus and à la carte selections. Long a favorite with visitors, it offers fresh ingredients turned into a wide array of tempting dishes such as grilled lamb chops with fresh thyme or preserved duck leg in a walnut sauce. The chef also prepares about four pasta dishes a day including fresh tagliatelle with prawns. Trout from the nearby mountains is also a regular feature, as is filet of halibut with baby vegetables.

In the Hotel Arcades, 13 av. paradis. ℭ **05-62-94-20-59.** Reservations recommended. Main courses 8.50€–14€; fixed-price menus 16€–22€. MC, V. Daily noon–2pm and 7–9pm.

PAU ★★★

768km (477 miles) SW of Paris; 196km (122 miles) SW of Toulouse

High above the banks of the Gave de Pau River, this year-round resort is a good place to pause in your trek to the Pyrénées. The British discovered Pau in the early 19th century, launching such practices as fox hunting, a custom that lingers. Even if you're just passing through, follow boulevard des Pyrénées, an esplanade erected on Napoleon's orders, for a famous panoramic view.

Pau is the most cosmopolitan city in the western Pyrénées, the capital of the Pyrénées-Atlantiques *département* (ministate). It was once the capital of the Béarn region, the land of the kings of Navarre, the most famous and beloved of whom was Henri IV. At one time the English made up 15% of the population; its population of approximately 82,000 still observes some English traditions, such as afternoon tea.

Essentials

GETTING THERE Pau-Uzein airport is 12km (7½ miles) north of town; call ✆ **05-59-33-33-00** for flight information. There are good **train** connections from Biarritz (six per day, taking 1½ hr.); the one-way fare is 17€. For train information, call ✆ **36-35. Driving** to Pau is relatively easy because of its location along the N117 roadway, which is directly accessible from Toulouse. From Paris, take A10 south to Vierzon, changing to N20 south to Limoges, continuing on N21 south to Tarbes, and finally turning west along N117 to Pau.

VISITOR INFORMATION The **Office de Tourisme** is on place Royale (✆ **05-59-27-27-08;** fax 05-59-27-03-21; www.tourismepau.com).

SPECIAL EVENTS In late May and early June there's the **Grand Prix de Pau** (✆ **05-59-27-31-89;** www.grandprixautomobilepau.com), when race cars compete for speed records in what may remind you of a small-scale replica of the Grand Prix in Monaco.

Exploring the City

The heart of the commercial district is **place Clemenceau,** out of which radiate at least five boulevards. At the western end of town stands the **Château de Pau ★**, 2 rue du Château (✆ **05-59-82-38-00**), dating from the 12th century and steeped in the Renaissance spirit of the bold Marguerite de Navarre, who wrote the bawdy *Heptaméron* at age 60. Marguerite commissioned the great staircase hall, and Louis XV ordered the bridge that connects the castle to the town. Around 1840, Louis-Philippe had the apartments redecorated. Inside are many souvenirs, including a crib made of a single tortoiseshell for Henri de Navarre, who was born here, and a splendid array of Flemish and Gobelin tapestries. The great rectangular tower, **Tour de Gaston Phoebus,** is from the 14th century.

Another intriguing area within the château is **La Salle aux 100 Couverts,** site of some of the enormous receptions that were held here during the building's heyday. The château is open for visits mid-June to mid-September daily 9:30am to noon and 1:30 to 5:45pm, and mid-September to mid-June daily 9:30 to 11:45am and 2 to 5pm. Guided tours (conducted in French and broken English, with an English-language pamphlet to supplement the tour guide), depart at 15-minute intervals during open hours. Admission is 5€ for adults, 3.50€ for students 18 to 25, and free for ages 17 and under.

The **Musée des Beaux-Arts ★**, rue Mathieu-Lalanne (✆ **05-59-27-33-02;** http://musee.ville-pau.fr), displays a collection of European paintings, including Spanish, Flemish, Dutch, English, and French masters such as El Greco, Zurbarán, Degas, and Boudin. It's open Wednesday to Monday 10am to noon and 2 to 6pm. Admission is 3€ adults, 1.50€ students, and free for children 18 and under.

Shopping

Pau affords ample opportunities for you to buy authentic regional specialties, such as chocolates, sweet jams, and Basque antiques. The pedestrian **rue Serviez** and **rue des Cordelières** harbor an array of boutiques and shops that carry these items, as do **rue Louis-Barthou, rue Henry-IV,** and **rue du Maréchal-Foch.**

Pau is home to some of the best antiques shops in the region, such as **Antiquites Delan,** 4 rue Gassion (✆ **05-59-27-45-62** or 06-08-07-82-40). The area around the château is the antiques center.

One of the best-known shops in Pau is **La Féerie Gourmande,** 48 rue du Maréchal Joffre (✆ **05-59-27-69-51**), which attracts gourmets from throughout the region. The owner, M. Francis Miot, has been voted best jam and candy maker in France several times. In addition to jams made from every Pyrénéan berry, the shop also stocks a selection of bonbons. The star and centerpiece, M. Miot's own creation, is a *coucougnette,* or jam-filled chocolate.

If you're interested in seeing where these confections are made, head for the suburbs of Pau, about 1.5km (1 mile) southeast of the center, to the residential hamlet of Uzos. Here you'll find **Musée de la Confiture** (✆ **05-59-35-05-56**), where exhibits display the history of jams from medieval times to the present. It's open Monday to Saturday 10am to noon and 2 to 4pm; admission is 4.60€ adults and 3€ ages 3 to 12; closed in December.

Where to Stay

Best Western Hôtel Continental   The centrally located Continental is one of the most prominent hotels in Pau. Renovated several times since its original construction around 1900, it's one of the two best hotels in town (the Gramont is another top choice). Rooms are functionally decorated, modernized, and soundproof. About 60 have midsize bathrooms with tub/shower combinations; the rest have showers.

2 rue du Maréchal-Foch, Pau 64000. ✆ **05-59-27-69-31.** Fax 05-59-27-99-84. www.hotel-continental-pau.com. 75 units. 70€–100€ double. AE, DC, DISC, MC, V. Free parking. **Amenities:** Restaurant; room service. *In room:* TV, hair dryer, minibar, Wi-Fi (free).

Hôtel de Gramont   In the heart of Pau, on a gracefully designed 18th-century plaza whose every architectural detail has been classified as a historic treasure, this hotel was built around 1880 in a style that complements the medievalism of the château nearby. Its management spent lots of money restoring the elegant woodwork in the street-level salons and outfitted the guest rooms with late-19th-century (mostly English) antiques. Each room has a comfortable bed and is decorated differently, but in a style that evokes grand-scale country living. About half of the medium-size bathrooms contain tub/shower combos; the others have showers. Many restaurants are a short walk away.

3 place Gramont, Pau 64000. ✆ **05-59-27-84-04.** Fax 05-59-27-62-23. www.hotelgramont.com. 34 units. 77€–126€ double; 140€–180€ suite. AE, DC, DISC, MC, V. Closed Dec 23–Jan 5. **Amenities:** Bar. *In room:* A/C (some rooms), TV, minibar, Wi-Fi (free).

Where to Dine

Au Fin Gourmet ★★ 🍴 BASQUE   This restaurant, on the southern periphery of Pau near the rail station, is maintained by Christian, Laurent, and Patrick, sons of the retired founder, Clément Ithurriague. The postmodern, circular dining room, with soaring windows overlooking a park, opens onto a terrace for warm-weather dining. The cuisine is based on regional ingredients. Some of the best menu items include grilled scallops with fennel, preceded by an appetizer of duckling foie gras with mushrooms. Rack of lamb with fresh herbs from the Pyrénées is an always-reliable course, as is the braised stuffed trout. Dessert may include four variations of caramel arranged on the same platter, or ice cream with rum.

24 av. Gaston-Lacoste. ✆ **05-59-27-47-71.** www.restaurant-aufingourmet.com. Reservations recommended. Main courses 22€–25€; fixed-price lunch 27€–76€, dinner 38€–76€. AE, DC, MC, V. Tues and Thurs–Sun noon–2pm; Tues–Sat 7:30–9:30pm.

Chez Pierre ★★ BEARNAISE/FRENCH   Year after year, we have our finest meal in Pau at Chez Pierre, which spins regional products into creative dishes. Established in 1924, it's a 5-minute walk west of the château. One dining room resembles a salon in an English men's club, another abounds with plants like a greenhouse, and the third (upstairs) affords a sweeping view over the gardens attached to the local branch of La Banque de France. Chef Raymond Casau, who spent years apprenticing with some of the most successful chefs in France, is among the finest around. His specialties are sole braised with wine, fresh salmon braised with Jurançon (a sweet, golden Pyrénéan wine), and a Béarnaise version of cassoulet (with different sausages than the Toulouse version, with a greater emphasis on confit of goose). One of the most attractive bars in town, outfitted like the club room of a golf course, is adjacent to the dining rooms.

16 rue Louis-Barthour. ✆ **05-59-27-76-86.** www.restaurant-chez-pierre.com. Reservations required. Main courses 22€–32€; fixed-price menu 36€. AE, DC, MC, V. Tues–Fri noon–2pm; Mon–Sat 7–10pm. Closed 2 weeks in early Jan and 2 weeks in mid-Aug.

Chez Ruffet ★★ BEARNAISE   This is the most famous restaurant in the Pau region, a gastronomic destination that sets it apart from most of the other restaurants in the region. It's on the southern outskirts of Pau, within an old-fashioned stone-built house with a slate roof and a bell tower. Many guests opt for one of the set-price menus that tend to revolve around "themes" of whatever is fresh at the time of your arrival, and which tend to be included in some way in each of the five courses associated with the meal. Essential "building blocks" for these menus in the past have included, among others, asparagus, tomato, scallops, exotic fruits, autumn truffles, and avocados. The menu changes regularly and often, but examples of food served here include sea scallops that are first smoked, then grilled, and served with chicken-stuffed ravioli and a sweet pepper–and–mango sauce; braised sweetbreads with a butter-flavored cream sauce and vanilla-flavored brioches; and line-caught sea bass glazed with miso.

3 av. Charles Touzet, Jurançon. ✆ **05-59-06-25-13.** www.restaurant-chezruffet.com. Reservations required. Fixed-price menus 26€, 40€, and 80€. AE, DC, MC, V. Tues–Sat noon–2pm and 7:30–10pm.

Where to Stay & Dine Nearby

Some of the world's most discerning people head to the town of **Eugénie-les-Bains,** about 53km (33 miles) north of Pau, in search of the marvelous domain (hotel, restaurant, and spa) of Michel Guérard. The town has no rail station, so most people drive from Pau. To get here, take N134 north to Garlin, follow the unmarked road west to the town of Geaune, and follow signs to Eugénie-les-Bains.

Les Prés d'Eugénie (Michel Guérard) ★★★ BASQUE   This Relais & Châteaux property is the creation of Michel Guérard, the chef whose *cuisine minceur* started a culinary revolution in the early 1970s that emphasized presentation over portion size. It attracts a stream of diners who appreciate the calm surroundings and the much-publicized cooking. The menu includes both *cuisine minceur,* so that calorie counters can still enjoy well-seasoned flavors and fresh ingredients, and the heartier *cuisine gourmand,* influenced by Basque and classic French recipes. Dishes are constantly evolving, usually tapping into regional sentimentality, as in the case of "bourgeois style" veal chops fried "over low flame in a corner of the fireplace." Specialties include cream of crayfish soup, freshwater crayfish roasted with limes, whiting in white-wine sauce, lamb steamed with fennel, and a variety of simply steamed fish with fresh vegetables.

Those unwilling to pay the stratospheric prices in the main restaurant sometimes book a table in a satellite restaurant operated by M. Guérard, **La Ferme aux Grives.** The cuisine focuses on rural specialties of the region, offering a single fixed-price menu for 46€. Comfortable and rustically elegant, it's open for lunch and dinner Thursday to Monday. A typical specialty is brochettes of free-range chicken cooked on a skewer.

In addition to the restaurants, there are a variety of accommodations. The most comfortable are the eight high-ceilinged units in an outlying annex, **Le Couvent des Herbes.** They cost 340€ to 380€ for a double, 450€ to 550€ for a suite. Slightly less glamorous are the 29 units in the main building, which rent for 350€ to 520€ for an apartment. Rooms are decorated in the style of a country manor house. Less expensive, and geared to the family trade, are the 30 units in **La Maison Rose,** where doubles go for 120€ to 200€, and suites cost 200€. Some units contain kitchenettes.

If you're planning on truly experiencing the spa, you won't really get an insight into its methodologies unless you come for a full-immersion sojourn of a week or more. About 25% of the clientele opt for an R & R, health, and revitalization routine, the cost of which, with full board, is 2,184€ per person weekly.

Eugénie-les-Bains, Beaune 40320. ☎ **05-58-05-06-07.** Fax 05-58-51-10-10. www.michelguerard.com. Reservations recommended. Main courses 45€–85€; fixed-price menu 156€–185€. AE, DC, MC, V. July 15–Aug daily noon–2pm and 7:45–10pm; Sept–Dec and Apr–July 14 Sat–Sun noon–1:30pm, Tues–Sun 7:45–10pm. Closed early Dec to mid-Mar.

Pau After Dark

Whereas nightlife in Pau always centered around **Le Triangle,** an area in the town center that's flanked by the rue Emile Garet, rue Lespy, and rue Castetnau, in very recent years it's been augmented with a rash of openings along **boulevard des Pyrénées** near the place Clemenceau. The best of the newcomers includes **Le Winfield,** 20 bd. des Pyrénées (☎ **05-59-27-80-60**), a rustic, sudsy, Australia-inspired pub that's arguably the best pickup joint in town. Outfitted with road signs from the Outback and warning signs not to kill the kangaroos, it charges no entrance fee and a beer costs around 3.50€.

Within the borders of Le Triangle you'll find another two-fisted contender, **Le Garage Bar & Buttery** (☎ **05-59-83-75-17;** www.legaragebar.com). Set within the echoing premises of what was conceived in the 1930s as an auto repair shop, it retains many of its original industrial-looking fixtures, plus a collection of antique traffic lights, road signs, mopeds hanging from chains in the ceiling, and vintage auto-related nostalgia. Most people come here just for the bar, but if you want food, platters cost 6.50€ to 13€ and include such items as English-style fish and chips, American-inspired burgers, and all-French versions of *bavette de boeuf* with garlic sauce and french fries. There are also fixed-price menus priced at 10€ and salads. It's open Monday to Friday noon to 1:30am, Saturday and Sunday 3pm to 1:30am.

The best of the town's two leading discos is **El Barrio Libre** (© **05-59-81-14-43;** www.elbarriolibre.com), which occupies a somewhat banal-looking shopping center (Le Centre Commercial Quartier Libre) in the suburb of Lescar, about 8km (4¾ miles) south of Pau's historic core. Here, a sometimes raucous sports-oriented crowd of 20-somethings moves restlessly between the metallic, high-tech interior and a large terrace every Wednesday to Sunday from 10pm till at least 3am. There's a cover charge of 11€ per person, although good-looking women sometimes manage to squeak in for free. Its most viable competitor is within Pau's Le Triangle, **L'Esprit,** 11 place du Foirail (© **06-75-38-59-99**), where bright lights flash above a shadowy dance floor that's flanked with a busy bar patronized by usually attractive 20- to 30-somethings from Pau and the surrounding farmlands and factory towns. Entrance, depending on the night of the week, ranges from free to 11€. It's open Wednesday to Saturday beginning around 10pm, getting busy at around 11pm. Both El Barrio Libre and L'Esprit rock and roll till around 5am, depending on business.

BAYONNE ★★

770km (478 miles) SW of Paris; 184km (114 miles) SW of Bordeaux

Bayonne is the leading port and pleasure-yacht basin of the Côte Basque, divided by the Nive and Adour rivers. A cathedral city and the capital of the Pays Basque, it's characterized by narrow streets, quays, and ramparts. Enlivening the scene are bullfights, *pelote* (jai alai), and street dancing at annual fiestas. You may want to buy some of Bayonne's famous chocolate at one of the arcaded shops along rue du Port-Neuf, and then enjoy coffee at a cafe along place de la Liberté, the hub of town.

Essentials

GETTING THERE   Seven TGV **trains** per day link Bayonne and Paris (trip time: 5 hr.; one-way fare: 84€). Nine trains per day arrive from Bordeaux (trip time: 90 min.; 26€ one-way). For train information and schedules, call © **36-35.**

There's **bus** service from Biarritz, 15 minutes away. Bus no. 1 departs from Biarritz at 12-minute intervals throughout the daylight hours, depositing passengers on place de la Mairie in Bayonne; the one-way fare is 1.20€. There's also bus service between Bayonne and outlying towns and villages not serviced by train. For bus information in Bayonne, call © **05-59-59-04-61.**

Bayonne is near the end of the N117 roadway, easily accessible by **car** from Toulouse and other cities in the south of France. From Paris, take A10 south to Vierzon, and then N20 south to Limoges. Continue on N21 south to Tarbes, and turn west along N117 to Bayonne.

VISITOR INFORMATION   The **Office de Tourisme** is on place des Basques (© **08-20-42-64-64;** fax 05-59-59-37-55; www.bayonne-tourisme.com).

SPECIAL EVENTS   During the 4-day **Fête de Bayonne,** the last week in July, a frenzy of outdoor concerts and dancing fills the streets. The celebration is intense.

For **free concerts** on fair-weather Thursday evenings in July and August, head to the gazebo on place de Gaulle, where styles range from jazz to traditional Basque. Contact the Office de Tourisme (see above) for more information.

Exploring the town

Vieux Bayonne, the old town, is inside the ramparts, on the left bank of the Nive. The early-13th-century **Cathédrale Ste-Marie (© 05-59-59-17-82;** www.cathedrale-de-bayonne.fr.st) dominates this part of town on rue d'Espagne and rue des Gouverneurs. The spiny 19th-century steeples are the best-known landmarks in Bayonne. The cathedral is worth half an hour of your time and is a good retreat on a hot day. It was begun in 1258 when Bayonne was under British control; it fell to the French in 1451. That explains the cathedral's ornamentation, mixing such elements as the English coat of arms (three leopards) with the fleur-de-lis of France. Some of the stained glass dates from the Renaissance, but the best statuary was smashed during the French Revolution. Don't miss the gorgeous 14th-century cloisters. They're like a secret garden from the Middle Ages. The cathedral is open daily 7am to 12:30pm and 3 to 7pm.

Atelier de Chocolat de Bayonne Andrieu   Bayonne is as well known for its chocolates as it is for its hams and pork products, and this combination museum and sales outlet is a good place to gather what you'll need to understand how they're made. Come to this industrial-looking neighborhood near Bayonne's railway station for a history of how and where the industry developed, and an insight into the complicated process of gathering together the ingredients for one of the world's most sought-after confections. In the showroom that's adjacent to the exhibits you'll find one of this organization's specialties: a "bouquet of chocolates," wherein chocolates flavored with, among others, vanilla and *"les piments d'Espelettes"* (spicy peppers from a nearby Basque village that's famous for producing them) are gathered together into forms and wrappings that resemble a bouquet of flowers.

7 allée de Gibéléou, Zone Artisanale Sainte-Croix. © **05-59-55-70-23.** www.atelierduchocolat.fr. Entrance 5.60€ adults, 2.80€ children 4–12. Mon–Sat 9:30am–12:30pm and 2–6pm.

Musée Basque ★★   Bayonne's major museum showcases the traditions, architecture, and decorative arts (including textiles and furniture) of the Basques in a state-of-the-art format that's more advanced and sophisticated than any equivalent museum in the Basque-speaking world.

37 quai des Corsaires. © **05-59-59-08-98.** www.musee-basque.com. Admission 5.50€ adults, 3€ students and children 6–17, free for children 5 and under; includes entrance to the Musée Bonnat (see below). July–Aug daily 10am–6:30pm; Sept–June Tues–Sun 10am–6:30pm.

Musée Bonnat ★★   This museum owns one of the best collections of paintings in France. It's hardly the Louvre, but it encompasses hundreds of canvases (far too many to display in its limited space). A sampling of works from some of the greatest European masters is showcased. If anybody's the star, it's Peter Paul Rubens (1577–1640), who has an entire salon devoted to his paintings. The collection's strongest point is its 19th-century art. Otherwise, it's like Art History 101, with works by David, Degas, Goya, Ingres, Leonardo da Vinci, El Greco, Tiepolo, and Rembrandt—an overview of European art from the 13th to the 20th centuries. Check

THE BASQUE COUNTRY

Bayonne

out the often-overlooked collection of antiquities in the basement, a museum within a museum with everything from Egyptian amulets to Greek vases.

5 rue Jacques-Lafitte. ✆ **05-59-59-08-52.** www.museebonnat.bayonne.fr. Admission 5.50€ adults, 3€ ages 6–17. May–Oct Wed–Mon 10am–6:30pm; Nov–Apr Wed–Mon 10am–12:30pm and 2–6pm.

Shopping

Most of Bayonne's specialty shops and boutiques lie inside the ramparts of the old town, Grand Bayonne. The pedestrian streets of **rue Port-Neuf** (aptly nicknamed the "street of chocolate shops"), **rue Victor-Hugo,** and **rue Salie** are major shopping destinations. For antiques, walk along the **rue des Faures** and the edges of **place Montaut,** behind the cathedral. Most of the modern shops and French chain stores are on **rue Thiers** and **quai de la Nive,** outside the old town. Visit **Maison de Jean Vier Shop,** carrefour Cinq Cantons (✆ **05-59-59-16-18**), to get your Basque bath, kitchen, and bed linens. **Cazenave,** 19 rue Port-Neuf (✆ **05-59-59-03-16**), specializes in *chocolats de Bayonne,* which include rich, dark, strong chocolate nougats; stop in the tearoom here for warm chocolate mousse.

The accessories of one Basque tradition have become something of a fine art. In olden days, the *makila* was used as a walking stick, a cudgel, or—when equipped with a hidden blade—a knife. Today, carved *makilas* are sold as collectors' items and souvenirs. For safety's sake, they almost never come with a blade. One of the best outlets in town is **Fabrication de Makhilas,** 37 rue Vieille Boucherie (✆ **05-59-59-18-20**). Another famous product of the Basque country is its cured hams, which taste best shaved into paper-thin slices and consumed with one of the region's heady red wines and perhaps a loaf of bread and (if you prefer) a smear of butter. An establishment that prepares and sells these hams is **Saloir et Séchoire à Jambon Pierre Ibaialde,** 41 rue des Cordeliers (✆ **05-59-25-65-30**), where the hams are sold either whole or in thin slices. Also available is an impressive roster of sausages, pâtés, and terrines.

Bayonne has been known as a centerpiece for the fabrication of chocolates since the days of the Spanish Inquisition, when Spanish and Portuguese Jews were driven out of Iberia by the Catholic monarchs, bringing the craft of chocolate making with them to France. For one of the best views in the region of the complicated process of chocolate making, head for **La Fabrique du Chocolatier Puyodebat,** 66 rue d'Espagne (✆ **05-59-59-20-86**).

Where to Stay

Best Western Grand Hôtel ★   The best hotel in town was built in 1835 on the ruins of a medieval Carmelite convent. In 1991, it attained government-rated three-star status, a position it admirably maintains. Rooms have modern fittings but retain an antique feel. Each midsize bathroom has a tub and shower.

21 rue Thiers, Bayonne 64100. ✆ **800/528-1234** in the U.S. and Canada, or 05-59-59-62-00. Fax 05-59-59-62-01. www.bw-legrandhotel.com. 54 units. 75€–149€ double. AE, DC, MC, V. Parking 13€. **Amenities:** Restaurant (breakfast only); bar; room service. *In room:* A/C, TV, hair dryer, minibar, Wi-Fi (free).

Mercure Bayonne Centre   The second-best choice in Bayonne, the six-story Mercure provides well-furnished rooms with views over the river Nive. Drinks are served on the terrace, which was carved out of a wooded setting beside the river, a

10-minute walk north of the cathedral. Rooms are in typical chain-hotel style, and each well-kept bathroom has a tub and shower.

Av. Jean-Rostand, Bayonne 64100. ☏ **05-59-52-84-44.** Fax 05-59-52-84-20. www.mercure.com. 109 units. 102€–150€ double. AE, DC, MC, V. Parking 8€. **Amenities:** Restaurant; bar; outdoor pool. *In room:* A/C, TV, hair dryer, minibar, Wi-Fi (9.90€ per day).

Where to Dine

Brasserie Aviron Bayonnais BASQUE   Very few restaurants that we know of are as passionately associated with local sports teams as this one, where regional rugby is viewed with something akin to obsession. Near the town's sports stadium and the river, within a 10-minute walk from the cathedral, it occupies a second-story dining room that's modern, minimalist, and lined with photos of local athletes. The same building contains the administrative headquarters for the town's rugby team, Aviron Bayonnais. Come here for two-fisted, no-nonsense platters of local charcuteries, among which, of course, will be paper-thin slices of *jambon de Bayonne*; garlicky tartines piled high with peppers, tomatoes, and onions; massive chunks of beefsteak prepared for two diners at a time; calamaris (*chiperones*) in a creamy garlic sauce; and oven-baked hake from nearby St-Jean-de-Luz prepared with olive oil and garlic "in the Spanish style."

In the Garage de la Nive, 1 rue Harry Owen Roe. ☏ **05-59-58-27-27.** Reservations recommended. Main courses 16€–25€; set-price menu 29€. DC, MC, V. Mon–Tues and Thurs–Sat 9am–2am; Wed 9am–3pm. Closed 2 weeks in Aug.

François Miura ★ 🎒 FRENCH   A few steps from the Eglise St-André, this restaurant occupies a late-19th-century cloister built for Visitandine nuns. The cuisine is the most eclectic and personalized in town. Menu items are sophisticated and composed with intelligence. They include flavorful, complicated dishes such as twice-cooked pigeon in regional wine stuffed with foie gras, and stuffed squid served with confit of pigs' feet flavored with squid ink and essence of crayfish. Less daring examples include warm calamari salad with two kinds of peppers, and braised rack of lamb with fresh vegetables and coriander sauce. Desserts may include a soufflé with pear liqueur.

24 rue Marengo. ☏ **05-59-59-49-89.** Reservations recommended. Main courses 19€–24€; fixed-price menus 21€–32€. AE, DC, MC, V. Thurs–Tues noon–2pm; Mon–Tues and Thurs–Sat 8–10pm.

La Cidrerie TTiPia ★ 🍶 BASQUE   This restaurant has become famous throughout Bayonne for its resuscitation of the cider-making traditions of the Basque country. Owned and managed by an amiable Basque nationalist known simply as Isabelle, and set within a rustic, three-story 19th-century warehouse in the heart of Old Bayonne, it serves two brands of (mildly alcoholic) cider, and a very limited array of old-fashioned Basque food. This is configured into a "one choice fits all" set-price menu whose four courses include omelets with morels; grilled steaks; and a slab of local goat's cheese with walnuts. It also includes as much cider as you can drink and coffee. More than most other restaurants in town, this place gets boisterous and gregarious, with lots of after-game sports fans sometimes singing over their cups after important matches.

27 rue des Cordeliers. ☏ **05-59-46-13-31.** http://titipia.364.fr. Set-price menu 29€. MC, V. Tues–Sun noon–2pm; Mon–Sat 8–11pm (till midnight Fri–Sat).

Le Cheval Blanc ★★ BASQUE The finest restaurant in Bayonne occupies a half-timbered Basque-style house built in 1715 in the heart of the historic center. Menu items vary with the season, but may include slices of foie gras with caramelized endive and pine nuts, ravioli stuffed with wild boar and flavored with local red wine and confit of baby onions, and corn blinis with flap mushrooms. Dorado may be simmered in garlic and served with *crépinette de marmitako* (diced tuna with red and green peppers, bound in a pig's stomach). One of the best desserts is a Grand Marnier soufflé.

68 rue Bourgneuf. ℰ **05-59-59-01-33.** Reservations recommended. Main courses 18€–35€; fixed-price menu 30€–80€. AE, MC, V. Tues–Fri and Sun noon–1:30pm; Tues–Sat 7:45–9:30pm. Closed Feb.

Bayonne After Dark

Nightlife centers on the neighborhood known as Petit Bayonne, the town's historic core. **Rue des Tonneliers, rue Pannecau,** and **rue des Cordeliers** are the liveliest areas after dark. **Katie Daly's,** 3 place de la Liberté (ℰ **05-59-59-09-14**), serves endless pints of Guinness; the drinkers really pile in on weekends. Expect a carefree group of rowdies and a lot of fun. For a taste of local color, try **Le Cabaret La Luna Negra,** rue des Augustins (ℰ **05-59-25-78-05;** www.lunanegra.fr), where the 6€-to-10€ cover charge includes cabaret, jazz, or blues performances and popular French songs.

BIARRITZ ★★★

779km (484 miles) SW of Paris; 193km (120 miles) SW of Bordeaux

One of the most famous seaside resorts in the world, Biarritz was once a fishing village. Favored by Empress Eugénie, the village near the Spanish border soon attracted her husband, Napoleon III, who truly put it on the map. Later, Queen Victoria showed up often, and her son, Edward VII, visited more than once.

In the 1930s, the Prince of Wales (before he was, and then wasn't, Edward VIII) and the American divorcée he loved, Wallis Simpson, did much to make Biarritz more fashionable as they headed south with these instructions: "Chill the champagne, pack the pearls, and tune up the Bugatti." Biarritz became the pre–jet set's favorite sunning spot. Although those legendary days are long gone, the resort is still fashionable and has become the surfing capital of France, with plenty of surf shops, snack bars, and even some reasonably priced hotels.

Essentials

GETTING THERE Seventeen **trains** arrive daily from Bayonne (trip time: 10 min.), which has rail links with Paris and other cities in the south of France. The one-way fare is 2.30€ to 3€. The rail station is 3km (1¾ miles) south of the town center, in La Négresse. For information, call ℰ **36-35.** Bus no. 2 carries passengers from the station to the center of Biarritz; the one-way fare is 1.20€. You can also take a cab for around 13€ to 20€. If you're **driving,** Biarritz is at the end of the N117 roadway, the major thoroughfare for the Basque country. From Paris, take A10 south to Vierzon, and then N20 south to Limoges. Continue on N21 south to Tarbes, and then head west on N117.

VISITOR INFORMATION The **Office de Tourisme** is on square d'Ixelles (ℰ **05-59-22-37-00;** fax 05-59-24-14-19; www.biarritz.fr).

SPECIAL EVENTS If you're in town in September, check out the modern dance and ballet performances during the 2-week festival of **Le Temps d'Aimer.** Cultural events take place in parks, churches, and auditoriums throughout town. Tickets cost 40€ for adults or 15€ for ages 5 to 15 (free 4 and under). For reservations and ticket sales for the festival, contact the tourist office above.

Biarritz is the surfing capital of France, and each year, in mid-July, cadres of enthusiasts descend on the town for the 5-day **Roxy Jam,** an event known as the **Women's International Festival of Long Board Surfing.** It's centered around the waves offshore from La Plage de la Côte Basque, with plenty of advertising depicting the kind of buffed and suntanned women you might have expected in California. A Hawaiian spirit permeates the town as surfers re-create the search for endless summer. You don't need to buy a ticket, as viewing is free and visible from most points along the waterfront of the above-mentioned beach. For more information, contact the tourist office. Biarritz also devotes more of its landscape and energy to golf than any other city in France. Ten courses lie within a short drive of the town. A good practice setting is the **Centre d'Entraînement d'Ilbarritz-Bidart,** avenue du Chateau, Bidart 64210 (✆ **05-59-43-81-30**); you can play 9 holes for 23€ to 36€. Passionate golfers might consider visiting in the third week in July during the **Biarritz Cup,** a nationwide competition attended by mostly French golfers. The series of playoffs takes place at the Golf du Phare, avenue Edith-Cavell (✆ **05-59-03-71-80;** www.golfbiarritz.com). Information on both festivals is available from the tourist office.

A Day at the Beach

Along the seafront facing the Casino is the **Grande Plage.** During the Belle Epoque, this was where Victorian ladies promenaded under parasols and wide-brimmed veiled hats. Today's bathers don't dress up in billowing skirts. Sometimes they don't even wear tops. The beach is also popular with surfers.

Promenade du Bord de Mer, along the coast within the city limits, is still a major attraction. The paths are often carved into cliffs, and sections have been designed as rock gardens with flowers, turning the area into a public park. From here, you can head north to **Pointe St-Martin,** where you'll find more gardens and a staircase (look for the sign DESCENTE DE L'OCEAN) leading you to allée Winston-Churchill, a paved path going along **Plage Miramar.**

La Perspective de la Côte des Basques, a walk that goes up to another plateau, leads to one of the wildest beaches in France: **Plage de la Côte des Basques,** with breakers crashing at the base of the cliffs. This is where surfers head.

If you like your beaches calmer, the safest beach is the small, horseshoe-shaped **Plage du Port-Vieux,** along the path from plateau de l'Atalaye. Its tranquil waters, protected by rocks, make it a favorite with families.

Exploring the town

Eglise St-Martin, rue St-Martin (✆ **05-59-23-05-19**), is one of the few vestiges of the port's early boom days. In the 12th century, Biarritz grew prosperous as a whaling center. The mammals' departure from the Bay of Biscay marked a decline in the port's fortunes. The church dates from the 1100s and was restored in 1541 with a Flamboyant Gothic chancel. It's in the town center between two of Biarritz's major arteries, rue d'Espagne and avenue de Gramont and is open daily 8am to 7pm. Admission is free.

Biarritz's turning point came with the arrival of Queen Hortense, who spent lazy summers here with her two daughters. One of them, Eugénie, married Napoleon III in 1853 and prevailed on him to visit Biarritz the next year. The emperor fell under its spell and ordered the construction of the **Hôtel du Palais** (p. 678). The hotel remains the town's most enduring landmark, though it was originally dubbed "Eugénie's Basque folly." Edward VII stayed there in 1906 and again in 1910, only days before his death. In a commanding spot on Grande Plage, the hotel is worth a visit even if you're not a guest. You can view the palatial trappings of its public rooms.

Before the Revolution of 1917, members of Russian nobility arrived—so many, in fact, that they erected the **Eglise Orthodoxe Russe,** 8 av. de l'Impératrice (✆ **05-59-24-16-74**). Across from the Hôtel du Palais, this Byzantine-Russian landmark was built in 1892 so that wintering aristocrats could worship when they weren't enjoying champagne, caviar, and Basque prostitutes. It's noted for its gilded dome, the interior of which is the color of a blue sky on a sunny day. It can be visited only on weekends: Saturday 3 to 6pm and Sunday 4 to 7pm.

After you pass the Hôtel du Palais, the walkway widens into **quai de la Grande Plage,** Biarritz's principal promenade. This walkway continues to the opposite end of the resort, where a final belvedere opens onto the southernmost stretch of beach. This whole walk takes about 3 hours.

At the southern edge of Grande Plage, steps will take you to **place Ste-Eugénie,** Biarritz's most gracious old square. Lined with terraced restaurants, it's the most popular rendezvous. Right below place Ste-Eugénie is the colorful **Port des Pêcheurs** (fishers' port). Crowded with fishing boats, it has old wooden houses and shacks backed up against a cliff. Here you'll find driftwood, rope, and plenty of lobster traps along with small harborfront restaurants and cafes.

The rocky **plateau de l'Atalaye** forms one side of the Port des Pêcheurs. Carved on orders of Napoleon III, a tunnel leads from the plateau to an esplanade. Here a footbridge stretches over the sea, to a rocky islet that takes its name, **Rocher de la Vierge (Rock of the Virgin),** from the statue crowning it. Since 1865, this statue is said to have protected the sailors and fishers in the Bay of Biscay. Alexandre-Gustave Eiffel (designer of the tower) directed construction of the footbridge. The walk out onto the edge of the rock, with crashing surf on both sides, is the most dramatic in Biarritz. From the rock, you can see all the way to the mountains of the Spanish Basque country, far to the south.

Here you can visit the **Musée de la Mer,** 14 plateau de l'Atalaye (✆ **05-59-22-33-34;** www.museedelamer.com), which houses 24 aquariums of fish native to the bay. The seals steal the show at their daily 10:30am and 5pm feedings. The museum also houses *requins* (sharks) that are fed on Tuesday and Friday at 11am and Wednesday and Sunday at 4:30pm. Admission is 7.80€ adults, 5€ students and children 4 to 16, and free for children 3 and under. It's open in July and August daily 9:30am to midnight, June and September daily 9:30am to 7pm, and October to May Tuesday to Sunday 9:30am to 12:30pm and 2 to 6pm. Closed 2 weeks around the end of January.

The only remaining building in town designed according to the tastes of the Empress Eugénie is **La Chapelle Impériale,** rue Pellot (✆ **05-59-22-37-10**).

Built in 1864, it combines Romanesque-Byzantine and Hispano-Moorish styles. Open July and August Tuesday, Thursday, and Saturday 2 to 7pm. Admission is 3€.

Musée Asiatica, 1 rue Guy Petit (© **05-59-22-78-78;** www.museeasiatica. com), has an unusual collection, mostly from India, Nepal, Tibet, and China. The art dates from prehistory to the current age. Admission is 7€ for adults, 5€ for ages 13 to 25, and 2€ for children 8 to 12; free for 7 and under. From September to June, it is open Monday to Friday 2 to 6:30pm, Saturday and Sunday 2 to 7pm. In July and August, it's open daily 10:30am to 6:30pm.

Shopping

The major boutiques, with all the big designer names from Paris, are on **place Clemenceau** in the heart of Biarritz. From this square, fan out to **rue Gambetta, rue Mazagran, avenue Victor-Hugo, avenue Edouard-VII, avenue du Maréchal-Foch,** and **avenue de Verdun.** Look for the exceptional Biarritz chocolates and confections, and textiles from the Basque country.

The finest chocolatiers are **Pariès,** 1 place Bellevue (© **05-59-22-07-52),** where you can choose from seven kinds of *tourons* (nougats) ranging from raspberry to coffee and **Henriet,** place Clemenceau (© **05-59-24-24-15** or 05-59-24-58-80), where the house specialty is *rochers de Biarritz* (morsels of candied orange peel and roasted almonds covered in dark chocolate). The owners also run the **Musée du Chocolat,** 14–15 av. Beaurivages (© **05-59-23-27-72;** www.planetemusee duchocolat.com), where exhibits illustrate chocolate making and its history. There's also a sales kiosk. During July and August, it's open daily 10am to 12:30 and 2 to 6:30pm; the rest of the year, it's open Monday to Saturday 10am to noon and 2:30 to 6pm. Admission fees are 6€ adults, 5€ students 12 to 18, 3€ children 4 to 12, and free for children 3 and under. At the other end of the gastronomic spectrum, try **Mille et Un Fromages,** 8 rue Victor Hugo (© **05-59-24-67-88),** specializing in, as the name suggests, a myriad of tasty French cheeses, as well as a host of hearty wines to accompany them.

Virtually every souvenir shop and department store in the region sells **espadrilles,** the canvas-topped, rope-bottomed slippers. A simple off-the-shelf model begins at around 15€, and made-to-order versions (special sizes, special colors) rarely top 70€.

Where to Stay

Château de Brindos ★★ 🏠 This is one of the most architecturally and culturally unusual homes in the southwest of France, with a history entrenched in the Jazz Age. Built by American heiress Virginia Gould in 1920, it occupies 11 hectares (27 acres) of inland park and garden. With a facade inspired vaguely by the architecture of Spain, and an interior loaded with architectural remnants such as fireplaces and staircases from the Gothic age, this is the most romantic stopover on the Côte Basque. Rooms are spacious, with antique furnishings and modern fittings. Fishing on the private lake can be arranged. The superb restaurant overlooks the lake.

1 allée du Château, Anglet 64600. © **05-59-23-89-80.** Fax 05-59-23-89-81. www.chateaudebrindos. com. 29 units. 275€–600€ double; 250€–330€ suite. AE, DC, MC, V. From town center, follow AEROPORT signs; after the 2nd roundabout *(rond-point),* follow signs to château; it's about 2.5km (1½ miles) north of Biarritz. Closed last 2 weeks of Feb. **Amenities:** Restaurant; bar; exercise room; heated outdoor pool; room service; sauna. *In room:* A/C, TV, hair dryer, minibar, Wi-Fi (free).

Hôtel Atalaye   For economy with a bit of style, head to this simple government-rated two-star lodging. In the heart of town on a tranquil spot overlooking the ocean, this early-20th-century hotel gets rather sleepy in winter. Rooms are well maintained and traditionally furnished; most of the small, tiled bathrooms have showers. Breakfast is provided anytime you request it. The location is right off place Ste-Eugénie near the beaches, lighthouse, and casino.

6 rue des Goelands, Plateau de L'Atalaye, Biarritz 64200. ℂ **05-59-24-06-76.** Fax 05-59-22-33-51. www.hotelatalaye.com. 25 units. 42€–68€ double; 59€–98€ triple. MC, V. Closed mid-Nov to mid-Dec (and last week of Jan). *In room:* A/C, TV.

Hôtel du Palais ★★★ ☺   There is no finer hotel palace along the Basque coast. The Hôtel du Palais has been the grand playground for the international elite for over a century. Napoleon III built it in 1854 as a private villa for Eugénie so she wouldn't get homesick for Spain. He picked the ideal beachfront, in view of the rocks and rugged shoreline. Of course the hotel has elaborately furnished suites, but even the double rooms have period furniture and silk draperies, plus spacious private bathrooms with luxurious tubs and showers. Try to get a room facing west to enjoy the sunsets over the Basque coast.

1 av. de l'Impératrice, Biarritz 64200. ℂ **800/223-6800** in the U.S. and Canada, or 05-59-41-64-00. Fax 05-59-41-67-99. www.hotel-du-palais.com. 154 units. 375€–575€ double; 700€–1,750€ suite. AE, DC, MC, V. **Amenities:** 3 restaurants; bar; children's program and playground; exercise room; outdoor seawater pool; room service; sauna; spa. *In room:* A/C, TV, hair dryer, minibar, Wi-Fi (free).

Mercure Plaza Hotel ★   Near the casino and beach, this hotel is a gorgeous Art Deco monument. Built in 1928, it has remained virtually unchanged, except for discreet renovations, so it's classified as a historic monument and a civic treasure. Rooms retain their original Art Deco furnishings; they tend to be large and have high ceilings, and some open onto private terraces. Those overlooking the back and side cost less than those with seafront views. The hotel has direct access to the beach.

10 av. Edouard-VII, Biarritz 64200. ℂ **05-59-24-74-00.** Fax 05-59-22-22-01. www.groupe-segeric. com. 69 units. 136€–236€ double. AE, DC, MC, V. Parking 17€. **Amenities:** Bar; room service. *In room:* A/C, TV, hair dryer, minibar, Wi-Fi (15€ per day).

Villa Vauréal ★ 🌶   This is our favorite guesthouse in Biarritz, lying within walking distance of the center and close to the seaside. Owner Christine Rannou Ader has named each of her accommodations after a type of fruit—raspberry, peach, mango, plum, and cherry. Breakfast is served outside on a terrace shaded by lime trees. Christine makes the peach and apple jams served with your breakfast. Her rooms are neat and tidy, furnished in a traditional way, each with a little kitchenette.

14 rue Vauréal, 64200 Biarritz. ℂ **06-10-11-64-21.** Fax 05-59-22-64-19. www.villavaureal.com. 5 units. 108€–187€ double. AE, MC, V. Parking 5€. **Amenities:** Garden. *In room:* TV, kitchenette, Wi-Fi (free).

ON THE OUTSKIRTS

Ferme Hégia ★★ 🎁   Surrounded by the mountains of the Pyrénées, a farmhouse from 1746 has been turned into the best *restaurant avec chambres* in the area. Just 34km (21 miles) inland from Biarritz, and 6km (3¾ miles) south of Hasparren along D152, this retreat is the domain of Michelin-starred chef Arnaud Daguin and his wife, Veronique. Ancient wooden beams and timbers have been lovingly restored, but the interior is done in a strikingly modern design. Guests enjoy a glass of champagne in the open kitchen, watching Daguin cook his elaborate dishes. The cuisine is among the finest in the Basque country. The chef, for example, takes incredible care with his ingredients. He takes almost as much care with the other ingredients that go into his market-fresh cuisine. The bedrooms are beautifully designed and spacious, but lack such "distractions" as phones or TV.

Chemin Curutxeta Celhay, 64240 Hasparren. ℂ **05-59-29-67-86.** www.hegia.com. 5 units. 650€ double. Half board 325€ per person. AE, MC, V. **Amenities:** Restaurant. *In room:* Wi-Fi (free).

Where to Dine

The restaurant at **Château de Brindos** (see "Where to Stay," above) also serves excellent Franco-Basque cuisine.

Clos Basque ★★ BASQUE/FRENCH   The best regional specialties are showcased here in this Basque kitchen known for its savory offerings from both the land and sea nearby. The creative cuisine varies with the season, the availability of ingredients, and the chef's inspiration on any given day. One of the best fish dishes is a local Atlantic whitefish known as *maigre*. Sea scallops frequently appear on the menu, as does fresh sea bass. Their codfish platter with chorizo and artichokes reflects inspiration from neighboring Spain. Rack of lamb and duck are often featured as well.

12 rue Louis Barthou. ℂ **05-59-24-24-96.** Reservations recommended as far in advance in summer as possible. Main courses 13€ each; fixed-price menu 24€. MC, V. Tues–Sun noon–1:30pm and Tues–Sat 8–9:30pm. Closed June 25–July 6, Oct 22–Nov 9, and Feb 18–Mar 18.

Negresse & Co. ★ 🌶 BASQUE/FRENCH   This restaurant takes its name from a 19th-century slave who escaped from an American plantation by hiding in the bottom of a French ship returning home. She established an inn in Biarritz, which was used by Napoleon's army en route to Spain. Inside the decor is somber and dignified, opening onto a summer terrace. At lunch typical brasserie food is served including grilled salmon or duck, as well as tender beef with the vegetables of the day. At dinner the menu is more gastronomic, where traditional recipes are mixed with more-modern cooking, including a delectable platter of scallops with polenta or roast capon, perhaps filet of the catch of the day with ravioli stuffed with fresh mushrooms. Menus change every month for the relatively young and fashionable crowd that flocks here.

44 rue Luis Mariano. ℂ **05-59-41-28-51.** www.negresseco.com. Reservations required. Lunch main courses 13€–20€; dinner main courses 20€; fixed-price lunch 13€; fixed-price dinner 34€. AE, DC, MC, V. Mon–Fri noon–2:30pm and Tues–Sat 7–9:30pm.

Biarritz After Dark

Start the night with a stroll around **Port des Pêcheurs,** an ideal spot for people-watching, with its sport fishermen, restaurants, and fascinating crowds.

Fortunes have been made and lost at **Le Casino Municipal,** 1 av. Edouard-VII (ℂ **05-59-22-77-77**), where you can easily catch gambling fever. The less formal section, containing only slot machines, is open daily 10am to 3am (until 4am Saturday). Entrance is free, no ID is required, and there's no dress code. The more elegant section (for *les jeux de table,* or table games) is open Sunday to Thursday 8pm to 3am, Friday and Saturday 8pm to 4am. This section requires a passport or photo ID. "Correct" dress for this section means no shorts or sloppy attire—jackets for men aren't required.

The hippest nightclub in town is **Le Copa,** 24 av. Edouard-VII (☎ **05-59-22-29-43;** www.lecopa.fr), which plays Latin (particularly Cuban) salsa, and virtually every other kind of dance music. **Le Play Boy,** 15 place Clemenceau (☎ **05-59-24-38-46**), appeals to a diverse crowd ranging in age from 20 to 40. More appealing is **Disco Le Caveau,** 4 rue Gambetta (☎ **05-59-24-16-17**), where a well-dressed and attractive crowd of gay and straight people mingle with ease. **Le Carré Coast,** 21 av. Edouard VII (☎ **05-59-24-64-64**), is open nightly between 7:30pm and 4am June and September, but closed Sunday to Wednesday the rest of the year. It combines a view of the sea, an outdoor terrace, a minimalist decor with lots of burnished steel, and a dance floor. It can get very crowded in here with the emotionally unattached (and sometimes the attached masquerading as the unattached) from the surrounding region. Entrance is free, but a whiskey with soda begins at around 10€.

ST-JEAN-DE-LUZ ★★

791km (492 miles) SW of Paris; 15km (9⅓ miles) S of Biarritz

This Basque country tuna-fishing port and beach resort is ideal for a seaside vacation. St-Jean-de-Luz lies at the mouth of the Nivelle, opening onto the Bay of Biscay, with the Pyrénées in the background. Tourists have been flocking here since the 19th century, when H. G. Wells "discovered" the town.

Essentials

GETTING THERE   Eight to 10 **trains** per day arrive from Biarritz (trip time: 15 min.; one-way fare: 3€–5€), and 10 trains per day arrive from Paris (trip time: 5½ hr.; one-way fare: 88€). For train information and schedules, call ☎ **36-35. Buses** pulling into town from other parts of the Basque country arrive at the Gare Routière (☎ **05-59-26-06-99**), in front of the railway station. St-Jean-de-Luz is a short **drive** from Biarritz along N10 south.

VISITOR INFORMATION   The **Office de Tourisme** is on 20 blvd. Victor Hugo (☎ **05-59-26-03-16;** fax 05-59-26-21-47; www.saint-jean-de-luz.com).

SPECIAL EVENTS   In July and August on Wednesday after 10:30pm and Sunday after 10:30pm, people pile into place Louis-XIV to take part in **Toro de Fuego,** a celebration of the bull. Revelers take to the streets to dance and watch fireworks. The highlight of the festivities is a snorting papier-mâché bull carried around place Louis-XIV. Between June 22 and June 26, the city celebrates the **Festival of St-Jean** (*Fêtes Patronales de la Saint Jean*) with concerts and a series of food kiosks along the harborfront. For 4 days during the first half of October, a small film festival, **Festival International des Jeunes Réalisateurs** (☎ **05-59-51-65-30**), showcases the work of filmmakers from southwestern France. For information about festivals, contact the Office de Tourisme (see above).

Fun on & off the Beach

THE BEACH   The major draw here is the gracefully curving stretch of the white-sand **La Grande Plage St-Jean-de-Luz;** it's one of the best beaches in France, and consequently very crowded in July and August. The beach lies in a half-moon-shaped bay between the ocean and the source of the Nivelle River.

THE PORT TOWN Though tourism accounts for most of the revenue around here, fishing is still important. In fact, this town is the major fishing port along the Basque coast, even though it's less important than in days past. Eating seafood recently plucked from the sea is one of the reasons to visit, especially when Basque chefs transform the big catch into intriguing platters. This port's many narrow streets flanked by old houses are great for strolling.

Exploring the town

In the town's principal church, the 13th-century **Eglise St-Jean-Baptiste ★★**, at the corner of rue Gambetta and rue Garat (② **05-59-26-08-81**), Louis XIV and the Spanish Infanta, Marie-Thérèse, were married in 1660. The interior is among the handsomest of all Basque churches. Surmounting the altar is a statue-studded gilded retable (altarpiece). The interior is open to visitors Monday to Saturday 9am to noon and 2 to 6pm, and Sunday 3 to 6:30pm.

La Maison Louis XIV is more richly furnished with antiques and mementos than La Maison de l'Infante, more interesting, and more densely loaded with souvenirs. It also has wax figures representing the important figures of the drama associated with this late-17th-century Franco-Spanish alliance.

La Maison de l'Infante L'Infante Marie Thérèse d'Espagne lived within this elegant building (aka La Maison Joanoenia) at the time of her marriage to young Louis XIV in June 1660. It was designed and built by wealthy weapons merchant Johannot de Haraneder. Its pink facade, made from bricks and local stones, evokes an Italian palazzo. Inside, one floor above street level, is a "grand" reception room with a 17th-century fireplace, and ceiling beams richly adorned and painted.

Quai de l'Infante. ② **05-59-26-36-82.** Admission 3€. June–Oct 15 Tues–Sat 11am-12:30pm and 2:30-6:30pm.

La Maison Louis XIV One of the most beautiful and elegant buildings (aka La Maison Lohobiague) in Saint-Jean-de-Luz was constructed between 1644 and 1648, beside the port. It's a good example of Louis XIII domestic architecture. Built of chiseled gray stone, it housed Louis XIV for 3 months prior to his marriage. His wedding night with L'Infante Marie-Thérèse took place here. The ceremony had been held in the nearby l'eglise Saint-Jean-Baptiste de Saint-Jean-de-Luz on June 9, 1660.

Place Louis XIV. ② **05-59-26-01-56.** Admission 5€ adults, 3€ students and ages 5-15 (free 4 and under). July-Aug Mon-Sat 10:30am-12:30pm and 2:30-6:30pm; Apr–June and Sept–Oct Wed–Mon visits only at 11am, 3, 4, and 5pm.

Shopping

You'll find the best shopping along pedestrian **rue Gambetta** and around the Eglise St-Jean-de-Luz. There you can find anything from clothes and leather handbags to books and chocolates to dishes and linens.

You can also ramble around the port, sip pastis in a harborfront cafe, and debate the virtues of the beret. Then scout out **Maison Adam,** 49 rue Gambetta (② **05-59-26-03-54**), which has sold almond-based confections from this boutique since 1660. Specialties include sugared macaroons, *tourons* (almond-paste candies flavored with everything from chocolate to confit of berries), and *canougat* (soft caramels). The boutique is closed mid-January to mid-February and for 1 week in November.

A final star in a town loaded with culinary stars is **Confiserie Pariès,** 9 rue Gambetta (✆ **05-59-26-01-46**). Well known for its chocolates and its pastries, it's especially famous for its canougat, a soft and easily chewable caramel that literally melts, with explosions of flavor, in your mouth.

Where to Stay

Hôtel Golf de Chantaco ★★　 This mansion has enough memorabilia from its Art Deco heyday to remind you of a time when aristocrats from around Europe made it one of their preferred hotels. Surrounded by an 18-hole golf course and parklands, it's 10 minutes by car from the beach or from the center of town. It resembles the eclectically designed country château of an erudite and somewhat eccentric industrialist. Rooms are luxurious, with personalized touches. Each plush bathroom has a tub/shower combination. Breakfast is served beneath the wisteria-covered arches of a patio.

Rte. d'Ascain, St-Jean-de-Luz 64500. ✆ **05-59-26-14-76.** Fax 05-59-26-35-97. 23 units. 160€–250€ double; 270€–750€ suite. AE, MC, V. Free parking. Closed Nov–Apr. Take D918 1.5km (1 mile) from the town center. **Amenities:** Lounge w/bar service; babysitting; golf course; outdoor pool; room service; tennis court. *In room:* A/C, TV, hair dryer, minibar, Wi-Fi (free).

Hôtel Hélianthal ★ 🦋　 Efficient, well designed, and comfortable, this hotel dates from the early 1990s, and is the most health-conscious hotel in the area, with cardio machines, a top-rated spa, and healthy food. It sits atop a restaurant that has been a city monument since the 1920s. Rising above the commercial heart of town, near the beach, it earns three stars from the local tourist office and has some of the amenities you'd associate with a more expensive property. Unfortunately, none of the Art Deco–style rooms overlook the sea, but many have terraces, bay windows, or balconies. Each room has an immaculately kept bathroom with tub and shower. The big-windowed restaurant, L'Atlantique, offers a terrace overlooking the sea.

Place Maurice-Ravel B.P. 469, St-Jean-de-Luz 64540. ✆ **05-59-51-51-00.** Fax 05-59-51-51-54. www. helianthal.fr. 100 units. 118€–248€ double. AE, DC, MC, V. Parking 6€–12€. **Amenities:** Restaurant; bar; babysitting; health club; pool; room service; sauna. *In room:* A/C, TV, hair dryer, minibar, Wi-Fi (free).

La Devinière ★★ 🦋　 This small establishment is the best-furnished moderately priced hotel in St-Jean-de-Luz. It occupies a former private town house where Rabelais once lived and the unsold inventories of its antiques-dealer owner helped it attain its present level of 18th-century elegance. Rooms are comfortable, well maintained, and—like the rest of the hotel—filled with attractive antiques. Each midsize bathroom has a shower and tub.

5 rue Loquin, St-Jean-de-Luz 64500. ✆ **05-59-26-05-51.** Fax 05-59-51-26-38. www.hotel-la-deviniere.com. 10 units. 120€–180€ double. MC, V. Parking 10€–15€. **Amenities:** Lounge. *In room:* TV, Wi-Fi (in some; free).

Le Parc Victoria ★★ 📱　 The most secluded and tranquil hotel at the resort is a white 19th-century villa, saved from destruction and lovingly restored by its owner, M. Larralde. Surrounded by flowering beds and luxuriant trees, the house is furnished with antiques in keeping with its original style. The chandelier-lit salon of the main building, decorated in Napoleon III fashion, sets the tone. Guest rooms hold antiques and comfortable, tasteful Art Deco furnishings, and the marble-clad bathrooms are completely up-to-date. The restaurant's cuisine and wines are first class.

5 rue Cepé, St-Jean-de-Luz 64500. ✆ **05-59-26-78-78.** Fax 05-59-26-78-08. www.parcvictoria.com. 18
units. 140€–240€ double; 280€–715€ suite. AE, DC, MC, V. Free parking. Closed mid-Nov to mid-Mar.
Amenities: 2 restaurants; bar; babysitting; outdoor pool. *In room:* A/C, TV, hair dryer, minibar, Wi-Fi (free).

Where to Dine

You may also like to check out L'Atlantique, the restaurant at the **Hôtel Hélianthal**
(see above).

Auberge Kaïku ★ BASQUE/FRENCH   On a narrow street off place Louis-XIV,
Auberge Kaïku is the best restaurant in town outside the hotels. The structure, with
hand-hewn beams and chiseled masonry, dates from 1540, and is said to be the oldest in town. Examples of the cuisine are roast suckling Pyrénéan lamb, *parillade*
(mixed grill) of shellfish, John Dory with fresh mint, filet of beef with essence of
truffles, and duckling in honey.

17 rue de la République. ✆ **05-59-26-13-20.** Reservations recommended. Main courses 20€–25€;
fixed-price lunch 25€; fixed-price dinner 32€. MC, V. July–Aug daily 12:15–2pm and 7:30–10pm; Sept–
June Thurs–Mon 12:15–2pm and 7–10pm.

Chez Kako BASQUE   "Kako who?" you might ask. He's Jean-Claude Ascery
(which translates from the Basque as "fox"), whose childhood nickname, Kako, is
known to virtually every longtime resident of St-Jean-de-Luz. You'll find his rustic,
artfully old-fashioned bodega within Les Halles, point of sale for the town's freshest
meats and produce, in a setting that turns even the most jaded newcomers into
moderate Basque nationalists. Come to this woodsy, heavily beamed bodega for
beefsteaks which in some cases are prepared only for two diners at a time, tapas
inspired by the cuisine of nearby Spain, very fresh fish—especially hake—and slices
of aromatic goat cheese from local farmsteads. There's a full list of French and Spanish wines, but many diners here prefer bottles of the moderately alcoholic local cider
instead.

18 rue du Maréchal Harispe at the Place des Halles. ✆ **05-59-85-10-70.** Reservations recommended.
Main courses 15€–20€; set-price menu 43€. AE, MC, V. Tues–Sat noon–2:30pm and 7:30–10pm (till 11pm
Fri–Sat). Open Mon in summer.

Chez Maya (Petit Grill Basque) ⚐ BASQUE   This small *auberge* is highly
acclaimed for quality and value, with specialties that include delectable fish soup
and paella. Don't expect urban glitter—things are too conservative and old-fashioned
for that. The fixed-price menu is the best deal in town. The chefs cook as their
grandparents did, preparing all the old favorites, such as squid cooked in its own ink
and a local version of fish soup known as *morro*.

4 rue St-Jacques. ✆ **05-59-26-80-76.** Reservations recommended. Main courses 15€–22€; fixed-price
menu 20€–29€. AE, DC, MC, V. Fri–Sun and Tues noon–2pm; Thurs–Tues 7–10pm. Closed Dec 19–Jan 25.

La Vieille Auberge BASQUE/LANDAISE   On one of the oldest streets in St-
Jean-de-Luz, this tavern specializes in seafood, and the owners claim that the fish
soup is second to none. They offer a good-value fixed-price menu. The food, especially mussels *à la crème,* goes well with the *vin du pays* (local wine). A *parrilladas* of
fish is particularly appealing.

22 rue Tourasse. ✆ **05-59-26-19-61.** Reservations required. Main courses 12€–24€; fixed-price menu
13€–30€. MC, V. May–Sept daily noon–3pm and 7–10:30pm; Oct–Nov and Feb–Mar Wed–Sun noon–
3pm, Wed–Sat 7–10:30pm. Closed mid-Nov to mid-Dec.

St-Jean-De-Luz After Dark

You can start by taking a walk along the promenade to watch the sunset. Around **place Louis-XIV,** you'll find a hotbed of activity at the cafes and bars.

A fun spot in the center of town is **Pub du Corsaire,** 16 rue de la République (© **05-59-26-10-74**), for unpretentious merrymaking accompanied by copious amounts of alcohol and rock 'n' roll. For dancing to recorded music, many night owls head northeast of town along RN10 to the neighborhood known as A Côte.

No one ever implied that to be Basque meant being celibate, or even particularly faithful to the concept of hearth and home. The hot pickup joint that's crowded with scantily clad and sometimes nubile wannabe *vedettes, starlettes,* and *princesses* is **Le Brouillarta,** promenade de Jacques Thibaud (© **05-59-51-29-51**). There's a view of the sea, a crowd of tourists and locals whose age ranges from 18 to around 55, platters of Basque food priced at 8€ to 18€ per main course, and a separate bar area where, frankly, no one really cares if you ever migrate onward to dinner at all. It's positioned about 3 blocks from the rue de la République, with a view of the sea and, let's say, a reputation as a place where you can make friends if you're so inclined.

BORDEAUX & THE ATLANTIC COAST

From La Rochelle to the Bordeaux wine district, the southwest of France is often a quick stopover for visitors driving from Paris to Spain. However, this area is noted for its Atlantic beaches, medieval and Renaissance ruins, Romanesque and Gothic churches, vineyards, and charming inns serving splendid regional cuisine.

On our journey to this intriguing region, we detour inland for some cognac in Cognac and for trips to nearby art cities such as Poitiers and Angoulême. If you can manage it, it's great to allow a week here—enough time to sample the wine, savor the cuisine, and see some of the sights.

POITIERS ★★

333km (207 miles) SW of Paris; 177km (110 miles) SE of Nantes

History fills this city, the ancient capital of Poitou, the northern part of Aquitaine. Everybody has passed through here—from Joan of Arc to Richard the Lion-Hearted.

Poitiers stands on a hill overlooking the Clain and Boivre rivers—a strategic location that tempted many conquerors. Charles Martel chased out the Muslims in A.D. 732 and altered the course of European civilization. Poitiers was the chief city of Eleanor of Aquitaine, who had her marriage to pious Louis VII annulled so she could wed England's Henry II.

For those interested in history, this is one of the most fascinating towns in France. The Battle of Poitiers was fought on September 19, 1356, between the armies of Edward the Black Prince and King John of France. It was one of the three great English victories in the Hundred Years' War, distinguished by the use of the longbow in the skilled hands of English archers.

After decades of slumber, the town has really come alive, with the opening of **Futuroscope,** a cinema theme park. The thriving student population (25,000 of Poitiers's 90,000 residents are students) adds vitality as well.

Essentials

GETTING THERE   **Rail** service is available from Paris, Bordeaux, and La Rochelle. Around 15 fast TGV trains arrive daily from Paris Gare Montparnasse (trip time: 90 min.; one-way fare: 50€). Another 17 (regular) trains arrive daily from Bordeaux (trip time: 2 hr.; one-way fare: 36€), and 12 TGV from La Rochelle (trip time: 1¾ hr.; 22€). For train information, call ☎ **36-35. Bus** service from Poitiers is so badly scheduled it's virtually nonexistent. If you're **driving,** Poitiers is located on the A10 highway; from Paris, follow A10 south through the cities of Orléans and Tours, on to Poitiers.

VISITOR INFORMATION   The **Office de Tourisme** is at 45 place Charles-de-Gaulle (☎ **05-49-41-21-24;** fax 05-49-88-65-84; www.ot-poitiers.fr).

SPECIAL EVENTS   The liveliest time to visit is from mid-June to mid-September during the **Poitiers l'Eté,** a festival of free live jazz, theater, opera, rock, and fireworks. Colored lights illuminate the facade of Notre-Dame La Grande for 15 minutes every evening at 10:30pm; free concerts and theater pieces, both in and out of the streets, take place at various parks and churches around the city. Check with the tourist office for schedules.

For about 8 days in late September, during the **Concerts Allumés,** recitals feature the organs in some of the town's most important churches. Most performances are free; otherwise tickets cost from 12€ for adults or 10€ for students. For information, contact the tourist office, or call ☎ **05-49-39-29-29** or visit www.concerts-allumes.org.

Exploring the City

Guided tours, mostly in French with some English commentary, are conducted in July and August daily at 11am. At 3pm daily there is a 2-hour tour going for 5.50€. During the rest of the year, tours depart every Wednesday and Saturday at 2:30pm, lasting 2 hours and costing 5.50€. Be prepared for a strong dose of French medieval history and lots of crumbling Romanesque stonework. For more information and details, refer to the tourist office above.

Baptistère St-Jean ★   From the cathedral, you can walk to the most ancient Christian monument in France. It was built as a baptistery in the early 4th century on Roman foundations and extended in the 7th century. It contains frescoes from the 11th to the 14th centuries and a collection of funerary sculpture.

Rue Jean-Jaurès. No phone. Admission .75€ adults, .50€ children 11 and under. July–Aug daily 10:30am–12:30pm and 3–6pm; Sept and Apr–May Wed–Mon 10:30am–12:30pm and 3–6pm; Oct–Mar Wed–Mon 2:30–4:30pm.

Cathédrale St-Pierre ★   In the eastern sector of Poitiers is the twin-towered Cathédrale St-Pierre, begun in 1162 by Henry II of England and Eleanor of Aquitaine on the ruins of a Roman basilica. The architecturally undistinguished cathedral was completed much later. The interior, 89m (292 ft.) long, contains some admirable 12th- and 13th-century stained glass.

Place de la Cathédrale. ☎ **05-49-41-23-76.** Free admission. Daily 8:30am–7pm (until 6pm in winter).

Eglise Notre-Dame-la-Grande ★★   This church, built in the Romanesque-Byzantine style and richly decorated, is from the late 11th century. See in particular its western front, dating from the mid–12th century. Surrounded by an open-air market, the facade, carved like an ivory casket, is characterized by pine cone–shaped

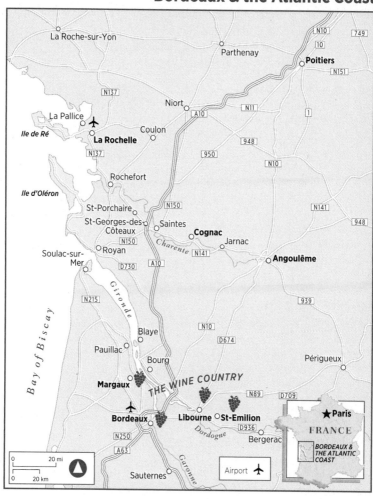

towers. It was thoroughly cleaned and restored in 1996. Carvings on the doorway represent biblical scenes.

Place Charles-de-Gaulle. ℂ **05-49-41-22-56.** Free admission. Mon–Sat 9am–7pm; Sun noon–7pm.

Futuroscope ★★ ☺ This science amusement park in a suburb of Poitiers is a wonderland of technology that lets you experience sounds, images, and sensations with the world's most advanced film-projection techniques and largest screens. Exhibitions include **Kinemax** (a rock crystal covered with mirrors with a 400-seat cinema); **Omnimax** (which projects films onto a gigantic dome with a special fish-eye lens, putting you into the heart of the action); and **Le Tapis Magique,** a film that shows you what it's like to fly above the world's most impressive monuments and sites of natural beauty. Another part of the park is Océan Oasis, which leads you on an underwater exploration of a reef off the coast of Baja California. In July and August every night until 10pm, *les nocturnes* are staged with illuminated fountains, lights, and recorded music. French families festively promenade through the attraction at this time.

Jaunay-Clan. ℭ **05-49-49-30-80.** www.futuroscope.com. Admission 35€ adults, 25€ children 5–16, free for children 4 and under. Daily 10am–dusk. Bus: 9. From Poitiers, take N10 or A10 about 9km (5¾ miles) north.

Musée Ste-Croix   On the site of the old abbey of Ste-Croix, this museum has a fine-arts section devoted mainly to painting—especially 16th- and 17th-century Flemish art and 16th- to 18th-century Dutch pieces. Several works by Bonnard, Sisley, and Oudot are on display, along with a bronze sculpture, *The Three Graces,* by Maillol. A separate archaeological section documents the history of Poitou, from prehistoric times through the Gallo-Roman era and the Renaissance, to the end of the 19th century. Admission includes the **Musée Rupert de Chièvres,** 9 rue Victor-Hugo (same phone). You'll find a small collection of 17th- and 18th-century Italian, Flemish, and French paintings. It's in the old town of Poitiers, within a 10-minute walk of the larger and more comprehensive Musée Ste-Croix.

3 rue Jean-Jaurès. ℭ **05-49-41-07-53.** www.musees-poitiers.org. Admission 3.90€ adults, free for ages 17 and under. Both museums June–Sept Tues–Fri 10am–noon and 1:15–5pm, Sat–Sun 10am–noon and 2–6pm; Oct–May Tues–Fri 10am–noon and 1:15–5pm, Sat–Sun 2–6pm.

Where to Stay

Hôtel de l'Europe ★ 🏨   Originally built in the 1930s, this hotel sits behind a facade of chiseled stone. The main core holds renovated high-ceilinged rooms decorated in vaguely Art Nouveau fashion or even African or Chinese styles; these units have either showers or tubs. Somewhat more modern and more comfortable rooms are in an annex built in the mid-1980s. These have a contemporary, conservative style and tub/shower combinations. Breakfast (the only meal available) is served in an old-fashioned dining room in the original building, in front of tall windows and an elaborate fireplace.

39 rue Carnot, Poitiers 86000. ℭ **05-49-88-12-00.** Fax 05-49-88-97-30. www.hotel-europe-poitiers. com. 88 units. 60€–95€ double. AE, MC, V. Parking 6€. **Amenities:** Room service. *In room:* TV, hair dryer, minibar (some rooms), Wi-Fi (free).

Hôtel du Plat d'Etain 🗡   One of the best bargains in Poitiers, this renovated hotel is on a narrow alley close to the landmark place du Maréchal-Leclerc. The much-renovated, much-simplified building dates from 1895. It's named after the medieval inn, the "Pewter Plate," that stood on the site. (That inn became infamous for unwittingly housing Ravaillac, the deranged monk who fatally stabbed King Henri IV in 1610.) Rooms are compact and simply but comfortably furnished, and most have a small bathroom with a shower unit. Many restaurants and sights are nearby.

7-9 rue du Plat-d'Etain, Poitiers 86000. ℭ **05-49-41-04-80.** Fax 05-49-52-25-84. www.poitiers-le platdetain.com. 20 units. 31€–76€ double with bathroom. AE, MC, V. Parking 5€. Bus: 2A. *In room:* TV, minibar, Wi-Fi (free).

Le Grand Hotel   It's the most imposing Art Deco monument in town, with an exterior that aficionados of the architectural style identify as "pure 1920s" and bedrooms that have maintained the same style in spirit through the frequent use of high-quality reproductions. With four stories and a location in the heart of the city's commercial core, it has hosted more French actors and entertainers than any other hotel in town, thanks to a good reputation for solid quality and a position that's only a few steps from the Théâtre National de Poitiers, a venue for both pop music and haute theatrics and drama. There isn't a restaurant on-site, but there's an expansive terrace, where breakfasts are served on clement summer mornings, overlooking a quiet inner courtyard. The rue Carnot, the street which contains it, has a denser concentration of restaurants than anywhere else in town. Bedrooms, depending on what floor you're on, may come with modernized 1920s-inspired decors and monochromatic color schemes.

28 rue Carnot, Poitiers 86000. ✆ **05-49-60-90-60.** Fax 05-49-62-81-89. www.grandhotelpoitiers.fr. 47 units. 78€–86€ double; 113€ suite. AE, DC, MC, V. Parking 6€. **Amenities:** Bar; room service. *In room:* TV.

Where to Dine

Alain Boutin ★ FRENCH/SEAFOOD   The name of the restaurant and the name of the chef are the same. Boutin has awakened the sleepy taste buds of the town with his market-fresh cuisine combined with his culinary imagination. A regional influence enhances his clever dishes, especially when he uses produce of the area, as he does most effectively. You might begin with a shellfish soup flavored with saffron with a rouille sauce, or else quail with braised raisins. Main-course delights are likely to include filet of zander or veal kidneys with a piquant sauce and a flan made with zucchini. Located near the Jardins de Blossac, the restaurant has one large dining room, plus another smaller one seating only 15.

65 rue Carnot. ✆ **05-49-88-25-53.** Reservations required. Main courses 12€–23€; fixed-price menus 15€–36€. MC, V. Tues–Sat noon–1:30pm; Mon–Fri 7:30–9pm. Closed 1st week of Sept and 1st week of Jan.

Poitevin 🍴 FRENCH   Much of Poitevin's lunch business comes from shoppers and office workers who descend on it at midday. Evening meals are less rushed. You'll have a choice of six cozy dining rooms. One room contains an 18th-century fireplace transported here from a demolished building nearby; another abounds with butterflies (on the carpets, curtains, and napery, and mounted in frames). Menu items include *mouclade Charentaise* (mussels in white wine–and-cream sauce); scallops with sauterne sabayon; and an unusual stewpot containing filets of eel and sole, served with lemon sauce. For dessert, try a semisoft slice of unctuously oozing chocolate cake.

76 rue Carnot. ✆ **05-49-88-35-04.** Reservations recommended. Main courses 16€–40€; fixed-price menu 26€–40€. AE, DC, MC, V. Daily noon–2pm; Mon–Sat 7–10pm. Closed 2 weeks at Easter, 3 weeks in late July and Aug, and 2 weeks at Christmas.

Vingélique ★ 🍴 CLASSICAL FRENCH   Established in the heart of historic Poitiers and contained within an ultramodern pair of fresco-ringed dining rooms, this is one of the best-recommended dining rooms in town. The chef focuses on fresh produce from local sources to create dishes, which include lobster salad with avocados and lime; "barely cooked" scallops with a chantilly of herbs and a salad of wild greens; filet of sea bass with a sea urchin sauce; and sweetbreads with a foie gras sauce. The only dining choice here involves the set-price menus, but because of the wide choice of seasonally adapted dishes available, that is just fine.

37 rue Carnot. ✆ **05-49-55-07-03.** Reservations recommended. Lunch *plat du jour* with dessert 11€; set-price lunches and dinners 27€–37€. AE, MC, V. Mon–Fri noon–2pm; Mon–Sat 7:30–10pm. Closed Aug.

LA ROCHELLE ★★★

467km (290 miles) SW of Paris; 145km (90 miles) SE of Nantes; 183km (114 miles) N of Bordeaux; 142km (88 miles) NW of Angoulême

Once known as the French Geneva, La Rochelle is a historic port and ancient sailors' city, formerly the stronghold of the Huguenots. It was founded as a fishing village in the 10th century on a rocky platform in the center of a marshland. Eleanor of Aquitaine gave La Rochelle a charter in 1199, freeing it from feudal dues. After becoming an independent city-state, the port capitalized on the wars between France and England. It was the departure point for the founders of Montreal. From the 14th to the 16th century, La Rochelle was one of France's great maritime cities. It became the principal port between France and the colony of Canada, but France's loss of Canada ruined its Atlantic trade.

As a hotbed of Protestant factions, it armed privateers to prey on Catholic vessels but was eventually besieged by Catholic troops. Two men led the fight: Cardinal Richelieu (with his Musketeers) and Jean Guiton, formerly an admiral and then mayor of the city. When Richelieu blockaded the port, La Rochelle bravely resisted. It took 15 months to starve the city into submission, during which time 25,000 citizens perished from hunger. On October 30, 1628, Richelieu entered the city and found only 5,000 survivors.

Today La Rochelle, a city of 140,000, is the cultural and administrative center of the Charente-Maritime *département* (ministate). Its famous city lights have earned it the title "City of Light." While many of La Rochelle's sights are old, the city is riddled with high-rise condos and home to the largest pleasure-boat basin in Europe. In summer, the city is overrun with visitors.

Essentials

GETTING THERE   The La Rochelle–Ile-de-Ré **airport** (⏣ **05-46-42-30-26**) is on the coast, 4km (2½ miles) north of the city. Take bus no. 7 to reach it. Rail connections from Bordeaux and Nantes are frequent. Six to eight **trains** from Bordeaux and Nantes arrive daily (trip time: 2 hr.; one-way fare: 25€). There are five daily fast TGV trains from Paris's Gare Montparnasse (trip time: 3 hr.); the one-way fare is 65€. For train information, call ⏣ **36-35. Buses** serve the Gare Routière, place de Verdun (⏣ **05-46-00-95-15** for information). If you're **driving** to La Rochelle, follow A10 south from Poitiers to exit NIORT/ST-MAIXENT, and then take N11 west to the coast and La Rochelle.

VISITOR INFORMATION   The **Office de Tourisme** is on Le Gabut (⏣ **05-46-41-14-68;** fax 05-46-41-99-85; www.larochelle-tourisme.com).

SPECIAL EVENTS   The busiest month is July; the **Festival International du Film de La Rochelle** rolls in at the beginning of the month. It attracts a huge following of fans, press, actors, directors, and, of course, paparazzi. Screenings are held around town; a pass for 10 screenings costs 45€. For information, contact the festival office in the Maison de la Culture, rue St-Jean de Perot (⏣ **05-46-51-54-00** or 01-48-06-16-66; www.festival-larochelle.org). For a week in mid-July, the music festival **Les Francofolies** features big names as well as not-so-famous groups, most of them international pop musicians. The town is overrun with groupies and fans, and a party atmosphere prevails. Tickets range from 20€ to 35€. Call ⏣ **05-46-52-28-96**

for details (www.francofolies.fr). The Office de Tourisme can also provide details on both festivals.

La Rochelle is also the site of the biggest showcase of boats and yachts in Europe, **Le Grand Pavois Salon Nautique.** It's a 5-day extravaganza in mid-September. The action is based in and around La Rochelle's Port de Plaisance (better known as the Bassin des Yachts, or Yacht Basin). Sellers and buyers of boats and marine hardware, as well as weekend sailors from everywhere, usually attend. For information about dates and venues, call ✆ **05-46-44-46-39** or check www.grand-pavois.com.

Exploring the City

There are two sides to La Rochelle: the old and unspoiled town inside the Vauban defenses, and the tacky modern and industrial suburbs. Its **fortifications** have a circuit of 5.5km (3⅓ miles) with a total of seven gates.

The town, with its arch-covered streets, is great for strolling. The port is a fishing harbor and one of Europe's major sailing centers. Try to schedule a visit in time to attend a fish auction. The best streets for strolling, each with a 17th-century arcade, are **rue du Palais, la Rue du Temple, rue Chaudrier,** and **rue des Merciers,** with its ancient wooden houses (seek out the ones at nos. 3, 5, 8, and 17).

Aquarium de La Rochelle ★ La Rochelle's blockbuster crowd pleaser rises from a portside position near the Port des Minimes, north of the old city. Inside are guided walkways stretching over two floors of massive and bubbling seawater tanks loaded with approximately 10,000 species of flora and fauna from the oceans of the world, living in what look like natural habitats. It's hard to miss this place; there are signs for it all over town.

Bassin des Grands Yachts, B.P. 4, Le Vieux Port. ✆ **05-46-34-00-00.** www.aquarium-larochelle.com. 13€ adults, 10€ students and children 3–17, free for children 2 and under. Use of English-language audio guide 3.50€. July–Aug daily 9am–11pm; Apr–June and Sept daily 9am–8pm; Oct–Mar daily 10am–8pm. Bus: 10.

Hôtel de Ville (City Hall) ★ The town's 14th-century showcase is built in Flamboyant Gothic style, with battlements. Inside you can admire the Henry II staircase with canopies and the marble desk of the heroic Jean Guiton. You must visit as part of a guided tour (in French only); advance reservations are not necessary.

Place de la Mairie, in the city center. ✆ **05-46-51-51-51.** Admission 4€ adults, 1.50€ students and children 4–18, free for children 3 and under. Guided tours July–Aug daily 3 and 4pm, June and Sept daily 3pm, Oct–May Sat–Sun 3pm (and some holidays at 3 and 4pm).

Musée des Beaux-Arts ★ The museum is in an Episcopal palace built in the mid–18th century. The art spans the 15th to the 19th centuries, with works by Eustache Le Sueur, Brossard de Beaulieu, Corot, and Fromentin. Twentieth-century pieces include works by Maillol and Léger.

28 rue Gargoulleau. ☎ **05-46-41-64-65.** Admission 4€ adults, free for children 17 and under. Oct–Mar Mon and Wed–Fri 9:30am–12:30pm and 1:30–5pm, Sat–Sun and holidays 2:30–6pm; Apr–Sept Mon and Wed–Sat 10:30am–12:30pm and 2–6pm, Sun and bank holidays 2:30–6pm.

Muséum d'Histoire Naturelle   Set within an enormous (2,500 sq. m/26,909 sq. ft.) once-private mansion in the heart of town, and reopened in 2007 after a 13-year closing, this museum stockpiles everything of interest, ethnographically and anthropologically speaking. Stuffed animals, African masks, maps of prehistoric migrational patterns, and everything brought back by La Rochelle's 17th-century traders from around the world are on display.

28 rue Albert 1er. ☎ **05-46-41-18-25.** www.museum-larochelle.fr. Admission 4€; free for 16 and under. Oct–Mar Tues–Fri 10am–6pm, Sat 10am–9pm, Sun 10am–6pm; Apr–Sept Tues–Fri 10am–7pm, Sat 10am–10pm, Sun 10am–7pm.

Musée du Nouveau-Monde ★   In an 18th-century town house rich with architectural details, this is one of the most intriguing museums in La Rochelle. It's rich with evidence of the city's prominent role in the colonization of Canada. The displays trace the port's 300-year history with the New World. Exhibits start with LaSalle's discovery of the Mississippi Delta in 1682 and end with the settling of the Louisiana territory. Other exhibits depict French settlements in the West Indies, including Guadeloupe and Martinique.

In the Hôtel Fleuriau, 10 rue Fleuriau. ☎ **05-46-41-46-50.** Admission 4€ adults, free for children 17 and under. Oct–Mar Mon and Wed–Fri 9:30am–12:30pm and 1:30–5pm, Sat–Sun 2:30–6pm; Apr–Sept Mon and Wed–Sat 10am–12:30pm and 2–6pm, Sun 2:30–6pm.

Musée Maritime   Comprised for the most part of two permanently docked boats, one a meteorological frigate, one an antique *chalutière de peche* (some kind of fishing boat), this museum evokes the grand days of La Rochelle as a maritime power and its commerce with the New World.

Quai Sénac de Meilhan. ☎ **05-46-28-03-00.** Admission 8€ adults, 5.50€ for students and children 4–16, free for children 3 and under. Apr–June and Sept daily 10am–6:30pm; July–Aug daily 10am–7pm.

Musée Orbigny-Bernon ★   The most important artifacts pertaining to the history of ceramics and of La Rochelle are in this collection, which includes painted porcelain. Established in 1917, the museum also houses a superb collection of Far Eastern art. The exhibits and photographs of La Rochelle in World War II are especially fascinating.

2 rue St-Côme. ☎ **05-46-41-18-83.** Admission 4€ adults, free for children 17 and under. Oct–Mar Mon and Wed–Sat 9:30am–12:30pm and 1:30–5pm, Sun 2:30–6pm; Apr–Sept Mon and Wed–Sat 9:30am–12:30pm and 2–6pm, Sun and holidays 2:30–6pm.

Tour de la Chaîne   During the 1300s, this tower was built as an anchor piece for the large forged-iron chain that stretched across the harbor, closing it against hostile warships. The unusual exhibits focus on the history of medieval naval warfare.

Quai du Gabut. ☎ **05-46-34-11-81.** Admission see above. Tues–Sun 10am–12:30pm and 2–5:30pm.

Tour de la Lanterne ★   Built between 1445 and 1476, this was once a lighthouse but was used mainly as a jail as late as the 19th century. A low rampart connects the cylindrical tower to the Tour de la Chaîne. During the Wars of Religion, 13 priests were tossed from its summit. You climb 162 steps to the top hold; in clear weather, the panoramic view extends all the way to Ile d'Oléron. On the way up, you can still see graffiti scrawled by former prisoners.

Opposite Tour St-Nicolas, quai du Gabut. ☎ **05-46-41-56-04.** Admission see above. Tues–Sun 10am–12:30pm and 2–5:30pm.

Tour St-Nicolas ★   The oldest tower in La Rochelle, Tour St-Nicolas was built between 1371 and 1382. It originally guarded the town against surprise attacks. From its second floor you can enjoy a view of the town and harbor; from the top you can see only the old town and Ile d'Oléron.

Quai du Gabut. ☎ **05-46-41-74-13.** Admission see above. Tues–Sun 10am–12:30pm and 2–5:30pm.

Where to Stay

France-Angleterre et Champlain ★★   Close to the major parks and the old port, this is the most gracious choice in La Rochelle. It was formed by uniting two smaller hotels many years ago. It's furnished with a winning combination of antiques and art objects and has a genial staff. Rooms are tasteful and dignified; many have a nautical theme. The midsize bathrooms hold tubs or showers. One of the best aspects of the hotel is its romantic garden, brimming with flowers, shrubbery, and shade trees. Breakfast is the only meal served.

20 rue Rambaud, La Rochelle 17000. ☎ **800/528-1234** in the U.S. and Canada, or 05-46-41-23-99. Fax 05-46-41-15-19. www.hotelchamplain.com. 40 units. 95€–140€ double; 135€–160€ suite. AE, DC, MC, V. Parking 8€. **Amenities:** Room service. *In room:* A/C, TV, hair dryer, minibar, Wi-Fi (free).

Les Brises ★ 🗲   This nautically decorated seaside hotel opposite the Port des Minimes, 1.5km (1 mile) north of the old city, offers a view of a soaring 19th-century column dedicated to the Virgin. You can enjoy the view from the front balconies of the six-story building as well as the parasol-shaded patio. The immaculate rooms have cherrywood furniture, comfortable beds, and compact, neatly organized bathrooms with shower units. Breakfast is the only meal served.

1, Chemin de la Digue de Richelieu, La Rochelle 17000. ☎ **05-46-43-89-37.** Fax 05-46-43-27-97. www.hotellesbrises.eu. 48 units. 90€–129€ double; 122€–200€ family room for 4. AE, DC, MC, V. Free parking. **Amenities:** Room service. *In room:* A/C, TV, hair dryer, minibar, Wi-Fi (free).

Masqhotel ★   Near the train station and the old harborfront, this is the most sophisticated modern hotel in town, the creation of a local architect, Michel Dufour, who wanted to create an avant-garde building in his hometown. The design is cutting edge, and Dufour isn't afraid of orange or apple green. He wanted to decorate the hotel as if it were his own home—simple yet chic and subtle. In that he succeeded admirably. From the lounge bar to the bedrooms, the hotel is high tech with top-quality furnishings and bedding, plus a lounge bar.

17 rue de l'Ouvrage a cornes, La Rochelle 17000. ✆ **05-46-41-83-83.** Fax 05-46-07-04-43. www.masqhotel.com. 76 units. 98€–168€ double. AE, DC, MC, V. **Amenities:** Bar; room service. *In room:* A/C, TV, hair dryer, Wi-Fi (free).

Where to Dine

Bar/Bistro André ✦ SEAFOOD
Seafood is an expensive item anywhere in France, but usually it's worth it. Here you can get a big meal even by choosing something from the lower end of the price scale. Traditional menu items include savory versions of fish soup; all kinds of shellfish; an unusual version of *cabillaud fumé* (home-smoked codfish) served with garlic-flavored cream sauce; curried mussels (*mouclade*); and a saltwater fish not very common in other parts of France, filet of *maîgre,* served with chive-flavored cream sauce. The restaurant is between the square overlooking the port and one of the oldest streets in town.

5 rue St-Jean/place de la Chaîne. ✆ **05-46-41-28-24.** www.barandre.com. Reservations recommended. Main courses 19€–32€. Fixed-price menus 34€–37€. AE, DC, MC, V. Daily noon–2:30pm and 7–10:30pm.

Chez Lulu FRENCH/INTERNATIONAL
Located a 3-minute walk from La Rochelle's Old Port, within a street-level dining room capped with stone vaults, this unpretentious and sometimes fun restaurant opened in 2007. Its owner, Betty Rechaux, quit her job as a financial auditor in Paris to return to her childhood home of La Rochelle to set up this place, naming it after her recently deceased paternal grandmother, Lulu. Inside, you'll sit on armchairs or on sofas, some of them upholstered in faux zebra skin. You may dine to the tune of a live pianist who performs some nights, on an irregular basis, beginning around 8pm. The best menu items include foie gras with pear chutney and a confit of eggplant; stuffed rabbit with autumn fruits served with a tatin of fennel and caramelized carrots; brochettes of crayfish with cannelloni; and roasted shoulder of lamb served with a confit of olives.

19 ter Place du Maréchal Foch. ✆ **05-46-50-69-03.** www.chezlulu.net. Main courses 16€; fixed-price menu 37€. MC, V. Mon–Sat 11:30am–3pm and 7–11pm.

Comptoir des Voyages ✦ FRENCH/INTERNATIONAL
This restaurant in the old town has a cost-conscious, lighthearted format that celebrates the cuisines of most of France's neighbors, the former colonies, and France itself. Surrounded by hardwood paneling and big windows, you'll have a choice of five starters, eight main courses, and six desserts. The frequently changing menu may include Martinique-style codfish fritters, lamb chops dredged in Indian spices, and buckwheat crepes stuffed with poached pears and Breton-style liqueur. Almost all the wines are from outside France.

22 rue St-Jean du Pérot. ✆ **05-46-50-62-60.** Reservations recommended. Main courses all 16€–24€; fixed-price menu 19€. AE, DC, MC, V. Daily noon–2pm and 7:30–10pm.

Richard et Christopher Coutanceau ★★★ MODERN FRENCH
This is not only the most glamorous and prestigious restaurant in La Rochelle, but also one of the finest along the coast. Delectable cuisine is served in a circular concrete pavilion in a pine-filled park, with big bay windows overlooking the sea. Clearly an artist, Richard Coutanceau, the owner and genius chef, prepares "modernized" cuisine. For

SAILING THE PORTS OF LA ROCHELLE

La Rochelle has always earned its living from the sea and from the ships that make its harbor their home. Four distinct harbors have grown up over the centuries, each a world unto itself, rich with local nuance and lore. They include the historic **Vieux-Port,** the **Port de Plaisance** (a modern yacht marina), the **Port de Pêche** (the fishing port), and the **Port de Commerce,** which is mostly used by large container ships.

The best way to appreciate them is to visit the tourist office (see "Essentials," earlier in this chapter), which acts as a clearinghouse for the outfitters (Croisières Inter-Iles, Navipromer, Cap à l'Ouest, and Ré Croisières) that conduct tours of the harbors. Tours combine a look at the modern facilities of one of France's largest ports with a waterside view of the historic ramparts—which, despite their girth and height, did not protect the city's 17th-century Protestants from starvation and eventual annihilation.

The company with the most frequent departures is the **Croisières Inter-Iles** (✆ 08-25-13-55-00; www.inter-iles. com). Every day from April to October, there are about a half-dozen cruises into each of the six ports. In winter, they're offered less frequently, usually only on school vacations. Tours last 70 to 180 minutes each, are conducted in French, and average 19€.

Another waterborne option—but only during July and August—involves taking a ferry from the Vieux-Port of La Rochelle to Ile de Ré. The island, 26km (16 miles) off the coast of La Rochelle and ringed with 69km (43 miles) of sandy beaches, holds nature preserves crisscrossed with bike and hiking paths. Croisières Inter-Iles (see above) serves the island. If you want to get here during July or August, and if you don't have a car, we recommend taking the ferry for a round-trip fare of 21€.

You can also drive your car across the bridge that connects the Ile de Ré to the French mainland. It's accessible from a point 3km (1¾ miles) south of La Rochelle. The toll is 16€ in summer, 9€ in winter. The local bus company, **Cie. Aunis Saintonges** (✆ 05-46-97-52-06; www. aunis-saintonge.fr), charges 3.50€ to 15€ each way for the trip from La Rochelle to several stops along the island, with departures several times a day year-round.

an appetizer, two of the most famous starters in France are combined: frogs' legs and snails roasted in parsley and garlic and served with truffle-laced creamy potatoes. The signature fish dish is line-caught sea bass cooked within its own crusty skin and served with stewed tomatoes and chorizo. Among the meat dishes, we prefer the roasted pigeon kabob with asparagus and tomato jelly, made even more alluring with truffles and a slightly bitter Choron sauce.

Plage de la Concurrence. ✆ **05-46-41-48-19.** www.coutanceau.com. Reservations required. Main courses 39€–62€; fixed-price menus 52€–95€. AE, DC, MC, V. Mon–Sat noon–2pm and 7:30–9:30pm.

La Rochelle After Dark

From July to September, head for **quai Duperré, cours des Dames,** and **cours des Templiers.** Once the sun starts to set, this becomes one big pedestrian zone peppered with street performers. It's a fun, almost magical area that sets the tone for the rest of the night.

COGNAC

478km (297 miles) SW of Paris; 37km (23 miles) NW of Angoulême; 113km (70 miles) SE of La Rochelle

The world enjoys 100 million bottles a year of the nectar known as cognac, which Victor Hugo called "the drink of the gods." It's worth a detour to visit one of the château warehouses of the great bottlers. Martell, Hennessy, and Otard welcome visits from the public and even give you a free drink at the end of the tour.

Essentials

GETTING THERE Cognac's rail station is just south of the town center. Five **trains** per day arrive from Angoulême (trip time: 40 min.), and six trains pull in from Saintes (trip time: 20 min.). For train information and schedules, call ⏺ **36-35,** or 08-92-35-35-35 from outside France. **Bus** travel is scarce in this part of France. For information, contact La Gare Routière (⏺ **05-45-82-01-99**), next to the railway station. If you're **driving** to Cognac, the best route from Saintes (which lies along the major route A10) is N141 east.

VISITOR INFORMATION The **Office de Tourisme** is at 16 rue du 14-Juillet (⏺ **05-45-82-10-71;** fax 05-45-82-34-47; www.tourism-cognac.com).

SPECIAL EVENTS Cognac grapes are among the last picked in France. Harvest time usually begins in mid-October.

Cognac is home to several annual festivals, the best of which is **Blues Passion,** a jazz festival that in 2010 celebrated its 17th anniversary. Performers come from throughout France and the world, and in the past have included Ray Charles. Conducted over a 5-day period in July, it presents most of its musical events in the outdoor amphitheater known as Théâtre de la Nature. Entrance to most individual events costs between 30€ and 40€, although a *passeport* granting access to all the concerts in the venue sells for 120€. For information about ticket reservations and venues, call ⏺ **05-45-36-11-81** or check www.bluespassion.com.

More closely tuned to Francophonic audiences is the annual **Coup de Chauffe/ Festival du Théâtre de la Rue,** wherein for a 3-day period in September, street performers present social or political satires in the open air without any admission charges. Although a working knowledge of French is useful at this event, the nature of many of the presentations is more "performance art" than traditional drama, and as such, many of them can be appreciated for their visuals. For information, call ⏺ **05-45-82-17-24** or visit www.avantscene.com.

Exploring the Town

Many visitors don't realize that this unassuming town of some 22,000 people is actually a community and not just a drink. Cognac may be beautiful to drink, but it's not beautiful to make. A black fungus that lives on the vapors released by the cognac factories has turned the town's buildings an ugly gray. But while the fumes discolor the houses, they also fill the air with sweetness.

If you'd like to visit a distillery, go to its main office during regular business hours and request a tour, or visit the tourist office for assistance. On a tour, you'll see some brandies that have aged for as long as 50 or even 100 years. You can have a free taste and then purchase a bottle or two. As far as we're concerned, **Otard** offers the most informative and insightful tours, partly because of the sheer majesty of its headquarters, in the late-medieval **Château de Cognac,** 127 bd. Denfert-Rochereau (© **05-45-36-88-86;** www.otard.com). The tour is half historical overview of the castle, half a technical explanation of cognac production. Parts of the château are appropriately baronial (King François I was born here), and enormous other sections hold tens of thousands of bottles of cognac. Tours last about 1 hour and cost 7€ for adults, 3.50€ for students 12 to 18, and are free for children 11 and under. From April to June and September to October, tours depart at frequent intervals daily from 11am to noon, and between 2 and 6pm. During July and August, tours depart frequently, daily between 11am and noon and 1:30 and 7pm. During November to March, tours depart only Monday to Friday, specifically at 11am, 2pm, and 4pm. Call the tourist office or the company several days in advance to check times, which rotate according to the number of visitors and availability of guides. The château lies within a 10-minute walk from the town center near the Hôtel de Ville (city hall).

Other distilleries that conduct tours are **Hennessy,** 1 quai Hennessy (© **05-45-35-72-68;** www.hennessy.com); **Camus,** 21 rue de Cagouillet (© **05-45-32-72-96;** www.camus.fr); and **Martell,** place Edouard-Martell (© **05-45-36-33-33;** www.martell.com). **Rémy Martin** maintains a battered but authentic-looking distillery in the countryside, at the domaine de Merpins, route de Pons (© **05-45-35-76-66**), and a glossier, more media-hip information center and sales outlet in the heart of Cognac. Known as the **Musée Rémy Martin,** it's at 20 rue de la Société Vinicole (© **05-45-35-76-66**), giving the most expensive tour of the lot. Priced at 25€ for adults and 14€ for persons 12 to 18, and 7€ for children 11 and under, it punctuates its insights into the world of Rémy Martin with frequent dégustations of esoteric cognacs and lots of bite-sized canapés to accompany them. Call in advance for reservations.

If you're short on time, a good retail outlet is **La Cognathèque,** 8 place Jean-Monnet (© **05-45-82-43-31**), which prides itself on having the widest selection from all the distilleries, though you'll pay for the convenience of having everything under one roof.

No one ever accused the cognac industry of not knowing how to promote its products. The **Musée des Arts de Cognac** lies in the town center at Place de la Salle Verte (© **05-45-36-21-10**). Within, you'll find exhibits showcasing everything associated with the cognac trade, from cultivation of grapes to bottle and barrel making to insights into global marketing and sales. Entrance costs 4.50€ for adults, 3€ for students. Admission is free for anyone 17 and under. It's open as follows: July to August daily 10am to 6:30pm; April through June and September to October Tuesday to Sunday 11am to 6pm; and November through March every Tuesday to Sunday 2 to 5:30pm. Accessible through an interconnecting door is **L'Espace Découverte en Plays du Cognac** (© **05-45-36-03-65**), which, through slides, photos, and videos, showcases touristic and oenophilic attractions of the surrounding region. There's no additional charge for access.

Within a 15-minute walk lies the **Musée d'Art et l'Histoire de Cognac,** 48 bd. Denfert-Rochereau (© **05-45-32-07-25**), with exhibits on popular arts and traditions, archaeological exhibits, and a fine art collection of paintings, sculpture, decorative arts, and furniture. Accessible with the same ticket that's valid for access to the above-noted Musée des Arts de Cognac (and vice versa), it's open as follows: July to August daily 10am to 6:30pm; April to June and September to October Tuesday to Sunday 11am to 6pm; November to March Tuesday to Sunday 2 to 5:30pm.

Cognac has two beautiful parks: the **Parc François-1er** and the **Parc de l'Hôtel-de-Ville.** The Romanesque-Gothic **Eglise St-Léger,** rue de Monseigneur LaCroix (✆ **05-45-82-05-71**), is from the 12th century, and its bell tower is from the 15th. Admission is free; it's open daily 8am to 7pm.

Where to Stay

Domaine du Breuil ★★   This tranquil 18th-century manor house, studded with magnificent windows, is in a 7.2-hectare (18-acre) landscaped park 2 minutes from the center of Cognac. Rooms are simple but well furnished and well maintained. Cognac aficionados and those in town to do business with the factories head here for the hospitality, the well-appointed rooms, and the excellent cuisine from the southwest of France. The food is reason enough to visit, and, naturally, you'll finish your meal with a cognac in the bar to aid digestion.

104 rue Robert-Daugas, Cognac 16100. ✆ **05-45-35-32-06.** Fax 05-45-35-14-15. www.hotel-domaine-du-breuil.com. 24 units. 65€–90€ double. AE, MC, V. Free parking. Closed Dec 20–Jan 5. **Amenities:** Restaurant; bar; outdoor pool; room service. *In room:* TV, hair dryer (in some), minibar (in some), Wi-Fi (free).

Hostellerie Les Pigeons Blancs ★   This stylish hotel is named after the white pigeons that nest in its moss-covered stone walls. The angular farmhouse with sloping tile roofs was built in the 17th century as a coaching inn. For many years, it was the home of the Tachet family, which transformed it into a hotel and restaurant in 1973. It's 1.5km (1 mile) northwest of the town center and offers elegant guest rooms outfitted in styles that range from Louis XV to Directoire. The midsize-to-spacious rooms are comfortably furnished, and each average-size bathroom has a combination tub/shower. The restaurant serves modern French cuisine and is reviewed below.

110 rue Jules-Brisson, Cognac 16100. ✆ **05-45-82-16-36.** Fax 05-45-82-29-29. www.pigeons-blancs.com. 6 units. 85€ double. AE, MC, V. Free parking. **Amenities:** Restaurant; room service. *In room:* TV, hair dryer.

Where to Dine

The restaurant at **Domaine du Breuil** (see "Where to Stay," above) serves worthwhile meals.

Hostellerie Les Pigeons Blancs ★★ MODERN FRENCH   This restaurant, run by the Tachet family, has two elegant dining rooms with exposed ceiling beams and limestone fireplaces. Menu offerings depend on the availability of ingredients, but may include warm oysters with mushrooms and champagne-flavored cream sauce, lobster with champagne sauce and bay leaves, slices of warm gooseliver with pears and white wine, and particularly succulent duck steak with warm mandarin oranges and caramelized vinegar. The charming chef, Jacques Tachet, uses cognac vapors to steam many of his raw ingredients, including excellent line-caught sea bass with spices. There's also superb filet of French beef with spices, cognac, and crème fraîche; and rack of lamb with freshly grated truffles.

110 rue Jules-Brisson. ✆ **05-45-82-16-36.** Reservations recommended. Main courses 16€–39€; fixed-price lunch 22€–59€. AE, MC, V. Daily noon–2pm; Mon–Sat 7–10pm.

Where to Stay & Dine Nearby

Moulin de Cierzac ★ 🎁   This 19th-century former mill house sits beside a flowing stream at the southern periphery of a village (St-Fort-sur-le-Né) 13km (8 miles) south of Cognac. Loaded with character and charm, owner-chef Georges Renault's property is best known as a superb restaurant. Many diners do opt to spend the night, particularly after a wine-and-cognac-soaked dinner. The cuisine makes abundant use of local products, especially foie gras, vegetables, nuts, berries, lamb, and cognac. Come for dishes that include slow-cooked foie gras marinated in a mixture of cognac, sauterne, and white port, wrapped in a napkin *("au torchon")*, and poached and half-cooked in boiling water. Also appealing are slow-cooked pork-based pâté flavored with cognac; pikeperch served with a compote of cabbage; and apple crumble.

The seven quaint, charmingly decorated guest rooms overlook a park that's traversed by a stream. They have big ceiling beams and TVs; the flowery decor evokes a British country house. The double rate is 54€ to 84€.

Rte. de Cognac, St-Fort-sur-le-Né 16130. ✆ **05-45-83-01-32.** Fax 05-45-83-03-59. www.moulindecierzac. com. Reservations recommended. Main courses 18€–35€; fixed-price menus 13€–38€. AE, MC, V. June–Sept Tues–Sun noon–2pm, daily 7–9pm; Oct–May Tues–Sun noon–2pm, Tues–Sat 7–9pm. Closed mid-Nov to Dec 3. From Cognac, drive 13km (8 miles) south of town, following the signs for Bordeaux and Barbezieux.

ANGOULEME ★★

443km (275 miles) SW of Paris; 116km (72 miles) NE of Bordeaux

The old town of Angoulême hugs a hilltop between the Charente and Aguienne rivers. You can visit it on the same day you visit Cognac. The town was the center of the French paper industry in the 17th century, a tradition that carries on today: Angoulême (pop. 46,000) remains the center of French comic-strip production. Rolling off the presses are the latest adventures of Tintin, Astérix, and Lucky Luke. During 3 days in January, Angoulême is the site of the **Festival de la Bande Dessinée (Festival of Cartoons),** the centerpiece of which is the **Cité Internationale de la Bande Dessinée et de l'Image (CNBDI);** see "Exploring the Town," below. During its run, cartoon artists from around the world gather to present examples of their work and lecture about their art. For more information, contact the festival (✆ **05-45-97-86-50;** www.bdangouleme.com), or the tourist office (see below).

Essentials

GETTING THERE   There are 12 regular **trains** (trip time: 1½ hr.) and 8 to 10 TGV trains (55 min.) every day from Bordeaux; the one-way fare is 22€. There are also 10 trains daily from Saintes (trip time: 1 hr.) and another five from Poitiers (trip time: 45 min.). From Paris's Montparnasse Station, seven TGV trains make the trip daily (trip time: 3 hr.); the one-way fare is 62€. For train information and schedules, call ✆ **36-35** or 08-92-35-35-35. **Citram,** place du Champ de Mars, Angoulême (✆ **05-45-95-95-99;** www.citram.fr), runs eight **buses** per day between Cognac and Angoulême. The trip takes 1 hour and costs 7.45€ each way. If you're **driving** from Bordeaux, take N10 northeast to Angoulême.

VISITOR INFORMATION   The **Office de Tourisme** is at place des Halles (✆ **05-45-95-16-84;** www.angouleme-tourisme.com).

Exploring the Town

The hub of the town is **place de l'Hôtel-de-Ville.** The town hall was erected from 1858 to 1866 on the site of the palace of the ducs d'Angoulême, where Marguerite de Navarre, sister of François I, was born. All that remains of the palace are the 15th-century Tour de Valois and 13th-century Tour de Lusignan.

Cathédrale St-Pierre ★, 4 place St-Pierre (🕿 **05-45-95-20-38**), was begun in 1128 and restored in the 19th century. Flanked by towers, its facade boasts 75 statues, each in a separate niche, representing the Last Judgment. This is one of France's most startling examples of Romanesque-Byzantine style. The 19th-century architect Abadie (designer of Sacré-Coeur in Paris) tore down the north tower and then rebuilt it with the original materials in the same style. In the interior you can wander under a four-domed ceiling. It's open Monday to Saturday 9am to 7pm, Sunday 10am to 6:30pm.

Angoulême is the European capital of the cartoon industry, with strong historical and creative links to many of the pop-art and cartoon themes that are part of the French cultural experience. The art form's focal point is the **Cité Internationale de la Bande Dessinée et de l'Image,** 121 rue de Bordeaux (🕿 **05-45-38-65-65;** www.cnbdi.fr), which has a museum devoted to famous (and usually original) cartoons and their creation, a cafe, a library, a bookshop, and creative people who come here for insights into the entertainment industry. It's open in July and August Tuesday to Friday 10am to 6pm and Saturday and Sunday 2 to 7pm; and September to June Tuesday to Friday noon to 6pm, Saturday and Sunday 2 to 6pm. Entrance costs 4€ for adults, 3€ for students, free for children 17 and under.

Finally, you can walk along the panoramic **promenade des Remparts ★**, a path that flanks the site of the long-gone fortifications that once surrounded the historic core of Angoulême. The most appealing section of the 3km (1¾-mile) walkway is the 1km (⅔-mile) section that connects the cathedral with Les Halles (the covered market). Views from here stretch over the hills that flank the River Charente almost 75m (246 ft.) below.

Where to Stay

Mercure Hôtel de France ★★ This 19th-century grand hotel stands in the center of the old town on extensive grounds. Rooms are generally spacious, with high ceilings and French Provincial furnishings; each comes with a fair-size bathroom. Beds are comfortably firm. A formal restaurant serves excellent food complemented with polite service; specialties include foie gras, sole meunière, and trout with almonds. Lunch is served Monday to Friday; dinner is offered nightly.

1 place des Halles, Angoulême 16000. 🕿 **05-45-95-47-95.** Fax 05-45-92-02-70. www.mercure.com. 89 units. 109€–141€ double. AE, DC, MC, V. Parking 8€. **Amenities:** Restaurant; bar; babysitting; room service. *In room:* A/C, TV, hair dryer, minibar, Wi-Fi (free).

Where to Dine

Mercure Hôtel de France (see above) serves first-rate cuisine.

La Cité FRENCH   Set at the northern edge of Angoulême's medieval core, within a neighborhood devoted to the city's bureaucratic civic administration, this small and intimate restaurant is pleasantly outfitted in tones of terra cotta and pale green, offset with white napery and a hardworking staff. The best menu items include foie gras with apples; sautéed crayfish tails; and an enduring house specialty, a brochette of seafood, where crayfish, scallops, and mussels are spit-roasted and served with a creamy garlic sauce. Most of the menu is devoted to fish, but there are a handful of meat dishes on the menu, including beefsteak and *magret* of duckling with orange sauce.

28 rue St-Roch. © **05-45-92-42-69.** Reservations recommended. Main courses 14€–16€; fixed-price menus 15€–29€. AE, MC, V. Tues–Sat noon–2pm and 7–10pm. Closed in Aug.

La Ruelle ★★ FRENCH   This first-class restaurant, in the oldest part of town, is Angoulême's best. Guillaume Severine Veyssiere is the only shining light in a dim culinary scene. Count on classic French recipes with a modern twist. The best specialties include ravioli stuffed with confit of duckling, served with vegetable bouillon with herbs; oysters in puff pastry in red-wine sauce; filet of fried red snapper with polenta and star-fruit sauce; shoulder of lamb cooked with herbs and baby vegetables; and semisoft warm chocolate cake served with coffee liqueur and essence of oranges. The space was originally part of a pair of houses separated by a narrow alleyway *(une ruelle)*. Vestiges of the 17th-century structure are visible in the dining room's stonemasonry and painted ceiling beams.

6 rue Trois-Notre-Dame. © **05-45-95-15-19.** www.restaurant-laruelle.com. Reservations recommended. Fixed-price menu 35€–60€. AE, DC, MC, V. Tues–Sat noon–2pm and 7:30–10pm. Closed Jan–Feb and 2 weeks in Aug.

Where to Stay & Dine Nearby

Hotellerie du Maine-Brun ★★   Originally a flour mill, this property (part of a chain noted for its tranquillity) is the premier place to stay and dine in this area. It's surrounded by 32 hectares (79 acres) of lowlands (including a garden, a creek, and open fields), about half of which are devoted to the production of cognac. The maître d'hôtel's preferred brand is the one made nearby, Domaine du Maine-Brun. These are the most luxurious accommodations around, larger than the lodgings at many competitors; each has a terrace. Rooms are individually decorated with 18th- and 19th-century French furniture. The restaurant serves splendid fare. Specialties include terrine of foie gras with cognac, and Porée charentaise, a combination of fish in a creamy Pineau wine sauce. Main courses range from 30€ to 40€.

RN 141, Lieu-Dit la Vigerie, Asnières-sur-Nouère 16290. © **05-45-90-83-00.** Fax 05-45-96-91-14. www. hotel-maine-brun.com. 20 units. 120€–130€ double; 170€ suite. AE, DC, MC, V. Hotel and restaurant closed mid-Nov to mid-Apr. Take RN 141 7km (4⅓ miles) west of Angoulême and turn right at Vigerie. **Amenities:** Restaurant; bar; outdoor pool; room service. *In room:* TV, hair dryer, minibar, Wi-Fi (free).

BORDEAUX ★★★

578km (359 miles) SW of Paris; 549km (341 miles) W of Lyon

On the Garonne River, the port of Bordeaux, capital of Aquitaine, is one of the world's most important wine-producing areas. It attracts visitors to the offices of wine exporters, most of whom welcome guests. (For details of a trip through the Bordeaux wine country, see "The Wine Country," later in this chapter.)

It may not exude the *joie de vivre* of Paris, but Bordeaux is a major cultural center and a transportation hub between southern France and Spain. Bordeaux is a city of warehouses, factories, mansions, suburbs, and wide quays 8km (5 miles) long. Now the fifth-largest city in France, Bordeaux belonged to the British for 300 years and even today is considered the most "un-French" of French cities.

With a population of some 700,000, the historic core of Bordeaux looks better than it has in years, thanks to the restoration of many of the city's 18th- and 19th-century buildings. This inner city is hailed as one of the great urban aesthetic triumphs of western France. In 2007, the town center of Bordeaux was classified as a World Heritage Site.

Essentials

GETTING THERE The local **airport,** Bordeaux–Mérignac (✆ **05-56-34-50-50** for flight information; www.bordeaux-aeroport.fr), is served by flights from as far away as London, Dublin, Madrid, and Barcelona. It's 15km (9⅓ miles) west of Bordeaux in Mérignac. Paris is an hour's flight away. A **shuttle bus** connects the airport with the train station, departing every 45 minutes from 7:45am to 10:45pm (trip time: 40 min.) and costing 7€ one-way. Children ride free. A taxi (✆ **05-56-96-00-34**) between the airport and the rail depot costs about 40€.

The railway station, Gare St-Jean, is on the west bank of the river, within a 30-minute walk (or 5-min. taxi ride) of the center of the old town. Some 15 to 25 **trains** from Paris's Gare Montparnasse (trip time: 3 hr. by TGV) arrive each day. They stop, en route, at Paris Charles de Gaulle airport to pick up additional passengers. The one-way fare is 66€. For train information and schedules, call ✆ **36-35** or 08-92-35-35-35.

Bordeaux is easy to reach by **car.** From Paris, follow A10 south through Orléans, Tours, and Poitiers into Bordeaux (trip time: about 5 hr.). Be aware that the streets of Bordeaux are fraught with hazards: narrow 18th-century alleys, massive traffic jams on the quays beside the Garonne, and simply too many cars and people. Easily available parking within the city's historic core is scarce. Whenever possible, head for one of the blue-and-white P signs that indicate public garages.

GETTING AROUND Three lines of a new modern tram system—labeled A, B, and C—have made traveling around Bordeaux easier than at any time in its history. Service is daily from 5am to 1am, with individual tickets costing 1.40€. A Tickarte costs 4.10€ for 1 day of travel, 5.20€ for 5 trips, or 10€ for 1 week.

Once aboard, you must validate your Tickarte, which is sold in *tabacs* and other outlets. The combined bus and tram system (✆ **05-56-57-88-88;** www.infotbc. com) serves both inner Bordeaux and its suburbs, with maps available at the train station. The most central information office is at 9 place Gambetta, open Monday to Friday 8am to 7:30pm and Saturday 9:45am to 12:25pm and 2 to 6pm.

VISITOR INFORMATION The **Office de Tourisme** is at 12 cours du 30-Juillet (✆ **05-56-00-66-00;** fax 05-56-00-66-01; www.bordeaux-tourisme.com), with a branch office in the Gare St-Jean (✆ **05-56-91-64-70**).

Exploring Bordeaux

Wine exporters welcome guests to sample wines and learn about the industry. In section 6, "The Wine Country," later in this chapter, we suggest a tour of the region. Plan your trip with maps, guides, and advice about local wines, available free from the **Maison du Vin (House of Wine),** 1 cours du 30-Juillet (✆ **05-56-00-22-88;** www.vins-bordeaux.fr), opposite the tourist office. To make the rounds of the vineyards, consider alternative forms of transport: bus, bicycle, or even walking.

STROLLS THROUGH TOWN The prettiest and most historic neighborhood in Old Bordeaux is the "golden triangle," defined by cours Clemenceau, cours de

Bordeaux

Legend:
- Church ✝
- Information ⓘ
- Post Office ✉

To Angoulême

Bus Station

place J.-Juarès

To Cap-Ferrat →

cours de l'Intendance

place Gambetta

VIEUX BORDEAUX

place de la Bourse

To Périgueux →

place Col. Raynal

Hôtel de Ville

To Périgueux

Pont de Pierre

place de Bir-Hakeim

place Canteloup

place de la Victoire

place du Maucaillou

To Gare St-Jean

↓ To Bayonne & Toulouse

0 — 1/4 mi
0 — 0.25 km

★ Paris
FRANCE
● Bordeaux

Abbatiale Ste-Croix **9**
Basilique St-Michel **11**
Basilique St-Seurin **1**
Cathédrale St-André **3**
Esplanade des Quinconces **6**
Fleche St-Michel **10**

Grand Théâtre **7**
Maison du Vin **5**
Musée des Beaux-Arts **2**
Place de la Bourse **8**
Place de la Comédie **4**
Pont de Pierre **12**

20

BORDEAUX & THE ATLANTIC COAST

Bordeaux

l'Intendance, and les allées de Tourny. You can traipse around the old town on your own, because it's fairly compact, or take advantage of the 2-hour **walking tour** the tourist office (see above) arranges daily at 10am (year-round) and 3pm (mid-July to mid-Aug only). Conducted in both French and English, tours take in all the most important sites and begin at the tourist office. Cost is 7.50€ for adults, 6.50€ for students, 5€ for children 13 to 18, and free for children 12 and under. We strongly recommend the tours, which correspond to the opening hours of each of the monuments listed below. Reserve in advance and call to confirm. Additionally, from April 1 to November 15, every Wednesday and Saturday at 10am, a bus tour (7.50€) with

French and English commentary departs from in front of the tourist office. The 2-hour tour includes 30 minutes of walking through narrow alleyways.

If you go it alone, your tour of Old Bordeaux can begin in the heart of this old city at **place de la Comédie,** a busy traffic hub that was once the site of a Roman temple. On this square, one of France's great theaters, **Grand Théâtre ★★**, place de la Comédie (✆ **05-56-00-85-95;** www.opera-bordeaux.com), the city's cultural symbol, was built between 1773 and 1780 as testimony to the burgeoning prosperity of Bordeaux's emerging bourgeoisie. This is one of the last remaining 18th-century theaters in the world, rivaling those of Naples, Stockholm, and Milan. A colonnade of 12 columns graces its facade. Surmounted on these are statues of goddesses and the Muses. If you'd like to visit the richly decorated interior, phone the tourist office to ask about the schedule of weekly guided tours. They cost 6€ for adults and 5€ for children.

From here you can walk north to **esplanade des Quinconces.** It was laid out between 1818 and 1828, and covers nearly 12 hectares (30 acres). A smaller but lovelier square is **place de la Bourse ★**, bounded by quays opening onto the Garonne. It was laid out between 1728 and 1755; the fountain of the Three Graces is at its center. Flanking the square are the Custom House and the Stock Exchange.

CHURCHES   The largest and most ostentatious church in Bordeaux is the **Cathédrale St-André ★★**, place Pey-Berland (✆ **05-56-52-68-10**), near the southern perimeter of the old town. The sculptures on the 13th-century Porte Royale (Royal Door) are admirable; see also the 14th-century sculptures on the North Door. Separate from the rest of the church is the 47m (154-ft.) **Tour Pey-Berland** (✆ **05-56-81-26-25**), a belfry begun in the 15th century. Foundations date from 900 years ago. The church is open July to September daily 10 to 11:30am and 2 to 6:30pm. Off season, hours are daily 8:30 to 11:30am, Monday to Saturday 2 to 5:30pm. The tower is open Tuesday to Sunday June to September 10am to 1:15pm and 2 to 6pm, October to May Tuesday to Sunday 10am to noon and 2 to 5:30pm. Tower admission is 5€ for adults and 3.50€ for those 25 and under. Organ recitals are sometimes held in July and August, usually on Thursday at 5pm. Admission is free.

Bordeaux, always a magnet for power, money, and ecclesiastical zeal, has four other important churches. For information about the churches described below, you can call the **Presbytère de l'Eglise St-Michel** (✆ **05-56-94-30-50**), but most of the people who answer speak only French. The churches' hours vary slightly but are usually Monday to Saturday 2 to 5pm.

Foremost among the "secondary" churches is the **Basilique St-Michel ★**, place St-Michel (part of place Canteloup; no phone). The church itself, constructed in stages from the 14th to the 16th century, is incredibly charming. More impressive is the **Fleche St-Michel ★** across the street. This tower, erected in 1472, is the second-tallest stone tower in France (after the cathedral at Strasbourg), rising 112m (367 ft.). The tower is open for visits June to September, daily 2 to 7pm, for 3€. You climb 228 steps to the top, where you have sweeping views over the port and the Garonne. The rest of the year, unless you receive special permission from the tourist office, you'll have to appreciate the architecture of the tower from the ground. During July and August, every Friday from 5 to 7pm the bells in the tower are rung as part of a free carillon concert that can be heard throughout the neighborhood.

Another historic church is **Basilique St-Seurin,** place des Martyrs de la Résistance (☎ **05-56-93-89-28**). Its most ancient sections, such as its crypt, date from the 5th century. See the porch left over from an earlier church; it has some capitals from the Romanesque era. In summer, hours are Tuesday to Sunday 9:30 to 6:30pm; off-season hours are Tuesday to Sunday 8:30am to 7:30pm. On Sunday the basilica may shut down at 1pm.

Abbatiale Ste-Croix, place Pierre-Renaudel (☎ **05-56-94-30-50**), gained attention in musical circles when its organ, a marvel built by a monk, Dom Bedos, was restored to its original working order in 1996. The church, a severe Romanesque structure from the 11th and 12th centuries, is revered for its stately dignity. In July and August, free organ concerts are presented Wednesday at 6:30pm; otherwise, the church is open only Thursday 10am to noon.

MUSEUM   **Musée des Beaux-Arts ★★**, 20 cours d'Albret, Jardin du Palais-Rohan (☎ **05-56-10-20-56**), has an outstanding collection from the 15th to the 20th centuries. Works by Perugina, Titian, Rubens, Veronese, Delacroix, and Marquet are on display. The museum is open Wednesday to Monday 11am to 6pm. Admission is 5€ adults, 2.50€ students, and free for ages 17 and under.

BOAT RIDES   The **pont de Pierre,** with 17 arches, stretches 478m (1,568 ft.) across the Garonne and is one of the most beautiful bridges in France. Built on orders of Napoleon I in 1813, the bridge can be crossed on foot for a view of the quays and the port. For an even better view, we suggest a **tour of the port,** which lasts about 90 minutes and goes up the river and all around the harbor. It departs from the Quai des Chartrons, in the center of town. It's available year-round. The cost is 10€ for adults and 8€ for children 9 and under. For exact times and a description of other cruises, call the tourist office (see "Essentials," above) or **Bateaux Ville de Bordeaux,** Quai des Chartrons (☎ **05-56-52-88-88**). Ask about the occasional floating concerts at night. Note that tours may be canceled without warning.

Shopping

If you want antiques, concentrate your search around **rue Bouffard, rue des Remparts,** and **rue Notre-Dame,** where you'll find a market area known as **Village Notre-Dame** (☎ **05-56-52-66-13**), housing about 30 antiques shops. Another destination is the neighborhood around **Eglise St-Michel,** particularly the passage St-Michel, a narrow alleyway a few steps from the church.

For fashion, go to the couture quarter around **place des Grands Hommes** as well as the **cours Georges-Clemenceau,** with its many upscale, trendy, and classic emporiums. For the greatest concentration of shops, head to the **rue Ste-Catherine,** the longest pedestrian street in France. It has at least 100 boutiques, from the most luxurious to the cheapest. Better-known choices include the ready-to-wear boutique of the hip Bordeaux designer **Jacqueline Dourthe,** 18 rue Lafaurie-de-Monbadon (☎ **05-56-52-35-78**), for creative, expensive designs. More elegant and esoteric, and definitely worth a look, is **La Soierie (Chantal Olivier),** 54 cours Georges-Clemenceau (☎ **05-56-51-23-75**), which carries a complete line of women's inner and outer garments made mostly of fabric from the silk mills of Lyon.

Despite a fire in 2003 that destroyed some artwork, **Galerie Condillac,** 24 rue Condillac (☎ **05-56-79-04-31**), is one of the classier art houses that specializes in

If you've come to Bordeaux to buy wine, try to choose one that carries personal significance because you've visited the vineyard, or consult the experts at the wine shops. We recommend **La Vinothèque,** 8 cours du 30-Juillet (✆ **05-56-52-32-05;** www. la-vinotheque.com), and **Badie,** 62 allées de Tourny (✆ **05-56-52-23-72**). The best red bordeaux wines come

from small houses such as **Château Lesparre,** Beychac-et-Caillau, 39km (24 miles) north of Bordeaux (✆ **05-57-24-51-23**); **Château Bel Air,** Naujan-et-Postiac, 40km (25 miles) east of Bordeaux (✆ **05-57-74-62-01**); and **Château les Bouzigues,** Saintes Gemmes, 76km (47 miles) south of Bordeaux (✆ **05-56-61-80-77**).

---

mostly local artists who paint with strong, vibrant colors. For a sugar rush, head over to **Cadiot Badie,** 26 allées de Tourny (✆ **05-56-44-24-22**), where the specialty for many decades has been sinfully flavorful chocolates, chocolate truffles, and pralines.

Where to Stay
EXPENSIVE

Hôtel Burdigala ★★ This is the best and most appealing hotel in Bordeaux's core. Well manicured, tasteful, and experienced at welcoming international travelers (many of them wine buyers), it rises five floors above a neighborhood that's otherwise devoted to commerce. Built in 1988, and frequently renovated, it feels like a modern-day grand hotel. Conservative, contemporary-looking guest rooms are relatively spacious, and the bathrooms are plush.

115 rue Georges-Bonnac, Bordeaux 33000. ✆ **05-56-90-16-16.** Fax 05-56-93-15-06. www.burdigala. com. 83 units. 210€–320€ double; 440€–550€ suite. AE, DC, MC, V. Parking 12€. Tram: A to Mériadeck. **Amenities:** Restaurant; bar; babysitting; access to nearby health club and pool (20€ per day); room service. *In room:* TV, hair dryer, minibar, Wi-Fi (free).

The Regent Grand ★★★ Located opposite the Opéra National de Bordeaux, The Regent Grand has been restored to its former glory, bringing true government-rated five-star luxury to the heart of Old Town. Rooms still evoke the 19th century, with their elegant damasks and reproduction Napoleonic furniture. Black lacquer wrought-iron lamps and pleated silk shades add more elegance. Rooms have all the modern amenities. Le d'Argent is the most elegant hotel dining room in town, offering market-fresh seafood is an atmospheric setting.

2-5 place de la Comédie, 33000 Bordeaux. ✆ **05-57-30-44-44.** www.theregentbordeaux.com. 260€–345€ double; from 455€ suite. AE, DC, MC, V. **Amenities:** Restaurant; bar; room service; spa. *In room:* A/C, TV, hair dryer, minibar, Wi-Fi (free).

Seeko'O Hotel ★★ This is the most daringly modern hotel ever to open in Old Bordeaux. Its jagged glistening white exterior evokes a block of ice. It's got enough electronic gadgetry to launch itself into space—well, almost. The location of this sci-fi hotel is near the gritty Hangars des Marques, a waterfront development undergoing massive gentrification. Bedrooms have been likened to a space-age bachelor pad, with some circular beds and color schemes of black and white with red splashes like a woman would "slash on" her lipstick. Most of the bedrooms are in essence junior suites, and bathtubs are designed for two.

54 quai de Bacalan, Bordeaux 33300. ☎ **05-56-39-07-07.** www.seekoo-hotel.com. 45 units. 189€–229€ junior suite; 380€ panoramic suite. AE, MC. Parking 10€. **Amenities:** Bar; room service; Turkish bath. *In room:* A/C, TV, hair dryer, minibar, Wi-Fi (free).

MODERATE

Best Western Bordeaux Le Bayonne Etche-Ona ★★   In 1997, two antique, stone-fronted town houses, Le Bayonne Hôtel and its neighbor, Hôtel Etche-Ona, were radically upgraded and joined to form this entity. The aura of the 1930s has been retained and many features added, most notably soundproofing and comfortable furnishings, along with midsize bathrooms. Rooms are medium to generous in size. Many attractions, including restaurants, the cathedral, place de la Bourse, the quays, and the Grand Théâtre, are nearby. Breakfast is the only meal served.

15 cours de l'Intendance (entrances at 4 rue Martignac and 11 rue Mautrec), Bordeaux 33000. ☎ **05-56-48-00-88.** Fax 05-56-48-41-60. www.bordeaux-hotel.com. 63 units. 152€–187€ double; 295€–345€ suite. AE, DC, MC, V. Parking 18€. **Amenities:** Bar; room service. *In room:* A/C, TV, hair dryer, minibar, Wi-Fi (free).

Mercure Bordeaux Centre ★   This hotel, in a sleek building facing a shopping mall in the Mériadeck business district, is a 5-minute walk from the town center. The well-furnished rooms with modern amenities and comfortable beds attract winegrowers and wine merchants from abroad as well as other business travelers and groups. The renovated accommodations are on the third and fifth through seventh floors. La Brasserie du Festival, the main restaurant, is one of Bordeaux's finest hotel grills.

5 rue Robert-Lateulade, Bordeaux 33000. ☎ **05-56-56-43-43.** Fax 05-56-96-50-59. www.mercure. com. 196 units. 140€–160€ double; 220€ suite. AE, DC, MC, V. Overnight parking 2€; hourly charge for daytime parking. Bus: 7 or 8. **Amenities:** Restaurant; bar; room service. *In room:* A/C, TV, hair dryer, minibar, Wi-Fi (free).

Mercure Château Chartrons ★★   This is one of Bordeaux's leading hotels, located near the landmark place Tourny. The medium-size rooms are standard chain-hotel accommodations, decorated with memorabilia of the wine trade. Each comes with a midsize modern bathroom. The bar has an impressive array of local vintages available by the glass. The restaurant serves bistro-style fare.

81 cours St-Louis, Bordeaux 33300. ☎ **05-56-43-15-00.** Fax 05-56-69-15-21. www.mercure.com. 145 units. 90€–190€ double; 210€ suite. AE, DC, MC, V. Parking 10€. **Amenities:** Restaurant; bar; babysitting; room service. *In room:* A/C, TV, hair dryer, minibar, Wi-Fi (free).

INEXPENSIVE

Hôtel Continental ★ 🗝   To get a certain class, charm, and elegance in Bordeaux at this price is a rarity. In the center of the golden triangle, on a semipedestrian mall dotted with boutiques, this 18th-century town house wins new fans every year. You'll get a warm welcome and a fine dose of Bordelaise hospitality. Rooms, although a bit small (especially the singles), are warmly decorated and furnished, each with a compact bathroom; a few have tiny balconies.

10 rue Montesquieu, Bordeaux 33000. ☎ **05-56-52-66-00.** Fax 05-56-52-77-97. www.hotel-le-continental. com. 51 units. 85€–104€ double; 105€–190€ suite. AE, DC, MC, V. Parking 2.30€. **Amenities:** Room service. *In room:* A/C (in some), TV, hair dryer (in some), minibar, Wi-Fi (free).

Hôtel de Sèze 🗝   This boutique hotel occupies an 18th-century building in a historic neighborhood. The hotel is such a well-known value that you should make

reservations as early as possible. Rooms are comfortable and well furnished; the cheapest has only a bed and bathroom.

5 rue Sèze, Bordeaux 33000. ℰ **05-56-81-72-42.** Fax 05-56-48-98-00. http://hotelsezemedoc.free.fr. 24 units. 58€–68€ double. AE, DC, MC, V. Parking 12€. *In room:* A/C (in some), TV, minibar, Wi-Fi (free).

Where to Dine

You can also try the restaurants at **Mercure Château Chartrons** and **Mercure Bordeaux Centre** (see "Where to Stay," above).

EXPENSIVE

La Tupina ★★ 🎁TRADITIONAL FRENCH One of Bordeaux's most talented chefs runs this cozy spot with a summer terrace near quai de la Monnaie. It's been called "a tribute to country kitchens and the grandmothers who cooked in them." Jean-Pierre Xiradakis's specialty is duck, so your meal may begin with croutons spread with duck rillettes, and the kitchen often uses duck giblets, skin, and livers in salads. Other specialties are roasted shoulder of lamb *en confit* with garlic and white beans, lamprey eel à la Bordelaise, and steaks grilled and barbecued at the table. Desserts usually include pears marinated in red Bordeaux wine.

6 rue Porte de la Monnaie. ℰ **05-56-91-56-37.** www.latupina.com. Reservations recommended. Main courses 14€–55€; fixed-price lunch 16€–65€, dinner 60€. AE, DC, MC, V. Daily noon–2pm and 7–11pm.

Le Chapon-Fin ★★★ MODERN FRENCH Dating from 1825, one of the city's most prestigious restaurants today occupies an early-20th-century monument that critics have referred to as "organic rococo." Designed by architect Alfred Duprat and crafted from distressed rocks into an Art Nouveau–style grotto, it soars almost 7.5m (25 ft.) to a skylight that floods the interior with light. Owner Nicolas Frion features artful renditions of fresh foie gras of duckling; lobster salad; Pauillac lamb grilled with peppers and mushrooms; sea bass with pecans, celery leaves, and cream; and succulent crayfish and scallops braised in spices and wine. The restaurant is in one of the city's upscale neighborhoods, between place Gambetta and the Marché aux Grands Hommes.

5 rue Montesquieu. ℰ **05-56-79-10-10.** www.chapon-fin.com. Reservations required. Main courses 33€–44€; fixed-price menus 36€–90€. AE, DC, MC, V. Tues–Sat noon–1:30pm and 7:30–9:30pm.

Le Pavillon des Boulevards FRENCH Small, intimate, and charming, this is an impeccably managed restaurant where the skillful chef (Denis Franc) and the head of the dining room (his wife, Nelly Franc) provide sophisticated food for discerning customers. Menu items include a dollop of caviar from local sturgeon, served with chestnut-flavored cream sauce; grilled crayfish with grilled blood sausage and cider; Breton lobster sautéed with vanilla beans with sauterne sauce; filets of turbot with Parmesan-flavored risotto; and fried crayfish tails served with fried blood sausage and apple juice. The cuisine is attuned to the changing seasons.

120 rue Croix-de-Seguey. ℰ **05-56-81-51-02.** Reservations recommended. Main courses 30€–38€; fixed-price lunch 40€, dinner 70€–100€. AE, MC, V. Tues–Fri noon–1:30pm; Mon–Sat 8–9:30pm. Closed last week in Dec and 3 weeks in Aug. Bus: 14.

MODERATE

Fernand (Bistro Bordelais) ★★FRENCH More and more serious foodies are flocking to a marvelous bistro, **Fernand,** next to the place de la Bourse on the waterfront in the Old Town. Here you get traditional French food in an atmospheric setting. The chef specializes in fresh wild fish along with an array of succulent oysters and other fish straight from the day's market. The homemade foie gras is remarkable. Depending on the season, you can enjoy fresh French lamb, even game in the autumn. Two especially enticing specialties are fricassée of scallops in a wild mushroom sauce or Chateaubriand sautéed with foie gras.

7 quai de la Douane. ✆ **05-56-81-23-40.** Reservations recommended. Main courses 17€–37€; fixed-price menus 30€–40€. AE, MC, V. Mon–Sat noon–2:30pm; Sun noon–3:30pm; and daily 7–11pm.

Le Mably ★ 🍴 FRENCH   In the heart of 18th-century Bordeaux, surrounded by art galleries and shops, this restaurant attracts gastronomes, hipsters, politicians, journalists, and locals interested in the fun, elegant atmosphere of a *brasserie de luxe*. Both old-fashioned rooms have late-19th-century decor. The duck-intensive menu lists salad of duck necks stuffed with pistachios, confit of duckling, *magret* of duckling, and, of course, duck liver. Recommendable nonduck items are veal kidneys with fresh coriander, blanquettes of veal, boeuf bourguignon, and several kinds of fresh fish. Pay special attention to the comprehensive wine list, rich in esoteric burgundies. There's additional seating on an outdoor terrace during warmer weather.

12 rue Mably. ✆ **05-56-44-30-10.** Reservations recommended. Main courses 15€–24€; fixed-price menu 22€–32€. AE, MC, V. Tues–Sat noon–2:30pm and 7:30–11pm. Closed 3 weeks in Aug.

Le Vieux Bordeaux ★ MODERN FRENCH   Nearly a neighborhood institution, this restaurant ranks among the top five in a highly competitive market. Specialties include roasted sea bass on a gratin of pulverized black olives, thin-sliced escalopes of duck foie gras with coffee-flavored sauce, and "Oriental" (sweet-and-sour) pigeon with lime sauce.

27 rue Buhan. ✆ **05-56-52-94-36.** http://le-vieux-bordeaux.com. Reservations recommended. Main courses 15€–32€; fixed-price lunch 30€, dinner 40€–52€. AE, DC, MC, V. Tues–Sat noon–2pm and 8 10:30pm. Closed last 2 weeks in Feb and 3 weeks in Aug.

INEXPENSIVE

Le Quai Zaco FRENCH/SPANISH   Its solid stone walls were originally built 200 years ago as a warehouse, and just before it became a restaurant, it functioned as a sales outlet for sporting goods. Today, it's a hardworking and conscientious restaurant with two distinctly different dining rooms, each with a decor that accents the antique masonry with jazzy artwork, molded plastic chairs, and industrial-looking tables. The cuisine is derived from southwestern France and northern Spain, and it might, on the day of your arrival, include a spicy gazpacho with ravioli stuffed with goat cheese; piccata of veal with stuffed tomatoes; sweetbreads with foie gras, endive salad, and pine nuts; a fricassee of artichoke hearts with oxtail; and stingray with caper-flavored butter. Desserts are plentiful and imaginative. How about a lemon-flavored pannacotta accented with a "carpaccio" of spiced and sliced oranges? You'll find this place about 1km (⅔ mile) north of the Gare St-Jean, immediately beside the wharves of the Garonne River.

80 quai des Chartrons. ✆ **05-57-87-67-72.** Reservations recommended. Main courses 16€–26€; fixed-price lunch 16€. AE, MC, V. Mon–Fri noon–1:30pm; Mon–Sat 7:45–11pm. Bus: 51.

L'O de l'Hâ ★ 🍴 FRENCH/INTERNATIONAL   The owners got the inspiration for this fashionable restaurant during a visit to New York and the innovative French restaurant Bouley. L'O de l'Hâ is on a narrow cobbled street whose name commemorates a long-gone medieval prison. Antique masonry, roughly textured plaster, and polished concrete decorate both fashionable dining rooms. Menu items are innovative and intriguing. Examples include crabmeat lasagna with coconut flakes; *brandade* of sweet potatoes with sweet peppers; large Dover sole with spinach, walnuts, and chanterelles; and braised lamb chops with tomato marmalade. From Thursday to Saturday, a DJ spins disco from 8 until around 11pm.

5 rue de l'Hâ. ✆ **05-56-81-42-21.** www.o-delha.fr. Reservations recommended. Main courses 8€–26€; fixed-price lunch 14€–17€. AE, DC, MC, V. Tues–Fri noon–2pm; Tues–Thurs 8–10pm; Fri–Sat 8–11:30pm. Tram: A to Musée d'Aquitaine.

Bordeaux After Dark

Pick up a copy of *Clubs et Concerts* at the Office de Tourisme or *Bordeaux Plus* at a newsstand; both detail the goings-on in and around town.

A play or an opera could make a good start to your evening. **Grand Théâtre,** place de la Comédie (✆ **05-56-00-85-20**), has a busy, diverse performance schedule.

You'll find gambling, drinking, dining, and people-watching at **Casino de Bordeaux,** in the Hôtel Sofitel Bordeaux Lac, rue Cardinal Richaud (✆ **05-56-69-49-00**). Rooms containing slot machines operate daily 10am to 4am. There's no admission charge. To enter the more formal gaming rooms (site of the roulette and blackjack tables), you must present a passport or an identity card. They're open every night 10pm until 4am. Live entertainment of some kind usually begins around 8pm Friday. The casino has an informal brasserie on the street level, where fixed-price menus cost 25€, and a restaurant one floor up, where fixed-price menus begin at 35€.

Animated street life rules the inner core of Bordeaux by night. Head to **place de la Victoire, place St-Pierre, place du Parlement, place Camille Jullian,** and **place Gambetta;** the latter swarms with students. Night owls in Bordeaux gravitate toward quai du Paludate, where restaurants, bars, and discos remain open until the wee hours.

The hottest drinking spot in Bordeaux is a red-and-black enclave of Cuban music, photographs, and posters, all of it richly lubricated with your choice of mojitos and some of the best-looking and most uninhibited people in town. Named after the street in Miami where many of Cuba's emigrants settled after Castro's takeover of Cuba, it's **Le Calle Ocho,** rue des Piliers de Tutelle (✆ **05-56-48-08-68**), open nightly from 6pm till dawn.

Two trendy, glamorous bars are **L'Absolute Lounge,** rue de la Devise (✆ **05-56-48-80-00**), which occasionally schedules live "electro-jazz"; and **La Casa Latina,** 59 quai Chartrons (✆ **05-57-87-15-80**), where merengue, salsa, and bachata might make you think that you've landed in the Dominican Republic or Brazil.

The leading gay bar, **BHV (Bar de l'Hôtel de Ville),** 4 rue de l'Hôtel de Ville (✆ **05-56-44-05-08**), is in the heart of town, across from the town hall. The handsomest men of Bordeaux, or so it is said, turn up here Tuesday to Sunday 6pm to 2am. Drag shows take place from October to June on Sunday at 10:30pm.

A good choice for dancing is **La Plage,** 40 quai de Paludate (✆ **05-56-49-02-46**), with its 1970s decor and just as classic 25- to 45-year-old crowd.

THE WINE COUNTRY

The major Bordeaux wine districts are Graves, Médoc, Sauternes, Entre-deux-Mers, Libourne, Blaye, and Bourg. North of the city of Bordeaux, the Garonne River joins the Dordogne to form the Gironde, a broad estuary. More than 100,000 vineyards produce some 70 million gallons of wine a year, some of which are among the greatest reds in the world. (The white wines are less well known.)

Some of the famous vineyards welcome visitors, providing you don't arrive at the busy harvest time. However, most vineyards don't have a permanent staff to accommodate sightseers. Don't just show up—call first or check with local tourist offices about appropriate times to visit. A typical tour includes information about the wine-making process and a tour of the cellars. Most châteaux have historical artifacts on display. Tours end with a tasting, in which visitors 18 and older may participate.

Before heading out on the Wine Road, or Route des Grands-Crus, make sure you get a detailed map from the Bordeaux tourist office (see "Essentials" under the "Bordeaux" section, earlier in this chapter), because the "trail" isn't well marked. From Bordeaux, head north toward Pauillac on D2, the Wine Road.

Libourne

This is a sizable market town with a railway connection. At the junction of the Dordogne and Isle rivers, Libourne is roughly the center of the St-Emilion, Pomerol, and Fronsac wine districts. In the town, a large colonnaded square still contains some houses from the 16th century, including the **Hôtel-de-Ville** (town hall). The town hall is open Monday to Friday 8:30am to 12:30pm and 1:15 to 5pm. During that time you can enter without an appointment to see the building's two showcase rooms (if they're not in use). The **Salle des Mariages** and the **Salle des Conseils** contain some antiques from the 1400s; most of the decor and design are from the 16th to the 18th centuries. You can also explore the remains of 13th-century ramparts. In the town center is the **Office de Tourisme,** 45 allée Robert Boulin (© **05-57-51-15-04**), where you can get details on visiting the vineyards.

WHERE TO DINE

Chez Servais ★★ ✆ FRENCH   The setting for our favorite restaurant in Libourne is an antique (probably 19th-c.) house whose sculpted facade occupies a prominent position in the town center. In the dining rooms—one small and intimate, the other more convivial—a hardworking professional staff serves items from a menu that changes at least every 6 weeks. Our favorite dishes include sautéed foie gras with white grapes; roasted sea bass with herbs, butter sauce, and flap mushrooms; scallops with salsify chips; and *magret* of duckling with sweet-and-sour sauce concocted from red seasonal berries.

14 place Decazes. © **05-57-51-83-97.** Reservations recommended. Fixed-price menu 27€–39€. AE, MC, V. Tues–Sun 12:30–2pm; Tues–Sat 7:45–9:30pm. Closed 1st week of May and 2 weeks in Aug.

Médoc ★

The Médoc, an undulating plain covered with vineyards, is one of the most visited regions in southwestern France. Bordeaux and the Pointe de Grave mark its borders. Throughout the region are many châteaux producing grapes; only a handful of these, however, are worthy of your attention. The most visited château is that of Mouton-Rothschild, said to be second only to Lourdes among attractions in southwestern France.

EXPLORING THE AREA

Château Lafite-Rothschild   This site is second in number of visitors only to the nearby Château Mouton-Rothschild. Count on spending at least an hour here. The *vinothèque* contains many vintage bottles, several dating from 1797. The Rothschilds purchased the château in 1868.

Rte. des Château, Pauillac. © **05-56-59-26-83.** www.lafite.com. Tours by appointment only; minimum 1-week notice required. Free admission. Tours Mon–Fri 2 and 3:30pm. Closed Aug–Oct.

Château Margaux   Known as the Versailles of the Médoc, this Empire-style château was built in the 19th century near the village of Margaux. The estate covers more than 263 hectares (650 acres), of which 80 hectares (198 acres) produce Château Margaux and Pavillon Rouge du Château Margaux; almost 12 hectares (30 acres) are devoted to producing Pavillon Blanc du Château Margaux. To see the vat rooms and wine cellars, make an appointment by letter or phone.

On D2, south of Pauillac, Margaux 33460. © **05-57-88-83-83.** www.chateau-margaux.com. Vat rooms and wine cellars by appointment only. Mon–Fri 10am–noon and 2–4pm. Closed Aug–Oct.

Château Mouton-Rothschild ★   Thousands of tourists visit this château, 1km (⅔ mile) north of Pauillac, one of many former homes of the baron Philippe de Rothschild and his American-born wife, Pauline. Today their daughter, Philippine de Rothschild, carries on their work. The reception area is furnished with sculptures and paintings that portray wine as art. An adjoining museum, shoehorned into the former wine cellars, features 18th- and 19th-century art and objects from the Rothschild family collections, as well as a historically important 16th-century tapestry, all of which focus on the cultivation of vines. To tour the cellars, make an appointment well in advance; for a tour that does not include the cellars, call a week ahead.

Le Pouyalet, Pauillac 33250. © **05-56-73-20-20.** Tours by appointment only. Tour 6€ without tasting, 18€ with tasting. Year-round Mon–Fri 9:30–11am; Mon–Thurs 2–4pm; Fri 2–3pm.

Société Duboscq   Duboscq, a wine packager and wholesaler established in 1952, occupies the stately premises of the late-19th-century Château Haut-Marbuzet. The staff will follow your visit to the cellars with a complimentary *dégustation des vins* (wine tasting) of whichever product you request. The château is 5 minutes north of Pauillac by car.

Château Haut-Marbuzet, St-Estephe 33180. © **05-56-59-30-54.** Free admission. Mon–Sat 9am–noon and 2–5pm by appointment only. Tours in English on request.

WHERE TO STAY & DINE

Cordeillan-Bages ★★   In a region obsessed with fine wine and fine food, this emerges as the most consistently celebrated restaurant and hotel. The setting is a 17th-century *chartreuse,* which the staff defines as something larger than a manor house and smaller than a château. Virtually everyone comes here for the restaurant, usually opting to spend the night after drinking wine with dinner. Fixed-price menus cost 90€ for lunch, 170€ for dinner. A la carte main courses go for 32€ to 60€. Menu items may include a simple but elegant version of foie gras served on confit of peaches with a reduction of port wine; roasted sea bass with essence of cockles and braised, licorice-flavored leeks; and a platter of suckling lamb cooked three ways (the shoulder *en confit,* the chops grilled, the neck stuffed and baked). The establishment's most famous dessert is an eggplant crystallized in sugar and served with anise-flavored cream sauce and basil-flavored sorbet. The restaurant, but not the hotel, is closed all day Monday and at lunch on Tuesday and Saturday.

The spacious guest rooms are decorated in a style that emulates the Hôtel Ritz in Paris, with formal curtains, upholstered walls, a scattering of antiques, and—other than the bouffant-style curtains—an airy minimalism. About half are contemporary, with monochromatic color schemes; the rest are in traditional country-house style.

Rte. D2, Pauillac 33250. © **05-56-59-24-24.** Fax 05-56-59-01-89. www.cordeillanbages.com. 28 units. 199€–292€ double; 392€ junior suite; 517€ 2-bedroom apt for 4. AE, DC, MC, V. Closed Dec 15–Feb 14. **Amenities:** Restaurant; bar; exercise room; outdoor pool; room service; sauna. *In room:* TV, hair dryer, Wi-Fi (free).

St-Emilion ★★

Surrounded by vineyards, St-Emilion is on a limestone plateau overlooking the valley of the Dordogne; a maze of wine cellars has been dug beneath the town. The wine made in this district has been called "Wine of Honor," and British sovereigns nicknamed it "King of Wines." The town, constructed mostly of golden stone and dating from the Middle Ages, is also known for its macaroons.

St-Emilion maintains the ancient tradition of La Jurade, a society dedicated to maintaining the highest standard for the local wine and promoting and honoring it around the world. Members of this society wear silk hats and scarlet robes edged with ermine, and members of the Syndicat Viticole, which watches over the quality of wine, have been around the world to promote the wines with this appellation.

ESSENTIALS

GETTING THERE   St-Emilion lies 35km (22 miles) northeast of Bordeaux between Libourne, 8km (5 miles) away, and Castillon-la-Bataille, 11km (6¾ miles) away. **Trains** from Bordeaux make the 45-minute trip to St-Emilion three times per day; the one-way fare is 7.50€. Trains from other parts of France usually require transfers in either Bordeaux or Libourne, a 10-minute train ride from St-Emilion. For train information in St-Emilion, call © **36-35,** or 08-92-35-35-35 from outside France.

VISITOR INFORMATION   The **Office de Tourisme** is on place des Créneaux (© **05-57-55-28-28;** fax 05-57-55-28-29; www.saint-emilion-tourisme.com).

EXPLORING THE TOWN

At the heart of St-Emilion is the medieval **place du Marché,** renamed **place de l'Eglise Monolithe,** between two hills. St-Emilion abounds with unusual monuments, some of them dug, for defensive reasons, into the limestone bedrock that adds such verve to the vineyards.

Foremost among the monuments is the **Eglise Monolithe ★**, place de l'Eglise Monolithe (© **05-57-55-28-28**), the largest underground church in Europe, carved by Benedictine monks during the 9th to 12th centuries. Three 14th-century bay windows mark its facade. A 14th-century sculpted portal depicts the Last Judgment and Resurrection of the Dead. The church is 11m (36 ft.) high, 20m (66 ft.) wide, and 38m (125 ft.) long. It can be visited only as part of an organized tour. Tours last 45 minutes, and English-language tours are regularly scheduled between May and September at 11:30am and 2:20pm, with an additional 4:30pm tour in July and August. For the rest of the year, English-language tours are by appointment. Each tour includes a visit to the church, its underground Benedictine catacombs, the 13th-century Chapelle de la Trinité, and its underground grotto—a site known as the Hermitage—where St-Emilion sequestered himself during the latter part of his life. The entire complex was kept alive during the heyday of its use by underground springs, which were surrounded in the 1500s by ornate balustrades (the monks charged admission). The tour, which lasts 45 minutes, costs 6.50€ for adults, 4.10€ for students, 3.20€ for children 12 to 17, and is free for children 11 and under.

You can visit two additional monuments without an organized tour. The first is the **bell tower** (*clocher*) of the Eglise Monolithe (see above). It rises on place des Créneaux, near place de l'Eglise Monolithe. Built between the 1100s and the 1400s, it's the second-highest tower in the La Gironde region and for years after its construction was the only aboveground landmark that indicated the position of the underground church. You can climb the bell tower and take in the panoramic view daily between 9am and 6pm every day except Christmas and New Year's Day for a 1€ fee. To do this, go to the tourist office, where someone will give you a key to the tower door in exchange for an ID card. (When you return the key, you'll get your ID back.)

You may want to visit the **Château du Roi** (✆ **05-57-24-72-09**), founded by Henry III of the Plantagenet line during the 13th century. Don't expect a full-fledged castle. The tower was the first section built, and the construction that followed was either demolished or never completed. Until 1608, this building functioned as the town hall. From its summit, you can see as far away as the Dordogne. You can climb the tower (the procedure is the same as for visiting the bell tower) during daylight hours every day except Christmas and New Year's Day, 10am to 12:30pm and 2 to 6pm (to 6:30pm Apr–Sept), for 1€.

WHERE TO STAY & DINE

Hostellerie de Plaisance ★★   This 200-year-old stone building, on 14th-century foundations, is the best lodging-and-dining choice in this medieval town. The stylish rooms, some with views of stone monuments and towers, accommodate sophisticated wine tasters and buyers from all over the world. Some rooms are small, but the best doubles have terraces where you can enjoy breakfast. The cuisine served here is the best known and most praised in the area. Chef Philippe Etchebest works with the region's bountiful seasonal ingredients, especially game, usually available October to February. Otherwise, menu items include salad of grilled quail with avocados, civet of sturgeon cooked with local red wine, and filet mignon of veal with wild mushrooms. Top it all off with a warm soufflé flavored with pear liqueur and served with nougat ice cream and chocolate sauce. Fixed-price menus cost 58€ at lunch, 40€ to 135€ at dinner.

Place du Clocher, St-Emilion 33330. ✆ **05-57-55-07-55.** Fax 05-57-74-41-11. www.hostelleriedeplaisance. com. 21 units. 350€–510€ double; 670€ suite. Half board 80€. AE, DC, MC, V. Parking 15€. Closed Dec 21–Feb 11. **Amenities:** Restaurant; bar; room service. *In room:* A/C, TV, hair dryer, minibar (some units), Wi-Fi (free).

THE DORDOGNE & PERIGORD: LAND OF PREHISTORIC CAVES, TRUFFLES & FINE WINE

Lovers of foie gras and truffles, not to mention nature lovers, have always sought out the Dordogne and Périgord regions of France. Our first stop, Périgueux, was the capital of the old province of Périgord. After following the trail of the Cro-Magnon people to prehistoric caves, we visit Cahors, the ancient capital of Quercy, then Montauban, where the painter Ingres was born.

But the towns aren't the stars: The fertile countryside holds the fascination. In some villages the Middle Ages seem to live on. It's said that no discoveries are left to be made in France, but you can disprove that by taking time to visit a region too often neglected by tourists.

PERIGUEUX ★

485km (301 miles) SW of Paris; 85km (53 miles) SE of Angoulême; 113km (70 miles) NE of Bordeaux; 101km (63 miles) SW of Limoges

This is the city of foie gras and truffles. Capital of the old province of Périgord, Périgueux stands on the Isle River. In addition to its food products, the region is known for its Roman ruins and medieval churches.

The city is divided into three sections: the Cité (the old Roman town), Le Puy St-Front (the medieval town) on the slope of the hill, and, to the west, the modern town.

Périgueux (pop. 35,000) is a sleepy provincial backwater. Its attractions probably won't hold your interest for more than a day, but it's a gateway to the Dordogne Valley and the cave paintings at Les Eyzies.

Essentials

GETTING THERE **Trains** run frequently from Paris, Lyon, and Toulouse, plus many regional towns. Twelve trains per day arrive from Paris from either Montparnasse or Gare d'Austerlitz (trip time: 4–6 hr.; one-way fare: 78€); 12 trains from Bordeaux (trip time: 1½ hr.; one-way fare: 20€); two trains from Lyon (trip time: 6–8 hr.; one-way fare: 52€ to 82€); and eight trains from Toulouse (trip time: 4 hr.; one-way fare: 39€). For train information, call © **36-35** or 08-92-35-35-35. There is no bus service. If you're **driving** from Paris, take A10 south to Orléans, and then A71 south to Vierzon. Continue along A20 south to Limoges, and then pick up N21 south to Périgueux.

VISITOR INFORMATION The **Office du Tourisme** is at 26 place Francheville (© **05-53-53-10-63;** fax 05-53-09-02-50; www.tourisme-perigueux.fr).

Exploring the Town & Environs

You may want to rent a bike and explore the countryside; a map is available from the tourist office. Rent from **Cycles Cumenal,** 37 rte. De Bergerac (© **05-53-53-31-56**), which charges 13€ per day.

Périgueux is a treasure-trove of Gallo-Roman antiquities. The most visible is the **Tour de Vésone,** a partially ruined site that stands 26m (85 ft.) tall, just southwest of town, beyond the railway station. Here you'll see the remains of a Roman temple dedicated to the goddess Vesuna, but you can't enter the site. **Jardin des Arènes,** an amphitheater that held as many as 22,000 spectators, is another reminder of Roman days. Now in ruins, the amphitheater, with a diameter of 394m (1,293 ft.), dates from the 2nd or 3rd century. This site is open May to August daily 7:30am to 9pm, September to April daily 7:30am to 6:30pm. Admission is free. Near the arena are the remains of the **Château Barrière,** rue Turenne, built in the 11th or 12th century on Roman foundations.

Year-round, Périgueux's tourist office conducts organized walking tours of the city. These tours, each lasting 1½ to 2 hours, are a worthwhile means of exploring the historical and architectural nuances of Périgueux. The cost is 5€ for adults, 3.80€ for students, and free for children 11 and under. Between mid-September and mid-June, tours run Monday to Saturday at 2:30pm, alternating every day between tours focusing on Gallo-Roman Périgueux and tours focusing on medieval Périgueux. But during high season, from mid-June to mid-September, tours are given every Monday to Saturday at 10:30am (Gallo-Roman tours) and at 3pm (medieval tours). Also during that period, a Sunday tour is conducted, but only at 3pm, covering whatever venues are most demanded by the participants. The tourist office also arranges a limited number of bike tours of the city and its environs. Priced at 5€ per person, adult or child, and lasting 1½ to 2 hours, they are scheduled June through August on Tuesdays at 10am.

The Dordogne & Périgord

Gastronomy reigns supreme in Périgueux, especially when it comes to smooth, melt-in-your-mouth foie gras. Stores that sell this delicacy abound. The best is **La Maison Léon,** 9 place de la Clautre (© **05-53-53-29-96**). Fresh foie gras, either in its natural state or in terrines and pâtés, is a specialty of Périgueux. Many of the vendors, including Maison Léon, are in the neighborhood around place St-Louis. If you want an adventure, head for a goose farm that makes its own foie gras, such as **A la Ferme de Puy Gauthier,** about 15 minutes south of town in Marsaneix (© **05-53-08-87-07**). To get there, follow signs to Brive.

🎁 BIKING THROUGH THE DORDOGNE

The Dordogne's rivers meander through countryside that's among the most verdant and historic in France. This area is underpopulated but dotted with monuments, châteaux, 12th-century villages, and charming churches.

As you bike around, the rural character of the area unfolds before you. Unlike in other regions of France, no château, hotel, or inn treats you disdainfully if you show up on two rather than four wheels. (*Au contraire,* the staff will probably offer advice on suitable bike routes.) If you're ever in doubt about where your handlebars should lead you, know that you'll rarely go wrong if your route parallels the riverbanks of the Lot, the Vézère, the Dordogne, or any of their tributaries. Architects and builders since the 11th century have added greatly to the visual allure of their watersides.

The SNCF makes it easy to transport a bike on the nation's railways. However, if you don't want to bring your own wheels on the train, there are plenty of rental shops throughout the region. (We recommend rentals in this chapter's sections on Périgueux and Les Eyzies-de-Tayac.)

Le Comité Départemental du Tourism, 25 rue du Président Wilson, Périgueux 24000 (✆ **05-53-35-50-24;** fax 05-53-09-51-41; www.dordogne-perigord-tourisme.fr), provides information about all the towns in the *département* and will help you organize bike, hiking, kayaking, and canoeing trips. Two of the best outdoors outfitters are **Canoë Loisir,** Residence Vigneras 24200 (✆ **05-53-31-22-92**), and **Canoë Dordogne,** Le Bourg, La Roque Gageac 24250 (✆ **05-53-04-24-08**).

Those who enjoy outdoor marketplaces should head for the **market** between place du Codert and place de la Clautre on Wednesdays and Saturdays from 8am to around 1pm. Other markets, especially those focusing on new and used clothing, housewares, and secondhand furniture, are on Wednesday 8am to around 5pm in Esplanade du Théâtre.

Cathédrale St-Front ★ In Le Puy St-Front (the medieval quarter) rises this cathedral, the last of the Aquitanian-domed churches and one of the largest in southwestern France. Built from 1125 to 1150, it was dedicated to a local bishop. The cathedral's bell tower rises nearly 60m (195 ft.), overlooking the marketplace. With its five white domes and colonnaded turrets, St-Front evokes Constantinople. The interior is built on the plan of a Greek cross, unusual for a French cathedral. Only qualified students of art history or architecture, with special permission, are admitted to the crypt and cloisters, which date from the 9th century.

Place de la Clautre. ✆ **05-53-53-23-62.** Free admission. Daily 9am–7pm (closes at dusk in winter).

Eglise St-Etienne-de-la-Cité ★ Périgueux's other remarkable church—this one in the Cité area—was a cathedral until 1669, when it lost its position to St-Front. The church was built in the 12th century but has been much damaged since. It contains a 12th-century bishop's tomb and a carved 17th-century wooden reredos depicting the Assumption of the Madonna.

10 av. Cavaignac. ✆ **05-53-06-48-10.** Free admission. Daily 8am–6pm.

Musée du Périgord ★   Built on the site of an Augustinian monastery, this museum has an exceptional collection of prehistoric relics, sculptures, and medieval and Renaissance treasures. Many of the artifacts were recovered from digs in the Périgord region, which is rich in prehistoric remains.

22 cours Tourny. ℂ **05-53-06-40-70.** Admission 4€ adults, 2€ students, free for children 17 and under. Apr–Sept Mon and Wed–Fri 10am–5pm, Sat–Sun 1–6pm; Oct–Mar Mon and Wed–Fri 10am–5pm, Sat–Sun 1–6pm.

Musée Gallo-Romain Vesunna   One of the most talked-about museums in central France opened in July 2003 within a mostly glass shell that was designed by the well-known architect Jean Nouvel. A short walk from the center of Périgueux, it's positioned directly above excavations, which revealed an extensive, albeit ruined, ancient Roman villa, replete with mosaics and many of the workaday artifacts of everyday life in the ancient Roman provinces. Visitors are intrigued by the juxtaposition of the hypermodern shell and the ancient artifacts within.

Rue du 26e Régiment d'Infanterie. ℂ **05-53-53-00-92**. Admission 5.50€ adults, 3.50€ students and children ages 6–25, free for children 5 and under. Oct–Mar Tues–Fri 9:30am–12:30pm and 1:30–5pm, Sat–Sun 10am–12:30pm and 2:30–6pm; Apr–June and Sept Tues–Fri 9:30am–5:30pm, Sat–Sun 10am–12:30pm and 2:30–6pm; July–Aug daily 10am–7pm. Closed 2nd and 3rd week of Jan.

Where to Stay

The **Château des Reynats** (see "Where to Dine," below) also has rooms.

Hôtel Bristol   This modern hotel, the best in the town center, is centrally located and offers recently renovated comfortable rooms, often with sleek styling. It's your best bet in a town with a limited, lackluster selection. Bathrooms are a bit small but come with a combination tub/shower. Breakfast is the only meal served, but it's only a 5-minute walk to the town's best restaurants and major points of interest.

37-39 rue Antoine Gadaud, Périgueux 24000. ℂ **05-53-08-75-90.** Fax 05-53-07-00-49. www.bristol france.com. 29 units. 69€–76€ double; 82€ triple. AE, MC, V. Free parking. Closed Dec 23–Jan 10. **Amenities:** Room service. *In room:* A/C, TV, hair dryer, minibar, Wi-Fi (free).

Where to Dine

Château des Reynats ★★ MODERN FRENCH   This slate-roofed 19th-century manor has a yellow and soft-red Empire dining room in which you can enjoy the finest *cuisine du marché* in the entire region. Someone on the staff may relay stories of the role the château played during France's disastrous exit from its former department of Algeria, when it functioned as a kind of refugee center for French citizens booted off their estates. Menu items are likely to include salmon with caviar, foie gras with mango tartar, and a well-prepared version of scallops with velvety chestnuts.

The château also rents 37 beautiful rooms. Thirteen of the rooms lie in the château, the rest in l'Orangerie, a guesthouse of comfort but less grand, of course, than the château. Rooms in the château range from 125€ to 190€ in a double, 230€ to 260€ in a suite, whereas doubles in the guesthouse go for 85€ to 96€.

15 av. des Reynas, Chancelode 24650. ℂ **05-53-03-53-59.** Fax 05-53-03-44-84. www.chateau-hotel-perigord.com. Reservations recommended. Main courses 29€–40€; fixed-price menus 28€–75€. AE, MC, V. Tues–Fri 12:30–1:30pm; Mon–Sat 7:30–9pm. Closed (restaurant) 3 first weeks of Jan.

Perigueux After Dark

If the weather is clement, begin your evening with a stroll in the streets and alleyways surrounding the **place St-Silain, place St-Louis,** and **place du Marché.**

Each of those three points within the town's historic core boasts high concentrations of bars, restaurants, and nocturnal diversions. One of the town's best and most frequented wine bars is **Le Cercle,** 3 rue Eguillèrie (*C* **05-53-53-34-79**). Their selection of cheese and fresh oysters is worth the trip, and their cellar contains many excellent vintages. A roughly equivalent place to drink and socialize, in this case within a deep underground cellar whose masonry vaults evoke medieval Périgueux, is **LuBu,** 3 rue des Jacobins (*C* **05-53-09-29-02**).

For the disco-crazed and high-energy crowd, the historic core's leading disco is **La Reg,** 16 rue Chancelier de l'Hôpital (*C* **05-53-53-10-55**). It's open only Thursday to Sunday nights from 11pm till dawn, with a cover charge of 5€. For bright lights, drinks, dialogue, and endless cups of coffee, consider the **Café Le St-Louis,** place St-Louis (*C* **05-53-53-53-90**); or the somewhat more media-hip and gastronomy-conscious **Garden Ice Café,** 7, allee de L'Empereur (*C* **05-63-63-06-21**).

LASCAUX (MONTIGNAC) ★

496km (308 miles) SW of Paris; 47km (29 miles) SE of Périgueux

The **Caves at Lascaux,** 2km (1¼ miles) from the Vézère River town of Montignac in the Dordogne region, contain the most beautiful and most famous cave paintings in the world. Unfortunately, you can't view the actual paintings (the caves have been closed to the public to prevent deterioration), but a replica gives you a clear picture of the remarkable works.

Four boys looking for a dog discovered the caves in 1940, which opened to the public in 1948, quickly becoming one of France's major attractions and drawing 125,000 visitors annually. However, the hordes of tourists caused atmospheric changes in the caves, endangering the paintings. Scientists went to work to halt the deterioration, known as "the green sickness."

Essentials

GETTING THERE The easiest way to reach Montignac is to **drive** northeast from Les Eyzies on D706 for 19km (12 miles).

Rail service is to the neighboring hamlet of Condat-Le-Lardin, 9.5km (6 miles) northeast. From there, taxis (*C* **05-53-51-80-46**) take visitors to Montignac for 20€. If no taxis are waiting, a railway station employee will call one for you. There's infrequent **bus** service from Sarlat, near Les Eyzies, but no bus connections from Condat to Montignac. For train information, call *C* **36-35.**

VISITOR INFORMATION The **Office de Tourisme** in Montignac is on place Bertrand-de-Born (*C* **05-53-51-82-60;** fax 05-53-50-49-72; www.bienvenue-montignac.com).

Exploring the Caves & Other Attractions

Public visits to Lascaux I ceased in 1963. Permission to visit for research purposes is given only to qualified archaeologists. Apply to **Direction Régionale des Affaires Culturelles (DRAC),** Service Régional de l'Archéologie, 54 rue Magendie, 33074 Bordeaux (*C* **05-57-95-02-02**). Scholars such as art historians of a less rigidly scientific bent should address a different bureaucracy within Périgueux: Semitour, 221 bis rte. d'Angoulême, B.P. 24001, Périgueux (*C* **05-53-05-65-65**). If you want to contact the staff at the cave, call ☎ **05-53-51-95-03.** For tickets, call ☎ **05-53-51-96-23.** *Be forewarned:* It's not easy to get around the protocol regarding visits to the interior.

Lascaux II   A short walk downhill from the real caves is Lascaux II, an impressive reproduction of the originals, duplicated in concrete and molded aboveground. The 39m-long (128-ft.) reproduction displays some 200 paintings so that you'll at least have some idea of what the "Sistine Chapel of Prehistory" looks like. You can see majestic bulls, wild boars, stags, "Chinese horses," and lifelike deer, the originals of which were painted by Stone Age hunters 15,000 to 20,000 years ago. Try to show up as close to opening time as possible—the number of visitors per day is limited to 2,000, and tickets usually sell out by 2pm. During the winter, you can buy tickets directly at Lascaux II, but from April to October, you must purchase them from a kiosk adjacent to the Montignac tourist office, place Bertran-de-Born. For information, call the number below.

2km (1¼ miles) from Montignac, off D706. ☎ **05-53-51-95-03.** Admission 8.80€ adults, 6€ children 6–12, free for children 5 and under. Mar, Oct–Nov 14 daily 10–11:45am and 2–4:45pm; Apr–June 30 and Sept daily 10am–noon and 2–5:30pm; July–Aug daily 9am–7:30pm. Closed Nov 15–Feb.

Le Thot ☺   This attraction includes a zoo with live animals, two projection rooms showing short films on the discovery of cave art at Lascaux, and exhibitions relating to prehistoric communities in the Dordogne. After your visit to Le Thot, walk out on the terrace for a view of the Vézère Valley and the Lascaux hills.

Thonac, 7km (4⅓ miles) southwest of Montignac along D706 (follow the signs pointing to the hamlet of Les Eyzies). ☎ **05-53-50-70-44.** Admission 5.80€ adults, 3.80€ children 6–12, free for children 5 and under. Combination ticket to Le Thot and Lascaux II 12€ adults, 7.80€ children 6–12, free for children 5 and under. July–Aug daily 10am–7pm; Sept 3–30 daily 10am–6pm; Oct 2–Nov 15 daily 10am–12:30pm and 2–6pm; Feb 6 to late Mar Tues–Sun 10am–12:30pm and 2–5:30pm; Apr–June daily 10am–6pm. Closed Nov 15–Feb 5.

Site Préhistorique de Regourdou ☺   About 450m (1,480 ft.) uphill from Lascaux I, a minor road branches off and runs through a forest until it reaches this site, discovered in 1954 and believed to be a center for a prehistoric bear cult. Found at the site were the sepulcher and skeleton of a Neanderthal man, surrounded by the sepulcher and skeletons of several bears. Also on the site is an archaeological museum, and about 20 semiwild bears that roam around a naturalized habitat that's barricaded against humans. The only way to experience this site (including the museum) is on a guided tour, conducted in both French and English. Tours depart at frequent intervals.

☎ **05-53-51-81-23.** Admission 5€ adults, 3€ children 6–12, free for children 5 and under. July–Aug daily 10am–7pm; Sept–Nov and Feb–June daily 11am–6pm. Closed Dec–Jan.

Where to Stay & Dine

Hostellerie la Roseraie ★ 🍴   In the heart of the medieval village, this little charmer is both affordable and cozy. It was converted from a comfortable home built for one of the town merchants in the 19th century on the banks of the Vézère. The midsize bedrooms have individual character and well-kept bathrooms with either a tub or shower. Adding to the charm is a rose garden in back. There is a pleasant terrace to enjoy in the summer months and the restaurant is one of the better choices in town, serving a traditional French menu. Nonresidents can also dine here, where menus cost from 28€ to 49€.

11 place d'Armes, Montignac 24290. ✆ **05-53-50-53-92.** Fax 05-53-51-02-23. www.laroseraie-hotel. com. 14 units. 80€–150€ double; 174€–204€ family room. Rates include breakfast. AE, DC, MC, V. Parking 8€. **Amenities:** Restaurant; bar; Internet; outdoor pool; terrace. *In room:* TV, hair dryer, Wi-Fi (in most; 3€ per 2 hr.).

Hôtel Le Relais du Soleil d'Or ★   In the heart of Montignac, this place functioned as a postal relay station during the 1800s, providing food and lodging to travelers. Today, it offers traditionally furnished rooms and a landscaped garden. The larger, better-decorated accommodations with more contemporary tub/shower bathrooms lie in a modern annex built in the 1980s, a short walk from the original building. Units in the hotel's core are very comfortable, albeit a bit less stylish; each has a compact shower-only bathroom. The main restaurant serves traditional Dordogne fare such as stewed snails with garlic and *magret* of duckling prepared with three different flavorings: cèpes (flap mushrooms), morels, and truffles. Dessert may be a slice of walnut cake with vanilla-walnut sauce. The less formal Le Bistrot offers salads, snacks, and simple platters. Set dinners in the main restaurant range from 28€ to 56€. In July and August half board is compulsory, costing 156€ to 240€ (for two persons).

16 rue du 4-Septembre, Montignac Lascaux 24290. ✆ **05-53-51-80-22.** Fax 05-53-50-27-54. www. le-soleil-dor.com. 32 units. 74€–154€ double. AE, DC, MC, V. Closed Feb. **Amenities:** 2 restaurants; bar; Internet; outdoor pool; room service; Wi-Fi (free). *In room:* TV, hair dryer, minibar.

LES EYZIES-DE-TAYAC ★★

533km (331 miles) SW of Paris; 45km (28 miles) SE of Périgueux

When prehistoric skeletons were unearthed here in 1868, the market town of Les Eyzies-de-Tayac (known as Les Eyzies) suddenly became an archaeologist's dream. This area in the Dordogne Valley was found to be one of the richest in the world in ancient sites and deposits. Some of the caves contain primitive drawings made 30,000 years ago. The most beautiful and most famous are at Lascaux (see above), but many caves around Les Eyzies are open to the public.

Essentials

GETTING THERE   Local **trains** run from Le Buisson, 19km (12 miles) away. The several daily trains from Périgueux are more direct. For information, call ✆ **36-35.** To **drive** from Périgueux, start along D710 southeast to Le Bugue, and then follow the rural road east for a short distance. Look out for the road sign pointing to Les Eyzies-de-Tayac.

VISITOR INFORMATION   The **Office de Tourisme** (✆ **05-53-06-97-05;** fax 05-53-06-90-79; www.tourisme-terredecromagnon.com) is open year-round at 19 rue de la Préhistoire (place de la Mairie).

Exploring the Area

Many of the caves in this area limit the number of daily visitors they admit; you can call ahead for reservations up to a year in advance. We recommend that you do so, especially if you plan to visit in the summer.

If you want to pedal around the countryside, you can rent bicycles at the tourist office. Prices begin at 8€ per half-day, 14€ per full day. A 20€ deposit is required; no credit cards are accepted.

Whether you're biking or driving, the loveliest villages include Beynac-et-Cazenac, 15km (9⅓ miles) southeast of Les Eyzies, and Sarlat-la-Canéda, 7km (4⅓ miles) northeast of Beynac. Smaller villages, including Castelnaud, La Roque-Gageac, Domme, and Montfort, lie beside the road that meanders through the Dordogne Valley. Throughout the region, routes are country roads marked only with signs leading to the above-mentioned destinations.

Make a special effort to relax within the shadow of the foreboding **Château de Beynac,** Beynac 24220 (✆ **05-53-29-50-40**), a 13th-century curiosity that opened its doors to visitors in 1961. The Grosso family has been renovating the monument for almost 40 years. Once it was the gathering place for the aristocracy of Périgord; today, the view over the valley and sense of history make a visit here worthwhile. It's open April through September daily 10am to 6:30pm, and October to March daily 11am to sundown. One-hour guided tours (in French and English) begin once or twice an hour. There are no guided tours from December to February. Admission, with or without the tour, costs 7€, or 3€ ages 5 to 11. There's a worthy restaurant in the nearby **Hôtel Bonnet** (✆ **05-53-29-50-01**), which occupies the site of a converted forge and blacksmith's shop in the center of Beynac.

Grotte de Font-de-Gaume ★ This is one of the few authentic caves still open to visitors, though access is limited in summer. Some of the markings you see aren't from the Magdalenian (Stone) ages but from British students on a holiday in the 18th century. Here depictions of bison, reindeer, horses, and other animals reveal the skill of the prehistoric artists.

Note: Only 140 visitors per day are permitted in the caves. In midsummer, demand far exceeds the supply of tickets, so call and reserve far in advance if you're coming between April and September.

On D47, 1.5km (1 mile) outside Les Eyzies. ✆ **05-53-06-86-00.** Admission 7€ adults, free for ages 25 and under. May 15–Sept 15 Sun–Fri 9:30am–5:30pm; Sept 16–May 14 Sun–Fri 9:30am–12:30pm and 2–5:30pm.

Grotte des Combarelles Discovered at the turn of the 20th century, the Grotte des Combarelles, on the southeast edge of town, has many drawings of animals, including musk oxen, horses, bison, and aurochs (wild oxen). Think of it as a gallery of Magdalenian art. Advance reservations are vital—only 60 visitors per day are admitted.

On D47, 17km (11 miles) north of Bergerac. ✆ **05-53-06-86-00.** Admission 7€ adults, free for ages 25 and under. May 15–Sept 15 Sun–Fri 9:30am–5:30pm; Sept 16–May 14 Sun–Fri 9:30am–12:30pm and 2–5:30pm.

Grotte du Grand-Roc (Cave of the Big Rock) ★★ Geologically, this is the most fascinating cave. Upon entering, you'll come on a tunnel of stalagmites and stalactites. The cave is about 1.5km (1 mile) northwest of Les Eyzies on the left bank of the Vézère (signs point the way on D47). There are no limits to visitors at this venue.

48 av. Préhistoirie, Les Eyzies 24620. ✆ **05-53-06-92-70.** Admission 7.50€ adults, 3.50€ children 6–12, free for children 5 and under. July–Aug daily 9:30am–7pm; Sept to mid-Nov and Easter to June Sun–Fri 10am–6pm. Closed mid-Nov to Easter.

Musée National de la Préhistoire ★★★ On a cliff above the village, this $30-million museum became the major cultural event of the French world when it opened in the summer of 2004. Designed by Florentine architect Jean-Pierre Buffi, this strikingly modern building stands next to a fortress-castle from the 16th century.

To prevent deterioration of the art, a limited number of visitors are allowed into the caves of **Les Eyzies-de-Tayac** each day (specifically Font-de-Gaume and Combarelles). Tickets are available up to 3 months in advance, and we advise you to reserve that far ahead if possible.

This museum is hailed for its treasure-trove of Ice Age artifacts, one of the two or three greatest collections in the world. Only 18,000 objects of the five million artifacts owned by the museum are displayed at any given time. Highlights of the collection include a small **15,000-year-old bison** ★ carved in bone, its head licking its flank. Its collection of **30,000-year-old stone engravings** ★★ are among the world's most ancient objects of art. The statue of the 3.2-million-year-old "Lucy" is a fake resin composition skeleton of a 3-year-old child (aged 50,000 years), but fascinating nonetheless. Also on display are the first replicas of the first-known human footprints, dating from around 3.6 million years ago.

1 rue de Musée ℂ **05-53-06-45-65.** Admission 5€ adults, 3.50€ students and ages 18–25, free for children 25 and under. July–Aug daily 9:30am–6:30pm; June and Sept Wed–Mon 9:30am–6pm; Oct–May Wed–Mon 9:30am–12:30pm and 2–5:30pm.

Where to Stay & Dine

Hostellerie du Passeur 🍴 This is the best bet for the frugal traveler—a well-maintained hotel containing simple, cozy rooms, each with a small but tidy bathroom with shower. The family-run restaurant serves well-crafted cuisine. The fixed-price menus, costing 30€ to 47€, are some of the best in town and contain such dishes as roasted rabbit with liquefied truffles and cèpes; roasted beefsteak with wild mushrooms; and scallops also served with flap mushrooms. Dessert may be frozen walnut soufflé. During good weather, you can dine on a shaded terrace.

Place de la Mairie, Les Eyzies-de-Tayac 24620. ℂ **05-53-06-97-13.** Fax 05-53-06-91-63. www.hostellerie-du-passeur.com. 19 units. 89€–120€ double; 170€ suite. AE, DC, MC, V. Closed early Nov to early Apr. **Amenities:** Restaurant; bar; room service. *In room:* A/C, TV, hair dryer.

Hôtel Cro-Magnon 🍴 This is the second-best hotel in town after Le Centenaire and is exceedingly comfortable, with affordable prices. The hotel may be named for a primitive man, but there's nothing rustic about the ambience and the tasteful accommodations provided. Rooms are midsize to spacious, and well furnished, with modern bathrooms with tub and shower. The breakfast buffet is quite generous.

54 av. de la Préhistoire, Les Eyzies-de-Tayac 24620. ℂ **05-53-06-97-06.** Fax 05-53-06-95-45. 15 units. 80€–90€ double. AE, MC, V. Free parking. Closed Oct to early Mar. **Amenities:** Restaurant; bar; outdoor pool; room service. *In room:* TV, hair dryer, minibar, Wi-Fi (in some; free).

Hôtel Le Centenaire ★★★ Nothing in this area equals the charms of this oasis, which is even better known for its cuisine than for its accommodations. A Relais & Châteaux member, it has undergone extensive renovations. The good-size, comfortable rooms are conservatively modern; bathrooms have tub/shower combinations and tiled surfaces. The chef, Roland Mazère, creates light, modern French cuisine, the finest of any restaurant mentioned in this chapter. Even if you're not a guest, consider a visit to the hotel's restaurant, where fixed-price menus cost 88€, 108€, and 140€. Specialties include gooseliver pâté and goose confit terrine—both equally divine—spider crab-and-apricot cake with scampi fritters, and a Périgord black-truffle risotto.

Rocher de la Penne, Les Eyzies-Tayac-Sireuil 24620. ✆ **05-53-06-68-68.** Fax 05-53-06-92-41. www. hotelducentenaire.fr. 24 units. 110€–180€ double; 180€–210€ suite. AE, DC, MC, V. Closed Nov–Mar. **Amenities:** Restaurant; bar; exercise room; heated outdoor pool; room service. *In room:* TV, hair dryer, minibar, Wi-Fi (free).

Hôtel Les Glycines ★ 🎁 We'd stay here just for the flower garden. Since 1862, this establishment has offered regional cuisine, comfortable accommodations, and charming touches such as drinks on a veranda with a grape arbor. Rooms are quaint with a regional charm and touches of designer style. Each is midsize to spacious; most of the compact bathrooms have a combination tub/shower. Restaurant specialties include foie gras, cèpes, and truffles; veal roasted with cured ham and truffled polenta; *confit de canard* with truffle juice; and roasted lobster with truffle risotto. Fixed-price menus range from 39€ to 95€.

Rte. de Périgueux (D47), Les Eyzies-Tayac-Sireuil 24620. ✆ **05-53-06-97-07.** Fax 05-53-06-92-19. www.les-glycines-dordogne.com. 23 units. 92€–162€ double; 186€–232€ junior suite. AE, DC, MC, V. Closed Nov to late Mar. **Amenities:** Restaurant; bar; babysitting; outdoor pool; room service. *In room:* A/C, TV, hair dryer, Wi-Fi (free).

SARLAT-LA-CANEDA ★★

9.5km (6 miles) E of Les Eyzies-de-Tayac; 530km (310 miles) SW of Paris; 60km (37 miles) NW of Cahors

The capital of Perigord Noir (Black Perigord), Sarlat is the best-preserved medieval town in southwestern France, actually a living museum. Its inner core is filled with so many ancient buildings that it's like stepping back into another age as you wander past stone structures of ocher color along cobblestone streets.

Sarlat goes back to Gallo-Roman times with a charter dating from 1298. At the time of Charlemagne, it was an ecclesiastical center. The zenith of its fame came in the 14th century, when it was known as a bustling center of artisans, painters, and students. Old Sarlat, called **Vieille Ville ★★★**, the main reason to visit, is split by the 18th-century main street, **rue de la République,** which is the commercial heart of town, the center of shops and restaurants.

With more medieval buildings than in any town in France, Sarlat is often a movie backdrop. Robert Hossein's *Les Misérables* was shot here in 1982, as was Danny Huston's *Becoming Colette* in 1991. In 2000 Johnny Depp took to the streets to film the internationally popular *Chocolat.*

Essentials

GETTING THERE Sarlat has good rail links with Bordeaux (trip time: 2½ hr.). If you travel here from Paris, you will most often have to change **trains** in Bordeaux. For train information and schedules, call ✆ **36-35.** The terminus in Sarlat lies 1km (½ mile) south of the old town. You can walk it in 15 minutes or else take a taxi.

Voyage Belmons (✆ **05-65-37-81-15**) also runs **buses** from the train station at Soulliac, a stop on the Paris-Toulouse line. Motorists **drive** the A10 autoroute from Paris, going by way of Poitiers, Angoulême, and Périgueux to reach Sarlat. Or else you can take the A89 from Bordeaux. Sarlat lies 180km (117 miles) east of Bordeaux.

VISITOR INFORMATION The Office de Tourisme, 3 rue Tourny (✆ **05-53-31-45-45;** www.ot-sarlat-perigord.fr), sells maps of the area and offers English-language tours from April to September.

SPECIAL EVENTS We like to visit Sarlat in July and August when the streets are bustling with people, many here to attend the **Féstival des Jeux de Théâtre de Sarlat** (✆ **05-53-31-10-83;** www.festival-theatre-sarlat.com). During the month of August and into the first week of September, Sarlat also hosts the **Féstival de Musique du Périgord Noir** (✆ **05-53-51-61-61**). The November film festival, **Le Féstival de Film de Sarlat** (✆ **05-53-29-18-13;** www.ville-sarlat.fr/festival) is the biggest such event in France after Cannes and Deauville.

Exploring the Town

Start your tour of Old Sarlat at **Place du Peyrou** ★, and allow at least 2 hours to wander around. Opening onto Place du Peyrou is the **cathedral,** which enjoyed its greatest prestige when it was an Episcopal seat between 1317 and 1790. The cathedral has a Romanesque bell tower, but most of the structure dates from the 16th and 17th centuries. Much of the interior is in the late Gothic style. The structure stands to the right of the tourist office (see above). Leave by the south doorway.

Behind the cathedral is the **Lanterne des Morts,** or "Lantern to the Dead" ★★, which was reputedly built in the 1100s to honor St. Bernard's pilgrimage to Sarlat. This is one of the finest examples of early medieval sepulchral architecture. Today it's visited mainly for its panoramic views.

Also opening on the Place du Peyrou, **Maison de la Boétie** ★ stands opposite the cathedral. You can admire its facade, as it's the most charming Renaissance house in Sarlat. Dating from 1525, the house has mullioned windows and a painted gable. It was once inhabited by the town's most famous son, Etienne de la Boétie, who was born about the time the house was completed. A criminal magistrate, he had a lifelong friendship with Montaigne, who was at La Boétie's bedside when he died in 1563. That death inspired Montaigne's famous essay "Friendship."

The second square to visit is **Place aux Oies** ★, known for its bronze statue of three geese by Lalanne. For centuries, this market sold live fowl, and the statue commemorates that long-ago role. The most stunning Renaissance facade on this square belongs to the Hotel Chassaing.

Our candidate for Sarlat's most colorful medieval street is **rue des Consuls** ★★, whose greatest buildings include the **Hôtel Plamon,** its Gothic windows making it look like a church. Beyond the doorway of Plamon is a series of five arcades on the ground floor opening onto a covered market. A trio of Gothic bay windows on the second floor has been restored to its original appearance.

If you follow the **Jardin des Enfeus** (behind the cathedral), you reach **Rue Montaigne** ★ where the great 16th-century philosopher was born and once lived. The buildings along this street are extremely photogenic.

Feel free to roam the back streets of Sarlat. You can allow yourself to get lost, as you'll invariably wind up back at the **place de la Liberté** in the center of town and the 18th-century Hotel de Ville, or city hall.

Sarlat is celebrated by French gastronomes for its foie gras and truffle market, **Le Marché aux Truffles et au Gras,** held in the place Boissarie every Saturday from 9am to noon December to February. Sarlat is also known for its wines, and the best selection is found at **Julien de Savignac,** Place Pasteur (✆ **05-53-31-29-20**).

> ## Abode of the Fabled Dame Blanche ("White Lady"), a Ghost
>
> The Dordogne is riddled with châteaux and one of our favorites, **Château de Puymartin** ★★ (📞 **05-53-59-29-97**), lies 8km (5 miles) from Sarlat, found along the curvy road between Sarlat and Les Eyzies, the D47. You can not only stay here (see below), but can visit it as a sight. The present owner, Countess de Montbron, shares her family home and will relate the story of the famous ghost, Dame Blanche, who, or so it is said, has been seen wandering the castle at night. The château is furnished with family heirlooms and has been in the Montbron family since 1450. It can be visited daily: April 8 to June and September 10am to noon and 2 to 6pm; July and August 10am to 6:30pm. In October it is also open daily but from 2:30 to 5pm. Admission is 7€ for adults, 5€ for students, and 3.50€ children 6 to 12.

Where to Stay

The most sumptuous way to live in and around Sarlat is at the **Château de Puymartin** (see above), which rents two of the most elegant guest rooms in the entire area. Surrounded by antiques, you get to live like a count (or countess) of medieval times but with all the modern comforts. The cost of a double is 135€ a night; MasterCard and Visa are accepted.

Hôtel des Récollets ★ 🍴 West of the rue de la République, you can enjoy some of Sarlat's medieval past by lodging in the old town at this time-honored hotel. It stands by the Chapelle des Récollets, dating from the 16th century. Behind an ochcr-colored stone facade, the hotel centers around the early medieval cloister of the convent, an idyllic spot for breakfast. On a summer day, a generous breakfast is served here among the flowers. Rooms are old-fashioned with exposed stone walls, and they are simply but comfortably furnished.

4 rue J. J. Rousseau, Sarlat 24200. 📞 **05-53-31-36-00.** Fax 05-53-30-32-62. www.hotel-recollets-sarlat. com. 18 units. 43€–63€ double; 69€ triple; 79€ quad. MC, V. Free private parking. *In room:* A/C, TV, fridge, Wi-Fi (free).

Hôtel Restaurant La Couleuvrine ★ Its sense of medieval history surpasses that of virtually every other hotel within the region. Capped with crenellations and museum-quality statues of the Virgin, it occupies the solid, once-fortified premises of what functioned as part of Sarlat's barricades during the 12th and 13th centuries. Bedrooms are cozy and in some cases rather small, with exposed stone and timbers. Philippe and Isabelle Lebon-Henault, the articulate and congenial owners, maintain an on-site boutique loaded with the best of the region's gastronomic bounty, and both of the restaurants here are reviewed below. The hotel's name, incidentally, derives from the long cannon (*les couleuvrines*) that used to be fired at attackers from the hotel's crenellations. The restaurant is closed Friday and Sunday.

1 place de La Bouquerie, Sarlat 24200. 📞 **05-53-59-27-80.** Fax 05-53-31-26-83. www.la-couleuvrine. com. 27 units. 59€–72€ double; 85€–105€ suite. AE, DC, MC, V. **Amenities:** 2 restaurants; bar, Wi-Fi (free). *In room:* TV.

La Madeleine It isn't as old as the also-recommended Hotel La Couleuvrine (see above), but with a pedigree more than 200 years old (it was originally built as an inn) and a three-star rating from local tourist authorities, it's a comfortable and well-managed place to stay. It's well positioned at the northern entrance to medieval Sarlat, and some locals refer to it as the grande dame of the town's hotels. The owners devote lots of time and attention to meals served within the dining room (reviewed below). Bedrooms are high ceilinged and large, with conservative, traditional furniture and good taste, and a history of housing French film stars during Sarlat's annual film festival.

1 place de la Petite-Rigaudie, Sarlat-la-Canéda 24200. ✆ **05-53-59-10-41.** Fax 05-53-31-03-62. www.hoteldelamadeleine-sarlat.com. 39 rooms. 73€–108€ per person. AE, DC, MC, V. Parking 10€. Closed mid-Nov to Feb. **Amenities:** Restaurant; bar. *In room:* TV, Wi-Fi (free).

La Maison des Peyrat ★ 👜 Away from the crowds that flock to Sarlat in summer, this is the most tranquil retreat in the area, lying only 1.6km (1 mile) from the center. The oldest section of this one-story stone structure dates from 1343 when it was a hospital for victims of the Black Death. Those unhappy memories are long gone now. In 1843 a local baron turned it into a hunting lodge. Today as a small hotel, it preserves much of its original character with simply furnished bedrooms in pastel and rattan furnishings. Exposed beams and original artwork add to the character. On a terrace shaded by chestnut trees, breakfast and dinner are served.

Le Lac de la Plane, Sarlat 24200. ✆ **05-53-59-00-32.** http://maisondespeyrat.com. 10 units. 55€–100€ per person. MC, V. Closed Nov 15–Apr 1. **Amenities:** Restaurant; outdoor pool; Wi-Fi (free). *In room:* TV, hair dryer.

Le Mas de Castel ★ 👜 Francine Charpenet Mottet has transformed the family farm into a tranquil retreat for guests who'd like to enjoy the countryside 3km (1¼ miles) south of the historic core of Sarlat. Standing on a hillside, the hotel lies in a residential area. Its old-world charm was retained as it was turned into a country inn that has many niceties, except a restaurant. Some of the rooms have outdoor tables for a picnic. The standard rooms are decorated in a provincial fashion and are most comfortable; if you pay slightly more you can get a "superior room," which is a bit larger with a terrace. All guests enjoy the garden and pool; next to the pool is a *borie*, a cone-roofed structure built without mortar. These flat stone huts existed in the south of France in ancient times.

Le Sudalissant, Sarlat 24200. ✆ **05-53-59-02-59.** Fax 05-53-28-25-62. 14 units. 48€–74€ double; 68€–96€ family room for 4. MC, V. Closed mid-Nov to Apr 3. **Amenities:** Outdoor pool. *In room:* TV, Wi-Fi (in most; free).

Where to Dine

La Madeleine FRENCH This is the well-managed dining room of one of Sarlat's most respected hotels (see above), a 200-year-old inn positioned at the northern periphery of the medieval core. The chef prepares flavorful and generous portions of dishes such as scallops of foie gras with raspberry sauce; omelets with truffles; and a *civet* (stew flavored with red wine) of goose. Caramelized apple tart with ice cream makes a worthwhile dessert.

1 place de la Petite-Rigaudie. ✆ **05-53-59-10-41.** Reservations recommended on weekends. Main courses 25€–42€. AE, DC, MC, V. Wed–Sun noon–1:30pm; daily 7–9:30pm. Closed mid-Nov to Feb.

Le Présidial DORDOGNE/FRENCH Its setting is a showstopper: a bulky Renaissance-era courthouse erected by that most promiscuous of French kings, Henri II, in

1558. Within an appropriately baronial dining room, or within a flowering garden, you'll select meals concocted from ingredients linked to the region, with ample use of foie gras, duckling, and truffles. Consider a pasta studded with sweetbreads and kidneys; roasted rack of spring lamb with mountain herbs; salmon in champagne sauce; medallions of veal in basil-flavored cream sauce; and some of the most succulent *mille-feuille* pastries in this part of France. Be warned that some diners have found the service lacking and the staff undertrained.

6 rue Landry. ✆ **05-53-28-92-47.** Reservations recommended. Set menus 35€–60€. AE, MC, V. Tues–Sat noon–1:30pm; Mon–Sat 7:30–10pm. Closed mid-Nov to Mar.

Le Quatre Saisons FRENCH   Only in a town as rich in medieval monuments as Sarlat could a well-recommended restaurant be tucked into a 14th-century stone tower whose origins and history aren't particularly well known. But that's exactly the case with this stone-and-masonry charmer run by the Delpech family, with Evelyne managing the dining room, and father-son team of Jean-Paul and Eric tending to the ovens in back. You'll climb an exterior stairway to reach the dining room, which is rather daringly outfitted in a minimalist contemporary style in tones of gray and soft orange. A separate corkscrew-style staircase leads upstairs to a terrace with additional tables and a view over town. Menu items might include scallops with creamy small peas sauce; foie gras with caramelized apple; lamb with an herb-and-corn-flavored cream sauce; a brochette of duck strips, each stuffed with foie gras; and a dessert specialty of deliberately undercooked chocolate cake served with licorice-flavored ice cream. You'll find this place across the town's main street (rue de la République) from the cathedral, a 2-minute walk from the restaurant.

2 côte de Toulouse. ✆ **05-53-29-48-59.** Reservations recommended. Set-price menus 26€–34€. AE, DC, MC, V. Thurs–Mon 12:15–1:30pm; Thurs–Mon 7:15–8:30pm (daily July–Aug). Closed 1 week in Jan and 1 week in Mar.

Restaurant La Couleuvrine/Côté Bistrot La Couleuvrines ★ FRENCH   The more formal dining venue with this previously recommended hotel is "the Restaurant," which occupies a baronial hall with 13th-century stonework, massive ceiling beams, a fireplace big enough to roast an ox, and a distinct sense that this room used to function as the meeting place for Sarlat's town council. Menu items reflect local ingredients, and might include a platter with both green and white asparagus and splashes of truffle-studded vinaigrette; foie gras of duckling with pear chutney; and a fricassee of scallops with prune liqueur and baby vegetables. Desserts usually include a brochette of fresh fruit with a creamy Sauterne-based sabayon.

If you happen to arrive at lunch, you'll be directed to "the Bistrot," where less complicated and less expensive platters of grilled fish and meat are featured, including meal-size salads and steaks with fried potatoes and creamy peppercorn sauce.

1 place de La Bouquerie, Sarlat 24200. ✆ **05-53-59-27-80.** Reservations recommended in the restaurant. Restaurant main courses 16€–29€; set menus 19€–32€; Bistrot main courses 10€–19€. AE, DC, MC, V. Restaurant daily 7:30–9pm; Sun noon–2pm. Bistro Mon–Sat noon–2pm.

ROCAMADOUR ★★★

541km (336 miles) SW of Paris; 66km (41 miles) SE of Sarlat-la-Canéda; 55km (34 miles) S of Brive; 63km (39 miles) NE of Cahors

Rocamadour reached the zenith of its fame and prosperity in the 13th century. Make an effort to see it, even if it's out of your way. The setting is one of the most unusual in Europe: Towers, old buildings, and oratories rise in stages up the side of a cliff on the slope of the usually dry gorge of Alzou. The population has held steady at around 5,000 for many years.

The faithful continue to arrive today as they did more than 8 centuries ago. As a pilgrimage site, Rocamadour is billed as "the second site of France" (Mont-St-Michel ranks first). Summer visitors descend in droves, and vehicles are prohibited. Park in one of the big lots and make your way on foot.

Essentials

GETTING THERE   The best way to reach Rocamadour is by **car.** From Bordeaux, travel east along N89 to Brive-la-Gaillarde, connect to N205 east into Cressensac, and continue on N140 south to Rocamadour.

Rocamadour and neighboring Padirac share a **train** station, **Gare de Rocamadour-Padirac,** that isn't really convenient to either—it's 4km (2½ miles) east of Rocamadour on N140. Trains arrive infrequently from Brive in the north and Capdenac in the south. For train information and schedules, call ⓒ **08-92-35-35-35. Bus** service in and out of town is so infrequent it's almost nonexistent.

VISITOR INFORMATION   The town maintains two separate **tourist offices** in the Hôtel de Ville, rue Roland-le-Preux (ⓒ **05-65-33-62-59**), and another well-signposted branch office within l'Hospitalet, in the old town (ⓒ **05-65-33-22-00;** fax 05-65-33-22-01; www.rocamadour.com).

Exploring the Town

The **site ★★★** of this gravity-defying village rises abruptly across the landscape. Its single street, lined with souvenir shops, runs along the side of a steep hill. It's best seen when approached from the road coming in from the tiny village of L'Hospitalet. Once in Rocamadour, you can take a flight of steps or an elevator from the lower town (Basse Ville) to the town's **Cité Réligieuse,** a cluster of chapels and churches halfway up the cliff.

To help people negotiate the town's steep inclines, the town maintains two elevators. One goes from the Basse Ville to the Cité Réligieuse, midway up the rocky heights of Rocamadour. The ride costs 2€ one-way, 3€ round-trip. The other goes from the Cité Réligieuse to the panoramic medieval ramparts near the hill's summit; it costs 2.50€ one-way, 4€ round-trip.

Château de Rocamadour perches on a rock spur above the town center. You can reach it by way of the curvy "chemin de la Croix." It was built in the 14th century and restored by the local bishops in the 19th century. Its interior is off-limits, except for guests of the church officials who live and work here. You can, however, walk along its panoramic **ramparts ★★★**, which open at 8am daily year-round. Closing times vary: 11pm in July and August, 6pm October to April, and 9pm in May, June, and September. Admission to the ramparts costs 2€.

The most photogenic entrance to the Basse Ville is the **Porte du Figuier (Fig Tree Gate),** through which many of the most illustrious Europeans of the 13th century passed.

One of the oldest places of pilgrimage in France, Rocamadour became famous as a cult center of the black Madonna. Zacchaeus, who entertained Christ at Jericho, supposedly founded it. He reputedly came here with a black wooden statue of the

Virgin, although some authorities have suggested that the statue was carved in the 9th century.

Basilique St-Sauveur   Against the cliff, this basilica was built in the Romanesque-Gothic style from the 11th to the 13th century. It's decorated with paintings and inscriptions recalling visits of celebrated persons, including Philippe the Handsome. In the **Chapelle Miraculeuse,** the "holy of holies," St. Amadour is said to have carved out an oratory in the rock. Hanging from the roof is one of the oldest known clocks, dating to the 8th century. The Romanesque Chapelle St-Michel is sheltered by an overhanging rock; inside are two 12th-century frescoes. The venerated **Black Madonna** ★ occupies a chapel—**Chapelle de Notre-Dame**—devoted almost exclusively to it. It was built in the 12th century, with many 19th-century additions and alterations, and lies adjacent to the Basilique St-Saveur. Above the door leading to the Chapelle Notre-Dame is an iron sword that, according to legend, belonged to Roland.

Place St-Amadour. ✆ **05-65-33-23-23.** Free admission. Daily 9am–11pm.

Cité Réligieuse   This cluster of chapels and churches is the town's religious centerpiece, visited by both casual tourists and devoted pilgrims. Site of many conversions, with mystical connotations that date to the Middle Ages, it's accessible from the town on the **Grand Escalier,** a stairway of 216 steps. Even today, although rarely, devout pilgrims make this journey on their knees in penance. Climbing the weathered steps will lead you to the **parvis des Eglises,** place St-Amadour, with seven chapels. Schedules of tours change frequently, based on saints' holidays and local church schedules. Three to five 1-hour tours take place each day (depending on the season); times are prominently posted at the entrance.

✆ **05-65-33-23-23.** Free admission; donations appreciated. Suggested donation for tour 6€ adults, 3.50€ children 8–18.

Where to Stay & Dine

Grand Hôtel Beau-Site ★   With its entrance evoking a medieval hall, this is the town's finest inn, a place with original character. The stone walls were built in the 15th century by an Order of Malta commander, Jehan de Valon (1440–1516). Today the rear terrace provides a view of the Val d'Alzou. The reception area has heavy beams and a cavernous fireplace. Rooms (23 of which are in the air-conditioned main building, the rest in a less desirable annex) are comfortable; each has a midsize bathroom, most with a combination tub/shower.

The restaurant serves regional cuisine prepared by the Menot family, which has owned the place for generations. Specialties include foie gras of duck with dark truffles, raw marinated salmon with green peppercorns, and braised and roasted duck served with truffled mashed potatoes. Dessert may be a slice of country-style fruit pie, served with caramel and whortleberry sauce, or a cake of caramelized walnuts. Fixed-price menus cost 26€ to 56€.

Cité Médiévale, Rocamadour 46500. ✆ **800/528-1234** in the U.S. and Canada, or 05-65-33-63-08. Fax 05-65-33-65-23. www.bw-beausite.com. 38 units. 75€–108€ double. AE, DC, MC, V. Free parking. Closed mid-Nov to mid-Feb. **Amenities:** 2 restaurants; bar; Internet (free); outdoor pool; room service. *In room:* A/C, TV, hair dryer.

Where to Stay & Dine Nearby

Château de Roumégouse ★ If you prefer to be away from the tourist bustle, try this Relais & Châteaux property in Roumégouse. The 15th-century château overlooking the Causse is surrounded by 4.8 hectares (12 acres) of parkland. Each spacious room is unique in both decor and architecture, and outfitted with antique furniture and paintings. Fixed-price menus at Roumégouse range from 38€ to 55€.

N140, Rignac, Gramat 46500. © **05-65-33-63-81.** Fax 05-65-33-71-18. 15 units. 140€–250€ double; 300€–480€ suite. AE, MC, V. Closed Jan–Apr. Take N140 to Roumégouse, 6.5km (4 miles) southeast of Rocamadour. **Amenities:** Restaurant; bar; babysitting; room service. *In room:* A/C, TV, hair dryer, minibar.

Hôtel Domaine de La Rhue ★ 🎒 The charming owners, Christine and Eric Jooris, gutted a 19th-century stable and turned it into a series of spacious rooms, each individually decorated in superb taste. Some have terraces, some have mini-bars, and all are equipped with compact bathrooms, mainly with shower units. On the lower level is an inviting reception and breakfast room with a welcoming fire-place. The Joorises, who speak English, are most helpful in directing you to the best places for dinner in the center of Rocamadour, a few minutes' drive away. Christine enjoys mapping out tours of nearby villages and plotting the best direction from which to approach each town or castle to ensure a commanding view and to take advantage of afternoon sun for photographs. Eric is a pilot and takes guests for a 45-minute hot-air balloon ride over the canyon of Rocamadour.

Rocamadour 46500. © **05-65-33-71-50.** Fax 05-65-33-72-48. www.domainedelarhue.com. 14 units. 75€–135€ double. MC, V. Closed Oct 20–Apr. Follow D673, then N140 signposted RHUE for a total of 5km (3 miles) from town. **Amenities:** Outdoor pool; Wi-Fi (free). *In room:* A/C (in some), hair dryer, kitchen-ette (in some).

CAHORS ★★

541km (336 miles) SW of Paris; 217km (135 miles) SE of Bordeaux; 89km (55 miles) N of Toulouse

The ancient capital of Quercy, Cahors was a thriving university city in the Middle Ages, and many antiquities from its illustrious past remain. Today, Cahors is best known for the almost-legendary red wine that's made principally from the Malbec grapes grown in vineyards around this old city. Firm but not harsh, Cahors is one of the most deeply colored fine French wines.

Since the mid-1990s, the city of Cahors has funded the redesign and replanting of at least 21 municipal gardens, most of them laid out in medieval patterns, using historically appropriate plants. The most spectacular of these gardens lie immedi-ately adjacent to Town Hall. Overall, they function as a magnet for horticultural societies throughout France.

Essentials

GETTING THERE To **drive** to Cahors from Toulouse, follow A62 north to the junction with N20 and continue on N20 north into Cahors.

Trains serve Cahors from Toulouse, Brive, and Montauban. You may have to transfer in neighboring towns. For train information and schedules, call © **08-92-35-35-35.** There's infrequent **bus** service from some of the outlying villages, several of which are of historical interest, but it's vastly easier to drive.

VISITOR INFORMATION   The **Office de Tourisme** is on place François-Mitterrand (✆ **05-65-53-20-65;** fax 05-65-53-20-74; www.tourisme-cahors.fr).

SPECIAL EVENTS   The **Festival du Blues** turns this town upside down for 3 days in mid-July, when blues groups, including some from the United States, descend. Most of the performances are open-air affairs, many free, with bands playing at cafes along the boulevard Gambetta. Formal concerts are usually at the **Théâtre des Verdures,** an open-air courtyard in the heart of the medieval city. Tickets are 15€ to 40€. For exact dates and information, contact the Office de Tourisme (see above). For tickets, contact **Cahors Blues Festival** (✆ **05-65-20-87-83;** www.cahorsbluesfestival.com).

Exploring the Area

The town is on a rocky **peninsula** ★ almost entirely surrounded by a loop of the Lot River. It grew near a sacred spring that still supplies the city with water. At the source of the spring, the **Fontaine des Chartreux** stands by the side of the **pont Valentré** ★★ (also called the pont du Diable), a bridge with a trio of towers. It's a magnificent example of medieval defensive design erected between 1308 and 1380 and restored in the 19th century. The pont, the first medieval fortified bridge in France, is the most eye-catching site in Cahors, with crenelated parapets, battlements, and seven pointed arches.

Dominating the old town, the **Cathédrale St-Etienne** ★, 30 rue de la Chanterie (✆ **05-65-35-27-80**), was begun in 1119 and reconstructed between 1285 and 1500. It was the first cathedral in the country to have cupolas, giving it a Romanesque-Byzantine look. One remarkable feature is its sculptured Romanesque north portal, carved around 1135 in the Languedoc style. It's open daily from 9am (the scheduled hour for daily Mass) to 6 or 7pm, depending on the season. Adjoining the cathedral are the remains of a Gothic cloister from the late 15th century. The admission-free cloister is open during the same hours as the cathedral.

Where to Stay

Hôtel de France   This 1970s hotel, positioned midway between pont Valentré and the train station, provides some of the best rooms in the town center. They're well furnished and modern. Each unit comes with an average-size bathroom, most with a shower unit. The room service is efficient, but breakfast is the only meal served.

252 av. Jean-Jaurès, Cahors 46000. ✆ **05-65-35-16-76.** Fax 05-65-22-01-08. www.hoteldefrance-cahors.fr. 39 units. 67€–94€ double. AE, DC, MC, V. Parking 7€. *In room:* A/C, TV, hair dryer, minibar, Wi-Fi (free).

Hôtel Terminus ★   On the avenue leading from the railway station into the heart of town, this hotel oozes the turn-of-the-20th-century character of its original stone construction. Rooms are conservative yet tasteful, with floral prints, fresh flowers, and firm beds. Bathrooms are average size, most with a combination tub/shower. On the premises is Le Balandre, the town's best restaurant. It specializes in regional dishes from the surrounding Périgord-Quercy district. Even if you don't opt for a meal in its Art Deco dining room or on the outdoor terrace, you may want to stop into the 1920s-style bar for a drink.

5 av. Charles-de-Freycinet, Cahors 46000. © **05-65-53-32-00.** Fax 05-65-53-32-26. www.balandre. com. 21 units. 70€–100€ double; 130€–160€ suite. AE, DC, MC, V. Parking free in courtyard, 7€ in garage. Closed last 2 weeks in Nov. **Amenities:** 2 restaurants; bar; room service; Wi-Fi (free). *In room:* TV, hair dryer, minibar.

Where to Dine

Le Balandre, the restaurant at **Hôtel Terminus** (see above), serves well-recommended cuisine.

Le Rendez-Vous ★ FRENCH One of the most appealing restaurants in Cahors's historic core occupies the stone-walled, ocher-colored premises of a 13th-century private house. It turns out an array of well-prepared and reasonably priced dishes that guarantee an animated crowd. Menu items change with the season, but may include fried foie gras with spice bread; *tarte fine* (brandied tart) layered with anchovies and confit of onions; superb farm-raised veal; roasted slow-cooked lamb; scallops, and grilled duck and foie gras with lentils.

49 rue Clément Marot. © **05-65-22-65-10.** www.le-rendez-vous-cahors.com. Reservations recommended. Main courses 14€; fixed-price lunch 18€–24€, dinner 24€. MC, V. Tues–Sat noon–2pm and 7:30–9:30pm.

L'O à la Bouche ★ 🍴 MODERN FRENCH One of Cahors's best brasseries lies within a historic 14th-century building whose dining room is lined with medieval masonry and capped with massive ceiling beams. The only way meals are choreographed at this popular spot involves full fixed-price menus, each with a choice of at least four food items per category (that is, a minimum of four starters, four main courses, and four desserts). So you'll find a wide enough variety to please any palate. Menu items include a creamy, mussel and lobster salad with noodles; homemade foie gras with quince jam; and fresh fish "bouillabaisse." Cheese may be substituted for any desserts on the menu, and if so, expect an esoteric type that may have derived from a small farm nearby.

134 rue St-Urcisse. © **05-65-35-65-69.** Reservations recommended. Fixed-price menu 27€. MC, V. Tues–Sat noon–1:30pm and 7–9:30pm.

MONTAUBAN ★

644km (400 miles) SW of Paris; 72km (45 miles) NW of Albi; 50km (31 miles) N of Toulouse

This pink-brick capital of the Tarn-et-Garonne *département* is the city of the painter Ingres and the sculptor Bourdelle. Montauban, on the right bank of the Tarn, dominated by the fortified Eglise St-Jacques, is one of the most ancient of southwest France's towns. The most scenic view of Montauban is at the 14th-century brick bridge, pont Vieux, which connects the town to its satellite of Villebourbon.

Jean-Auguste-Dominique Ingres, an admirer of Raphael and a student of David, was born in 1780 in Montauban. His father, an ornamental sculptor and painter, recognized his son's artistic abilities early and encouraged him. He was noted for his nudes and historical paintings, now considered fine examples of neoclassicism. One of his first exhibitions of portraits in 1806 met with ridicule, but later generations have been more appreciative. With the exception of one work displayed in the town's cathedral, Montauban's work by Ingres is in the Musée Ingres (see below).

Essentials

GETTING THERE If you're **driving,** RN20 (Paris-Toulouse-Andorra, Spain), RN113 (Bordeaux-Marseille), and the A61 motorway run through the Tarn-et-Garonne. Seven **trains** arrive here daily from Paris Gare d'Austerlitz (trip time: 5–6 hr.) costing 70€ to 90€ one-way; trains arrive every hour from Toulouse (trip time: 25 min.), costing 8.50€ one-way. For train information and schedules, call © 08-92-35-35-35. For **bus** information, call © 05-63-63-60-60.

VISITOR INFORMATION The **Office de Tourisme** is at place Prax Paris (© 05-63-63-60-60; fax 05-63-63-65-12; www.montauban-tourisme.com).

SPECIAL EVENTS The major cultural happening, the **Festival Alors Chante** (© 05-63-63-66-77; www.alorschante.com), takes place during Ascension Week, which begins 40 days after Easter. The event showcases contemporary French music and song, and offers performances by both stars and talented unknowns. Tickets cost 10€ to 45€. The **Festival de Jazz à Montauban** (© 05-63-63-56-56; www.jazzmontauban.com), typically held the second week of July, fills the outdoor venues with blues and jazz concerts.

Exploring the Area

Shoppers may want to pick up some foie gras at the **Conserverie Artisanale Larroque,** 1300 av. de Falguières (© 05-63-63-45-40). Or visit **Pecou,** 10 rue de la République (© 05-63-63-06-38), for a supply of *montauriol* (chocolate-covered cherries with a shot of Armagnac) and *boulet de Montauban* (chocolate-covered roasted hazelnuts) candies.

A specialty of the town is *pigeonniers miniatures*—models of pigeon coops that were built on local farms to attract pigeons for their "fertilizer." The **Librairie Deloche,** 21 rue de la République (© 05-63-63-22-66), carries 30 models of various architectural styles and a selection of books on pigeonniers.

Head for the **Cathédrale Notre-Dame,** place Roosevelt (© 05-63-63-10-23), a classical building constructed in 1692 and framed by two square towers. In the north transept is the monumental painting the church commissioned from Ingres, *Vow of Louis XIII.* It's open Monday to Saturday 9am to noon and 2 to 7pm. Masses are conducted Sunday from 10am to noon.

Musée Ingres ★★ Upon his death in 1867, the artist bequeathed to Montauban more than two dozen paintings and some 4,000 drawings (more than any other museum except the Louvre). They're on display at this 17th-century bishops' palace. One painting is *Christ and the Doctors,* a work Ingres completed at 82. The *Dream of Ossian* was intended for Napoleon's bedroom in Rome. On the ground floor are works by Antoine Bourdelle, who was influenced by Rodin. The busts Bourdelle sculpted of Ingres and of Rodin are particularly outstanding.

1 rue de l'Hôtel-de-Ville. © **05-63-22-12-91.** Admission 6€ adults, 3€ seniors, free for children 17 and under. July–Aug daily 10am–6pm; Apr–June and Sept–Oct Tues–Sun 10am–noon and 2–6pm; Nov–Mar Tues–Sat 10am–noon, Tues–Sun 2–6pm.

Where to Stay

Restaurant La Cuisine d'Alain et Hôtel Orsay (see below) also rents rooms.

Hôtel Mercure Montauban ★   In a town not known for its inns, this is a shining light. One of the most dramatic hotel renovations in the district occurred in 2001, with continuing renovations every year since then. Today, it's the most appealing modern hotel in town, with relatively large rooms and comfortable beds. All units come with midsize bathrooms. The restaurant, La Brasserie Bourdelle, named after the local sculptor, serves fixed-price menus costing 13€ to 35€, with main courses going for 9€ to 21€.

12 rue Notre-Dame, Montauban 82000. 📞 **05-63-63-17-23.** Fax 05-63-66-43-66. www.mercure.com. 44 units. 104€–137€ double. AE, DC, MC, V. Parking 8.50€. **Amenities:** Restaurant; bar; room service. *In room:* A/C, TV, minibar, hair dryer, Wi-Fi (free).

Where to Dine

The **Hôtel Mercure Montauban** (see above) has a decent restaurant.

Les Saveurs d'Ingres ★★ FRENCH   In a vaulted dining room in the center of town, Cyril Paysserand showcases his culinary wares. It's close to the Ingres Museum and makes an idyllic luncheon stopover. His cuisine uses market-fresh ingredients, and his cooking is sublime, often with imaginative touches. One of our favorite dishes is the sauté de foie gras with mango chutney and cashew nuts. You might follow with a delectable plate of sweetbreads with artichokes and truffles. In season, woodcock is a special feature.

11 rue de l'Hôtel de Ville. 📞 **05-63-91-26-42.** Reservations required. Main courses 25€–28€; fixed-price menus 25€–70€. MC, V. Tues–Sat noon–1:30pm and 8–9:30pm. Closed last week of Jan, 1 week in May, and 1 week in Aug.

Restaurant La Cuisine d'Alain et Hôtel Orsay ★ MODERN FRENCH   This is the best restaurant in town. Chef Alain Blanc is talented and inventive. Try terrine of lentils flavored with the neck of a fattened duck *en confit,* filet of beef with foie gras and apple flan, or warm escalope of foie gras with apples. The amazing dessert cart offers plenty of choices. Built a century ago, the well-kept Hôtel Orsay has 20 pleasantly decorated but unpretentious rooms, with doubles running 55€ to 75€.

29, rue Salengro, Face Gare (across from the train station). 📞 **05-63-66-06-66.** Fax 05-63-66-19-39. www.hotel-restaurant-orsay.com. Reservations recommended. Main courses 20€–35€; fixed-price menus 22€–58€. AE, MC, V. Tues–Fri noon–2pm; Mon–Sat 7:30–10pm. Closed 1 week in May, 2nd and 3rd weeks of Aug, and Dec 23–Jan 8.

Montauban After Dark

The town's most crowded nightlife venue is **La Bonne Mousse,** 2 rue Voltaire (📞 **05-63-63-55-26**). Here, within a bleak-looking industrial zone 3km (1¾ miles) north of Montauban's historic core, is a sprawling, beer-soaked pub with *ambience musicale.* Drinks flow readily at a rambling bar area, and from an elevated stage, local bands, on a rotating basis, do their best to liven things up. Opening days and hours of this sometimes highly erratic concert hall vary with the season, but in most cases are Thursday to Saturday 9pm till 1am; it's best to call before you go.

One of the busiest and most widely visited nightclubs in Montauban is **Le Caïpi-rhina,** a warm and rustic vaulted cellar beneath a Mexican restaurant, **Le Santa Maria,** 2 sq. Bourjade (📞 **05-63-91-99-09**), close to Musée Ingres. Open Thursday to Saturday, it gets busy beginning around 10pm. Entrance is usually free unless a live band is entertaining that night or if a special theme night is in effect.

THE MASSIF CENTRAL

n your race south to Biarritz or to the Rhône Valley to the Riviera, you'll pass through the Massif Central. This is the most undiscovered part of France, much of the region wild, mountainous, even inaccessible and not arable. Here you'll find ancient cities, lovely valleys, and wonderful provincial cuisine. With its rolling farmlands, countryside, and châteaux and manor houses (many of which you can stay and dine in), this is one of the most unspoiled parts of France—your chance to see a life too rapidly fading.

From the spa at Vichy to the volcanic *puys* of the Auvergne, the Massif Central offers much of interest and much to learn about the art of good living. We begin in George Sand country, in the province of Berry, and proceed to the Auvergne Limousin.

BOURGES ★★★

238km (148 miles) S of Paris; 69km (43 miles) NW of Nevers; 153km (95 miles) NW of Vichy; 282km (175 miles) NW of Lyon

Once the capital of Aquitaine, Bourges lies in the heart of France; you can easily visit it from Orléans, at the eastern end of the Loire Valley (see chapter 8). The commercial and industrial center of Berry, this regional capital is still off the beaten path for most tourists, even though it boasts a rich medieval past. Its history extends far beyond the Middle Ages: In 52 B.C., Caesar called it the finest city in Gaul. Today Bourges remains a rather sleepy provincial town, awakened only by the life surrounding the Institut Universitaire de Technologie.

Essentials

GETTING THERE There are good road and rail connections from Tours and other regional cities. Five to eight **trains** arrive daily from Paris's Gare d'Austerlitz (trip time: 2 hr.; one-way fare: 30€); the trip sometimes requires a transfer at nearby Vierzon. Twelve trains a day arrive from Tours, taking 1½ hours, a one-way fare costing 21€. For information and schedules, call ✆ **36-35** or 08-92-35-35-35. If you're **driving** from Paris, take A10 south to Orléans and A71, and then RN20 to Vierzon, where you pick up Route 76 east into Bourges. From Tours, head east along RN76.

VISITOR INFORMATION　The **Office de Tourisme** is at 21 rue Victor-Hugo (www.bourges-tourisme.fr).

SPECIAL EVENTS　The energy level really picks up between April and August, thanks to several colorful music festivals. The **Festival Printemps de Bourges,** during 5 days in late April, includes dozens of concerts ranging from traditional French music to international pop and rock. Most events cost 24€ to 35€, though any number of spontaneous performances pop up along the sidewalks and in the bars for everyone to enjoy at no charge. For tickets and more information, contact the **Association Printemps de Bourges,** 22 rue Henri-Sellier (✆ **02-48-27-28-29;** www.printemps-bourges.com). At the beginning of June, a younger, high-impact music scene explodes during the **Festival Synthèse,** which has attracted groups such as U2 and some of the best performers in France. For information, call ✆ **02-48-20-41-87. Un Eté à Bourges** runs from mid-June to mid-September. During this time, the streets fill with musical performers and actors; more-structured performances also take place in churches and public monuments, with free tickets (usually). For information, call ✆ **02-48-24-93-32,** or contact the tourist office.

Seeing the Sights

Cathédrale St-Etienne ★★★　On the summit of a hill dominating the town, this is one of the most beautiful Gothic cathedrals in France. Construction began at the end of the 12th century and wasn't completed until a century and a half later. Flanked by asymmetrical towers, it has five magnificent doorways, including one depicting episodes in the life of St. Stephen. The cathedral has a vaulted roof and five aisles, and is remarkably long (122m/400 ft.); it's distinguished by its stained-glass windows, best viewed with binoculars. Many of the windows were made between 1215 and 1225. One impressive scene, *A Meal in the House of Simon,* shows Jesus lecturing Simon as Mary Magdalene repents at his feet. To climb the north tower for a view of Bourges, buy a ticket from the custodian. The same ticket allows you to explore the church's 12th-century crypt, the largest in France. In the crypt is the tomb (built 1422–38) of Jean de Berry, who ruled this duchy in the 14th century. Fanatically dedicated to art, he directed a "small army" of artisans, painters, and sculptors. The recumbent figure is the only part of the original tomb that has survived.

After your visit, you may want to wander to the **Jardins de l'Archevêché,** the archbishop's gardens, credited to Le Nôtre. From these gardens you'll have a good view of the eastern side of the cathedral.

Place Etienne-Dolet. ✆ **02-48-65-49-44.** Free admission to cathedral; tower 5€ adults, 3.50€ ages 18–25; crypt 7€ adults, 4.50€ ages 18–25, free for children 17 and under. Cathedral daily Apr and Sept 9:45–11:45am and 2–5:30pm; May–June 9:30–11:30am and 2–5:30pm; July–Aug 9:30am–12:30pm and 2–6pm; Oct–Mar 9:30–11:30am and 2–4:45pm. Crypt closed until 1pm Sun for Mass.

Hôtel Lallemant　The Renaissance Hôtel Lallemant, a 5-minute walk north of the cathedral, has been transformed into a museum of decorative art. The mansion

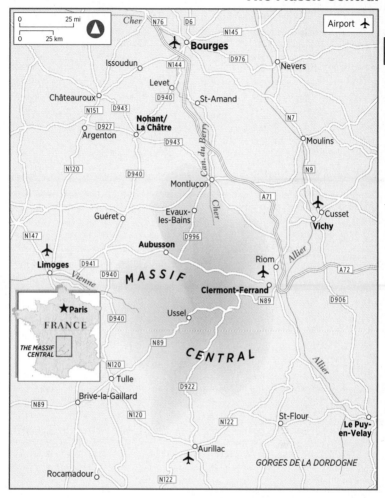

was built for a textile merchant; today its galleries display a colorful history of Bourges. Exhibits include china, objets d'art, ceramics, and antique furniture.

6 rue Bourbonnoux. ⓒ **02-48-24-56-21.** Free admission. Tues–Sat 10am–noon; Tues–Sun 2–5pm.

Musée du Berry   This museum is inside the Hôtel Cujas, built about 1515. On display is a collection of Celtic and Gallo-Roman artifacts; the 280 funerary sculptures are impressive. Some rooms are devoted to finds from Egyptian archaeological digs, along with medieval masterpieces of sculpture from around 1400; some rooms on the second floor have ethnological exhibitions.

4 rue des Arènes. ⓒ **02-48-70-41-92.** Free admission. Mon and Wed–Sat 10am–noon; Wed–Sun 2–5pm.

Palais Jacques-Coeur ★★ This is one of the country's greatest secular Gothic structures. Take a 1-hour guided tour—the only way to see the palace—through the four buildings surrounding a central court, constructed around 1450 by the finance minister and banker Jacques Coeur. M. Coeur never got to enjoy the palace, however. After a trial by a jury of his creditors, the wealthy financier was tossed into prison by Charles VII and died there in 1456. His furnishings no longer remain, but the decor and wealth of detail inside the palace allow a remarkable view of 15th-century opulence. In the dining hall is a monumental chimney piece, and in the great hall are sculptures from the 15th and 16th centuries. The mandatory tour is in French; English speakers receive a printed translation of the commentary.

10 bis rue Jacques-Coeur. © **02-48-24-79-42.** Admission 7€ adults, 4.50€ ages 18–25 and over 60, free for children 17 and under. Combination ticket (to crypt and tower only) and Palais Jacques-Coeur 10€ adults, 6.50€ students. 6 tours depart daily on a schedule that changes weekly.

Where to Stay

Grand Hôtel Mercure Hôtel de Bourbon et Abbaye St-Ambroix ★★ This
is the finest hotel in Bourges, and its cuisine is the best in the area. In the early 1990s, the Mercure chain converted a 17th-century abbey and a stately home into this first-class hotel. The cheerful rooms are well appointed and comfortable (except for the half-timbered units beneath the sloping mansard roof on the third floor, which are a bit cramped). The stonework of the exterior and the public areas is beautiful and artfully cadenced to reflect the site's historic origins. The setting, almost adjacent to the rail station, is convenient for train travelers.

The cuisine at Abbaye St-Ambroix is prepared by chef François Adamski. Menu items change with the seasons, but may include scallops cooked in tarragon butter with French caviar; foie gras fried with dried fruit, fresh pears, and a reduction of red wine; or roasted John Dory with vegetable lasagna.

Bd. de la République, Bourges 18000. © **02-48-70-70-00.** Fax 02-48-70-21-22. www.hoteldebourbon. fr. 58 units. 110€–205€ double; 185€–235€ suite. AE, DC, MC, V. Free parking. **Amenities:** Restaurant; bar; room service. In room: A/C, TV, hair dryer, minibar, Wi-Fi (free).

Le Christina 🍷 This is a standard but comfortable inn, built in the 1930s and renovated many times since. It rises three or five stories (depending on which part of the hotel you're in). The bigger and renovated rooms have private safes and are outfitted in a vaguely Louis XVI style. Other units don't have private safes, are a bit smaller, and have decors loosely based on Louis XV or a streamlined internationally modern style. Regardless of their style, each is cozy and comfortable, with warm colors. The location, a few steps from the cathedral and the Palais Jacques-Coeur, is convenient. Breakfast is the only meal served, but several simple brasseries lie within walking distance.

5 rue de la Halle, Bourges 18000. © **02-48-70-56-50.** Fax 02-48-70-58-13. www.le-christina.com. 71 units. 58€–85€ double. AE, MC, V. Free parking. In room: A/C, TV, Wi-Fi (free).

Where to Dine

The **Abbaye St-Ambroix** at the Grand Hôtel Mercure (see above) also offers fine cuisine, with fixed-price menus costing 32€ to 90€.

Jacques-Coeur ★ TRADITIONAL FRENCH This tavern serves traditional bourgeois cuisine, though the food at Abbaye St-Ambroix (see above) is better.

Although keeping the old name and atmosphere, Stephane Philippon has taken over this restaurant, changing the menu seasonally to take advantage of the best shopping at local markets. For an appetizer, you might try ravioli filled with langoustines or else an escalope of foie gras, followed by such mains as veal kidneys in Madeira sauce or roasted scallops in Noilly Prat. The desserts are homemade and tempting, and service is efficient. The featured wines include Quincy and Menetou-Salon, two excellent but not well-known regional vintages. Of the two medieval Gothic-style dining rooms, the one on the upper floor is more interesting, with exposed beams and plaster impressions of scallop shells on its ceiling (ca. 1947).

3 place Jacques-Coeur. © **02-48-26-53-01.** www.restaurantjacquescoeur.com. Reservations required. Main courses 20€–30€; fixed-price menu 20€–54€. MC, V. Tues–Fri noon–2pm; Mon–Sat 7:15–9:15pm. Closed 1 week late Dec and 1 week late Jan.

Bourges After Dark

Most of the best clubs are in Bourges's old town. Try **Le Pub Birdland,** 4 av. Jean-Jaurès (© **02-48-70-66-77**), an old-fashioned establishment with a wood interior, a young crowd of heavy-duty beer drinkers, and jazz and rock. **Beau Bar,** rue des Beaux-Arts (© **02-48-24-40-49**), pulls in a bohemian crowd—artists, poets, songwriters, and the like. For something a little different, head to **La Soupe aux Choux,** part of the restaurant Le Guillotin, place Gordaine (© **02-48-65-43-66**), where you can take in an evening of *cafe-théâtre.* Shows can be anything from musical performances to stand-up comedy; tickets run 8€ to 15€.

NOHANT/LA CHATRE

290km (180 miles) S of Paris; 31km (19 miles) S of Châteauroux

George Sand was the pen name of Amandine Lucile Aurore Dupin, baronne Dudevant, the French novelist born in 1804. Her memory is forever connected to Nohant, the little Berry hamlet near the Indre Valley.

In her early life, she wrote bucolic tales of peasants, but she also penned romantic novels in which she maintained that women were entitled to as much freedom as men. Among her 80 novels, some of the best known were *François le Champi* and *La Mare au Diable.* She was also known for her love affairs; her two most notorious were with the poet Alfred de Musset and the composer Frédéric Chopin. By the time of her death in Nohant in 1876, George Sand had become a legend.

Essentials

GETTING THERE If you're **driving,** it's a 1-hour trip from Bourges to La Châtre on D940 south. The closest **train** station is in Châteauroux, 36km (22 miles) from La Châtre; connecting bus service (no. 15) links Châteauroux to Nohant/La Châtre. Nohant and La Châtre are 6km (3¾ miles) apart. From Bourges, you can buy a combination train and bus ticket to La Châtre via Châteauroux. Five daily trains make the run to Châteauroux, where you transfer to a bus to complete the 2-hour trip. For complete train information, call © **36-35,** or 08-92-35-35-35 outside France.

VISITOR INFORMATION The nearest **Office de Tourisme** is 134 rue Nationale in La Châtre (© **02-54-48-22-64;** fax 02-54-06-09-15; www.pays-george-sand.com).

In The Footsteps of George Sand

Le Domaine de George Sand ★   At the Château de Nohant, known today as La Maison de George Sand, the novelist learned the ways and thoughts of the peasants. During her time here, she entertained some of the intellectual and artistic elite of Europe: Flaubert, Balzac, Delacroix, Liszt, and Gautier. The building, which its guides define as a *maison bourgeoise,* is in its own park. It was constructed of stone in 1763 and purchased in 1793 by the family of George Sand. Today, it houses mementos of Sand and her admirers and friends, with testimonials to the literary conceits and eccentricities of one of France's most enduringly famous writers. The only way to visit is on a 45-minute guided tour in French (non-French speakers can follow along with a printed text). You can see the boudoir where she wrote the novel *Indiana,* published when she was 28. You can also visit her bedchamber and study. At Nohant, George Sand staged theatricals, dramatizing several of her novels—not very successfully, according to reports. Today, over 3 weekends in June, *fêtes romantiques de Nohant* are sometimes staged, with an impressive list of musical performers.

36400 Nohant-Vic.℗ **02-54-31-06-04.** Admission 7€ adults, 4.50€ students and ages 18–25, free for children 17 and under. July–Aug tours daily at 10, 10:45, 11:15am, noon, and 2pm, then every 30 min. (or 45 min.) until 6pm; Apr–June and Sept–Oct tours daily 9:30, 10:30, 11:15am, 2, 3, and 4pm; Nov–Mar tours daily 10, 11:30am, 2:30, and 3:30pm.

Where to Stay & Dine

Auberge de la Petite Fadette ⚓   This compound of interconnected 19th-century ivy-covered buildings abuts a château and is the focal point of one of the smallest villages in the region. Five generations of the Chapleau family have owned the renovated compound since 1890. A scattering of antiques decorates the interior. Rooms are cozy and comfortable, each outfitted with 19th-century antiques and the aura of a private home. The restaurant, open daily for lunch and dinner year-round, charges 31€ to 42€ for its fixed-price meals.

Place du Château, Nohant 36400. ℗ **02-54-31-01-48.** Fax 02-54-31-10-19. www.auberge-petite-fadette.fr. 9 units. 70€–120€ double. AE, MC, V. **Amenities:** Restaurant; bar; room service. *In room:* TV, hair dryer.

Château de la Vallée Bleue ★★   This is the area's most prestigious address. Dr. Pestel built the small, charming château in 1840 so that he could be close to his patient George Sand. It's now a hotel and restaurant owned by Gérard Gasquet. The rooms bear the names of the doctor's guests, including Musset, Delacroix, Flaubert, Chopin, and Liszt. All rooms have dignified, sometimes antique, furniture, and six have a complete bathroom with tub/shower combination (the rest have showers). There's also a 4-hectare (10-acre) wooded park. The excellent regional specialties are characterized as *cuisine actuelle,* with an accent on presentation; they include goat cheese and carp with lentils, and chicken à la George Sand (with crayfish sauce). Fixed-price menus are 24€ and 44€. For dessert, try a delectable pear baked in pastry.

Rte. de Verneuil, St-Chartier, La Châtre 36400.℗ **02-54-31-01-91.** Fax 02-54-31-04-48. www.chateau valleebleue.com. 15 units. 95€–145€ double; 150€–195€ suite. AE, MC, V. Hotel closed mid-Nov to mid-Mar. **Amenities:** 2 restaurants; room service; outdoor pool. *In room:* TV, minibar, hair dryer, Wi-Fi (free).

VICHY ★★★

348km (216 miles) S of Paris; 53km (33 miles) NE of Clermont-Ferrand; 174km (108 miles) NW of Lyon

This world-renowned spa on the northern edge of the Auvergne, in the heart of Bourbon country, is noted for its sparkling waters, which reputedly alleviate liver and stomach ailments. It looks much as it did a century ago, when princes and industrial barons filled its rococo casino. (The casino you'll visit today isn't the one that thrived during the spa's 19th-c. heyday. That edifice, at 5 rue du Casino, now functions as a convention hall.)

Since 1861, when Napoleon III was a frequent visitor, much has been done to add to the spa's fame. During the 1980s, the hotels and baths of Vichy underwent a modernization program to keep up with the times and the other baths of France, much to the pleasure of their clients and their ever-changing tastes.

The Perrier craze that has swept most of the world has aided the city's reputation for health and relaxation. The Perrier Company has a contract to bottle Vichy water for sale and runs the city's major attractions. Vichy is a sports and recreation center, boasting a casino, theaters, regattas, horse racing, and golf. The **Parc des Sources,** a promenade with covered walks, is the center of Vichy's fashionable life, which is at its peak from May to the end of September.

Essentials

GETTING THERE Vichy lies on the heavily traveled Paris–Clermont-Ferrand rail line. Some 20 **trains** per day arrive from Clermont-Ferrand (trip time: 35 min.). Ten trains per day arrive from Paris's Gare de Lyon (trip time: 3 hr.); the one-way fare is 45€. For train information and schedules, call ℭ **36-35** or 08-92-35-35-35. **Bus** service into town is usually not as convenient or well orchestrated as the train. The Gare Routière (ℭ **36-35**) lies adjacent to the rail station. If you're **driving** to Vichy from Paris, take A10 south to Orléans, and then connect to A71 south. At the Gannat/Vichy exit, follow N209 east to Vichy.

VISITOR INFORMATION The **Office de Tourisme** is at 5 rue du Casino (ℭ **04-70-98-71-94;** www.vichy-tourisme.com).

Where to Stay

Best Western Aletti Palace Hôtel ★★ ☺

This early-1900s hotel, the largest and, in some ways, stateliest in town, preserves the grand vistas and elegant accessories of the Belle Epoque. The high-ceilinged rooms are comfortably furnished. Many have balconies overlooking the wooded park and casino, and all come with spacious bathrooms with tub/shower combinations. If you ask, the staff will tell you about the role of this monument (under a different name, the Thermal Palace) during the tenure of the collaborationist Vichy government: It housed the headquarters of Vichy France's Ministry of War. These days, the hotel has a good restaurant and offers a bar and a terrace with a view of Vichy.

3 place Joseph-Aletti, Vichy 03200. ℭ **800/528-1234** in the U.S., or 04-70-30-20-20. Fax 04-70-98-13-82. www.bestwestern.com. 129 units. 128€–160€ double; 195€–230€ suite. Children 11 and under stay free in parent's room. AE, DC, MC, V. **Amenities:** Restaurant; bar; babysitting; children's activities; outdoor heated pool; room service. *In room:* A/C, TV, hair dryer, minibar, Wi-Fi (free).

Hôtel Chambord 🥄

This government-rated two-star choice is one of the best bets for a spa holiday on a budget. The pleasant hotel, built near the rail station in

Choosing a Spa Vacation

For a sojourn at a spa and health farm, contact the **Centre Thermal des Dômes,** at the Novotel Thermalia (☎ **04-70-97-39-59**), or the **Centre des Célestins,** at the Hôtel les Célestins (☎ **04-70-30-82-00**). For questions about Vichy's spas and hydrotherapy facilities, call ☎ **04-70-97-39-59** or 0800/30-00-63 within France.

the 1930s, has high ceilings and more space than you may find in newer buildings. Its rooms are renovated, each tastefully and comfortably furnished. The Escargot Qui Tette restaurant offers well-prepared meals in a sunny setting with reasonable prices.

82-84 rue de Paris, Vichy 03200. ☎ **04-70-30-16-30.** Fax 04-70-31-54-92. www.hotel-chambord-vichy. com. 28 units. 48€–85€ double. AE, DC, MC, V. **Amenities:** Restaurant; bar. *In room:* TV, Wi-Fi (free).

Where to Dine

The restaurant in the **Hôtel Chambord** (see above), Escargot Qui Tette, serves excellent regional and French cuisine.

Brasserie du Casino TRADITIONAL FRENCH   In business since 1921, with its original decor in place, this is the leading brasserie in Vichy, a preferred stop for actors and musicians visiting from Paris to perform at one of the local theaters. The restaurant, known for its sheathing of copper and Art Deco mahogany, is busy at lunch. Specialties include duck breast with a confit of figs, paupiette of rabbit with shallots, veal kidneys with fresh spinach and truffle sauce, monkfish with an essence of fennel, and veal liver with fondue of onions.

4 rue du Casino. ☎ **04-70-98-23-06.** Reservations recommended at lunch. Main courses 15€–21€; fixed-price menu 16€–25€. MC, V. Thurs–Mon noon–1:30pm and 7–9:15pm. Closed 2 weeks in Mar and Oct 20–Nov 20.

L'Alambic ★ MODERN FRENCH   This small restaurant has only 12 seats, and because L'Alambic has some of the best food in Vichy, they fill up quickly. Since 1989, Jean-Jacques Barbot has appealed to what one food critic called "the jaded palates of Vichy." Within a pale green, warmly appointed dining room, which locals say is ideal for intimate dialogues, you can order from an array of ever-changing dishes, which may include cream of mussel and scallop soup flavored with saffron; a ravioli of sea snails served with a chicken-and-herb-flavored mousse and a lentil-flavored cream sauce; codfish stuffed with a confit of oranges, tomatoes, olives, and capers; a supreme of guinea fowl stuffed with an herb-flavored mousse; and a frozen *verveine*-flavored soufflé. Incidentally, the oil paintings that line the dining room were painted by chef Barbot's longtime companion, Marie-Ange Tupet, who supervises the service in the dining room.

8 rue Nicolas-Larbaud. ☎ **04-70-59-12-71.** Fax 04-70-97-98-88. Reservations required. Main courses 16€–24€; fixed-price menu 26€–47€. MC, V. Wed–Sun noon–1:30pm; Wed–Sat 7:30–9:30pm. Closed mid-Feb to early Mar, 3 weeks in Aug, and Dec 23–Jan 3.

Vichy After Dark

If you're in the mood to meet the locals, head for the town's most animated bar, **Le Vichy,** 15 rue Burnol (☎ **04-70-97-05-70**). Here, within a mostly blue-toned setting punctuated with a long bar and a karaoke setup, you can babble and jive with a clientele aged 23 to 50. The town also contains two casinos, both of them modern, contemporary-looking affairs, and both of them accessorized with dining and drinking facilities. The larger, better accessorized, and more appealing of the two is the **Casino des Quatres-Chemin,** rue Lucas (© **04-70-97-93-37**). Inaugurated in 2004 within the Centre Commercial des Quatres Chemins, it replaced the grand, neoclassical casino (Casino Elysée Palace, now closed) whose clients included Napoleon III in the 19th century. The newer setting is glassy, glossy, and Vegas-ish. An area devoted exclusively to slot machines, with free entrance and virtually no dress code, is open daily 10am to 3am. A more formal area for blackjack and roulette (games referred to as *les grands jeux*) is open daily 8pm to 3am (until 4am Fri–Sat). To access *les grands jeux,* you must present a driver's license, ID card, or passport. Whereas *les grands jeux* are closed in February, the slot machines remain open here year-round, and there's a restaurant on-site.

Le Grand Café, 7 rue du Casino (© **04-70-97-16-45**), is a less impressive place to gamble, this one only with slot machines, and lies within a modern annex of the old casino. Entrance is free, and it's open daily 10am to at least 2am (slot machines room open until 3am on Sat), and sometimes later, depending on business. A cafe-bar and restaurant are on the premises, as well as a disco, **Le Loft** (© **04-70-97-16-46**), which is modern, reverberating with pulsating electronic dance music, and noted as the town's most popular drinking and dancing joint. The disco is open Wednesday to Saturday from 9:30pm to 3am; admission is free.

CLERMONT-FERRAND ★★

399km (248 miles) S of Paris; 177km (110 miles) W of Lyon

This city in south-central France was the ancient capital of the Auvergne. Clermont-Ferrand has seen a long parade of history. It was created in 1731 by a merger of two towns, Clermont and Montferrand. The city is surrounded by hills, and in the distance stands one of the great attractions of the Auvergne, the volcanic mountain Puy-de-Dôme.

Today Clermont-Ferrand (commonly called Clermont) is hardly celebrated for its ancient appearance and medieval streets. Much of the town looks as if it were created in the stark 1960s and 1970s. It's not a town in which we'd choose to linger, but it's an important rail hub in this region and has a number of attractions that do bring in visitors. Its population numbers 150,000 for the city and 260,000 for the city and its surrounding region.

Essentials

GETTING THERE **Rail** lines converge on Clermont-Ferrand from all parts of France, including Marseille, Toulouse, and Paris's Gare de Lyon. The one-way fare from Paris is 53€; the trip takes 3½ hours. Trains from small towns in the Auvergne usually require a connection. For train information and schedules, call © **36-35** or 08-92-35-35-35. Clermont-Ferrand is best approached by **car** from two cities. The 4-hour drive from Paris begins along A10 south to Orléans, continuing south along A71 to Clermont-Ferrand. From Lyon, take A47 west to St-Etienne, traveling northwest on A89 to Clermont-Ferrand.

Aéroport de Clermont-Aulnat (☎ **04-73-62-71-00**), about 4km (2½ miles) northwest of the town center, receives about 80 flights a day from all over France as well as Italy, Switzerland, and Belgium. **Air France** (☎ **08-20-82-08-20**) flies here from Paris round-trip. Buses meet every flight and take passengers to town, the bus station, or the rail station. The one-way fare is 4€. For bus information, call ☎ **04-73-84-72-57.**

Train travel into Clermont-Ferrand is, overall, more convenient and efficient than bus service. **Buses** serve the **Gare Routière,** boulevard François-Mitterrand (☎ **04-73-93-13-61** for information), on the southern periphery of town.

VISITOR INFORMATION The **Office de Tourisme et des Congrès** is on place de la Victoire (☎ **04-73-98-65-00;** fax 04-73-90-04-11; www.clermont-fd. com). It's unique in France because it also houses a free museum in its basement called the **Espace Art Roman.** An interactive presentation combines a slide show with photographs and archaeological remnants depicting the Auvergne as a rich repository of Romanesque architecture and artifacts. The short film takes 45 minutes, and it's worth spending another hour digesting all the additional information. From May to September, the tourist office and the museum are open Monday to Friday 9am to 7pm, Saturday and Sunday 10am to 7pm; October to April, hours are Monday to Friday 9am to 6pm, Saturday 10am to 1pm and 2 to 6pm, and Sunday 9:30am to 12:30pm and 2 to 6pm.

SPECIAL EVENTS If you're in town at the end of January, check out one of the 40 screenings during the **Festival du Court Métrage.** Ten sites, mostly on boulevard François-Mitterrand, show works by up-and-coming directors. Tickets are 3€, with discounts for packages of 30 showings (56€), and can be purchased through **Sauve Qui Peut le Court Métrage,** La Jetée, 6 place Michel de l'Hôpital (☎ **04-73-91-65-73;** www.clermont-filmfest.com).

Exploring The Environs: A Spectacular Volcanic Landscape

The region surrounding Clermont-Ferrand is one of France's most geologically distinctive. In 1977, the government designated 382,800 hectares (946,000 acres) as the **Parc Naturel Régional des Volcans d'Auvergne.** The park contains 186 villages as well as farms with herds of cows and goats that produce the Auvergne's cheeses and charcuterie. Scattered among them are at least 90 extinct volcanic cones *(puys)*, which rise dramatically and eerily above the pine forests.

One of the highest and oldest of these is **Puy-de-Dôme ★★★** (1,440m/4,724 ft. above sea level), a site used for worship since prehistoric times by the Gauls and the Romans. In 1648, Pascal used this mountaintop for his experiments that proved Torricelli's hypothesis about how altitude affects atmospheric pressure. And in 1911, one of the most dramatic events in French aviation occurred at Puy-de-Dôme when Eugène Renaux, with a passenger, flew nonstop from Paris in just over 5 hours, to land precariously on its summit and collect a prize worth 15,200€ in today's currency. From the summit you'll have a panoramic view: On a clear day, you can see as far east as Mont Blanc.

Shuttle buses run from the base to the summit daily 10am to 6pm in July and August, and Saturday and Sunday in May, June, and September 12:30 to 6pm; the fare is 4€ round-trip. You can drive your car to the summit, but be aware that the road has many sharp curves, many steep drop-offs, and lots of potentially lethal hazards, especially when it's mobbed with visitors. If you opt to take your own car on days when the shuttle bus is operating, local authorities will let you do so only between 6pm and 10am the next day. The road and the parking lots remain open through the night. On the way up, you'll pay a toll of 6€ year-round; downhill passage is free. Frankly, unless you really want to see the summit by moonlight, it's better to take one of the shuttle buses. From November to March, the road is closed completely because of snow. Dial © **04-73-62-21-46** for more information.

The different areas of the park contain radically dissimilar features. **Les Puys** (also known as Monts Dômes) are a minichain of 112 extinct volcanoes (some capped with craters, some with rounded peaks) packed densely into an area 4km (2½ miles) wide by 31km (19 miles) long. Each dome is unique: Some were built up by slow extrusions of rock; others were the source of vast lava flows. Those with craters at their summits were the sites of violent explosions whose power contrasted with the region's peace and quiet today. The geological fury that created these hills ended between 5,000 and 6,000 years ago, but the rectangle of extinct volcanoes traces one of the most potentially unstable tectonic areas in France, the San Andreas Fault of the French mainland.

This region is relatively lightly populated, so you may not be aware of the park's boundaries during your explorations. Details about trekking and camping are available from the **Parc Naturel Régional des Volcans d'Auvergne,** Montlosier, Aydat 63970 (© **04-73-65-64-00**), 20km (12 miles) southwest of Clermont-Ferrand. You can buy at least half a dozen guidebooks covering specific hikes and walks (2–6 hr. in duration).

Seeing the Sights in Town

Begin your tour in the center of Clermont, the bustling **place de Jaude,** where you can sample a glass of regional wine at a cafe. Later, walk north on the all-pedestrian rue du 11-Novembre, which branches off from the main plaza. This street leads to the all-pedestrian **rue des Gras,** the most historic and evocative artery of Clermont.

Most of the appealing buildings are in **Vieux-Clermont,** whose focal point is **place de la Victoire,** site of the black-lava **Cathédrale Notre-Dame de l'Assomption ★★** (© **04-73-98-65-00**). One of the great churches of central France, it dates to the 13th and 14th centuries. Structural additions were made in the 19th century. Its outstanding feature is the series of stained-glass windows from the 13th and 14th centuries. Admission is free; it's open year-round Monday to Friday 7:30am to noon and 2 to 6pm, Saturday and Sunday 9:30am to noon and 3 to 7:30pm.

After leaving the cathedral, explore the buildings in this neighborhood. In particular, look for the **Maison de Savaron,** 3 rue des Chaussetiers, constructed in 1513. It's noted for the beauty of its courtyard and its Renaissance vaulting. Today it's a crêperie, **Le Quinze-Treize** (© **04-73-92-37-46**), where you can enjoy a meal-size (savory) or dessert-style (sweet) crepe beneath the artfully crafted vaulting. It's open Monday to Friday noon to 3pm and 6:30pm to midnight, Saturday and Sunday noon to midnight.

Several blocks northeast of the cathedral is the finest example of Auvergnat Romanesque architecture, made of lava from volcanic deposits in the region, the **Basilique Notre-Dame-du-Port ★★,** rue du Port. Dating from the 11th and 12th centuries, the church has four radiating chapels and a transept surmounted by an octagonal tower. The crypt holds a 17th-century black Madonna. UNESCO lists the complex as a World Heritage Site. Admission is free; it's open daily from 8am to 7pm (until 8pm June to mid-Oct).

Between the two churches stands the Renaissance **Fontaine d'Amboise,** place de la Poterne. Its pyramid supports a statue of Hercules. Nearby is **square Pascal,** commemorating the birth of mathematician Blaise Pascal in 1623 in a house on rue des Gras. Regrettably, the house was demolished in 1958, but a statue stands in honor of the native son.

Musée d'Archéologie Bargoin   The collection here consists of objects excavated from Auvergnat sites founded by the Gallo-Romans and their predecessors: pottery shards, bronzes, woodcarvings, and an array of works noteworthy for anyone interested in France's prehistoric and pre-Roman origins. There's also an unusual collection of antique Oriental carpets; in the same building, the **Musée du Tapis d'Art** displays around 80 rare Middle Eastern and East Asian carpets. Each is artfully lit and suspended from walls and ceilings, and together they represent the evolution of the carpet as a prayer aid and a decorative work of art. Don't expect anything French in this place—it completely omits the carpets produced in nearby Aubusson.

45 rue de Ballainvilliers. (℃ **04-73-42-69-70.** www.clermont-ferrand.fr/-Musees-.html. Joint admission 4.50€ adults, 3.50€ seniors, free for children 17 and under and students. Tues–Sat 10am–noon and 1–5pm; Sun 2–7pm. Closed Jan 1, May 1, Nov 1, and Dec 25.

Musée d'Art Roger Quilliot   This museum is in a suburb 3km (1¾ miles) northeast of Clermont's center, in an award-winning building erected in 1992. This is the cultural showcase of the Auvergne. When it was created, multiple works of art were culled from other museums throughout the Auvergne and then reassembled into a format that displays European art and culture in chronological order. Visitors make their way in a circular pattern through rooms devoted to French, Italian, and Flemish works, progressing from the 7th to the 20th century.

Place Louis-Deteix, Montferrand. (℃ **04-73-16-11-30.** http://museedart.clermont-ferrand.fr. Admission 4.50€, free for students and children 18 and under. Tues–Sun 10am–6pm. Closed Jan 1, May 1, Nov 1, and Dec 25. From the center of town, follow av. Michelin east until you see the signpost pointing north to Montferrand.

Where to Stay

Hôtel Le Kyriad   This is not the best hotel in town, but it's still a good value. Built in unassuming 1970s style, it has well-maintained rooms that are comfortably furnished though somewhat uninspired. The small bathrooms are tidily organized; each has a shower. The hotel is a popular overnight stop for farmers and sales representatives of companies selling farm equipment, so as a casual visitor you may feel somewhat in the minority. The simple bistro offers affordable meals.

51 rue Bonnabaud, Clermont-Ferrand 63000. (℃ **04-73-93-59-69.** Fax 04-73-34-89-29. www.hotel-kyriadcentreclermont.com. 80 units. 60€–105€ double. AE, DC, MC, V. Parking 12€. **Amenities:** Bistro; bar; room service. In room: TV, hair dryer, minibar, Wi-Fi (free).

Le Mercure Centre ★   A favorite of the business traveler, this early-1970s hotel is the best of a fairly lackluster lot. Its location near the Jardin Lecoq is great for jogging and strolling. Most of the well-furnished rooms are spacious. Each midsize bathroom has a tub/shower combination. Everything is functional and businesslike, not necessarily exciting. The restaurant, L'Eau à la Bouche, is a worthwhile choice.

82 bd. François-Mitterrand, Clermont-Ferrand 63000. (℃ **04-73-34-46-46.** Fax 04-73-34-46-36. www.mercure.com. 123 units. 75€–190€ double. AE, DC, MC, V. Parking 14€. **Amenities:** Restaurant; bar; room service. In room: A/C, TV, hair dryer, minibar, Wi-Fi (free).

Where to Dine

L'Eau à la Bouche, in the **Mercure Centre** hotel (see above), serves regional specialties and classic French cuisine.

Brasserie Danièle Bath ★★ 🍴 MODERN FRENCH   Lots of superb flavors go into the locally inspired yet grandly creative cuisine. Begin with such delights as tarte of scallops with black truffles; rabbit, shrimp, and tomato strudel; or perhaps a small lasagna of salmon with black olives. The excellent fish changes seasonally, and you can also count on any number of savory meat dishes, including roast lamb with glazed turnips. Pigeon is another specialty, served with roasted foie gras.

Place St-Pierre. 🕐 **04-73-31-23-22.** Reservations required. Main courses 13€–25€; fixed-price lunch 18€; fixed-price dinner 27€–36€. AE, DC, MC, V. Tues–Sun noon–2pm and 7–10pm. Closed Feb 5–Mar 10 and 2 weeks in Aug.

Emmanuel Hodencq ★★★ FRENCH   The namesake of this restaurant is the town's culinary king, having topped even the longtime favorite, Jean-Claude Leclerc (see below). The dynamic chef is equally at home with traditional or *moderne* cookery, and his delectable dishes almost waltz out of the kitchen and onto your table. Local "wheeler-dealers" (a reference to Michelin tires) and politicos hang out here. The menu features the best of local produce—perhaps foie gras in caramel vinegar or roasted pigeon with chanterelles. Grilled red mullet is a perfect dish, as is medallion of veal in grainy mustard sauce.

Place St-Pierre. 🕐 **04-73-31-23-23.** www.hodencq.com. Reservations required. Main courses 33€–63€; fixed-price menu 37€–105€. AE, MC, V. Tues–Sat noon–2pm; Mon–Sat 7:30–10pm.

Jean-Claude Leclerc ★★ FRENCH   One of the best-known restaurants in Clermont-Ferrand occupies a modern dining room in a late 19th century town house in the center of Clermont's oldest neighborhood. It features ultracontemporary decor, large-scale oil paintings, and an emphasis on creative cuisine that's carefully tuned to the seasons. Our favorite dishes are roasted lobster served on rémoulade of celery and apples; truffle-studded turbot served with creamy mashed potatoes; and faux-filet of Salers beef served with gravy that's enriched with foie gras and truffles.

12 rue St-Adjutor. 🕐 **04-73-36-46-30.** www.restaurant-leclerc.com. Reservations recommended. Main courses 30€–40€; fixed-price menu 28€–65€. AE, MC, V. Tues–Sat noon–1:30pm and 7:30–9:30pm. Closed 3 weeks in Aug and 1st week in Jan and May.

Clermont-Ferrand After Dark

Most French nightclubbers begin their evenings on the town by heading to the **boulevard Trudaine,** a thoroughfare in the town center that's very close to the Eglise Notre-Dame-du-Port. It's lined with at least 20 bars and restaurants catering to the young and the restless.

B. Box, La Pardieu (🕐 **04-73-28-59-74;** www.bboxclub.com), is the biggest nightclub in Clermont. Expect mass consumption of alcohol and a bevy of attractive people. Cover ranges from 10€ to 15€ and includes your first drink. It's open from 11pm to 5am Thursday to Saturday only. Two other dance clubs are **Le Frog,** 12 rue des Petits Gras (🕐 **04-73-37-99-73**), and **Le Symbol,** 11 rue de Serbie (🕐 **04-73-31-01-01;** www.lesymbol.com). Both attract a crowd over 25, including lots of single, divorced, and nominally married people looking for a dance and perhaps a fling. A popular gay bar is the **Bar d'O,** place de la Victoire (🕐 **04-73-91-43-14**), which tends to be busy during the late afternoon and early evening (4–9:30 or 10:30pm); it's open Monday to Saturday 7:30am to 1am. After that, but only Wednesday to Saturday after 10pm, gay men and, to a lesser extent, women, head for **L'Enigme,** 32 rue Fontgieve (© **04-73-31-07-63;** www.l-enigme.com), the town's (and the region's) busiest and most animated gay disco. Entrance ranges from free to 10€, depending on the night of the week, and the dancing usually continues until at least 4am.

AUBUSSON

380km (236 miles) S of Paris; 89km (55 miles) E of Limoges; 95km (59 miles) NW of Clermont-Ferrand

In the Creuse Valley, the little market town of Aubusson enjoys world renown for its carpets and tapestries. Aubusson abounds with clock towers, bridges, peaked roofs, and turrets—all of which inspired the painter Gromaire's widely reproduced cartoon *View of Aubusson.* Against the gray granite, rainbow-hued skeins of wool hang from windows. The artisan's workshops spread throughout the town; many are open to the public (just ask). The origin of the industry is unknown. Some credit the Arabs who settled here in 732. Others think the craft came from Flanders in the Middle Ages. For years, the favorite subject of the reproductions created for sale was *The Lady and the Unicorn,* the original of which was discovered in the nearby Château de Boussac. Many tapestry reproductions of the works of 18th-century painters such as Boucher and Watteau have been made. Since World War II, designs by painters such as Picasso, Matisse, and Braque have been stressed.

Essentials

GETTING THERE Aubusson has **rail** service, much of it indirect, from Clermont-Ferrand and Paris, among other cities. About 10 trains a day depart from Paris's Gare d'Austerlitz for Limoges, where passengers board an SNCF bus for the 90-minute ride on to Aubusson. Bus fare from Limoges is 13€ each way. For bus information, call © **05-55-66-13-28.** Total transit time from Paris to Aubusson is about 4½ hours; the one-way fare is 55€. From Clermont-Ferrand to Aubusson, an early-afternoon train departs daily for a nearly 4-hour trip (with at least three stops and at least three changes en route); the one-way fare is 24€. For information, call © **36-35** or 08-92-35-35-35. Most **bus** service into town originates in the area, with inconvenient connections from other parts of France. For information, call Aubusson La Gare Routière (© **05-55-66-13-28**). If you're **driving** from Clermont-Ferrand, take D941 west to Aubusson. The trip takes between 1 and 1½ hours.

VISITOR INFORMATION The **Office de Tourisme** is on rue Vieille (© **05-55-66-32-12;** fax 05-55-83-84-51; www.ot-aubusson.fr).

Exploring the Town

Aubusson is the site of at least 15 carpet manufacturers, many of which spend their entire production year fulfilling advance orders—thereby accumulating very few inventories of unsold goods, disappointing many visitors in the process. To alleviate this, the tourist office, between March and October, maintains a carpet showroom inside its premises with about 20 carpets from different manufacturers on display and for sale. And depending on which style of carpet you like from the samples on display, the office will guide you directly to the sales staff at the manufacturer. There, if you don't mind waiting for the carpet of your dreams (it takes approx. 2 months of eye-straining labor to produce 3 square feet (.9 sq. m). of completed carpet), you may eventually receive your very own Aubusson, crafted in whatever style and color palette you've indicated at the time of its original commission, at prices substantially less than what you'd have paid in a retail outlet in, say, Paris or New York.

The **Musée Départemental de la Tapisserie,** avenue des Lissiers (✆ **05-55-83-08-30;** www.creuse.fr), has exhibits related to the 600-year-old tradition of the Aubusson carpet- and tapestry-weaving industry. The displays also highlight the 20th-century rebirth of the Aubusson carpet and the art of tapestry weaving. The museum is open September to June Wednesday to Monday 9:30am to noon and 2 to 6pm; and July to August Wednesday to Monday 10am to 6pm, Tuesday 2 to 6pm. Admission is 6€ for adults, 4€ for students, and free for ages 17 and under.

Maison du Tapissier, accessible directly from the tourist office, rue Vieille (✆ **05-55-66-32-12**), contains a collection of antique carpets and a replica of a carpet-weaving studio from the early 19th century. It's open in June and September daily 9:30am to 12:30pm and 2 to 6pm, and October to May Monday to Saturday 9:30am to 12:30pm and 2 to 6pm. Admission is 6€ for adults and free for children 11 and under.

Where to Stay & Dine

Hôtel Le France   This is the best and most appealing hotel in a town whose visitors are mostly business travelers, buyers, and decorators from other parts of Europe. It sits behind a 200-year-old facade of thick granite blocks in the heart of this "overgrown village" of 400 souls. Each of the guest rooms is different. Some rooms—especially the pricier ones—hold antiques and *baldaquin* (canopy) beds, with hanging draperies romantically positioned on all sides. Rooms are not air-conditioned, but the masonry walls tend to keep things temperate. The likable manager, M. Morel, knows a lot about the town and the surrounding region.

6 rue Déportés, Aubusson 23200. ✆ **05-55-66-10-22.** Fax 05-55-66-88-64. www.aubussonlefrance. com. 21 units. 59€–95€ double. Free outdoor parking; indoor parking 8€. AE, DC, MC, V. **Amenities:** Restaurant, brasserie; bar; room service. *In room:* TV, hair dryer, Wi-Fi (free).

LIMOGES ★

396km (246 miles) S of Paris; 311km (193 miles) N of Toulouse; 93km (58 miles) NE of Périgueux

Limoges, the ancient capital of Limousin in west-central France, is world famous for its exquisite porcelain and enamel works. Enamel production is a medieval industry revived in the 19th century and still going strong today. In fact, Limoges is the economic capital of western France. Occupying the Vienne's right bank, the town has historically consisted of two parts: La Cité (aka Vieux Limoges), with its narrow streets and old *maisons* on the lower slope; and La Ville Haute (aka "Le Château"), at the summit.

Essentials

GETTING THERE   Limoges has good **train** service from most regional cities, with direct trains from Toulouse, Poitiers, and Paris. Fifteen trains depart daily from Paris's Gare d'Austerlitz for Limoges (trip time: 2½ hr.); the one-way fare is 52€. For complete train information, call ✆ **36-35** or 08-92-35-35-35. **Bus** transit in and out of the small towns and villages nearby can be arranged through the **Régie des**

Transports de la Haute-Vienne, place Charentes. If you're **driving** from Aubusson, take D941 west for the 1-hour trip.

VISITOR INFORMATION The **Office de Tourisme** is at 12 bd. de Fleurus (© 05-55-34-46-87; fax 05-55-34-19-12; www.tourismelimoges.com).

Exploring the Town

If you'd like to see an enameler at work or an operating porcelain factory, ask at the tourist office (see above) for a list of workshops, or go directly to the famous **Pavillon de la Porcelaine** (see below).

Thanks to the rich deposits of kaolin (known locally as "white gold"), found near Limoges in the 18th century, more than 30 manufacturers of porcelain have set up operations through the years. Many maintain factory outlets, sometimes offering good-quality seconds at reduced prices. In the center of town, you'll find **Raynaud**, 14 ancienne rte. d'Aixe (© 05-55-01-77-55), and **Porcelaines Philippe Deshoulières-Lafarge,** 20 rue Armand Dutreix (© 05-55-50-33-43). Largest of all, with the best publicity operation, is **Bernardaud,** 27 av. Albert-Thomas (© 05-55-10-55-50), where a small-scale museum (focusing on past porcelain-related triumphs) and a tearoom adjoin the showroom.

Cathédrale St-Etienne The cathedral was begun in 1273 and took years to complete. The choir was finished in 1327, but work continued in the nave until almost 1890. The cathedral is the only one in the old province of Limousin built entirely in the Gothic style. The main entrance is through Porte St-Jean, which has carved wooden doors from the 16th century (constructed at the peak of the Flamboyant Gothic style). Inside, the nave appears so harmonious it's hard to imagine that its construction took 6 centuries. The rood screen is of particular interest, built in 1533 in the ornate style of the Italian Renaissance. The cathedral also contains some admirable bishops' tombs from the 14th to the 16th centuries.

Place de la Cathédrale. © **05-55-34-53-81.** Free admission. Summer daily 10am–6pm; rest of year daily 10am–5pm.

Eglise St-Michel-des-Lions Construction of this church began in the 14th century and continued into the 15th and 16th centuries. Although the church is not as interesting as older Romanesque churches in other parts of the Auvergne, it's the headquarters of the cult of St-Martial, a Limoges hometown bishop who died in the 3rd century. The church is the home of what's reputed to be his skull, stored in an elaborately enameled reliquary. Les Ostensions is a religious procession, established in 994, that occurs every 7 years from February to November. The skull, La Chasse de St-Martial—which some adherents credit with mystical powers—is removed from storage and exhibited as part of religious ceremonies that attract as many as 100,000 devout adherents. The next such procession is scheduled for 2016.

Place St-Michel. © **05-55-32-26-98.** Free admission. Mon–Sat 8am–6pm; Sun 8–11:45am and 4–6pm.

Musée Municipal de l'Evêché-de-Limoges Adjoining the cathedral in the Jardins de l'Evêché—which offer a view of the Vienne and the 13th-century pont St-Etienne—the old archbishops' palace is now the Musée Municipal. The elegant 18th-century building has an outstanding collection of Limoges enamels from the 12th century, as well as some enamel paintings by Leonard Limousin, who was born in 1505 in Limoges and went on to win world acclaim and the favor of four monarchs. Limoges was also the birthplace of Auguste Renoir, and the museum displays several of his works.

Place de la Cathédrale. © **05-55-45-98-10.** Free admission. June–Sept daily 10am–noon and 2–6pm; Oct–May Wed–Mon 10am–noon and 2–5pm.

Musée National de la Porcelaine Adrien-Dubouché ★★ This museum, in a 19th-century building, has the largest public collection of Limoges porcelain. Its 12,000 pieces illustrate the history of glassmaking and ceramics (porcelain, earthenware, stoneware, and terra cotta) throughout the ages. In France, its porcelain collection is second in quantity only to that of Sèvres. The main gallery contains whole dinner sets of noted figures and some contemporary Limoges ware.

8 bis place Winston-Churchill. © **05-55-33-08-50.** www.musee-adriendubouche.fr. Admission 4.50€ adults, 3€ ages 6–18. Wed–Mon 10am–12:25pm and 2–5:40pm.

Pavillon de la Porcelaine Haviland has been exporting its porcelain to the United States and other countries since 1842, when a group of American entrepreneurs immigrated to France from Boston to found the first American-owned company ever established in Europe. Over the years, it has used the designs of artists such as Gauguin and Dalí. In the museum, you can see masterpieces as well as original pieces created for the U.S. White House. A video screening can tell you more about the manufacturing process, and a large shop also sells the porcelain at factory prices.

40 av. John-Kennedy. © **05-55-30-21-86.** Free admission. July–Aug daily 10am–6:30pm; Sept–June Mon–Sat 10am–1pm and 2–6:30pm.

Where to Stay

Efficient, no-nonsense lodgings, favored by visiting businesspeople, can be found at the **Best Western Hotel Richelieu,** near the town center at 40 av. Baudin, Limoges 87000 (© **05-55-34-22-82;** fax 05-55-34-35-36; www.hotel-richelieu.com). Doubles go for 100€ to 112€.

Hôtel Royal Limousin ★ This is the town's leading inn, built in the 1960s adjacent to a parking lot in the center of Limoges. The large, modern, chain hotel–style rooms have midsize bathrooms, mostly with tub/shower combinations. Accommodations on the noisier avenue Carnot side cost less than those on the quieter place de la République. The only drawback is that a lot of tour groups stay here. There's no restaurant, but the staff refers hotel guests to the restaurant next door.

Place de la République B.P. 280, Limoges 87007. © **05-55-34-65-30.** Fax 05-55-34-55-21. www. mercure.com. 76 units. 102€–130€ double. AE, DC, MC, V. **Amenities:** Room service. *In room:* TV, hair dryer, minibar, Wi-Fi (free).

Where to Dine

Le Versailles FRENCH Set on a busy commercial boulevard near the center of town, this is a deeply entrenched staple of conservative French cuisine that's always mentioned as one of the town's most visible, most professional, and most consistent dining spots. The rooms that contain it haven't changed much (especially the wood paneling and mirrors) since it was built in 1928. Since the restaurant opened in 1932, it seems everybody in town has been here at least once. Today, the menu remains relatively conservative but with long lists of flavorful and freshly made food. The best examples include sweetbreads with morels; a cassoulet of veal kidneys with sweet red wine; a long list of grilled meats from nearby purveyors, served with your choice of Béarnaise, pepper, garlic-butter, or wine sauce; a stewpot of scallops with flap mushrooms; sole meunière; and medallions of monkfish with salted ham and stewed tomatoes.

20 place d'Aine. ✆ **05-55-34-13-39.** Reservations recommended. Main courses 15€–32€; Mon–Sat set-price menus 16€ and 22€–29€. AE, MC, V. Daily noon–2:30pm and 7:30–11:30pm. Bus: 4 or 10.

Where to Stay & Dine Nearby

IN ST-MARTIN-DU-FAULT

La Chapelle St-Martin ★★★   This is the best place in the area if you enjoy early-1900s living and superb food in the tradition of the Relais & Châteaux group. The hotel is in a private park with two ponds. The tasteful rooms are individually decorated with a 19th-century theme, usually Directoire or Empire. The restaurant offers excellent French food, with fixed-price menus ranging from 40€ to 66€.

87510 Nieul. ✆ **05-55-75-80-17.** Fax 05-55-75-89-50. www.chapellesaintmartin.com. 13 units. 80€–190€ double; 260€–360€ suite. AE, DC, MC, V. Free parking. Hotel closed Jan 1–Feb 7. Reserve well in advance. Restaurant closed Mon July–Aug. Take N147 and D35 11km (6¾ miles) northeast from Limoges. **Amenities:** Restaurant; outdoor pool; room service; tennis court. *In room:* A/C (in some), TV, hair dryer, minibar, Wi-Fi (free).

IN NIEUIL

To get to Nieuil from Limoges, take N141 west of the town center (signposted ANGOULEME). The town of Nieuil is signposted at the town of Suaux. Follow the signs for about 1.5km (1 mile) east of the village toward Fontafie. Nieuil lies 64km (40 miles) northwest of Limoges.

   Note: Don't confuse Nieuil with La Chapelle St-Martin (see above) at Nieul, near Limoges, 55km (34 miles) away, with a slightly different spelling.

Château de Nieuil ★★   This fabled old inn comes with quite a pedigree. The château, built in the 16th century as a hunting lodge for François I, became the first château-hotel in France in 1937. Restored by the *comte* de Dampierre early in the 1800s after its destruction in the Revolution, it has remained in the antiques-collecting Bodinaud family since around 1900. Rooms are beautifully furnished and magnificently comfortable, with elegant bathrooms. Today, 160 hectares (395 acres) of park and forest surround a series of beautifully maintained gardens.

   The restaurant, La Grange aux Oies (the Goose Farm), is in a stone-walled annex constructed in the late 19th century as stables. The cuisine focuses on classic and regional recipes. Main courses cost 21€ to 25€; fixed-price menus are 26€ to 46€ at lunch, 70€ at dinner; there is a kids' menu for 17€. Nonguests may dine here if they call ahead.

Nieuil 16270. ✆ **05-45-71-36-38.** Fax 05-45-71-46-45. www.chateaunieuilhotel.com. 14 units. 130€–275€ double; 255€–420€ suite. AE, DC, MC, V. Closed Nov–Apr. **Amenities:** Restaurant; bar; outdoor pool; room service; tennis court. *In room:* A/C, TV, hair dryer, minibar, Wi-Fi (free).

LE PUY-EN-VELAY ★★★

523km (325 miles) S of Paris; 129km (80 miles) SE of Clermont-Ferrand

Le Puy-en-Velay (usually shortened to Le Puy) is one of the most extraordinary sights in France. Steep volcanic spires, left over from geological activity that ended millennia ago, are capped with Romanesque churches, a cathedral, and medieval houses that rise sinuously from the plain below. The history of Le Puy centers on the cult of the Virgin Mary.

Le Puy today is a provincial city of steep cobblestone streets with lots of rather shabby buildings (many of which are being restored). Much of the population of approximately 21,000 lives off the tourist trade, and today's visitors follow in the footsteps of Charlemagne, Le Puy's "first tourist." Le Puy remains a major pilgrimage destination, although it is not as famous as Lourdes.

In France, Le Puy is defined as the capital of lentils. Lentils produced within a specific distance of Le Puy are categorized in a way that emulates the classification of the country's most prestigious wines, as A.O.C. (Appellation d'Origine Contrôlée). The town is also the point of departure for pilgrims who follow the road to Santiago de Compostela in northwest Spain. A blessing in honor of pilgrims takes place every morning at 7am in the cathedral (see below). Because of the numbers of pilgrims who have stopped at Le Puy and its cathedral, UNESCO lists the town, as well as the entire length of the chemin de St-Jacques de Compostelle, as a site of importance to the universal patrimony.

Essentials

GETTING THERE   Passengers arriving in Le Puy from anywhere in Europe must change **trains** at St-Georges d'Aurac. From there, 10 small trains, timed for convenient connections, travel along the 28km (17-mile) spur route that connects Le Puy's railway station to the rest of the lines of the SNCF. For information, call ✆ **36-35** or 08-92-35-35-35. **Bus** service is of use only in and out of the small villages in the Auvergne. Even buses from Clermont-Ferrand take at least 3 hours to cover the relatively short distance. For **bus** information, contact La Gare Routière at ✆ **04-71-07-42-36.** If you're **driving,** the best way to reach Le Puy is from St-Etienne, traveling southwest along N88. From Clermont-Ferrand, drive south along N88 to Lempdes, continuing southeast along N102 to Le Puy.

VISITOR INFORMATION   The **Office de Tourisme** is on place du Clauzel near La Mairie (town hall; ✆ **04-71-09-38-41;** fax 04-71-05-22-62; www.ot-lepuyenvelay.fr).

Seeing the Sights

Le Puy is the historic center of the French lace industry; you'll find lace shops on every block. But to be assured of handmade authenticity, look for the words DENTELLE DU PUY. Under a 1931 local government ordinance, the display of this mark is a privilege reserved for the real thing. The best selections of local lace are at **Spécialités du Velay,** 1 bd. St-Louis (✆ **04-71-09-09-34**); **Valois Dentelles,** 28 place du Plot (✆ **04-71-09-60-69**); and **Aux Souvenirs du Puy,** 60 rue Raphaël (✆ **04-71-05-76-71**).

Cathédrale Notre-Dame ★★★   This Romanesque cathedral was conceived as a shelter and prayer site for medieval pilgrims heading to the religious shrines of Santiago de Compostela in northwestern Spain. Marked by vivid Oriental and Byzantine influences, it's worth a visit. The cloisters contain carved capitals dating from the Carolingian era. Occupying the cathedral's original treasury, and accessible from inside the cathedral, is **Le Musée d'Art Religieux.** It contains fabrics, religious icons, and gold and silver objects, including an unusual enameled chalice from the 12th century, that have been associated with the church for many centuries.

Place du For. ✆ **04-71-05-98-74.** Free admission to cathedral; to cloisters, Chapel of Relics, and museum 5€ adults, 3.50€ students and ages 18–25, free for children 17 and under. Cathedral Mar–Sept daily 7am–7:30pm; Oct–Feb daily 7am–6:30pm. Cloisters, Chapel of Relics, and museum Oct–Mar daily 9am–noon and 2–4:30pm; Apr–June daily 9am–12:30pm and 2–6pm; July–Sept daily 9:30am–6:30pm.

Chapelle St-Michel-d'Aiguilhe ★★ This 10th-century chapel, perched precariously atop a volcanic spur that rises abruptly from hilly terrain, is one of the city's most dramatic sights. It sits on the northwestern perimeter of Le Puy. Reaching the summit requires a long climb up rocky stairs. When you get here, you'll be struck by the Oriental influences in the floor plan, the arabesques, and the mosaics crafted from black stone. On view are some 12th-century murals and an 11th-century wooden depiction of Christ.

Atop the Rocher St-Michel. ✆ **04-71-09-50-03.** Admission 3€ adults, 2.50€ students, 1.50€ children 13 and under. Visits daily: Mid-Mar–Apr 9:30am–noon and 2–5:30pm; May–July 9 9am–6:30pm; July 10–Aug 25 9am–6:45pm; Aug 26–Sept 30 9am–6:30pm; Oct to mid-Nov 9:30am–noon and 2–5:30pm; mid-Nov to mid-Mar 2–5pm.

Musée Crozatier Celebrating the history, culture, and geology of the region, this museum contains exhibits of handicrafts, especially lace, some of which date from the 16th century. It also has a collection of minerals, crystals, pottery shards, and bones from nearby archaeological excavations, architectural embellishments from the Romanesque era, and paintings from the 14th to the 20th centuries.

In the Jardin Henri-Vinay. ✆ **04-71-06-62-40.** Admission 3.20€ adults, 1.40€ students and ages 18–25, free for children 17 and under. June 15–Sept 15 daily 10am–noon and 2–6pm; Mar–June 14 and Sept 16–30 Wed–Mon 10am–noon and 2–6pm; Feb and Oct–Nov Mon and Wed–Sat 10am–noon, Wed–Mon 2–4pm. Closed Dec–Jan.

Where to Stay

Hôtel Régina In no way is this 1905 hotel grand, but it's the finest in town and well located right in the heart of town. A radical renovation brought it into its current condition, offering simple but thoughtfully decorated rooms containing midsize bathrooms. One entire floor has air-conditioning. The in-house brasserie offers affordable platters of food. In the afternoon, it turns into a tea salon that attracts many local retirees and shopkeepers.

34 bd. du Maréchal-Fayolle, Le Puy-en-Velay 43000. ✆ **04-71-09-14-71.** Fax 04-71-09-18-57. www.hotelrestregina.com. 25 units. 60€–88€ double; 95€–110€ suite. AE, DC, MC, V. Parking 6.50€. **Amenities:** Restaurant; room service. *In room:* A/C, TV, hair dryer, Jacuzzi (in some), minibar, Wi-Fi (free).

Where to Dine

Le Chamarlenc FRENCH/AUVERGNAT The kitchen is devoted to the traditions of the region, preparing dishes that utilize Auvergne's robust wines, as well as regional lentils, which crop up in appealing and flavorful ways. You might start with the delectable terrine of the house or a freshly made soup of the day. The main meat and poultry dishes are forever changing, as are the vegetables, based on seasonal adjustments. The homemade desserts tend to be luscious.

19 rue Raphaël. ✆ **04-71-02-17-72.** www.lechamarlenc.fr. Reservations recommended. Fixed-price menus 12€–20€. MC, V. Tues–Sat noon–2:30pm; Thurs–Sat 4–10pm.

FAST FACTS

FAST FACTS: FRANCE

Area Code All French telephone numbers consist of 10 digits, the first two of which are like an area code. If you're calling anywhere in France from within France, just dial all 10 digits—no additional codes are needed. If you're calling from the United States, drop the initial 0 (zero).

ATM Networks & Cash Points See "Money & Costs," p. 56.

Business Hours Business hours are erratic, as befits a nation of individualists. Most banks are open Monday through Friday from 9:30am to 4:30pm. Many, particularly in small towns, take a lunch break. Hours are usually posted on the door. Most museums close 1 day a week (often Tues), and they're generally closed on national holidays. Usual hours are from 9:30am to 5pm. Refer to the individual listings. See "Holidays," below, for a list of recognized holidays.

Generally, offices are open Monday through Friday from 9am to 5pm, but always call first. In Paris or other big French cities, stores are open from 9, 9:30, or (often) 10am to 6 or 7pm without a break for lunch. Some shops, delis, cafes, and newsstands open at 8am and close at 8 or 9pm. In some small stores, the lunch break can last 3 hours, beginning at 1pm. This is more common in the south than in the north.

Car Rentals See "Rentals" in section 3 of chapter 3. Also see "Airline, Hotel & Car-Rental Websites," later in this chapter.

Currency See "Money & Costs," p. 56.

Drinking Laws The legal age for the purchase and consumption of alcohol is 18. But you'll rarely be carded. Still, it's smart to carry an ID (your own!). The police are very strict about driving while intoxicated. If convicted, you face a high fine and possibly jail time.

Driving Rules See "Getting There & Getting Around," p. 50.

Electricity Electricity in France runs on 220-volt, 50-cycle AC current. U.S. electricity is 110-volt, 60-cycle current. If you are bringing anything electric, you will need a plug adapter and possibly a voltage transformer. Some appliances have dual voltage, which means that you will only need a plug adapter to run your hair dryer or razor, for example; a switch on the appliance will allow you to change voltages. Adapters and converters are for sale at Radio Shack and luggage and travel stores.

Embassies & Consulates If you have a passport, immigration, legal, or other problem, contact your consulate. Call *before* you go—they often keep odd hours and observe both French and home-country holidays. The Embassy of the **United States,** 2 av. Gabriel, 8e (📞 **01-43-12-22-22;** http://france.usembassy.gov; Métro: Concorde), is open Monday to Friday from 8:30am to 5pm. The Embassy of **Canada** is at 35 av. Montaigne, 8e (📞 **01-44-43-29-00;** www.international.gc.ca/canada-europa/france/menu-en.asp; Métro: F-D-Roosevelt or Alma-Marceau), open Monday to Friday from 9am to noon and from 2 to 5pm. The Embassy of the **United**

Kingdom is at 35 rue du Faubourg St-Honoré, 8e (✆ **01-44-51-31-00;** http://ukin france.fco.gov.uk; Métro: Concorde or Madeleine), open Monday to Friday from 9:30am to 1pm and from 2:30 to 5pm. The Embassy of **Ireland** is at 4 rue Rude (✆ **01-44-17-67-00;** www.embassyofireland.fr; Métro: Etoile), open Monday to Friday from 9:30am to 1pm and from 2:30 to 5:30pm. The Embassy of **Australia** is at 4 rue Jean-Rey, 15e (✆ **01-40-59-33-00;** www.france.embassy.gov.au; Métro: Bir Hakeim), open Monday to Friday from 9:15am to noon and from 2:30 to 4:30pm. The embassy of **New Zealand** is at 7 ter rue Léonard-de-Vinci, Paris 75116 (✆ **01-45-01-43-43;** www.nzembassy.com; Métro: Victor Hugo), open Monday to Friday from 9am to 1pm and from 2:30 to 6pm. The embassy of **South Africa,** 59 quai d'Orsay, 7e (✆ **01-53-59-23-23;** www.afrique sud.net; Métro: Invalides), is open Monday to Friday 9am to noon.

Emergencies   In an emergency while at a hotel, contact the front desk. Most staffs are trained in dealing with a crisis and will do whatever is necessary. If the emergency involves something like a stolen wallet, go to the police station in person. Otherwise, you can get help anywhere by calling ✆ **17** for the police, ✆ **18** for the fire department (*pompiers*), or ✆ **15** for medical emergencies.

Etiquette & Customs   **Gestures:** If invited to someone's home, bring flowers, but never in the number of 13, which is said to bring bad luck. Don't bring any white flowers (for weddings), red carnations (bad will), or white lilies or chrysanthemums (for funerals). You can also bring wine, but make sure it's an expensive bottle; anything else is considered insulting.

Avoiding offense: Always try to arrive exactly on time if invited to a French house for dinner. Also, dress well.

Eating & drinking: Don't begin eating until the host or hostess has said, *"Bon appétit."*

Business etiquette: Say *"bonjour"* or *"bonsoir"* (good morning or good evening), with either a monsieur or madame, when meeting someone, even a shopkeeper. Upon leaving, say *"au revoir"* (goodbye), even if leaving a shop where you didn't buy anything. Business cards are exchanged after the initial intro.

Gasoline (Petrol)   See "Getting There & Getting Around," p. 50.

Holidays   In France, holidays are *jours fériés.* Shops and many businesses (banks and some museums and restaurants) close on holidays, but hotels and emergency services remain open.

The main holidays include New Year's Day (Jan 1), Easter Sunday and Monday, Labor Day (May 1), V-E Day (May 8), Whitmonday (May 19), Ascension Thursday (40 days after Easter), Bastille Day (July 14), Assumption of the Blessed Virgin (Aug 15), All Saints' Day (Nov 1), Armistice Day (Nov 11), and Christmas (Dec 25).

Hospitals   Dial ✆ **15** for medical emergencies. In Paris, the **American Hospital,** 63 bd. Victor-Hugo, in the suburb of Neuilly-sur-Seine (✆ **01-46-41-25-25;** www.american-hospital.org; Métro: Pont-de-Levallois or Pont-de-Neuilly; bus no. 82), operates a 24-hour emergency service. The bilingual staff accepts Blue Cross and other American insurance plans. Hospitals in other major cities include **Hôpital Rouen,** 1 rue de Germont (✆ 02-32-88-89-90; www.chu-rouen.fr), in Rouen; **Hôpital Bretonneau,** 2 bd. Tonnellé (✆ 02-47-47-80-29; www.chu-tours.fr), in Tours; **Hôpital Civil de Strasbourg,** 1 place de l'Hôpital (✆ 03-88-11-67-68; www.chru-strasbourg.fr), in Strasbourg; **Hôpital Edouard Herriot,** 5 place Arsonval (✆ 08-20-08-20-69), in Lyon; **Hôpital de Avignon,** 305 rue Raoul Follereau (✆ 04-32-75-33-33), in Avignon; **Hôpital St-Roch,** 5 rue Pierre Dévoluy (✆ 04-92-03-33-33), in Nice; and **CHU de Rangueil,** av. du Prof. Jean-Poulhes (✆ 05-61-32-25-33), in Toulouse.

Insurance   **Medical Insurance**   For travel overseas, most U.S. health plans (including Medicare and Medicaid) do not provide coverage, and the ones that do often require you to pay for services upfront and reimburse you only after you return home.

As a safety net, you may want to buy travel medical insurance, particularly if you're traveling to a remote or high-risk area where emergency evacuation might be necessary. If you require additional medical insurance, try **MEDEX Assistance** (✆ **410/453-6300;** www.medexassist.com) or **Travel Assistance International** (✆ **800/821-2828;** www. travelassistance.com; for general information on services, call the company's **Worldwide Assistance Services, Inc.** at ✆ **800/777-8710;** www.worldwideassistance.com).

Canadians should check with their provincial health plan offices or call **Health Canada** (✆ **866/225-0709;** www.hc-sc.gc.ca) to find out the extent of their coverage and what documentation and receipts they must take home in case they are treated overseas.

Travelers from the U.K. should carry their European Health Insurance Card (EHIC), which replaced the E111 form as proof of entitlement to free/reduced cost medical treatment abroad (✆ **0845/605-0707;** www.ehic.org.uk). Note, however, that the EHIC only covers "necessary medical treatment," and for repatriation costs, lost money, baggage, or cancellation, travel insurance from a reputable company should always be sought (www.travelinsuranceweb.com).

Travel Insurance   The cost of travel insurance varies widely, depending on the destination, the cost and length of your trip, your age and health, and the type of trip you're taking, but expect to pay between 5% and 8% of the vacation itself. You can get estimates from various providers through **InsureMyTrip.com** (✆ **800/487-4722**). Enter your trip cost and dates, your age, and other information, for prices from more than a dozen companies.

U.K. citizens and their families who make more than one trip abroad per year may find an annual travel insurance policy works out cheaper. Check **www.moneysupermarket. com** (✆ **0845/345-5708**), which compares prices across a wide range of providers for single- and multitrip policies.

Most big travel agencies offer their own insurance and will probably try to sell you their package when you book a holiday. Think before you sign. **Britain's Consumers' Association** recommends that you insist on seeing the policy and reading the fine print before buying travel insurance. The **Association of British Insurers** (✆ **020/7600-3333;** www.abi.org.uk) gives advice by phone and publishes *Holiday Insurance,* a free guide to policy provisions and prices. You might also shop around for better deals: Try **Columbus Direct** (✆ **0870/033-9988;** www.columbusdirect.net).

Trip-Cancellation Insurance   Trip-cancellation insurance will help retrieve your money if you have to back out of a trip or depart early, or if your travel supplier goes bankrupt. Trip cancellation traditionally covers such events as sickness, natural disasters, and State Department advisories. The latest news in trip-cancellation insurance is the availability of **expanded hurricane coverage** and the **"any-reason"** cancellation coverage—which costs more but covers cancellations made for any reason. You won't get back 100% of your prepaid trip cost, but you'll be refunded a substantial portion. **TravelSafe** (✆ **888/885-7233;** www.travelsafe.com) offers both types of coverage. Expedia also offers any-reason cancellation coverage for its air-hotel packages. For details, contact one of the following recommended insurers: **Access America** (✆ 866/284-8300; www.accessamerica.com); **Travel Guard International** (✆ 800/ 826-4919; www.travelguard.com); **Travel Insured International** (✆ 800/243-3174; www.travelinsured.com); and **Travelex Insurance Services** (✆ 800/228-4602; www. travelex-insurance.com).

Internet Access There are hundreds of cybercafes all over France. For a list of Internet cafes, go to www.cybercaptive.com or www.cybercafe.com. The most popular in Paris seems to be **Luxembourg Micro,** 81 bd. Saint-Michel, 5e ((© **01-46-33-27-98;** www.luxembourgmicro.com; Métro: Luxembourg); it's open daily from 9am to 11pm. See "Internet & E-Mail" under "Staying Connected," in chapter 3.

Language English is increasingly understood in France, especially among young people who have studied it in school. People are more likely to understand English in such centers as Paris and the Riviera than in the more remote provinces. Service personnel in hotels tend to speak English, at least at the front desk. A staff member at most restaurants will speak a bit of English. However, many people you encounter in France do not speak English, and you may want to carry a Berlitz handbook. For some basic vocabulary, refer to the "Useful Terms & Phrases" chapter.

Legal Aid If you get into any legal troubles, contact your consulate. See "Embassies & Consulates," above, for contact information.

Lost & Found To speed the process of replacing your personal documents if they're lost or stolen, make a photocopy of the first few pages of your passport and write down your credit card numbers (and the serial numbers of your traveler's checks, if you're using them). Leave this information with someone at home—to be faxed to you in an emergency—and swap it with your traveling companion. Be sure to tell all of your credit card companies the minute you discover your wallet has been lost or stolen, and file a report at the nearest police precinct. Your credit card company or insurer may require a police report number or record of the loss.

Use the following numbers in France to report your lost or stolen credit card: **American Express** (call collect U.S. (© **336/393-1111**); **MasterCard** ((© **08-00-90-13-87;** www.master card.com); **Visa** (© **08-00-90-11-79;** www.visaeurope.com). Your credit card company may be able to wire you a cash advance immediately or deliver an emergency card in a day or two.

If you need emergency cash over the weekend when all banks and American Express offices are closed, you can have money wired to you via **Western Union** ((© **800/325-6000;** www.westernunion.com). **Travelers Express/MoneyGram** is the largest company in the U.S. for money orders. You can transfer funds either online or by phone in about 10 minutes ((© **800/MONEYGRAM** [666-3947]; www.moneygram.com).

Identity theft and fraud are potential complications of losing your wallet, especially if you lose your driver's license with your cash and credit cards. Notify the major credit-reporting bureaus immediately; placing a fraud alert on your records may protect you against liability for criminal activity. The three major U.S. credit-reporting agencies are **Equifax** (www.equifax.com), **Experian** ((© **888/397-3742;** www.experian.com), and **TransUnion** ((© **800/680-7289;** www.transunion.com).

If you've lost all forms of photo ID, call your airline and explain the situation; your carrier may let you board the plane if you have a copy of your passport or birth certificate and a copy of the police report you've filed.

Mail Most post offices in France are open Monday to Friday from 8am to 7pm and Saturday from 8am to noon. Allow 5 to 8 days to send or receive mail from your home. Airmail letters within Europe cost .85€; to the United States and Canada, .90€. Airmail letters to Australia and New Zealand cost .90€.

You can exchange money at post offices. Many hotels sell stamps, as do local post offices and cafes displaying a red TABAC sign outside.

Newspapers & Magazines Copies of the international edition of the ***International Herald Tribune*** are distributed all over France and are sold at newspaper kiosks and at newsstands in the lobbies of first-class or deluxe hotels. Copies of ***Time*** and

Newsweek are also widely sold. A far larger selection of U.K. magazines and newspapers is available. London newspapers arrive in Paris an hour or so after publication.

Passports   See www.frommers.com/planning for information on how to obtain a passport.

For Residents of Australia   Contact the **Australian Passport Information Service** at ✆ **131-232,** or visit the government website at www.passports.gov.au.

For Residents of Canada   Contact the central **Passport Office,** Department of Foreign Affairs and International Trade, Ottawa, ON K1A 0G3 (✆ **800/567-6868;** www.ppt.gc.ca).

For Residents of Ireland   Contact the **Passport Office,** Setanta Centre, Molesworth Street, Dublin 2 (✆ **01/671-1633;** www.irlgov.ie/iveagh).

For Residents of New Zealand   Contact the **Passports Office** at ✆ **0800/225-050** in New Zealand, or 04/474-8100, or log on to www.passports.govt.nz.

For Residents of the United Kingdom   Visit your nearest passport office, major post office, or travel agency or contact the **United Kingdom Passport Service** at ✆ **0870/521-0410** or search its website at www.ukpa.gov.uk.

For Residents of the United States   To find your regional passport office, either check the U.S. State Department website or call the **National Passport Information Center** toll-free number (✆ **877/487-2778**) for automated information.

Pharmacies   If you need a *pharmacie* during off hours, have the front-desk staff at your hotel get in touch with the nearest Commissariat de Police. An agent there will have the address of a nearby pharmacy open 24 hours a day. French law requires that the pharmacies in any given neighborhood display the name and location of the one that remains open all night. In Paris, one of the most central all-nighters is **Pharmacy Les Champs "Derhy,"** 84 av. des Champs-Elysées, 8e (✆ **01-45-62-02-41;** Métro: George V).

Police   Call ✆ **17** anywhere in France.

Smoking   In 2008 France banned smoking in cafes, restaurants, and nightclubs. In fact, smoking is banned everywhere but in private homes and in the streets.

Taxes   As a member of the European Union, France routinely imposes a value-added tax (VAT in English; TVA in French) on many goods and services. The standard VAT is 19.6% on merchandise, including clothing, appliances, liquor, leather goods, shoes, furs, jewelry, perfumes, cameras, and even caviar. Refunds are made for the tax on certain goods and merchandise, but not on services. The minimum purchase is 184€ at one time for nationals or residents of countries outside the E.U.

Telephones   The French use a *télécarte,* or phone debit card, which you can purchase at rail stations, post offices, and other places. Sold in two versions, it allows you to use either 50 or 120 charge units (depending on the card) by inserting the card into the slot of most public phones. Depending on the type of card you buy, the cost starts at 10€ and goes up from there. You must use this card when making calls within France; coins are no longer accepted. You can use a major credit card in much the same way as a *télécarte,* but there's a catch: To do so involves a minimum charge of 20€. The phone system gives you 30 days to use up this 20€ credit. If possible, avoid making calls from your hotel; some establishments will double or triple the charges.

Time   The French equivalent of daylight saving time lasts from April to September, which puts it 1 hour ahead of French winter time. France is usually 6 hours ahead of U.S. Eastern Standard Time, except in October, when U.S. clocks are still on daylight time; then France is only 5 hours ahead. The rest of the year, when it's 9am in New York, it's 3pm in France.

23

FAST FACTS

Time

Tipping The law requires all bills to say *service compris,* which means the total includes the tip. But French diners often leave some small change as an additional tip, especially if service has been exceptional.

Some general guidelines: For hotel staff, tip 1.05€ to 1.50€ for every item of baggage the porter carries on arrival and departure, and 1.50€ per day for the maid. In cafes, service is usually included. Tip is included in fee. In theaters and restaurants, give cloakroom attendants at least .75€ to 1.20€ per item. Give restroom attendants in nightclubs and other establishments about .50€. Give cinema and theater ushers about .50€. For guides for group visits to museums and monuments, 1.50€ is a reasonable tip.

Toilets If you're in dire need, duck into a cafe or brasserie to use the lavatory. It's customary to make a small purchase if you do so. Paris Métro stations and underground garages usually contain public restrooms, but the degree of cleanliness varies. France still has some "hole-in-the-ground" toilets, so be warned. For reviews and recommendations of the tidiest toilets in France and other places, visit **www.thebathroomdiaries.com**.

Useful Phone Numbers U.S. Dept. of State Travel Advisory (📞 **202/647-5225,** staffed 24 hr.); U.S. Passport Agency (📞 **202/647-0518**); U.S. Centers for Disease Control International Traveler's Hotline (📞 **404/332-4559;** www.cdc.gov).

Visitor Information Before you go, your best source of information is the **French Government Tourist Office** (www.franceguide.com), which can be reached at the following addresses:

- **United States:** 825 Third Ave., 29th Floor, New York, NY 10022 (📞 **514/288-1904;** fax 212/838-7855); 205 N. Michigan Ave., Chicago, IL 60601 (📞 **514/288-1904**); or 9454 Wilshire Blvd., Ste. 715, Beverly Hills, CA 90212 (📞 **514/288-1904**).
- **Canada:** 1800 av. McGill College, Ste. 490, Montreal, QC H3A 2W9 (📞 **514/288-2026;** fax 514/845-4868).
- **United Kingdom:** 178 Piccadilly, London W1J 9AL (📞 **09068/244-123** [60p per min.]; fax 020/7493-6594).
- **Australia:** 25 Blight St., Sydney, NSW 2000 (📞 **02/9231-5244;** fax 02/9221-8682).

Although AAA has maps of France, the best are *cartes routiéres* (road maps) published by Michelin. Both map books and fold-outs are available at almost any large bookstore in Paris and other French cities, and are sometimes available at news kiosks. The Michelin maps offer alternative *routes de dégagement,* which you can travel to skirt big cities and avoid traffic-clogged highways. We recommend the *France Tourist and Motoring Atlas* (No. 20197).

Water Drinking water is generally safe, though it's occasionally been known to cause diarrhea. If you ask for water in a restaurant, it'll be served bottled (for which you'll pay) unless you specifically request *l'eau du robinet* (tap water). Your waiter may ask if you'd like your water *avec gas* (carbonated) or *sans gas* (without bubbles).

USEFUL TERMS & PHRASES

GLOSSARY OF FRENCH-LANGUAGE TERMS

It's often amazing how a word or two of halting French will change your hosts' dispositions in their home country. At the very least, try to learn a few numbers, basic greetings, and—above all—the life raft, *"Parlez-vous anglais?"* As it turns out, many French do speak passable English and will use it liberally if you demonstrate the basic courtesy of greeting them in their language. Go out, try our glossary on, and don't be bashful. *Bonne chance!*

24

BASICS

English	French	Pronunciation
Yes/No	Oui/Non	**wee/nohn**
Okay	D'accord	**dah-*core***
Please	S'il vous plaît	**seel voo *play***
Thank you	Merci	**mair-*see***
You're welcome	De rien	**duh ree-*ehn***
Hello (during daylight hours)	Bonjour	**bohn-*jhoor***
Good evening	Bonsoir	**bohn-*swahr***
Goodbye	Au revoir	**o ruh-*vwahr***
What's your name?	Comment vous appellez-vous?	**ko-mahn voo za-pell-ay-*voo*?**
My name is . . .	Je m'appelle . . .	**jhuh ma-*pell* . . .**
Happy to meet you	Enchanté(e)	**ohn-shahn-*tay***
Miss	Mademoiselle	**mad-mwa-*zel***
Mr.	Monsieur	**muh-*syuh***
Mrs.	Madame	**ma-*dam***
How are you?	Comment allez-vous?	**kuh-mahn tahl-ay-*voo*?**
Fine, thank you, and you?	Très bien, merci, et vous?	**tray bee-ehn, mare-ci, ay *voo*?**
Very well, thank you	Très bien, merci	**tray bee-ehn, mair-*see***
So-so	Comme ci, comme ça	**kum-*see*, kum-*sah***

English	French	Pronunciation
I'm sorry/excuse me	Pardon	**pahr-*dohn***
I'm so very sorry	Désolé(e)	**day-zoh-*lay***
That's all right	Il n'y a pas de quoi	**eel nee ah pah duh kwah**

Getting Around/Street Smarts

English	French	Pronunciation
Do you speak English?	Parlez-vous anglais?	**par-lay-voo ahn-*glay*?**
I don't speak French	Je ne parle pas français	**jhuh ne parl pah frahn-*say***
I don't understand	Je ne comprends pas	**jhuh ne kohm-*prahn* pas**
Could you speak more loudly/more slowly?	Pouvez-vous parler un peu plus fort/plus lentement?	**poo-vay-voo par-lay un puh ploo for/ploo lan-te-*ment*?**
Could you repeat that?	Répetez, s'il vous plaît?	**ray-pay-*tay,* seel voo *play***
What is it?	Qu'est-ce que c'est?	**kess kuh *say*?**
What time is it?	Qu'elle heure est-il?	**kel uhr eh-*teel*?**
What?	Quoi?	**kwah?**
How? or What did you say?	Comment?	**ko-*mahn*?**
When?	Quand?	**kahn?**
Where is . . . ?	Où est . . . ?	**ooh eh . . . ?**
Who?	Qui?	**kee?**
Why?	Pourquoi?	**poor-*kwah*?**
Here/there	ici/là	**ee-*see*/lah**
Left/right	à gauche/à droite	**a goash/a drwaht**
Straight ahead	tout droit	**too drwah**
I'm American/Canadian/British	Je suis américain(e)/ canadien(e)/anglais(e)	**jhe sweez a-may-ree-*kehn*/can-ah-dee-*en*/ahn-glay (*glaise*)**
Fill the tank (of a car), please	Le plein, s'il vous plaît	**luh plan, seel voo *play***
I'm going to . . .	Je vais à . . .	**jhe vay ah . . .**
I want to get off at . . .	Je voudrais descendre à . . .	**jhe voo-*dray* day-son-drah ah**
I'm sick	Je suis malade	**jhuh swee mal-*ahd***
airport	l'aéroport	**lair-o-*por***
bank	la banque	**lah bahnk**
bridge	pont	**pohn**
bus station	la gare routière	**lah gar roo-tee-*air***
bus stop	l'arrêt de bus	**lah-*ray* duh boohss**
by means of a bicycle	en vélo/par bicyclette	**ahn *vay*-low/par bee-see-*clet***
by means of a car	en voiture	**ahn vwa-*toor***
cashier	la caisse	**lah *kess***

English	French	Pronunciation
cathedral	cathédral	**ka-tay-*dral***
church	église	**ay-*gleez***
dead end	une impasse	**ewn am-*pass***
driver's license	permis de conduire	**per-mee duh con-*dweer***
elevator	l'ascenseur	**lah-sahn-*seuhr***
stairs	l'escalier	**les-kal-*yay***
entrance (to a building or a city)	une porte	**ewn port**
exit (from a building or a freeway)	une sortie	**ewn sor-*tee***
fortified castle or palace	château	**sha-*tow***
garden	jardin	**jhar-dehn**
gasoline	du pétrol/de l'essence	**duh pay-*trol*/de lay-*sahns***
ground floor	rez-de-chausée	**ray-de-show-*say***
highway to . . .	la route pour	**la root por**
hospital	l'hôpital	**low-pee-*tahl***
insurance	les assurances	**lez ah-sur-*ahns***
luggage storage	consigne	**kohn-*seen*-yuh**
museum	le musée	**luh mew-*zay***
no entry	sens interdit	**sehns ahn-ter-*dee***
no smoking	défense de fumer	**day-*fahns* de fu-may**
on foot	à pied	**ah pee-*ay***
1-day pass	ticket journalier	**tee-kay jhoor-nall-ee-*ay***
one-way ticket	aller simple	**ah-*lay* sam-pluh**
police	la police	**lah po-*lees***
rented car	voiture de location	**vwa-*toor* de low-ka-see-on**
round-trip ticket	aller-retour	**ah-*lay*-re-*toor***
second floor	premier étage	**prem-ee-*ehr* ay-*taj***
slow down	ralentir	**rah-lahn-*teer***
store	le magasin	**luh ma-ga-*zehn***
street	rue	**roo**
subway	le Métro	**le *may*-tro**
telephone	le téléphone	**luh tay-lay-*phone***
ticket	un billet	**uh *bee*-yay**
ticket office	vente de billets	**vahnt duh bee-*yay***
toilets	les toilettes/les WC	**lay twa-*lets*/lay vay-*say***
tower	tour	**toor**

Necessities

English	French	Pronunciation
I'd like . . .	Je voudrais . . .	jhe voo-*dray* . . .
a room	une chambre	ewn *shahm*-bruh
the key	la clé (la clef)	la *clay*
I'd like to buy . . .	Je voudrais acheter . . .	jhe voo-dray ahsh-*tay* . . .
aspirin	des aspirines/des aspros	deyz ahs-peer-*eens*/deyz ahs-*prohs*
cigarettes	des cigarettes	day see-ga-*ret*
condoms	des préservatifs	day pray-ser-va-*teefs*
dictionary	un dictionnaire	uh deek-see-oh-*nare*
dress	une robe	ewn robe
envelopes	des envelopes	days ahn-veh-*lope*
gift (for someone)	un cadeau	uh kah-*doe*
handbag	un sac	uh sahk
hat	un chapeau	uh shah-*poh*
magazine	une revue	ewn reh-*vu*
map of the city	un plan de ville	unh plahn de *veel*
matches	des allumettes	dayz a-loo-*met*
necktie	une cravate	eun cra-*vaht*
newspaper	un journal	uh jhoor-*nahl*
phone card	une carte téléphonique	ewncart tay-lay-fone-*eek*
postcard	une carte postale	ewn carte pos-*tahl*
road map	une carte routière	ewn cart roo-tee-*air*
shirt	une chemise	ewn che-*meez*
shoes	des chaussures	day show-*suhr*
skirt	une jupe	ewn jhoop
soap	du savon	dew sah-*vohn*
socks	des chaussettes	day show-*set*
stamp	un timbre	uh *tam*-bruh
trousers	un pantalon	uh pan-tah-*lohn*
writing paper	du papier à lettres	dew pap-pee-*ay a let*-ruh
How much does it cost?	C'est combien? / Ça coûte combien?	say comb-bee-*ehn*?/sah coot comb-bee-*ehn*?
That's expensive	C'est cher/chère	say share
That's inexpensive	C'est raisonnable/C'est bon marché	say ray-son-*ahb*-bluh/say bohn mar-*shay*
Do you take credit cards?	Est-ce que vous acceptez les cartes de credit?	es-kuh voo zaksep-*tay* lay kart duh creh-*dee*?

Numbers & Ordinals

English	French	Pronunciation
zero	zéro	**zare-*oh***
one	un	**uh**
two	deux	**duh**
three	trois	**twah**
four	quatre	***kaht*-ruh**
five	cinq	**sank**
six	six	**seess**
seven	sept	**set**
eight	huit	**wheat**
nine	neuf	**nuf**
ten	dix	**deess**
eleven	onze	**ohnz**
twelve	douze	**dooz**
thirteen	treize	**trehz**
fourteen	quatorze	**kah-*torz***
fifteen	quinze	**kanz**
sixteen	seize	**sez**
seventeen	dix-sept	**deez-*set***
eighteen	dix-huit	**deez-*wheat***
nineteen	dix-neuf	**deez-*nuf***
twenty	vingt	**vehn**
twenty-one	vingt-et-un	**vehnt-ay-*uh***
twenty-two	vingt-deux	**vehnt-*duh***
thirty	trente	**trahnt**
forty	quarante	**ka-*rahnt***
fifty	cinquante	**sang-*kahnt***
sixty	soixante	**swa-*sahnt***
sixty-one	soixante-et-un	**swa-*sahnt*-et-*uh***
seventy	soixante-dix	**swa-sahnt-*deess***
seventy-one	soixante-et-onze	**swa-sahnt-et-*ohnze***
eighty	quatre-vingts	**kaht-ruh-*vehn***
eighty-one	quatre-vingt-un	**kaht-ruh-vehn-*uh***
ninety	quatre-vingt-dix	**kaht-ruh-venh-*deess***
ninety-one	quatre-vingt-onze	**kaht-ruh-venh-*ohnze***
one hundred	cent	**sahn**
one thousand	mille	**meel**
one hundred thousand	cent mille	**sahn meel**
first	premier	***preh*-mee-ay**
second	deuxième	***duhz*-zee-em**

English	French	Pronunciation
third	troisième	*twa*-zee-em
tenth	dixième	*dees*-ee-em
twentieth	vingtième	*vehnt*-ee-em
thirtieth	trentième	*trahnt*-ee-em
one-hundredth	centième	*sant*-ee-em

The Calendar

English	French	Pronunciation
Sunday	dimanche	dee-*mahnsh*
Monday	lundi	*luhn*-dee
Tuesday	mardi	*mahr*-dee
Wednesday	mercredi	*mair*-kruh-dee
Thursday	jeudi	*jheu*-dee
Friday	vendredi	*vawn*-druh-dee
Saturday	samedi	*sahm*-dee
yesterday	hier	ee-*air*
today	aujourd'hui	o-jhord-*dwee*
this morning/this afternoon	ce matin/cet après-midi	suh ma-*tan*/set ah-preh-mee-*dee*
tonight	ce soir	suh *swahr*
tomorrow	demain	de-*man*

GLOSSARY OF BASIC MENU TERMS

Note: To order any of these items from a waiter, simply preface the French-language name with the phrase *"Je voudrais"* (jhe voo-dray), which means, "I would like . . ." *Bon appétit!*

Meats

English	French	Pronunciation
beef stew	du pot au feu	dew poht o *fhe*
marinated beef braised with red wine and served with vegetables	du boeuf à la mode	dew bewf ah lah *mhowd*
brains	de la cervelle	duh lah ser-*vel*
chicken	du poulet	dew poo-lay
rolls of pounded and baked chicken, veal, or fish, often pike, usually served warm	des quenelles	day ke-*nelle*

English	French	Pronunciation
chicken, stewed with mushrooms and wine	du coq au vin	**dew cock o vhin**
chicken wings	des ailes de poulet	**dayz ehl duh poo-lay**
frogs' legs	des cuisses de grenouilles	**day cweess duh gre-*noo*-yuh**
ham	du jambon	**dew jham-bohn**
haunch or leg of an animal, especially that of a lamb or sheep	du gigot	**dew *jhi*-goh**
kidneys	des rognons	**day *row*-nyon**
lamb	de l'agneau	**duh lahn-*nyo***
lamb chop	une cotelette de l'agneau	**ewn koh-te-lette duh lahn-*nyo***
rabbit	du lapin	**dew lah-pan**
sirloin	de l'aloyau	**duh lahl-why-*yo***
steak	du bifteck	**dew beef-*tek***
filet steak, embedded with fresh green or black peppercorns, flambéed and served with a cognac sauce	un steak au poivre	**uh stake o *pwah*-vruh**
double tenderloin, a long muscle from which filet steaks are cut	du chateaubriand	**dew *sha*-tow-bree-ahn**
stewed meat with white sauce, enriched with cream and eggs	de la blanquette	**duh lah blon-*kette***
sweetbreads	des ris de veau	**day *ree* duh voh**
veal	du veau	**dew *voh***

Fruits/Vegetables

English	French	Pronunciation
cabbage	du choux	**dew *shoe***
eggplant	de l'aubergine	**duh loh-ber-*jheen***
grapefruit	un pamplemousse	**uh *pahm*-pluh-moose**
grapes	du raisin	**dew ray-*zhan***
green beans	des haricots verts	**day ahr-ee-coh *vaire***
green peas	des petits pois	**day puh-tee *pwah***
lemon/lime	du citron/du citron vert	**dew cee-*tron*/dew cee-tron *vaire***
orange	une orange	**ewn o-*rahnj***
pineapple	de l'ananas	**duh lah-na-*nas***

English	French	Pronunciation
potatoes	des pommes de terre	**day puhm duh *tehr***
potatoes au gratin	des pommes de terre dauphinois	**day puhm duh tehr doh-feen-wah**
french fried potatoes	des pommes frites	**day puhm *freet***
spinach	des épinards	**dayz ay-pin-*ards***
strawberries	des fraises	**day *frez***

Beverages

English	French	Pronunciation
beer	de la bière	**duh lah bee-*aire***
milk	du lait	**dew *lay***
orange juice	du jus d'orange	**dew joo d'or-*ahn*-jhe**
water	de l'eau	**duh lo**
red wine	du vin rouge	**dew vhin *rooj***
white wine	du vin blanc	**dew vhin *blahn***
coffee	un café	**uh ka-*fay***
coffee (black)	un café noir	**uh ka-fay *nwahr***
coffee (with cream)	un café crème	**uh ka-fay *krem***
coffee (with milk)	un café au lait	**uh ka-fay o *lay***
coffee (decaf)	un café décaféiné (slang: un déca)	**un ka-fay day-kah-fay-*nay* (uh *day*-kah)**
coffee (espresso)	un café espresso (un express)	**uh ka-fay e-*sprehss*-o (un ek-*sprehss*)**
tea	du thé	**dew *tay***
herbal tea	une tisane	**ewn tee-*zahn***
drinks not included	boissons non compris	**bwa-sons nohn com-*pree***

Index